THE WORLD'S GREATEST

Gun Digest

2011

65th Edition

EDITED BY

Dan Shideler

Published by

Gun Digest® Books, an imprint of F+W Media, Inc.
Krause Publications · 700 East State Street · Iola, WI 54990-0001
715-445-2214 · 888-457-2873
www.krausebooks.com

To order books or other products call toll-free 1-800-258-0929
or visit us online at www.krausebooks.com, www.gundigeststore.com
or www.Shop.Collect.com

CAUTION: Technical data presented here, particularly technical data on handloading and on firearms adjustment and alteration, inevitably reflects individual experience with particular equipment and components under specific circumstances the reader cannot duplicate exactly. Such data presentations therefore should be used for guidance only and with caution. Gun Digest Books accepts no responsibility for results obtained using these data.

ISSN 0072-9043

ISBN 13: 978-1-4402-1337-3
ISBN 10: 1-4402-1337-2

Designed by Dave Hauser and Patsy Howell
Cover design by Tom Nelsen

Edited by Dan Shideler

Printed in the United States of America

John T. Amber
LITERARY AWARD

We're proud to note that this year's winner of the John T. Amber Literary Award is one of our longest-running contributors, the inestimable Jim Foral, for his 2009 Gun Digest feature, the "Age of Mobilubricant."

Jim has a knack for uncovering forgotten chapters in our shooting heritage and reacquainting us with them with his witty, readable prose. How many of us knew that, in the age before jacketed bullets were perfected, serious marksmen typically dipped their bullets in a can of automotive grease? I didn't, and perhaps you didn't either. But I enjoyed discovering this bit of esoterica, as I suspect you did.

As its name implies, the John T. Amber Literary Award recognizes not only a writer's knowledge but his ability to express it. We again note, with all regrets that may be necessary, that as a craft, gunwriting is a vanishing art. In this day of the blog, the flamer, the spammer and the unmoderated bulletin board, it's easy to forget that the best gunwriters, the ones who have endured, not only know their subject but know how to entertain the reader. Jim Foral is one of these.

Jim is a humble man. When asked to provide us with a biography, he responded with the following:

A weakly credential man doesn't embellish. Here 'tis.

A once wider field of youthful passions has narrowed as I've gotten older. Some have slipped loose and are gone entirely, but the zeal for the history of the shooting sports hasn't shifted. My stuff has now been printed in twenty different periodical and annual titles, but my greatest publishing satisfaction has come from being allowed an annual presence in Gun Digest, whose subtitle "The World's Greatest Gun Book" is not just an uninspired cliche or a groundless boast.

Jim Foral

I've always regarded its readers as my peers, and I'm grateful for the opportunity to contribute. My bride Kathy and I live in Lincoln, Nebraska, where I work in the commercial floor covering field, and bowfish - another passion - more than any man should be allowed."

Thanks, Jim. And we hope you will honor us with your contributions for years to come.

Dan Shideler
Editor
Gun Digest

Less being better than more, the easiest way to get in trouble was to dunk the whole clip into the can of Mobilubricant.

We're delighted to offer another fascinating piece of scholarship by one of Gun Digest's favorite authors, this one dealing with a nearly-forgotten chapter in the story of the 1903 Springfield.

The age of Mobilubricant
BY JIM FORAL

Frankford Arsenal 1921 Match cartridge with "Tin Can" bullet (Gary Muckel collection)

WELCOME

to the 2011 Edition of *Gun Digest*!

When *Gun Digest* was founded in 1944, it had been a scant 33 years since the U. S. Army's adoption of what many have called the greatest pistol of all time, the Model 1911. And now here we are, on the threshold of the centennial of that truly remarkable pistol. Today, of course, there are dozens of companies who make 1911 and 1911A1 pistols, offshore and domestic, and in shooting most of them, I haven't yet found one that wasn't, at the least, a sturdy, serviceable pistol. Some of course have been a great deal more than that.

This edition of *Gun Digest* contains an excellent overview of the history of the 1911 and its commercial variants by — who else? — *Gun Digest*'s venerable Contributing Editor for semi-auto pistols, **John Malloy**, whose familiarity with the 1911 is second to no one's. From the pre-1911 Model 1905 to today's Colt Rail Gun, John literally knows the 1911 inside and out.

Of course, other things are happening in the world of shooting besides the 100th anniversary of the 1911. Our chronic ammunition shortage, especially in regard to self-defense ammo, seems to be abating as hoarding and hysteria wane, so it's now possible to feed that .380 and .40 and bang away just as you used to, at only slightly higher prices. Of course, our able Contributing Editor for ammunition, **Holt Bodinson**, gives you the inside scoop on the last ammo-related developments a bit later in these pages, and our good friend and Contributing Editor **Larry Sterett** helps us get the most out of the consequent boom in reloading in his remarkable profile of the latest reloading components and tools.

The hottest area in the gun market today seems to be in small, CCW pistols. Contributing Editors **John Malloy** and **Jeff Quinn** cover these in their respective sections — and hoo-boy, is there a lot to cover! But sporting rifles and shotguns are enjoying their fair share of innovation, too, and well-known gunscribe and. Contributing Editor **Tom Tabor** shares his in-imitable perspectives on today's rifles — and there's more out there than ARs, folks — while our good friend and Contributing Editor **John Haviland** lines up his bead on today's shotgun market.

Of course, not all guns go "*Bang!*" or "*Boom!*" — some go "*Pffft!*," either intentionally or not, so we are indebted to Contributing Editors **Tom Caceci** and **Wm. Hovey Smith** for their insights on airguns and blackpowder rifles, respectively. Women's issues are ably covered by one of our favorite gunslingers and firearms trainers, **Gila Hayes**. And for those who love adorned and special-order guns — and who doesn't? — we're grateful to Contributing Editor **Tom Turpin** for his breathtaking pictorial on custom and engraved guns.

With so many guns entering the market, sooner or later someone's going to have to fix them, so we welcome gunsmith and Contributing Editor **Kevin Muramatsu**'s report of what's new in the tricks and tools of the gunsmithing trade. Contributing Editor **Wayne Van Zwoll**, who's looked through more scopes than I've looked through martini glasses, sorts out the burgeoning scopes and sights market for you in a way that our old catalog section never could.

Of course, what would *Gun Digest* be without the usual assortment of pieces about oddball handguns, custom rifles, great gunwriters of the past, and controversies? All of this can be found in these pages along with much more that I hope you'll find as entertaining and intriguing as I did.

Speaking of Which. . .

You may notice that the catalog in this edition of *Gun Digest* may look different to you unless you're a very long-time reader. We've reverted to a format that *Gun Digest* used back in the mid-sixties. Aside from providing a nice retro touch, the new layout allows us to keep the picture of a gun closer to its description, which we hopes eliminates the page-jumping and other contortions readers formerly had to endure. As always, guns are presented by major type, then in alphabetical order. Prices shown are representative, of course; a 10-minute visit to the internet or your neighborhood gunshop will show you that, truly, there is no such thing as "suggested retail price." Some manufacturer's don't even provide them — and if a manufacturer doesn't provide good photos of his products, there's a good chance they won't appear in our catalog section.

You will also notice that we have shortened or eliminated entirely the catalog sections that formerly dealt with optics, reloading presses and literature. We have left the former two categories in the capable hands of **Wayne Van Zwoll** and **Larry Sterett**, respectively — and this for a simple reason: were we to include all shooting-related wares in this book, the book would have to be twice as big, twice as expensive, and would include no feature articles, which we feel have always been the heart and soul of *Gun Digest*. As for including periodical literature or books, we have discovered to our dismay that many retailers of this specialized literature have suspended operations, so if you are looking for a particular out-of-print book on guns or shooting, we refer you to www.amazon.com. If a book exists, you'll find it there.

A Call for Papers

Gun Digest remains what it has always been: the world's leading firearms annual. Many of the pieces written in the pages were not written by profesional gunwriters but gun just plain folks. We have never met a gun owner who didn't have something interesting to say, so if you would like to write something for possible future publication in *Gun Digest*, be our guest! All materials must be submitted in electronic format (e.g., MS-WORD or .rtf files) and must be accompanied by a suitable number of in-focus, high-resolution images (300 dpi or greater) in digital format (.jpg or .tif).

If you have such a manuscript, or an idea for one, contact us at: **Editor, *Gun Digest***
Gun Digest Books
700 East State Street, Iola, Wisconsin 54990

Please include your full name, street address, telephone number and email address with your submission.

Dedication

This edition of Gun Digest is cheerfully and respectfully dedicated to you, the reader, who has made Gun Digest the world's leading firearms annual since 1944.

Acknowledgments

This edition could not have been completed without the support of Jim Schlender, Gun Digest Books's guiding hand, and of David J. Blansfield, our strongest corporate sponsor. Dave Hauser, Tom Nelsen and Patsy Howell lent their peerless layout talents, without which this book would never have been completed or look so attractive.

And a final word of thanks to those who prefer to be known only as EGH, EC, NA and JW, without whose help and support I would have been quite out to sea.

Cordially,
Dan Shideler, Editor
GUN DIGEST

About the covers

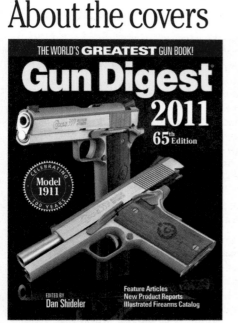

FRONT COVER Today, without serious question, the 1911 is the King of the Hill of semi-auto pistols. A few of us remember one of the first major departures from the "traditional" 1911: the Coonan Model B of the late 1970s. Chambered for the .357 Magnum, the Coonan Model B was a solid performer from a smaller firm, but it happened to appear just as the "wondernine" phenomenon was taking off. The Coonan faded into obscurity, leaving behind a hard-core cadre of True Believers.

Today, glory be, The Coonan Model B has been reborn in two incarnations by Coonan Inc. of Blaine, Minnesota. The new Coonan .357s are available in two configurations: the full-size Coonan Classic, with 5-inch barrel and seven-round magazine; and the Commander-sized Coonan Compact, with 4-inch barrel and six-round magazine. Both Coonans feature frames and slides made of 17-4PH stainless steel, and both are 100% made in the USA. A number of custom options are available. For more information, visit www.coonaninc.com.

BACK COVER In this, the 1911's centennial, we thought it fitting to tantalize you with two noteworthy examples of the greatest pistol of all time: the Kimber Centennial Edition (top) and Remington's new 1911 R1.

The Kimber Centennial Edition is limited to a run of 250 pistols with a suggested retail price of $4,352. It's all Kimber, meaning top-of-the-line, and is of course made here in the USA with special finishing work by Turnbull Restoration. For more information, visit www.kimberamerica.com.

Though Remington Arms never mass-produced the 1911 or 1911A1 until now – that distinction belonging to affiliated office equipment manufacturer Remington Rand – it is awfully nice to see again the name of Remington on a handgun. At press time we know but little about Remington's plans for the 1911 R1, but next year we expect to have a full report. For breaking news, visit www.Remington.com.

Gun Digest Staff

EDITOR Dan Shideler

CONTRIBUTING EDITORS

Holt Bodinson: Ammunition, Ballistics & Components; Web Directory
Wm. Hovey Smith: Black Powder
John Haviland: Shotguns
John Malloy: Handguns: Autoloaders
Tom Tabor: Rifles
Jeff Quinn: Handguns: Revolvers and Others

Tom Turpin: Custom and Engraved Guns
Wayne Van Zwoll: Optics
Gila Hayes: Women's Perspective
Kevin Muramatsu: Gunsmithing
Tom Caceci: Airguns
Larry Sterett: Reloading Components and Equipment

TESTFIRE

TABLE OF Contents

TR's "BIG (FIRE) STICK"

President Roosevelt's Holland & Holland Double Rifle

BY **TOM CACECI**

TR and his son Kermit, who also carried an H&H double rifle on Roosevelt's famous safari.

President Theodore Roosevelt was a man whose life was lived on the stage of world affairs on a grand scale. In a speech at the Sorbonne in Paris, on April 23, 1910, he remarked:

… credit belongs to the man who is actually in the arena, whose face is marred by dust and sweat and blood; who strives valiantly; who errs, who comes short again and again, because there is no effort without error and shortcoming; but who does actually strive to do the deeds; who knows great enthusiasms, the great devotions; who spends himself in a worthy cause; who at the best knows in the end the triumph of high achievement, and who at the worst, if he fails, at least fails while daring greatly, so that his place shall never be with those cold and timid souls who neither know victory nor defeat.

TR was a rancher, politician, statesman, soldier, historian, and Nobel Laureate (he received the Nobel Peace Prize in 1906 for his mediation of a settlement of the Russo-Japanese War), a strong-willed leader of men who lived the credo he preached. Less than three weeks after leaving the White House in March of 1909 after more than 40 years "in the arena" of public life, this vigorous and virile man took up a new challenge: a massive safari to collect specimens of African wildlife for the Smithsonian Institution and the New York Zoological Society. His year-long trek is perhaps the best-known and certainly one of the best-chronicled hunting trips in history, a grand adventure on a scale to suit the tastes and abilities of America's 26th President.

Hunting was in TR's blood, a passion he indulged during his days in the western US, and in more sedate settings in the east. He had an abiding love of the outdoors, expressed in the preface to *African Game Trails*, the book that describes his safari:

…there are no words can tell the hidden spirit of the wilderness, that can reveal its mystery, its melancholy, and its charm. There is delight in the hardy life of the open, in long rides rifle in hand, in the thrill of the fight with dangerous game. Apart from this, yet mingled with it, is

Royal Grade Double Rifle with Case and Accessories, Presented to Theodore Roosevelt, 1909. Holland & Holland, Ltd. English (London). .500/.450 Nitro Express Caliber. Serial Number 19109. Frazier International History Museum. Museum Purchase, 2001.32. Holland & Holland, Ltd. Photo courtesy Frazier International History Museum.

the strong attraction of the silent places, of the large tropic moons, and the splendor of the new stars; where the wanderer sees the awful glory of sunrise and sunset in the wide waste spaces of the earth, unworn of man, and changed only by the slow change of the ages through time everlasting.

These are words of a romantic, a semi-mystic who is also a visionary. TR was all of these things and more. His love of the outdoors life led him to become the founder of the National Parks System and a founding member of the Boone & Crockett Club as well as the New York Museum of Natural History, testimony to both his love of the hunt and his respect for the hunted. He is justly recognized as one of the fathers of the modern conservation movement. As a hunter, he well understood the basic principle that preservation of wildlife requires that economic value be afforded to it, game and non-game species alike; that a species' very survival depends on its value to man. He undertook his safari with this vision in mind:

Wise people…have discovered that intelligent game preservation, carried out in good faith, and in a spirit of common-sense as far removed from mushy sentimentality as from brutality, results in adding to the state's natural resources…. Game laws should be drawn primarily in the interest of the whole people, keeping in mind certain facts that ought to be self-evident…. Almost any wild animal…if its multiplication were unchecked…would by its simple increase crowd man off the planet; and that far short of this…a time comes when the existence of too much game is incompatible with the interests of the cultivator. There should be…sanctuaries…where game can live and breed absolutely unmolested; and elsewhere…allow a reasonable amount of hunting on fair terms to any hardy and vigorous man fond of the sport…. Game butchery is as objectionable as any other wanton form of cruelty or barbarity; but to protest against all hunting of game is a sign of softness of head, not of soundness of heart.

Planning such a safari necessarily started well in advance, as it was a complex logistical and scientific undertaking as well as a grand adventure. He was accompanied by scientists and specialists from the museums involved, as well his 19-year-old son Kermit, then a freshman at Harvard University. Many of the arrangements were made through two of the world's most famous big game hunters, Edward North Buxton and Frederick Courteney Selous. Other famous hunters who joined him on arrival included R.J. Cuninghame and Leslie Tarleton, hard-bitten Englishmen who were Old Africa Hands. The expedition's ponderous equipment included motion picture cameras and technicians, too, as this was the first safari to be filmed. The equipment and supplies for such a trip required no fewer than 150 porters and assorted gun-bearers, askaris, and of course their camp followers, all of whom had to be fed on the march. TR, in charge, had his work cut out for him and had no lack of hunting opportunities.

Among his preparations was the assembly of his famous African Battery: a pair of Winchester rifles in .405 caliber; Springfield rifles in the then-new Army caliber, .30-06; and the most powerful rifle in his collection, a "Royal" grade double rifle made by Holland & Holland of 98, New Bond Street, London, recognized then as now as "The Royal Arms Maker," whose elite list of customers included not only Presidents, but King Edward VII, numerous Indian Rajahs, many members of the European Royalty and the American plutocracy, and those lesser notabilities who could afford their prices, people who demanded – and got – the best.

TR's rifle is now on display at the Frazier International History Museum in Louisville, Kentucky, the centerpiece of a fabulous assemblage of artifacts focused on American and British arms of the Colonial to modern period. In addition to the collection of guns

The first animal to fall to TR's H&H double: the Kilimakiu rhino.

from the frontier and western eras on this continent, one floor houses a stunning array of weapons from Britain, a collaborative effort with the Royal Armouries in Leeds. The Frazier is one of the premier arms museums in this country and for anyone with an interest in history and the role arms played in this nation's development, a visit there is an absolute must.

"Best Gun" double rifles are rightfully considered the very apex of the gunmaker's art. While double rifles were and are made elsewhere, English ones are universally considered superior to all others; and H&H is ac-

knowledged to be the "Best of the Best" maker of this unique type of firearm. The firm's origins go back to 1848 when Harris John Holland set up shop as a gunmaker in London. By 1876, he had been joined by his nephew, William Harris Holland, and the new firm, Holland & Holland, was located at 98, New Bond Street, London W1—as fashionable a shopping district as could be found in Victorian times. Holland & Holland are still very much in business today. While the names of their clientele may be different, neither the quality of their guns nor their stratospheric prices have changed. They are still the "Royal Gun Makers" in every sense. TR's "Royal" grade double, serial number 19109, was a product of the best efforts of the best craftsmen in the world, a monument to H&H's artisans, their skill, and the firm's traditions, as much as to its one-time owner's passion for the hunt.

Working through the office of the Honorable Whitelaw Reid, Ambassador to the Court of Saint James, and with Mr. Buxton acting as liaison to H&H, President Roosevelt placed the order for the rifle in the Spring or Summer of 1908. It was, of course, stocked to fit his personal measurements, which had been taken in America in August of that year and sent to the firm. A copy of the original order is present in the Frazier's records. It specifies:

A best quality .450 bore double Royal H'less non-ejector Cordite Rifle, long top strap cheek piece pistol hand stock recoil heel plate, loops for sling, pull to be light, say right 3-1/2 pounds, to measurements rec'd 21/8/08.

As you'd expect, the workmanship is flawless. According to the documentation, this rifle weighs over 10 pounds, but as with any fine double, it feels much lighter and is perfectly balanced. I took the very considerable

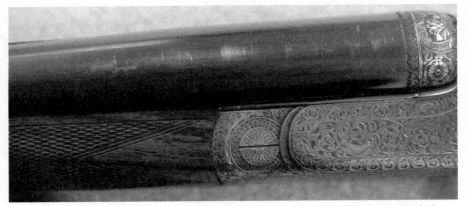

Scratches on the barrel show that this is a working gun and was used as intended.

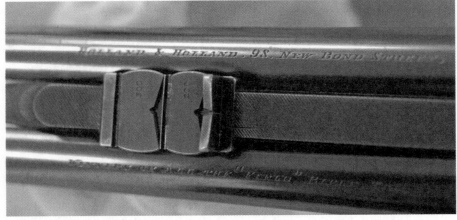

The flip-up rear sight leaves, made to TR's directions. Express-caliber double rifles are meant for close-in work on big animals; a 300-yard leaf (especially for a man who admits "At long range...I never was really good for anything") is pure optimism on someone's part! Note also the barrel inscriptions. The *Field* was an important sporting publication of the day.

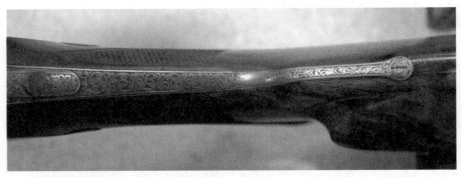

The elongated tang of TR's double rifle, intended to strengthen the stock against the battering of the .450/.500 round. Note the cast-off of the stock, which brought the barrel group in line with TR's right eye. (TR was blind in his left eye, the result of a recreational boxing injury he incurred while President.)

TR's special-order front sight.

liberty of raising it to my shoulder and found it pointed as fluidly and as instinctively as a shotgun.

It's a hammerless sidelock with small floral and scroll pattern engraving on the locks and the receiver, all of which were left in the white. The engraving is elegant but subdued, and actually as functional as it is decorative: it effectively breaks up the highly polished steel with what amounts to a matte finish from a distance. Despite the profuse coverage, there is very little in the way of embellishment otherwise. The cocking indicators are inconspicuous bands of gold inset into the ends of the hammer pivots, and the word SAFE is inlaid in gold on the top tang but there is no other ornamentation. Per TR's specifications, the "long top strap" tang extends halfway down the length of the stock, a way to strengthen the wrist against the very substantial recoil of the cartridge it fires. The heavily-engraved grip cap has a spring-loaded lid, inside which is a spare set of strikers.

The stock is a stunning example of the woodcarver's art, although again, it isn't ornate. The beautifully grained walnut has no cracks or splits, and its "London Finish" is a bit worn, but it's completely sound. As with the barrels, the stock shows handling marks, especially on the wrist, whose left side checkering is noticeably worn. TR was right-handed; there is a cheekpiece on the left side and the proper amount of cast-off to bring the sights into alignment with his dominant right eye. The pull length is 14-3/8 inches to the front trigger, with a drop at the heel of 2-1/2 inches.

Inlet into the left side of the stock is a golden medallion bearing the Presidential Seal and the initials "TR," which I believe to be a post-1909 addition. I'm certain the butt plate is a replacement: it's an incongruous red rubber pad that would be more at home on a double shotgun from Sears, Roebuck than a London Best Gun. I contacted H&H about this matter of the butt plate because correspondence in the files indicates that it was sent back to H&H for work in 1986. (In 1989, a film was released "starring" the Roosevelt double: *In The Blood* tells the story of TR's great-grandson and his hunting experience in Africa. The film, directed by George Butler, interweaves documentary footage from the original expedition with modern images, tracing the route TR followed and bridging the time span of four generations.) The medallion may

Load data was also engraved on the bottom of the rifle's receiver.

have been inlet at the same time. I was told by a Mr. Guy Davies that H&H have no record of installing either the medallion or the butt pad, but I'm absolutely positive the latter isn't original. I can't believe that H&H would have put something like it on a gun like this one.

The fore-end assembly isn't original either. It too was replaced in 1986. The correspondence from that time indicates that the original was in very bad condition and couldn't be salvaged. Not only did H&H replace the wood, they made new metal parts as well, later "distressing both to match the level of wear the rest of the rifle." I never would have guessed this from my examination: H&H's craftsmen matched the level of "distress" of the new and old parts perfectly.

The sights are an example of how a customer for a London Best Gun gets what he wants. The front sight is an elongated gold bead on a short matte rib. The bead is rather small to my way of thinking, but TR had specified the sights he wanted in a note (on White House stationery) to Mr. Buxton:

I have never used a peep sight. I do not know whether it is just a prejudice of mine, or whether it is really that my eyes are not suited to one. At long range, I am sorry to say, I never was really good for anything. I enclose you the type of front sight I like most. The rear sight I like very open, but with a little U that takes the bead of the front sight.

The rear sight, also on a matte rib, was made exactly to this description and the sketch provided in the note. It's a 3-leaf type with one fixed leaf for 100 yards, and flip-up leaves for 200 and

(with amazing optimism) 300 yards.

The blued 26-inch barrels bear H&H's name and address and the inscription, "Winners of All The 'Field' Trials, London." Despite coming from the workshop of the premier Bespoke Gun Maker and being as perfect an example of "Best Gun" standards as could be imagined, this is indeed a working rifle. Moreover, it's one that has obviously been used as its maker intended: both barrels have scratches in the finish, the sort of wear-and-tear you'd get from leaning it against various dead mud-crusted pachyderms or carrying it in a scabbard. However, it's still in remarkably good condition, fully functional, with the action crisp and tight. Although TR carried and used it extensively for a year in very remote places, where access to proper cleaning equipment was limited to what his bearers could carry and conditions were not those the modern hunter enjoys, one could run a patch or two down the bores and it would be ready for

The engraved grip cap holds two extra strikers in case of emergency.

action. Moreover, H&H can still supply the correct Cordite-loaded rounds they intended it to use: these are made by Kynamco, successors to the famous firm of Kynoch, who made TR's ammunition.

TR had much experience with dangerous animals in North America. Moreover he had the advice of professional ivory hunters who well understood the essential requirements for a weapon to be used on very large animals that not infrequently fight back; undoubtedly he took their counsel seriously. Although Terry Wieland's *Dangerous Game Rifles* and John "Pondoro" Taylor's *African Rifles & Cartridges* were published long after TR's death, this rifle meets these authors' criteria perfectly in all respects. Both are strongly of the opinion that a rifle for dangerous game should have neither ejectors or an automatic safety. Ejectors are complicated mechanisms prone to malfunction; and if the hunter is facing a charge and must hastily reload, the safety will be on from the moment he opens the breech. He is under the stress of mortal danger and an automatic safety may well get him killed. TR's rifle has a non-automatic safety catch and extractors, not ejectors. (Correspondence implies that originally TR wanted a hammer gun – of which choice "Pondoro" would have heartily approved – but H&H had no hammer action on hand. To build one from scratch would have delayed the safari for a year or more.)

Double rifles are fiendishly expensive in part because each is essentially not one, but two rifles, joined together by a common stock. The real art of building one is to get both of the barrels to shoot to the same point of impact at some specified distance. This process of "regulation" is laborious but essential, and it demands that only ammunition with specific performance characteristics be used. The ammunition for this rifle was made to H&H's specifications. Pasted inside the case (and engraved on the underside of the action) is the specific load for which this rifle is regulated: a 480-grain .450 caliber bullet fired with a charge of 70 grains Cordite. The production records include a notation that the rifle was test-fired with this load on December 12, 1908, five days before delivery, and achieved the accuracy H&H considered acceptable: a group of 2-1/8 inches by 1-1/2 inches at 100 yards. This is about 2 MOA, which even today is pretty good, and for a rifle to be used on dangerous game at close range,

entirely adequate…especially out of two separate barrels using open sights!

H&H was seriously concerned lest any other ammunition be used, with inferior results in terms of accuracy or point of impact: the ammunition label carries the warning that "H&H will not guarantee the accuracy of this rifle unless their ammunition be used," and another informing the owner that ammunition could be obtained from "Messrs. Walter Locke & Co., Ltd., Calcutta & Lahore." That ammunition was available several thousand miles away in India probably wasn't much of a comfort to TR, so he brought a substantial supply.

As with the matter of the safety catch, extended top tang and extractors, the caliber was selected with care and upon expert advice. The ".500/.450 Nitro Express" is based on the 3-14-inch long .500 Nitro Express case, necked down to hold a smaller .450 bullet: the standard British nomenclature for this caliber is ".500/.450-3-1/4," and it's still catalogued as the ".500/.450 Nitro Express" by Kynamco. It's still regarded by modern hunters as an outstanding choice for dangerous game. People who hunt big animals understand that it is bullet momentum and, above all, deep penetration that make a rifle effective, not high velocity. Taylor speaks highly of the .450-calibers in general and the .500/.450 NE in particular, noting that its roomy necked-down case causes it to develop much lower chamber pressures than comparable rounds, a matter of very real importance in tropical countries. Standard chamber pressure of the .500/.450 NE is 15-1/2 tons per square inch, a little more than half that of a .30-06.

The .500/.450 NE cartridges Kynamco makes today are identical in performance to TR's. Only one loading is available, a 480-grain bullet with a muzzle velocity of 2175 fps out of a 28-inch barrel (it would be a bit less from the 26-inch barrels on TR's gun). To Americans who are geared to think in terms of lighter bullets at higher velocity, +/- 2000 fps isn't very impressive, but that big bullet has better than 5,000 foot-pounds of muzzle energy. Taylor measured a rifle's effectiveness by what he referred to as "Knockout Value," noting that, "…it's the weight of the bullet that matters when it's a case of knocking down some beast at close quarters." The .500/.450 NE has momentum and penetration to spare and served TR well in some very

tight spots.

The complete order included a heavy "best leather" case, in which were stored two slings, cleaning jags and a cleaning rod, a funnel, a bottle of sight black, and sundry other accessories. Inside the well-beaten-up but still intact case remain two sets of jags in small leather pouches, the cleaning rod, a bottle of "Rangoon Oil" and a jar of "Rangoon Jelly," plus two wide slings with narrow ends for the 1-1/4-inch swivels. A Kynoch cartridge carton contains two fired shells and one live cartridge.

The rifle was a gift to the retiring President from many of his friends and admirers: a large label pasted into the lid contains a list of the names of all the individuals who subscribed to the fund. The names are a Victorian-era Who's Who, many of the names still remembered today. In addition to F. Courtney Selous, various Dukes and Duchesses, the Earl of This and That, are many names of people who would play major roles on the world stage in the coming decade: Sir Edward Grey (Foreign Minister at the time of the First World War), Lord Curzon (Viceroy of India), and a name any reader of famous hunting stories will recognize: Colonel J.H. Patterson, author of *The Man-Eaters of Tsavo*.

This is a rich man's gun: H&H was paid 85£/13s/6d for it, about $500 at the then-current rate of exchange. This was the equivalent of a year's wages or more for an English working stiff. Prices have gone up a bit, but H&H will be happy to build a duplicate today for anyone who has about a half a million dollars to spend.

African Game Trails, the delightful book that showcases TR's prowess (not only as a hunter but as a man of letters), is a nearly day-by-day account of his progress through eastern Africa. In it he recounts numerous kills he made, including those with the Holland & Holland. Here is his recounting of the first kill made with his "Big Stick":

A Wakamba man came running up to tell us that there was a rhinoceros on the hill-side three-quarters of a mile away…I immediately rode in the direction given…In five minutes we had reached

The case for TR's .450/.500 double, showing all supplied accessories.

the opposite hill-crest…. The huge beast was standing in entirely open country, although there were a few scattered trees of no great size at some little distance from him…. I cannot say that we stalked him, for the approach was too easy. The wind blew from him to us, and a rhino's eyesight is dull. Thirty yards from where he stood was a bush…it shielded us from the vision of his small, pig-like eyes as we advanced towards it, stooping and in single file, I leading. The big beast stood like an uncouth statue, his hide black in the sunlight; he seemed what he was, a monster surviving from the world's past, from the days when the beasts of the prime ran riot in their strength…. So little did he dream of our presence that when we were a hundred yards off he actually lay down.

Walking lightly and with every sense keyed up, we at last reached the bush, and I pushed forward the safety of the double-barreled Holland rifle which I was now to use for the first time on big game. As I stepped to one side of the bush…the rhino saw me and jumped to his feet with the agility of a polo pony. As he rose I put in the right barrel, the bullet going through both lungs. At the same moment he wheeled, the blood spouting from his nostrils, and galloped full on us. Before he could get quite all the way round in his headlong rush to reach us, I struck him with my left-hand barrel, the bullet entering between the neck and shoulder and piercing his heart…Ploughing up the ground with horn and feet, the great bull rhino, still head[ing] towards us, dropped just 13 paces from where we stood. This was a wicked charge, for the rhino meant mischief and came on with the utmost

determination…. [T]he vitality of the huge pachyderm was so great, its mere bulk counted for so much, that even such a hard-hitting rifle as my double Holland – than which I do not believe there exists a better weapon for heavy game – could not stop it outright, although either of the wounds inflicted would have been fatal in a few seconds.

Of course, the Holland was also used on elephant, occasionally with some assistance:

…looking over the heads of my companions, I at once made out the elephant…. The leader was the biggest, and at it I fired when it was sixty yards away, and nearly broadside on, but heading slightly toward me. The recoil of the heavy rifle made me rock, as I stood unsteadily on my perch, and I failed to hit the brain. But the bullet, only missing the brain by an inch or two, brought the elephant to its knees; as it rose I floored it with the second barrel…. Reloading, I fired twice at the next animal. It stumbled and nearly fell, but at the same moment the first one rose again, and I fired both barrels into its head, bringing it once more to the ground. Once again it rose – an elephant's brain is not an easy mark to hit under such conditions – but as it moved slowly off I snatched the little Springfield rifle and this time shot true, sending the bullet into the brain.

During the expedition, TR personally killed 13 rhinos, his son Kermit taking another seven. Eleven elephant – eight of them by TR's hand – fell to his double rifle. Many more animals were killed with this and the other guns in his battery, either for the Museums or as food for the hunting party. The Holland

did yeoman service in the taking of thousands of animals over the year-long trip.

Upon Rosevelt's return to America, the Smithsonian Institution received almost 800 examples of various African animals, large and small. One of them, a white rhinoceros TR killed at a place called Kilimakiu, is the only one on display today, in the Hall of Mammals. A sign placed next to it identifies its donor. A comparison of the original photo taken at the time of the kill, and the horns of the animal on display, confirms that they are the same beast.

A hundred years have passed since Roosevelt made his grand safari. The world has changed greatly in the century since: two world wars – the first of which claimed Kermit's life – have been fought as well as several smaller ones and innumerable regional conflicts. The world of 1909 with its political and economic issues, its imperialist conquests, its good and bad, all of it, has vanished into the mists of the past. Yet the H&H double still is here, a tangible link to that world and its mighty figures.

This rifle symbolizes in its substance not just a hunt, but the twilight period of the only sort of world in which such a hunt could be made. It is emblematic of the exploitation of Africa and its resources, but as well, of the embryonic environmental conscience of western societies, embodied in the rationale for the hunt itself and the words of its commander. TR's safari may be considered in some sense the watershed event in the development of modern-day conservation and preservation ethic. The rifle's true value is therefore as a historical artifact joining today's hunter/conservationists with those who came before them, by virtue of its one-time ownership by a major player in the history of America and the world. It is the best-known and best-documented firearm ever made, beyond any conceivable monetary valuation; a unique example of the pinnacle of the gunmaker's craft, a symbol of a lost era, and a tribute to a man whose legacy lives on still in our game laws.

Resources & References

Roosevelt, Theodore. 1910. *African Game Trails.* Syndicate Publishing Company, New York.

Taylor, John. 1948. *African Rifles & Cartridges*, Special Edition for the Firearms Classic Library (1995).

Wieland, Terry. 2006. *Dangerous Game Rifles*. Country Sports Press (Camden, ME) ISBN 0-89272-691-1.

The Innovative Winchester Model 59

This close-up view of the right side of the receiver shows the carrier lock button located below the ejection port. The button in the anterior bow of the trigger guard is the cross bolt safety.

BY BERNARD H. DiGIACOBBE, M.D.
PHOTOS BY ROSEMARIE V. DVORCHAK

Supposedly, if you build a better mouse trap the world will beat a path to your door. However, this was not the case with the Winchester model 59 autoloading shotgun. While it was certainly a better mouse trap, the shooting public ignored it. Sales were so poor, in fact, that Winchester stopped production in 1965 after selling only 82,085 of them. As so often happens, shortly after production ceased the gun enjoyed near-cult status, especially among upland game hunters.

Then as now, if a shotgun barrel becomes obstructed with mud or snow, it is likely to burst when the gun is fired. Sometimes this causes the muzzle to split. Other times it causes the barrel to split all too close to the shooter's hand or face. Increasing the thickness of the walls of the barrel would make the barrel stronger. Unfortunately, the extra weight would ruin the gun's balance. To try and solve this dilemma, the Winchester engineers experimented with aluminum alloy and titanium barrels. While these

metals allowed for stronger barrels, they could fragment, resulting in an even more dangerous situation. After more than five years of research and development, the engineers settled on a then new material, fiberglass. This material had recently demonstrated its strength and durability in boats and car bodies. Each barrel had a full 500 miles of glass fiber wound circumferentially around a 0.020-inch steel liner. The glass fiber was then bonded under heat and pressure in a polyester matrix. To achieve a conventional appearance, the outer surface of the barrel was wrapped with color impregnated fiberglass cloth. This outer layer was then machined to a smooth finish. The finished barrel, although shiner and slightly larger in diameter, closely resembled a

conventional shotgun barrel.

In addition to serving as a mandrel for winding the glass fiber, the steel liner also later protected the fiberglass from the intense heat of the burning powder and the abrasion of the shotgun pellets. Remember, this was before shells were

This photo demonstrates the spatial relationship of the floating chamber to the barrel and the receiver.

loaded with plastic shot cups, which is today the norm. As an added bonus the steel liner also contained the interrupted threads for attaching the barrel to the receiver!

In fiberglass boats and car bodies, the glass fibers are randomly arranged. This results in the fiberglass being of equal strength and – unfortunately – equal weakness in all directions. However, on the Win-Lite barrel (as Winchester called it) the strength was maximized circumferentially where it was needed the most. This resulted in a barrel with almost twice the hoop strength of a conventional steel barrel but with only about half the weight! As an added bonus, in the unlikely event of catastrophic failure, the circumferentially wound glass fibers restricted fragmentation. Factory testing revealed that when the barrels were deliberately blown up, they would split lengthwise without fragmenting. This gradually released the contained pressure.

The fiberglass also offered some more practical advantages. Like fiberglass boats and car bodies, these barrels were dent resistant. The impregnated color also made the scratches less visible. Unfortunately, the chamber area could turn yellow in color with sustained usage. Reportedly, the muzzles could

start to unravel if subjected to continual abuse. But then again the muzzle of any abused shotgun can be a sorry sight. At this point one has to wonder: was the Win Lite barrel the inspiration for today's high-tech carbon fiber rifle barrels?

While the model 59 was available only in 12 gauge, different barrel lengths were available initially. The improved cylinder barrels were 26 inches while modified choked barrels were 28 inches. Full choke barrels were available in 28 or 30 inches. However, by 1961 only 26 inch barrels were available. Earlier barrels

had the front sight mounted directly on the barrel in conventional fashion; later barrels had a pad placed at the muzzle to mount the front bead slightly higher. Surprisingly, none of the

Win-Lite barrels was fitted with a top rib. Presumably one could have been easily glued to the barrel. This would have been considerably easier than soldering a top rib to a conventional steel barrel.

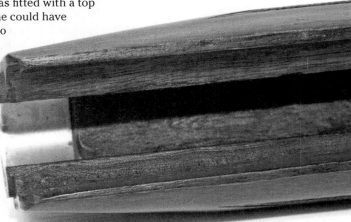

Not only were the receiver and trigger assembly made out of aluminum to save weight, but even this small stock reinforcement was made of aluminum. All this resulted in a gun that weighed less than the trigger pull on many other guns!

The external fiberglass surface of the barrel made it virtually impossible to install one of the then-popular aftermarket external collet type external chokes. Remember the PolyChoke? To compensate for this, in 1961 Winchester introduced a removable/interchangeable choke, threaded into the muzzle end of the steel liner of the barrel. An inch or so of the removable choke extended beyond the muzzle. The external portion had a series of transverse slots serving as a muzzle brake, as was common with many of those external collet chokes. While modified chokes were fitted as standard, extra Versalite (as Winchester called them) choke tubes were available in improved cylinder and full constrictions, for an extra $4.95 each. They were supplied with a flat stamped sheet metal wrench for easy removal. In actual practice they could be easily changed by hand. Yes, the model 59 introduced the now ubiquitous choke tubes! And after the passing of the Model 59, that idea lay dormant for decades.

In addition to its lightweight barrel, the Model 59 also had a lightweight aluminum receiver. These advances resulted in a 12 gauge autoloader that weighed only a little over 6 pounds! The gun's predecessor, the Model 50, weighed about 7-3/4 pounds. Incidentally, there was also a lightweight version of the Model 50 with an aluminum receiver, which weighed a little less.

The 59's receiver was not only streamlined in size and shape but was also devoid of external screws and pins. The sides of the receivers featured a roller-impressed hunting scene: perhaps a bit crude by today's standards, but in all fairness it was Winchester's first use of the technique. As with other aluminum receivers of the time, those receivers were prone to developing cracks at points of stress. On the Model 59 this was most likely to occur on the

right side just behind the slot for the operating handle. If buying a used Model 59, be sure to inspect this area very carefully! Fortunately the engineers at Winchester learned to solve this vexing problem by peening (stress relieving) the receiver in this area. Reportedly, the receivers could turn white after hard use. While I have observed at least one cracked receiver, I can't remember ever having seen a receiver that turned white.

The remainder of the Model 59 was a carry-over from its predecessor, the standard-barreled Model 50. However the Model 50 was also a very innovative gun. It was probably the only shotgun to use the floating chamber system of operation. Back then, gas operated shotguns were available, the first successful

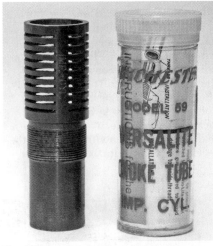

The Model 59 introduced the now ubiquitous concept of interchangeable choke tubes.

The quick detachable trigger mechanism featured several design features that resulted in one of the best trigger pulls ever offered on an autoloader. Unfortunately the complex shapes of the components meant that they could not be economically stamped from sheet metal but rather had to be investment cast. This significantly increased the cost of production. Why did Winchester color the assembly gold? Perhaps they just wanted to flaunt some of the many innovations in the mechanism.

one having been the High Standard Supermatic, released under the J. C. Higgins brand name. Unfortunately those guns were unreliable, especially if their gas pistons weren't cleaned regularly. This problem was exacerbated by the fact that their gas pistons were difficult to dissemble and clean.

The more successful autoloading shotguns of the time were recoil operated, generally utilizing the long recoil system of operation. The old "hump back" Browning A-5 is a good example of that system of operation. The barrel would telescope approximately 5/8 of an inch into the receiver. This relatively long motion of the barrel would result in an undesirable "double-shuffle" pattern of recoil. The barrel travel also complicated the fitting of a top rib. Worse yet the gun had to be adjusted when switching to or from magnum loads by removing the barrel and reversing the friction ring.

On the Models 50/59, however, the floating chamber, which included the forcing cone, telescoped into the chamber end of the barrel. The bolt locked directly to an extension at the back of the floating chamber. Thus immediately after firing, the floating chamber and bolt would recoil backward while still locked together. After .09 of an inch of rearward travel, an abutment within the receiver prevented further rearward

travel of the floating chamber. By that time, the cam of the bolt carrier would have unlocked the bolt from the floating chamber. The unlocked bolt was then free to continue traveling rearward. A small coiled spring and plunger within the receiver would return the floating chamber to its full forward position. Compared to the previously described long recoil system, the short travel of the lightweight floating chamber didn't have enough inertia to cause the undesirable "double shuffle." It didn't even have enough inertia to operate the gun! To increase the bolt's momentum, it was connected via a rod to a weight contained within the buttstock. The rearward motion of these components was resisted initially and subsequently reversed by the recoil spring, which was also contained within the buttstock. The combination of the light weight barrel in conjunction with the extra weight in the buttstock resulted in a uniquely muzzle light balance. This resulted in a very responsive swing that some hunters, especially quail and grouse hunters, preferred.

The system would work with all standard American 2-3/4-inch shells, including 2-3/4-inch magnums, without external adjustment. Malfunctions could occur with light loads or shells with a

slow pressure buildup. This was more common with European loads, and Model 50s sold in Europe ultimately had to be modified for reliable operation. According to the physicists, you don't get something for nothing. It took a fair amount of energy to operate the mechanism and compress the recoil spring. Fortunately this energy came from the recoil generated from firing the gun. According to Winchester, the gun had 20% less recoil! In addition, the recoil was more comfortably distributed over a long (relatively speaking) push as opposed to a sudden jolt. Extending the recoil pulse has the effect of decreasing the shooter's perception of recoil.

So, while lighter guns generally kick more, the Model 59 actually kicked less. The effect was further enhanced by the muzzle brake configured into the Versa Lite choke tubes. As such it was an ideal beginner's gun, light to carry and shoot with the effectiveness of a 12 gauge! And of course the same features endeared it to experienced hunters. Supposedly, the gun would jam if debris accumulated between the exterior surface of the floating chamber and the corresponding surface of the barrel.

Certainly any gun can jam if enough debris accumulates in the wrong place. However, one of the 59s that I examined for this piece had quite a bit of crud lying within the bottom of the receiver. When questioned, the owner stated that he couldn't remember the gun ever jamming. The U. S. Treasury Department, however, found a definite problem with the floating chamber. Shortly after the Model 50 was introduced, they discov-

The right side of the gun. It seems ordinary enough until you pick it up.

ered that the gun could be fired without the barrel attached. As such the gun could be used as a sawed off shotgun. To prevent this, Winchester was required to recall their initial production and modify them so that they couldn't shoot without the barrel attached.

The floating chamber system was also used in some other firearms. It was used in the Colt Ace, a .22 rimfire adaption of the Colt 1911. In that gun, the floating chamber was utilized to increase the recoil of the .22 cartridge, allowing it operate the heavy slide of the gun. In the Remington Model 550 autoloading rifle, the floating chamber selectively boosted the recoil of the .22 Short cartridge, allowing .22 Short, Long and Long Rifle cartridges to be used interchangeably. These guns, as well as the floating chamber itself, were the brainchildren of the legendary Marsh "Carbine" Williams. He is, however, best remembered for having developed the short stroke gas piston used in the M-1 carbine of World War II. He was a genius at understanding the momentum dynamics of autoloading guns and went on to perfect the short recoil system of operation. Surprisingly, he wasn't a formally trained engineer. In fact he had little formal education at all. However he managed to work out the principles of operation of those guns while serving out his prison sentence at the Caledonia Road Camp in North Carolina! Even more amazing is the fact that the warden allowed him to build and modify the guns needed to prove their system of operation.

Some of the earlier autoloaders were plagued by the uncomfortable positioning of their triggers. The Models 50 and 59 maintained the feel and trigger location of the beloved Model 12 pump action. This can be traced back to the fact that back in 1945 Winchester modified a Model 12 as a prototype to test the floating chamber concept. Like the Model 12 and most other repeating shotguns, the Models 50 and 59 had a conventional crossbolt safety located in the anterior portion of the trigger guard. Removing the aluminum assembly reveals some of the innovations of the firing mechanism. A novel feature for the time was how easily it could be removed. Simply drift out the two transverse retaining pins located above the trigger guard and then depress the carrier lock button. The trigger assembly can then be pulled out of the bottom of the receiver.

The Model 59 was known for its quality trigger pulls. The lack of creep and slack was actually a feature of the design. The sear was integral with the trigger, which virtually eliminated any free travel. The distance from the pivot pin to the sear was maximized in relation to the distance from the pivot to the trigger. This in turn shortened the trigger pull and minimized the shooter's perception of the still-present creep. Unfortunately, this made the earlier versions prone to misfiring. The short length of pull also made them prone to doubling. To prevent this, an additional or back-up sear was configured into the hammer ahead of the main sear notch. Thus, if the trigger were not pulled back far enough, this extra sear notch would block the fall of the hammer.

Unfortunately for Winchester, a number of guns were already sold before this system was adopted. To address this potential problem, Winchester sent a "Blue Book" to gunsmiths throughout the U. S. and Canada explaining how to rectify this potential problem.

With the trigger assembly removed, the complex shapes of the various components of the feeding assembly become apparent. These were also designed by Marsh Williams. He "whittled" them through trial and error until they functioned flawlessly. However, this resulted in shapes that were difficult to manufacture. The then relatively new technique of investment casting helped, but only somewhat. However, they were still nowhere as easy to make as the stamped sheet metal components in modern repeaters. Fortunately the springs were all simple wire springs rather than the more expensive and less reliable leaf springs.

Surprisingly, the magazines of the Models 50 and 59 only held two shells, plus of course one in the chamber. (While this is certainly no disadvantage nowadays, shooters of the time placed an excessive value on firepower.) The ejector was also simple and reliable: a sturdy rod sliding lengthwise within the bolt with the rear portion of the ejector protruding out the back of the bolt. When the bolt reached the end of its rearward travel, the ejector struck an abutment within the rear of the receiver. This then transmitted the force forward, forcibly ejecting the shell. The system is simple and effective, as there were no small parts to break or malfunction because of congealed lubricants.

Unlike the Model 50, which was available in 12 or 20 gauge, the Model 59 was available only in 12 gauge. However, a

The Win Lite barrel, although slightly larger in diameter and shinier, closely resembles a conventional shotgun barrel. Note the interrupted threads at the breech and the interchangeable choke tube at the muzzle.

deluxe version called the Pigeon Grade was manufactured in 1962 and 1963. It featured hand-honed internal components and engine-turned bolts and bolt carriers as well as better-grade stocks built to customer specifications. In 1962 this grade listed for $249.65 while the standard grade sold for $149.50. To put these prices into perspective, the competing Browning A--5 "Hump Back" listed for $129.75 with a plain barrel or $149.75 with a venti-lated rib. So the Model 59 was competitively priced. Yet sales of the Model 59 were so poor that Winchester even resorted to a free trial offer. Prospective buyers could take a Model 59 hunting for a day, free of charge. Still, sales lagged to the point that production was terminated in 1965.

Unfortunately, things are different today. Today Model 59s are scarce and people willing to part with one are even more scarce. Even if they are too old to hunt with them, they still retain a definite affection for them. If you can locate one in need of repair, replacement parts are occasionally available from the Guns Parts Corporation of West Hurley, New York. However if you are thinking of converting an old lightweight Model 50 (which had an aluminum receiver) into a 59, the Win-Lite barrels are seldom if ever available.

So the Model 59 was definitely a better mouse trap. Yet the shooting world failed to beat a path to Winchester's door. Why this was so remains a mystery. Perhaps the shooters of the time weren't as sophisticated as the gun. Despite their short production runs, the Models 50 and 59 sired many innovations that continue to live on in other guns. That's not a bad epitaph for any gun.

On the upper face of barrel, the model number marking.

The French Service Revolver Models of 1873 and 1874

BY RAYMOND CARANTA

Just as the Civil War has been called the major military event of the 19th century in the United States, the Franco-Prussian war of 1870 is considered in France to be the landmark for armament evolution during the last thirty years of that period.

As a matter of fact, for instance, 1870 marked the bridge between the muzzle-loading and breech-loading eras for military firearms. In this connection, if we consider handguns, immediately after the war, most cavalry departments shifted from traditional muzzle-loading horse pistols to the most up-to-date metallic cartridge revolvers.

FRENCH CAVALRY HANDGUNS BEFORE THE WAR

In the French cavalry, the handgun was considered, up to the war, quite as a secondary weapon, after the saber and the lance. It is for this reason that, in 1870, the "1822 T Bis" horse pistol, a flintlock single shot design converted to percussion in 1860, was still the basic service handgun.

It was a conventional side-lock single shot 69-caliber gun, 13.7 inches long and weighing 43 oz. with a 7.8-inch barrel. Officers were either armed with single shot flintlock "1822 T" horse pistols converted in 1840 to percussion (overall length 13.4 inches; weight 35 oz. with 7.8-inch barrel) or with the Officers Model of 1833 (same caliber; overall length 14.3 inches; weight 32 oz. with 7.8-inch barrel). However, most cavalry officers used personal handguns, such as the Lefaucheux 12mm pinfire revolvers.

Also, it can be added that, while the converted "1822 T" Officers pistols were only improved basic trooper handguns, the Model of 1833 was much closer to an aristocratic continental duelling pistol. Nevertheless, if we refer to 1855 French military literature ("*Maximes, conseils et instructions sur l'art de la guerre.*" Paris, Leneveu, Libraire – Editeur. 1855), our top brass did not rely too much on handguns: "...A pistol shot, if not fired at very close range, will miss 99 times out of one hundred; however, never rest the muzzle against the object aimed at, for fear of bursting the barrel...."

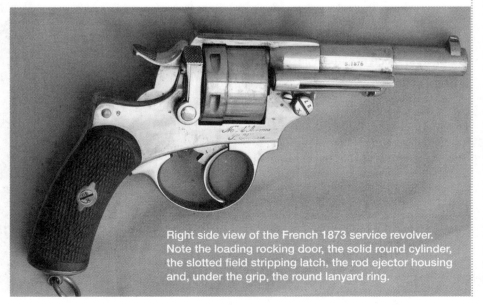

Right side view of the French 1873 service revolver. Note the loading rocking door, the solid round cylinder, the slotted field stripping latch, the rod ejector housing and, under the grip, the round lanyard ring.

BEYOND THE FRANCO-PRUSSIAN WAR

After the Sedan disaster of September 2, 1870, which saw the capitulation of the Emperor Napoleon III, the National Defence Government, which became in charge of the war effort, was in urgent need of war materiel. Therefore it purchased, among others, many surplus guns of the American Civil War, resulting in the import of excellent, but obsolescent, single action muzzle-loading revolvers. When the peace was restored, most European Armies realized therefore that, for properly arming horsemen, it was time to adopt modern double action metallic cartridge revolvers.

So, in France, a Military Commission was placed in charge of selecting a new service model for general distribution, which was required to feature a solid frame. Among the miscellaneous guns tested were the new central fire Lefaucheux adopted by the Navy in 1870, together with special Galand and Chamelot-Delvigne prototypes. (See *L'aristocratie du pistolet* by Raymond Caranta and Pierre Cantegrit. Crépin-Leblond, Paris. 1997.) In the end, it was the Chamelot-Delvigne product that was selected.

Belgian J. Chamelot was a gunsmith residing in Liège and Henri Gustave Delvigne, a French Captain residing in Paris, was well known for his activity in the field of ballistics. The two united their efforts in 1862 and designed several revolvers covered by twelve patents by June of 1873. Most of these were pinfire guns, the double action Model 9 of 1864 having already being tested by the military in 1867.

THE CHAMELOT-DELVIGNE FOREIGN SERVICE REVOLVERS

The first successful revolver of the new solid-frame Chamelot-Delvigne line was the 10.4mm rimfire model, adopted by Switzerland on April 24, 1872. These guns were first made in Belgium for the Swiss Army by Pirlot Frères in Liège, in 1873. Later, they were converted into centerfire in 1878, at the Bern Waffenfabrik facilities in Switzerland.

After the French, the Italian Army adopted also a similar Chamelot-Delvigne design as their model of 1874, in service up to 1889. It was chambered in 10.35 mm centerfire, now called the "Italian service caliber" with a 177-gr. lead bullet at 735 fps).

THE 1873 CHAMELOT-DELVIGNE FRENCH CAVALRY MODEL

This is a superb solid-frame fixed-barrel revolver 9.68 inches long, weighing 43.7 oz. with a 6-shot cylinder and a 4.48-inch barrel of .44 caliber. Rifling is four right hand lands and grooves at a 13.78:1 pitch. The oval trigger guard is nicely shaped, the rod ejector being protected by a housing parallel to the barrel's right side. The grip butt features a steel round cap fitted with a swivelling lanyard ring.

All components are individually marked with the revolver serial number, which is not a mere luxury, as they are not interchangeable without fitting. The gun can be entirely disassembled by hand, using the beak of the cylinder axis head as a key for releasing the side-plate lock screw.

In our opinion, the models of 1873 and 1874 are, from a mechanical standpoint, the finest of our French service revolvers.

THE FRENCH 11MM SERVICE AMMUNITION

The original loading consisted of a centerfire rimmed cartridge featuring a hollow base 179-gr. sharp pointed pure lead

The hammer at the safety notch.

To remove the cylinder, depress the field stripping latch, with the ejector rod unlocked, and pull out the rod. With the loading door opened and hammer at the safety notch, the cylinder can be easily removed.

In front of the hammer, at the frame rear end, the rear sight "V" notch.

In the frame rear hump, on the left side, the side-plate slotted attachment screw.

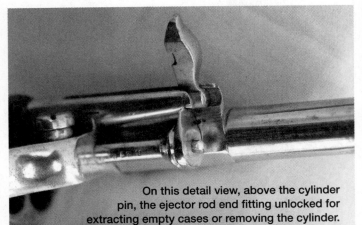

On this detail view, above the cylinder pin, the ejector rod end fitting unlocked for extracting empty cases or removing the cylinder.

bullet propelled by 10 grains of black powder at a laughable 426 fps muzzle velocity for a muzzle energy of only 72 ft./lbs. If we compare with the .44 SW American loading of 1871 (180 grains bullet at 649 fps) intended for shooting in a top-break revolver, one wonders why a "solid frame" was required!

Obviously, French military engineers were later ashamed of such performance, as they increased the muzzle velocity to 623 fps in 1890! As a matter of fact, it is this later improved loading that was used during both World Wars.

SHOOTING THE 1873 SERVICE MODEL

With its circular grip, the gun – which balances at 42% of its overall length, under the cylinder rim, i.e. above the trigger with the hammer lowered – is very comfortable in the hand, as it is slightly muzzle-heavy, and points naturally.

The trigger lies a bit too far forward for double action shooting but is adequate for single action. However, the sights are too high at 1.57 inches above the hand and the "V" notch is quite narrow in relation with the bead for slow fire shooting at 25 meters.

Thanks to the grip rear hump, the gentle recoil is easily controlled. In fact, the only problem with this gun is its trigger pull (8.8 lbs. in single action and 15.4 lbs. in double).

Thanks to the fact that these Chamelot-Delvigne revolvers are now legally considered in France to be "antiques," many people are using them, without licence, for competitive shooting, off-hand, at 25 meters (about 28 yards). As their only flimsy component is the trigger return spring, we now have French craftsmen who make spares, and as our modern shooters do not use their guns on horseback, such springs can be lighter than the originals, bringing the single action pull down to about 5 pounds, which is quite perfect!

THE ACCURACY REQUIREMENTS OF THE TIME

According to the "Shooting Regulations for Cavalry" of 1894 ("*Règlement sur l'instruction du tir des troupes de cavalerie,*" dated september 15, 1894), the shooting distances were 15 and 30 meters (49 and 98 feet) at circular targets of respectively 20 and 40 centimeters in diameter (8 and 16 inches). The larger target featured an internal 8-inch-diameter ring counting for two points and an outer one for one point.

At 30 meters, shooting was performed single action only (12 rounds) and, at 15 meters, both in single and double action (12 rounds each) for a total of 36 rounds. The larger targets were used at 30 meters only and the smaller ones, at 15 meters.

With scores reaching or exceeding 24/36, shooters were rated first class; at 12/36, they rated second class; and, under 12/36, third class. (Now, 115 years later, we shoot at 25 meters single action only, at the ISU international circular target featuring a 2-inch ten ring.)

JAMS AND COMPONENT FAILURES

The French 1873 cavalry revolver was quite a rugged gun for its time. Using the regular 1890 service ammunition, misfires were rare in single action, but return trigger spring breakages were quite common. In double action, to the contrary, firing pin spikes could occur and, more rarely, cylinder jams. The Cavalry manual instructions concerning combat use of the 1873 revolver gave the following advice (*Manuel du cavalier – 15ème régiment des chasseurs.* Belfort, 1876):

> ### The Revolver: Its Use In Mêlée
>
> *Same maintenance than for the rifle; daily check of lock and ratchet.*
>
> *The revolver is a very efficient weapon in mêlée, but its use should be limited to very close range.*
>
> *Accordingly, the cavalryman armed with it must hold the saber in his bridle hand and use his revolver against a threatening opponent, an enemy out of reach, or gunners sheltered behind their cannons.*
>
> *Moreover if he is unhorsed, he can defend himself from infantry men…*

PRODUCTION FIGURES AND COSTS

The Saint-Etienne arsenal manufactured 325,885 Model 1873 revolvers (including 67 pre-production guns) by 1884. 176 of these revolvers were rebuilt in 1884, using salvaged components.

When, in 1877, the French Navy abandoned their former Lefaucheux Model 1870 in favor of the 1873 revolver, this particular version was delivered blued, for improving its resistance to salt water. A total of 12,868 guns in the Navy configuration was delivered from 1877 to 1886. Many of them were still in service during World War II.

The 1873 service revolvers were charged to the Government from 41,30 Francs (about $8.26) in 1884, to 62,96 Francs (about $12.59) in 1886.

After World War II, this writer purchased a brand new second-hand example around 1952 at 1000 Francs (about $4 USD). They are now much more highly prized than that in Europe. Currently, as legal antiques, they are worth 1000 Euro ($1450 USD) in the same condition! As for the rarer Navy models marked with the anchor, if they retain their original blue finish, you may have to pay up to 2000 Euro ($2900 USD)!

1874 CHAMELOT-DELVIGNE FRENCH OFFICERS' MODEL

In 1874, while the army was testing the first 67 production model 1873 troopers' revolvers, the Saint-Etienne arsenal released the new, more lighter and compact "Officers Model of 1874."

Basically, the action was the same as the M1873's, but the cylinder was fluted and slightly shorter; the overall length was reduced by one inch (8.58 inches instead of 9.68 inches); the barrel was shorter (4.33 inches instead of 4.48

inches); the sights were improved; and the trigger pulls were smoother. Moreover, the guns were now blued, with the action components light yellow heat-treated. In short, it was now a gentleman's handgun intended for general distribution among all French Army officers.

From the practical standpoint of the user, the "V" notch was slightly more opened and deeper than on the original 1873 version for troopers, and the front sight bead was .01 inch smaller.

In single action, the trigger pull was now in the 7 lbs. range but, in double action, it was similar to that of the 1873 model, as officers were also riding horses and facing the same dangers as basic cavalrymen.

Two current handloaded cartridges for 25-meter shooting with .450" caliber commercial lead round balls, a small cardboard wad and 13.8 grains of Swiss black powder No. 2.

If one translates these improvements into reality at the shooting range, given equal skill, the officer was quite advantaged comparatively to the private, a condition which was perhaps not much democratic but which did preserve the hierarchy.

This writer had the privilege to own and use, with original Gevelot commercial cartridges, a mint 1874 revolver in 1954. In single action, the trigger pull was perfectly clean at approximately 6 lbs. and, at 25 meters (28 yards), the gun was able to group all impacts in the 7 ring of the international "P50" target (7.87 inches diameter). Shooting double action (approximately 15 lbs. pull) at a row of five Olympic silhouettes at the same range, the gun was pleasant to use, with a one-inch trigger stroke, but much slower than a modern Colt or Smith & Wesson revolver. The recoil was negligible.

In the hands of modern competition shooters,

Inside the grip, the key which is activated to relax or bend the mainspring.

off-hand scores are in the 90/100 range (4-inch diameter bull), using handloaded ammunition.

PRODUCTION FIGURES AND COSTS

From 1875 to 1885, the total military production of the 1874 model was 31,920 guns, at a maximum price of 63,22 Francs (approximately $12.64 USD) in 1875 and a minimum of 43,37 Francs, or $8.67 USD, in 1880.

In this connection, I had to pay 25,00 Euro ($5 USD) for my exceptional sample in 1954, while it would be worth of, at least, 1500 Euro ($2175 USD) now. Remember, these are European values.

A less ambitious sample may cost, these days, about 1200 Euro (approximately $1,740 USD).

FRENCH SERVICE REVOLVERS: SPECIFICATIONS

French Service Model of 1873

Manufacturer: Manufacture d'Armes de Saint-Etienne
Year of manufacture for test specimen: 1876
Caliber: 11 mm (.44) French Revolver Model 1873
Cylinder capacity: 6 shots
Length overall: 9.68 inches
Total height: 5.75 inches (at stock ring pin axis)
Thickness: 1.77 inches (at cylinder)
Empty weight: 43.7 oz.
Loaded weight: 47.20 oz.
Barrel length on test specimen: 4.48 inches
Rear sight: fixed "V" notch .08 inch wide at top and .02 inch deep on frame
Front sight: bead type of .09 inch diameter on barrel
Height of rear sight top above the hand: 1.89 inches
Trigger pull: Single action: 8.8 lbs. / Double action: 15.4 lbs.
Safety devices: Double action: safety notch on hammer
Frame material: steel
Finish: polished white
Action type: double action Chamelot-Delvigne 1871/1873 system (patents
    29664 dated 11/21/1871 – 31924 dated 02/15/1873
    32848 dated 06/30/1873) – fixed firing pin

French Service Model of 1874

Manufacturer: Manufacture d'Armes de Saint-Etienne
Year of manufacture for test specimen: 1875
Caliber: 11 mm (.44) French Revolver Model 1873
Cylinder capacity: 6 shots
Length overall: 8.58 inches
Total height: 5.75 inches (at stock ring pin axis)
Thickness: 1.77 inches (at cylinder)
Empty weight: 35.6 oz.
Loaded weight: 39 oz.
Barrel length on test specimen: 4.33 inches
Rear sight: fixed "V" notch .11 inch wide at top and .04 inch deep, on frame
Front sight: bead type of .08 inch diameter on barrel
Height of rear sight top above the hand: 1.57 inches
Trigger pull: Single action: 7 lbs. / Double action: 16.3 lbs.
Safety devices: Double action: safety notch on hammer
Frame material: steel
Finish: blued with trigger and hammer light yellow heat treated
Action type: double action Chamelot-Delvigne 1871/1873 system (patent
    29664 dated 11/21/1871 – 31924 dated 02/15/1873
    32848 dated 06/30/1873) – fixed firing pin

The N-Frame S&W Revolver

BY PAUL SCARLATA

PHOTOS BY JAMES WALTERS AND BUTCH SIMPSON

Ever since I first became interested in firearms (no, I'm not going to tell you how long ago that was!) I have associated certain periods in history with particular firearms. For example, when I think of the Thirty Years War in Germany (1618-1648) the firearm that comes to mind is the matchlock musket. Nor can I discuss the American Revolution (1775-1781) without mentioning Daniel Morgan's Virginians and their long rifles. When the Napoleonic Wars (1804-1815) are the subject, I envision red coated infantry marching in formation with flintlock Brown Bess muskets, while the American Civil War (1861-1865) is exemplified by muzzleloading, rifled muskets such as the M1861 Springfield. And I doubt there is a gun fancier in the world who does not connect the settling of America's western frontier with the Winchester lever action carbine and Colt SAA revolver.

As a historian and gun collector, I find the period most interesting to be that thirty-year stretch between 1884 and 1914. During this time we saw the invention of smokeless gunpowder and small bore rifle cartridges, the perfection of bolt action repeating rifles, semiautomatic pistols and fully automatic firearms. From the groundbreaking 8mm Lebel cartridge and Mauser's Gewehr 98 rifle to the Colt 1911 pistol and Maxim machine gun, many of the greatest advances in firearms technol-ogy occurred during this three-decade time span.

But another firearm was perfected during this era that has garnered little of the attention lavished upon its contemporaries: the double action (DA) revolver. While DA revolvers were nothing new, having been around since the 1850s, in the 1890-1910 period the newly perfected swing-out cylinder unloading/reloading system was combined with improved DA trigger mechanisms to produce the modern revolver as we know it today. In fact, I believe I'm on firm ground when I state that except for magnum cartridges and the use of high tech metals, there is little about the modern DA revolver that a firearms engineer from 1900 would find remarkable.

And of all the revolvers developed during this time, none of them is more interesting than the heavy-caliber, large-frame wheelguns from the Springfield, Massachusetts, firm of Smith & Wesson.

Smith & Wesson introduced their first large frame (referred to as the N-frame), swing-out cylinder, DA revolver, the .44 Hand Ejector – also known as the 'Triple Lock" or "New Century" – in 1907 to compete with Colt's New Service revolver. Up until this time all of S&W's large-caliber revolvers had been of the hinged-frame, top-break variety, and, while popular, they were never viewed as quite rugged enough or chambered for powerful enough cartridges to be a real threat to Colt's predominance in the American military and civilian markets.

S&W brought out their first swing-out cylinder revolver, the .32 Hand Ejector, in 1896 followed by the 38-caliber Military & Police revolver in 1899. The .44 Hand Ejector used the same basic mechanism as these smaller caliber revolvers. The cylinder was locked by a rod that passed through the ejector system and latched into a recess on the face of the breech while a second lock was provided by a spring loaded stud in a lug underneath the barrel that snapped into the forward end of the ejector rod. But S&W felt that a stronger system would be required with the powerful cartridges they intended to use, so additional locking was provided by a bolt housed in the ejector rod shroud that locked into a mortise on the cylinder yoke.

The .44 Hand Ejector could be ordered with 4-, 5-, 6- or 6.5-inch barrels, with wooden or hard rubber grips and a choice of blue or nickel finish.

S&W also introduced a new cartridge that was to become as famous, if not more so, than the revolver itself: the .44 S&W Special. This was based upon their popular .44 Russian but used a case 0.2 inch (5mm) longer and loaded a 246-gr. lead bullet moving at 755 fps. In addition to becoming popular for law enforcement and self defense, it quickly earned a reputation for accuracy and preempted the .44 Russian as the dominant target shooting cartridge of the day. While .44 Special guns accounted for the majority of sales, the Triple Lock revolver was also offered chambered for the .44-40, .45 Colt and, for the British market, .450 Boxer and .455 Webley.

When World War I broke out in 1914, the British government placed large orders with S&W for revolvers. In addition to producing purpose-built .455 revolvers, many 44-caliber guns were retrofitted with .455 cylinders and barrels to supply the anxious British. But in the brutal conditions of trench warfare it became obvious that the Triple Lock was far too finely made a revolver: the third lock and the ejector rod shroud often became clogged with mud or debris, preventing the cylinder from closing.

S&W rectified these problems by the

The .38-44 Heavy Duty was designed for serious police work and fired a special heavy-duty .38 Special loads that came close to equaling the .357 Magnum.

weapons and while they were committed to the 1911 Colt pistol, it soon became obvious that not enough could be produced to meet demand. In 1916, the Army approached S&W about a "substitute standard" handgun and were offered the Hand Ejector, Second Model. But while the Army was not

provide clearance for the half moon clips and wider cylinder stop stud to keep the cylinder in place when swung open. When the U.S. declared war on April 2, 1917, S&W began production and delivered the first Smith & Wesson Revolver, Caliber .45, Model 1917 on September 6, 1917.

While the Army's original intention was to issue these revolvers to rear echelon and support troops, shortly after the first M1917s reached France, they began appearing in the trenches. It proved to be a rugged, powerful fighting handgun capable of standing up the vile conditions of trench warfare with aplomb and were soon much in demand by American doughboys. By the time contracts were canceled in 1918, S&W had delivered 163,476 Model 1917 revolvers to the U.S. Army,

S&W continued to produce the Second Model after World War I. Once again, the most popular caliber was the .44 Special with the .45 ACP a distant runner up while smaller numbers were produced in .38-40, .44-40, .45 Long Colt and .455 Webley. Another variation, the .44 Hand Ejector, Third Model was produced in 1926 on special order from the Wolf & Klar Company, a firearms distributor in Fort Worth, Texas. It was basically a .44 Special caliber Second Model with an ejector rod shroud and proved popular enough that limited numbers were produced up until 1950.

In 1937 the Brazilian government placed an order for 25,000 Second Models in .45 ACP. Known as the Modelo 1937 they were – except for the fact that some were fitted with checkered rather then smooth grip panels – identical to U.S. issue M1917s.

During World War II the army and

S&W pioneered the "half-moon" clip with their famed .45 caliber M1917 revolver (right). The new Performance Center M625 revolver continues this tradition with "full-moon" clip loading.

simple expedient of removing the offending parts. The modified revolver, dubbed the .455 Hand Ejector, Second Model or .455 Hand Ejector, Mark II, went into production in 1915. All British issue Mark IIs had 6.5-inch barrels and boasted a commercial-grade blued finish. The big Smith proved popular and by 1918 more than 68,000 had been supplied to British and Canadian forces.

As it became obvious that the United States would soon be entering the conflict on the Allied side, the U.S. Army began casting about for additional

adverse to using revolvers they insisted upon one precondition: any substitute standard handgun MUST use the issue .45 ACP cartridge! This presented a problem as the rimless ACP cartridge would not function with the standard revolver ejector system. Working in conjunction with Springfield Armory, S&W's engineers developed what has become known as the "half moon clip," a semicircular piece of flat stamped steel with cutouts into which three rimless .45 ACP cartridges could be snapped. This allowed the rimless cases to be ejected by the extractor bearing on the clip and had the secondary advantage of allowing very fast reloading.

The only modifications required to the design were a shorter cylinder to

The Performance Center Model 625 took honors for handling and accuracy.

France, 1944. 1st. Lt. John Upchurch covers a group of surrendering Germans with a S&W M1917 revolver. (Photo courtesy of Bruce Canfield)

The famous S&W Model 1917 pioneered the use of half moon clips to allow firing rimless pistol cartridges in a revolver.

The Model 327 TRR8 was designed for police service and has the ability to mount many different types of lights, optical sights and lasers.

The Model 327 TRR8's eight round cylinder can be loaded with loose rounds of full moon clips.

USMC issued M1917s once again. While primarily used by military police and support troops, quite a few turned up in combat where they again gave a good account of themselves. In addition, large numbers were supplied to our British and Chinese allies.

Production resumed after World War II as the .45 Hand Ejector Model of 1917. In 1950 S&W began offering two slightly updated revolvers, the .45 Hand Ejector Model of 1950 with fixed sights and the .45 Hand Ejector Model of 1950 Target with a ribbed 6.5-inch barrel and adjustable sights. The latter was superseded two years later by the heavy-barreled .45 Hand Ejector Model of 1955 which, after 1957, was known as the Model 25.

Lest we get too far ahead of ourselves and become confused, let us backtrack for a moment. The post-World War I years saw a massive switch by U.S. police to medium-frame revolvers chambered for the .38 Special cartridge, and S&W's .38 Military & Police soon became the "standard" revolver in the holsters of most police officers in the Western hemisphere.

The 1920s and 1930s were times of great social change and economic unrest which led to the rise of a new breed of violent criminals. The proliferation of the automobile, combined with poor communications and lack of coordination between police agencies, provided these lawbreakers with the means to commit crimes, escape quickly, and elude pursuit. In addition, the heavy gauge steel auto bodies of the day provided excellent protection for these highly mobile *banditti*.

Gunfights between police and automobile-mounted robbers led to a call for a handgun cartridge capable of defeating auto bodies. In response, several ammunition companies loaded the .38 Special with a 200-gr. lead bullet at a velocity of 730 fps for 236 ft/lbs. of energy. Often referred to as "Super Police" or "Highway Patrol" loads, they nevertheless proved inadequate. Also, medium-frame revolvers tended to loosen up or go out of time when fed a steady diet of them.

In 1930 S&W came to the rescue with a revolver that, over the years, has been known by several names: .38/44 Heavy Duty, .38/44 Hand Ejector or .38/44 Super Police. It was in fact, little more than the fixed-sight .44 Hand Ejector rebarreled and chambered for the .38 Special and fitted with an ejector rod shroud. It proved to be a rugged, no-frills handgun capable of digesting a unlimited diet of heavy-bullet .38 Specials and became especially popular with rural sheriff's departments and Highway Patrol agencies in the western and southern states.

In 1931, Remington developed a high-performance .38 Special loaded with a 158-gr. hardened lead bullet which, when fired from a 6.5 inch barrel, attained a velocity of 1175 fps, producing an impressive 460 ft/lbs.of muzzle energy. While Remington called it the .38/44 S&W Special Hi-Speed, it quickly became known simply as the ".38/44." It was also available loaded with a 150-gr. metal pointed bullet at the same velocity, a round that had no trouble whatsoever penetrating auto bodies, walls and the primitive bullet proof vests of the day. *[This .38/44 load is not to be confused with the earlier, similarly-named .38-44 S&W, a special target cartridge chambered in a variant of the S&W Model 3 large-frame, top-break revolver. –DMS]*

That same year, S&W offered a second version designed for sportsmen and target shooters. The .38/44 Outdoorsman came with a 6.5-inch barrel, a fully-adjustable rear sight and a patridge front sight. The .38/44 revolvers retained their popularity throughout the 1930s and '40s although production ended in 1941 so S&W could concentrate on war orders. Production resumed after the war and in 1957 the .38/44 was rechristened the Model 20 while the Outdoorsman became the Model 23. But the increasing popularity of the .357 revolver led to declining sales, and manufacture of both ceased in 1967.

One of the more notable events in firearms history occurred in 1935 when S&W's Philip Sharpe, in cooperation with Winchester's Merton Robinson, introduced the .357 S&W Magnum cartridge. Based on the venerable .38 Special case lengthened by one-eighth of an inch, the original load propelled a 158-gr. bullet to approximately 1500 fps (from an 8-3/4-inch barrel), qualifying as the most powerful handgun cartridge of its era. (Note: the velocity of factory-produced .357 ammunition was later reduced to the 1200-1300 fps range.)

The first revolvers available chambered for the .357 were based on S&W's N-frame and were dubbed, appropriately enough, the .357 Magnum Hand Ejector. S&W's new Magnum revolver was a deluxe item featuring the highest levels of craftsmanship and finish. All .357 Magnums were custom-made and were fitted with a fully adjustable rear sight while the buyer had the options of seven different front sights, any length barrel from 3-1/2 to 8-3/4 inches and several different styles of grips.

In an obvious attempt to attract the attention of the law enforcement community, S&W's president presented revolver serial #1 to FBI director J. Edgar Hoover on May 10, 1935. But while the .357 Magnum was beyond the budget of most 1930s police agencies, the cartridge's performance quickly earned it an enviable reputation and in pre-World War II years it became a status item among both civilian shooters and law enforcement personnel. And while some affluent agencies issued them, many more were purchased with private funds by officers wanting the "best." In the post-war years .357 Magnum Hand Ejector production continued and in 1957 it was rebaptized the Model 27. (It's worth noting that the first 5,500 .357 Magnums were registered to their original purchasers. Today these guns are called "registered Magnums," and their value is somewhat higher than non-registered Magnums of the same vintage, all other factors being equal.)

In 1954, so as to satisfy demand for a more affordable magnum revolver, S&W introduced the .357 Highway Patrolman (in post-1957 nomenclature, the Model 28). While this N-frame lacked the external finish and cosmetic beauty of the .357 Magnum, its lower price made it an instant hit and it became one of the most popular American police handguns of its day. By the early 1960s the Model 27 and 28 were outselling the .38/44, .44 Special and .45 ACP caliber N-frame guns by a wide margin, leading to S&W quietly dropping them from their catalog.

By the early 1950s the renowned writer, shooter and hunter Elmer Keith had spent several years hot-rodding the .44 Special and was advocating the development of a revolver cartridge capable of taking big game. Between 1954 and 1955, in cooperation with Remington, S&W engineers developed the .44 Remington Magnum cartridge. This was based upon the .44 Special case lengthened 0.125 inch and loaded with a 240-gr. jacketed bullet that was pushed to 1180 fps for 741 ft/lbs. of muzzle energy, making it the hands-down, most powerful, smokeless powder revolver cartridge of all time.

Introduced in 1955, the massive S&W .44 Magnum Revolver (post-1957, the Model 29) was an expensive specialty item that sold in limited numbers to big game hunters. But with the release of Clint Eastwood's hit 1971 film *Dirty Harry*, the Model 29 became the most sought-after handgun on the American market, causing prices to skyrocket as the limited numbers available quickly sold out. While the pace of production at

Designed for concealed carry and home defense, the new Night Guard line features Scandium alloy frames, stainless steel cylinders and special night sights.

Possibly the most famous revolver cartridges of all time were all designed for S&W N-frame revolvers. Left to right: .357 S&W Magnum, .41 Remington Magnum and the .44 Remington Magnum.

A replaceable, hardened steel shim prevents frame "cutting" from the gases of powerful Magnum cartridges.

Recoil with the Hwy Patrolman, self-explanatory.

Recoil with the M29, stiff but controllable.

S&W's factory was stepped up, it still took several years to catch up to demand. S&W's marketing types wisely conducted an advertising campaign that used *Dirty Harry* movie posters to extol the virtues of their most powerful revolver. The Model 29 became so well know to the general public that even those persons who have no interest whatsoever in firearms can tell you in an instant what type of revolver Detective Harry Callahan carried!

"Magnum mania" was now sweeping the handgun world and it seemed that everyone with R&D or production facilities was either trying to develop a new magnum cartridge or market a revolver chambered for one. In 1963 S&W had announced a new N-frame, the Model 57, chambered for the .41 Remington Magnum cartridge, which was intended to provide sufficient power for hunting big game but with lower levels of recoil than the big .44. The following year, in an attempt to popularize the .41 Magnum with police, S&W introduced the Model 58 revolver which, with its 4-inch heavy barrel and fixed sights, harked back to the .44 Hand Ejector Third Model. Despite the development of medium-velocity .41 Magnum loads, the concept never quite caught on with American police although a loyal group of big game hunters evolved that kept the .41 Magnum cartridge and Model 57 revolver commercially viable propositions.

The next trendsetting move by S&W occurred in 1963 with the introduction of the J-frame Model 60, the first all-stainless steel revolver. As the practicality – and popularity – of stainless steel grew, S&W expanded the option to most of their N-frame guns. Over the next several years, the market saw the introduction of the stainless steel Models 629 (.44 Magnum), 657 (.41 Magnum), 624 (.44 Special), 627 (.357 Magnum), 625 (.45 ACP) and 610 (10mm Auto). The two latter guns use full moon clips to handle the rimless pistol cartridges and, because of their rapid reloading capabilites, once dominated dominate those action shooting sports where revolvers are used such as ICORE, bowling pin shooting, IDPA and IPSC.

With the burgeoning popularity of semiauto pistols, in recent years the market for revolvers has shrunk, leading to S&W's dropping several models. But that being said, over the past few years S&W's Performance Center has introduced a number of limited edition and custom N-frame revolvers. Six of the newest are the Model 625 5.25-inch competition revolver in .45 ACP; the classically styled, blue steel Model 251 .45 Hand Ejector in .45 Colt; the Model 28 in .357 Magnum (an eight-shooter, no less!); the Heritage Model 25-12, a reincarnation of the Model 1917 in .45 ACP; and two tricked-out hunting revolvers, the Model 647 Comped Hunter in .41 Magnum and Model 629 7.5-inch Stealth Hunter in .44 Magnum.

The newest kids on the block are the S&W Night Guard revolvers, which utilize a frame constructed from a special alloy that contains a small amount of Scandium, a rare metal that has the ability to transmit its strength and flexibility when alloyed with other metals – in the case of the Night Guard revolvers, aluminum. This allows the construction of lightweight frames capable of standing up to the operating pressures of magnum cartridges.

But the Night Guards differ from S&W's other light weight revolvers in that a replaceable blast shield made of thin, hardened steel is positioned above the cylinder/barrel gap where it prevents hot powder gases from "cutting" the frame's top strap. While it would have been possible to use titanium cylinders to reduce weight even further, S&W decided to fit the new revolvers with stainless steel cylinders featuring a Physical Vapor Deposit (PVD) matte black finish that provides increased

(top) This side view shows the Triple Lock's locking bolt housed in the bottom of the ejector rod shroud...

(above) ...that locked into a mortise on the front of the cylinder crane.

protection against salts, solvents, powder residue, abrasion and just about any other problem they may encounter.

Night Guards also feature what just might be the most practical set of sights I have ever seen on revolvers intended for service use. The XS Sight Systems 24/7 Big Dot front sight has a tritium insert surrounded by a large, white ring making it equally visible in the dark or bright light conditions. The rear sight is a Cylinder & Slide Extreme Duty fixed unit whose generously-proportioned U notch allows a fast sight picture and alignment under a variety of light conditions.

The Night Guard line includes three N-frame guns: the M327NG (eight shot .357), M329NG (.44 Mag) and the M325NG (.45 ACP). As it would be unprofessional of me to pass judgement upon these handguns without actually test firing them, I amassed a varied selection of N-frame revolvers and my friend Butch Simpson and I ran them through their paces. My test guns ran the gamut from oldest to newest: a British contract .455 Triple Lock (converted to .45 Auto Rim, and so marked on the left side of the barrel but restored by the present owner with an original .455 cylinder; a .357 Highway Patrolman; a .44 Magnum Model 29; and a Performance Center Model 625 5.25-incher. The intended purposes of these four handguns run the gamut from military service (Triple Lock*), to big game hunting (M29), to action pistol competition (M625) and, finally, to police service (Highway Patrolman). Test ammo consisted of the following: Federal .357 Magnum, 158-gr. Nyclad; PMC .44 Magnum, 180-gr. JHP;. Lawman .45 ACP, 230-gr. FMJ; and Fiocchi .455 Mk. II, 262-gr. LRN. Ably assisted by my good friend

SPECIFICATIONS OF TESTED N-FRAMES

.44 Triple Lock
Caliber .... .44 Special
Barrel length .... 4", 5", 6", 6.5"
Overall length .... 11.75" (6.5" barrel)
Weight (unloaded) .... 38.5 oz.
Capacity 6
Grips .... checkered walnut
Front sight .... blade
Rear sight .... groove in top strap

US Model 1917
Caliber .... .45 ACP
Barrel length .... 5.5"
Overall length .... 9.6"
Weight (unloaded) .... 34 oz.
Capacity 6
Grips .... smooth walnut
Front sight .... blade
Rear sight .... groove in top strap

.38-44 Heavy Duty
Caliber .... 38 Special
Barrel length .... 4", 5", 6.5"
Overall length .... 10.4" (5" barrel)
Weight (unloaded) .... 40 oz.
Capacity 6
Grips .... checkered walnut
Front sight .... blade
Rear sight .... groove in top strap

Highway Patrolman
Caliber .... 357 S&W Magnum
Barrel length .... 4", 6"
Overall length .... 9.25" (4" barrel)
Weight (unloaded) .... 41.75 oz.
Capacity 6
Grips .... checkered walnut
Front sight .... blade
Rear sight .... fully adjustable

Model 29
Caliber .... .44 S&W Magnum
Barrel length .... 4", 6", 6.5", 8-3/8"
Overall length .... 11.4" (6" barrel)
Weight (unloaded) .... 47 oz.
Capacity 6
Grips .... Magna walnut
Front sight .... blade with insert
Rear sight .... fully adjustable

Performance Center Model 625
Caliber .... .45 ACP
Barrel length .... 5"
Overall length .... 10.5"
Weight (unloaded) .... 42 oz.
Capacity 6
Grips Hogue Laminate Combat
Front sight .... gold bead
Rear sight .... fully adjustable

Model 327 TRR8
Caliber .... 357 Magnum
Barrel length .... 5"
Overall length .... 10.5"
Weight (unloaded) .... 35.2 oz.
Capacity 8
Grips .... Hogue rubber
Front sight .... interchangeable brass bead
Rear sight .... fully adjustable

Model 329NG Night Guard
Caliber .... .44 Magnum
Barrel length .... 2.5"
Overall length .... 7.75"
Weight (unloaded) .... 29.7 oz.
Capacity 6
Grips .... Pachmayr
Front sight .... interchangeable brass bead
Rear sight .... V notch

purpose – were more or less equal. Each displayed strong and weak features: the Triple Lock had an excellent DA trigger pull but its grips and sights were too small for fast shooting; the M29 was, once again, pleasingly accurate but its recoil was stiff; the Highway Patrolman was the handiest of the four although muzzle blast from the .357 cartridge was heavy; finally, while the M625 proved the most accurate, Butch and I both felt that replacing its smooth wooden grips with a set of modern, finger groove, synthetic grips would enhance handling even further.

In conclusion, I believe I'm safe in saying that the job description of the large frame, heavy caliber revolver has not changed all that much, if at all, in the last century. For this reason, a S&W N-frame wheelgun is sort of an ageless entity. In fact, it might be fair to say that a present-day law enforcement officer, soldier or outdoorsman would be equally well served with an 80-some-thing year old S&W .44 Triple Lock as he or she would be with a modern M627 revolver.

Note: I would like to thank the following persons and organizations for supplying revolvers, ammunition, photos and much needed information used in the preparation for this article: Roy Jinks, Ken Jorgensen, Lois Chase, Vincent Scarlata, Butch Simpson, Bonnie Young, Daniel Hecht, Smith & Wesson, Inc., Fiocchi USA, PMC and Blount, Inc.

Select Bibliography

Boothroyd, Geoffrey. *The Handgun.* New York: Bonanza Books, Inc., 1967.

Canfield, Bruce. *U.S. Infantry Weapons of World War II.* Lincoln, RI: Andrew Mowbray Publishers, 1996.

Canfield, Bruce. *U.S. Infantry Weapons of the First World War.* Lincoln, RI: Andrew Mowbray Publishers, 2000.

Ezell, Edward Clinton. *Handguns of the World.* New York: Barnes & Noble Books, 1981.

Hogg, Ian V. and Weeks, John. *Pistols of the World.* Northfield, IL: DBI Books, Inc., 1982.

Jinks, Roy G. *History of Smith & Wesson.* North Hollywood, CA: Beinfeld, Publishing, Inc., 1977.

Myatt, Major Frederick. *Pistols and Revolvers.* London: Salamander Books, Ltd., 1980.

Neal, Robert J. and Roy G. Jinks. *Smith & Wesson 1857-1945.* Livonia, NY: R&R Books, 1975.

Nonte, George. *Combat Handguns.* Harrisburg, PA: The Stackpole Books, 1980.

Smith, W.H.B. *Book of Pistols and Revolvers.* Seacaucus, NJ: Castle Books. 1968.

Stebbins, Henry H., Albert J. Shay and Oscar R. Hammond. *Pistols, A Modern Encyclopedia.* Harrisburg, PA: The Stackpole Company, 1961.

Butch Simpson, I fired each gun for accuracy from a rest at 50 feet.

While firing large caliber revolvers from a rest can be a trying process, our quartet of big Smiths proved controllable and accurate. As luck would have it, all four printed more or less to point of aim, even the fixed-sight Triple Lock. Neither of us was surprised when honors went to the finely made Performance Center Model 625, which put six rounds of Speer hardball into a pleasing 1-5/8-inch group. Somewhat surprisingly, the runner-up was the heaviest recoiling of our test guns, the Model 29, with a beautifully centered 1-3/4-inch group. Even thought it had the shortest barrel, the Highway Patrolman was no slouch with a half dozen .357s in 2-1/8 inches, while the greybeard of the bunch, the Triple Lock, showed it could still do what was needed to be done with six Fiocchi .455s in 2-3/8 inches.

Butch then set up a series of D-1

target at ten yards and we performed the following drills with each revolver. As we did not have holsters suitable (i.e., big enough) for our test guns, each drill began with the shooter holding the revolver at the low ready position (45 degree angle to the ground). The test protocol was as follows:

1. Six rounds, slow aimed fire.

2. Three sets of rapid fire, double taps.

3. Six rounds as fast as we could obtain a flash sight picture.

We were gratified to find that all four of the N-frames performed these tasks with aplomb. In fact, except for a few hits in the outer scoring zones caused by the Triple Lock's rather minuscule sights, all four of our targets had nicely centered groups in their respective X and 10 rings. Except for the differences in felt recoil the performances of these revolvers – each of which was produced in a different era, fired a different cartridge and was designed for a different

The Mighty(?) 9mm Rimfire

BY **PHILLIP PETERSON**

"**Y**ou collect 9mm *what*?"

I get that a lot when the subject of collections comes up. I have been collecting (accumulating, really) 9mm rimfire firearms for about twenty years now. There are seventeen resting in my safe at this time. Many American shooters have never heard of a 9mm rimfire shotgun. They were made as inexpensive "garden guns" and will be found in a variety of action types and makers. While Winchester is the only U.S company that ever made a 9mm shotgun, the Model 36, many famous European gun makers have offered them at one time or another. Most that we see were brought to the U.S. by immigrants or by US servicemen returning from the World Wars.

The name most commonly associated with the 9mm RF guns is "Flobert," and many sellers describe these guns as such. But a bolt-action or a break-open gun is not a Flobert; a gun may fire a Flobert cartridge and still not be properly termed a Flobert. Flobert was credited with patenting the rimfire cartridge and there is a specific action design that bears his name.

SMALL ORIGINS

The rimfire or Flobert cartridge was invented in 1846 by France's Louis Nicholas Auguste Flobert (pronounced flow-BARE) and consisted of a primed brass cup topped with a round ball, loaded without powder. These little cartridges were made in several sizes: 4mm, 5mm, 6mm (.22), 7mm, 8mm and 9mm. The rimfire cartridge is Flobert's biggest and most enduring contribution to the gun world. Using his case and priming design, the 6mm/.22 was developed further in the U.S. by Smith & Wesson and others by lengthening the case and adding gunpowder. The resulting cartridge, the .22 Short, quickly became the most common and widely distributed

Top to bottom: Fabrique Nationale, Herstal Belgique, marked "FL 9m/c" with 17.5-inch barrel; Simson Prazislans Karbiner Simson & Co. Suhl with spoon bolt, 24.75-inch barrel marked "Flobert"; JG Anschutz GmbH Waffenfabrik, Ulm, Germany, 21.75-inch barrel marked "Kal 9mm Glatt"; Anschutz Model 1365, German proof marked 1969, 25.4-inch barrel marked "Kal 9mm Glatt."

(circle) 9mm Rimfire ammunition, 9mm Parabellum cartridge shown for size comparison. Top row, left to right:RWS shotshell, brass/paper construction; Winchester shotshell, brass/paper construction; Fiocchi brass shotshell. Bottom row, left to right: Remington ball cap; RWS ball cap; Fiocchi conical bullet cap.

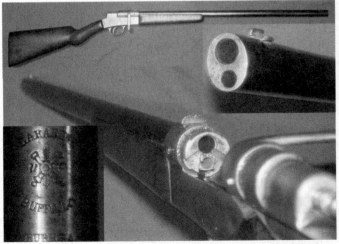

The unique Carabine Buffalo bolt action over/under 9mm/.22 combination gun.

cartridge in the world. Flobert's rimfires were originally used in handguns for indoor or "parlor" shooting and soon became extremely popular. Shortly after use of the ball loading became common, ammunition manufacturers started loading Flobert-style shotshells. These used the ball loadings' brass cap as a cartridge head but also incorporated a cardboard tube of varying length loaded with shot. Other rimfire cartridges in the 6mm-12mm range were developed during the first fifty years of fixed ammunition but only the .22/6mm and 9mm remain in widespread use.

The various 9mm rimfire shotguns quickly became known as "garden guns" because they were considered ideal for potting small varmints that raided the family garden. In America, they became popular with farmers, who used them to dispatch barn pigeons without blowing hard-to-fix holes in the roof.

A FLOBERT FLOBERT

There is also a firearms design that carries Floberts' name. My parlor pistol, for example, is a true Flobert in that it has a Flobert action: a single shot with a breechblock that rocks open when the hammer is pulled back. The hammer locks the breech closed at the moment of firing. This arrangement is very similar to the Remington Rolling block action. However, the Flobert design is not as strong and has been made only for low-power cartridges.

Flobert firearms in .22 and .32 caliber rimfire are fairly common in the United States. They rarely have any markings except the word "Belgium" stamped somewhere on the barrel and perhaps the telltale "crown over ELG in an oval" proofmark. Many were low-price imports from Belgium that were sold through Sears-Roebuck and other mail order catalogues in the late 19th and early 20th centuries. Prices as low as $1.99 were advertised for these types of guns, most of which were bought by poor farmers who did not have the money to get an American-made gun. When these Floberts survive into the modern era, they are frequently in rough condition. They were, after all, bought as tools and used as such. To make matters worse, this was in the era of black powder cartridges with mercuric primers, a combination that almost invariably led to bore erosion.

Other Flobert guns were brought home by American GI's from service in WWI or WWII. Among these there were various 9mm shotguns and rifles.

The Bernardelli Giardino 9mm rimfire semiautomatic shotgun and a box of the brass-cased ammunition made for it.

IT'S NOT A FLOBERT

Yet another single shot design, sometimes mistakenly referred to as a "Flobert," is the Warnant.

The Warnant system consists of a pivoting breech that swings up and operates the extractor, similar to the U.S. "Trapdoor" Springfield. Part of the hammer locks the breech closed upon firing. There are single shot, side by side, and over/under examples of the Warnant design that are occasionally encountered.

This Anshutz 9mm action shows the U-shaped extractor that rides in a slot beneath the bolt on many 9mm shotguns. This piece is sometimes missing as it can fall out if the bolt is removed.

BOLT ACTIONS

The single shot bolt action is the most common type of 9mm rimfire firearm found. These are usually very simple guns. Some have rifle sights and some have a simple bead sight; some cock on opening, others on closing. Some have a manual cocking piece. Many do not have a safety. Most have a simple U shaped extractor sliding in a slot underneath the bolt. (Note: Make sure the extractor is present in any 9mm bolt action you might be considering buying.. They can fall out if the bolt is removed and are frequently lost or broken.)

Many well-known European arms makers have offered 9mm rimfire guns in their product line. Germany seems to be the most prolific nation of origin. Some noted manufacturers from Germany include Alfa, Anschutz, Erma, Geco, Muchler and Simson & Co. Other continental makers include Fabrique Nationale and Bayard (Belgium), Webley & Scott (England), St. Etienne (France), Bernardelli and Beretta (Italy), and Husqvarna (Sweden).

While most 9mm shotguns seen in the United States were manufactured between 1900 and 1940, the design remained popular in Europe after WWII and a few firms still produce them today, the vast majority of which are single shots. I have never seen or heard of a magazine-fed 9mm bolt action garden gun.

OUR AMERICAN COUSIN

The sole American-made firearm chambering the 9mm rimfire is a bolt action: the Winchester Model 36. Introduced in 1920, there were about 20,000 units made by the time production stopped in 1927. The Model 36 used basically the same action as the popular Winchester Models 1900, 1902 and 1904 single shot boys' rifles in .22 caliber. The action was originally designed by John Browning and has a small bolt handle and short action. It sported an 18-inch barrel and a gumwood stock. Winchester marketed this model as a "Garden Gun" for use on small pests and birds at close ranges. Unfortunately, the Model 36 did not have a definite niche within the U.S. market. In most cases a single shot .22 would have been a better choice for up-close use and a centerfire shotgun would have worked better in the open field.

Other designs of 9mm shotguns include a variety of break-open actions. Some feature a side lever; others use an under-lever. One of my 9mm doubles has an underlever action. I once saw a beautiful French made side by side 9mmx.22 hammerless Cape Gun that had the typical box lock action with lever on top of receiver. It was fully engraved. The owner was not interested in selling. Believe me, I tried.

One of the most interesting 9mm garden guns guns I have seen was the Carabine Buffalo. This was made at St. Etienne, France, in the early 20th century. It is a 9mm/.22 over/under. The barrel is a solid piece with two bores drilled through. The muzzle is oval shaped and the gun has a unique bolt action design. The front section of the bolt covers the chamber end of the barrel and has locking lugs that match lugs on the barrel.

GARDEN GUN?

As previously noted, this European term refers to firearms made for close range control of small pests such as cats, rats, moles, and birds. The effective range of the 9mm shotshell is about 25 feet. These low-powered guns can be used around the yard or inside a barn.

The only ballistic information I was able to find on the 9mm rimfire shotshell comes from the current production brass-cased Fiocchi 1-3/4-inch brass shell with a 1/4-oz. load of # 6, #7, #8, or #9 shot. Fiocchi lists a muzzle velocity of 600 fps and an impressive 87 foot pounds of energy. In comparison, the Winchester Super-X .410 2-1/2-inch load lists a half-ounce charge of shot with a muzzle velocity of 1225 fps.

According to an Edwardian English gun writer, the 9mm shotshell was certainly up to its intended purpose:

> "With a mini-gun like this it is necessary to start thinking in feet rather than yards. This is not unreasonable for something that might be used around buildings and on farm trackways and lanes, which are only 12ft or so wide.
>
> A starting point was 6ft from the muzzle. At this distance most of the shot was contained in a 3/4in hole. At 12ft the pattern was nice with a 3in circle and at 18ft there was still a good pattern.
>
> At 24ft (eight yards) there was still the potential for bowling a rodent over, but by 30ft the small amount of shot was very thinly spread."

A RIFLE?

Two of my guns have rifled bores. The engraved Warnant single shot has deeply cut rifling and one barrel of the underlever double has wide, shallow rifling. As for the 9mm ball loads, I could find no data on any of them. All I do know is that I can see the ball leaving the barrel. Even though many of these guns feature rifle sights, there is little relationship to where a single ball shot will hit. No grouping at all. You really can shoot these in a basement or parlor. Just don't fool yourself into believing that doing so will improve your shooting – this is one case in which the gun really can't shoot better than you can hold.

STILL AVAILABLE

There are still 9mm garden guns being made in Europe. Despite the very small market it seems the old Flobert 9mm will leave a mark in three separate centuries. One model found

Two-barrel garden guns, top to bottom: Warnant system 6mm/9mm over/under, no maker's mark; Warnant system 9mm side by side marked Mariette Brevete, with Belgian-proofed 29-inch barrel, no caliber markings; side by side 9mm underlever break-open action, no maker's mark, German proof, 23.9-inch barrel, has no caliber markings.

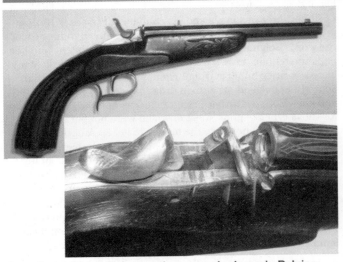

9mm Parlor Pistol. Flobert action, no maker's mark, Belgian proofed, 8-inch barrel, no caliber marking.

online at an English shooting website is the Falco, which is made in Italy. This is a break-open single shot that uses a pivoting trigger guard as the opening lever. The gun can be folded almost in half and there is a groove in the forearm for the trigger guard to rest in when the gun is fully folded. They are offered in 9mm and .410. This is similar to a Beretta-made single shot that was imported to the U.S. in the 1970s. Some Falco products are currently imported to the U.S. but not the 9mm shotgun.

Another current production 9mm shotgun is made in Italy by Vincenzo Bernardelli. They call it a "Giardino," which is Italian for "gardener." This is a semiautomatic with a three-round box magazine. It uses a simple blowback action, just like .22 LR rifles. This model appears in the 2010 *Standard Catalog of Firearms* with a value range of $100- $600, depending on condition. [*Editor's Note: A fine book! We're personally acquainted with its author. –DMS*] It is in the U.S. catalogs of a few importers and

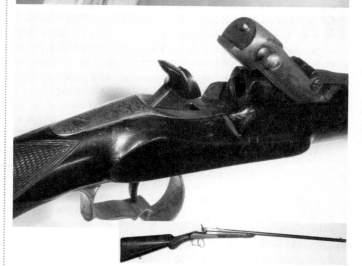

German Warnant system side by side. The left barrel in smoothbore, the right barrel is rifled. Note the folding leaf sight.

has a MSRP of close to $800, the weak US dollar being mostly responsible for the seemingly unreasonable high price.

HOW MUCH?

There are very few 9mm rimfire firearms listed in the price guides, possibly only the Winchester Model 36 and the Bernardelli Giardino. I have found no evidence that there has ever been a commercial importation to the United States of any bolt action 9mm shotguns. Many here in the U.S. were brought home as souvenirs from WW I and II. Other used guns have been imported recently from Sweden. Some U.S. entrepreneurs bought up thousands of used sporting guns there when citizens tired of the ever-increasing regulation of firearms and sold them rather than go through more paperwork to keep them. Lots of 9mm shotguns were included. I have six guns that came from one importer, including the Belgian Warnant SxS.

9mm bolt actions typically sell in the $150-$400 range with the name brands like Anshutz bringing the most. The Winchester Model 36 has a price range of $225-$750 in the 2010 *Standard Catalog of Firearms*.

Side by side, over/under, Flobert and Warnant guns are valued mostly as curiosities. Price will be determined by condition, maker, and quality. Single shots generally sell for $150-$300. Two-barrel guns can be $300-2500. A finely made hammerless double could bring a lot more.

LOADING UP

9mm rimfire shot shells are still made by Fiocchi with limited importation to the US. These function fine in the semiautomatic Bernardelli, for which they are made. These shells will fit and fire safely in most of other guns but some have a problem with extraction. The full-length brass sticks in the chamber, requiring extra effort to remove. A cleaning rod from the front works best.

The old loads were paper-walled, often with odd-looking

A Belgian-made Warnant 9mm rimfire with a rifled bore and 23-inch octagon barrel.

floral or leaf designs printed on them, looking something like brass-capped Chinese firecrackers. There are not any paper 9mm shotshell loads currently being imported to the U.S., but some small manufacturers might still produce them for the European or South American market. 9mm rimfire ball caps are currently made by Fiocchi and RWS and are available from specialty importers and retailers such as Midway USA (midwayusa. com), where they're currently priced at $22.99 for a box of 50.

That seems a reasonable price to pay to keep one of these strange old shotguns shooting. If you have a 9mm garden gun, especially an older one, the best advice is to have it checked out by a competent gunsmith before firing it. Then the only thing you'll have to worry about are the people who ask you, "What the heck is *that*?"

SMITH & WESSONS OF THE GREAT WAR

BY TOM OSBORNE

Smith & Wesson Hand Ejectors such as these saw service with British, Canadian and American forces during the First World War. In skilled hands they proved to be very effective weapons for close-quarter, trench combat. Bottom to top: .455 First Model, .455 Second Model, Model 1917 .45 ACP.

World War I brought dramatic changes to the way nations waged war. The development of the machine gun abruptly rendered horse-mounted cavalry obsolete and relegated open-field, frontal infantry assaults to little more than mass suicide missions. Technical advances in artillery enabled German and Allied forces to shell each other from unprecedented distances with deadly accuracy. This conflict signaled the inception of mechanized warfare, with the introduction of armored tanks by Great Britain and the ever-expanding use of aircraft by both sides.

It was a war in which Allied troops spent miserable weeks in trenches awaiting the order to attack. When the command came, the men who went over the top faced murderous machine gun fire and the threat of poison gas. Those who survived the carnage of no-man's-land and made it to the enemy entrenchments at times found their four-foot-long bolt action rifle, topped by another fifteen inches of bayonet, to be a greater liability than asset in the close-quarter fighting that followed.

Within the confines of the trenches, a stout club often proved more useful than an unwieldy rifle. On exhibit in London's Imperial War Museum is a collection of brutal looking, improvised clubs used by British soldiers for hand-to-hand trench combat during the First World War. Britain's military leadership

astutely concluded that while a club might be handier than a rifle under these constrictive battle conditions, it was still not the ideal tool for such work. But the English eschewed the shotgun as a weapon of war and the submachine gun had yet to be invented.

Traditionally, the British regarded handguns as being of minor tactical importance in warfare. They were

considered strictly defensive weapons and the few soldiers who carried them received minimal training in their use. However, the engagement in which England found herself from August of 1914 until November of 1918 was anything but traditional. Representing a rare departure from conventional military wisdom, the combat status of the handgun was

Half-moon clips enabled Smith & Wesson's Model 1917 revolver to function with .45 ACP ammunition, making it an effective substitute for the Model 1911 pistol. These revolvers played a significant role in the First World War. Displayed with the gun are an Army-issued canvas pouch holding six loaded clips and a World War I vintage ammo package containing eight loaded half-moon clips.

upgraded. A large caliber revolver was deemed the logical offensive weapon for fighting in the trenches.

Yet, useful as the revolver was for close-quarter combat, it certainly could not replace the Lee-Enfield rifle as the primary fighting implement of the British Army. Nor was it feasible to equip infantrymen with both rifles and revolvers for several reasons, not the least of which was the problem of securing the long gun when the handgun was deployed. Instead, handguns were worn by commissioned officers, who normally did not carry rifles. British infantry raids on German trenches were typically led by lieutenants armed with revolvers. Not surprisingly, the battlefield attrition rate of British lieutenants during the First World War was severe. Handguns were also carried by both officers and en-listed men in such assignments as Field Artillery, where rifles were impractical.

In 1914 the standard side arm of the British Army was the top-break Webley revolver in either Mark IV or Mark V configuration. The Mark VI version of the Webley was formally adopted for use by both British and Commonwealth forces on May 24th, 1915. All three models were chambered in .455 Webley, which had been their service caliber in various black and smokeless powder incarnations for some 23 years.

The first of the .455 Webley series of cartridges, the Mark I, was designated as Britain's official military handgun round in 1891. With a case length of .855 inch, the Mark I cartridge held a meager 18 grains of black powder. That con-servative charge expelled a 265-grain, hollow base, lead bullet from a 6-inch revolver barrel at a lethargic 600 fps. In 1897 it was succeeded by the Mark II round, which retained the same 265-grain lead bullet but substituted 7 grains of cordite as the propellant. Because the more efficient cordite required less volume to achieve the same power as black powder, case length of the Mark II cartridge was reduced to .760 inch. Even though the Mark II round was nearly one tenth of an inch shorter than its predecessor, the chambers of all Webley .455 revolvers were bored long enough to accept the original Mark I cartridge.

Throughout World War I the regula-tion revolver ammunition used by British land forces was the .455 Mark II. Generating a muzzle velocity of only 620 fps, the Mark II round might seem to have been woefully inadequate for combat. But it proved effective in battle,

delivering greater short-range stopping power than its modest ballistics would suggest.

While Britain's military leadership had come to recognize the handgun's value, there simply weren't enough Webley revolvers available to supply those soldiers who required them. Com-pounding the problem, Webley & Scott was unable to manufacture them in suf-ficient numbers to satisfy the demand. Members of the Commonwealth found themselves turning to outside sources to meet their handgun needs. Anticipating her impending entry into the war that was already raging on the Continent, in the summer of 1914 England contacted Smith & Wesson, seeking a suitable double action revolver chambered for the .455 round.

THE .455 FIRST MODEL HAND EJECTOR

Smith & Wesson had been producing their .44 Hand Ejector model since 1908. Also referred to as the "New Century" model, this gun was the original N-frame revolver. A distinctive feature of the New Century was a third locking lug located at the front of the yoke, or crane, that engaged a spring-loaded pin in the ejector rod shroud. This engineering nicety earned the gun its popular title of "Triple Lock."

The New Century could easily be adapted to the .455 cartridge, but the British found the yoke-mounted locking lug and full ejector rod shroud objectionable, fearing their close toler-ances would make the gun susceptible to binding from dirt and mud. Despite

these concerns, the need for additional handguns was so pressing that the Brit-ish agreed to accept Triple Locks until Smith & Wesson could re-design the revolver and eliminate the undesirable features. The urgency of the situation prompted Smith & Wesson to begin converting existing .44 Special cylinders to .455 caliber for use in British Contract guns. According to Smith & Wesson historian Roy Jinks, some 5,600 Triple Locks in .455 caliber were eventually manufactured before production of the re-designed revolvers began.

During the First World War Smith & Wesson revolvers were supplied to Eng-land through the Remington Arms-Union Metallic Cartridge Company, which served as the American purchasing agen-cy for the British Commonwealth. Like all Smith & Wesson firearms, the British Contract guns underwent standard factory proof testing prior to shipment. Before the revolvers were issued for service however, British inspectors also tested them, stamping their own proof marks in various locations on the guns.

The .455 First Model in my collection has a tiny "London View Mark" (a crown over the letter 'V') stamped in each of the cylinder flutes. The frame and barrel also bear this same stamping. On my example the English proof marks are unobtrusive and do not detract from the overall appearance of the revolver. In fact some might argue they impart a degree of character to the piece. That is not always the case with Commonwealth proofed revolvers. I have observed some that looked like they had fallen victim to a deranged inspector using a sledge hammer and cold chisel. Such guns usu-

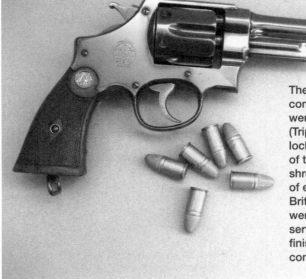

The initial 5,600 British contract Hand Ejectors were .455 First Models (Triple Locks). The third locking lug, at the juncture of the frame and ejector rod shroud, was a minor marvel of engineering. However, the British felt the tolerances were too close for a military service revolver. Fit and finish of these guns rivaled commercial production.

ally have more "character" than suits my pedestrian tastes.

Occasionally a British Contract revolver will be encountered that also displays personal markings such as a soldier's name and assignment. These generally imply private ownership, as the Government disapproved of anyone purposely defacing His Majesty's revolvers. Identifiable personal markings can add to the history (and sometimes the value) of a gun, if they help establish its provenance. The .455 First Model in my collection has what may be a previous owner's name faintly stamped on the left side of the frame below the thumb-piece, but it was struck so lightly that only a few letters can be discerned. This gun is in excellent condition and retains nearly all of its original bright blue finish. Even though it was built under military contract, it is as beautifully fitted and polished as any commercial revolver made by Smith & Wesson.

Fortunately, my First Model Hand Ejector is still chambered for the .455 cartridge. Many of the British Contract guns that found their way back to the United States following World War I were subsequently re-chambered to .45 Colt, or .45 ACP, either by Smith & Wesson or other enterprising individuals. This alteration involved milling down the back of the cylinder to accommodate the thicker rims of .45 Colt ammunition or clips for the rimless .45 ACP cartridge. If modified for the .45 Colt, the chambers required lengthening as well. From a practical standpoint there may have been some justification for these conversions, as both replacement rounds were much more readily available in this Country than .455 ammunition, but the modifications definitely destroyed the originality of the guns.

Background research by Roy Jinks on the .455 First Model in my collection indicates that it left the factory on January 21, 1915, and was delivered to the Remington Arms-Union Metallic Cartridge Co. in New York City. The gun obviously made it to England, as evidenced by its British proof marks. Beyond that, little is known regarding the service it saw. What is apparent from the condition of the revolver is that whoever had it treated it well.

Though there is little doubt that many of the .455 First Model Hand Ejectors saw use in combat, few documented accounts of their service are known. One such anecdotal example, however, can be found in Elmer Keith's book *Sixguns*

By Keith. On page 40 Keith relates the story of a Canadian soldier who was taken prisoner at night by three German troops and was being escorted back to their lines. In the darkness the Germans had overlooked a Triple Lock revolver the Canadian had under his tunic. When the four of them sought sanctuary in a shell crater during an artillery barrage, the captive took advantage of the light from exploding flares to locate the position of each of the German soldiers. He then drew his revolver and shooting double action, dispatched his captors before they had time to react.

The story recounted by Keith may very well be factual. In 1991 Mr. David Penn, who was the Keeper of Exhibits and Firearms at London's Imperial War Museum, gave a presentation to members of the Smith & Wesson Collectors Association. A transcript of his lecture was published in the SWCA 1992 Winter Newsletter. According to Mr. Penn: "The First World War was the only period in which British forces treated the revolver as an offensive weapon. It was very effective for trench fighting in skilled hands and by the end of the war, training was very sophisticated indeed, with a plethora of rapid fire, long range, trench clearance, quick draw and quick reloading techniques being taught at the Southern Revolver School at Wareham. The final test was a trench clearance at night, the only illumination being provided by exploding thunderflashes." Apparently "thunderflashes" is another term for flash grenades or some similar type of ordnance.

THE .455 SECOND MODEL HAND EJECTOR

Eliminating the ejector rod shroud and yoke-mounted locking lug of the First Model brought the .455 Hand Ejector into conformance with the British concept of a proper military handgun. Smith & Wesson quite logically labeled the re-designed revolver the ".455 Second Model." Other changes incorporated into the Second Model included a slight increase in the diameter of the cylinder, with a corresponding enlargement of the cylinder recess in the frame. Additionally, the recoil shield on the left side of the frame was contoured to better accommodate the center pin of the cylinder. Finally, a more subdued satin blue replaced the high-luster finish of the First Model. Among characteristics shared by both the First and Second Models were the 6-1/2-inch barrel, finely

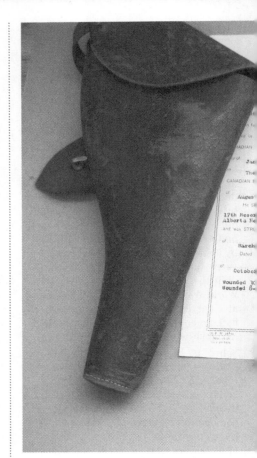

A Canadian contract S&W .455 Second Model and holster which once belonged to Lt. Martin H. Bluethner of the 5th Canadian Mounted Rifles Battalion rest on a copy of Lt. Bluethner's Certificate of Service (discharge form). Martin Bluethner served over four years with the Canadian Expeditionary Force and was honorably discharged March 20, 1919.

checkered walnut stocks and a lanyard ring in the butt of the grip frame.

A total of 69,755 Second Models were manufactured in .455 caliber. Roy Jinks' book *History of Smith & Wesson* states that when production peaked in December of 1915 the factory was turning out 5,690 British Contract, Second Models per month. That production level was maintained until mid-September of 1916 when the contract was completed.

England wasn't the only Commonwealth nation that turned to Smith & Wesson in quest of handguns during World War I. Due to its position as the senior dominion in the British Empire, Canada immediately found itself drawn into the hostilities with Germany upon England's declaration of war. Faced with an acute shortage of serviceable handguns, Canada also contracted with Smith & Wesson for revolvers. Figures listed in

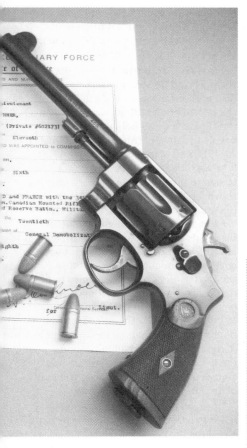

Smith & Wesson 1857-1945, by Robert J. Neal and Roy Jinks, show that 14,500 of the .455 Second Models were purchased by the Canadian Government, to be issued to soldiers of the Canadian Expeditionary Force (CEF).

Much more crucial than the shortage of handguns, however, was Canada's critical lack of fighting men. In early 1914 the Canadian Army comprised some 3,000 regular soldiers, supported by a militia of volunteers. Recognizing that war was imminent, in the summer of that year Canada launched a recruiting drive to form an expeditionary force. Whether motivated by a sense of patriotism, a desire for adventure, or the princely sum of $20 a month military pay, many young men enlisted. The Canadian Army eventually numbered nearly 600,000 strong. Of those, some 418,000 soldiers served overseas as members of the Canadian Expeditionary Force. Fighting under terrible conditions in France and Belgium, Canadian forces distinguished themselves in several major battles, at times incurring heavy casualties.

The .455 Second Model in my collection is the most interesting of the three Smith & Wessons discussed in this article, simply because more is known of its history. This gun and a companion

leather holster were offered for sale on-line by a licensed dealer in New Jersey. One of several photos displayed on the seller's website was a close-up of the revolver which showed the letter "C" enclosing a double broad arrow, stamped on the frame near the thumb-piece. The "C" told me the gun had originally been the property of Canada. The double broad arrow inside the "C" indicated that at some point the revolver had been an "out of store" purchase, meaning it had been sold to someone by the Canadian Government.

Additional photos showed there was a large chip in the base of the gun's left stock panel and someone had carved the initials "MHB" in the bottom of that panel. Otherwise, the revolver appeared to be in very good condition and most importantly, it was still in its original chambering.

But what really caught my attention were the photos of the old military holster. Even though its exterior was in pretty rough shape, what made the holster so intriguing was the hand-printed inscription on the underside of the flap, which read:

Lt. M H Bluethner
5th C.M.R. Bn.

By this time curiosity was getting the best of me. Leaving the seller's website to access the computer's search engine, I typed in "5th C.M.R. Bn," to see what might be learned. The resulting information revealed that the abbreviation stood for "5th Canadian Mounted Rifles Battalion." A website dedicated to the Battalion's history reported that the 5th Canadian Mounted Rifles had been formed in 1915 as a horse-mounted infantry unit of the Canadian Expeditionary Force and was comprised of volunteers from Quebec's Eastern townships. In late 1915 the 5th Canadian Mounted Rifles Battalion shipped out for England. There the unit was converted to an infantry battalion attached to the 8th Canadian Infantry Brigade, 3rd Canadian Division, CEF. Between 1916 and 1918 the Battalion saw action in both France and Belgium. Posted on the website was an impressive list of campaigns in which

soldiers of the 5th Canadian Mounted Rifles fought, as well as battle honors accorded to the unit.

While the condition of the revolver alone seemed good enough to justify its purchase, the added bonus of the holster, coupled with the prospect of linking both items to a major chapter in history, were too much to pass up. Enticed by the possibility that further research might uncover additional details of their provenance, I bought the gun and holster. Upon receiving them, an inquiry was sent to Roy Jinks, who advised that the revolver was a Canadian Government Contract gun and had been shipped to Ottawa, Canada, on May 19, 1916. Having ascertained the factory background of the gun, the next step was to see what could be learned about Lieutenant M. H. Bluethner. Who was he? Had he been actively involved in combat, and if so, had he survived?

A bit more computer sleuthing led to the website of LIBRARY AND ARCHIVES CANADA, a Government-sponsored resource offering a wealth of information on a variety of subjects, including soldiers of the Canadian Expeditionary Force. A phone call to their offices in Ottawa confirmed that Martin Herman Bluethner, born April 26, 1892, had indeed been a member of the CEF. Furthermore, for a very reasonable processing fee, copies of his complete military records were available. Little time was lost in placing a request for Martin Bluethner's

Holster flap, w/ cap badge: This Inscription on the underside of the holster flap prompted me to purchase the .455 Second Model revolver and holster that once belonged to Lt. Martin H. Bluethner. The 5th Canadian Mounted Rifles cap badge shown here is a highly collectible item in its own right.

files. With a planned vacation trip to Europe just a few weeks away, the hope was to have the records in hand before leaving. Depending on the information contained in them, it might be possible to visit places where Martin Bluethner had been some ninety years earlier. If he had fought in France or Belgium, his files might list those locations. In the event he had not survived the War, perhaps they would disclose his resting place.

The package that arrived contained 44 pages of material. Included in the documents were copies of Martin Bluethner's attestation (enlistment) papers, medical history, casualty (injury) forms, regimental and company conduct sheets, pay records and his dispersal (discharge) certificate. The following summary of his military service was chronicled from the documentation:

Martin Herman Bluethner enlisted in the Canadian Over-Seas Expeditionary Force on January 11, 1915, at Stratford, Ontario. He was 22 years old, 5 feet, 7-1/4 inches tall, and weighed 135 lbs. According to his attestation form, he had brown hair and blue eyes. Martin's civilian occupation was "clerk" and his religion Lutheran. Upon his enlistment, Recruit Bluethner was given Regimental (military ID) Number 602173 and was assigned to the 34th Battalion.

Martin H. Bluethner at age 43. This photograph, which was affixed to his "Declaration of Intention to Become a U.S. Citizen", is the only picture of Martin Bluethner I was able to obtain. The application form was submitted on October 18, 1935. Martin was naturalized as a United States citizen on April 29, 1938, in Federal Court at Newark, NJ.

After completing cadet training, Private Bluethner shipped out for England, arriving there on November 1, 1915. While stationed with the Canadian forces at Bramshott, England, he was transferred to the 17th Reserve Battalion, CEF on March 15, 1916. On April 9, 1916, he was transferred to the 5th Canadian Mounted Rifles Battalion and embarked for France.

Throughout the 35 months that Martin Bluethner was a member of the 5th Canadian Mounted Rifles, the Battalion experienced some of the heaviest fighting of the War, in France and Belgium. The Somme, Flers-Courcelette, Ancre Heights, Vimy, Passchendaele, The Hindenburg Line and Canal du Nord were just a few of the battles in which soldiers of the 5th CMR saw intensive action.

On June 24, 1916, Private Bluethner was recommended for promotion. Corporal Bluethner was wounded on October 30, 1917. Although the records do not specify the nature of the injury, or where he was when it occurred, The 5th Canadian Mounted Rifles Battalion suffered an exceptionally high casualty rate during the costly campaign of Passchendaele, in Flanders, which took place from July 31 to November 10, 1917. The odds are very strong that Corporal Bluethner was wounded in this protracted engagement. Presumably, the injury was fairly minor, as nothing in his files indicates that he was hospitalized.

On January 1, 1918, Corporal Bluethner was promoted to sergeant. He was promoted to the rank of lieutenant on August 6, 1918. On November 8, 1918, Lieutenant Bluethner sustained a bullet wound in his right thigh. Once again, the injury apparently was not serious enough to cause him to be removed from the roster, and he was listed as remaining "at duty."

The war officially ended November 11, 1918. The 5th Canadian Mounted Rifles remained in France until February 13, 1919, when they proceeded to England. On March 8, 1919, Lieutenant Bluethner departed Liverpool, aboard the H.M.S. Carmania*, for his return to Canada. He was "struck off strength" (discharged) on March 20, 1919, In Ottawa, upon demobilization of his unit.

From his military record it appears that Martin Bluethner served honorably with the Canadian Expeditionary Force for over 49 months, 35 of those months as a member of the 5th Canadian Mounted Rifles. During the more than

four years he spent in the military, Martin Bluethner earned three field promotions and was twice wounded in the service of his Country.

What service Martin Bluethner's revolver and holster might have seen during the war was already in France. His records reflect that twice during his tour in France and Belgium, he returned briefly to England (August 8 to August 18, 1917, and March 23 to April 8, 1918). It is possible that the revolver was issued to him on one of those occasions. However, the greater probability is that the gun was privately purchased from the Canadian Government by Martin Bluethner upon his promotion to lieutenant. During the First World War it was customary for commissioned officers of the British and Canadian Armies to buy their personal sidearms from Government stores. This hypothesis seems to be supported by the title "Lt. M. H. Bluethner" inscribed on the underside of the holster flap. In all likelihood, the double broad arrow marking was stamped on the gun's frame at the time of its purchase by Lt. Bluethner.

Reconstructing Martin Bluethner's military career led to a natural curiosity about his life following the War. Also there was the question of how his revolver and holster had found their way to a firearms dealer in New Jersey, nine decades after the gun was made. Returning to the computer, an internet search was conducted for any descendants or family members who might know "the rest of the story." The Canadian Province of Ontario seemed the logical place to start, since Martin Bluethner's military records listed the town of London, Ontario, as his home. Because Bluethner is not an especially common surname, a good chance existed that someone with that last name might be related to Martin. The search turned up one listing for the name. Ironically, the gentleman who answered my phone call identified himself as Martin Bluethner.

Most cordially, Martin explained that although he believed Martin Herman Bluethner was his great uncle, after whom he had been named, he had never known the man and was unable to provide any details about his later life. Upon hearing what my research had discovered, Martin's own curiosity became piqued. Exchanging e-mail addresses, we both agreed to look further into the matter and keep each other updated on any progress made.

Over the next several weeks, a more

complete picture of Martin H. Bluethner's post-war, civilian life began to emerge. After his discharge from the Army, he was employed by the Canadian Bank of Commerce. He married Dorothy Florence Harvey on June 25, 1921, in Toronto. The wedded couple lived in Montreal, where two daughters were born to them. Martin immigrated to the United States on October 30, 1927, and established residence in Essex County, New Jersey. Six months later, on May 1, 1928, the rest of the Bluethner family joined him, making their home at 280 Gregory Avenue, in West Orange, New Jersey. On April 29, 1938, Martin Bluethner became a naturalized U.S. citizen in the Federal District Court at Newark. He continued in his banking career, starting as an auditor, and eventually attaining the position of Vice President with the Bronx Savings Bank. Martin lived out his final years in the town of Rye, in Westchester County, New York, where he died in May of 1982. He had survived one of the bloodiest conflicts in modern history and lived to a full 90 years of age.

The only remaining loose end was to determine how the revolver and holster came into the possession of the dealer who sold them to me. Through a phone call to the dealer it was learned that he bought the gun and holster from a friend. The dealer said it was his understanding that they had belonged to his friend's father. The dealer put me in touch with the friend, who told me that several years ago his father worked for a bank in the Bronx. The bank provided the gun to his father for use when he transported large sums of money via the New York subways (that must have been MANY years ago) and the man's father had retained the revolver and holster when he retired. This information would seem to fill the final gap in the story, assuming that the man's father was an employee of the Bronx Savings Bank where Martin H. Bluethner served as a Vice President.

THE MODEL 1917 HAND EJECTOR

Smith & Wesson's Model 1917 revolver can perhaps best be described as an expedient that actually worked. When President Woodrow Wilson addressed Congress on April 2, 1917, requesting a declaration of war against Germany, the official side arm of the United States Military was the semiautomatic Colt Model 1911 pistol. Much like their Commonwealth allies, American forces were faced with a severe shortage of handguns as they entered the conflict. Furthermore, the Colt factory was unable to produce Model 1911s in anywhere near the numbers sought by the military. To bolster production, Remington-UMC was awarded a contract for manufacture of the pistols. The U.S. Army's Springfield Armory also undertook the job of producing Model 1911s. But tooling up for such a project was no small task, and neither source was able to build the guns fast enough in the quantities needed.

Procuring revolvers to supplement the semiauto pistols seemed a reasonable solution to the handgun deficit. However, the Army's requirement that revolvers submitted for testing use the same rimless .45 ACP ammunition as the Model 1911 posed an engineering challenge. Smith & Wesson had been working on a Hand Ejector capable of firing the .45 ACP round and submitted samples to the Army for evaluation. The problem of extracting the rimless cartridges from a revolver cylinder was solved by means of a three-round "half-moon" clip, the design of which has been credited to Smith & Wesson President Joseph Wesson.

Following tests conducted in early June of 1917, the Army found Smith & Wesson's submission to be satisfactory for military use. The company was initially awarded a contract for 100,000 model 1917s, but according to Army records, Smith & Wesson ultimately delivered 163,634 of the revolvers to the U.S. Government between 1917 and 1919.

Utilizing the half-moon clips developed by Smith & Wesson, Colt Firearms adapted their New Service revolver to fire the .45 ACP round as well. After testing, it too was deemed an acceptable alternative to the Model 1911 pistol, and Colt was also awarded a Government contract. Like Smith & Wesson's Hand Ejector, Colt's New Service revolver was labeled the Model 1917. While there is some difference of opinion among firearms historians regarding the exact total, At least 154,802 Colt Model 1917 revolvers were delivered to the U.S. Government during the course of World War I.

Smith & Wesson's Model 1917 revolver was essentially a modified version of the .455 Second Model Hand Ejector that the company had built in large numbers for the Commonwealth nations. In addition to chambering the revolver for the .45 ACP round, modifications to the gun included shortening the barrel to 5-1/2 inches and slightly reducing bore size to better fit the .451" diameter .45 ACP bullet. Other changes were mainly cosmetic. Gone was the commercial grade finish of the .455, replaced by a faster, more utilitarian soft blue. Instead of being finely checkered, the walnut stocks of the Model 1917 were left smooth, another concession to increased production speed.

Those measures taken to expedite manufacture of the Model 1917 didn't diminish the gun's functional qualities. It proved to be a rugged, reliable substitute for the 1911. Packing the same ballistic punch as its semi-auto counterpart, and quickly re-loadable by means of the half-moon clips, Smith & Wesson's service revolver apparently was the side arm of choice for some U.S. troops. In the December 1999 issue of the NRA periodical *Man At Arms*, firearms historian Charles Pate presents a detailed study of the Smith & Wesson Model 1917. Author Pate writes that Military Police units reportedly preferred the Model 1917 revolver to the 1911 pistol.

In his article, Pate also discusses distribution and usage of the Smith & Wesson revolver, saying, "World War I use of the M1917 was fairly extensive, but primarily by combat support and combat services support troops rather than infantrymen or the cavalry…many thousands were shipped directly to ports of embarkation for subsequent shipment to Europe, and the revolvers clearly played a significant role in the war."

Background research on the Model 1917 in my collection shows that it was shipped from the Smith & Wesson Factory to the Springfield Armory on June 8, 1918. The gun has the standard stampings of "UNITED STATES PROPERTY" on the underside of the barrel and "U.S. ARMY MODEL 1917" on the bottom of the grip frame behind the lanyard ring. It bears the usual Government inspector's markings. These include a small provisional acceptance stamp on the left side of the frame behind the trigger, as well as the Ordnance insignia final acceptance stamp (a flaming bomb) on the left side of the frame in front of the hammer. Although this Model 1917 has obviously seen use, the overall condition of the gun is excellent. Regrettably, other than the information obtained from Smith & Wesson factory records, little is known about the history of this particular firearm. What role this revolver may have played in the War effort will probably forever remain a mystery.

RANGE TESTING THE GUNS

Even though the three World War I-era revolvers presented in this article are in great shape, none of them can be described as "mint." In this writer's opinion that makes them all eminently shootable. As well as being an enjoyable diversion, a range session with these three Hand Ejectors, using ammunition that replicates the performance of the original military rounds, should also provide some practical insight into the power and accuracy of the handguns used by Allied forces in the Great War.

Finding modern .45 ACP ammunition that duplicates the load used by the American doughboys is not a problem. The classic loading of a 230-grain round nose, jacketed bullet, propelled at a muzzle velocity of approximately 800 fps, is still produced by several ammo makers.

Obtaining modern .455 Webley Mark II ammunition is a little more problematic. Due to low consumer demand in the U.S., for many years this archaic round was not offered by any domestic manufacturer. The Italian firm Fiocchi was about the only commercial source of new, non-corrosive .455 Mark II ammo. Bullet weight of the Fiocchi loading is 262 grains, rather than the nominal 265 grains of the original round, but such a slight weight difference should be of no consequence.

Hornady recently added .455 Mark II ammunition to their product line. To the best of my knowledge, this is the first American company to catalog the old British chambering in well over half a century.

In years past, the British firm Kynoch also marketed .455 Mark II ammunition. However, their present website lists only centerfire rifle rounds for sale, and it is unclear if they currently make handgun ammunition in any caliber.

At one time, Canadian Industries Limited (CIL) loaded .455 Colt ammunition under their Dominion label. Although this cartridge is approximately one tenth of an inch longer than the .455 Webley Mark II case and its muzzle velocity is over 150 fps faster than the Mark II load, .455 Colt ammo can safely be used in First and Second Model Hand Ejectors. This is because like Webley & Scott, Smith & Wesson also bored the chambers of their .455 revolvers deep

enough to accept the greater case length of the original .455 Mark I black powder round. Case dimensions of the .455 Colt are similar to those of the .455 Mark I. But from what I can determine, .455 Colt ammunition is no longer made.

While World War I military surplus .455 Mark II ammunition is quite rare, occasionally quantities of surplus .455 Mark VI ammo from the Second World War are encountered. Unfortunately, World War II military surplus .455 ammunition has also become quite collectable and using it for recreational shooting is not really cost effective.

Inventorying the .455 Mark II ammunition I have accumulated over time yielded usable amounts of Fiocchi, Hornady, and Kynoch brands, as well as a handfull of World War II Mark VI Canadian surplus ammo. Modern, commercial .455 Mark II ammo is loaded with hollow base, lead bullets, much like the original military ammunition. A sample bullet was pulled from each of the three brands of .455 Mark II ammo to be used for the range tests, along with a World War II Mark VI jacketed round. The diameter of each bullet was measured with a micrometer, and each bullet was weighed. The following data was obtained:

Manufacturer	Type	Bullet Dia.	Bullet Weight
Fiocchi	(lead)	.454"	262.3 grains
Hornady	(lead)	.452"	264.6 grains
Kynoch	(lead)	.445"	265.3 grains
WWII Mark VI	(jacketed)	.454"	266.7 grains

The Hornady bullet has an unusual post swaged into the center of the base cavity. Evidentally the post is meant to facilitate obturation of the bullet's skirt.

All three brands of .455 ammo, and

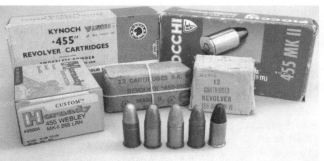

Commercial .455 Mark II ammunition used in the range tests included Fiocchi, Hornady and Kynoch brands. Also shown are a string-tied 2-pack of military .455 Mark II ammunition, dated 1922 and a World War II box of .455 Mark VI Ammo, both of Canadian manufacture. The front row comprises assorted military & commercial rounds.

a box of commercial Remington-Peters .45 ACP 230-grain ball ammunition, were used in testing the vintage revolvers at a local range. To eliminate human error, a Ransom Rest was employed for the accuracy tests. Bullet speeds were measured with a ProChrono brand digital chronograph positioned 10 feet from the muzzle. Although distances in close-quarter trench combat were probably much shorter, the target was placed at 25 yards.

For the tests, each revolver was clamped into the Ransom Rest and a dozen rounds were run through the gun to settle it into the grip inserts. Once the revolver was solidly secured in the machine rest, 18 rounds (three cylinders full) of each brand of ammunition were fired in the gun. Accuracy was determined by measuring the extreme spread of each six shot group, center-to-center, and then calculating the three-group averages.

The testing process began with the .455 First Model. Eighteen rounds each of Fiocchi, Hornady and Kynoch ammunition were fired in the gun. While the Hornady product delivered the smallest average group size of 2.81 inches, it also turned in the lowest velocity, clocking an average 566 fps from the Triple Lock.

preserve my small remaining stock of Kynoch .455 ammunition, only Fiocchi and Hornady brands were tested in the Second Model Hand Ejector. The Fiocchi ammo produced the smaller average group size of 4.56 inches, as well as the higher velocity, averaging 615 fps.

An older box of commercial Remington-Peters 230-grain, .45 ACP ball ammo was used in testing the Model 1917. The rounds were loaded into half-moon clips, much the same as ammunition used by American Doughboys in World War One. The three group average for the Model 1917 measured 4.49 inches and bullet speed averaged 807 fps.

Full results of the 25 yard range tests are listed in the accompanying table:

Ballistics Test Results

Revolver	Ammunition	Velocity	Average group (")
.455 1st Model	Fiocchi .455 Mk II	629 fps	3.87
	Hornady .455 Mk II	566 fps	2.81
	Kynoch .455 Mk II	627 fps	3.11
455 2nd Model	Fiocchi .455 Mk II	615 fps	4.56
	Hornady .455 Mk II	546 fps	5.12
Model 1917	R-P .45 ACP (Ball)	807 fps	4.49

Upon completion of the Ransom Rest tests, I decided to try a little off-hand shooting before leaving the range. The gun selected was the .455 Second Model, as I was curious to see how the revolver might have felt to Lt. Martin Bluethner 90 years ago. Filling the cylinder with a half-dozen rounds of the Fiocchi ammo, I took a six o'clock hold on a 10-inch-tall rock about 35 yards out. The rock, which was located at the base of a safe, earthen backstop, approximated the size of a man's head. Shooting was done from a standing position, using a two hand grip, firing single-action (probably not the way Lt. Bluethner was taught). Despite the narrow, rounded front sight blade, I had little trouble keeping all my shots on the rock. This would seem contrary to the showing the gun had just given from the machine rest. I can't explain it, but that's what happened.

In addition to being pleasantly surprised at the off-hand accuracy of the gun, I was favorably impressed by how mild the recoil of a 262-grain bullet traveling at 600 fps feels when fired from a 37-ounce revolver. Light recoil means faster recovery time between shots, a definite plus in short-range fighting. The British may have had something after all, with their affinity for heavy, slow-moving bullets.

Though I tried to approach the range session objectively, with no precon-ceived notions or expectations, the test results proved somewhat surprising. Perhaps subconsciously I assumed the old Hand Ejectors would deliver better accuracy than they did. Prior to this, the only .45 caliber Smith & Wesson revolver I had tried in the Ransom Rest was my Model 25-2 chambered in .45 ACP. With select loads, that gun will regularly group under 1-1/2 inches at 25 yards. Past experience with the Model 25-2 may have influenced my thinking, creating unrealistic expectations of the vintage Smiths.

I suppose it's possible that the .455 Mark II service ammunition issued in the First World War might have shot better in one or both of my .455 revolvers than the commercial ammo used in these informal tests. In regard to the Model 1917, limiting the test to a single brand of .45 ACP ball certainly limits the validity of the findings as well. It is not at all unusual for a handgun to shoot admira-bly with one brand of ammunition and abysmally with another.

Still, the lackluster performance of the three Hand Ejectors prompted a search for information about the handgun accuracy standards of either the British, or U.S. Armies during World War One. Checking the assorted reference mate-rial on my bookshelves proved relatively unproductive. Charles Pate's excellent and very comprehensive book, *U.S. Handguns of World War II*, contains cop-ies of United States Army specifications for secondary pistols and revolvers used in the Second World War. On Page 327 the accuracy requirements for .38 caliber revolvers, both .38 Special and .38-200, are described in a memorandum dated January 26, 1944. The memo reads: "Revolvers shall be tested for accuracy by firing six shots at a 2-¾ inch bull's-eye, 15 yards from the muzzle. An arm rest shall be used, and sights held at six o'clock. All the shots shall be in or cutting the bull's-eye. Full loads shall be used."

While this circa 1944 memo was helpful, it didn't address the question of military handgun accuracy standards during the First World War. Failing to find reference to the subject in my re-sources, I consulted one of the foremost authorities on such matters, firearms historian and author, again Charles Pate. Mr. Pate graciously informed me that in all of his research he had never come across any documentation dealing with World War One military standards of handgun accuracy for either revolvers, or the Model 1911 pistol. I asked him if the U.S. Army had a set of criteria for rejecting Model 1911s. He said they did, but poor accuracy wasn't one of them.

From all indications, in 1917 the United States Army wasn't overly concerned about pin-point accuracy from their sidearms. Apparently, if a handgun could reliably place a disabling hit on a man-size target at trench-fighting distances, it was considered acceptable. There is no question that the three World War I-era Hand Ejectors demonstrated that capability. As a point of interest, the official handgun qualification target currently used by many law enforcement agencies is the NRA, TQ-19, man-size silhouette. On the TQ-19 the area of the torso where a hit is considered disabling measures 11-1/2 inches wide, by 15 inches high (not including the neck and head). The kill zone (heart and upper thorax) measures 6-1/2 inches wide by 4 inches high. All three of the Hand Ejectors kept their hits within those parameters. Even though the vintage revolvers might not win any competitive matches, they certainly posses a level of functional accuracy adequate for their intended purpose.

CONCLUSION

These three Smith & Wesson revolv-ers and their contemporaries are tangible pieces of history, having earned this distinction through stalwart service with British, Canadian and American forces during the first global conflict of the 20th century. Their duties long completed, the guns now quietly reside in my modest collection. Occasionally they are brought out to be admired for the craftsmanship that went into their manufacture, or to be subjects of conjecture over their role in past world events. However, this was the first time in untold years that they have actually been fired. Shooting the old Smiths was both enjoyable and enlightening. The experience also evoked a sense of personal connection with the Allied soldiers who fought, and in too many cases, made the ultimate sacrifice during the Great War.

Their range session finished, the three World War I veterans were packed up to be taken home, given a good cleaning and put away. Most assuredly they will not be forgotten, nor will the generation of young men who carried them. Over nine decades have passed since peace was declared on that first Armistice Day, November 11th, 1918. Virtually all those who fought in the "War to End All Wars" are now gone. But these three revolvers and others like them remain as an unforgotten link to that time and those men.

THE LITTLE BROWNIE THAT CHALLENGED THE WORLD:

The Mossberg·Brownie (1919-1932)

BY JACK A. MYERS

HOW THE BROWNIE CAME TO BE

Before the world-wide sales success of its little Brownie pistol launched the O.F. Mossberg & Sons company to its well deserved world-wide recognition, Oscar F. Mossberg had already gained knowledge and experience in the field of gun manufacturing and sales.

Oscar was an industrious young Swede of 22 when he immigrated to America in 1866. And 53 years later, in 1919, he introduced his Brownie pistol, the first and only handgun his small company ever produced. That small company continues today and now holds the distinction of being America's oldest surviving, family-owned, gunmaking company. In my opinion, the little Brownie is as much an example of the American gunmaker's art as Sam Colt's earliest revolver or Oliver Winchester's first lever action rifle.

A truly unique little pocket pistol, Mossberg's Brownie was a four-barrel double-action handgun that weighs in at just 10 ozs. and is 4.5 inches overall, with a cluster of four 2.5-inch barrels. A single pull of the trigger cocks and fires the first barrel and on the same stroke revolves the firing pin to the next barrel's chamber. It is chambered for the .22 Short, Long, or Long Rifle cartridge. Every Brownie left the shop with a small manual extractor rod fitted in a small well behind the left grip. The top of the gun has a very small rectangular opening at top left to accommodate this rod. (Extractor rods are usual missing from the older guns, but new reproduction rods that cannot be distinguished from the originals are readily available on the internet.) Although all of the estimated 33,404 Brownies produced shared the same appearance, with a rich, blued finish and ridged black walnut grips, some were roll stamped with different patent information on the right side of the barrel cluster.

Contemporary writers have reported that due to its diminutive size, ease of concealability, and near superiority to other designs available at the time, the Brownie was an attractive and appealing all-purpose handgun. It was named after a similarly-endowed mythical character which was very popular in that era's literature: the Brownie, a fictitious elfin character created in the late 1800s by Canadian illustrator Palmer Cox (1840-1924). Though perhaps hard to appreciate today, Cox's Brownies were as popular in late-Victorian America as Smurfs would be a century later, and their name inspired a number of popular consumer products. The very popular Kodak "Brownie" camera is a good example; another is the junior division of the American Girl Scouts, founded in 1912, which added a branch for younger girls in grades two and three called "Brownies" with this explanation: "Our Brownie age level gets its name from folk tales of little brownies that would enter homes and help the occupants with housework. This sets the tone for Brownie Scouts who are learning to help others."

The information we share here will not be a detailed report of the company's early years, but more a synopsis of discoveries about the variations of Brownies that have surfaced over the ensuing years. Both collectors and dealers want to know more how they can recognize an unusual, rare, scarce, or oddball Brownie from the more commonly found specimens, than to study the company history. I feel sure there are more discoveries to come of heretofore unrecognized variations of the Brownie.

Early writers have described Oscar's involvement with the design and production of other small, easily concealed handguns sold by the the the C.S.Shattuck Co., stating he was first awarded a patent in 1906 for a four-barrel pistol which came to be known as the Shattuck "Unique" or "Invisible Defender." We know the name "Novelty" has also been used in connection with those early pistols. Those early researchers have also detailed how he toiled alone in his one-man shop in a loft at Hatfield, Massachusetts, to produce those guns for his employers. Mossberg subsequently worked for the Stevens Arms Company and Marlin-Rockell in a variety of production management positions.

In 1919, at the tender age of 75, Oscar –

An original Brownie, as drawn by Canadian illustrator Palmer Cox (1840-1924).

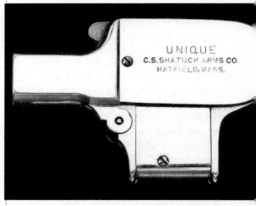

"Unique" palm pistol made by Mossberg for C. S. Shattuck. Note misspelling of "Shattuck" on roll marking.

under the auspices of his newly-formed company, O.F. Mossberg & Sons – started producing his new Brownie pistol, almost a full year before receiving the patent for it. Oscar filed an application for his Brownie with the U.S. Patent Office on Aug. 28, 1919. His patent (number 1,348,035) was awarded July 27, 1920. It's interesting to note that unlike most such patent applications of that era, the guns he produced actually matched the drawings he had submitted! It is recorded that Oscar moved his gun production facilities to New Haven, Connecticut and still later moved again into larger facilities in New Haven and hired a few mechanically knowledgeable helpers from among his Swedish friends.

NUMBER OF BROWNIES PRODUCED

Since there are no known surviving factory records to verify the actual number of units produced in Oscar's 13 years of fabricating Brownies, guesstimated figures for a total number range from 32,000 to 37,000. Since I've been keeping a database on observed and reported serial numbers on these guns, the highest serial number I would consider reliable is 33,404, found on a gun in Florida. And although I was told of a serial numbered gun lower than any other reported, I never saw it except in a couple of photos, and the person who reported it did not answer my request for additional photographic proof. Therefore, the lowest number I can personally attest to is in my collection and is number 212.

This leads to some interesting speculation. Oscar Mossberg began production of the Brownie in 1919, before receiving the patent he had applied for in August of that year and which was not granted until nearly a year later, on July 27, 1920. Now, do the math. For Oscar to have produced my estimated 33,404 units from 1919 to 1932, as reported, the output of his shop facilities would have to have averaged 2,569 units annually. That averages out at 214 units per week, or 31 units per day. Therefore my Brownie numbered 212 could conceivably have been produced the first or second week of production and was handled by Oscar himself!

However, when one considers the amount of time Oscar probably spent on preparation and experimentation with various production methods, it's doubtful #212 left his shop until sometime

in perhaps the first month. Previous reports are not clear on how many helpers, if any, Oscar hired at the very beginning. Though the name of the company includes "& Sons," his boys were aged 21 and 23 at the time, so is very probably that he hired some more experienced help for his assembly process.

TOUGH TIMES DEMANDED TOUGH SALES TACTICS

Early Brownie ads were primarily aimed at the outdoorsman type of prospective buyer such as hunters, trappers, fishermen and such. As that dark decade of the 1920s inexorably moved toward the Great Crash of 1929 and resulting mass unemployment, many men were resorting to such outdoor vocations in order to feed their families. The initial price of the Brownie was $5. Six years later, probably due to Oscar's improved production methods, Taylor Fur of New York was offering the Brownie for just $3.45 in their 1926 advertisements!

The Brownie ads state they would be shipped "postpaid" anywhere in the U.S.. The Brownie was delivered in a small, very plain, boxed unmarked in any manner. The boxes in my collection measure 4.75" X 3.5" X 1" deep, just big enough to accommodate the Brownie, wrapped in brown oiled paper, and accompanied by factory papers. Other writers have reported that these fragile boxes were produced in blue, red or black solid colors with no particular color being more common than any other. The specimens I have are solid black, and the only other two I've been told of were also black. The boxes, being composed of paper, have a much lesser degree of survivabilty than the guns they contained and are therefore more rare to find than the guns themselves. The current price of these guns in Very Good to Excellent condition, with their original box and papers, is quite high. One such specimen advertised nationally in a gun publication in 2007 for $799 was already sold when I inquired about it.

It's interesting to note that the boxes

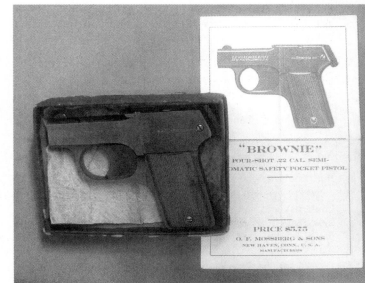

Brownie in original factory box.

I've handled were of simple cardboard construction, but were then covered with the colored paper that has a somewhat "pebbled" texture to it. It had to have been more expensive to use a plain box with that extra step of production necessary to glue that colored and textured paper over every surface of the box, except most of the interior! I've not yet resolved that puzzling feature.

VARIATION #1

The information stamped into the right side of the barrel cluster on these earliest guns is shown in the photo at left. In italicized type it reads: PAT. APPL'D.FOR. There are no spaces between the abbreviated words.

The location of the serial numbers on this variation may be found in five

Location of serial numbers on Variation #1.

different locations: 1) under the right grip, on the edge of the gripstrap, down at bottom; 2) with gun open, on right side of the barrel cluster, down near the hinge; 3) with gun open, look up under the little "ears" on the front of the barrel latch lever which lies along the top of the gun; 4) & 5) on back of both metal side plates on receiver section of the gun. Some of the earlier guns also had the serial number written in pencil on the back of the wooden grips. We estimate this model was produced from 1919 until mid-1923 and that there were probably between 10,000 and 11,000 produced.

NOTE 1: So far there have been only 50 of the Variation #1 reported to our database. This is 32.25% of the total production, not quite one third.

NOTE 2: Due to the length of some serial numbers and the limited space available on some parts, only the last three or four digits of the whole number may be found. These are typically found in locations 2) and 3) shown in the photo, and on back of grips.

NOTE 3: The muzzle of the barrels has not been chamfered (beveled) as on later guns. The face of the muzzle is completely flat.

NOTE 4: Unlike some later Brownies, there is no pin at top center of the metal plate on the right side. Below are photos of the two types of sideplate. Earlier Variations #1 and #2 had no pin.

Location of the pin that identifies later variations. Variation #1 (front) has no pin.

Warning Regarding Disassembly

The metal side plates on the Brownie have a single screw towards the rear holding them to the frame. When you remove that screw, *do not pry up* on the plate. This usually results in the sharp edges of both the plate and the frame being marred beyond repair. These metal side plates are beveled into the frame at the front edge. After removing the screw *gently* loosen the plate by lifting it and/or moving it up and down to loosen it from the frame. Once loose, slide it to the rear for removal. CAUTION: There are some variations with an alignment pin through the metal plate on the right side. On these Brownies, once the screw is removed you must gently lift the rear of the plate until it just clears the top of the pin before sliding it to the rear.

VARIATION #2

Variation #2 differs from Variation #1 only in that the stamped patent information on the right side of the barrel cluster reads: PAT'D.JAN.27,1920. That is the date which was discovered to be in error. The patent papers are plainly marked as July, not January. I've had only six Variation #2 specimens reported to the database. These represent just under 4% of the total number reported. This would indicate 1,260 units probably were produced from mid-1923 to early in

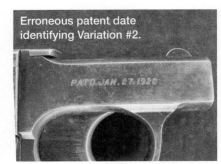

Erroneous patent date identifying Variation #2.

1924, a guesstimated total of 1,260 units. Personally, I have a hunch it may have been even less.

VARIATION #2.5

Variation #2.5 differs from Variation #2 in ways which strongly indicate it to be a short-run transitional piece to the later Variation #3, which the company seems to have eventually settled on and produced in greatest volume. The serial numbers can be found in the same locations as on Variations #1 and #2. The only visible external clue that this is not one of those two earlier variations is that no alignment pin is found in the metal plate on the right side, even though it has the correct patent date stamped on it, which would immediately identify it as a Variation #3. The patent info reads: PAT. JULY 27, 1920. It's interesting to note that the stamped patent information on Variation #2.5 has a space separating each word or group of numerals.

Alignment pin absent

July patent date

No external serial number on butt

Identifying characteristics of Variation 2.5.

This particular example of Variation 2.5 is a very recent discovery and only three specimens have been observed thus far. They represent only 1.3% of the total production, or less than 400 units produced, probably for only 30 days or so early in 1924. The serial numbers on the reported specimens are just 725 apart, which if Oscar followed the usually consecutive numbering of each piece, would mean there may be at least another 723 units out there. Whichever figures one uses, this means that Variation #2.5 is currently the rarest of the Brownie family and should, especially in the future, demand a premium in its selling price.

VARIATION #3

Variation #3 had the longest production period and therefore the most units of production, making it the most often encountered Brownie variation found. The stamping found on the right side of the barrel cluster of this variation is the same as the previous Variation #2.5: PAT. JULY 27, 1920. An estimated

Brownie Variation #3.
Note alignment pin, which
distinguishes it from Variation #2.

20,977 units were produced from 1924 until the end of its production in 1932. Both of the boxed specimens I've managed to obtain are the Variation #3. It stands to reason that since these were the most recently made guns, the better their chance to have survived in Very Good, or Excellent, and even New condition. (Unfired, pristine guns with their original box and factory papers have come to be commonly known as NIB, or New In Box.) Only four boxes have been reported thus far.

Variation #3 is easily identified by the small alignment pin through top center of the right side metal plate. Its serial numbers are stamped into the bottom of the butt; on right side of the barrel cluster down near the hinge; and under the small "ears" on front of the barrel latch lever along the top of the gun.

NOTE: The full serial number is on butt while the other two stampings may only be the last few digits due to space available, and, these latter two locations can only be seen when the barrel cluster is lowered for loading.

OTHER VARIATIONS?

There is a very good possibility that there are even more variations of this little pistol than the four reported here. Variation #2.5 was discovered only because I had learned to start observing every survivor for the slightest difference from any Brownie heretofore known. I then noticed there was a specimen that had the patent date of one variation but lacked the pinned side plate of that variation. Possibly parts

from two different variations joined, I thought? Soon after that a similar survivor became available. The main difference was that the later one was in excellent condition and not likely to be a hodgepodge of parts from different guns.

In the fairly recent past I've observed other, more startling types of Brownies but have passed them off as home-made fabrications involving some original factory parts and a lot of imagination, mainly because none of them had their particular unusual feature ever advertised as available from the factory. There is also a possibility they were experimental display pieces to show and learn if there was a demand for their particular feature. However, nothing has ever been noted in print from that era about such experimental items. Now I'm not so sure. I may have erred and passed up a great opportunity to unearth and disclose a fifth variation. The moral of the story is: keep your eyes open and keep looking. Maybe you will be announcing the finding of a new Brownie!

A WORD OF ADVICE

For those who would like to fire one of these old-timers, be advised they were designed in an era before the advent of our modern steels and higher velocity ammunition. Therefore a real danger exists that the gun may be damaged, and/or the shooter injured, when firing one of these guns using modern hi-vel ammo. I have owned one such Brownie which had a large chunk of metal blown out of the area between the chambers! And as always, with all older guns it's a good idea to have it inspected by a reliable and competent gunsmith before firing it.

Mystery Mossberg?

The 1979 issue of Gun Digest heralded the coming of a Mossberg "Combat Model" .45 pistol which would be ready for delivery "at the end of this year" for just under $350. One stainless steel prototype automatic pistol evidently was available for display at the NRA show that year. It would be interesting to know at this late date exactly what became of that prototype and why the production of that gun never proceeded.

That same Gun Digest article goes on to state that this was not the only Mossberg entry into the handgun field. It outlines how Security Industries of America had a small-frame 5-shot revolver they'd been developing but to which Mossberg had obtained the rights "and will be producing it soon." Oh, yeah?

Interesting to note, in that article the author calls our beloved Brownie "anything but a howling success," and notes that "it soon disappeared from the scene." The author further says of the Brownie, "Today it's a lesser collector's item."

The author finishes his story with this statement: "This time Mossberg seems to have taken a more likely tack and we expect to see a good shooter response to these two guns." Hmmmmm.... That was written just 30 years ago. The author obviously did not have access to a crystal ball.

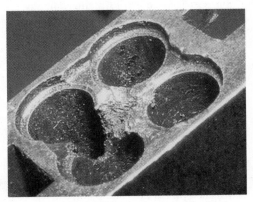

Brownie chamber blowout caused by high-velocity ammunition.

The ARs of Olympic Arms

BY **STEVE GASH**

The AR-15 rifle is one of the most popular rifle designs of all time, and for good reason. It is reliable, accurate, durable, and can be had in an almost unbelievable array of configurations. Demand is at an all-time high, and everybody, it seems, is building ARs.

Olympic Arms, Inc., unlike some other AR companies, makes all their major components in-house, rather than getting them from outside sources. Olympic has direct and total control over their manufacturing processes, which results in high-quality end products. Couple that with very competitive prices and you have a recipe for business success. A comprehensive and highly varied product line doesn't hurt, either, and it would be surprising if Olympic doesn't make an AR that trips your trigger.

The firm that is now Olympic Arms has been in the gun business since 1956, but it did not start out building ARs. Company founder Robert Schuetz began manufacturing gun barrels as the Schuetzen Gun Works in Colorado Springs, Colorado. In 1975, the company moved to its current location in Olympia, Washington, and in 1982, changed its name to Olympic Arms.

Olympic is still a family-run business. Robert's son Brian serves as Vice President and oversees manufacturing. Robert's daughter, Diane Haupert, handles the administrative side of things as Chief Financial Officer. The company's 16,000 square-foot plant in Washington employees about sixty people, and their casting facility in Costa Mesa, California, employs another twenty folks.

Olympic's manufacturing processes utilize state-of-the art CNC machines that finish parts in a single operation and eliminate "tolerance stacking" that can occur when several machines perform operations on a single part. Remember that the AR is an "assembled" gun, not a "fitted" gun. Top-quality component parts are the key to quality.

Upper receivers come either with a carry handle with a rear sight, or a flat top with Picatinny rails. Gas blocks can have an A2 front sight that is compatible with the carry handle rear sight, or can be flat top so as to not interfere with the optics. Heavyweight bull barrels with a crowned muzzle or more slender military weights with an A2 flash suppressor are made in lengths from 16 to 24 inches, and more than one twist rate is available.

As expected, lowers are pretty much interchangeable with different uppers so that the user can swap out a varmint upper to make a big game rig or vice versa. All of the controls are in the familiar places, and operate like you expect them to. And Olympic AR triggers are some of the best I've ever tested.

I count about 23 different models of ARs in the current Olympic line. The exquisite "Ultramatch" (UM) and "Servicematch" (SM) models come with true .223 Remington chambers while virtually all of the other .22-caliber ARs have mil-spec 5.56mm chambers. (Both of my Olympic ARs are 5.56, and shoot all .223 loads with no problems whatsoever.) Standard twist for the UM model is 1:10-inch, but a 1:8-inch is avail-

The pin-point accuracy of this Olympic K8 target model is enhanced by the superlative Burris 4.5-14x40 Fullfield II Tactical scope. The Ballistic Plex reticle aids in long-range shooting. The Tactical rings of the proper height are also from Burris.

The "Gamestalker" rifle is new for 2010 is chambered to the .300 Olympic Super Short Magnum (OSSM). Olympic says it's designed for North American big game hunting. The efficient little round duplicates .30-06 ballistics out of a 22-inch barrel. You can't get much more American than that. (Photo courtesy of Olympic Arms.)

able. This is reversed in the SM rifle, where 1:8-inch is the standard and 1:10 the option. For the majority of the 5.56 models, 1:9-inch is standard.

An interesting variant is the 16-inch barreled K3B-FAR, which has A2 sights and flash suppressor, and a six-position collapsible stock. The K7 is similar but comes with a fixed A2 stock. The K4B also has A2 everything, but comes with a 20-inch barrel. This model is also available in 6.8 Remington SPC. The Model K74 in 5.45x39 Russian features the collapsible stock. The LT series has ACE FX skeleton stocks, ERGO grips, and free-floating four-rail aluminum handguards that surround 16-inch barrels. The GI-16 is a military look-alike with a collapsible stock. The K3B-CAR has an 11.5-inch barrel, but has a permanently-attached A1 flash suppressor so it's legal for civilians.

To my way of thinking, the K16 is the most practical AR around. With a crowned 16-inch match stainless bull barrel, 1:9-inch twist, A2 stock, flat tops, and free-floated handguard, it's a gem. It's also available in 6.8 SPC (as the model K1668).

Lovers of pistol cartridges in ARs are not forgotten, with the K9, K10, K40, and K45 models. in 9mm Parabellum, 10mm, .40 S&W and .45 ACP, respectively. They have 16-inch barrels, collapsible stocks and a specially designed pistol-caliber flash suppressor. There are even 6.5-inch barreled "pistols" in 5.56m (the OA-93 and K23P models).

For those of us on a budget, Olympic makes what they call their "Plinker Plus" models in 5.56. Of standard configuration, the MSRP on the 16-inch barreled model is only $713.70 and $843.70 for one with a 20-inch barrel. ARs don't get any less expensive than that, folks.

For big game, the K8-MAG is available in .223, .243, and .25 WSSM calibers. These models are available with 24-inch, 1:10-inch twist barrels, and flat-top everything, so they're optics ready from the get-go.

For those who think a big game caliber ought to start with (at least) a "3," there is the brand new Gamestalker rifle in the equally new .300 Olympic Super Short Magnum (OSSM). Accordingly to company literature, this little gem propels a 150-gr. bullet at about 3,000 fps and is ballistically superior to the .30-06. The Gamestalker has a 22-inch barrel with a 12-inch twist. Hunter Shack Muni-

The versatile ARs are now well accepted as legitimate hunting arms, after years of opposition from those who resisted hunting with what they viewed as "military arms."

tions (HSM) makes loaded ammunition, but the case is easily formed from .25 WSSM brass. Hornady makes the dies, and Hodgdon has load data in the works, so handloaders will have a field day with this one. For those who already have a complete AR, an upper in .300 OSSM is also available; I have one on order and can't wait to try it.

At a SHOT Show a few years back, I decided that I would concentrate on ARs, and (if possible) pick one that, as Goldilocks said, was not too hot, not

One of the (many) beauties of the AR platform is the almost endless variety of configurations that are possible. For example, a 5.56mm plinker or target model can quickly and inexpensively be converted to a great hunting gun by simply swapping out the uppers, producing a rifle similar to this K8-MAG in .25 WSSM.

Olympic Arms makes a comprehensive array of ARs in many calibers that are suitable for hunting, target shooting, home defense, and law enforcement. Here are, at top, a 16-inch barreled model K16 in 5.56mm. and, below, the "Target-Match" model K8 with a 20-inch barrel. Both models feature stainless steel barrels with a 1:9-inch twist.

too cold, but just right. I didn't know what I was in for. ARs were everywhere: long ones, short ones, fat-barrelled and skinny ones, odd-looking sights, and various appliances hanging off of the multitudinous rails that decorated the receivers and handguards. I was in a serious funk.

Then, as if by divine guidance, I happened upon the Olympic Arms exhibit. Affable Tom Spithaler thrust out his hand and said, "Hi, what can I help you with?" Tom is Olympic's Sales Director, and as such is a veritable walking encyclopedia on their ARs. I gave him my by now well-rehearsed spiel: no

sights, target-type barrel, 9-inch twist, nice trigger, and a cost that didn't break the bank. I explained that I was a merely recreational shooter (that's gun writer code for "clod-busting plinker").

I figured he'd start off with the same tired litany I'd heard a dozen times, like "Well, we usually go with a XRM-Q laser sight, a water-cooled, belt-fed action with a collapsible flash-and-dash thing-a-ma-bob on the barrel, and a gross of 45-round teflon-coated camo magazines for back-up, just in case." Instead, Tom just said, "No problem. Would you like that with a 16- or 20-inch barrel?" At last, someone who offered what I wanted!

Tom showed me their K16 and K8 models in 5.56mm – both appeared (to me, at least) exactly the same except for barrel length. When I fondled the K8, it was lust at first glance: a 416 stainless steel "Ultra Match" barrel with a 9-inch twist, flat top everything, no sights, and a very nice trigger. It reeked of quality, and the price was quite reasonable (MSRP $908.70). I ordered one, and it has exceeded my expectations. (I later bought a K16 in 5.56, too. It also sports a 416 stainless match barrel.)

In about 2007, the then-new 6.8mm Remington SPC was introduced at the behest of the U.S. military. (Its military

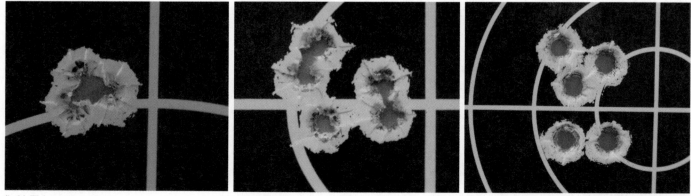

(left) This ragged hole was made with the K8 and the 50-gr. Hornady V-MAX over 25.8 grains of IMR-8208XBR. Velocity was 3,052 fps. (middle) My favorite Olympic AR is the K16 in 6.8 SPC, as it delivers accuracy and power in a compact package. The 85-gr. Barnes Triple Shock-X and 31.0 grains of AA-2230 produced this great group. Velocity was a peppy 2,711 fps. (right) The .25 WSSM AR doted on a diet of the 110-gr. Hornady InterBond spiced up by 46.3 grains of Reloder 19 at 2,891 fps.

designation is 6.8x43mm.) The 6.8 is based on the old .30 Remington case, and at 2.26 inches in length, it fit into AR-15 magazines like a glove. "SPC" stands for "Special Purpose Cartridge," and that purpose, of course, is that when the bad guys are shot, they stay shot.

When I learned that the Olympic Model K16 was available in 6.8, I ordered one. It also has a stainless steel barrel and is undoubtedly the pick of the AR litter. The 6.8 cartridge is a terrific performer. It is really just a "short" .270, as the bullet diameter is the *uber*-popular .277 inch. Let's face it, the 6.8 is what the .223 would be if it could. It shoots heavier bullets and packs more down-range punch. And it's accurate.

A recent assignment brought to my door yet another Olympic AR, this one a Model K8-MAG in .25 WSSM. It has a portly 24-inch barrel, and consequently it's a little heavy, but does it shoot! And the .25 WSSM rivals the lovely old .25-06 ballistically. What's not to like?

In the past 30 years or so, I have tested and written-up literally dozens of bolt-action rifles and have come to the realization that big game rifles that shoot 1-inch groups are the exception, not the rule. After shooting the Olympic ARs and other makes, and from observing friends' ARs in action, I have come to the sobering conclusion, shared by multitudes of AR shooters, that almost any box-stock AR will shoot rings around the average factory bolt gun.

A K16 in 6.8 SPC Remington dressed for success: A Leupold 6x scope, high rings for a proper cheek-weld, and a C Products 17-round magazine stuffed with handloads featuring the new 110-gr. Nosler AccuBond bullet.

I have shot all three of my ARs and the .25 WSSM loaner with a variety of factory and handloads, and have experienced exactly zero problems – nary a malfunction, save the occasional too-light starting handload common to any gas-banger, and accuracy with all of them has been very good to excellent. I have tried most of the new varmint .22 bullets and .223 factory fodder with excellent results. Here are a few of (the many) shooting highlights.

SHOOTING IMPRESSIONS

I got the K8 first, so let's start with it. With its heavy 20-inch barrel, the K8 sits like a rock on the bags, and just punches out ragged holes. It is a death-ray in prairie dog towns. While a host of loads perform well, I'd probably have to pick either the 55-gr. Nosler Ballistic Tip over 24.0 grains of Ram Shot's X-Terminator or the 60-gr. Hornady V-MAX ahead of 23.6 grains of Hodgdon's new super powder IMR-8208XBR. The K8's nine-inch twist allows it to handle bullets up to the stellar 69-gr. Sierra MatchKing, and the Federal factory load with it averages .74 inch. Sierra's 63-gr. Semi Spitzer and 65-gr. Spitzer Boat Tail bullets are also terrific. If you need a load with deep penetration for bigger small game, check out the 62-gr. Barnes Triple Shock-X with 23.1 grains of IMR-8208XBR.

The K16, with a barrel four inches shorter than the K8's, actually gives up little in velocity, and it is fully as accurate. The 40-gr. Nosler Ballistic Tip is super at 3,494 fps with 24.2 grains of Vihtavuori N-130 powder, and is a ground-squirrel vaporizer. But loads with 50- to 55-gr. bullets get the most use, and the Hornady 50-gr.V-MAX really cooks with 26.2 grains of Varget. The Nosler Ballistic Tip of the same weight favors 25.3 grains of X-Terminator. Both clock over 3,000 fps, and accuracy is all you could ask for. These handloads compare nicely with Hornady's 53-gr. BTHP Match load at 2,925 fps and group

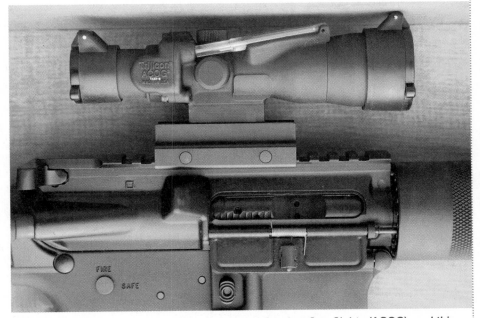

Trijicon has sold over one-half million Advanced Combat Gun Sights (ACOG), and this one makes a perfect sight for a K16 in 5.56mm for either law enforcement or home defense. The ACOG's reticle is specially calibrated for the 5.56mm's trajectory.

under an inch.

As I have noted, the 6.8 SPC is a superbly balanced cartridge. An excellent selection of bullet weights from 90 to 115 grains is available, and while some 130-gr. bullets shoot fine, their velocities are a bit low for reliable expansion. This is no impediment, as the tough Barnes 85-and 110-gr. Triple Shock-Xs and Nosler 110-gr. AccuBond bullets make the little 6.8 perform all out of proportion to its size.

For the lighter TS-X, a load of 31.0 grains of AA-2230 delivers 2,711 fps and consistently groups under an inch. A charge of 30.0 grains of IMR-8008XBR gives the 110-gr. Hornady V-MAX a velocity of 2,497 fps. For pure paper punching, look to the 115-gr. Sierra MatchKing over the same powder charge. Most handload velocities equal or exceed those of factory loads in my rifles.

The most recent Olympic Arms AR to cross my path is the .25 WSSM K8-MAG

Big game hunters will favor this accurate and powerful Model K8-MAG chambered in .25 WSSM, shown here with the excellent Vortex Crossfire illuminated reticle 3-9x40 scope, secured in a Weaver Tri-Rail mount. The K8-MAG is also available in .223 and .243 WSSM calibers.

Olympic Arms AR Rifle Range Tests

Model: K8, caliber 5.56mm, 20-inch barrel, 1:9-inch twist

Powder	Charge	Primer	Bullet	OAL(")	Vel. (fps)	SD	Group (")
IMR-8008XBR	26.7	F-205M	Sierra 40-gr. BlitzKing	2.215	3,117	6	.77
IMR-8008XBR	25.8	F-205M	Hornady 50-gr. V-MAX	2.250	3,052	8	.46
IMR-8008XBR	25.3	F-205M	Nosler 55-gr. Ballistic tip	2.250	2,952	15	.55
X-Terminator	24.0	F-205M	Nosler 55-gr. Ballistic tip	2.250	2,992	10	.94
IMR-8008XBR	23.6	F-205M	Hornady 60-gr. V-MAX	2.300	2,724	19	.30
Viht. N-140	23.6	R-P 7½	Hornady 60-gr. V-MAX	2.300	2,625	6	1.18
IMR-8008XBR	23.1	F-205M	Barnes 62-gr. Triple Shock-X BT	2.300	2,750	10	.87
IMR-8008XBR	23.1	F-205M	Sierra 63-gr. Semi Spitzer	2.270	2,700	17	.39
Viht. N-140	23.6	R-P 7½	Sierra 63-gr. Semi Spitzer	2.270	2,586	16	.47
IMR-8008XBR	23.8	F-205M	Sierra 65-gr. Spitzer BT	2.270	2,726	6	.51
IMR-8008XBR	23.8	F-205M	Hornady 68-gr. BT HP	2.260	2,731	4	.59
Hornady 53-gr. BTHP Factory Load				2.255	2,995	21	1.01
Federal 69-gr. Sierra HPBT Match Factory Load				2.205	2,731	23	.74

Model: K16, caliber 6.8mm SPC, 16-inch barrel, 1:10-inch twist

Powder	Charge	Primer	Bullet	OAL(")	Vel. (fps)	SD	Group (")
AA-2230	31.0	F-210	Barnes 85-gr. Triple Shock-X	2.250	2,711	21	63
IMR-8208XBR	30.5	F-210	Barnes 85-gr. Triple Shock-X	2.250	2,491	14	.53
X-Terminator	31.0	F-210	Barnes 85-gr. Triple Shock-X	2.250	2,613	13	1.00
X-Terminator	29.0	F-210	Speer 100-gr. Soft Point	2.250	2,457	9	.64
IMR-8208XBR	30.0	F-210	Hornady 110-gr. V-MAX	2.250	2,497	11	.47
AA-2230	30.0	F-210	Nosler 110-gr. AccuBond	2.250	2,557	7	1.06
X-Terminator	29.0	F-210	Nosler 110-gr. AccuBond	2.250	2,485	11	.78
IMR-8208XBR	30.0	F-210	Sierra 115-gr. MatchKing BTHP	2.250	2,390	10	.47
COR-BON DPX 110-gr. Barnes Triple Shock-X Factory Load				2.253	2,481	22	1.38
Silver States Armory 110-gr. Sierra SP Factory Load				2.251	2,451	20	.70
Hornady 110-gr. V-MAX Factory Load				2.242	2,510	31	.87
Hornady 110-gr. BTHP Factory Load				2.230	2,493	12	.81

Note: Remington cases were used for all 6.8mm handloads.

Note: Accuracy is the average of at least three, 3-shot groups at 100 yards from a bench rest. Velocities were measured with an Oehler M-35P chronograph with the front

For proper functioning, all AR rounds must be held to an cartridge overall length of 2.25 inches, such as these .25 WSSM handloads.

Here are just four of the over-achievers for which Olympic ARs are chambered (from left): the ubiquitous .223 Remington; the 6.8 SPC Remington; the hot new .300 Olympic Super Short Magnum; and its parent cartridge, the .25 Winchester Super Short Magnum.

noted above. It continues to astound with its pure accuracy and excellent power. Antelope and deer beware.

Basically, about every load performed well, but here are a few favorites. Big game is the role of the .25 WSSM, and bullets weighing 100 grains and up are just the ticket, and all six shot well. The Nosler Partition bullet clocks almost 3,000 fps out of the .25 WSSM over 44.1

grains of IMR-4007SSC. Another winner is the 110-gr. Hornady InterBond with 46.3 grains of Reloder 19 at 2,824 fps.

A main attribute of the .25 caliber is its ability to shoot heavier bullets than a 6mm. Here, the 120-gr. Speer Grand Slam cooks along at 2,755 fps with 44.1 grains of H-4350. This makes a terrific bigger big game load.

All in all, it is hard not to find a particular model and caliber set up in the Olympic Arms AR line that isn't appealing. They are competitively priced, functionally reliable, very accurate, and they accept a wide range of handloads without a whimper. In the crowded AR market, collectively they represent solid value.

Model: K16, caliber 5.56mm, 16-inch barrel, 1:9-inch twist

Powder	Charge	Primer	Bullet	OAL(")	Vel. (fps)	SD	Group (")
H-322	24.8	R-P 7½	Hornady 40-gr. V-MAX	2.215	3,388	12	.69
Viht. N-130	24.2	R-P 7½	Nosler 40-gr. Ballistic Tip	2.215	3,494	14	.71
Reloder 7	23.3	R-P 7½	Speer 45-gr. Soft Point	2.215	3,322	12	1.00
Varget	26.2	R-P 7½	Hornady 50-gr. V-MAX	2.250	3,026	11	.90
X-Terminator	25.3	R-P 7½	Nosler 50-gr. Ballistic Tip	2.250	3,093	15	.86
X-Terminator	24.0	WSR	Sierra 55-gr. Soft Point	2.250	2,961	9	.61
Hornady 53-gr. BTHP Factory Load				2.255	2,925	18	.98

Note: Federal cases were used for all 5.56mm handloads.

Model K8-MAG, caliber .25 WSSM, 24-inch barrel, 1:10-inch twist

Powder	Charge	Primer	Bullet	OAL(")	Vel. (fps)	SD	Group (")
AA-2230	31.0	F-210	Barnes 85-gr. Triple Shock-X	2.250	2,711	21	63
Big Game	47.5	WLR	Sierra 87-gr. Spitzer	2.250	3,036	17	.73
IMR-4007SSC	44.1	WLR	Barnes 100-gr. TS-X BT	2.250	2,906	15	.88
IMR-4007SSC	44.1	WLR	Nosler 100-gr. Partition	2.250	2,946	21	1.04
H-4350	47.0	WLR	Speer 100-gr. Hot Cor	2.250	2,990	19	1.25
IMR-4007SSC	44.1	WLR	Sierra 100-gr. Spitzer	2.250	2,903	8	.91
IMR-4007SSC	44.1	WLR	Swift 100-gr. A-Frame	2.250	2,923	24	.98
Reloder-17	45.0	WLR	Swift 100-gr. Scirocco II	2.250	2,966	6	1.22
Reloder-19	46.3	WLR	Hornady 110-gr. Interbond	2.250	2,824	12	.74
Hunter	47.5	WLR	Nosler 110-gr. AccuBond	2.250	2,891	9	1.32
Varget	37.2	WLR	Nosler 115-gr. Ballistic Tip	2.250	2,679	3	.71
W-760	47.0	WLR	Hornady 117-gr. BTSP	2.250	2,905	6	.98
IMR-4007SSC	41.0	WLR	Sierra 117-gr. Spitzer BT	2.250	2,696	7	.87
Reloder-17	43.0	WLR	Nosler 120-gr. Partition	2.250	2,771	8	1.07
H-4350	44.1	WLR	Speer 120-gr. Grand Slam	2.250	2,755	9	.98
Ball-C(2)	39.3	CCI-250	Speer 120-gr. Hot Cor SP	2.250	2,642	23	1.26
N-560	44.0	WLR	Swift 120-gr. A-Frame	2.250	2,537	18	1.08
Winchester 110-gr. AccuBond Factory Load				2.34	2,989	19	1.50
Winchester 115-gr. Ballistic Silvertip Factory Load				2.34	3,022	14	1.06

Note: Reformed Winchester cases were used for all .25 WSSM handloads.

screen 12 feet from the guns' muzzle. Abbreviations: SD, standard deviation; OAL, cartridge overall length; F, Federal; R-P, Remington-Peters; BT, boattail; HP, hollow point.

ON THE TRAIL OF "SMALL DEER" WITH

Allyn Tedmon

Champion of Stevens rifles, hunting ethicist, defender of the Second Amendement – Allyn H. Tedmon was all of these and more.

BY CLARENCE ANDERSON

"When one gets down to a real honest confession of his good times, he usually ends up telling himself it was the little, inexpensive hunting trip he enjoyed most." Every important gunwriter has on occasion addressed small game hunting, but how many became so enamored of it as to declare that "most of the shooting fun for the most of us has been had with small game"? Well-read riflemen are familiar with the work of Charles Landis, who made a science of squirrel and woodchuck sniping, and perhaps also Paul Estey, another 'chuck specialist, but the name of their contemporary, and author of the preceding assertions, Allyn Henry Tedmon, is unknown to most twenty-first century shooters.

Republication of the books of Landis and those of other shooting authorities of the time – Crossman, Whelen, Sharpe – has perpetuated their reputations, but because Tedmon's work, prolific though it was, appeared almost exclusively in magazines, his name has receded into obscurity and has been preserved from oblivion only by his unique association with a marque still venerated by many, the J. Stevens Arms Co.

Why resurrect the career of a writer whose work is unavailable except to collectors of vintage sporting magazines? Interest in shooting and collecting Stevens single-shots, and single-shots in general, which began to wane after WWI, has expanded enormously since Tedmon's day. But absorbing as this may be to Stevens afficionados and small-game devotees, no less significant is his tireless, impassioned advocacy of good sportsmanship – the ethics, that is, of hunting – along with his seemingly obsessive concern with threats to the Second Amendment. Tedmon was not, of course, the only writer of the time to treat these subjects, but he was singular in his vehement insistence on them over a publishing career that commenced in 1914, if not earlier, and continued intermittently until 1959.

"GANGLING PRODUCT OF THE WEST"

Local history collections in the Denver and Ft. Collins, Colorado, areas record almost nothing of the career of their nationally-known native son Allyn Tedmon but contain good deal of that of his entrepreneur father, Bolivar, who arrived in Ft. Collins in 1878. Perhaps it was Bolivar's upbringing under the hardscrabble conditions of farm life in the unforgiving Adirondack Mountains of New York that fueled an unflagging desire to better himself, but for whatever reasons, he became a highly successful frontier businessman and civic leader, owning real estate, insurance, mining, and grocery interests as well as erecting northern Colorado's earliest three-story brick building, the Tedmon House Hotel in Ft. Collins. After the latter property was sold in 1882 for a substantial profit, Bolivar's political connections reportedly gained him appointment as Colorado's Deputy Superintendent of Insurance, resulting in the family's

Allyn H. Tedmon
Photo courtesy Jim Foral

moving to Denver, where Allyn was born Nov. 11, 1884. Most of Bolivar's business enterprises foundered in the Panic of 1893, compelling him in the late 1890s to accept a position with the Columbia Investment Co. of New York.

But this personal and financial calamity for his father proved to be a providential turning point in the life of Allyn, "gangling product of the West," he called himself, setting the stage for his evolution into a shooting authority of national repute. Allyn was enrolled by his father in the college preparatory Dwight School of Manhattan, which suggests that his father's losses, if crippling, were not ruinous. At Dwight, Allyn established a lifelong friendship with another student, Charles Hopkins, whose accounting and managerial skills eventually earned him the position of Treasurer of the J. Stevens Arms Co.

Like father, like son: two Stevens-equipped generations of Tedmons after a day's hunting.

PRAIRIE DOGS HIT WITH THE .25 STEVENS RIM FIRE GO DOWN RIGHT NOW, AND STAY DOWN

deer" were relatively abundant.

Had the family never been uprooted, his father's gift of a rifle and his initial exploits as a hunter could of course have taken place as easily in Colorado as in the Greater New York metropolitan area. The experience that would have been difficult to replicate elsewhere, however, was Allyn's exposure to organized shooting activity, especially schuetzen-style competition, of an intensity probably unmatched anywhere in the country. "A worker in my father's office" who was himself a schuetzen competitor seems to have been largely responsible for introducing Allyn, as a spectator only, to this demanding discipline. Curiously, references to his own father as a shooting mentor, beyond providing the hardware, are conspicuously absent from his later writings: a pointed contrast to Allyn's intense involvement in coaching his own two sons.

"I well remember as a boy of 16 or 17... the old Greenville Schuetzen Range," he wrote in "Those Stevens Rifles," where "my brother and I met Dr. Hudson and numerous other noted target shooters of the time." Likewise recalled with pleasure were "visions of the old Zettler Brother's Gallery." Born into the kind of rural culture which accepted guns as everyday objects of utility and sport, his exposure to the sophisticated world of schuetzen competition revealed a scientific dimension to riflery that a lifetime of shooting back on the ranch would have been unlikely to reveal. His "shooting consciousness" had been permanently enlarged.

HOME AGAIN

By 1904, Bolivar's financial health had revived sufficiently to allow the family to return to Ft. Collins, where Bolivar, ever the entrepreneur, had purchased another real estate and insurance business. Having by this time graduated from Dwight, Allyn enrolled that same year in the Colorado Agricultural College of Ft. Collins and graduated in 1908 with a B. S. in Agricultural Science. His new degree was not the immediate passport to worldly success he probably envisaged, and because he evidently entertained no desire to join his father in business, he spent the next several years ranching with his brother in Wyoming – a meager living, but one

This happy convergence of interests greatly facilitated Allyn's research, decades later, into the history of the arms maker he came to esteem above all others. The first fruit of that research, and also the earliest detailed examination of the firm to appear in print, was "Those Stevens Rifles" in the Dec. 1926 issue of *The American Rifleman*, but several similar studies followed.

The germ of Allyn's infatuation with Stevens, however, was implanted by his own father, whose Christmas gift in 1900 was "the first rifle I ever owned... a Stevens Ideal No. 44...to me, yet, the most beautiful rifle ever produced in this country." So emphatic a sentiment, expressed 20 years later and after much

grown-up shooting experience, leaves no doubt as to the impression that "first rifle" made on 16-year-old Allyn.

The family apparently resided, at least seasonally, in northern New Jersey during some part of their "Eastern exile," as a letter of Allyn's published in the July, 1902, issue of *Recreation* identifies his address as Ridgefield, N. J. This brief response to another reader's query, very likely his first appearance in print, further extols the "good work" of both the Model 44 and the .32 Long Rifle cartridge, which, he took pains to explain, was, unlike other rimfire ammunition, "inside lubricated" (i.e., the bullet's grease grooves were inside the case). It also provides evidence that opportunities for the pursuit of "small enlivened with plenty of shooting. Once he remarked that, so as to reserve their beef for market, prairie-dog potpie ("the equal of any grey squirrel") became a staple of their diet. By the mid-teens, however, he finally secured a position with the Wyoming Dept. of Agriculture in Big Horn and Washakie Counties, reportedly becoming that state's first professional agricultural agent. Neither his professional position nor college education would have been deduced by readers of his early articles, however, as Allyn seemed to go out of his way to cultivate the impression that he was merely an ordinary cowpuncher.

Allyn played no part in WWI, owing, he once mentioned fleetingly, to a visual problem. This condition would account for his early interest in riflescopes – although for one suffering impaired vision, he reported many impressive accounts of good shooting on moving targets with aperture sights. (Ordinary open sights he derided as worthless.) Possibly the birth of Allyn's first child, Allyn, Jr., in 1917 also had something to do with his escape from the trenches. Bolivar, Jr., followed in 1920, and both boys became "featured players" and frequent photographic subjects in their father's articles of the '20s and '30s. Finally, in 1921, Allyn returned to Colorado to stay, having obtained the job of Arapaho County Agricultural Agent. He settled his family in the county seat of Littleton, a peaceful ranching community some ten miles south of Denver.

Although Allyn never brought up his career or professional duties in his own writing, "An Agricultural History of Littleton," published by that city, paints a picture of an energetic young man full of ideas new to this community. As "the new agent from the college in Ft. Collins," he "tried to persuade farmers that only through livestock could they succeed. This paid off...and in the 1920s Littleton was considered 'The Pure-Bred Livestock Center of the West.'" The position of County Agent presumably meshed very nicely with the interests of a sportsman, for Allyn was probably a welcome guest at every farm and ranch within his district. The job, however, brought little financial satisfaction, if his complaints of penury were true. Discussing reloading in 1923, he remarked that he had done so for years without a powder scale, using only an Ideal powder measure, because "$10 is a lot of money to have sitting on a shelf, for me at least." Though an early proponent of

telescopic sights, he lamented in 1927 that he had been "without one for years simply because I couldn't afford one." A thoughtful reader is tempted to suspect such comments were actually references to his early post-college, prairie dog-eating years, not his late '20s circumstances, but even if true, it seems clear his college education never provided him with the financial means of his father, who lived until 1937.

HIGH-VELOCITY FEVER

That his special relationship with Stevens rifles culminated in his being anointed "Godfather of Stevens Rifles" in the May, 1940, *The American Rifleman* by J. V. K. Wager would have been surprising to readers of his earliest articles, because Allyn, like so many of his contemporaries in the 'teens, had been bewitched by high-velocity and firepower. The spell, in his case, had been cast by a Model 99 Savage chambered for the sensational new .250-3000 cartridge. Having learned through C. E. Howard, a Colorado friend who collaborated with Charles Newton in designing small-bore, high-velocity cartridges such as Savage's .22 High-Power, that the .250 was "in the works," Allyn arranged to lay hands on one of the first to become available in 1915.

That cartridge proved to be a revelation. All his previous shooting experience, which included a hard-worked Model 99 in .303 Savage, had conditioned him to expect a perceptible lag-time between discharge and bullet impact, but the .250 "just simply reaches out and grabs them before one can think," he marveled in *Outdoor Life* in 1915, the first of at least seven pieces celebrating this cartridge. "I have never shot an arm which gives such an impression of power." Constant practice on running jack-rabbits honed skills he enlisted in the eternal war waged by most cattlemen against their common foe, the ubiquitous coyote, and reloading expanded the .250's versatility to include

Belief in the .25 Stevens was something of a genetic trait in the Tedmon family, as this photo of one of Allyn's sons shows.

The .25 Stevens Sure Stops 'Em

another hereditary rancher's enemy, the prairie dog. By the Nov. 1, 1922 issue of *Arms and the Man*, he believed "I have done more really good shooting with my Savage .250 than with all the rest put together."

The new job in Colorado, however, and its scarcity of the kind of shooting opportunities he had enjoyed in Wyoming, soon led to a cooling of his enthusiasm for his Savage .250 and a resurgence of interest in the guns of his youth, the Stevens single-shots. Cash-strapped as usual, he had sold his .303 to finance the new .250 but evidently never considered parting with his cherished Stevens 44, converted by this time into an even more useful .32-40 after sustaining cleaning-rod damage to its bore. (Stevens made a particular specialty of such reboring.) Although his fondness for "Those Stevens Rifles" had crept into earlier pieces, it was with that nicely researched treatise of 1926 that his initial reputation as a high-velocity advocate waned, and his public identification with the guns of Chicopee Falls began to take shape. (Lest his unsolicited nickname of "the Godfather of Stevens Rifles" be interpreted as somehow self-serving, he felt compelled to conclude the piece with a disclaimer: "Don't take me for a Stevens salesman, for what I have are not for sale.")

The Godfather reviewed and applauded Stevens scopes for their good value in the July, 1927, *The American Rifleman* and lamented the passing of Stevens' acclaimed Model 44 ½ falling-block action in the July, 1930, issue. The following year of 1931 proved to be, in retrospect, one of particular significance for him, as the magazine published three interrelated pieces that established unmistakably the special niche he was to occupy in the shooting world the remainder of his life. "Small Deer Rifles," in the March issue, recounted and analyzed his trials of innumerable cartridges, from rim-fires to down-loaded high-power rounds, on

a variety of small game species. "The .25 caliber rifles vamped me," he declared, referring principally to the .25 Stevens RF and the two .25-20s. Note that in Ted-mon's usage, the term "small deer," an Elizabethan expression, referred to any wild mammal. Allyn made this quaint phrase, used once before in a 1921 *Arms* piece, his very own as effectively as if it had been trademarked.

"Sighting 'Small Deer' Rifles," following in the August issue, was a plea for small-game riflemen to recognize the futility of obtaining a clear aiming-point with metallic sights on targets so small as to be obscured by the blade or bead of a front sight. "Nothing less than a good telescopic sight is fit to put on a really good 'small deer' rifle.... You can't afford not to have one." This argument correlated perfectly with two other favorite themes: the fine value represented by Stevens scopes relative to others selling at twice the price, and the ethical hunter's moral imperative to strive to avoid crippling, "the agonies of gunshot fever."

The latter consideration became his principal thesis in the final part of his 1931 *The American Rifleman* trilogy, "Rim Fires and Game," in the November issue. The object

of that theme was the .22 RF cartridge, which Tedmon passionately insisted was the single greatest contributor to unnecessary suffering among small game of all varieties. "I know that many squirrels are killed with the .22 LR; on the other hand, many...crawl away wounded to die a lingering death not due these game little beasts." That he was speaking from bitter personal experience he did not conceal: "During those thoughtless and heartless days of a man's life, I shot dozens of prairie dogs with the .22 LR. Today I get little pleasure and plenty of regret when I recall how many were hit, only to crawl gamely into the burrow to die, victims of my thoughtlessness."

ETHICAL CONCERNS

Extreme as Tedmon's feelings may seem to contemporary readers, he was by no means alone in holding such views: "I have for years joined with Col. Whelen and others in condemning the .22 RF for shooting game; that is, anything larger than rats...English sparrows and the like." In the August 1, 1922, issue of *Arms and the Man*, sightmaker "Trim Nat" (Tom Martin) enlarged upon this point: "Why will some men insist that the .22 LR hollow-point is amply large enough for such game [woodchucks]? It is not, and it is only trade selfishness and cruelty to advocate its use. The main effort is to sell the .22 LR as being just the thing for woodchuck hunting."

But who would be so irresponsible as to make such a claim? A U. S. Cartridge Co. advertisement of the period confirms that these rimfire critics were not setting up straw men to knock down. *Arms and the Man*, in the March 1, 1920 issue, published a claim by Ozark Ripley, a very well known sporting writer into the 1950s, of clean kills with .22s on geese, turkey, deer, and a timber wolf. Plenty more of the same foolishness can be found by anyone who cares to review the literature of this period. Clearly, hyperbolic advertising, aided and abetted by the fatuous braggadocio of accomplices in the sporting press, promoted the abuses that inflamed Tedmon and others who took seriously their ethical responsibilities as hunters.

Discouraging the use of .22 RFs for hunting (but not, of course, for practice and target shooting) was but half of "Rim Fires and Game"; the other half was a ringing endorsement of Tedmon's ideal small-game rimfire, the Stevens .25 Long. "After having spent a lifetime shooting at small game and seeing it

"I HAVE SHOT QUITE A GOOD MANY OF THESE HI-SPEED AND SUPER-X CARTRIDGES IN MY STEVENS MODEL 47 RIFLE"

Stevens was an early advocate of telescopic sights, especially when they were mounted on Stevens single-shots.

murdered by others, I can only repeat what I have said time and again before: the .25 RF is by far the best small game rim fire cartridge we have today." Such sentiments were echoed by almost everyone who wrote about this cartridge, including Whelen ("the only rim-fire to use for hunting"), but everyone complained of its unreasonable cost: well over twice the price of .22 LRs. "There is your answer," explained Tedmon; "Humanity is a hollow term where the average man's pocketbook is involved."

For his own use, Tedmon inclined toward the .25-20 Single Shot, experimenting with loads that stretched the potential of this venerable round, but his words in this piece were aimed at the great mass of casual shooters who did not reload. It should go without saying, moreover, that he was not addressing himself to small-bore riflemen in the class of Charles Landis, who hunted with match-grade rifles and target scopes and whose marksmanship and skill in range estimation were fruits of a lifetime of practice and study of the technical minutiae of their sport.

No Ph.D. in psychology is needed to trace the origin of Tedmon's unusual compassion for small game animals. Repeatedly, as if in contrition, he lays bare harrowing memories: "I emptied the magazine [of a M1906 Winchester] into that badger. . . . He probably lingered for a day or more, suffering untold pangs of death, while I, brainless yap that I was, rode off forgetful of it all." That act of thoughtless cruelty seared itself into his memory, and helps to explain later outbursts of vitriol, such as this passage from "Mountain Marmot Stalking in Colorado in *Sports Afield*, July, 1936: "For those sportsmen who must kill, kill, kill, I recommend a job on the killing floor of a slaughter house."

SECOND AMENDMENT ACTIVIST

Game hogs, slob hunters, and fools misled by advertising into believing their four-pound .22 repeaters were good medicine for 250-yard varmint hunting were perennial targets of Tedmon's invective, but another menace loomed larger in his consciousness as the century wore on: "the white-livered busybodies" agitating "to take this right [to keep and bear arms] from us." This impassioned warning about legislative assaults on the Second Amendment was delivered in "What Would Pat Garrett Have Done?" in the Jan. 1, 1923, *Arms and the Man*. In the June 1 issue (following the renaming of the publication as *The American Rifleman*), "A Law for the Outlaw" predicted with farsighted imagination how the back of the Second Amendment might be most easily broken – not by bans or confiscation, but by taxation. This same year, he was accorded the unusual privilege of presenting two editorials denouncing gun control hysteria, in the June 1 and Dec. 15 issues.

Modern shooters may wonder what all the fuss was about in those pre-Brady days, but Tedmon was by no means raising a false alarm: the national crime wave resulting, indirectly, from Prohibition precipitated a frenzied outcry from big-city politicians and newspapers for more restrictive firearms legislation, particularly the banning of privately owned handguns. Proposals modeled on New York's Sullivan Law were introduced in several state legislatures, and the National Firearms Act of 1934, banning such mobster's favorites as Marble's Game Getters, and "trapper" carbines, became the law in force today. After the repeal of the Volstead Act, much of the clamor for new restrictions subsided – temporarily. Tedmon never again wrote expressly about gun control for *The American Rifleman* but he remained vigilant about this threat for the rest of his life.

Yet another pet Tedmon theme was the moral obligation of sportsmen to invest time in teaching children the sporting use of firearms: "If you and I don't teach our boys the love of the rifled barrel...who is going to do it?" His own boys were made test cases with their progress charted in many of his articles, beginning with "Start the Boy Out Right," in *Outdoor Life* of July, 1920. "Boys and Rifles" appeared in *The American Rifleman* of Nov. 1927, and "Rifles and Guns for Little Boys," was a stand-in for Whelen's regular *Outdoor Life* column of Oct., 1935. Both of the latter offered advice for remodeling rifles for shooters as young as five or six. The failure of most draft-age men at the beginning of WWII to possess even rudimentary rifle-handling skills was because their parents had waited for "government social workers" to exercise that responsibility, as he facetiously claimed in "Give Uncle Sam a Boy Who Can Shoot" in the Jan., 1943, *The American Rifleman*.

OTHER INTERESTS

Tedmon occasionally indulged in a genre of writing that has fallen out of favor since the 1950s, but once enjoyed widespread popularity: the largely fictional comic yarn. "Them Awful Boys," in the Dec. 1925 *Outdoor Life*, "Mystery Lead," in the Dec. 1944 *The American Rifleman* , and "Precocious Pellets," in the Dec. 1946 *The American Rifleman* , are characteristic examples. Modern readers are apt to find these tales rather more tedious than entertaining, but they serve to illustrate something perhaps unexpected about the personality of Tedmon: far from being the humorless moralist which the occasionally scalding vehemence of his tirades might suggest, a broad sense of country-boy humor percolated through much of his work, particularly that of the '20s and '30s. Refined wit it wasn't, but rather the kind of good-natured cornpone that made *Hee-Haw* a hit TV show in the '70s. He also occasionally ventured into fiction, as two known examples in *Ace-High* magazine attest.

Whether because he believed he had said enough, or because his editors thought so, Tedmon wrote less about small deer and sporting ethics in the years after WWII. In five pieces published between 1945 and 1952, he promoted a new (or rather, revitalized) interest – offhand, free-rifle competition, a modern derivative of the Schuetzen matches that had captivated him as a youth but had since died out due to anti-"German" sentiment.The last published work of his known to this collector was, most fittingly, a return to a "favorite" subject, "The Stevens Favorite Rifle," in 1959. He permanently left the range on November 28, 1969, at 85 years of age, and now lies among other family members in Grandview Cemetery of Ft. Collins.

Allyn Tedmon originated the tell-it-as-I-see-it, "straight talk express" the first time he put pen to paper; he never mastered the fine art of equivocation. For this reason, his charismatic voice would probably prove unpublishable today, or not, at any rate, without editing so severe as to oppress his distinctive spirit. Fortunately for anyone who cares to sample that spirit, much of his work appeared in *Arms and the Man* and *The American Rifleman*, which – because they tended to be preserved by NRA members – remain the most widely available today of pre-WWII sporting periodicals.

PARTIAL BIBLIOGRAPHY OF ALLYN H. TEDMON

1902   "Recommend No. 44 Stevens," *Recreation*, July.

1914   "Differs from 'Antipop,'" *Outdoor Life*, Jan.

1915   "That New Rifle," *Outdoor Life* (reprinted in *Gun Writers of Yesteryear* by Jim Foral).
"Horse Play Out West," Outing, Dec.

1916   "Rifle Notes," *Outdoor Life*, Feb.

1917   "On the Trail of the .250-3000," *Outers' Book*, Nov.

1919   "Random Hunting Reflections," *Outdoor Life*, March.
"Rifle Notes," *Outdoor Life*, April.

1920   "The .250-3000 Savage on Big Game," *Arms and the Man*, June 1.
"Looking Backward," *Outdoor Life*, July.
"Start the Boy Out Right," *Outdoor Life*, July.
"What You and I Can Do with an Inexpensive Arm," *Outdoor Life*, Aug.
"Rifles What Was," *Arms and the Man*, Dec. 1.

1921   "Small Deer," *Arms and the Man*, Oct.1.

1922   "Lest We Forget," *Arms and the Man*, Feb.15.
"Hunting the Little Bears of the West," *Arms and the Man*, May 15.
"The Fable of a Rifle Nut," *Arms and the Man*, June 1.
"There Were Others," *Arms and the Man*, June 15.
"Coyotes," *Arms and the Man*, July 1.
"The Days of Real Sport," *Arms and the Man*, Aug. 1.
"The High Power," *Arms and the Man*, Sept. 15.
"Milkin' Her Dry," *Arms and the Man*, Nov. 1.

1923   "What Would Pat Garrett Have Done?," *Arms and the Man*, Jan.1.
"Canis Latrans," *Arms and the Man*, Jan.15.
"Ramblings of a Nut," *Arms and the Man*, April 1.
"If You Can't Buy It, Make It!," *Arms and the Man*, May 15.
"A Law for the Outlaw," *The American Rifleman*, June1.
"Beyond the Dollar Sign," *The American Rifleman*, Sept.1.
"The .250-3000 on Lion and Bear," *The American Rifleman*, Sept.15.
"Truth is Mighty and Shall Prevail," *The American Rifleman*, Dec. 15.

1924   "Popping Prairie Poodles with Chauncy Thomas," *Outdoor Life*, Feb.
"The Single Shot Rifle, *Outdoor Life*, Feb.
"Not for Pistol 'Antis,'" *The American Rifleman*, Sept.15.

1925   "It Reminded Me," *The American Rifleman*, March 1.
"Them Awful Boys," *Outdoor Life*, Dec.

"Those Stevens Rifles," *The American Rifleman*, Dec.

1927   "Not an Hour Off, But an Off Hour," *The American Rifleman*, April.
"The Scope Sight You Can Afford," *The American Rifleman*, July.
"Boys and Rifles," *The American Rifleman*, Nov.

1928   "Where Peterson Barrels Were Born," *The American Rifleman*, Jan.
"A Man at Stake," *Ace-High Magazine*, August 1.

1929   "A Red Letter Day," *The American Rifleman*, March.

1930   "The Stevens Ideal 44 1/2 Action," *The American Rifleman*, July.
"Riders of the Crescent," *Ace-High Magazine*, July 15.

1931   "Two Favorites," *The American Rifleman*, Feb.
"Small Deer Rifles," *The American Rifleman*, March.
"Sighting Small Deer Rifles," *The American Rifleman*, August.
"Rim Fires and Game," *The American Rifleman*, Nov.

1932   "On Safety in Shooting and Other Matters," *The American Rifleman*, Jan.
"The Front Sight on Small Game," *The American Rifleman*, Nov.

1933   "Butt-Plates to Order," *Field and Stream*, Feb.
".25-20 Super Speed," *The American Rifleman*, Nov.
"Thoroughfare Bear," *The American Rifleman*, Dec.

1935   "Rifles and Guns for Little Boys," *Outdoor Life*, Oct.
"A Good Rifle Rest," *The American Rifleman*, Dec.

1936   "Mortgaged Marmots," *Outdoor Life*, June.
"Mountain Marmot Stalking in Colorado," *Sports Afield*, July.
"Specter Buck," *Outdoor Life*, Sept.

1937   "C. W. Rowland Has Left the Range," *The American Rifleman*, Jan.
"The .25 Stevens Rim Fire," *The American Rifleman*, March.
"Hunting Marmots in the Rain," *The American Rifleman*, June.
"The .25-20 and Its Grandchildren," *The American Rifleman*, Dec.

1938   "Stevens 44 ½'s Still Favorites," *Outdoor Life*, Jan.
"Try Jackrabbit Shooting," *The American Rifleman*, Dec.

1939   "There is a Limit," *The American Rifleman*, Jan.
"C. E. Howard–Rifleman," *The American Rifleman*, Feb.
"When You Can't Lie Down," *The American Rifleman*, June.
"Johnny Chuck–Game or Varmint?," *National Sportsman*, Aug.
"Duplicate Bucks," *The American Rifleman*, Oct.

1940   "The Savage Model 1899," *The American Rifleman*, Feb.
"Why Not a Savage .35?," *The American Rifleman*, March.

1941   "Chauncy Thomas," *The American Rifleman*, Dec.

1943   "Give Uncle Sam a Boy Who Can Shoot," *The American Rifleman*, Jan.
"Short Range Backlog," *The American Rifleman*, July.
"An Old Timer's Story of .22 Caliber Hunting," *The American Rifleman*, Dec.

1944   "That Man Peterson," *The American Rifleman*, Jan.
"Mystery Lead," *The American Rifleman*, Dec.

1945   "Offhand, I'd Say," *The American Rifleman*, March.
"Air Guns for Aerial Targets," *The American Rifleman*, Oct.
"Postwar Shooting," *The American Rifleman*, Nov.
"The Offhand Rifle," *The American Rifleman*, Dec.

1946   "That Modern Single Rifle," *The American Rifleman*, Jan.
"Precocious Pellets," *The American Rifleman*, Dec.

1948   "Sport with the Free Rifle," *The American Rifleman*, Jan.

1949   "Tatar Cellar's Junior Coach, *The American Rifleman*, Aug.

1952   "So You Want Better Offhand Scores," *The American Rifleman*, July.
"The American Free Rifle," *The New Official Gun Book*,
Charles R. Jacobs, Ed.

1953   "The Blake .400." *The American Rifleman*, Jan.
"The Stevens Model 44 Action," *The Single Shot Rifle News*, April.

1956   "He Splits Cards at 100 Yards," *Guns Magazine*, March.
"Single-Shots of Yesterday," *Gun Report*, Sept.

1957   "Stevens Tip-Up Rifles," *Gun Report*, May.

1959   "The Stevens Favorite Rifle," *More Single Shot Rifles*, James Grant.

Custom and Engraved Guns

BY TOM TURPIN

(right) This photo shows the new USA-made Searcy "rising bite" double flanked on either side by an original Rigby double shotgun featuring the rising bite they offered to the market at the turn of the 20th century. This pair of original Rigby doubles were made in 1903. The Searcy was finished in 2010. Photo by Steve Helsley.

(opposite) A close-up photo of the Searcy-produced Rigby Bissell "rising bite" locking system. Due to the complexity and difficulty of manufacture, to my knowledge, none have been made in more than a half-century, probably closer to 75 years or so. Photo by Steve Helsley.

Shane Thompson FN 98 Mauser.
Photo by Gene Wright.

Shane Thompson

Shane Thompson is a very talented young gunmaker. He does both stock and metalwork and he does each with equal meticulousness. The rifle shown here is a good example of his work in both materials. He started with a very early FN Model 98 Mauser action that he blueprinted, truing all the surfaces. He recontoured and reshaped a 1909 Argentine set of bottom metal and fitted it to the action. He fabricated scope rings and bases from bar stock in his shop and fitted them to the action. He chambered the barrel for the 270 Winchester cartridge, fitted a three-position safety and finally hand polished the action and barrel.

The stock on this rifle is a bit unusual. It is fabricated from a piece of mesquite that grew on the client's ranch. The client cut and sealed the wood many years ago. He insisted on using it for the stock. Shane whittled out the stock and fitted it with a genuine horn forend tip and grip cap. He checkered it in a point pattern 24 and added a mullered border. He finished his work by mounting a Leupold 3-9 variable scope. The finished rifle weighs 7 lbs., 11 ozs. W/O scope, and 8 lbs., 10 ozs. with scope. The astute viewer might note that the rifle is a right hand action, but stocked for a southpaw. That's the way the client learned to shoot, and the way he wanted it done. Finally, Gary Griffiths engraved the rifle.

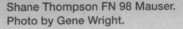

Simillion Winchester M70 .375 H&H Magnum. Photo by Gene Simillion.

Gene Simillion

This 375 H&H rifle is from the Colorado shop of Gene Simillion. Starting with a Winchester Model 70 Classic action, a Krieger barrel, and a very nice stick of Turkish walnut, Gene went to work. He first blueprinted the action and fitted Blackburn bottom metal to it. He fitted and chambered the Krieger barrel, working on the feeding until it is flawless. He machined custom bases for the Talley scope rings he used to mount the Swarovski variable scope. He also fitted an adjustable rear sight to the barrel. He then whittled the stock from the blank of Turkish walnut and checkered it in a point pattern, 26 LPI. The finished rifle with scope weighs 9-3/4 pounds.

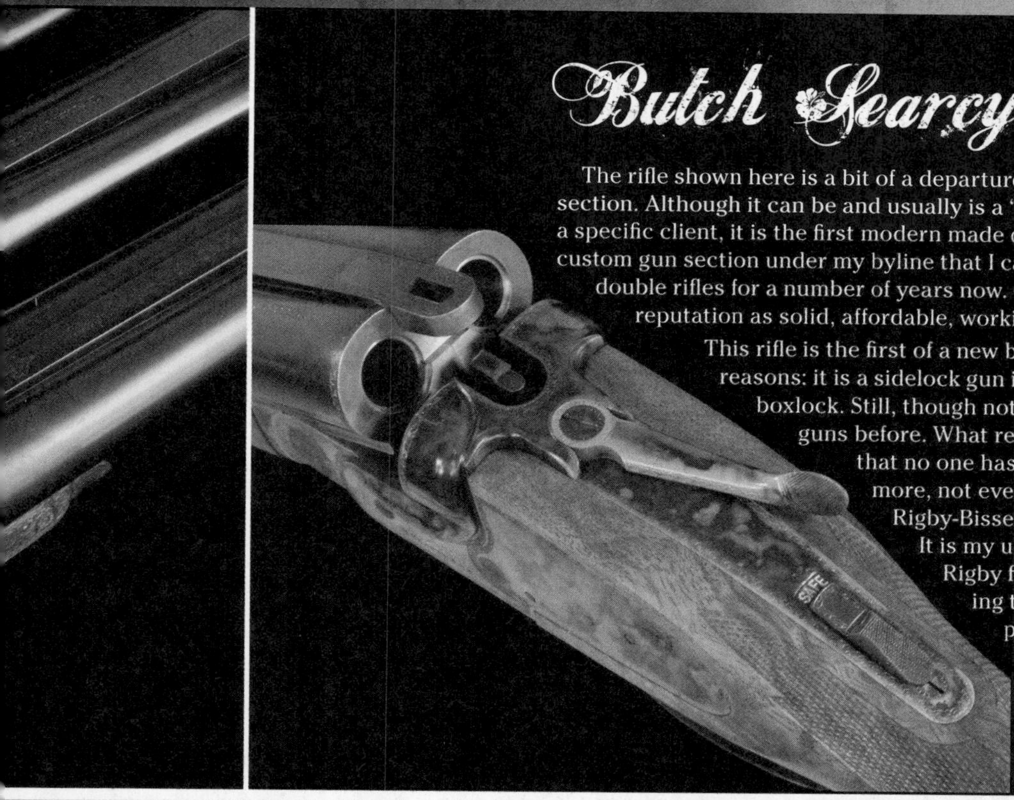

Butch Searcy

The rifle shown here is a bit of a departure from those normally found in this section. Although it can be and usually is a "bespoke" gun, and therefore made for a specific client, it is the first modern made double rifle that has appeared in the custom gun section under my byline that I can recall. Butch Searcy has been making double rifles for a number of years now. Over time, his rifles have developed a reputation as solid, affordable, working double rifles.

This rifle is the first of a new breed of Searcy double, and for two reasons: it is a sidelock gun instead of the more often encountered boxlock. Still, though not common, Butch has produced sidelock guns before. What really sets this one apart, and something that no one has produced in at least a half-century or more, not even the Brits, is that this rifle features a Rigby-Bissell patent (1879) rising bite third-bite. It is my understanding that the "new" London Rigby firm is producing a Rigby double featuring this locking system as well. I've seen photos of it "in the works," but don't know if it is finished as yet. At any rate this rifle is complete and chambered for the .470 NE cartridge.

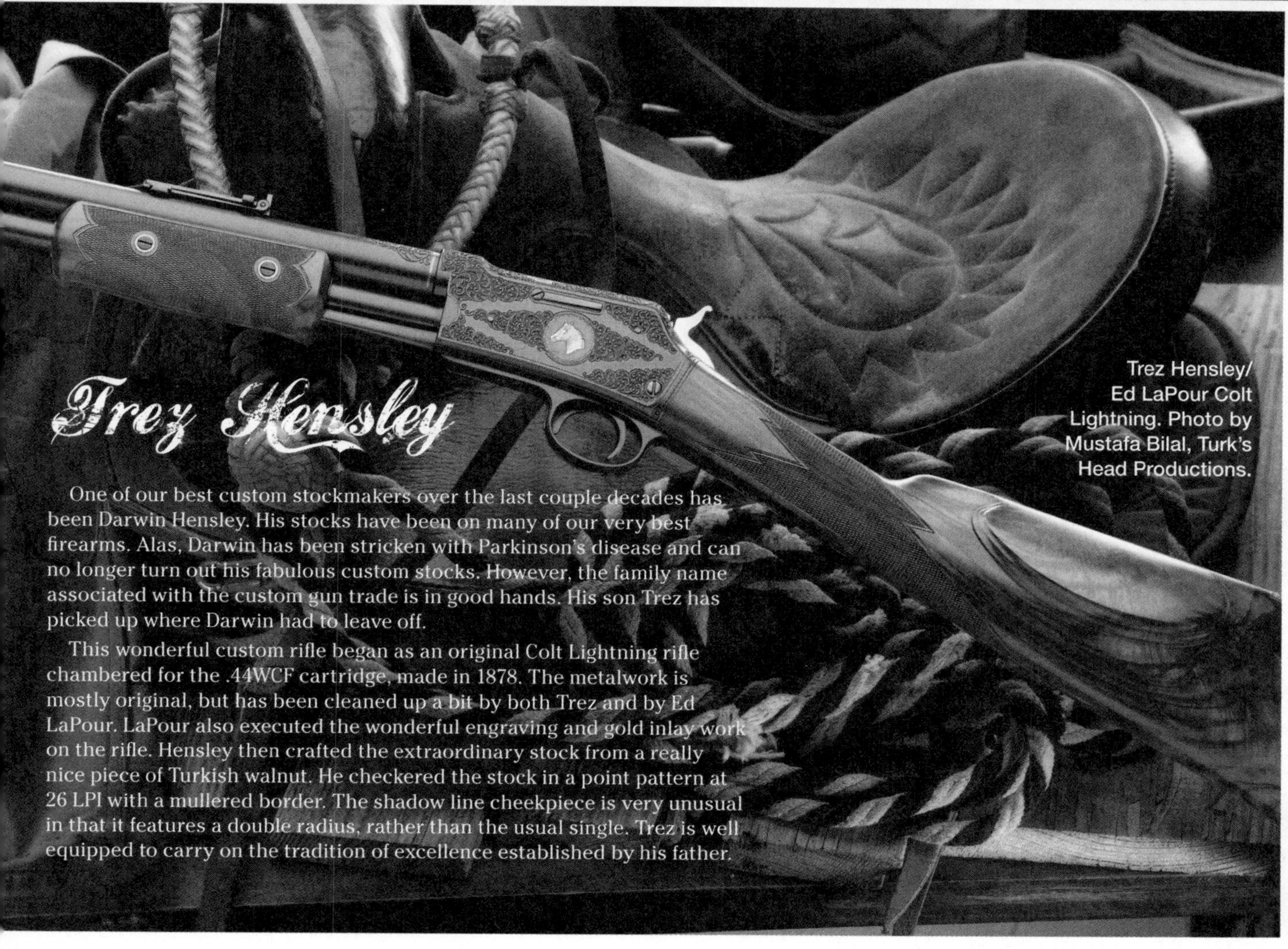

Trez Hensley

Trez Hensley/ Ed LaPour Colt Lightning. Photo by Mustafa Bilal, Turk's Head Productions.

One of our best custom stockmakers over the last couple decades has been Darwin Hensley. His stocks have been on many of our very best firearms. Alas, Darwin has been stricken with Parkinson's disease and can no longer turn out his fabulous custom stocks. However, the family name associated with the custom gun trade is in good hands. His son Trez has picked up where Darwin had to leave off.

This wonderful custom rifle began as an original Colt Lightning rifle chambered for the .44WCF cartridge, made in 1878. The metalwork is mostly original, but has been cleaned up a bit by both Trez and by Ed LaPour. LaPour also executed the wonderful engraving and gold inlay work on the rifle. Hensley then crafted the extraordinary stock from a really nice piece of Turkish walnut. He checkered the stock in a point pattern at 26 LPI with a mullered border. The shadow line cheekpiece is very unusual in that it features a double radius, rather than the usual single. Trez is well equipped to carry on the tradition of excellence established by his father.

Hans Doesel

Hans Doesel is a relatively young German engraver who studied under my old friend Erich Boessler. I believe that he apprenticed under Erich as well as studied for his Master certificate under him. He's been a Master engraver for several years now and is turning out some fastidious work. He is very versatile and can do traditional Germanic sculpting in deep relief, as well as delicate bulino work. Shown here are two examples of his artistry.

(top) Doesel Sauer Model 202 action featuring rather typical Germanic gold line inlay work in combination with much less common bulino game scenes. Framing both is profuse scrollwork. All the work is beautifully done. Photo by Hans Doesel.

(bottom) Doesel Floorplate from a Model 70 Winchester that is mostly bulino work depicting an African scene featuring three Cape buffalo. Included is moderate gold line inlay and larger scroll decoration, including a fleur de lis motif. Photo by Hans Doesel.

Roger Ferrell and Mark Swanson

Ferrell/Swanson Frank Wesson No. 1 Long Range Rifle in .45-100. Photos by Tom Rowe.

This rifle was commissioned by a collector of Frank Wesson rifles with a goal of creating a quality reproduction of the original Wesson No. 1 Long Range rifle as a tribute to Frank Wesson. The owner of this rifle is also writing a book on Wesson rifles. The Wesson design is based on Alexander Henry's falling block action. The most unique feature on the rifle is the treatment of the octagon flats at the breech of the action. All work, including the exquisite American Black Walnut stock, was done in the Georgia shop of Roger Ferrell except for the engraving. Mark Swanson executed that portion of the project. The tang and heel sights are exact reproductions of original Wesson sights that the owner had fabricated specifically for this project. The front sight is from Montana Vintage Arms. The rifle is chambered for the .45-100 cartridge.

Barry Lee Hands

Shown here are two examples of the artistry of Montana engraver Barry Lee Hands. Considering that he's about the same age as my son, it's remarkable that he has progressed so much in such a short time. A very versatile engraver, he can do most any style of engraving, and do it very well indeed.

This little Colt .25 auto is a perfect canvas for Barry's exquisite floral and gold pattern, on both steel and pearl. This work is as good as it gets. Photo by Barry Lee Hands.

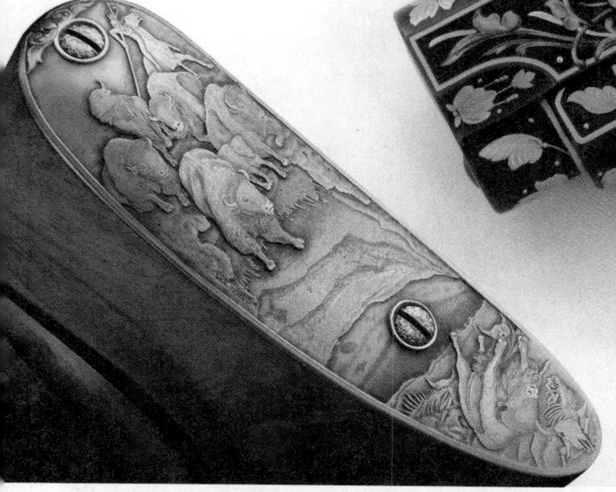

It is probably unfair to show just the buttplate engraving on this rifle. The scene depicts the annual collection of winter's meat by the plains Indians, driving buffalo off a cliff and then collecting their rewards. This scene is done in high relief and is immaculate. Photo by Barry Lee Hands.

Terry Wieland and James Flynn

This rifle is the brainchild of outdoors writer Terry Wieland. Terry is a Canadian by birth, and an avid Anglophile. In addition to being a fantastic writer, he is also a history buff and delights in doing themed projects. This rifle is such a project, and is called his Beau Brummell rifle. Brummell, for those unaware, was the arbiter of English men's fashion in the late 18th century and into the early 19th century. His motto was "if people turn to look at you on the street, you are not well dressed." He left behind an England where men dressed in austere but superbly cut clothing, a style still followed there today.

Wieland/Flynn
"Beau Brummel Rifle"
on FN Supreme Mauser action.
Photo by Terry Wieland.

Wieland, in collaboration with Louisiana gunmaker James Flynn, transferred Brummell's concept in clothing to the making of this rifle. Their object was to demonstrate the time, effort, and skill that go into making a custom rifle functional and aesthetic perfection, like a Beau Brummell dinner jacket. Starting with a FN Supreme Mauser action, a Danny Pedersen 25-caliber cut-rifled barrel, they had Bill Dowtin of Old World Walnut personally select the blank of walnut for the project. James Flynn then fashioned all the components into a functional masterpiece that would fully fit Beau Brummell's sense of styling. I like to call it quiet elegance.

Reto Buehler

Reto Buehler began this project with a Granite Mountain Arms Magnum Mauser action, a custom contoured PacNor barrel, and a fabulous stick of Turkish walnut. He first extended the tangs to the action and to the bottom metal. He also machined the quarter rib from bar stock. The GMA action was worked over to feed the big .500 Jeffery cartridges like a hot knife through butter. He then fashioned the terrific stock in the English styling. He checkered the stock in 20 LPI flat topped checkering. Reto finished the job by rust bluing the metalwork and nitre bluing the ejector and extractor spring. It just doesn't get any better than this.

Reto Buehler .500 Jeffery on GMA action. Photo by Mustafa Bilal, Turks Head Productions.

Mike Dubber

Mike Dubber from Indiana is a super-talented engraver. Over the past several years that I've known him, he has matured from a really good engraver into a really great one much more quickly than most I have known. This photo is a recent example of his exemplary work. He started with a 2nd Generation Colt SAA, and a theme of the Lakota Sioux last buffalo hunt. He even had a pencil drawing of the last Sioux buffalo hunter, drawn by an unknown artist in the 1800s. The 5-1/2 inch barrel revolver has been heavily inlaid with gold and platinum, and has been fitted with custom sambar stag grips. It is chambered for the .45 Colt cartridge and is finished in French Gray.

Mike Dubber 2nd Gen SAA in .45 Colt. Photo by Tom Alexander.

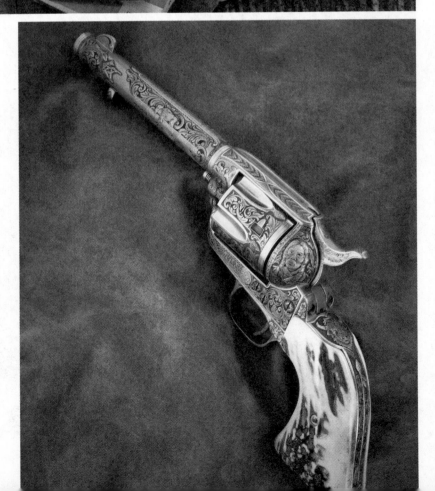

Gary Goudy

A lovely custom rifle from the shop of stockmaker Gary Goudy. The rifle was a Model 70 Featherweight .30-06, and the barrel was so accurate that it was retained. Gary fitted an ancient set of Ted Blackburn bottom metal to the action. Note that it does not use a straddle floorplate, something that Ted hasn't produced in years. The stock is checkered in a very nice point pattern with mullered borders. Bob Evans engraved the rifle.

This is most likely the most unusual custom rifle that you'll ever come across. Gary Goudy's client wanted a custom BB gun for his grandson. Gary came up with a brand new Daisy Red Ryder BB gun and stocked it with a magnificent piece of Turkish walnut. I've been around the horn a time or two, but this is the only custom BB gun that I've ever come across.

Paul Lindke

Stockmaker Paul Lindke started this project with a pre-'64 Model 70 barreled action, chambered for the .270 Winchester cartridge. The factory barrel was so accurate that it was retained. He picked up a very nice stick of California English walnut from Steve Heilmann, and added a McFarland steel skeleton buttplate, a Leupold VX-3 2.5-8 scope, and Leupold double dovetail mounts. He stocked the rifle, adding an ebony forend tip, and checkered the stock in a 24 LPI fleur de lis pattern with ribbons.

Bob Strosin

What's the old saw about the shoemaker's kid's shoes never getting done? When engraver Bob Strosin decided he needed a new elk rifle, he pulled out the stops. He had Joe Bautz work over the 1909 Argentine Mauser action, doing the blueprinting and adding a three-position safety, Talley quick-detachable mounts, and a raised and checkered bolt stop pad. Bautz turned the metal over to Toby Leeds who crafted the superb stock, with a steel buttplate. Strosin then used the rifle as a canvas for his embellish-ment. He also did the bluing and French Gray finishing.

Strosin/Bautz/Leeds 1909 Argentine Mauser. Photos by Tom Alexander.

Lee Griffiths

Lee Griffiths is a very talented and versatile engraver. Shown here are two examples that emphasize the wide range of engraving styles that he is more than capable of execut-ing to perfection. The first photo is of a L.C. Smith double 12-gaugeshotgun, which Griffiths engraved in traditional scrollwork, bulino scenes, and gold line inlay work. There is also heavy chiseled sculpting on the fences and the breaking lever. The second example, a Perazzi O/U, features much more contemporary styled engraving, combining traditional scrollwork with a heavily sculpted trigger guard bow, and multi-metal inlay work, including gold, platinum, silver, and copper inlays. Both pieces are exquisitely done.

(above) Lee Griffiths LC Smith 12-gauge. Photo courtesy of Lee Griffiths.

(left) Griffiths Perazzi O/U. Photo courtesy of Lee Griffiths.

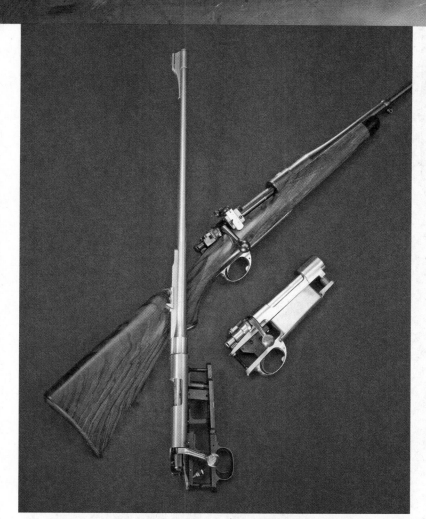

David Norin

Chicago-area gunmaker David Norin can and does do everything on a custom gun except the engraving. Shown here are some examples of his work. The action is a Standard Model, which came out of the great Oberndorf Werke in the 1930s. Norin fitted a Fisher round bottom magazine and trigger guard assembly, added a new bolt knob, suitably checkered, and polished, ground and stoned the action to the stage shown in the photo. The barreled action is a Dakota .22 RF to which has been added a sculpted bolt knob, a quarter-rib with express sights, and added stoning and polishing. This barreled action will be stocked as a mini-African stalking rifle. Finally, the completed rifle is a Mauser action 7x57, fitted with Fisher round bottom magazine and trigger guard assembly, an Oberndorf style bolt knob, three-position safety, Blackburn trigger, and a Lyman 48 peep sight. The rifle is stocked in a very nice stick of Turkish walnut and checkered in a point pattern at 22 LPI. The rifle is intended to be a deep woods deer rifle.

The artistry of David Norin.
Photo by Tom Alexander.

Al Lofgren

Al Lofgren is a superb stockmaker and long-time member of the American Custom Gunmakers Guild (ACGG). Al delights in crafting fine custom stocks in the Germanic style. He has crafted many stocks using the reinforcing side-panels, so reminiscent of Mauser factory stocks from the early twentieth century. In preparing for this job, looking through Michael Petrov's fine book, *Custom Gunmakers of the 20th Century*, he came across an example of a Sauer made rifle with metal side-plates inletted into the reinforcing panels of the stock. He decided to incorporate metal side-plates into this stock job, using a nice stick of walnut from Paul and Sharon Dressel. Steve Nelson did much of the metalwork, including the square-bridging work on the rear bridge. He also did the quarter-rib and installed the 3-position safety, Talley scope mounts and the Weaver 3x scope.

Lofgren Mauser with metal sideplates.
Photos by Tom Alexander.

Glenn Fewless

The rifle shown here is a very early Gibbs 1870 Farquharson, serial number 92. It is a well-traveled rifle. It went from England, where it was manufactured, to India, and from there to New Zealand, and from Kiwi land to the USA. The rifle is chambered for the .500 3-inch Black Powder Express. It was not in the best of condition when it arrived at the Wisconsin bench of metalsmith Glenn Fewless. He completely rebuilt the rifle including fitting a 26-inch full ribbed barrel. When Glenn finished the metalwork, he shipped the rifle to Illinois stockmaker Doug Mann. Doug crafted the magnificent stock from a superb stick of Turkish Exhibition grade walnut. Working from the blank, he whittled out the stock keeping in mind the original Gibbs styling for the stock. He added the leather covered pad, ebony forend tip, and checkered the finished stock in a 24 LPI point pattern. The rifle as shown is still in the white, awaiting finishing instructions from the client.

Glenn Fewless Gibbs Farquharson in .500 BPE, still in the white. Photos by Tom Alexander.

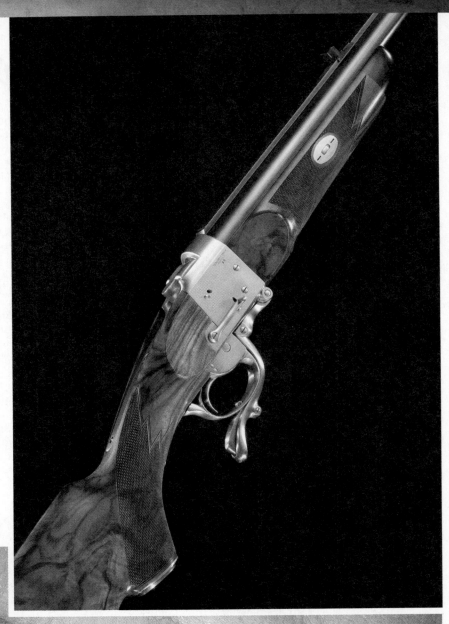

Joe Rundell

Joe Rundell is a multi-talented guy. He crafts wonderful custom stocks, does superb metalsmithing, but above all, he is a master engraver. While I don't normally run photos of anything other than custom guns here, I liked this custom knife so well that I thought it would be permissible. Knives and guns go together like biscuits and gravy anyway. Scott Sawby, using Damascus steel forged by Devin Thomas, crafted this custom Damascus folder. The client for this knife wanted nudes on the scales, and selected Joe Rundell to do the execution. He did a masterful job.

Photo by Tom Alexander.

Roger Sampson began studying engraving under the watchful eye of Emma Achleithner, who had been trained in Ferlach, Austria. Roger became a member of the Firearms Engravers Guild of America (FEGA) in 1985, and has been a professional member since 1989. He currently serves on the board of FEGA. Although Roger has specialized for years in adorning miniature firearms, the one shown here is a full-size rifle. It is an original early Winchester Model 1885, built in 1888. The rifle was built by Jim Westberg and checkered by Don Klein. Roger than engraved the rifle in a lovely scroll pattern. The rifle is currently in the white, awaiting a decision from the client on the final finish option.

Roger Sampson original Winchester Model 1885, still in the white. Photo by Tom Alexander.

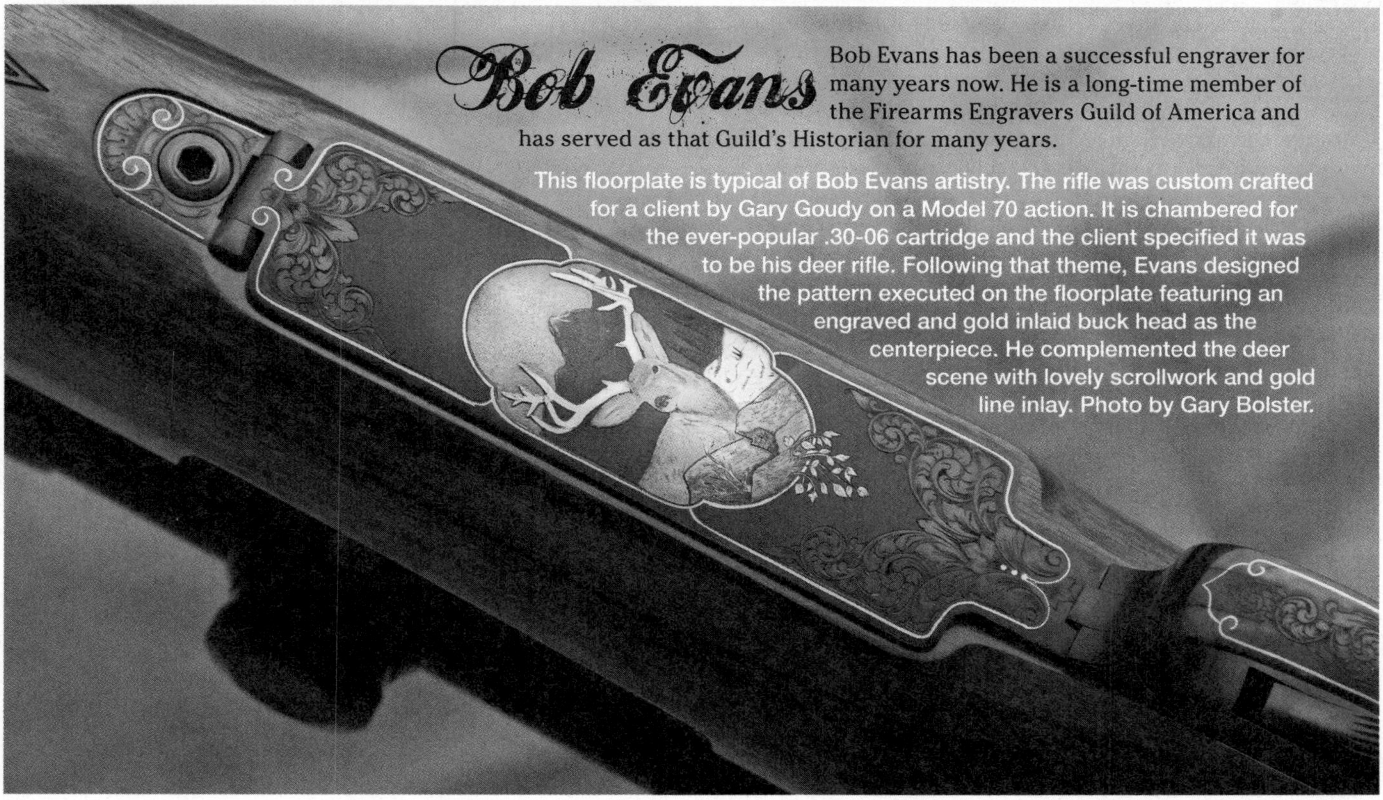

Roger Sampson

Bob Evans

Bob Evans has been a successful engraver for many years now. He is a long-time member of the Firearms Engravers Guild of America and has served as that Guild's Historian for many years.

This floorplate is typical of Bob Evans artistry. The rifle was custom crafted for a client by Gary Goudy on a Model 70 action. It is chambered for the ever-popular .30-06 cartridge and the client specified it was to be his deer rifle. Following that theme, Evans designed the pattern executed on the floorplate featuring an engraved and gold inlaid buck head as the centerpiece. He complemented the deer scene with lovely scrollwork and gold line inlay. Photo by Gary Bolster.

THE "OTHER" AUTOLOADERS

Though popular today, gas-operated shotguns had – and have – some stiff competition. BY NICK HAHN

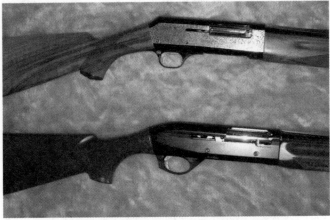

Top: Franchi 48 AL Eldorado Grade: long recoil system;
Bottom: Benelli Montefeltro Ultralight, inertia system.

Despite the tremendous popularity of the over/under shotgun and the resurgence of the classic side by side, when it comes to shotguns, in the U.S. the repeaters are ahead in popularity. There are many reasons for the repeaters' dominance, its lower price being one of the most important. Whatever the reason, the repeating shotgun sees the most widespread use among shooters, and there are basically only two categories that really matter: the pump (slide action) and the autoloader (semi-automatic). The autoloader is preferred by many today.

Among today's autoloaders, the vast majority are of the gas-operated variety. Some of the most popular brand names are gas-operated. Only the Benelli and its subsidiaries Franchi, Breda and Stoeger still continue to market non-gas-operated autoloaders. Today's gas-operated autoloaders are very reliable, soft shooting, versatile, and well balanced, a far cry from the early versions which had problems handling different loads. As one noted shotgun authority put it recently, the autoloader has reached the zenith of its development in reliability and handling qualities.

The gas-operated autoloader gained its popularity with the appearance of the Remington 1100 in 1963. Prior to that, they were either not reliable or could not handle high and low velocity loads interchangeably. There were the Remington 58 and the 878, the Beretta and LaSalle. The High Standard Supermatic, which was first marketed as the J.C. Higgins Model 60, made its first appearance in 1956. However, the early gas-operated autoloaders tended to be either heavy and bulky like the J.C. Higgins, or incapable of handling all loads like the early Remington and Berettas. The recoil operated autoloader still ruled the roost.

The basic difference between the gas-operated autoloader and the recoil-operated version is that in the former, the operation of the gun uses gases that are bled through a small hole (or holes) at the bottom of the barrel located about midway between the chamber and the muzzle. These gases push the gas piston, which in turn pushes the action bars rearward to cause the ejection of the empty and the subsequent reloading of a fresh round. In the recoil-operated autoloader – whether long recoil, short recoil, inertia, or floating chamber – all of these actions are operated by the force of recoil rather than by escaping gas.

Some today are unfamiliar with the recoil-operated autoloader since many of the older models have been discontinued and are found only in the used gun racks. Compared to the slick and shiny new models found today, the old-timers look downright plain if not shabby! But for many years, ever since its introduction in 1903, the recoil-operated autoloader was the king, especially if it was a Browning made by FN. One could say without reservation that the granddaddy of all autoloaders is the old Browning, more commonly known as the A-5 (aka Auto-5).

Browning A-5 with the long recoil system, the granddaddy of them all. The very first successful autoloading shotgun. This one is the legendary Sweet Sixteen model.

The Browning A-5, the brainchild of John Moses Browning, utilizes what is known as the long recoil system. The operation of the action is dependent upon the recoiling barrel, which moves the full length of the action, ejecting a spent case and reloading a fresh round just as the movement of a pump handle on a pump gun would do. In short, the recoiling barrel (which rides on a heavy spring wrapped around a magazine tube) performs exactly the same function that the forward arm of a shooter does on a pump gun. It is a very simple system that when properly set up (i.e., with its friction rings installed correctly) can be extremely reliable, as millions of Browning A-5s and its progeny have proven.

Browning's A-5 with its long recoil system produced a whole bunch of look-alikes and outright copies. Remington produced its famous Model 11, which was almost exactly like the A-5 with some modifications, under Browning license and Savage produced its 700 series, also under Browning license. In 1948, Remington streamlined the receiver of their Model 11, kept its long-recoil action, and simplified the friction ring system and *voila!* The new Model 11-48 was born. This was a very successful design and, although displaced by the 1100 in 1963, it continued to sell well into the 1970s as the budget priced "Mohawk" model.

Overseas, the Italians in particular took to the long-recoil autoloader and produced several versions of the old A-5 that were somewhat modified. Luigi Franchi came out with a lightweight, more streamlined version in 1948. Franchi's version is sold to this day as the Model 48 AL. Breda made a finely finished autoloader that could be completely disassembled without tools and had interchangeable chokes as early as the late 1940s.

There were other offshore autoloaders that were never imported into the U.S. The Japanese made several versions. Miroku made a simplified A-5 clone (it was actually made by KFC for Miroku) that was marketed under the Charles Daly label in 1960s. SKB made models 300 and 900 (not the XLs, which were gas operated) which were mechanically almost identical to the Franchi, imported from 1960s into the 1970s. Even the Russians of the old Soviet Union produced their version of the recoil-operated autoloaders, the Models MU21 and MU22. [*Editor's note: The Germans also got into the act with an unmarked A-5 knockoff bearing German proofs that was marketed briefly before WWII. Of course Winchester had its own take-down variation on the A-5 long recoil theme, the notorious M1911 "Widowmaker." – DMS*]

The long recoil autoloader first introduced in 1903 by Browning is still being produced, not as a Browning (the A-5 was discontinued in 1998), but as the Franchi 48AL, over 100 years after its first appearance! However, despite the fact that Robert Stack won the world 20 gauge Skeet Championship with a Remington Model 11, except for the streamlined 11-48s in smaller gauges – especially the 28 and .410 – the recoil operated autoloaders never really caught on with trap and skeet shooters.

From 1903 until the 1950s, there were no other autoloaders in the U.S. that were successful other than those based on the long recoil system. In 1953, John Browning's son Val came up with a design that was very different from the standard long recoil-operated autoloader. Val tweaked the existing short recoil system that had been used in the Johnson Automatic rifle, a rifle of questionable reputation that was used by some Marine and Army units during WWII. In the short recoil system, the barrel moves but about an inch or so, only far enough to start the breech block moving, then the breech block takes over on its own inertia and completes the cycle of ejecting the empty and reloading a fresh round. It is a very simple and extremely reliable system that does not require any friction rings and can fire both low and high velocity loads interchangeably.

Browning called its new short recoil autoloader the Double Automatic. It was designed to fire only two rounds. Lacking a magazine tube and all the stuff that goes with it, the Double Automatic had a balance that was as close as one could get to that of a double gun. It was extremely well made and began to arrive in large numbers by 1955. But alas, because it was but a two-shot and had a loading port on the left side of the receiver,

Browning Double Automatic "Twelvette" Model with short recoil system. A beautifully-made, superbly-handling gun that just never caught on.

it never really caught on, although some recognized its qualities and latched onto it. It was mass-produced only in 12 gauge although a couple of experimental 20 gauges were built. The Double Auto sold fairly well but not well enough, so it was discontinued after an 18-year run. Incidentally, it was also with the appearance of this new gun that the old humpback was renamed the "Automatic Five" or "A-5," to differentiate it from the newer Double Automatic. Prior to that, the old humpback was simply called the Browning Automatic, as indicated on its butt plate.

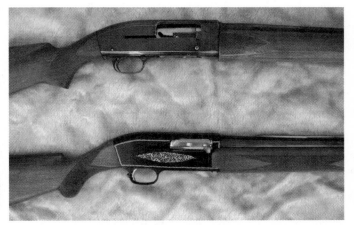

Top: Winchester Model 50, slipping or floating chamber; Bottom: Browning Double Automatic, short recoil system.

At about the same time, Winchester introduced an autoloader that was also quite innovative. Actually, although the Browning Double Auto was developed in 1953, the Winchester appeared earlier in larger numbers in 1954. The new Winchester Model 50 employed a "floating chamber" that previously had been used in a .22 caliber pistol, the Colt Ace, and the Remington .22 rifle Model 550. The Colt Ace had been in production since 1935, so the Model 50's was not a new concept. Still, it was new when it came to shotguns. In this system, the barrel is stationary, does not move at all. Instead, the chamber is a separate piece of tube that is sleeved into the barrel and slides back and forth. At the shot, the recoil forces the chamber to jab backward and moves the breech block, which completes the cycle on its own inertia, ejecting the empty and reloading the chamber with a fresh round. This was a very simple and effective method of harnessing the recoil energy. Unfortunately the gun did not catch on. The Model 50 with a steel receiver was very butt-heavy because it had its recoiling mechanism in the buttstock. Most shooters found it to be not just butt-heavy, but simply too heavy overall. The Model 50 in 12 gauge weighed close to 8-½ pounds and in 20 gauge it was around 7-½ pounds! Although it was made in trap and skeet versions, it never gained popularity because it lacked proper balance for clay target shooting.

Winchester tried to change that and came out with a better version, the Featherweight Model, with an alloy receiver. This made the gun lighter and shifted some weight to the front. It was an excellent gun, but still it did not sell well. It was trying to compete with the Browning A-5, which had been in production for over 50 years and had become a legend with field shooters. Among newer guns, the Remington 11-48 was a sleek looking, popular autoloader especially with skeet shooters. And Savage's take on the Model 11-48, the Model 755, was selling well in its own right.

Winchester tried harder and came out with the Model 59, which used the same system but had a barrel that even today would be considered revolutionary. The Winchester Model 59 used a thin steel liner that was wrapped with 500 miles of fiberglass thread to make what they called a Win-lite barrel. Together with the alloy receiver, this made for an excellent upland gun weighing in at 6-½ pounds in 12 gauge. But the Model 59 with its revolutionary barrel didn't make it, either. One good thing came out of that attempt. Winchester introduced screw-in chokes for the Model 59 in 1961, calling it the Versalite chokes. The concept eventually caught on. (Contrary to popular belief, Winchester was not the first with the interchangeable choke tube. A Massachusetts gunsmith by the name of Sylvester Roper patented a choke device that attached to the end of the barrel back in 1866, and the Italian gun maker Breda had a choke tube system called "Quick Choke," which made its appearance in the 1940s. The Simmons Choke, very similar to Breda's "Quick-Choke" came out a year before Winchester, and Armalite had a similar system on their revolutionary AR-17. If you include choke tubes that did not attach directly to the barrel, but to a recoil chamber, then you can go back to 1922 when the Cutts Compensator first appeared. But Winchester could rightly be given credit for having made the first commercially successful "internal" or "screw-in" choke tubes in the U.S.)

Ironically, although the Winchester choke system survived, later to be reborn as the "Winchoke," the floating chamber action did not, at least not in a shotgun. Like the short recoil system, the floating chamber system could be very reliable, providing the gun was cleaned and maintained properly. Most of the problems found associated with this system were simply caused by lack of maintenance and cleaning!

The Winchester Model 50 lasted only seven years. Introduced in 1954, a year after the Browning Double Automatic, it was discontinued in 1961. The Model 59 was introduced in 1958 and lasted until 1965. The Browning Double Automatic outlasted both Winchesters by staying in production until 1971. With the discontinuance of the Double Automatic, the choice in autoloaders was reduced to either the old long recoil or the newer gas operated system.

In 1967, a relatively little known company in Italy – Benelli – introduced their version of an inertia-driven system in an autoloader, the M-1. In 1983 Benelli further refined the system by providing a rotating bolt head. The first of the early Benelli shotguns began to appear in the U.S. around mid 1970s; these

guns were brought in initially either individually or by small importers, but in 1977 Heckler & Koch began importing the Benelli shotguns in larger numbers. The Benelli is an extremely reliable, well-made, well-finished gun. In the Benelli system, the barrel is stationary as in the floating chamber, and only the breech bolt moves back at the shot and completes the cycle.

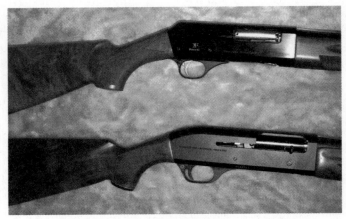

Top: Franchi 48 AL: long recoil system; Bottom: Benelli M-1: inertia system.

The inertia system, in different variations, has been around a long time. It seems that the Italians tinkered with it more than anybody else. In one form or another, it's been in existence since the 1920s. Benelli is constantly tweaking the system, coming out with different variations almost annually. The Benelli is very popular here in the U.S. with hunters and seems to have caught on with the Sporting Clays shooters as well.

Today, except for Benelli's inertia and Franchi 48AL's long recoil system, there are no other non-gas operated shotguns available to the American shooters, except on the used-gun market. The Beretta UGB 25 Xcel, which operates on the short recoil system, for all practical purpose can be counted

Bernardelli
Automatico VB – inertia system.

out of the equation, since it is made only as a trap gun. So essentially what we have today among autoloading shotguns is the inertia-driven and the long recoil-operated shotguns of Benelli and Franchi. All the rest are gas-operated. Are there other recoil operated systems? Yes, but their manufacture is not widespread.

In the 1930s the German company of Walther experimented with an autoloader that employed the toggle system like the famous Luger pistol and there was also the Scandinavian Sjogren. In the 1960s Stoeger imported a Vincenzo Bernardelli produced autoloader that employed a different type of inertia breech bolt system on a one piece-stocked, box magazine-fed shotgun that looked more like a rifle. Named the Automatico V.B., it was well-made but never caught on with the public, not here, not in Italy. It was made in 12, 16, and 20 gauges, but the smaller-gauge versions are extremely rare in the U.S.

The Cosmi is another non-gas operated system that has been around in Europe since the 1930s. It was developed as early as 1925 and has always been a strictly in-house, hand-made gun. Most shotgunners will never see a Cosmi, let alone handle one. It uses an inertia system on an action body that can be opened with a top lever like any break action gun! The magazine is contained in the buttstock. It is made in 12, 16, and 20 gauges and is, perhaps needless to say, very expensive.

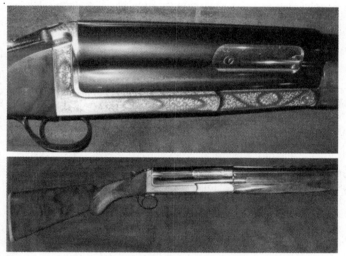

The Cosmi: a unique inertia system with a break-open action. Expensive, too.

The earlier mentioned Armalite Corporation came out with a rather unique autoloading shotgun, the AR-17, which they called the "Golden Gun," a lightweight gun made of "space-age" materials that weighed 5-½ pounds in 12 gauge. It worked on the short recoil system but unlike the Browning Double Auto, which had a loading port on the side, the AR-17 loaded from the bottom in conventional fashion and had interchangeable choke tubes. Unfortunately, it never caught on. It was, perhaps, a bit too futuristic looking with its gold anodized coloring and plastic stock. Parts for this gun were made between 1956 and 1962, enough for 2000 units. However, only a total of 1,200 units was sold during its lifetime.

Currently, the only shotgun that operates on a short recoil system is the rather expensive, previously-mentioned Beretta UGB25 Xcel. The UGB, like the Cosmi, has the unique break-open barrel like a double gun or a single shot, yet it also has a round that is held on the side, somewhat like the Browning Double Auto, and operates on short recoil. It is made only as a 12 gauge trap gun.

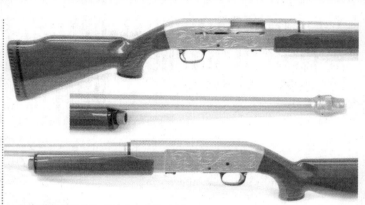

Armalite AR-17, short recoil system.

So, now we come to the question of, what possible advantage could non-gas-operated autoloaders hold over gas-operated guns. Most will agree that dependability is no longer the big issue with gas-operated guns, so that is not an advantage for non-gas guns. Possibly the biggest difference between the gas and the non-gas autoloaders is their respective handling characteristics, their dynamics. Some gas-operated autoloaders may very well weigh less than their non-gas-operated counterparts, but their balance points will be different and chances are their forearms will be thicker.

By their very nature, the gas-operated guns require more hardware up front in the forearm area. It is amazing how balance can shift with something as seemingly insignificant as the gas piston. That is one reason why the floating chamber Winchester Models 50 and 59 are light up front. The Browning Double Auto also owes its excellent handling qualities to the lack of a magazine. The Franchi 48AL solves this problem by having a lightweight alloy magazine tube, so the weight up front is considerably less than, say, that of the Browning A-5. Still, the A-5 has a much livelier feel and thinner forearm than a gas-operated autoloader because it has less material up front. Some of the gas-operated autoloaders today, those designed as "upland" guns, do employ alloy magazine tubes to reduce weight. But there's still all that hardware up front that has to be there for the gun to function.

Perhaps someone other than Beretta will attempt to revive the floating chamber system or the short recoil system. Browning attempted to bring back the short recoil system in its ill-fated A500R. However, the gun was very short-lived owing to its ugly design and mechanical problems. Recently Benelli came out with their radically different Vinci model. This rather unusual looking shotgun uses a different inertia system, eliminating the action spring that is usually found in the buttstock. Being of modular design, the Vinci contains its entire bolt mechanism, including the action spring, in the receiver. The buttstock contains no mechanical parts. It is an ingenious system but not entirely new. The earlier mentioned Automatico VB by Bernardelli employed a similar system. It was not exactly like the Vinci, but similar in application.

The modern gas-operated autoloader is a far cry from the early versions. Today they are beautifully put-together and extremely reliable. But as long as they are dependent on all that hardware to make the gun cycle, they will never have that desired "between-the-hands" feel, and they will always be, just a bit, even if tiny bit, more susceptible to stoppage.

And that's why there will always be a market for the "other" autoloaders.

A TRIO OF UNUSUAL REMINGTON MILITARY ROLLING BLOCK RIFLES

BY GEORGE J. LAYMAN

Perhaps it is a stroke of providence that an author may, without warning, be deluged with an entirely unexpected crop of examples of a specific commodity that serve to make a work of nonfiction an even better finished product. Such has been my experience during my research on my latest book, *A Collectors Guide to the Remington Rolling Block Military Rifle and its Variations* (2009: Mowbray Publishing Company, Woonsocket, RI).

This latest work is the most intriguing study of an antique firearm that I have ever encountered, and it didn't reach its climax until the final nine months preceding publication. Never before did so many of the rare, unknown, and unexpected variations of the Remington military rolling block rifle make a showing in so short a span of time. From the practically unheard-of Remington Model 1902 in 7.62x54 mm caliber, to the Remington Cadet No. 206 in .45-70 caliber, to one of six known remaining examples of the Springfield-Remington Transformation rifles tested by the St. Louis Board, to solving the puzzle behind the Remington Greek Contract Model, never has such a roller coaster of a book ever confronted me!

In the following pages I'll share a few of the more interesting portions of this work. The trio of of military rolling block rifles and carbines featured herein are perhaps the first or the very few seen by a majority of collectors, both tyro and advanced alike. The very presence of these three Remingtons – which include a two-band .50-70 Government caliber rifle found in Cuba that smacks of the little known Civil Guard Model with a hybrid No. 1-1/2 and No. 1 frame in a unique caliber; a .50 caliber rimfire carbine with Cambodian markings; and a nearly nonexistent Model 1902 7mm Mauser caliber rifle of El Salvador contract – make for a rare gathering of the elusive and esoteric. Therefore let us take a truly international journey amongst a few of the many military rolling blocks that have taxed this author's bank of knowledge to the utmost!

A REMINGTON CIVIL GUARD MODE OR SINGLE ROLLING BLOCK VARIATION UNTO ITSELF

A majority of antique military rifle collectors and students of the rolling block family of firearms have seldom been able to acquire one or more examples of a breech-loading single-shot rifle that was once catalogued by E. Remington & Sons as the Civil Guard Model. Primarily associated with early purchases of the rolling block by Spain, this elusive variant listed in Remington factory literature between 1874 and 1884 was often described as a two-band, military rolling block rifle in .43 Spanish caliber, having a 30.5-inch barrel that was coupled with a saber bayonet lug as standard equipment. Introduced during Spain's first contract of 1869, it was intended to arm the Guardia Civil or Spanish Civil Guard, an organization which today remains an active para military-police organization serving throughout the peninsula of Spain.

Exact delivery numbers to the Spanish government are unclear at best, with a majority having been sent to Cuba to arm the *Ejercito Ultramar*, which was Spain's overseas colonial armed forces. The most common number given by historians has been estimated at 3,000 pieces received by Spanish quartermasters in colonial Cuba. A very small number of these rifles have been retained by the Remington Museum, not to mention those few that had been sold during the late 1940s downsizing of the museum's inventory.

The November 1, 1920, Remington Museum inventory list compiled by Melbourne Chambers displays a disappointing total of four, with two very unique examples that are now stored in the museum archive room. One is in a very peculiar .42 Berdan caliber, with another specimen in the proper .43 Spanish caliber but made up with a New York State action and a rubber butt plate. The author purchased one of the other Civil Guard Models that were sold off in the 1940s, which was a .58 Berdan-caliber example that had two barrel bands and a Turkish crescent moon and star stamped on the left hammer flat. Identified by a brass tag with inventory number 146, this particular Civil Guard Model has neither the correct .43 Spanish chambering, nor the standard saber bayonet lug.

None of the past or present Civil Guard Model rifles in the Remington museum is a "catalog correct" representation. The Schuyler Hartley & Graham shipment records of 1868 to 1900 list a mere 1,130 of the .43 Spanish-caliber Civil Guard Models as having been shipped to Argentina. No others of this variation are noted on this listing and recorded as shipped to any other nation in the Spanish-speaking Americas, nor even to Spain itself.

In the past 45 years of military rolling block research and collecting, the author has examined a total of four genuine catalog-correct Civil Guard Model Remington rolling block rifles, and has owned one example which was British proof-marked. It was discovered in British Honduras in the mid-1990s. All rifles of this genre observed to date have displayed evidence of having performed hard but honest service and all appeared to be in very good condition as a whole.

During the course of completion of my latest book, it was in early in 2009 that a most inscrutable Remington-manufactured military rolling block rifle was obtained. This particular arm may be described as a special order variation of Remington's Civil Guard Model, appearing to be in a singular category

These views of the full length Cuban rifle from both left and right side indicate it is in excellent condition overall. The rifle's barrel is covered with a fine pitting from the muzzle to the breech. This is primarily noticeable on the left side of the rifle. The right side of the frame has a minimum of fine pitting; however, it is noticeable to a small extent.

Partial case colors are visible on the right frame as well along with the butt plate that has faded case colors which are very brilliant internally when the plate is removed. The right side of the two barrel bands shows a clear, crisp, deeply-struck Spanish crown.

The right breech block flat has a small tri-leaf cartouche which was a standard marking on Remington Spanish contract rifles and carbines.

all to itself. A genuine pre-1898 antique, it was discovered in Cuba, of all places, and purchased from a Russian acquaintance who is a collector and purveyor of international military antiques. Since Russian citizens may travel to Cuba and export a variety of commodities, it is a rare stroke of fortune to have friends with such privileges!

What I had purchased was a two band, Remington-made military rolling block in .50-70 Govt. caliber, with two Spanish crown-marked barrel bands that was manufactured with the smaller, No. 1-1/2 action such as found on the Lightweight "Baby Carbine," albeit cosmetically similar to a scaled-down, Civil Guard Model minus the saber bayonet lug. Stamped on the right breech block flat is a tri-leaf cartouche, which is often present on the early, first contract Spanish Model rolling block rifles in .43 caliber which were often issued to the colonial garrisons in Cuba, Puerto Rico, and perhaps the Philippines as well. This remarkably well-maintained rifle, together with an

unknown number of others of its ilk, was evidently supplied to a specific unit(s) in the colonial Spanish period. It could also perhaps have been a straw purchase by insurgents in that island nation prior to or during the War of 1898.

Though not a Civil Guard Model in the classical catalog-specified sense of the word, this two-band rifle using the full house .50-70 center fire cartridge has the E. Remington & Sons address on the tang with the last patent date of March 1874 and is equipped with a rotary extractor. Upon removal of the forearm, a cartouche of A.F.G. can be seen on the rear flat. A genuine anomaly among rolling block rifles in .50-70 Govt. caliber, it would almost fill the bill as the elusive but scantily advertised Cadet Model 301 once sold by Charles Godfrey in New York City; however, it is physically quite

different. The presence of tang markings indicating production prior to the 1886 receivership of the Remington company is one of the physical traits which give this rifle a full-size look, in addition to its very uncommon smaller frame. Further research suggests that the A.F.G. cartouche has an affiliation with the pre-1898 Spanish Customs and Tariff Service located near present day Guantanamo, Cuba. In the nineeenth century, this region was one of the main ports where Spain received all incoming military goods shipped to Cuba. It was

also one of the main offices of the Spanish "Aduanero," which is the customs branch. Thus it appears that the customs officers were armed with rifles and revolvers different in caliber and sometimes type from those issued to the army.

A view with the action opened reveals the rotary extractor cut on the left side of the breech block, which appears unfired by virtue of the absence of brass pressure ring residue on the face and the shiny, unblemished bore. The butt stock and forearm on this light version of a Civil Guard Model retains a raised grain appearance especially noticeable on the former. When the forearm is removed, it reveals "A. F. G." stamped to the rear, along with a clean, blue finish on the barrel in this protected area. (Photo by Stuart Mowbray.)

Unlike the tri-flat upper receiver design of the Cadet Model 206 in .45-70 (which, by the way, was the only Remington military rolling block sold commercially in this chambering) this unique .50-70 has a rounded upper receiver, a la the Light "Baby Carbine." In addition, the rear sling swivel is located on the buttstock and not on the front of the trigger guard, a common feature unique to the various cadet models including a small number of full-size United States martial rolling block rifles and carbines. The mere presence of this esoteric military rolling block rifle provides a degree of certainty that Cuba may still retain a substantial inventory of military rolling block rifles.

Returning to the Civil Guard Model in its basic configuration, the one point that puts it out of place with mainstream Spanish military rolling block rifles is the presence of the saber bayonet lug. Many collectors are aware that among the rolling block rifles sold to Spain from Remington, including those domestically produced by the Spanish under license, all official military versions were manufactured to accept only the angular bayonet. That is to say, except for the small numbers of Spanish-made musketoons and the so called "Royal Bodyguard" Models – the latter having a lug made to accept a 27-inch saber bayonet – makes all of this an exception and not the rule. It may well be assumed that the standard, catalog-specified Civil Guard Model many collectors are quite familiar with may have been a failure from a marketing standpoint and ended up being sold off to customers enthralled by its catchy nomenclature. Thus this first-to-be-seen, and obviously rare, No.1-1/2 size Civil Guard style rifle, chambered in .50-70 Government and adapted to an angular bayonet, may indeed be an independent, unknown variation that accidentally slipped through the cracks.

The possibility may also exist that documentation of this model could have disappeared among the many natural calamities that over the years have robbed historians of much vital data pertinent to Remington history and its products. Should Cuba ever become opened for free trade in the future and permit American citizens the opportunity of unrestricted travel, the research of military rolling block history will be an area we simply must look into.

Shown below is a chart of the dimensions of this scarcity as compared to both the No.1 and No.1-1/2 size actions:

A SADDLE RING CARBINE FROM SOUTH-EAST ASIA

The presence of the Remington rolling block in Asia has normally been confined to China and Japan as far as general knowledge is concerned. Since the publication of the author's most recent work on the military rolling block, this region has proven that those countries using this particular single shot-military rifle was more widespread than previously thought.

One Asian country that had never been thought of as a user of the Remington rolling block system is the one-time French Protectorate of Cambodia, which is bordered by Siam (the name of Thailand prior to 1939), Viet Nam, and Laos. Just two years after the end of the Viet Nam war in 1975, this .50 caliber rimfire Remington saddle-ring carbine was found in Thailand in an area not far from the Laotian capital of Vientiane.

One of the great surprises of this carbine was that after its forearm was removed, it revealed a WWII vintage ten peso, Japanese occupation note from the Philippine Islands! How this ended up hidden under the forearm in between the barrel is truly puzzling – especially since Cambodia is a good distance over water from the Philippines. It may well be that this carbine was taken as a souvenir by a Japanese soldier in Cambodia or Thailand during the war who had been previously stationed in the Philippines and took an occupation note as a souvenir and hid it in the rifle. Other than this, it could be anyone's guess!

This carbine was brought back by an Army officer to the United States as an antique war trophy in 1977, which is probably the first time this rolling block had returned stateside in over a century! The carbine is identified by its Cambodian Sanskrit markings, as well as the presence of a twelve-bladed "Chakra," an ancient pin-wheel like symbol representing blades of fire. Most unique is that its chamber dimensions equate to an all-but-unknown .50 caliber rimfire cartridge with a case measuring 1.5" in length and a bullet diameter of .577"; aside from its length, it has a distinct resemblance to the .56-50 Spencer rimfire.

The action on this carbine is, in its entirety, a factory-correct Remington product, right down to placement of the saddle ring and staple. One feature that appears somewhat peculiar when compared to other Remington rolling block carbines is the presence of a ramrod stop at the front of the trigger guard. With this being an early Remington New Model action with rimfire breech block, it may originally have been designed as a two band, full stock, saddle ring carbine, all of which were equipped with a short cleaning rod. Regardless of its original configuration, it is a genuine first in the military rolling block collecting field.

A strong French colonial influence in this region of the world may be the reason why this carbine found its way to Southeast Asia. For many years, Siam and Vietnam treated Cambodia as a buffer state, but with France gaining more and more favoritism and becoming opportunistic with the Cambodian king, they began encroaching deeper into Siamese and Vietnamese territories. A tug of war between Siam and France ensued and slowly weakened Cambodia, eventually throwing the country into civil strife. It was at this time that France supplied Cambodia with arms and ordnance to help authorities protect the country from the scores of bandit and rebel groups that resulted from all the civil strife. Most, if not all, military and police small arms supplied to Cambodia, Laos, and Vietnam from 1884 on originated from France. Furthermore, most Remington rolling block rifles and carbines supplied to Cambodia's gendarmes and military organizations were taken from the left-over, obsolescent Franco-Prussian War surplus.

As earlier noted, the caliber of this carbine has a unique identity crisis. The fully round, unmarked, 20-inch barrel is similar to either a Whitney or an 1865 Spencer carbine barrel, having what appears to be Burnside style three-groove rifling. However, the chamber has ample free bore in order to accommodate a nearly 1-3/4- inch cartridge. The lower butt stock has a plugged sling swivel inlet, carbine butt plate, and Cambodian Sanskrit markings on the lower butt stock that appear to be the number "3" at the far right led by what appears as the number "seven" and a compound word using a "T"-sounding consonant. Next is what seems to resemble an obliterated cartouche or royal insignia of sorts, struck in a square, block-print configuration.

The most significant of all markings,

	No. 1	No. 1-1/2	Cuban No. 1-1/2
Average Action Width	1.312" - 1.323"	1.140" - 1.143"	1.221"
Average Receiver Wall Thickness	.290"	.172"	.245"

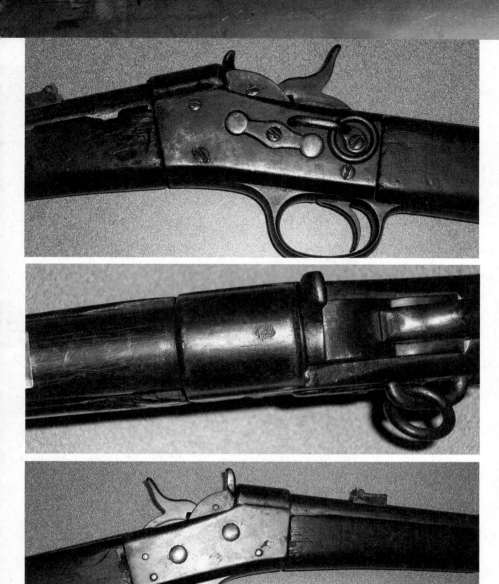

however, is the Chakra over the receiver ring, which genuinely identifies this carbine as having been issued within this region of the world – more importantly, by the French Protectorate of Cambodia. As previously mentioned, this pinwheel-like design is a symbol representing a number of meanings from several other countries in this surrounding part of Asia. It is also the royal marking of the house of Thailand, something that stems from a time well before the country's name was changed to Thailand. Furthermore, the Chakra represents the ancient bladed weapon of the Khmer gods.

The tang markings on this well-used example are the earliest found on the New Model Rifle Remington rolling block action, ending with the date April 17 1866. The left side of the frame displays a cryptic "B " stamping adjacent to the extractor screw. This carbine is equipped with the standard 100- to 500-yard carbine rear sight. Its nearly black, oil-soaked stocks, with assorted gouges and dings, are evidence of hard use. Mechanically sturdy, the action is tight, appearing well-maintained, but the bore rates only fair.

In conversing with several military rolling block specialists and collectors, I found that none has observed a military rolling block having Cambodian or Sanskrit markings or even knew they existed. Removal of the butt stock reveals two matching sets of the alphanumerics D8 2162, stamped on the upper and lower left flats of this carbine, which could be coded serial or casting numbers. The author is still not certain if this is one of the 21,117 Remington rolling block carbines in various calibers purchased by France in the period of 1870-71. The full round barrel is common to the Transformation Conversion Rifle. Another possibility exists that a .58 caliber rifle musket barrel could have been modified and installed on the action.

The mere presence of this carbine, coupled with such an exotic and enigmatic set of markings, is *ipso facto* assurance that the collector of military rolling block firearms can expect no foreseeable end of variety in the near future. This Cambodian example once again proves that this now highly specialized field of collecting is chock full of ample, unlimited potential.

Without question, this is one military rolling block with a set of markings that few collectors would have thought ever existed – one stamped with crisp, prominent Sanskrit letters identifying it as the former Cambodian military or police property. The appearance of this Remington carbine is another indicator that French influence was still very prevalent throughout Southeast Asia in the nineteenth century. Such an early Remington military carbine with a Type 2 action in any rimfire chambering is considered a rare find. Note the concave axis of the rimfire breech bloc, and the six o'clock position of the firing pin. Externally, the barrel sides of the chamber are completely round, something reminiscent of the Whitney rolling block, but the barrel displays no markings. The closeup of the seven-bladed Chakra stamped over the receiver ring shows it to be deep and everlasting:a number "3" next to two similar consonants with a "T"-like pronunciation. The square-like cartouche at the end, which appears to be an Arabic "L" or a "C," may also be an obliterated royal inspector's stamp or yet another Sanskrit mark. The sling swivel channel on the lower butt stock behind these markings has the texture of hard rubber or an ebony-like filler. (Author's collection.)

THE EL SALVADOR MODEL 1902: A RARE ROLLING BLOCK RESPONSIBLE FOR A NICKNAME

Mexico and El Salvador are so far the only Latin American nations of the smokeless powder era to have their national crests roll stamped over the receiver ring, including the only known variant having the words "MODELO 1902" marked at the bottom. They are seldom encountered in any quantity due to smaller production numbers.Those that are found are often in very rough, well-used condition.

The 1901 El Salvador contract, which actually commenced delivery the following year, is undoubtedly responsible for creation of the popular and widely used term "Model 1902." Essentially a *deja vu* of Mexico's "special order" of three years earlier, the Republic of El Salvador was the first quantity purchaser of this new, "improved" Model 1897. Unlike Mexico's earlier contract of 14,000-plus rifles and carbines, El Salvador's New Model Small Bore Military Rifles were equipped with the Albert Day-patent, automatic rotary extractor of October 22, 1901. In addition to the national crest, the Salvadoran Model 1902 was equipped with a very unique hand guard that has a longitudinally grooved inlet extending from the front of the receiver ring to the middle barrel band. Those who may discover one of these in very good or better condition, together with an unblemished national crest, should consider themselves very fortunate, as the bulk of surviving examples display excessive wear. This variation is also an important addition to any collection of post-1900-era military rolling block rifles.

For the record, it is worth mentioning that the Remington Museum archive room at Ilion, New York, has fortunately retained a single sample of the Model 1902 Salvadoran contract in near new condition, the only one known to the author in such condition. Though production numbers of the El Salvador contract Model 1902 were less than half the total of the larger quantities of the Mexican contract of Model 1897 rifles, the reason so few have appeared on the surplus market is due to many having been discarded by the Salvadoran government sometime after 1934. During this time, a large, anti-government revolt was in progress which saw some 10,000 to 30,000 peasants and revolutionaries massacred in an event known as the *La Matanza*. Many of the anti-government factions used obsolete military rifles and machetes during their struggle, and it was reported that thousands of their weapons were dumped in the Gulf of Fonseca following the government's victory. No doubt many rolling block rifles were among them.

The receiver ring on these rifles has an elaborate roll stamped crest marked, "Republica del Salvador-Modelo 1902" with "CAL. 7mm S.M." (Spanish Mauser) marked ahead of the upper hand guard. Butt stocks may also be found with an assortment of rack numbers as well.

All in all, this variation should be classified as a special order affair in its entirety. Surviving Salvadoran defense records show that the first deliveries of the 5,550 rifle contract (but no carbines) began in the spring of 1902. In reality, this may perhaps make El Salvador the first customers of the so-called Model 1902 Remington rolling block featuring the improved automatic rotary extractor. The other half of the story is that the very presence of this marking may be the reason why all of the new rolling block rifles with this feature were responsible for the unofficial title of Model 1902. It should also be noted that some Model 1902 Remington rolling block rifles displaying those special features of the Salvadoran Model, such as the grooved upper hand guard minus the national crest, in many cases represent an "overrun" variation totaling somewhere in

(left) A perfect example of one of the Remington Model 1902 El Salvador contract rifles shipped without the roll stamped national crest on the receiver ring. This specimen was found by the author in a wooden crate of 10 identical rifles. Discovered in 1995 in an abandoned warehouse near Quantico, Virginia, once leased by Hunters Lodge (Ye Olde Hunter) a few miles to the north in Alexandria during the 1960s, the site yielded some interesting leftovers of the past. With the help of an acquaintance, the author obtained the entire case of 7mm Remington rolling block rifles. Each rifle was equipped with a Remington marked knife bayonet and metal scabbard and leather frog, all having a "Ye Olde Hunter" shipping label and tag banded to the buttstock. Handwritten on each tag was, "Salvadoran Remington Rolling Block Rifle w/ Bayo and Scabbard, VG Condition, $19.95." All tags were dated "8-17-68," a time somewhat past the golden era of the '50s and '60s milsurp years.

As seen here, the condition of the rifles rates about very good: nice bores, and all stocks have the abundance of the usual dings of the past. Each bayonet appears to be in far worse condition than the rifles, with all blades showing deep pits that smoothed out quite well after cleaning. The absence of the Salvadoran national crest is very obvious; however accompanying paperwork in the case specified all were imported directly from that Central American country, with customs clearance from the port of Norfolk, Virginia. Entry into the United States was granted in May of 1968. Following the acquisition of this case of rifles, the author has since assumed that El Salvador may well have been one of the last countries south of the border to clean out their armories and unload the final shipments of 7mm Remington rolling block ordnance. Rumors still persist that Nicaragua has about 3,000 remaining in the Managua arsenal, and at least a half a dozen have trickled in through Canada since 1988. The question is: how many still remain?

As to why this misplaced case of ten rifles were never returned to Hunter's Lodge main warehouse, no one has any idea. All this author knows is that the developer of the property where they were stored in 1995 told my friend to "clean the place out and take what you wish, otherwise it will all end up in a landfill!" There truly is nothing better than good friend! (Author's collection. Photos by Tony Matias.)

(below) This variation should be classified as a special order affair in its entirety. The roll stamping of the Salvadoran crest is the only other smokeless powder-era Remington to have a national crest other than the Mexican Contract Model 1897. it is believed that the Salvadoran Contract variant was responsible for the unofficial title of "Model 1902." Surviving Salvadoran defense records show that the first deliveries of the 5,550 rifle contract (but no carbines) began in the spring of 1902. In reality, this could make El Salvador the first customers of the so called, Model 1902 Remington rolling block that featured the improved automatic rotary extractor patented in October of 1901. Collectors should note that any Model 1902 Remington rolling block rifles displaying the aforementioned special features of the Salvadoran Model minus the national crest total no more than an estimated 800 pieces. Early documentation suggests that these rifles were not stamped and were ultimately held back by Remington because of a default. An unknown number were later purchased by El Salvador without the crest and were perhaps therefore a bit lower in cost. Such unmarked rifles indeed occasionally do appear and are of great interest to the rolling block specialist.

the range of an estimated 800 to 1,000 pieces. Furthermore, an unknown number were purchased by El Salvador in 1903 without the crest and were perhaps significantly lower in cost due to the absence of the marking. Such unmarked rifles do occasionally appear and are of interest to the collector. However, distinguishing an overrun piece from a genuine second order Salvadoran version is practically impossible. Surviving import records from the now defunct "Hunters Lodge" (also known as "Ye Olde Hunter") of the 1950s and '60s do indicate that several hundred Model 1902 Salvadoran-type contract rifles without the national crest were imported into the United States from both Honduran and Panamanian sources. These too may be considered contract overruns; however, their early origins cannot be determined.

Hard usage and the humid jungle climate took their toll on all the old military rifles. Thus those few 7mm Salvadoran rolling block rifles that made it to *del Norte* ("The North") as surplus are normally discovered in rough, pitted condition. It is a fortunate collector who uncovers one of these prizes in anything better than good condition.

THE Bull Dog PACK: Variations of the Breed

BY GORDON BRUCE

Editor's Note: Last year we presented George Layman's piece on bulldog revolvers, written primarily from an American perspective. This year we offer yet another piece on Bulldogs, written by our British friend Gordon Bruce.

Since the creation of Webley's compact little calibre .450 revolver named The British Bull Dog, its basic design has been copied and produced by many other gun manufacturers during the latter part of the nineteenth century.

The name had been registered as an official trade mark in Britain by Henry Webley himself, on behalf of the Birmingham firm, P. Webley & Son, on 12 March 1878. On that occasion, it was claimed to have been in regular use for the revolver since 1873. Webley had specified the title of BULL DOG as two separate words, rather than a single word, or joined by a hyphen. Thereafter, in firearms circles, it has become a generic term for nearly all short-nosed pocket revolvers.

The general styling and construction of the Webley, with its small grip shape, double-action mechanism and swing-out ejector, became the basis for most subsequent designs.

Perhaps the examples that adhered more closely to the original were those produced in Liege, Belgium, a major centre of pistol manufacturing at the time and from where many thousands of the little pistols were constructed for export.

Much of the Belgian handgun production at that period was directed towards the American continent, where the little Webley model had enjoyed considerable success during its initial sales period and so it was not long before Liege manufacturers sought a larger share of the gun trade in that region.

Ever conscious of an expanding market, the Belgians made full use of appropriate titles on their Bull Dog models in order to attract customers. Names such as Western Bull Dog, California Bull Dog, Southern Bull Dog, Texas Bull Dog and Frontier Bull Dog had been devised to give a suitable connotation to the weapons and were soon adopted. These variations on the original Bull Dog title were usually stamped, or sometimes engraved, onto the top strap, in similar manner to that employed on the Webley.

Development of the American West, with all its associated traumas in the face of Indian attacks, saloon bar brawls and general crime, had become a lucrative outlet for gun sales.

General travellers, prospectors, railway men, saloon keepers, bankers and gamblers were all competing for a share of the growing prosperity throughout the region. In such a volatile environment, it was only natural that, sooner or later, serious confrontations would arise and many felt a need to be armed for self protection.

One of the most popular and effective forms of self-defence for those individuals was the handgun, and there had been a general adoption of such weapons as a normal items of personal equipment. Single-shot and double-shot pistols of the more basic Deringer pattern already enjoyed a wide distribution throughout the United States as they were normally of an effective .41-inch calibre and, furthermore, could also be easily concealed about the person. Despite being effective at close quarters,

their main disadvantage was that only a single shot could be fired, compared with several rounds from a normal holster revolver. Of course, multi-chambered pistols that were small enough to be carried conveniently in the pocket were then usually of minimum calibre as a concession to lightness.

The original calibre .44 Webley Bull Dog revolver had been designed specifically to overcome this discrepancy in a compact form of self-defence giving several shots of reasonable power.

As its name implied, it was small yet powerful for its size. Possessing a handgun of that calibre and one emanating from such a prominent handgun manufacturer may well have added to a general feeling of security for each purchaser. Attendant to that concept was the knowledge that shots fired from a .44 revolver would certainly have more detrimental affect on any wild animal than those fired from a pistol of lesser power.

CONTINENTAL VERSIONS

At first, the Belgian gun manufacturers still adhered to the larger calibres and most of the Bull Dogs from Liege were chambered for the .450 cartridge. The construction and quality of these weapons, while perhaps not quite up to the standard of the British product, were perfectly adequate and this, together with the more reasonable purchase price, created a huge demand for Bull Dog models generally amongst the transient American workforce. Prices ranged from as low as $6 to $7, in comparison to a $12 charge for the Webley, thus presenting a serious challenge to the British product.

Bull Dog models imported from Belgium were normally stamped with Liege proofhouse marks, consisting of the letters E L G arranged above a star and contained within an oval, to denote definitive proof. (This mark was valid until the year 1893, when the oval was surmounted by a Crown.) Other marks that may be encountered include the letter R beneath a Crown, indicating a rifling test, plus other capital letters beneath a star as the bench mark of a particular Inspector.

While the external appearance of the Belgian versions remained fairly similar to the original, items of the lock mechanism and its arrangement were frequently altered by various Liege gun makers. The hammer of the British Webley was raised to a cocked position by an arm pivoted at the rear end of the trigger; a sprung sear then engaged a notch under the hammer to hold it in position until disengaged by the trigger being pulled back. Lock mechanism of the Liege product usually differed from the Webley in having a small, spring-influenced, arm hinged to the front face of the hammer, from where it was engaged by a rearward extension of the trigger. Those examples having a half-cock safety notch, also featured an additional lever positioned beneath the hammer. Others that were provided with a rebound feature had a similar lever to hold the hammer away from the cartridge primer. No spring was provided but the lever had a hook at its rear end, which extended behind the lower rear part of the hammer. When the trigger returned forward after firing, the lower rear surface of the trigger cammed against the upper forward end of the rebound lever, forcing the rear hook to pull the hammer back slightly.

British Bull-Dog: Title is stamped onto top strap and upper flat surface of barrel and is also marked CLEMENT ARMS Co. Weapon has Liege proof marks and was possibly manufactured by Charles Clement at turn of 19th century.

Grip plates are of hard rubber with vine design at upper and lower extremities. Other examples of this type are known to be marked N.Y. ARMS Co., reported to be trade name used by Crescent Firearms Company (1888-1893). Courtesy Homer Ficken.

Perhaps one of the more distinctive features of the Belgian models was an alteration to the frame for providing a more effective hold on the weapon when firing. This appeared on several Bull Dog types, on which a projection was formed at the upper rear of the stock to offer an abutment for the hand when the weapon recoiled at each shot. Another item that varied from the norm was the mainspring, which replaced the standard Webley double-limb component with a single leaf spring held to the inner face of the stock by a single screw. This made installation and removal a fairly simple process and less hazardous for the owner.

Several important Liege gun makers were involved in the manufacture of Bull Dog revolvers and they each employed a different title for their product. Most obvious was an adoption of the original term "British Bull Dog" with the last two words either separated, or joined by a hyphen. On some models, this was stamped onto the top strap, while others had the title engraved by hand at the same location.

A more abrupt title of "The Bull-Dog" was also used as an alternative by Liege gun makers and, in similar fashion, could be either stamped or engraved onto the top strap.

While the use of assorted titles for the Bull Dog models was quite prevalent during the latter part of the nineteenth century, an identification of the manufacturer was seldom applied. On the rare occasions that it took place, there was either a small trade mark of some form, or simply the initial letters of a maker's name. It had even been common policy for Liege gun makers to register the names of fictitious companies as trademarks for use on their weapons.

The Bull Dog: Five-shot calibre .44 S&W model with italics THE BULL DOG engraved onto top strap. Birmingham proof mark, plus letters J and C stamped on left side of grip frame. Addition at lower front corner of cylinder acts as friction brake. Link at side of ejector swivel is spring with small stud to provide friction on ejector rod. Serial No.520. Courtesy Homer Ficken.

Five-shot Calibre .450 model with THE BULL-DOG stamped onto top surface of top strap. Liege Inspection mark of star above letter D on right-hand side. Stock plates are light brown wood. Initials T and J appear at left side suggest probable Trade Mark of Liege gun maker Joseph Tholet. Note reinforced area on frame for loading gate hinge. Serial No. 12 (Royal Armouries, Leeds).

In an attempt to make the pocket revolver even more compact, the Belgians decided to eliminate the trigger guard entirely and employ a folding trigger. Revolvers of this pattern were produced by Leopold Ancion-Marx, Edouard Schroeder, Henri Sauveur, Auguste Lebeau, Manufacture Liegeoise d'Armes a feu, etc. and offered in a variety of forms under an assortment of titles, one of which was "Belgian Bull Dog." It was usually equipped with vulcanised stock plates, moulded with an elaborate foliate decoration, or furnished in mother-of-pearl as an optional extra. A thumb-operated safety device could also be provided to secure the hammer.

In March 1890, the firm Manufacture

Liegeoise d'Ames a feu had registered a trade mark of the letters ML beneath a Crown, which was sometimes applied at the left side of the frame together with alternative markings on the top strap.

Elaborately decorated versions were popular option offered by many Liege gun makers.

As sales within certain regions of the United States increased, so also did the variety of names for the Bull Dog models as an enticement for those seeking to purchase a revolver. Amongst the first to appear in this category was the title of "California Bull Dog" on a revolver chambered for the calibre .44 Webley and .44 Bull Dog cartridges but which would also accept .44 S&W or even the .44 Russian rounds.

This model was quite distinctive in having fancy black rubber stock plates with moulded neo-classical head (sometimes referred to as Thunder God), accompanied by branch and leaf decoration. Stock plates of this pattern were widely adopted by Liege gun makers and have been observed on various other Bull Dog style revolvers, notably on those produced by Joseph Tholet, who operated in Liege between the years 1886 and 1900, producing pocket models of the bull dog type.

The California model was also sold marked "Texas Bull-Dog" and remained virtually identical although, in contrast to the standard form, its title was sometimes applied to the right-hand side of the frame, rather than appearing on the top strap.

Distribution of both types was fairly widespread throughout the United States. On the Western coast, the Texas version retailed in San Francisco by the firm of Shreve & Wolf, who were in partnership from 1881 until 1886. Revolvers of that same pattern were also advertised in the 1886 catalogue of John Moore's Sons at the Eastern side of America in New York City. The version offered on that occasion was nickel-plated in .44 calibre and could be purchased at just $6.65 with either 3.5-inch or 4.5-inch barrel.

Both the CALIFORNIA and TEXAS titles were registered as official Trade

Marks on 7 July 1881 by the Belgian gun maker, Pierre Deprez, who was a descendant from one of the oldest established gun-making families of Wandre, then a small town about ten kilometres from Liege itself.

California Bull-dog: Calibre .44 five-shot model marked CALIFORNIA BULL-DOG on top strap. Barrel length on this model is 2.75-inches and weapon is nickel-plated. Courtesy Homer Ficken.

Texas Bull Dog: Calibre .44 five-shot model engraved with TEXAS BULL DOG at right side of frame. Barrel length on this model is 3.5-inches and weapon is nickel-plated. This version was sometimes marked as WESTERN STAR. Courtesy Homer Ficken.

An equally suitable title for the Texas market was STAR, a word which had been registered as a Belgian trade mark by Liege gun maker, Louis Muller, in 1889. (Whether or not he was ever involved with the manufacture of the Star Bull Dog model is still unresolved.) However, that particular version had certainly been produced by Neumann

Star Bull Dog: Calibre .44. model with 2.5-inch octagonal barrel and title stamped onto top strap. Also marked with star emblem on left side of frame and at bottom of stock plate. Serial No.646. Courtesy Homer Ficken.

Brothers of rue Saint-Remy, Liege, where the firm had been in the business of gun making since 1863. Examples from that source carried the symbol of a hunting horn combined with the initial N, a trade mark registered by Neumann on 30 December 1893.

That particular version differed from the usual Belgian models in having an octagonal section barrel and was without the Liege style of lock work incorporating a hammer rebound action.

Although the names of those American states may have been used to good effect in broadening the appeal of Bull Dog models amongst Californians and Texans, other titles were introduced to widen the field of interest even further. In fact, whole regions were incorporated into the names stamped onto weapons which were often virtually indistinguishable from their contemporaries.

The version marked Western Bull-Dog continued to feature a recoil abutment at the rear of the stock that had been introduced on the earliest types. Some examples also had a prominent raised boss on the left side of the frame to strengthen the loading gate pivot area. Without that rectangular support, the drilling for the gate screw was very close to the outer surface of the frame and a possible source of fracture.

Most specimens in this category were marked with pre-1893 Liege proof marks, although few calibre .44 versions had any positive identification of their manufacture. Amongst the notable exceptions were weapons with the initials L & T contained within a small rectangle, representing the Liege gun makers, Lambin and Theate. That particular firm had developed from the original business of Leon Lambin and which had made various firearms between the years 1877 and 1894. There has been no other identification found on "Western Bull-Dog" models to confirm manufacturer. Most examples continue to display the usual Belgian proof marks, although some may also be found with Birmingham proofs.

Other versions that were marked SOUTHERN BULL DOG followed the Webley design more closely in having the sear extending through into the trigger guard area and were without any provision for hammer rebound. It was otherwise typical of the Belgian production.

Both the "Western" and "Southern" versions were produced by various Liege gun makers, none of whom had made an official registration for either of the two names used for these specific Bull Dog revolvers. (It might be relevant to note that Joseph Janssen of rue Saint-Laurent, Liege, had registered Trade Marks for the Southern Arms Company and also for the Western Guns Manufacturing Company during October 1893).

Perhaps the most bizarre adoption of the term Bull Dog could apply to a large Belgian-made revolver with a 5.375-inch barrel. This version was advertised by the Boston firm of Turner & Ross in 1883 under the title of FRONTIER BULLDOG and priced at $8. The generous size of this weapon did not necessarily merit its inclusion within the Bull Dog category, although the full title was indeed stamped upon the flat surface of the top strap. Initial production types had no sighting groove, since a raised sight notch had been provided at the rear. It was, of course, much larger in appearance than the average models, being almost a copy of the Webley Royal Irish Constabulary model firing a calibre .44-40 CF Winchester cartridge. This was clearly a big advantage to those already owning a .44 Winchester rifle, as it enabled them to use just one type of ammunition for both weapons, thus making the revolver a very desirable addition for the trade in the American west.

Frontier models also differed in having a cylinder capacity of six rounds rather than five and, in common with other Liege versions, the lockwork featured a rebounding action.

Southern Bull Dog: Virtual copy of Webley model but with different title stamped onto top strap. Walnut stock plates cut with chequered pattern.

Considerable emphasis had been placed on the shape and finish applied to the stock, which was usually of hard rubber with a moulded decoration and was claimed to give an exceptionally firm grip when shooting. Earliest models were also provided with a finger support on the trigger guard to give even more improvement, although this was soon eliminated on later models.

Most examples incorporated a usual sighting groove on the top strap with the title arranged on either side. In some instances, these were also provided with a military-style lanyard ring.

An indication of manufacturer does not normally appear on the weapon in any form and Frontier models appear to have been produced in Liege by several different gun makers. In general construction and appearance it was the same as calibre 44-40 revolvers marked FRONTIER ARMY.

Use of the word "Frontier" was most appropriate, as the weapon was certainly destined for markets throughout the frontier regions of the United States. It was a title first used in identifying the Colt .44-40 single-action revolver of 1875.

The 1892 catalogue of the New York firm of Schoverling, Daly & Gales advertised an improved version which was also similar to the final pattern of Webley R.I.C. revolver. The new model differed in having a fluted cylinder and lanyard ring attachment but otherwise remained much the same as its predecessor.

While not totally conclusive, there is some evidence that revolvers of this type were imported by the New York agency from the Belgian arms manufacturer Jules Pire & Company of Antwerp. That firm was established in 1885 to produce weapons of all types, including several revolver models. The son of Jules Pire later became a manager with Schoverling, Daly & Gales and was responsible for the distribution of Belgian guns throughout the United States.

In 1895, the catalogue of Montgomery Ward & Company, a nationwide retail and mail-order business, listed the Frontier Bull Dog at $3.85, a price which then compared very favourably with that of a Colt single action Frontier model at $16. By that time, of course, solid frame revolvers had become rather outdated due to the introduction of hinge-frame, self-extracting models at very similar prices. Many of these revolvers with the alternative title of FRONTIER ARMY, although similar in design to the Bull Dog versions, were still being offered by U.S. mail-order houses in 1900.

In addition to the Frontier model, the Boston company of Turner & Ross also offered "The New British Bull Dog" model as a 5-shot model in .44 centre fire. It was rather ominously described as "The revolver with which Guiteau assassinated the President," a clear reference to the shooting of President James A. Garfield on 2 July, 1881, by Charles Guiteau. In a slightly less ominous promotion, the pistol was otherwise recommended for express messengers, mail clerks, bankers, watchmen, miners and even members of the police force.

Revolvers of this pattern were first produced in Belgium during the early 1880s by Neumann Brothers, who had also been responsible for manufacture of the Star Bull Dog.

Finished in nickel plating and with hard rubber stock plates, this model was priced at $7 in the Turner & Ross catalogue of 1883 and appeared later in the 1884 catalogue of Meacham Arms Company. At that period, barrels could be obtained in either round or octagonal section.

While the general style remained typical of other Bull Dog revolvers, it was distinctive in having a raised portion of the frame at the upper rear area of the stock. Moulded within a circular border at the top end of each stock plate, was the head of a bull dog, while the remaining surface was finely chequered and bordered. A title of NEW BRITISH BULL DOG was stamped onto the top strap and further identified by a hunting horn symbol applied at the forward left side of the frame. At the centre of the horn was the initial N. Both the Bull Dog face and horn symbol were inaugurated as Belgian trade marks on 30 December, 1893, although it had clearly been used several years previously.

New British Bull Dog: Manufactured in Liege by Neumann Brothers, New British Bulldog in calibre .44 was popular sidearm throughout American West.

In their 1883 catalogue, Turner & Ross offered the New British Bull Dog in the following variations:

• Calibre .44 with round or octagonal barrel, rubber stock and full nickel plating, for $7

• Calibre .44 with octagonal barrel

Typical example with THE BRITISH BULL DOG on top strap and with initials of Southern Pacific Rail Road Company on barrel flat, plus weapon number 87. Courtesy Homer Ficken.

The English Bull Dog: Calibre .450 five-shot Lieg model of The English Bull Dog retailed in England by Mitchell & Company of Manchester.

The Ulster Bull Dog: Calibre .450 five-shot example of THE ULSTER BULL DOG produced by James Braddell & Son of Belfast. Brazing additional butt onto standard Webley model produced more comfortable grip when weapon was fired. Serial No. 5039. Courtesy W.C.Dowell.

Example with ratchet cylinder probably manufactured in Liege. London proof marks and retailed by J. Braddell & Son, Belfast. Models in similar style to this and within same serial range were also produced by P. Webley & Son. Serial No. 20503. Courtesy Imperial War Museum, London.

and chequered ebony stock, for $6 (The same model was also offered in calibre .38 as the imported "American" Bulldog at $7.)

• Calibre .32, .38, or .44 with chequered walnut stock, round barrel and plain cylinder, for $5.

It was also stated that, in recent times, many hundreds of these models had been sold throughout the western regions to places such as Deadwood, Cheyenne and Virginia City.

Included amongst all the other Bull Dog titles, with their deliberate inclination toward the American market, was a usage by Belgian gun makers of the full phrase stamped on the original Webley model, THE BRITISH BULL DOG. (As well as being a British trade mark, it had also been registered in Belgium by the firm P. Webley & Son in May 1881).

At this point, it is worth noting that the Webley firm had resorted to having some of their Bull Dog revolvers made by others in order to cope with an increasing demand from abroad. These were duly returned to the Birmingham for finishing and to receive a British proof mark. However, it had been customary for the Webley firm to identify their products with the "Flying Bullet" symbol in addition to the title stamping and so it may have been an infringement of the Webley Trade Mark registration for the Belgian models to be marked in that way .

In any event, adoption of that title was obviously put to good effect in boosting sales within the United States, where the Webley model had already been acclaimed as "the famous and much celebrated Bull Dog."

It is known that models in this category were acquired by the Southern Pacific Rail Road Company to be carried by some of their employees. Origins of that company can be traced back to 1868, when it operated from San Francisco through New Mexico to New Orleans, establishing many "way stations" as it traversed the Western states of America. Revolvers were issued to various agents and also acquired by foremen of maintenance crews working in the more remote areas. Examples have been identified with the mark of Societe Dumoulin Freres, which had operated in Liege since 1877 and later in association with gun makers Albert Simonis and Joseph Janssen.

Examples marked with an alternative title of "English" Bull Dog were also of Liege origin and used much the same

casting as those marked "British" or others marked "Western."

Application of the new name was made in three different forms: one stamped with capital letters as THE ENGLISH BULL DOG on the top strap; another engraved in serif italic lettering simply as ENGLISH BULLDOG (two words) on the top strap; a third with serif lettering in a single line on the top strap as ENGLISH BULL DOG (three words). The latter version was chambered for a calibre .44 cartridge and featured a fluted cylinder and octagonal barrel section.

At various times, the firm of P. Webley & Son had supplied limited quantities of revolvers to other manufacturers in Britain, or to retailers who simply added their own name to the weapon without necessarily claiming its manufacture. In such instances, it was not an easy matter to distinguish exactly which maker may have been responsible for any particular weapon, even one bearing another trade mark. This was compounded by such an influx of Bull Dog style revolvers from Belgium, where manufacture in the multitude of Liege workshops had been prolific.

A typical example occurred with a version that incorporated all the regular features of the Webley pattern, plus one distinctive addition, yet failed to display a positive mark of its manufacture.

One of the main criticisms of Bull Dog models had been the lack of a firm hold when shooting, due to the small size of its grip frame. This was overcome to a large extent on the introduction of the American versions, which were constructed with bigger frames but it became most noticeable on a variety produced to special order by the Irish gun makers, Joseph Braddell & Son of Belfast. These weapons were altered by having an extension brazed onto the butt, leaving the original grip frame intact to provide a fulcrum for the mainspring. The brazing took place at the front and rear straps. It was an addition that increased the handle length by a further inch (25mm) and certainly produced a much improved hold when firing, although in doing so, it sacrificed much of its "pocketable" qualities. Examples have been observed with foliate engraving at the rear strap as an attempt to cover any visible joint in that area.

Models in this category are not only identified by their much longer handle but also by a title of THE ULSTER BULL DOG engraved onto the top strap. It is not absolutely clear if this extension was added at the Webley factory or the work undertaken by Braddell, who certainly had the facilities to do so. In all probability, it was indeed the latter. Company literature claimed no fewer than five workshops at the Braddell establishment in Castle Place, Belfast, employing up to 20 men engaged in the production of revolvers, rifles, shotguns and assorted sports equipment.

At certain occasions in its own production series, the Webley factory also introduced models with slightly longer grips, although not so long as those on the "Ulster." An extension of approximately half an inch was added by the Birmingham firm, who were obviously conscious of a niche in the market to be exploited with that alternative to their normal version.

It is significant to note that not all models marked THE ULSTER BULL DOG featured the longer grip and so it did not become a standard pattern from that source. In addition to those with plain cylinders, there were also examples with ratchet cylinder stops and even some with a smaller grip size. Unlike those known to have been produced in Belgium, the "Ulster" versions adhered more closely to the regular Webley format in having exactly the same lockwork with trigger-operated sear. Some difference did occur with the barrel rifling, however, which had been reduced from nine grooves to just five wide grooves and narrow lands.

The next model to be produced in Europe was certainly the oddest of Bull Dog designs, featuring a frame that hinged upward in front of trigger guard to eject and reload. It is reputed to have been based upon a design patented by the Birmingham gun maker, William James Hill (1860-1897), although no patent has been located under that name.

A slight mystery also surrounds the use of the name Stanley. In fact, the Stanley Arms Company was a trade name used by Dumoulin Freres, Liege (1877 - 1894), where manufacture of this particular model may have taken place. The same hinged frame design also appears on other continental revolvers.

Earliest examples were marked Hill's Patent Self extracting "BULL DOG" on one side of the barrel, while later models displayed just "THE STANLEY" BULL DOG at the same location. These versions all bear the trade mark of William J.Hill, depicting a winged hourglass beneath the entwined initials WJH,

applied at the left-hand side of the frame behind the cylinder. This mark had been officially registered by Hill in 1880. Weapons of this type were available in calibres ranging from .320, .380, .442 to .450, although not all were necessarily identified as Bull Dogs.

Single-shot and double-shot pistols of the more basic Deringer pattern had enjoyed a wide distribution amongst travellers, frontiersmen, miners and gamblers throughout the United States during the period of its formation. Small pocket pistols of this pattern had been produced by the Colt company since 1870 and had become highly popular, due to their combination of compact design with a large calibre bullet. As a weapon for personal defence, they were reasonably effective at close quarters but not accurate over any greater distance.

In England, the Webley company had recognised the value of such a weapon and even produced similar examples prior to its introduction of the Bull Dog types. While the first Bull Dog revolvers held more cartridges than the Deringer pistols, they were still only chambered for rounds of a similar calibre. Subsequent versions were made for the calibre .450-inch centre fire rounds, giving a slightly more hefty punch for use in awkward situations. However, for those individuals demanding the maximum effect, it inevitably became possible to obtain the same weapon with a heavier and more powerful round. Although those versions were of much the same size and design, they were considerably heavier, adding approximately a further seven ounces to the average weight.

Weapons in this category were identified with the appropriate title BEHEMOTH BULLDOG, the two words separated in typical fashion by the sighting groove on the top strap. Because of its unusual calibre, comparatively few of these models were manufactured. The use of much smaller calibres had gradually became more prevalent for other Bull Dog models, which could be purchased in .38, .32 or even .22 rim-fire calibre.

In Britain, revolvers of the standard Bull Dog pattern, while not marked with a specific Bull Dog title, were also being produced in small quantities by various English gun makers, including Charles Pryse, David Bentley, Thomas Bland and others, the majority of whom followed the same pattern already established by Webley. Of these individuals, it was

Nickel-plated presentation model awarded to John Brewster, City of Derry Rifle Club, in 1875. Serial No. 53927. Courtesy Frank Michaels.

The Stanley Bull Dog: Five-shot calibre .45 model marked "THE STANLEY" BULL DOG at left side of barrel. Depressing lever under front of frame allows barrel to hinge back until curved arm is operated to eject all cartridges simultaneously. Serial No. 371. Courtesy Reg Milson.

Behemoth Bulldog: Calibre .50 five-shot model with title stamped onto top strap. Cylinder on this model measures 1.75-inches in diameter and barrel is slightly longer than usual at 2.75-inches. Barrel rifling is just four grooves with right-hand twist.

Tower Bull Dog: Calibre .450 five-shot model of THE TOWER BULL DOG. Produced by David Bentley and retailed by Thomas Turner of Birmingham, England (1834-1890). Serial No. 222. Courtesy W.C.Dowell. Thomas Turner was a gun maker in his own right and also had his own trade mark since the year 1876.

Calibre .32 six-shot solid frame revolver by Forehand & Wadsworth. BULL DOG title is stamped onto top strap, while patent dates of 1861 and 1871 appear on left side of barrel. This example is fitted with ebony grip plates and has patented ejector system held by catch underneath cylinder spindle.

Forehand & Wadsworth Bull Dog Revolvers: Upper: Calibre .32 six-shot BULL DOG revolver. Lower: Calibre .38 five-shot version with modified cylinder spindle. BULL DOG title appears on top strap, plus patent dates of 1861, 1871 and 1875 at other side of barrel.

BRITISH BULL-DOG: Calibre .450 five-shot model by Forehand & Wadsworth with swivel ejector and rebounding hammer. This version is nickel plated and has ivory stock plates. Courtesy David B.Smith.

Indian Bull-dog: Calibre .44 five-shot INDIAN BULL-DOG model by Forehand & Wadsworth was virtually identical to "British Bull-Dog" model made by same company.

actually the Birmingham gunmaker David Bentley who chose to add another specific Bull Dog title to his particular model.

Arranged at either side of the sighting groove on the top strap was a new name, THE TOWER BULL DOG, engraved in backward-sloping letters, while his "London Tower" trade mark was applied at the left side of the frame. This has been officially registered by Bentley on 28 April 1876 but was later acquired for renewal by the Webley company in 1890.

His version was distinctive in having a portion of the frame extended rearwards to form a sharp angle with the grip, thus presenting an improved hold when the weapon was fired. A different style of grip plates was also featured, with each hardwood plate being mortised to fit under the upper end of the frame opening and retained by a single screw and clip at the butt, rather than with the usual screw at the centre.

Bentley had manufactured revolvers at his Aston works between the years 1871 and 1883, by which time, revolvers of his Bull Dog pattern retailed in Britain at a price of fourty-two shillings each. Registration of the "Tower" trade mark was renewed by the Webley firm in 1918 and again in 1932.

AMERICAN VERSIONS

The earliest type of revolver manufactured in the United States to bear the words BULL DOG is represented by a little six-shot model with spur trigger produced by Forehand & Wadsworth of Worcester, Massachusetts. It was not of the Webley pattern but followed the same style as the Colt New Line series of 1872 with two patented features incorporated. The first was for a method enabling the cylinder stop to be operated by the trigger and had been patented by Ethan Allen in 1861 (U.S. Patent 33509), while the second was for a convenient means of housing a removable ejector rod inside the cylinder spindle, where both were retained by a spring catch at the front of the frame. In essence, it allowed the revolver to be emptied and loaded without the inconvenience of having to remove the cylinder. That particular arrangement was patented by Sullivan Forehand and Henry C.Wadsworth in 1871 (U.S. Patent 116 422). References to both patents were stamped onto the left-hand side of the barrel.

A second version of the spur trigger

Bulldog dispensed with the removable ejection rod feature but otherwise remained much the same in general appearance. The only difference was the addition of a third patent date at the left-hand side of the barrel referring to a hammer rebound feature, although this was not incorporated onto that particular weapon.The additional design featured a mechanism to remove the hammer nose from contact with the cartridge primer while the cylinder remained held by the stop lever, an arrangement patented by Messrs. Forehand & Wadsworth in 1875 (U.S. Patent 162 162).

Forehand & Wadsworth were also the first to produce an American duplicate of the original British model with a swivel ejector, although it differed slightly in having a "saw-handle" grip as opposed to the usual "parrot beak" shape and was provided with a fluted cylinder in place of the initial plain variety. These were almost indistinguishable from other European versions and bore the marking BRITISH BULL-DOG on the top strap, plus a manufacturer identification on the upper surface of the barrel. (For some reason, the Bull Dog name used previously on the spur trigger models had now become hyphenated). An improvement had also been added to the lock mechanism to permit a rebound of the hammer after firing, in order to prevent it from making contact with the cartridge primer.

It has been reported that introduction of the American-made version occurred during the late 1870s, when it was available in three sizes: a seven-shot .32 model, a six-shot .38 S&W model and a five-shot model for the .44 Webley cartridge. Of those three calibres, the latter appears to have been the most popular.

Revolvers of that pattern were advertised by the manufacturers Forehand & Wadsworth in their catalogue of c. 1880. They were eventually listed by the San Francisco gun dealers N.Curry & Brother in 1884 and also appeared in a catalogue of that same year by E.C.Meacham, St. Louis. In order to distinguish the American model from others, it was claimed that only genuine examples were marked with the Forehand & Wadsworth trade mark (depicting the head of a Bulldog stamped onto the left side of the frame). However, not all examples were marked thus, as some were without the trade mark but displayed the company name on the barrel flat and so it seems that mainly the earliest examples had the "dog's head" stamp.

Grip plates were normally of hard rubber cut with an overall chequered pattern and shaped to suit an additional lump at the top of the grip.

The F&W British Bull-Dog appeared in the 1886 catalogues of New York gun dealers G. W. Caflin and John P. Moore's Sons and continued to be offered in the J. H. Johnston gun lists of 1888.

Due to the increasing popularity of hinged frame self-extracting models on the American market, most solid frame revolvers had become somewhat outdated and, as a result, prices for the little Bull Dog were being seriously reduced. In the 1889 catalogue of Folsom, it was offered at just $2.77. Despite this, Clabrough & Golcher of San Francisco continued to list the Forehand & Wadsworth British Bull-Dog in 1890, while J. H. Johnston also listed it in their 1895 catalogue.

Forehand & Wadsworth's Firearms Manufactory continued in operation at Worcester until 1890, when Henry Wadsworth retired from the partnership and the business was reformed as the Forehand Arms Company. Concurrent with manufacture of the BRITISH BULL-DOG, a similar type of revolver was produced by Forehand & Wadsworth during the 1880s and marked with the alternative title of INDIAN BULLDOG. (Note: This time the latter name was without hyphen.) Both these American models followed much the same configuration as those made in Belgium by Joseph Tholet.

Those revolvers that departed most radically from the original Bull Dog concept were undoubtedly the models manufactured in the United States with the purpose of introducing a more patriotic version for the domestic market.

Early entrants to the scene with a revised design were the gunmakers Iver Johnson & Martin Bye of Worcester, Massachusetts, where the first American version was produced. It differed mainly from its British counterpart in not being provided with a swivel case ejector but, instead, having a quickly removable cylinder to make ejection and loading more convenient. A large-diameter extension of the cylinder spindle had been cross-knurled for this purpose. The method used was virtually identical to that employed on the earlier spur trigger model and most other American pocket revolvers at that time.

A further change also occurred in the lock mechanism with an elimination of the Webley double-limb mainspring and its replacement by a single-leaf component. In other respects, the double-action lock arrangement was much the same as on the Webley Bull Dog with the exception of pins, rather than screws, being used for the trigger and sear pivots. The latter item also served to retain the trigger guard. Although the guard itself still remained as a separate unit from the frame, it had been extended to form the front grip strap and was held at its base to the butt. Stock plates were of hardened rubber with a chequered pattern.

Manufactured versions had the title BRITISH BULLDOG stamped onto the top strap, which did not have a sighting groove but was provided with a small recess at the rear for the hammer rest. Lettering in this instance was quite small and positioned centrally, reading from muzzle to breech.

The weapon was available in either .44 Webley or .38 S&W calibre, the larger version being the only one provided with a hinged loading gate behind the cylinder at the right-hand side of the frame. In calibre .38 it had a 2.5-inch barrel and weighed 16 ounces, while in calibre .44 it featured a 2.75-inch barrel and was three ounces heavier.

According to official sources, production was apparently quite brief, beginning in 1881 and terminating just over one year later, when the original partnership with Martin Bye was dissolved and the Iver Johnson Arms Company formed. As a consequence, serial numbers are reported to have reached no more than five digits.

Under a somewhat incongruous heading of American "British Bull-Dog," the weapon was still being advertised for sale in the 1884 catalogue of E. C. Meacham, St. Louis, Missouri. It was then available in nickel plated finish and either calibre could be purchased for $3 each. By that time, the Iver Johnson company had commenced manufacture of an improved model with the more acceptable title of AMERICAN BULL-DOG.

While still retaining the same basic features of the British Bull-Dog, subsequent American models employed an extended frame section at the rear to give improved handing qualities. A change in the grip contour also introduced a new style of grip plate moulded in hard rubber with a symbolic American eagle design. Standard finish was nickel-plating.

There has been some reports of early

American British Bull-dog: Calibre .44 Centre-fire, five-shot model manufactured by Johnson and Bye Gunsmiths. BRITISH BULLDOG is stamped onto top strap. Barrel measures 2.5 inches but this example has no rifling grooves, only supplementary rifling notches at muzzle. Courtesy Homer Ficken.

American Bull-Dog: Calibre .44 five-shot First Model made by Iver Johnson Arms Company with Bull Dog title stamped on top strap. Lock mechanism remained similar to previous version made by Johnson & Bye.

Cylinder spindle is held to front of frame by its own spring catch. Note: Subsequent variation of First Model American Bull Dog was also available with octagonal barrel section.

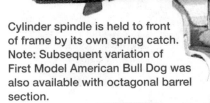

American Bull Dog: Calibre .44 five-shot Second Model by Iver Johnson with title stamped onto barrel flat. Note smoother frame contour, plus changes to cylinder spindle and stock plates.

American Bull Dog with extra-long barrel. Examples of this type were sometimes marked as ARMY BULL DOG.

Boston Bull-Dog: Calibre .38 six-shot model of BOSTON BULL-DOG manufactured by Iver Johnson as lightweight version of American Bull Dog. Serial No. 7028. Courtesy William Goforth.

Boston Bull-Dog versions were not fitted with hinged loading gate and catridges were simply guided through shielded groove in frame.

XL Bull Dog: Representative example of XL model in Calibre .32 Rim Fire with 3-inch barrel and hardened rubber stock plates as standard. Note lever at forward side of frame to release cylinder spindle.

production examples of this pattern fitted with wooden grip plates and marked as BRITISH BULL-DOG. The 1882 catalogue of Philadelphia gun dealer Joseph C. Grubb & Company quoted the American Bulldog in six calibres ranging from .22 short rimfire to .44 Webley centre fire and prices from $8 to $10.

A second pattern of the American Bull Dog emerged in 1884 with a slightly modified frame contour, which had been smoothed to a more rounded shape at the rear. Stock plates were finely chequered and incorporated the moulded head of a bull dog at the point of attachment, while the front grip strap was altered to be formed as an integral part of the frame, rather than being an extension of the trigger guard. Other than a slight restyling of certain components, the lock assembly remained almost unchanged.

As manufacture progressed, certain minor changes began to be introduced. Extending from the front of the frame, a noticeable reduction had been made to the diameter of the cylinder spindle, which was given a series of small knurled sections and a change had also been made to the spindle locking lever.

In conjunction with the alterations, it had also been decided to introduce an alternative barrel of an octagonal section. This appeared initially on somewhat bizarre large frame calibre .44 models fitted with a six-inch barrel, half of which was octagonal, while the remainder was round. Weapons of this type were stamped with AMERICAN BULL DOG, the words arranged at either side of the sighting groove on the top strap. They continued to feature hardened rubber stock plates moulded with an American Eagle design and also retained the standard finish in nickel-plating.

Manufacture of all versions except those of calibre .38 had ceased before the turn of the century, although sales continued in retail stores throughout America for several years thereafter.

Also in this series were examples marked BOSTON BULL-DOG on the barrel flat. This version was virtually identical to the Iver Johnson Second Model of American Bull Dog, except for the name and different style of stock plates, which had an "I J" monogram moulded around the stock screw in place of the dog's head. Intended as a lighter weapon, it was only made for the smaller calibres .22, .32 and .38, each of which had a different frame size.

Arrangement of the lockwork components remained much the same as on the American Bull Dog and continued to be without any means for rebounding the hammer. The system on both Bull Dog models relied upon the shooter engaging the hammer in a safety notch, which held it well back from the cartridge.

Production appears to have been between the years 1887 and 1899, although it was not listed in the catalogues of the principle Iver Johnson retailer, J. P. Lovell of Boston, until after 1890.

An illustration of the model subsequently appeared in the 1895 catalogue of Hartley & Graham, New York, and could be obtained in a variety of calibres ranging from .22 rim fire to .38 centre fire advertised at a mere $2.25. Various options of finish, such as Ivory stock plates, Pearl stock plates, or engraving, were also available.

Among the many different handguns produced by the well-established firm of Hopkins & Allen in Norwich, Connecticut, was yet another version of the Bull Dog variety, this time marked as the XL BULLDOG. General styling of the new model closely followed the same pattern that had been set previously by the Iver Johnson Arms Company. In typical fashion, the pivoting ejector had been omitted, allowing the cylinder to be removed for reloading, although in this case it was released by operating a large lever at the left side of the frame. It was an extremely well-made weapon whose title was included with other wording arranged on the top strap at either side of the sighting groove: HOPKINS & ALLEN MFG Co. Pat. MARCH 28 1871 at one side and XL. BULL DOG 32 CAL. RIM FIRE on the other. The patent referred to U.S. No.113053, which was obtained by Samuel Hopkins and had included a method of retaining the cylinder axis. That same arrangement was actually employed on several other revolver models produced by that firm.

The XL version of the species enjoyed sales throughout the eastern states of America during the final years of the nineteenth century. An 1880 catalogue of Merwin, Hulbert & Company in New York advertised the XL Bulldog as "made by Hopkins & Allen" and in later years the same firm continued to list it in four versions. Six-shot models were available in calibre .32 Rim Fire and .32 Central Fire, while five-shot versions were offered in calibre .38 Central Fire. All were fitted with 3-inch octagonal section barrels, while the latter model was also offered with a five-inch barrel. Stock plates were available in hard rubber, ivory and pearl, or even in a wide variety of exotic stone. (A calibre .44 version had been listed by G. W. Claflin of New York in 1886, although that type seems to be rare.) The May 1887 catalogue of Merwin, Hulbert & Co. at 28 West 23rd street, New York City, continued to include the XL Bulldog as one of six other solid frame revolvers, each with the prefix "XL."

Another notable American gun maker, Harrington & Richardson, had also decided to add a Bull Dog model to their series of double-action revolvers by the year 1887. It was introduced in two versions, a six-shot calibre .32 rimfire and a five-shot calibre .38 rimfire, as virtual copies of the Iver Johnson model.

The H&R company had been in business producing various firearms since 1875 at their factory premises in Worcester, Massachusetts and were most prominent in the manufacture of hinged frame revolvers. The Bull Dog series was simply a variation of the H&R American Double Action revolvers that the company had produced in previous years.

Despite its strong similarity to the Second Model American Bull Dog, there were certain minor alterations that made the new version more identifiable. Barrels were still provided in both round and octagonal section but all were fitted with half-round foresights in place of an angular form. Vulcanised rubber stock plates were chequered and moulded with decorated patterns at top and bottom in a design unique to Harrington & Richardson. Of course, chequered wooden stock plates could still be obtained as an optional extra.

Stamped onto the top strap and separated by the sighting groove were the words, THE H.&R. and BULL DOG, reading from barrel-to-breech. At the rear of the top strap, a T-shaped recess had been cut to receive the hammer. The trigger guard also followed the second type American Bull Dog in being separate from the frame and held by a pin at each end. There was no hinged loading gate at the right-hand side and the H&R models simply had a channel cut from the frame with part of the recoil shield removed to aid in chambering cartridges. However, a loading gate was available as an optional extra for all models and could be fitted if required. At the opposite side of the weapon, a flatter recoil shield replaced the more substantial Iver Johnson form. Otherwise, there was very little difference between the two versions.

A weapon similar to the H&R Bull Dog but with a barrel length of two inches was advertised in the 1899 catalogue of Harrington & Richardson Arms Company with the title YOUNG AMERICA BULL DOG and continued to be listed alongside the H&R Bull Dog.

These early weapons were clearly intended for black powder cartridges and so Second Models of the two named versions were introduced in 1905 to cope with more modern smokeless powder charges. Serial numbering of both patterns occupied the same range as certain other revolvers produced at the same factory with each number being applied at the bottom of the butt strap, or at the left side of the frame beneath the stock plate. By 1923, after 36 years of production, the rimfire versions had been discontinued.

LATEST ADDITION TO THE BULL DOG PACK

While the Bull Dog term has become part of the gun vocabulary, it is seldom applied to modern handguns, the majority of which are now of a semi-automatic type. An exception exists in a new version recently produced by the Charter Arms Corporation of Stratford, Connecticut. Named as the BULLDOG PUG, it differs from the more usual form in featuring a swing-out cylinder released by movement of a sliding catch at the left-hand side. Although still a relatively small weapon, a large single-piece wooden or rubber stock surrounds the grip frame to ensure a good firm hold on the weapon when fired. This calibre .44 Special model is acknowledged to have the highest power-to-weight ratio of any similar-sized pocket revolver. At a weight of only 20 ounces and with a barrel of 2.5 inches it falls well within the standard "Bull Dog" range.

© Gordon Bruce. (The author wishes to thank Homer Ficken, Frank Michaels and William Goforth for the kind help given during the preparation of this article.)

The H&R Bull Dog: Calibre .32 six-shot model produced by Harrington & Richardson. Note absence of hinged loading gate from behind cylinder and use of pins to hold trigger guard.

Young America Bull Dog: Calibre .38 Rimfire five-shot model with two-inch barrel. YOUNG AMERICA BULL DOG is stamped on top strap while full address of Harrington & Richardson Arms Company appears on left side of barrel.

Charter Arms Bulldog Pug: Calibre .44 five-shot model produced by Charter Arms Corp. Title and calibre are stamped onto left side of barrel, while company address appears on right side of barrel. Weapon is nicely blued and has London Proof marks. Serial No. 972787. Courtesy Imperial War Museum, London.

Revolvers used to gather data. Clockwise from top right: Freedom Arms and Mag-Na-Port custom Stalker single action revolver in .454 Casull with Bushnell Elite 2-6 scope; Ruger, a double action Super Redhawk in .480 Ruger with Simmons 2-6X scope; another DA Ruger but a Redhawk in .44 Magnum with a Burris 1-½X4 scope; .460 S&W with Burris 1-½X4 scope; and .500 S&W DA customized by Mag-Na-Port with a Trijicon Reflex sight.

life begins

BY DR. GEORGE E. DVORCHAK, JR.

As we're all aware, big bore firearms are known for their stopping ability, which is why we like them. On the negative side, they are also known for their recoil. Yet there are many big bores, meaning 40-caliber-plus, that depending on the round, load and firearm, will not bite the hand that feeds them. Also in this category there are cartridges that cannot reach out there as effectively as some others and are at their best at shorter range.

When it comes to handguns, we have single and double action revolvers that are usually chambered for cartridges designed for use in a cylinder. Then there are the single shots which, although they do chamber traditional handgun cartridges, can also be chambered in what most would think of as rifle cartridges.

It's not always easy to categorize big bore cartridges as being "for" one application but not "for" another. Some cartridges such as the .45 ACP have a

major role in pistols for both defense and target use, yet I've found that this round also makes for a great close-range varmint number. On the other side of the spectrum, the .450 Marlin was designed for lever action carbines for big game. Today the T/C Encore, which can safely handle high pressure cartridges, is also chambered for the .450, and it is a handful. Then we have other cartridges as the .45 Winchester Magnum, which most would think of as a competition cartridge but which is a great cartridge for game such as whitetail. (Unfortunately it's slowly slipping into oblivion.)

The following is a summary of some popular – and some not-quite-so-popular – big bore cartridges that are found in revolvers and single shot handguns. All are effective for the jobs they were designed to perform.

(Note: For some bullets, two sizes are listed, an apparent ambiguity which is due to which make of bullet is available for a specific cartridge. This is

an example of why it is important to use the loading data developed for a specific make of bullet and follow such guidelines closely. Variations also occur in bullets from the same company, depending on whether they're lead or jacketed.)

.44 REMINGTON MAGNUM

(0.429" or 0.430") This revolver cartridge, which was introduced in 1955-56 as a joint venture by Smith & Wesson and Remington, is likely one of the most well-known revolver cartridges of all time. Even those who know nothing about guns have heard about this cartridge and the S&W Model 29 because of the popular *Dirty Harry* movies of the 1960s. The positive aspect of the publicity was that the name got out there; the bad, at least for me at that time, was that to purchase a Model 29 for hunting, if a store had one at all you could expect to pay $100 or more than the list price. The other "bad" aspect was that the .44

Examples of four 40+ calibers in the T/C Encore and Contender. From top: SSK barrel in .444 Marlin on a Contender with a Bushnell 2-6 scope; ribbed SSK T/C Contender in .45-70 Government with Bausch & Lomb 4X scope; T/C Encore barrel in .480 Ruger with T/C 1.25X4 scope; T/C Encore in .450 Marlin with T/C 2.5X7 scope.

Magnum had a reputation of being Mr. Punishment, especially when it came to recoil. What that did was scare people away from using this fine cartridge and revolvers for hunting.

Yet by the standards we have today, this is a middle-of-the-road cartridge when it comes to power and recoil. But when introduced, it was the most powerful handgun cartridge of all time. In reality, in a single action or double action handgun, the recoil is not that bad. What's bad is the blast! This I feel is what causes one to flinch and close one's eyes when the trigger is pulled, not the recoil. I have dispatched many whitetail with it and it was quite effective. But then, with a 2X scope or an electronic dot sight and most all shots within 20 to 70 yards, what a nice handgun and cartridge to use! My experience is with 180- to 300-grain bullets with a preference being a 200- or 240-grain. Shot capsules are also available which if used within 10 or so feet, drop a snake with a head shot.

.444 MARLIN

(0.429" or 0.430") This "rifle" cartridge is kind of like a .44 Magnum case that took vitamins and got taller. In a joint venture with Remington in 1964, Marlin introduced a new big bore lever action rifle appropriate for short to moderate ranges, and the .444 Marlin hit the

market. In 1965, I bought one and used it until 1989, when JD Jones at SSK Industries made me a Thompson/Center Contender barrel so chambered. On introduction, the .444 cartridge lacked an effective bullet, since the thinner jacketed 240-grain .44 Magnum bullets were all we had available, and they

Cartridges reviewed, from left: the .500 S&W, the .460 S&W Magnum, the .454 Casull, the .45 Colt, the .45 Winchester Magnum, the .45 ACP, the .480 Ruger and the .44 Magnum.

To interchange cartridges, as long as the bullets' diameter is the same, Freedom Arms makes accessory cylinders available that can be switched in less than a minute. For the .454 Casull, for example, extra cylinders are available for the .45 ACP, .45 Colt and .45 Winchester Magnum, the latter of which is popular in Europe.

.45 ACP

(0.451" or 0.452") This 45-caliber is likely the most popular semiauto pistol cartridge of all time. With a 230-grain bullet, it found its place in the Model 1911 pistol as adopted by the military. A fine military, police and target round, I started to use it for small game in an S&W revolver years ago since in my state, semis are not permitted for hunting. Recoil is tolerable but as the handgun so chambered is reduced in size and weight, recoil begins to climb. In a revolver it is a pleasant cartridge to shoot. Yet even though a great military round, it is not recommended for game as large as or larger than deer. It will do the job, but I am afraid that more game will be wounded since it does not have the velocity, or really suitable bullets, for use at hunting ranges. Shot capsules are also available for this cartridge, again for snakes up close.

.45 WINCHESTER MAGNUM

(0.451") Around 1979 this rimless case, with bullets comparable in weight to those of the .45 ACP, was introduced by Winchester. Designed originally for silhouette shooting, my first experience with it was in a Wildey gas-operated handgun owned by a friend who was serious about knocking over steel targets. What it did for the semiauto was to give it .44 Magnum ballistics. My next experience was in a Freedom Arms revolver chambered for the .454 Casull for which a special cylinder had to be fitted by Freedom. (If you want to fire the .45 ACP round in the Freedom Arms .454, buy an extra cylinder from the company and you are ready to go.)

Unfortunately, today it is even hard to find factory loaded ammunition for what the .45 WM, one of the most powerful semiauto cartridges. Due to the lack of ammunition, if you want a revolver with low recoil, then get a .44 Magnum or semiauto. A plus for this cartridge was that it was easy to fire due to its moderate recoil in the stout Thompson/Center Contender, the Wildey semiauto or the Freedom Arms revolver. When gathering data for this review, I called my friend to borrow his firearms so chambered but with silhouette on the decline I found he had quit the sport and then sold all but his revolver, which he now seldom fires. This goes to show that even if one has the handgun, the next hurdle is the ammunition if you do not handload.

couldn't stand up to the .444's increased velocity. Then Hornady in 1967 introduced a 265-grain bullet specifically for this cartridge, one that generated higher velocities than the .44 Magnum. I have used 240- and 300-grain bullets but in my handloads back then and with factory ammunition today, the 265-grain is what I prefer for deer and black bear. If your T/C Contender or Encore is ported or has a special brake, this cartridge's recoil is in the 44 Magnum class.

.45 COLT

(0.451", 0.452" or 0.454") Back when I was a kid in the 1960s when few had .44 Magnum handguns, the .45 Colt was popular with handgun hunters. Adopted by the army in 1873 for their Colt Single Action Army revolver, the original black powder load was both accurate and effective with its 255-grain lead bullet. Today this cartridge is gaining in popularity due to Cowboy Action competitions, though I have seen a few hunters using it for deer with hand-loaded ammunition. For hunting, there are good bullets available but not much in factory loaded ammunition. Again, the new magnums and other cartridges such as the .454 made this cartridge less popular than it used to be. You can fire a .45 Colt in a .454 Casull cylinder BUT if you do that, make sure you thoroughly clean the cylinder's chambers, especially the shoulders. This is critical since fouling can result in a tight chamber for the longer .454 round, with a hazardous increase in pressure. According to Bob Baker at Freedom Arms, this is one reason why they recommend an extra cylinder chambered in .45 Colt if you plan on firing a lot of .45 Colt ammunition in your .454.

.454 CASULL

(0.451" or 0.452") Note: When loading this cartridge and you desire maximum loads, you must use a bullet with a thick jacket, so check your manual's recommendations carefully.

As the .44 Magnum raised handgunning up a notch, in 1957 the Freedom Arms single action revolver and 454 Casull cartridge took it up two notches. At a SHOT Show years ago when I was speaking with Dick Casull, he told me that he got started when he had the idea to push .45 Colt loads above and beyond what was thought possible in what I believe were modified Colt single actions. To safely chamber this new cartridge, Freedom Arms then built what was and still is a premium single action revolver. Bob Baker, who is now the president of Freedom Arms and with whom I have hunted deer over the years, has taken deer, pronghorn and many elk that I know of with the .454.

What is interesting about the .454 is that until 1998 it was a proprietary cartridge available only from Freedom Arms. The premium Freedom Arms revolver, when coupled with the then most powerful revolver cartridge available, set the handgun hunting world on fire. My friend Lynn Thompson of Cold Steel Knives fame has used this combination with open sights to harvest the biggest and baddest game Africa has to offer. This is quite a revolver cartridge but one that is easy to control as long as the handgun has a Mag-na-brake from Mag-Na-Port, and as long as you use hearing protection, even when hunting. 250-, 260- and 300-grain factory loaded ammunition is available.

.460 S&W MAGNUM

(0.452") Note: When loading this cartridge and you desire maximum loads, you must use a bullet with a thick jacket, so check your manual's recommendations carefully.

This cartridge followed in the footsteps of a truly big bore of S&W revolvers, the .500 S&W Magnum (see below). The .460, introduced in 2005, was dubbed the .460XVR. From its name designation, you may think that it uses a bullet different in diameter from that of the .45 Colt or .454 Casull but in reality it does not; therefore, the .45 Colt and .454 Casull cartridges can be fired in any revolver chambered for the .460. Like the .454, this is an extremely high pressure cartridge that must be loaded with bullets appropriately designed. When it comes to recoil, due to the weight and design of the S&W revolver, its bark is worse than its bite. Again, if you can handle a .44 Magnum, you can handle this one. The factory loads I use include 200- (Cor-Bon), 260- and 275-grain bullets.

.45-70 GOVERNMENT

(0.458") As an official military cartridge back in the 1880s, the .45-70-500 was a 45-caliber boomer loaded with 70 grains of black powder, which pushed a 500-grain bullet. It was the 1980s when Ruger, Marlin, SSK Industries (who made T/C Contender barrels so chambered) and Thompson/Center Arms in 1990 that brought this fine big bore back from the road to extinction. For hunting and taking shots from short to moderate ranges, say, 150 yards, I prefer the 300-, 325- or 350-grain bullets. Recoil in T/C handguns – especially if they have muzzle brakes from SSK, T/C or Mag-Na-Port – is moderate and again in the .44 Magnum class. In fact, I prefer firing the .444 Marlin, .45-70 and .450 Marlin in handguns to firing them in carbines since, to me, they're actually easier to control in a handgun. In carbines, the shoulder takes the hit; in handguns, the recoil raises the firearm and if you hold on and don't let the blast cause flinching, the energy generated doesn't knock you around.

.450 MARLIN

(0.458") This cartridge originated from another joint venture with Marlin and Hornady in 2000. The result was a .45 suitable for big game at moderate ranges in the Marlin carbine. Then Thompson/Center chambered it in their Encore carbine and handgun. Now, in the handgun, even with a T/C muzzle brake, this one is a handful. In fact, its recoil is the most of any of the cartridges I cover here. Yet it is surprisingly controllable, though certainly not for the faint of heart. Common bullets I used are the 325- and 350-grainers. Today this chambering in the Encore is available only from T/C's custom shop.

.480 RUGER

(0.475") Back in 2001, big news at the SHOT show was that Hornady and Ruger had worked together on a project, the result of which was the introduction of the .480 Ruger. Like many of the cartridges that can be fired in the cylinders of others, this cartridge can be fired guns chambered for the .475 Linebaugh. This is possible because the Ruger cartridge is simply a shortened Linebaugh.

For Additional Information:

Black Hills Ammunition: **www.black-hills.com**
Cor-Bon/Glaser: **www.corbon.com**
Federal Ammunition, ATK: **www.federalpremium.com**
Freedom Arms Inc.: **www.freedomarms.com**
Hornady Manufacturing Co.: **www.hornady.com**
Mag-Na-Port International: **www.magnaport.com**
Remington Ammunition: **www.remington.com**
Ruger Firearms: **www.ruger.com**
Smith & Wesson: **www.smith-wesson.com**
SSK Industries Inc.: **www.sskindustries.com**
Thompson/Center Arms: **www.tcarms.com**
Winchester Ammunition: **www.winchester.com**

Again, if you do this, thoroughly clean the cylinder's chambers so as not to increase the pressures of the longer cartridge. Although a step up from the .44 Magnum, I do not see it (or the .44 Magnum, for that matter) as a 200-yard revolver cartridge. In a Ruger revolver, the .480 cartridges I have fired were loaded with 325- and a 400-grain bullets. The most pleasant to fire was with a 325- grain bullet and that only makes sense. Recoil in the well designed Ruger is moderate: in the 44 Magnum class, and that is not bad.

.500 S&W MAGNUM

(0.500") Introduced in 2003, this was the first big bore cartridge for the new S&W Model 500 revolver, built on their massive X frame. Weighing in at 72.5 ounces with an 8-3/8-inch barrel, this 5-shot revolver had to be massive to handle the new cartridge (and, later, the 460 Magnum). With a muzzle energy of around 2600 foot pounds, this double action handgun's new Hogue designed Sorbothane rubber grip and factory recoil compensator did a lot to tame this cartridge's ferocious recoil. Adding Mag-Na-Ports afterward reduced that even more! Although I feel most could handle the recoil, shop owners tell me that when a customer wants a handgun for deer and bear, they recommend the .460 over the .500 since it generates less recoil. In factory loads, I have used the 300-, 350- and 400-grain bullets and prefer the 300 for general use.

In my experience over the years, the best way to get the handgun/caliber best suited to you is to start with the firearm rather than with the cartridge. If possible, handle a single shot, a single action and a double action revolver while keeping an idea in your mind as to what its use will be. To effectively do this, know the average muzzle velocities of the various cartridges and then check out which bullet weight and designs are available, as well as factory loads. Now select the action type that feels the most comfortable and can handle the cartridge you prefer.

Last tip: purchase a .22LR rimfire

in the same type of handgun as your centerfire and if you are going to put a scope or dot sight on that big bore, then do the same with the rimfire. Now shoot the rimfire a lot and when you go over to the much more expensive big bore to practice, you will be surprised just how effective you already are.

From mild to wild, cartridges larger than 40-caliber are hotter than ever and here to stay. The big bores are anything but boring!

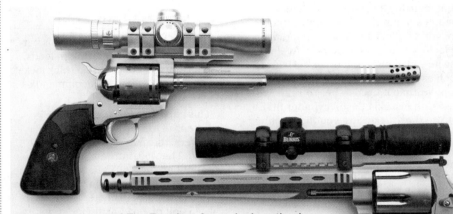

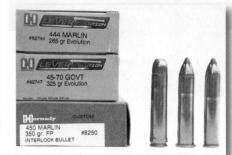

How things change! The Freedom Arms single action in .454 Casull can also fire the shorter 45 Colt cartridge. The double action Smith & Wesson below in .460 S&W Magnum can safely fire not only the .460 cartridge cartridge but the shorter .454 Casull and even shorter .45 Colt. Both guns customized by Mag-Na-Port, Inc.

In single shots as those from Thompson/Center Arms, the .444 Marlin, .45-70 Government and .450 Marlin are great performers. Note that Hornady LeverEvolution loads, with their spitzer or "pointed" bullets, gives big bores a bullet that can reach out father without shedding velocity as fast as a blunt nose bullet will.

Factory Ammunition: Comparative Ballistics

Cartridge	Muzzle Velocity (fps)	Handgun	Factory Ammunition
.44 Magnum	1182 fps	Ruger Redhawk 7-1/2" barrel[1]	Federal Vital Shok 225-gr. Barnes Expander
.444 Marlin	2022 fps	T/C SSK Contender 14" barrel[3]	Hornady LeverEvolution 265-gr. Evolution
.45ACP	1001 fps	Freedom Arms 10" barrel[2]	Black Hills 230-gr. JHP
.45 Win. Magnum	1366 fps	Freedom Arms 10" barrel[2]	Black Hills 250-gr. JHP*
.45 Colt	977 fps	Freedom Arms 10" barrel	Black Hills 255-gr. SWC*
.454 Casull	1870 fps	Freedom Arms 10" barrel	Winchester 260-gr. DJHP Bonded
.460 S&W Mag.	1888 fps	S&W 460XVR 10-1/2" barrel	Federal Premium 275-gr. Barnes Expander
.45-70 Govt.	1606 fps	T/C SSK Contender 14" barrel[3]	Hornady LeverEvolution 325-gr. Evolution
.450 Marlin	1899 fps	T/C Encore 15" barrel[4]	Hornady 350-gr. FP Interlock Bullet
.480 Ruger	1346 fps	Ruger Super Redhawk 7-1/2" barrel	Hornady 325-gr. HP/XTP Mag
.480 Ruger	1440 fps	T/C Encore 15" barrel[4]	Hornady 325-gr. HP/XTP Mag
.500 S&W Mag.	1920 fps	S&W Model 500 8-3/8" barrel[1]	Hornady 300-gr. Evolution

* No longer in production [1] Mag-Na-Port [2] Mag-Na-Brake [3] SSK Arrestor [4] T/C Muzzle Tamer

a robert hillberg cornucopia

Editor's Note: In our opinion, Robert L. Hillberg – former head of research and development for High Standard Manufacturing – is a national treasure, being one of the few surviving masters of post-WWII American firearms design. Many of his countless creations, including the Whitney Wolverine, the Wildey gas-operated .45 pistol and the COP four-shot derringer, are avidly sought by collectors today, as are his more conventional designs. Here, the esteemed Mr. Hillberg offers his insights on the early history of High Standard and the development of the Ithaca Model 49 single-shot rifle, the Savage 101 pistol and the Browning BPS shotgun.

BY ROBERT HILLBERG

Firearms designer extraordinaire and emeritus Bob Hillberg holding the Olympic arms copy of the Whitney Wolverine pistol.

CREATION OF THE BROWNING BPS SHOTGUN

When we take a close look at the splendid line of shotguns offered by Browning, we observe a high quality line of guns ranging from the expensive single shot Trap guns, to the popular over/under double guns such as the beautiful Citori line In the autoloading field, Browning has been a popular choice of shooters ever since John Moses Browning invented the first autoloading shotgun way back in 1911. This world-famous gun was produced in Belgium by Fabrique Nationale as the Browning Auto 5, and by Remington in this country as the Remington Model 11 and the Savage Model 720 *et al.*

Bob with the original BPS design blueprint drawing in the background.

Oddly enough, there was not a pump shotgun in the company's line since Mr. Browning sold the manufacturing rights for the initial design of a pump action shotgun to Remington in 1915 (patent 1143170, originally issued to John M. Browning). In fact, the pump shotgun was missing from the Browning sales inventory until the introduction of the BPS in 1977 – an absence from the rapidly-growing pump action gun market for 62 years!

Remington introduced the 1915 Browning design as the Model 17 pump action shotgun. Remington sold a total of 72,644 Model 17s before discontinuing it in 1933. When the Browning patent expired, the Ithaca Gun Co. was free to copy the basic Model 17 Remington. They promoted it as the Ithaca Model 37; it was designed in 1933 and put in production in 1937. This fabulous pump shotgun is still manufactured today and it has been the cornerstone of Ithaca's production since its inception.

The great market potential for the pump action shotgun was recognized by both manufacturing giants Remington and Winchester. The popular Winchester Model 12 pump was designed by T.C. Johnson, a Winchester engineer who spent many years designing a pump action that did not infringe on the Browning patent. This highly successful shotgun was accepted as one of America's premier shotgun designs. Nearly two million were sold from 1912 to 1963, when production was discontinued.

Remington also recognized the tremendous sales and market appeal potential for a reliable, top-quality pump gun that could be competitive in cost with the Winchester Model 12. They designed the famous Remington Model 870, which was first sold in 1950. The 870 was exceptionally successful and it turned out to be the world's highest-volume shotgun ever produced. Sales of the 870 had reached two million by 1973 and over seven million by 1996! It is still being manufactured today by the Rem-

ington Arms Co. in Ilion, New York, using the very latest technology in materials and methods.

Onserving the vast sales potential for a pump action shotgun and the complete absence of this type of shotgun in Browning's line of guns, I couldn't help but wonder if a well-designed, premium-quality Browning pump gun that offered advanced features could compete with the legendary Winchester and Remington. I was further tantalized by the fact that it would be a natural move for Browning, since John M. Browning pioneered the very first pump action shotgun with several advanced features not even found today on the Remington 870.

The more I thought about developing and presenting a proposal for an advanced, premium quality pump shotgun to Browning, the more enthusiastic I became. It seemed to me to be a natural, considering the early patent and history of the first Browning-designed pump. I reviewed the past history of the pump action shotgun with my boss Howard Johnson, president of the Bellmore Johnson Tool Company (BJT) of Hamden, Connecticut. I was employed as BJT's chief engineer at the time, and in 1970 I persuaded Howie to let me design a prototype of the proposed shotgun, later known as the BPS (Browning Pump Shotgun). He became equally enthusiastic about the possibility of selling the BPS and gave me permission to design the gun's layout in detail prior to the actual presentation to Browning.

I proceeded to set up the design project objectives for the new project as follows:

1. The gun must be completely ambidextrous and favor both right and left hand shooters. Bottom ejection was essential, and the side ejection receiver ports would be eliminated.

2. The safety must be thumb operated, centrally located on the receiver tang and easily controlled by the thumb on the trigger finger right or left hand.

3. It must be loaded from the bottom ejection port opening without depressing the lifter and with no restriction or finger pinching by the lifter during the loading operation.

4. Twin action bars must be employed for smooth non binding slide operation.

5. The receiver must be machined from quality high strength steel. All components should likewise be quality materials. (No die-cast parts.)

6. Smooth, streamlined receiver, stock, and forearm shape. (No humpback shape to rear of receiver.)

7. Best quality balance and user-friendly stock dimensions in accordance with Browning's high standards.

8. Absolute top quality to be employed in all components with no substitutes in materials or methods.

9. Tremendous reliability of function and smoothness of operation to be absolutely mandatory.

10. Addition of a trigger disconnector to positively eliminate the possibility of accidentally firing when shucking the slide while holding the trigger to the rear.

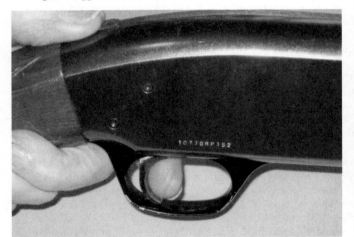

This illustrates the thumb engaging the central position of the BPS's ambidextrous safety without moving the trigger finger to operate the safety for a fast shot, as is necessary with a conventional crossbolt safety.

With these project objectives now clearly established, I was at last ready to start the new design layout with a clean sheet of paper. This was the beginning of many decades of long, laborious hours of detailed design work for me. It also involved an intensive study of the competition to analyze their good and bad features.

I was then engaged in making the largest and most complete design layout I have ever made. After countless design studies following the project objectives, the layout consisted of detailed sectional drawings of the action in the locked firing position, the eject position, and the loading position. Full scale outlines of all the action components were illustrated along with a complete parts list and heat-treat specifications.

When the design layout was finally complete, Howie and I were ready to make a presentation to the Browning executives

at their beautiful corporate headquarters at Morgan, Utah, in the foothills of the rugged Wasatch mountain range.

We were well received by company president John V. Browning and the owner, Mr. Val A. Browning, a well-known Utah industrialist and son of the great John Moses Browning. Val's father acquired 126 firearms patents in his lifetime and created a myriad of the world's most famous commercial and military guns of all types. Needless to say, it was a prestigious moment for me to meet these people. The meeting couldn't have gone better because they were intrigued by the proposal of adding a quality pump shotgun with a touch of the original Browning heritage in its design. They were well pleased with my design layout.

Val Browning was a Cornell law and engineering graduate and a gun designer in his own right with 48 patents. He pored over my proposed BPS design layout and understood exactly what I was trying to accomplish. Howie and I were more than pleased at their interest, and we all agreed the next step would be to build a prototype for test. Building new model guns from scratch was old hat to us at BJT. We had for years built many first model and experimental guns for Hi-Standard, Winchester, Marlin, Colt, the CIA, and the Springfield Armory. We had a staff of the area's best tool and die makers. It was agreed that we would make detailed engineering drawings from the layout and actually fabricate and preliminary test the gun. This was right up our alley as we had done this successfully many times before. For this phase, Browning agreed to our building the prototype at their expense. We also agreed on a royalty to be paid on each gun sold in production.

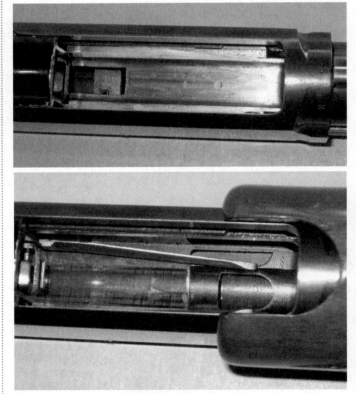

(top) The bottom loading and ejection port opening showing the retracted lifter and the bottom of the locked bolt with an unobstructed access for loading a fresh round with the bolt and slide in the foreword or firing and loading position.
(above) The bottom port opening showing the lifter in the down or eject position with the slide and bolt in the rear position.

Howie and I returned to BJT elated at our success, and we made plans for the final phase of our agreement, the actual building and test of the prototype. This required many hours of concentrated effort by carefully-chosen tool makers. Once again our good fortune held. The prototype went together as planned, and it performed beautifully right from the start. Quite frankly, I was very proud and grateful to the many individuals who made it happen. Usually a new prototype generally requires parts redesign and fabrication due to malfunction, worn or broken parts in test, awkward assembly, etc. – but the BPS required absolutely no rework.

Our involvement in the BPS program was virtually over at this point; it was up to Browning to put the final approval on the gun and get it manufactured in quantity production. For many years Browning guns were manufactured by Fabrique Nationale de Herstal in Liege, Belgium. The Browning Company was required to seek an outside contractor to manufacture the BPS because they lacked the large facility necessary to build the production guns in the U.S.A. A decision was made to make the BPS in production by the Miroku Firearms Mfg. Co. in Japan to Browning's exacting quality standards. Browning sent an early sample of the production gun to BJT for our examination. We were highly pleased with the performance and high quality of this production gun. Howie gave me the gun as a souvenir for proposing and designing the BPS.

Things had progressed from a dream to a reality. BJT kept their word and shared one half of the Browning royalties with me during the first production phase. Unfortunately for BJT and me, that arrangement would come to an early termination.

The Browning Arms Company was established in the United States in 1927 a year after the death of John M. Browning. Half a century later, in 1977, the Belgium firm of Fabrique Nationale acquired the company. At that time the BPS was in full production and our BJT royalty was in full effect. The new organization wanted to continue to produce the gun but did not want to pay the royalty to BJT. As a result, Browning offered BJT a lump-sum cash buyout to eliminate the royalty agreement. We accepted this offer and our participation and all future communications with Browning regrettably came to a close. I have worked for numerous firearms companies and the

military over the years as a designer, court expert witness and consultant, but I have never enjoyed working for anyone more than I did Browning. To me, they have always been a class organization in every respect.

The BPS saga did not die at the ending of our involvement. In fact, it was only the beginning, and the BPS is still being made today with numerous options to meet public demand. It is now available in 10, 12, 28, 20, and .410 gauges with high-post full-vent sighting ribs, Invector choke tubes, various barrel lengths, select model walnut stocks, and engraved receivers. These additions were all added by Browning. My prototype gun consisted of only the basic functional action.

The current BPS suggested retail price ranges from $519 to $780, depending on model. Market sales have steadily improved, and expert critics have given the BPS a top rating for its exceptionally smooth function and reliability, with Browning's typically fine workmanship and finish.

CREATION OF THE HIGH STANDARD MANUFACTURING CORPORATION

The complex history of High Standard generated from the elementary designs for .22 caliber single-shot and semi-automatic pistols by a Hartford, Connecticut, inventor, Lucius N. Diehm, who patented a series of firearms from 1916 to 1925. The Hartford Arms & Equipment Company was established primarily to produce several of the Diehm-designed pistols. This small company was only mildly successful and produced about 5,000 pistols between 1925 and 1930 before suffering bankruptcy and going out of business. Needless to say, these early Hartford Arms Diehm-designed pistols have become a very scarce rarity for pistol collectors.

The early birth and growth of the High Standard Company in Connecticut was all due to the guiding genius and drive of one man, a very talented and energetic Swede and New Haven, Connecticut, resident, Carl Gustav Swebilius. He was instrumental in the entire concept and the initial achievements of the High Standard Company.

Swebilius had a very extensive background in the firearms business. The son of a Swedish watchmaker, he learned his trade as a young man working as an apprentice toolmaker and designer for

the Marlin Firearms Co. in New Haven. During World War I he was instrumental in converting a Colt .30 caliber machine gun into an aircraft weapon. He is also credited for developing a synchronous fire control permitting a machine gun to fire through the moving blades of an aircraft propeller. He became experienced and well-respected at Marlin, both as a tooling expert and as an accomplished designer.

After the war was over, Swebilius joined a Hamden wire company for which he designed machinery for manufacturing insulated wire. In 1921 Marlin rehired him back as the chief engineer for a short time until they temporarily ceased operations in 1923. Swebilius then joined Winchester as a senior gun designer. During this period of unrest in the firearms industry, Swebilius wanted to start and control his own gun company, and he subsequently resigned from Winchester and started his own business in 1926.

This company, the High Standard Arms Manufacturing Company of Hamden, Connecticut, produced deep-hole drills for making rifle barrels and specialty items for the local firearms factories. This was the actual birth of the fabulous High Standard Company. It started out as a small shoestring operation, but then Swebilius purchased the now-bankrupt Hartford Arms Company for less than $1,000. This was the beginning that started High Standard in the handgun manufacturing business, and it allowed Swebilius to produce a clone of the Diehm-designed Hartford Arms Model 1925 .22 semi-automatic pistol. It was ultimately to became the very successful High Standard Model B and the beginning of a long list of various High Standard .22 models. At the time of Swebilius's death from cancer in 1948, High Standard had produced over a quarter of a million .22 pistols of various models. It can be truly said that High Standard's birth and growth were largely due to the dynamic energy, dream and guidance of Carl Gustave Swebilius.

His rapid success was due to his ability to recognize and select key men of outstanding ability to build the framework of the rapidly expanding gun company. In one of his first moves in the new company, he hired George Wilson, Sr. from the defunct, recently-purchased Hartford Arms Co. Wilson was a very experienced and capable gun designer with years of know-how in the manufacturing business. His addition to the newly-formed High Standard Co. to manufacture handguns came from his previous experience at Hartford Arms producing Diehm pistols.

Swebilius had a burning desire to produce and aid the allied forces with their war effort at the outset of World War II. To this end, Swebilius enlisted the help of Jack Owsley, who had many influential contacts in England. He was able to convince the British Purchasing Commission that High Standard could be a major supplier to their desperately-needed .50 caliber machine gun program. They responded immediately, and High Standard was awarded a contract for 12,000 Browning aircraft guns with an advance of $6 million. With very large contracts in their pocket, High Standard was able to secure local bank financing to build a new factory on Dixwell Avenue in Hamden. They were able to purchase the very latest machine tools and equipment for massive machine gun production. Needless to say, this was all they needed to greatly expand in rapid order from a small, modest, pistol manufacturer of 250 employees to one of the largest and most respected players in the gun industry with a work force of 4,000!

The US Army soon became High Standard's main customer and the company responded by outproducing all other suppliers of .50 caliber Browning Aircraft machine guns. This included such giants as Colt, Savage, and General Motors. At the same time they also supplied the army with .45-caliber barrels for the 1911-A1 service pistol and thousands of model HD B .22 pistols for training and recreation purposes. They also manufactured and supplied over 2,000 Model HD-MS pistols equipped with silencers for the Office of Special Services. The OSS guns were used for clandestine operations. Wartime production of High Standard was 228,000 .50-caliber aircraft machine guns.

During the war Swebilius was the second highest salaried citizen in the United States. A congressional investigation revealed that High Standard's price to the government for the .50 caliber machine gun was considerably less than any of the other contractors for the same gun. Suffice it to say they must have done something right!

After the end of the war, the massive buildup of military equipment slowed to a virtual standstill. At that time, High Standard's management decided to become a major player in the commercial arms business by increasing their own handgun product line and to establish a long-time agreement to produce an economy line of shotguns and rifles for the Sears, Roebuck Co. Sears was unusally successful in promoting these products through their massive coast-to-coast merchandising network under the trade name of J.C. Higgins. *[Editor's note: "J C Higgins" was not a made-up brand name, like "Betty Crocker" or "Aunt Jemima." John C. Higgins (1908-1964) was the head of Sears, Roebuck's Chicago accounting office and their chief comptroller. – DMS].* The agreement with the Sears, Roebuck Company was for them to invest a substantial sum of capital annually in the Research and Development group to design, build, and test new Sears firearms products and to create the new tooling required to produce these guns.

Carl Swebilius hired an old friend from Winchester, Fred Humiston, to head the newly-formed High Standard research department. Fred was a gun designer from the old school who created his new designs on milling machines and lathes rather than on the drawing board. The modern age of CAD-CAM and computers had not yet arrived, of course.

(Historical footnote: The heavily-publicized Hollywood film *Carbine Williams* film starring Jimmie Stewart gave credit exclusively to David "Marsh" Williams for designing the US M1 Carbine. Not so. The carbine was hurriedly designed by several members of the Winchester engineering group with Fred Humiston as the key designer. It was actually the Humiston-designed carbine and not the Williams design that was tested and approved by the government for wartime mass production and use. Knowledgeable Winchester engineering personal and executives know that Fred Humiston and not Williams was actually the main person in the carbine's development and acceptance. An excellent report in a June 6, 1951, article by Edwin Pugsley, the chief of engineering of Winchester at that time, clearly establishes and verifies the carbine's true story and the extent of Williams's involvement.)

Humiston's High Standard Research and Development department was started with three designers and two excellent ex-Winchester tool makers. Their initial duty was concerned with manufacture and design of Sears product. After about a year, in 1956, the gifted Fred Humiston passed away from cancer, and vice president George Wil-son Sr. appointed me as his replacement.

The R&D workload increased considerably as High Standard took on experimental government contracts from Springfield Armory and the Detroit Tank Arsenal for the design of the T-152 and T-153 tank machine gun. A new design of the T-3 double action 9mm pistol with a twin stack feed was also required for the armed services. In addition to the added military research, the R&D department was required to continue with the Sears commercial gun design program. This expansion obviously required increased R&D personnel, so the workforce was expanded to 10 designers and six tool makers, plus the use of subcontractor tool companies. It was during this period that I designed, built and tested the world's first gas-operated autoloading shotgun. This unique shotgun was produced by High Standard as the Supermatic and the Sears JC Higgins Model 60.

Many thousands of the Higgins Model 60 Sears guns were sold. It employed the patented hollow gas piston which surrounded the magazine feed tube, thus allowing greater magazine capacity without lengthening the forend stock. High Standard enjoyed a fine reputation for creative design and excellent workmanship in that era.

The momentum and drive of the of the original High Standard company were sadly missing with the deaths of Carl Swebilius, George Wilson Sr., Fred Humiston, and a number of management and key employees who either resigned or retired at that time. I went to the Bellmore Johnson Tool Co. as chief engineer, in which capacity I designed the .22 caliber Whitney Wolverine sporting pistol, the 12-gauge Browning BPS pump shotgun (see above), and the .45 Winchester Magnum Wildey gas-operated pistol. Harry Sefried, after designing the popular Sentinel .22 revolver in the High Standard R&D department, went to the Sturm-Ruger Co. as the Chief Engineer and designed a number of Ruger's finest guns, including the famous 10-22 rifle, several of the Ruger revolver models and the Mini-14 .223 caliber rifle.

In 1968 the original High Standard top management had changed and they decided to sell the company. It was acquired by the Leisure Group, a non-firearms company selling sporting goods equipment. A turbulent period followed. The original High Standard facilities in Hamden were moved to the Leisure Group location in East Hartford in 1976.

in 1978 the property changed again with a buyout of the Leisure Group. In 1984 the assets were sold by the buyer.

Corporate stagnation followed until 1993 when a progressive, up-to-date company bought High Standard and completely reorganized it. The new owner is the High Standard Manufacturing Company, Inc., of Houston, Texas. This new owner invested in facilities and the very latest technology and equipment. In 1994 They began to ship the newly manufactured High Standard .22 pistols. They are dedicated to returning the High Standard reputation and quality back to equal or better than the excellent pre-1968 standards. I pray that the new organization will continue with the legacy, spirit, and success of the Swebilius area.

DESIGN OF THE ITHACA MODEL 49 RIFLE

After the Whitney Wolverine pistol development with the Bellmore Johnson Tool Company in the early 1950s, I took a close look at the various firearms manufacturer's product lines to determine if there were any opportunities for market-

Gun Digest editor-in-chief John T. Amber personally reviewed the Ithaca M49 .22 in the 1962 edition.

able products. I was aware that many progressive sales departments were undoubtedly searching for the same thing. One company stood out as obviously in need of new product design: the Ithaca Gun Company of Ithaca, New York. They were well-known for producing a very high quality product that often needed precision hand-fitting by highly skilled workman. This type of labor, while greatly admired, was gradually placing itself out of the competitive price range. Other companies were using advanced designs with newer machines and the latest technology. This ultimately limited Ithaca's competitive abilities.

Ithaca had for a long time lacked an aggressive design staff. Aside from their excellent old double guns, their greatest design achievement had been the redesign of the Browning-designed Remington Model 15 pump shotgun as the Ithaca model 37. It was universally accepted by the shooting public and it even outsold and outlasted the fabulous Winchester model 12 pump gun! Unfortunately it wasn't enough to sustain this early landmark company, which was founded way back in 1880.

World War II provided some relief for the financially troubled Ithaca. They produced

a number of .45 Colt 1911-A1 service pistols and M3 grease guns between 1943 and 1945. This activity served only as a temporary band-aid, however. They were hurting for a new product to augment their only winner, the rock-solid Model 37 pump gun. Ithaca's president, Sheldon Smith, and his brother and director of manufacturing, Charles Smith, made a valiant attempt to create a business turnaround after the great war by producing a .22 autoloading rifle which developed numerous function problems, and they also made an ill-fated attempt to have MIT personel design a semi-automatic shotgun for them. As one might expect, it was a brilliant study but thoroughly impractical to mass produce as a competitive sporting shotgun.

These post-war failures made Ithaca understandably cautious despite the fact that they were extremely anxious to produce a single-shot .22 rifle that I designed, the BJT Saddle Gun, after witnessing a flawless demonstration of the prototype rifle. The Smiths personally contacted a large number of leading firearms merchandisers and surveyed their estimate of the volume sales at different price levels. Because of the extremely low direct labor and low cost material to produce the rifle, the retail price was established at an amazingly low $21.95. This price was established extremely low to dramatically produce a very high sales volume at a minimum profit. This was in stark contrast to prior Ithaca sales philosophy. In 1960, the Ithaca Model 49 sold for $21.95 – and the Ithaca single barrel trap gun sold for $2,500!

In setting up the project objectives for the first presentation of what became the Itaca Model 49 rifle, I figured it must be compatible with Ithaca's current capabilities and finances. With this in mind I established the following objectives.

1. It must include the lowest possible tooling expense.

2. It should require an absolute minimum of direct labor to produce.

3. It must be unique in design and appeal to a vast new potential market.

4. It must have eye appeal.

5. It must be safe, accurate, and durable.

From a design point of view these project objectives were extremely difficult to achieve. A high-cost, expensive and complicated mechanism would be infinitely easier

New — Ithaca's Forty-Nine, a lever action single shot 22 rimfire that has the Western look.

New — Jefferson 260 autoloader in 22 RF Magnum.

they'll ever get.

The concept of the annual model changes hasn't enveloped the gun industry yet, at least to any substantial degree—let's hope it never does.

Colt Pat. F.A. Mfg. Co.

Rifles—Once again Colt has modified its line of hunting rifles. The 1961 series will all be made on the Sako action and all barrels will be 12-grooved. The short Sako action will be used in 222 and 222 Magnum, the medium action for calibers 243 and 308; 270 and 30-06, as well as the 264, 300 and 375 Mag-

of heat and cold, parts entirely free of lubricant, and immersion in sand or mud, this light rifle performed beyond the usual military requirements.

Colt looks upon the AR-15 as the ideal combat-assault-sniper rifle, and foresees a big sale to police and military units—the gun may also be ordered in caliber 7.62 NATO. For complete data write to Colt.

Shotguns—Colt enters the competition for U.S. shotgun dollars this year for the first time since 1900 or so. Two types will be available late in 1961— conventional in form and styling (full

You'll find data on all of them however, in our catalog pages.

Ithaca

Easily one of the big hits of the year is Ithaca's Model 49 Saddlegun—as you can see from the illustration on these pages, it has all the looks of the traditional lever action repeating rifle, even to size. Actually, this trim little carbine—it's only 38¼ inches over-all —is a single shot handling 22 S, L, LR cartridges. The lever actuates a modified form of Martini action, that is, a pivoting breechblock.

43

to design, but it obviously would never be compatible with Ithaca's immediate requirements. To meet these five objectives I reasoned that a low-cost single shot "boy's first rifle" with the eye appeal and look of "the gun that won the west" would add considerably to its sales appeal. The legendary Winchester 94 was Hollywood's standard equipment for the western lawmen and the bad guys. It would have great appeal to the movie-going teenage shooters. If the price of the rifle was rock bottom and the gun was accurate and safe, it should be a winner!

To meet the cost objectives, the single shot and safety requirement seemed the most logical answer. To preserve the Model 94 look, the lever action would be used for loading, extraction and ejection only. Lever function would not cock the hammer. For safety reasons, the hammer had to be manually cocked for each shot. With the hammer forward in the down or fire position, the gun would not discharge if the gun were dropped or suffered a hard blow on the hammer. This required the shooter to perform deliberate, separate motions to load and fire the gun.

To meet the low cost objectives, a concentrated effort was centered on reducing the direct labor wherever possible. The two main components that presented the greatest cost savings were the bolt and the receiver. The bolt did not move horizontally but its front end swung vertically, Martini fashion, thus exposing the barrel breech for loading and ejection. This normally would require a complex bolt that was expensive to machine from a solid bar. A tremendous cost saving was employed here by using a new process utilized by Chrysler and Ford for certain engine parts at great savings: the forming of parts by compacting powdered iron under tremendous pressure and then sintering them under high heat. The advantage of this process is extreme accuracy and very low cost. The cost saving for the bolt was substantial and the strength was more than adequate, as attested by the performance of many thousands of rifles. The powdered metal process today is common and utilized by many industries.

The receiver was fabricated from die-cast zinc, and it saved a lot of difficult machining from a forging or bar stock. This cost savings realized by the resulting elimination of many direct labor operations was tremendous. The construction of the barrel, however, did not save any direct labor. It was fabricated the same way all quality barrels have been made for many years. This became evident when the Model 49 demonstrated excellent accuracy over many thousands of rounds.

The western-styled wooden forend and stock were in keeping with their famous big brother, the Model 94 Winchester.

The overall appearance of this rifle and Ithaca's low sales price of $21.95 was sensational. When the BJT prototype was first demonstrated to Sheldon and Charles Smith, they were extremely impressed with its appearance, performance, and low cost. They immediately opened negotiations with us to purchase the rifle.

Since this was the very first of many firearms which were designed to and built for outside production, instead of asking for a royalty we negotiated for a lump sum cash payment to cover our expenses for the designing and fabricating the prototype plus a nominal profit. Ithaca accepted this approach and Bellmore Johnson and I agreed to split the profit equally. This was virtually the end of our connection with Ithaca and we observed the initial activity and the successful introduction of the Ithaca Model 49 BJT-designed rifle.

Ithaca successfully produced many thousands of guns before they were consumed by debt and bankruptcy from previous indebtedness. They were faced with a demand to remove hazardous materials from the site by the New York State Environmental Protection Agency and the city of Ithaca. This was the result of over a century of manufacturing. A federally-mandated cleanup program to dispose of land containing thousands of tons of lead-contaminated soil cost Ithaca $4.8 million dollars! Besides the cleanup, the factory itself was in a sad state of disrepair. It was obvious the grand old factory had to be sold or go out of business. Unfortunately, the low volume of the trap gun, the steady sales of the Model 37 and the large sales volume of the Model 49 all failed to revive the troubled company. They were forced into bankruptcy and the only saleable things left of interest for other investors were the timeless Model 37 pump shotgun and the new Ithaca Model 49 rifle.

The rifle was eventually sold to Savage and it was marketed as the Stevens Model 89. A total of 31,841 guns were shipped by Savage during the next few years. By then the direct labor costs to manufacture the rifle had increased, as had the price of zinc, the material for the major die-cast components. The rifle had lost its momentum and no longer offered the sales and profit advantage it originally enjoyed. This would be the sad ending of this fine little rifle, the Ithaca Model 49.

The Model 49 Ithaca .22 rifle ended with the sale to Savage. The price was right, and its workmanship and accuracy were very acceptable. I designed it to be a Honda, not a Cadillac. (Note: the M49's design, whichI did not patent, was later produced by Agawam Arms of Agawam, Massachusetts.)

(Note also that the solid design and performance of the Ithaca Model 37 were not about to be forgotten, however. After surviving several sales and bankruptcies, the remaining company was sold. The new owner, David Dlubak, is an avid sportsman, hunter and businessman. Dlubak purchased Ithaca Guns USA, LLC in June of 2007 and he created a new and up-to-the-minute facility in Upper Sandusky, Ohio, using the very latest and finest manufacturing technology. Receivers and other parts are now fabricated on CNC machines from solid billets of the finest steel. Dlubak insists that all operations of the new factory are to be of the very highest quality and all parts are to be fabricated entirely by U.S. manpower. This type of operation ensures top performance and quality equal to or better than the original Ithaca's very high standards.)

THE SINGLE-SHOT SAVAGE MODEL 101 PISTOL

The concept for this unique handgun came as a result of the spine-tingling early struggles between heroic lawmen and despicable bad guys as shown on TV in the 1950s. This universal theme was that honesty and fair play always win. These scenarios made a deep impression on young Americans and entertained many oldsters as well. The numerous handgun conflicts which erupted always involved the rock-solid legendary Colt single action pistol. This was Hollywood's standard equipment for the good guy's and bad guy's handgun, which, in truth, was close to being historically correct. The lasting romance of this famous old six-shooter is still with us today. It had excellent balance combined with a superb universal grip. It was well built and rugged and it always functioned.

Loading the single action Colt revolver to fire in a single shot mode is not a simple operation, however. A live cartridge has to be placed in an empty chamber and the cylinder manually rotated to the proper position to align with the barrel when ready to fire by cocking the hammer. This is not a simple, straightforward operation. It is not a maneuver for an inexperienced shooter. A simple, safer, and inexpensive concept for loading and extracting a single-shot had to be devised.

I therefore imagined a new "lookalike" single-shot version of the famous old Colt. If produced at an extremely low sales price, would have an immediate sales appeal as a boy's first handgun. I have always considered that the safety and simplicity of a single-shot was mandatory for a novice's first gun. Too many careless and unnecessary accidents have been caused by beginners with repeating firearms.

The solution to this problem was to load the pistol directly by passing the barrel through a false, non-rotating cylinder. This combined unit was rotated to the right side of the frame for easy and safe extracting or loading. When the unit is rotated back to the firing position, the hammer remained in the safe rebound position and had to be be manually cocked to fire. I made the layout and the finished detail drawings for this design and enlisted the excellent tool makers of the Bellmore Johnson Tool Co. to build the prototype for the proposed production gun.

I had become very familiar with Savage through several previous design projects and also as a Savage expert witness in several court cases. I decided to present this proposal to their top management. When I demonstrated the pistol to Jack Knode, the VP and chief engineer of Savage, he was enthusiastic over the design prospectus and decided to make the tooling in-house. I had recommended subcontracting the die-cast frame to Alcoa, the contractors for my Whitney Wolverine pistol frame. They had a large engineering office and a huge manufacturing facility. Jack decided to save money and hire a moonlighter to design the tooling and produce the die castings in-house at their own facility. I was hired by Savage to work with this individual in the Savage engineering department until the tooling for the die-cast frame was complete. Fabricating the frame from an aluminum die casting saved Savage a considerable amount of direct labor in machining and polishing. The hammer and trigger were formed and hardened by the sintered metal process from a subcontractor, and this further eliminated large machining and finishing costs. The plastic-impregnated wood segments for the grips were subcontracted with the typical Savage molded Indian head logo embedded.

Savage was able to produce and market the newly-christened Model 101 pistol in 1960 at the very low price of $19.50! This single shot pistol was well-made, accurate, and economical. It made a lot of sense for a beginner's first handgun, or for a safe, reliable, and inexpensive general-purpose .22 pistol for just about any shooter.

Of possible interest to collectors is the fact that I had Savage make up about a dozen 101 pistols which couldn't be loaded and fired. They were marked "DUMMY" on the bottom strap of the grip. I gave four of them to my neighborhood kids to play with as cowboys and Indians. The rest were used by Savage as salesmen samples.

SAVAGE MODEL 101
CALIBER: 22 S, L, or LR, single shot.
BARREL: 5½ inches with ejector rod.
LENGTH: 9".
WEIGHT: 20 oz.
STOCKS: Compressed wood.
FEATURES: Integral barrel and cylinder swings out for loading and ejection.
SIGHTS: Blade front and movable notch rear.
PRICE: Blued $19.50

SHERIDAN KNOCABOUT Model D
CALIBER: 22 S or LR, single shot.
BARREL: 5" Tip up type.
LENGTH: 6¾"
WEIGHT: 24 oz.
STOCKS: Black plastic.
SIGHTS: Fixed, ramp front, square notch rear.
PRICE: Blued $17.95

SMITH & WESSON 9mm Model 39
CALIBER: 9mm Luger, 8 shot clip.
BARREL: 4"
LENGTH: 7⅜"
WEIGHT: 26½ oz.
STOCKS: Checkered walnut.
SIGHTS: ⅛" serrated ramp front, adjustable rear.
SAFETIES: Magazine disconnector and positive firing pin lock and hammer release.
FRAME: Lightweight alloy, with checked arched mainspring housing and lanyard loop.
ACTION: Locked-breech, short recoil with dropping barrel, double action. Top matted slide stays open on last shot. Nickeled $95.00
PRICE: Blued $85.00

WHITNEY 22 AUTOLOADER
CALIBER: 22 LR, 10 shot.
BARREL: 4⅝ inches.
LENGTH: 9 inches.
WEIGHT: 23 oz.
STOCKS: Checkered plastic, walnut finish. Grooved trigger.
SIGHTS: Patridge type, ⅛" blade front.
PRICE: Blued .... $39.95 Nickeled $44.95

209

The 1961 Gun Digest featured two Hillberg-designed pistols on the same page: the Whitney Wolverine and the Savage M101.

Because of the horrendous recoil of the .500 Jeffery it was decided that a second lug attached to the bottom of the barrel would provide an additional amount of support. Both lugs were glassed in and the standard two cross-bolts were added.

BY TOM TABOR

John Taylor wrote glowingly about the .500 Jeffery in his books and should get a certain amount of credit for keeping the caliber alive over the decades. But, even without Taylor's assistance it is not difficult to see the merits of this fine old warrior. Prior to the .460 Weatherby Magnum entering the scene in 1958, the .500 Jeffery was considered the most powerful magazine rifle cartridge in the world. But even though the Jeffery is no longer considered the "biggest of the big," I believe that when facing an animal intent on eating, stomping or goring me, I would much prefer to have a Jeffery in hands than virtually any other caliber.

There is a lot of history behind the .500 Jeffery, but unfortunately the records of its origin are blurred. We know that it is a proprietary cartridge of rebated rimless design and that it is very similar to the 12.5x70mm Schuler. We also know it was designed for use in the German Mauser bolt-action rifles. Schuler was probably the originator of the cartridge, but that is an arguable point.

I had dreamed of building a custom big bore rifle for decades and within that time I had pawed over mountains of writings before finally settling on building a .500 Jeffery. Then, once I had made my mind up that the Jeffery was the rifle for me, I wondered why it took me so long to reach that conclusion. To my way of thinking the Jeffery outshines virtually any of the other historic English and European calibers and when compared to the modern rounds like the Dakotas and A-Squares, the Jeffery has nothing to be ashamed of.

Once the parts were received, Dan Coffin of Coffin Gunsmithing started putting the rifle together.

RESURRECTION OF THE .500 JEFFERY

My dream came to reality shortly after being confronted by a couple of Cape buffalo bulls while hunting plains game in South Africa. Immediately upon returning to the States I stopped into Coffin Gunsmithing's shop in Victor, Montana, where Dan Coffin and I ironed out plans for a brand new custom big-bore rifle. Ever since 1990 Dan has been in the employment of the country and western singer, Hank Williams, as Hank's private gunsmith. Recently, however, Dan has been taking on additional work building both bigbores and varmint rifles. He has a tremendous amount of experience constructing bigbores and soon we had the beginnings of a rifle plan on the table. I agreed to do much of the leg work in obtaining component parts, which primarily came from the mail order house of Brownells, while Dan would see to getting the CZ 550 action and the Montana Rifleman barrel ordered.

The CZ 550 action was going to take a consider amount of work, and Dan indicated he would get started on it as soon as it arrived. The bolt face would need to be opened, the ejection port enlarged, the magazine converted over to a single stack feed and the trigger modified. The single stack feed was necessary to ensure proper and reliable feeding of the huge .500 cartridges and the trigger modifications would elimi-nate the set trigger design that CZ seems to be so proud of. Dan would also move the trigger further back, giving it a more pleasing appearance inside the trigger guard. To provide an added degree of support Dan recommended that we add a second lug that would attach to the underside of the barrel. This would provide a little more surface area and strength to guard against stock cracking as a consequence of the expected heavy recoil of the .500.

I normally prefer the appearance of black walnut, but due to the demands placed on the stock by the .500, I decided that a piece of the typically stronger, French walnut might be a better choice. Before long we had a nicely figured, solid, AA-Grade French walnut blank waiting to be roughed in, after which Dan would do the fitting and finish work.

Whenever you try to send a big 570-gr. bullet out the muzzle between 2,300 and 2,400 fps you can, as a consequence, ex-pect a considerable amount of recoil. For this reason I wanted to leave the contour of the barrel heavy, which wound up to be close to one inch in diameter as it met the forearm of the stock. The most common barrel length for a rifle like this is probably 24 inches, but I was looking for a fast handling rifle for those tight spots on dangerous game that no one wants to be faced with, but appreciates being prepared for. A barrel of 22 inches seemed to fit that bill perfectly. In order to provide better overall balance and at the same time reduce the felt recoil, two 1-lb. mercury recoil reducers were placed in the butt stock. This resulted in a terrifically well-balanced rifle that would swing quickly. Eventually the rifle hit the target weight of just under 12 lbs. with scope.

One thing I fear possibly as much as being mauled by a hungry lion or stomped by an angry elephant is the

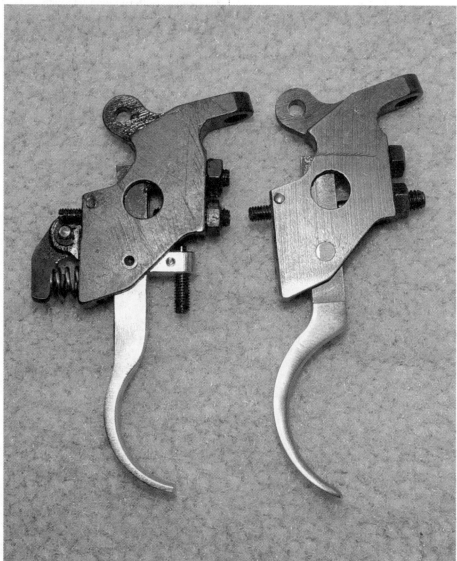

We felt the CZ stock trigger (left) needed modifying. Our newly revised trigger (right) eliminated the set trigger mechanism and moved the trigger farther back.

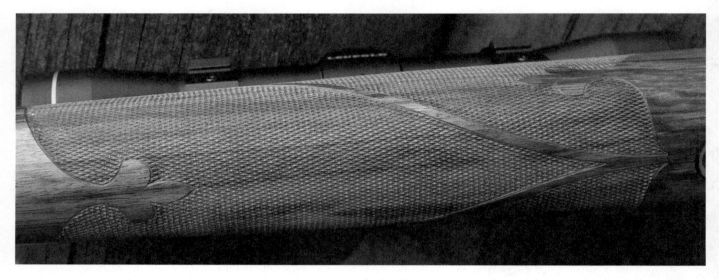

idea of getting hit in the eye with the scope from a caliber like the .500 Jeffery. I have been the recipient of such a blow but from a much smaller caliber and I do not want to repeat that experience, especially if it is the consequence of sending the equivalent of a 1-1/3-oz. fishing sinker speeding to its destination. For this reason I took the advice of a close friend and retired South African professional hunter and got the scope away from my eye. We mounted the long eye relief Leupold scope 10 inches out on the barrel and anchored it with a modified set of Leupold quick detachable QRW mounts.

A critical point in constructing any custom firearm in either a wildcat caliber, or in this case what some people might consider an obsolete caliber, is ammunition. And in the case of the .500 Jeffery, if you're going to shoot it, you're going to load for it. Working with the chamber reamer manufacturer Pacific Tool and Gauge and the custom reloading die shop of Hornady I was able to get the two parties together in order to ensure that the chamber dimensions would match precisely the reloading dies.

Once the metal work was well underway I was able to turn my mind to the finish work. Who would do the stock checkering, a much needed part of any beautiful custom rifle? And did I want any metal engraving done? Eventually it was decided that Pam Wheeler would do the checkering. Pam was well known

(above) The wrap-around fleur de lis checkering pattern, complete with ribbons, is a work of art and adds a significant bit of elegance to the overall appearance of the rifle.

(below) Gouse Freelance Firearms Engraving completed the metal engraving project by adding a Cape buffalo on the magazine floor plate.

in the business and over the years has checkered for companies such as Kimber, Cooper, Weatherby, Ljutic and even the famous late custom shotgun maker Tommy Sietz. Pam is exceptionally flexible and has the ability to provide you with virtually any pattern and style you prefer. Before long we had agreed to a moderately fancy ribbon fleur de

The .500 Jeffery/.500 Schuler Controversy

BY JAMES TUCKER

Sifting through the sands of time is a daunting task! In this case, and I do mean case, I'm referring to an eighty-year-old controversy over the cartridges we know today as the .500 Jeffery and the 12.7X70mm (.500 Schuler).

In books and articles that I have read over the last thirty years, most of the controversy seems to be over who originally developed the cartridge. The year 1927 is when Schuler and Jeffery introduced their cartridges to the public. The first mention of August Schuler Waffenfabrik's new cartridge appeared in a German gun magazine that year. They named and promoted it as the .500 Schuler. It wasn't until 1940 that RWS renamed it the 12.7x70mm. The records of the firm W. J. Jeffery show that they sold their first .500 in 1927.

While this is of interest to many with a historical outlook, those who build and shoot the Schuler/Jeffery cartridges need to know that they are NOT the same cartridge. They are two separate cartridges although nearly everything in print says they are the same. Having worked on six rifles chambered for the ".500 Jeffery" and been involved with two others, I can tell you that the two cartridges are definitely different.

The important difference between the two cases is the shoulder angle. This is very important because for rimless cartridges, as both of these are, the headspace length is determined by the distance between a point on the shoulder and the base of the cartridge. When the angle of the shoulder is changed, the length of the headspace is also changed. If you put a cartridge with a shorter headspace length into a longer barrel chamber, you instantly create a condition known as "excessive headspace." This may result in a case rupture and can cause serious damage to the rifle and shooter.

The Jeffery has a longer shoulder angle of roughly 12.5 degrees. The Schuler utilizes a shorter, steeper angle of a bit over 19.5 degrees. The consequence of putting a .500 Jeffery cartridge in a .500 Schuler chamber is that you create excessive headspace. And, conversely, putting a .500 Schuler cartridge in a .500 Jeffery barrel makes it difficult or impossible to close the bolt.

C.I.P. (*Commission Internationale Permanente pour l'Epreuve des Armes à Feu Portatives*, the European equivalent to SAAMI) standardized the dimensions for the "12.7x70mm (.500 Schuler)," its official name, in 1998. The "500 Jeffery" received C.I.P. approval the following year. Both were slightly revised in 2002. A quick look at the dimensions shows that while similar, they are different in nearly every dimension. With C.I.P. standardization of the two cartridges coming ten years ago you would think, "What's the problem?"

The problem is that with the longtime misrepresentation, many people have the mistaken idea that they are the same cartridge! This translates into rifles being marked .500 Jeffery that have the Schuler chamber. Chamber reamers have been marked .500 Jeffery/Schuler. Brass has been headstamped .500 Jeffery that won't fit into the chamber of a .500 Jeffery rifle. This can be very frustrating, costly, and potentially dangerous.

If you have a .500 Jeffery rifle and are experiencing difficulty opening the bolt after firing and/or the primers are flattened, STOP. Do not continue to fire your rifle. These are signs of excessive pressure. Take your rifle and ammo to a knowledgeable gunsmith and have it thoroughly inspected. You are probably firing .500 Jeffery ammo in a .500 Schuler chamber.

David Little of Kynamco Ltd., makers of Kynoch ammo, pushed for and got the CIP standardization of the .500 Jeffery cartridge. He provided the best explanation as to the design of the .500 Jeffery and backed it up with physical evidence. To paraphrase:

While both gunmakers built rifles using Mauser actions, Schuler's design incorporated a straight stack magazine to accommodate their cartridge while Jeffery stayed with the Mauser double stack design. Also, the German bullets of the time came apart and failed to penetrate deeply on thick skinned game. W. J. Jeffery used a longer shoulder angle for feeding, a thicker jacketed bullet for better penetration, and cordite powder to create the .500 Jeffery. Jeffery was not an ammunition manufacturer and probably had Kynoch do all or most of this on his behalf. It is likely they got Schuler "basic brass" cases from the German manufacturer and then formed and loaded it to Jeffery's specifications. It seems obvious that Schuler came up with his cartridge first. It is equally obvious that Jeffery did not "steal" Schuler's cartridge and put his name on it, as some have said.

The .500 Jeffery is an excellent cartridge for dangerous game. It is not a 12.7x70 mm (.500 Schuler). Treating them as the same can be dangerous to humans and fine rifles.

.500 Jeffrey (left) and .12.7X70mm/.500 Schuler (right). Note the difference in shoulder angle.

lis pattern similar to one she had done recently on a friend's custom .416 Rigby rifle.

To add a little more flare I decided to have some metal engraving as well. Michael Gouse of Gouse Freelance Firearms Engraving was contacted and a decision was made to have him do a modest amount of scroll engraving, and seeing how a couple of Cape buffalo brought me to this point, he would appropriately include an engraved Cape buffalo head on the floor plate.

In cases like the .500, finding reloading data can sometimes be a problem, but I was fortunate to find data on a couple of websites as well as in a reloading manual put out by A-Square. This provided a good point to start from and eventually I compiled my own data. (See table below.)

Big bores are notorious for not being accurate. Two-inch groups at 100 yards are often considered adequate, but when author shot this three-shot group using 570-grain Barnes Banded Solids he was elated.

Quite astonishing to me was the fact that virtually all of the tested loads impacted at the same point on paper at 100 yards; even the Barnes Banded Solids cut paper at the same point as the Triple Shock bullets. This is an important consideration when contemplating going after dangerous game. The rifle consistently held all of its rounds within 1-1/2 inches and on several occasions they cut a single 3-shot ragged hole. This is considered exceptional by any big bore standard. Extreme accuracy and beauty, all in one firearm – what more could a shooter ask for?

CONTACTS

Coffin Gunsmithing, LLC *(Gunsmithing)*
375 Sweathouse Creek Rd.
Victor, Montana 59875
E-Mail: coffingunsmithing@yahoo.com

Pam Wheeler *(Checkering)*
P.O. Box 827
Stevensville, Montana 59870
Telephone: (406) 381-1484

Gouse Freelance Firearms Engraving *(Engraving)*
708 Adirondac
Hamilton, Montana 59840
Telephone: (406) 363-0254
E-mail: create@mtart.com
Web: http://www.mtart.com

Pacific Tool & Gauge *(Chamber reamers)*
598 Avenue C
Medford, Oregon 97503
Telephone: (541) 826-5304

.500 Jeffery Rimless Reloading Data

Bullet	Case	Powder	Primer	Muzzle Velocity/fps
Barnes Banded Solid 570 gr.	Bertram	IMR4895/103.0 gr.	Federal GM215M	2,288 fps
Barnes Banded Solid 570 gr.	Bertram	IMR4895/105.0 gr.	Federal GM215M	2,359 fps
Barnes Banded Solid 570 gr.	Bertram	H4895/102.0 gr.	CCI-250	2,223 fps
Barnes Banded Solid 570 gr.	Bertram	H4895/104.0 gr.	CCI-250	2,311 fps
Barnes Triple Shock 570 gr.	Bertram	H4895/102.0 gr.	CCI-250	2,228 fps
Barnes Triple Shock 570 gr.	Bertram	H4895/104.0 gr.	CCI-250	2,277 fps

Note: All of these loads shot to the same point the in the author's test rifle at 100 yards. No signs of excessive pressure were noted and all rounds functioned flawlessly.
Starting point references: 1) http://www.accuratereloading.com/500jef.html; A-Square Reloading Manual.
Warning: Even though these loads were felt to be safe in the author's current rifle, ALWAYS start 5-10% below listed charge and work yourself up to a safe maximum level in your firearm. The author or this publication takes no responsibility for any result using these loads.

THE OLD AND NEWER WINCHESTER MODEL 88 RIFLE and CARBINE

BY **BERNARD H. DiGIACOBBE, M.D.**
AND **GEORGE E. DVORCHAK JR., M.D.**
PHOTOS BY **GEORGE DVORCHAK**

On examining the Winchester Model 88, it becomes obvious even to the non-collector that its concept and design were advanced for a rifle that was first introduced back in 1955. Previously, lever action rifles were restricted to low pressure cartridges and further limited to the use of blunt-nose bullets which shed velocity faster than "pointed" varieties. These bullet types were what could only be safely used since there was obviously a safety concern of "pointed bullet tips on primers" in the tubular magazine varieties of lever action carbines. In addition, most of these earlier designs were ill-suited to the use of telescopic sights. One notable exception was the Savage Model 99. While this design with its rear lock-up was already over half a century old, it could handle, or more importantly extract, such

(left) Although old and used hard by a previous owner, with rust outside and inside, our test Model 88 still had some life left in it. Co-author George Dvorchak fired two groups at 100 yards. The first shot was low, then with a few clicks up and left, three shots with Winchester 168-gr. BS ammo printed a 1.25-inch group. The second group fired with Remington 180-gr. CLPSP ammo grouped two inches with two shots touching each other. For a once rusted-up old rifle, it still shoots well!

(below) Shown is some of the increased complexity which greatly contributed to the manufacturing cost of the model 88.

The original Model 88 with its hand-cut checkering but topped with a modern scope, a Buris 3X-9X Fullfield II and Millett ScopeSite rings.

high pressure cartridges as a .250-3000 (now simply called the .250 Savage) and .300 Savage. It was also readily adaptable to the use of a scope mounted to the top of its action. This lever action thus became an increasingly popular choice with hunters and was in a position to challenge Winchester's domination of the level action rifle market at that time.

Back in the mid-'50s, shooters were also showing an increasing preference for bolt-action rifles that were not only ideally suited for high pressure cartridges with pointed bullets but were also readily adaptable to the use of scopes. This was also the era when scope sights were becoming increasingly popular since they were now better made and affordable. The management at Winchester must have anticipated that the generation who just witnessed the development of the jet plane and atomic bomb would be ready for a rifle that was every bit as powerful and streamlined as the new high performance cars that were selling in ever-increasing numbers. Certainly the public would want something more advanced than the already half-century-old lever action designs then available. To maintain their dominance of the lever action market, Winchester would fashion a compact rifle that included just about every new feature available.

While this is usually the formula for a technically advanced but impractical disaster, the Model 88 was one of those rare cases where everything fit together just right!

A TRULY UNIQUE DESIGN

Like the most advanced bolt actions of the time, the front-locking, rotating bolt of the New Model 88 featured a recessed bolt head with a plunger-type extractor. This would not only fully support the cartridge head, but also simplify manufacturing by eliminating the need to cut and index the extractor groove in the rear face of the barrel. The bolt head also offered the then-novel feature of three locking lugs – this before bolt action rifles offered this feature. This would not only reduce the amount of rotation necessary to operate the mechanism but was also significantly stronger. It offered a larger restraining surface than a conventional two-lug Mauser-type bolt action rifle and was more stable, just as a tricycle is steadier than a bicycle.

These three lugs were also cut with a slight pitch at the rear surface to provide the necessary mechanical advantage of "primary extraction" in removing a swollen case. Now, combining the rotation and recto-linear motion of a bolt action with the perpendicular motion of a lever is actually easier than it sounds. This can be readily accomplished with the use of a cam and bolt carrier mechanism and of course, the extra lever travel necessary to operate the cam and bolt carrier. But that's not how Winchester did it! They did it with a short lever travel of a mere 60 degrees. To achieve this seemingly impossible task, they relied on additional levers and of course the necessary linkage along

The Model 88 was chambered in the following four calibers, from left to right: the big .358 Winchester; next, the versatile .308 Winchester; then the good but underrated .284 Winchester; and last, what has become a first caliber for many young hunters, the .243 Winchester. This rifle, along with the Model 70, was used to introduce these then new calibers.

side the main lever to multiply the motion of the main lever. The Model 88 may thus be more accurately referred to as a "levers-action" rifle.

Integrating this train of levers and their linkage into the already tight spacial constraints of the 88 is perhaps one of the greatest feats of engineering in lever-action rifle design. Despite this complexity, this rifle is surprisingly smooth in operation. However, like other

These photos show the large opening in the stock as required by the design as well as a close-up of the grooved magazine catch conveniently located to the front of the magazine well. The large rectangular opening required by the design was also a weakness of this rifle, which was partially compensated for by the recoil block discussed in the article.

lever actions, it is best operated briskly to ensure smooth, reliable feeding. For those interested, this feat of engineering can be readily appreciated by visualizing the lever train, located along side the main lever, and exposed during the normal routine operating of the lever. Unfortunately, what the engineers achieved through ingenuity most shooters undo with unfamiliarity. In actual practice, many shooters still un-shoulder a lever action rifle and operate the lever from the hip before re-shouldering and re-sighting the rifle for a follow-up shot.

At this point, it's worth noting the presence of a pivot between the finger loop and the trigger guard portion of the lever. This does not function as a grip safety as in, say, the model 336 Marlin but as a catch to keep the lever closed. There is a small hook along the top hidden surface of the finger lever that locks into a catch within the receiver. Another novel feature of the 88

was the location of the trigger pivot within the lever itself. The trigger thus remained in close contact with the shooter's finger throughout the course of operation. With other lever actions, the trigger remains attached to the receiver and is thus prone to stabbing the shooter's trigger finger when chambering a round. After the first time you get pinched, you soon learn to reposition your finger when using those systems. It's one of those mistakes you make just once! Now, with the hammer remaining in the receiver and the trigger mounted on the lever, some sort of additional sear or interrupter mechanism was required between the hammer and trigger. To prevent accidental firing while reloading, the 88 was fitted with an interrupter mechanism that required the trigger to be fully released forward before re-firing. All of this complexity does have its cost, both in terms of manufacturer's cost and quality of trigger pull. It's one of those things that you might notice initially but quickly adapt to, particularly on a rifle designed to hunt big game and not varmints.

The quality of the trigger pull is fortunately aided somewhat by a trick used by the Winchester engineers on their Models 50 and 59 shotguns. By maximizing the distance from the trigger pivot point to the sear surface, they were able to minimize the amount of trigger travel and hence amount of "creep" transferred to the shooter's finger. In reality, this is something you are aware of but quickly adapt to during actual use and is therefore no problem, at least to us. The Model 88 we evaluated had a trigger pull measuring a crisp 5.5 pounds.

The internal hammer arrangement of the 88 does prevent the use of the conventional half-cocked position of the hammer as a safety. While some will prefer the external hammer safety arrangement, this system is also prone to accidental discharge when operated with cold or inexperienced thumbs. The 88 was fitted with a crossbolt safety conveniently located along the anterior bow of the trigger guard/lever. This was similar to the safety mechanism used on pump action and other shotguns and hence was familiar to most shooters. A less obvious safety feature was a cam machined into the rear surface of the firing pin that prevented the firing pin from projecting past the bolt face until the bolt lugs were fully engaged and the action completely locked.

The Model 88 was also the first lever action rifle offered with a one-piece stock. This, in conjunction with the interior hammer, certainly contributed to the overall streamlined and modern appearance of the rifle. It also contributed to the overall light weight of the 88, which generally weighs between 6-1/2 and 7 pounds. In addition, many agree that a one-piece stock is more conducive to accuracy and tuning for accuracy then a conventional two-piece stock. This one-

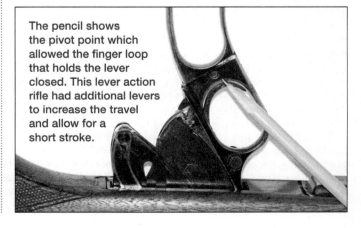

The pencil shows the pivot point which allowed the finger loop that holds the lever closed. This lever action rifle had additional levers to increase the travel and allow for a short stroke.

piece stock arrangement did, however, require a very large rectangular opening to accommodate the trigger mechanism and box magazine. This is one of the weaknesses of the 88. Because of the length of this opening and the thinness of the sidewalls of the stock, they are prone to cracking, particularly about the rear of the receiver. This probably explains Winchester's fitting of a recoil block that remains permanently affixed to the rear of the stock, similar to the method of construction of the M-1 Carbine (which was also a contemporary Winchester development).

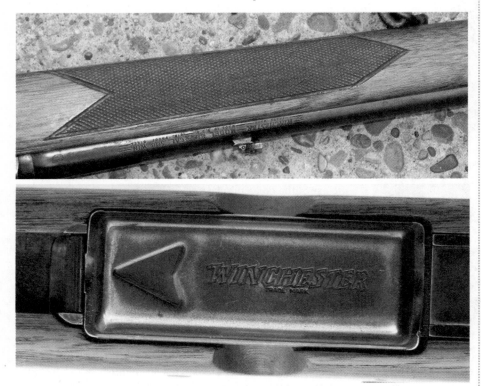

(top) The cut-checkered walnut stock was standard on the pre-'64 Model 88. Later versions had the much-maligned impressed basket weave pattern. (above) Differences in the magazines. The pre-'64 model magazine was a little shorter than later ones with both being marked with the words Winchester, Trade Mark.

To remove the barrel and action, one needs to remove the forend screw and then lift the barrel and action out of the stock while pivoting the rear of the receiver against the recoil block. On 88s manufactured before 1957, the rear of this recoil block was fitted with a three-bumped figure or "cloverleaf" configuration with a very short tang. This was later modified into an entirely rounded shape to mitigate against splitting of the stock. According to master gunsmith Ted Neal of Altoona, Pennsylvania, this is why "it is important when restocking these rifles to pay close attention to the grain pattern of the stock in this area as

well as the bedding of the recoil block."

Despite the complexity of the 88, it remained competitively priced with its competition, the new Remington 760 pump action and Winchester Model 70 bolt action rifle. To achieve this feat, the Winchester engineers relied on numerous clever cost-saving measures, most obvious being the commonality of parts between the 88 and the later-introduced Winchester 100 autoloading rifle. In an era when parts were machined with jigs and fixtures and subsequently inventoried, this commonality greatly reduced production cost. Furthermore, the majority of these parts were components which could be easily manufactured from sheet metal or with simple lathe technology. With the exception of the magazine's spring, for example, all were simple wire springs that were not only cheaper to manufacture but significantly less prone to breakage than a flat spring.

With its front locking, rotating bolt and one-piece stock, the 88 should have been as accurate as a conventional bolt action rifle and it generally was – but isn't. To understand that statement you need to remember that today's accurate out-of-the-box bolt action rifles are

the combination of many independent technologies that more or less coalesced after the end of production of the 88. As with other rifles with one-piece stocks, the 88 often responded to tinkering and tuning of the bedding. Overall, the 88 is inherently as accurate as a bolt action rifle. Perhaps the biggest thing that contributed to the accuracy of the Model 88 by 1950s and '60s standards was its adaptability to the use of telescopic sights. In addition to the side ejection, the solid top receiver was actually pre-tapped for scope mounting.

As with any mass-produced rifle, there are conflicting opinions as to the rifle's performance and reliability. Some maintain that the complexity made it susceptible to malfunctions and feeding problems. This may be, but the older 88 pictured in this article was bought by our friend Steve Hamilton second-hand and was literally rusted shut. After being cleaned up by a gunsmith, it has given decades of trouble-free service despite being treated little better by its present owner, who is a hunter who hunts in all-weather conditions no matter how severe. He feels that if he can take it, his equipment should also, since both are around the same age. While we don't recommend using such a rare rifle under these conditions, that this rifle has performed flawlessly under severe winter/sleet conditions is perhaps the best indicator of its reliability.

CALIBERS

The 88 was literally designed around the compact dimensions of the .308 Winchester cartridge and was offered only in this caliber during its first year of production, 1955. By 1956, it as well as its sister, the Model 70 bolt action rifle, introduced two new cartridges based on the .308 case, the .243 and .358 Winchester. While the .358 chambering was discontinued in 1962 due to a lack of sales, the .243 chambering remained available until termination of the 88's production in 1973.

In 1963, the Model 88 and Model 70 bolt action rifle were again used to introduced a new Winchester cartridge, the .284 Winchester. This was perhaps the first American cartridge to offer a rebated rim. Since this concept had already been introduced decades earlier in Europe, it was rather novel to American shooters. While this cartridge had a full half-inch diameter magnum case, it was fitted with a reduced rim diameter, the same as that of a .308 cartridge. This

As with any long runs in firearms, there were numerous versions of butt plates. The bottom of the butt plate on the earlier version has the word WINCHESTER, with TRADE MARK in smaller letters underneath. An example from a newer version we examined lacked any wording.

allowed for the increased performance of a short magnum case while utilizing the same bolt machining as for the .308 family of cartridges. It did, however, result in some reduction in magazine capacity: from four shots to three, plus, of course, one in the chamber (3+1). With a total of 42,340 guns in .284 Winchester being manufactured, these are the rarest calibers in the 88 line and hence the most desirable from the collector's point of view.

MODIFICATIONS

As with any gun enjoying a long production run, there were several modifications along the line to this one, with most of the engineering reworks being completed by 1957. As most gun enthusiasts know, there were the infamous cost-cutting measures implemented at Winchester in 1964. While the mechanism remained essentially unchanged in the post-'64 Model 88, the hand-checkered stock was replaced with an impressed checkering basketweave pattern combined with an oak leaf motif as seen in our photo of a newer model. These 88s are every bit as functional as the pre-64 Model 88s and might even be appreciated by those who still value their old polyester leisure suits.

The post-64 Winchester stocks are somewhat thicker through the mid-section than their pre-'64 counterparts, which might actually be a desirable feature. A more appreciated variation were the approximately 28,330 carbines manufactured the five years following 1968. In addition to their shorter 19-inch barrels (as is opposed to 22-inch for all the rifle counterparts), they were fitted with barrel bands and smooth stocks devoid of checkering. That these so infrequently come up for resale may be an indication of their rarity or, perhaps, the value their owners place on them.

EPITAPH

Production of the Model 88 ceased in 1973 after 19 years and production of 255,545 Model 88 rifles and 28,330 carbines. This should not, however, be regarded as unflattering to the 88. While the Winchester 94 and 92 lever action rifles literally sold in the millions, the 88 represents the third largest production run of any of Winchester's modern lever action rifles, excluding the 293,816 military sales of the Model 95 muskets sold to Czarist Russia. Production of the Model 88 actually exceeded that of the Winchester 95 lever action rifle and even the much-lauded Model 1886. Winchester cited increasing cost production as the reason for dropping production of the 88. While this may seem like the usual and customary cop-out, in the case of the 88 it might actually be true. All the 88's technical advancements resulted in a complicated design that not only required many small parts but also critical dimensioning and meticulous fitting of them to assure reliable functioning.

To get an idea of just how complex the design is, one need only retract the bolt and remove the magazine. Shining a powerful light into the bottom of the receiver with the bolt forward and later retracted will reveal just how complicated the design actually is. Removing the barrel and receiver assembly from the stock will reveal that the "one-piece" receiver is actually an assembly of many small, intricately-fitted components. (Incidentally, when removing the barrel assembly from the receiver, one should not fully retract the lever assembly as it will jam in this position. We know – we did this ourselves, but after some time and having had a lot of practice at problem-solving, we got it back in place. While some sources have cited the need to have a gunsmith reassemble

the action, the action can be closed by carefully massaging and pressing on the rear portion of the lever train.)

As is apparent, this complexity made the rifle very expensive to produce. This flaw was exasperated by the high cost of American labor. Worse yet, the Winchester factory had developed around the rise of the traditional lever-action repeater, which hardly required modern production technology: the competing Winchester 94 and Marlin 336 were much simpler to produce. Even the Savage 99 had significantly fewer and larger, easier-to-manufacturer parts and thus offered a much higher profit margin, which, after all, was and is the name of the game.

Perhaps the biggest reason for the cessation of production of the 88 was a matter of demand. Apparently the generation that had just witnessed the development of the jet plane and the atomic bomb was not ready for a truly advanced design but rather preferred the nostalgia of the classic lever-action rifle. These, based on the traditional Browning-derived styling with external hammers and lesser degrees of technical sophistication, continue to sell well. For example, the Winchester Models 1892, 1895, and 1886 have been reintroduced; the Model 1894 lasted until 2006; and sales of the Marlin Model 336 continue unabated. The ultra-modern Browning lever action rifle and Savage 99, regrettably discontinued, sell somewhere in between. The Model 88 has nevertheless achieved a cult status amongst enthusiasts, which keeps interest in it at a high level. As with Parker shotguns and pre-Model 70 Winchester rifles, the Model 88 is in constant demand by collectors and, hence, gun dealers.

Those who recognized the technical merits of the 88 back in the '50s and '60s and were smart enough to purchase one may have actually cheated time. Winchester produced a rifle that was not only a half-century ahead of itself in technology but was also one of the all-time great lever-action rifles.

Now the question is whether Winchester will ever reintroduce the Model 88. The answer, as we see, it is likely "no," since the Winchester product line has been greatly scaled back and its parent company Browning still offers the competing Model 81 BLR. But then, why not have two good levers available from one company?

THE COLT 1911

The First Century

BY JOHN MALLOY

Students of firearms are aware of the significance of the year 1911. In that year, a century ago, the Browning-designed Colt Model 1911 was adopted as the sidearm of the United States military forces. Perhaps no single semiautomatic handgun is better known, or has had more influence on pistol design, than the 1911. Now, 100 years later, the Colt/Browning 1911 design lives on, little changed, and it remains amazingly popular.

Since its introduction, the 1911 has proven itself as the United States military pistol in two World Wars and a number of other conflicts. Other countries produced the Colt/Browning design, made under license. Still other countries made unauthorized close copies of the pistol.

Civilian use of the big Colt pistol reinforced its value. By the midpoint of the 1900s, the 1911 was on its way to becoming one of the winningest target pistols in use. In the latter part of the century, law enforcement agencies were won over to the semiautomatic pistol, and many went with the time-tested 1911.

For almost half its history, the 1911 reigned supreme as the premier semiautomatic pistol in America. During that time, no other big-bore pistol was even produced in quantity in this country. In the latter part of the 20th century, other companies made competing semiautomatic pistols of more modern design,

New names keep coming up for companies offering new 1911s. Legacy Sports now offers their Citadel 45 in full-size and compact versions.

but the 1911 retained its popularity. With patent protection long gone, other firms began to make nearly exact copies—part-for-part-interchangeable 1911-type pistols—under their own names. New names, some now almost forgotten, entered the firearms lexicon. By the closing decade of the 1900s, other producers such as Springfield, Para-Ordnance and Kimber achieved major positions as 1911 manufacturers.

By the beginning of the 21st century, even companies that were making pistols with more modern features decided to get on the gravy train and began making their own 1911 pistols. Companies such as Smith &Wesson, SIG-Sauer and Taurus introduced 1911s.

The 1911 design, now a century old, seems to be at a peak of popularity.

HISTORICAL BACKGROUND

In the 1890s, the semiautomatic pistol was successfully introduced to the firearms world in Europe. In 1893, the Borchardt became the first commercially-successful autoloader, followed by designs of Mauser, Bergmann, Mannlicher and Luger. To these European developments was added one with an American name — Browning. John M. Browning's 32-caliber pocket pistol was introduced in 1899 by Fabrique Nationale (FN) in Belgium. Early developments were relatively small in bore size, ranging from less than 30-caliber to an upper limit of 9mm. Around the turn of

the 20th century, the concept of a larger-caliber semiautomatic pistol had been experimented with in several countries, including Great Britain. However, it took a design of American inventor John M. Browning to bring a truly successful big-bore pistol into being.

Browning, along with his handgun work for FN, had provided designs to Colt. Colt saw promise in military sales and introduced a Browning-designed 38-caliber automatic in 1900. This caliber appeared to be a favorable one, as the US military was by then using 38-caliber revolvers.

However, the need for a larger-caliber handgun became evident during the Spanish-American war of 1898 and the subsequent Philippine Insurrection. When the United States acquired the Philippine Islands from Spain as a result of the war, it was an unpleasant surprise to find that many Filipinos did not like American control any more than they had enjoyed Spanish rule.

The resulting insurrection was officially over in 1901, but deadly conflict, especially in the southern islands, continued well into the next decade. These southern islands were inhabited by fierce Moro tribes that had been converted to a form of Islam. The service sidearm of the time, the double-action .38 Long Colt revolver (marginal even in "civilized" warfare), proved to be inadequate to stop a charging Moro. Old Single Action Army 45-caliber revolvers were withdrawn from storage, had the barrels shortened to 5-1/2 inches, and were sent back into service. A quantity of 1878 double-action Colts, modified with a strange long trigger and enlarged guard, were also issued.

The stopping power of the old big-bore .45s proved to be far superior. However, they were stopgap measures. An effective standard modern handgun was needed.

What was needed? The famous Thompson-LaGarde tests, which involved shooting live stockyard cattle and human cadavers, provided one part of the answer: the new handgun would be a 45-caliber. Thus, the search for a new sidearm began in the early 1900s. Although semiautomatic pistols were coming into use, the cavalry still firmly favored the dependable revolver.

The stage was set that any "automatic" considered must have reliability equal to that of the revolver and be a .45. A series of tests, to begin in 1906, was contemplated by the Army.

PRIOR TO THE TEST TRIALS

Two 45-caliber cartridges would be used: a rimmed one for revolver use, and a rimless one for the automatic pistols.

The rimless version was essentially similar to a commercial round produced by Winchester for Colt since the spring of 1905. The Winchester ammunition was made for Colt's new 45-caliber autoloading pistol, which had been introduced in the fall of 1905.

The 1905 Colt .45, developed by John M. Browning, was a logical development of the locked-breech 38-caliber Colt/Browning pistol. The new .45 had a five-inch barrel, which gave it an overall length of about eight inches. It weighed about 33 ounces. Capacity of the magazine was seven rounds. The cartridge, in its original loading, pushed a 200-grain bullet at about 900 feet per second. It was a potent load for a semiautomatic pistol of the time.

To today's shooters, the 1905 pistol might seem strange. It had no grip safety and no thumb safety. The shooter just cocked the hammer when he was ready to shoot. The hammer itself was of a rounded burr shape. The recessed magazine release was at the bottom of the grip frame. The only visible control was the slide stop on the left. It worked well, and a contemporary writer called it "a good fighting pistol." It was the only .45 automatic in commercial production, a fact that gave it a decided advantage when the tests began.

It is worth commenting on the slide of the early Colt automatics. We are so used to semiautomatic pistols having slides that it is difficult to realize now what an innovation Browning had introduced. The earliest high-power auto pistols — the Borchardt, the Bergmann, the Mauser, the Mannlicher and the Luger — had exposed barrels with the locking mechanism completely behind the barrel. Browning designed the slide as a totally new concept, a moving breechblock that extended forward over the barrel. Not only did this make a much more compact pistol for any barrel length, but the slide and barrel could have mating lugs to form the short-recoil locking mechanism.

The Colt .38 automatics had been linked to the frame at both the front and rear of the barrel. Lugs on the barrel mated with recesses in the slide. Thus, the barrel and slide were locked together during firing. Then, as the barrel moved down after firing, the slide was free to move rearward, ejecting the empty case and feeding in a new cartridge on its return cycle. This same system was used with the 45-caliber Model 1905.

THE 1907-1911 TEST TRIALS

The initial tests were scheduled for 1906, then rescheduled for early 1907.

When the board convened on January 15, 1907, eight applicants had submitted nine designs. Three were revolvers, and six were automatic pistols. The revolvers, Colt, Smith & Wesson and Webley-Fosbery, were soon dropped from consideration.

The autoloaders, at that early stage of history, represented a variety of concepts in competition for the first time. Having the 1905 already in production made Colt the front-runner. However, besides the Colt, the Army also tested pistols from Bergmann, Knoble, White-Merrill, Luger, and Savage. Three of

In the early post-WWII decades, the only 45-caliber semi-automatic pistols available to give the Colt Government Model any competition were the Spanish Llama (upper) and Star (lower) pistols. Neither design was a part-for-part copy of the 1911, but the guns were look-alikes of comparable size and weight.

The 1905 Colt was the first successful 45-caliber semiautomatic pistol. Having a gun already in production gave the Colt company a head start when the U. S. military tests began in 1907.

In 1971, Colt brought out the Combat Commander, the same size as the original lightweight Commander, but with a steel frame.

Revolvers had been made of stainless steel for some years, but in 1977, AMT brought out the first 1911-style 45 automatic made of stainless steel. The AMT Hardballer was essentially a stainless copy of the Colt Gold Cup National Match.

the entries — the Bergmann, Knoble and White-Merrill pistols — were rejected early in the tests as being unsuitable. The Colt was considered the best and the Savage worthy of additional testing. The Board authorized the purchase of 200 each of the Colt and Savage pistols for field tests. Colt, of course, readily accepted, but the fledgling Savage company, then just 12 years old, was unwilling to tool up for such a relatively small production run, so the contract was offered to the third-place Luger. The German DWM company (*Deutsche Waffen- und Munitionsfabriken*), the maker of the Luger/Parabellum pistols, accepted the contract but then backed out. Apparently, the larger Luger .45 could not have been made on existing production machinery, and the German firm may have also been reluctant to redesign production tooling for a small contract. Also, DWM may have wanted to put more resources into the final development of its 9mm pistol. This pistol was indeed shortly thereafter adopted by the German Army as the Pistole '08 (P08).

The failure of DWM to supply 45-caliber Lugers for the field tests gave Savage a chance to reconsider. A semiautomatic pistol would give the company a chance to expand its product line, which then consisted only of the hammerless lever-action rifle designed by Arthur Savage. Savage accepted the contract.

The competition of the Savage was a good thing. During the field tests, which ran from 1907 into 1911, the Savage was good enough to show that the original 1905 Colt design could use substantial

improvement. Browning, 52 years old at the beginning of the tests, worked with Colt, making changes to the design as the continuing testing indicated they were needed. The result of the changes was an increasingly superior Colt pistol.

The final test was a 6000-round endurance test, held during March 1911. Pistols would cool after every 100 shots, and would be inspected, cleaned and oiled every 1000 shots. Both pistols fired over 1000 rounds without problems, but as the shooting continued, the Savage developed problems with malfunctions, and parts defects appeared. The refined Colt fired shot after shot, 100 after 100, 1000 after 1000, until the full 6000 rounds were completed without a stoppage or parts problem.

The tests were a milestone in the development of the semiautomatic pistol. The end result of four years of extensive testing was the most reliable large-caliber pistol in the world. The final report on the Colt stressed "its marked superiority…to any other known pistol."

ADOPTION OF THE 1911

The Colt design was adopted, on March 29, 1911, by the US Army as the Model 1911 pistol. Colt would be the supplier. The Navy and Marine Corps also adopted the 1911 within a short time.

As adopted, the 1911 pistol had a 5-inch barrel and weighed about 38 ounces. The unlocking was still accomplished by downward movement of the barrel, but the barrel had only one

link at the rear, with the muzzle supported by a barrel bushing. It had both thumb and grip safeties. A pushbutton magazine release had been added. For better pointing characteristics, the grip-to-bore angle had been changed from a straight 84 degrees to a slantier 74 degrees.

Colt immediately discontinued the 1905, and as its replacement, put the Model 1911 into commercial production also. With what was then probably the most thoroughly tested pistol in the world, Colt not only offered the 1911 as a commercial model, but additionally looked for other markets beyond the United States.

FOREIGN VARIATIONS

Norway was the second country to adopt the 45-caliber Colt 1911. Because guns based on Browning's patents could not be handled in Europe by Colt FN in Belgium made the arrangements. In 1912, the Norwegians standardized the Colt design to their liking and adopted it. The modifications apparently consisted primarily of changing the checkering pattern on the hammer and applying Norwegian markings. Only about 500 Model 1912 pistols were made. Minor changes were suggested in 1914, and in 1919, after World War I had ended (Norway was neutral during World War I), these were incorporated into the Model 1914 Norwegian pistol. The most noticeable change involved a redesigned slide stop, with the thumbpiece lower and slightly rearward. Having a small army, Norway produced about 22,000 1914 pistols, felt this to be adequate, and stopped production.

While Norway sat out World War I as a neutral nation, Great Britain had been one of the principal participants. The British were poorly prepared for war, and had shortages of most small arms. In 1912, the British had adopted a large-bore autoloading pistol, the Mark I Webley self-loader. The pistol was chambered for the .455 Webley Self Loading cartridge (also called .455 Eley). Independently designed, the round was similar in dimensions and power to the .45 ACP cartridge.

The precisely-fitted Webley autoloader proved unreliable in conditions of sand or grit. The 1912 Webleys were restricted to sea duty, and the British looked for another type of .455 pistol. The one they acquired was the 1911 Colt. The first of the 455-caliber Colts was reportedly shipped in mid-1915. It is believed that about 13,500 were shipped to Great Britain for military use.

The next country to adopt the Colt 1911 was Argentina, in 1916. The Colt was adopted as the Pistola Automatica Sistema Colt, Calibre 11,25mm Modelo 1916. Essentially, the Argentine 1916 was identical to the commercially-made US Colt except for markings.

UNITED STATES USE THROUGH WWI

As they became available to the American military, 1911 pistols were sent to the Philippines, where fighting with native tribes continued. The new .45s were also used in the1916 Punitive Expedition, led by General John J. Pershing, that went into Mexico after Pancho Villa.

Colt made all the early 1911 pistols. However, the U. S. Government, previously content to manufacture only long guns (and to purchase handguns from commercial manufacturers), reconsidered. The Ordnance Department wanted an arrangement by which it could manufacture the 1911 at Springfield Armory if it so desired. After some negotiation, Colt conferred the right to manufacture the pistol to the government for a royalty of $2.00 each. After a contract for 50,000 Colt-made pistols, the government could manufacture pistols at the rate of one pistol for every two ordered from Colt.

The Springfield pistols were essentially identical to the Colt-made pistols except for markings. Visually, they could be recognized by the sharper (less-gradual) termination of the scallop at the front of the slide.

World War I had broken out in Europe in 1914. In hindsight, it was only a matter of time until the United States was drawn into the war. America entered on the side of the Allies on April 6, 1917. At that time, apparently without any actual analysis, Ordnance believed that Colt "…would be able to take care of the entire pistol program…." However, the new conditions of trench warfare caused military planners to increase the distribution of sidearms. At first, 10% were to be armed with the 1911, then, up to 60%. Eventually, up to 72% of front-line troops were authorized to carry pistols as well as rifles.

The United States was not prepared to achieve this kind of pistol production. Because of the need for more rifles, Springfield Armory stopped pistol production during 1916 and 1917. (It did resume Model 1911 production in 1918, after the use of the 1917 Enfield had eased the need for 1903 Springfield rifles.)

In 1917, Colt delivered pistols at a monthly rate of about 9000 guns. In 1918, production increased from about 11,000 to a monthly peak of over 45,000 by the end of the war. This was not enough.

Even by the winter of 1917, it had become obvious that Colt production alone could not supply enough pistols. A new source was found in Remington-UMC. Remington had been manufacturing 3-line Mosin-Nagant rifles for Russia, but the contract ended when Russia withdrew from the war in 1917. By mid-1918, with full cooperation from Colt, Remington-UMC began production of the 1911. By September, completed pistols were being shipped. By the end of 1918, Remington-UMC was up to 4500 pistols a month. The total made was 21,676. Except for markings, they were the same as the Colt pistols.

Even with the Remington pistols (and with .45 ACP-caliber 1917 Colt and S&W revolvers), there were still just not enough handguns. Orders were placed with a number of other firms. However, the end of the war came in November 1918 before any additional production was established. One instance of actual pistols being made took place in Canada. The North American Arms Co. (in the Ross rifle plant) made some finished 1911 pistols, although probably fewer than 100 were made.

The 1911 pistol proved itself in combat during World War I. Many instances of excellent performance of the 45 were reported. The exploits of Corporal Alvin York are probably the most memorable use of both rifle and pistol. York almost single-handedly captured 132 German soldiers. His actions stopped a German counterattack in France's Argonne Forest. (And, yes, I know — the Gary Cooper movie depicted York as using a captured German Luger. However, that was only because the moviemakers could not get the 1911 to work with blanks! York used a 1911.)

BETWEEN THE WARS

After any war, military development generally slows down. Pistol development during the decades of the Roaring Twenties and the Great Depression was relatively minor.

Use in the World War had pointed out a few minor complaints concerning the 1911. Soldiers with small hands had experienced some trouble gripping the pistol and controlling the trigger properly. The hammer spur sometimes pinched the fleshy web of a shooter's hand against the tang of the grip safety. The fine sights were difficult to see under conditions of low light. It tended to point low during instinct shooting.

Accordingly, subtle changes were made to the pistol to answer these

Taurus, a 1911 manufacturer since 2005, makes a variety of 1911 pistols, including this rail-equipped variant.

Kimber, one of the major forces in the 1911 world, recently introduced the SIS variant, in several different sizes.

situations. The trigger was shortened, and the frame was recessed on the sides near the trigger to provide better access. The tang of the grip safety was lengthened. The sights, although still small by today's standards, were made with a larger square notch at the rear and a wider square front sight. The flat mainspring housing was replaced by an arched housing. Subtle changes were also made to the rifling.

These changes were approved in 1923, and by 1925, Colt had put them into production. In June 1926, the nomenclature was changed to Model 1911A1.

With the adoption of the 1911A1, much of the 1911 tooling at Springfield became obsolete. No more 45-caliber pistols were made at Springfield. Only that tooling able to produce spare parts common to 1911 and 1911A1 pistols was retained.

Colt, of course, changed its commercial offering as soon as the military specifications were implemented. The military pistols were marked Model 1911A1, but the commercial pistols were, for the first time, marked "Government Model."

Mexico had adopted the 1911 after WWI and had purchased pistols directly from Colt. After about 1926, pistols with the 1911A1 modifications were supplied.

Argentina, as noted previously, had adopted the 1911 as their Modelo 1916. After 1927, Colt supplied 1911A1 pistols. Markings on the Argentine Colts remained the same, except that the modified pistol became known as the Modelo 1927. In the early 1930s, Colt agreed to license manufacture by the Argentine government. The Argentine-made Colts were made at Fabrica Militar de Armas Portatiles (FMAP) in Rosario, Argentina. Unlicensed modified pistols, the Ballester-Rigaud and Ballester-Molina, were also made in Argentina.

During the 1920s, the automobile had become common, and had become widely used by criminals. Law Enforcement found that bullets from the traditional .38 Special revolver, and even the big .45 automatic, would not reliably penetrate car bodies. In 1929, Colt introduced its Super 38 pistol. The Super 38 was a Government Model modified to use a high-powered version of the old .38 ACP cartridge introduced in 1900. With a velocity of almost 1300 feet per second (fps), the new Super 38's 130-grain jacketed bullet earned a good reputation for penetration.

A 22-caliber pistol based on the 1911 design would be a good training and

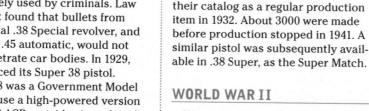

World War II Model 1911A1 pistols, like this Ithaca-made specimen, were standardized with parkerized finish, plastic grips and flat hammers. (This pistol, bought through the DCM, was the author's first 45 automatic.) Ithaca, now located in Upper Sandusky, Ohio, is once again making 1911s.

target pistol. In 1931, Colt introduced a .22 Long Rifle blowback pistol, the Ace. Later, about 1937, Colt incorporated the floating chamber designed by David Marshall Williams ("Carbine Williams"), and the new pistol became the Service Model Ace. The Ace was discontinued in 1941, but the Service Model Ace was used for training during World War II.

Target shooting with handguns, previously a sport for single-shot pistols and revolvers, saw the use of semiautomatic pistols becoming more common. At the 1930 National Matches, Colt introduced its National Match 45-caliber pistol. Based on the Government Model, it had a match-grade barrel, honed action, and could be supplied with fixed sights or with Stevens adjustable sights. Barrels and slides were fitted and numbered to each other. The National Match pistol was well-received, and Colt put it into their catalog as a regular production item in 1932. About 3000 were made before production stopped in 1941. A similar pistol was subsequently available in .38 Super, as the Super Match.

WORLD WAR II

World War II began officially on September 1, 1939, with the German invasion of Poland. The success of the German blitzkrieg surprised even the Nazis. The Germans needed additional arms to supply their occupation troops, and began a program of producing

and utilizing the suitable firearms of captured countries

Norway had been neutral during WWI, and reaffirmed neutrality during WWII. However, Nazi Germany viewed Norway as a base of operations against the Allied blockade, and as a possible staging area for an attack on Great Britain. German forces attacked Norway on April 9, 1940, and the country fell within two months. When production of the 1914 Norwegian Colt resumed, it was under German, not Norwegian, control. Apparently issued only in Norway to occupation troops or subservient Norwegian troops, about 10,000 additional Norwegian 45s were produced before the German surrender in May of 1945.

When the United States was forced into World War II by the Japanese attack on Pearl Harbor on December 7, 1941, we were again poorly prepared for war. However, many of the production problems experienced during WWI were avoided. It had been realized that manufacturers other than those making firearms could be utilized for pistol production. About two million 1911A1 pistols were made during the war. Colt, involved with other war production, was not the largest producer of the WWII .45. That honor went to Remington-Rand, the typewriter and business-machine manufacturer.

About 1,032,000 pistols were made by Remington-Rand. This amounted to almost 55% of production. In the year of 1944 alone, the company produced over one-half million pistols. Historian Donald Bady called this "the largest annual production by a single manufacturer in the history of firearms."

Colt produced about 480,000 pistols, over 22% of the total production. Ithaca Gun Company, a shotgun maker, manufactured about 369,000, amounting to almost 20%. Union Switch & Signal Co. made 55,000 guns. The Singer (sewing machine) Manufacturing Co. was given an "educational order" of 500 pistols.

Production was aided by the early determination of a "standard" pistol to be made by all companies. Essentially all WWII 1911A1 pistols were "Parkerized" (a rust-resistant phosphate finish), had brown plastic grip panels, and had flat-sided hammers. The trigger/stirrup unit was made from stamped components, and grooving replaced checkering on some parts. Colt worked with the other manufacturers, and this cooperation assisted production.

In addition to production of new 45s, a number of old Model 1911 pistols that had been placed in storage were refurbished for WWII use. They were parkerized, and if parts were needed, 1911A1 parts were installed. Work was done at Augusta Arsenal, and such pistols were stamped with the letters "AA."

Again, the Colt/Browning 45 pistol proved itself as a reliable, powerful sidearm. It stood apart from other handguns used during the Second World War.

POST-WAR, THROUGH THE 1950S

The basic 1911 handgun had gone through its second world war with an exemplary record. Essentially every American serviceman held the pistol in high regard. This feeling was well-represented in the 1959 novel, *The Pistol*, by James Jones. The novel follows the movement of a 45-caliber pistol among U. S. servicemen after Pearl Harbor, in which every man who has any contact with the pistol wants it for his own personal protection.

Still, after 1946, for the first time in almost four decades, U. S. military planners considered the possibility of a lighter pistol, and also began to consider a change to the 9mm Parabellum (9mm Luger) ammunition used by both wartime adversaries and allies.

Colt investigated the possibilities of a lighter Government Model, and developed an association with ALCOA Aluminum. A number of frames were made of aluminum alloy, and test pistols were made. To further reduce weight, the barrel length was shortened to 4-1/4 inches, and the slide shortened accordingly. A rounded "burr" hammer was used, which also allowed use of a shorter-tang grip safety. The test pistols were made in the by-then traditional .45 ACP and .38 Super, and — with an eye to possible military tests — also in 9mm Luger chambering.

Eventually the military reconsidered, realizing that plenty of 45-caliber 1911A1 pistols were on hand. In June 1950, the United States became involved in a "police action" in Korea (it was not called the Korean War until later). The 45-caliber pistols, along with the rest of America's WWII armament, went back into service. Consideration of a 9mm pistol was dropped, at least for the time being.

Colt had already made a decision to market the shorter, lighter version of the Government Model. In early 1950, it was introduced as the Commander Model. Calibers were .45, .38 Super and 9mm. The Colt Commander was a landmark pistol. At 26-1/2 ounces, it was our first big-bore aluminum frame pistol. Often overlooked is the fact that the Commander was the first pistol ever commercially produced in America in the 9mm chambering.

By the end of the 1950s, the position of the 1911 had evolved. Now, almost half a century old, from being a splendid military pistol, it was becoming everyman's pistol.

After the end of WWII, all shooting sports increased in popularity. A joke of the time was that returning servicemen were only interested in two things — and the second one was shooting.

Bullseye pistol shooting benefited from this renewed interest and became very popular. The National Match Course had sections for 22-caliber, Centerfire and 45-caliber pistols. Everyone wanted a .45.

The National Matches, closed during WWII and Korea, resumed in 1953. Military "National Match" pistols were made from .45s on hand beginning in 1955. Most were made at Springfield Armory (thus getting the facility back into providing pistols, if not actually manufacturing them), and were stamped NM. Originally fitted with high fixed sights, they were made with adjustable sights in 1961. Colt furnished parts for such work.

However, the maker of the first, the original pre-war National Match pistol, could hardly have been satisfied without a match pistol of its own. Colt, in 1957, brought out an improved version of its early National Match 45, called the Gold Cup National Match. It was a highly-developed pistol for competition shooting. It became the standard by which .45 target pistols were judged.

Surprisingly, it was not the only newly-made target-oriented .45 autoloader available. The Spanish Llama pistols (copies of the 1911, but not part-for-part copies), were imported by A. F. Stoeger since 1951. In 1957, the Llama line also introduced a target version in .45 caliber. Before that time, a number of gunsmith shops had begun specializing in "accurizing" .45s for target competition.

As the 1950s went on, then began what has been called "the Golden Age of Surplus." As countries around the world updated their military equipment, they cleaned out their armories. Military equipment, including firearms, was sold on the world market. A large portion of the guns came to the country with the greatest degree of personal freedom — the United States. Some of the pistols that came in as surplus were 1916 and 1927 Argentine .45s. Many were "accurized" and used for target shooting. Norwegian 1914 .45s also made their appearance. Also coming in were a smaller number of the British 455-caliber Colt 1911s. To make the .455s more salable, they were advertised, "Will shoot .45 ACP." (Yes, they would, but not very accurately.)

Traditional Bullseye shooting was not the only pistol sport to gain popularity. A new handgun sport was developing in California. Popularized by the writing of Col. Jeff Cooper, the two-handed action-style pistol shooting was called "practical" shooting. Shooters found it to be fun as well as practical, and the new sport grew. These informal matches grew into the alphabet soup of IPSC, USPSA, PPC and NRA Action shooting of today. Based on the concepts of Accuracy, Power and Speed, the pistol that fit Cooper's ideas best? The 45-caliber Government Model.

THE 1960S

The 1960s started as a continuation of the 1950s, but by the end of that decade, things had changed dramatically in the

Military National Match pistols used at Camp Perry had the trigger weighed and a tape placed on the trigger guard to show it met specifications. This gun was fired at Camp Perry in 1967 by the author, and still has the 1967 tape on the trigger guard.

United States firearms scene.

In the early years of the '60s, the popularity of the 1911 got a boost when the Ordnance Department, through the Director of Civilian Marksmanship (DCM) made surplus 1911 and 1911A1 pistols available to members of the National Rifle Association (NRA). The August 1960 issue of *American Rifleman* gave the details. Price was $17, including packing and shipping. Pistols were classed "unserviceable," which meant they may have had minor defects, but were safe to fire. (The Ithaca 1911A1 I got had a cracked slide stop, which cost me a dollar to replace.) The influx of inexpensive .45s was a shot in the arm to the pistol-shooting sports.

Spare parts for the 1911-type pistols were also available. Enterprising small manufacturers made new frames, and gunsmiths assembled new 1911s from the parts.

Those military-surplus 45-caliber pistols sold during the 1960s were the last pistols sold by the U. S. government to civilians. Soon, national tragedy, politics, and the growth of the anti-gun movement would adversely affect the firearms scene.

For those who wanted to buy a .45 and were willing to wade through the onerous restrictions of the Gun Control Act of 1968, Colt had something new. The loose fit of the average military

1911 had given rise to the idea that the 45 was "not accurate." Colt investigated possibilities, and determined that a new barrel bushing, a collet-type with spring-steel "fingers" to position the barrel, would increase accuracy. Without publicity, Colt began fitting pistols with this experimental new system in 1969. About 750 were reportedly made. They can be identified by the letters, "BB," stamped near the correct serial numbers.

THE 1970S

The new "accurizer" barrel bushing system worked well, and in 1970, Colt brought it out as a standard item for its 1911 line. New nomenclature then became Colt's Mk. IV / Series '70. The collet-type bushings were used in the Government Model and Gold Cup National Match pistols. The Commander continued to use its original shortened solid bushing.

The next year, 1971, a Combat Commander was added to the Colt line. The same size as the original lightweight Commander, the pistol had a steel frame and weighed 33 ounces. 1971, the Centennial of the National Rifle Association, also saw a special Centennial Gold Cup made to commemorate the anniversary.

In 1973, things took a bad turn for Colt. A strike lasting from April through August took place. With Colt production

curtailed for almost half a year, the "lookalike" Llama and Star pistols from Spain (modified copies of the 1911) got more attention. The Spanish pistols listed at ten to twenty dollars less than a Colt Government Model, which sold for $135.

The Colt Commander had provided a more compact 45-caliber handgun, but there was interest in a .45 in an even smaller package.

In 1975, the Spanish firm producing the big Star pistols brought out the Star PD. The new small Star was a shortened and lightened .45 with an aluminum frame. With its 4-inch barrel and weight of 25 ounces, the Star was, for a short time, the smallest .45 available.

In 1976, the year of America's Bicentennial, the 1911 was miniaturized in America by the new firm calling itself Detonics. Originally using Colt parts modified by them, and then manufacturing their own, Detonics brought out a compact steel .45, weighing 31 ounces. It was of innovative design, and had a 3-1/2-inch barrel. The Detonics pistol introduced the cone-barrel positioning system, orienting the short barrel in the slide without a bushing.

Until the 1970s, Colt had been the sole source of newly-made traditional U. S. 1911-style pistols, but during that decade, the market for similar .45s made by other firms grew.

About 1977, the AMT (Arcadia Machine & Tool) Hardballer was introduced. The pistol was essentially of Gold Cup configuaration, a target-grade pistol with adjustable sights. However, the AMT Hardballer was manufactured of stainless steel. It was apparently the first stainless-steel 1911 ever offered. The AMT line grew, with fixed sight pistols and Commander-size pistols soon offered. Within a short time, they were joined by the striking Long Slide Hardballer, a similar adjustable-sighted pistol, but with a 7-inch barrel and correspondingly longer slide.

As the decade went on, Practical shooting (sometimes called "West Coast Shooting") spread across the country. Practical shooting was joined by other pistol sports, such as Bowling Pin shooting. Reliable quick-shooting pistols using powerful cartridges were in demand.

New companies sprang up across the country. In the closing years of the 1970s, 1911s were made, often in now-trendy stainless steel, by small companies such as Crown City (New York) and Vega (California).

In 1978, M-S Safari Arms began making striking 1911s with some of their own features. Most noticeable was a projection on the front strap of the grip to position the finger below the trigger guard. (M-S Safari was acquired, in 1987, by Olympic Arms, which made 1911s under the Safari and Schuetzen names, and still makes Olympic 1911-style pistols.)

Custom pistolmakers began to thrive. Wilson Combat had opened by 1978 and continues in business.

THE 1980S

The growth of new interest in the 1911 that had begun in the '70s had a tremendous increase in the 1980s. In fact, there was a growth of interest in handguns of all types. A category called the "wondernines" gained popularity. They were full-size double-action 9mm pistols with magazine capacities up to 19 rounds,

In 1983, Colt added a firing-pin safety to the 1911 design. This prevented the firing pin from moving until the trigger was pressed. The new variant became the Mark IV / Series '80. In 1985, Colt also added stainless-steel versions of the Series '80 pistols.

During the 1980s, it became very clear that Colt was no longer the only maker of 1911 pistols. By 1981, the ODI (Omega Defensive Industries) Viking pistol, a 1911 fitted with the Seecamp double-action trigger system, was introduced. That same year, Auto-Ordnance, owned then by Numrich Arms, brought out the GI-style Thompson 1911A1 pistol. A number of guns from different companies appeared, based on modified 1911 designs. Representatives of this category were the Coonan, Arminex and Grizzly pistols.

Randall, a company first involved in making replacement stainless magazines for 1911s, in 1983 introduced a line of stainless-steel 1911 pistols. Early stainless autoloaders had developed problems with galling, developed as the stainless slide rubbed across the stainless frame. Randall believed they had solved those problems, and advertised the Randall as "the only stainless steel fit for duty." The most striking Randalls were the left-hand versions, which were completely left-handed—even the rifling turned the opposite way! About 7% of Randall's pistols were left-handed. The Randall Curtis E. LeMay pistol, honoring Air Force General LeMay, was a

4-1/4-inch barrel and a 6-shot finger-rest magazine. After making about 10,000 guns, Randall became overextended and the company failed in 1985.

Faring better was Springfield Armory, a new commercial company that had acquired the name of the former government facility. Springfield began in 1985 with pistols that were essentially recreations of the WWII 1911A1. It continues as one of the major 1911 manufacturers. A few other 1911 pistols, such as the MP Express from Meister Products, were made for a short time and then went out of production. Interarms, the large importer, built over a thousand 45-caliber 1911 pistols on new frames using surplus GI parts. With a sly reference to Colt's Gold Cup, the new pistols were marked and sold as the Interarms Silver Cup.

In 1985, a stir was created by the U. S. military selection of a 9mm service pistol. A version of the Beretta 92, with a 16-round magazine, was chosen. Even in the period of the wondernines, some old-timers were less than enthusiastic about the choice of cartridge. Thinking of the performance of the .45 during WWII, one remarked, "Now we have the pistol cartridge used by the countries defeated during the war."

1986 arrived, Colt's 150th anniversary. However, the sesquicentennial was not a good period for the company. In 1986, a bitter strike against Colt began and dragged on for four years. The

company economized during its time of limited production. Although it was not officially dropped until 1988, no mention of the collet-type "accurizer" bushing apparently was made after 1986.

Although 1986 meant hard times for Colt, other things happened.

The futility of gun-control laws was becoming obvious. In 1986, the Firearms Owners Protection Act was passed. One of the provisions was to allow importation of surplus firearms again, thus reversing one of GCA '68's many restrictions.

In 1986, the Falcon Portsider was introduced, a left-handed pistol made to enter the niche abandoned when Randall went out of business. Falcon made only a small number of pistols, and was gone by 1990.

About 1988, Para-Ordnance, a Canadian company making "non-gun" dye-marking guns, introduced a sideline of large-capacity frames and magazines for the 1911. Standard 1911 parts could be fitted to the frames to create the first large-capacity 1911-type 45s. Soon, in 1990, the company began making complete pistols. Para-Ordnance, today simply called Para, grew to become a major supplier of 1911 pistols.

Other companies made 1911s before the decade ended. Federal Ordnance made the Ranger, a basic GI-style 1911A1. Michigan Armament (distributed from, of all places, California) made somewhat

The Randall 45 was introduced in 1983 as "the only stainless steel fit for duty." Gaining great publicity for its left-hand pistols, most of Randall production consisted of traditional right-hand 1911s. The company had financial problems and went out of business in 1985.

fancier variants. Custom maker Ed Brown started business in 1988.

In spite of its labor problems, Colt was still active during this time. The 45-caliber Officers ACP was introduced in 1985. The new Colt compact pistol had a 3-1/2-inch barrel, weighed 34 ounces, and had a 6-shot magazine in a shortened frame. The 10mm Delta Elite variant of the full-size Government Model came out in 1987. By the end of the decade, the double-action stainless-steel Colt Double Eagle had become a production item, at least for a few years.

In 1988, Florida enacted a "shall issue" license-to-carry law that became a model for similar laws in other states. The growth of legal concealed carry across the country increased the demand for handguns of various types. The 1911 became even more popular among ordinary citizens for personal protection.

THE 1990S

If interest in the 1911 had increased in the 1980s, it can be said to have exploded in the 1990s.

At the beginning of the decade, Colt carried out a plan to get back into the basic 1911 market. Its enhanced offerings had become fancier, and the market for basic "wartime" pistols had grown. By 1991, the Colt 1991 A1 was introduced, actually continuing the serial number range of the company's 1911 A1 pistols of World War II. With a matte finish and simple features, the new Colt was competitive in its niche. Commander (4-1/2-inch) and Compact (3-1/2-inch) variants were offered in 1993.

By 1998, Colt introduced an even smaller pistol with a 3-inch barrel, the Defender. The 23-ounce .45 used a cone-barrel system to orient the barrel in the slide.

Early in the decade, in 1991, a new name, Norinco, was added to the list of 1911 companies. The Chinese entity made a surprisingly good copy of a 1911. The Norinco got good reviews until president William J. Clinton prohibited importation of firearms from China in 1995.

The popularity of the 1911 design grew. Other names were added to the list of companies offering 1911 pistols: McMillan (1992), STI (1993), Rocky Mountain Arms (1993 – trying a third time for the left-hand market), and Mitchell (1994). Because Para-Ordnance high-capacity pistols were gaining popularity, Mitchell's new 45s were offered in double-column configuration — 13+1 — as well as the traditional single-column style. Springfield and Llama also offered large-capacity 13+1 pistols that same year.

1994 was a poor time to offer large-capacity pistols. In that year, the so-called "Assault Weapons Ban" was passed into law.

Among other absurd restrictions, the ban limited magazine capacity of all detachable magazines to 10 rounds or less. High-capacity staggered-column .45 magazines could no longer be made. Obviously, no other pistols of other calibers could have magazines of greater than 10 rounds, either. The high-capacity "wondernine" magazines, holding up to 19 rounds, were no longer legal to make. Compared to a 10-round 9mm, a traditional 1911 .45 holding seven or eight rounds began to look a much better choice. 45-caliber pistols became more popular. As firearms authority J. B. Wood wryly noted, "If you can't make as many holes, make bigger ones." Interest in the .45, and in particular, the 1911, boomed.

From the midpoint of the 1990s, the demand for, and production of, 1911 pistols grew. In 1995, Ithaca brought out a 50th Anniversary edition of its WWII .45. Even more new names appeared: Brolin (1995), Kimber (1995), BUL and GAL (both imported from Israel in 1996), Armscor (imported from the Philippines by KBI in 1996), Griffon (1997, South Africa), Entreprise Arms (1997), Rock River's first 1911 (1998), Valtro (1998, from Italy), and Shooters Arms Manufacturers, "S.A.M" (1999, from the Philippines). The Charles Daly name, formerly associated with shotguns, was introduced on a pistol for the first time in 1998, when KBI used the name on its 45-caliber 1911.

In 1999, Auto-Ordnance was acquired by Kahr Arms. Kahr rejuvenated the Auto-Ordnance/Thompson 1911 pistol line. Galena industries acquired the right to produce the AMT 1911 line and some other AMT pistols (but sadly went out of production by 2002).

For decades, gunsmiths had been making custom-built pistols based on the 1911. Such guns started as one-of-a-kind handguns. With time, it was realized that many customers wanted similar features. A relatively small number of different customized pistols would satisfy the majority of customers.

Smith & Wesson entered the 1911 field in 2003 and markets an extensive line, including variants of the full-size SW1911.

By the end of the 1990s, this making of "production custom" 1911s was a booming business. Companies such as (alphabetically) Briley, Ed Brown, Les Baer, Nowlin, STI, Strayer-Voigt, Wilson and others had offered such special 1911s.

THE NEW CENTURY

With the flurry of interest in the 1911 that had exploded in the closing decades at the end of the 20th century, the production of 1911-style pistols had been spread among a large and growing number of different companies Colt was no longer the primary producer. Three relatively new companies — Kimber, Springfield and Para-Ordnance — vied for that position. Kimber advertised their company as "first in the number of 1911 pistols made and sold." Not to be outdone, Springfield claimed "the greatest selection of 1911 pistols." Para-Ordnance introduced features that set its offerings apart.

As the new century began, Colt again fell on hard times. In the year 2000, the company discontinued most of its handgun line. Only the Single Action Army and the 1911 were left. The 1911 was offered in 45 caliber only. Within a few years, however, Colt's fortunes improved.

Not everyone had liked the Series '80 firing pin safety. Colt decided to go back to its roots with new 1911 offerings. The Series '80 continued in the line, but by 2002, Colt had reintroduced its Series '70 pistol, without the firing pin safety. Actually, it could have been considered a "pre '70" Government Model, as it also did not have the fingered barrel bushing. The "new" Series '70 has modern higher sights, and improved barrel ramping.

Reception was good, and in 2003, the original WWI-era Model 1911 was reintroduced. The pistol was a faithful recreation of the .45 as made around the year 1918.

Colt remained a 1911 manufacturer in an increasingly large group of 1911 manufacturers.

New names continued to enter the world of the 1911. New companies appeared to offer their versions of the 1911. In the first few years of the 21st century, one could see new 1911 pistols bearing the names of Dan Wesson (a revolver company making its first autoloaders), High Standard (the resurrected company expanding its product line), Peters Stahl, Rock River, Century, Firestorm, Casull, Pacific Armament, DPMS (prototype only), Bond Arms, Lone Star, Ed Brown, Guncrafter, Uselton and Detonics USA (the latest incarnation of the original Detonics).

In 2003, the familiar old name of Smith & Wesson was also added. Apparently figuring "if you can't beat them, join them," S&W introduced the SW1911, and plunged into an extensive line of 1911-design pistols within a few years. A year later, in 2004, SIGARMS (now SIG-Sauer) also decided to get into the 1911 business. SIG brought out its GSR (Granite State Revolution) line of 1911 pistols, which soon became known by "Revolution."

In 2004, a bright spot appeared for firearms owners: the absurd "Assault Weapons Ban" was allowed to sunset. High-capacity pistols and magazines in all calibers could again be made. Of course, smaller calibers could be made with larger magazine capacities.

New high-capacity 9mm pistols were offered. However, the popularity of the 1911 had grown to the point that it was not threatened by new designs.

After the AWB sunset, in the last half of the new century's first decade, firearms developments continued. The pace of 1911 development was breathtaking.

The largest additional entry into the 1911 field was Taurus, in 2005. Billing itself as the "World's Foremost Pistol Maker," Taurus quickly marketed a full line of 1911 pistols. The Brazilian maker joined Smith & Wesson and SIG, all of which had just joined frontrunners Kimber, Springfield and Para as new major players in the 1911 world.

In 2006, the U. S. military called for tests of 45-caliber pistols due to questions of the 9mm's efficacy during the Desert Wars in Iraq and Afghanistan. Exactly 100 years after calling for tests to consider a .45 in 1906, the military wanted to again consider a .45 in 2006. The traditional 1911 was not invited, however; .45s to be considered would be double-action, polymer-frame pistols. As before, the tests were postponed and at the time of this writing have not been resumed. The companies that had been preparing pistols instead offered them to the commercial market, in competition with the 1911.

The 1911 seemed not to notice the new competition. The 2005 introduction of the Taurus 1911 showed that major companies still saw potential in the design.

The Taurus was not the only new entry of this recent period. Just within the last few years, new 1911 pistols with new names were introduced by Double Star, Iver Johnson, Rock Island (RIA), U. S. Fire Arms (1911s with the wide grips of the 1905), Nighthawk, American Classic, Tisas (the first Turkish 1911), EMF (the Cowboy arms company, branching into 1911s), and Legacy Sports (offering their Citadel 1911). Dan Wesson was acquired by CZ-USA, giving the Czech company access to 1911 sales.

Colt remains a major player in the 1911 field, offering new variants as well as traditional models. In 2007, Colt introduced the Concealed Carry model, followed by the New Agent in 2008. Colt decided to cash in on the trend of accessory rails on the front of a 1911 frame, and came out with a gun for that niche in 2009. What to call it? Colt kept it simple: the Colt Rail Gun.

Colt, the original manufacturer, has made the 1911 continuously since its introduction in 1911. The amazing growing interest in the century-old pistol now has, quite literally, dozens of other companies simultaneously making their versions of the same design. These guns are being made in the United States and in a growing number of foreign countries. This situation is unprecedented in the world of firearms.

CONCLUSION

A complete description of every 1911 made by every maker would be a huge volume of information, beyond the scope of this presentation. What is here presented is the basic history of the development of the 1911 design, and the amazing growth in the popularity of the design with the passing of time.

Now, one hundred years from its beginning, we have no idea where we really are in the story of the 1911. Has the 1911 reached its peak, and will it start a decline? Or, is it about to begin a new phase of popularity?

What words can summarize the amazing story of the 1911 at the event of its centennial, its 100th year? We can try a few:

The Colt/Browning 1911 design has completed its first century. It has stood the test of time. It has proved itself in military combat, law-enforcement use, target competition of many types, personal protection and recreational shooting.

It has been scaled down, both in size (3-inch barrels) and in caliber (22-caliber). It has been scaled up, both in size (7-inch barrels) and in caliber (50-caliber). Millions upon millions have been made, many of them close to the original specifications, others gussied up with a number of modifications and accessories.

In its early days, the 1911 was so good that it discouraged competition. It was then considered the best pistol ever designed. One hundred years later, there are many who say that it still is.

The .38 S&W:

THE LITTLE ROUND THAT REFUSES TO DIE

BY DAVID J. LaPELL

1942 Vintage Smith & Wesson .38-200 British Lend Lease revolver.

It has been known by many names throughout its long life: the .380/200, the .38 New Police, the Belgian 9mm revolver, but it first started off as the lowly .38 S&W.

In 1876 Smith & Wesson began producing their new First Model "Baby Russian" revolver chambered in a new cartridge, the .38 S&W. Given its nickname because of the resemblance to the larger Smith & Wesson No. 3 Russian, the First Model was a five-shot single action revolver that was offered with either a 3-1/2 inch or 4-inch barrel and was ideal for concealing in a vest or pants pocket. Both the revolver and the new .38 caliber cartridge proved to be an instant success. All of the small, concealable handguns prior to that were chambered mostly in .22 and .32 rimfire, leaving much to be desired in the realm of stopping power. The Smith & Wesson First Model and the .38 S&W bridged the gap between the little underpowered pocket guns and the larger, more powerful revolvers that were too difficult to conceal.

Originally loaded with just over 9 grains of black powder and a 146-grain lead bullet, the .38 S&W had an average muzzle velocity of 740 fps and a muzzle energy of around 175 ft. lbs. While not anything to write home about in this day and age, it was far superior to the bal-listics of the .32 Long, which delivered a 90-grain bullet at a little over 900 fps.

With the popularity of the .38 S&W cartridge and the First Model, Smith & Wesson wasted no time in bringing out their Double Action First Model in 1880, which resulted in a whole series of small revolvers that in one form or another would be produced until 1940. These little pocket-sized guns proved so successful that their basic premise was copied by Iver Johnson, Hopkins & Allen, Harrington & Richardson, and a whole host of others in America and abroad. In fact, one such revolver was used in an attempt to cut short the life of one of America's greatest Presidents.

On October 14, 1912, Theodore Roosevelt was in Milwaukee, Wisconsin, campaigning for a return to the White House after four years out of office. Teddy had just left his hotel when a bartender named John Schrank stepped out from his hiding place and fired a single shot from a .38 S&W revolver. Schrank later claimed that the ghost of President William McKinley told him to kill Roosevelt because no man should have more than two terms in office as President. (Roosevelt was trying for a third.)

Schrank was quickly tackled before he could get another shot off, and when Roosevelt's aide asked if he had been hurt, Teddy replied, "He plinked me, Henry." That single bullet had passed through Roosevelt's overcoat, his folded speech that was in his pocket, and his metal eyeglass case before stopping three inches deep into his chest. True to form, the former Commander in Chief refused medical attention and delivered his speech despite the fact he was bleeding profusely. When he later went to the hospital doctors found that the bullet was too close to Roosevelt's heart to remove. Despite his wound, the Bull Moose was back out on the campaign trail only six days later.

Smith & Wesson continued to make break open pocket revolvers in .38 S&W, and in 1917, began producing their .38 S&W Regulation Police, a five shot Hand Ejector built on their I-frame line. The I-frame revolvers were too small for the then fairly new .38 Special but were perfect for the shorter .38 S&W. The Regulation Police came with fixed sights and a 4-inch barrel.

In 1936, Smith & Wesson began making a 2-inch barreled version of the Regulation Police called the Terrier. These guns proved to be very popular for concealed carry, and are still quite popular to this day in some circles.

Yet no matter how well liked these new guns were, the .38 S&W was still primarily found in the small break-open pocket revolvers. With new cartridges like the .357 Magnum being introduced in 1935 along with small semi-automatic pistols like those from Colt, the .38 S&W appeared to be on a short road to obsolescence. Then a savior came from the most unlikely of places, the British Empire.

For the latter part of the nineteenth and early part of the twentieth centuries the British supplied Her Majesty's soldiers with large-caliber revolvers. After the end of WWI someone in charge of British Ordnance came to the conclusion that a 200-grain bullet in .38 caliber would be just as effective in combat as their tried-and-true 260-grain .455 Webley. So in 1922 the new Enfield No. 2 top break revolver was unveiled and chambered in the British version of the .38 S&W. The British round differed from the American .38 S &W with its heavier 200-grain lead round-nose bullet that was backed with 2.8 grains of "Neonite" powder for a muzzle velocity of 630 fps and a muzzle energy of 175 ft. lbs. The new round was dubbed the .380/200 Cartridge Revolver Mk I. Prior to World War II, however, the British feared that the 200-grain lead bullet of the .380/200 violated the Hague Convention of 1899's ban on "exploding bullets," so they replaced them with a 178-grain jacketed round-nose bullet. This new round was called the Cartridge Pistol .380 Mk IIz.

The British continued to use the older .380/200 rounds for training purposes, but when World War II broke out both the 200- and 178-grain loads were issued to the troops as ammunition was in short supply.

The outbreak of the war found the British also lacking in handguns, so they quickly turned to the United States for help. This came in the form of the Smith & Wesson Military & Police revolver. The British had originally contracted Smith & Wesson to produce a lightweight 9mm semi-automatic rifle. The gun proved to be unreliable and the idea and the rifles were scrapped. To make up for the money that had been advanced to Smith & Wesson, a deal was struck to provide the British with Military & Police revolvers at the rate of $20 each.

In March, 1940 Smith & Wesson began producing Military & Police revolvers chambered in .38 S&W, and these were so marked on the right side of the barrel. Other than the caliber, these

These two photos show the United States property markings that are found on British Lend Lease revolvers.

guns were mechanically identical to the .38 Smith & Wesson Special guns that were already being turned out. Soon the entire factory was dedicated to the production of revolvers that were to be shipped to England. By December of 1940, 112,584 Military & Police revolvers chambered in .38 S&W had been manufactured and sent overseas as part of the Lend-Lease program. While these guns have the look of the Smith & Wesson Victory model revolvers with their lanyard rings and plain finish, they lack the V and SV serial number prefixes that did not start until April of 1942 at serial number 1,000,000. These earlier Lend-Lease revolvers were marked with "UNITED STATES PROPERTY" and "U.S. PROPERTY" on the top strap with ordnance markings on the butt.

Throughout the war, the .38 S&W

Small .38 S&W-chambered revolvers like this one from US Revolver Company were made by the hundreds of thousands

Military & Police revolvers were used by British, Canadian, New Zealand, and Australian armed forces. Some of the Australian M&Ps were in service long after the war, remaining in use until the 1980s.

Other countries enjoyed the use of surplus .38 S&W revolvers as well. The Royal Hong Kong and Royal Singaporean Police were both supplied with Webley Mk III and Mk IV .38 S&W revolvers that were not retired until the 1970s. The Ordnance Factory Board of India to this day still manufactures ammunition for surplus .38 S&Ws in the form of the 178-grain .380 Mk IIz cartridge.

After World War II, Smith & Wesson continued production of the .38 S&W Military & Police revolvers and sold them to British Commonwealth countries. The gun was never officially catalogued but did become known as the Model 11 in 1957. Production finally stopped in 1965, and now any post-WWII Military & Police .38 S&W revolvers are desirable collector's items.

Smith & Wesson continued to produce their smaller I-frame Terrier and .38 Regulation Police revolvers (later the Model 32 and Model 33, respectively)

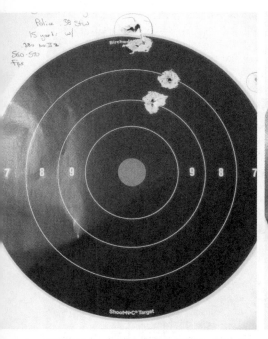

Five-shot group from 15 yards with vintage Military .380 Mk IIz rounds.

Five-shot group from 15 yards with Remington 146-grain lead bullets.

Five-shot group at 15 yards with handloads using 3.1 grains of Unique and 146-grain lead bullets.

in the little cartridge, but with the introduction of the Smith & Wesson Chief's Special in 1950 and the rival Colt Detective Special both chambered in .38 S&W Special, there was not much interest in the little .38 S&W revolvers anymore. They soldiered on until 1974, when Smith & Wesson made their last .38 S&W handgun.

Yet while the .38 S&W has been on the brink of extinction at one time or another, it just refuses to throw in the towel. This is in no small part due to the sheer multitude of handguns around the world chambered for it. Not counting the more than half million Military & Police revolvers produced for the British, Smith & Wesson made over 1,000,000 handguns of the little pocket variety over a period of 60 years. Then there were the countless thousands of revolvers made by various other companies all over the world. .38 S&W ammunition is still very easy to obtain, with Remington and Winchester both offering loads using the venerable old 146-grain lead bullet that is advertised at 685 fps and has a muzzle energy of 150 ft. lbs. These modern smokeless loads can be safely used in the break-open revolvers as long as the gun itself is in safe working order.

A word to the wise on some of the old .38 S&W pocket revolvers: those from Smith & Wesson were the best quality break-open guns of all that were produced, with the possible exception of the Webleys. The copies of those little S&W handguns range from excellent to barely functional, so if you have an old .38 S&W revolver and are considering shooting it, have it checked by a competent gunsmith first.

More powerful ammunition can also be had for the stronger revolvers like the Smith & Wesson M&Ps and the I-frame revolvers. Fiocchi loads their 145-grain lead bullet at 780 fps, which will work just fine in the swing-out cylinder revolvers but are too hot for the break-open guns. Surplus military ammunition can still be found, and more often than not it is the full metal jacketed .380 Mk IIz.

A word of warning when it comes to shooting .38 S&W ammunition out of guns that are chambered in .38 Special: *Don't even think about it.* The .38 Special has a bullet diameter of .358 whereas the .38 S&W's is .361. Even though a large number of the surplus British M&P revolvers have been rechambered to .38 Special, their bores are oversized and accuracy won't be the greatest. Some of these guns were not converted properly

and can even be dangerous to shoot. Stick to guns that are original .38 S&W guns; you will be happier and safer in the long run.

Recently I decided to take an original .38 S&W Smith & Wesson Military & Police revolver to the range with some factory ammunition as well as some handloads to see what I could make of the old warhorse and the cartridge. This particular Military & Police was part of the first batch of pre-Victory Model revolvers in 1940. It was shipped to the U.S. Government Hartford Ordnance Depot in Springfield, Massachusetts, but somehow ended up here in the states for the duration of the war.

I managed to scrounge up some original military ball ammunition, which was the 178-grain jacketed round-nose .380 Mk IIz loads. Velocity was less than what I expected, averaging only 560 fps from the Smith's 5-inch barrel. Shot from a rest at 15 yards, the shots grouped at 2-½ inches but were a couple inches high with one flyer skewing off to the right.

Next I decided to try a vintage box of Remington factory ammo. These were the same 146-grain lead round-nose bullets that are still offered to this day. Velocities with these were much better, running about 650 fps from the muzzle. From the same range of 15 yards, these also grouped at 2-½ inches but hit a bit low and off to the right.

I followed these up with a few of my handloads. The first were 146-grain lead bullets over 2.3 grains of Winchester 231. These turned out to be a disappointment, with a muzzle velocity of only 500 fps despite the fact that some of my manuals listed it as being much more. Groups were fairly ragged and a few inches low.

Next I brought along some loads using the same 146-grain lead bullets with 3.1 grains of Unique. These proved to be very accurate, hitting at nearly point of aim at 15 yards and having a velocity of 640 fps. Of all the loads I shot that day, these were the best overall with a 2-¼ inch group.

I then decided to see what kind of punch the little .38 S&W cartridge had. I didn't want to waste a perfectly good surplus military helmet, so instead I found an old round metal kid's sled that

Vintage Remington Kleanbore .38 S&W rounds (left) with modern, nickel plated-cased rounds (right).

appeared to be just as thick. (Sorry for those of you that may be nostalgic over these.) I first decided to shoot some .38 Specials from a 5-inch-barreled Model 27 Smith & Wesson for a comparison. These were nothing more than standard 130-grain FMJ ammunition. The three .38 Specials I fired went right through with little difficulty. For the .38 S&W I used some vintage .380 Mk IIz loads from the same distance out of my 5-inch-barreled Smith & Wesson Military & Police revolver. Again I fired three shots, just to the right of the .38 Specials. Two .38 S&Ws went through, but one only tore the metal as it bounced off of the metal sled. I can see why the little .38 was not exactly seen as a manstopper during World War II.

What the .38 S&W really has going for it is its inherent accuracy combined with almost no recoil. In the K-frame sized gun, it had little more recoil than a revolver of the same sized chambered in .22 Long Rifle. With the right handloads and in the right gun, it makes for a very handy small game cartridge. Rabbits and squirrels would certainly be within the .38 S&W's limits in either an old Smith & Wesson M&P or a Regulation Police. It has enough power to get the job done on game animals without destroying too much meat like more powerful calibers.

The .38 S&W, despite being written off at one time or another, is still hanging on even though no handguns have been produced for it for 35 years. I have little doubt that while it has been on the ragged edge of retirement more than once, the .38 S&W won't be going away any time soon.

THE WEST AND THE GUN

BY JIM FORAL

CHAUNCEY THOMAS.

Chauncey Thomas (1872-1941) at age 39. Talented, cultured and articulate, he self-eulogized: "Whether my writing will live I do not know. Time is my sole critic so it is idle to speculate. Anyway, I have had a good time doing the work I had to do." His name lives on in Mt. Chauncey, a 9500-ft. peak located a hundred miles west of Denver and named for him by the U.S. government.

After the Civil War, America moved westward across the continent. In the two decades to follow, civilization gradually but steadily stretched from ocean to ocean. The old emigrant trail had given way to the iron horse and the settler made certain that the savage made room for him. Cattle grazed where the buffalo once roamed, and regions formerly devoid of humanity were how inhabited.

In 1890, the Director of the Census announced that an unbroken frontier line in the West no longer existed. Lawless territories were tamed and granted statehood. The times were changing. By 1900, the Indian had been overpowered and his threat eliminated. The days of the open range were a far-gone memory and distances were abridged by the railway and the trolley. All of this had happened during the short lifetime of many individuals, and these were sad times for older men. That the West and its times had finally faded was a crushing and unpleasant thought. Their West, a unique period of about 40 years, the likes of which men never saw before and will never see again, was vanishing into history and folklore just as the bison and plains grizzly had vanished.

Against this backdrop of vanishing frontier and fading memories, a fanciful image of the old West had arisen. The wild misconception was that every mining or cow town, every lumber or farming community west of Omaha was afoul with rustlers, cutthroats, assorted thieves and bunko artists, were saturated with sixgun and sawed-off shotgun-toters, were enveloped in a perpetual smog of black powder smoke, and were thoroughly dangerous places to be. This appears, in the minds of many, to be the popular image of the West just before WWI. Hollywood capitalizes on this erroneous notion still. Even though old timers aplenty stepped forward and insisted on setting folks straight, for the most part they were not successful in dispelling the myths.

There was, early in the twentieth century, a new generation of *Outdoor Life* readers who had formulated the misguided opinion concerning conditions of the old frontier West. The media played a major role. Sensationalistic newspaper accounts of the tabloid variety were especially to blame. Publishers relied on this twaddle and other literary garbage to increase sales and circulation. The young were also heavily influenced by the popular Western dime novel hairraiser directed at them, many of which had been authored by writers who had never ventured west of Akron. The timing of the public unleashing of these sort of things could not have been better. The popular idea of the Old West, constructed in the press, was that the men – all of them – were armed and drunken gamblers who shot one another at the slightest provocation. Each woman was a dance hall girl with a public nickname. Each tree and boulder hid a lurking grizzly. Horses, even the plow mules, were unbreakable bucking broncos.

Chauncey Thomas did his best to straighten out the record and was instrumental in pooh-poohing the rampant misconceptions surrounding the Old West that were implanted firmly in the minds of the latter-day tenderfeet. Thomas knew whereof he spoke. Born on the banks of Cherry Creek, Colorado, in 1872, as a boy he saw Leadville in its heyday, Cripple Creek from the beginning, and herds of bison and the Indian, all free on the plains. Young Chauncey was trained as a journalist by his father, a veteran newspaperman. Later, he drifted from one eastern editorial office to another, finally returning to Denver in 1908. In demand as a lecturer, he was regarded as an authority on frontier history.

Some of the absurdity generated by this loose type of journalism, especially as it pertained to the extent of the use of guns on the frontier, unavoidably found its way into the various departments of *Outdoor Life* magazine. A fair percentage of the readership was convinced that the gun was the only tool that figured prominently in opening the West, subduing the Indian, and wiping out the wolf and buffalo. Thomas endured these opinions for a while before he spoke out. He had been an eyewitness, he pointed out, and this is not what he saw.

Contrary to romance and what the tabloid media would have people believe, Thomas maintained that the gun had little to do with the West's settlement. He spelled out the drab and disillusioning reality: "If not a pioneer after 1860 had had a gun, the West would have been settled just the same, neither better nor worse, as guns did not cut much figure either way. But the stamp mill and the irrigation ditch did – and therein lies the real romance of the West." The real winners of the West, he wrote, were the pick and the shovel: the pick in the mountains, the irrigation shovel in the valleys. To these we might

The Old Henry Rifle

By CHAS. N. EASTON

Forty-five years ago, when the old man was young
The old Henry rifle was new;
A white-covered wagon creaked, rumbled, and swung
And swept a broad trail in the dew;
The pioneer strode by the side of his team,
Or hunted the coverts for game;
His newly-wed wife dropped her needle to dream,
Or walked by her man's stalwart frame.
And Life smiled before them and Love smiled between,
The prairie smiled up at the sky;
Wild roses and phlox breaking up the bright green
With patches of vividest dye;
Then sweet were the songs that the bobolinks sung,
And warm was the love of the two,
Forty-five years ago, when the old man was young
And the old Henry rifle was new.

Forty-five years ago, when the old man was young
The old Henry rifle was new;
And thru all the years has the pioneer clung
To the gun as a friend proven true,
For the Henry has shortened the wolf's thieving life,
And taken its toll of the deer;
And in troublous times it protected the wife
And babes of the young pioneer.
Now life lies behind them—yet Love smiles between—
The glow of the sunset grows dim,
But warm is the light and the prairies are green
In the place where she's waiting for him. . . .
. . . .
The rifle comes down from the antlers where hung,
Together they pass in review;
The forty-five years since the old man was young
And the old Henry rifle was new.

Occasionally the old-timers would even bang out a poem or two. Charles N. Easton contributed this one to the September of 1916 issue of Outers Book.

that had been to points West under a variety of circumstances. Reminiscent Western gentlemen recalled past nineteenth century experiences and described the guns that had tagged along. Many submitted photographs. This habit, apparently encouraged by the publishers, marched to the dreaded drumbeat of progress throughout the Edwardian era. It lasted through the outbreak and duration of the War in Europe and a little beyond, until the old geezers eventually died out, or belatedly stepped into the twentieth century.

Taken as a whole, the contributors were not spinning rambling yarns. Most accounts were concise and direct treatments describing a weapon or artifact. An overview of this trend, and a sampling of a few examples, may be as useful and entertaining to modern day readers of the New Millennium as our gun crank predecessors found it a hundred years ago.

In the Spring of 1911, the editor of *Outdoor Life* allowed 10 valuable pages for a feature article that author and

ad the ore cart, the spike driving sledge, the ox-yoke, the twin bladed axe, the branding iron and other mundane implements symbolic of exertion.

Despite Thomas' qualified insistence that the proper function of the firearm of the West was grossly overplayed, the mainstream of *Outdoor Life*'s readership refused to accept the apparent heresy. Guns, after all, had been fixed in the minds of so many as being as closely associated with the true old-time Westerner as the cowboy was to the horse. Journalists, armed with their creative licenses, had seen to that. None of the readers of the outdoor magazines appeared to have an interest in hearing tales of the instruments of farming, ranching, railroading, mining or any of the truly genuine components of Western history, but they were entranced by the notion of the guns and had a special fascination with the rifles and revolvers that certainly must have seen use on the plains and in the mountains.

By about the year 1908, the real Old West was a not-too-distant memory in the hearts of the men who had lived it. Even at this late date, some gloomy

die-hards rejected the thought that their West was gone, and refused to let it be relegated to the past. They embraced the futile hope that the old West hadn't been buried just yet.

About this time, a distinct and unique episode in the history of sporting journalism began to unfold. Some of the gray-haired men sent to magazine editors descriptions of their old guns. In many cases they provided anecdotes that shed a genuine and captivating light on weapons

Most likely, this old Westerner did not write his own caption. A sharp-eyed reader of Recreation magazine noted that the rifle was not a Ballard, but a Maynard.

TINKERING HIS OLD BALLARD.   PHOTO BY W. E. CARLIN.

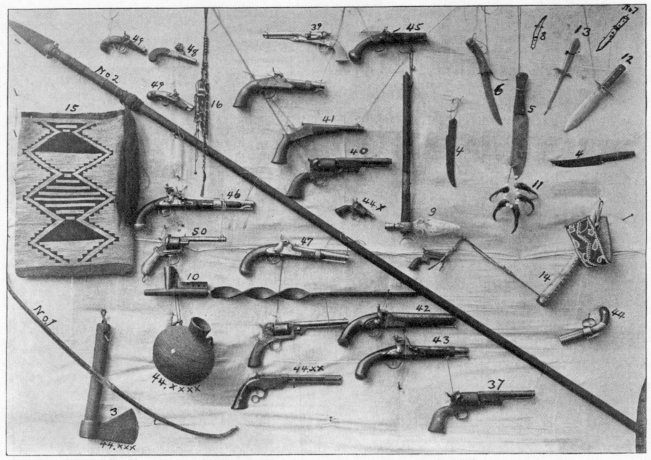

PLATE NO. 1.—FROM DON MAGUIRE'S PRIVATE COLLECTION OF OLD WEAPONS.

artifact accumulator Don Maquire was pleased to title "Frontier Weapons." Mr. Maquire, incidentally, seems to have initiated the popular, but far too infrequent, mass exhibitions of Old West guns and relics. His presentation is the first of its type that I have noticed. Other collections may have varying levels of appeal, but they paled to Maquire's 50-item display.

In the years that went by between 1870 and 1900, Don Maquire spent his time in various places in the West. His collection of Indian artifacts was extensive and important. The assembly included an assortment of lances, scalping knives, peace pipes and claw necklaces – and, of course, guns of all sorts.

Maquire's collection of long guns included a representative gathering of pioneer and immigrant guns of the common sort. Some of these had seen their first service in foreign lands. One such was a matchlock brought over by a naïve Chinese merchant who must have had no idea what to expect on the plains but recognized the need for a gun of some type. A Swiss Army rifle, the .41 caliber

Vetterli, and other out of date European military weapons were also included.

There were others. American guns were represented by the Jennings, the rare Colt Model 1855 revolving rifle, the proven and ever-present Remington Rolling Blocks and the .45 caliber Springfields which were cheap, plentiful and frequently seen in the company of a pioneer family. No worthwhile collection of Western items is complete without a Sharps rifle, and Maquire's was an early conversion to fire metallic cartridges. Confederate and Union rifles that had made their way westward with discharged or deserted veterans were reminders of these guns in the overall picture of the American West's settling. Maquire didn't consider the shotgun to be deadly enough for "men of our class," but one specimen merited a place in is collection. This was a double barreled hammer gun carried by Niel House, who used it to ride Express guardsman for Wells Fargo to Virginia City from Sacramento in the early days.

Several other accumulations of Western artifacts were profiled during this

(above and opposite) Don Maguire's collection of western artifacts and weapons as profiled in the June, 1911 issue of Outdoor Life.

period. One of the more significant was the 47-year weapon collection of George Shull. In 1873, Shull's collection started as an innocent gathering of working guns and wound up as an assemblage of remnants of the Western tradition. His guns included Civil War battlefield pick-ups, brass framed Winchesters, Spencers, even Evans rifles and the rest, totaling nearly 50 reminders of better times. A white-goateed Mr. Shull posed with his assortment of mementos for a picture taken at his Iowa home, and it was published on page 51 in the January, 1920 number of the *Magazine of the West*.

Jas. N. Sterling submitted a photo and brief descriptions of his 30-year gatherings in December of 1917. In the collection were three Sharps rifles, the first a bona-fide killer of bison. Chambered for the massive .45-120-550 case, it tipped the scales two ounces over 17 pounds. The aristocratic brother of the Sharps buffalo gun and champion at

PLATE NO. 2.—FROM DON MAGUIRE'S PRIVATE COLLECTION OF OLD WEAPONS.

the thousand-yard line was the Sharps Creedmoor. Mr. Sterling's elegant example sported a wind gauge front sight, and two vernier rears, one of which was mounted on the rifle's heel for use in the supine, or back position.

Among the quality relics of buffalo days were two Remington percussion revolvers and a pair of .44 caliber cap and ball Colts. There were a couple of Spencers, one of which was a dazzling long-barreled factory sporting rifle . The lever action was represented by the 1866 Model Winchester, and a Henry nice enough to command six figures on today's market.

An entire page of the January 1916 *Outer's Book* was devoted to a stunning photograph of the Colt collection of Charles W. Parker of Concord, California. Nearly every model and every variation of sixgun and revolving rifle that was ever assembled at a Colt plant was represented. Sadly, only the photo was published. For the Western history buff, missing were the details of individual pieces and how they might have figured in the struggle to win the West.

The muzzle loader of the Kentucky class got its fair share of attention and exposure. A fair number of readers furnished reports on the gunsmith crafted flintlock and cap lock arms they had manage to retain, inherit, or acquire. During this era, many guns made by artisans such as Jas. Golcher, Simon Miller, John Shell, Isaac Palm, all famous in their time, were brought to the attention of the readers across the pages of *Outdoor Life* and the other outdoor magazines. Mark Woodmansee, as one example, submitted a delightful photo of his five Kentuckys, together with their accouterments for his fellow enthusiasts to enjoy. One of these was retrieved from where it was dropped by one of Pickett's Virginia rebels at the Battle of Gettysburg, July 3, 1865.

However, all the wishing in the world wouldn't bring back the frontier conditions of the early West or its spirit. A Missourian who chose to sign his namee "L 'Encuerado" shed some interesting light on the use of the Henry rifle, both in the Civil War and on the plains of the West. In April of 1908, he furnished

Outdoor Life readers with an anecdote involving a tiny band of steely-nerved Rebel veterans and a larger group of Indians being exposed for the first time to the repeating rifle. The incident took place somewhere in the Northwest.

At one of their camps, they were attacked by a band of hostile savages who feigned a charge, hoping to draw the fire of the white men. The Indians intended to rush them before their guns could be reloaded. They succeeded in drawing the anticipated fire, and charged the defenders furiously, only to be met by a murderous and rapidly successive fire at a range close enough to see the flabbergasted expressions on the faces of the red men. The few survivors retreated at full speed. L 'Encuerado was later given one of the Henrys associated with the lopsided battle as a memento.

A sketch of three seldom-seen pistols was presented in *Outdoor Life* for March of 1917. Don Maquire provided the opportunity as well as a couple of photographic cuts. Of the three, he seemed to be the most proud of a pristine Sharps single shot breechloading pistol

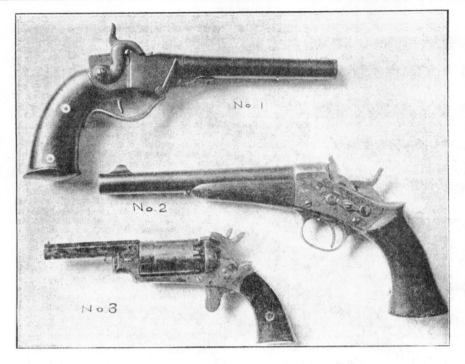

No. 1

No. 2

No. 3

Don Maguire's three relic pistols pictured and described in the March, 1917 issue of Outdoor Life. From top: Sharps 44-caliber single-shot breechloading percusssion pistol; 58-caliber Remington rolling block pistol; Walsh Firearms Co. five-chambered, 10-shot revolver. The loads were superimposed in each chamber. The right hammer fired the front charge through a tube in the cylinder wall. The left hammer fired the rear load. Needless to say, the Walsh never really caught on.

patterned after the Sharps side-hammer rifle principle. Its inventors had hopes that this arm would fall into favor of the military when it was brought out in the mid-1850s. The Colt revolver was a formidable competitor, however.

The second was a particularly well preserved specimen of a Remington 58-caliber rolling block pistol that Mr. Maquire had acquired at a sale of government surplus items. Maquire told how this model was issued to cavalry-men who discovered that it was just the thing for "riding close to buffalo." Gal-loping alongside a bison and shooting it from atop a fast mount was considered to be grand sport for a horse soldier stationed on the range.

The third rarity was a dual-hammered Walsh ten-shot revolver of 1859 vintage. The inventor of this gimmick must have had visions of superseding the Colt sixshooter. There were a few bugs in the design and the gun wasn't a success, although a few made their way into the holsters of Confederate troopers during the Civil War. Maquire's example was retrieved on the battlefield of Corrinth in October of '62, from the person of a Rebel captain who, as war trophy seek-ers have remarked throughout history, "no longer had a need for it."

Dr. B.J. Ochsner was one of the great surgeons of the West and one of its most devoted handgun cranks. His pistol collection was profiled in the December 1916 issue of Outdoor Life. There were pistols of all descriptions, from French duelers to the ultra-modern Luger.

Included were two scarce Pope-barreled handguns, a Smith and Wesson .38 and a Stevens. The high point of the collection to the Old West buffs certainly, was the brace of Colt Navies, presented by a for-mer superintendent of the Mesa Verde National Park, and were known to have killed several men on the frontier. A. H. Hardy, Peters exhibition shooter and author of the piece, failed to mention whether the dead men were good guys or bad guys.

Correspondent Don Wiggins showed up in 1914 with a primitive-looking North and Savage revolving rifle of 1852 vin-tage that was a genuine Indian weapon. Harry Bennet, the rifle's proud owner in 1914, had secured it from the Hood River Indians 10 years previously. The buck who sold it to him passed along that his father had carried the gun while fighting under Chief Joseph. A number of brass tacks, about fifty, ornamented the stock in typical red man fashion. Hood River legend had it that each tack represented the scalp of a white man.

As the metallic cartridge came into common usage in the late 1870s, the percussion system was effectively obso-leted. The cartridge revolvers replaced the cap and balls, and some of their owners neglected their old sixshooters, allowing them to decay like a pair of old shoes. Sometimes the old guns were simply discarded and considered good riddance. It was maintained that the old system was an untrustworthy and dangerous one, and there was some risk associated in shooting them. In

an improperly managed cap and ball, wayward sparks at discharge would jump from cylinder to cylinder, detonat-ing some or all of the chambers with a single pull of the trigger. If the Colt revolving rifle was said to have been particularly bad in this respect, the Remington percussion revolver was the worst offender. Modern black powder enthusiasts are aware of this threat, and take steps to prevent an occurrence. It could be that the tough frontier sorts didn't put much stock in the danger, and tended to dismiss the phenomena as rumor – until it happened to them.

An eyewitness account which ap-peared in the February 4, 1905 issue of Forest and Stream gave some credence to the hearsay. Shortly after the Civil War, there was a small military encampment just north of new Orleans. A dozen soldiers, including our correspondent Cabio Blanco, took the afternoon off for a bit of pistol practice. When it came his turn to fire, a young trumpeter shooting one of the infernal Remingtons had three or four cylinders go off simultane-ously. With a still stinging hand, the boy flung the gun into the canal where it doubtlessly still remains. (He wound up compensating Uncle Sam for the govern-ment issue pistol; $13 was deducted from his pay.)

Mr. E.C. Phillips of Trinidad, Colorado, wrote in the December, 1912 issue of Out-ers Book that he had one of the personal weapons of famous scout and frontiers-man Kit Carson. This was an over/under double-barreled percussion rifle. There were two hammers, one on either side of the arm. Evidently, Carson saw the merit in having the extra shot at his command. Carlos Gove of Denver made the rifle entirely by hand for Carson in 1858. Re-portedly, Gove made two such rifles. The other was for noted scout and Indian fighter Tom Tobin. Tobin, incidentally, is reported to have captured the infamous Esponisa band of outlaws for the price on their heads. Tobin camped with the gang, and while they slept, killed them and cut off their heads. He then gathered the heads in a gunny sack and carried the grisly baggage to the authorities and claimed the rewards.

Phillips pointed out that the Carson rifle was a choice and rare specimen, and marked a step forward in the development of firearms. Also noted was the fact that the rifle was for sale. One has to wonder if the Carson story was not a scheme to enhance the price tag.

F.J. Carnes burst into the gun department of the period *Field and Stream* magazine and expounded on the subject of Colt revolvers. Although the Arms and Ammunition column editor Bob Nichols may not have approved of intruders in his magazine space, he allowed Carnes some ink to clarify a few inaccuracies. Responding to some misinformation spread through previous statements made in the column regarding the earliest of Colt revolvers, Carnes very ably proceeded to set a lot of people straight. Along with the text, Carnes published a photo of his Patterson Colt, as well as a Walker model Dragoon from his own collection. The latter was a well-worn example, with the company number of "D" co. 189. For the sole benefit of the reader, we must presume, Carnes appraised his rare Colt, assigning to it a value of $500. Nickols opined that the topic was an interesting one, and perhaps a bit more devotion to the old guns might induce folks to rummage through their attics and turn up more scarce Colts.

With old guns under such discussion during this period, the public's fascination and interest in the outlaw and other notable gunmen of the frontier grew exponentially, which sparked a fairly widespread side discussion on gunslinger topics. This seems to have peaked in the early 1920s. "Could the Bad Men of the West Really Shoot?" and "The Truth About Wild Bill" were among the juicy titles.

The bad man was the seldom seen but perpetually perceived image of the Wild Frontier. His willingness to use the gun and his alleged proficiency with it were a big part of the mystique. Most of us are able to relate to an attraction to and a fixation with the outlaw, though we may not be able to put our fingers on the reasons. Each of us as youngsters played cowboys and Indians. I can't recall any of my boyhood chums volunteering to be the village dolt that groomed horses

at the livery. Not one wanted to clerk at the dry goods store or perform coolie labor with the railroad gang. All of them wanted to be the good guy or the bad guy (depending). We all wanted to be the players who got to carry and shoot the guns.

Many gray-haired eyewitnesses, and some who would have liked to be so regarded, took up a pen and offered first hand accounts of their acquaintances, friendships, chance meetings, or narrow escapes with one of the West's celebrated desperados. Some of this must simply be taken with a grain or two of salt, but a percentage of the narratives are certainly to be considered reliable. Sifting fact from fiction is impossible. Nevertheless, this material makes mighty interesting reading.

A description of one person's relationship with Calamity Jane, as a good example, appeared in a *Hunter-Trader-Trapper* magazine in 1925. Regrettably, there is no mention of her guns. Old men who remembered well not being shot by Billy the Kid wrote with questionable authority during the same time. Wild Bill Hickok seems to have left an endless string of human beings that knew him well, judging from the printed evidence.

Not everyone was entranced by the common guns of the immigrant or pioneer farmer, the guns that really won the West. Everyone was, it seems, interested in the guns of the gunman. I daresay we still are. A few of these firearms that once were used by the infamous made their way into the hands of an individual or a family, where they had been closely held for two or three decades before

they were presented to readers of an outdoor magazine. Collectors had a few of them too.

Belle Starr's '73 Winchester .44-40 came to light in the July of 1920 *Outdoor*

Life. Belle was the daughter of a Methodist minister, a good girl gone astray. One of the West's great outlaw leaders, she ran with the James gang and Jim Cummings, and generally terrorized Oklahoma when it was known as Indian Territory.

Missourian Fred E. Sutton wrote in his brief note that Belle was killed at Younger's Bend in the I.T. (Indian Territory) on February 3, 1889. Edgar Watson was credited with the deed. After Belle hit the ground, her saddle mare Venus swam the river and was intercepted by U.S. Marshal James Boles, who lifted the carbine from its saddle scabbard. Sometime later he gifted the gun to Mr. Sutton, its owner in 1920. The photograph accompanying Mr. Sutton's essay indicated that BELLE STARR is rather crudely but conspicuously carved on the right side of the butt stock . On one side of the breech in her name in brass letters. On the other side is a brass figure of a bell and a star. One would suppose that this precious Winchester is in a major collection. On the other hand, it could still be reposing in a closet somewhere in Missouri.

The largest collection of old guns that was made public knowledge was that of C. Burton Saunders of Berryville, Arkansas. *Outdoor Life* editor J.A. McGuire judged that an account of Mr. Saunders' vast collection was sufficiently noteworthy to warrant a three-and-a-half page coverage in the October 1923 issue. Perhaps the centerpiece of Saunders' 700-plus guns was a Colt Navy once owned by Jesse James. Supporting the claim was a letter from the son of the

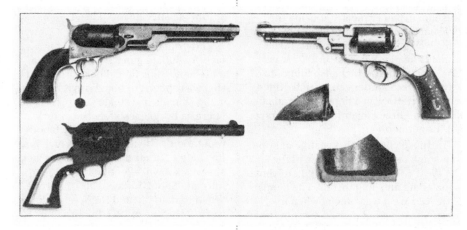

The Saunders collection contained at least three guns used by Jesse James: a .36 Colt Navy, a Starr, and a Colt M1873. From Outdoor Life of October of 1923.

man Jesse gave the pistol to in 1877. Thomas G. Davis had done James a favor of some sort, and the method of demonstrating his appreciation was to present Mr. Davis with a gun when he happened to be temporarily weaponless. The barrel is inscribed "Jesse James, Sep.12, [sic] Pilot Knob, Mo." Also worthy of mention is a Single Action Colt that was said to have been given to James' brother-in-law at Sonora, California. The relative later lent it to a forest ranger and the gun was ruined when his cabin burned. Saunders was later able to acquire it.

A 44-caliber Starr six-shooter was decorated by James himself with a copper dagger and an inverted letter "J" inletted into the grip. Driven into the grip was a number of small nails, each of which was believed to have represented a man fallen dead to the Starr. Included in this count were four law officers who tried to arrest Jesse in 1876 at the Miller Ranch, five miles out of Joplin. Legend has it that after the revolver was emptied, James threw it on a table and made his getaway. A servant woman present immediately dropped the gun into a jar of warm lard that was on the hearth. She later buried the jar together with the concealed gun, and it was preserved in this fashion until it was recovered at a later date. Ultimately, it wandered into the collection of C. Burton Saunders.

Joaquin Murrietta was a conscience-less Mexican bandit and gringo-hater who specialized in brutally plundering California mining camps. He lived by the sword, and at age 23, died the same way. He was decapitated, and his pickled head was kept on display at the Gordon Museum in San Francisco. During the 1906 earthquake/fire, the gruesome thing was lost and never found. Taken from his headless corpse in 1853 was his Colt Dragoon, which also found its way into the Saunders collection. Killed with Murrietta was a hopeless criminal known as Three Finger jack. Saunders got his gun too.

For those clinging to a vestige of hope that some remaining elements of the Old West still survived, a singular event signaled its finishing throes. The demise of the Old West was official when its personified symbol passed away in the Spring of 1917. Buffalo Bill Cody, Army scout, buffalo hunter, and the showman who took the frontier West around the world, died quietly in Denver, and with him the era of the frontier and the conquest of the plains and the mountains.

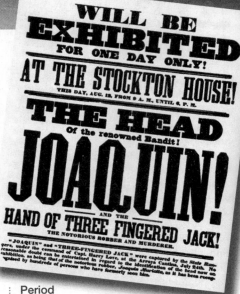

Period advertisement for Joaquin Murrietta's traveling head.

With his passing, the Old West was gone, hopelessly and irretrievably lost to a glorious and semi-mythical past.

Fittingly, Chauncey Thomas was the last man to interview Cody as he lay on his deathbed. Mr. Thomas' wordy account of his audience with Buffalo Bill appeared in the May, 1917 number of the *Magazine of the West*. In his last days, Bill and Chauncy talked guns and Western experiences. Cody spoke of his heavy buffalo guns, the type favored by bison killers who sniped them from a stand. Bill used two Sharps rifles, a ponderous .45-120-550 weighing 18 lbs. and an 11-lb. bottlenecked .44 caliber.

Cody liked to shoot his bison from a horse's back, galloping close to the herd and lung-shooting them at very close range. For this, a light powerful rifle was his weapon of choice. A Winchester 1873 was especially well liked, as was a Spencer carbine.

Cody smiled when he named his favorite buffalo gun: "Lucrezia Borgia," a breechloading 50-caliber Springfield that was special to him. With it he slew 4,250 animals in a single year. (The real Lucrezia Borgia, a sixteenth-century Italian socialite, had an equally bloody reputation.) The Indians had a nickname for Cody's Lucrezia. To certain red men, she was known, affectionately or fearfully, as "Shoot Today – Kill Tomorrow." When Buffalo Bill and the West he knew were both gone in 1917, Lucrezia Borgia remained draped across a set of elk antlers at the ranch, next to the knife Cody used to kill Yellow Hand.

When Cody died, the "real" Old West died with him. Today, we're fortunate that the recollections of those who really had "been there, done that" have survived in the yellowing pages of the old outdoor literature. The witty Chauncey Thomas, the orator most capable, delivered a succinct but sufficient eulogy for this unique period in American history: "The Old West is dead, and the frontier six shooter is a relic. Where the Indian roamed we have the suffragette; we run short of carfare instead of cartridges, and instead of pulling the .45, we are pulled by the 5:40."

Emerson Hough was an habitual *Forest and Stream* columnist through the peak of the frontier years and a familiar provider of sporting, natural history, and conservation material. When he contributed a short feature, unimaginatively titled "The West and the Gun" in the June 23, 1900, number, it must have struck his loyal followers as uncharacteristically reflective. When he published his observation, it was a trifle too early in the century for the sort of thoughts that were on his mind.

Mr. Hough spent the best part of his life in the West; for many years he was a New Mexican. He wrote that he lived through a time when seeing a sidearm strapped to a man's hip was the usual and expected thing. He once shot – informally at targets – with Pat Garrett, the sheriff of Lincoln County, the man who ended the career of Billy the Kid with a bullet.

While visiting a Chicago gun store during the first Spring of the twentieth century, Hough caught his initial glimpse of the new-fangled Colt .38 Automatic pistol and puzzled over its complex gadgetry. It was a curious, right angled, out-of-balanced affair. Hough had grown old enough to be resistant to change and to progress. With sad strokes of his pen, Mr. Hough foreshadowed the attitude that would preoccupy the minds and imaginations of Westerners for the next 20 years when he wrote: "These Browning boys, out in Ogden, Utah, who get up all these revolutionizing inventions in firearms, are Western men, and they must have an odd reflection now and then that there is no longer any West, no longer any Billy the Kids, no longer much use for guns, big or little."

By the time of the European War, the Wild West had been broken and tamed. The boom town was now a ghost town. The nester had fenced himself in and was there to stay. The bad man didn't come to town to drown his thirst any longer; law and order were on tap.

It was the third and last deer season in western South Dakota. That meant the air temperature was hovering around eight degrees above zero, and the winds off the Big Horn mountains were gusting to a strong 55 mph, with a constant breeze settling in at about 35 mph. Not the best day for deer hunting, but the only one our group of four hunters had. Tom Hanson, my friend and neighbor on our South Dakota mountain hideout, had been glassing several deer down on a wide flat half-cut winter cornfield about an hour north of home for better than an hour. With the time now approaching 8:00 a.m., Tom knew that very soon those whitetail would bed down about mid-field and at that point it would be time to move down against the stiff wind, walk the corn row edges, then glass between the quarter-mile long rows until a target could be located.

With a pair of hunters blocking the natural exit route downwind on the field, two more took up positions on each side of the field, but at a staggered pattern with a good 150 yards between each of them. This was to establish a safe fire zone and not shoot across that short cornstalk-infested flats and thereby hit the hunter on the opposite side. Now with everyone in position, it was time

to glass and comb those rows. Maybe with luck, some winter meat would be brought to the table.

Tom and another friend, Jerome Bressler, had already hunted the corn a week earlier. At that time the same system had netted four plump doe, and on this wind-driven morning, the system would be exactly the same. Now the hunt was about to progress. Jerome and I had drawn long straws, and it was my job to take the position on the back side of the corn field as Jerome walked the two-track roadside a full 200 yard to my rear. Glassing his half of the long clean rows of slightly snowdrifted corn stalks as I did the same on my side, we proceeded down the mile section toward our blocking partners, working as a team.

At about mid-field, a large doe stood up and walked directly across my end of the field. She was at or close to 200 yards and standing in a location that presented a clean, clear shot. I was using a set of Bog Pod shooting sticks, and they were extended to my full shoulder height. Moving back against a fence post so as to steady myself against the gusting wind, I locked down my crosshairs, dropped a half breath from my lungs, and touched off a round, which consisted of a 55-grain Norma

ORYX soft nose bullet. At the shot, the .22-250 Remington was sent downrange by the Savage Predator turnbolt rifle. The doe shuddered a bit, then turned away, breaking into a slow trot toward some higher-standing cornstalks.

Knowing the drill that had taken place all to often in my 50-plus years of hunting whitetail, I moved my rifle scope sight immediately to the far side of the thick cornstalk stand and waited for the old girl to emerge. Show up she did. Now the range had been extended another 50 to 75 yards yards, and I was wishing for my tried and true .25-06 pushing a 117-

The .223 round is a military lightweight and not a proven big game cartridge at all.

LIGHT CARTRIDGES FOR DEER:
A New Shooting Trend — or Impending Disaster?

BY L.P. BREZNY

Author zeroing his .22-250 Savage from a bench rest table. Accuracy is very much required when using .22 centerfires for big game.

The S&W M&P-15-T performs well as a coyote rifle, and the author also took deer with it.

In effect, the 55-grain softnose bullets were not energy-effective against the 155-pound animal. The ratio of bullet mass to body mass just didn't compute in this very direct and obvious test scenario. Tom had dropped a pair of adult does in the same field by way of his handloaded 55-grain Ballistic Tip .224 bullets that were turning up about 3200 f.p.s. velocity. Shooting his R-15 by Remington topped by Burris 4.5 X14 glass sights, he had elected to take head/neck shots on the two animals and thereby dropped both in their tracks with the light-caliber rifle. Here was the classic example of bullet placement getting the job done.

Jerome, with his DPMS AR Hunter in .243 Winchester and the 95-grain Winchester boattail, still elected to shoot neck shots on the cornfield at under 150 yards. As Jerome says, when in doubt take the best shot possible regardless of the rifle being put to work. Good advice in any big game harvesting situation! Was the data returned by my two partners valuable? Of course it was, as any kill can be a learning curve of sorts. With accuracy being a given – all the local Dakota hunters I have spent time with afield can shoot for sure – the next element to success is body area placement. Light bullets and small calibers require placement in areas of the body that will result in immediate neurological takedown, versus a more prolonged death caused by blood loss.

About two days after the cornfield hunt I was at home working in my office when my wife Colleen indicated that a wounded buck was walking through our back forty. Glassing the deer I could see a full left hind quarter was just about shot away, or eaten away. As we have big cats here in the northern foothills of western South Dakota's Black Hills, I was not at all surprised. Getting a call into my local game warden I was given the green light to take the animal down. My weapon of choice in this case was the S&W M&P-15-T that was standing in the hallway with a loaded five-round magazine in the receiver well. (Out here in the wild west it is common practice to keep a rifle in the kitchen.)

Heading outside and reaching a large tree trunk, I steadied myself and then touched off a round with the Gem Tech-suppressed quiet gun, and the 36-grain Black Hills brand Barnes

grain Sierra boattail bullet as loaded by Federal Cartridge. This was my go-to load in most cases on the wide-open western South Dakota prairies, but today I was in a test mode, and as such the .22-250 had gotten the call that cold windy morning.

Pushing the muzzle of the Savage Predator into the slightly angling high wind that was coming from my left, I reset my sights for added windage and touched off round number two. Again the doe seemed to shudder and shift her weight a bit. However, again she turned away and proceeded to move on down the field in the general direction of the blockers waiting at the other end.

With the doe out of sight and nothing going on in the direction of the blockers, Jerome and I both started to converge on the location at which I had made the second hit on the deer. We were lucky that we had fresh snow and short corn to deal with. In effect, if that deer was hit anywhere close to the vitals, we could stay on her track all day if necessary. With about 100 yards of a zig-zagging trail we located the deer. She was down and stone dead, laying directly between two rows of corn stubble. Two bullets had entered her left side vitals, but no exit wound or blood trail was visible. The small .224 bullets had entered the animal, leaving the hide to close over the entry wound, then causing all the blood given off by one bullet to the liver and a second hit to the lung to pool in the lower portion of the chest cavity.

The .223 can take deer humanely, given perfect shot placement, but there are better choices for the task.

This fancy dressed AR is a big part of the reason some have lobbied for light rifles in the field. However, at what price in wounded game?

Varmint Grenade did the rest of the job. At 170 yards, and with bullet placement at the base of the head/neck, the hurting old buck never knew what hit him. That VG bullet made of dusted or sintered copper coring and a solid copper jacket just turned to a gas inside his head and upper spine area. With a muzzle exit velocity of almost 3700 f.p.s., this little fast mover did the job with both velocity and accuracy.

With my partner's kills and the example I just related to you, am I saying that the .224 or any light bullet is appropriate for taking big game animals the size of deer or even antelope cleanly? Yes – but only if all the conditions regarding bullet placement location, range, and rifle accuracy have been met. In South Dakota we often hunt rolling, open prairie land, flat grain or crop fields, or other areas that allow a good visual and ideal tracking conditions on an animal that takes a hit. Lacking these conditions, the net effect can be a lost animal.

EASTERN STATES AND .22S FOR DEER

While we can and do get away with shooting very light rifles on deer and antelope out here in the wide-open west – again, due for the most part to being able to locate an animal after the shot – I don't believe the same can be said for areas of the country that contain whitetail in heavy cover. Based on what I have seen and will elaborate on a bit later, I tend to believe that it is asking for trouble to allow a hunter into the woods in, say, Minnesota with a .223 Remington loaded for deer. How can I make that judgment, being a Dakota hunter? Because I spent about 50 years of my life hunting whitetail not just for trophies, but in old-school meat events in Minnesota, Wisconsin, and Iowa. Believe me, friends, I know what I am talking about here, and slapping a bullet into a big northern Minnesota swamp buck's vitals and then tracking him through black willow, swamp bottoms, and heavy buck brush ain't my idea of a good day at the office. The bottom line here is that you're going to lose game. Woodland states that enact legislation that allows the use of light cartridges such as the .223 for big game seem to be missing the obvious, and according to some I have discussed this issue with, seem to care less about wounding the critters. I think the .22 as a big game cartridge in these conditions, or for the most part in almost *all* conditions, is nothing but a careless stunt!

Yes, I have observed a professional hunter with hundreds

of kills under his belt take down even trophy whitetail with a .220 Swift and a medium Winchester 55-grain pointed softpoint bullet. However, now we're getting back to range, bullet placement, and just plain know-how, which in turn moves us into the second phase of this discussion: the suitability of heavy-hitting .22s beyond the .223 Remington or even the .22-250 Remington as big game harvesting tools.

INCREASED FIREPOWER, OBVIOUS RESULTS

Staying with the .224 caliber bullets in weights well below 100 grains, I undertook several hunts at one point in my rather detailed study of the newer Winchester Super Short .223 WSSM. Targets were antelope and deer in combination, with an additional goat hunt in western South Dakota.

Moving to the .223 WSSM gave me the opportunity to experiment with several variables. In addition to increased velocity and energy, different bullet designs were employed in the field, such as a Barnes 62-grain TSX and a 53-grain TSX flatbase, thereby increasing accurate range and retained energy. I could have turned to the new Norma 55-grain soft point ORYX pills loaded in the .220 Swift, which moves at about the same velocity as the .223 WSSM, but I didn't have a Swift on hand, and I did have a .223 WSSM in a Winchester Model 70 Feather Weight. That rifle and those paired cartridges had already chalked up positive history of several goats and whitetail deer.

With antelope being the primary target, and having several doe kid tags to fill, my target weights were at or near 100 pounds. Now I was setting out in northern Harding country South Dakota, with the first in my pair the handloaded Barnes 62-grain bullets. The handload pushed the Barnes TST at 3628 fps behind a burning mass of Varget in a 38.5 grain charge. This load was max for Varget and the Barnes bullet but was able to stay close to the Swift even at its increased grain weight. As an example, the .220 Swift when loaded with a 53-grain Barnes TSX FB bullet leaves the muzzle at a maximum velocity of 3882 if pushed by a 43.5 grain charge of AA 2700. "Yes, a couple of hundred feet faster," you're saying – but also a bullet nine grains lighter with less kinetic energy on target after the speed thing begins to dry up a bit down range. In my book it all balances out when comparing very high velocity loads and modest grain weight changes back to back. Speed kills, and with light bullet and small calibers you can't get them moving fast enough. Even a slight change in grain weight can return major dividends at the target in terms of raw energy, which translates into killing force.

My first goat taken with the .223 WSSM was a young buck within legal kid goat size (horn length). He was angling across a shallow draw and moving directly across me from right to left at a bit under 100 yards. He had just cleared a fence and seemed to be more interested in what was following him than he was in me. Shooting off a set of Bog Pod sticks, I saw my shot hit just behind the shoulder, about mid-body. The antelope reacted much like those whitetail had during the late season doe hunt in that cornfield, and after hunching up a bit, he just trotted over the ridge and out of sight. Moving up the draw quickly so as to get another crack at him, I now observed the animal going up a steep rise right to left. knowing that game in general won't go uphill when hit hard, I clearly understood that this guy required an additional shot in the vitals. Round two hit him higher, and with the addition of that second bullet he went down hard. Both bullets had exited the back side of the critter, with the first hit taking out a lower section of lung and

This whitetail buck can be taken at reasonable range limits, but bullet placement is everything when shooting light rifles.

the second the top of his heart. In this case a shot inside 150 yards maximum (the second shot) had done a good job. Now, however, the question still remained: did the first round make him sick enough to fall to the second hit? I guess we will never know, but a subsequent pair of goats a few weeks later did shed some additional light on the subject.

Glassing a water hole on my friend Randy Routier's ranch hunting operation at Buffalo, South Dakota, I had been camped out on a ridge top for two days and had been sitting in wait for a good buck to show up with his harem of doe goats. It was well into the first season at this point, and these animals were skittish to say the least. About mid afternoon on the second day of my hunt, 11 goats came walking up a draw and onto the water hole. Seeing no trophy buck in the bunch, I set aside my .25-06, a go-to system for long-range trophy work, and looked down the .223 WSSM at a good-sized (over 100 pounds) goat. The .223 WSSM was loaded with the Barnes 53-grain TSX flatbase at the same velocity as the Swift (3913 f.p.s.) via 40.5 grains of Varget. Aiming again at the point again just behind the left shoulder and a bit high, I caught the doe's heart and one lung with the Barnes. At the shot my doe just walked off the edge of the stock tank, then proceeded to fall over within about 15 yards. Like the previous .223 WSSM kill, no bullet was recovered. At a range of 125 yards, everything in the bullet department was moving just too fast for the small-frame animal to hold that pill in place.

It should be pointed out at this time that handloading Barnes bullets in a .223 WSSM with a bore twist rate of 1 in 9 inches means keeping the grain weight under that of the tested 62-grain TSX bullet. My rifle, however, while not being known to shoot accurate groups with that heavy bullet, did return game harvesting accuracy. In most cases, it is best to stay with the published game plan for the .223 WSSM in a factory rifle and shoot the 53- to 55-grain or lighter bullets. As a final note, remember: it is always advisable to test on paper extensively before going afield.

Over the course of three hunts I elected to turn to the .223 WSSM, which resulted in two of my own goats, an assist on a third for a friend, and and an additional whitetail. In each case the fast moving .22 caliber got the job done, but not always within easy walking distance from the point at which the animal was first hit by the light bullets.

MORE POWDER AND MORE BULLET

When my partner Mr. Bressler elected to turn to his DPMS .243 on that cornfield hunt and subsequent hunts later in the season, he was eliminating the possible loss of an animal because of underachieving ballistics downrange as applied to lighter bullets and rifles. After spending almost two full years with the .224 caliber bullets in a variety of cartridges that ranged from high velocity to very high speed varmint type separators, I came to the conclusion that when you can use medium calibers that offer state-of-the-art ballistics performance, why even bother with the small stuff? The move to a .25 WSSM, 25-06, and, yes, even the 243 Winchester clearly illustrated a major step forward in performance. In terms of selection, about equal time was split between the .25 WSSM and .25-06 with an industry cull hunt using the 243 Winchester stuck right in the middle. It was a convenient series of hunts, and I managed to get a great deal accomplished in terms of some back-to-back comparisons.

Shooting a new Speer test bullet at 100 grains during the cull hunt, I was assigned to a tower stand on a very wide open trail that was boarded by heavy pine forest, and then given a list of what to take and exactly where to place the shots. In all cases the .243 out to 235 ranged yards did a good job of cleanly taking my test subject with single well-placed shots. Shooting

involved right angle vital shooting, sharp angle shots from back to front, and head-on shooting for vital penetration testing. Special metal-sensing systems used in detecting land mines (no, I'm not kidding) were employed to locate bullets that had not passed through the targets.

That deer shoot had been the official type event, but then I headed back to South Dakota and a few other states, hunting on my own for some detailed review time with the .25 WSSM and .25-06 Remington. With a buck license on a wide-open prairie unit and a second doe tag as well, I went to work with my Model 70 Winchester chambered in .25 WSSM. The bullet was the 110-grain Accu Bond in a Winchester factory wrapper. Bullet choice was Winchester factory or handloads, due in fact to the cartridge being loaded only by Winchester at the time of that test shooting. Federal was making brass for a period of time, or at least some of it crossed my reloading dies with their headstamp on them, but the WSSM line in all calibers is a exclusive product of the Winchester folks.

My first South Dakota kill involved a nice buck at 225 yards. I had been belly-crawling this guy all mid-morning for a clean, clear shot. He was courting three doe whitetail and was paying very little attention to the green and brown blob that was crawling toward him out on the open prairie. When I got set for my shot, he was clear of the does and now presented a solid left-to-right broadside vital area bullet contact point. At the shot, the deer, which I judged to be about three years old, dropped to his belly, never moving even a foot forward. The Accu Bond 110-grain bullet had done its job, and I was gaining more interest in this short, fat super-cartridge that had been thought up by Winchester. With two additional deer taken with the .25 WSSM, I was seriously wondering why anyone would

Author with a full-size deer target when setting up his Savage Predator .22-250 for taking big game with the .224-caliber bullet.

even start to take up the .224 caliber bullet as a serious deer harvesting system. To me it was much like shooting waterfowl with a 28 gauge. It just didn't fit the proper profile of a game harvesting gun system.

With some additional hunting with my old and well-used .25-06 matched with Federal 117-grain Sierra bullets, it was clear that under almost all conditions – with the exception of some ultra high wind and long range work with

Norma supplied many of the bullets used in this review. For a general-purpose round in the .223 Remington, the Norma Oryx 55-grainer is hard to beat.

a .300 Win Mag– the .25-06 family of cartridges could meet the requirements of a very good deer round each and every time. For the most part I had not even moved into the 7mms or the 30-calibers, for I found enough solid performance from those 6mms and .25s to fit any ballistics requirement for whitetail deer.

WHAT ARE THEY THINKING?

In most cases I would be the last guy to ever come down as dictating guns and loads for sport hunting. I don't like the massive shooting restrictions encountered so often especially in many of the eastern states. However, as illustrated in the main body of this review, the .224 caliber family of cartridges tends to come up short in the delivered performance department even at close range when the smaller .222 Mag and .223 Remington have been used afield. The more you move up the energy and velocity, as with the .22-250, .220 Swift or .223 WSSM, the more happens in the energy contact department. However, often the reaction of the animal to a hit is a "walk off" – not good when it comes to tracking time, as penetration is poor and blood trail faint. Under these circumstances, a day can become very long indeed.

Trying to get a good reason for turning with these light calibers is like pulling teeth. I would suspect that the main popularity of many small-bore "big game guns" centers around the fact that so many hunters own .223 Remington-chambered rifles of the " black gun" type nowadays. Another factor may be that so many so-called "ladies' and youth" bolt guns are chambered in light .22 centerfires. Even so, shooting a Model 70 Feather Weight in .25 WSSM, or even a .243 Winchester in a Remington Model Seven, doesn't increase weight much if at all, and as for recoil, well, if you can't handle a .243 or .25 you're better off taking up some other form of outdoor activity.

Currently I have been shooting an outstanding H.S. Precision ultra lightweight turn bolt chambered in .25 WSSM that is nothing less then a one-hole tack-driver off the bench rest. With this rifle there is a big bang, with no follow-up recoil. The complete scoped rifle weighs no more (under seven pounds net weight) than a lightweight .223 Remington as offered by many companies. Will I give up on lightweight cartridges for general use? No way! But I'll go with something a bit bigger, thank you, when I'm taking out after whitetail, mule deer, or even speed goats.

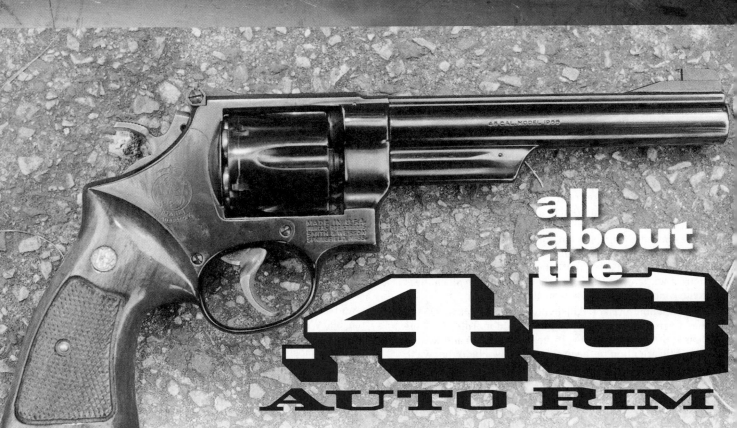

all about the .45 AUTO RIM

The author's much-appreciated Smith and Wesson .45 Auto Rim revolver. This is possibly the most versatile big bore ever produced.

BY ROBERT H. CAMPBELL

I enjoy firing a number of pretty odd handguns simply for their own sake. Like many of you, I find calibers both new and old a challenge to fully develop in terms of accuracy and power. But when it comes to real work, such as harvesting game or winning competition, logic dictates the proper choice.

Among the handgun calibers I enjoy the most are those that give results out of proportion to their paper ballistics. The .44-40, .45 Colt and .45 Auto Rim are relatively mild to fire. The big, heavy bullets they use don't break any speed records. But their effect on the target – be it a game animal, falling plate or the inoffensive ten pin – is impressive. I do not enjoy firing hard-kicking magnums nearly as much as the milder big bores. When I need more power than is available from a six-inch barrel .45 Auto Rim revolver, I consider a rifle rather than a longer, heavier, more powerful handgun. The man who masters the .500 Magnum has my respect, but when I feel the game outclasses my handguns, a rifle such as the Mauser Engineer's carbine is much handier, and easier on me, than a hard kicking Magnum. But that's me.

I am sure my affinity for the big bore revolver is related in some manner to my appreciation for the 1911 .45 caliber semi-auto. But the die was cast at an early age. Let's just say I owned a big

The 25-5 revolver, top, is heavier and has better sights than the 1917, bottom, but either can serve well in their intended roles. Note Ahrends grips on the 1917.

bore revolver before high school and the 1911 came along after I was driving and owned my own vehicle. No matter how many 1911s I eventually own, I can never change the fact that my first .45 was a humble and well-worn 1917 revolver.

Even today, my battery includes several 45 ACP handguns that are not autoloaders. These revolvers are more versatile than any semi-auto and can be loaded with a wider selection of bullets. The edge in power goes to the revolver for reasons we will cover in due course. I am not, however, going to argue that the .45 Auto Rim, a companion to the .45 ACP in revolver chamberings, is more efficient than the .44-40 or the .45 Colt. The differences are probably conversational at best. But the .45 ACP/AR revolver is the ideal big bore revolver for the man who also owns .45 caliber self-loaders.

An observation that I must make is that the .45 Auto Rim is among a very few revolver cartridges designed from the start for use with smokeless powder. The .44-40, .45 Colt and the .44 Special are longer cases, designed to perform well with bulky black powder. The .45 Colt in particular demands attention to detail. The .45 AR is much more straightforward, with good results with practically any powder. The .45 AR can be a miser with powder, producing good results with light charges of fast burning powder. But each cartridge has its place.

If you're not familiar with the .45 Auto Rim, perhaps bit of history is in order.

IN THE BEGINNING

The .45 AR is something of an accident, but it was also a fortunate turn of events for the handgunner.

The .45 AR came to life in 1920, using a short cartridge case that is simply a thick-rimmed .45 ACP case. This gives the .45 AR a tremendous advantage in the use of controlled amounts of faster-burning powder. A full powder burn, limited muzzle flash and blast and mild recoil are more easily realized with the .45 Auto Rim than with any other big bore cartridge.

The story of the 1917 revolvers is well-known but must be told again. Considering the material shortages across the nation as we entered World War I, it is a surprise Krag rifles were not sent to Europe! The Springfield was in short supply but a production line in full swing, supporting the British, supplied the Enfield 1917. In like fashion, Colt and Smith and Wesson production lines were producing large-frame .455 caliber

Big and heavy, this old Colt New Service 1917 is also very smooth and accurate.

revolvers for the British. Production of these handguns, which were based on the Colt New Service and S&W New Century respectively, was diverted to the US Army. The Army did not wish to use .455 caliber revolvers; neither did they wish to use the .45 Colt cartridge. The .45 Colt is designed for button-ejecting single action revolvers and does not translate as well to double action star-ejecting revolvers. The big .45's case rim has a tendency to hang under the ejector star. Most of all the Army did not wish to have two handgun cartridges in the inventory, anyway. A solution was developed to allow the revolvers to chamber the .45 ACP cartridge.

Chambering a revolver for the .45 ACP cartridge isn't a problem. Ejecting the rimless .45 ACP cartridge presented more difficulty. The now-famous moon clip solved this difficulty. The thin sheet metal clip was originally issued in pairs, with two three-round clips needed to fully load the revolver. After the gun load was fired, a rap on the ejector rod threw all six cases out at once. Naturally, fired and unfired cases would be ejected simultaneously. This system created the most efficient loading and ejecting system ever used in a revolver. No matter what the angle of the muzzle, there was no possibility of the spent cases jamming under the ejector star. All were ejected at once.

Also, a moon-clipped revolver is the fastest revolver of all to reload. Whether the muzzle is pointed up or down, it is possible to quickly load the .45 ACP

Smooth, reliable, hand-fitted. The original 1917 is a good revolver, among the best choices for personal defense.

The author often totes this 1917 Smith and Wesson when hiking or simply spelunking.

This photograph illustrates the three types of .45 ACP/AR headspacing. The cartridges at the top are .45 ACP rounds, held by a two-round moon clip. On the bottom left are two .45 ACP cartridges simply loaded in the chamber, and finally two .45 AR cartridges. The author feels the .45 AR solution makes the most sense.

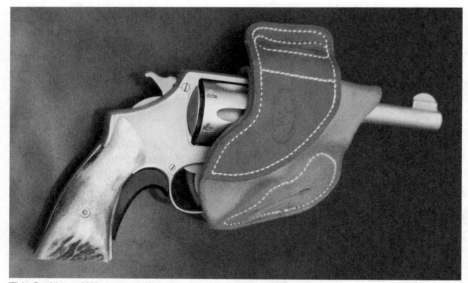

This Smith and Wesson 1917 is fast handling and powerful. The revolver has been Meta Life plated and fitted with Ajax stag grips. Carried in a Tucker belt slide, this is as good as it gets in a defensive revolver.

revolver with moon clips and remain in business. It seems doubtful this system would have been developed outside the crucible or war, but it worked well. How much use the 1917 revolvers saw is another matter. Used they were, by military police, drivers, and tank personnel, while front line troops received the lion's share of 1911 self loaders. If I could not have gotten my hands on a 1911, I would not have felt naked with a good 1917. I am sure a few doughboys preferred the familiar revolver.

After the war, many 1917s were sold as surplus. Some went to bank guards, others went to the fledging US Border Patrol, and quite a few were used by outdoorsmen. After all, here was a good double action big bore revolver at a modest price.

Most of the shooting public, however, did not care for moon clips. They were seen as a nuisance at best. Since the .45 ACP cartridge headpaced on the case mouth and not on the rim, the 1917-pattern revolvers could be fired without the clips, but the cases had to be picked out one at a time, a tedious process. Remington introduced a solution in 1920: the .45 Auto Rim. The .45 Auto Rim is basically a rimmed .45 ACP, with a rather thick head in relation to the short case. It is not interchangeable with the dimensionally similar .45 Schofield. Enterprising handloaders (is there any other type?) learned the .45 AR offered a couple of advantages over the .45 ACP, other than the obvious simplicity of chambering without the aid of moon clips: the case head is stronger and offers more support, allowing heavier loads, and the .45 AR is well-suited to lead bullet loads, something that could not always be said of the .45 ACP round as fired from the 1911. The original .45 AR factory loading produced 830 fps with a 230-grain round nose lead bullet. Today, to the best of my knowledge, the .45 Auto Rim is loaded by Georgia Arms on a standard basis and is available from custom maker Quality Cartridge as well. (Note that as of this writing, most ammunition makers are experiencing heavy delays and backorders.) The tried-and-true Remington loading has, regrettably, disappeared from Big Green's catalog, and it is doubtful whether it will ever reappear.

The best news to come along in some time is the availability of .45 Auto Rim brass from at least one manufacturer: Starline. With these high quality cartridge cases, the .45 Auto Rim fan has a reliable resource and may reasonably stretch his .45 AR to accommodate heavy loads.

The bulk of .45 Auto Rim ammunition was fired in the 1917 revolvers. Elmer Keith designed a semi-wadcutter bullet just for the short chambers of this revolver (238-grain Lyman #452423 – now sadly out of production but occasionally available on the used market). Short chambers are the one real failing of the .45 AR. The 1917s and even some

The Star Bullets 185-gr. SWC HP performed beyond expectation. This is excellent expansion at low velocity.

Left to right, the 185-gr. Star bullet with experiments in seating depth, the 200-gr. Speer Gold Dot in .45 AR brass, the 240-gr. Sierra JHP and the 230-gr. XTP, all good loadings for specific uses.

The Sierra bullet at left has been deep seated; no need to worry about feed reliability in the revolver. But be certain to reduce powder charge when experimenting with deeper seating of heavy bullets.

At maximum velocities, the Speer Gold Dot, left, gave good results and the Sierra 240-gr. JHP shows uneven expansion. The 230-gr. weights are best suited to standard .45 ACP velocity.

.45 AUTO RIM LOAD DATA

Note: All loads loaded on RCBS equipment, all primers standard Winchester Large Pistol primers. All brass is Starline. All handloads listed were fired for testing in the Smith & Wesson 1955 target revolver.

JACKETED BULLETS

Bullet	Grains/Powder	Muzzle Velocity	5-shot group/ 25 yards (")
Nosler 185-gr. JHP	5.5 Titegroup	956 fps	1.9
Nosler 185-gr. JHP	8.5 Unique	1066 fps	2.5
Sierra 185-gr. JHP	8.5 Unique	1099 fps	2.1
Sierra 185-gr. FMJ	7.5 Unique	956 fps	1.2
Sierra 185-gr. JHP	6.5 Bullseye	1023 fps	1.6
Speer Gold Dot 185-gr. JHP	7.0 HP38	990 fps	2.0
Speer Gold Dot 185-gr. JHP	5.5 Titegroup	970 fps	2.2
Hornady 200-gr. XTP	7.5 Unique	965 fps	1.6
Gold Dot 200-gr.	8.2 Power Pistol	980 fps	1.9
Sierra 200-gr. FMJ	7.4 Unique	941 fps	1.5
Sierra 200-gr. FMJ	8.2 Power Pistol	1001 fps	1.8
Hornady 230-gr. XTP	7.2 Unique	923 fps	1.8
Hornady 230-gr. XTP	7.0 Power Pistol	878 fps	1.7
Sierra 230-gr. JHP	6.8 Unique	876 fps	1.5
Sierra 230-gr. MATCH	5.2 Bullseye	829 fps	1.8
Sierra 240-gr. JHP *	7.0 Unique	907 fps	1.0
Montana Gold 230-gr. FMJ	6.8 Unique	909 fps	1.2

* This is a good load, very accurate, but the bullet is designed for the .45 Colt. I don't believe you will see any expansion on game at this velocity. But just the same it is among the most accurate .451-inch bullets, not only in the .45 AR but in my .45 ACP and .460 Rowland pistols as well. It certainly has enough penetration for most purposes.

LEAD BULLETS

Bullet	Grains/Powder	Muzzle Velocity	5-shot group/ 25 yards (")
185-gr. Star SWC HP	5.4 Unique	680 fps	2.0
	3.6 Bullseye	701 fps	2.2
	5.0 Bullseye	899 fps	2.6
BallistiCast 207-gr. nominal			
200-gr. SWC	5.8 Accurate #2	901 fps	1.7
200-gr. SWC	7.8 Accurate #7	860 fps	1.9
200-gr. SWC	6.5 Unique	926 fps	2.1
200-gr. Oregon Trail	4.5 Bullseye	808 fps	1.25
225-gr. FP Oregon Trail	5.0 Bullseye	824 fps	1.6
	7.0 Unique	932 fps	1.5
	4.2 231	670 fps	2.0
Accu Cast 250-gr. SWC	5.0 Accurate #2	790 fps	1.8
	6.0 Unique	860 fps	1.9
Dry Creek 255-gr. SWC 6.5	Accurate #5	780 fps	2.0
	6.0 Unique	840 fps	1.6
	7.0 Unique	933 fps	2.0
	13.0 2400*	1029 fps	1.5

modern 625s will not accept the longer 250-grain bullets, so the 200- to 240-grain SWCs are used. The 1955 Targets usually accept heavier bullets. Also, some of the modern runs of 625s will not function properly without moon clips when firing the .45 ACP. They simply will not headspace correctly unless .45 AR or clipped .45 ACP cartridges are used.

When the heavy barrel 1955 models came along, handloaders worked up combinations that gained a new respect for the .45 AR. With its heavy barrel, target stocks and full length ejector rod housing, the new revolver was heavier and more pleasant to use than any 1917. The .45 AR's stronger head and the fact that the cartridge case is better supported in the revolver than the .45 ACP in the 1911 autoloader allowed the cartridge to considerably outperform the .45 ACP. The .45 AR is about as strong as a safe load in the Colt SAA in .45 Colt. For medium game and as a defense load, this is an outstanding caliber.

I appreciate the combat advantages of a .45 ACP revolver with moon clips, and have used this combination successfully in bowling pin shoots. But with top accuracy and hunting more my focus these days, I use the .45 AR for the most part. For informal shooting I sometimes use the more common .45 ACP brass without clips, although some revolvers lose accuracy potential when fired in this manner due to inconsistent headspacing. I have read comments from writers in the popular press who have stated that it is good to have a 1917 revolver on hand to shoot up your off-spec .45

A fine set of adjustable sights goes a long way in achieving consistent accuracy. Smith and Wesson micro sights offer a good sight picture and excellent adjustment.

These cartridges are clipped into two-round moon clips from Ranch Products. When loading a 50-round box for use in the .45 ACP revolver, these moon clips allow easy loading for immediate use – a good idea!

ACP handloads. This is one short step up from lunacy. First, who wants to make up poor handloads? The revolver is more tolerant of light loads and a less than perfect crimp, true, but a high primer or less than perfect headspace is detrimental to revolver function. Pull those bad handloads and try again!

Some of the 625s are accurate but I maintain the 1955s (marked 25-5 in modern production) are the most accurate .45 AR revolvers. Remember, some revolvers will not use heavy bullets such as the 250-grain XTP or some 255-grain SWCs, so make up a dummy round or two before beginning your loading program.

I have used a large number of cast bullets in my revolvers. A handgun that is going to live with me must digest lead bullets. This proletarian diet offers good economy and accuracy. I have made use of the .45 AR's great versatility in producing a number of gallery loads. Hornady's .457-inch lead ball, intended for black powder revolvers, works just fine over 3.0 gr. of Bullseye or 5.0 gr. of

Unique, for 550 to 650 fps, respectively. The round nose bullet doesn't have much range but its power is respectable. At 15 yards, this load will cut one ragged hole. Be careful in ensuring that you crimp the round ball properly or you will sacrifice bullet pull and ignition will be erratic as a result. The neat 160-grain SWC offered by Hunter's Trail performs well, too. For teaching a novice to shoot, this is a fine bullet with good accuracy but little recoil. 4.0 gr. of Bullseye is all that is needed. This is a hard-cast bullet that will not lead if loaded a bit hotter, but I have not done so. It is a good light bullet for target use at moderate range and really does the business.

These light bullets are really trick bullets but that's fine – they serve a real purpose. The more appropriate weights begin at 185 grains. I have to say that a special bullet that has impressed me is the Star 185-grain SWC HP. I have used quite a few in the .45 Auto. It's a swaged bullet, and its accuracy is outstanding with leading not too bad if velocity is kept below 900 fps. I wondered if the hollowpoint was for balance or if the bullet would expand in ballistic media. Only when I began to load these bullets in the .45 AR did I test expansion. I was surprised! Beginning at 750 fps the bullets expanded, and at 850 fps expansion was impressive. This would be a fine small game bullet, even a defense bullet for home use. As a bonus, accuracy is excellent and recoil light. Unlike jacketed bullets, you do not have to push this bullet hard to achieve expansion.

200-grain SWCs are nearly always accurate, and if driven fast enough they can be good hunting bullets. Ejected from my BallistiCast mold at 205 grains, the 200-grain SWC is especially accurate. When I go the store-bought route, Oregon Trail and Leadhead have given fine results.

A heavier bullet is the 225-grain flat-point so popular in the .45 ACP. This bullet is murder on bowling pins, far more effective than the 230-grain RNL. That little flat on the nose simply does the business. The 225-grain FP is a compromise, as a true SWC often is a bit harder to stuff in the cylinders quickly when using moon-clipped .45 ACP ammunition in competition. When shooting IDPA I use RNL bullets, but for pins you have got to have a flat point or SWC for effect. Simply because they are available and inexpensive, I have used many 230-grain RNL bullets in the .45 AR, always with good results. The last batch was from Magnus bullets. Heavier are the 250-grain bullets from Oregon Trail. Designed for the .45 Colt, I have enjoyed these bullets to no end. They hit hard even at moderate velocity and give a resounding WHACK! on meeting steel plates. I like that. The 255-grain Dry Creek Bullet Works SWC is efficiency in lead at its best, an accurate bullet that gives good accuracy. While all of these bullets have good points and some are more fun than others to use, if I were limited to only one or two, the 200-grain SWC and the 225-grain FP would get the nod.

If you are using one of the 1917 revolvers, sight regulation is an issue and the lighter and heavier bullets may not be viable, even if the heavy bullets will work in the short 1917 cylinder. The 230-grain bullets will generally strike an inch or two high at 25 yards while the 200-grain bullet will strike to the point of aim. Lighter bullets can be really low, on the order of four inches, with no easy way to adjust the sights, unless you wish to permanently sight the gun by file work for the lighter bullets. There are none of these problems with the 1955 target models. You may be able to raise bullet impact in a fixed-sight revolver by increasing barrel time, i.e., by lowering velocity, but in doing so you necessarily degrade performance a bit. Conversely, you can usually lower point of impact by increasing the velocity, provided you don't exceed published load data and don't mind the possibility of increased leading.

In jacketed bullets, the 185-grain bullets may offer excellent accuracy and good expansion. I have enjoyed excellent results with the 185-grain Sierra in both regards. I admit to less experience with the Nosler but it too has given good results. The original bullet weight Browning envisioned when working with the fledging .45 ACP was 200-gr.s, but the Army demanded a 230-grain bullet. The 200-grain bullet often offers good balance betweeen the two. The 200-grain Hornady XTP, at 1000 fps, will penetrate 16 inches or more of ballistic media and open to .68 caliber. Bill Wilson of Wilson Combat prefers this bullet to any other and offers a special load from his shop using this bullet. Accuracy is good. The standard 230-grain weight bullets are still the best choice in jacketed hollowpoints for all around use. The XTP offers the most penetration, the Sierra opens the quickest, and the Gold Dot offers a good balance of expansion and penetration. A largely overlooked choice is the Winchester 230-grain JHP, offered in bulk quantities. This bullet expands like a heavy Silvertip, with excellent repeatability – it works from 800 fps with best results about 860 fps. I would feel very comfortable with this bullet in a personal defense load. For a general defense and hunting load, the 230s offer a fertile field. I think the hunter will probably prefer the XTP but the others offer considerable utility.

The Montana Gold bullets in both FMJ and hollowpoint form are designed for match grade accuracy. I am working my way through several thousand at this point. While I originally intended to use most in my GI .45s, the bullets have proven accurate in my .45 AR loads. I prefer a bullet that can be crimped for heavy AR loads, in case the bullet would jump the crimp and tie the cylinder up, but so far nothing I have used in the .45 AR has generated this type of recoil. So, the RNL bullets have performed fine.

Moving to the heavy weights we find the Sierra 240-grain JHP as the heaviest jacketed bullet we can feasibly use in the .45 AR. Designed for the .45 Colt, the Sierra bullet features a crimping groove. At the velocities we obtained with this bullet, expansion is simply not there. Still, accuracy is excellent and there is some expansion of the nose, along with deep penetration. For hunting thin-skinned game I prefer a heavy SWC but the Sierra could serve at moderate range.

When all is said and none, I could easily get by with a handful of standard loads. A good 200-grain SWC load for the 1917s, a 225-grain FP for bowling pins, a 230-grain JHP for defense and a heavy SWC for game would do the business. But

SOURCES FOR MOON CLIPS

A note on moon clips: These devices are readily available, along with tools to unload the clips that make life a lot easier for the .45 ACP revolver fan. If you shoot in competition that requires a revolver speed load, these are the way to go.

TK Custom offers a demooning tool that removes spent cases from the clips, making a nasty chore much easier. Beckham produces a polymer clip for less serious use that works just fine in my revolvers.

Ranch Products offers a bewildering array of clips, including a neat two-round clip that allows the .45 ACP revolver shooter to have a box at ready in standard form but all mooned up.

Ranch Products
PO 145, Malinta Ohio 43535
www.ranchproducts.com

RMZ Beckham Design
866-726-2658

Quality Cartridge
www.qualitycartridge.com
888-643-8023

TK Customs
404 Fox Ridge Road, Rantour Illinois 61866
www.moonclips.com

I enjoy an experiment and also enjoy my light gallery or plinking loads – if you call a load and handgun combination that's accurate well past 50 yards plinking!

The .45 AR has a lot going for it. Accuracy, economy, comfort and real power are just a start. If you have a .45 ACP revolver that has been languishing for lack of proper loads, break it out and give it an honest appraisal. You just may find my favorite revolver cartridge has much merit.

BY JIM DICKSON

THE RETURN OF THE KRIEGHOFF LUGER

2006 marked the return of the Krieghoff Luger to production after a lapse of over 60 years. A limited edition of 200 guns was begun, built by hand to the Best Quality standards of a Dickson, Purdey, or Holland & Holland double, with the sole exception that the WWII finish is applied instead of the finish of a Best Quality double. The parts were all hand-fitted and finished by one man, master gunsmith Frank Kaltenpoth, the same way a Best Quality double is made. The enormous hours of handwork are reflected in the Best Quality price of $17,545 and the fact that production is still underway as I write this in 2009.

This is the only Best Quality production run of a pistol in history. It is fitting that this tribute to the Luger is being made by Krieghoff because they made the finest Lugers of all time during WWII. Krieghoff was the only Luger manufacturer to achieve 100% interchangeability of parts without any hand-fitting: a monumental achievement and a milestone in the history of mass production.

Krieghoff is no stranger to Best Quality guns. Their Essencia is a handmade traditional Best Quality sidelock shotgun built to be the equal of anything made by the best British makers. The Luger is the only pistol worthy of this level of treatment simply because it is the only pistol that has a service life measured in the millions of rounds. This is because it is a miniature pistol version of the Maxim machinegun, the only machinegun design that can fire 10 million rounds and still be good to go. Of course we are talking about regular barrel changes along the way here. The Luger also is one of the designs that works better if precisely fitted. The higher the quality of the fit of the parts, the better it works – just like a Best Quality double. Some designs work best with lots of slop in the parts, while others like just a !little and some like everything as tight as possible for the best reliability under all conditions. The Luger is one of the latter.

A LITTLE BACKGROUND

The pistol popularly known as the Luger began to take shape in 1893 when Hugo Borchardt, inspired by the success of the Maxim machinegun, built his toggle action automatic pistol. But this was not Maxim's heavy, robust, virtually jam-proof design with plenty of places for dirt to hide. The Borchardt featured a toggle that was very lightweight and bottomed out on the bottom of the pistol, where enough dirt can jam the gun. It's an overcentered, toggle-leveraged action, which means the toggle lock was over the centerline of the cartridge. This mechanism is an inclined plane so the action doesn't open on itself.

The longer the cartridge and the greater the mass of the gun, the better the Borchardt worked. In a lightweight gun with a

Krieghoff 1-of-200 Luger, action open. Note the exquisite finish and straw coloring on the trigger and safety.

The quality of the Krieghoff Essencia hand-made Best Quality sidelock shotgun rivals that of the finest British doubles. The Krieghoff Lugers are made to precisely the same standards.

short cartridge, you get too fast a cycle time for proper feeding. The slower burning the powder, the slower the breechblock goes back, thus partially offsetting a fast action cycle. Therefore Hugo Borchardt decided to put a 7.63 bullet of 85 grains in a bottlenecked case with slow burning powders for a velocity of 1,280 fps. Mauser would later take this cartridge and increase the velocity to 1,410 fps for his M1896 Mauser military pistol. The Borchardt had a vertical grip, so there was virtually no drag on the cartridges as they were fed through the magazine, which contributed greatly to its reliability.

Reliable or not, the Borchardt was a clumsy, strange-looking gun. If it were ever to sell, something had to be done. The rights to the Borchardt pistol were owned by Ludwig Loewe of DWM (*Deutsche Waffen und Munitionsfabriken*). Ignoring the original designer, he turned the redesign over to Georg Luger. It was time for the ugly duckling to turn into a beautiful swan, a swan that combined ergonomic and esthetic perfection in a remarkably lightweight all-steel gun of just 30 ounces.

Georg Luger had considered well the needs of a combat shooter: the beautiful new gun had the fastest possible toggle release. The toggle stayed open on the last shot; you changed the magazine and gave the toggle a quick tap with the hand that inserted the magazine and you resumed firing. The bulge at the bottom of the front of the frame was hollowed out to facilitate loading a magazine that might be jammed in at the wrong angle by a soldier under fire with his eyes on the enemy instead of the gun. The lanyard loop is in the perfect position above the hand to steady the gun in firing. In addition, the magazine release was so perfectly designed and positioned that it was copied on the M1911 .45 automatic.

The new gun was a beauty, the belle of the ball. Everywhere people were entranced by its striking appearance and the new-found ease of hitting the target with a pistol that it offered. The Luger's legendary handling qualities took the shooting world by storm. Switzerland was first to adopt it in 1900, with Germany adopting it in 1908 (hence the P08, or *Pistole 08*, nomenclature). Many more nations adopted it and still more bought large qualities. At last there was a pistol that seemed to accurately aim itself!

The transition of Borchardt to Luger without the input of Hugo Borchardt

was not perfect, though. The Borchardt lock was carefully balanced to the recoil impulse of the 7.63 Borchardt cartridge. Luger used the same lock with shorter, higher-intensity rounds without adding the mass to the lock to compensate for them, which resulted in excessively fast action cycling times. This became a critical problem when the grip angle was changed from the vertical Borchardt grip to the steeply angled Luger grip, where the drag on the cartridge reduced the magazine spring's efficiency to only 60%. A powerful magazine spring that is strong enough to require the use of a loading tool was needed on the Luger to be sure that the magazine could feed the cartridge up to the proper position before the breech closes prematurely, jamming the gun. This is the cause of almost all Luger malfunctions.

You really can't have a Luger's magazine spring too strong. American

Like all Lugers, the Krieghoff has an immediately-identifiable profile.

gun designer Max Atchisson once managed to get a spring in a Luger magazine so powerful that even with a loading tool he could only load five rounds. That gun was unjammable, cycling the hottest loads effortlessly. British Best Quality gunmaker Giles Whittome once put one coil spring inside another in a Luger magazine, resulting in a magazine that was a beast to load but effortlessly cycled the hot "For Submachinegun Use Only" British Sterling SMG ammo at over 1400 fps. The need for a powerful magazine spring is the reason that the WWI Luger magazines with their wooden bottoms were later replaced with extruded magazines with aluminum bottoms that could accomodate stronger springs for greater reliability. Overall cartridge length is important also. The steep angle of the magazine is only 1.070 inches front to back, which dictates a maximum overall cartridge length of 1.180 inches with very little under that acceptable.

While the Luger likes a slow push recoil, the Browning-design pistols of today like a hot primer and a sharp recoil. Consequently most of today's ammo is made for their functioning needs, which are the exact opposite of the Luger's. Also, their overall length does not always lie within the Luger's

operating lengths. Like the M16, the Luger is sensitve about the ammo used in it.

To keep the lock from cycling too fast, the WWI German Army Luger load was a 115-grain bullet at 1,025 fps. A slow-burning, single-base nitrocellulose powder with a high silica content that slowed ignition coupled with slightly underpowered low-flame primers gave a slower burning curve and a slower push, resulting in a slower cyclic time to allow proper feeding and reliability. WWII ammo was also slower burning but with a 124-grain bullet and, later, a 130-grain bullet. Mauser Werke altered the spring strength of the German Army's Lugers for this ammunition. Ammunition marked for machinepistol use (MP-38, MP-40) was loaded with extra-hot primers that make the Luger cycle too fast for reliability. The best American powder for Lugers is Red Dot shotgun powder as it most closely equals the WWI powder's burning and acceleration rate. 4.1 grains of Red Dot and a 115-grain bullet will give 997 FPS and 3.9 grains of Red Dot and a 124-grain bullet will give 1,025 FPS. Winchester primers are the best American primers for Lugers because they are the least likely to be pierced by the Luger's long firing pin. When that happens, gas can go back through the firing pin hole, pushing the firing pin and spring back and ripping the back out of the breechblock. The extractor may also be forced up and torn out of the breechblock.

Prior to WWII, Germany put three relief grooves in the firing pin to let the pressure from a pierced primer go past the firing pin instead of driving it as a piston backwards. The Finns drilled a hole in the bottom of the breechblock into the firing pin area to bleed gas off in their guns.

Materialkarte P08

Laut	X	Nummer:
Hülse	X	
Hintergelenk	X	Kunde: _Krieghoff Ammond_
Abzugstange		
Abzugstangenbolzen		Sonderwünsche:
Abzugstangenfeder	X	
Auswerfer	X	
Kammer		
Schlagbolzen		
Schlagbolzenfeder		
Federkolben		
Bolzen Ka/VG		
Auszieher		
Auszieherfeder	X	
Auszieherstift	X	
Vordergelenk	X	
Bolzen VG/HG		
Bolzen HG/Hü		
Griffstück	X	
Sperrstück	X	
Sperrstückfeder	X	
Kammerfangstück	X	
Kammerfangfeder	X	
...riegel	X	
...ebel	X	
...ebelstift	X	
...riss...	X	
...riffs...enschrauben		
...agazi...		
...eckplatte		
...bzugwinkelhebel	X	
...bzugshebelstift		
...upplungshebel		
...upplungshebelstift	X	
...upplungsstange		
...chließfeder	X	
...agazinhalter	X	
...agazinhalterfeder	X	
...orn	X	
...eder Abzugstange	X	
...chlüssel	X	

A grouping of unfinished Krieghoff Luger parts from the bench of master gunsmith Frank Kaltenpoth.

The 9mm Parabellum cartridge has always presented problems for gun designers because its tapered case can give uneven pressures in an automatic.

The tapered case grips the chamber and if there is dirt in the vicinity, the tapered case wedges in it and jams instead of pushing it forward into the chamber as a straight case does. As a result, no 9mm Parabellum can function reliably with a rough or dirty chamber. The 9mm Parabellum also has a high chamber pressure of 36,000 psi, which can rise into the low 40,000 psi range if a bullet is bumped and set back into the case. This is not the sort of pressure the light Borchardt toggle liked and, remember, it was not beefed up in mass when it became the Luger.

The tapered 9mm cases also gave feeding problems in the Luger's sharply-inclined magazine where they tend to tilt and create extra drag in addition to the side drag, resulting in a magazine that has difficulty feeding cartridges to the super-fast toggle action before the bolt rides into the top side of the cartridge instead of the cartridge base because the cartridge hasn't had time to rise up to full feeding position. The problem was compounded by the Luger's incredibly light weight of 30 ounces, which lets the muzzle flip up more in recoil as the cartridges in the magazine are simultaneously driven down by that flip – this on a magazine whose angle of feed dictates that it be so precisely positioned that a worn magazine catch or a magazine that hangs too low will cause feeding jams.

Georg Luger had originally designed his gun for the .30 Luger cartridge, which was well balanced to the design. Someone took the case and opened it up to 9mm for a bolt action "garden gun" cartridge, in which role its tapered case was an aid to extraction. About this time, the German police experienced several failures of the 93-grain .30 Luger to stop a determined assailant, so DWM ordered Georg Luger to chamber the Luger for the new 9mm cartridge as this would only require rebarreling. Georg pointed out the aforementioned objections plus the fact that the heavier bullet would have a larger recoil impulse than the lightweight toggle had sufficient mass to resist. Bottom line: business cost-cutting overruled the designer and Georg's protests fell on deaf ears.

To his credit, Georg Luger made the gun work with a less than perfect cartridge for it. When you consider the initial strikes against it and the final outcome, you realize that this is one of the finest triumphs of German firearms engineering.

The Luger was inspired by the Maxim Machinegun and indeed Hiram Maxim referred to it as a Maxim machinegun in pistol form. (He also considered it a patent infringement.) Like the Maxim, the Luger is an incredibly long-lived gun. According to Alfred Gallifent, a Swiss Federal Certified Armorer who was qualified to work on the Swiss Army's Lugers, the five most common Luger repairs in order of frequency were 1) the grip screws were buggered up by someone with an ill-fitting screwdriver; 2) the L-shaped spring that retains the takedown lever would break; 3) the leaf spring on the M1900 would break; 4) the receiver forks would break when some idiot dropped it on concrete; and 5) the transfer bar from the trigger to the sear was buggered up by people tinkering with it and bending it in an attempt to get a better trigger pull.

When these are the most common repairs on guns in continuous service since 1900, you have a most excellent design.

Precision machining at its finest.

The Krieghoff Luger in its high-tech case, itself something of a work of art.

The Krieghoff Luger, disassembled.

THE NEW KRIEGHOFF

An enormous amount of research went into ensuring that the new Krieghoff Lugers were absolutely perfect continuations of the WWII production run. Krieghoff's production drawings did not all survive the war intact but the Bavarian Main State Archives, Department 4, War Archives in Munich had the "Dimension Tables" for the P08. Original Krieghoff P-code pistols were carefully studied to ensure exact duplication of the technical details unique to the Krieghoff Luger. Precise duplicates of the original marking stamps such as the Krieghoff "sword/anchor logo" were made. Molds were made to produce duplicates of the original military brown bakelite grips and tooling produced to once more make the WWII Krieghoff PO8 magazine and aluminum magazine bottom. Original gun barrels were copied to make the correct land and groove pattern on the new barrels. This is unheard-of attention to technical detail in a recreation.

Great attention was given to getting the precise bluing colors of the original, a job complicated by new environmental laws banning some of the original ingredients in the blueing formulas. However, Krieghoff succeeded with true Teutonic precision. Every color is absolutely the

same. The full attention of this German industrial giant was devoted to getting every detail exactly right. The finish has no tool marks except for the obligatory milling machine swirls in the safety area which also had to be exactly reproduced. A Luger without these would just not be an authentic Luger.

The parts all begin as precision forgings for maximum strength. The original alloys are used where they are still available and when new ones had to be substituted, careful chemical experimentation was done to be sure the bluing was exactly the same as the originals on the new alloys. Most people would not be able to tell the difference, but Krieghoff could, and only perfection was acceptable. The forgings were then sent to a modern five-axis CNC milling center to make the pieces that will be hand fitted together. The machine requires custom tools and contoured cutters.

The Krieghoff Luger's frame has more than 600 points where measurements are taken. A 13-pound forging is milled and broached down to a half-pound semi-finished frame. It takes 7.5 hours to reduce 20 to 25 pistol frames to this stage with the most modern production equipment. The rear cuts to hold the trigger sear flat spring proved a difficult problem to solve, as did many others in the 100-year-old design. This gun was not intended for easy modern production. Specialized broaches like the one used to cut the slide guides in the side of the frame had to be made. It should be noted that it is a huge financial undertaking to tool up to make the Luger or any other gun, and Krieghoff has not done that – nor could anyone – for a mere 200 guns. What they could do was machine it to a point that a master gunsmith could take over with his hand files and hand-make it the rest of the way in the same manner that Best Quality doubles are hand-filed from forgings provided by a blacksmith. Believe me, it is a long way to go. You are paying one of the world's greatest gunsmiths to hand-make you a pistol just as he would hand-make a Best Quality double shotgun or rifle. You are getting every cent's worth of the price. Indeed, Krieghoff cut profits to the bone on this tribute to their old friend the Luger. The guns are only sold direct to the customer without a middleman to keep the price below $20,000. This is a true labor of love by Krieghoff.

The artist doing all the hand work on the Krieghoff Luger is Frank Kaltenpoth.

While the English gun trade has tended to keep their gunmakers at the bench and away from the fame they are due as individual artists, this attitude has actually worked against them, as today most people imagine "Best Quality" guns to be mostly machine-made. Nothing could be further from the truth, and that mistake is not to be repeated with the Krieghoff P08.

Frank Kaltenpoth was born on October 20, 1963, the son of a lockmaker. He started his apprenticeship as a gunsmith at Ferlach in 1980, graduating with honors in 1984. He then spent four years in military service as armorer in charge of all hand-held weapons and the main gun of the Leopard 1 tank in Panzer Battalion 134 of the German Army stationed in Wetzlar, Germany. He began working as a gunsmith at Kettner in Augsberg in October of 1988. After four years, he was eligible for the two-year master gunsmith course in Ulm, where he graduated with honors in June of 1993. He then worked for Kirstein, remodeling and custom-building M1911-A1 pistols. There he learned to use CNC machines to rough out a part to a point where he could hand-file and hand-fit a gun to Best Quality standards. Combining the latest machining techniques with traditional Best Quality handwork is a great skill and one that few men have. As befitting a great master, Kaltenpoth is technically self-employed but since 1999 has done work only for Krieghoff.

Krieghoff's production of the Luger pistol dates back to 1934, when they were awarded a Luftwaffe contract for 10,000 pistols. The last of these were delivered in 1937. Most significantly,

they delivered on the Luftwaffe's contract clause that required interchangeability of parts. Previously all Lugers were hand-fitted. Furthermore, they did this with a massive reduction in rejected parts during production, reducing Mauser's 40% rejection rate to a more acceptable 10% rejection rate. This heightened standard of machine production raised the bar for Mauser and the other German firms. For Krieghoff, it resulted in lucrative contracts to make the MG 15 and other weapons.

Both Mauser and Krieghoff remedied a problem found in the 1920s-vintage Lugers made by Simson. The top rear of the ear on either side of the Luger's frame must be of sufficient thickness to prevent the head of the rear toggle link axle being completely exposed as the toggle cycles. If fully exposed, the axle

The Luger is a natural pointer. Fully extend your arm, lock your eyes on the target, nestle your chin on your shoulder, and squeeze. Chances are you'll hit what you're aiming at.

Holsters for the Luger, left to right: Strong Leather pancake with thumb-break snap, post-war East German military, and fast-draw pancake without safety strap from El Paso Saddlery.

(or pin, if you prefer) can drift out during recoil and prevent the toggle from returning to battery. This was found to occur only on Simson Lugers, which had the most metal removed from this area. Mauser and Krieghoff both increased the thickness here beyond even that of the DWM Lugers to make sure this would not happen to a German soldier in combat. To draw attention to their fix, Mauser added an extra machining cut to produce a slight bulge over the area needing more thickness, a sight that many former Simson users found comforting.

The Luger is a gun well worthy of such attention to detail. It is the easiest pistol of all to hit with; nothing points faster or more accurately. It is the most accurate service pistol ever issued. Most Lugers will shoot 10mm groups or less at 25 meters, and the only repeating pistols that I know of that have shot a 1-inch minute of angle group at 100 yards are the Luger and the 8-3/4-inch-barreled S&W .44 Magnum, although the latter hardly qualifies as a service pistol because of its huge size, recoil, and inability to fire rapid fire. Despite the many slanders leaped on it by gun writers over the years, when given the correct ammo and a magazine with a powerful spring, the Luger is also one of the most reliable pistols in the world – the number one spot being held, of course, by the M1911-A1 .45 automatic.

These virtues enabled the Luger to become one of the top three gunfighting pistols of all time based on the number of kills made. The other two are the M1873 Colt Single Action Army revolver and the sainted M1911-A1. The latter

is the gun I carry but the fact remains that the Luger points better and is more accurate. It's the pistol I use for varmints and trick and fancy shooting.

The Luger was one of the most popular military pistols in the world in the first part of the 20th century. Many nations adopted it and used it in far-flung corners of the world, but its greatest combat use was by the German Army. The German soldier was not a pistoleer and did not know about instinct shooting without sights. In the rough and tumble brawl of trench raiding and close-quarters fighting, the P08's handling qualities gave him all the lessons he needed. It was quickly found that if you looked at the target and pointed the Luger at it, you usually hit exactly where you were looking. In the close confines of a trench, the Luger was a far more deadly weapon than the bolt action rifle and bayonet of his adversaries. The Luger continued to rack up its score through WWII, where German officers who intended to actually shoot someone with their pistol went for the Luger and those who wanted a pistol as a badge of rank opted for .32s. A good example was the SS officer who, as legend has it, was presented one of the first Walther P38s but continued to carry his Luger because he could hit better with it.

The Luger was often slandered by contemporary American gunwriters, perhaps out of an admirable sense of national pride or perhaps because they could do so without offending an advertiser. They attacked "the enemy's gun," the Luger, calling it unreliable and saying things such as, "If your Luger jams, use hot ammo. Lugers like hot ammo" and "The Luger's magazine spring is unnecessarily strong and makes it too hard to load. Clip a few coils off to make it easier." The truth is that Lugers don't like hot loads and they won't work with a weak magazine spring. Today, perhaps as many as nine out of 10 Luger magazines in the country have been shortened, causing jams.

As previously noted, the Luger is very ammo-sensitive and requires the strongest magazine spring possible. Give it this and it is reliable. As for its not working in the dirt, it performed perfectly in the maelstrom of flying mud and dirt of WWI while the vaunted S&W Triple Lock revolvers jammed in the mud. So much for revolver vs. automatic reliability! WWI settled that issue quite nicely. After WWI, the Luger was rather popular with the American cowboys.

It perfectly fit the chaps pocket, a notorious dirt and sand trap infamous for tying up revolvers with sand in their guts. When WWII came along, the Luger continued to shine.

The Luger was always carried in a holster designed for maximum protection from the elements. The German officer was expected to have the pistol in prime operating condition instead of trying to do a fast draw every time an enemy popped up. For modern civilian carry, I have never found anything better than the pancake holster design. It offers the best combination of concealability, comfort, and fast draw available. I have used this design ever since it first appeared many years ago. Here are two companies' versions:

Strong Leather Co. makes a classic molded thumb break pancake holster of the very highest quality for the Luger pistol that will meet any civilian or police needs. I have never been able to find fault with their work. Contact Strong Leather Co., P.O. Box 1195, 39 Grove St., Gloucester, Massachusetts, 01930.

A quick-draw pancake holster without a retaining strap is offered by El Paso Saddlery Co., 2025 East Yandell Dr., El Paso, Texas, 79903. This company began in the days of the Wild West and made holsters for the deadliest old West gunfighter of them all, John Wesley Hardin. They have the longest history of making fast-draw holsters of anyone. This is the holster to wear when action is imminent. It may not have a securing top strap for normal duty use, but, man, it is fast!

As we have seen, the Luger is one of the finest pistols ever made, and the new Krieghoff is the finest Luger ever made. As the late great Col. George Chinn, whose monumental five-volume series *The Machinegun* is the definitive work on machinegun mechanisms, once told me, "As long as nitrocellulose is our propellant, all possible mechanisms have already been invented. All that remains is to reconfigure existing systems into different guns." Pistols don't offer as many different tactical design configuration possibilities as shoulder arms, so the pistol got perfected early. Once you reach the summit, all roads lead downhill regardless of how new they are. So if you want the ultimate pistol, you get a M1911-A1 .45 automatic. If you want the best pointing, easiest to hit with, and most accurate pistol, you get a Luger.

And if you want the finest Luger, you get a new Krieghoff.

This blade type front sight is mounted in a dovetail slot. Drifting this sight to the right will move bullet impact to the left and vice versa. To raise point of impact, the sight is filed down. To lower point of impact, a taller front sight must be installed.

The British soldier was well-trained and immensely brave, willing to march through flames for his stalwart commanders. Then why is it that the mighty redcoats of the then greatest army in the world were slaughtered by American citizen-soldiers at the Battle of New Orleans in January of 1815? Sir Edward Michael Pakenham was one of the Queen's best, the leader of 8,000 crack men, while our own Andrew Jackson had 3,500 to 4,000 under him. Statistics vary, but they do not depart far from 385 Brits killed, 1,186 wounded and 484 captured, while the Americans suffered 13 dead, 58 wounded and 30 captured. You may read that the British soldier fought in rank and file while Jackson's boys sniped from trees and behind rocks. Not so, according to best records.

The Americans did have heavy artillery established in earthworks (bulwarks) called "Line Jackson" after the Major-General of the Tennessee Militia. That 32-pound gun, along with one 18-pounder, three 12s, three 6s, and one 6-inch howitzer, had to have a telling effect. However, the Brits knocked out several of these. Detailed specifics of the battle remain obscured in time's dark shadow, but General Pakenham's death by a volley of grape shot had to affect troop morale.

Regardless, I submit that the arrival of Tennessee Sharpshooters from Kentucky bode strong in the rout. These lads carried *rifles with iron sights*. The original Brown Bess musket I once fired weighed 11 pounds and was pole vault long, with a lump of metal at the end of the barrel pretending to be a front sight with no true rear sight for alignment.

Smoothbores had their advantages: faster to load in the heat of battle and easier to clean than rifled long guns. And the 75-caliber round ball from the Brown Bess was vicious – when that big hunk of lead found the mark. But putting that spherical bullet exactly on target was more wishful thinking than reality. The 19th century American rifle, on the other hand, "barked" tree squirrels for supper and pricked the enemy "a way off yonder." Rifling caused round bullets to spin on their axes, promoting equalization of discrepancies as well as stabilizing conical projectiles. But without good sights, the rifle would prove no more effective than smoothbore musket. Knowing this, early rifle makers developed a multitude of iron sight designs. W.W. Greener, in the 1910 Ninth Edition of his famous book, *The Gun and its Development*, illustrated several.

Greener writes of one example: "A favourite back-sight with South African sportsmen is the combined leaf, and tangent sight, for it is suitable both for game-shooting and target practice." This Cape Sight had two folding leaves along with a standard plate for ranges up to 300 yards plus an adjustable slide for shooting up to 1,000 yards.

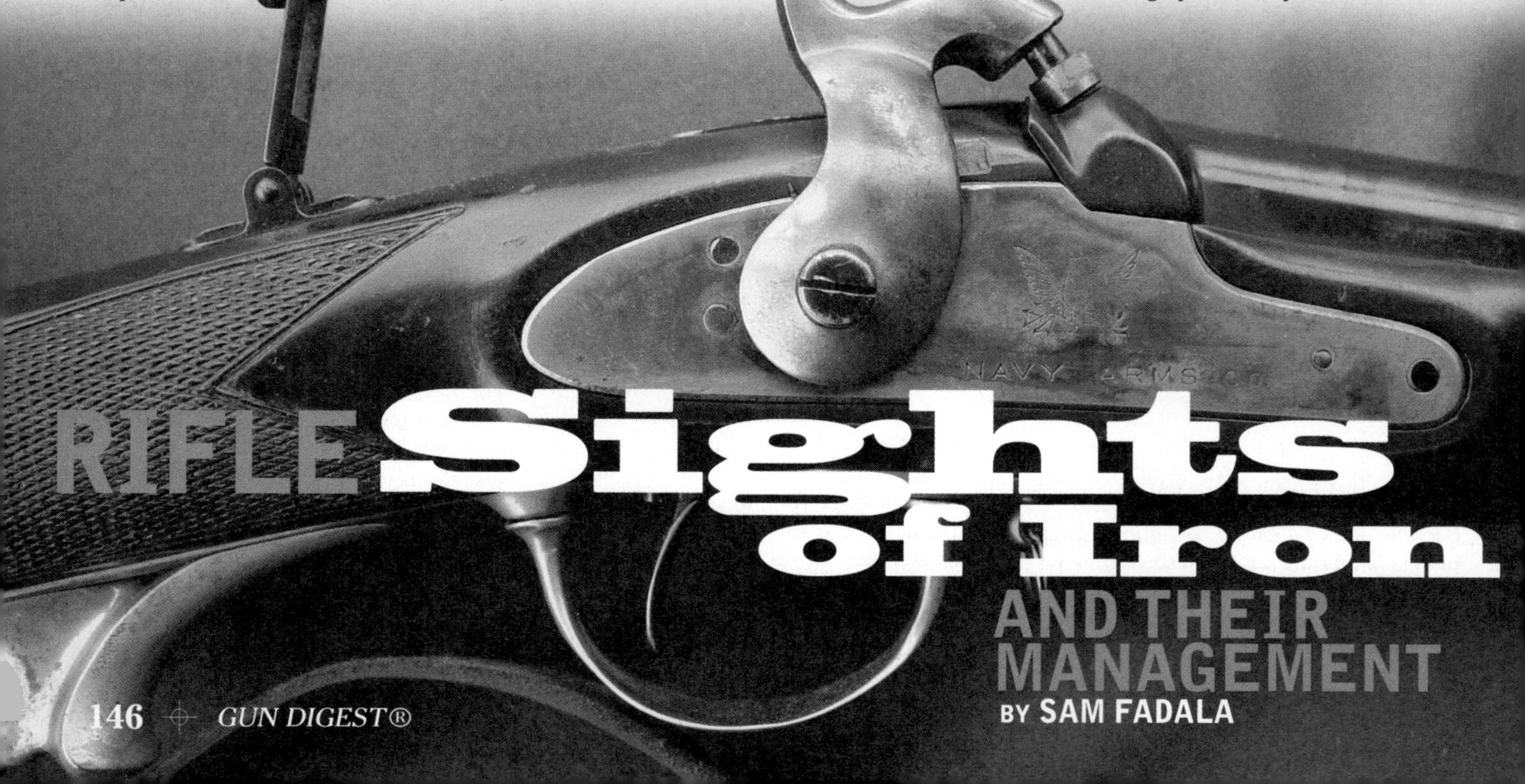

The tang sight on this muzzleloading rifle illustrates another type of "peep" sight. The tang sight allows use of open iron sights on this rifle.

RIFLE **Sights** of Iron
AND THEIR MANAGEMENT
BY SAM FADALA

Our own Lyman Company had a big hand in viable early iron sights, including a popular double-leaf model. Both leaves were regulated for the same elevation. But one was open V while the other was straight bar with ivory reference triangle. Lyman's Sporting Tang Sight was joined by the company's No. 1 aperture or "peep." Lyman continues to offer precision micrometer aperture sights, such as the Model 66-A, friendly on the Model 94 Winchester with quarter-minute "clicks." The dizzying variety of iron sight choices that lay before the 19th century shooter continues today.

Match rifles of the early 1900s were privy to countless options, including the Orthoptic Back-sight with Vernier Scale and Lyman's Disc Peep for Match Shooting. Greener had his own Orthoptic Wind-gauge aperture sight plus a Miniature Cadet Sight. He also introduced a front sight that flipped to combine barleycorn and bead, barleycorn being a thick upside down V. My mentor Jack O'Connor, writing on the subject, corralled iron sights into four categories. Rear sights he noted as a notch in V or U shape "cut in a piece of iron." Jack included the hole or peep sight, adding a flat un-notched bar with white centerline stripe (rare). Finally, he applauded the Patridge sight – not the first-day-of-Christmas bird in the pear tree but named for E.E. Patridge who developed the design in the 1880s for exhibition shooting—a square rear notch optically matched to a flat-topped blade front sight.

The simple V or U notch, still popular, works better than its simplicity suggests. Countless tons of prime game meat have been brought to table with rifles sporting this sight. I have seen O'Connor's flat bar with white line in Africa. It is intended for close encounters of the Cape buffalo kind. It is simple and fast for bullet placement at very close range when a hunter's starched shorts are at risk of being sullied and the target is a broad skull or hearty shoulder. The Patridge is much more precise when it has a frame of reference, as explained below, especially effective with the six o'clock hold.

Taking nothing away from any of these open sights, it is the peep (aperture) that rules the world of rifle iron sights when precise bullet placement is called for.

Last season, partly for the SCI meat donation program, I hunted big game exclusively with my Marlin 336T Texan .30-30 carbine, the one closely resembling Winchester's famous Model 94. The original open iron sight missed nothing, only one second shot required on an antelope buck taking a bullet on angle. And yet, the open iron and bead front on that carbine are now replaced with a White Stripe front matched to a Ghost Ring aperture (peep) from XS Sight Systems. The promise of an extra margin of bullet placement was fulfilled with this peep sight. Groups proved the .30-30's potential as a mid-range cartridge, as evidenced by Hornady's LeverEvolution ammo and my own handloads (160- to 165-grain bullets at 2,450 feet per second from 20-inch barrel, a blip faster out of the 24-inch tunnel.

Nineteenth century iron sights proved so useful that they remain with us today. Consider the Marble Arms threesome of full buckhorn, semi-buckhorn, and flat-top rear sights. Dovetailed into the barrel, these open irons are adjusted for windage by drifting left or right, elevation accomplished via a double step elevator (ladder). You drift the front sight left to hit right, right to hit left, rear sight up for higher, down for lower bullet impact. Simple and effective. All three have white enamel diamonds for center reference with reversible U- or V-notches. The Marble open rear sight is a prime example of the family. But there are scores of others on new rifles as well as myriad

A good look at an elevator bar, also called a ladder, beneath an open iron sight. The notches are used to change the height of the sight, going up to hit higher, down to hit lower. The notches do not have a specific value.

The justly-renowned receiver-mounted Lyman Peep Sight.

after-market choices.

Rifle iron sight variation over time is an interesting study. But management of these sights is imperative for in-the-field results. The glass sight magnifies the image, which in turn increases perceived rifle movement. The rifleman immediately discovers that if he or she wants to hit that target, a better stance with greater control is demanded — sitting, kneeling, prone, hasty sling (carry strap or sling slipped through arm) or, better, a solid rest, be it the top strut of a packframe or over a log or boulder. The iron sight can give a false sense of rifle steadiness because it lacks magnification, leading the shooter to "hold sloppy." I once found a dandy Marlin half-magazine 336 in .32 Winchester Special. Groups were OK with original irons. Adding a Lyman micrometer "peep" provided honest 1.5-inch and smaller patterns at 100 yards.

As a young firefighter on the Arizona/Mexico border I met two old miners who loved to show off their .30-30 skills. They were good. Both said they never "saw" their sights. They relied on "snap-shooting." Fact is, the bullet can only go where the sights are "looking." These two marksmen, experts through years of practice, were certainly seeing their sights. They also knew that if their carbines fell prey to wagging this way and that way, the result would be an errant bullet. Even offhand, they respected the equation of "shaky equals miss – steady equals hit." The iron-sighted rifle must be treated to the same control rules as the scoped rifle. This is the rule: best possible rifle control followed by clear and precise sight picture, and finally the same careful trigger squeeze given the scoped rifle.

Here is the Ghost Ring Rear sight mounted on an older Model 336 Marlin Texan .30-30. It is a highly effective and very fast iron sight option.

Proper sight picture means a bold *contrast* between the front sight and the target — be that target a bull's eye or bull moose. The front sight must be clearly distinguishable, not blended into the target. Two types of sight picture are six o-clock and dead-center. Six o'clock has top of front sight optically "sitting" directly below the intended point of impact. Dead-center has front sight optically right on top of the target. I prefer six o'clock with peep, dead-center with open irons.

Front sight coloration can be important for contrast. Colors include gold (copper alloy), white, ivory, and black, along with every imaginable hue from orange to red, blue, yellow, and pink. Bead size is also important. Prevalent dimensions are 1/16-, 3/32-, and 1/8-inch, the latter fast at very close range, but too coarse for distance because it covers too much target.

An example of front sight color importance is the White Stripe from SX Sight Systems, which is visible against all backgrounds: from plains, tundra, thickets, black timber, mountain canyons, swamps to the treeless tops of sheep country. Lighted from behind, the white stripe stands out. Lighted from the front, the whole sight appears solid black. The sight picture of this peep/post combination prints point of impact two to three inches above the top of the post at 100 yards for .30-30-class muzzle velocities. Place the top of the post mid-chest on deer-sized game at 100 yards and the bullet strikes a little high, but well within the vitals. At 200 yards, given modern .30-30 ballistics, the flying missile falls a hand-width below the top of the post, but again within the chest region. While today's marksmen consistently hit targets at 1,000 yards and beyond with iron-sighted rifles, as

witnessed at any blackpowder cartridge match, my personal outside limit is about 200 yards with irons on big game, rangefinder verified when practical.

The open iron demands triple "visual accommodation," the eye focusing on three planes: rear sight, front sight and target. Smart shooters learn to clearly focus on only two of the three: front sight/target. Of course the front sight must be optically centered in the notch of the rear sight for alignment. But with training and practice, the shooter learns to deal with a slightly blurred rear sight while maintaining a sharp front sight on target picture. When a SWAT team commander trained me to be a better marksman, he had me repeat "front sight-target; front sight-target; front sight-target" as the key to precise bullet delivery with open iron sights. Frame of reference is important. If the front sight optically overfills the rear sight notch, it is impossible to align it properly. It's best to have a glint of light, if ever so minute, on either side of the front sight as it appears in the notch in order to assure that it is centered.

The peep sight requires only two points of visual concentration: front sight/target. Newcomers to the aperture sight work hard trying to optically locate the front sight in the center of the hole. This conscious level of aiming with the peep tramples on its simplicity and effectiveness. The human eye naturally seeks out the point of brightest light, pinpointing the front sight in the hole "automatically." Ghost Ring rear sights come with a 191-inch and .230-inch inside diameter apertures. These are big. But as O'Connor pointed out, he removed the disc from his Lyman peep sights entirely, leaving a huge hole with negligible diminishment of group size. The nam Ghost Ring, tells it all. The rear sight

The famous Lyman folding rear sight is standard on many factory rifles.

A good example of a semi-buckhorn sight on an old-time Model 94 Winchester. The horns almost make it to full buckhorn status, but not quite.

(aperture) becomes nothing more than a halo to be ignored. It is supposed to look fuzzy. Simply line up that front sight on the target and squeeze off the shot. Work hard, and you lose. Let your natural eyesight take over, and you win.

When sighting in, even when going for the dead-center hold, I begin with six o-clock because it offers a more specific aiming point: a bull's eye sitting on top of a front sight. For dead-center sighting, the group falls just below the bull's eye. Sighting in to zero at the base of the bull, the rifle will be sighted in for the dead-center hold. The true six o'clock hold, with bull's eye optically "sitting right on top of" the front sight, the bullet strikes just above the aiming point. This allows the target to remain visible, rather than be covered by the front sight. Aperture sights on my Marlin rifles in .30-30, .32 Winchester Special, and .38-55 are sighted to group about three inches above the front sight at 100 yards, which provides a hold-on for deer-sized game out to 200 yards.

So everyone should immediately abandon the glass sight and go iron? Not in a millennium! The premier sight of all times is the scope. My PH rifle for Africa, a Marlin .45-70 with big bullets going faster than the old warhorse's originators imagined in their wildest dreams, wears a Leupold 1.75-6X scope. My Marlin XLR .35 Remington is dressed with the same glass sight. My Morrison .30-06 is graced with the super high-tech Swarovski X6i 2X-12X with lighted reticule. I go iron for only four reasons, but they are good ones. First is the challenge. I have to get a little closer to that buck, bull, or boar with irons. (It's called stalking.) Second is success. In those wonderful whitetail haunts where the shot normally comes no farther than three first downs to boot toe, the simpler iron sight works just fine.

Third is appropriateness. My lever-action carbines wear iron sights that promote fast-handling at brush and timber ranges. Fourth is maintaining the simple lines of simple rifles, especially those "cowboy" lever actions.

The famous Springfield Model of 1903 went to war with essentially a Patridge type sight system: square post with U-notch, ideal for six o'clock hold with flat blade level at top of notch. The M-1 Garand (pronounced Gare´-end, not Gah-rand´, by the way) had an aperture sight adjustable to 1,200 yards. Most gunners today still

The Ghost Ring front sight is usually, but not always, coupled with a White Stripe front sight from the same manufacturer.

learn with iron sights. The modern shooter is smart to add iron sight savvy to his or her body of knowledge because, geriatric as they may be, irons are here to stay. They are effective, light in weight, rugged, reliable, and they retain the sleek lines of rifles when that is important cosmetically or for rattlesnake speed in tight spots.

Buy a new rifle today and you may very well find it outfitted with iron sights. All my short- to medium-range rifles are iron-sighted. But not those long-range rascals. They wear scope sights. You bet.

IRON RIFLE SIGHTS OVER TIME

In the late 19th century, as an 1895 catalog reveals, all Winchester Models 1873, 1875, 1886, plus .22s and the Winchester Single Shot, came with open iron sights. Likewise Marlin's Model 1891 and 1893. In the 1920s, open irons continued to rule. Same in the '30s. By 1940, the Model 70 Winchester could be purchased with Lyman 48WJS and 57W micrometer receiver sights, the Model 71 with optional 98A peep. The Model 94 continued with open irons.

The standard Savage 99 wore open iron sights in this time frame, while the 99K had a tang peep, the 99-RS a Lyman aperture sight. Marlin's 36, forerunner of today's 336, came with open irons in the '40s. Today, Marlin lever-actions continue with factory open iron sights, as does the Browning's Lightning, while Remington, Winchester, Savage, and Ruger offer both open and aperture sights, factory-wise. And sometimes scope-ready, too, with no sights at all.

(left) This Ghost Ring rear sight is provided with a large aperture to give the "ghost image" picture of sharp front sight on target with "ghostly" image in the aperture.

(above) The dovetail slot into which a rear sight would be placed. The dovetail slot allows the drifting of a rear sight from right to left for changing bullet impact on the target from right to left.

MILITARY RIFLE ACCURACY: A COMPARISON

BY JOHN T. BUTTERS

This article chronicles the results of an enjoyable project that grew out of a series of more or less unrelated events starting in the year 2000 with the acquisition of a very nice SMLE No. 4 MK2 rifle. I had always wanted to find out for myself what my father, who served in the British Army in WWI, found so praiseworthy about the SMLE.

Admittedly, he was issued the No. 1 rifle in one or another of its earlier versions but the No. 4 model was more appealing to me due to its better trigger arrangement and heavier barrel. I immediately discovered that his observation that it was "the same size from muzzle to butt plate" was indeed close to being literally correct. Thankfully, I did not have to check on the truth of his comments regarding its handiness as a club carrying an oversized butcher knife on the other end. He believed that "cold steel is the answer" and "the rifle is designed for disciplined and commanded musketry and is best employed under strict unit control."

On the other hand, I was trained by American GIs with European and Asian theater combat experience who emphasized individual marksmanship at reasonable ranges within the constraints of "fire discipline." Fighting with sharpened entrenching tools, rifle butts and bayonets was recognized as a part of the job to be avoided if at all possible. As one bestriped and beribboned old master Sergeant told us, "if you can stop 'em when they are 300 yards away that's 10 times better than 30 yards away. That doesn't mean you need to mess with 'em at a thousand yards unless you're told to. One of the SOBs may have a mortar." Dad and I never reconciled our philosophical differences over the question of individual marksmanship versus unit musketry exercises.

I once saw the movie *Enemy at the Gates*, in which the Russian protagonist used a Moisin-Nagant long rifle. As a kid I had been exposed to the comments of a gunsmith who bad-mouthed the Moisin-Nagant in the belief that it was "weak

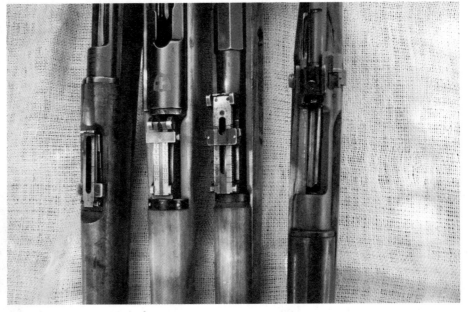

and dangerous." In the '50s and '60s the Communist Nations of the Eastern European Block used the Moisin-Nagant long rifle in the international military rifle competitions when it was their turn to host the matches. Russian, Romanian, East German and Bulgarian shooters and others shot some remarkable scores against our best marksmen in those so called "CISM" (*Commite Internationale Sport Militaire*) matches.

Guns were supposedly chosen by lot to ensure an even footing and ammunition was said to be a "common issue." All was purportedly equal although suspicious minds darkly hinted that some guns and ammo were "more equal than others," especially when shot by the host countries! Even so, I wanted to see for myself how a really good Moisin-Nagant would shoot. When the Finnish M39 Moisin-Nagant in 7.62x54R became available with a new 1942 rebuild by the Finnish "B" factory (Valmet?) I ordered one.

Others followed in quick succession: the Swiss K31 in 7.5 x 55 Schmidt-Rubin, the Swedish M96 Mauser in 6.5x55, the Yugoslav M48A in 8x57, the M1909 and 1891 Mausers in 7.65x53 Argentine, and

Rear sight comparison. Left to right: M96 Carl Gustav Swedish Mauser, M31 Schmidt-Rubin, M39 Finnish Moisin-Nagant, 1903 A3 Springfield.

the Arisaka M38 in 6.5x50 Japanese came my way. I already had a DCM 1903A3 by Smith Corona that was a proven performer so I was all set to make a military bolt rifle performance comparison that spanned the late 19th through the mid 20th centuries.

For the shooting phase of the project, I chose to shoot from prone with issue sights, a coat, a glove and a tight sling, as I felt that off-the-shoulder performance would be more uniform than off the bench and more in keeping with field usage. Except for chronograph sessions, all shooting was "personalized" match-type using U.S. military and US NRA targets at ranges out to 880 yards.

Observation and opinions of individual characteristics were noted and compared within the group. Ammunition included both handloads and "issue grade" where available. All rifles were inspected for structural soundness of the action and bolt and correct function of the firing mechanism and all were checked for proper headspace. After all, some of these "old soldiers" are a century old and, while yet still eminently serviceable, deserve "some respect"! The rifles I used were all in great shape but there are those out there that are not. Let the shooter beware!

As the rifles and ammunition for test firing were assembled it became obvious that the ordnance officers of the various nations were in broad agreement in some areas but differed significantly in others. Only the 98 Mauser types (48A Yugoslav and 1909 Argentine), the Moisin-Nagant and the 1903-A3 were cock-on-opening actions. All the rest cocked on closing. All safeties locked the firing pin and all had positively controlled feed. The M91 Mauser's, the Arisaka's, the Moisin-Nagant's and the Swiss Schmidt-Rubin's safeties locked the bolt closed on "safe" while the rest could theoretically at least be manipulated to unload the chamber on "safe." All had rapid reload features and mechanical intercepts preventing firing out of battery.

Only the SMLE and the Schmidt-Rubin had removable magazines. The 03 A3 and the 48A Mauser had one-piece trigger guards and floor plates; the rest had removable floor plates which again, at least theoretically, enabled unloading the ammunition in the magazine without running it through the loading/ejection port.

All the countries represented issued both carbine length and "long" rifles except the U.S. and Britain, who got along with the nominal two-foot barrel length, as did Switzerland after 1931 and Sweden after 1938. The Arisaka and the Mausers (except for the Swedes) had "barleycorn" inverted V-front sights. The rest had square top posts, the width of which was remarkably close to the width of a man's shoulders as seen through the sights at 300 yards. Only the 1903 A3 and the SMLE had peep rear sights; the rest, except for one Kokura arsenal Arisaka, had open notch rear sights.

Finally, the ordnance departments were divided into three main groups with regard to size of bullet and power of cartridge. First, the small bore proponents were represented by the 6.5x50mm Japanese and the 6.5x55 Swede. (To this group may be added the 6.5 Mannlicher types as used by Austria and Greece but which were not included in this test series.) Next in line came the 308W/7.62x51 group, represented by the .303 Brit, the 7.5x55 Schmidt-Rubin and the 7.65x53 Argentine. All use 174-grain bullets at close to 2,550 fps.

Next the big boys on the block checked in with the 8x57 Mauser, the 7.65x54 R and the .30-06. They all step up a rung with more bullet energy than the other two groups.

The tests I ran showed that as issued they all could be made to shoot well enough to meet minimum "match rifle" standards, and with a little tuning some managed to afford a number of pleasant surprises. Issue ammunition, with two remarkable exceptions, was a disappointment, yielding a dull four minute of angle average. This no doubt was the result of economies of production and quality control, which were in keeping with a planned "dispersal on target" which would prevent an excited and stressed soldier from emptying his magazine into one small spot on the battlefield when the objective of his superiors was that he "spread it around and share it a little."

Every rifle tested would shoot into at least 2-1/2 minutes of angle with tailored handloads. The 6.5 Swedes would cut that in less than half and were the over-achievers in the class. It is well worth noting that without exception, the best performance with all was with service weight bullets at service pressures and velocities. The old bald-heads running ordnance knew what was safest and most accurate because they worked hard and smart at finding it out. Respect that knowledge and be instructed thereby.

NO. 4 MARK 2

The old No. 4 Mark 2 .303 Brit was made at the Fazakerly Factory near Liverpool in February of 1950 and if it was ever issued it didn't get shot much. It came with a short stock and a capricious performance that quickly earned it the name "Crazy Albert." It was tantalizingly finicky, shooting 3 or 4 shots into a 2-½ or 3 inch group at 200 yards, then scattering the next 3 or 4 from 7 ring to 7 ring, high low, right, left – who the

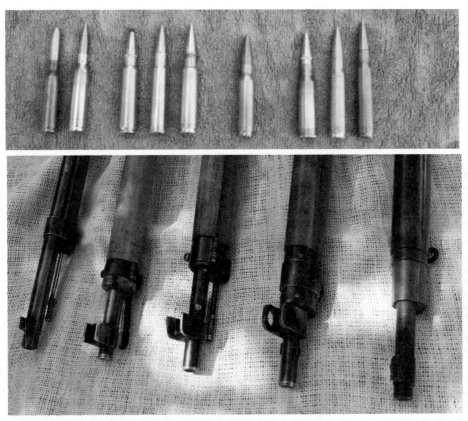

(top) Cartridge comparison (not all tested). Left to right: 6.5X50 Japanese Military, 6.5X55 Swedish, 7.65X53 Belgian (Argentine), 7.7X56R (.303 British), 7.5X55 Schmidt-Rubin (Swiss), 7.62X51 NATO (308 Winchester), 7.62X54R Russian, 7.92X57 (8mm Mauser), .30-06 Springfield (7.62X63).

(above) Front sight comparison, left to right: M96 Carl Gustav Swedish Mauser, M31 Schmidt-Rubin, M39 Finnish Moisin-Nagant, No.4 Mk 2 Short Magazine Lee Enfield, 1903 A3 Springfield.

hell knows where next? – before settling down in the original group. A recurring skinned place on my forehead above my right eye was cured by the purchase and careful fitting of an "L" or long version of the issue stock.

Frustration at the inconsistency of performance on target was eventually cured under the tutelage of "Les" Karas of Ontario, Canada, who graciously provided directions for tuning Crazy Albert and curbing its tendency to scatter shots all over the target. In brief, it involved careful fitting and glass bedding to keep the barrel free-floated and the front band from touching the front sight. It also helped to use a paint mark on the cartridge case head to index fire-formed and neck-sized cases in the chamber the same way each time. (It seems the Brits were more interested in getting the bolt to close on anything that was stuck in the chamber than in facilitating the re-loading of fired cases.) Trigger pull was smoothed by polishing the roughness from engaging surfaces but not reduced from the 6-pound, two-stage pull it came with. In this condition, it was shot in a high power match at Camp Bullis in the Spring of 2001.

Things went pretty well until the 600-yard stage, when elevation problems caused by having to hold off for about 4 minutes of wind one way to 6 minutes the other way resulted in a 168. The low comb on the stock also prevents an effective "spot weld" when the rear sight is elevated for 600 yards.

Back to "Les" Karas, who offered a chuckle and some sympathy, along with some leads on a source for a windage-adjustable rear sight. Several weeks later "Bertie" was sporting a very nice fully adjustable A. J. Parker rear with an adjustable aperture. This sight was designed to mount directly on the No. 4 rifle with no machining required. It works great and although the rifle is no longer "showroom stock," it is a fun gun with a mild recoil that has put 22 rounds into a 24"x36" group at 880 yards, scoring a 188 on a frame mounted 1000 yard target. I believe it would have done better with target pulling service to help in doping the wind and mirage between shots.

The ammunition was South African Berdan primed 174-grain non-corrosive MK VII issue ball reseated .015 inch. Without reseating to break the seal, vertical dispersion increased by over a minute of angle. A handload using IMR 4320, a Winchester case and primer and the Hornady 174-grain .3105 FMJBT bullet at 2480 fps shot into less than 2 minutes of angle and had the same point of impact as the GI loading all the way from 200 yards to 500 yards. No comparison has been made yet at 880 yards. (Why 880 and not 900? Because I can't get 900 from my firing line without a mammoth earthmoving project!)

The old SMLE no longer deserves to be called "Crazy Albert." It has had its problems fixed as well as may be reasonably done and will shoot as accurately and as reliably as the run-of-the-mill National Match M-1. It would make an easily portable and effective service rifle due to its light weight, handy configuration and smooth bolt operation. While it didn't have "target accuracy" as received, it probably had sufficient battlefield accuracy, particularly when used as described by my old Brit Infantryman Dad.

MOISIN-NAGANT

The Moisin-Nagant was a hexagonal-actioned rifle picked up out of the snow by the Finns during the winter war of 1939-1940 after the Russians threw them away so they could run faster. Being no dummies and recognizing the value of the salvage, the Finns brought the rifles home and reworked the ones they liked, rebarreling them with a 27-1/2 inch tube and restocking them with an extended forend. Sights were replaced with the Finnish military standard rear leaf and a windage adjustable front set with two opposing screws graduated to move the service bullet impact the width of one ring on the 300-meter international/Scandinavian target for each increment of adjustment.

The one I got was rebarreled and rebuilt in 1942 by "B." I understand that

B decimal target with 500-yard slow fire group using handloads reproducing the .30-06 National Match cartridge using the M72 FMJBT 173-grain bullet, shot with 1903-A3 Springfield.

880-yard slow fire group with No.4 Mk2 SMLE using South African GI 7.7x56R (.303B) Mk 7Z 1980 Ball with 174-grain FMJBT bullet reseated .015 deeper than issued. Note two sighters at 11 o'clock.

means Valmet. If it had been shot since it was proofed, I saw no evidence of it with a Hawkeye borescope. This rifle was big, tough, heavy and clumsy but all business. It got known as "Ivan the Terrible" or just "The Brute" for short. The trigger was almost 7 pounds with two stages but was amazingly uniform. Despite the weight of pull, the second stage was sharp and predictable, making it quite usable. I can see how such a trigger would be no drawback at -30° F in blowing snow while wearing gloves.

A variety of steel case Eastern Bloc ammo with 154-, 174- and 197-grain bullets was quite uniform in performance – all bad – with 8 inch to 10 inch groups at 200 yards and getting worse at 300 yards. The barrel however was really nice inside, appearing to have been carefully lapped to a very uniform .3105 diameter. The first load of 4320 with the Hornady 174-grain .3105 bullets in Lapuan 7.62 x 54R brass chronographed 2660 fps and grouped into just over 1 MOA at 200, 300 and 500 yards, impacting right on the 200 meter, 300 meter and 500 meter settings. Would it work as a sniper's rifle? Hell yes!

Especially if the shooter was tough. Everything about this rifle is tough. The recoil is tough, the trigger is tough, the bolt operation is tough. This is a big, heavy combat rifle designed to take it and to dish it out with .30-06 class ballistics. I like the old pig but I have

to feel like experiencing a little recoil when I go out to shoot it and be willing to manhandle the bolt and trigger in the bargain.

M48A 8X57

The Model 98 Mauser clan was represented by a Yugoslav M48A 8x57 short rifle and a pair of 1909 Argentine 7.62 x 53s, one short rifle and one long rifle. The 48A was like new inside and out and was finished almost as nicely as a new commercial Mauser.

Cheap Turkish 1938 Berdan-primed 154-grain ball, guaranteed to be corrosive by its vendor, shot into 4 MOA out to 300 yards. It all shot, though, and chronographed quite uniformly at 2970 fps with an extreme spread of 44 fps. I pulled some of the bullets and reseated a Sierra 150-grain flat base soft point instead of the original full metal jackets. I was rewarded with 2950 fps "Munich Match" that grouped into about 1-1/2 MOA all the way out to 500 yards.

The barleycorn front sight gave me trouble with elevation, though. It would fade out at the point no matter how hard I concentrated on it and would give me vertical changes that I did not experience with the more visible flat top front posts. It was also more difficult to define the point of the barleycorn so as to level it with the top of the rear sight notch. For me, a good sized rear peep and 8

minute wide flat top front post seemed to give the best results in both bright and dim lighting. It was easier to see the sights and take a uniform picture with a peep and flat top post.

All that said, I used the 48A and "Munich Match" to cull a spike buck out of my "Range Ravine" at about 350 yards in the dusk just before dark one evening as I was gathering up my gear. The 8x57 is a powerful cartridge and gives away little in terminal ballistic effect to the 30-06.

As a photographer friend of mine once said, "You take the picture with the camera you've got." Much the same is true of rifles: the handier the gun, the more likely you are to have it in hand. Such is the case with the 23.6 inch-barreled Model 48A. It is relatively light and quick to the shoulder with a better than average stock shape for a military rifle. The trigger pull was pretty good, a two-stage generic Mauser military type, and a pull weight very close to 4-1/2 pounds. The general impression was quite favorable, probably one of the best all-around bolt rifles for a soldier to carry day in and day out.

M1909 ARGENTINE

The same comments apply to the M1909 Argentine short rifle except that it had a bore diameter of .313 inch and, although in very nice shape, it would not shoot better than about 2-1/2 MOA with

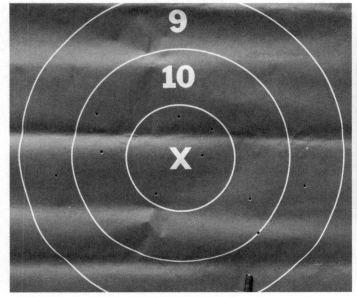

880-yard No.4 Mk 2 targets with sighters pasted.

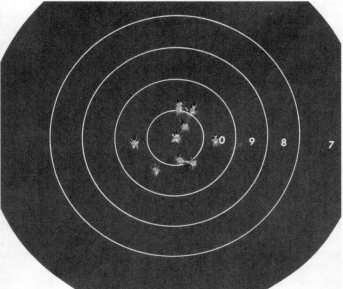

M96 Swede 200-yard slow fire group on MR52 decimal target (600 yard reduced for 200 yards). Score100/5X. Closer is easier but the skinny comb on the issue M96 stock makes a consistent "spot weld" and head position more difficult and contributes to left and right sighting errors.

"Upgraded" rear sights. M. Soderin Aperture Type, M96 Carl Gustav Swedish Mauser (left); A. J. Parker Type 4/47, No.4 Mk 2 SMLE (right).

anything that was tried. The Argentine 184-grain surplus ammunition wouldn't shoot any better than 6-inch 100-yard groups even though the bullets miked .313.

The M1909 Argentine long rifle had a fine .3105 barrel but wouldn't shoot the surplus issue stuff either. However, 150-grain Hornady spire point .311 bullets at 2668 fps with IMR 4895 performed very well, approaching 1 MOA out to 300 yards. The 174-grain Hornady FMJ boat tail .3105 bullets with IMR 4064 at 2560 fps were also nearly MOA performers all the way to 500 yards. The barleycorn front sight on the long rifle didn't seem to cause as much sighting elevation error as it did on the shorter rifles. The 20 percent longer sight radius probably helped.

The nicest thing about the DWM built Argentine Mausers, after their commercial grade finish, was the 7.65x53 Argentine (or Belgian, if you prefer) cartridge. It loads with ease and is very comfortable to shoot, performing about like a strong .308W. After loading for and shooting a number of examples I am surprised that the 7.65x53Argentine/Belgian Mauser cartridge is as well kept a secret as it seems to be. Try it – you'll like it!

A M91 short rifle and a M91 long rifle

in 7.65x53 were also tested and shot quite well except with the Argentine issue ammunition. The long rifle had a .313 diameter barrel and might have done better than 2-½ to 3 MOA if the correct bullets had been available. The carbine, which appeared to have been an arsenal rework of a long rifle, had a .312 barrel and shoots 150-grain .312 spire points into about 2 inches at 100 yards. Not inspiring, but good enough for a rifle to carry behind pig chasing dogs in the Louisiana low country. It's short, light, handy and cheap enough to sacrifice some finish on it. If need be, it's a good "rain and mud gun" if you don't mind the cock on closing.

Neither of the M91s qualified as a first rank infantry or sniper rifle in my opinion. They were serviceable but not outstanding.

ARISAKAS

The Arisakas were a ho-hum lot, with grossly oversize chambers that complicated reloading. I am sure that some Type 38 Arisaka long rifles would turn out fine accuracy but I was unable to find any. Norma factory 140-grain soft points were not only expensive but erratic as well. Sierra 140 Matchkings could be driven no faster than about 2150 fps before pressure signs started to appear. 2-1/2 to 3 minutes of angle was the best I could get despite stories told by WWII veterans about snipers who "after a while you began to think couldn't miss." Trigger pulls were rough and upwards of 10 pounds.

A finely-finished Kokura long rifle had peep sights for both "battle ranges" and long range that gave good sight pictures. Some Koishikawa long rifles, in contrast, all had open rear sights. The light recoil generated by the 6.5x50 cartridge was easy to take and if the rifles could have been made to shoot would have invited longer range sessions. I quickly tired of errant shots and spread-out groups. So much for the Arisakas I tested.

I may be fairly accused of saving the best for last with reports on the K31 Schmidt -Rubin, the 03-A3 Smith Corona Springfield and the M96 Swedes. They all shot, some a little better than others, but every one was trouble-free fun.

K31

The K31 came with dinged-up wood, perfect metal work and a card under the butt plate with the name, address and telephone number of the Swiss trooper from Basel who was sent home with his rifle in 1958. He must not have shot it much because a borescope inspection showed no discernable throat wear and a mirror finish rivaling the product of some U.S.-based master barrel makers. Slugging it revealed an exceptionally round and uniform .3070 bore. Swiss issue 1911 type 174-grain full metal jacket boattail ball shot so well that I thought that my first 10 rounds at 200 yards were an anomaly. They weren't, and they scored an easy possible with about half x's on the 200 yard NRA "A" target.

The next 10 were as good or better. The chronograph gave a muzzle velocity right at 2550 fps. Thinking I could improve on the GI issue stuff, I broke the bullet seal by reseating the out-of-the-box ammo by about .015 inch. Wrong. It made no discernable difference. Next step was to load some 168-grain Sierra Matchkings to the service load velocity. No help there, either. The 168s weren't quite as good as the Swiss issue, still cleaning the 200 yard "A" but with far fewer x's and noticeably more dispersion. I gave up and ordered another case of 7.5 x 55 Swiss GI. "'Arf a crown and no regrets!" to quote the Picadilly Lily!

Schmidt Rubin sights have a cleverly diagonaled slot in which the square top post front is mounted. Windage corrections are made by driving the front sight fore and aft, which also moves it right and left – simple. Swiss ordnance likewise gave the rifleman few choices in sight elevation. Only cardinal 100-meter changes selection from 200 to 1500 meters are possible with no "in between" detents.

To take advantage of the undoubtedly well-planned coincidence of bullet impact and elevation settings, I got out some old "D" -type military silhouette targets with "V's" and 5's as high scores. At 300 yards, the top of the front sight was "shoulder width" on the target, very visible and easy to hold for elevation on the horizontal lower edge of the black.

Slow fire "V's" were the order of the day. Seventy-second standing-to-prone rapid fire exercises starting with four rounds in the magazine and reloading with six from that funny tin and cardboard Swiss clip were really fun.

Once I got over trying to lift up on the straight-pull bolt T-handle, I found a smooth rhythm of operation that was as satisfying and fast as any fine turnbolt or semi-auto match rifle. After the first uninterrupted rapid fire string I shot I lay there and watched the timer count off an unused 12 seconds that I hadn't needed.

The K-31 will shoot but had beautiful closely machined parts clearances that I suspect would suffer if the rifle were taken into the sand or the jungle. So what? The Swiss weren't going either place. From a tall Swiss hill, the K31 would have been capable of "delivering a large volume of accurate fire" and is said to have figured in Germany's decision to let the Swiss alone in WWII.

Bottom line: great rifle. Swiss GI 174-grain ball shoots better than my hand-loads and will give you x-ring groups at least out to 500 yards. I'm keeping mine to play with some more.

1903-A3

About fifty years ago in Dallas, there were five shooters who got caught up in the local competition scene and who participated in what was called "military rifle" matches in which any issue military rifle could be used. The course of fire was the national match course and it attracted a wondrous array of WWI and WWII rifles and cartridges. One of the five ordered a Springfield from the Director of Civilian Marksmanship. When it arrived it came into the form of a "U.S. Smith Corona 1903-A3" with a "C" stock, sheet metal hardware and a slick four groove SC-7-43 barrel.

All the five used "the rifle," which turned out to be a shooter, in those military matches. It was variously owned, sometimes several times and for varying periods, by at least three of the five. Miraculously it avoided being sporterized by one or another of us. Only two of the five are still alive and only one of those still shoots. The old 03-A3, however, has not aged. Indeed, its users over the years have lovingly and meticulously cared for the old rifle inside and out. Its dark American walnut wood has the deep luster and sheen imparted by a few drops of linseed oil rubbed in by hand after each use. Admittedly its forend and butt plate have places where "firm grip"

deposits betray the rifle's past but their piney scent and roughened texture are part of its character.

If a shooter ever had the equivalent of a "Proustian Madeleine" surely this must be it, a sweet memory of things past. Damned old gun shoots! It'll give you inside x-ring groups with "white box" match all the way to 600 yards right today if you do your part. It shoots 125s, 150s, 168s, 173s, 180s, and 190s. You get the feeling that it would shoot copper doorknobs as well if you had enough of 'em to work up a load. The sights don't have enough "in between" elevation graduations to accommodate all of the "non-GI" combinations at all ranges and it's possible to run out of windage adjustment in challenging conditions, but the peep rear is the right size and distance from the eye and the skinny front post is made to order for the small-bull "A", "B", and "C" targets with "V" rings.

The bolt runs slick and there's enough stock comb to let you maintain a consistent sight picture. More recoil than with an M-1 but just remember that you're shooting a .30-06 with all the power you'll ever need. Damned old gun shoots!

SWEDE M96

If the Swedes are to be known for something besides their goofy socialist politics and their beautiful women, I would suggest the combination of the M96 Mauser rifle and the 6.5x55 Swedish cartridge. It was everything the Arisakas I tested could have been and weren't.

Three Model 96s, one Model 38 short rifle and a CG63 arsenal-built, Olympic-type 300-meter competition rifle, all with trigger pulls in the 4-pound range, were tested using 144-grain full metal jacket boattail Swede FFV bullets made in 1954 for use in Olympic competition. The best accuracy was found at very close to 2600 fps from a 29.1 inch barrel. The worst any of them shot was about 1-1/2 MOA; the best was right at half that. Both open and peep rear sights worked well with the aperture type of course being better by far.

One of the M96 long rifles was a literally unfired "Swedish National Match" with a sturdy M. Soderin receiver-mounted peep with highly repeatable windage and elevation settings. Only the bolt and receiver parts had matching numbers but the rifle obviously had been expertly rebuilt with a new select barrel at the Carl Gustaf Factory, probably in the '50s

or '60s. That gun and the CG63, also with a used but good barrel and Soderin rear sight, will shoot 3/4 MOA. The M96 "National Match" has a flat top post front sight and the CG63 has a hooded front with Anschutz post and globe inserts. Happiness is being confident that no matter how bad your shot is it will come on call!

The Swede military stocks are long and skinny but reasonably good cheek support can be had with a careful "spot weld." Light recoil and a long sight radius helps also. Care must be taken not to use too much sling tension. The long slender rifle can be bent 3 or 4 minutes left if you use more sling tension than is necessary for a good stable hold.

Light recoil helps in that department too. A National Match M-1 may be "horsed" pretty hard, and must be to keep a good stable position, without causing an impact shift toward 9 o'clock. The CG63 stock lets its barrel float so is also fairly immune to sling tension bending. Don't do it with the limber long guns like the M96 issue Swedes, though. They don't tolerate it well.

CONCLUSIONS

Well, it's taken about five days to generally summarize about five years testing of about a dozen different rifles, all of the above being brought about by a couple of idle questions arising out unbridled curiosity. Somebody said, I forget who, that the Brits built the battle rifles, the Germans built the hunting rifles and the Americans built the target rifles, and then everybody issued them to their troops. I'd have to call that a tempting oversimplification but in the spirit of the thought would add the Swede to the target rifle classification. When you have a cartridge that you can shoot all day long without undue fatigue and which will deliver a 140-grain bullet into an x-ring group at 600 yards under the same conditions that will drift a 174-grain 30 caliber bullet from one edge of the 10 ring to the other, you have a cartridge with a target advantage. After all, as the old Sarge said, "You can't miss 'em hard enough to hurt 'em."

My favorites overall: the Swedes, the Swiss and the 03-A3 with honorable mention to the No. 4 rifle and the 7.65x53M1909 long rifle. Just don't make me choose between my 03-A3 and the M96 Swede with the Soderin peep!

Too many hunting cartridges?
No! Still, some are superfluous. Wayne thinks these indispensable.

The Top 20

BY WAYNE VAN ZWOLL

One rifle-maker I know chambers for about eighty cartridges. If reamers were mortgages, he'd qualify for a bail-out. But he's not selling any. "Customers appreciate the choice," he says. "Some want a round no one else is shooting." New cartridge designs have come in quick succession over the last decade, with the proliferation of short rimless magnums. Some riflemen would argue we have a surplus now – that there's a lot of duplication in the middle and utterly useless numbers at the extremes.

Wildcatting hit its stride after World War II, when returning GIs fashioned their own high-octane cartridges from .30-06 and .300 H&H hulls. A ready supply of 1903 Springfields, 1917 Enfields and 1898 Mausers made experimenting cheap. Improved optics put affordable scopes in easy reach, so barrels didn't need iron sights. Those were the days of Mashburn and Ackley and myriad lesser-known pioneers, whose designs prospered. When Winchester rolled out the first of a series of short (.30-06-length) belted magnums – the .458 – in 1956, wildcatters fell upon it like wolves. The subsequent .264, .338 and .300 Winchester Magnums, and Remington's 7mm, soon filled the obvious voids. The new magnums confirmed the merits of Roy Weatherby's proprietary .257, .270, 7mm and full-length .300, introduced during World War II!

Since 1962, several wildcats have been adopted by ammunition firms. Remington, for example, was first to offer the .22-250, .25-06 and .35 Whelen. Meanwhile benchrest competitors Lou Palmisano and Ferris Pindell were winning matches with their stubby .22 and 6mm PPCs. "Short and fat" found its way into hunting cartridge design during the late '90s. The Winchester Short Magnum line debuted in 1999, in a .308-length .30 with more punch than a .300 H&H. Remington's Short Action Ultra Mags followed. John Lazzeroni announced even more potent short-action cartridges; both he and Remington also marketed full-length rimless magnums. Hornady designed the .375 Ruger to beat .375 H&H performance in .30-06-length actions, and new propellants enabled Hornady to give .300 and .338 Ruger Compact Magnums high speeds in short barrels. And while Federal necked up the .308 Winchester to deliver its potent .338, Hornady applied the latest powders and FlexTip bullets to its muscular .308 and .338 Marlin Express for lever guns.

Even if you ignore the behemoths – the .458 Lott, Weatherby's super-charged .416, Remington's heaviest Ultra Mags and big-bore British Express cartridges from Norma – a shooter can go daffy trying to finger twenty cartridges as "best." To reduce the angst, I've not listed cartridges pre-dating the .30-06. So you won't see the .30-30 or 9.3x62, the 6.5x55, 7x57 or 8x57, the .30-40 Krag or .303 British – early smokeless rounds with distinguished records on game. In parentheses you'll find close ballistic matches, also-rans for reasons as trivial as chronology. Had the .280 beaten the .270 to market, it probably would have claimed the spotlight. Given more space, I'd add the .260 Remington, .340 Weatherby, .358 Norma….

Honestly, though, the first quarter of the twentieth century produced all the cartridges most of us need!

Loads listed are representative of those I like; the best load for any specific application may differ. Here, then, in kind of ascending order:

.22-250 REMINGTON

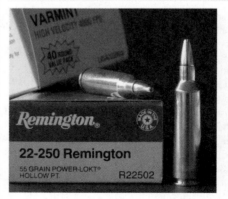

Now over seventy years old, the .22-250 remains hugely popular – not only among shooters who wreak havoc in prairie dog towns, but among coyote hunters and, particularly in Texas, deer hunters. The .22-250 has weathered competition from other fast-stepping .22s: the .220 Swift, .225 Winchester, .224 Weatherby and .223 WSSM. None has come close to unseating it.

The .22-250's parent case is the .250 Savage, developed by Charles Newton in 1913. During the 1930s, Harvey Donaldson, J.E.Gebby, J.B. Smith, John Sweany and Grosvenor Wotkyns necked the hull to .22. A version by Gebby and Smith, circa

1937, became the "Varminter" – a name copyrighted by Gebby. But not until 1965 did the Varminter go commercial, when Remington adopted it in M700 rifles. The .220 Swift's larger case allowed 4,110 fps with 48-gr. bullets. But the Varminter wasn't far behind. Now the Swift has faded, while the .22-250 is chambered in every varmint-class rifle I can think of.

With a 50-gr. bullet at 3,800 fps, the .22-250 carries more than 500 ft-lbs of energy to 400 yards. That bullet starts as fast as a 40-gr. spitzer from a .223, but it bucks wind better and at 400 yards trounces the .223's by 270 fps. For deer the 6mms excel – though 55- and 60-gr. bullets in the .22-250 have taken boxcar loads of whitetails and, in the Far North, caribou. A 60-gr. .22-250 bullet at 3,600 fps beats a 75-gr. .243 bullet off the blocks by 200 fps and is still moving faster at 400, where it carries 627 ft-lbs to the .243's 768. A Varminter softpoint through the slats is deadly on deer, if not legal everywhere.

Handloaders charge the .22-250 with powders mid-range in burn rate: AA2520, H335, IMR 3031, RL-15, Viht 140. Loaded ammo is offered by Black Hills, Federal, Hornady, Remington and Winchester.

50-GR. ACCUTIP (REMINGTON), 200-YARD ZERO

	Muzzle	100 Yds	200 Yds	300 Yds	400 Yds
Velocity, fps	3800	3339	2925	3546	2198
Energy, ft-lbs	1603	1238	949	720	536
Arc, inches	-1.5	+0.8	0	-4.9	-15.2

6MM REMINGTON (.243 WINCHESTER)

The 1955 introduction of the .244 Remington paralleled the debut of Winchester's .243. The .244, based on the .257 Roberts hull (derived in turn from the 7x57), had more capacity than the .243, a necked-down .308 Winchester. But short rifle actions required deep seating of long bullets in the .244, so the ballistic advantages of factory loads were minimal. Remington chambered the round in its M722 bolt rifle. Its 1-in-12 twist proved the correct spin for bullets of 75 to 90 grains. But riflemen wanted heavier bullets for deer and pronghorns. They turned to 100-gr. softpoints in the .243. Winchester's M70 barrels were rifled 1-in-10. Still, not all tales of twist are true. I owned a Remington 722 in .244 and managed minute-of-angle groups with 100-gr. handloads.

In 1963 Remington reinvented the round, replacing the 90-gr. bullet in .244 ammo with a 100-gr. Core-Lokt. Barrels and case heads came off the line stamped "6mm Remington."

Dimensionally, the cartridge was and is the same as the old .244, but 6mm barrels feature 1-in-9 rifling.

Like the .243, .250 Savage and .257 Roberts, the 6mm Remington shoots flat and has mild recoil. Varmint hunters know it bucks wind better

than fast .22s. It shines on deer-size game. I once clobbered a pronghorn buck at just over 400 steps with a 90-gr. Remington softpoint. The 6mm is factory-loaded to an overall length of 2.91 inches. Handloaders find it superior to the .243 (OAL 2.75) in actions like the mid-length Ultra Light, whose magazine swallows 3-inch cartridges.

While you can accelerate 55-gr. bullets to over 4,100 fps in the 6mm case, you'll deliver more energy at distance with 75- or 80-gr. hollowpoints clocking 3,500. A 100-gr. factory load at 3,100 fps is 140 fps faster than a comparable .243. Hornady's Light Magnum ammo puts the 6mm close to Weatherby's .240.

100-GR. POINTED SOFTPOINT (HORNADY LIGHT MAGNUM), 200-YARD ZERO

	Muzzle	100 Yds	200 Yds	300 Yds	400 Yds
Velocity, fps	3250	3003	2769	2547	2335
Energy, ft-lbs	2345	2001	1702	1440	1211
Arc, inches	-1.5	+1.2	0	-5.7	-16.8

.257 ROBERTS

Charles Newton developed our first high-speed 25-caliber cartridge in 1912. It fired a 100-gr. bullet at around 2,800 fps, an 87-gr. bullet at 3,000. Savage called it the .250/3000. Ned Roberts bested it during the 1920s by necking down the 7x57 Mauser case. The .257 Roberts was apparently a joint venture with F.J. Sage and A.O. Neidner – who had necked the .30-06 to form the .25 Neidner, forerunner of the .25-06. Roberts liked the more compact (efficient) 7x57 hull and trimmed it 1/16 inch. Townsend Whelen recommended a 15-degree shoulder. By 1930 Griffin & Howe was chambering rifles in .25 Roberts. Mr. Griffin convinced Ned Roberts to dispense with the trimming. In 1934 Remington adopted the round as the .257 Roberts, using a groove-diameter name to distinguish it from other 25s. Remington moved the shoulder ahead, increasing its angle to 20 degrees.

The .257's civil disposition prompted Jack O'Connor to predict at the close of World War II that the cartridge would soon rank among the top three in bolt rifles. He was wrong. The Roberts slipped partly because light bullets didn't shoot accurately enough for varmint hunters, and blunt factory-loaded big game bullets lost enthusiasm quickly. By the early 1950s, when Winchester-Western fielded an accurate 87-gr. varmint bullet and Remington a 100-gr. pointed Core-Lokt, the .243 was about to debut. It would all but bury the Roberts. O'Connor still praised the .257 as a wind-bucking varmint cartridge and as a top pick for deer. Warren Page wrote that it was too short to stay with the .25-06 ballistically, too long for short actions.

The .257 offers plenty of punch for big game. Federal pushes 120-gr. Nosler Partitions to 2,780 fps, while Hornady lists a Light Magnum 117 SST at a scorching 2,940 fps. Winchester starts its 117-gr. Power Point at 2,780, but it decelerates fast. Ditto for Remington's 117 Core-Lokt, which holds up better but leaves the gate at just 2,650 fps. Handloaders add speed and reach with long spitzers like the Barnes 100-gr. TSX, Nosler's 110 AccuBond and the 117 Sierra GameKing.

120-GR. NOSLER PARTITION (FEDERAL), 200-YARD ZERO

	Muzzle	100 Yds	200 Yds	300 Yds	400 Yds
Velocity, fps	2780	2560	2360	2160	1970
Energy, ft-lbs	2060	1750	1480	1240	1030
Arc, inches	-1.5	+1.9	0	-8.2	-24.0

.25-06 REMINGTON

Soon after the Great War, A.O. Niedner necked the '06 case to 25 caliber, with no other changes. That 1920 version has endured longer than various other hot-rod .25-06s. But it wasn't until 1969 that the round was commercially loaded, when Remington chambered it in the M700 rifle and put the first .25-06 factory ammunition in green boxes. The .25-06 won't match sales of the .270, which appeared five years after Neidner's .25 but nearly 45 years before Remington adopted it. Still, the .25-06 counts many fans. It is faster than a .257 Roberts, is more efficient than a .257 Weatherby Magnum and can do everything a .270 can do while beating the .243 at its own game.

Conceived as a long-range multi-purpose round, the .25-06 is loaded mostly for deer-size animals. The lighter bullet weights once common on every list have largely been abandoned. At this writing, only Winchester still catalogs woodchuck loads – an 85-gr. Ballistic Silvertip in its Supreme line, and a 90-gr. Super-X softpoint. Its 110-gr. AccuBond at 3,100 fps (also a Federal load) ranks among the best big-game picks. It's faster than the long 117s and 120s that set the upper limit for .25 bullets. A pal of mine handloads 100-gr. Hornadys. He's shot 20 elk with them and never lost one.

Factory-loaded 85-gr. bullets from the .25-06 clock nearly 3,500 fps at the muzzle, while 120s plod at 2,990. In-between, 100- and 110-gr. bullets chronograph 3,210 and 3,100. Those middle-weights offer a useful combination of heft, sectional density and velocity. Just match bullet construction to the task.

100-GR. BARNES TRIPLE-SHOCK (FEDERAL), 200-YARD ZERO

	Muzzle	100 Yds	200 Yds	300 Yds	400 Yds
Velocity, fps	3210	2970	2750	2540	2330
Energy, ft-lbs	2290	1960	1675	1425	1205
Arc, inches	-1.5	+1.2	0	-5.8	-17.0

.270 WINCHESTER (.280 REMINGTON)

The .270 Winchester came along in 1925, but a similar cartridge pre-dated it. In 1917 the brilliant Wilhelm Brenneke introduced his 7x64, which powered a 173-gr. bullet 500 fps faster than the 7x57. Both became popular with European hunters and proved the lethality of sub-.30 bullets. The cartridge being essentially a necked-down .30-06., the .270's .277 bullet is .007-inch smaller than that of most 7mms. Winchester's name helped sell it to U.S. hunters. So did Jack O'Connor, who began his gun-writing career during the .270's infancy. When in 1937 it became a charter chambering in the Winchester Model 70, the .270 became even more popular. Only the .30-06 has enjoyed a larger production run in this rifle.

First paired with 130-gr. bullets at 3,000 fps, the .270 was soon accused of ruining venison. Hunters used to the modest damage inflicted by .30-30 bullets called for a milder load. Winchester complied with a 150-gr. softpoint at 2,675. Nobody bought it. Improved bullets and demand for cartridges of great reach sealed the .270's popularity. Strong 140- and 150-gr. bullets driven fast made the round more versatile. Clean and sleek in profile, .270 hulls stack neatly in magazines and glide silkily up feed ramps. Mild recoil helps you shoot a .270 well. Standard rifling twist is 1-in-10.

Competition was inevitable. Beginning in 1957, the wildcat 7mm-06 was loaded commercially as the .280 Remington. Stoked to 47,000 psi to function reliably in Remington pump and

autoloading rifles, it got a peppier 150-gr. load in 1979, when it became the 7mm Express. The name didn't stick. Remington revived the .280 designation. Ballistically, modern loads match those of the .270. The 7mm Remington Magnum wooed many western hunters when it was announced in 1962. Still, the .270 remains among the five most popular elk rounds in hunter surveys I've conducted over a decade. It excels for long shots at deer and sheep. O'Connor used his on moose. Alaskan guide Hosea Sarber is said to have dropped grizzlies with a .270. Federal and Hornady catalog 140-gr. bullets in High Energy and Light Magnum lines. Varmint hunters can detonate sodpoodles with Remington's 100-gr. load. A list of .270 factory loads would total nearly fifty, including excellent options from Fiocchi, Norma and RWS. Remington even fields a Managed-Recoil load. Roll your own? Mid-range powders like RL-15, IMR 4895, H380 and AA 2520 work with 130-gr. bullets. I prefer RL-19 and 4350 but have used lots of surplus H-4831. Yes, you can dump H-4831 into a .270 hull, card it off at the mouth, seat a 130-gr. bullet, then lay deer low. You'll get better accuracy with a scale, though.

130-GR. BALLISTIC SILVERTIP (WINCHESTER), 200-YARD ZERO

	Muzzle	100 Yds	200 Yds	300 Yds	400 Yds
Velocity, fps	3050	2828	2618	2416	2224
Energy, ft-lbs	2685	2309	1978	1685	1428
Arc, inches	-1.5	+1.4	0	-6.5	-18.9

.270 WEATHERBY MAGNUM

When it appeared in 1943 the .270 Weatherby must have wowed hunters. Roy claimed a starting velocity of 3,375 fps with 130-gr. bullets – 300 fps faster than the .270 Winchester! This flat-shooting cartridge was the first of Weatherby's magnums to gain commercial status. Developed on the heels of his .220 Rocket, it featured a .300 H&H hull trimmed to 2.55 inches to fit .30-06-length actions. The .257 and 7mm Weatherbys followed on the abbreviated case; the full-length .300 Weatherby arrived in 1944, a year before Roy started his rifle business.

The .270 Weatherby Magnum is, to my mind, the quintessential long-range big game round. You could say as much about the 7mm Weatherby. But few others qualify. The hugely popular 7mm Remington and badly mistreated .264 Winchester Magnums have similar cases, but neither matches the .270 Weatherby as Norma loads it – with 130-gr. softpoints and 140 Ballistic Tips that kill deer like the hammer of Thor. The 130 Barnes TSX, with 130 Partition, 140 Accubond and 150 Partition bullets (all factory-loaded) offer reach, punch and penetration

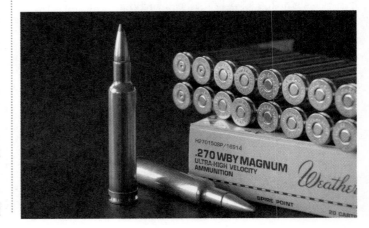

aplenty for elk. A Montana bull I shot a couple of years ago took a 140-gr. AccuBond at 300 yards, sprinted hard downhill, then skidded on his nose. He was dead in seconds, though I found the bullet had struck farther back than I'd have liked.

Weatherby lists nine Norma loads, from 100-gr. softpoints at 3,760 fps to 150-gr. Partitions at 3,245. If you want to shoot 100-gr. bullets, get a .25-06 – or a .257 Weatherby Magnum. Roy's powerful .270 is best paired with 130- to 150-gr. spitzers. Its 140- and 150-gr. bullets fly from the roost 140 fps faster than do bullets of the same weight from the 7mm Remington. They hold up a little better downrange too. This sizzling .270 will carry a ton of energy past 400 yards with 140 AccuBonds. Several factory loads let you zero at 300 yards without putting sight-line more than 3-1/2 inches below bullet arc at 200! Though Winchester's .270 Short Magnum is a ballistic twin to the Weatherby, the WSM doesn't feed as smoothly. Despite its lethal sting, the .270 Weatherby Magnum is civil in recoil.

140-GR. ACCUBOND (NORMA-LOADED, WEATHERBY), 300-YARD ZERO

	Muzzle	100 Yds	200 Yds	300 Yds	400 Yds
Velocity, fps	3320	3113	2916	2727	2547
Energy, ft-lbs	3427	3014	2644	2313	2016
Arc, inches	-1.5	+2.8	+3.4	0	-8.1

7MM-08 REMINGTON (7X57 MAUSER)

It was not the first modern 7mm round designed for use in short-action rifles – though that was the claim in 1980 when the 7mm-08 appeared. The .284 Winchester pre-dated it by 17 years. But the 7mm-08 might be considered the first successful modern short-action 7mm. Based on the .308 Winchester case, with no change except neck diameter, the 7mm-08 was first loaded with 140-gr. pointed Core-Lokts. Remington now lists a 120-gr. hollow-point and a 140 AccuTip as well – plus a Managed Recoil load with 140-gr. pointed Core-Lokts. Other major ammo firms offer many other options. The first rifles chambered in 7mm-08 were the Remington M788 and M700. Now it's in most short-action bolt guns, plus Browning's BLR. While case capacity is slightly less than that of the 7x57 Mauser (its 2.04 inch hull is .2 inch shorter than the Mauser's), the 7mm-08 is typically loaded to higher velocities.

With a 140-gr. softpoint at 2,860 fps, the 7mm-08 matches the speed of a 150-gr. bullet in the .284 Winchester. Even more ambitious are Hornady's Light Magnum offerings, with 139-gr. SST and Interbond bullets exiting at 3,000 fps. Efficient case design, and bullets suitable for most North American big game, make the 7mm-08 a fine choice for all-around hunting. Civil in recoil, it's a perfect match for lightweight rifles. It's also a favorite on metallic silhouette ranges, where its 140-gr. bullets reach 500-yard targets faster and with as much energy as 150-gr. .308s. Though 160-gr. bullets would be useful in some applications, their length would require deep seating in many rifles.

The 7x57, developed in the nascent years of smokeless powder, ranks as one of the most useful big game rounds ever. Armies around the world adopted it soon after its 1893 introduction. Hunters in the far reaches of the British empire shot mountains of game with it. Even elephants fell to its long, blunt 173-gr. solids. Most popular now with 139- to 150-gr. softpoints, it remains a stellar choice for deer-size game. The slightly shorter 7mm-08 is a better fit for .308-length actions, and the longer .270 offers a little more punch; still the 7x57 endures, a deadly, light-recoiling round for most of the game most people hunt.

139-GR. INTERLOCK (HORNADY LIGHT MAGNUM), 200-YARD ZERO

	Muzzle	100 Yds	200 Yds	300 Yds	400 Yds
Velocity, fps	3000	2759	2530	2312	2106
Energy, ft-lbs	2777	2348	1975	1650	1368
Arc, inches	-1.5	+1.5	0	-7.0	-20.5

7MM REMINGTON MAGNUM (7MM WEATHERBY MAGNUM)

In 1892 Peter Paul Mauser and his brother Wilhelm designed a turn-bolt military rifle for the 7x57 Mauser cartridge. The 1893 Mauser and its smokeless round quickly filled arsenals the world over. Hunters liked it too. Meanwhile, England, F.W. Jones designed a 7mm round for Sir Charles Ross and ammunition giant Eley. But the Ross rifle was flawed, and bullets failed at impact speeds of nearly 3,000 fps. In 1907 John Rigby introduced the .275 Rimless, a 7x57 clone. The .280 Rimless Jeffery came in 1915, with a 140-gr. bullet crowding 3,000 fps. Two years later in Germany, Wilhelm Brenneke offered the similar 7x64.

During the 1920s and '30s, wildcatters concocted several 7mms on the belted .300 Holland case and on Charles Newton's rimless .30. The Western Cartridge Company produced, briefly, John Dubiel's .276. An improved version came from Griffin & Howe. The .280 Dubiel, with its .288 bullet, got higher speeds from full-length .300 H&H brass, as did A.E. Mashburn. *Field & Stream* shooting editor Warren Page took a lot of game with his 7mm Mashburn. Charlie O'Neil, Elmer Keith and Don Hopkins came up with a .285 OKH. Holland's .275 Belted Rimless Magnum Nitro was loaded to uninspiring levels by Western Cartridge until 1939. Five years later Roy Weatherby announced his 7mm, on a Holland hull trimmed to 2.55 inches.

The 7mm Weatherby Magnum as loaded by Norma is a full-throttle round, lanching the 120-gr. Barnes TSX at 3,430 fps and 160-gr. Nosler Partitions at 3,200. Weatherby lists nine loads, with bullets as heavy as 175 grains. Truly a versatile cartridge, this 7mm got a lukewarm reception at first, because only Weatherby rifles chambered it. Then, in 1962, Remington announced a similar round. The 7mm Remington Magnum came with the introduction of Remington's M700 rifle. Both were instant hits. Wyoming outfitter Les Bowman blessed the new 7mm as a top pick for elk and mule deer. It had the reach of a .270 but more punch. Subsequently, it has appeared in every rifle built for short belted magnums. In my surveys, the 7mm Remington Magnum is as popular as the .30-06 among elk hunters. With 150-gr. bullets at 3,110 fps, this belted 7 is truly versatile. Pointed 150- and 160-gr. bullets carry a ton of energy past 300 yards. Federal's Trophy Bonded 175s at 2,900 fps excel for deep penetration in tough game.

150-GR. SIERRA GAMEKING (FEDERAL), 200-YARD ZERO

	Muzzle	100 Yds	200 Yds	300 Yds	400 Yds
Velocity, fps	3110	2920	2750	2580	2410
Energy, ft-lbs	3220	2850	2510	2210	1930
Arc, inches	-1.5	+1.3	0	-5.9	-17.0

.300 SAVAGE

Born June 13, 1857 in Kingston, Jamaica, Arthur Savage went to school in England and the United States. Immediately after college he sailed for Australia, where he found work on a cattle ranch. Arthur also found a wife, Annie Bryant, and started a family. One of his sons was born in a wagon on a wilderness trek. At the end of his 11-year stay in Australia, he reportedly owned the biggest ranch on the continent. He sold it to explore other frontiers, notably in the munitions field. With another inventor, he developed the Savage-Halpine torpedo. It was later sold to the Brazilian government. In 1892, when Savage was 35 years old, he designed an infantry rifle, a hammerless lever-action. Submitted it for testing at the 1892 ordnance trials, it was beaten by the Krag-Jorgensen. Turning next to sportsmen, Arthur Savage refined the rifle and developed a new cartridge for it – the .303 Savage. In 1894 he formed Savage Arms Company in Utica, New York.

Savage's Model 1895 was offered only in .303. In 1900, a year after the improved rifle was dubbed the Model 1899, it became available in .30-30; in 1903 the .25-35, .32-40 and .38-55 arrived. The .303 and .30-30 lasted till World War II. The .250/3000 Savage, designed by Charles Newton in 1913, remained a signature chambering throughout the 99's long life. The .25-35, .32-40 and .38-55 were dropped by 1920, when the firm introduced its .300 Savage cartridge, intending to duplicate .30-06 performance in short actions. Falling short of this lofty standard, the round still proved popular. When in the early 1950s the U.S. Army considered replacing the .30-06 in battle rifles, they turned to the .300 Savage. Its neck proved too short for reliable functioning in machine guns, so they lengthened it. Result: the military 7.62 NATO, or .308 Winchester.

The .300 Savage is now almost lost in the shadow of the .308 and other more potent rounds. Still, it is a fine deer cartridge, with lighter recoil than the .308. Now nearly 90 years old, the .300 Savage once ranked among the top choices among elk hunters. I've shot mule deer, pronghorns and caribou with 150-gr. pointed Core-Lokts, which fly flatter than bluff-nosed 180s.

.300 SAVAGE, 150 SP (FEDERAL), 225-YARD ZERO

	Muzzle	100 Yds	200 Yds	300 Yds	400 Yds
Velocity, fps	2630	2350	2100	1850	1630
Energy, ft-lbs	2305	1845	1460	1145	885
Arc, inches	-1.5	+3.0	+1.0	-8.3	-27.2

.308 MARLIN EXPRESS

It was designed to match the .308 Winchester ballistically, yet fit and feed in a loop-belly carbine with a 47,000 psi pres-

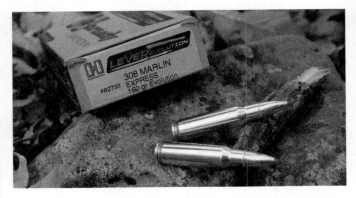

sure lid. Tall order. But in 2004 Hornady's Dave Emary had just finished developing lever-action ammo with pointed bullets. LeverEvolution .30-30 cartridges shot much flatter than traditional rounds, but as the bullet tips were of soft polymer, they were still safe in tube magazines.

The .308 Marlin Express derived from the .307 Winchester, a rimmed cartridge introduced for the Winchester M94 in 1980. The .307 lags behind the .308 Winchester by about as much as it beats the .300 Savage: 100 fps. The .308 Marlin Express case is a .307 shortened from 2.015 inches to 1.920. A mere .050 inch longer than the .300 Savage, it outperforms both the Savage and the .307.

New ball powders enabled Dave Emary and company to get more from the .308 ME case than was possible earlier with the .307. And Hornady's flex-tip bullets held onto that velocity down-range. The 160-gr. bullet fashioned specially for this round has a long ogive (.140 inch longer than on the .307). In fact, that shallow curve forced Hornady's team to shorten the case. They moved the Interlock band is as far forward as possible, for high weight retention. From a 22-inch barrel rifled 1-in-10, the .308 Marlin Express clocks an honest 2,660 fps and passes the 300-yard mark at over 2,000. It carries 1,200 foot-pounds to 400 yards!

The cartridge is inherently accurate. Scoped with a Leupold variable, my Marlin XLR punched out a three-shot group miking an even inch. That first season in New Mexico, I used it on elk, triggering a shot as the six-point bull quartered to me at 70 yards. The Hornady bullet smashed his scapula. The animal went down shortly as I followed up with the fast-cycling Marlin 336. A post-mortem showed either bullet would have been lethal. For all-around big game hunting, the .308 ME delivers! It hits like a .308 Winchester but keeps pressures to levels that will never give you a sticky case!

160-GR. EVOLUTION (HORNADY), 250-YARD ZERO

	Muzzle	100 Yds	200 Yds	300 Yds	400 Yds
Velocity, fps	2660	2438	2226	2026	1836
Energy, ft-lbs	2513	2111	1761	1457	1187
Arc, inches	-1.5	+3.0	+1.7	-6.7	-23.5

.308 WINCHESTER

Shortly after World War II, ordnance officers began looking for an infantry cartridge to replace the .30-06. The short neck of the .300 Savage made it incompatible with machine guns. The chosen alternative: a similar case with a longer neck and gentler shoulder. The T-65 experimental round became a sporting cartridge first, when in 1952 Winchester (which helped in its development) dubbed it the .308 Winchester. Three years

later the U.S. Army adopted it as the 7.62 Nato.

Chambered in M88 and M100 lever-action and autoloading rifles, as well as in the Model 70, the .308 quickly drew a following. Remington listed the .308 in its M722 beginning in 1956. Since then, every modern bolt gun I can think of has been bored for this cartridge – plus pump rifles, autoloaders and lever-actions like the Browning BLR and Savage 99.

Factory loadings for the .308 include bullets as light as 110 grains, which Hornady stokes to 3,165 fps. But it and Remington's 125-gr. Managed Recoil offering are both less versatile than the many 150- and 165-gr. loads. In my view, 180-gr. bullets belong in a bigger case; still, the .308 gives them lethal speed. A top pick among heavy payloads is Federal's potent High Energy package, with a 180 Partition at 2,740. Hornady sells high-octane performance in the 150-gr. category with its Light Magnum Interlocks at 3,000. I like Federal's Trophy Bonded 165 for tough game. Norma catalogs its fine 180-gr. Oryx, plus Nosler and Swift bullets from 150 to 180 grains. Black Hills lists three hunting loads, besides match ammo with 155-, 168- and 175-gr. BTHPs. A 168-gr. or 175-gr. Sierra MatchKing offers all the accuracy you can use to 600 yards and suffices at 1,000 until wind gives the edge to faster .30s. The .308 is factory-loaded to 52,000 CUP (62,000 PSI), high enough that you won't want to handload much hotter.

mouths and could cause pressure spikes. An alloy of zinc and copper, 5-95 or 10-90, solved this problem. It became known as gilding metal. World War I demonstrated the value of high ballistic coefficients, so the Army replaced the 150-gr. bullet with a 173-gr. spitzer at 2,646 fps. This M-1 cartridge plagued troops to 5,500 yards. In 1939 the Army reduced recoil with the M-2 load, a 152-gr. spitzer at 2,805 fps. We used it to win World War II.

As a hunting cartridge, the .30-06 is a fine choice for any North American big game and for all but a few ponderous beasts abroad. It is the all-around cartridge, chambered in more rifles than any other round except, now, the .308. During the first 25 years of M70 production, Winchester sold the rifle in 18 chamberings. More than a third of these M70s (208,218) were .30-06s! Ballistically, the '06 nearly matches the 7mm Remington Magnum – in fact, high-octane loads from Hornady and Federal beat the big 7.

The .30-06 has kept company with some well-known shooters, from Teddy Roosevelt to present-day globetrotters whose '06s have salted the pages of Boone & Crockett and Safari Club records books.

Jack O'Connor used 53 grains of IMR 4320 behind 150-gr. bullets for 2,950 fps; Townsend Whelen launched 165-gr. boattails with 58 grains of 4350; Warren Page claimed fine accuracy with 180-gr. bullets and 55 grains of 4350.

168 BALLISTIC SILVERTIP (WINCHESTER SUPREME), 200-YARD ZERO

	Muzzle	100 Yds	200 Yds	300 Yds	400 Yds
Velocity, fps	2670	2484	2306	2134	1971
Energy, ft-lbs	2659	2301	1983	1699	1449
Arc, inches		+2.1	0	-8.6	-24.8

.30-06 SPRINGFIELD

The .30-06 cartridge dates to 1900, when engineers at Springfield Armory started work on a rifle to replace the .30-40 Krag-Jorgensen. Their prototype emerged in 1901. Two years later the 1903 Springfield appeared. Its 30-caliber rimless round featured a 220-gr. bullet at 2,300 fps – a ballistic match for the 8x57 and its 236-gr. bullet at 2,125 fps. A year after the .30-03's debut, Germany switched to a 154-gr. 8mm spitzer at 2,800 fps. The Americans countered with the Ball Cartridge, Caliber .30, Model 1906. It hurled a 150-gr. bullet at 2,700 fps from a case shortened .07, to .494. All .30-03 rifles were recalled for rechambering.

The first .30-06 bullets were jacketed with an alloy of 85 percent copper, 15 percent nickel. It did not hold up at .30-06 velocities, and fouling rendered rifles inaccurate. Tin plating reduced fouling, but over time, tin "cold-soldered" to case

180-GR. ACCUBOND CT (WINCHESTER SUPREME), 200-YARD ZERO

	Muzzle	100 Yds	200 Yds	300 Yds	400 Yds
Velocity, fps	2750	2573	2403	2239	2082
Energy, ft-lbs	3022	2646	2308	2004	1732
Arc, inches	-1.5	+1.8	0	-7.9	-22.8

.300 REMINGTON SHORT-ACTION ULTRA MAG (.300 RUGER COMPACT MAGNUM)

It was the beginning of the 21st century. While Remington was completing its Ultra Mag cartridge line, Winchester was introducing its .300 Winchester Short Magnum. Remington followed quickly with its .300 and 7mm Short-Action Ultra Mags – but too late to upstage the .300 and .270 WSMs.

The rush to short rimless cases started on the benchrest circuit. Lou Palmisano and Ferris Pindell, both accomplished shooters, stumbled upon the .220 Russian, a necked-down 7.62x39. They reshaped it to form what would become the .22 PPC. That was in 1974; a 6mm PPC would soon follow. Base to shoulder, these hulls measured barely an inch. Palmisano expected a shorter powder column to yield better accuracy. It did. By 1980, fifteen of the top twenty had a PPC on the line. In 1989 all of them used PPCs.

John Lazzeroni was next to champion short cases, in powerful hunting rounds based on the .404 Jeffery case. Then, in 1999 came the .300 WSM. Though it beat Remington short magnums to market, it did not make them irrelevant. SAAMI determined then that Remington's .300 and 7mm cartridges differed enough in name and dimensions from the Winchester rounds to warrant production of both groups. Slightly shorter than the .300 WSM, Remington's .300 Short Action Ultra Mag delivers the same performance, and it fits in the firm's compact Model Seven action. My chronograph shows 180-gr. Partitions at 2,940 fps.

Most recently, Hornady has joined the competition with .300 and .338 Ruger Compact Magnums, They have an edge on WSM and SAUM rounds in carbine-length barrels, thanks to proprietary propellants. I killed an elk with a lightweight Remington Model Seven Alaskan in .300 SAUM and a moose with a Ruger 77 Hawkeye carbine in .300 RCM. Magnum performance from short, lightweight rifles: Bravo!

180-GR. PARTITION (REMINGTON), 200-YARD ZERO

	Muzzle	100 Yds	200 Yds	300 Yds	400 Yds
Velocity, fps	2960	2761	2571	2389	2214
Energy, ft-lbs	3501	3047	2642	2280	1959
Arc, inches	-1.5	+1.5	0	-6.8	-19.7

.300 H&H MAGNUM

In 1925 the British firm of Holland and Holland came out with "Holland's Super .30," a necked-down .375 H&H Magnum. The long (2.85-inch) tapered case had an 18-1/2-degree shoulder, which helped it slide eagerly into the chambers of magnum Mausers. Almost immediately, Western Cartridge Company began loading the round in the U.S. as the .300 H&H Magnum. It drove a 180-gr. bullet 200 fps faster than could a .30-06. Competitive shooter Ben Comfort used a rifle in this chambering to win the 1,000-yard Wimbledon Cup Match in 1935. By that time it had become popular in custom sporters by Griffin & Howe. A charter chambering in the Winchester Model 70 (1937), it later appeared in Remington's M721 (1948). Because it required a magnum action, the .300 Holland could not be as widely adopted as its contemporary, the .270. The advent of Weatherby's .300 in 1945, and the 7mm Remington and .300 Winchester Magnums in the early 60s, put the skids on this fine cartridge.

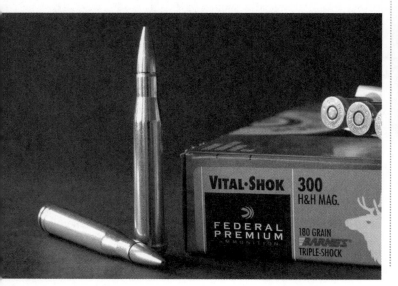

Ballistically, Holland's Super .30 falls squarely between the .30-06 and .300 Winchester Magnum. It seems no more violent in recoil than the '06, but offers 400 more foot-pounds of energy at the muzzle. At 300 yards, the margin is still nearly 300 foot-pounds. I killed my first elk with a .300 H&H. I have owned several and regret parting with every one I've sold. They all shot well (One M70 punched a 7/8-inch group at 200 yards). The .300 H&H has a stellar reputation on big game the world over. I used it to down a huge eland bull with one 180-gr. Core-Lokt in front of 69 grains H4831.

Once loaded by several firms with 150-, 180- and 220-gr. bullets at 3,190, 2,880 and 2,620 fps, the .300 H&H is now offered only by Federal, with 180-gr. Nosler Partition and Barnes Triple Shock bullets. Handloaders are well served with powders like RL19, H4350, AA 3100, IMR 4831, VIHT N-160.

180-GR. BARNES TRIPLE-SHOCK (FEDERAL), 200-YARD ZERO

	Muzzle	100 Yds	200 Yds	300 Yds	400 Yds
Velocity, fps	2880	2680	2480	2290	2120
Energy, ft-lbs	3315	2860	2460	2105	1790
Arc, inches	-1.5	+1.7	0	-7.3	-21.3

.308 NORMA MAGNUM (.300 WINCHESTER MAGNUM)

The .308 Norma Magnum – a product of A.B. Norma Projectilfabrik of Amotfors, Sweden – came to the U.S. in 1960, a year after the .358 Norma Magnum. Oddly enough, both rounds arrived in the form of unprimed cases only! Loaded ammunition would follow 18 months later; but the lag did nothing to endear the new rounds to American shooters. A shortened, blown-out .300 H&H Magnum, the .308 has almost identical capacity. But it is 2.56 inches long, not 2.85; so it fits standard-length actions. A "re" stamp on the first case heads meant they were Boxer-primed, thus reloadable. (Berdan priming once prevailed in Europe.)

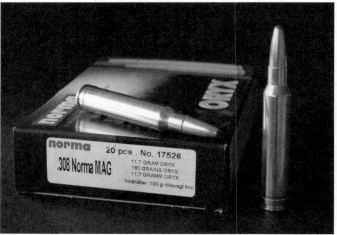

Shultz & Larsen and Husqvarna built rifles for the new Norma cartridges right away. Browning's High Power rifles was also chamberd for the .308 Norma Magnum; it arrived in 1959, just in time for the Norma chamberings. The High Powers were lovely indeed, with fine walnut and deep blue. As a youngster, I wanted one badly. Alas, the series was dropped in 1974, to be replaced eventually by the A-Bolt. The Norma chamberings did not carry over.

The .308 Norma is essentially a .30-338, a wildcat that hunters adopted after the .338 Magnum's debut in 1958. The Norma case is insignificantly longer, its rim insignificantly smaller. Its case is almost .1 inch shorter than the .300 Winchester's; but the .308 Norma has a .318 inch neck, compared to the .300's .264 inch neck. The slightly greater capacity of the Winchester's case delivers a negligible ballistic edge. The .308 Norma can kick 180-gr. bullets at nearly 3,100 fps from a 24-inch barrel. I zero for 200 yards, shade six inches high at 300 and eighteen at 400 – where this .30 still carries a ton of energy.

The last elk I took with the .308 Norma fell at just 40 yards in Idaho timber to a Norma load with a 180-gr. Nosler Partition. Handloaders use powders of medium to slow burn rate. I prefer IMR 4350 and H4831, RL-19, RL-22 and H1000. Heavy bullets do well with IMR 7828.

200-GR. NOSLER PARTITION, 71.0 GR. RL22, 27" DOUGLAS BARREL (NEAR-MAXIMUM LOAD!), 200-YARD ZERO

	Muzzle	100 Yds	200 Yds	300 Yds	400 Yds
Velocity, fps	2955	2760	2575	2390	2225
Energy, ft-lbs	4040	3515	3045	2630	2255
Arc, inches	-1.5	+1.7	0	-6.8	-20.4

.338 MARLIN EXPRESS

For more than a century, bullets for tube magazines have worn blunt noses. Pointed bullets resting against primers posed a hazard in recoil. Then Hornady came up with "flex-tip" bullets that fly like hard-tipped spitzers but are safe in tube magazines. LEVERevolution ammunition added reach to the .30-30 and similar cartridges and revived interest in lever-action rifles. But Dave Emary and his fellow engineers did not

Author killed this pronghorn with an iron-sighted Marlin 1895 XLR in .338 Marlin Express.

stop at the bullet tip. They experimented with new powders to boost muzzle velocities. Then Hornady announced the .308 Marlin Express, which offered .308 Winchester performance at pressures compatible with rear-locking, lever guns. In 2007 the .338 ME met an even more ambitious goal: it matched the .30-06.

Winchester's M71 rifle in .348 Winchester once held title as the most potent tube-fed lever-action, but its blunt bullets lost enthusiasm fast. Marlin's Model 1895 in .450 Marlin hits hard inside 100 yards, but even pointed .45 bullets lack the ballistic coefficient to stay with bullets of smaller diameter. Federal's .338 operates at pressures too high for traditional lever rifles. The Hornady team turned to the .376 Steyr, which Hornady already manufactured, and changed dimensions to come up with a new .33. Emary and company re-engineered their 200-gr. .338 Winchester Magnum bullet, installing a thinner jacket and a flexible tip.

Factory loaded, the .338 Marlin Express measures 2.60 inches. The 1.89-inch semi-rimmed case has a 25-degree shoulder and a base diameter of .553. At 2,565 fps, the .338 ME's pointed 200-gr. bullet matches the velocity and energy of the .348 Winchester bullet at the muzzle, then quickly leaves it behind. Out of the gate, the .338 Marlin Express bullet can't quite equal the punch of the .450 Marlin's. But they land with equal authority at 100 yards. Beyond that, the ballistically superior .338 takes over. It very nearly duplicates the arc and payload of a 210-gr. Nosler Partition from the .338 Federal, but at lower pressure. The flight path and energy package match those for a 180-gr. spitzer from a .30-06.

200-GR. FTX (HORNADY), 250-YARD ZERO

	Muzzle	100 Yds	200 Yds	300 Yds	400 Yds
Velocity, fps	2565	2365	2174	1992	1820
Energy, ft-lbs	2922	2484	2099	1762	1471
Arc, inches	-1.5	+3.0	+1.2	-7.9	-25.9

.338 FEDERAL

You'll look hard to find a more practical, versatile cartridge than the .338 Federal, though it's not yet five years old. You'll find none that crams so much power into a .308 case, though we've had that hull for more than 50 years. This compact round begs comparison with the .30-06 and even the .338 Winchester Magnum. The .338 Federal launches 180-gr. bullets more than 100 fps faster than standard loads in the .30-06 and packs an additional 300 foot-pounds of muzzle energy.

Winchester's .338 Magnum has been around for nearly half a century now, and while it didn't set sales records initially, many elk hunters now consider it the ideal mix of reach and bone-crushing power, in a case compatible with standard rifle actions. While the .338 Federal has less authority than the magnum, it also has considerably less recoil. And there's less difference downrange than you might think. With a 180-gr. bullet, the .338 Federal shoots as flat as the Magnum with a 210 Partition. At the muzzle, a 210 in the .338 Federal clocks the same as a 250 from the Magnum and strikes within a vertical inch of it at 300 yards.

The commercial success of Federal's new .33 is still in question. Weatherby's introduction a few years ago of the excellent .338-06 should have sucked buyers from the woodwork. But though the .338-06 ranks as one of the most popular American wildcats, it has not sold well as a Mark V chambering. Perhaps if ammunition firms Stateside had followed Norma in loading the round, and domestic manufacturers had offered it in ordinary rifles, its fortunes would have improved. In my view, the .338 Federal deserves more attention than do many cartridges introduced in the last decade. Like the .338-06, it is effective on game as big as elk out to the ranges most hunters can hit vitals. It's efficient in barrels of modest length, manageable in recoil, easy to handload. Magazines hold more .338 Federal rounds than they will any short magnums.

185-GR. BARNES TRIPLE-SHOCK (FEDERAL), 200-YARD ZERO

	Muzzle	100 Yds	200 Yds	300 Yds	400 Yds
Velocity, fps	2750	2550	2350	2160	1980
Energy, ft-lbs	3105	2660	2265	1920	1615
Arc, inches	-1.5	+1.9	0	-8.3	-24.1

.338 WINCHESTER MAGNUM

The first belted magnum from Winchester appeared in 1956. It pushed a 500-gr. bullet at 2,130 fps. Muzzle energy exceeded 2 1/2 tons. But if you didn't have elephants among the melons, or the jack for a 21-day safari, you didn't really need a .458. Two years later Winchester announced a necked-down belted magnum, the .338. Like the .458, its hull was 2.50 inches long, .35 shorter than that of the parent .375 H&H Magnum. So the

.338 fit .30-06-length rifle actions – as had Roy Weatherby's .257, .270 and 7mm rounds fifteen years earlier. Still over-powered for most game (Winchester named its .338 rifle the Model 70 Alaskan), the new cartridge started slowly. In 1964, when Winchester overhauled its M70, .338 ammunition listed for $6.30 a box, a buck and a half more than '06 cartridges. You could choose Winchester or Western ammo with 200-, 250- and 300-gr. softpoints, at roughly 2,950, 2,650 and 2,450 fps. The 300-gr. round-nose factory load soon expired, but more useful 225-gr. bullets later became options, at 2,800 fps.

As I recall, most hunters in the early 1960s thought of the .338 Magnums as a specialized cartridge for truculent bears and 70-inch moose. Now such magnums are considered do-all cartridges for the recoil-tolerant. Bullets of all types, Ballistic Tips to solids, have appeared for this .33. Hornady Heavy Magnum ammo features 225-gr. Interlock bullets at 2,950 fps. This stellar long-range elk load shoots flatter than a 180-gr. .30-06 and brings 2,100 ft-lbs to 400 yards, as much as most '06 bullets claim at 200. The .338 Magnum roars past the rimmed .33 Winchester, a forebear that, in 1902, hurled 200-gr. flat-point bullets at 2,200 fps from lever guns. The .340 Weatherby, which followed the .338 in 1962, outperforms it – from a longer action. Ditto the rimless .338 Lapua, a Finnish sniper cartridge that

arrived in 1983, and the .338 Remington Ultra Mag, circa 2000. The .338 Winchester Magnum remains the most versatile of the big .33s.

225-GR. BARNES TRIPLE-SHOCK (FEDERAL), 200-YARD ZERO

	Muzzle	100 Yds	200 Yds	300 Yds	400 Yds
Velocity, fps	2800	2610	2430	2260	2090
Energy, ft-lbs	3915	3405	2950	2545	2185
Arc, inches	-1.5	+1.8	0	-7.7	-22.3

.35 WHELEN (.350 REMINGTON MAGNUM)

Shortly after the .30-06 appeared in 1906, wildcatters began reshaping the case. James V. Howe of Griffin & Howe may have fashioned the first .35 Whelen, naming it after firearms guru Colonel Townsend Whelen. The round may also have been Whelen's. In 1922, when it surfaced, Whelen was the commanding officer at Frankfort Arsenal; Howe was a toolmaker there. No doubt the two collaborated. The .35 Whelen served hunters who wanted heavier bullets than offered by the .30-06 but flatter flight than possible with Winchester's .405. Because the only change in the '06 case was an expanded neck, the .35 Whelen cycled in any rifle designed for the .30-06. Many Depression-era barrels pitted by potassium chlorate primers were rebored to .35 Whelen. But after Winchester declared in 1937 that it would chamber the M70 in .300 and .375 H&H, interest in .35s waned. The .35 Winchester and .35 Newton were last factory loaded in 1936.

The .350 Remington Magnum appeared in the M660 rifle, here camouflaged by the owner.

The .35 Whelen remained a handloading proposition until 1988, when Remington chambered it in the M700 and began making ammo. But twenty years earlier, Remington had developed its own .35 magnum on the familiar Holland case. The .350 Remington Magnum, first available in 1965, was sized to fit the 2.80-inch magazine of the new Model 600 Magnum rifle. In 1966 a 6.5 Remington Magnum appeared, also for .308-length actions. The company listed 200-gr. Core-Lokts from the .350 at 2,710 fps, faster by 200 fps than the 250. My shooting logs show original 200-gr. loads clocking 2,650 from a 22-inch tube. In 1968 Remington replaced the 600 and 600 Magnum with new versions called 660s. But by end of 1971, they'd been dropped. Remington continued loading 6.5 and .350 Magnum cartridges. The .350 made an eight-year run in the Model 700; it fell from that list in 1974. You could still buy Remington factory loads in 1997.

In 2003 Remington revived its .350 Magnum in a rifle reminiscent of the 600. The Model 673 (6 for ancestry, 7 for the Model Seven action, 3 for the year of introduction) wore a stock of beech and walnut laminates, as had the 660 Magnum; but the profile is more appealing. I killed an elk with a 673.

The .350 Remington Magnum edges the .35 Whelen ballistically, but both excel where you might need deep-driving bullets to penetrate quartering animals that weigh as much as refrigerators. I've killed a moose with a Model 700 in .35 Whelen and a superb mule deer. A Remington M78 with a 26-inch Douglas barrel in .35 Whelen Improved gives me 2,750 fps with a 225 Partition. I dropped an elk with that rifle and a 250-gr. Speer. Remington's two Core-Lokts are still the only commercial .35 Whelen loads.

250-GR. POINTED CORE-LOKT (REMINGTON), 200-YARD ZERO

	Muzzle	100 Yds	200 Yds	300 Yds	400 Yds
Velocity, fps	2400	2197	2005	1823	1652
Energy, ft-lbs	3197	2680	2230	1844	1515
Arc, inches	-1.5	+2.8	0	-11.3	-33.2

.375 H&H MAGNUM (AND .375 RUGER)

Holland and Holland introduced the .375 Belted Rimless Nitro Express in 1912. It migrated to the U.S. from England in 1925, when Western Cartridge Company began loading it and its spawn, a belted .30, under the label, "Holland and Holland

Author with Heym double rifle. The .375 H&H Magnum is a popular chambering in doubles.

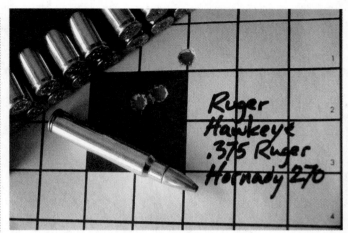

.375 Ruger, 100-yard group.

Magnum." About 1926, New York's Griffin & Howe began offering the .375 in magnum Mauser rifles. In 1937 Winchester put the cartridge on its charter roster of Model 70 chamberings. Remington listed it in the Model 725 Kodiak, fewer than 100 of which were built, all in 1961. Even Weatherby took an occasional order for a .375 H&H rifle, though Roy's line of high-velocity rounds included a blown-out version of the cartridge. All rifles bored for the .375 must have a full-length action to accommodate the 2.85-inch case. Overall SAAMI cartridge length is 3.60 inches.

Originally loaded with 270- and 300-gr. bullets, the .375 H&H has benefited from new bullets like Nosler's 260-gr. AccuBond, which carries more punch to 200 yards than the .30-06 musters at the muzzle. Drop at 300 yards is about the same. The .375 quiets big African beasts with the bone-mashing momentum of controlled-upset 300-gr. softpoints from Nosler and Barnes, Hornady, Winchester and Trophy Bonded. While some professional African hunters rate it as marginal for elephant and close-cover buffalo, the .375 has taken tens of thousands of both. New solid-bullet loads from Norma and Hornady confirm this as a dangerous-game cartridge.

Three years ago, Hornady upstaged the .375 H&H with the .375 Ruger, a shorter rimless cartridge that uses the same bolt face but whose case body starts out at belt diameter. Slightly greater capacity gives the .375 Ruger a ballistic edge of 130 fps. And it will snuggle into a .30-06-length action. The new Ruger round feeds well, if not quite as silkily as the long, tapered .375 H&H. Ruger Hawkeye rifles in .375 Ruger feel gunny – as did the first Winchester 70s bored for the .375 Holland & Holland.

260-GR. NOSLER ACCUBOND (FEDERAL), 200-YARD ZERO

	Muzzle	100 Yds	200 Yds	300 Yds	400 Yds
Velocity, fps	2700	2510	2330	2160	1990
Energy, ft-lbs	4210	3640	3130	2685	2285
Arc, inches	-1.5	+2.0	0	-8.5	-24.5

So there you have it: my picks for the top twenty rifle cartridges. If you had a brace of good rifles chambered for them, you'd be well turned-out to hunt anything in the world, from the tiniest prairie dog to the biggest bear. Your sentimental favorite may not appear on my list, but, to paraphrase Sen. Patrick Leahy, "You get fifteen hunters in a room, and you get twenty opinions!"

AN INSIDE LOOK AT AN AMERICAN CLASSIC

BY STEVE GASH

Gliding metal is received in rolls that weigh about 3,000 lbs. It is fed into a press that punches out "cups," the beginnings of bullet jackets. Gilding metal is composed of copper and zinc, usually 95:5%, but this ratio can vary considerably, depending on the type of bullet for which it is intended.

ranges were littered with spent .22 rimfire cases, and Vernon had an idea. He designed and built a machine that ironed out the rims of .22 cases and formed them into bullet jackets. It worked, and soon Speer was making .22-caliber jacketed bullets. An interesting adjunct to this story is that another handloading pioneer, Joyce Hornady, was Speer's partner in this enterprise for a while.

In 1944, Vernon Speer moved from Lincoln, Nebraska, to Lewiston, Idaho, bought some property along the Snake River, built a factory, and started making bullets. Speer produces bullets in that facility to this day. Speer Bullets became part of Alliant TechSystems (ATK) in 2001. This was an important development, as ATK also owns a host of other shooting-sports companies.

The ATK folks are justly proud of Speer Bullets and are not bashful in showing it off. Thus, in July of 2009, they invited several gun writers to Lewiston

Speer bullets have long been a staple of handloaders worldwide, but behind the name lies a fascinating history of a small-town entrepreneur who realized the American dream through hard work, innovation, and dedication to his customers.

As is true of many companies, necessity was the impetus behind Speer Bullets. Vernon Speer was a dedicated reloader, and in the early 1940s, he started making his own bullets. In those days, the military effort soaked up virtually all of the basic materials needed to make bullets, and copper was in especially short supply. But rifle

for a tour of the Speer plant and related company facilities in Lewiston. It was quite an experience. If you've got a few minutes, let me tell you about it.

While the Speer Bullets factory still overlooks the picturesque Snake River, Vernon would probably not recognize it today. The plant has been expanded and updated with state-of-the-art equipment and processes, where highly-trained engineers and technicians scurry about, assembling a vast array of specialized products – not only component bullets, but also handgun ammunition, as well.

With minor variations, Speer makes four basic types of bullets. Hollow-points for varmints and boat-tail match bullets are traditional "cup and core" bullets. The Hot-Cor and Grand Slam are standard big game bullets that utilize a molten-core process. Then there are the electroplated Uni-Cor and the Gold Dot bonded bullets. Each type has specialized design features for its intended purposes. Plus, Speer is offering some exciting new bullets that build on proven technology. More on these later.

Junk science not withstanding, lead is a basic requirement of most bullet making, and Speer uses lots of it. The factory receives foundry-certified lead alloy in 2,000-lb. blocks. Their antimony content varies from .85% to 3.0%, depending on the eventual use of the lead. Blocks are lowered into gigantic furnaces, melted at 820° F and re-cast into 305-pound cylindrical billets. The billets are then extruded in a huge press into wire for bullet cores. The diameter of the wire varies, depending on what caliber of bullet is it for. The wire is then fed into a machine that whacks off little cylinders of the appropriate length. These will become bullet cores.

(top) All operations are done under the watchful eyes of operators so everything goes according to plan. Here the billets are being processed into wire for bullet cores. (right) The wire is collected on spools and identified as to antimony content and diameter.

Meanwhile, in another part of the plant, huge spools of gilding metal are unrolled and pulled through a press that punches out cups that will become bullet jackets. A series of additional drawings lengthens the jackets and trims them to the proper length. The cores are seated and the bullet is swaged to its final form. Manufacture of the Hor-Cor jacket is similar, but in the Hot-Cor process, 100-lb. "pigs" of lead are melted and the molten metal is poured into the jacket, cooled, and then swaged to shape. The advantage of the Hot-Cor process is that it eliminates voids and air bubbles between the jacket and core and effectively locks the two together.

This prevents the jacket from slipping during expansion.

The Grand Slam bullet was introduced in 1975 and has become a favorite of many hunters. It uses a core made of a three-component alloy that is injected into the jacket at 900° F. The heavy jacket itself contains internal fluting to initiate expansion and "heel folds" near the jacket's base. When the core alloy cools in this "heel pocket," the two are locked together permanently.

Elsewhere in the sprawling complex, another high-tech operation is under way. Lead (with the proper antimony content) is formed into the cores of the Uni-Cor handgun bullets. These shiny little gems are very precisely made. For example, those destined to become 9mm

Tubs containing thousands of pre-formed cups dot the factory floor.

These neat little lead slugs will become cores for traditional "cup and core" bullets that have been the mainstay of reloaders for decades.

The innards of Uni-Cor bullets start out as a "pig" of lead alloy, like this one being lowered slowly into the melting furnace.

bullets measure exactly .349 inch in diameter. After the .003-inch jacket is electrochemically applied (to each side), the bullets mike the requisite .355 inch. The "jackets" are applied in huge tanks with special electroplating solutions in them. A large quantity of copper-alloy "slugs" and finished cores are placed in the tanks and gently rotated while a high-voltage current is transmitted

through the system. After a specified period of time, the almost-finished bullets emerge from the tanks with their new coats. This process, of course, permanently locks the core and jacket together with a chemical bond. After a quick bath, they're off to final swaging.

Construction of the Gold Dot bullet is somewhat similar to a traditional cup and core bullet, except that the jacket is bonded to the core to positively prevent separation. Gold Dots are made in various configurations for law enforcement and personal protection, as well as hunting versions, plus special loads for snub-nosed handguns. Speer also produces an extensive line of their Lawman and Gold Dot handgun ammunition in the Lewiston plant, in addition to the Blazer centerfire ammunition for CCI (also a part of ATK). A total of 68 difference loads is in the current lineup.

Lastly, the finished bullets and ammo are neatly boxed and readied for shipment to eager customers. This part of the operation is also a delight to watch as the colorful labels are applied

to the boxes and they are readied for shipment. The sight of these huge quantities of bullets made this dedicated handloader swoon.

Throughout the plant, everyone I met was a dedicated professional, and they went about their appointed tasks with enthusiasm and vigor. It was also reassuring to see many younger faces at work. This bodes well for the future.

Never one to rest on its laurels, Speer is actively expanding its component and ammunition lines for this year, and at the July fete, I had a chance to learn about, see and shoot one of their newest offerings.

The ATK/Speer honchos running this show assembled our gaggle of gun scribes at the Jack O'Connor Hunting & Heritage Hertitage Center in Lewiston for a pow-wow. There they presented a concise overview of the current Speer line and outlined plans for future developments. There was both good and (what I consider) bad news relayed here. The good news started with the announcement that the entire Speer brand will be updated and enhanced with new products. One of these was announced at the gathering, and was so new then that it hadn't even been named. Well, this new hunting bullet has now been christened, and it is called "DeepCurl." DeepCurl will be available in most popular weights and calibers, and the new bullet builds on Federal's Fusion technology. Consequently, it delivers

Speer's latest development is the "DeepCurl" hunting bullet, which provided fine accuracy, controlled expansion, and deep penetration in our tests. (No, they will not be offered for 7mm in 225-gr. weights, as shown on this mock-up SHOT Show box!)

excellent accuracy, deep penetration, reliable expansion. The "fusion" part means that the jacket will never, ever, separate from the core, period. Plus, it is to be "popularly priced." (This is marketing parlance for "inexpensive.") Some noises were made to the effect that DeepCurl might ultimately replace the Hot-Cor. This elicited howls of anguish from the audience, as the Hot-Cor has been whacking deer, elk, and various critters for decades.

The Gold Dot handgun line will also be expanded to include more specialized bullets for hunting and personal protection. Also anticipated for the very near future is a .20-caliber bullet for prairie dogs.

I was distressed to hear that the Grand Slam bullet might be discontinued at some future date. I told the Speer folks in no uncertain terms that they could not stop making the Grand Slam as long as I am alive. It is a highly effective big game bullet, and one of my all-time favorites. I doubt that this stern admonition made them quake in their boots, but at the 2010 SHOT Show, an ATK official told me that currently "there are no plans to discontinue the Grand Slam." And, I am pleased to report, the

Here your humble correspondent assembles some .327 Federal ammo on an RCBS Pro 2000 progressive press.

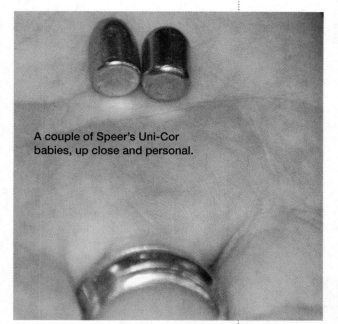

A couple of Speer's Uni-Cor babies, up close and personal.

entire lineups of Grand Slam and Hot-Cor bullets appear prominently in the latest Speer Bullets catalog. O joy!

Best of all, we got to shoot! At a beautifully appointed range nestled in the Idaho hills a short distance from the Snake River plant, Speer engineers were ready for us to test their wares.

There were reloading presses in place as well as adequate supplies of various components for us to assemble into test rounds, and we loaded up a bevy of neat numbers. I concentrated on the new .327 Federal Magnum and Speer's new 115-gr. Gold Dot .32-caliber bullet over 10.0 grains of Alliant's 2400 powder. Velocity was around 1,160 fps, and accuracy was excellent out of the Ruger SP-101 test gun. Other scribes worked on the stalwart .44 Magnum and everybody's favorite, the .30-06. A couple of big-bore fanatics loaded and then shot a .416 Rigby with Federal Premium's newly re-designed 400-gr. Trophy Bonded Bear Claw (TBBC).

We shot the .30-caliber, 180-gr. version of the then unnamed (DeepCurl) bullet out of a .30-06, first at paper targets, where one-inch groups were the rule, then into ballistic gelatin at 100 yards. It penetrated a total of 19 inches, and expansion was picture perfect. The retained weight of the bullet was 175.6 grains. As the bullet started out at 179.1 grains, this amounts to a loss of a whopping 3.5 grains (less than 2%).

We also loaded and fired the .30-caliber, 180-gr. version of Federal's new version of the TBBC bullet out of the .30-06. This sleek bullet is called the "Trophy Bonded Tipped," or TBT for short. Its most conspicuous feature is the brilliant nickel-plated jacket. Extensive tests by Federal engineers showed conclusively that the nickel plating actually fouled less than traditional jacket material and was more accurate over the long haul. The new bullet has a comely translucent polycarbonate tip, a demure crimping cannelure, and a sexy boattail. The shank of the bullet has three "bourrelet" grooves that give the metal displaced by the rifling a place to go. These aid accuracy and make the bullet more forgiving of variations in the rifle's bore diameter, reduce bullet yaw, and increase in-flight stability. The TBT will be available in popular diameters and weights in both Federal factory loads and as components for handloaders.

The 400-gr. TBBC out of the .416 Rigby bullet left no doubt that the biggest game in the world is in serious jeopardy. Over a stiff dose of Alliant's Reloder 19, the huge slug plowed through both 16-inch gelatin blocks, but the bullet was found on the ground behind just beyond the goo. It, too, expanded perfectly, and did not separate.

The tour of the Speer plant was extremely educational, and the informational seminar made it clear that the company is dynamically poised to remain a force in the reloading marketplace with new products and processes. I think Vernon Speer would pleased to see his legacy.

Clockwise, from the top:
NAA .22 Long Rifle, Charter Dixie
Derringer, NAA The Earl,
NAA .22 Magnum Pug,
NAA .22 Magnum.

the smallest revolvers

BY JEFF QUINN

for many years now, folks who have the need to go armed, but to do so in situations where discretion is of the utmost importance, often rely upon the handy little five-shot revolvers that have come to be known as mini guns. Having very little in common with the Minigun that is in use world-wide by the military, these diminutive revolvers are well-built, and all are made of stainless steel for corrosion resistance and durability.

These little weapons are usually carried in a pocket, or a svelte holster close to the skin, and are almost always subjected to sweat. In such an environment, stainless is a good choice of material. Stainless steel can corrode, but is much more resistant to corrosion than high carbon steel, and these little guns hold up quite well as a constant pocket companion.

Once also made by Freedom Arms, these small revolvers are now manufactured by North American Arms (NAA) of Provo, Utah, and by Charter Arms of Shelton, Connecticut. Both are solid American companies that have been making quality firearms for several years. NAA specializes in these mini revolvers, along with some compact pocket semi-auto pistols. Charter is famous for manufacturing compact, affordable revolvers such as their .44 Bulldog and five-shot .38 Special pocket guns but have been producing their Dixie Derringer mini rimfire revolvers for a couple of years now. Freedom Arms makes some of the world's most powerful hunting revolvers and single shot pistols, built to a degree of perfection unmatched in the gun industry, but their mini revolvers can still be found in the used gun market and command a

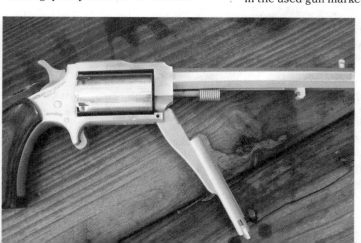

(farl left) NAA Pug Tritium front Night Sight.

(left) NAA The Earl has a unique base pin retainer lever.

premium from collectors

These smallest examples of the revolver maker's art have long been relied upon as last-ditch weapons for uniformed law enforcement officers, hidden away in a pocket or boot, used as an up-close-and-personal defensive weapon in the event that the officer lost the use of his primary duty gun. These compact five-shot rimfires are also carried daily by thousands of people who cannot, for whatever reason, conceal a larger weapon, or carried in addition to a larger handgun as a back-up gun.

Some scoff at the impotency of these 22-caliber handguns, and while they do not possess the power of a big-bore handgun, one of these tiny revolvers in the pocket is much better than a .45 that is left at home. The basic premise of carrying a handgun for protection is that it is ALWAYS within reach. Always. The need for a defensive firearm is, by definition, a response to an imminent or in-progress attack. When you need your defense handgun, you need it immediately. There is no time to go get it. It needs to be within reach. If you can't reach it, it is of no use to you.

As law-abiding citizens, we carry a defensive handgun as we go about our daily lives, doing the things that we do routinely every day. If we were expecting trouble, we would choose to not be in that place or would be armed with a fighting shotgun or rifle. If I were certain that trouble was coming, a .22 caliber rimfire revolver that is no bigger than a pack of smokes would be way down on my list of preferred weapons. Somewhat higher on the list, but still not near the top, would be a larger handgun. That, however, is where the compromise comes in: we must choose a balance between portability, concealability, and firepower. While way down on the firepower chart, the mini revolver is at the top of the easy-to-carry, easy-to-hide list. Also, especially in .22 Magnum caliber, these little guns can do quite well in a pinch, and I would much rather have one of these in my pocket than a knife as a defensive tool. In my experience, a .22 Magnum penetrates better than a .38 Special, and with any small caliber handgun projectile, penetration is paramount.

Another use for which these little revolvers really shine is as a snake gun. Every time I write about killing snakes, I get several emails from those who proclaim that we should never kill a poisonous snake and condemn me for promoting such practices. I get the

feeling that these folks most likely live in the city somewhere and never encounter a poisonous snake outside the confines of the local zoo. They certainly do not live out in the woods of the South or the deserts of the Southwest. I never kill a harmless snake, but around here, cottonmouths and copperheads are shot on sight. Tree-huggers tell us that a cottonmouth will not attack a human unless cornered, but they have failed to

(right) Most of the mini revolvers have a pushpin-type base pin.
(below) The NAA belt buckle "holster."
(bottom) The Charter Dixie Derringer and .22 Magnum NAA Mini conversion models have auxiliary .22 Long Rifle cylinders.

longer-barreled handgun, but the .22 Magnums still manage to exceed 1000 fps from these tiny guns. For defensive purposes, I like to stick with the hyper-velocity Long Rifle cartridges, such as the CCI Stinger, or better yet, one of the .22 Magnum loads, like the PMC Predator or Winchester Dynapoint hollowpoints.

You load all these little five-shot revolvers by removing the cylinder, poking out the empties with the base pin, inserting fresh cartridges one at a time and then replacing the cylinder. You won't win any speed-shooting contests with such a gun, and a quick combat reload is not in the cards. With these small handguns, five shots is pretty much all you're going to get in a fight, so the Magnums definitely have the edge in power.

I gathered a few samples of the current mini guns on the market for review here: four from NAA and the Dixie Derringer from Charter. The standard NAA Mini in .22 Magnum, as well as the Dixie .22 Magnum, came as convertible models, both having auxiliary .22 Long Rifle cylinders. These convertibles offer a lot of versatility, being able to chamber and fire .22 Short, Long, Long Rifle, and Magnum cartridges in the same gun. Again, given the choice, I like the Magnums for serious purposes, but the Long Rifle option offers a lot of inexpensive practice, simply by switching cylinders.

The Dixie Derringer has a crossbolt safety, while the NAA guns have notches between the chambers. Both methods

The NAA Mini is dwarfed by the compact Ruger LCP.

work well to keep the hammer away from the cartridge rims in the event that the revolver is dropped. All of these guns fire in the single action mode, meaning that the hammer much be manually cocked before the trigger can be pulled to fire the weapon.

Holsters are available for the mini revolvers from North American Arms or Simply Rugged Holsters, among others. NAA also has a dandy little belt buckle that holds their .22 Long Rifle Mini inside, giving the wearer the look of a rodeo cowboy but releasing the Mini into the palm quickly when needed.

While most of these small guns have short barrels, The Earl from NAA is unique among the breed, wearing a four-inch octagon barrel and having an underlever to retain the base pin, replicating the look of the old Remington revolvers from the nineteenth century. Besides being a very handy way to retain the base pin, it just plain looks cool, and I fell in love with The Earl at first sight. (That is a phrase that I never thought would enter my mind, by the way.)

The longer barrel and resulting longer sight radius make hitting with The Earl easier than with most of the mini revolvers, but they can all do pretty well. You won't see a mini revolver on the line at the National Matches at Camp Perry, but at defensive ranges, they can hold their own. The small sights are pretty hard to see with my fifty-year-old eyes, but the NAA Pug wears a Trijicon tritium front sight and an express rear sight, and seeing those sights, especially at night, is much easier. Firing the Pug, I could easily keep a cylinder full of ammo on a human silhouette target at 25 yards and a quick five into the head area of the same target offhand at seven yards. For defensive purposes, that is quite good enough. Most gunfights happen very quickly and within arms' reach, but it is good to know that the mini revolvers can still be used across a large room or down a hallway if needed. These small revolvers all weigh between one quarter and one-half pound each, depending on barrel length and chambering.

I fired all of the mini revolvers with a wide variety of Long Rifle and Magnum ammo, and all five guns functioned perfectly. They vary in small details such as the base pin style and barrel length, but they are all basically dandy little single action hideout guns. They ride easily in the pocket or a small holster, and can always be with reach. That is their most endearing trait, besides just being a lot of fun to shoot. These mini guns fill a niche that needed filling, and they offer the opportunity for a fighting chance in a tiny package.

The NAA Pug in .22 Magnum put a cylinderful on a silhouette at seven yards.

BUYING BULLET ALLOY ON THE INTERNET

BY KENNETH L. WALTERS

In the pre-internet days when you bought bullet metal, you purchased it from companies specializing in this stuff. Several firms had been around for decades and they advertised in the gun magazines regularly. All had excellent reputations. Order linotype and that is exactly what you got. But the internet changed all that. Now these firms are long gone, replaced by either online auction sites or online shooter supply firms.

There are problems with buying bullet metal at an online auction site. First, much of their bullet alloy is NOT what it is cracked up to be. You may think that you are buying linotype but you are probably just getting wheelweights. I'll explain what these alloys are shortly. Second, because these are auction sites their prices fluctuate wildly. Finally, you have to be very careful when you read the ads. I've seen some that suggest that you are bidding on a 50-pound lot but you aren't. If you read the fine print carefully you'll see that you are bidding on a per pound basis. You really need to pay close attention here. The one advantage of online auction sites is that they always have a lot of bullet metal for sale.

Dealing with the online shooter supply firms also has drawbacks. These shooter supply firms don't specialize in bullet alloy. They just have it as a catalogued item, one of many. And they don't carry much. If you want to buy hundreds of pounds you are just out of luck. Also, because they are low-volume sellers, their prices are REALLY high. This isn't price gouging. Their high prices simply reflect the fact that this is a low-volume item. It is really more of a customer service than anything else. The advantage of online shooter supply firms is that you get what you pay for. Order linotype and that is exactly what you will get.

There is one oddity about buying from an online shooter supply firm, incidentally. As near as I can tell they buy their bullet alloys in 56-lb. chunks consisting of eight 7-lb. ingots. They catalogue this stuff in multiples of these 7-lb. ingots. So there will be a price for 7 pounds, another for 28 and a third for 56. Catalogued items like this only disappear when they are sold out. The next time they get another shipment, usually at a higher price, they do not update the older listings, they just add new ones. The oddity here is that they may well have two absolutely identical catalogue items with vastly different prices. The 56-pound listings, for example, are the most expensive and, probably because of that, the slowest to sell out, so it is not uncommon to find several listing in these online catalogues for 56 pounds of linotype with considerably different prices. If you are going to buy bullet alloy from an online shooter supply firm ALWAYS compute the price per pound for every entry they have. Do not, for example, just compare the prices for the 56-pound lots. Compare them all and order the lots that have the lowest price per pound. This can save you a substantial amount of money!

How do you pick between online shooter supply firms and online auction sites? If you want to buy a small amount of bullet alloy, buy from one of the online shooter supply firms. You'll pay a very high price but you'll get what you ordered hassle-free. Order linotype from an online shooter supply firm and you'll get linotype. If you want to buy a lot of bullet metal, however, you are going to have to go to an online auction site.

Dealing with the online auction sites is an art form. It takes time and effort. If you are willing to spend the time and effort you can do well but this is NOT a hassle-free environment. You have to know what you are doing or you'll get taken!

Here's how to deal with an online auction site. Watch the online auction site listings for bullet alloy for some time before making your first purchase. You are looking for potential sellers that have been around for a while and who have a reasonable chance of being there in the future. You are going to make a considerable investment in time and effort in picking your seller so you want to be sure that after you do that that he will still be around. You also want to know what a reasonable price is for his alloys. Once you've picked a potential seller, e-mail him. All the auction sites allow this. Tell him that you are not interested in bidding on one of his large lots but would like to place a small order, twenty pounds or so. Offer to pay him what you know to be a fair price. You know what a fair price is because you have been following his auctions. Don't be cheap and don't offer too much. Just offer the going rate plus shipping. Most auction site sellers will sell you a small amount. Once you get your order, analyze it. If it is what it was claimed to be, buy more. I'll explain how to buy more while minimizing your cost shortly. If it isn't what it is suppose to be, don't buy from this seller again.

[Editor's Note: Some online auction sites prohibit bidders from making any kind of outright offer to buy from a seller who has ongoing auctions. In this case, you might ask the seller to start a separate auction for a small quantity at a reasonable "But It Now" price. –DMS]

Make sure that you know exactly what you are buying. Some sellers list "bullet alloy." I have no idea what the chemical composition of "bullet alloy" is. I'd steer clear of someone who isn't specific as to what he is selling. Many ads, however, indicate that the alloy is linotype, lead or wheelweights. These are bullet metals whose chemical composition can be confirmed. There are other bullet alloys, of course, but you almost never see them on the auction sites. I have no idea why. They are, however, readily available from the online shooter supply firms.

It isn't quite right to say that I can show you how to analyze an unknown alloy. What I can do is show you how to confirm an alloy's composition. If you are buying linotype, 30:1 (30 parts lead to one part tin by weight) or pure lead, I can show you how to confirm that you got what you paid for. I will also show you how to spot wheelweights. As a lot of linotype sold on the online auction sites these days is actually wheelweights, this too is useful.

Linotype is the Rolls-Royce of bullet alloys. A bit expensive and maybe unnecessarily hard for some applications, this is the best bullet alloy you can get. It works particularly well in applications where you need a hard alloy, for semi-automatics or high-pressure rifles for example. The chemical composition of linotype is 4% tin, 12% antimony and 84% lead by weight. Anything else isn't linotype. I originally switched to linotype decades ago in the hopes that I could avoid alloy buildup in my pistol and rifle barrels. I haven't seen any lead fouling since. Also, linotype yields excellent cast bullets. The problem of incomplete bullet mould fill-out with linotype, for example, can be easily eliminated, usually by just increasing your furnace temperature slightly.

Wheelweights are the other extreme. Their main appeal is that they are, or at least should be, cheap. If you have a friend who owns a gas station or tire store you should be able to get them for nothing. If you have to buy them from a local tire shop, they should still be inexpensive. Wheelweight bullets, in my opinion, do not stand up well to high pressure, which limits their usefulness, but they are readily available and inexpensive. Never buy wheelweights on the internet, incidentally, because you should be able to find them locally at very reasonable prices. It may take some time to find a local gas station or tire store that will sell you wheelweights, but look until you find one.

RCBS 50-515-FN

Maker	Mould	Alloy	Average Weight (grains)
RCBS	50-515-FN-1	Linotype	513
RCBS	50-515-FN-2	Linotype	510
RCBS	50-515-FN-3	Linotype	508
RCBS	50-515-FN-4	Linotype	510
RCBS	50-515-FN-2	Lead	557
RCBS	50-515-FN-3	Lead	558
RCBS	50-515-FN-2	WW	541
RCBS	50-515-FN-1	30/1	553

A WEIGHT-BASED APPROACH TO ANALYZING ALLOY

The first analytical technique we will examine is a weight-based approach. The mould I used is RCBS 50-515-FN. I have four of these moulds. To keep the data from these four separate I've scratched a –1, -2, -3 and –4 into the sides of the mould. Look at the accompanying RCBS 50-515-FN table **(above)**. Note that the weights vary quite a bit as I changed alloys. Linotype will always yield the lightest bullets because it has the lowest lead content. Pure lead bullets will always be the heaviest. 30:1 bullets will fall somewhere in between. All these alloys (lead, linotype and 30:1) have exact chemical compositions, so the weight of these bullets made from these alloys does not change!

Suppose you buy a batch of what is advertised as linotype at an online auction site. Cast up several dozen visually acceptable RCBS 50-515-FN bullets using your alloy and weigh them. You want an average weight from several dozen bullets so that any weight imperfections are averaged out. Weighing just one bullet will not cut it. If the average weight falls between 507 and 513 grains then you've got linotype. If the visually acceptable bullets average weight falls between 554 and 560 grains then you have pure lead. If the visually acceptable bullets average weight falls between 538 and 544 grains you have wheelweights.

How much weight variation can you expect? Look at the table. I had four of these moulds. With linotype the weight spread between my four moulds was 6 grains. So I averaged the weights shown for the various alloys in the table and then used a weight spread of plus or minus 3 grains from that average.

There will be weight differences between bullets cast from different alloys for any cast bullet. That is true whether you are talking about a 22-caliber bullet or a 50-caliber bullet. But with a heavy bullet it is far easier for these weight differences to be seen. Would any mould casting a heavy bullet work? Yes! The largest conventional bullet mould I know of, made by NEI (Northeast Industrial), casts a linotype projectile weighing right at 3500 grains.

What could this really big NEI mould do that the RCBS 50-515-FN cannot? For 30:1 (30 parts lead to one part tin by weight) the average weight of a bullet from my RCBS mould is 553 grains. That's close enough to the average weight of a pure lead bullet, 557 grains, that you cannot use this RCBS mould to tell the difference between pure lead and 30:1 alloy. Why not? Because the weight spread for pure lead would be the average weight from the table, 557 grains, plus or minus 3 grains. That yields a weight spread of 554 to 560 grains. And the weight spread for 30:1 is the average from the table, 553 grains, plus or minus 3 grains. That weight range is 550 to 556 grains. These two weight ranges overlap so you cannot tell which alloy you have. The problem here, of course, is that 30:1 is almost pure lead. But that huge NEI mould casts bullets that are more than six times heavier so the weight difference between 30:1 and pure lead using it would be roughly 25 grains. That's a big enough difference that you could tell these two apart. Size matters!

Do you have to buy this RCBS mould for this weight-based technique to work? If you want to use my weight standards, yes! You could, of course, make up your own. To do that you would need a mould yielding a bullet weighing at least 500 grains and you would need to buy samples of each metal you wanted weight standards for from one of the online shooter supply firms. Buying all these alloys will cost you more than buying this one RCBS mould.

What do you do if you get a weight of 528 grains from a batch of metal that you thought was linotype? Remember I said that this technique could confirm an alloy's composition. In this case this technique absolutely confirms that you did not buy linotype because you did not get a weight of between 507 and 513 grains. Remember the average weight for a linotype bullet from the table was 510 grains. The weight spread for linotype would be 510 plus or minus three grains. So what alloy has a weight of 528 grains? I have no idea but it sure isn't linotype. If your internet seller told you that this stuff was linotype I would not buy from him again!

A HARDENING-BASED APPROACH TO ANALYZING ALLOY

The second technique for analyzing bullet alloys uses an entirely different approach. It looks for differences in the way things harden. The scientific name for this is a phase change. What's a phase change? Water turning to ice occurs at a phase change. As you'll see shortly this is a graph-based approach.

There are differences in how phase changes happen. A chemical element, like lead, will change from a liquid to a solid at one specific temperature. Lead is not an alloy. It is a chemical element. Some alloys, called eutectics, also change from a liquid to a solid at one specific temperature. Linotype is a eutectic alloy. Linotype is, in fact, the only eutectic alloy that a bullet caster is likely to run into. Non-eutectic alloys change from a liquid to a solid over a wide temperature range. This is what happens with wheelweights.

So how an alloy turns from a liquid to a solid tells you something about what it is. Use a casting thermometer and a 20-pound furnace. Turn the furnace on and melt up all the alloy. Then turn the furnace off and record the temperature at EXACTLY one-minute intervals. Plotting these temperatures yields a cooling curve. The minimum amount of alloy you want to use is 20 pounds. Anything less and much of the detail in the cooling curve will be lost.

Look at the graph titled "Bullet Casting Alloys" **(above)**. Pure chemical elements, like lead, and eutectic alloys, like linotype, will have a very specific cooling curve. The temperature will drop initially, on the left, as the liquid cools. Then there will be a large central flat, a constant temperature where the liquid is turning into a solid. And finally, on the right, the temperature will drop

slowly once again as the solid metal cools. Only pure elements, like lead, or a eutectic alloy, like linotype, will do this. Nothing else will.

Do you need a highly accurate thermometer to do this? No. Two things can identify a phase change: the exact temperature at which the phase change happens or the shape of the cooling curve. You'd need an accurate thermometer for thexact temperature but you do not need an accurate thermometer to see the shape of the curve. Any inexpensive casting thermometer will do. You really luck out with this approach, incidentally, because the temperatures at which lead and linotype turn from a liquid to a solid are far apart. So even if your thermometer is way off it just doesn't matter. Just make sure that you take your temperature readings at EXACTLY one minute intervals and that the thermometer needle does not drag on the surface behind it.

Look at the Figure entitled "Linotype Dragging Needle Study" **(below)**. This cooling curve doesn't have a central flat even though it is linotype. The central flat disappeared because the needle was dragging on the surface behind it and

that threw off the temperature readings. You absolutely have to avoid having that happen!

How do you avoid this? You can actually see the needle jerk if it is dragging on the surface behind it so spotting this problem is easy. The solution is easy, too. Just take off the glass plate in front of the needle and bend the needle outward. A really simple fix!

How about wheelweights? The shape of the cooling curve in the graph titled "Bullet Casting Alloys" is typical. Note that wheelweights DO NOT turn from a liquid to a solid at one constant temperature. The phase change for wheelweights here starts after about 20 minutes at a temperature of about 570° F and continues until about the 65-minute mark at a temperature of about 460°. There is no single large central flat in this cooling curve where the temperature is constant. There is, obviously, a small region of constant temperature around the 60-minute mark but that is not what we are looking for. Do these exact temperatures matter? No. Will they be the same for any batch of wheelweights? No. Look at the series of cooling curves in the graph titled

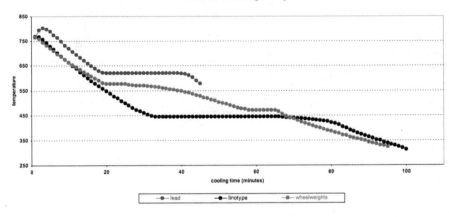

Bullet Casting Alloys

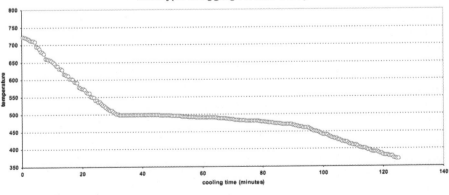

Linotype Dragging Needle Study

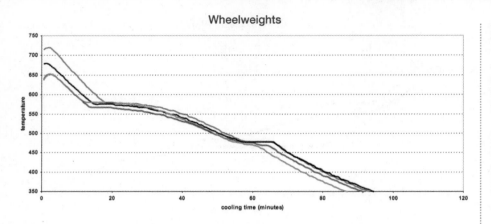

Wheelweights

"Wheelweights" **(above)**. These plots are similar but not identical. That's because the chemical composition of each batch of wheelweights is a little bit different. But because we are looking for the shape of these curves and not the exact temperatures at which things happen, these minor variations don't matter.

How do you make practical use of cooling curves? Look at the graph titled "Mystery Alloys" **(below)**. Mystery alloy #1 was supposed to be linotype. Is it? No, it was just wheelweights but wheelweights sold at linotype prices. I never bought from this seller again. Mystery

alloy #2 was "bullet alloy." I hate that description and normally would have avoided a seller using it but friends had bought some of this stuff and like it. So I called the guy.

He was a real estate developer who had bought a piece of land that had an old building on it. He couldn't tell what the building was because it had been abandoned for decades and was covered over with vines. He couldn't even find the doors. He had to get a power saw and cut through a wall. He found an old print shop. There was literally tons of metal lying all over the place. He called

all this stuff "bullet alloy" because he had no idea what it was. He was going to take it to the dump until a friend convinced him to try selling it on the internet. What was he selling? Look at the graph. This is linotype. He had over five tons of it.

This story, incidentally, is not unique. I have a friend whose father died. When he was younger he owned a small print shop. Try as I might I could not convince her to sell his old type. Tons of it went to the dump. She literally threw thousands of dollars away!

Mystery alloy #1 was wheelweights but was being sold as linotype. Though he sold me a small initial sample, if I wanted more I'd have to bid on it. And those auctions were running the price WAY up. No thank you!

Mystery alloy #2 was linotype but it was being sold as "bullet alloy." I asked for a 600-pound non-auction price. Got a really good deal. The guy didn't want to fool around with this stuff and he was glad to get rid of it in large blocks so he sold it to me at less than what he was getting on his auctions. I bought another 1200 pounds and analyzed it. It was all linotype. I wish that I could have afforded the entire five tons. This was linotype at wheelweight prices!

Now let's consider how accurate this technique is. Look at the graph titled "Lead + 2% Tin" **(bottom)**. Remember, lead should turn from a liquid to a solid at one, and only one, constant temperature. Said another way, the cooling curve for pure lead is going to have a central flat, a long region where the temperature remains constant. (We saw this for pure lead in the graph titled "Bullet Casting Alloys.") The alloy used here, however, is slightly different. I took pure lead and added enough pure tin to it to come up with a mixture that was 98% lead and 2% tin by weight. The reason for doing this was that I wanted to see if this minor change in composition would cause a detectable change in the lead cooling curve. It did. The arrow shows where the central flat broke down. This very little "dip" in this graph means that this is NOT pure lead. Because the cooling curve for pure lead is thrown off by the addition of only 2% tin means that this technique can spot a difference in composition as little as 2%.

These cooling curves, then, are a very accurate way to confirm an alloy's composition. If the lead or linotype you buy is off by only a couple percentage points, your cooling curve will catch

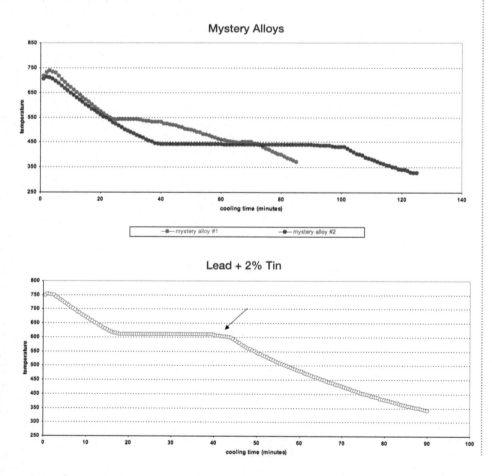

Mystery Alloys

—●— mystery alloy #1   —●— mystery alloy #2

Lead + 2% Tin

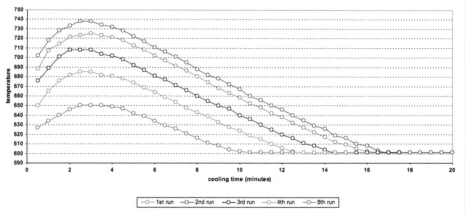

Thermometer Abuse Studies

that very minor difference. This is a very accurate chemical analysis!

Casting thermometers, incidentally, work well here. The graph titled "Thermometer Abuse Studies" **(above)** shows a series of lead cooling curves done with an RCBS casting thermometer. Before each run I whacked the thermometer on my workbench. Obviously this abuse had no effect.

WHICH APPROACH IS BEST?

Now let's compare these two techniques. I've used both for years and on several occasions I've used both to analyze a single batch of bullet alloy. Doing that was really informative. What I found was that the first technique, the one based on weight, is by far the more accurate and also the easier to do and that the second, the one based on the graphs, is less accurate and is a lot more work. So you would want to use the weight-based approach because it is easier and more accurate, right? Maybe not!

Remember we noted earlier that the graph-based approach could spot an alloy whose chemical composition was off by as little as 2%. Said another way, the graph-based approach will not spot a difference in composition that is off by less than 2%. A 2% difference isn't important. Such a difference has no practical significant when casting bullets or when shooting them. I'm absolutely sure about that because I've shot tens of thousands of such bullets without experiencing any troubles whatsoever. So the graph-based approach is insensitive to minor, unimportant changes in composition. Statisticians like the word "robust" to describe something that works well even when things are a little bit off. So the appeal to the graph-based approach is that it is insensitive to minor, unimport-

ant compositional differences. It is, in my opinion, just better suited to the real world.

Now let's suppose that you have found a seller on the internet. You have bought a small batch of his bullet metal. You have analyzed it and you liked what you got. How do you go back to this fellow and buy more at an attractive price?

Never bid on an auction. Instead call and make him an offer. Knowing what his recent auctions have been going for helps. Pick a price below what he has been getting recently. That way you have room to move up if you have to. Order as much as you can possibly afford. The larger the order the more likely you are to get a volume discount. Specifically ask for a volume discount if you are buying several hundred pounds. Ask him how much he'll need beyond shipping charges for packing this stuff.

Packing this stuff is an art form and he should be paid for doing it. Ask him to pack the boxes very tightly, filling up any air spaces with tightly compressed newspaper. Also ask him to cut up pieces of thick cardboard and line all six sides of the boxes with it. Also ask him to put in L-shaped thick cardboard pieces in the corners. And you want the boxes wrapped with clear plastic tape. All this will drive up his handling charges but it is money well spent because it minimizes ruptures. You also want insurance. Tell him that you'll probably order more later. That gives him another reason to be helpful.

Selecting a shipper is also important. The most recent linotype supplier I found is in California. As I'm writing this he can ship a 70-lb. box of linotype from California to Arizona for about $25 via UPS. It would cost a lot more, obviously, if I lived on the east coast. I've never had a problem with UPS and I've used them a

lot. Another possibility is to use the Post Office flat box rate. Currently you can ship up to 70 pounds to anywhere in the country for about $10 using this flat box rate. The Post Office supplies special boxes for this service and they are free. Obviously it is a lot cheaper to use the Post Office.

But there are serious problems with shipping bullet alloy using the Post Office. The Post Office clearly never thought that anyone could fit 70 pounds into one of their flat rate boxes. Many post offices refuse to take such heavy boxes. Others will take them but only if they contain no more than 40 pounds. And complaints from the Post Office staff are commonplace. Deliberate, willful damage is also common. If you ship very much bullet alloy this way, expect a call from your local Postmaster. Mine was actually quite nice about it. Even made special arrangements for the deliveries. But this is atypical. Most Postmasters really get very angry when you ship large amounts of bullet metal this way. Some go so far as to claim that bullet alloy cannot be shipped via the post office. That is just a flat-out lie.

Though potentially substantially cheaper than UPS, don't use the Post Office. They are just way to difficult to deal with. After years of trying to use the Post Office, I've switched to UPS. UPS is much more expensive but the service is far better.

Remember there are two kinds of online internet alloy sellers. Shooter supply firms are an excellent source if you want a small amount and you are not concerned about the cost. The good news is that you can be absolutely sure that you'll get what you pay for. It will be a hassle-free purchase. The bad news is that this is a very expensive way to buy bullet alloy and these firms don't carry much so a large order isn't possible. If you are going to buy a lot of bullet alloy you will need to use an online auction site. This is *not* going to be a hassle-free purchase.

You have to select your seller with care. You have to know exactly what he claims to be selling. You need to read his ad with extreme care. You need to be very specific about how you want this stuff packaged and shipped. You have to analyze the alloys you get and buy in bulk *only* if your analysis shows that you got what you paid for. But if you are willing to do all this, you can actually get linotype at wheelweight prices.

That "Other" 1911–
THE WINCHESTER MODEL 1911 SHOTGUN

BY JOHN MALLOY

The year 1911 is a significant one for students of firearms. In that year, the Browning-designed Colt Model 1911 semiautomatic pistol was adopted as its service sidearm by the U. S. Government. It came to be considered by many as the best pistol ever made. One hundred years later, it is still produced by Colt and a constantly-growing number of other companies.

There was another firearm introduced in 1911 by a major manufacturer. In that year, the Winchester Model 1911 semiautomatic shotgun was presented to the public. Winchester Repeating Arms Company (WRA) had offered a successful line of semiautomatic rifles within the previous eight years, and had great expectations for its first autoloading shotgun. However, the Winchester 1911 was not particularly successful and has been largely forgotten.

The story of the Winchester 1911 is an interesting one, though. It should be better known by those with an interest in firearms history.

Like the story of the Colt 1911, the story of the Winchester 1911 begins with John M. Browning.

It is well known that recognition of Browning's genius was established during his relationship with Winchester. For a number of years, Winchester bought the rights to every design Browning invented. Browning's ideas were made and marketed by Winchester. Included were the Winchester Single Shot rifle, and other rifle models 1886, 1892, 1894, 1895, and 1900, the shotgun models 1887, 1893 and 1897 — and all the variants based on these models. Winchester bought every rifle and shotgun design that Browning developed, even if they were not interested in producing the designs as Winchester products. Although Browning was working with Colt and the Belgian firm

of Fabrique Nationale (FN) on pistol designs, Winchester could not afford to let other manufacturers begin producing Browning rifle and shotgun designs. WRA had their experts work with Browning to develop solid patents. Then the company bought each patent outright.

By the 1890s, Browning had begun working with automatic mechanisms, in which the energy of one shot would provide the power to operate an action for the next shot. His pistol designs were produced by Colt in the United States and Fabrique Nationale (FN) in Belgium. A machinegun of Browning design was made by Colt in 1895.

Browning had turned his attention to an autoloading shotgun design. In March 1899, he wrote Winchester's president, T. G. Bennett, that he had developed an autoloading shotgun to show him. The following month, he brought the new gun to Winchester's New Haven, Connecticut, office.

Winchester's practice with all Browning-designed models was to test it for operational performance and to check the mechanical operation for possible patent infringement. The company's experienced patent lawyers and firearms designers, under the leadership of Thomas C. Johnson, found a potential problem with the lifting arrangement in the Browning shotgun. They tried to buy the rights to the other patent (which had been awarded to noted firearms designer Hugo Borchardt) but had no success.

Browning was able to work out a different lifter arrangement, one that did not violate the Borchardt patent. However, the new system required other mechanical changes, and the shotgun was returned to Browning for further work. The problems were remedied during 1901 and in January of 1902 Browning returned to talk to Winchester about the new gun.

Browning met personally with Winchester head T. G. Bennett. Winchester had bought the rights to every gun he had ever designed. However, this time, Browning was not satisfied with the usual outright purchase agreement. He saw great possibilities for the autoloading shotgun and wanted a royalty agreement. Bennett, however, did not want to break Winchester's tradition of buying rights outright. He obviously felt that such a change in arrangements would create problems with the company's design staff and with other people who

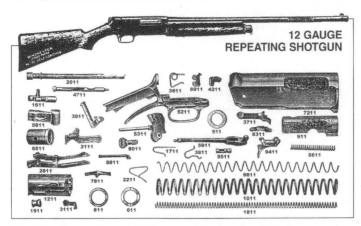

The Winchester Model 1911, seen here in an early parts drawing, was an ill-fated competitor to Browning's wildly successful Auto-5 autoloading shotgun.

might offer ideas from outside the company. He flatly refused Browning's request for a royalty agreement. The meeting came to an awkward close. Neither man wanted it to end, but neither man would give in. Browning picked up the shotgun and walked out.

Browning then made an appointment with Marcellus Hartley, head of Remington Arms Company, to show him the new shotgun. He was waiting in Hartley's office when word came that Hartley had died suddenly at a luncheon meeting.

Browning, shocked, began to think about taking the gun to Fabrique Nationale. He had sold pistol designs to the Belgian company but had never actually been there. Apparently, on the spur of the moment, Browning booked passage to Belgium. The new shotgun was reportedly carried on board under his arm. When he arrived in Europe, Browning was heartily welcomed by FN officials. They were glad to deal in person with the man who had given them the opportunity to manufacture the best-selling pistol in Europe — the Browning 32-caliber autoloading pistol. The new shotgun was well-received by FN officials, and arrangements were made to manufacture it. Reportedly, 10,000 were sold within the first year. By 1905, arrangements were made with Remington to offer it, under the Remington name, to the US shooting market.

Even before the American Remington introduction, Winchester officials watched with regret as the Browning automatic shotgun became a best seller throughout the world. It became obvious that Winchester needed to offer a competing semiautomatic shotgun.

The job of coming up with one fell to creative Winchester engineer Thomas C. Johnson. Unfortunately for Johnson, he had been in charge of the Browning shotgun patent application and had made the patent essentially "iron-clad." He later once remarked wryly that the patent was so strong that it took him almost a decade to come up with another autoloading shotgun that would not be an infringement.

Johnson, at age 41, was only seven years younger than Browning. Johnson had also started working with semi-automatic firearms by the turn of the century. He was the originator of the Winchester autoloading rifle line that began with the 22-caliber Winchester Model 1903 and went through the 32- and 35-caliber Model 1905, the 351-caliber 1907, and the most powerful version, the 401-caliber Model 1910. Con-

currently, he worked on the autoloading shotgun design.

The rifles were all of blowback operation, but the blowback mechanism would not work with the shotgun design. Johnson found it difficult to work around the Browning patent that he himself had helped write. It is to his credit that he was able to come up with a credible rival to the Browning. It was introduced as the Winchester Self-Loading Shotgun, Model 1911, in October of that year. However, there were some features of the Browning patent he could not duplicate. The rights to such a simple part such as the bolt retracting handle could not be overcome. The Winchester 1911 had no handle on the bolt. The new WRA shotgun had to be cocked by pulling the barrel back, and a portion of the barrel near the muzzle was knurled for this purpose.

The Model 1911 shotgun held a special place in Winchester's product line. It was, of course, their first self-loading shotgun. Following the 1893 and 1897 outside-hammer pump guns, the Model 1911 was also Winchester's first hammer-less shotgun. In 12 gauge, chambered for the 2-3/4-inch shells then becoming standard, the 1911 was offered with 26- and 28-inch barrels, choked either full, modified or cylinder bore. Barrels with a matted top surface were available at extra cost. The 1911 shotgun was never furnished with raised or ventilated ribs. All barrels were made with the knurled area between the muzzle and the front of the forearm to provide a gripping area for cocking the gun.

Similar to the Browning, the Winchester self-loader had a five-shot tubular magazine.

The stock of the 1911 was a departure for Winchester. The company traditionally had used high-grade walnut for stocks, even on its less-expensive guns. The Model 1911 (which, at $38 for the standard version, was the most expensive gun in the Winchester line) was offered with a birch stock. The stock construction was of three-piece laminated type, and the forearm was also birch, but with an elm insert. Apparently, Winchester found this laminated wood gave better resistance to recoil. Felt recoil could be heavy, because both the barrel and breechblock recoiled for each shot. (The friction-ring system of the Browning was firmly protected by patent and was not used for the 1911.) Walnut stocks were available at extra cost for those who had to have them, but only the densest pieces of walnut were

used for 1911 stocks.

Heavy recoil was apparently a characteristic of the Winchester 1911. Recoil was designed to be reduced by friction between the recoiling barrel and a buffer under the barrel in the receiver. At the rear of the receiver, another buffer slowed and stopped the breechblock during its rearward travel. However, as the guns were used, wear on the parts and excessive oiling would reduce the effectiveness of this system, and the gun had a reputation for harsh recoil.

The Model 1911 became the Model 11 after World War I, after serial number 52,000. At the same time, Winchester simplified the terminology for all their rifle and shotgun models, dropping the full year of introduction as a model designation, and using two-digit numbers.

Winchester made every effort to produce a fine gun. The 1911 was a dependable shotgun. It was made of good steel, and the guns were finished with excellent polish and bluing.

Thomas C. Johnson continued working with Winchester. A year after the introduction of the Model 1911, the Johnson-designed hammerless slide-action gun, the Winchester Model 1912, was introduced. Within a few years, the "Model 12" had earned the title, "the perfect repeater."

The Model 1911 self-loader, the older Model 1897 and the newer Model 1912 were made concurrently, and became the Model 11, Model 97 and Model 12, respectively, after World War I. Production of the Model 11 continued into 1925 and ended with serial number 82,774. The two pump guns continued into the decades after World War II, with millions of guns made.

Although the Model 1911 autoloader was considered a prestige gun and had moderately good sales, Winchester did not consider it particularly satisfactory. It would be 15 more years before Winchester made its second entry into the autoloading shotgun field. The Model 40 was introduced in 1940. However, it was discontinued the next year, in 1941, when war production began to take up most of Winchester's manufacturing capacity.

The old Model 1911 shotgun is largely forgotten today, unknown to all but dedicated students of firearms. However, because of its interesting history, the story of that "other" 1911 deserves to be better known.

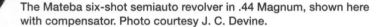

The Mateba six-shot semiauto revolver in .44 Magnum, shown here with compensator. Photo courtesy J. C. Devine.

Revolvers

BY JEFF QUINN

The past year has certainly been an interesting one for gun owners. We have in our nation the finest selection of firearms available anywhere in the world, yet we also have politicians vowing to rip those guns from our possession. However, on most fronts, I think we're winning.

Just in the last few months, several new concealed-carry guns have hit the market, and more are on the way. I have seen prototypes of some very interesting and useful compact revolvers that should be available by the time this *Gun Digest* goes to press. While many choose a semiauto for concealed carry, the compact revolver still holds

its own, with many knowledgeable citizens recognizing the advantages of a reliable revolver as a last-ditch fighting gun. While revolvers can break, it is a rare occurrence. I have never heard of a revolver having a failure to feed or having a cartridge case hang up halfway through ejection. Another plus is that a revolver does not leave your empty brass lying on the ground. Many of us choose revolvers for personal defense for these reasons, and while there are some good semiautos that are used for hunting, most handgun hunters choose either a revolver or a quality single-shot, for reasons of accuracy, power, and reliability.

Let's take a look at some of the better offerings of revolvers, derringers, and single-shot pistols that are available today. With modern revolvers now having capacities from five to twelve rounds in their cylinders, 2011 is a good year for those who choose to purchase and enjoy "Revolvers and Others."

AMERICAN WESTERN ARMS

AWA is best known for their line of 1873 single action revolvers, which are some excellent Colt replica sixguns. Offered in most popular chamberings and barrel lengths, the AWA line consists of their Classic revolvers, made very much like the sixguns of the late nineteenth

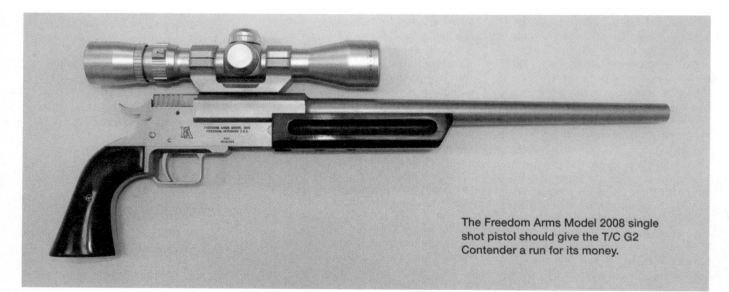

The Freedom Arms Model 2008 single shot pistol should give the T/C G2 Contender a run for its money.

One big honkin' single action revolver: the Magnum Research BFR .45-70.

and Others

Bond Arms Snake Slayer .45 Colt/.410 shotshell derringer. An extremely well-built derringer of the Remington pattern.

Is this cute or what? The North American Arms .22 Magnum mini-revolver with LaserLyte laser sight.

Taurus Judge .45 Colt/.410 shotshell polymer-frame revolver, a new twist on the well-established Judge lineup.

century, and their Ultimate series with upgraded coil springs and various stock options. These revolvers have a reputation for smooth actions and quality production. Less well-known among the AWA-distributed products are the semiautomatic Mateba revolvers. These futuristic-looking revolvers feature interchangeable barrels and are chambered for the .357 and .44 Magnum cartridges, as well as the .454 Casull. The Mateba fires from the bottom chamber in the cylinder, lowering the center of the recoil in relation to the shooter's hand, for a more straight-back recoil impulse, lessening muzzle jump and making target acquisition between shots faster. While many uninformed shooters think of the revolver as antiquated, this Mateba is as modern as you can get.

BERETTA

Beretta has been cranking out some very good-looking Old West style firearms for a few years now, since their

single action, which should be safely carried with an empty chamber under the hammer. Beretta offers not only the 1873 Single Action Army style but a modified Bisley style sixgun as well.

There is also the Stampede Marshall, which has a Thunderer-style birdshead grip frame. Beretta revolvers are chambered for either the .357 Magnum or .45 Colt cartridges.

BOND ARMS

Bond Arms has been producing high-quality two-shot derringers for several years now and have reached the apex in derringer design. Their derringers are often regarded as the best that money can buy, and Bond offers an extensive variety of chamberings, from .22 Long

Rifle up through .45 Colt/.410 shotshell, covering many popular chamberings in between. Bond derringers are built primarily of stainless steel, and they exhibit first class craftsmanship and are built with quality materials. My personal favorite is the Snake Slayer. I have one that I carry often. Besides its intended use against venomous reptiles, it is also a fine personal defense arm for use against carjackers and other two-legged predators. Loaded with #000 buckshot or Winchester's new buck and birdshot load, it would be a very effective close-range defensive weapon. The Bond Arms derringers offer a lot of versatility, with the barrels being interchangeable, so one can switch calibers as needed. Bond Arms also offers some high quality

Author with Colt .45 SAA.

corporate acquisition of Uberti. Building on the quality firearms produced by Uberti, Beretta markets their Single Action Army replicas with some high-grade finishes such as a brilliant carbona-type blue, along with authentic-looking case coloring and an antique finish that makes the gun look like an original, well-worn gun from the late nineteenth century. Beretta adds a transfer bar safety system to their revolvers that allows the firearm to be carried fully loaded, with a live cartridge under the hammer – unlike the original style 1873

leather holsters in which to carry your derringer. I particularly like the horizontal driving holster. It is ideal to wear while riding in a vehicle or on an ATV or motorcycle, placing the handgun within reach for a fast and comfortable draw.

CHARTER ARMS

Charter Arms has built their reputation upon providing very useful gun designs that are affordable for the common man. I have many times relied upon a Charter revolver for various needs, mostly a .38 Special riding in a boot or pocket for protection, and at other times packing their handy little .22LR Pathfinder as a trail gun while just bumming around in the woods. The Charter revolvers are available in blued steel or stainless, and recently they have added alloy frames to the lineup for those who want to carry the lightest possible package.

The latest innovation from Charter is the finishes that they apply to their alloy-frame guns. Made in a variety of colors, their pink finish has proven to be extremely popular with women in Charter's Pink Lady variation of their five-shot .38. They also have a couple of revolvers with a mottled finish. I refer to them unofficially as their "Cat" revolvers. The Cougar has a pink mottled finish, and the Panther a medium-dark bronze mottled finish. I have handled and shot both of these, and they are indeed good-shooting, lightweight revolvers. Both have exposed hammers and black synthetic grips, and they draw a crowd when brought out in public. Some love the finish while others hate it. No one seems to be neutral on these flashy new finishes from Charter Arms. Personally I like them, especially the bronze mottled finish.

Besides these, Charter still builds their legendary .44 Special Bulldog revolvers. These powerful belly guns fill a needed niche in the market as they have for the past few decades. The Bulldog

The eye-catching Cougar and Panther from Charter Arms.

is lightweight and easy to conceal yet carries five .44 Special cartridges in the cylinder. Recoil is stiff with heavy loads, but not really painful at all. These stainless revolvers are not much bigger than a compact .38 Special but pack a hefty punch. In addition to their popular .38 Special and .44 Special revolvers, Charter still has their rimfire Pathfinder line in .22 Long Rifle and .22 Magnum, along with revolvers chambered for the .32 H&R Magnum, .327 Federal Magnum, and .357 Magnum. Charter also makes a true left-handed snubnose revolver called the Southpaw. The Southpaw is a mirror image of their standard revolver design with the cylinder latch on the right side; the cylinder swings out to the right as well.

Also of interest to us here is the Charter Dixie Derringer. The Dixie is a five-shot .22 Long Rifle or .22 Magnum mini-revolver with a crossbolt safety. Construction is stainless steel throughout. Weighing in at just six ounces, the Dixie Derringer can hide just about anywhere and is pretty effective at close range, especially the .22 Magnum version.

CHIAPPA

Chiappa is a relatively new name in the firearms business but is the outgrowth of the well-established Armi Sport company. Chiappa has entered the market with several quality replica firearms, but the one of interest here is not a replica of an Old West gun at all but a thoroughly modern revolver. The Chiappa Rhino is a unique sixgun that fires its cartridges from the bottom barrel in the cylinder, resulting in a lower bore axis in relation to the shooter's hand, and greatly reduced muzzle jump upon firing. Much like the Mateba in design, the Rhino is more compact but does *not* share the Mateba's semiauto design. I have not yet been able to fire the new Rhino, but have seen and handled a few examples in various barrel lengths. It appears to be well-crafted of quality materials. The Rhino is chambered for the 357 Magnum cartridge. It certainly has a very unconventional appearance but feels really good in my hand. I have high hopes that it will work very well in reducing the muzzle jump and felt recoil of the .357 Magnum cartridge.

CIMARRON

For many years now, Mike Harvey and the gang at Cimarron Firearms in Fredericksburg, Texas, have been at the forefront of marketing quality replicas of Old West style rifles and handguns. Of concern here is their extensive line of authentically reproduced historic sixguns. Cimarron has not only 1873 Single Action Army replicas, but has also delved into other lesser-known but very historic firearms of the nineteenth century. Cimarron offers replicas of most of the major players in the cap and ball sixgun business of that era, such as the Walker, Dragoon, Army and Navy guns, as well as the Remington and even the Leech & Rigdon guns. Cimarron covers the transition from cap and ball to cartridge with their conversion revolvers and the 1872 Colt replica. The company also offers the Remington 1875 and 1890 cartridge revolvers, as well as a variety of the Smith & Wesson break-open sixguns such as the Russian and Schofield models.

Besides these authentic single action

The EAA .45 Colt single action Bounty Hunter.

Rossi .38 Special revolver is a competent concealed-carry piece.

An awesome snubbie: the Smith & Wesson Model 25 .45 ACP

Chiappa Rhino .357 Magnum revolver.

replicas, Cimarron has a selection of two-shot derringers. They are small and easily concealed and are chambered for the .22 Long Rifle and Magnum rimfire cartridges, as well as the .32 H&R Magnum and the .38 Special.

The .22 Long Rifle and .22 Magnum Plinkerton revolvers are priced to get most anyone into the single action revolver game. These guns are built from a non-ferrous alloy but have steel-lined chambers and barrel, and they shoot surprisingly well. The Plinkerton would make a good understudy to Cimarron's centerfire sixguns, but it's also a handy and reliable plinker.

One new attention-getter from Cimarron is the so-called "Holy Smoker," modeled after Russell Crowe's revolver in the film *3:10 to Yuma*. It has a tastefully-rendered, gold-plated sterling silver crucifix on each grip panel.

COBRA

Cobra Firearms of Utah manufactures some small and reliable two-shot single action derringers. These compact derringers are made in .22 Long Rifle, .22 Magnum, .38 Special, 9mm Luger, .25 Auto, .32 Auto, .380 Auto, and .32 H&R Magnum. Their Titan model is built of stainless steel, and is offered in 9mm Luger and .45 Colt/.410 shotshell. These derringers are available in a variety of colors, and each sells at an affordable price. Brand new from Cobra this year is their Shadow +P-rated five-shot .38 Special revolver. This one has a concealed hammer and looks very much like a Smith & Wesson Model 642. It has a stainless cylinder and barrel with an aluminum frame for an overall a weight of fifteen ounces. I have not yet had the opportunity to fire one of these, but I have handled a couple of them, and they

appear to be well-made from quality materials. I look forward to trying one out soon.

COLT

Colt has been producing revolvers for almost 175 years now. In fact, if it were not for Sam Colt, we might not have revolvers. His first successful revolver, the Paterson, set the stage for all revolvers that have followed. That design, while it worked pretty well, was delicate and underpowered, but it led to the big Colt Walker, which packed a lot of punch and set the Colt company on its way to success. Through the years, Colt has produced some very good revolver designs, but today has only one Colt revolver in its stable, that being the Single Action Army. The SAA is probably the most recognized handgun in the world, and is certainly the most copied

Ruger LCR polymer-framed .38 Special, one of the hottest revolvers on the market.

revolver design ever produced. Colt still produces the SAA, and the latest sixguns that they have been shipping for the past few years are as good as any that Colt has ever produced. Available in three barrel lengths (4.75, 5.5, and 7.5 inches), the Single Action Army is chambered in a choice of .357 Magnum, .44 WCF, .45 Colt, .38 Special, .32 WCF (.32-20) and .38 WCF (.38-40). The SAA is available in blued/case-hardened or nickel finishes. Through the Colt Custom Shop, many options are available such as non-standard barrel lengths and hand engraving.

EUROPEAN AMERICAN ARMORY

EAA Corp. has a line of Single Action Army replica revolvers called the Bounty Hunter. These sixguns are available chambered for the .22 Long Rifle and .22 Magnum cartridges, with an alloy frame and a choice of six or eight-shot cylinders. The available centerfire chamberings are the .357 and

.44 Magnums and the .45 Colt. These sixguns are built with all-steel frames in a choice of nickeled, blued, or case-hardened finishes and have the traditional half-cock loading feature but include a modern transfer bar safety action that permits carrying them fully loaded, with a live round under the hammer without fear of firing if accidentally dropped.

The double-action Windicator revolvers are chambered for the .38 Special cartridge with an alloy frame, or the all-steel .357 Magnum version. Both revolvers have a synthetic rubber grip and a businesslike matte blue finish, with a choice of two- or four-inch barrel.

FREEDOM ARMS

Freedom Arms of Freedom, Wyoming, is best known for its fine, sturdy, and super-accurate revolvers. It is often said that a Freedom Arms revolver is built like a fine Swiss watch. I disagree. A Swiss watch has a lot of tiny, delicate parts, and can get screwed up beyond

Blackhawk Ruger eight-shot .327 Federal Magnum Blackhawk with Barranti Leather rig. The term "six-shooter" is obviously inadequate to describe it.

repair if dropped hard. The Freedom Arms revolver is tough. It is built to very close tolerances but can also take a lot of abuse. Chambered for such powerful cartridges as the .454 Casull and the .475 Linebaugh, the Freedom revolvers will withstand a lot more punishment than most shooters can endure. The Freedom Arms revolvers are meticulously fitted and finished to perfection. The chambers in the cylinder are precisely aligned with the bore, and every detail of these revolvers follows the same precise standard of quality.

The large-frame Model 83 is the flagship of the Freedom Arms line and is chambered for the aforementioned .454 Casull and .475 Linebaugh cartridges, in addition to the .357 Magnum and .500 Wyoming Express cartridges and the

.41 and .44 Magnums. It's available with fixed sights or rugged adjustable sights. The adjustable-sight guns also accept a variety of scope mounts.

The Model 97 is Freedom's compact frame single action revolver. Built to the same tight tolerances as the Model 83 revolvers, the Model 97 is a bit handier to carry all day and is chambered for the .17 HMR and .22 Long Rifle/Magnum rimfire cartridges, as well as the .327 Federal, .357 Magnum, .41 Magnum, .44 Special, and .45 Colt centerfire cartridges. In addition to these standard handgun cartridges, the Model 97 is also available in Freedom Arms' own .224-32 cartridge, which is a fast-stepping .22 centerfire based on the .327 Federal cartridge case.

First introduced to the public last year, the Freedom Arms Model 2008 Single Shot pistol is the first single shot handgun that ever stirred any interest in me. There have been several very good single shot pistols on the market for years, but the Freedom Arms is the only one that is built like a Freedom Arms revolver. I have fired a couple of these chambered in the 6.5x55 and 6.5 JDJ cartridges, as well as one chambered for the .375 Winchester cartridge. Current chamberings offered are the .223 Remington, 6.5 Swede, 7mm BR, 7mm-08, .308 Winchester, .357 Magnum, .357 Maximum, .338 Federal and .375 Winchester. Standard barrel lengths are 10,15, and 16 inches, depending on caliber, but non-standard lengths are available as well for a nominal cost.

What makes this single shot so comfortable to shoot is the single action revolver grip style. Shooting the pistol allows the gun to recoil comfortably, with no pain at all to the hands as is encountered with some single shot pistols. The barrels are interchangeable, with extra fitted barrels available from Freedom Arms, allowing the shooter to switch among any of the available barrel and caliber options all on one frame. The Model 2008 weighs in around four pounds, depending on barrel length and caliber. The barrel is drilled for a Freedom Arms scope mount, and the scope stays with the barrel, allowing the interchange of the barrels without affecting the sight adjustment. These new single shot pistols have handsome impregnated wood grips and forends and are shipping now.

LEGACY SPORTS

Legacy Sports is best known for their Howa and Puma rifles, but they also have made a big splash in the market last year with their Bounty Hunter Model 92 lever action pistol. The Bounty Hunter resembles a sawed-off Model 92 lever action rifle, but is built from the start as a pistol, so it needs no special NFA tax stamp for approval. It can be purchased just like any other pistol, and has become quite popular for its nostalgic appeal, as well as its reliable function and accuracy. Legacy also markets a couple of good holster rigs for this "mare's leg" pistol, made by Bob Mernickle exclusively for Legacy Sports. The holster and belt combo is a beautiful rig and makes a necessary addition to the Bounty Hunter, completing the nostalgic package.

Legacy also has their 1873 Colt replica sixgun called the Puma Westerner. These are reliable and well-built sixguns, chambered for the .357 Magnum, .44 WCF, and .45 Colt cartridges, with 4.75-, 5.5-, or 7.5- inch barrels. They are very high-quality Colt SAA replicas. These sixguns are offered with a blued and case-hardened finish with walnut grips, nickel finish with walnut grips, or with a stainless finish and white synthetic ivory grips. The Puma line also includes a very affordable single action replica chambered for the .22 Long Rifle or .22 Magnum cartridge that would make a good trainer for the larger bores, but will be a lot less costly to shoot.

MAGNUM RESEARCH

Magnum Research of Minneapolis, Minnesota, has been producing their quality BFR revolver for many years now. These robust single action revolvers are built for hunting the largest, most dangerous game on the planet. In addition to their venerable .454 Casull revolvers, the BFR is available in other high-performance calibers like the .460 and .500 Smith & Wesson Magnums, the .475 Linebaugh and .480 Ruger revolver cartridges, as well as the .30-30 Winchester, .444 Marlin, and .45-70 rifle cartridges. The BFR is also available chambered for the ever-popular .45 Colt/.410 shotshell combination, which offers a lot of versatility in a handgun.

NORTH AMERICAN ARMS

The North American Arms mini-revolvers are well-established in the market place, being in production for a long time now, but they seem more popular than ever. These little five-shot miniature revolvers are more often than not bought as a deep-concealment hand-gun. They're small enough to fit into most any pocket, and are handy enough to always be with you, no matter what the attire or climate. Chambered for the .22 Short, .22 Long Rifle, or .22 Magnum cartridges, these little jewels are easy to carry and surprisingly accurate within their intended range. The small sights and short sight radius makes hitting at a distance a challenge with most of them, but there is one model – the Pug – available with a really good set of high-visibility sights, and now LaserLyte makes a laser sight just for the NAA revolvers, adding to their usefulness and versatility.

ROSSI

Rossi has been producing reliable and affordable revolvers for decades. These double-action sixguns are available chambered for the .38 Special and .357 Magnum cartridges, in either blued steel or stainless finishes. Rossi was acquired by Taurus a few months ago, and all of

The oddly-named and somewhat angular Windicator .38 Special.

the Rossi revolvers are now produced by Taurus in Brazil. They are quality, reliable revolvers built for concealed carry or as a duty/hunting gun. Available with short barrels and fixed sights for concealment or longer barrels and adjustable sights for precision shooting, the Rossi line still means a quality product at an affordable price.

RUGER

Sturm, Ruger builds some of the strongest and most reliable revolvers available today. The company's Single-Six and Blackhawk lines are running strong, with the welcome addition of the New Model Flattop Blackhawk introduced a couple of years ago. Ruger now offers as a regular catalog item the Flattop .44 Special. This is a long-awaited .44 Special built on the frame that is sized like that of the original .357 Blackhawk. The .44 Special Flattop is also available in a Bisley model this year, with a blued finish, and also as a regular Flattop made

of stainless steel. These new Flattop models have proven to be wildly popular among single action sixgun enthusiasts.

Ruger has also taken the .327 Federal cartridge that they introduced a couple of years ago in the SP-101 compact revolver and chambered it in the Blackhawk. This stainless Blackhawk has an eight-shot cylinder and is strong enough to exploit the full potential of the .327 Federal cartridge. This little cartridge really performs, offering high velocities and deep penetration. The Ruger's cylinder is long enough to handle the long 120- and 135-gr. .327 bullets (which actually measure from .312 to .313 inch diameter).

In their double action revolver line, Ruger also chambers the relatively new .327 Federal in their GP-100 revolver. This revolver is also built from stainless steel, wears a four-inch barrel, and has a seven-shot cylinder. Of course, Ruger still has the GP-100 in .357 Magnum. This is one of the strongest, most reliable, and most durable double action .357 Magnum sixguns ever built. Ruger got started in the double action revolver business with their excellent Six series guns back in 1971. My first handgun was a blued steel four-inch .357 Magnum Ruger Security-Six. I learned to shoot with that superb sixgun. It was strong, reliable, and just the right size and balance for a .357 Magnum revolver.

The Six series has given way now to the GP-100 series, and the GP is a worthy replacement, probably better in many ways than my old Security-Six. The GP-100 has proven

itself already, selling in large numbers since its introduction in 1986. This year Lipsey's, a large Ruger distributor, has a special high-polish blued steel GP-100 that is the best-looking double action .357 Magnum to ever leave the Ruger factory. Moving up in size a bit is the Ruger Redhawk, chambered for the .44 Magnum and .45 Colt cartridges. The Redhawk is bull-strong and as reliable as an anvil. Though it has been around for over thirty years, I have never seen a worn-out Redhawk. They can withstand a lifetime of shooting and never miss a beat. At the top of the heap, at least in size, is the Super Redhawk, chambered for the .44 Magnum and the .454 Casull. The .454 can also chamber and fire .45 Colt cartridges – as long as the shooter takes care to scrub the chambers clean afterwards – and is a very versatile handgun. Built for hunting, the Super Redhawk comes supplied with scope mounts and is a superb choice for hunting large game with teeth and claws.

At the other end of the size scale, Ruger introduced their polymer-framed LCR five-shot .38 Special revolver last year, and it has been a runaway success. Ruger has sold many thousands of these little pocket revolvers the first year, and demand is still outpacing supply. Mine has proven to be strong, reliable, and accurate. Look for other additions to the Ruger defensive revolver line this year. They have some promising new handguns in the works.

SMITH & WESSON

Smith & Wesson has been in the revolver business for over 150 years. No longer producing any single action revolvers, with the one exception of their Performance Center engraved Model 3 Schofield, S&W is probably the most prolific producer of double action revolvers in the world. From the .22 Long Rifle up through the formidable .500 Smith & Wesson Magnum, if a revolver cartridge exists, chances are that S&W has at least one revolver chambered for it. The small J-frame five-shot .38 Special revolvers are some of the most popular self defense guns ever produced. The Model 642 is probably the best-selling revolver in the S&W line. It is a compact, reliable five-shot revolver with a concealed hammer and a lightweight frame. It's easily slipped into the pocket, where it rides comfortably, day in and day out, ready for action when needed. While not my first choice if headed for a fight, I often carry a lightweight .38 S&W in my pocket. It can just be placed there and

Smith & Wesson Performance Center .460 S&W Magnum revolver. This may be the largest production revolver currently built.

forgotten, but is always ready should a need arise.

Moving up in size, the S&W K&L frame revolvers (K = medium frame; L = "medium-plus") are the mainstay of the Smith & Wesson duty line. These revolvers have served well for generations of sixgun users, both for defense and for hunting. The larger N-frame guns are the epitome of what a Smith & Wesson revolver should be. The classic Models 27 and 29 are back in the lineup and are beautiful and functional examples of the timeless double action revolver. The N-frames are now available in snubbie configurations, something unimaginable even a decade ago. Large but well-balanced, these .357 and .44 Magnum sixguns define the double action revolver to many shooters; with their typically crisp single action trigger pulls and butter-smooth double action trigger pulls, they are reliable and accurate.

Moving up again in size to the S&W X-frame gun, we find the most powerful double action revolvers ever produced. The .460 and .500 S&W Magnums are at the upper limits of what most would ever consider possible in a hand-held revolver. Just thirty years ago, the .44 Magnum was considered to be the "most powerful handgun in the world, and would blow your head clean off," as Dirty Harry Callahan phrased it. The

.44 Magnum now pales in comparison to the power of the .460 and .500 Magnums. Of course, even back when the Dirty Harry movies were made, that was not a true statement, but it made for good theatre. However, today there is no doubt that the big S&W Magnums are powerful enough to take any game animal on Earth.

On the other end of the scale in both size and power, Smith & Wesson has just introduced a small polymer-frame revolver. I have only briefly fired two examples of them, but both shot very well. The Bodyguard 38 is a five-shot .38 Special revolver with a built-in laser sight. The cylinder release is ambidextrous and rides at the top rear of the frame. Just to the right of that is the activation switch for the laser. I am a firm believer in laser sights for defensive weapons. At night, it is hard to see the regular notch and blade sights on a handgun. Tritium sight inserts are good, but in a conflict, your attention will be on the target. The laser sight places the dot on the target, making solid hits much more likely under stress. The built-in laser sight is a good idea. In addition to the integral laser on the Bodyguard, S&W also offers the excellent Crimson Trace Lasergrip on many of their defensive handguns, which is a welcome option.

TAURUS

Taurus USA has many different revolvers available for use for concealed carry, target shooting and hunting. From their small lightweight pocket revolvers up through their 454 Raging Bull, Taurus has a wide selection of revolvers from which to choose. Their small-frame snubnose revolvers are available chambered for the .22 Long Rifle, .22 Magnum, .32 H&R Magnum, .327 Federal, .38 Special, and .357 Magnum calibers. They are available in blued, nickel, or stainless finishes, mostly with fixed sights, but a couple of models have fully adjustable rear sights. Their duty-size

four- and six-inch .357 Magnum revolvers are still in production, with a wide variety of models available. The Raging series of hunting handguns chamber powerful cartridges like the .44 Magnum and .454 Casull and are good choices for hunting big game.

Still probably the hottest-selling revolvers on the planet now are the many variations of the Taurus Judge. Folks have really taken to these versatile handguns. They are available in all-steel or lightweight versions, with two-, three-, or six-inch barrels, depending on model. Available chambered for the 2-1/2- or 3-inch .410 shotshell, both also chamber and fire the .45 Colt cartridge. These are formidable close-range defensive weapons, firing .45 Colt, .410 birdshot and .410 buckshot. They will also fire .410 slugs, but if a solid projectile is desired, the .45 Colt cartridge is a much better choice. I really like the personal defense loads that are now being sold by Winchester, Hornady, and Federal. These loads are tailor-made for the Judge series of handguns and are very effective for social work. New for this year is the Taurus Judge with a short barrel and a polymer frame, making for a relatively lightweight and compact package.

THOMPSON/CENTER

Thompson/Center is responsible for making the single shot hunting pistol popular. Starting with their Contender model decades ago, the T/C pistols have evolved into the Encore and Contender G2 designs, but both are just improvements and refinements of the original Contender pistol. The Contender is offered in just about any chambering that one would want, from .22 Long Rifle up through powerful rifle cartridges such as the .45-70 Government and all the magnum handgun cartridges, including the .460 and .500 S&W Magnums. Thompson/Center offers wooden and synthetic stocks and a variety of barrel lengths. The barrels are interchangeable within the same frame group, and these hand-rifles come pre-drilled for scope mounts to take full advantage of their power and accuracy potential.

UBERTI

Uberti Firearms has been producing quality replicas of nineteenth century American firearms for decades now. While manufacturing replica rifles and handguns for other companies such as Beretta (Uberti's parent company) and Cimarron, Uberti also markets their own line of replica firearms. The Uberti Cattleman series replicates the Colt Single Action Army design and includes the brand-new Callahan Model that is chambered for the .44 Magnum cartridge, probably a first for an SAA clone. This Magnum is offered with original-style fixed sights or as a flattop style with adjustable target sights. In addition to the Callahan, Uberti offers this 1873 style sixgun in .45 Colt, .357 Magnum, and .44 WCF (.44-40) cartridges. Finish options run from a standard blued/case-hardened to nickel and even a bright charcoal blue finish.

The Uberti Stallion is a slightly scaled-down version of the Single Action Army and is chambered in a choice of six-shot .22 Long Rifle or .38 Special, or a ten-shot .22 Long Rifle. There are also Bisley and birdshead grip models available. Uberti also has fans of the old Remington revolvers covered with their Outlaw, Police, and Frontier models, replicating the 1875 and 1890 Remington revolvers. Uberti has several variations of the S&W top-break revolver, including the Number 3 Second model, as well as the Russian, in both nickel and blued finishes as well as fully hand engraved models. These are available in .38 Special, .44 Russian, and .45 Colt chamberings. Uberti has not forgotten the fans of the early cap and ball sixguns and

offers authentic replicas of the Colt and Remington cap and ball revolvers.

U. S. FIRE ARMS

USFA of Hartford, Connecticut, builds some of the best 1873 style Single Action Army revolvers that money can buy, crafted to precisely replicate one of the finest sixguns ever designed but built on modern CNC machinery and hand-fitted by American craftsmen. I own a few of the USFA revolvers, and each one that I have owned and fired has been very accurate and well-fitted. USFA offers an extensive choice of calibers and options, from hand engraving to ivory or fancy walnut stocks. Caliber choices include .45 Colt, .22 Long Rifle, .32 WCF, .38 WCF, .44 WCF, .38 Special and .44 Special. Standard barrel lengths of 4.75, 5.5, and 7.5 inches are available, as well as non-standard custom shop lengths. Abbreviated barrel lengths are available on some models.

One very unique USFA sixgun that I love is their Snubnose model. This sixgun has a two-inch barrel, a modified Thunderer style grip, and is the ultimate single action big bore belly gun. Offered in blue or nickel, it wears a full-size rounded grip and for a touch of class, it has a lanyard loop on the butt. [*Editor's Note: The USFA Snubnose, as well as its big brother the Omnipotent, seem to be modeled after the Colt Model 1878 Double Action but are single action only. -DMS*] Another USFA that I love is their John Wayne "Red River D" sixgun. This gun replicates the Single Action Army revolver that John Wayne carried in most of his western movies, and it has his Red River D cattle brand tastefully applied to the gun. The John Wayne revolver has a special serial

number range, simulated ivory grips, and a quality western holster and belt rig.

USFA now offers a slightly scaled down version of the SAA frame that is chambered for the .327 Federal cartridge. Called the Sparrowhawk, this eight-shot revolver wears a blued finish and a 7-1/2-inch barrel. It has a fully adjustable rear sight and a post front sight. The sights are just like the ones on their .357 Magnum Shooting Master revolver.

As I stated at the beginning of this piece, last year was certainly an interesting one for gun owners, and this next year looks to be exciting as well. Gun manufacturers are reporting all-time high sales numbers, as well as strong profits, all in this time of deep financial recession. As we cross into this second decade of this new millennium, revolver sales are still very strong. The semiauto fans have tried to put the nail into the coffin of the antiquated revolver for decades now, but it refuses to die. No need for such rivalry! While semiauto designs are more popular than ever, many shooters, hunters, and those who carry concealed still prefer the reliable, accurate, and easy-to-use revolver. At the same time, the derringer is still running strong, providing a compact, simple design with plenty of power for close-range performance. The single shot pistol is still very popular with hunters, offering rifle-like accuracy with rugged reliability and simplicity. 2011 is shaping up to be a banner year for gun sales of all types, with revolver sales continuing to be red-hot.

S&W 63: Smith & Wesson Model 63 .22 Long Rifle.

If it were possible to lay my hands on the old Savage Model 110 that I hunted with as a youth and place it next to one of the rifles I currently use today, on the surface few people would notice a great deal of difference. But while the basic firearm design concepts haven't changed significantly in recent decades, the gun manufacturers have without a doubt made significant inroads when it comes to accuracy, performance and dependability. I suppose that is why people such as I get so excited each year when the new models are brought out. No matter what shooting discipline we choose to participate in, we are eager to take advantage of anything that could result in improving our shooting performance. The following is just a sampling of some of the innovative rifles that are now available t o world's sportsmen.

The new Anschutz Model 1770 represents the first totally newly-designed Anschutz action in over thirty years.

BY **TOM TABOR**

RIFLES

The Italian-made, desmodromic Sabatti SAB92SF side by side rifle, imported by EAA, blends Old-World charm with a price tag that's hard to beat.

Author shown with an Asian water buffalo taken in the Northern Territory of Australia with a custom rifle using a CZ action chambered for .500 Jeffrey.

ANSCHUTZ

The Model 1770 is the latest addition to Anschutz's hunting rifle line and is currently offered in only .223 Remington. This rifle represents the first time in over thirty years that Anschutz has introduced a totally new action. The design includes a six locking lug, a short 60-degree bolt lift and a single stage match trigger, which is set at the factory to 2.5-lbs. pull, but can be adjusted from 2 to 4.5 lbs. The German style Meister grade stock comes with an oil finish, semi-oval cheek piece, Schnabel forend

and rosewood pistol grip cap. The stock is checkered at the pistol grip and forend. The medium weight barrel is cold hammer forged and 22 inches long. Overall length of the Model 1770 is 41.73 inches and the weight without a scope is 7.48 lbs. The MSRP for the new Model 1770 is $2,495.

BENELLI U.S.A.

Benelli is possibly best known for their semiautomatic shotguns, but recently the company has announced a new combat carbine rifle that is not

only used and appreciated by the U.S. military forces but now can be the centerpiece of an effective home defense plan and in some cases for hunting and target shooting. The new MR1 fires the 5.56mm NATO (.223 Remington) and uses the ultra-reliable, battle-proven ARGO (Auto-Regulating Gas-Operated) system. This is the same system developed by Benelli for the M1014 and used for over a decade in multiple conflicts by the U.S. Marine Corps. The ARGO system incorporates a gas port located just forward of the chamber where the

Benelli's new MR1 combat carbine is not only used and appreciated by our armed forces but can now be the centerpiece of an effective home defense plan or in some cases used for hunting and target shooting.

The new Blaser bolt-action, detachable-magazine R8 Rifle blends elegance with versatility.

The new BRNO Effect single-shot rifle comes attractively engraved with high country game scenes on the receiver.

The latest addition to Browning's A-Bolt is the TCT Varmint with a Bell and Carlson stock specifically designed for shooting from the prone position.

After several years of being out of production, the Browning T-Bolt is now available once again in all sorts of flavors.

CZ-USA's Model 455 rimfire rifle. Some consider it a classic, and who are we to argue?

gases are hotter and cleaner, resulting in less fouling and more reliable cycling. The stainless steel, self-cleaning piston operates directly against the rotating bolt, thereby eliminating the need for complex linkages. The Picatinny rail allows mounting of both conventional and night-vision sights, while still retaining the capabilities of the metallic-sight. And, an optical Picatinny tri-rail forend kit is available that permits the mounting of a laser sight. The rifle comes from the factory equipped with a five-round magazine, but it will also accept any standard M16 magazines.

BLASER U.S.A.

For years Blaser has been recognized for their versatile interchangeable-barrel rifles, but the company has carried this trait one step further with their new Blaser bolt-action, detachable magazine R8 Rifle. The R8's magazine and trigger assembly have been merged together into a single compact module. The magazine buttons are positioned just above the trigger guard. For safety reasons, when you remove the magazine the R8 automatically de-cocks, keeping the cocking slide from engaging. The new Blaser Precision Trigger breaks at a trigger pull of 1-5/8 lbs. with an extremely short release time and does not rely on a spring to reset the trigger after firing. The desmodromic trigger mechanism offers reliability in extreme conditions such as freezing rain and blowing dust. [*Editor's Note: "desmodromic"? No, Tom didn't just make up that word. It refers to mechanisms that use different types of controls in order to function. Who knew? –DMS*] A wide variety of R8 models are available to select from, including even an individually engraved version.

BRNO

The new BRNO Effect single-shot rifle comes with a select walnut stock and is available in full-length style. The rifle weighs only a mere 6-pounds and comes engraved with high country game scenes on the receiver. It also comes with a single set trigger, automatic safety and iron sights and includes the scope base for mounting optics. Currently the Effect is available in .308 Winchester and .30-06 and carries a MSRP of $1,699.

BROWNING

Years ago, Browning's inventory consisted of only two guns: the Superposed and the Auto-5 shotguns, but today that line has been expanded to include approximately 300 flavors of shotguns alone, about 350 different models of rifles and around 30 different pistols. Included with that vast array of noteworthy firearms today is the T-Bolt™ .22 rifle. After dropping this innovative straight-pull design years ago, Browning decided to bring it back recently and now offers several different stock variations and finishes, including composites, sporters and target/varmint styles. The short-throw action makes the T-Bolt quick to load from the unique 10-round "Double Helix" magazine. MSRP for the T-Bolts range from $705 to $789.

Another Browning rifle that has experienced a great deal of success has been the A-Bolt. Like the T-Bolt, this rifle is offered in many different variations and styles including the recent TCT Varmint. (Sad to say, the "TCT" has nothing to do with the author's own initials.) This particular A-Bolt comes with a glass bedded receiver that is matte blued and drilled and tapped for a scope. The barrel is free-floating, 22 inches long and fluted and is also matt blued with a target crown. The composite stock is a hand-laid fiberglass Bell and Carlson that is specifically designed for shooting from the prone position and comes with aluminum bedded block for improved accuracy. Currently the TCT Varmint is available chambered for .223, .22-250 and .308 and weighs 10 lbs., 6 oz. MSRP is $1,299.

COOPER FIREARMS OF MONTANA

When compared to many other rifle manufacturers, Cooper Firearms of Montana isn't a large company, but over the last two decades they have earned a reputation for making rifles of exceptional high quality that possess unsurpassed tact-driving accuracy. Cooper changed ownership in 2009 and since that time the company has focused their attention on better customer relations, improved products and a shorter order turnaround time.

In the past the company has concentrated primarily on rimfire and the smaller centerfire chamberings that lend themselves for use by varmint hunters and predator hunters and for moderate-range target shooting. This has included both the normal production cartridges as well as a broad array of wildcats. This year the company entered a new era of production by offering a short-action repeater called the Model 54. This totally newly-designed rifle was specifically developed for the classic .243-.308 family of cartridges. Currently it is available in .22-250 Remington, .243 Winchester, .250 Savage, 7mm-08 Remington, .308 Winchester and .260 Remington, but the company plans to add to those choices in the near future. The Model 54 comes in a wide variety of stock configurations including several classic styles and varmint designs. All of the Model 54s come with fully adjustable single stage triggers of the Cooper design, Sako style machined extractors, plunger style ejectors machined from solid bar stock and the three front bolt locking lugs that Cooper has become known for. The basic MSRP for the Classic and Varmint Laminate is $1,695 and that of the Western Classic is $3,895. Because Coopers is essentially a custom shop, custom features can be added to any of their rifles. Prices for those are available upon request.

CZ-USA

The CZ 455 is a new generation of rimfire bolt-action rifles that will eventually consolidate all of the receivers currently used in the Model 452 line into a single platform. This combination, with CZ's new interchangeable barrel system, will allow the user to easily change the stock configuration as well as the caliber. The American Model is the first to see the benefits of this change, but other configurations will soon follow. The Model 455 comes with an adjustable trigger, hammer forged barrel and billet machined receiver and is available in .22 LR, .22 WMR and .17HMR. The MSRP for the American CZ 455 is $463 to $504.

EUROPEAN AMERICAN ARMORY - SABATTI

Quality double rifles often come with five-figure price tags. On the other hand, European American Armory (EAA) is importing a high-quality, Italian-made

Elegance, accuracy and quality are what Cooper's new, first short action repeater, the Model 84, is all about.

double that not only carries an attractive price tag but it is chambered in a wide variety of cartridges, ranging from the tried-and-true .45-70 all the way up to the big .500 Nitro Express. [*Editor's Note: Yes, but is it desmodromic? –DMS*] The Sabatti SAB92SF comes with all the quality features and characteristics that are common in doubles today including a beavertail forend, European styled checkpiece, deep cut checkering, high grade walnut stock, tang mounted safety, chrome-moly barrels, very attractive full engraving and a chrome-steel receiver. For quick target acquisition, modern fiber optic sights have been added. MSRP on the Sabatti SAB92SF is just over $6,000. For more information you can visit http://www.ussginc.com/index.html, or contact EAA Corp. at 411 Hawk St., Rockledge, FL 32955 or at (321) 639-4842.

HI-POINT

Hi-Point Carbines may not be exactly what all shooters are looking for, but these lightweight, low-cost, very versatile rifles fills a nice niche in the firearm field that few others seem to be filling at this time. Currently the Hi-Point Carbine comes chambered in 9mm Luger or .40 S&W, which allows the shooters the benefits associated with using the same ammunition for both their rifle and sidearm. This makes these rifles an excellent choice for either law enforcement or for home defense applications. The robust all-weather black molded polymer skeletonized stock is both tough and lightweight. The forearm has a grabby surface that permits the shooter to wear gloves or shoot bare handed in all types of weather. The simple blow back design feeds the cartridges from the compact

single stack 10-round magazine, which is interchangeable with those of the Hi-Point series semi-auto pistols of same caliber. The metal finish is a special high-durability black powder coat and the stock is a black molded polymer construction. The carbine comes equipped with both an upper and lower Picatinny rail, so you can hang no end of stuff off it if you want. Depending on caliber, the barrel length varies from 16-1/2 to 17 inches and the weight runs about 7 lbs. The Hi-Point Carbine's MSRP is remarkably low at only $249 to $299.

HOWA

Howa has extended its Howa/Hogue Model lineup recently to include the newly developed .375 Ruger powerhouse cartridge. It includes a Hogue Overmolded™ stock in either black or OD green color, a 20-inch #2 contour barrel, Hi-Vis #3 front and rear sights and is available in either blued or stainless.

KIMBER

Kimber has now added to their line of fine Model 84s with a brand new long action rifle, appropriately called the Model 84L. It comes in two styles: the Classic Select Grade and the Classic. The Classic Select Grade Model is available in .25-06 Remington, .270 Winchester and .30-06 Springfield. The stock is French walnut with an ebony forend tip. The Classic Model 84L is available in .270 Winchester and .30-06 Springfield and comes with a Claro walnut stock. The weight is the same for both the Classic Select and Select Grade at a mere 6 lbs., 2 oz. Both come with 24-inch barrels and are equipped with all-steel trigger guards and floorplates. MSRP for the Classic Select is $1,359 and $1,179 for the Classic.

MOSSBERG

Mossberg has recently released two new centerfire bolt action rifles in the company's Maverick Series: a Long-Action Rifle and a Super Bantam Short-Action Rifle. The standard features include such niceties as a free-floating button-rifled barrel, a recessed muzzle crown, factory installed Weaver-style two-piece scope bases and a 4+1 cartridge capacity. They are offered in four popular calibers. The long action model comes in either .30-06 Springfield or .270 Winchester and the short action Super Bantam comes in either .243 Winchester or .308 Winchester. Both come with a matte blued finish and a black synthetic stock, but in the case of the Super Bantam the stock is adjustable in order for it to grow as the youngster grows. Adding or removing inserts at the butt permits the stock to be lengthened or shortened as needed to fit the shooter.

NOSLER

Nosler has made a significant addition to their current Model 48 line of rifles with the introduction of the Model 48 Trophy Grade Rifle (TGR). The new TGR features a free-floating 24-inch chrome-moly barrel and a crisp 3-lb. Basix trigger. Targeting those hunters who face wet and inhospitable conditions, the TGR includes a custom aluminum bedded Bell & Carlson composite stock and the exterior metal surfaces are protected by a special application of Cerakote. The interior working parts have a corrosion-resistant coating of Micro-Slick, too. Nosler officials indicate that hunters can expect sub-MOA performance at 100 yards with the TGR. It is available in nine big game calibers, with the addition of two new choices in the Model

The Howa/Hogue Model lineup is now available chambered for .375 Ruger.

The utilitarian Hi-Point Carbine comes chambered in either 9mm Luger or .40 S&W.

The stylish Kimber 84L Classic Select Grade.

Mossberg's Super Bantam Short-Action Rifle comes with the ability of "growing" in stock length as the young shooter grows.

Ruger's 10-22 VLEH Target Tactical rifle.

One of the more unique new designs comes from Rossi/Taurus. The Circuit Judge blends a revolver design into a rifle and is capable of firing either .45 Colt or .410 shotgun ammunition.

Sako offers economy in their new modestly-priced Model A7 bolt-action rifle.

Savage has added to its very successful Model 10 BAS-K and 10 BAT/S-K line with yet another long range offering, the Model 110 BA chambered in .338 Lapua and 300 Win. Magnum.

Savage is offering their new Model 111 Long-Range Hunter chambered for 6.5x284 Norma, which has a reputation as being very successful in competitions out to 1,000 yards.

Thompson Center's HotShot™ Youth Rifle chambered for .22LR is sure to be a hit with young shooters by mirroring mom & dad's T/C Pro-Hunter rifles.

Weatherby's Vanguard® Youth rifles features a removable elongated spacer system that is adjustable to fit the shooter.

The John Browning-designed Model 1895 and 1886 are once again available from Winchester, honoring a historic time in our history.

48 Varmint
Rifle: .204 Ruger
and .223 Remington. The
MSRP for the Model 48 TGR runs from
$1,745.95 to $1,895.95.

OLYMPIC ARMS, INC.

Olympic Arms continues to build top quality ARs in a wide variety of configurations. The usual 5.56mm, 6.8 SPC and .7.62x39 are available, as well as some pistol calibers. Unique to Olympic is the Model K8-MAG that is offered in .223, .243 and .25 WSSM. New for 2010 is a new cartridge developed by Olympic called the .300 Olympic Super Short Magnum (OSSM). This new hotrod produces ballistics exceeding those of the .30-06 out of a 22-inch barrel. Winchester .25 WSSM brass is easily necked-up to make the cases. Hornady makes the dies, Hodgdon will have load data available soon, and HSM supplies factory loaded ammo. Complete rifles, as well as uppers ready to go on your existing AR, are available. The complete rifle is called the "Gamestalker" and it's a real looker with its camo finish, ACE skelton-buttstock and ERGO Sure Grip. It comes with no sights, but its flattop design allows shooters to arrange it in any optics configuration that they see fit. The aluminum handguard is free-floated and the 22-inch stainless-steel barrel is of a lightweight hunting contour. Overall weight is a comfortable 7.5 lbs.

ROSSI/TAURUS

Possibly one of the most unique new rifles making its debut is the Rossi/Taurus Circuit Judge. [*Editor's note: The Circuit Judge also pops up in our Shotguns section. –DMS*] The rifle combines the design of the Taurus revolvers with that of a long gun. This shotgun/rifle crossover offers the ability to shoot .410 2-1/2- or 3-inch magnum shotshells or .45 Colt ammunition in any order or com-

bination without the need of changing barrels. The Circuit Judge is available in either a smooth bore or a rifled barrel version and comes with a blued finish, hardwood Monte Carlo style stock, single-action/double-action trigger, fiber-optic front sight, yoke detent, recoil pad, transfer bar and the Taurus Security System. The barrel measures 18.5 inches long, the overall firearm length is only 38 inches and total weight is only a mere 4.75 lbs. MSRP is $618.00.

RUGER

It wasn't long after Ruger appeared on the firearm/shooting scene in 1949 that shooters throughout the world began to appreciate the quality of the products that this company produces. Over the six-plus decades that followed, Ruger has established a reputation as a very progressive company that seemingly has the inherent ability to supply exactly the type of firearms that shooters are looking for. And there is no better example of this than a couple of newly released rimfires.

First there is the SR-2 that combines the visual features of an AR rifle with the fun and economy of shooting a .22 LR. The SR-22 uses a standard 10/22 action inside a top-quality, all-aluminum chassis that faithfully replicates the AR-platform dimensions between the sighting plane, buttstock height and the grip. It includes a Picatinny rail optic mount and a six-position telescoping M4-style buttstock on a mil-spec diameter tube, plus a Hogue Monogrip pistol grip. The round, mid-length handguard is mounted using a standard-thread AR-style barrel nut, which allows a vast array of rail-mounted sights and accessories to be used. The 15-1/8-inch barrel is precision-rifled and constructed of cold hammer forged alloy steel and comes capped with a SR-556/Mini-14 flash suppressor.

The second new addition to Ruger's rimfire rifles is the 10/22® VLEH Target Tactical rifle. This rifle offers many of the inherent features used in the Hawkeye® Tactical bolt-action rifle but in a semi-auto rimfire action. It builds on many of the features of the Ruger 10/22 Target Model, beginning with the same precision-rifled, cold hammer forged, spiral-finished barrel, but cut to the shorter length of 16-1/8 inches in order to reduce the weight and improve the handling. The .920-inch OD match-grade barrel is capped with a target crown to protect the rifling at the muzzle, and

the barreled action is mounted in a non-slip, rugged Hogue OverMolded stock. The trigger of the 10/22® VLEH Target Tactical rifle is the same as used on the 10/22® Target Model and an adjustable bipod comes with each rifle. The rifle, minus the bipod, weighs 6-7/8 lbs.

SAKO

For the economy-minded shooter, Sako has merged many of the desirable Sako features into their Model A7 bolt-action rifle, yet kept the price down. The A7 comes in wide variety of the most popular calibers ranging from .243 up to the .300 Win. Mag. It is available in either blued or stainless steel and includes such features as a cold hammer forged match-grade barrel, single stage adjustable trigger (adjustable from 2 to 4 lbs. pull), detachable magazine, two-position safety with separate bolt release button, Weaver-style scope bases and a lightweight synthetic stock. Depending on caliber, the weight ranges from 6-3/8 to 6-5/8 lbs. with barrel lengths from 22-7/16 to 24-3/8 inches. Each rifle is guarantee to place five shots into a 1-inch group at 100 yards. MSRP for the blued model is from $850 to $900 and the stainless model runs from $950 to $1,000.

SAVAGE ARMS

In the last decade Savage Arms has substantially improved both the quality of their products and expanded their firearms lines. The company's newly developed AccuTrigger and AccuStock come stock on many of those products, and this has provided Savage with a significant edge over their competition. This year the company followed up their very successful 2009 release of the radical Model 10 BAS-K and 10 BAT/S-K tactical/target rifles with yet another: the Model 110 BA. Chambered for .338 Lapua and .300 Win. Mag., this considerably extends the range of these great precision rifles. The BA modular platform is built around an aluminum stock that features Savage's innovative three-dimensional bedding system. Buttstock and pistol grips are easily interchanged and a three-sided accessory rail adds versatility. The 110 BA features a five-round detachable magazine, high-efficiency muzzle brake and a Magpul PRS adjustable stock. MSRP is $2,267.

Another great addition at Savage is their new Model 111 Long-Range Hunter with a new chambering for 2010, the 6.5x284 Norma. The 6.5x284 Norma has been very successful in competition out to 1,000 yards and is a favorite of those who appreciate 26-calibers. The new Long-Range Hunter features a 26-inch fluted magnum sporter barrel, AccuTrigger, AccuStock with Karsten adjustable cheekpiece and a matte blued finish. MSRP is $934 to $972.

SMITH & WESSON

Smith & Wesson is best known for their high-quality handguns, but over the last few decades the company has very successfully moved into the rifle and shotgun market. Recently the company released a great new addition to their line of rifles, the .22LR-platform Model M&P 15-22, which mirrors the AR-style centerfire rifles. The M&P 15-22 comes with a 25-round detachable magazine and a six-position collapsible CAR stock that's capable of collapsing to an overall length of 30.5 inches or extending to 33.75 inches. The match-grade precision barrel is 16 inches long with a 1:16 twist. The weight is a moderate 5.5 lbs. and the sights are an adjustable A2-style post in the front and an adjustable dual aperture in the rear. In addition, the M&P 15-22 comes with a functioning charging handle, quad rail handguard, threaded barrel with an A1-style compensator, and lightweight, high strength polymer upper and lower receivers. They come from Smith and Wesson with a lifetime service policy and carry an MSRP of $569.

THOMPSON/CENTER ARMS

In the recent years Thompson/Center Arms (now a Smith & Wesson company) has become a major player in the area of sporting firearms. Answering the calls of predator hunters, in January 2010 the company added yet one more member to their Venture family of rifles, the T/C Venture Predator. At the core of the T/C Venture Predator is its 22-inch precision barrel with 5R "offset" rifling and target grade crown. T/C guarantees these rifles to have MOA accuracy. Just a few of the many inherent favorable features include a trigger with an adjustable pull from 3.5 to 5 lbs, a nitrate-coated bolt with a 60-degree lift, a roller-burnished receiver (which helps to provide quick follow-up shots), and a classic styled composite stock with inlaid traction grip panels. The T/C Venture Predator comes from the factory with a drilled and tapped receiver and ships complete with Weaver-style scope bases already installed. Currently the rifle is available in .204, .22-250, .223 and .308 and comes with a single stack 3+1 detachable nylon box magazine. The Venture Predator is entirely made in the U.S. and is backed by Thompson/Center's lifetime warranty for a retail price from $549 to $599. Sounds like a helluva deal to us.

To be available in April of 2010 from T/C is the new .22LR HotShot Youth Rifle. Designed to mirror mom and dad's T/C Pro-Hunter, the HotShot includes many features that are favorable to a youngster, like an easy to operate break-open system, a weight of only 3 lbs. (!) and an overall length of 30-1/4 inches. With the rifle's single shot design and hammer block trigger, the HotShot will not fire until the hammer is cocked. It's available in three colors (black composite, Realtree AP camouflage and pink AP camouflage). The HotShot is made totally in the United States and is also backed by T/C's lifetime warrantee at an anticipated retail price ranging from $229 to $249 (again: !).

WEATHERBY

Weatherby has long been a supporter of our youth and the company's introduction of their new Vanguard® Youth Rifle further emphases that dedication of getting youngsters involved in shooting sports. The Vanguard Youth features a removable elongated spacer system that is adjustable to fit the shooter. Installing the spacers creates a longer length of the pull, allowing it be changed from 12-1/2 up to 13-5/8 inches. The rifle weighs only 6-1/2 lbs. and comes with a #1 contour 20-inch barrel. It's equipped with a black synthetic stock, fully adjustable trigger, a cold hammer forged barrel and the proven Vanguard short action. It has an injection molded Monte Carol style stock and is currently only available in a right-hand version. Available calibers include .223 Remington, .22-250 Remington, .243 Winchester, 7mm-08 Remington and the

Ruger combines the AR platform with economy in their .22LR-chambered SR-22.

Olympic Arms' Model K8-MAG is now offered in a new cartridge developed by Olympic, the .300 Olympic Super Short Magnum (OSSM).

The latest addition to Nosler's line of fine rifles is the Model 48 Trophy Grade Rifle (TGR).

.308 Winchester. The Youth Vanguard Weatherby carries a MSRP of $529.00.

A number of shooters appealed to Weatherby, requesting that the company produce a detachable magazine rifle. Weatherby responded with a couple of new offerings in their Vanguard line: the Synthetic DBM (stands for detachable box magazine) and the Sporter DBM. The magazines are made of a durable polymer, which helps to reduce the overall weight of the rifles. The magazines hold three rounds and come with a unique cartridge counter for easy reference in the field. Other features of the Synthetic DBM include a black injection-molded composite Monte Carlo stock, matte black metalwork and a low-density recoil pad. The Sporter DBM has a raised-comb Monte Carlo walnut stock with a satin urethane finish, a rosewood forend and low-luster, matte-blued metalwork. Both rifles weigh 7 lbs. and are available in .25-06

Remington, .270 Winchester and .30-06 Springfield and come with a 24-inch #2 contour barrel, but, again, only in a right hand. configuration

WINCHESTER REPEATING ARMS

Winchester has expanded its line of rifles once again to include a couple of John Browning-designed models from our distant past: the Grade I Model 1895 and the extra light Model 1886. Both of these lever action models have deeply blued receivers and blued steel end caps and are equipped with straight buttplates. Both come with top tang safeties and adjustable buckhorn rear sights. The 1895 is available in .405 Winchester, .30-06 and .30-40 Krag, while the 1896 is available only in .45-70. The Grade I 1895 carries a MSRP of $1,179 and the Grade I 1896 is $1,269. Also new from Winchester is a takedown version of the 16-inch-barrelled Model 1892 Trapper Carbine, a finely-machined little honey that's expected to be vailable in short, short, short supply sometime this year.

Semi-Auto Pistols

BY JOHN MALLOY

The big news in the semiautomatic pistol world for 2011 is, of course, that the Colt/ Browning 1911 design has been in continuous — and growing — production for a full 100 years!

Few manufactured items of any kind are made continuously for a century. It is even rarer for a century-old item to be the leader in its field. This position, however, has been achieved by the Colt/Browning 1911 pistol design.

As the 1911's centennial approached, the venerable design gained, rather than lost, popularity. With the passing of the years, more and more companies added 1911s to their product lines. In the year 2010 alone, over half a dozen firms added their names to those offering a 1911. To celebrate the 100th anniversary, 1911 centennial commemoratives will be offered by a number of companies.

Not only has the original centerfire locked-breech 1911 design remained popular, but 22-caliber versions — blowback pistols styled after the 1911, and with many 1911 features — have been offered. Several new ones appear this year alone.

Even with the historical importance of the centennial, the news is not all 1911. The recent trend of very small 380-caliber pistols continues into this year. A number of new little .380s are added this year, offered by both major firms and smaller companies.

22-caliber pistols are always of interest, whether they look like 1911s or not. Several new .22 semiautomatic pistols appear this year. Also, more new conversion kits to allow larger-caliber pistols to handle .22 Long Rifle ammunition are being introduced. .22 pistols are regularly used for training, competition, hunting and recreational shooting.

Polymer-frame pistols remain strong sellers. Slowly gaining popularity over the years, polymers have become a mainstay in the world of autoloading pistols. A number of new polymer-frame guns, from a variety of companies, and in a variety of calibers, are being introduced.

Pistols varying greatly from traditional designs are being made, and the usefulness of carbines chambered for traditional autoloading pistol cartridges has been demonstrated. So, in this report, I'll continue to cover unconventional pistols and pistol-caliber carbines.

There are a lot of very interesting things going on in the world of semiautomatic pistols. Let's take a look at what the companies are offering:

AKDAL

The Turkish-made Akdal pistols have found a home in America. They will be imported by American Tactical Imports. (See ATI.) Akdal pistols were introduced by ATI in January 2010. These pistols, first mentioned on these pages last year, are polymer-frame pistols in 9mm and .40 S&W, designed to compete in the Glock niche. These new pistols may be wearing new names when they reach the production stage.

AMERICAN CLASSIC

American Classic 1911 pistols are imported by Import Sports, a New Jersey company. The original 1911-A1 "Mil-Spec" version has been joined by enhanced American Classic II (full-size 5-inch) and Commander (4.25-inch) variants. Both of these pistols are available with either deep blue or new hard chrome finishes.

The new top-of-the-line Trophy Model is a full-size 5-inch gun available in hard chrome finish only. It has a number of enhancements, including adjustable Novak-type rear sight, dovetailed fiber-optic front sight, front and rear slide serrations, full-length guide rod and eight-round magazine.

ARMSCOR

Armscor is a Philippine manufacturing company with U. S. headquarters in Nevada. The company produces pistols patterned after the 1911 and CZ-75 pistols. In the United States, 1911-type guns are sold under the Rock Island Armory (RIA) name. With the current interest in 22-caliber 1911 pistols, a new RIA 22-caliber pistol was displayed at the 2010 SHOT Show. Of "open-top" slide design, the new .22 pistol has a fixed barrel. Production models were scheduled for summer of 2010.

ATI

American Tactical Imports, a relatively new player in the semiautomatic pistol field, seems to have a larger presence with the passing of time.

The line of ATI ported double-action pistols introduced last year, made by the Tisas firm in Turkey, is now in full production. These are striking-looking pistols, with true functional barrel porting, and also decorative porting on the sides of the slides.

There is also a new high-capacity 9mm with similar mechanism, but styled somewhat after the Browning Hi-Power 9mm pistol. It is designated the American Tactical HP9. The HP9 has a 5-inch barrel and carries an 18-round magazine. It is available in black, chrome and two-tone finishes.

And, if we have a pistol that favors the Hi-Power, why not one that looks a bit like the Beretta 92? ATI is also marketing a new 9mm AT92. The AT92 can be had in a full-size version with 4.9-inch barrel, and a compact with 4.3-inch barrel. Capacity is 15+1.

GSG (German Sporting Guns) firearms are also imported by ATI. So new it didn't get into the catalog is the GSG 1911 22-caliber pistol. Made as a .22 rimfire pistol, the frame and all other parts below the slide are all big-bore 1911. The .22 magazine is the same thickness as that of the original 45. ATI describes it as having "the same weight and feel of a 1911 pistol with many interchangeable parts."

And, now, as of January 21, 2010, ATI will also offer full-caliber 1911 pistols. A few prototypes on display at the 2010

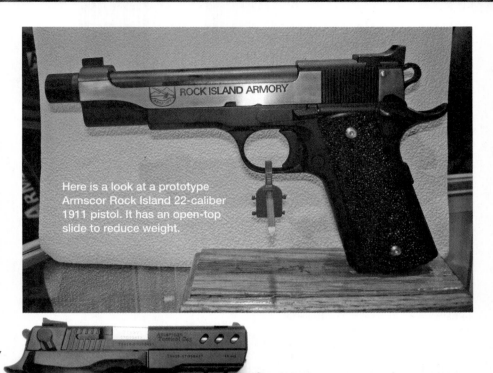

Here is a look at a prototype Armscor Rock Island 22-caliber 1911 pistol. It has an open-top slide to reduce weight.

The largest of ATI's line of Turkish-designed double-action ported pistols is the .45 ACP Model C45.

American Tactical's HP9 pistol looks a bit like one might expect a double-action Hi-Power to look. The double-column magazine holds 18 rounds.

American Tactical Imports' Model 92 pistol has a familiar shape, similar to that of a Beretta 92.

In the United States, Philippine-made Armscor 1911 pistols are marketed under the Rock Island Armory name.

SHOT Show were marked "American Tactical M1911 A1." A "Mil-Spec" 5-inch pistol will be one of the first variants offered. Pistols with rails, enhanced models, and short cone-barrel variants are also in the works. The popularity of the 1911 is stronger now than ever before, and now ATI will have a full line of 1911 pistols.

ATI also distributes the Guncrafter Industries 50-caliber conversion kit for Glock pistols. The kit consists of a complete top end and magazine, and fits Glock Models 20 and 21. When the kit is installed, the Glock can handle the powerful .50 GI cartridge, with 275- and 300-gr. bullets at 875 and 700 fps.

BERETTA

Beretta doesn't make a 1911, but they do have an anniversary. The Beretta 9mm pistol was adopted by the US military in 1985, so it has achieved its 25th year of service. Actually, the design dates back to 1975, when the Beretta Model 92 came into being. A variant of the 92 was adopted as the US service pistol on April 10, 1985, and became the M9. The commercial 25th Anniversary M9 pistol available to civilians is a close copy of the military M9, with military-style markings that are close to those of the actual military pistols. They have a unique M9 prefix to the serial numbers.

The Model 92 series has some new variants now. The most distinctive feature of the new 92A1 (9mm) and 96A1 (40) is the rail on the forward part of the frame. They also have higher-capacity magazines (17 rounds in 9mm, 12 in 40), and removable front sights. There are some internal modifications also, and — note this — the trigger guards are now rounded.

The PX4 Storm has a new variant in the series. A compact Storm is now between the full-size and sub-compact versions. The new Compact Storm has a 3.2-inch barrel, which gives it a 6.8-inch overall length and 5.2-inch height. It weighs about 27 ounces. Magazine capacity is 15 rounds in 9mm, and 12 rounds in .40 S&W.

The NEOS pistol now has a new carbine kit available. The kit has a grip frame that is moulded with a shoulder stock, and a longer barrel. These parts allow the conversion of the pistol into a handy carbine for informal shooting. Each kit comes with a warning against using the shoulder stock frame with the original pistol barrel.

BERSA

Acknowledging the presence of women in the shooting world is a good thing. A rather abstract way of doing this is to put colors generally related to the female sex on special pistols. In 2010, Bersa joined other companies by promoting the color pink. The Bersa Thunder 380 will now be available with optional pink grips.

A new line of Bersa polymer-frame concealed-carry pistols with a slim grip profile is in the works. Planned in 9mm (BP9cc) and .40 S&W (BP40cc), the new polymer-frame Bersas will weigh about 21 ounces, with 3.2-inch barrels. The new compact pistols look good. However, as of January 2010, the new pistols had not yet been approved by BATFE, so all I can do here is give you this advance notice.

BREN TEN

The Bren Ten is back! Really, the exact name, this time. In the last edition of this publication, recall that Vltor had already put into production an improved version of the original Bren Ten as the Vltor Fortis pistol. Since then, the company has acquired the rights to the name "Bren Ten." Pistols will now be marketed under the Bren Ten name. Bren Ten-marked pistols were planned for May 2010 availability. Standard, Vice and Special Forces variants are scheduled. They are made by Vltor and distributed by Sporting Products, LLC.

BROWNING

Browning doesn't have a 1911 in its line, but the Hi-Power, introduced in 1935, reached its 75th anniversary in 2010. Special Hi-Power pistols made during 2010 will have commemorative engraving on the top of the slide. Three variants were planned: a Standard model with walnut grips and fixed sights, a Standard model with walnut grips and adjustable sights, and a Mark III variant with composite grips with matte finish and fixed sights. The Hi-Power is available in 9mm and .40 S&W, but all the 75th Anniversary engraved versions will be in the original 9mm chambering only.

New lighter Buck Mark 22-caliber pistols have been added to Browning's rimfire pistol line. The pistols have fluted aluminum alloy barrels with steel sleeves. Available with 5.5-inch (28 ounces) or 7.5-inch (30 ounces) barrels, the guns are available with either matte grey or matte green finishes.

CANIK

A new line of Turkish-made pistols was introduced at the 2010 SHOT Show. Introduced as the Canik 55 series, the 9mm pistols are based on the CZ 75 double-action system. The basic "Standard" model is accompanied by the self-descriptive "Light" and "Compact" models. Variations from these offerings seem to be identified with sea-life names such as the Shark, the Piranha, the Stingray and the Dolphin. No importer had been named at the time of this writing.

CENTURY INTERNATIONAL ARMS

Century International Arms continues to offer its Arcus 9mm pistols (double-action versions of the Browning HP) and its line of Shooters Arms 45-caliber 1911 pistols, as well as other traditional semiauto pistols. This year, something a bit more unconventional is offered in the form of the Colefire Magnum pistol. The Colefire has the appearance of the Sterling 9mm submachinegun design but is a semiautomatic pistol chambered for the 7.62x25mm Tokarev cartridge. The unusual pistol uses a modified side-mounted Sten magazine that holds 25 rounds of ammunition. Why 7.62x25? Well, during the ammunition shortage that is still continuing at the time of this writing, surplus Tokarev ammo is one of the least expensive and most readily-available kinds of surplus pistol ammunition! The Colefire has a 4.5-inch barrel and is a bit over 13 inches long. It weighs well over four pounds, and should be easy to shoot for even long plinking sessions.

CHARLES DALY

A sad note. KBI, the parent company of Charles Daly and other firearms brands, went out of business on January 29, 2010. As of the time of this writing, arrangements were being made for another company to handle service for guns that had been offered by KBI. In its last year, KBI marketed handguns bearing the names Charles Daly and Jericho, as well as the new line of CD striker-fired pistols.

A company statement expressed hope that another firm will offer Charles Daly products in the future.

CHIAPPA

Introduced in prototype on these pages last year, the Chiappa 1911 22-caliber pistol is now a production item.

Styled after the popular 45-caliber 1911 pistol, the concept behind the Chiappa 1911 22 was to provide a 22-caliber semiauto pistol at a cost less than that of a conversion kit for a 45.

The black-finish production pistols fall into three categories, separated basically by sighting systems. The Standard Model 1911-22 has traditional fixed sights. The Tactical model has an angled rear sight that extends slightly to the rear of the rear sight dovetail. The Target model has a fully-adjustable rear sight. Other options are two-tone variants, which combine the black frame with a slide colored either tan or olive drab. All variants are supplied with double-diamond grips with the Chiappa logo in the middle. Barrels are 5 inches, weight is 32 ounces, and magazines hold 10 rounds of 22 Long Rifle ammunition. A sample target demonstrated by Chiappa showed impressive accuracy.

The Chiappa Model 1911-22 is distributed in America by MKS Supply. Essentially identical pistols, marked PUMA 1911-22, are also distributed by Legacy Sports International.

CIMARRON

For many years, Cimarron has been a leader in providing the superb replicas of historical rifles and revolvers favored by Cowboy Action shooters. Now, for the first time, the company will offer semiautomatic pistols.

Cimarron is working with Armscor to make a true 1911, representative of the period during which the "old west" was gradually becoming modernized. This transitional period is sometimes referred to as the "Wild Bunch" era, memorialized by motion pictures such as *The Wild Bunch*, *The Professionals*, and *Big Jake*.

A few prototypes were exhibited at the Cimarron display at the 2010 SHOT Show. They had true 1911 frames, without the recesses behind the trigger area. The slides were marked with the original patent dates to 1913 and carried the Cimarron name. Production versions will have, of course, double-diamond wood grips. A company representative said they were looking ahead to a 100-year commemorative version.

C.O. ARMS

New 1911-style pistols have recently been introduced by C.O. Arms, a company based in Millington, Tennessee. The Scorpion model is a full-size model with forged stainless-steel slide and frame. The Stinger variant has a short 3.25-inch

Century International Arms markets the 9mm Arcus pistol, a Bulgarian-made double-action modification of the Hi-Power pistol.

(left) Beretta's series of PX4 Storm pistols now has a new compact version. The new rotating-barrel handgun has a 3.2-inch barrel.

The Chiappa 1911-22 duplicates the look and feel of a full-size 1911 pistol and is chambered for the .22 Long Rifle cartridge.

The appearance of Century International's new Colefire semiautomatic pistol shows its origins in the Sterling submachinegun design. It is chambered for inexpensive 7.62x25mm ammunition.

A new Tennessee company, CO Arms, offers several variants of the basic 1911 pistol.

The new polymer-frame CZ 75 P-07 Duty pistol can be easily recognized by its unusual large trigger guard.

Five years ago, CZ-USA brought out a 30-year commemorative for the 1975 CZ 75 design, and possibly the company will also have a similar 35-year commemorative.

(left) The Dan Wesson Valor, a 5-inch 1911 pistol, here with a brushed stainless-steel finish, is new for 2010.

FNH-USA's FNP-45 Tactical pistol is a polymer-frame military-style handgun with an elongate threaded barrel.

Ed Brown Products has brought out a special commemorative 45-caliber 1911 to recognize Massad Ayoob.

barrel and slide, but has a full-size aluminum grip frame length, giving it 9+1 capacity. Caliber? .45 ACP, of course.

COBRA

Cobra Enterprises, a Utah company, offers personal-protection semiautomatic pistols in calibers from .32 ACP to .45 ACP. Small variations slip into the catalog with little fanfare. A new finish is now offered for their Patriot 45, a 19-ounce polymer-frame double-action-only (DAO) pistol. Previously available with the stainless-steel slide covered in a matte black finish, it is now offered in polished finish for those who like a bright slide on a two-tone pistol. The Patriot has one of the best DAO autopistol triggers I have tried — much like a good revolver double-action trigger.

COLT

Needless to say, Colt is taking the 100th anniversary of its Colt/Browning 1911 design seriously. All guns made during the year of 2011 will have special markings. The company is not just going to put a new roll-stamp on existing products, however. Colt has a number of new variants of the basic 1911 offered, in order to cover as many niches as possible.

The Colt Rail Gun, introduced on these pages last year as a stainless-steel pistol, is now also available with a blackened finish. The 9mm chambering, popular with many women, and with men who want a lower-recoiling pistol, is now offered in its small Defender (3-inch, stainless-steel carry pistol with white-dot sights) and New Agent (3-inch, blued carry pistol with trench sight system).

The New Agent 45 is now also available in a new double-action-only version. Colt is coming back into the double-action world with relatively little fanfare, as its Double Eagle offering of the past did not take the firearms world by storm. The full-size 5-inch Government Model is also available in a double-action-only variant. This variant is of additional interest because it is also put together with a lightweight aluminum-alloy frame.

In addition, the standard single-action Government Model is also now available with the lightweight frame. A number of shooters have expressed interest in a lighter full-size 5-inch Government Model as a good carry pistol. In some modes of carry, the forward weight distribution of the longer barrel actually allows easier carry, as well as slightly improved ballistics The reduced weight can make carry easier.

Colt also is making a pitch for parts sales via the internet. A customer can go to www.coltsmfg.com and order original-equipment spare parts and accessories direct from the factory, at what the company describes as "unbeatable prices."

COONAN

Coonan is back! Regular readers of this report will recall Coonan Arms as a manufacturer of modified 1911 pistols that would handle the .357 Magnum revolver cartridge. Some years ago, they had expanded the product line to include the .41 Magnum, but then financial problems caused the company to close. Now Coonan is back, with the guns in full production in .357 chambering. Standard 5-inch, and more compact 4-inch versions are offered. Will the .41 again be available? A company official said it is a possibility.

CZECHPOINT

Czechpoint, Inc. (easy to remember the name), operating from Knoxville, Tennessee, distributes firearms manufactured in the Czech Republic. Along with a number of rifles, Czechpoint also offers the .32 ACP Scorpion pistol. Recall that the original "Skorpion" was a tiny .32 ACP submachinegun developed by the Czechs for clandestine use while the country was under Communist control.

The newly-made Scorpion pistol is the same size as the original (10.6 inches long, 4.5-inch barrel, weight 39 ounces) but is semiautomatic only and has no provision for the wire shoulder stock of the original. The mechanism is straight blowback, and the gun is fed from either 10- or 20-round detachable magazines.

With each Scorpion pistol comes a hard case, one 10-round and two 20-round magazines, a magazine pouch, a holster, and — a nice touch — a CD with the owner's manual and the history of the gun. Grips can be one of four different styles of wood or plastic.

CZ-USA

The latest pistol to be imported by CZ-USA is the CZ 75 P-07 Duty, announced on these pages last year. It is a conventional double action, steel-slide, polymer-frame pistol. Barrel length is 3.7 inches. The overall dimensions are roughly 5x7 inches, placing the P-07 in the compact class. Weight is about 27 ounces. The capacity of this 9mm pistol is 16+1. Unlike the other CZ 75 variants,

the P-07 is shipped as a decocker-only, but parts are available for an owner-installed conversion to permit cocked-and-locked operation. Perhaps the most noticeable feature of the P-07 is its unusual extra-large trigger guard, with a long vertical front portion. Because the front of the frame has a moulded accessory rail, it seems almost as if the trigger guard was designed as an index for an attached accessory. Originally introduced in 9mm, the P-07 will soon be available in .40 S&W, with 12+1 capacity.

A limited edition stainless-steel variant of the CZ 75 B (the B indicates the new firing-pin safety) was offered in early 2010. It is a full-size pistol with 4.7-inch barrel, in 9mm, with 16+1 capacity. The stainless pistol is fitted with an ambidextrous safety, which the standard CZ 75 B does not have.

The CZ Custom Shop offers several competition and target variants that do not appear in the general CZ lineup. Although the pistol dates back to 1975, I have not yet heard of a 35-year commemorative edition, but one may be in the works. The company brought out a special 30-year commemorative, and at this time, when commemoratives are in the air, we might yet see a 35th year pistol.

We are in a period of great interest in accessory rails on pistols. Relatively few shooters regularly use the rails for light or laser attachment, but the rails can be put to such use when desired. Now, CZ gives us another use. The company offers a bayonet suited to attachment on the rails! The bayonet also has a rail, so an additional accessory can be placed below the mounted bayonet. A real attention-catcher.

DAN WESSON

Dan Wesson (recall that the DW company is now under the ownership of CZ-USA) produces 1911-type pistols that extends CZ's line of double-action autoloaders. Two new models were introduced in early 2010. The Valor is a stainless-steel full-size 5-inch 1911, available in brushed stainless finish, or a matte black "Duty" finish. The new 45-caliber Valor has a match barrel with 1:16 twist, and features Heinie "straight eight" night sights.

Another introduction, the Dan Wesson Guardian pistol, is designed as a lighter "Commander-size" carry pistol. It comes in 9mm chambering, the only 9mm pistol in the Dan Wesson lineup. It is built on an aluminum-alloy frame, which has a

"bobtail" treatment at the lower rear portion of the grip frame. The 29-ounce pistol has ambidextrous thumb safeties.

DETONICS

Since the beginning of its history, Detonics has always had the knack of coming up with features outside the mainstream. An innovation for its traditional small 45-caliber CombatMaster is putting the front sight on the barrel itself. This arrangement allows an interesting new way to index the slide and barrel together on the forward travel of the slide.

DIAMONDBACK

Florida has become a major player in the firearms industry, with a number of companies providing a wide range of firearms. The latest addition is Diamondback Firearms, of Cocoa, Florida. Their product is a small new 380-caliber locked-breech pocket pistol, the DB 380. The compact polymer-frame pistol is only 3/4-inch wide and weighs 8.8 ounces. It has a 2.8-inch barrel. Capacity is 6+1. Two 6-round magazines are available, one with a flush base and one with a finger-rest base. Trigger mechanism is double-action-only, with a reported 5-pound pull. The trigger activates a striker firing system. The three-dot sights are adjustable for windage on the rear sight. I am not sure how the company name was established; however, having grown up in Florida, I can attest to the fact that the state is home to some spectacular diamondback rattlesnakes. At the time of this writing, RSR, of Grand Prairie, Texas, is the exclusive distributor of the Diamondback DB380.

DOUBLESTAR

The DoubleStar .45 pistol was introduced on these pages two years ago and went into production last year. Now, a new "Combat Pistol" is being offered. The new gun offers the basic pistol with new options. The Combat Pistol offers Novak three-dot sights, a Novak 8-round magazine, and 25-lpi checkering and other features. Although relatively new to the 1911 world, DoubleStar will offer a 100-year commemorative variant.

ED BROWN

People who have made great contributions to the honorable use of handguns for sport, personal defense and law-enforcement purposes deserve to be recognized for what they do. In January 2010, Ed Brown Products announced that they would honor Massad Ayoob with a special Massad Ayoob Signature

Edition 1911. The limited edition pistol will be a 4.25-inch Commander-size pistol with bobtail frame and double-diamond grips. Made of stainless steel, the commemorative pistol weighs about 35 ounces. The sights are three-dot night sights. Ayoob specified that the trigger have a 4.5-pound pull and that the pistol be able to group jacketed-hollow-point ammunition into two inches or less at 25 yards. What makes the pistol special as a commemorative is a facsimile of Ayoob's signature on the right side of the slide. A copy of Ayoob's book, *The Gun Digest Book of Concealed Carry*, is included with each pistol.

Thinking ahead, Ed Brown announced that the company will put out a 100-year commemorative to acknowledge the unique record of the Colt/Browning1911 design during the past century.

EMF

Last year, EMF got back to its "Early and Modern Firearms" beginnings. They added, to their western-style guns, a line of 1911 pistols and a new polymer-frame 9mm pistol.

Now, the polymer-frame pistol, the FMK, is in full production. The 1911 line, made in Tennessee, has several variants, including the original 1911 A1, an enhanced Combat model, and a new Nightstalker 1911, in black with a rail. Slides are now marked "Hartford Model 1911."

This year, EMF has also added a line of pistol-caliber carbines. The new JR Carbine is a straight blowback, offered in 9mm, .40 S&W and .45 ACP. It looks a little bit like an AR-15, but is much simpler. However, it will accept many AR aftermarket items, and is loaded with rails that allow all sorts of additions. The construction is interesting, in that calibers can be changed with only a magazine well, bolt and barrel change. The carbine can be ordered with either right- or left-handed controls, and the bolt handle and ejection of empty cases can be on either side. The carbines are initially furnished with appropriate Glock magazines, but the magazine well is modular and can be adapted to other magazines. Looks as if a lot of thought has gone into this design.

FNH USA

A number of new pistols were introduced by FNH USA this year. Let's start with the largest first.

The FNP-45 Tactical pistol is a .45 ACP polymer-frame conventional double action arm that pretty obviously had its origin in FN's design program for military testing. The pistol is described as "completely ambidextrous," with decocker/safety, slide stop and magazine release operable from either side. The 5.3-inch barrel extends forward of the slide and is threaded. The flat dark earth frame has an accessory rail moulded into its forward portion. Interchangeable backstraps are furnished. The slide has high night sights front and rear. The top of the slide is cut and threaded for an electronic sight, and a plate is furnished to cover the mounting holes. The FNP-45 Tactical pistol comes with three 15-round magazines in a fitted Cordura nylon case.

The new FNX-40 and FNX-9 pistols are polymer-frame guns that have four interchangeable backstraps. Each FNX has a 4-inch barrel. The 40-caliber version weighs 24 ounces and uses a 15-round magazine. The 9mm weighs 22 ounces and uses a 17-round magazine. Each pistol comes with three magazines and a lockable hard case.

The Five-seveN pistol, chambered for the 5.7x28 cartridge, is now available with low-profile fixed combat sights, as well as the adjustable sights previously offered. The Five-seveN pistols are available in black, dark earth and olive drab. Magazines of 10- and 20-round capacity are available, and three magazines come with each pistol.

GIRSAN

Girsan, a Turkish manufacturer, has made 9mm pistols based on the open-slide Beretta 92 design. At the 2010 SHOT Show, Girsan displayed several new models of closed-slide 9mm pistols with front frame rails, including their MC 27 and MC 27E (a ported variant). The MC 21 is a .45 ACP pistol made with a similar configuration.

Of great interest to us here is a new line, the Girsan MC 1911. As you might have guessed, it is a full-size .45 ACP based on the Colt/Browning 1911 design. Prototypes displayed at the SHOT Show were of the general WWII 1911A1 configuration. Interestingly, at least one early prototype had a true 1911 frame, with no frame recesses behind the trigger. The MC 1911 S is the standard "Government Model" style, but with a forward frame rail.

I was told that an American firm would import the Girsan 1911s but could not get any definite details.

GLOCK

Glock has introduced the Generation 4 (generally referenced as Gen4) series of Glock pistols. The new features include three interchangeable grip backstrap options, a non-slip texture on the grip frame, a reversible magazine release, and a new dual recoil-spring system.

Each larger backstrap adds 2 millimeters to the linear distance between the trigger and the rear of the backstrap. The more-aggressive grip frame texture is a series of polymer pyramids (Glock calls them "polymids"); Models 17, 19, 22 and 23 are now available with this surface. Glock calls this the RTF, or "Rough Textured Frame." The reversible magazine catch is somewhat larger than former ones, and Glock apparently will provide information for shooters who want to make the change to left-hand operation. The new dual recoil springs are considered an "assembly." The first Gen4 pistol is the 40-caliber Model 22. The model number on the slide reads, "22Gen4." Other versions will obviously become available.

GSG

German Sporting Guns (GSG) has introduced a new 22-caliber 1911 pistol. The lower portion is completely 1911, with a fixed barrel and blowback operation of the slide up above. The GSG – 1911 will be handled by American Tactical Imports. (See ATI.)

GUNCRAFTER

Guncrafter Industries makes 1911-type pistols in their own proprietary .50 GI cartridge. This year, they offer a new Model 3, a Commander-style pistol with a 4.25-inch barrel and a "bobtail" frame treatment. Guncrafter offers a new load for the .50 GI with solid copper hollow-point bullets that open up into four "wings."

This year, Guncrafter offers — of all things — a standard .45 ACP 1911. The 1911 .45 went into the catalog before a name was chosen for it. It is known, for the time being, as the "no-name" pistol.

A conversion kit to convert the Glock Models 20 or 21 to .50 GI is offered. Such items are available through American Tactical Imports. (See ATI.)

HK

Heckler & Koch has offered their P30 pistol in 9mm chambering, and by January 2010, had also offered the basic pistol in .40 S&W. The 40-caliber version has a 13-round magazine and has a 3.85-

inch barrel. The longer 4.45-inch barrel available as an option for the 9mm is not offered for the 40-caliber P30.

HK feels that the P30 pistol holds up pretty well. On display at the 2010 SHOT Show was a 9mm P30 that had shot 75,000 rounds. Yes, there were nine stoppages, but the HK people are working to correct that.

HIGH STANDARD

The "Space Gun" is back! One of the most recognizable 22-caliber target pistols of all time, the long-barrel High Standard Olympic Trophy is back in production. Its long barrel, muzzle brake, and extra weight under the barrel gave it a distinctive appearance, and it was generally referred to as the "Space Gun." The rear sight was mounted on the barrel, not on the slide, to prevent misalignment. The Olympic Trophy was a winner on the firing line in decades past.

Now, it is back again, in an updated version. The frame is now stainless steel, with a black Teflon coating. Barrel lengths offered are 6.75, 8 and 10 inches. Optional weights are 2-ounce or 3-ounce. I was fortunate to have the new Olympic Trophy demonstrated to me by Bob Shea, who started working with High Standard way back in 1942, and who still serves as an advisor to the present organization.

Not enough nostalgia yet? High Standard plans were to reintroduce the affordable Dura-Matic 22-caliber plinking pistol of years past. The new Dura-Matic was scheduled for May 2010 introduction at the National Rifle Association (NRA) convention.

HI-POINT

Hi-Point continues to offer its line of affordable pistols and pistol-caliber carbines. Nothing new is being offered in the pistol line this year, but the carbines are wearing new stocks. Regular readers of this publication may recall that I sneaked a picture of prototype number 1 of the new stock design into this report last year. Now, they are standard. The new stocks have rails on the top of the receiver cover, rails under the forearm, and rails on the sides of the forearm. There is plenty of space to hang just about anything a shooter wants on the Hi-Point carbine now. A recoil-reducing butt pad is attached. Available in 9mm and .40 S&W, the carbines come with sling, swivels, scope base, adjustable aperture rear sight and trigger lock.

One of the new FNH polymer-frame guns with interchangeable backstraps, the 9mm FNX-9, here is shown with a black slide and a flat grip backstrap.

(right) Guncrafters Industries offers a kit to convert a Glock Model 20 or 21 to use the big-bore 50 GI cartridge.

A new 22-caliber 1911. The new .22 has been introduced by German Sporting Guns.

The High Standard Olympic Trophy, often called the "Space Gun," is back in production. Here, the reintroduced pistol is demonstrated by Bob Shea, who started working for High Standard in 1942. Shea knows these guns well.

Interstate Arms Corporation's new Regent 45 is a "Series '70" pistol, made for IAC by Tisas in Turkey.

A new small 380-caliber pistol, the I.O. Hellcat, has been introduced by I.O., Inc. Here is a peek at prototype X2.

(right) The new manual-safety version of the Kahr PM9 also has a loaded chamber indicator.

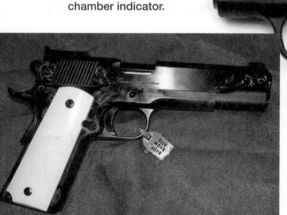

(left) To commemorate the 100 years of the 1911 design, Kimber, a leading producer of 1911-type pistols, is offering a limited-edition commemorative pistol.

(right) The new Kriss pistol. Well, all right, this is really the Kriss submachinegun with the stock removed. However, this is how the Kriss pistol will look, but it will be semiautomatic only.

Legacy Sports International has expanded its Citadel 1911 line. The new .38 Super version is offered now, with several finish options.

(below) Les Baer's new offering is the Boss 45, an enhanced two-tone pistol.

Hi-Point firearms are backed by the company's no-questions-asked lifetime warranty. They are distributed by MKS Supply.

INTERSTATE ARMS

A new 1911! Interstate Arms Corp. (IAC) is offering the new Regent 1911 A1 "Series '70" pistol. The new pistol is manufactured for IAC by the Tisas firm in Turkey. The new pistol looks good, and production models are said to have a consistent 5.5-pound trigger pull. (See TISAS.)

ISSC

The 22-caliber Austrian ISSC pistol, first mentioned on these pages in the last edition of this publication, is now in production. Looking much like a hammer-fired Glock, the ISSC can be used as a training understudy for those using Glock pistols, as well as other uses. The new 22s now have an accessory rail. "ISSC – USA" will be the new markings on the pistols.

ITHACA

Ithaca Gun Company produced Model 1911A1 45-caliber pistols during World War II. Ithaca was the third-largest producer of 45s during that conflict, making close to 20% of the total pistols made. A total of about 369,000 were manufactured by Ithaca back then.

Now, Ithaca is back in the 1911 pistol business. For the 100th anniversary of the 1911 design, Ithaca is making a commemorative pistol, as close to WWII specifications as possible. The only changes in the slide markings are that Ithaca has changed its business location, and "Upper Sandusky, OH" appears in place of the original "Ithaca, NY." Ray Rozic, who worked on the development of the new Ithaca .45, explained that CNC machining allowed much closer clearances now. Made of 4140 certified steel, a prototype with .002-inch slide/frame clearance fired 1000 rounds in about an hour without problems.

The only other WWII manufacturer still making 1911 pistols is, of course, Colt. It is good to have Ithaca back.

IVER JOHNSON

It seemed as if the Iver Johnson 1911 pistols would be stuck in limbo, but they are now a production reality, in time for the 100th anniversary of the 1911 design. Both .45 ACP and 22-caliber pistols were scheduled for full production by mid-2010. A number of different variants, from basic GI style to deluxe enhanced guns, full-size and commander-size, are offered.

Iver Johnson also offers conversion kits to make any 45-caliber 1911 into a .22.

IO, INC.

IO, Inc., of Monroe, North Carolina, provider of many surplus items and US-made AK-style rifles, has introduced a new small US-made .380 pistol. A company representative noted that IO had seen the popularity of small 380-caliber pistols and had combined the best features of existing offerings and made improvements to make a new pistol. The Hellcat .380 is a polymer-frame double-action-only pistol with a 2.7-inch barrel. Weight is only 6.6 ounces. Size is 5.5 inches long by 3.6 inches high — it will almost, but not quite, hide under a common 3x5 index card. I did not get a chance to shoot one, but tried the trigger, and it was decent in double-action. Capacity is 6+1. Each pistol will come with two six-round magazines and an inside-the-pants holster.

KAHR

Kahr Arms has a new version of their PM9. Recall that the PM9 is a subcompact 9mm with black polymer frame and matte stainless slide. It has a 3-inch barrel, measures 5.3x4inches, and can use either six- or seven-round magazines. Weight is about 16 ounces.

The new variant has an external manual thumb safety, and also a loaded chamber indicator, one that rises above the top level of the slide. These new features allow sale of the PM9 in states (such as Massachusetts) where the standard model is prohibited. However, the standard model PM9 will remain in the company's product line.

Another new addition to the PM9 lineup is a variant that comes with a Crimson Trace laser sight.

The little P380, introduced here last year, has a new variant. The original small .380 had a black polymer frame and stainless slide. The new "black" variant has the stainless slide coated in black to produce a less-noticeable pistol for discrete carry.

KBI

A noted above, KBI is no longer in business, as of early 2010. (See Charles Daly.)

KEL-TEC

Kel-Tec's big news is their new PMR-30, a light 30-shot pistol chambered for the .22 Winchester Magnum Rimfire (.22 WMR) cartridge. It is a full-size pistol, measuring almost 6x8 inches, but is light, only 13.6 ounces unloaded (going only to 19.5 ounces fully loaded with 30 rounds). Barrel length is 4.3 inches, and Kel-Tec records a velocity of 1230 fps with a standard 40-grain .22 WMR load.

Kel-Tec harnesses the relatively high-pressure .22 WMR cartridge by what they call a "hybrid blowback/locked breech system." Apparently, a problem using the .22 Magnum in a blowback system is that the case begins to move out of the chamber while still under substantial pressure. Kel-Tec uses a fluted rearward-moving barrel that stays in contact with the breechblock during the time of highest pressure. This appears to be similar to the system used by the FN Five-seveN pistol, and the origin of the mechanism dates back to the French MAB Model R pistol of the 1950s.

The PMR-30 has slide and barrel made of 4140 steel, and the basic frame is 7075 aluminum. Other parts, including the magazine, are glass-reinforced nylon (Zytel). The magazine has an internal rib that separates the rims of the cartridges, avoiding rim-over-rim problems and aiding smooth feeding. The magazine has view holes, so that the shooter can tell how many rounds are loaded. The pistol has fiber-optic sights,\ and a surprisingly good trigger. Introduced at the January 2010 SHOT Show, the PMR-30 was expected to be available by mid-2010.

KIMBER

Kimber has built a good part of its reputation on its 1911 pistols, and you can bet that the firm is going to recognize the 100th anniversary of the 1911. The Centennial Edition comes from Kimber's Custom Shop. In .45 ACP (of course), the Centennial has a special casehardened finish by Turnbull Restoration. Engraved slides, true elephant ivory grips and other features make the Centennial special. Only 250 of the cased guns will be offered.

Also from the Custom Shop, a new line of carry pistols has been introduced. The fist thing that caught my eye about the Super Carry series was the rounded butt treatment – not really a "bobtail," but reminiscent of the smooth curve of the old Colt pocket pistols of 1903. The Super Carry Custom is a full-size 5-incher, the Pro has a 4-inch bushingless barrel, and the Ultra goes down to 3 inches, with a shorter grip frame. With

aluminum frames, weights are 31, 28 and 25 ounces, respectively.

Kimber deserves praise for its support of the shooting sports. Setting aside a portion of sales of certain guns, the company has donated to the U.S. Shooting Team, to the time of this writing, a total of $675,000. Thank you, Kimber.

KRISS

Kriss firearms are offered by Tranformational Defense Industries (TDI). Introduced here in this publication two years ago, the Kriss semiautomatic .45 ACP 16-inch carbine (an outgrowth of the earlier Kriss .45-caliber submachine-gun) was joined last year by a 45-caliber "short-barrel rifle" and a 40-caliber carbine.

Now, in early 2010, the Kriss semiautomatic pistol has joined the family. The new pistol has a 5.5-inch barrel, and is, in essence, the short-barrel rifle without any provision for a stock. It is BATF-approved, but cannot be made available in some states or municipalities, perhaps because it has an unusual appearance.

LEGACY

In 2009, Legacy Sports International introduced its Citadel line of 45-caliber 1911 pistols, in full-size 5-inch and Concealed Carry 3.5-inch variants. The line expanded in 2010. The Citadel line now offers both versions with one-piece wraparound Hogue grips of various colors. In addition, finishes may now be matte black, brushed nickel or polished nickel. Brand new is the Citadel .38 Super, a full-size 5-incher. It can be had with black, brushed nickel or polished nickel finishes, all with double-diamond wood grips.

Joining the centerfire 1911 pistols is the new Puma 1911-22. Roughly the same size, and with similar operating characteristics, the Puma 22 Long Rifle pistol has a 5-inch barrel, a 10-round magazine and weighs 32 ounces. Made by Chiappa Firearms, it is mechanically the same pistol as the Chiappa 1911-22 marketed by MKS Supply. (See Chiappa.)

The polymer-frame 9mm BUL pistols introduced last year by Legacy have quietly slipped out of the catalog for 2010.

LES BAER

A .45 autoloader named after a car? Les Baer Custom admits that owner Les Baer is an aficionado of powerful automobiles as well as powerful handguns. The new "Boss 45" introduced this year harks back to the Ford Mustang Boss

429 of yesteryear.

The pistol has a chromed frame and blued slide, with grasping serrations only at the rear. An adjustable rear sight and red fiber-optic front sight allow accurate sighting. The Boss 45 is guaranteed to shoot 3-inch groups at 50 yards.

MAGNUM RESEARCH

Magnum Research now has a 1911! The Minnesota company will offer a full-size 5-inch and Commander-size 4.3-inch "Desert Eagle" 1911 pistols. A prototype Government-size pistol at the 2010 SHOT Show was marked "Desert Eagle 1911 G. / Magnum Research, Minn, MN." The Commander-size pistols will carry 1911 C. markings. The pistols will be enhanced models, with beavertail tang, ventilated hammer and trigger, lowered ejection port, and special sights. The new 1911s are reported to be manufactured by BUL in Israel.

The "Baby Desert Eagle" name has been applied to new additions to the Magnum Research line, polymer-frame "fast action" pistols. The new guns will be offered in 9mm and .40 S&W. Capacity of the 9mm is 15+1, the .40 is 12+1.

The little 380-caliber Micro Desert Eagle, introduced last year, now is offered in three finishes. The 14-ounce pistols will be available as blued, nickel or two-tone blue/nickel.

MASTERPIECE ARMS

Masterpiece Arms, of Braselton, Georgia, makes a line of "MAC-10" pistols and carbines in 9mm and .45 ACP. Both traditional top-cocking, and (new for 2010) side-cocking variants are offered. Pistols may have 3-, 6-, or 10-inch barrels, and the carbines carry 16-inch barrels. In addition to the new side-cocking option, two new calibers have now been introduced, going both lower and higher in power levels.

For those who like low recoil and low cost, the MPA 22T is offered in .22 Long Rifle. The new .22 is built on the 9mm frame and comes with a long 27-round magazine. With its unconventional looks, it may be the dream plinking pistol for some people.

For those who want more power than the .45 ACP offers, MPA now can offer pistols and carbines in .460 Rowland caliber. Both pistols and carbines come with muzzle brakes and have 30-round magazines.

PARA

The Para GI Expert (Product Code GI45) introduced last year as a lower-price "basic" 1911 with some updated features many shooters want, now has two additional variants. The same gun is now offered in a stainless-steel version (GI45S) with the same features. The additional new variant has the same finish as the original GI Expert, but is enhanced with a beavertail tang with a bump on the grip safety portion, an adjustable trigger, and fiber-optic front sight. This new gun gets the Product Code GI45ESP. Each GI Expert comes with two 8-round magazines.

RUGER

Ruger's first striker-fired centerfire pistol, the 9mm SR9, now has a compact variant. The new SR9c has shortened the barrel from the SR9's 4.14 inches to 3.5 inches. The grip frame has been shortened to accommodate a 10-round magazine, instead of the original 17-rounder. The SR9c has pared the weight of the original down from 26.5 ounces to 23.4 ounces.

Although the SR9c has a 10-shot magazine, there are options. The magazine comes with two interchangeable bases: one flush and one with a finger grip extension. Actually, the 17-round magazine can also be used with the compact pistol, and Ruger offers a grip extension adapter to fill in the extra space. The compact pistols ship with one 10-round and one 17-round magazine, the two bases and the extension for the longer magazine.

Many features of the larger SR9, such as three-dot sights and reversible backstrap, are also included with the compact version.

SIG-SAUER

A number of new things from SIG-Sauer this year. Let's start with the updates from items introduced last year.

The new 380-caliber P238, a pretty little thing in its original form, now can be had in seven different versions. All are mechanically the same, and all have black anodized frames. The differences are in different materials and colors of grips, and different color finishes on the slides and small parts. They make an attractive group.

The long-range P556 pistol introduced last year now has a 22-caliber understudy. The new P522 is roughly the same general size as the 223-caliber P556, but is chambered for the .22 Long Rifle cartridge. With a 10-inch barrel, the overall length is a bit over 20 inches, and weight is about 5.5 pounds. The P522 pistol comes with a 25-round magazine. A 10-round magazine is also available.

The modular P250 is an interesting design. A single frame containing the entire trigger and firing mechanism can be used with polymer grip frames of various sizes, and barrels and magazines for different calibers can be used. So, the owner of a P250 can have several different guns by switching parts. How to do this? Well, SIG has made it easier with its P250 2SUM kit. The kit contains a full-size P250, and also everything needed to convert it to a P250 subcompact. A lot better than having a pistol and ordering a bunch of extra parts to convert it.

New E2 (Enhanced Ergonomics) variants of the P226 and P229 are available. The new one-piece grip frame reduces the area of the backstrap, and reduces overall circumference. The modular grip snaps into place, eliminating screws. The E2 models also have a reduced-reach trigger and feature SIG's Short Reset Trigger (SRT) system. The company believes these characteristics will allow these 9mm pistols to better fit a wider range of shooters' hands.

SMITH & WESSON

S&W has had good success recycling old revolver names onto their new items. Following the reuse of Chief's Special and Military & Police, now we have totally new guns that bear the Bodyguard name. The company developed two small new handguns that would wear the Bodyguard designation — a laser-sighted .38 revolver and a laser-sighted .380 pistol. Both guns were designed from the start to have integral lasers. The revolver is interesting, but you'll read about it elsewhere. Let's take a look at the 380.

The little pistol is double-action-only, but has second-strike capability. It also has a manual safety. It is tilting-barrel recoil-operated and is not a blowback. The gun has a stainless-steel slide and barrel (coated with Melonite) and a polymer frame. The 6+1 pistol is hammer-fired, and weighs less than 12 ounces. The integral laser sighting system is part of the frame, and has ambidextrous controls. The laser has three positions—constant, pulse, and off. The new bodyguard pistols were introduced on January 19, 2010, and scheduled for May 1 production.

Incidentally, the original Bodyguard revolver will remain in production with a unique model number, a separate series from the new Bodyguard guns.

Smith & Wesson also has introduced a new "Pro-Series" line of pistols. According to a company representative, these guns will bridge the gap between standard production and Performance Center guns. Included are three M&P polymer-frame pistols and two SW1911 pistols. The M&P guns are in 9mm and .40, with enhancements in sights and trigger pulls. The 1911 guns include a 5-inch full-size variant in 9mm, and a 3-inch subcompact .45, with special sights and other features.

SPRINGFIELD

The Springfield XD(M) line, introduced on these pages in the last edition, now has two new additions. The XD(M)–3.8 is a new shorter-barrel variant in 9mm, with 19+1 capacity and .40 S&W, with 16+1 capacity. The 3.8 designation refers to the 3.8-inch length of the barrel. The XD(M)–4.5 features the new slip-resistant slide serrations. By the beginning of 2011, a new .45 ACP version of the XD(M) is planned to also be included in the Springfield line.

Every XD(M) comes with a case that contains the pistol, two magazines, a lock, paddle holster, magazine loader, double magazine pouch, and three interchangeable backstraps.

STI

STI International has an anniversary of its own. The Texas company is celebrating its 20th year and has produced an eyecatching 20th Anniversary pistol to commemorate the occasion. The special commemorative pistol is marked on the slide "20th Anniversary, 1990-2010." The grasping grooves on the slide include a distinct XX, the Roman numerals for 20.

The company has introduced its patented 2011 frame, a metal/polymer composite. STI claims the new frame is appropriate for the 100th anniversary of the 1911 design, taking it into a new century. The metal frame/polymer grip system allows lighter weight and a grip thickness hardly larger than the original. A number of STI guns are now using this frame.

The lightest pistol in STI's lineup is the Escort. At 22.8 ounces, the 3-inch .45 has a Commander-size frame.

STI pistols tend to be eyecatchers. One of the most striking pistols the firm offers is the Elektra. In several variants, the one most likely to attract attention is the Electra Pink version. With its

Magnum Research has entered the 1911 world. Here is the Desert Eagle 1911 G., a full-size .45.

(left) Masterpiece Arms has introduced a new 22-calber version of its "MAC-10" style pistols. The 22 pistol comes with a 27-round magazine.

A compact version of the company's 9mm SR9 pistol, Ruger's new SR9c has a 3.5-inch barrel and shortened grip.

SIG SAUER's P522 is a 22-caliber unconventional pistol with a 10-inch barrel and a 25-round magazine.

The 380-caliber SIG SAUER P238 is now available in seven different finishes. This striking specimen has the "rainbow" metal finish.

STI has passed its 20-year anniversary, and has put out a special pistol to commemorate the event. Notice the Roman numeral XX, used to represent 20, in the slide grasping grooves.

pink grips and pink filling of the slide lettering, it seems appropriate for either a man or woman shooter.

STOEGER

The Stoeger Cougar pistol is now available in .45 ACP chambering. The new Cougar 45 is only slightly larger than the 9mm and 40-caliber versions previously offered. Designated Model 8045, the .45 has a 3.6-inch barrel.

Recall that the Cougar design was originally introduced by Beretta, a mid-sized pistol with a rotating-barrel locking system. A few years ago, Stoeger took the design over. Now, it is made

in Turkey and imported by Stoeger.

The .45 that I examined had an all-black finish. However, the 9mm and .40 pistols in the Cougar line are now offered in several other finishes. They can be had as all silver with black grips, or with a silver frame and black slide and grips.

TACTICAL INNOVATIONS

Shown for the first time at the 2010 SHOT Show, the COHORT pistol is offered by Tactical Innovations. The new 22-caliber pistols are based on a modified Ruger 10/22 platform. Made in Idaho, the new pistols have aluminum receivers and a Ruger-style bolt. However, one can see a big difference right away—the

action is rear-charging, with a bolt retraction system patterned after that of the AR-15. A rail allows any sighting system desired by the shooter.

Barrels are stainless steel, with various lengths and configurations. Threaded muzzles (with caps) are standard. A 25-round Tactical magazine is furnished with the Cohort pistol, and an AK-style magazine release is used. The laminated stocks come in a variety of colors. Matched with different colors of triggers and trigger housings, the Cohort can become a very colorful, and very individualized, gun.

The Bodyguard .380 from Smith & Wesson has its controls on the left, but its double-action-only mechanism is suitable for use with either hand.

TAURUS

Taurus' new offerings were dominated by an amazing lineup of "Judge" .45/.410 revolvers, but you'll have to read about them elsewhere. Although overshadowed by the big revolvers, interesting semiauto pistols have been introduced by Taurus.

Carrying through on the renewed interest in small 380-caliber pistols that began last year, the Taurus 738 TCP is now a production item. The small 6+1 pistol weighs about 10 ounces (9 ounces in the Titanium version).

The 24/7 G2 series of polymer-frame pistols is the culmination of Taurus experience with the 24/7 series and the 800 series lines. The new 24/7 G2 offers a choice of single-action, conventional double-action, or double-action-only triggers. The double-actions offer "strike two" capability. Slide stops, decockers and manual safeties are ambidextrous. Calibers are now 9mm, .40 S&W, and .45 ACP. Along with the traditional 4.2-inch barrel, there are now a compact version with a 3.5-inch barrel and a long slide variant with a 5-inch barrel.

The 800 series now has a compact of

its own. The larger 4-inch 800 pistols have been scaled down to a compact size appropriate for a 3.5-inch barrel. The 809 compact is available in 9mm, .357 SIG, and .40 S&W.

The 700 "Slim" pistol series, introduced in the 9mm chambering, has gone both up and down. The slim single-column pistols are now available in both .380 and .40 S&W versions.

Taurus has had a hard time coming up with a satisfactory 22-caliber pistol for target, plinking and recreational shooting. Several worthy prototypes have been introduced over the years, but none made it to full production status. Now, the company thinks a new .22 on the 800 frame will do the trick. The Model 822 will be available with either 4.5- or 6-inch barrels. The hammer-fired guns will be conventional double action, and will have "strike two" capability. 822 pistols will have adjustable sights. A conversion kit, allowing any 800-series pistol to shoot .22 Long Rifle ammunition, will also be offered.

TISAS

The Turkish firm Tisas introduced a 45-caliber 1911-style pistol on these pages a few years ago. Now, the new 1911 is offered in the United States by Interstate Arms as the Regent pistol. (See Interstate Arms.)

USELTON

Uselton Arms, a maker of 1911-style pistols since 1999, planned for a special gun to commemorate the 100th year

Tactical Innovations has just introduced the Cohort pistol, based on the Ruger 10/22 design, but with rear-charging operation.

anniversary of the 1911 design. The result is a striking-looking handgun. The frame is case colored, and the slide is polished mirror bright. Engraved on the right side of the slide (and effectively using roman numerals) is this legend in a three-line display: MODEL 1911 / MCMXI-MMXI / COMMEMORATING 100 YEARS. The Uselton 100 Year Commemorative will be available in full-size Government Model, and also in compact Officers Model versions.

VLTOR

The pistol based on the Bren Ten design, and offered for the first time last year as the Vltor Fortis, is now available under the original Bren Ten name. (See Bren Ten.)

VOLQUARTSEN

Volquartsen Custom makes an amazing number of interesting 22-caliber pistols, most based on the original Ruger design. Last year, Volquartsen introduced a prototype of a new design of .22 target pistol, which they named the V-10X. The frame was CNC-machined from aluminum billet material, and the barrel was a taper fit into the aluminum frame. Finger grooves were machined into the frame, and followed the contour of the grips. The laminated wood grips themselves were available with either right or left thumb rest.

Now, a year later, the company also offers new variations with built-in muzzle brakes, and with rails mounted top and bottom for attaching various types of sights and accessories. Traditional open

Volquartsen's new machined aluminum V-10X pistol is in production, in several different colors, including black.

sights are, however, furnished with each pistol. Trigger is set at about 2 pounds and has pretravel and overtravel adjustments. Want a special color? The V-10X is available hard-anodized in black, silver, red, green, blue and purple.

WALTHER

The Walther PK380, introduced on these pages last year, is now a production item, and already has several new variants. The PK380, at 5.2x6.5 inches, is larger than the current offerings of small 380s, but is roughly the same size as Walther's P22, the firm's small 22-caliber pistol. The PK380 has a 3.7-inch barrel and weighs about 21 ounces.

Along with basic black, other variants now available are: a First Edition (serial numbers 1 through 2000 are reserved) which comes with an extra magazine and a nylon holster, a nickel slide version, and a black gun with an attached laser. All variants of the Walther PK380 use an eight-round single-column magazine.

WILSON

The Wilson Sentinel, a small steel-frame 9mm with a 3.6-inch barrel, was introduced last year in this publication. It quickly achieved a certain popularity, and its suitability as a lady's carry pistol was examined. The result was a new variant named appropriately, if somewhat tongue-in-cheek, Ms. Sentinel.

The Ms. Sentinel pistol was specifically designed to be carried equally well in a purse or in a holster. The configuration of some of the controls is subdued to avoid snagging. A round butt frame was used. A shortened trigger, better suited to smaller hands, was installed. To reduce weight, an aluminum frame and a fluted 3.5-inch barrel were used. The result, Wilson feels, is a 9mm pistol that will be a very good choice for a woman's protection pistol.

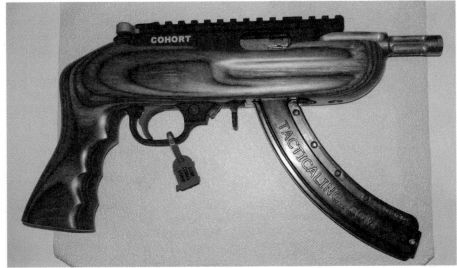

GUNS AND GEAR FOR WOMEN

BY GILA HAYES

When savvy shooting women shop for guns and gear, they ask two simple questions:

1. Does it work?
2. Does it fit?

Feminized packaging may add eye appeal as illustrated by colored pistol frames, pink or pearl grips, color-laminated long-gun stocks, pink-o-flage clothing, brightly colored hearing protection and safety glasses and more. While female-oriented marketing campaigns may catch women's attention initially, ultimately how well guns

Stag Arms left-handed AR puts the controls under the lefty's thumb where they belong.

and shooting equipment fit and function is the determining factor in a woman's long and successful experience with the gear.

How well are gun and shooting gear manufacturers meeting the less glamorous requirement of reliability and functionality? Products displayed at the 2010 SHOT Show, the industry's premier convention where manufacturers show their wares to media and retailers, reveal a continued availability of woman-friendly designs, ranging from hunting and tactical clothing for ladies, to shotguns and rifles that

Jennie Van Tuyl's short, light DPMS Panther Arms AR15 is outfitted with an LE Entry Tactical Stock from Brownell's.

fit smaller shooters, pistols that fit small hands and accommodate women's more challenging concealment needs as well as a few holsters, and a lot of holster handbags.

Gone, we fervently hope, are the days when the woman braving the local gun shop was automatically pointed toward the fake pearl-gripped .25 caliber semiauto or, if its operation seemed too daunting, a double action revolver! Still, beginners of either gender are well served by a quality .22LR handgun or rifle, simply because it provides lots of trigger time with little recoil and does so with minimal expense. For years, Ruger's Mark II pistols ruled the market in .22 semiautos, while a great variety of kit guns from Smith & Wesson, Taurus and other revolver manu-facturers, some of whom have come and gone and come back again, made choosing a begin-ner's revolver not an issue of availability, but one of de-ciding between all the options! HKS even makes speed loaders for .22s, making an introduction to speed loading drills possible!

Not all women are fond of the stiff, long trigger pull characteristic of the double action revolver, however. For these beginners, the plethora of .22LR caliber semiautomatic pistols provides the ability to practice all the steps to operate a full-sized self-defense pistol, again with the lighter recoil and cheaper ammunition. Options include traditional favorites like the Ruger Mark II, Browning Buck Mark, Smith & Wesson's .22 pistols, Beretta's pocket models as well as their Neos plus a variety of high-end competition pistols. With operations closer to those of full-sized handguns, Sig Sauer's Mosquito, full-sized CZs and EAAs in .22, Walther's P22 and conversion kits for 1911s and Glocks are also good choices for beginners for whom shooting skills will eventually address self-defense concerns.

While beginning shooters of either gender may prefer to start with a small

caliber gun and its easy operating characteristics, with good training, both men and women graduate quickly to guns in reasonable defense calibers, if that is their reason for taking up shooting. These advancing shooters may still cherish their .22LR rifles and handguns for plinking, practicing, and pleasure, but with a bit of diligence, the pursuit of highly suitable revolvers, pistols, rifles and shotguns in more effective calibers yields a variety of choices.

HANDGUNS "FIT" FOR A QUEEN

The trend toward adjustable backstrap inserts makes fitting a pistol to small-handed shooters far easier than it was even five years ago, though sometimes the backstrap inserts seem merely a way to increase a medium-sized grip to sizes large and extra large! The latest and possibly most celebrated manufacturer to offer the adjust-able grip option is Glock. In the smallest varia-tion, Glock's

Author admits to a yearning to own a SIG P238 with the Titanium rainbow-colored slide.

the subject of destructive grip recon-touring and refinishing as shooters have struggled to slim down that ubiquitous handgun to improve trigger reach.

For those for whom this size

Walther's pistol options include the .22LR P22, the .380 PK380, and for concealed carry the very minimalist PPS in 9mm.

fourth generation pistol's grip is about 1/8 inch smaller in circumference. It is currently available in Models 17 and 22, and Glock insiders predict the 4th Generation Model 19s and 23s should be out around May of 2010.

The large-gripped polymer-framed Glock has long been

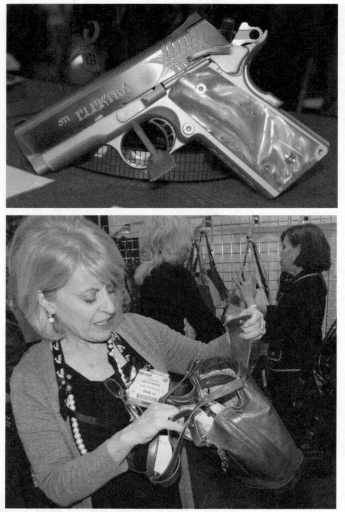

(top) STI's Elektra model is a carry-sized 9mm with pink grips indicating their marketing plan for sales to women. It also comes in black.

(above) Carol Rutherford of Woolstenhulme Designer Bags shows a nicely accessorized blue gun purse.

reduction makes a sufficient difference, the fourth generation of Glocks eliminates that after-market expense.

SIG-Sauer took a different route when they tackled the need for a more individualized pistol fit. Their Model 250 is extremely modular, allowing choices in caliber, frame size, barrel length and more. A one-piece polymer grip is available in compact and full size. For some, the backstrap to trigger reach will still be too long, and SIG's short trigger offers help.

Other models of handguns are perennial favorites with women, because from the very beginning, their grips were small enough for a good fit. Kahr Arms' many models in 9mm Parabellum, .40 and even .45 come immediately to mind in this class, as does Walther's model PPS, and more historically, the single column 1911 design in its many variations and calibers.

Of the latter, the popularity of models chambered in alternatives to the traditional .45 ACP cartridge continues to increase. In addition to expanding ammunition options for the small-hand-friendly 1911, this classic handgun type is served by a tremendous variety of after market options and accessories, including thin grip panels to further reduce bulk, night sights,

high visibility sights, laser sights, triggers of varying lengths, grip safeties of varying geometry, extended, bobbed, minimalist and ambidextrous thumb safeties, modified magazine releases and more!

9mms and .40 S&W caliber 1911s are no longer rare, whether emblazoned with the logos of Kimber, Para Ordnance, STI, Springfield Armory, Taurus and even Colt's Manufacturing! Colt's, of course, marketed a 9mm Parabellum Commander now and again in the years after WWII, though in recent decades, they've become somewhat rare. Thus, at the 2010 SHOT Show, I was delighted to see a 9mm Colt Defender on display. The new Defender is a lightweight subcompact with an alloy frame, a 3-inch barrel, and the traditional single action semiautomatic manual of arms. In my opinion, the pistol just cried out for a pair of slim grip panels and a short trigger. Still, I predict it will prove a solid foundation for many a customized women's self defense pistol and I was glad to see it.

As we strive to customize and modify a handgun to fulfill individual needs and desires, we often begin to impinge on reliability. Unfortunately, the 1911 has long been subject to excessive gunsmithing, often to the detriment of its dependability. In addition, a common rule of thumb to bear in mind: the short-barreled concealment pistols are frequently finickier about ammunition, the strength of the shooter's grip during the firing cycle and other variations that interrupt the relationship and interaction between the recoil spring, the weight of the slide, and the pressure of the cartridge. A sometimes delicate balance is required to shuck out the empty case and feed in a fresh one. Sometimes the snubbiest semiautos use very stiff recoil springs, and while vital to reliability, this feature may make it challenging for some female shooters to manually cycle the action.

ITSY, BITSY, TEENY WEENY...UM, HANDGUN

Overall gun size is always a challenge when women gear up for self defense. Gun weight has been reduced – in my opinion, to unrealistic extremes – in the alloy framed revolvers. That's right, I'm no fan of the super light, 11- and 12-oz. snubbies, because with high-performance defense ammunition, they are simply beastly to shoot. A pistol's overall dimensions, however, contribute or detract considerably from whether or not women will find it a realistic choice for daily carry for self defense.

Pistols like the Defender, Springfield EMP, Glock 26 and 27, Springfield XD subcompact, Ruger's new subcompact SR9,

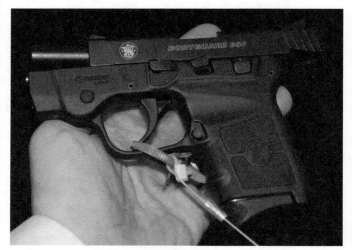

Smith & Wesson's tiny .380 Bodyguard semiautomatic.

Short stocks make these small-statured shotgunners smile! On the left, women's gun columnist Diane Walls holds her Remington 11-87 fit with custom-made Choate stock, while Rivendell Consulting owner Jennie Van Tuyl's Remington 1100 has a traditional wooden stock that is cut down considerably.

and many others of similar size are the preferred choices because they are just large enough to afford a good shooting grip, moderate recoil control, and a reasonable sight radius. But what to carry during hot summer days, at dress-up affairs, and under other circumstances when even those chopped-down variations are too big to conceal? In times like these, a .380 that men consider a backup, deep-concealment hideout or a pocket pistol is likely to become the primary defense gun for many a lady.

While these are the guns to which many default in challenging concealment conditions, they are poorly suited to the beginner who is learning the lessons of sight alignment, trigger control and gun manipulation like loading and malfunction clearing. Not only does the pistol's small, light size amplify even the .380 ACP's recoil, the miniaturized frame often compromises a strong grip somewhat, and the miniaturized controls and levers – when they are even present – can be slow and fumble-prone. Still, the genre continues to be among the most popular pistols a gun shop can stock.

It is ironic that concurrent with

the worst .380 ACP ammo shortage in my memory, gun manufacturers have introduced more miniaturized .380 pistols than ever before. No longer does shooting a .380 mean lugging around a Beretta Cougar or Bersa Thunder, guns nearly as large as a 9mm Glock 26/27 and much bigger than a Kahr Arms PM9! Nowadays, the deep concealment .380s are half that size, with measurements of slightly more than 3-1/2 inches by 5 inches for the Ruger LCP and its ilk.

In 2001, North American Arms debuted their .380 Guardian, a slightly larger echo of their earlier .32 ACP all-steel micro pistol based on the venerable Seecamp design. Its continuing popularity gives shooters who worry about polymer's durability a valued option. Not long thereafter, Kel-Tec beefed up their madly popular polymer-framed .32 ACP semiauto to chamber .380 ACP ammo and the result was the P3AT. The eight ounce .380 has proven amazingly durable, though the sights are rudimentary. Both alternatives were the mainstays of the pocket pistol crowd until two years ago when Ruger reworked the Kel Tec design into their polymer-framed LCP.

That same year Kahr Arms introduced their P380, which just continues to become more and more popular. The simple, DAO mini is less than 5 inches long, and, at just under 4 inches, is a bit longer through the grip. Unlike most other pocket pistols, the Kahr P380 comes from the factory equipped with the manufacturer's conventional drift-

adjustable bar-dot combat sights. Many years ago, the folks at NAA put a set of Novak pistol sights on my Guardian 380, achieving the same effect. Now Kahr Arms does it from the start.

This year, Smith & Wesson joined the pocket semiautomatic market in a big way with their Bodyguard line. A partially polymer revolver of J-frame size and a .380 mini semiauto were on display at the 2010 SHOT Show, attracting a lot of attention. Both are manufactured with integral lasers from Insight Technology.

The S&W Bodyguard 380 takes the double action semiauto pocket gun concept to a new level. While the forerunners – Seecamps, Guardians and Kel Tecs – cut back on bulk by eliminating operating levers like slide stops and thumb safeties, the Bodyguard 380 has

Outdoor gear like this camouflage by Foxy Huntress gives ladies a choice in hunting clothing.

a full complement of controls – a thumb safety, a slide lock, and a take down lever, all tucked in flush to frame. While unobtrusive, these controls make gun operation far more user-friendly. The .380 Bodyguard is just over 4 inches high, 5-1/4 inches long, and weighs just less than 12 ounces unloaded. It holds six cartridges, plus one in the chamber.

SIG-Sauer's P238, a redux of the old single action semiauto Colt .380s, caught my eye at SHOT Show last year, so in 2010 it was a delight to see several new variations, including one breath-takingly beautiful option with a rainbow Titanium finished slide equipped with SIGLITE® night sights atop a matte black frame and wearing pretty rosewood grips. The P238s weigh 15 ounces, and are just under 4 inches tall and 5-1/2 inches long, with a 2.7-inch barrel. Other finish options included a two-tone scheme, as well as an all matte black option. Interestingly enough, the single action trigger weight is set between 7-1/2 to 8-1/2 lbs., considerably heavier than the double action only LCR, Kel Tec or Bodyguard.

SO MANY PISTOLS, SO LITTLE TIME

Handgun selection, while vastly assisted by the plethora of models and variations marketed, can also become a confusing and potentially expensive adventure. Two questions – highlighted at this article's beginning – must guide handgun selection. First, is the handgun reliable? If unable to shoot and test reliability yourself, you will be dependent on anecdotal reports, though in the age of the Internet, such accounts probably outnumber the stars in the firmament. Certain handgun brands, however, like Glock pistols for example, are designed for reliability before any other consideration. The second question, of course, concerns fit. If you find a reliable gun that fits properly, search no further!

Before leaving the subject of handgun fit and function, I'd like to add that several decades ago, semiauto pistol reliability was suspect, patchy and unpredictable. The pistols were often ammunition-sensitive, and at worst, it was expected that a gunsmith's services were required to guarantee a reliable semiauto. If you wanted a totally reliable handgun, you simply bought a revolver! While we still occasionally run into pistols that won't function reliably, that hassle is far less prevalent nowadays.

At the same time, revolvers are a fine handgun choice for shooters of either gender, though ladies rankle at the suggestion that women find them more suitable owing to their simple operation! Really, skillful handgun operation results from full familiarity and training with the gun, regardless of its design. Still, the choice between revolver and semiautomatic asks how much strength is required to manually cycle a semiauto's slide versus the stiffness of the revolver's trigger pull. Both can be impediments to skill with a handgun, so we welcome the lighter springs of many 9mm handguns compared to the stiffer spring often required to keep a heavy-caliber pistol running, especially in the short-barreled concealment configurations. New approaches to revolver design have changed trigger geometry, but too often these innovations show up in the super lightweight polymer and alloy revolvers that are too light for much recoil absorption, so the recoil batters the shooter with each discharge, and practice is painful.

THE HOLSTER HASSLE

Gun fit issues pale in comparison to the thorny issue of holsters for women. Gun purses are available in profusion,

(top)Sig Sauer's P238 now comes in several options, including one with a Titanium rainbow colored slide.

(middle) Colt's 9mm Defender New Agent.

(bottom} Sig Sauer .22 LR Mosquito in a bold black and shocking pink design

the magic is in the fit

Given enough time and concentration, most shooters can coax accurate shots out of handguns, rifle or shotguns that do not fit them. While plinking at the range, a deliberate rate of fire – one shot every minute or two, for example – accommodates all manner of misfit gear. It is, instead, during high-intensity defense or duty training, or Heaven forbid, under the stress of a self defense emergency that ill-fit guns betray their unfortunate owners.

Instead of long seconds committed to getting the gun in just the right firing position, followed by a careful alignment of the sights or optics and slow, deliberate pressure applied to the trigger, under stress we find the gun extended toward target in an approximation of grip and stance, often fired while moving away from the threat or to cover. Trigger control must occur in an extremely compressed cycle, delivering multiple shots in a matter of seconds. Here, the shooter discovers that the compromised grip and shooting platform imposed by the ill-fitting gun interferes with accuracy, interrupts use of the sights (if there is even sufficient light to see and use them), and exaggerates muzzle flip and recoil. How much better it would be to solve gun fit problems at the time of the gun purchase!

HANDGUN FIT

With the pistol centered in the web of the hand, both the length of the fingers and the meatiness of the hand determine how well the trigger finger will be able to contact the face of the trigger. A mere tip of a trigger finger is a poor candidate for a smooth, straight-to-the-rear trigger pull, especially at speed.

A handgun that allows the crease of the trigger finger's first joint full contact with the

When the pistol is too big, as is this big Glock Model 29 for these small hands, the mere tip of the finger on the trigger is insufficient for a smooth pull.

face of the trigger while the gun is centered in the web of the hand gives the most natural pointing. Since babyhood, humans have locked out the arm and extended the index finger when emphatically pointing. A properly fitting handgun takes advantage of all those repetitions, and aiming it mimics that oft-repeated action.

An extremely small-handed shooter or one mandated to use an overly-large gun accommodates by moving the backstrap toward or even beyond the ball of the thumb. A gun gripped thus naturally points somewhat to the right for a right-handed shooter and to the left for a lefty. A strong isosceles-style stance combined with a hard two-handed grip brings the natural aim back to center when poor fit thus compromises natural pointing. This is harder to maintain if circumstances throw the shooter into one-handed shooting, though responsibility for a child, calling for help on a phone or radio, or other concerns may result in one-handed shooting in a fast-breaking situation.

FITTING LONG GUNS

Classically, we've considered stock fit on shotguns acceptable if, when the butt is held in the crook of the elbow, the trigger finger has a good purchase on the trigger. It is still a good standard, though we see the value of an even somewhat shorter stock when the small-statured shooter operates the pump-action shotgun, or needs to be able to mount and fire the rifle or shotgun rapidly. The shorter the stock, the easier, as illustrated by special response teams in law enforcement's use of the collapsible AR stock.

For shotgunners, recoil control and subsequently accurate, rapid fire is considerably improved when a short stock accommodates quickly mounting the shotgun, attaining a repeatable cheek weld, and having a strong flex in both the shooting and support arm to hold the shotgun firmly against the pectoral muscle.

While we love the collapsible AR stocks for their easy adaptability for short shooters, many don't encourage a good cheek weld, a factor that deserves consideration when setting up a rifle for a woman.

SPECIALTY NICHE

In a world where gun stores with high-volume sales tend to stock products purchased by the majority of their customers, who are men,

it can be a challenge for a smaller shooter to locate a good selection from which to choose. An industry that actively pursues the woman's market must surely be heartened by small businesses like the newly-opened Rivendell Sales & Consulting, a one-woman operation focused on custom orders for women who need personalized attention to detail to be sure they get a gun that fits.

Owner Jennie Van Tuyl was getting her new business started at the 2010 SHOT Show, meeting not only with resources to help with the businesses' operation, but identifying guns most likely to fit her customers.

It takes some extra effort to pull all the details together, but with determination and creativity, women can find a nice selection of pistols, shotguns and rifles that work reliably and fit them well.

When this small-handed shooter centers the tang of a Springfield EMP pistol in the web of her hand, the trigger finger has good contact with the trigger.

Great fit and the left-handed option will sell this Remington rifle to a number of female shooters.

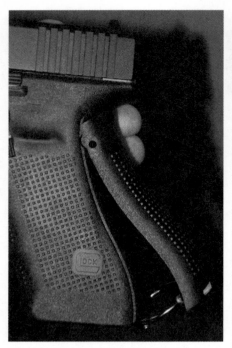

Glock's 4th generation pistol and the insert used to adjust grip size.

however, and some of them show considerable thought and ingenuity, with more and more designed by women who habitually carry guns for self defense. Galco has long been the leader, and Lisa Des Camps deserves a nod of appreciation for her guiding hand in developing a line of stylish and functional gun purses. The other big player in fashionable gun purses is Coronado.

Several start-ups that are bringing in more options in fashionable gun purses are Gun Tote'n Mamas and Designer Concealed Carry, with a variety of big, brightly colored bags with built-in holsters for concealed handgun carry.

For range work requiring belt holsters, Blade Tech's women's dropped and offset belt holster works well. Kramer Handgun Leather led the way in dropped and offset designs, and Kramer's women's belt scabbard continues to relieve holster discomfort for short-waisted women. Other alternatives include several of C. Rusty Sherrick's holsters, FIST holsters, and Del Fatti Leather's SLP/F model designed to be worn forward of the strong side hip. Its muzzle forward rake reminds me of one of the first women's holsters I saw, Mitch Rosen's Nancy Special, designed for short-barreled guns, and also using the muzzle forward orientation to get the grips away from the ribcage.

Another alternative that works extremely well is one-on-one work with smaller holster makers who are happy

to work up a custom holster solution for women. Sometimes – as in the case of *Concealed Carry Magazine* editor Kathy Jackson's experience with Ted Blocker Holsters of Tigard, Oregon – a couple of small but vital modifications yielded an extremely comfortable IWB holster worn in front of the strong side hip. Ladies who want to cash in on Kathy's success need only call this holster maker and ask for the LFI-OZC.

Up-and-coming holster maker John Ralston of 5-Shot Leather provided the same kind of service when he made a deeply canted IWB the author wears behind the strong side hip. Minimal in design, the Ralston holster is a take off on his stock item, the Inside Burton Scabbard.

Both the Blocker and Ralston holsters

are comfortably carried on contour cut belts from the makers of the holsters, and the contoured belts go far to increase the comfort of holsters worn for long hours at a time.

THE BIG WORLD OF LONG GUNS

If the backstrap to trigger measurement is the key to good handgun fit, on rifles and shotguns the critical element is the length of pull, measured from trigger face to the end of the stock. Women who like to shoot shotguns and rifles get help with stock fit from the so-called youth models, as well as variable length "collapsible" tactical stocks, or they find relief in replacement stocks in shorter lengths of pull. Fortunately the prevalence of 12- and 13-inch length of pull

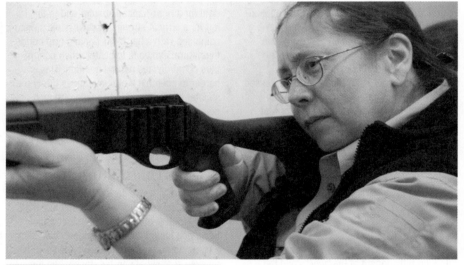

(above) Diane Walls likes the control her custom Choate pistol grip gives her Remington 11-87.

(left) Jennie Van Tuyl chose the Rock River Arms LE Entry Tactical Stock to tailor her DPMS Panther Arms AR-15 rifle to her shorter stature.

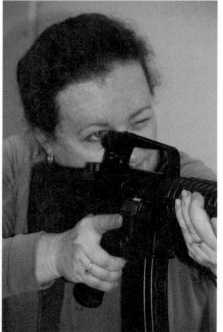

stocks, often in the mis-named "youth models," are a common variant among all the reputable shotgun and rifle lines.

When fitting rifles and shotguns to women, another factor can complicate gun selection. Women have higher incidences of cross-eye dominance than do men. The easiest cure is to shoot the rifle or shotgun from the shoulder corresponding to the dominant eye, which in the case of cross-dominance is usually the left side. Consider the plight of the woman eager to join her friends at the shotgun or rifle range, If left-eye dominant, she faces the further challenge of operating a gun designed for right-handed shooters with her less dexterous hand!

With shotguns, we value features like Mossberg's tang-mounted safety that make the gun more ambidextrous. With semiautomatic rifles, innovations like Stag Arms' fully left-handed AR-15 are welcome indeed. With nearly all of the AR-15s sold optimized for right-handed shooters, we are particularly apprecia-tive of Stag Arms fully adapted left hand AR-15! Though lefties can make do with the standard right-handed semiauto rifles, how nice it would be to have the "fire" and "safe" switch under the thumb where it is most ergonomic.

In bolt rifles, Remington, Savage, Browning and Ruger have a variety of excellent options for both short hunters and left handed ones, as well. The Ruger M77 Hawkeye comes in lefty and righty configurations, as well as models with the standard 13-1/2-inch length of pull and a compact version with a 12-1/2-inch LOP. A half dozen caliber choices run the gamut from .223 Rem. to .308 Win.

Kramer Handgun Leather was one of the first to make what became their wildly successful Women's Dropped and Offset holster, shown here with a S&W M640.

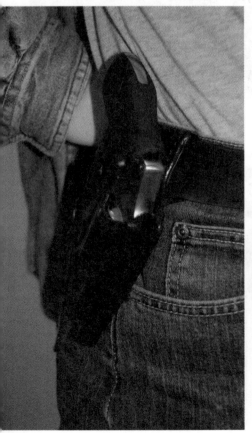

WHAT TO WEAR

Speaking of hunting, women's outdoor clothing has long been one area in which smaller manufacturers have excelled, with the options ranging from moderately reworked men's outdoor wear, to some very feminine fashions for outdoor wear. Smaller gloves, boots and socks, functional jackets, vests, trousers and even coveralls are marketed to female outdoors enthusiasts. At the 2010 SHOT Show, a feminine Henley short sleeved shirt that had its own protective recoil pad sewn into the shoulder area particularly charmed me.

There's probably a market for both pink, cutsie outdoorswoman clothing and toys, but for my money, I am consid-erably more heartened by clothing and products made to meet women's specific needs – proper fit for the smaller frame, true functionality like weather proofing and comfort – than I am by sheer, lacy pink camouflage negligees! [*Editor's Note: There is probably room for opinion on this point. -DMS*]

EOTAC, Fernando Coelho's tactical clothing company, has just added a line of women's tactical trousers for female shooters, competitors and the more serious needs of women in law enforce-ment. Featuring a shorter rise than EOTAC's men's tactical trousers, but still fitting through the seat and thigh, the pants are available in four colors of light weight rip stop fabric. Coelho predicted that future variations would include more fabric choices, shorts and maybe even capris!

(top) Foxy Huntress' shooting shirt in women's sizes and styles makes shotgunning more fun.

(right) Tina Coelho of EOTAC shows their tactical trousers specifically designed for women.

(left) Good fit comes first on these Wiley-X safety glasses; the pink accent color may attract the female customer.

The numbers and varieties of muzzleloading guns offered to American consumers continue to evolve. Some companies have reduced or eliminated traditional muzzleloaders to concentrate on newer muzzleloader or cartridge guns. Nonetheless, CVA has upgraded their entire line of muzzleloaders, Dixie Gun Works is importing two new Davide Pedersoli guns, Pedersoli continues to introduce new guns, Thompson/Center Arms has a new drop-barrel in-line and Traditions has new lightweight rifles and a hunter's pistol.

Although Knight Rifles has discontinued gun production and is looking for a buyer, the company maintains a repair and accessory sales office in Ohio. Some Knight guns were offered through Sportsman's Warehouse at discounted prices, and these guns sold out within days.

Navy Arms Co. no longer sells muzzleloading guns, and CVA and Thompson/Center have almost completely discontinued their side-lock rifles and smoothbores. However, there is still moderate interest in replica military smoothbores and shotguns.

WHY USE SMOOTHBORES?

Smoothbore muzzleloaders are a mystery to many shooters who hunt with in-line rifles. Users of the newer muzzleloaders often don't understand how an unrifled gun can shoot accurately enough to kill anything but small game with birdshot.

I don't shoot everything with smoothbore guns; I also hunt with muzzleloading rifles and pistols. I have taken ducks, geese, swan, quail, dove, guinea fowl, pheasant, squirrels, rabbits, deer, hogs, bison and a blue wildebeest with smoothbores. If there is something that I have not shot with a smoothbore, it is only because I haven't gotten around to it.

Smoothbore guns come in and out of the market. Some of those that I describe have not been made for decades. With the demise of Knight Rifles the most advanced muzzleloading smoothbore ever made, the TK-2000, is out of production. The bright side is that Davide Pedersoli and others still offer traditional military and sporting muzzleloaders for reenactors and hunters.

At present, Davide Pedersoli has a variety of sporting and military smoothbore guns that are sold by several importers; MDM has a 209-primed break-action shotgun; and Thompson/Center Arms' Custom Shop sells a muzzleloading turkey barrel for Encore-frame guns.

One source of original guns, a few of which are sound enough to be shot, is Atlanta Cutlery, who imported thousands of muzzleloaders from the Royal Arsenal of Nepal. Many were made in India or Nepal and are smoothbore versions of English-designed rifles, including the Brunswick and Enfield patterns.

Author with Earnst Dyason and buffalo.

MUZZLE LOADERS

BY WM. HOVEY SMITH

Pedersoli photo of
Gibbs Hunter.

WHS Trophy GA tom taken with Austin &
Halleck muzzleloading shotgun.

SMOOTHBORE GUNS, LOADS AND GAME TAKEN

Gun	System	Powder	Shot	Gauge	SG	P	D	G	S	Tk	BG
Tanegashima	Match	50[1]	½	.50	X						
Bess	Flint	100/95	1¼	11	X		X		X		X**
Mortimer	Flint	25 FFFg	1	12	X		X	X			
		50FFg	1-1/8	12	X		X	X			
Brunswick[3]	Perc.	80	1 1/8	14	X	X				X	
1842 Musket[4]	Perc.	100	1¼	11	X		X	X	X		X**
T/C Mountain	Perc.	100	1¼	12	X		X	X	X	X	
D.P. Slug	Perc.	100	1¼	12	X		X		X		X**
Austin&Halleck[2]	209	85 T7	1 3/8	12	X	X	X	X	X	X	
TK-2000[2]	209	120	1½	12	X	X	X	X	X		

Abbreviations: T7=Triple Seven, SG=Small game, P=Pheasant, D=Ducks, G=Geese, S=Swan, Tk=Turkey, BG=Big Game

Notes:
1) Powder is GOEX FFg black powder unless otherwise designated.
2) With the Austin & Halleck and TK-2000 I use 1-1/4-ounce by volume of HeviShot for waterfowl or the approximately equivalent

1-3/8-oz of lead shot for turkey.
3) Atlanta Cutlery sells guns only as collector's items. Many are unsafe to shoot. Only exceptional guns that have been shot with proof charges should be used.
4) Powder charges are increased for round ball loads used on big game.

A JAPANESE MATCHLOCK

Tanegashima, or Tagie for short, is a Japanese matchlock that I recommend to anyone who wants the maximum hunting experience but does not want to clean much game. I have not been lucky enough to have a deer in front if it when it was inclined to shoot.

With a patched .50-caliber round ball and a load of 85 grains of FFg black powder, this gun will shoot 4-inch groups at 50 yards once its numerous eccentricities are mastered. Matchlocks, this one included, also sometimes fire spontaneously. This is the heaviest charge that I can use in this gun with a degree of comfort.

BROWN BESS MUSKET

Bess, a .75-caliber flintlock musket, was imported from Japan by Dixie Gun Works and is now made by Davide Pedersoli. This "Indian Gun" variation of the Brown Bess musket has a shortened browned barrel, robust lock and is .75-caliber or 11 gauge. The instant I saw it, I thought that this gun had the potential of being a serious waterfowler. This proved to be correct, and it has taken a variety of game. One accomplishment was killing the first "flintlocked" swan in living memory at Lake Mattamuskeet, North Carolina.

Bess has also taken two deer with single shots. Shooting round ball with a gun that has no rear sight takes skill in that the face must be positioned in exactly the same spot on the stock for consistent results.

A FLINTLOCK FOWLER

Davide Pedersoli's Mortimer 12-gauge fowler was a difficult gun to figure out. It had a very tight barrel, making it difficult to load standard 12-gauge plastic

wads, and I once tipped over a johnboat in freezing water trying to reload it. The best-shooting load was a duplex load employing 25 grains of FFFg followed by 50 grains FFg and 1-1/8-ounces of shot – a 16-gauge load. If you overload this gun it will shoot a hollow-centered pattern that you could throw a goose through.

With conventional paper and fiber wads I have used it to take dove, quail and small game and have employed bismuth loads for ducks. Bismuth shot in this gun will kill close-range waterfowl, but I prefer HeviShot loads contained in plastic shot cups which enabled me to successfully use this gun on snow geese.

BRITISH 1842 PERCUSSION MUSKET

As might be supposed for the percussion version of the British Brown Bess,

Pedersoli Mississippi Hunter.

Dixie Gun Works Spanish Musket.

the 1842 can use the same loads. My best work with this gun was on decoying geese near Wisconsin's Horicon Marsh. In this instance the big birds were coming in close. Shooting a cylinder-bored gun was advantageous compared to the others who where shooting silver-dollar-sized patterns at 15 yards from their tightly-choked semiautos.

This gun was made around 1850 for the British East India Co. by Wilkinson Sword. Although it had some rust pits on the outside of the barrel, it was in good condition compared to similar guns sold by Atlanta Cutlery. I re-proofed the gun before using it using proof charges from Dixie Gun Works' catalogue.

BRUNSWICK SMOOTHBORE

This relic was in poor condition when received. I replaced a spring and restored it to shooting condition because I wanted to shoot a 69-caliber, or 14-gauge, gun. The 14 was popular as a muzzleloading gauge but dropped out of favor when cartridge guns came along. I first took it on a preserve hunt for pheasant, where it did well, and then killed a turkey with it. Having done these hunts, I disabled it and gave it to a friend as a wall hanger. My conclusion was that the muzzleloading 14-gauge killed well and was economical in its use of powder and shot.

Wads for 14-gauge guns are available from Dixie Gun Works These wads can also be used in replica 69-caliber muskets to convert these into usable shotguns for hunting upland game. Should you already own a replica musket in this caliber, there is no reason why it cannot be used as a hunting gun.

I do not recommend the "buck and ball" military loads for deer. If you hit with the 69-caliber ball you won't need the three .30-caliber buckshot. If you hit with only the buckshot, that will likely only wound the deer.

DAVIDE PEDERSOLI SLUG SHOTGUN

I chose to purchase Davide Pedersoli's slug-shotgun because the flip-up rear sight and cylinder-bored barrels offered the potential of using it as a shotgun and double-barreled round-ball gun.

Experimenting with both patched round balls and balls contained in plastic Winchester 1-1/4-ounce Red Wads, I found that both did well. I chose the plastic-wadded load to take deer in

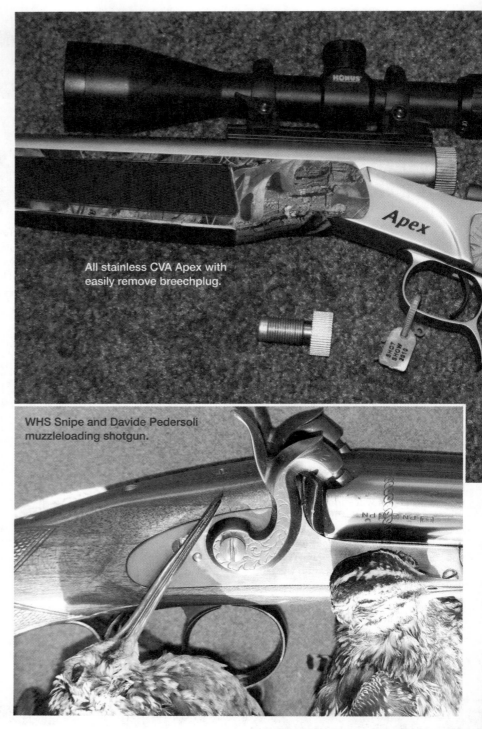

All stainless CVA Apex with easily remove breechplug.

WHS Snipe and Davide Pedersoli muzzleloading shotgun.

the U.S. and a blue wildebeest in Africa. I used a load of 135 grains of GOEX FFg in the U.S. and a 155-gr. charge of WANO black powder in Africa. With the WANO load and shooting offhand at 35 yards, I put a left and right within two inches of the bull which is good shooting with any double gun, rifled or not.

In Georgia, I often use this as a ball and shot gun with one barrel loaded with shot and the other with a round ball. This way I am ready for anything.

THOMPSON/CENTER MOUNTAIN RIFLE SHOTGUN

This contradictory-sounding title results because this gun was the shotgun version of the now-discontinued T/C Mountain Rifle. This gun was made in when the advantages of musket-cap ignition were re-appreciated, but before the use of 209 primers in muzzleloading guns. This gun was meant to be a lightweight muzzleloader for mountain

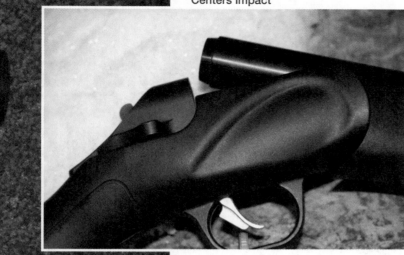

Barrel shroud lock in Thompson Centers Impact

use. As a shotgun, it was too light until I increased its weight with some lead shot and beeswax poured into the buttstock.

This was also the first muzzleloader that I experimented with that had interchangeable chokes. I would have liked a longer barrel, but did fine with the gun using it for small game, ducks, geese, swan and turkey.

AUSTIN & HALLECK 12-GAUGE BOLT ACTION

I had three problems with this now-discontinued gun. The first one was that it weighted only 6 pounds. This was too light for a shotgun to take 1-1/4-ounce waterfowl loads. I loaded its butt with lead shot and beeswax and installed a solid steel ramrod. This helped make the gun much more shooter-friendly. Another problem occurred because the machined projection on the end of the firing pin was too small reliably fire the 209 primers. This was complicated by a coil spring that weakened over time and failed to fire on the gun's first swan hunt. I ordered another firing pin

and strengthened the spring by putting washers on the firing pin spindle.

With these modifications, it worked fine on a Canadian snow goose hunt, Nebraska pheasant hunt and North Carolina brant hunt. The firing pin must be carefully adjusted to ensure that it will fire the 209 primer.

KNIGHT TK-2000

Without question, the best use of the Knight TK-2000 is to scope it and use it as a turkey gun. With its capability of shooting loads containing up to 2-1/2-ounces of shot and producing tight patterns, this muzzleloader is as capable a turkey slayer as any cartridge shotgun. This capability comes at the costs of considerable recoil which may be acceptable for one or two shots at a turkey, but not for waterfowling.

The heavy shot charges pattern low, and I had to use the adjustable iron sights to compensate. I did some serious killing on wild-flushing pheasants in West Virginia with 1-1/2-ounce loads of lead #5s and 120 grains of GOEX FFg. I still had iron sights on the gun when I took it for its swan hunt. When a good swan flew nearby I had trouble finding its head in my sights. I had to stand with one leg on the seat and shoot

over the back of the blind.

The bird fell with the shot, and I also fell from my unstable perch. The gun knocked my glasses off, cut my nose and the recoil kicked me to the other side of the blind. The charge caught the swan in the head and there were over 20 hits in the bird's head and neck at about 40 yards.

Based on this experience, I removed the rear sight and reduced the load to 120 grains of FFg equivalent and 1¼-ounces of shot.

HUNTING WITH A POOR MAN'S DOUBLE RIFLE

Many double rifles in African calibers are priced at $10,000 and up. When I saw Traditions' no-longer-made Rex over/under .50 caliber rifle, I immediately thought of Africa. The gun's 12-pound weight made it heavier than a deer rifle needed to be, but I reasoned that this weight could soak up the recoil from a black-powder load that was potent enough for Cape buffalo.

This proved to be the correct. I worked up a load of 150 grains of Hodgdon's White Hot pellets and PowerBelt's 530-grain steel-tipped Dangerous Game Bullet that developed 1,316 fps and 2,038 ft./lbs. of muzzle energy. I used as few of the discontinued steel-pointed bullets as possible to zeroed the scope at 50 yards while shooting the fixed barrel. The second, adjustable, barrel shot this heavy bullet 3-inches high.

Another difficulty was that the gun sometimes doubled with this load. This meant that I could only shoot one barrel before opening the gun and priming the second barrel. My plan was to fire the top barrel first and carry a priming tool in my left hand to slap a primer into the lower barrel when needed. The result was that I was carrying two single-shots rather than achieving the rapid left-right shots offered by a double gun.

The hunt offered additional difficulties. Earnst Dyason, of Spear Safari, could fit me in for a South African hunt the first week in April. This was at the

Boutet Empire pistol 45 caliber smoothbore.

end of the rainy season on a property that was very thickly vegetated.

On the third day of the hunt we cut fresh tracks of a lone "Dugga Boy." After tracking through sometimes head-high brush and weeds we found him at about 20 yards. We waited until he offered the clearest possible shot at its shoulder. I aimed as low as I could see and fired. The bullet penetrated the near-side shoulder, passed through the ribs and broke the off-side leg. Despite this injury, the buffalo ran. After multiple encounters, the buffalo charged and Dyason stopped it with a brain shot at 4-5 yards.

When the buffalo was butchered, the bullet had performed well, but hit too high in the chest cavity to intersect the lungs. I now know more about shooting Cape buffalo than I did, and I mentally

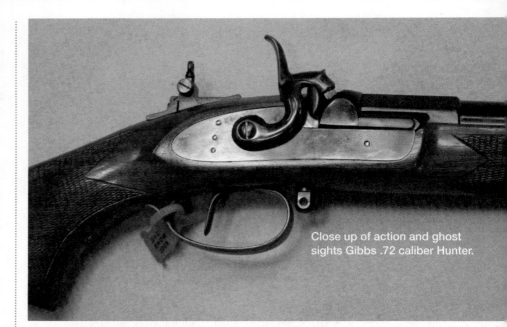

Close up of action and ghost sights Gibbs .72 caliber Hunter.

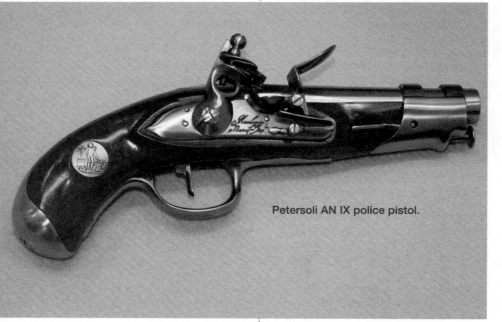

Petersoli AN IX police pistol.

GOOD OLD BOY HUNT

An adjunct to my buffalo hunt was a hunt in the Cape Province that was arranged by WhiteSmoke Forum (www.whitesmoke.co.za) moderator Willem O'Kelly. A few days before my arrival the first shipment of Bobbiejanbutts (baboon butt) smoothbores had been received from India's Delhi Gun Works, and forum members were eager to try them out.

These guns were replicas of the long-barreled flintlock smoothbores that the Dutch settlers used in South Africa from the late 1600s-1870s and most resemble America's Hudson River Fowlers. With the assistance of many individuals, I was hosted on a farm owned by Johan von Rensburg and participated in some "buckskinning" Afrikaans style.

replayed my shot on every other buffalo that I saw.

Dyason and I also stalked ostrich. I used the same 150-grain charge, but with the .444-grain PowerBelt bullet. The huge bird took over 2,000 pounds of muzzle energy and stayed on its feet. Another shot was needed to kill it. The bullets expanded to about .70-caliber and remained in the animal. This copper plated lead bullet would have been too soft to offer sufficient penetration on Cape buffalo. This experience confirmed PowerBelt's Michael McMichael's observation that these bullets did not offer deep penetration on buffalo-sized animals.

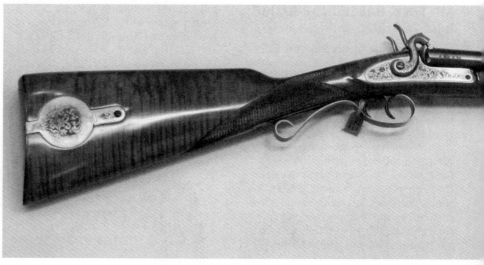

(above) South African hunters in period dress with their replica smoothbores.
(left) Exposed ignition in Thompson Centers NorthWest Explorer.

Although no big game was taken by the smoothbores on this trip, they did gather some springhairs and rabbits with their new guns using loads of pink Sannadex power, a South African-made black-powder substitute.

New Guns

CVA

Almost every gun in the CVA line received an upgrade for 2010. The Apex, Accura, and Optima are now all stainless steel guns. They, along with the other drop-barrel guns in the line, are now fitted with the new QRBP (Quick Release Breech Plug), to allow easer than ever cleaning and unloading.

The bolt-action Elkhorn Pro has an exposed nipple for musket and #11 caps for use in those states that require exposed ignition while the least expensive gun in the line, the Buckhorn at under $200, has 209-ignition in a simple striker-fired gun. CVA's best-selling gun, the Wolf break-action, is still priced at under $250 and also comes with the new QDBP system.

DAVIDE PEDERSOLI

This Italian gunmakers' muzzleloading and black-powder cartridge guns are marketed through various outlets, including Cabela's, Dixie Gun Works, Traditions and others. Three new guns attracted my attention. These were a

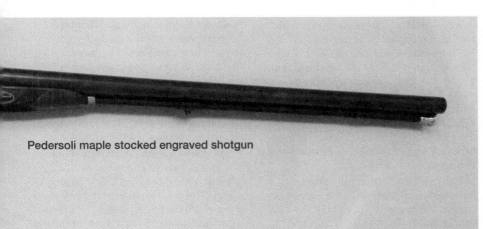

Pedersoli maple stocked engraved shotgun

maple-stocked 12-gauge "Old English" muzzleloading double shotgun with engraving and browned barrels ($1,718); the commemorative Gendarme AN IX flintlock pistol in 15.2mm caliber ($694); and a half-magazine round-barreled 1886 Winchester lever action. The '86 will be available in June for about $1,600.

Other new guns included the White Hawk, which is a falling-barrel "parlor rifle" that shoots lead BBs or .177 pellets powered by 209 primers ($300) and a Derringer Guardian which also uses 209 primers ($220). One model of the Guardian also fires .177-size projectiles. Another new pistol is an elegant replica of a .45-caliber smoothbore flintlock pistol made by Nicholas-Noel Boutet, who was gunmaker to Napoleon and had his workshop at Versailles ($1,180).

Additional models were also offered of the company's replica Sharps and Winchester single-shot cartridge guns. Expanded offerings were also made in the Mississippi Hunter rolling block which is now chambered in .22LR ($754), .357 Magnum, .38-55, .45 Colt and .45-70 ($888).

This year the company also launched an on-line magazine, "Pedersoli No. 1," which will feature articles about muzzleloading events, guns and hunting – including some by the author. Free subscriptions are available at www. davide-pedersoli.com.

DIXIE GUN WORKS

Two new muzzleloaders are being offered by Dixie. The most unusual is the Gibbs African Hunter rifle with a .72-caliber rifled barrel, ghost-ring adjustable sights with a 1:75 round-ball twist that will sell for about $1,640. The recommended load for this gun is a 100-grain charge of FFg black powder and a patched round ball and bullet (Pedersoli mold U309-720). I prefer to use about 150 grains of FFg and a hard-lead 12-gauge ball for African plains game and larger bores for bigger animals.

The African Hunter does not come with a ramrod, which detracts from its utility as a hunting gun. Installing a heavy steel ramrod would improve this gun's over-all usefulness and the added weight would enhance the user's ability to more comfortably shoot heavier loads.

Dixie also introduced a .69-caliber Spanish Musket for reenactors who wanted a gun that resembled those used in Spanish-America about the time

of the Revolutionary War. This gun uses a 1-inch flint and a .680 patched round ball. It has a recommended retail price of $1,400.

THOMPSON/CENTER ARMS

A new design of break-action muzzleloader, the Impact, was introduced by Thompson/Center Arms. With a competitive price of $249 for the blued-finished model, this gun will appeal to many hunters. The barrel is closed by a manually retracted barrel shroud, reminding me of the locking mechanism used by Remington and Valmet, among others. The gun is polymer stocked and at 6.5 pounds is very light.

The gun also has an adjustable buttstock and uses the same trigger as the more-expensive Omega ($330-$550) and Triumph ($430-$650). The Impact would be an ideal beginner's rifle. Initially, loads as low as 55 grains of FFg and a patched round ball could be

(top) Traditions Vortek rifle with easy remove breech plug.

(above) Traditions new Vortek 50-caliber pistol.

used for targets and turkey hunting. As a youngster grew, the loads, length and weight of the gun could be increased to 100 grains and 240-grain saboted bullets. For maximum performance with heavier loads, the gun needs to have some additional weight added to the buttstock and a solid steel ramrod, both of which are easy user modifications.

As does CVA and Traditions, Thompson/Center also has a version of its Omega, called the NorthWest Explorer ($327-$407), which has a cut-away section of the barrel to provide an exposed ignition and a 1:48-inch twist for full-caliber bullets. These modifications make this gun legal to use in Washington, Oregon and Idaho.

TRADITIONS

Traditions continues to carry a number of side-lock flintlock and percussion rifles in its line. Three new additions to the Vortek line include the Ultralight and Northwest Edition rifles and a pistol.

The Vortek .50-caliber muzzleloading rifles have drop-out triggers, CeraKote finishes and Accelerator Breech Plugs. The Northwest edition has the rear of the barrel milled out to expose the primer. These guns weigh 6.25 pounds and have 28-inch barrels. Both rifles sell for between $439-$499, depending on options.

The pistol version is also a .50-caliber break-barreled gun, but with a 13-inch barrel and CeraKote finish for $369. Although I have not shot this gun, I am impressed by how it feels, by the quality of its iron sights and by its general design. I would prefer a few more inches of barrel and a steel ramrod, but this pistol has all appearances of being a winner.

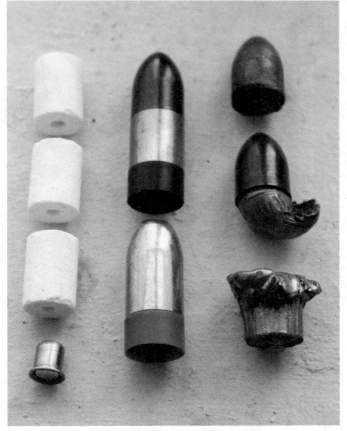

PowerBelt bullets and Hodgdon WhiteHot pellets.

Powders, Bullets and Accessories

Alliant, the maker of Red Dot powder, will be launching Black Dot powder, which is advertised as a cleaner burning, virtually non-corrosive black-powder substitute. This powder may be used in muzzleloaders (including flintlocks) and in cartridges loaded by Cowboy Action shooters.

Muzzleloading shooters going to South Africa will find this country's home-grown Sannadex to be acceptable in both flint-lock and percussion guns, although there are apparent problems in batch-to-batch uniformity. If you ever have occasion to use it, allow some range time to determine what charge corresponds to your gun's black-powder load.

IMR's White Hot pellets worked very well in the Traditions's double that I used and in other guns. This powder has a low residue and cleans up easily with soap and water.

Both Thompson/Center Arms and Traditions now offer low-cost saboted lead bullets for use in sighting in. Thompson/Center calls its bullets Cheap Shot Sabots and Traditions has named their sighting-in bullets Plinkers ($9.99 for 20). Both are 240-gr. hollow-pointed lead bullets which are also effective close-range deer and wild hog killers.

Sannadex Powder on Giraffe skull.

Gavin Margrate is a fine craftsman who produces black-powder accessories sold under the Bushbuck Trading label. Besides offering hand-made brass cappers, flask and shot bags, he also makes powder horns using horns from African antelopes. Should you like a powder horn made from an antelope that you shot, he can produce a custom horn and/or bag to make a unique African trophy. His telephone numbers are 0444-883-1113 or 082-469-3236, or he may also be contacted by E-mail at plumcrazy@absamail.co.za.

New Book

X-treme Muzzleloading: Fur, Fowl and Dangerous Game with Muzzleloading Rifles, Smoothbores and Pistols is now available (about $20, AuthorHouse, Amazon.com and others). Based on a lifetime of hunting with many muzzleloading guns in North America, Europe and Africa, this book describes the author's sometime zany, sometimes dangerous experiences with these front-loading guns.

In cover, a 3-9x variable works fine – if you keep it at 3x! This hunter takes aim with a Redfield.

OPTICS

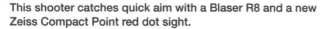

This shooter catches quick aim with a Blaser R8 and a new Zeiss Compact Point red dot sight.

Author fires a Blaser R8 with a Zeiss 6-24x56 scope, one of three new Victory Diavaris this year.

BY WAYNE VAN ZWOLL

Yes, I found plenty of new hardware at January's SHOT (Shooting, Hunting and Outdoor Trade) show. The Las Vegas Convention Center, SHOT's traditional home, was, alas, not available. Hundreds of exhibitors converged on the town's Venetian and Palazzo Hotel complex and the rat-runs of conference rooms opened to add square feet to the refurbished Sands Convention Center. "Plenty of traffic…. Better than I expected…. Needed more space" pretty much summed it up. The recession has surely influenced the choices of hunters and shooters; but it has hardly kept them home. They're buying rifles, ammo and optics. Dealers and distributors are writing orders. Product lines continue to grow – especially those that deliver value for the dollar.

An upbeat SHOT Show can trigger irrational exuberance – the marketing of products with no real utility. Alas, such items appear even in somber times. In this report I'll try to winnow that chaff and separate the worthy from the merely recent.

AIMPOINT

Since its start in 1974, Aimpoint has worked to offer the best red dot sights. Early on, that was easy, because red dot sights were then new. In fact, Gunnar Sandberg's first "single-point sight" had no optical tunnel. You couldn't look through this sight; you looked into the tube with one eye while your other registered a dot superimposed on the target. Sandberg refined the device and founded Aimpoint to produce it. Hunters liked the illuminated dot, suspended in a wide field they could see from almost any place behind the sight. The front lens of a modern Aimpoint is a compound glass that corrects for parallax – unlike most red dot sights, whose reflective paths shift with eye position. Aimpoint's doublet brings the dot to your eye in a line parallel with the sight's optical axis, so you hit where you see the dot, even when your eye is off-axis. A 1x Aimpoint gives you unlimited eye relief too. Advanced circuitry on the newest models reduces power demand. Batteries last up to 50,000 hours with a mid-level brightness setting.

The lightest of Aimpoint's 9000 series weighs just 6.5 ounces. Each windage and elevation click moves point of impact 13mm at 100 meters. The newest Hunter series comprises four models: long and short tubes, 34mm and 30mm in diameter. They all feature 1x images, 2-minute dots, half-minute clicks. A 12-position dial lets you fine-tune dot intensity – low for dim light, high under sunny skies. One CR-2032 battery lasts five years if you never turn the sight off! Hunter sights are waterproof. Fully multi-coated lenses (43mm up front on the 30mm sight, 47mm on the 34mm tube) deliver a sharp image, and as with all Aimpoints, the internal design gives you unlimited eye relief with zero parallax. Sturdy enough for military use, Aimpoints have been adopted by armed forces in the U.S. and France. They serve sportsmen in forty countries. One of every ten moose hunters using optical sights in Sweden carries an Aimpoint. I've killed moose with these optics in dark timber, then shot golf-ball-size groups on paper at 100 yards. The company's line includes a Micro H1, ideal for bows and handguns. (Aimpoint.com.)

ALPEN

A young optics company, Alpen has surprised everyone over the last few years with "great buy" credits from such venerable sources as *Outdoor Life*. While 2010 brings only a few new products to the catalog, many established optics in the Alpen line deserve another look. In short-summary fashion, then:

The Rainier 20-60x80 spotting scope accommodates a camera adapter for photography at long range. AR riflescopes for air guns were designed to endure double-shuffle recoil. Carriage-class Rainier binoculars now come in 8x32 and 10x32 versions that are 20 percent lighter than the 42mm originals but still wear BAK4 lenses, phase-corrected coatings, a locking diopter dial and twist-out eyecups. The AlpenPro Porro series includes an 8x30 that's ideal for the woods. Alpen's energetic

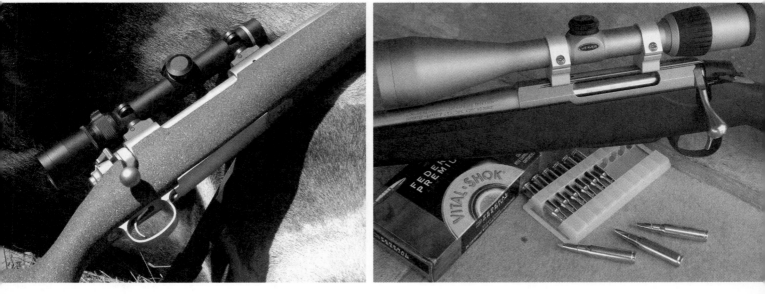

Author took this Montana rifle with a 1.5-5x Leupold to Africa, shot game from 12 to 250 yards.

This Weaver Grand Slam scope, one in a big stable of fine variables, tops a Tikka T3 rifle.

Vickie Gardner is busy "scrambling to fill back-orders from 2009!" Why? "Alpen offers great value; the riflescopes and binoculars truly are great buys."

Also, some 2009 introductions were premature; stock didn't arrive until late in the year. Wings binoculars, for example. Choose 8x42 or 10x42, with ED glass as an option. The 8x42 has impressed me in the field; so has a new Apex rifle-scope on a bolt-gun in the rack. The four Apex sights just cataloged include three with turret-mounted parallax dial and new bullet-drop-compensating reticle. "We've also upgraded our 20-60x80 spotting scope with a fine-focus knob," says Vickie. Shift focus quickly with the standard dial, then refine the image with this new adjustment. (Alpenoutdoors.com.)

BARRETT

While Barrett is known for its 50-caliber rifles, it also markets an optic that helps shooters hit at long range. The Barrett Optical Ranging System – BORS – is a sight attachment, a 13-ounce device you pair with a scope. It incorporates a small ranging computer powered by a CR-123 lithium battery. There's a liquid crystal display with a four-button keypad. Factory-installed cartridge tables tailored to your loads enable the computer to deliver precise holds for long-distance shooting. The BORS includes an elevation knob and a knob adapter. A set of steel rings mounts the unit to any M1913 rail and are secured with hex nuts that endure the beating from Barrett rifles in .50 BMG. Press the 6-o'clock power button, and you're ready

to engineer a shot. The screen shows your zero or sight-in range and indicates any cant (tipping of the rifle), which at long range can cause you to miss. To determine range, you specify target size, then move the horizontal wire of your reticle from top to bottom on the target. The range appears in yards or meters. Now you can use the elevation knob to dial the range. The BORS unit must know your load, of course. You provided that data earlier; the unit stores it as a ballistics table. It can hold up to 100 tables for instant access. At the end of this process – which takes longer to explain than to do – you can hold dead-on at any range. The BORS automatically compensates for vertical shot angles. You can adjust the scope for up to 90 degrees of inclination and declination, in increments of 2 degrees. Temperature and barometric pressure come on-screen when you press the 9-o'clock button. If the battery dies, you can use the scope as if the electronics were not there. Paired with a Leupold Mark 4 LR/Tactical 4.5-14x50 scope, the BORS unit on my Barrett rifle shrugs off the .50's blast and recoil. (Barrettrifles.com.)

BURRIS

When variables started to gain traction with hunters, the 3-9x became the logical leader. Not only did 3x afford fast sighting; 9x was all you needed for any big game – and even coyotes at long range. The three-times power range seemed adequate. As shooters chased power, though, four-times magnification appeared, in 3-12x and

4-16x 30mm scopes. Burris was among the first with six-times magnification. Its 2-12x scope is surely versatile! Like the Euro Diamond and Black Diamond lines, both Six Series sights (40mm and 50mm up front) feature 30mm tubes and 4 inches of eye relief. Signature Select and Fullfield II models have 1-inch tubes. The Fullfield II 6x40 and 3-9x40 have impressed me as fine values – also the 2-7x35. Burris Ballisic Plex and Ballistic Mil-Dot reticles are available in the Euro Diamond and Black Diamond scopes, and the Signature Select and Fullfield II lines. Illuminated reticles define the Fullfield II LRS scopes, which have flat battery housings on the turret. Fullfield 30s (3-9x40 and 3.5-10x50) feature 30mm tubes at affordable prices. The biggest news at Burris in 2010 is the Eliminator, a programmable laser range-finding scope. You enter the ballistic path of your cartridge (drop figures at 500 yards, with a 100- or 200-yard zero) to get instant reads for correct hold when you see game. The sight (at its core a 4-12x42 LaserScope) tells you the exact distance. You get accurate data to 800 yards on reflective objects, 550 on deer and elk. At 26 ounces, the Eliminator is heavy, but not burdensome.

If long shooting isn't a priority, compact scopes should be. Burris' 1-inch Timberline series, from 4x20 to 4.5-14x32 AO, fills this slot. The firm recently improved its 1.6-ounce reflex-style red dot sight: FastFire II is now waterproof. Battery-saver mode extends the life of the lithium CR2032 battery to five years. FastFire mounts

Oldie but goodie: This Swarovski Habicht variable complements an Ultra Light rifle in .30-06.

In thickets, you want low magnification. Author has a 1.5-5x Leupold on this Montana rifle.

fit popular lever rifles; a mounting plate slipped between receiver and buttstock on repeating shotguns gives you Speed-Bead. I tried this sight on a Remington 1100; the clay targets suffered that day! The company also lists a 1x, 5-ounce tube-style red dot sight, the 135. Like many optics firms, Burris has grown its tactical line. Fullfield II Tactical scopes and Fullfield TAC30 variables (3-9x40, 3.5-10x50 and 4.5-14x42) have been joined by a 3x AR-332 prism sight, and an AR-Tripler, which you place on a pivot mount behind a red dot sight for extra magnification. Binoculars and spotting scopes complete the extensive Burris line. (Burrisoptics.com.)

BUSHNELL

Last year the Elite 6500-series rifle-scopes – 2.5-16x42, 2.5-16x50 and 4.5-30x50 – introduced Bushnell fans to nearly-seven-times magnification, the broadest range in the industry. (I've since seen a scope with 10-times magnification. It wasn't a Bushnell, and at the top third of its range the image was noticeably soft.) The 6500 Elite still impresses me, now with the DOA (Dead On Accurate) reticle. It has the spaced bars common to many reticles. Minute-of-angle dots mark intersections with the bottom wire. DOA can also be ordered on Elite 3200 and Trophy sights. The Elite 4200 employs standard and lighted reticles. In this series, the 3-9x40, 2.5-10x40 and 4-16x40 appeal to me. I've found the images sharp and bright; you can also mount these scopes low. Target knobs and side-focus dials appear on

selected Elite scopes, like the 6-24x40. For hunters on a budget, Bushnell has up-graded the Trophy series. Trophy XLT scopes feature fully multi-coated lenses, fast-focus eyepiece, even flip-up lens caps. I like the 2-6x32, but there are alternatives, up to 6-18x50. Bushnell's 4-12x laser range-finding rifle-scope complements a long line of hand-held laser instruments.

For 2010, ED Prime glass and Rain-Guard HD coatings improve Bushnell's top-end Elite 8x42 and 10x42 binoculars. A step down in price, you'll find new Legend 8x36 and 10x36 binoculars. At 21 ounces, these roof-prism glasses are an ideal size for the trail. My pick: the 8x36, with its 4 1/2mm exit pupil. It has many Elite features, including ED glass and RainGuard. An Excursion spotting scope, with folded light path, comes in 15-45x60 and 20-60x80 versions. And there's a new 15-45x spotting scope compact enough to slip into a backpack. Dual-speed focus on this Legend HD allows for coarse and fine focusing, quickly. Bushnell's most field-worthy laser range-finder may be the Scout 1000 with ARC, technology that takes shot angle into account so you get corrected distance for accurate shooting at steep vertical angles. Single-button control makes this 6 1/2-ounce range-finder easy to use with one hand. In bow mode, it reads between 5 and 100 yards. Rifle mode sets it for 100 to 800 yards. (Bushnell.com.)

CABELA'S

Because it does not make riflescopes,

Cabela's markets those from other firms – branded items from Leupold, Nikon, Swarovski, Zeiss and other well-known manufacturers and imported optics – with its own Cabela's label. Its manufacturers also produce for "name" companies in optics. They own the best of machines and technology and negotiate modest labor costs. Cabela's enjoys an economy of scale that contributes to low prices, so it's no surprise that these optics are exceptionally good buys. The Alaska Guide series of rifle-scopes includes fixed-powers as well as eleven variables. Most useful for big game and varmint hunters are the 3-9x, 4-12x AO and 6.5-20x AO scopes, all with 40mm objectives and 1-inch tubes. They list for less than $400. A 4x Cabela's scope helped me take a mountain goat and a moose in British Columbia. If you're feeling the cruel pinch of want these days, consider the Pine Ridge line; it's less expensive still. There's also a series of Cabela's tactical scopes with inter-changeable turrets and left-side parallax knobs. The 2-7x32, 3-9x40, 3-12x40 and 6-18x40 start at less than $100, with fully multi-coated lenses, fast-focus eyepieces and adjustable objectives. A new Lever-Action scope features a reticle proportioned to help you determine and hold for distances that impose significant bullet drop. Five inches of eye relief help you aim fast. Cost: $100. Cabela's lists similar scopes for shotguns and muzzleloaders. (Cabelas.com.)

DOCTER

World War II brought big changes in

Author takes a bead with a Magnum Research rifle and Greybull-modified Leupold scope.

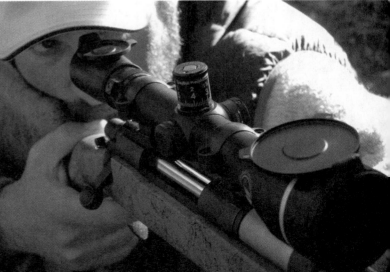

This Leupold 4.5-14x50 VX-3 has been modified for long shooting by GreyBull Precision.

the staid and respected German optics industry. Long after the ripples of that conflict subsided, new names attached themselves to old companies. In 1991 the Carl Zeiss Jena factory in Thuringia, Germany, began producing Docter optics. In 2006 Merkel USA became the U.S. importer. Docter Optic has since wooed hunters Stateside with rifle-scopes featuring 1-inch tubes and rear-plane reticles. The 3-9x40, 3-10x40, 4.5-14x40 AO and 8-25x50 AO Docter Sport scopes boast features of more expensive sights. Docter's line also includes 1-inch 6x42 and 8x56 fixed-power Classic models, plus 30mm Classic variables: 1-4x24, 1.5-6x42, 2.5-8x48 and 3-12x5 with fast-focus eyepieces, resettable windage/elevation dials and lighted reticles. In the Unipoint series, the electronically controlled rear-plane dot stays a constant size, while the first-plane main reticle varies with magnification (and stays in constant relationship with the target). Doctor catalogs three magnesium/alloy-frame binoculars: 8x42, 10x42 and a bright 8x58. They're of roof-prism design with center focus and four-layer achromatic front lenses. A central diopter dial with vernier scale ensures precise focus to just 3 feet! (Merkel-usa.com and docter-germany.com.)

GREYBULL PRECISION

Ballistic performance has many measures. Most venerated among hunters is reach – long-range accuracy and payload. Extending reach is, after all, a fundamental purpose for firearms. One shooter who has made long reach

a mission is John Burns, a Wyoming gun-builder who, with Coloradans Scott Downs and Don Ward, runs GreyBull Precision. They fashion mid-weight hunting rifles for hunters who expect to shoot far.

Optics are a key component of GreyBull rifles. The firm contracts with Leupold to install Greybull's own reticle in Leupold's 4.5-14x VX III sight. It's essentially a Duplex with a few fine horizontal lines for range estimation, and one-minute tics to help you shade for wind. The elevation dial is meant to move; each is cut for a specific load and marked so you can quickly dial the distance and hold center. Adjusting windage dials, most hunters agree, is unwise. Wind changes speed and direction, and you can get lost correcting yourself off zero. So GreyBull scope dials have numbers scribed above distance marks. They show minutes of adjustment needed in a 10-mph crosswind. Testing these scopes, I've found yardage and windage marks spot on. Of course, a laser range-finder is all but necessary to get accurate distance reads. I enjoyed the opportunity to test the Greybull scope on a Greybull rifle, and both performed magnificently. (Greybullprecision.com.)

LEICA

Best known for its superlative Ultravid binoculars and Geovid range-finding binoculars, Leica now offers 8+12x42 and 10+15x50 Duovid glasses. These aren't "zoom" or variable binoculars. Such mechanisms are too heavy and bulky

for binoculars, and those that have appeared from less prestigious firms show substandard images. The Duovid is an "either-or" instrument. Switch from 8x to 12x (or 10x to 15x) for a close-up view. At 37 and 44 ounces, Duovids aren't light. But they're relatively compact and certainly more portable than spotting scopes. Optical quality is excellent – so too that of the Geovid, now with 42mm objectives as well as light-gobbling 56s. Geovids have been up-graded with the HD fluorite glass of Leica's Ultravid HD binoculars. These fluorite lenses enhance brightness and resolution and can reduce overall weight. All four Geovids (8x42, 10x42, 8x56 and 12x56) have alloy frames and deliver accurate range reads to 1,200 yards. The Ultravid has replaced the time-honored Trinovid binocular. The line includes 8x20 and 10x25 compact models, and full-size roof-prism glasses from 8x32 to 12x50. HD versions feature fluorite in every lens, proprietary AquaDura coating on exposed glass.

The big news at Leica this year is two new riflescopes, the company's first under its own label. The 2.5-10x42 and 3.5-14x42 feature 30mm tubes, rear-plane reticles and AquaDura lens coating to shed water. This hydrophobic compound (also featured on Leica binoculars) beads water and makes lens cleaning easy. At 15 and 17 ounces, these rifle-scopes are lightweight. They're also good-looking and have plenty of free tube for mounting. Four inches of eye relief make the new scopes a logical choice for hard-kicking rifles. (Leica-sportoptics.com.)

Nikon's ProStaff scope and T/C's new Venture rifle are bargain-priced but perform at higher levels.

AR-style rifles have become the rage. AR-specific scopes like this Bushnell have followed.

LEUPOLD

Last year Leupold quietly bought the Redfield name. It is now producing a new line of Redfield riflescopes and binoculars. Hard to believe! During my youth, the two firms were fierce competitors. They represented, with Bausch & Lomb, the best of American-made hunting optics. The new Redfields are made at Leupold's Beaverton, Oregon, facility. Starting at $160, they're priced to sell! Choose from 2-7x33, 3-9x40, 3-9x50 and 4-12x40 "Revolution" scopes, all with fully multi-coated optics and finger-adjustable dials. Leupold VP Andy York joined me on an elk hunt last fall, to initiate the Redfield line. Alas, neither of us killed an elk; but Andy assures me the Redfield name had nothing to do with our luck! I like the 3-9x40's classic profile, sharp images, generous eye relief. The satin finish complements any rifle. Three knurled rings on the eyepiece are signature Redfield – as distinctive as Leupold's gold ring. Subdued red logos grace the turret and objective bell. A 4-Plex reticle (remember, it's not a Duplex unless it's a Leupold!) and a range-finding "Accu-Range" reticle are both standard. The latter is a plex with a circle at the field's center. At 4x, I found the circle subtends one foot at 100 yards. There's a dot on the bottom wire for precise aim to around 400 yards with most cartridges. These affordable 1-inch scopes should appeal to any hunter. Mount them in low rings, like the one-piece, lightweight Talleys I prefer.

Though it's hard to trump the new Redfield series for value, shooters who insist on the best optics still have many choices at Leupold. Two years ago, Leupold introduced its top-end VX-7 scopes. The low-profile VX-7L, with a concave belly up front, followed (3.5-14x56 and 4.5-18x56, complementing the VX-7 in 1.5-6x24, 2.5-10x45 and 3.5-14x50). These sights have European-style eyepieces and "lift and lock" SpeedDial turret knobs. Xtended Twilight glass features scratch-resistant DiamondCoat 2 lens coating. The power ring is matched to a "Ballistic Aiming System" so you can tailor magnification and reticle to the target and distance. Nitrogen was replaced by argon/krypton gas to better prevent fogging.

The VX-7 is still top-of-the-line. But it's being crowded by the VX-3 series introduced last year to replace the Vari-X III. Nearly 40 models are listed. Cryogenically treated stainless adjustments move 1/4, 1/8 and 1/10 m.o.a. per click in standard, competition and target/varmint versions. An improved spring system ensures precise erector movement. The fast-focus eyepiece has a rubber ring. These features also appear on the new FX-3 6x42, 6x42 AO, 12x40 AO and two scopes designed for metallic silhouette shooting: a 25x40 AO and 30x40 AO. Choose from 18 reticle options for the VX-3 and FX-3 series, and five finishes for the 1-inch and 30mm 6061-T6 aircraft alloy tubes.

To accommodate the AR-10 and AR-15 platforms, there's a new Mark AR series: 1.5-4x20, 3-9x40, 4-12x40, 6-18x40. The Mark 4 tactical line includes an ER/T M1 4.5-14x50 sight with front-plane reticle. As in European scopes, this reticle stays in constant relationship to the target throughout the magnification span, so you can range a target at any power. The smallest of Leupold's scopes – FX II 2.5x20 Ultralight – remains one of my favorites. It sits tight to the receiver in extra-low rings, slides easily into scabbards, weighs just 7-1/2 ounces and has all the power you need for big game to 200 yards. For bolt rifles with longer reach, I prefer the 4x33 and 6x36 FX IIs.

Long shooting at small targets calls for the 6.5-20x40 Long Range VX-3 – and other sights in the LR stable. New pocket range-finders, the RX-1000 and RX-1000 TBS, boast better light transmission – three times what you get from some others, according to Leupold. In open country last fall, I downed an elk far away with a VX-3 4.5-14x. The extra magnification helped. (Leupold.com.)

MEOPTA

Having produced high-quality optics for 77 years, Meopta has announced a line of 1-inch rifle-scopes specifically for the American market. The MeoPro sights, in 3-9x42, 4-12x50 and 6-18x50, have handsome profiles and plenty of free tube, with compact eyepieces that allow for the forward mounting I prefer. The 6-18x50 features a turret-mounted parallax dial. "MB550 Ion Assisted" lens coatings sound as if they belong in a science-fiction movie; in truth, they're excellent coatings that boost light transmission to the highest levels.

Author fitted this Clearidge 6-20x40 AO to a Savage M10 rifle in .308. Low cost. Good optics.

This T/C Venture wears a new Nitrex scope. ATK owns Nitrex, now under the Weaver label.

These scopes complement three new binoculars: 6.5x32, 8x42 and 10x42. That 6.5x, with its wide field and great depth of focus, is just what hunters need in cover – and has plenty of power for most hunting in the mountains. The Czech-made Meopta lines still include 30mm MeoStar variable rifle-scopes. The newest R1 series comprises seven scopes, from 1-4x22 to 4-16x44. There's also a 7x56 fixed-power. Four MeoStar binoculars include 20-ounce 8x32 and 10x32 glasses. Meostar S1 spotting scopes (75mm objective) come with standard or APO glass, straight or angled eyepiece, and 30x, 30x wide-angle or 20-60x zoom eyepiece. There's a collapsible 75mm scope, too. (Meopta.com.)

NIGHTFORCE

The name isn't descriptive. Nightforce has nothing to do with infrared imaging. This optics firm specializes in high-quality rifle-scopes for precision shooting. Since 1993, more world records in long-range Benchrest events have been set with Nightforce scopes than with any other. They're a top choice among 1,000-yard and 50-caliber marksmen. The 8-32x56 and 12-42x56 Precision Benchrest models have resettable dials with 1/8-minute clicks, as well as glass-etched illuminated reticles. Their four-times magnification range is shared by the NXS series, from the 3.5-15x50 and 3.5-15x56 NSX to the 5.5-22x50 and 5.5-22x56, the 8-32x56 and 12-42x56. Compact scopes for big game hunting recently joined that roster. The 1-4x24 and a 2.5-10x24 sights and, now, a 2.5-

10x32 weigh just over a pound with the 30mm bronze alloy tubes common to Nightforce scopes. Like all but the Precision Benchrest models, the new 2.5-10x has a turret-mounted focus/parallax dial. (The 8-32x56 and 12-42x56 bench scopes wear front-sleeve parallax rings.) A new 3.5-15x50 F1 with first-plane reticle caters to hunters who want the reticle to stay in constant relationship to the target throughout the power range. Nightforce rifle-scopes endure the toughest tests in the industry. Each sight must remain leak- and fog-proof after submersion in 100 feet of water for 24 hours, freezing in a box at a minus 80° F, then heating within an hour to 250° F. Every scope gets pounded in a device that delivers 1,250 Gs, backward and forward. Lens coatings must pass mil-spec abrasion tests.

Nightforce now offers eleven illuminated reticle options. They're distinctive and appealing because they cover so little of the field. The firm also markets accessories for competitive and tactical shooters. Mil radian windage and elevation knobs deliver .1 mil per click. Long-range shooters can specify a turret with 1-minute elevation and half-minute windage graduations, for big changes in yardage with short dial movement. A "zero-stop" turret has an elevation dial that can be set to return to any of 400 detents in its adjustment range. One-piece steel scope bases have a recoil lug to ensure the mount doesn't move. Five heights of steel rings let you install the scope in just the right location. Unimount, machined from

7075-T6 alloy, has titanium crossbolts and a 20-minute taper for long shooting. Nightforce's Ballistic Program for Windows, and the abbreviated version for Pocket PCs, helps you determine bullet arc at distance. The company assembles its carriage-class optics at its plant in Idaho. (Nightforceoptics.com.)

NIKON

While Nikon's optics line has grown this year, the company's biggest news may be its ballistics program, which you can access free from Nikon's website. Plug in a cartridge, the bullet type and velocity to get down-range speed and energy data instantly. Specify zero range, and you'll see the bullet's arc. Or work backward to find the sight-in range that gives you longest point-blank distance. Nikon has programmed in dozens of popular centerfire rounds. Manipulations are so simple even a cave man can do them. How does Nikon benefit? "We get a chance to show you how our optics help you hit," explains C.J. Davis. "Beyond that, it's just good business to do what we can for the industry and for our customers." Having played a little with the program, I can endorse it. While I've no interest in anything that extends my time at a computer screen, Nikon's ballistics program threatens to do just that!

As for hardware, Nikon riflescopes now include an M-223 series for AR shooters. The 1-4x20, 2-8x32 and 3-12x42 can be used on other rifles, of course; but BDC reticles for the 2-8x and 3-12x M-223 are tailored for popular AR-15

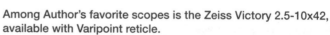

Zeiss Varipoint scopes feature a lighted rear-plane reticle, controlled by a left-hand turret dial.

Among Author's favorite scopes is the Zeiss Victory 2.5-10x42, available with Varipoint reticle.

loads. The Monarch line remains Nikon's flagship, with its "African" and "Long Range" subsets. The 1-4x20 has a 1-inch tube; the 1.1-4x24, available with an illuminated reticle, is a 30mm sight. Both provide four inches of eye relief for fast aim and "recoil space." They feature German #4 reticles and half-minute click adjustments. The African scopes round out a line tilted to high-power optics by the 2008 debut of an 8-32x50ED SF with 1/8-minute adjustments. The 5-20x44 affords great reach in a sight of reasonable size. For all-around hunting, the 2.5-10x42 is hard to beat.

The 4-16x50SF and 2-8x32, recent additions, pretty much cover the rest of the field. I've found Monarch optics to equal the brightest in the industry. The "Gold" and "X" series have 30mm tubes. "Coyote Special" rifle-scopes introduced last year (a 3-9x40 and a 4.5-14x40) still sell well. They feature BDC reticles and camouflage finish. A reflection-fighting screen hides the front lens. The Omega 1.65-5x36 scope for muzzleloaders is also a hit, as is the 1.65-5x36 SlugHunter. Both have a generous five inches of eye relief and BDC reticles suited to the trajectories of the most common bullets. Omega's parallax setting is 100 yards, that of the SlugHunter 75. The value-oriented ProStaff stable has a new entry for 2010: this 4-12x40 is an excellent scope that gives you bright images, a useful power range and a svelte tube that complements trim rifles. Nikon also lists two new range-finders this year, one for archers, the other for riflemen. There are new 42mm models in the mid-priced

Monarch ATB binocular line. Nikon's top-end EDG binoculars (7x42, 8x42, 10x42, 8x32, 10x32) with open-bridge design and a locking diopter are good glasses made better with ED lenses. Ditto the EDG Fieldscope, 85mm or 65mm. Its zoom eyepieces (16-48x and 20-60x) interchange with Nikon fixed-power eyepieces. (Nikonhunting.com.)

PENTAX

In 2010, Pentax is taking on the recession with a new series of value-priced rifle-scopes it calls the GameSeeker II line. There are six models, from the yeoman 3-9x40 to a 4-16x50 and a light-grabbing 2.5-10x56. They feature one-piece, 1-inch alloy tubes, fully multi-coated optics and finger-adjustable windage and elevation dials. Choose from a standard plex reticle or the Precision Plex BDC. GameSeeker scopes are priced from around $100, which should make them popular. Last year, Pentax added a 3-15x50 GameSeeker to that stable. Five-times magnification offers more versatility than you'll likely need for big game. I chose instead a 3-9x32 for a moose hunt. That 12-ounce sight was perfect for my Ruger carbine in .300 RCM. Its high level of resolution helped me shoot a bull when I picked out a sliver of antler deep in shadowed timber. You can choose from eight 1-inch variable GameSeekers, plus 4x32 and 6x42 fixed-power sights. The 30mm Lightseeker 30 series comprises 3-10x40, 4-16x50, 6-24x50 and 8.5-32x50 scopes. Pioneer II models, 3-9x40 and 4.5-14x42, feature 1-inch tubes, fully multi-coated optics. Among

Pentax spotting scopes, the compact PF-63 Zoom with fixed 20-50x eyepiece is particularly well suited to hunting, while the PF-80ED and PF-100ED excel when weight doesn't matter. Interchangeable eyepieces include 32x, 46x and 20-60x options for the 37-ounce PF-65ED, which also accepts a Pentax PF-CA35 camera adapter for 35mm SLRs.

Pentax binoculars include a 7x50 Marine model with built-in compass on a liquid bearing for fast dampening. Waterproof, with twist-up eye-cups and a click-stop diopter ring, the rubber-armored 7x50 has all the best features of the Pentax roof-prism DCF roof prism binoculars. These come in 8x, 10x and 12.5x, with 32mm to 50mm objectives, with phase-corrected prisms in alloy and polycarbonate shells. A Porro prism PCF line includes 8x40, 10x50, 12x50 and 20x60 binoculars. Among my favorite hunting glasses is an unlikely choice: the Pentax 9x28 BCF LV. Despite its modest exit pupil, this binocular gives me bright images, and at 13 ounces it's eminently portable. I like the twist-out eyecups, click-stop diopter. The surface is easy to grip. Other good choices for the trail: 8x36 and 10x36 DCF NV roof-prism glasses. (Pentaxsportoptics.com.)

SCHMIDT & BENDER

Long revered for excellence in rifle-scopes, Schmidt & Bender has hewed mainly to the European traditions of big tubes and first-plane reticles. Last year S&B announced its first 1-inch riflescope for the American market. The 16-ounce 2.5-10x40 Summit has a rear-plane

Kimber's 84L delivered excellent groups with a Leupold VX-3. A handsome outfit too!

Leupold has re-introduced the Redfield brand, with binoculars and rifle-scopes built in Oregon.

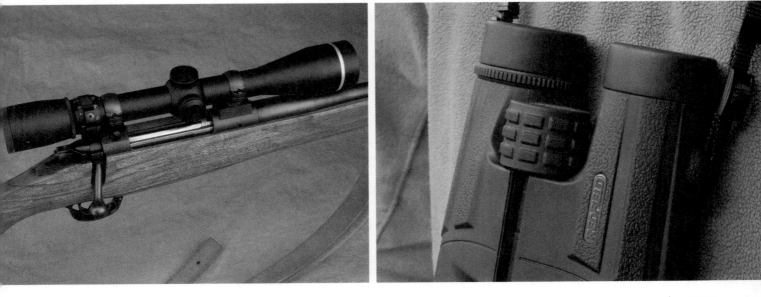

reticle. Optically, it seems to me the equivalent of higher-priced Classic and top-end Zenith lines. It has the right power range and profile for at least 99 percent of all big game hunting! Recent changes in S&B administration have not shifted its main focus. A small company by most standards, S&B still caters to people who want the very best in optical sights. Its roots lie in the hunting field, but it has brought innovation to the tactical table too. Three years ago a S&B 3-12x was adopted by the U.S. Marine Corps for its 30- and 50-caliber sniper rifles. Its 34mm Police/Marksman scopes rank among the most sophisticated LE sights around. Lighted mil dot reticles, as on S&B's 4-16x42 P/M II, come with 11-setting turret-mounted rheostats. The automatic shutoff saves battery while the previous setting automatically engages when you hit the illumination switch again. A side-mounted parallax adjustment hides the battery cage. Windows on windage and elevation knobs show you where the reticle is in its adjustment range. Flash-dot reticles incorporate a beam-splitter to illuminate a dead-center dot, which vanishes at a touch if you desire just the black reticle. The Police/Marksman line now comprises 17 scopes with 30mm and 34mm tubes. The latest is a 5-25x56 PM II with locking turrets.

For hunting, I've come to favor S&B's 3-12x42 Classic, a versatile, durable, good-looking 30mm scope that delivers brilliant, tack-sharp images. I like the 6x42 and 10x42 fixed-power Classics as well, available with 1-inch and 30mm

chassis. The Zenith series comprises four 30mm variables: 1.1-4x24, 1.5-6x42 (a great hunting sight!), 2.5-10x56, 3-12x50. They wear the P/M's "Posicon" windage and elevation dials. (Schmidt-bender.de or scopes@cyberportal.net [the website of its U.S. importer].)

SHEPHERD

The advantages and disadvantages of front- and rear-plane scope reticles are clear. A front-plane reticle grows in apparent size as you dial up the power but stays the same size in relation to the target. It does not move out of the optical center of the scope, and as a range-finding device it gives you the same picture no matter what the magnification. But at long range, where targets appear small and you want precise aim, the reticle can obscure the aiming point. Up close, when you power down for quick shots in thickets, the reticle shrinks, becoming hard to see quickly. A second-plane reticle stays the same apparent size throughout the power range, so it won't hide distant targets at high magnification, and it won't vanish when you turn down the power to find game quickly up close. But because its dimensional relationship to the target changes with every change in magnification, range-finding becomes a task best limited to one power setting.

Shepherd scopes offer both reticles. You get an aiming reticle that doesn't change size and a range-finding reticle that varies in dimension with power changes. Superimposed, the front- and rear-plane reticles appear as one. The

former comprises a stack of circles of decreasing diameter. To determine yardage, match a deer-size (18-inch) target with one of the circles. Correct holdover is factored in because the circles are placed to compensate for bullet drop. A trio of range-finding reticles suit the trajectories of popular cartridges. Vertical and horizontal scales are marked in minutes of angle so you can compensate for wind. The 6-18x M556 Shepherd is specially designed for AR-style rifles. I've used these sights; they work as advertised. An amigo has a 6-18x that he says "is really unfair to coyotes." (Shepherdscopes.com.)

SIGHTRON

Magnesium is 33 percent lighter than aluminum, so hunters should appreciate Sightron's SIIIMS line of binoculars. New for 2010, it includes 8x32, 10x32, 8x42 and 10x42 roof-prism, magnesium-frame glasses scaling 20 to 25 ounces. The 8x32 is my choice. All feature phase-corrected, multi-coated optics and twist-up eye-cups. The company is also listing a new ESD – Electronic Sighting Device. It's a 33mm red dot sight with a 5-minute dot. Choose from eight intensity levels. Recession got you? Sightron's S1 scopes are bargain-priced but feature multi-coated front and rear lenses. Pick from a broad selection of reticles, finishes and power ranges. SII and SIII series are up-grades. Like its competition, Sightron is now offering a range-compensating reticle with dots spaced out on the lower wire. Several high-power variables have joined the Sightron family this

Author bears down offhand with a Weatherby Vanguard rifle and Bushnell Elite 6500 scope.

Dave Anderson's Weatherby rifle sports a Zeiss Victory scope. Some now feature FL glass.

A Swarovski variable on an Ultra Light rifle helped Dori Riggs collect this fine warthog.

All told, the 2010 catalog lists more than 50 scopes in SI, SII and SIII series. Long Range models feature 30mm tubes, turret-mounted parallax dials and reticles that include a mil dot and an illuminated German #4A. Target knobs are tall for easy access. From the 3.5-10x44 to the 8-32x56, these scopes feature fully multi-coated optics in one-piece tubes, with resettable ExacTrack windage and elevation adjustments and a fast-focus eyepiece. External lenses wear "Zact-7," a seven-layer coating to reduce light loss. A hydrophobic wash disperses raindrops. Eye relief approaches four inches. An SII 1.25-5x20 Dangerous Game sight with over six inches of clear tube has replaced the 2.5x20 that has

year. A new SIII Tactical Fixed Power line comprises 10x, 16x, and 20x scopes with 42mm objectives, 30mm tubes.

served me well on hard-kicking rifles. High-power variables and 36x benchrest sights have front-end parallax sleeves. I like the dot reticle in these scopes, also available on the 5-20x42. Sightron's Hunter Holdover reticle for hunting scopes incorporates a couple of simple hash marks on the lower wire. Specify it on 3-9x42, 3-12x42 and 45.5-14x42 SIIs, and on the 3-9x40 SI. In my experience, Sightron scopes deliver great value for the dollar. (Sightron.com.)

STEINER

Aggressively pursuing hunting markets after decades of service to military units the world over, Steiner introduced last year the 21-ounce Wildlife Pro 8x30 binocular, its first center-focus Porro-prism glass in twenty years. For 2010, the firm has announced a laser range-finding binocular. The 10x50 LRF can reportedly range reflective targets to 1,600 yards, and with 1-yard accuracy to 500. The digital display comes up quickly; a scan mode helps you range moving targets. The LRF has HD glass and weighs 46 ounces. Also new from Steiner: 8x56 and 10x56 Predator C5 binoculars. While at 40 and 43 ounces these aren't as portable as smaller Steiners, they give you brilliant images in poor light. The 7mm and nearly-6mm exit pupils are all the average eye can use in the deepest shadow. I find these glasses very bright. The newest center-focus versions wear a thin rubber armor for a slim profile. Still the flagship of Steiner's line is the Peregrine XP. This center-focus, open-bridge binocular

Zeiss introduced its range-finding binocular a couple of years ago. It's a marvelous instrument!

Modestly priced, new Redfield rifle-scopes have finger-friendly dials, very good optics.

focuses as close as 6-1/2 feet. The large 30mm eyepieces have twist-up eyecups and flexible wings that fold back to prevent external fogging from face moisture. Outside lens surfaces feature a hydrophobic "NANO Protection." It beads water so you can see clearly in rain and snow. The Peregrine XP (8x44 and 10x44) is waterproof and lightweight, with a rugged magnesium frame. It comes with neoprene hood and a clever Click-Loc strap. The Peregrine XP has earned the NRA's coveted Golden Bullseye Award for excellence. (Steiner-binoculars.com.)

SWAROVSKI

After a decade of vigorous new-product development, Swarovski is tweaking its EL binocular. The Traveler 8x32 and 10x32 are the company's best hunting binos in casual dress. I like the open-hinge design. Swarovski has expanded its Z6 rifle-scope line to include 2.5-15x56 and 2.5-15x44 sights. They afford you the lowest practical magnification plus enough power to pester prairie dogs in the off-season. I've used the 1.7-10x42 afield, have only good things to say about it. The newest Z6 is a 2.5-15x56. As with other 30mm Z6 models, an illuminated reticle is an option. The switch, atop the eyepiece, has an automatic shutoff and two memory locations, one for daytime and one for night use. Turn the switch and the reticle delivers illumination for prevailing conditions. The 1-6x24 Z6 has the broadest power range of any "dangerous game" sight. At 4-3/4 inches, its eye relief is most generous.

Author killed this leopard in tall grass at 12 yards. Credit a Leupold 1.5-5x20 for the quick shot!

Nightforce specializes in high-power riflescopes. But hunting models have recently appeared.

Bright glass (here in a Leupold) can salvage a hunt when your only shot comes in dim light!

Swarovski's Z5 rifle-scopes offer five-times magnification in one-inch tubes. A 3-15x42 may be the perfect scope for shooters who want the greatest versatility in a relatively lightweight scope. Swarovski borrowed from subsidiary Kahles to produce a Ballistic Turret capable of storing several zero settings. You set those zeroes with ballistics tables or by live firing. Change load and zero; then return to your original in a wink. The Ballistic Turret is an option on selected Swarovski scopes. A simpler way to hit long-range targets is with the BR reticle. Its ladder-type bottom wire has 10 hash-marks. BR is available in three AV models and 1.7-10x42 and 2-12x50 Z6 sights. (Swarovskioptik.com.)

TRIJICON

The ACOG (Advanced Combat Optical Gunsight) established Trijicon as a leading innovator in rifle optics. More than half a million have been sold. But the ACOG's application is primarily military. The AccuPoint is Trijicon's flagship hunting optic, a scope with two sources of reticle illumination. The fiber optic window in the ocular bell, and tritium in the reticle itself, yield a bright aiming point without batteries. An adjustable cover lets you trim light from the fiber optic coil and tune reticle brightness. Last year AccuPoint came up with plex and crosswire-and-dot reticles, as alternatives to its original super-fast delta. Lost in the lumination hype, however, has been the quality of Trijicon optics. "It's definitely top-drawer," Trijicon's Andrew Chilkewicz reminds

me. I agree. Trijicon's fully multi-coated glass gives you brilliant, razor-edged images. And if you've shied from lighted reticles, this is the brand to try first. Choose a delta in amber, red or green, a dot in amber or green. Combine it with a black crosswire if you like. I prefer the crosswire and amber dot. My pick among Trijicon scopes is the 3-9x40. After decades in the field, it's still in my view the most practical for all-around big game hunting. But you can also opt for a 1.25-4x24 or a 2.5-10x56 with 1-inch tube. A 1-4x24 and a powerful 5-20x50 have 30mm tubes. For fast shooting in 'pole thickets, Trijicon markets reflex sights with lighted dots of various sizes. The RMR (Ruggedized Miniature Reflex) can be had with a light-emitting diode that automatically adjusts to incident light. It has an alloy housing, the Trijicon RedDot sight a nylon-polymer frame. Either can be paired with the ACOG. A battery-free RMR uses tritium and fiber optics only; the electronic version is powered by a 17,000-hour lithium battery. (Trijicon.com.)

TRUGLO

Luminescent shotgun beads and rifle-sight inserts, with tritium and fiber-optic elements, brought TruGlo early success. Now the firm offers red dot sights and rifle-scopes too. Waterproof and compatible with any Weaver-style mount, the red dot sights come in reflex (open) configuration or 1-inch and 30mm and 40mm tubes. Dual-Color (red and green) Multi-Reticles come standard in some models. All versions of the tube sight

have unlimited eye relief, multi-coated lenses, click-stop windage/elevation adjustments, an 11-level rheostat to control reticle brightness. Reflex red dot sights weigh as little as 2 ounces, carry a 4-minute dot with manual and light-sensitive automatic brightness modes. TruGlo markets several series of rifle-scopes, topped by the Maxus XLE in 1.5-6x44, 3-9x44 and 3.5-10x50. The Infinity 4-16x44 and 6-24x44 have adjustable objectives. To make long-range hits easier across a variety of loads, each comes with three replaceable BDC elevation knobs. Tru-Brite Xtreme Illuminated rifle-scopes feature dual-color plex and range-finding reticles. Pick a 3-9x44, 3-12x44 or 4-16x50. Muzzleloader versions are available. The 4x32 Compact scope for rimfires and shotguns, 4x32 and 1.5-5x32 illuminated sights for crossbows round out TruGlo's stable of 1-inch scopes. TruGlo line of illuminated iron sights includes a fiber optic AR-15 gas block front sight with protected green bead. (Truglo.com.)

VORTEX

New Razor scopes from Vortex reflect the growing interest in tactical sights. The 1.4-4x24 has a 30mm tube, the 5-20x50 a 35mm tube. Both scopes deliver brilliant images from extra-low-dispersion lenses. Lighted, etched-glass reticles lie in the first focal plane. A zero-stop mechanism in the elevation dial prevents it from spinning past sight-in setting, for fast return to zero. Vortex matches turrets with reticles; and you can specify mil-dot graduations,

Author banged this gong repeatedly from 540 yards with a Leupold/Greybull scope on a .243.

A BSA Catseye scope on a Kimber 84L in .30-06 produced these groups (and filled a deer tag).

or minutes of angle. More practical for most hunters are Vortex Vipers. Also available in tactical guise, they come in six versions and five power ranges. I prefer the 3-9x40 (14 ounces) and 4-12x40 (17 ounces). Choose from six reticles, including dot, BDC and mil-dot. The Viper line features both 30mm and 1-inch tubes. More affordable Vortex Diamondbacks have 1-inch tubes only, as do entry-level Crossfires. All boast fully multi-coated optics.

The widest selection in the Vortex family comes under the Crossfire banner. That line includes 2-7x32 and 4x32 sights for rimfires, a 2x20 handgun scope and a 3x32 for crossbows. As with the Vipers, you get tall target knobs (and 30mm tubes) on the most powerful scopes. Specify a mil dot or illuminated mil dot reticle on the 6-24x50 AO. Vortex also lists a red dot sight, the Strikefire, with fully multi-coated lenses. Choose red or green dot to suit conditions. The sight has a 30mm tube and weighs 7.2 ounces. It has unlimited eye relief, comes with a 2x optical doubler. The new, shorter Sparc red dot sight weighs just 5 ounces and features a one-piece, multi-height base, a 2-minute dot. Like the Strikefire, it is parallax-free beyond 50 yards and comes with a doubler. Fully multi-coated optics of course. In spotting scopes Vortex catalogs two Nomad models, both with your choice of straight or angled eyepiece. The 20-60x80 and the budget-priced 20-60x60 accept adapters for most pocket-size digital cameras. At the top end, there's the Razor HD spotting scope

with apochromatic lenses and an 85mm objective. It weighs 66 ounces with an angled 20-60x eyepiece. The die-cast magnesium alloy body is argon-gas purged. It has coarse and fine focusing wheels. (Vortex.com.)

WEAVER

Eight decades after Bill Weaver's 330 led a trend away from iron sights, Weaver is re-introducing the 330's progeny, the iconic steel-tube K4. More than any other scope, the K4 confirmed the value of optical sights for my generation of hunters. The new version has a Dual-X reticle that doesn't move off-center in the field when you adjust windage and elevation! While the K4 may be all you need on that '06, Weaver offers more for 2010. The Super Slam series now includes a 1-5x24 Dangerous Game sight with heavy Dual-X that should excel in thickets. Besides the Grand Slam, Classic V, Classic K and T-series scopes, there's now a Buck Commander line, with 2.5-10x42, 3-12x50 and 4-16x42 models. Prices start at just $280, retail. For close shooting, Weaver offers a red/green dot sight with five brightness settings. It has a 30mm tube, an integral Weaver-style base. Tactical sights will probably proliferate, as the shooting public is not that of Bill Weaver's day. Thus, the firm announced in 2009 a 4-20x50 Tactical scope with 30mm tube, front-plane mil dot reticle and side-focus parallax dial. But you can still buy a K-series fixed-power hunting scope (one of the most-overlooked bargains in rifle sights). Among target scopes, I like the

T-24. It offers a 1/2-minute or 1/8-minute dot reticle. Target adjustments on dual-spring supports ensure repeatable changes.

New Classic binoculars have been added to Weaver's line this year: 8x32, 8x36 (my pick), 8x42, 10x42. ATK, parent company to several shooting-industry brands, counts Nitrex as well as Weaver in its family. Early in 2010, Nitrex became part of the Weaver fold, although the lines remain separate. Nitrex TR One scopes (similar to Weaver's Grand Slam) are joined by TR Two (Super Slam) scopes with additional reticles: glass-etched EBX (ballistic), dot and illuminated. These sights boast five-times magnification – 2.5-10x42 to 4-20x50 – and turret parallax dials. Pull-up, resettable windage and elevation knobs need no caps. The TR One series includes a new 4-15x50 AO scope. (Weaveroptics.com, Nitrexoptics.com.)

ZEISS

Brisk sales of Conquest rifle-scopes several years after their introduction confirm their appeal to shooters keen for value. I like the 4x32; if you must have a variable, the 2-8x32 and 3-9x40 make sense. The 4.5-14x44 milks the reach of hot-rod cartridges but looks good on lightweight hunting rifles. Like the 6.5-20x50, it features a turret-mounted parallax dial. By the way, Zeiss has just cut the list price on its 3-9x40 Conquest from $499 to $399! While there's little new in the Conquest stable for 2010, the top-rung Victory series boasts an up-grade of the 6-24x72, a 34mm scope

The finger-friendly dial on Author's BSA Catseye scope delivers predictable, repeatable clicks.

The new Redfield 3-9x40 seems a great match for this Marlin 1895 rifle in .338 Marlin Express.

Author shot this elk with a Magnum Research rifle in 6.5 Creedmoor, Leupold/GreyBull sight.

introduced in 2005 but now with quarter-minute clicks and FL glass. Two new Victory scopes also incorporate fluorite lenses. I used a 6-24x56 recently, on a super-accurate Blaser R8 in .300 Winchester. At 600 yards, prone, it was no trick to reduce a plastic pail to splinters. The 4-16x50 is better suited to hunting rifles, and should be on your short list if you expect long shooting. But for all-around hunting there's no better sight than the Victory 2.5-10x42. With four other Victory scopes, it's available with Varipoint, an illuminated dot in the second focal plane complementing a black first-plane reticle. So the main reticle stays in constant relationship to the target (for easy ranging), while the dot subtends a tiny area even at high power. A left-side turret knob controls dot brightness on the 1.1-4x24 Victory. The 2.5-10x42T*, 2.5-10x50T*, 3-12x56T* feature automatic brightness control.

Zeiss has just introduced a Compact Point red dot sight. Its 3.5-minute dot has five brightness levels. Weight: less than 3 ounces with two 3V lithium batteries. The 8x45 and 10x45 T* RF binoculars introduced last year have proven themselves afield, with a laser range-finding unit that requires no "third eye" emitter but delivers 1,300-yard range on reflective targets. This unit is fast – you get a read in about a second – and the LED self-compensates for brightness. The binocular itself has peerless optics, with a rain-repellent LotuTec coating on ocular and objective lenses. You can program the RF with computer data to get holdover for six standard bullet trajectories. Zeiss still sets the bar for laser-ranging scopes, too, with its 3-12x56 Diarange. The Zeiss PhotoScope is a 20-60x80 DiaScope spotting scope with a 7-megapixel digital camera built in. The 15-45x power range affords you the equivalent of a 600-1800mm zoom in a 35mm camera – plus a 68-degree field at 15x, which Zeiss claims is 40 percent wider than normal. The camera uses a 7.4-volt lithium ion battery and SD card to deliver images in standard file formats. PhotoScope 85T* FL weighs 6-1/2 pounds. And yes, it does produce images that qualify for full-page prints! (Zeiss.com/sports.)

Author found this BSA scope a worthy hunting sight, despite its low price. Rifle: a Kimber 84L.

S H O T

BY **JOHN HAVILAND**

Ithaca's Mike Farrell his holding his company's Phoenix 12-gauge over-and-under that is in production after a year and some of final development.

Except for hunting pronghorn antelope at long-range, a shotgun in various forms of dress works fine for every type of hunting in North America. With one receiver a hunter can clamp on a rifled barrel to shoot slugs and hunt big game from deer and elk to bears and hogs. That barrel can be switched out for a smoothbore barrel that accepts various screw-in choke tubes to hunt feathered game from waterfowl and turkeys to grouse and quail and stay tuned up on clay targets all year. Many of us, though, are not quite so utilitarian and like a separate shotgun for each shooting game. Let's see what the shotgun

companies have for both practical and particular shotgunners this year.

BENELLI

Last year Benelli built up the suspense to the unveiling of their Vinci shotgun with advertisements of fashion models running through the street, carrying an oblong parcel containing the shotgun and looking with concern over their shoulders like international secret agents were on their trail. Once Benelli opened the box in early spring I got my hands on a Vinci and I've been shooting it ever since.

The Vinci comes from the box in three pieces: barrel/receiver, trigger group/forearm and buttstock. The barrel/receiver mates with the trigger group/forearm and a turn of the forearm cap locks them together. The front of the buttstock locks into the rear of the trigger group/forearm and a clockwise partial turn of the buttstock fastens them. Once the gun is together its profile does have a rather bulbous belly forward of the trigger guard.

The Vinci action uses the In-Line Iner-

GUNS

Browning Cynergy Mossy Oak Breakup.

tia Driven operating system. Its two-lug bolt is similar to other Benelli autoloaders. However, the bolt's rearward spring and guide rod compress against a plate inside the receiver, instead of extending into the stock like the Inertia Driven system in other autoloading Benellis. The In-Line Inertia Driven system cycles very reliably and the Vinci fired several hundred 1- and 1-1/8-oz. target loads without a single blip, leaving just a slight amount of grime inside of the action after all that shooting.

The Vinci's ComforTech Plus recoil reduction system is gentle on the shoulder and cheek when shooting that many target loads and hunting loads. The smooth insert on the comb allows the cheek to slide during recoil. Vertical rows of gel inserts in the buttstock allow the buttstock to flex and absorb recoil and a soft recoil pad caps it off. Several days in the duck swamps I shot the Vinci with Winchester Xtended Range Hi-Density waterfowl loads with 1-1/4 and 1-3/8 oz. of shot. The recoil was much less than with my old Benelli Super 90.

The Vinci weighs six lbs. 14 oz. with a 28-inch barrel. That's fairly light for a three-inch 12-gauge, so I carried it into the mountains for blue grouse and along the creek bottoms for ruffed grouse. I shot handloaded 1-1/8 oz. of 7½s for the grouse and if I do say so myself, I shot rather well with the gun.

This year the turkey version of the Vinci is available. It has a SteadyGrip vertical grip stock and 24-inch barrel, camouflaged muzzle to toe.

On the light and handy side, Benelli's Legacy autoloader is chambered in 28 gauge. The gun weighs five pounds with either a 24- or 26-inch barrel with a carbon fiber ventilated rib. Benelli states it is the lightest autoloader in the world. Its walnut stock and forearm are covered with WeatherCoat finish to protect the wood from the rain and snow. An acid-etched bird hunting scene covers the lower receiver and an Aircell recoil pad soaks up what little recoil the 28 gauge generates.

BERETTA

Shotgun companies continue to develop mechanical methods to reduce the brutal recoil of 12-gauge

3½-inch magnum shells. My solution is to simply not shoot shells the size of a Roman candle.

Beretta's autoloading A400 Xplor is for bird hunters who want a portable 3-inch 12-gauge shotgun, but with the option, if the silly notion ever overtakes them, to shoot 3-1/2-inch shells. The Xplor weighs 6.6 pounds, slightly less than Beretta's AL 391 3-inch 12-gauge. To reduce recoil, the Xplor uses the Kick-Off system that incorporates two hydraulic dampers in front of the recoil pad and a third inside the stock bolt to check the slam of the bolt against the rear of the receiver. In addition to lessening the sharp stab of recoil, that third damper reduces wear on the internal parts.

Often a 3-1/2-inch gun has a difficult time cycling target loads. An elastic band on the gas piston in the Xplor, though, prevents propellant gases from escaping from the gas valve so all the gas operates the action. The elastic band also scrubs gas residue off the inside of the cylinder. I shot Federal 1-1/8 oz. target loads one after another through an Xplor without a single hiccup. Recoil was only a slight jump of the

Gail Haviland struts her stuff with a Beretta Tx4 Storm autoloader 12-gauge.

Gail Haviland is shooting an Ithaca Model 37 Ultralight with Ladies Stock.

gun in my hands. The silly notion to fire 3-1/2-inch shells in the gun momentarily overtook me. I came to my senses and fired just one. The recoil was *ouch!* there but no more than from other guns weighing a couple more pounds.

The Beretta Tx4 Storm autoloader is a home-defense 12-gauge. The Storm weighs slightly under 6-1/2 pounds with its 18-inch barrel ported at the muzzle. The length of pull of the buttstock can be adjusted with half-inch spacers. Rubber grip inlays on the synthetic stock and forearm ensure a firm grasp. An adjustable ghost ring sight mounts on a rail on the receiver top to aim in conjunction with a high front sight with protective ears.

My wife shot the Storm with buckshot loads at 25 yards. The paper target was a sieve when she finished shooting and I plan to stay on her good side.

BLASER

The over-and-under F3 SuperTrap uses interchangeable single or over-and-under 12-gauge barrels. The barrels are free-floating and adjustable to move pattern impact of each barrel. The tall rib is also vertically adjustable to fine tune pattern placement. A barrel weight system keeps the gun's weight the same whether one or two barrels is in the receiver. The stock is set with cast for left or right-handed shooters and the comb is adjustable for height.

The F3 frame is also available in 28 gauge with 28-inch Competition or 28-inch Game barrels. The Competition barrel features the identical weight, balance and rib as all the other F3 Competition barrels in 12 and 20-gauge. A variety of Briley choke tubes comes with each barrel.

BROWNING

The Maxus Hunter is a good looking version of the camouflage Maxus autoloader introduced last year. The Hunter wears a walnut stock and forearm and the nickel finish on its aluminum receiver is engraved with a mallard and a pheasant. The barrel is blued with a flat ventilated rib and comes with full, modified and improved cylinder Invector-Plus choke tubes.

The Maxus Sporting Carbon Fiber has a silver and carbon fiber finish on its receiver and stock and forearm and carbon fiber finish on its barrel. It comes with five screw-in choke tubes and an Inflex Technology recoil pad.

As always, there are new Citori over-and-unders.

The Citori 625 Feather Three Barrel Set comes in a leather-trimmed case with 26 or 28 inch lightweight profile barrels in 20 and 28-gauge and .410-bore. The aluminum receiver has a walnut forearm with a Schnabel tip.

Browning Maxus Sporting Carbon Fiber.

A leather case holds the Citori 625 Sporting Four Barrel Set with 30-inch barrels in 12, 20 and 28 gauge and .410. Each barrel set has five screw in choke tubes and a HiViz fiber optic front sight. The 12-gauge barrels have a tapered floating top rib. The 20, 28 and .410 have a ventilated top and side rib. The 12 and 20-gauge barrels are ported.

Remington 870 Express Tactical A-TACS Camo.

Remington 870 Super Mag Turkey-Predator Camo.

Remington 870 Bone Collector.

Browning Cynergy Classic Feather Combo.

Mossberg Slugger with LPA trigger.

Ithaca's Phoenix 12-gauge over-and-under. The gun has no soldered parts.

Blaser F3 Super Trap.

Browning Citori 625 four-barrel set.

Browning Citori Micro.

Browning Citori WHite Lightning.

Browning Citori 625 three-barrel set.

The Winchester SX3 All-Purpose.

The Citori 625 Sporting Golden Clays is chambered in 12 gauge with a 2-3/4-inch chamber. Its steel receiver is finished in silver nitride with gold engraving of a game bird transforming into a clay target. The stock has a gloss oil finish on high grade walnut with tight radius grip. Lengthened forcing cones go along with five choke tubes.

The Citori Lightning's steel receiver has a blued finish and engraving and a gloss finish on its walnut stock and forearm. The Lightning is chambered in 12, 20 and 28 gauge and .410 and comes with three choke tubes. The Citori White Lightning is pretty much the same gun with a silver nitride finish on the receiver.

The Citori Micro has a steel receiver. Its 24 or 26-inch barrels are chambered in three-inch 20 or 12-gauge. The stock is short with a 13-3/4-inch length of pull to match the slender forearm.

More than a few Browning guns are now stocked with a Dura-Touch Armor Coated composite stock and forearm covered with camouflage:

• *The Gold Light and National Wild Turkey Federation's Gold Light 10-Gauge are covered with Mossy Oak Break-Up Infinity.*

• *The 12-gauge 3 and 3½-inch Browning Pump Shotguns are also covered with Break-Up Infinity camo. The BPS Rifled Deer 12-gauge has a composite stock while the 20-gauge version has a wood stock. Both guns have 22-inch barrels and a cantilever base for mounting optics.*

• *The Cynergy over-and-under 12-gauge with a 3-1/2-inch chamber likewise has a composite stock covered with Mossy Oak Infinity or Duck Blind camo.*

Browning's Cynergy line of over-and-unders is starting to rival the number of its long-established Citori models. The Cynergy Classic Feather Combo has an aluminum receiver and comes with 27-inch barrels in 3-inch 20 gauge and 2-3/4-inch 28 gauge. Three choke tubes come with each barrel set and the whole package fits in a leather case. The Cynergy Classic Field has a steel receiver with a silver nitride finish. The 12 gauge model has engraved pheasants on the left side of the receiver and mallards on the right. The 20 and 28 gauges and .410 are engraved with quail and grouse. The Cynergy Classic Sporting with Adjustable Comb has all that plus ported barrels and ventilated top and side ribs.

The Winchester SX3 Comact.

Browning Citori 625
Sporting Golden Clays.

Mossberg Mini
Super Bantam.

Benelli Vinci – just as it comes from the box.

The innovative
Rossi Circuit Judge
revolving shotgun.

Benelli Xplor. A fine-handling
shotgun.

Mossberg Combo
with LPA trigger.

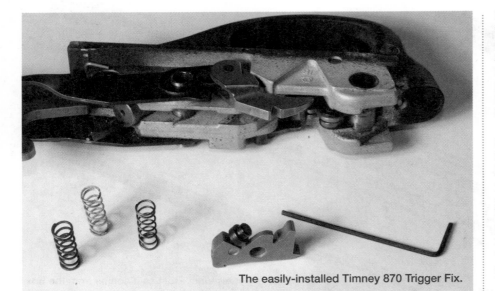

The easily-installed Timney 870 Trigger Fix.

ITHACA

Ithaca is putting its Ladies Stock on its Model 37 pump 20 gauges. The stock has a little less pitch on the butt, a bit more toe out and drop of the comb heel to fit a woman. The gun comes with a 14.25-inch length of pull, but Ithaca will cut the stock to any length requested when ordering a gun. Ithaca's Mike Farrell said, "I rejected the first four forearms they brought into my office because they were all too big." The forearm Farrell finally approved is just large enough to fill the hand, yet keep the fingers away from the barrel.

My wife, Gail, picked up a Model 37 Ultralight with a Ladies Stock to shoot a few clay targets thrown by Farrell. Being a typical male, I coached her on fixing her focus on the target and to bring the gun up to the target and fire. Farrell leaned over and said, "Why don't you just let her shoot." As fast as Farrell could push the release button on the electric trap, Gail dusted nine targets in a row with the little Ultralight 20-gauge.

As Gail kept shooting, I took the hint and walked over to look at Ithaca's Phoenix 12-gauge over-and-under that is in production after a year and some of final development. Ithaca starts with a 15-lb. length of steel to make the over-and-under's barrels. Two pounds of steel remain by the time the barrels are final machined. All that machining leaves behind integral dovetails at the muzzle that lock the barrels together and stanchions for the replaceable rib that is held in place with one screw. The breech end of the barrels are held with a tubular connector. "There is no solder on these barrels," Farrell said, "and they

will never shoot loose or move or warp due to heat or just about anything else."

It was kind of noisy trying to talk with Farrell, as Gail was in the background, still busting targets with the Ultralight.

MOSSBERG

Mossberg has reduced the size of its Youth model pump and called it the 510 Mini. The .410 and 20-gauge Mini both have 18½-inch barrels and a length of pull of 10-1/2 or 11-1/2 inches, 1-1/2 inches shorter than the standard Youth Bantam models. The forearm is also scaled down from the traditional youth size and is easy for short arms to reach.

Mossberg first put its adjustable Lightning Bolt Action triggers on all its

bolt-action centerfire rifles. Now the trigger is available on its pump-action guns and is called the Lightning Pump Action (LPA) trigger. The LPA's pull can be adjusted from under three to seven pounds. The trigger is featured on the Mossberg 500, 535 and 835 Turkey, Slugster and Combo models.

The Just In Case Mossberg 500 pump breaks down into three pieces to store in soft case. To keep it compact, the gun has a synthetic pistol grip stock and 18-1/2-inch cylinder bore barrel. The grip attaches to the receiver with a slotted head bolt. Assembled, the gun measures only 28-3/4 inches in length and holds five rounds in the magazine and one up the spout. Such a compact package stores out of the way in a boat or truck, but is there just in case you need it.

REMINGTON

Remington continues to add models to its Model 887 Nitro Mag with three new pumps.

The Nitro Mag Bone Collector Edition has a 26-inch barrel with a HiViz fiber optic front sight and is emblazoned with that TV show's whitetail skull logo. The gun has a 12-gauge 3½-inch chamber and its pump action insures it will cycle every type of shot and slug load.

The 887 Nitro Mag Combo is made for waterfowl and turkeys. A 22-inch barrel for turkeys has HiViz fiber-optic rifle sights and a Super Full Turkey Rem Choke tube. The 28-inch waterfowl barrel has a front HiViz fiber optic sight and an Extended Waterfowl choke tube.

The forearm on the Ithaca Model 37 Ultralight with Ladies Stock is just big enough for the hand to hold and keep the fingers away the barrel.

The Model 887 Nitro Mag Tactical has an 18-1/2-inch barrel with a clamped on rail for mounting a flashlight or other accessories. A tube extension increases magazine capacity to six rounds. At the muzzle are a HiViz fiber optic sight and an extended, ported tactical Rem choke. Sling swivel studs are built-in the stock and on the forearm.

The 870 Express Super Magnum Turkey/Waterfowl is covered with Mossy Oak Bottomland camo. Its 26-inch barrel is chambered for 3-1/2-inch shells and has includes Wingmaster HD Waterfowl and Turkey Extra Full Rem choke tubes. A HiViz fiber optic front sight and receiver drilled and tapped for an optic sight tops it off.

The 870 SPS Super Magnum Turkey/Predator is mounted with a TruGlo 30mm Red/Green Dot Scope. The ambidextrous ShurShot vertical grip stock has soft molded-in panels for a sure hold and its 20-inch barrel has a Wingmaster HD Turkey/Predator Rem choke tube.

A black padded sling and Wingmaster HD™ Turkey/Predator Rem Choke are included.

The Tactical A-Tacs Camo dresses the Model 870 Express Tactical A-Tacs. The Tactical has an 18-1/2-inch barrel with an extended, ported Tactical Rem choke. The SpeedFeed IV pistol grip stock provides a firm grip and a SuperCell recoil pad dampens recoil. A fully adjustable XS Ghost Ring Sight is mounted on a Picatinny rail on the receiver rail with white bead front sight. The gun holds seven rounds of 2-3/4-inch shells with the two-shot magazine extension.

The Model 11-87 has been banging away in the duck swamps and pheasant fields for decades. This year the 11-87 returns to its roots with the Sportsman Field wearing a satin-finished walnut stock and forearm with cut checkering. A nickel-plated bolt and gold-plated trigger accent the satin blue barrel and receiver. The 12-gauge model has a 28-inch barrel with a ventilated rib and modified choke tube. The 20-gauge has a 26-inch barrel.

In Remington-speak, the word "Super" means a 12-gauge 3-1/2-inch gun. Remington has several new Super 11-87s. The 11-87 Sportsman ShurShot Super Magnum Turkey has a ShurShot pistol-grip stock and is covered with Realtree APG HD camo. Its 23-inch barrel has fully adjustable TruGlo rifle sights and a Wingmaster Turkey choke tube. The 11-87 Sportsman Super Magnum comes with HiViz front fiber optic sight with interchangeable light pipes on its 28-inch barrel. The 11-87 Sportsman Super Magnum Waterfowl includes an Adjustable Length of Pull Kit to vary pull one inch. It also has a HiViz front fiber optic sight with interchangeable light pipes on its 28-inch barrel. All 11-87 Supers now have rubber overmolded grip panels on the stock and forearm, SuperCell recoil pad and a black padded sling.

ROSSI

Rossi's sister company, Taurus, has been backordered on its Judge .410/.45 Colt revolver ever since it was introduced several years ago. Rossi has run with the Judge and made a long gun out of it and called it the Circuit Judge. The revolving cylinder gun is available with an 18-1/2-inch smoothbore or a rifled barrel and weighs 4-3/4-pounds. The Circuit Judge has a blued finish and a hardwood stock with a Monte Carlo comb. A fiber optic front sight, recoil pad and transfer bar safety system finishes it.

TIMNEY TRIGGERS

The 870 Trigger Fix lightens the pull and removes the creep from the trigger on Remington 870 pumps. The Trigger Fix comes with a sear, light, medium, or heavy pull weight springs and a hex head wrench. I put in the new sear and a spring in my 870 in about fifteen minutes. I drifted out the two pins that hold the trigger assembly in the 870 and then the pin that holds the sear in place. Then I slipped in the new sear with the light spring and tapped the sear pin back in place. The original sear and spring in the trigger produced a pull with a lot of mush and a four pound pull. The new sear and spring reduced the pull to two pounds and removed all the creep. A few turns in of the adjustment screw increased the pull weight to 2-1/2 pounds, just right.

WEATHERBY

The Synthetic Youth 20 gauge semiauto weighs 5-3/4 pounds and has a 12-1/2 inch length of pull and a 24-inch barrel. That light weight is the result of an aluminum receiver and a synthetic stock and forearm. The barrel bore is chrome lined and comes with improved cylinder, modified and full choke tubes.

The PA-08 Synthetic pump shotgun has a black injection-molded stock and metal with matte black finish. Like its partner the Upland, with walnut stock and forearm, the Synthetic is a 12 gauge with a 3-inch chamber and a 26 or 28-inch barrel and a weight of 6-1/2 pounds. Improved cylinder, modified and full choke tubes are supplied.

The PA459 pump is a home defense shotgun. Its vertical rubber grip buttstock makes it quick to point and shoot. Its forearm incorporates a rail to clamp on accessories such as flashlight. A second rail is screwed on the receiver and is mounted with a ghost ring sight adjustable for windage and elevation. The blade front sight has a fiber optic pin. The 19-inch barrel is chrome lined and fitted with an extended and ported cylinder choke tube.

WINCHESTER

Winchester has several new variations of its Super X3 autoloader for big game and bird hunting and target shooting. The Super X3 All-Purpose Field 12-gauge has a 3-1/2-inch chamber. Its gas-operated Active Valve System cycles target to magnum shells in combination with full, modified and improved cylinder choke tubes in 26- or 28-inch barrels. Its stock is adjustable with two length of pull spacers and drop and cast adjustment shims, which are included. Mossy Oak Break-Up Infinity camo, with Dura-Touch Armor Coating, covers the entire gun. The Super X3 Compact Field 12- and 20-gauge models have 26 or 28-inch barrels with a 13-inch length of pull on the stock. A supplied spacer increases that length to 13-1/4-inches. Cast and drop shims are also included. The gun's chamber and bore are chrome-plated and the bolt, slide and carrier are nickel-plated. An Inflex Technology recoil pad helps dampen recoil.

The Super X3 Rifled Deer Cantilever has a 22-inch rifled barrel and is covered in Mossy Oak Breakup Infinity on the metal and composite stock.

The Super X3 Sporting Adjustable has a walnut stock with an adjustable comb. The Sporting 12-gauge has a 2-3/4-inch chamber, ambidextrous safety and Pachmayr Decelerator recoil pad. Five choke tubes are included.

The Super X3 Walnut Field 20-gauge weighs 6-1/2 pounds with a 28-inch barrel. The 12-gauge model weighs only 7 pounds. That light weight is the result of an aluminum receiver and magazine tuber and slender barrel with a trim forearm. A Pachmayr Decelerator recoil pad is installed and two stock spacers can lengthen pull.

AIRGUNS

BY TOM CACECI

The 2010 SHOT Show had many new products of interest to anyone using an airgun. Modern airguns are serious, high-performance tools for target competition or sport hunting. New technology and production methods have created air weapons that are affordable, easy to use, and typically free from most of the restrictions imposed on firearms. At the same time, they're powerful enough to use effectively in pest control operations or serious small game hunting. What's out there today isn't a "kid's BB gun" any more.

AIR ARMS from the United Kingdom has introduced the EV-Z MARK IV rifle for target work. It has an adjustable palm rest and a poplar stock that can be finished in a wide variety of colors to suit the taste of the buyer.

BEEMAN, another UK manufacturer no stranger to US airgunners, has introduced the dual-caliber ELITE X-2 rifle with interchangeable barrels.

BELTFED is a brand-new name in the airgun world, with a product that is unique. Everyone loves full-auto fire: while BB guns and softair guns simulate it, this company's .22 is a CO_2-powered pellet gun, firing actual pellets at the astonishing rate of 12 shots per second or 720 rounds per minute. As the name implies, it's belt fed: the belt is enclosed in a drum-type housing that gives the Beltfed the look of a "Tommy Gun" to go with its performance. Power is provided by a large CO_2 reservoir that connects to a tank adapter. Magazine capacity is up to 125 rounds, and velocities are comparable to other CO_2 powered guns. No word yet on when this product will be on dealer shelves.

BSA is one of the best-known brands of airguns in the world, usually associated with pump-pneumatic and break-barrel rifles, but they have introduced a new line of PCP (precharged pneumatic) rifles to the American

The display screen used on Daystate rifles, and their patented Harper valve system.

HARPER PATENT
MAP COMPENSATED TECHNOLOGY

WP.230 BAR

Daystate

be determined but it will be among the lowest priced PCP rifles on the market, no doubt making it even more attractive to new airgun enthusiasts.

CROSMAN, America's most famous airgun manufacturer, displayed many new products, and an entirely new technology for break-barrel guns, the Nitro Piston Magnum power plant in their Trail NPXL series rifles, available in .177, .22, and now .25 calibers. The Nitro Piston mechanism replaces the conventional spring of the typical break-barrel gun. The heart of the Nitro Piston is a gas-filled cylinder, which offers numerous advantages compared to a spring. Crosman claims it is 70% quieter than a conventional spring, requires less cocking force to achieve the same level of power, and most importantly, can be cocked well in advance of shooting. In a spring-powered rifle, cocking too far in advance of the shot will result in the

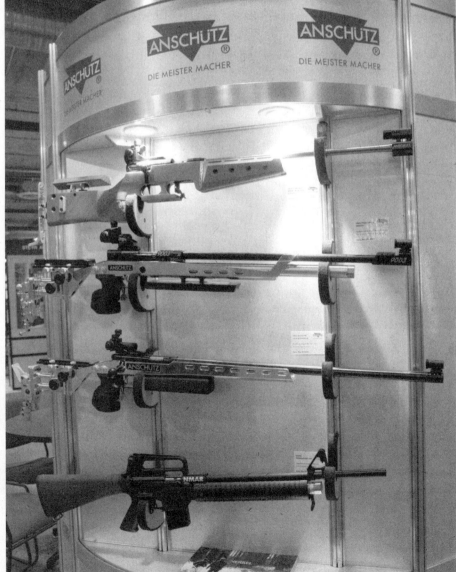

(top) Alan George, General manager of Air Arms, holds their EV-2 Mark IV rifle, a target gun with adjustable palm rest and a poplar stock that can be finished in many different colors.

(above) Dani Navikas of Beeman Precision Airguns displays the X12.5, a 1250 FPS rifle in their line.

(left) Anschutz is a major name in shooting, and have a line of airguns to complement their firearms, which have long dominated the field of biathlon competition. Anschutz expects the use of airguns in biathlon to continue to grow, as they permit younger shooters to enter the sport.

Top to bottom: The Air Wolf MCT, the Air Ranger, the Huntsman Midas Grade, and the Mk 4 from Daystate.

spring taking a "set" and the result is diminished power: not so with the Nitro Piston system. The gas cylinder is also unaffected by outside temperature so that velocities are consistent from shot to shot. Another advantage is a reduction in recoil compared to spring power.

Following up on the success of their BENJAMIN Discovery and Marauder series, Crosman has brought out a .25 caliber version of the Marauder, their top-of-the-line PCP rifle. The new Marauder operates at 2500 PSI, moving a heavy .25 caliber pellet at 850+ fps, generating 45 foot-pounds of muzzle energy, a significant increase over the .22 caliber version introduced last year. It has a "choked" (tapered bore) barrel to enhance accuracy and uniformity of velocity, will run on CO_2 as well as air (the so-called "Dual Fuel" option), and a built in pressure gauge. The handsome hardwood stock is checkered, and a two-stage, adjustable trigger is standard equipment. The .25 Marauder is intended for the varmint hunter and pest

Crosman introduced the Silhouette, a PCP handgun for target shooting.

control airgunner who needs high levels of power; the big pellet is more effective, with superior knock-down power for larger animals.

Crosman hasn't neglected the air-powered handgunners, either. They have introduced two new PCP pistols, the Silhouette and a one-hand version of the Marauder. The Silhouette is offered in .177, the Marauder pistol in .22. The 10-shot Marauder pistol utilizes the same internal technology and sophisticated trigger system that the rifle version does, and Crosman offers a detachable shoulder stock as an optional accessory. The smaller-caliber Silhouette has a barrel made by Lothar Walther and Crosman claims it will shoot quarter-inch groups at 30 meters. Velocity of the Silhouette is approximately 450 fps. It meets both International Handgun Metallic Silhouette Association and NRA standards for competition.

Crosman Corporation also has partnered with REMINGTON (which also owns Marlin) to produce new branded products. The MARLIN Cowboy is a traditionally-styled lever-action BB gun with an "Old West" look and feel that will appeal to kids. It has numerous safety features that guns of a previous era lacked, though: notably an anti-snap-back system to prevent the cocking lever from pinching hands if it's accidentally released. With a velocity of 350 fps, the Marlin Cowboy is an ideal entry point into shooting for young people.

A Remington-brand break-barrel rifle using Crosman's Nitro Piston technology will be available with a number of features to appeal to the small game hunter: a synthetic all-weather stock with a ventilated butt plate, enhanced trigger, and a Crosman CenterPoint 3-9x40 scope.

Crosman is also producing airsoft guns under the BUSHMASTER brand, with applications to gaming and law enforcement training. The Bushmaster Predator and Carbon 15 airsoft guns are very realistic electrically-driven rifles suited to law enforcement training scenarios. The Game Face airsoft line has also been expanded to include three very realistic models marketed to the gamers.

(top) Named for the Outdoor Channel's TV series, the "Bone Collector" is new from Gamo.

(left) The Hatsan rifles feature the "Quattro Trigger" for improved pull and crisper let-off than is typical of break-barrel rifles.

{above} Hatsan also has an extensive line of conventional spring-pistol break-barrel designs.

{below} The prototype for Cometa's new value-priced PCP rifle, which is slated to enter the US market in the Spring of 2010.

Crosman has introduced Verdict Marker Pellets for use in all airsoft guns. These are coated with a chalk-like substance that leaves a mark when it impacts a player at 60 fps or more – a feature especially useful in law enforcement training activities, where there must be confirmation of a hit. The Verdict pellets are seamless and environmentally friendly, as they are biodegradable. Biodegradable pellets are also sold under the Game Face label.

Located in the UK, DAYSTATE is one of the world's premier manufacturers.

They are offering rifles on the cutting edge of airgun technology that incorporate proven systems and first-class workmanship. This year they have introduced the Air Wolf MCT, a PCP rifle, available in both .177 and .22 caliber. In the UK, air rifles are limited by law to energy levels of 12 foot-pounds or less, but the Air Wolf is intended for the American market and is far more powerful, producing muzzle energy of 17

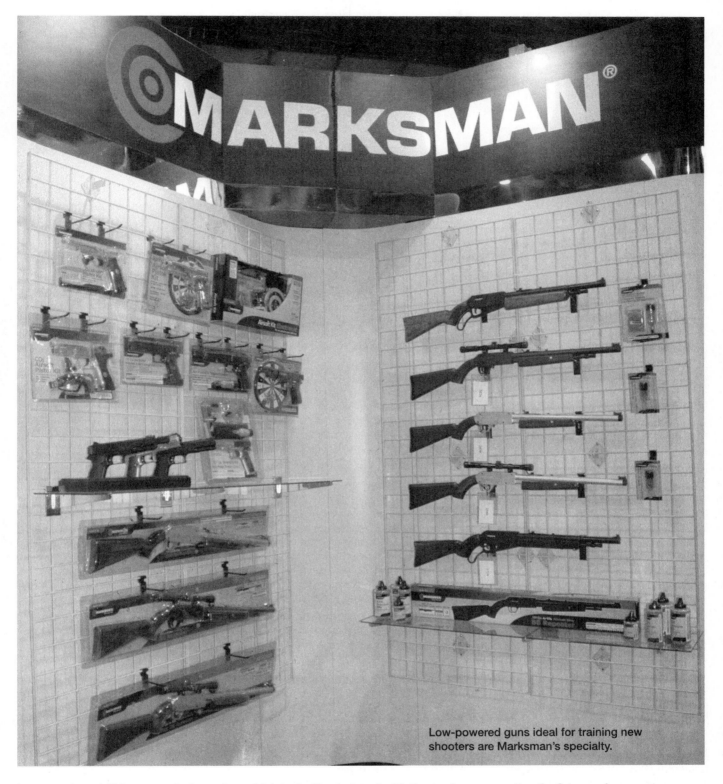

Low-powered guns ideal for training new shooters are Marksman's specialty.

foot-pounds and 40 foot-pounds depending on which caliber is chosen. The Air Wolf uses a patented Harper "slingshot" valve, designed to reduce the "hammer bounce" usually associated with PCP rifles and to permit very high power levels thanks to the use of what Daystate calls "Map Compensated Technology" (MCT) system. The Air Wolf is a very high-tech rifle, designed with the needs of the airgun hunter and field target shooter in mind.

The Air Wolf MCT is a 10-shot repeater with a 230-Bar (3335 PSI) air tank that can provide up to 70 shots at 40 foot-pounds and as many as 400 at 12 foot-pounds before a refill is needed. MCT uses an on-board computer to monitor the firing cycle on a micro-second basis, feeding the information back into the main firing valve control system to produce consistent velocity from one shot to the next, by adjusting the valve output and lock time. Continual regulation of the power output results in a flat power curve as well as absolutely controlled air release. No air is "wasted" by

Justin Biddle, Marketing Manager for Umarex USA, displays the new "EBOS" (Electronic Burst of Steel) CO2-powered full-auto BB gun.

this very precise, computer-controlled air regulation, producing more shots per tank. An LCD display screen shows the rifle's status continually.

The on-board computer also permits the shooter to choose one of eight distinct firing modes and to choose one of two pre-programmed power levels. Another version (cataloged as the Air Wolf MVT) permits the shooter can select the level of velocity and power desired. The Air Wolf is available in a left-hand model, as well as in rifle or carbine length. Other features include a sound moderator system, adjustable electronic trigger, and a keyed safety "Power Isolator" switch.

The MCT technology is also used in Daystate's MK4 iS-S and ST rifles, also available in rifle or carbine length. The MK4 series guns are fully programmable, and equipped with handsome walnut stocks, with the option of conventional (S) or thumbhole (ST) styles.

Also on display was the latest version of Daystate's famous Huntsman rifle, the Huntsman Midas LE Grade. This beautifully upgraded Huntsman is to be made in very limited quantities: only 100 will be produced for worldwide distribution. The number to be sent to the USA has not yet been determined. Airguns of Arizona, Daystate's importer, said they have ordered 25 of the Midas grade rifles but don't have a delivery date yet.

GAMO, one of the world's leading manufacturers, has several new break-barrel guns and high-tech pellets that provide a new level of performance. Chief among these is the Gamo Bone Collector, a break-barrel rifle designed in collaboration with Michael Waddell and Travis "T Bone" Turner of the Outdoor Channels TV series of that name. The Bone Collector rifles are a limited release, with a special Hunter Green synthetic stock handsomely accented with grey rubber inserts. The Bone Collector logo is emblazoned on each side of the stock. Bone Collectors are available in both .177 and .22, with muzzle velocities of up to 1250 and 950 fps respectively using Gamo's new PBA pellets (see below). The rifles are fitted with integral sound suppressors and a special 3-9x40 scope as well as open sights.

Gamo's new products also include the a new series, the SOCOM Tactical, Carbine, and Extreme guns. These all utilize an advanced power plant to drive pellets up to an amazing 1600 fps in the Extreme. The SOCOM Tactical, offered in .177, has an adjustable cheekpiece on its synthetic stock, a molded fore-end and a palm swell. It is fitted with a scope as well as open sights and includes as well a fully adjustable laser and light for night use. The SOCOM Carbine in .177 is a fast-handling high-powered rifle fitted with a scope only; it too has an adjustable stock. The SOCOM Extreme has taken the break-barrel rifle to a new level, with a completely redesigned power plant that has been tuned for maximum velocity with the PBA .177 pellets. The composite bull barrel reduces cocking force and the near vertical pistol grip assures excellent control. The 3-9x40 scope provided includes red, green, and blue illuminated reticles.

For hunters, Gamo has brought out the Rocket series, designed for high performance at moderate price. In .177, they generate velocities of 1250+ fps, and are fitted with 4x32 scopes from the factory. Stock options include black or camouflage synthetic. The light weight and high performance of these sporting guns make them ideal for the small game airgun hunter.

In keeping with the current trend towards big bores in airguns, Gamo has introduced their Hunter Extreme "Cannon" Big Bore in .25 caliber. This scoped rifle has a high-grade beech stock and a 3-9x40 scope, and claims 1000 fps with PBA ammunition. It's Gamo's ultimate product for hunting and varmint control.

High velocity is the key to airgun utility: the slogan of the airgunner is "Speed Kills," and Gamo has taken steps to produce special pellets with lower weight for enhanced ballistic performance. The heart of this new pellet technology is the Platinum Ballistic Alloy (PBA) introduced in 2005 and incorporated into several new pellet designs. PBA is lighter than lead, offering the potential for up to 30% higher speeds. Pellets made from PBA are available in several styles, including a domed all-PBA version, and two specially-tipped varieties. PBA pellets are made in .177, .22, and .25 and are suitable for use in all makes of guns.

In addition to the domed version, Gamo has brought out the tipped Blue Flame and Glow Fire pellets. The Blue Flame is made in .177 using the PBA alloy; the Glow Fire is a lead pellet. Both are made in .177 at this time. Both the Blue Flame and Glow Fire pellets incorporate a polymer tip, for reduced weight and higher velocities. The Blue Flame's tip initiate expansion on impact, coupling high velocity and high terminal energy for use on small and medium sized game. The Glow Fire lead pellet is intended for the night hunter: its polymer tip literally glows in the dark after exposure to light, to facilitate loading a rifle at night.

STOEGER is a new name in the airgun field, though not to American shooters. They are importing an attractively-priced line of break-barrel guns made in China. The Stoeger X-Series rifles run from the X-5 to the X-20, the numbers indicating top velocity levels. The X-5 is rated at 800 fps, the X-10 and X-20 at 1200 fps and the X-50 at 1500 fps (all ratings listed are with alloy pellets).

All the X-Series rifles are in .177 caliber, and have an ambidextrous safety catch, adjustable rear sights, and an adjustable two-stage trigger. Stock

options include wood, black synthetic, and Advantage Timber HD camouflage. The X-10 and X-20 can be fitted with an optional scope sight. This range of airguns is expected to cover the needs of new shooters, youths, and small game hunting.

UMAREX has teamed up with Ruger to produce a youth-oriented spring-air gun carrying the Ruger brand name. The

Ruger Explorer Youth rifle is light, moderately powered, and sized to smaller shooters; it incorporates several safety features that make it ideal for training new shooters. The Explorer weighs less than 4-1/2 pounds and is only 37 inches long, sized to fit smaller frames. Its synthetic thumbhole stock is ambidextrous; the power plant drives a pellet at under 500 fps and requires a cocking effort of

Walther of Germany makes a line of precision target air rifles as well as their famous firearms.

Produced by Crosman, this traditional Western-style Marlin BB gun is sure to be a hit with youngsters.

control gas release, and three modes of operation: single shot, a four-shot burst, and an eight-shot burst. In single-fire mode this gun generates 540 fps with BBs and boasts tactical railing, a removable forearm grip, and an adjustable rear sight. Power is provided by an 88-gram CO_2 capsule concealed in the gun's grip.

Also out under the Umarex brand is another tactical style BB gun, the Steel Storm, featuring a six-shot burst mode, a 300-shot reservoir, and tactical railing for mounting accessories. The Steel Storm uses a pair of 12-gram CO_2 capsules and can generate speeds up to 430 fps in single-shot mode.

Realism is part of the fun of shooting BB guns, and Umarex caters to that need with their new High Power Pistol (HPP), which routes some of the CO_2 propellant into a circuit to "blow back" the slide, producing a very realistic recoil feel. This is an invaluable training feature. Despite using gas to simulate recoil, the HPP moves a BB out at a very respectable 410 fps.

Umarex's entry into the "ultra-fast pellet" competition is the new RWS Hypermax alloy pellet, in .22 caliber.

16-1/2 pounds, half the normal amount. Importantly, the Explorer is equipped with a trigger barrel-safety system to prevent the barrel from slamming closed if the trigger is pulled while it's open, eliminating the chance of a finger injury. Very competitively priced, and with a "name" label, it should appeal to new shooters and their parents or coaches.

Umarex has also teamed up with BROWNING and has expanded their line of pistols with the Browning Model 800 Mag spring-air handgun in .22 caliber, complementing the .177 model already in the line. Like the .177 version, the Model 800 has an ergonomic ambidextrous grip and recoilless action which reduces the amount of recoil produced by the movement of the spring piston. It attains

a velocity of 600 fps in .22 caliber, and to reduce cocking effort, includes a cocking assist handle. Other features of the Model 800 Mag include an automatic safety, fiber optic sights, and a synthetic ergonomic pistol grip.

Umarex also makes CO_2 powered guns, with licensed branding from other famous companies. New this year is the MP5K-PDW in their HK-branded line, a tactical-style rifle shooting BBs at 400 fps. The COLT Defender is yet another CO_2-powered BB gun, a close copy of the scaled-down M1911-style Colt product. The Umarex copy has double-action-only lockwork and a maximum speed of 440 fps from its 4.3-inch barrel.

Umarex sells CO_2-powered guns under its own name as well, and has several new entries into this fun-shooting segment of the market. The tactical style Electronic Burst of Steel (EBOS) semi-automatic has an electronic trigger to

Predator International is importing the Polymag pellets, in various calibers: this one is not for 155mm howitzer, it's a display of their polymer-tipped product!

Sunny Sun of Xisico USA, with the bamboo-stocked Model 206.

This follows on the very successful .177 version and is intended for use in all brands of .22 caliber guns.

It's no secret that China is one of the largest sources of airguns. Given their enormous domestic market and their power in export sales, neither is it a surprise that new players and new companies come into the game every year. XISICO AIRGUNS is now competing in the USA, with a break-barrel rifle and pistol as new products.

The Model 206 break-barrel gun made by this company has a stock made from bamboo. Bamboo is an excellent stock material, thanks to its density and hardness: the arrangement of the fibers in this woody material give it extraordinary strength in compression. Bamboo is also capable of being worked almost like metal to facilitate inletting and precision fit. The companion piece to the Model 206 is a break-barrel pistol with a Picatinny rail and an automatic safety feature.

Xisico has an under-lever rifle, the Model 46U with a quick-release lever lock, an auto safety, and a pellet speed of 1000 fps.

They are also producing and exporting their first CO_2 powered gun, the Model 60C. The model designation is obvious when you look at it: it bears a startling external resemblance to the famous Marlin Model 60 autoloading .22

rifle! This too has an automatic safety and it boats an adjustable trigger.

Turkey has recently emerged as source of economically-priced, high-value firearms, and their industry is turning its attention to the airgun market as well. ARMED is producing two break-barrel guns, the Model 6 and the Model 6W, the latter having a wood stock. To date there is no importer bringing Armed guns to the USA but they hope to be selling here in the next year.

HATSAN, a Turkish company better known in the USA for its line of shotguns, is now producing break barrel rifles. The Hatsan Model 88 features a specially designed Quattro Trigger system for improved pull; and also a power plant with an integral recoil reduction system. The mechanically identical Model 88 TH has a thumbhole stock.

Stefan Gervasoni, Export Manager for Daystate in the UK, holds the Grand Prix, their top-of-the-line rifle for field target shooting.

With all due respect to my able Contributing Editors, I'd like to note a handful of new products that tripped my personal trigger during the last 12 months. You can read more about a few of them in other areas of this book, but this is my take.

EDITOR'S PICKS

BY DAN SHIDELER

CAD rendering of the new Merwin, Hulbert .44 Pocket Army. Note the historically-correct skullpopper butt.

RETURN OF THE MERWIN, HULBERT

One of the biggest news items, at least in my worldview, is the return of the famous Merwin, Hulbert large-frame revolver. The original M,H revolvers were made by Hopkins & Allen beginning around 1876 and marketed under the Merwin, Hulbert name until around 1890; they were the fourth best-selling large revolver in the days of westward expansion, trailing Colt, S&W and Remington.

The best-known Merwin, Hulbert is probably the .44 Pocket Army, a chunky little spud chambered in .44-40 which, like all Merwin, Hulbert large-frame double-action centerfires, features a unique – you better believe it's unique! – pivoting barrel assembly that acts as a simultaneous cartridge extractor. If you've ever examined an original Merwin, Hulbert Pocket Army, you're not likely to forget the experience.

And now, thanks to computer-aided machining technology, the Merwin, Hulbert .44 Pocket Army is being remanufactured by Michael Blank's Merwin, Hulbert & Company right here in the USA. According to my contact at M,H& Co., the .44 Pocket Army is the first model to be released, followed by the Frontier Army 2nd Model and 3rd Model Double Action. M,H&Co. also tell me that they have added A-Square safari rifles and ammunition manufacturing to their production mix, with the august personage of Col. Art Alphin himself heading their R&D/New Product Development effort. Heady stuff indeed!

The new Merwin, Hulberts are expected to hit the market in 2010 with a base retail proce of $1250, not bad at all as such things go. You can learn more – and even pre-order your new Merwin, Hulbert – at the company's website, http://www.merwinhulbertco.com.

The Minie Ball Pipe by J.M. Boswell.

J.M. BOSWELL MINIE BALL PIPE

My long-time readers (both of them) know that I am an inveterate pipe smoker. I will now pause for 30 seconds so you can berate me and cite a litany of dreadful statistics that show that pipe smoking is not good for me.

Point taken – and disregarded. I don't ask much of a pipe: it should stay cool all the way through the smoke; it should break in quickly; it should draw smoothly even if I've packed it too tightly. That's why I prefer Boswell pipes, handmade by J.M. Boswell and his son Dan of Chambersburg, Pennsylvania. J.M. has been making handcrafted and custom pipes for 35 years, and I'd say he's just about perfected his art. For my money, they're among the Top Ten finest makes in the world.

I own several Boswells, but one of my favorites is his Minie Ball Pipe. The story goes that during the Civil War, soldiers

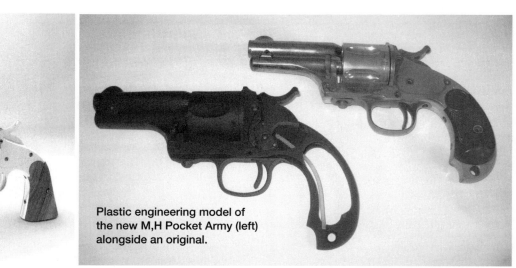

CAD modeling of the upcoming Merwin, Hulbert Model 2 Frontier Army.

Plastic engineering model of the new M,H Pocket Army (left) alongside an original.

The Rossi Model 720 in .44 Special, an appealing revolver on the used-gun market.

who were hard up for a smoke used to bore a hole in the hollow base of a lead 58-caliber Minie Ball, insert a straw or reed, and puff away happily. I can't say I particularly like the sound of smoking a lead pipe, so I was delighted to learn that J.M. has improved on the concept by making his Minie Ball Pipe out of briar and fitting a vulcanite churchwarden stem to it. It makes for a delightful short smoke.

J.M.'s pipe is also quite a bit larger than a real Minie ball, and its grease grooves are not quite to scale. But as a smoking pipe it's as clean and cool as a good Dunhill, and that's saying plenty. If you're a pipe smoker or a Civil War reenactor, you'll want to try this pipe. Prices hover around $90, and that includes an ounce of your choice of the Boswells' excellent blends. For more information, visit boswellpipes.com.

ROSSI 720 .44 SPECIAL REVOLVER

Last summer I stumbled onto what I consider an excellent little revolver, the Rossi Model 720 five-shooter in .44 Special. I'm the first to admit that early Rossis may have left a bit to be desired, but later-production Rossis strike me as well-built guns. (Rossi is now owned by Taurus, don'tcha know.)

The Model 720 has a 3-inch barrel and a fluted cylinder and is made from stainless steel throughout. Dimensionally, it approximates a S&W K-frame, though S&W never offered a .44 in that medium frame size. Some Model 720s left the Rossi factory with 3.5-inch barrels and

unfluted cylinders, probably an attempt to tamp down recoil a bit. Mine has an adjustable rear sight, but some had a fixed groove rear.

The Model 720 has been out of production, sad to say, for at least since 2003 but examples still turn up on the used-gun market. I got mine, a lightly-used example, for $225, which isn't at all bad for any steel-framed .44 Special. As you remember, the K-frame S&W Combat Magnum didn't really hold up well under the battering of full-house .357 loads, so I use the old 246-gr. pointed lead .44 Special load in my 720, or a 200-gr. Cowboy Action load. Recoil is gratifyingly stout, something like a .45 hardball out of a 1911.

.44 Special snubbies are a boutique item, with the market currently dominated by variations on the Charter Arms Bulldog. But if you for some reason want an adjustable-sight .44 carry gun with better than average fit and finish, don't automatically turn up your nose at a Rossi 720 at a good price. I used to, and I was just plain wrong.

DAISY MODEL 25 BB GUN

I have a soft spot for Daisy airguns, so I was happy learn that Daisy has brought back the hallowed Model 25 pump BB gun.

For those of you who came in late, the Model 25 was introduced way back when Hector was a pup, back in 1915. With a muzzle velocity of around 400 fps, it quickly gained a reputation as a hard-hitter. The grand old Model 25 had a run that lasted until 1979, with two commemorative editions being released in 1986 and 1994.

Now Daisy has brought back the Model 25 – not as a special-run promotional but as a legitimate production item. The "new" Model 25 is made offshore to Daisy's specifications and features all the goodies that we older kids remember: the scissors-jointed pump action

(which can pinch the unwary fingertip), the 50-shot magazine tube, the flip-up peep rear sight with choice of U-notch or aperture. Daisy lists the Model 25's velocity as 350 fps, which is just about perfect for small birds, rodents, aluminum cans and all sorts of paper targets.

The Model 25's buttstock and pump handle are made of an attractively-stained oriental mystery wood and its receiver is roll-engraved.

The reintroduced Daisy Model 25 50-shot BB repeater – a legitimate classic.

I admit that after I tore open the carton and monkeyed around with the Model 25 for a few minutes, I immediately ordered another one to set aside unopened. It really is that cool.

The Model 25 lists at $74.99 on the Daisy website (daisy.com) but can be had for substantially less from a number of online retailers and possibly some brick-and-mortar shops, too. At full-boat retail, the Daisy Model 25 is still an exceptional bargain, even in these days of "serious" upscale airguns.

CHIAPPA ARMS 1911-22 PISTOL

The Chiappa 1911-22 was introduced in the fourth quarter of 2009, so these attractive rimfire pistols have been around long enough for me to form an opinion of them. I like them.

The 2-lb., 1-oz. 1911-22 is a straight blowback pistol chambered in .22 LR and patterned after the 1911. In fact, my hands have a hard time telling the difference. The Chiappa is built on an alloy aluminum frame with a steel barrel and has all its essential controls in the same place as its centerfire counterpart. Its rear sight is drift-adjustable, though I have heard of, but not seen, a version with a fully-adjustable rear sight. The 1911-22 has a key-activated lawyer safety on the rear right side of the slide and dispenses altogether with the "real" 1911's grip safety, so it's by no means a perfect rimfire clone of the 1911 or even the sainted Colt Ace. Close enough for me, though.

The 1911-22 is intended to provide the 1911 shooter with an economical rimfire pistol that's price-competitive with a .22 conversion barrel/slide assembly. With a street price of well under $300, it succeeds in that role rather well. *Gun Digest* Contributing Editor Jeff Quinn reports one-hole groups from a good rest at 25 yards with his 1911-22; I haven't equalled that performance yet, but I have managed several 2.5-inch groups offhand at 25 yards. That's all I can reasonably expect, given my advancing years and receding abilities.

I have talked to a few shooters who have complained that the 1911-22 is prone to stovepipe jams. This was true in the case of mine, too, until 250 or 300 rounds slicked things up. It then proved remarkably

reliable and jam-free. Just shows what a good cleaning every now and then and six boxes of ammunition can do. Some shooters have broken in their 1911-22s using ammo with a little more oomph, such as CCI Stingers, but I used good old Remington Thunderbolt and Federal American Eagle. What my 1911-22 really prefers, though – in terms of both accuracy and reliability – is Remington Golden Bullet hollowpoints.

The 1911-22's trigger takes some getting used to. It's creepy, and you have to get into the habit of releasing it fully so it can reset. The gun's finish is rather thin, and I suspect that a few hundred more trips into and out of the holster will strip the bluing (or blacking, rather) off the slide pretty thoroughly. Still, for an extremely affordable plinker or as a training stand-in for a "real" 1911, these are petty gripes.

The Chiappa 1911-22 comes in a lockable hard case with two 10-round polymer magazines and a surprisingly well-written user's manual. As near as I can tell, it's made of offshore components that are assembled in God's Country (Dayton, Ohio). Never head of Chiappa? Sure you have – it used to be known as Armi Sport. For more information, visit chiappafirearms.com.

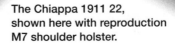

The Chiappa 1911 22, shown here with reproduction M7 shoulder holster.

The 50-caliber Shinsung Dragon Slayer PCP air rifle, shown with Leaper's scope and bipod.

Pyramyd and 3-inch groups with the solids. (When I opened the boxes, the pellets neither looked nor felt as though they weighed 200 grains, but my RCBS reloading scale says they did, right down to the half-grain.)

If you think that the Dragon Slayer is silent simply because it's an airgun, allow me to disabuse you. The Dragon Slayer sounded to me an awful lot like a Browning Baby or Colt Vest Pocket semiauto in .25 ACP being fired in a small room. That kind of report isn't going

SHINSUNG CAREER DRAGON SLAYER .50 AIR RIFLE

I'm either growing up or growing down, but I'm finally taking an active interest in air rifles. These are banner days for the airgun industry, and the hottest thing in an already-hot market is the pre-charged pneumatic (PCP) gun. In a PCP airgun, compressed air is held under extremely high pressure (up to 3,000 lbs.) in a tubelike reservoir usually located beneath the gun's barrel.

The ShinSung Career Dragon Slayer .50 is the Godzilla of PCP rifles, firing 200-gr. pellets at 600 fps, give or take. That's 160 ft-lbs. of energy, generally comparable to the old blackpowder loading of the .44 Russian revolver cartridge. Needless to say the Dragon Slayer .50 is capable of game a good deal larger than starlings or chipmunks.

The good folks at Pyramyd Air Gun Mall kindly lent me a Dragon Slayer .50 so I could see what this PCP fuss was all about. Contrary to my expectations, however, there's really nothing mysterious about operating this behemoth of an air rifle. You can charge the reservoir from a scuba tank or a heavy-duty hand pump that Pyramyd recommends. Living in the middle of Amish country, I didn't have a scuba tank handy and was rather put off by the array of fittings and adapters that might be needed to fill the reservoir in this manner, but the hand pump did the trick just fine, especially if you can pull a Tom Sawyer and trick someone else into doing it.

When the reservoir is full, cock the sidelever near the breech, insert the pellet, and seat it by closing the lever. You're now ready to go.

My Dragon Slayer had about a 5.5-lb. trigger pull with zero staginess, and considering that the rifle weighs around 11.5 lbs. when duded up with a Leapers 4-16x50AO scope and a bipod, you're not likely to have too many called fliers due to the jitters. My Dragon Slayer turned in consistent 2.25-inch groups at 50 yards with the swaged hollowpoint pellets supplied by

to deafen children or break windows, but it's quite noticeable.

Pyramyd Air retails the Dragon Slayer Combo (with scope, hard case, and bipod) for a cool $799. Add another $238 for the hand pump and you can see that owning the Mother of All Airguns entails quite an investment. The Dragon Slayer is a remarkably well-crafted airgun that shoots like there's no tomorrow, but I suppose my uses would be better served by the new Benjamin Marauder 25-caliber PCP airgun that's scheduled to appear as this edition of *Gun Digest* goes to press. Still, if the biggest and baddest is your cup of tea, you might want to pay an online visit to Pyramyd Air at pyramydair.com and check out the Dragon Slayer (and about a thousand other fascinating airguns).

200-gr. 50-cal. pellets for the Dragon Slayer, with a .357 Magnum for scale.

GUNSMITHING PRODUCTS

BY KEVIN MURAMATSU

"There's nothing new under the sun." Maybe so, but there seems to always a bigger hammer, nicer house, faster car, more expensive rifle, or higher capacity pistol.

Gunsmithtown is like that. Many companies come out with something new, like parts or sights for just one or few firearms, and then spend the next two years expanding the line to cover all the common models. This is a good thing, as a well-intentioned and -manufactured product should be applied to the limits of its applicability. The original idea is expanded until it is improved, flatteringly copied, or, sometimes, outright stolen. Then maybe something new comes along, but frequently it is really the same thing but looks a bit different to meet someone else's idea of perfection. Those are two of the great things about freedom: free enterprise and free markets. If someone wants something, someone else will make it. [*Editor's Note: . . .and, most likely, someone else will rip it off. -DMS*]

A perfect example of this phenomenon is the vast assortment of aftermarket parts and upgrades for the AR-15 series of rifles, particularly pistol grips and handguards. Many of these items are effectively user installable, many are not, and even the easy ones are often taken to a smith to install anyway.

On the flip side of the coin are even cooler, and unfortunately, less common examples. New tools that only a gunsmith could (or even should) appreciate can be seen in the pages of catalogs from places like Brownells. A sear polishing jig means nothing and is worth nothing to the average American, but it can be the centerpiece of a gunsmith's source of income. An AR-15 action wrench just looks like a weird metal stick to my cousin, but to the armorer's eyes it is a tool of indispensable value.

Every year we are blessed with a small new assortment of those unique tools, a few not so unique but still very useful tools, and an absolute glut of new parts to meet some dude's pseudoscientific value assessment for "the best of the best."

There are always new cleaning utensils and liquids every year, so we shall begin by discussing a few of those new residents in Gunsmithtown.

THE TOOLS OF CLEANING

The boys at **Battenfeld Technologies** have developed two little handy accessories. The first is called a Patch Trap. A "why didn't anyone think of that sooner" tool, it simply straps onto the muzzle and catches patches and splatter as they are pushed out of the bore. Gunsmiths have been taping or rubber banding water bottles for years onto rifle muzzles, but this little inexpensive doohickey replaces that system with a little elegance and a lot of sanitary thinking. It reduces clean up times and dimes involved in wiping solvent and crud off the floor, bench, and face.

In conjunction with the trap, they have also developed a little tool called a Rapid Bore Guide to replace the third hand that you weren't born with. Taking a standard bore guide (which everyone with a brain ought to be using to clean a rifle) they have added a little attachment to make it easier to center a patch on a jag while pushing the rod through the bore guide into the barrel, using only two hands. The leading attachment grasps the patch perpendicularly to the bore, and you just shove the rod and jag through the attachment into the bore, taking the patch with it. Now this isn't

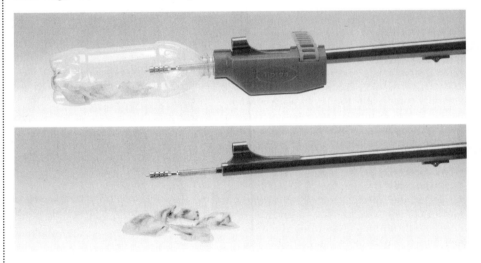

Tipton Patch Trap. Catch it or clean it up. Your choice. (Photo courtesy Battenfeld Tech.)

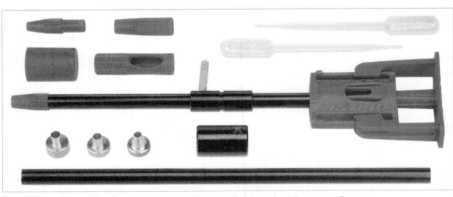

The Tipton Rapid jag/patch assist is like a third hand with seven fingers. (Photo courtesy Battenfeld Tech.)

a difficult task without this tool, but it does quicken it up, and in combination with the bore guide keeps the patch on the jag as it goes through the receiver, where you have no opposable thumb to hold it on, and where the patch can often fall off. Oil or solvent can also be efficiently applied while the patch is being held.

An interesting, related developmental thread has resulted in tri-lobed cleaning patches from **Rigel Products** known as Triangle Patches. We all know that normal, square patches work well, but the surface area of the patches is not maximized, because the patches form folds that are not used effectively. These lobed patches, when pushed down the bore, offer similar amounts of surface area for cleaning but wrap around the brush better without jamming in the bore. This effectively grants the user a patch that hits the bore with more effective surface area and thus shortens the time used in bore cleaning and reduces the number of patches used.

The same outfit also makes bore brushes of two diameters called Jag Brushes. The smaller diameter frontal bristles hold the patch while the standard diameter brushes at the rear scrape away crud.

THE GOOPINESS OF CLEANING

A cursory look at the new cleaners and oils on the market reveals a trend transitioning to the synthetic. A great representative of this movement is from good old **Brownells**. Friction Defense Xtreme gun oil has a huge operating range; from -100°F to +550°F. Any oil with additives like Teflon, being suspensions rather than solutions, generally settle, needing to be shaken prior to use to resuspend the small particles or nodules composing the additives. An unsung benefit to this stuff is that it does not come out of suspension like other lubricants. Thus there's little need to vigorously shake the bottle prior to application, and anything that comes out today will be as good as the stuff that came out yesterday after sitting on the shelf.

...AND FROM THE BROWN CORNER...

Brownells also has a neat new bluing tank accessory that will reduce pain. Hot bluing salts hurt when they splash and burn a hole clear through your hand. The Bluing Shield is meant to act

Brownells' new torque handle. Hefty and tough. Here, it is seen magically turning a Remington action screw all by itself.

as a splash guard when adding hot salts to the hot tanks, thus keeping your skin intact by blocking any possible splash during these occasions. It is sized to fit the Brownells bluing tanks perfectly.

Welcomed is the Brownells Adjustable Torque Handle. From as little as five inch/pounds to well over seventy inch/pounds it is suitable for scope bases and rings, action screws, and anything else you could think of to torque. It is heavy and well made, and very ergonomic and easy to adjust, using the standard Brownells Magna-Tip inserts.

Brownells is also selling a four-inch Magna-Tip extension for the screwdriver sets. Sometimes the long driver handle is just not quite long enough, and for many of those times, this extension should calm the troubled storms of frustration caused by a driver being just a little bit too short.

TOOLS, TOOLS GALORE

Score High Gunsmithing has a wonderful new tool to assist in bedding

an action into a stock. Complementing their excellent adjustable pillar stock drilling jig and Pro Bed 2000 epoxy are their stock bedding blocks. These units are available for Remington 700 short and long actions, ADLs and BDLs, and replace the trigger guard and bottom metal during the bedding process, preventing damage or stuck-on compound on the trigger guards. The blocks come off the stock quickly and easily, with no cracking, and if release agent is used, do so every time.

A pocket-sized contraption called The Gun Tool has been produced by **Avid Design**. Essentially a folding pocket gunsmith toolbox, it can be easily carried in a range bag and contains some very useful items. Torx and hex head drivers, replaceable magnetic bits retained in a compartment, a choke tube wrench and scope adjustment blade, punch, and a small knife are all housed within its walls. Keep it in the range bag with a small hammer and any gunsmith worth his lathe should be able to fix three-quarters of the problems at the range and make despondent shooters there happy indeed.

Used in other fields such as camping and government activities are the products from the company known as **Loksak**. I've found that these tough waterproof, airproof, extreme temperature-resistant bags are excellent choices for long term storage of firearms. I have cleaned up for storage many antique or collectable firearms, and the idea of a flexible container with these properties is very appealing to me. Combined with active moisture fighters like the

The Avid Gun Tool is a pocket toolbox. Notable are the hex driver bits in the back that insert in the end.

vapor releasing Inhibitor VCI Pro Chips from **Van Patten Industries**, or even plain old desiccant packs, a gunsmith or gun owner can keep an old valuable heirloom safe and sound, not worrying about ambient moisture causing harm to the collection or keepsake. They are just now breaking into the firearms storage arena, and the bags come in many sizes and are surprisingly affordable. The glory days of cosmoline are over.

Not even available or even properly named as this column is written is a very useful upgrade to the Hawkeye borescope from **Gradient Lens Corporation**. The Hawkeye uses a small eyepiece and tube, and with the use of proprietary gradient lens technology, it allows the gunsmith to peer down the bore of a firearm with crystal clarity. Useful for determining bore condition and finding imperfections or damage, looking through the little eyepiece can nevertheless be somewhat straining, and only one person can see it at a time. Fortunately, any existing Hawkeye borescope can now be upgraded with video technology. It allows the user to run the scope down the bore and display the image in video form on a computer monitor. This is incredibly useful. Customers often look upon the gunsmith with suspicion, never believing that they, of all people, could damage their bores, crowns, or chambers with poor practices. It never quite clicks that there may be a series of pits in the bore too small to see clearly from the muzzle or heavy copper fouling in the grooves that is affecting accuracy.

This upgrade not only displays in video for a present customer, but also records the video so that the relatively computer-competent smith can save it to use as evidence of a problem. It should be easy to foresee the arguments reduced, the solutions more quickly reached, and the incredible reduction in eye strain made possible by this product.

The last entry in the general tools is from **Manson Precision Reamers**. A new revolver tooling reamer set is sure to make revolversmiths' lives more convenient. This set is designed to pilot off the shaft of the reamer itself, with some spring tension at the muzzle end pulling the reamer forward, while the hand turns the T-handle beyond the muzzle. This allows truly concentric cutting with minimized chatter. One reamer cuts the forcing cone, another trues and squares the rear of the barrel, and the third chamfers the corner between the two.

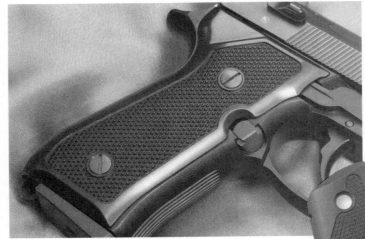

New slim Alumagrips for the Beretta 92. (Photo courtesy Alumagrips)

PARTS, PARTS, PARTS

There are some truly cool new gun parts. Possibly the most practical is the new trigger from **Timney Triggers** that replaces the crummy stock unit on the Mosin-Nagant rifles. These rifles are everywhere, cheap, and make great starter rifles for new gun owners. It's about time someone made an upgrade that went beyond the stock and scope mount fields to something that will really make tangible improvement to the rifle. It is also simple to install and is adjustable and has a convenient side mounted safety. Many folks look upon these rifles with scorn they do not deserve. Thankfully, Timney does not.

Why **Caspian** hasn't promoted their new ambidextrous 1911 safety more energetically is puzzling. It utilizes an oversized sear pin with a dovetail on the end to retain the right side piece. This means that the little tab (while still present), and corresponding cut-out in the right grip panel is unnecessary, and that the right side piece stays tightly onto the frame. Furthermore, the joint between the two safety pieces uses not the usual tongue-in-groove, but a square peg and hole, and the connection is actually inside the right frame wall rather than in the middle. These features result in a much smoother, well-fit, better-feeling upgrade to the standard ambi safety.

Alumagrips has continued their line of aluminum pistol grips. Added to the pot are units for Beretta 92 pistols and Para double stack 1911 pistols. Both are slim line to minimize the width of the pistol grips. The beauty of these grips, as was true of the previous incarnations of them, is the incredibly textured

(below) Para pistols also get a new Alumagrips treatment to look even better. (Photo courtesy Alumagrips.)

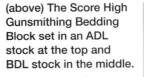

(above) The Score High Gunsmithing Bedding Block set in an ADL stock at the top and BDL stock in the middle.

(right) Dave Manson's reamer set for revolvers is a new, innovative, convenient way to work on your revolver's forcing cone. (Photo courtesy Manson Precision Reamers.)

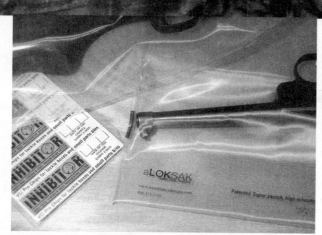

A great way to store guns for long periods, the Loksak bags combined with Inhibitor chips will keep your guns rust free for an extended time in the back of your closet or under your lawn.

Mega Arms' MTS monolithic single rail upper receiver, seen here on matching lower. A quad rail is also available for those needing to hang Christmas ornaments. (Photo courtesy Mega Arms.)

The Multitasker Series 2 with all the tools necessary to field repair the AR15 in a high quality package. (Photo courtesy Multitasker.)

checkering surfaces, providing a firm slip-resistant grip for even wet hands. The best part is that they look quite smart and definitely liven up the appearance of the handgun.

On a similar note, **Hogue** has expanded past the rubbery grips that they have been well known for and has introduced a line of grips made from G10. Varied checking patterns cut into these types of grips really take advantage of the appearance, setting off the laminated layers of multicolored material. This Extreme series also includes Damascus style steel, Titanium, and exotic wood insert grips as well.

Cylinder & Slide is producing replacement parts for the old Colt .380 (Type M) pistol. A quality replacement sear and hammer should work well in the old classics when the originals wear out and make great additions to the current line of parts for these collectables.

The last general part covered here is more of a representation of a positive trend than a note on a specific new part. The Winchester Model 70 allen-headed action screws from **NECG**, available from Brownells, are evidence of a growing drift toward non-traditional screw heads. This is the 21st century and there is no excuse to remain with flat heads and Phillips heads in screws. Let's get with the program. When we have hex heads, and even better, Torx headed screws available, then let us fully transition over. Hex heads, and Torx even more so, are much more difficult to bugger up; they prevent skipping and sliding off (which causes many blemishes on guns using flat headed screws); and they have a far higher torque resistance. Best

of all, they look a heck of a lot cooler. A few companies such as Remington have been using hex-headed action screws for some time now and the rest of the pack needs to jump on the bandwagon forthwith. Sure, Torx or hex heads are a few pennies more expensive. But chances are an awful lot of people would be pleased to pay those few pennies to get a better screw or bolt.

AR STUFF

Continuing to lead the pack of new gunsmithing products are those for the AR-15. Still very hot sellers, the accessories related to the AR craze continue on *ad infinitum*. Can't complain, though.

Joining the oodles of upper and lower receivers on the market, sold stripped for home-building pleasure, is the **Mega Arms** MTS upper receiver. This Monolithic Tactical System (monolithic meaning that the upper receiver and handguard are one solid machined unit) will fit any milspec lower receiver. Being one solid unit aids in stiffening what would normally be the upper/handguard interface, making the rifle more consistently accurate by removing a stress point where the handguard, barrel, and receiver meet. Enhancing that even further is that the barrel remains free-floated. The MTS uses standard off-the-shelf barrels, and with a proprietary barrel nut and wrench it's simple for anyone, from the old time gunsmith to the hobby builder, to construct a nice rifle. A really snappy-looking AR can be build using this product, available in quad rail or single top rail models, combined with the corresponding matching lower that Mega has been producing for several years. Both pieces are machined from a large billet of 7075 aluminum. Together, this is one of the most cosmetically attractive arrangements in the AR world and it is clear that Mega is into good looks.

In the "convenient tools to have" category are two by **Multitasker**. A leatherman-style folding model called a Series 2 has a pair of pliers and several more AR specific tools enclosed within it, such as a carbine stock wrench, front sight tool, and cleaning pick. The Ultralight model is much smaller, the size of a Swiss army knife, with the same specialty tools, but minus the pliers, knife, and file. They will just disappear into your pocket, and if you are a AR busy gunsmith, they'll serve you well with those impromptu repairs at the range.

HAND LOADING

BY LARRY STERETT

With the increased prices of factory loaded ammunition, interest in handloading should also increase – and apparently it has, judging from the recent backorder situations at many manufacturers of reloading tools and components. The major cost of a loaded cartridge is the brass case, and if the case can be reloaded five to ten times, or more, the cost per round decreases, after the cost of the reloading equipment is recouped. Plus, you can tailor your loads for varmint hunting, big game hunting, target shooting, tactical shooting or whatever the need. (Trapshooters often reload several thousand rounds of their favorite load each year in order to reduce the cost of shells needed for practice.) The equipment covered in this update doesn't cover everything available, but it should provide an idea as to what is currently available and what's new.

DATA

Reloaders need reliable reloading data. Thankfully, such data for factory, obsolete, and even wildcat cartridges is all over the place.

The hardbound volumes of data, such as those by Barnes, Hornady, Lee, Nosler, Speer, and others, or the large, softbound volumes of Lyman, Accurate Arms, etc., are enormously valuable. Their only downside is the lapse time between new editions. A recent trend is toward a smaller paper-bound manual or magazine-size volume of data issued yearly, often by powder manufacturers or distributors. One of the most informative, the *Hodgdon Annual,* is issued by the Hodgdon Powder Company and published by *Shooting Times.*

The latest *Hodgdon Annual* features one less than a dozen excellent articles on reloading by well-known writers,

The Hornady Auto Charge is a sophisticated digital powder measure. Note the drain plug on the right side.

The GSI Rotary Bullet Feed for Dillon XL650 and Super 1050 reloading machines.

plus the latest loading data for 135 rifle cartridges, from the .17 Ackley Hornet to the .50 BMG, and 72 handgun cartridges from the .22 Remington Jet to the .500 S&W Magnum. In addition there are a few other valuable features, including a table of Relative Burn Rates for powders, rated from the fastest (Norma R1) to the slowest (Vihtavouri 20N29); a table of Powder Usage for various pistol, rifle and shotgun powders; a description of many of the powders currently on the market; and a legend of the abbreviations used in the manual. (Data is provided for ten different 6.5mm cartridges, including two of the newest, the 6.5 Grendel and the 6.5 Creedmoor, but not for the older 6.5mm Remington Magnum.)

No loading data for shotshells is provided in this manual, but for each of the rifle or handgun cartridges, load data is provided as follows, for specified bullets (the bullet being listed by weight, brand name, bullet type, diameter and overall loaded cartridge length): powder, grains, velocity (instrumental) and pressure (CUP) for both starting loads and maximum loads. Other data provided for

the loads for a specific cartridge include the case used (Federal, Hornady, Remington, Sierra, Winchester, etc.), trim length, primer brand (type and size), barrel length and rate of twist. It doesn't get much better or more complete than this.

Lyman Products will have a new *Cast Bullet Handbook* available by the time you read this. This is the fourth edition and the first new one in thirty years. The entire Lyman line of pistol and rifle bullet moulds will be chronicled, along with data for some moulds by other manufacturers whose bullet designs will be of interest to reloaders of cast bullets. A number of new cartridges since the third edition will be featured, such as the .327 Federal, along with some new black powder loads for a number of the popular older cartridges, especially those regaining status among Cowboy Action. A number of authoritative "how to" articles are also featured.

LYMAN PRODUCTS

Other new Lyman products for handloaders include a Big Dipper Casting Furnace, Big Dipper Casting Kit, Cast Iron

Lead Pot, Magnum Inertia Bullet Puller, and a Universal Case Prep Accessory Kit. The Big Dipper Furnace has a 10-lb. capacity, features heavy-duty aluminum construction with a stable non-tipping design, and operates on 115 volts. Heat-up time is rapid, with control to +/- 10 degrees. (The Casting Kit contains the BD furnace, a casting dipper, ingot mould, Super Moly Bullet Lube and the *Lyman Reloading and Cast Bullet Guide* – everything needed to get started in casting bullets, except for a bullet mould of the required size.) The Cast Iron Lead Pot has a 10-lb. lead capacity and is flat-bottomed to reduce tipping. A heat source, such as an electric hotplate, is needed to melt the lead and keep it hot. (With the older iron pot I used to use a tripod, similar to what plumbers used at one time, over a single gas flame; it worked.)

To salvage the components when you make a reloading flub, the new Magnum Inertia Bullet Puller will be handy. With a full size handle for comfort, the Puller features a head design capable of handling case sizes from the FN 5.7x28mm to the largest magnum. Insert cartridge, secure cap, strike puller on a solid sur-

SOME OF THE QUALITY CARTRIDGE UNPRIMED CASES FOR THE J. D. JONES LINE OF WILDCAT CARTRIDGES.

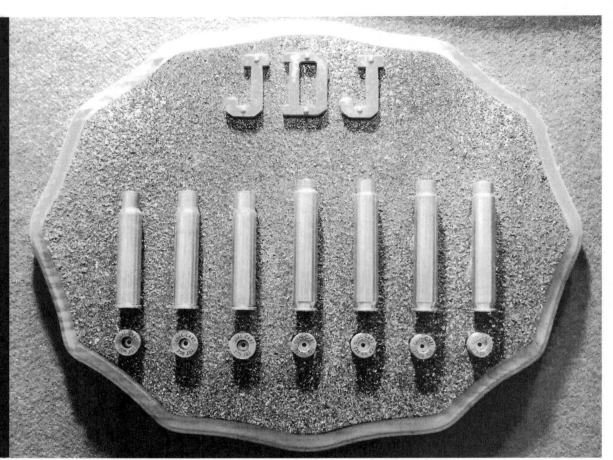

QUALITY CARTRIDGE UNPRIMED CASES FOR THE COMPLETE GIBBS SHARP SHOULDER, SHORT NECK, LINE OF CARTRIDGES.

ACKLEY CARTRIDGES, REGULAR AND IMPROVED, RANGED FROM .17 CALIBER TO .475 AND POSSIBLY HIGHER. THESE ARE A FEW OF THE UNPRIMED ACKLEY CASES AVAILABLE FROM QUALITY CARTRIDGE.

OBSOLETE CARTRIDGES COME IN ALL SIZES. THESE UNPRIMED CASES BY QUALITY CARTRIDGE REPRESENT ONLY A FEW OF THE MANY AVAILABLE.

Hornady's digital Sonic Cleaner literally blasts the dirt and carbon buildup from inside and outside the cartridge case.

face. (A 6x6-inch square, inch-thick plate of cold-rolled steel works very well as a surface on which to strike the Puller.) Then unscrew the cap and remove the bullet, powder and case. Depending on the cartridge, bullet seating depth, and crimp tightness, two or more strikes may be necessary, but it will eventually remove the bullet.

The Universal Case Prep Accessory Kit features eight small tools to fine-tune trimmed cartridge cases prior to reloading. Packaged in a folding zippered storage pouch are a pair each of primer pocket reamers (small and large), primer pocket cleaners, primer pocket uniformers, and inside and outside deburring tools to eliminate the sharp edges on a trimmed case mouth. A new Carbide Cutter Head for the Lyman Case Trimmer and a new Universal Carbide Case Trimmer are available. (The Carbide head holds its sharp edge much longer than the regular steel trimmer head.)

GSI INTERNATIONAL

If you reload using one of the Dillon XL 650 or RL 1050 or Super 1050 reloading machines, GSI International has a new Rotary Bullet Feed to speed up the reloading process. The Conversion Units contain all parts necessary for feeding one caliber of bullet, including the feed ring, bullet column, feed wheel, seat stems, bushing and GSI toolhead assembly. (XL 650 users will need to move some items from their regular toolhead to the GSI toolhead, such as the sizing die, powder die and system, powder check, if used, and the crimp die.) The GSI toolhead for the 1050, with the Bullet Feed Mechanism integrated into the left side, replaces the standard 1050 toolhead. The new system includes a new casefeed post and bracket which mount directly into existing machine holes. Also included are a camming plate for the bullet feeder's index lever and a gas spring to handle the added weight of the bullet and feeder. The 1050 Rotary system includes the GSI toolhead with feed mechanism, extended case feed post with brackets, clear plastic feed tub, an indexer camming plate, and gas spring with locating block. Items to be moved from the standard 1050 toolhead include the case feed cam, primer push-rod, ratchet cam, fasteners, sizing die, powder die and system, powder checker (if used), and the crimp die.

The GSI Rotary Bullet Feeder uses a small DC electric motor to rotate the feed ring counterclockwise. (For the USA, the 110 VAC input becomes, via a transformer, a 12 VDC output.) The feed rings are caliber specific, and many popular calibers such as 9mm, .40 S&W, .45 ACP, .223 Remington, etc., are currently available.

REDDING RELOADING EQUIPMENT

Redding Reloading Equipment has a number of new die sets available, plus some new calibers in the regular die sets. (The G-R Carbide Push-Thru Base Sizing Die to resize the base section of fired .40 S&W cases were mentioned last year, and it's a excellent die for reloaders of large quantities of .40 S&W ammunition using once-fired brass.) Now available in the regular Series D die sets for bottleneck case are full length and neck-sizing dies for the .260 Remington Improved (40°), 6.5 Creedmoor, .370 Sako Magnum, and .458 SOCOM cartridges. (Individual dies and Deluxe sets are available, but no trim and form dies for these cartridges.) Redding has new National Match Die Sets available for the .223 Remington, .308 Winchester, and .30-06 Springfield cartridges. These three-die sets, which list for over a pair of C-notes, include a full length sizing die, competition bullet seating die, and a taper crimp die. (Taper crimp dies are available for handgun cartridges that headspace on the case mouth, and for the following additional rifle cartridges: 6.5 Grendel, 6.8 Remington SPC, .30-30 Winchester, 7.62x39mm, .300 Winchester Magnum, and .300 Remington Ultra Magnum.)

Benchrest shooters and any other handloader interested in obtaining maximum accuracy from their handloads can now obtain an "Instant Indicator" Headspace and Bullet Comparator for two additional cartridges, the .204 Ruger and .338 Lapua Magnum. (The Instant Indicator, with or without the dial indicator, is currently available for 34 different rifle cartridges. It can be used on any family of cartridges that have the same shoulder angle.) It is supplied with the proper bore diameter bushing, surface contactor, shoulder contactor, headspace gauge, and complete instructions. Its use permits the sorting of bullets and sized cases for uniformity – uniformity of shoulder bump, bullet seating depth, trimmed case uniformity, and comparison of fired cases to sized cases for headspace differences. It can even be used to sort cases fired in different rifles, determine when cases need trimmed, and sort loaded ammunition for uniformity.

Any handloader with a loading press and a set of dies, but lacking other essentials, might check out the Redding Versa Pak Reloading Kit. It contains all the other items, powder measure, case trimmer, case lube and pad, powder funnel, powder scale, etc. that simplify the handloading process, including a new Hodgdon reloading manual and a DVD titled "Advanced Handloading Beyond the Basics."

RCBS

Bullet pullers and feeders seem to be the hot items at present for reloading equipment manufacturers. RCBS has a new Pow'r Pull kit and two two Bullet Feeder kits for their progressive presses. The Pow'r Pull features a rugged one-piece body, plus cap, and comes with three chucks to accommodate cases heads from the 5.7x28mm to the Winchester WSM and Remington RUM families. (By the way, NEVER attempt to pull bullets from rimfire cartridges using an inertia bullet puller.)

The RCBS Bullet Feeder kits are available in two sizes, one for 22- or 30-caliber rifle cartridges, and one

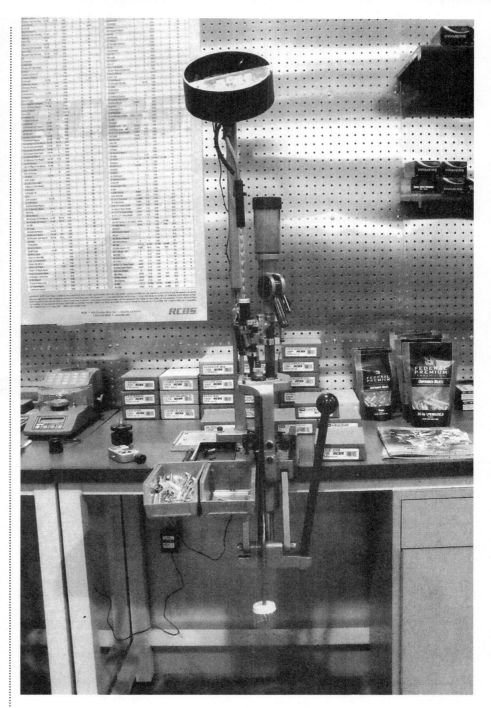

for handgun calibers from 9mm to .45 ACP. The Feeders operate on 110 VAC, with adapters for United Kingdom, Australian, and continental European use included. Designed to fit onto most 7/8"x14 threaded progressive presses, the Feeders orient the bullets to drop into the feed mechanism, but are for jacketed or FMJ bullets only and not for use with lead bullets, cast or swaged. Hopper capacities are approximately 250 (22-caliber) or 100 (30-caliber) bullets for the rifle caliber feeder and 200 for the handgun caliber feeder. The

The RCBS Bullet Feeder set up on the RCBS progressive loading press. It feeds the bullets, base down, directly into the feeding tube, ready to be dropped into the case mouth.

Feeders carry a two-year warranty and are said to increase the loading rate by as much as 50%.

Keeping loading presses, dies, etc., cleaned and lubed is a necessity for both successful and long-term operation. RCBS has a couple of Die/Press Lube Kits: one kit for loading dies and a

separate one for loading presses. These kits contain the necessary chemicals and brushes to permit proper cleaning and ensure equipment longevity.

RCBS has added six new calibers to their loading die lineup. These include the .30 T/C and .338 Marlin Express to the Group A line, and 6.5 Creedmoor, .30 Remington AR, .338 Norma Magnum, and .416 Ruger to the Group D line. Full-length die sets and neck sizer dies are available, but no trim dies at present. Not exactly new, but for those handloaders of the really big bore, RCBS has die sets for the .416 Barrett, .460 Steyr, and .50 BMG cartridges, in addition to a Safari Series line covering seven calibers from the .404 Jeffery to the .505 Gibbs. If what you need isn't available, RCBS does have a listing of nearly 650 "special order" die sets. (Note that the firm no longer produces one-of-a-kind custom die sets.)

HORNADY

In addition to having some new cartridge loads available, plus a couple of new cartridges for U. S. shooter, Hornady Manufacturing has several new components and a couple of great equipment items for handloaders. The Lock-n-Load Power Case Prep Center was introduced last year. Combining a power trimmer with primer pocket uniformer, cleaner, reamer, flash hole deburring

tool, case mouth chamfer and deburring tools, etc. , the Case Prep Center takes up little space on the reloading bench. The two new Hornady tools include the Lock-n-Load Auto Charge and the Sonic Cleaner.

The Auto Charge has a scale capacity of 1,000 grains and will weigh accurately to within 0.1 grains. Finished in Hornady red with a clear plastic hopper, the machine features an easy-to-use keypad with backlit display, manual and automatic dispensing options, plus trickle function, overcharge protection, and several other unique features. A side-mounted clean-out spout or drain makes emptying the hopper a real breeze. An electric Hornady powder scale with a 1,000-grain capacity should be available about the time you read this.

Sonic parts cleaners have been available and in use by the automotive industry and others for a good many years. Now Hornady has a Lock-n-Load Sonic Case Cleaner. The new Cleaning unit can hold up to one hundred .308-size cases, or two hundred cases of .223 size. Coupled with a unique cleaning solution called One-Shot Sonic Cleaner, available in one-quart containers, this device, which features a digital timer, uses ultrasonic action to literally blast away carbon and dirt building up from the outside, inside, and even the primer

Unprimed brass and a couple of loaded cartridges from TR&Z USA. Left to right: 6.5x51R; 7.7x58mm Japanese; 7.92x33mm Kurz; and 7.63mm Mauser.

pocket areas of the cases. (The cleaner can also be used on small parts.) No tumbling, no vibrating, just put in the One-Shot, place the dirty cartridge into the solution, set the digital timer, and the Sonic Cleaner will take care of the rest.

In addition to the the new Auto Charge and Sonic Cleaner for handloaders, Hornady will have unprimed brass available in 6.5 Grendel, .338 Marlin Express and 9.2 x62mm, with the same available as Lock-n-Load Modified "Series A " cases for the O.A.L. Gauges. Custom Grade, Series I two-die sets are available for the 6.5 Grendel, and a number of new FTX seating stems are available for use in seating dies. These FTX stems are available in five calibers, from .30 to .50, and for bullet weights up to 300 grains.

One handy item to have on the loading bench is the Die Maintenance Kit. This Kit includes spare decap pins, zip spindles, retaining rings, Sure-Loc ring, a decap retainer, and an Allen wrench. Another handy new items is the Universal Shellholder Extenstion. It isn't needed often, but it's worth its weight in gold when it is.

For the really dedicated handloader who wants to form a large number of standard cases into an improved design, without having to fireform, Hornady has the answer: a Hydraulic Form Die Kit. It's available in two basic sizes: for cases under 2.60 inches or less in length and for cases 2.601 to 2.999 inches in length. Prices are under $200. Custom dies are also available (form, size, seat, trim, etc.) as a single die, or up to a four-die set, depending on the cartridge.

It's not new reloading equipment, but new to the Hornady line is the 5.45x39mm loaded with a 60-gr. V-MAX in the Varmint Express line. No loading dies, yet. Another item, not related to handloading *per se*, is the Hornady Cartridge Introduction Board. Featured in a shadow box display are 21 the of the SAMMI cartridges which the Hornady firm has introduced since 1988, from the rimfire to the big bores.

SIERRA

Sierra, The Bulletsmiths, has a new laminated countermat that illustrates the entire Sierra line of bullets, including the Long Range Specialty Bullets, from .22 to .338. Other non-bullet items of interest to the handloader include four reloading videos, VHS or DVD, plus an advanced video, "Beyond the Basics." Handloaders wanting to check out exterior ballicstics can do so on the Sierra Infinity, Version 6, Computer Software.

Some Quality Cartridge unprimed brass cases, left to right: 6/5mm TCU; .351 Winchester Self Loading (SL); 357 Herrett; .240 H & H Magnum; .270 Ackley Magnum; .416 Taylor; .425 Westley Richards; .30 Gibbs; .358 STA; .416 ACC-REL; .500 Cyrus; and .366 DGW.

This software, which is available in CD-ROM format only, has the entire 5th Edition of the *Sierra Rifle and Handgun Reloading Manual* integrated into it. An Infinity Mobile program is also available for handheld computers, using the Windows Mobile Operating Sysem, Versions 5.0 and above.

NOSLER

Nosler has several new bullets for handloaders, including some lead-free BT (Ballistic Tip) .204, .224, and .243 designs for varmint shooters. Designed to perform best at high velocity (a minimum of 1600 fps is recommended with no upper limit), these bullets feature a fragmenting copper core. Nosler now has new unprimed brass for the 6.5x55mm Mauser, .300 WSM and .375 H & H Magnum cartridges, and custom loaded ammunition for the last two cartridges.

A new, expanded (848 pages) *Nosler Reloading Guide, No. 6,* features loading data for 117 cartridges. Each cartridge section begins with an introduction by a different well-known industry name or writer, relating personal experiences, advice, or anecdotes. "Comments From The Lab" are presented for many of the cartridges. Written by the Nosler ballistics team, they provide advice and insight for working up safe, effective and accurate loads. Load data for each cartridge is presented in a graphic format with easy-to-read bar graphs giving the reader a quick comparison of load velocities for each bullet weight. These graphs also permit a comparison between powders, making powder selection for a specific cartridge easier and faster than before. (Starting, intermediate and maximum loads for each powder listed are provided for each cartridge.)

MISCELLANEOUS NEAT STUFF

Not a loading manual, but a valuable reference for handloaders is *Ammo & Ballistics 4*, published by **Safari Press**. This large 438-page softbound volume provides ballistics data for over 160 centerfire cartridges of interest to handloaders, and similar data for some rimfire cartridges. Over 2400 factory loads for handguns and rifles are documented, and case dimensions are provided for most of the cartridges, including some for which dimensions are not easily found elsewhere. (Not that the dimensions for the .500 A-Square, .577 Tyrannosaur, or .700 Nitro Express are needed frequently.) This volume also contains some useful miscellaneous information, including a "How to Use This Book," along with four short feature articles, including one on handgun hunting and another on the great .470 Nitro Express cartridge.

Foster Products has a new 3-in-1 Carbide Case Mouth Cutter for either the original manually-operated case trimmer or the power case trimmer. It slides over the cutter shaft and secures in place with one set screw. The 3-in-1 feature comes from the fact the new cutter will perform three functions simultaneously in one pass. It trims the case to length, chamfers the inside case mouth to an angle of 14° and the outside of the case mouth to an angle of 30° — 3-in1. Three caliber choices (.224, .243, and .308) are currently available, with additional calibers to be added later. The cutter blades are made from U. S.-manufactured carbide steel, and if used exclusively on brass cases, should never need sharpening.

Barnes has more than twenty new bullets available, including a 300-gr. Tipped Triple-Shock X bullet for the .458 SOCOM

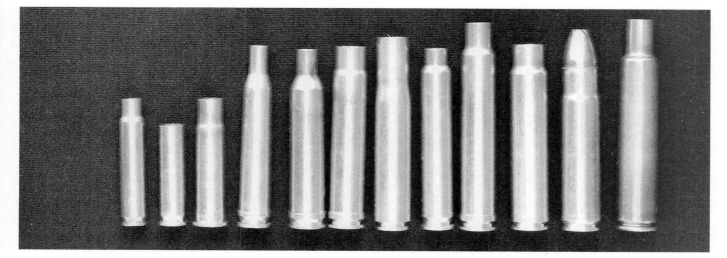

cartridge and four Barnes Buster Bullets for non-deflecting deep penetration, three for big-bore handguns and a 400-gr. for the 45-70 Gov't.

Barnes also has two clubs handloaders can join (www.bcarnesbullets.com). One, Club X, is free, while the Copper Club has a minimal annual fee. Club X members can view selected loads from the Barnes Ballistics Lab, peek at the latest products, receive an online newsletter, receive handloading tips, and even enter drawings for prices. The Copper Club members receive five gift packages, have access to all load data being developed for *Barnes Reloading Manual No. 5*, enrollment in Barnes University, and more.

Frankford Arsenal has new 20-round slip-top boxes to house handloaded cartridges in the .222 Remington size range, from the .17 Remington to the .222 Remington Magnum. These boxes are available in choice of blue or gray coloring. Another great Frankford box for container for handloads is the Ammo Vault. Available in two sizes to fit most cartridges, the Vault is constructed of impact-resistant material which will not break if dropped. A rubber molded bottom cushions the cartridges, and foam inserts hold the cartridges securely. Overall height adjustment accommodates different cartridges, and the two sections of the vault lock together to keep the lid from falling off. (Simply squeeze where it states "Press Here" and pull to separate the two halves and access the cartridges.) The RMD size Ammo Vault accommodates rounds from .222 Remington up to .35 Whelen size, while the RLG Vaults handle the Magnums — Remington, Weatherby, Winchester, etc. — and cartridges to the .50-110 Winchester or similar sizes.

Loading trays are a necessity for handloading and Frankford Arsenal has a Universal Loading Tray capable of handling most rifle case calibers from .17 to .458 and handgun caliber cases from 9mm to .500 Smith & Wesson. Unique stepped cavities accommodate several different size brass cases Handgun caliber holes are on one side, and the rifle case caliber holes are on the reverse side. The trays measure 11-1/4 inches long, by 5-1/2 inches wide and measure 1-1/4 inches deep. Capacity is 50 cases, either side. For handloaders with preference for loading trays to fit a specific cartridge case, Frankford has a dozen "Perfect Fit" trays to fit most cases from the .25 ACP to the .500 Nitro

Express. Except for the .500 Nitro tray, which has a 45-case capacity, the trays hold .50 cases.

Sinclair International features drop tubes for powder measures, R.F.D. Culver-style powder measures, neck sorting tools, flash hole cleaners, and a host of other products for handloaders. Sinclair manufactures some products and is a source for others, such as Forster, Lyman, RCBS, Redding, and Wilson. (Wilson manufactures stainless steel straight line neck sizing and bullet seating dies, while Sinclair produces an arbor press which works well with the Wilson dies and is small enough to take to the range.) Sinclair's Custom Press is C-type press machined from solid aluminum alloy. Capable of handling cases up to the .308 size, the press features a one-inch ram with a snap-in shellholder slot and is also small enough to take to the range.

Any handloader using Redding dies will appreciate the Sinclair Lock Ring Pliers. These machined aluminum split pliers clamp around the locking rings and lock nut on the Redding dies and make loosening a jammed ring easy. And the pliers do not damage the locking rings.

Western Powders Inc. publishes two Load Guides, one for Accurate powders and one for Ramshot powder. The latest editions are 3.4 and 4.4, respectively, and both feature new data for the 7.62 x39mm, 6.5x47mm Lapua, and the .308 Marlin cartridges. No dimensional drawings are in these guides, but they do include good loading data with a listing of bullet weight, make, type, starting load, maximum load, velocities, maximum load pressure, and cartridge overall length (COL). Other pertinent information includes test barrel length and rate of twist, primer used, and bullet diameter.

The Accurate guide provides loading data for twenty handgun cartridges from the 5.7x28mm FN to the .500 Maximum, and seventy rifle cartridges from the .17 Remington Fireball to the .550 Magnum. Loads for lead bullets are provided for some of the cartridges. In addition, a few loads are provided for Blackhorn 209 powder users in their muzzleloaders and for 22 cartridges used frequently by Cowboy Action Shooters. These CAS cartridges range from the .32 H & R Magnum to the .50-90. Some notes are provided for specific cartridges, such as using Dacron filler with the load for the .45-120 SS cartridge.

The Ramshot Guide includes loading data for two dozen handgun cartridges from the FN 5.7x28mm to the .500 Maximum, and 71 rifle cartridges from the .17 Remington Fireball to the .550 Magnum. The data is provided in the same manner in both guides but not all cartridges in production today are included. (Data for the .416 Remington Magnum cartridge is provided in both guides, for example, but no data is provided for the .416 Ruger or .416 Rigby cartridges.)The same Buckhorn 209 data is included in this guide, but there are loads for five popular CAS handgun cartridges using regular Ramshot powder and lead cast or swaged bullets.

Another handy reference volume for handloaders is the *Ammo Encyclopedia, 2nd Edition*, from **Blue Book Publications**. This 840-page softbound volume resembles one of older Sears, Roebuck & Co. catalogs in size. It does not feature loading data, but it does contain dimensioned drawings of cartridges from the .17 Remington Fireball to the .700 Nitro Express in the centerfire sporting rifle section, and additional cartridges under other chapter headings. (This tome contains 62 chapters, with cartridges — current, obsolete, sporting, military, proprietary, wildcats, rimfire, shotshells, etc. — featured in chapters 40 through 54. There are even a few cartridges listed as "Too New to Include….") Data for each cartridge includes alternate names and/or calibers, history, description, ballistics, current manufacturer if still in production, and comments, along with a dimensioned drawing. Dimensions are provided for most, but not all, cartridges. For example, the 5.8x42mm Chinese cartridge has dimensions provided, but the 5.8x21mm Chinese cartridge does not.

This volume provides information on primer, propellant, cartridge case, and bullet manufacturing, ballistics, history, formulas and much more. The case dimensions are all much of the same type, but not always to the same scale. In the first edition, not all cartridge drawings were of the same type and some computer-generated drawings were rather crude. In this edition it is much easier to compare cartridges, and there are nearly 600 handgun, rifle, and shotshell cartridges featured.

Shotshell handloaders should check out **Ballistic Products Inc.** (BPI).This firm, which has been in business since 1974, advertises it has "Everything for Shotgunners." It offers calls, books, choke tubes, and even more important to handloaders, loading presses, accessories and shotshell reloading components. At last count the firm had sixteen different reloading manuals, each devoted to a specific topic, such as "The Sixteen Gauge Manual," "The Mighty 10 Gauge," "Handloading Steel Shotshells," and "Handloading Hevi-Shot." Some of these manuals have gone through several revisions so the contained information is up-to-date.

Need a roll crimper, wads for reloading 8-gauge, 24- or 32-gauge shells? BPI has them. Roll crimpers for use in a drill press are available in six gauges, from 28 to 8, plus .410 (no 14-, 24-, or 32-gauge roll crimpers). Wads are available in the usual gauges, plus also for the small gauges, such as the 24, 28, and 32. BPI even has all-brass hulls for these smaller gauges, including the 32 but not the 14. To package those reloaded shotshells, especially if you purchase any once-fired hulls, BPI has new factory-style boxes in 5-, 10- and 25-round sizes. Constructed of select-grade heavy card stock, these boxes will outlast many factory boxes.

Handloaders looking for a new powder measure might check out the JDS Quick Measure (www.quick-measure.com) produced by **Johnson Design Specialities.** This measure is said to charge 100 cases in less than four minutes and not cut any powder. It may not be a beauty to behold, but efficiency is the key word, and if it works well, color, shape, etc., shouldn't matter.

If you handload for any unusual wildcat or obsolete cartridges for which your brass supply is running low, or are looking for suitable brass, the Hollywood, Maryland, firm of **Quality Cartridges** (http:/www.qual-cart.com) might jut have what you need. This firm loads for over 200 different cartridges, and has brass with the correct head-stamps on the cases. The firm does not sell single cases but in minimums of 20 rounds or more. The firm even has brass for some of the old smallbore English cartridges such as the .240 Holland & Holland (note that this is not the larger, and later, .244 H&H Magnum) and the .242 Vickers. Among the wildcat cases available, or loaded cartridges, are most of the Ackley line; the sharp-shoulder Gibbs; the Mashburn; and the list goes on. If you're loading for one of the early Winchester Self-Loading rifles and need .32 WSL, .35 WSL, .351 WSL, or .401 WSL cases, try Quality.

There are times when the ultimate

handloader can make use of a small lathe. (Most handloaders have a bit of experimenter in them, resulting in all sorts of wildcat cartridges and other related oddities.) **Sherline Products** (www.sherline.com) has two lathes, the Model 4000 (inch) and Model 4400 (inch), which operate on regular 100-240 VAC lines. Sherline also has several models, including metric sizes, in place of inch (English) measurements. The 4000 lathe has eight inches between centers, while the 4400 has 17 inches between centers. The Model 4000 weighs less than 24 pounds, which means it can fit easily onto most loading benches. Accessories are available including digital readouts, vertical mills, tool posts, stereo micsroscope, zero handwheels, live center, and more. Reducing the rim diameter or thickness on a cartridge case becomes a simple task, as does making a rimless case or a rebated-rim case out of a rimmed case. Capable of machining most materials from plastic to stainless steel, the Sherline lathe can even be used to produce small parts, although most work would probably center around cartridge case, bullets or possibly loading dies.

Wolfe Publishing Company has a new (5th) edition of *Propellant Profiles*. Featuring detailed descriptions of most of the current and discontinued powder, this 452-page volume is probably the most comprehensive book of its type available on the market today. It also includes some recommended loads and tips for improving your reloading procedures.

The Big Three (Federal, Remington, and Winchester) all offer unprimed brass cases for the most popular cartridges they manufacture, but for the obsolete and some of the less popular calibers brass for reloading may be difficult to locate. **Graf & Sons** (grafs.com), **Huntington Die Specialities** (www.huntingtons.com), and **Quality Cartridges** (www.qual-cart.com) are excellent places to start looking. For obsolete military caliber brass and some others, **TR&Z USA** Trading Corporation (www.ppu-usa.com) has some great new brass from Serbia. (The firm also had loaded ammunition in most calibers.) Looking for .22 Jet (remember this

revolver cartridge?) or 7.63mm Mauser (not 7.62mm Tokarev) brass and/or cartridges? TR&Z USA has them, and even .30 (7.65mm) Luger, along with the more popular 9mm Luger, .40 S&W, .45 ACP, etc. In the rifle line there are the 6.5x52mm Carcano, 6.5x55mm Swedish, 7.54x54mm French, 7.5x55mm Swiss, 8x50mm Lebel, 7.63x53mm Argentine, and 8x56mm Mannlicher, and for those who happened to obtain one of the new semi-auto MP-44s, 7.9x33mm Kurz, commonly called the 8mm Kurz. The firm also has 9.3x62mm Mauser brass and cartridges in addition to many of the regular American calibers. (No unprimed 5.45x39mm brass or cartridges yet.)

Annual reloading manuals, such as this one by the Hodgdon Powder Company, provide the most up-to-date handloading data.

Handloaders who are building their own wildcat rifle, and need or want to do their loading dies at the same time, can obtain 7/8"x14 tpi die blanks, in 12L-14 or 416 stainless steel, from **Newlon Precision** (www.newlonprecision.com). Available as body forming, sizing, and/or bullet seating dies, and ready to ream, with pilot holes from .17 to .338 caliber, these dies use standard Redding or Wilson bushings.

AMMUNITION, BALLISTICS and COMPONENTS

BY HOLT BODINSON

Developments in new ammunition and new calibers are the driving force in the firearms market today. There've been some big surprises this year. The Freedom Group, which owns Remington, bought Barnes Bullets, adding that successful, family-owned business company to the Group's long list of recent firearm company acquisitions. Hornady continues to be a hotbed of innovation, this year unveiling its extensive "Superformance" line of rifle ammunition that pushes velocities of standard cartridges up to 100-200 fps faster than traditional factory loads. Components from the major companies are beginning to flow again, and if there is a significant trend, it would be toward the "green" side of the business with more and more lead-free projectiles, primers and loaded ammunition making their appearance. Thankfully, from a shooter's viewpoint, the ammunition manufacturers are finally beginning to catch up with their back orders so once again the retail shelves are filling up with ammunition and components.

Swift's bonded A-Frame rifle and pistol bullets are widely loaded by the larger ammunition manufacturers.

Aguila predicts that the 5mm Remington Rimfire Magnum will be chambered commercially this year.

AGUILA

Introduced in 1970, the modern-looking, bottlenecked 5mm Remington Rimfire Magnum (RRM) arrived loaded with potential. Here was a fast, varmint cartridge capable of propelling a 38-grain, 0.2045-inch diameter hollowpoint bullet to 2,100 fps. Chambered in Remington's 5-pound, plinker-grade Models 591 and 592, the 5mm RRM fell flat on its face.

In 2008, Aguila revived the little 5mm with a 30-gr. JHP at 2,300 fps, and the firearms world was abuzz wondering which company would be the first to chamber the round in a quality firearm. It didn't happen in 2008 or 2009, but something's up in 2010 because Aguila gave me a wink and a nod at the SHOT Show. They're coming out with an additional jacketed soft-point loading with similar ballistics for the 5mm RRM this year. Something's up. Stay tuned.

ALLIANT POWDER

Having introduced five new spherical handloading powders this past year, Alliant is getting into the substitute black powder business. They will be marketing a very successful existing BP substitute, BlackMag Xp, under the label "Black Dot." Black Dot is compatible with all ignition systems, contains no sulfur and is non-corrosive and non-fouling. With an indefinite shelf life, Black Dot is also moisture resistant. A smaller-grained form of Black Dot, know as "Flash" under the BlackMag label, may also be marketed as a priming powder

for flintlocks. Alliant is also introducing a new shotgun powder designed specifically for reduced recoil loads (7/8- 1 1/8 oz.) in the 12-gauge. Called "Extra-Light" it is a clean-burning propellant with sufficient density so that normal wads and cases can be used for reloading. Data on Black Dot and Extra-Light is available at www.alliantpowder.com.

BALLISTIC PRODUCTS

Ballistic Products, the source for everything related to shotgun ammunition and components, is teaming up this year with RIO Ammunition, reportedly the world's largest manufacturer of shotshells. RIO, a Spanish firm dating back to 1896, has established an American manufacturing facility in McEwen, Tennessee, and will be focusing its marketing efforts on the independent dealer. RIO manufactures all the components for its shotshells: powders, primers, hulls, wads and shot. Under their business arrangement, Ballistic Products will be the source of RIO components as well as loaded shotshells. See Ballistic Products' wide line of components, tooling, literature, just about everything you need as a shotgunner, at www.ballisticproducts.com.

Craig Sanborn's black powder substitute, Black Mag Xp, will be marketed by Alliant under the "Black Dot" label.

BARNES BULLETS

The big story at Barnes this year is that they have been bought by the Freedom Group and are now part of the family of companies that includes Remington, Marlin, Dakota Arms, Parker Gun, Bushmaster, DPMS Panther Arms, H&R, L.C. Smith and others. The Freedom Group is now the largest manufacturer of commercial arms and ammunition in the USA. Building on the success of their "Tipped Triple-Shock X Bullet" that combines the accuracy and controlled expansion of the conventional Triple-Shock X with a polymer tip,

Barnes new Triple-Shock X bullet in .375 caliber (350-gr.) should be a terrific big game load.

there are seven new offerings in 2011 ranging from a .264 (100-gr.) to a .458 (300-gr.), the latter designed specifically for the SOCOM cartridge. The standard TSX line is upgraded with a .224 (50-gr.), a .338 (285-gr.) and a .375 (350-gr.). The Barnes tactical lines get a facelift with the addition of a TAC-X .308 (110-gr.) and a .338 (285-gr.). The tactical pistol line (TAC-XP) sees the addition of a 9mm (95-gr.) while the TAC-RRLP (Tactical Reduced Ricochet Limited Penetration) group gets a 6.8 SPC (85-gr.). For updated bullet specifications go to www.barnesbullets.com and www.barnesbullets.com/mle.

BERGER BULLETS

As we went to press, Berger announced that it was working on a .338 (250-300-gr.) hunting bullet with an extremely high ballistic coefficient in the range of 0.85-0.86. The rest of the line remains unchanged while production catches up with demand. See www.bergerbullets.com.

BERRY'S MANUFACTURING

Berry's offers an extensive line of copper-plated lead handgun bullets at very attractive prices. An upgraded line of competition bullets is being developed with thicker copper-plated jacket to insure flawless feeding in autoloaders. The heaver plated additions include a 9mm (124-gr.) hollow base, a .40 S&W (190-gr.) and a .45 ACP in either 185 or 200 grains. See Berry's full line of plated, non-plated and "cowboy" bullets at www.berrysmfg.com.

(above) Black Hills' .223 Rem ammunition featuring a 62-gr. Barnes TSX bullet at 3,100 fps is a devastating hunting or tactical load.

(below) Black Hills' .260 Rem. Gold Line target load features Lapua's sensational 139-gr. Scenar match bullet.

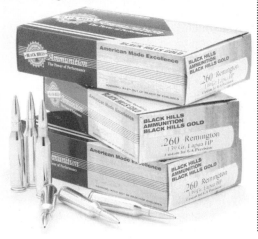

BLACK HILLS AMMUNITION

Consistently providing some of the most accurate ammunition on the market, Black Hills is offering three new loadings this year. At the top of the list is what could be considered the most efficient and effective .223 load on the market – a 62-gr. Barnes TSX bullet at 3,100 fps from a 24-inch barrel. The monolithic 62-gr. TSX expands immediately on impact to .45 caliber but continues to penetrate without loss of bullet weight. In the .223, it's a devastating hunting or tactical load. In the Gold Line, the .260 Rem. case is being loaded with Lapua's match bullet, the 139-gr. Scenar, for long range target and tactical use. Black Hills is the only company currently loading the .338 Norma Magnum. The .338 Norma Magnum with a 300-gr. Sierra MatchKing at 2,725 fps produces

the same or better ballistics than the .338 Lapua. The Norma case is both shorter and more efficient than the Lapua version, and long .338 projectiles with high ballistic coefficients can be loaded in the Norma case without intruding into the powder column. Expect to see more use of the excellent .338 Norma Magnum as a long range target and tactical round once loaded ammunition and components become more available. www.black-hills.com.

BRENNEKE USA

Long known for their advanced hunting shotgun slug designs, Brenneke is introducing two new tactical slug loadings for the 12 ga. 2 3/4-inch. The first is a reduced recoil slug weighing 438 grains with a velocity of 1,256 fps. Called the "Tactical Home Defense" slug load, it is designed to deliver maximum stopping power without over-penetration or projectile deformation. The second tactical slug load is known as the "Special Forces Short Magnum." Featuring a hardened 525-gr. slug at 1,418 fps, the SFSM is designed for maximum penetration without deformation and is quite capable of plowing through vehicles, doors and walls. In independent tests, the SFSM penetrated 34.9 inches of FBI-spec ballistic gelatin while its nearest competitor was stopped at 26 inches. See the interesting test data and graphic photos of these new tactical loads at www.brennekeusa.com.

CCI

CCI's rimfires have gone green! For the small game hunter, the popular .17 HMR now comes packed with a 16-gr. TNT Green bullet at 2,500 fps. For 22 LR fans, CCI is offering a "Short Range Green" lead-free plinking round featuring a 21-gr. copper/polymer mix bullet at 1,650 fps. It's great to see the rimfire line getting ahead of the non-lead curve. See the details at www.cci-ammunition.com.

CENTURY INTERNATIONAL ARMS

Century is in unique position to ferret out great ammunition deals from across the globe. They offer a variety of military and standard rifle and pistol calibers under their "Hotshot" brand at bargain basement prices. What caught my eye this year were offerings for H&K's weird experimental round, the petite 4.3x45mm, as well as the 9mm Flobert Long loaded with #9 and #10 shot, the 9mm Browning Long and the 9mm Largo. Stock up on these exceedingly hard-to-find rounds before they're gone forever. www.centuryarms.com.

FEDERAL PREMIUM

Introduced several years ago, Federal's proprietary "FliteControl" wad has a proven track record of delivering exceptionally uniform and dense shot patterns. This year the FliteControl wad technology coupled with FliteStopper shot is being introduced in two specialized loads. The first, labeled Black Cloud Snow Goose FS Steel, is designed specifically to reach up there in the clouds where the snow geese fly. In a 3-inch 12-gauge loading, the new shell packs 1-1/8 oz. of FliteStopper steel BBs or #2s at 1,635 fps. The second new shell, labeled Prairie Storm FS Lead, is designed to fold tough and wiry late season pheasants at extended ranges. The dual shot load consists of 30% nickel-plated FliteStopper lead shot and 70% copper-plated hard lead shot. Available in the 2-3/4/12-ga. (1-1/4 oz at 1,500 fps) and 3-inch 12-ga. (1-5/8 oz. at 1,350 fps) and 3-inch 20-gauge (1-1/4 oz. at 1,300 fps), Prairie Storm is loaded with #4, #5 or #6 shot.

With the Taurus Judge revolver now available with a 3-inch cylinder, Federal has generated two new 3-inch .410 loads for the Judge. One features five pellets of

Federal intends to supply a variety of fresh handloading components to the marketplace.

(above) Federal's Prairie Storm FS Lead ammunition is designed to fold tough and wiry pheasants.

(below) Federal's Black Cloud Snow Goose ammunition is designed to deliver a deadly pattern to the high-flying birds.

#000 buck at 960 fps and the other, nine pellets of #4 buck at 1,100 fps. Two interesting new loads featuring the Barnes Triple-Shock X bullet are a 110-gr. loading for the .30-'06 sporting a sizzling muzzle velocity of 3,400 fps and a 50-gr. load in the .22-250 Rem. at 3,750 fps. Going green receives some attention in the varmint line with Speer TNT Green bullets being loaded in the .22 Hornet (30-gr. at 3,150 fps) and the .204 Ruger (32-gr. at 4,030 fps). Target shooters should be pleased with three new loadings in the Gold Medal match line with 93-gr. and 123-gr. Sierra MatchKings being loaded in the 6.5x55 at 2,625 fps and 2,750 fps respectively plus a 250-gr. MatchKing for the long range .338 Lapua Magnum at 2,950 fps.

Handgun hunters will hail the addition of Swift A-Frame bullets in the .357 Mag., .41 Rem. Mag., .44 Rem. Mag., .454 Casull, .460 S&W and .500 S&W. Federal has done an outstanding job of feeding the big game hunting market with great loadings in all the classic American, British and metric calibers. This year those lines are being improved with the additional loading of Barnes Banded Solids and Triple Shock X bullets as well as Swift A-Frames. Finally, Federal is making a major effort to bring on line a host of new handloading components including Trophy Bonded Bear Claw and Sledgehammer Solid bullets. See the complete catalog at www.federalpremium.com.

FIOCCHI

With "ballistics to be determined," Fiocchi is fielding two new cartridges this year: a 28-ga. 3-inch and the 7mm Penna, a handgun cartridge designed for IPSC that will be chambered initially by STI. Fiocchi is highly focused on their new non-toxic lines that include rifle, pistol and shotgun ammunition. Fiocchi's answer is a proprietary "Tundra" composite composed of a mixture of Tungsten-Iron-Fluoropolymer. Fiocchi claims that their Tundra shot is softer than Bismuth, 115% heavier than lead and safe for

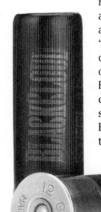

all chokes and older pre-steel barrels. As a bullet core material, it will appear in new loadings for the .223, .308 Win., .30-'06 and 9x19 EMB. By mid-year, Fiocchi will finally be offering a new line of paper hulled target loads for the 12-gauge. Still available for those classic British doubles in the 2-1/2-inch 24- and 32-gauges are high antimony lead field loads. See their latest lineup at www.fiocchiusa.com.

GRAF & SONS

Working with Hornady, Graf virtually revived old military cartridges like the 6.5 Carcano loaded with a proper 0.268-inch diameter bullet and the 8x56 Hungarian Mannlicher with its odd 0.330-inch bullet. When you need hard-to-find reloading components NOW, Graf usually has them on the shelf. The company is a great source for surplus ammunition and ammunition loaded by all of the European makers. See their online catalog at www.grafs.com.

HODGDON

Burning up the benchrest and varmint hunting circuits is Hodgdon's new small bore powder, IMR 8208 XBR. IMR 8208 XBR is a small grain propellant that is part of Hodgdon's "Extreme" family of powders that are uniquely insensitive to variations of temperature. The new powder is proving ideal in the centerfire .22s and compact-case cartridges up through .30 caliber. In the 6mm PPC, it's winning all the matches. Hodgdon has just released its new 5000+ loads reloading manual that does a good job of covering test reports on IMR 8208 XBR. The easy way to keep track of Hodgdon loading data and its three powder subsidiaries is through the web at www.hodgdon.com, www.goexpowder.com, www.imrpowder.com and www.wwpowder.com.

HORNADY

Hornady shook up the sporting ammunition industry this year with the introduction of their "Superperformance" line that carries the bragging tagline, "The new standard by which all ammunition will be judged." The secret is in the powder formulation that permits standard loading procedures to achieve velocities 100-200 fps faster than conventional factory loads without increases in pressure, recoil or pricing. The Superperformance line currently covers 18 centerfire rifle cartridges ranging from the .243 Win. to the .458 Win. Magnum.

NORMA SOLIDS
Professional Guide Ammo

Superperformance cartridges are loaded with either the SST or Hornady's new non-toxic monolithic game bullet made from gilding metal, called the "GMX." In fact, the GMX bullets and the equally revolutionary Flex Tip (FTX) bullets are being offered this year in a variety of calibers as handloading components. Responding to the need for "green" varmint ammunition, Hornady is loading its non-leaded NTX bullets in the .17 Mach 2, .17 HMR, .22 WMR, .204 Ruger and .223 Rem. NXT bullets are also being offered as handloading components.

Giving the AK and AKM shooters some real game loads, Hornady is loading V-Max bullets in the 5.6x39mm and the 7.62x39mm cartridges. The 6.5 Grendel and 6.5 Creedmoor get upgraded with a variety of new bullets, and the Critical Defense ammunition line is expanded with the addition of a .357 Mag. (125-gr.) FTX, .40 S&W (165-gr.) FTX and .45 ACP (185-gr.) FTX. See the complete Hornady catalog at www.hornady.com.

LAPUA

This year Lapua is producing two new precision-drawn cases for handloaders: the .22-250 Rem. and the .308 Win. Palma, which takes a small rifle primer. The full Lapua story is at www.lapua.com.

LIGHTFIELD

Known for its outstanding shotgun slug loads, Lightfield has expanded into the field of less lethal law enforcement and home defense ammunition. This year the focus is on home defense rounds in 12-gauge, 20-gauge and .410. Lightfield's proprietary rubber/poly-

Norma's new monolithic solids feature a flat meplat to insure deep, straight-line penetration.

mer balls, buckshot and spiny star projectiles will be loaded to a different specification for home defense use. The home defense rounds are designed for close-quarter engagements while avoiding the possibility of collateral damage. www.lightfieldslugs.com.

NORMA

Based on necked-up .300 Norma Magnum brass, the .338 Norma Magnum is finally making its debut but initially as component brass only. You'll have to load the exceptional cartridge yourself or go to www.black-hills.com for custom ammunition. This year Norma is teaming up with Blaser to develop a complete Blaser family of big game cartridges based on the .404 Jeffery case. The proprietary Blaser line will include cartridges in 7mm, .300, .338 and .375 calibers, and Blaser insisted that the new line deliver velocity/energy values superior to the 7mm Rem. Mag., .300 Win. Mag., .338 Win. Mag and the .375 H&H. Blaser fans will have something to look forward to! Famous for its African PH line of big bore cartridges, Norma has introduced a new monolithic flat-meplat solid that is plated with a black synthetic to reduce pressure and fouling. The improved solid is being loaded across the African PH line from the mild mannered 9.3x62 to the booming .505 Gibbs. Finally, through an improved production process, Norma is "double-press heading" its brass to obtain maximum strength in their cases. See Norma's extensive lines of hunting and match ammunition at www.norma.cc.

Going green, Nosler is introducing a new line of lead-free Ballistic Tips for varmint calibers.

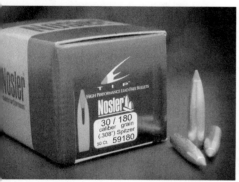

(below) Nosler's Trophy Grade hunting ammunition is match quality all the way.

Remington's Copper Solid big game bullets have developed an enviable reputation for performance in the field.

REMINGTON

Big Green is upping the power factor of their lightweight R-15 AR platform rifle for big game with a new .30

Remington is releasing its Premier Core-Lokt Ultra Bonded bullet line as reloading components.

NOSLER

There's a lot of "green" at the Nosler store this year. Leading the charge is a new line of lead-free Ballistic Tip varmint bullets including a .204-inch (32-gr.), .224-inch (35- and 40-gr.) and a 6mm (55-gr.). The big game E-Tip line, which is proving to be quite accurate, is being expanded with the addition of a .257 (100-gr.), a 7mm (140-gr.) and an 8mm (180-gr.). Over in the Nosler/Winchester Combined Technology corner are nine new offerings: a .204 (32-gr.), a 6mm (95-gr.), a .257 (115-gr.), two .270s (130- and 150-gr.), two 7mms (140- and 150-gr.), an 8mm (180-gr.) and – surprise! – a 300-gr. RN bullet for the .45/70. Over in the match bullet category, there are two new precision bullets: a 6.8mm (115-gr.) and a .308 (190-gr.).

Calling it "The World's Finest Manufactured Ammunition," Nosler will be expanding its Trophy Grade Ammunition line with the loads for the .223, .22-250, 6.5x55, 7mm Rem. Mag., .308 Win. and .300 Rem. Ultra Mag. See their catalog and the company store at www.nosler.com.

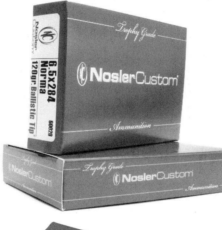

PMC is getting back into the cowboy and shotshell business.

PMC

PMC reports that because of the insatiable demand for rifle and handgun ammunition in 2009, they were forced to put new introductions on hold until later this year. Plans call for bringing back their shotshell and cowboy lines and introducing new frangible, tactical and target loads. Stay tuned at www. pmcammo.com

Remington AR load featuring a 150-gr. Core-Lokt PSP at 2,575 fps. Again, the "green fever" is catching, so Remington is adding its polymer-tipped Premier Copper-Solid bullets to the .30-30 (150-gr.), .30-'06 (165-gr.), .300 Win. Mag. (165-gr.) and .300 Ultra Mag. (165-gr.). Among the more unique offerings this year in the "Remington Rifle" ammunition line are the .338 Marlin Express with a 250-gr. SP at 2,189 fps and .450 Bushmaster with a 260-gr. AccuTip at 2,180 fps.

Recognizing the increasing popularity of the Taurus Judge revolver, Remington has loaded four Heavy Density #00 buck in a 2-1/2-inch .410 shell. With a velocity of 1,300 fps, it's a wicked little buckshot load. Labeled the "Disintegrator CTF," Remington is loading a highly frangible bullet composed of sintered copper and tin in the 9mm +P, .38 Special +P, .40 S&W and .45 Auto. While not announced yet, Remington engineers have developed 3-inch and 3-1/2-inch 12-gauge shotshells capable of delivering 1-1/8 to

1-3/8 oz. of steel shot at the unheard-of velocity of 1,700 fps. Be looking for this revolutionary shotshell in the second half of the year. Maybe the best news is that Remington components will once again be available in quantity including primers, bulk-packed rifle and pistol brass and bullets as well as Premier Core-Lokt Ultra Bonded, Core-Lokt and Premier AccuTip bullets. See Big Green's excellent website and catalog at www.remington.com.

RIO AMMUNITION

This old and respected Spanish firm is one of the largest manufacturers, if not the largest, of shotshells in the world and has recently finished an ultra-modern North American production facility in McEwan, Tennessee. Rio's a vertically integrated company manufacturing all the components that go into a shotshell itself and thus can assure a high degree of quality control and consistency of product. Currently its marketing focus is the independent sporting dealer rather than the large box stores. With a full line-up of game and target loads and with its latest affiliation with Ballistic Products, it's a product line well worth looking for. www.rioammo.com

SIERRA

Sierra reports they've had a hard time just keeping up with demand this year, much less introducing any new products. See the bulletsmiths at www.sierrabullets.com.

SPEER

"Deepcurl" is the moniker for Speer's latest lines of electro-chemically bonded rifle and pistol bullets. The rifle lineup extends from 6mm through .338-caliber while the handgun hunter gets every caliber from .38 through .475 and .500. Responding to the increasing popularity of the .204 Ruger, Speer is introducing a 32-gr. TNT Green bullet and a conventional 39-gr. TNT HP for the little 20-caliber.

Encapsulating a lead core in a FMJ is an ingenious technique to control lead. Speer's electro-chemical plating process gives the company an advantage since the end product is uniformly and completely bonded in a jacket. New this year is an expansion of the TMJ encapsulated rifle bullet line with offerings in .22, 6mm, .270, 7mm and .30 caliber. The justifiably famous Gold Dot bullet line is expanding with the addition of Gold

"Deepcurl" is the name of Speer's new line of electro-chemically bonded rifle and handgun bullets.

Dot HP's for the .327 Federal Magnum (100-gr.) and the .380 Auto (90-gr.). See the whole component list at www.speerbullets.com.

SWIFT BULLET COMPANY

Swift's A-Frame bullets have quite a reputation in the big game fields of the world for controlled expansion and weight retention. For calibers like the .505 Gibbs, .500 Jeffery, .500 Nitro or .50 Alaskan, Swift is introducing 535- and 570-gr. A-Frame bullets in .505-inch and .510-inch diameters. The A-Frame pistol bullet line is growing this year with the addition of a .357 caliber (180-gr.), a .41 caliber (210-gr.) and a .50 caliber (325-gr.). See them all at www.swiftbullets.com.

WINCHESTER AMMUNITION

Winchester has reinvented the classic buck-and-ball load as a personal defense shell.

Called the Supreme Elite PDX1 12, the 12-gauge 2-3/4-inch shell packs 3 pellets of #00 plated buckshot over a 1-ounce Power Point slug. Call it a Hammer Load! The other shotshell is designed for the Taurus Judge revolver to overcome the problem of the rifling engaging the shot wad/shot column and throwing it down and to the right. The new Supreme Elite PDX1 410/2 1/2" shell comes loaded with three flat "Defense Disk" projectiles and 12 plated BBs. It's a variation of the

buck-and-ball concept and should prove lethal at short distances.

Winchester's Bonded PDX1 handgun ammunition line has been expanded to include the .380 Auto and .45 Colt. Winchester, too, has come down with the green fever with the addition of lead-free Ballistic Silvertips in the .223 Rem. (35-gr.) and .22-250 Rem. (35-gr.) plus a .22 LR round loaded with a 26-gr. tin truncated HP bullet. Winchester's patented Dual Bond big game bullet delivering double-caliber expansion and 100% weight retention is now loaded in the .45-70 Gov't (375-gr.) and the .44 Magnum (240-gr.).

Marking 200 years since Oliver Winchester's birth, Winchester's collector's series of commemorative ammunition packaged in vintage boxes celebrates the .22 LR, .30-30 and .45 Colt this year. Finally, the Super-X Power Max Bonded centerfire rifle line, designed specifically for whitetail deer hunting, has been expanded to include the .243 Win. (100-gr.), 7mm Rem. Mag. (150-gr.), 7mm WSM (150-gr.), .30-'06 (180-gr.), .300 WSM (180-gr.) and the .300 Win. Mag. (180-gr.). See all these products and Winchester's new web-based Ballistic Calculator at www.winchester.com.

WOLF

No new cartridges or loads this year, but Wolf will be importing a complete line of rifle, pistol and shotgun primers at very attractive prices. www.wolfammo.com.

WOODLEIGH

Woodleigh has developed a radically new homogeneous, "hydrostatically stabilized" hollowpoint big game bullet. Machined from a copper alloy, the bullet is perfectly cylindrical from its base to the beginning of its short, hollow, cone-shaped nose. Woodleigh claims the new design delivers incredible straight-line penetration with massive wound cavitation. The new bullet is available in calibers ranging from .30 to .577, including all the classic British double rifle calibers. www.woodleighbullets.com.au.

(left) Woodleigh's "hydrostatically stablized" big game bullet has proven as effective as it is unusual.

Norma has designed a proprietary line of Blaser brand magnums based on the .404 Jeffery case.

Pappy's Squirrel Gun

BY STEVE GASH

All Christmases are special for kids, but sometimes the adults are even more thrilled. So it was in 1955 when, at the tender age of twelve, I saw what Christmas was really all about.

The entire Gash clan was assembled at my parental grandparent's modest home on Askew Street in Kansas City, Missouri, on that Christmas Eve. William Alfred and Elva Truma Gash had three children: my father, William Aubrey, Samuel Edward, and Glenva. Legend has it that I called my grandfather "Pappy" because as a wee tyke I couldn't say "Grandpa," and burbled out "Pappy" instead. It would remain my appellation of love and respect for this fine gentleman for over forty years.

William Alfred and Elva Truma Gash at their home in Kansas City, Missouri, in 1955. His friends and coworkers called him "Willie," but he was always "Pappy" to the author. He loved to hunt squirrels, both fox and grays, in the Missouri River bottoms with his Winchester Model 42 .410.

A fox squirrel nest in a tall oak tree. Pappy would sometimes sit patiently at the base of a nearby tree. Soon the quarry would show itself, the Model 42 would speak, and another dinner of fried squirrel was in hand.

Pappy built diesel engines for Greyhound buses for 20 years and started a well-earned retirement in 1963 (photo circa 1980).

Pappy's Model 42 Winchester was made in 1955 and has accounted for countless squirrels, a few rabbits, and even a quail. It served him well, as it will future generations.

Pappy and Grannie went all out for Christmas. Presents were plentiful, if not expensive, and they always laid on a big feed: turkey with all the trimmings. If Pappy couldn't find a turkey big enough, he bought two. All the aunts, uncles, cousins were there – and the grandkids, all seven of them.

After we'd eaten ourselves into a coma and had repaired to the cramped front room that afternoon, I noticed Grannie earnestly talking to my Dad's brother. His parents called him "Pard," as he was always his Pappy's "little partner." I called him "Uncle Butch," although I have no idea how that tradition got started. Grannie leaned over to Uncle Butch and said, "Do you know what this squirrel gun is that Dad wants?" Uncle

Butch assured her that he did, and I saw Grannie give him some cash; I was not privy to the exact amount. Grannie was a homemaker and did work outside the home, so she had obviously (if you'll pardon the eventual pun) squirreled away a buck here and there over the year to come up with this money.

In those days, the Sears, Roebuck store nearby at 15th and Cleveland was where you bought most everything, and they had a modest gun rack stocked with brand-new models. As he made preparations for the short drive to Sears in his 1953 Oldsmobile, I put up a howl and Uncle Butch, who was always kind to children and other small animals, graciously allowed me to ride along.

As we approached the gun counter, I stared wide-eyed at the array of gleaming wood and blued steel. My uncle pointed to a sleek, slender-barreled gun on the wall, and said, "That's the one." It was a brand new

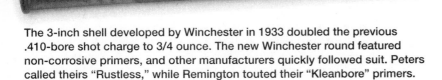

The 3-inch shell developed by Winchester in 1933 doubled the previous .410-bore shot charge to 3/4 ounce. The new Winchester round featured non-corrosive primers, and other manufacturers quickly followed suit. Peters called theirs "Rustless," while Remington touted their "Kleanbore" primers.

Pappy favored No. 4, 5, and 6 shot for squirrels, but an occasional 7-1/2 sneaked in, too.

Winchester Model 42 and was about the most beautiful sight my young eyes had ever seen. The retail price of a standard grade, plain barrel model 41 in 1955 was $81.70; not exactly chump change back then. The clerk put it in its box, accepted payment, and off the Modal 42 went to its new home.

The details of how the gun was spirited into the house, wrapped, and sneaked under the tree before Christmas morning are lost to the annals of time, but on Christmas morning, after the grandkids had ripped open their presents, it was the grownups' turn. One of us grandkids always played "Santa" by passing out the presents, but Grannie insisted on handing the flat box with her gift to Pappy herself. Puzzled, he gingerly tore at the paper. Soon the big red "Winchester" logo and "W" became visible. As the contents emerged, a grin a mile wide occupied Pappy's face, and the twinkle in his eye was a sight I'll never forget. No kid could be more surprised or happier than he.

Pappy was a passionate squirrel hunter and thought that the sun rose and set on the .410 bore. Heretofore he had used a break-action single shot .410. Now, the perfect squirrel gun was his, and bushy-tails in the tallest oaks

were in serious jeopardy for decades thereafter.

Winchester engineer T. C. Johnson designed the Model 12, which was introduced in 20 gauge in 1912; the 12 and 16 gauges came along two years later. Johnson's protégé William Roemer began design of the Model 42 in 1928, and in May of 1933, Winchester introduced the new gun in .410 bore.

The Model 42 was not just a "scaled-down" Model 12. From its inception, it was purely a .410 gun, and Roemer received two patents for the design in 1933. One covered the receiver and the other its internal parts. Economy of manufacture, aesthetic appeal, and technical superiority were hallmarks of the Model 42.

The new pump gun was actually ready in 1932, but, in a shrewd marketing move, Winchester president John Olin held up the launch until the development of the new 3-inch .410 shell. Up until 1932, .410 shells were loaded with only 3/8ths of an ounce of shot. The new 3-inch shell introduced by Winchester in 1933 doubled that to an astounding 3/4 ounce. Hunting with 3/4 ounce of shot gave another dimension to the .410 bore, and countless squirrels, rabbits, and various mountain grouse have gone to

their reward at its call.

In addition to the "standard" grade, the Model 42 was made in "Skeet," "Deluxe," "Custom" models, and even "Trap" guns. "Special Order" guns could be had with just about any feature your heart and pocketbook desired. By far the most common of the post-war units wore plain barrels, but guns with solid/matted ribs and ventilated ribs (of a couple of types) were also produced. Interestingly, many of the coveted "Skeet" versions had either plain- or solid-rib barrels. About 64% of the post-war barrels were 26 inches, with the remaining 36% being 28 inches in length. After 1960, only 26-inch barrels were offered, except on special order guns.

The actual production of complete guns is uncertain, but we do know that Winchester made 164,801 receivers through September 10, 1963. The serial number was stamped on the receiver when the it was made, not necessarily when the gun was assembled. As receivers (and other parts) were manufactured, they were placed in bins, and they were not used consecutively. Thus, a receiver may have lain at the bottom of the bucket, so to speak, for some time until it was used.

Several thousand (perhaps as many

The graceful little Winchester Model 42 .410 is as lively and functional today as it was 55 years ago and still provides an hono

as 6,000) receivers were reserved for the repair of existing guns; some were destroyed in production or simply "lost." It is known that Winchester sent 158,800 Model 42s out for sale.

In 1954, Remington introduced its Model 11-48, a slick little recoil-operated, semi-automatic in .410, and sales of the Model 42 declined precipitously. Production of the fine Model 42 ceased in 1963.

Pappy's Model 42 is a "Standard" grade with a 28-inch, full-choke barrel (Symbol No. G4204S). Its serial number is 138,529, indicating that its receiver was made between January 5 and February 3, 1955. It is in about 90% condition, as he carried and used it in the hardwoods for many years. The gun is typical of the post-war production. The bottom of the forend is flat, with 14 grooves just on the sides. Pre-war models had 18 grooves that circled the round forend. The pistol grip does not extend below the stock, also unlike the pre-war version.

The effects of age eventually overtake us all, and in 1982, Pappy and Grannie moved to Marshall, Missouri, to be near their daughter, Glenva. Pappy never hunted with the Model 42 after that, but shortly after the move, he and his granddaughter Kathy Peuster went to a friend's farm, and Pappy fired the Model 42 a few times. It was his last trip afield with it.

Pappy passed away in 1984. Soon thereafter, Aunt Glenva visited my parents in Pittsburg, Kansas, while my wife and I were there. As she came through the door, I noticed that she was carrying a tattered gun case. "I think Daddy would want you to have this," she said. In it was the Model 42, thankfully not damaged by its tenure in the dreaded leather tomb.

I reverently removed the gun and admired this marvel of miniature precision. Later I gave it a thorough cleaning and test fired it. As expected, it still functioned flawlessly. I have used the Model 42 for some small-game safaris, as it was designed and made to be used and enjoyed, just as Pappy did for many years.

All grandparents are special, and Pappy certainly was. I must agree with Aunt Glenva: I think Pappy would be pleased that I am now the temporary custodian of this piece of family and firearm history. I'm sure that a future generation will continue its legacy.

Acknowledgments

Special thanks to Glenva Peuster and her daughter Kathy Peuster for much assistance researching family photos and history.

My Nine-Lives Mauser 98

BY ANDY EWERT

Author believes that in a hunting rifle, form must follow function. His sporterized Mauser 98 scout rifle combines rugged reliability, power, accuracy, compactness and customized features for deep-woods deer hunting. Its beauty comes from its performance in the field. The fact that this one good gun was put together on a budget only adds to its allure.

The notion that form follows function has particular relevance to the hunting rifle. Reliability, accuracy, power, weight, handling, and safety are required prerequisites. An attractive – or at least easy-on-the-eyes – appearance is important to most of us. An interesting history, well, that's icing on the cake. My one good gun, a sporterized Mauser 98 "scout" rifle, has all of these attributes – and then some.

Sometimes nirvana comes right out of the box. Other times it must be achieved through personal initiative. My sporterized Mauser VZ-24/G.24t/Model 24/47 "nine lives" 7.92 X 57 mm scout rifle is a case in point.

My hunting rifle dates back 70-plus years to the famous Czech Republic arms producing city of Brno. Originally designated by the Czechs VZ-24, a variant of the extended Mauser 98 family, this particular battle rifle changed hands through the fortunes and misfortunes of three armies during World War II. At some point, it was acquired by the German Wehrmacht, becoming a

G.24t, and later captured by Yugoslavian partisans, arsenal refurbished at some point by its new masters, and redesignated Model 24/47. These changes in ownership are evident by markings on the rifle's receiver and barrel. For untold decades, this veteran rested peacefully in a warehouse, most likely somewhere in the Balkans, packed in Cosmoline, awaiting the next conflict.

I purchased the rifle for less than $200 more than a dozen years ago from the former Springfield Sporters in Penn Run, Pennsylvania. At that time, I suffered an acute obsession with military Mauser 98s, acquiring not only my Czech prize, but also German variants exported to Portugal, Argentina, and Brazil, among others. Fortunately for my finances, I'm in the recovery stage. Still, my pulse quickens at the sight of a 98 languishing in a dusty rack or display table.

For several years, I left the rifle as-is, enjoying casual shooting sessions with economical FN military surplus machine gun fodder. I'm sure my fellow riflemen at the range appreciated the bright

plumes of orange flame and baritone booms that followed each pull of the trigger. It shot well and cheaply. Yet in stripping the warhorse, I marveled at its quality workmanship, tight fit, smooth functioning, and elegant simplicity. Its bore shone. The bluing was even and subdued. But, as with many military free agents, its stock's varnish didn't exactly agree with a Cosmoline coating. So what? It had pedigree. After all, the rifle's receiver ring bore the Yugoslav Communist Party coat of arms, along with its latest model designation!

My gypsy's transition from occasional plinker to meat rifle came about unexpectedly after a chilly November Wisconsin deer hunt. I muffed an opportunity in a tract of unmanaged forest, due to the confluence of heavy brush, a 24-inch barrel, and slow reflexes. A handier, shorter-barreled weapon would have carried the day, so I reasoned.

This was the time Jeff Cooper's scout rifle was making press. I bought into it hook, line, and sinker, but the Steyr's hefty sticker price and unorthodox appearance kept me on the sidelines. Besides, I already had an elegant, brand name bolt gun that grouped phenomenally at the bench and proved itself time and again over 20 years in the field. Still, I wanted a scout rifle, but my way and on a budget. Maybe if I had sold all my 98s I could have raised the fare for the Steyr, but that was not an option. The Czech Mauser would become my scout rifle.

The first steps were to have the barrel cut down to 18 inches, the muzzle crowned, and the horizontal bolt bent down to sporter configuration. A local gunsmith accomplished these refinements satisfactorily for a bit over $100. Next was the long-eye-relief scope. Finding a Burris 2-3/4X scout scope was no problem. However, mounting it so it stayed put in recoil was quite another matter.

After a broken brand-name mount sent the Burris two feet vertical (a very lucky catch spared the glass), Dad fashioned a clever substitute using the rifle's original rear sight barrel-band mounting assembly, ground flat, as a base. He cut and shaped a steel plate that dovetailed neatly into the mounting's groove (that held the original rear sight assembly) and had it welded in place for a 10 spot.

Next he drilled and tapped the plate to hold a B-square mount and Weaver rings. The mount was secured to the plate by allen head screws. The assembly has held rock-solid ever since. Annual sight-ins are a predictable three-shots-and-out affair. Since Dad's handiwork, I've never had to adjust its zero, despite occasional encounters with tree trunks while conducting business afield.

The Mauser's smooth, delightfully predictable two-stage military trigger – undoubtedly arsenal honed to pleasing predictability – was left intact, as was the indigenous wing safety. An Ashley Outdoors ghost ring rear sight coupled with a New England Custom Gun Service banded ramp front sight completed the ensemble for an additional $120. The barrel handguard was chucked and the stock shaped by Dad to pleasing trimness and sanded to a gentle sheen without finish, thanks to the cosmoline-soaked wood.

My scout's military pedigree permits use of stripper clips for loading cartridges. This may seem trivial, but it does accommodate trouble-free loading in dawn darkness. Every bit helps.

All the flutter about controlled vs. push feed in bolt action rifles makes for spirited armchair debate if one feels the urge. I do not. I've jammed both types, but good. Both mishaps were my fault. Technique and practice eliminated the problem. My Mauser scout feeds reliably and smooth, even when bone dry and sprinkled internally with forest debris. Deep woods deer hunting takes its toll on a rifle that often must double as a walking stick and a foil against whipping branches. It isn't a place for the fragile in body or equipment.

Mounting a Burris long-eye-relief scope so it stays in place during recoil was key to the rifle's success. Author's father fashioned a steel plate that fitted into the Mauser's military rear sight assembly that serves as a foundation for anchoring the scope mount. The design provides a rock-solid hold that hasn't shifted zero since its inception years ago.

At the range, 150-grain Hornady spire points, backed by 50.5 grains of IMR 4895 (for about 2,700 fps) group within an inch plus a little off the bench at 100 yards – if I do my part. The first two shots from a cold barrel usually fall almost on top of each other. My ability to relax and not think about where number three will drop is the limiting factor.

The advantage of the long-eye-relief scope lays in rapid target acquisition and a full field of view, compared with traditional mounting, sighting, and more powerful magnification. This became immediately apparent to my 50-year-plus, bifocaled eyes in the forest. With a little practice at keeping both eyes open and focused on the target, then superimposing the moderately magnified, enlightened view with one's line of vision, remarkable things are possible.

The rifle's first test came the final day of a seemingly unsuccessful backwoods foray. Dad and a group of hunters congregated by a line of parked cars, magazines emptied, to enjoy a mid-morning coffee break and swap stories. I kept the Mauser loaded, wing safety up. As fate would have it, a doe – with typical female nonchalance – strode unconcerned across an opening, a measured 162 yards distant, three steps from the safety of a tree line. Offhand, I flipped the safety, brought crosshairs to bear, and squeezed the trigger, in less time than it takes to put it to words. The deer was slapped down for the count.

Though the distance was about five times greater than what I've experienced or expect in my annual Badger State deer hunt, the scout rifle concept proved itself decisively at one extreme of the range spectrum. I don't believe I could have equaled this performance in the aforementioned time frame with my full size, 4X scope-equipped bolt gun.

Three years later, the scenario was altogether different. This time the range was about 30 feet, in very thick cover, and low early morning light. A plump four-point buck crossed the gap between two mature conifers. Again I was forced to shoot offhand and out of alignment. Fortunately, I heard the deer's approach, had the crosshairs in the opening before he arrived, and directed the slug to the near shoulder, where it angled diagonally through the body cavity, exiting the offside rib cage. The buck bolted and in two bounds dropped for the count.

On reflection, there is only one shortcoming in my Cooper-inspired scout. With its stepped military barrel, standard-length 98 action, scope, and steel add-ons, it steadies nicely but, at a shade under 8 lbs., doesn't make the Colonel's weight by a pound and some ounces. I substituted a Butler Creek synthetic stock, but it still won't pass muster on the scale.

Big deal. It performs as required and looks distinctive (read "unusual"; it still draws impolite stares from the unenlightened). It's Mauser reliable. And it came my way on budget. I suppose I could invest in an aluminum magazine/trigger guard assembly, replace the military-issue barrel, and find a gunsmith competent in shaving steel with a milling machine, but really it would be solving a problem that doesn't exist – at considerable cost, to be sure.

By my count, this Czech/German/Yugoslav/American battle rifle/plinker/hunting rifle is on its fourth life. I'd love to be around if my one good gun ever reaches number five, but that seems unlikely. It's a burden someone else down the line will have to bear.

My Sporterized Mauser – At Last

BY **HARVEY T. PENNINGTON**

The main ingredients of author's military-to-sporter conversion were (top to bottom) a 24-inch, 7mm Douglas barrel; a semi-inletted stock blank from Bob's Custom Gun Shop, of Polson, MT; and the action of a Yugoslav Mauser.

Author credits the writings of Jack O'Connor, the shooting editor for *Outdoor Life* magazine from 1937 to 1973, with inspiring him to create a sporting rifle using the action of a military Mauser. This photograph of O'Connor (left) and author was taken in 1976 at the end of a visit with Mr. O'Connor at his home in Lewiston, Idaho.

I think the idea of sporterizing a military Mauser has been with me since I was in my early twenties. There is no doubt that it was the direct result of reading Jack O'Connor's books and articles. He, of course, was the shooting editor of *Outdoor Life* magazine from 1937 until 1973, and, without doubt, was one of the most influential gun writers of that time. Like many others of my generation, I greatly admired O'Connor's articles during the years when I was beginning to hunt, and could hardly wait for the next monthly issue of that magazine to arrive in the mail. Certainly, he had a lot to do with feeding my early passion for hunting and accelerating my love of fine sporting firearms, particularly the big-game rifles.

One type of rifle that he obviously admired was the custom sporting Mauser. For me, some of the pictures of his Mauser sporters were simply the stuff of a young rifleman's dreams, and I hoped some day that I could have one of my own. However, I understood that O'Connor's best Mausers were the products of the fine work of such master craftsmen as Alvin Linden, Al Biesen and W. A. Sukalle, and, as the years advanced, I knew that such custom work was far too costly for my budget. That left only one alternative: I would have to build my own.

Of course, I had no illusions of my work's ever comparing to that of some great rifle-maker. After all, I'm no custom gunsmith – just a retired prosecutor who happens to love good rifles, hunting and competitive shooting. But, somehow, it seemed important to me to have a sporterized Mauser with the lines of the classic style of a bolt-actioned hunting rifle of the 1920s, '30s or '40s. And, if all went well, the fact that I would have built it myself would simply make it more special, to me at least.

Now, tinkering around at home with

Here the Douglas barrel is being turned in a Smithy lathe to bring it to proper dimensions so that it would properly headspace the 7mm/08 Remington cartridge.

a surplus military rifle to make it more suitable for use as a sporting rifle – and to make it better fit the needs and taste of its civilian owner – is one of those hobbies that has occupied the time of many a rifleman/hunter. That pursuit probably achieved its greatest popularity in the years following World War II, when tons of U.S. and foreign military rifles were made available to the public. Shooting publications of the late 1940s, '50s, and early 1960s commonly ran pages of advertisements from companies such as Klein's, Winfield and Ye Old Hunter that promoted these low-cost, surplus rifles. Money was tight then for most average families, and the better military surplus rifles were seen as less-expensive alternatives for the big-game hunter. All that was needed was a little imagination and some time in the home workshop.

As a matter of fact, my first deer rifle was a Mark IV .303 British Short Model Lee Enfield (SMLE) that my dad bought for me from a discount store. The cost of the rifle was less than $20. Of course, it was my job to convert it into the sporting rifle I wanted.

I worked on that old .303 in our basement, usually at night and on weekends. I cut down the military stock, reshaped the forend, removed some unnecessary metal (such as the clip guide and military peep sight), shortened the barrel to 22 inches, and cold-blued the barrel and

action. It was slow work, and painful, too, when a tool would slip at the wrong time. But, I learned a lot about files, rasps, hacksaws and other simple hand-tools during the process. Of course, I did not feel competent about doing some of the work. On those occasions, I would enlist the help of a local gunsmith, such as the one who added a Williams front-sight ramp and a Williams 5-D receiver sight. (By the way, that 5-D sight actually did cost only five dollars back then; the year was 1960.)

My conversion of that .303 British was very inexpensive. It was also a little crude-looking. But it worked. In November of 1960, I harvested my first deer with that rifle using a 215-gr. .303 British Winchester factory load. Some time later, I got tired of the look of the .303's converted military stock and bought a semi-inletted, two-piece stock blank from Fajen. I took my time, carefully shaping and finishing the stock and even doing some follow-up metal work. The rifle now looks quite nice and still shoots well, either with 215-gr. jacketed bullets or with the heavier gas-check cast bullets such as Lyman's No. 308284 or their No. 311299.

After all the time and sweat I had in that old .303 British, perhaps it should seem that the last thing I would want to do much later in life would be to start another such project. But, as I said earlier, O'Connor's articles and photos had kindled that desire many years before, and now, after my retirement, I really wanted to try another military-to-sporter conversion, this time on a Mauser. And this time the conversion would be a more extensive one.

The basis of my conversion turned out to be a clean Yugoslav Mauser that I bought through my local gun dealer. The Yugo Mauser is a large-ring M98 variation with an intermediate-length action. When I got home, I disassembled it, and everything (including the stock and barrel) was discarded except for the action.

Before committing to a military-to-sporter conversion project, it is crucial to understand the rifle to be converted. There is probably no better source on the various Mausers, and how they work, than *The Mauser Bolt Actions – A Shop Manual,* by Jerry Kuhnhaussen (published and distributed by Heritage Gun Books). That book is filled with crucial information for the person who undertakes the home conversion of a

Right-side, full-length view of author's sporter conversion of his military Mauser. The lines given to the rifle are reminiscent of those of American and European bolt-actioned sporters of the early-to-mid 1900s. It is chambered for the 7mm/08 Remington cartridge.

Left-side, full-length view of Author's converted Mauser. With its 24-inch Douglas barrel, the completed rifle weighs about 7-3/4 pounds; having only iron sights, it is a delight to carry in the field.

military Mauser.

Of equal importance, the home gun-smith must understand his own limitations. Otherwise, the converted rifle may wind up in the trash, rather than in the hunting fields or on the target range. As an example, I wanted my converted rifle to have a streamlined bolt handle, rather than its unsightly military version. But, from the onset of this project, I knew I simply did not have the know-how, the experience, or the equipment necessary for that part of the conversion. Therefore, I farmed out that task to Bob Riggs, a nearby gunsmith who has had a lot of experience in such matters. As per my request, Bob cut off the old bolt handle and replaced it with a new handle which I had purchased from Brownells, the gunsmith supply house in Montezuma, Iowa. It was mounted to the Mauser's bolt at the same angle as used by Winchester on its Model 70 actions.

As to the rifle's new chambering, I gave some thought to one of O'Connor's favorites, the 7mm Mauser (7X57) but finally decided on the 7mm/08 Remington instead. Handloaded to their full potential, these rounds are nearly identical ballistically. However, factory loads for the 7mm/08 Remington are loaded to much higher pressures (and velocities) than 7mm Mauser factory loads because the 7mm Mauser is chambered in many older, weaker actions. Further, although I handload almost all of my ammunition, there is always the chance of being on a hunting trip and, in a pinch, for one reason or another, having to rely on factory ammo. Thus, the nod went to the Remington round, which I consider com-

pletely suitable for medium big-game and for heavier varmints as well.

Of course, I needed a new barrel, and for that I contacted Douglas Barrels, Inc., of Charleston, West Virginia. That company has been supplying fine quality barrels — at reasonable prices — since just after World War II. And, besides, that business was located just a couple of hours' drive from my home in Kentucky. A simple phone call to Douglas Barrels assured me that they could supply what I wanted. First, however, they wanted to test the hardness of my Mauser's action to make sure it was suitable for the conversion I had in mind. I took the action to them, and it passed the test.

Just a few days later I had a new Douglas XX, "air-gauged" premium barrel in hand. I had opted for a medium-weight sporter barrel 24 inches in length. The barrel was delivered in the white, threaded for the Mauser action, and was chambered for the 7mm/08. The rate of twist was one turn in nine inches.

Since I would be barreling the action myself, the folks at Douglas had deliberately cut the 7mm/08 chamber slightly deeper than necessary to allow for proper headspacing. Following the instructions accompanying the barrel, I managed to headspace the barrel and mount it to my action using my small Smithy lathe, depth gauges, headspace gauges, a barrel vise and wrench, and, most importantly, a lot of patience. It turned out just fine.

After the rebarreling process was completed, the metal surfaces of the barrel, action, floorplate and new bolt

handle were hand-polished down to a 400-grit finish using emery cloth. Although there was some pitting on the action, it was quite shallow, so the polishing was not quite as tedious as I had feared. I also thinned, contoured and polished the trigger guard, which added remarkably to the rifle's overall appearance.

As for sights on my new rifle, I wanted iron sights only. I felt they would better suit the type of rifle that I had in mind. Besides, to me there has always been a certain added degree of satisfaction that comes when hunting with iron sights that is not present when the rifle is equipped with a scope. And I liked some of the early hunting pictures of Jack O'Connor and his wife, Eleanor, armed with scopeless rifles that were equipped with receiver aperture sights. Consequently, I made contact with a Texas dealer who specializes in old, out-of-production iron sights, and was able to locate exactly what I wanted: a Lyman 48M receiver sight, designed specifically for the Mauser 98 action. (The famous Lyman 48 receiver sight was in production continuously from 1911 until 1974. My 48M sight was the third edition of that sight, introduced in 1947.)

Using levels, a small machinist's clamp and the drill press on my Smithy, I drilled and tapped the Mauser's receiver for the old Lyman sight. That job was completed without a hitch, and, to me, the sight complements the look of the rifle.

The front sight that I chose to use was the N.E.C.G. "Masterpiece" Banded Front Ramp. This is a ramp sight that attaches to the barrel by means of a barrel band. It is sold in conjunction with several different interchangeable front sight inserts. The insert I chose was a post with a sloping, brass face, reminiscent of the old Redfield "sourdough" front sight.

I found an unfinished, semi-inletted stock blank for my 98 through Bob's Custom Gun Shop of Polson, Montana. To ensure that the stock's holes for the guard screws would properly align with my "intermediate" length Yugo action, I shipped the action to them, and they cut the blank using the Yugo action as a guide. Once the action and stock were returned to me, I found the stock's wood to be a nicely-figured grade of dense, dark walnut. Also, per my request, the folks at Bob's had fitted a steel grip cap and one of the checkered-steel Neider buttplates to the stock, saving me many hours of labor. But there was still a lot of work to be done on my part before the stock would be completely fitted and finished.

To ensure that the stock would be tightly fitted to the action, I finished inletting for the barrel and action using the old lamp-black method. Simply put, I "smoked" the barrel and action over a kerosene lamp. (Actually, my kerosene "lamp" was a small, glass baby-food jar with a metal lid; I punched a hole in the center of the lid and slid in a round wick. The jar was then filled with kerosene and the wick was lighted and adjusted to a higher-than-normal position to allow it to smoke. This is much smaller and handier around the workbench than a regular kerosene lamp.) The action and barrel were held over the lamp's wick and, once sufficiently blackened, were then carefully placed in the stock, and tapped lightly with a rawhide hammer so that smudges would be left by the lamp black where the metal came into contact with the wood. The action and barrel would then be lifted from the stock, and a scraping tool was then used to remove the black marks that had been left on the wood. This process was repeated many dozens of times before the inletting was complete, but the result was an inletting job that was as perfect as I felt I could achieve.

I chose to "float" the barrel in the stock rather than have it bedded to contact the stock's forend. Floated barrels have given the best accuracy in my target and hunting rifles and have proven to give less change in the point of impact of the bullet in differing atmospheric conditions. Consequently, when the inletting was finished, I removed some of the wood of the stock from the flat under the front receiver ring and from the recoil lug recess to a point in the barrel channel about 1-1/2 inches ahead of the action. This allowed room for the bedding compound; I used Brownells' Acraglas Gel. After the Acraglas bedding process was completed, I then removed just enough wood in the remainder of the barrel channel so that a dollar bill could barely pass between the barrel and its channel in the stock. As a result, the only place the stock's forend and the barrel made contact was the first one and one-half inches ahead of the receiver ring.

I wanted my rifle to have the look of some of the older American and European bolt-actioned sporting rifles, so I cut the forend of the stock to a shorter length than is commonly seen today. I did not intend to use a "shooting" sling on this rifle; rather, I wanted only a carrying sling. The front swivel for that sling would attach to a stud that would be part of a barrel band that would be mounted about three inches in front of the tip of the forend. I located such a barrel band swivel stud (manufactured by Gentry) in the Brownells' catalog and ordered it.

When the remainder of the stock-shaping was accomplished, it was sanded to a smooth finish using 200-grit sandpaper and then #00 steel wool. The last stock work prior to applying the finish was to lightly moisten the stock with a damp cloth to raise the grain and sand it smooth again with the steel wool. This last process was repeated 4 or 5 times until the grain of the wood could no longer be raised.

Next, French Red stock filler was rubbed into the stock and allowed to dry overnight. It was rubbed off across the grain after drying completely. Once I was satisfied that the grain had been filled, the stock was ready for its finish. For that, I chose Birchwood Casey's Tru-Oil. I applied the Tru-Oil using #00 steel wool. I dipped a small "tip" or point of the steel wool into a tiny amount of Tru-Oil and rubbed it into the stock using small, circular motions. Each such application would cover only about a three-inch section of the stock, and, as soon as each application with the steel wool was completed, and while the oil was still wet, the excess oil was rubbed off across the grain using a clean, soft, lint-free cotton cloth. At that point, I began applying Tru-Oil, in the same manner, on the next three-inch section of the stock. Once the entire stock had

These Bausch & Lomb 6-power (6 X 30mm) binoculars are World War II-vintage, and were issued for use by the U.S. Navy. Later, when sold as war surplus, thousands were purchased for use by hunters. The author purchased these binoculars recently at the Log Cabin Gun Shop in Lodi, Ohio, after completing the work on his 7mm/08 Mauser. They were used on the Wyoming antelope hunt.

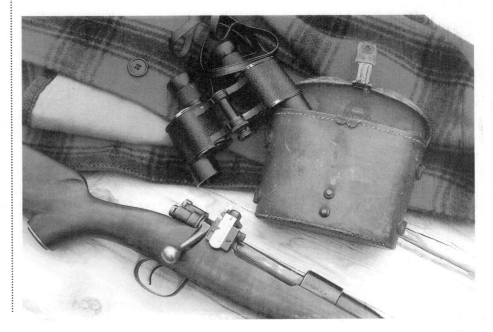

been covered in this way, the stock was set aside to dry for 24 hours. After that time, another coating was applied in the same manner.

I considered the stock's finish to be completed after the application of about five coats of oil. The finish obtained by the method I have described is a deep sheen, and, to my eyes, is much more attractive than the glaringly shiny, spray-on, acrylic finishes seen on some commercial gunstocks today. A hand-rubbed oil finish not only has a nice appearance, it is reminiscent of the time when gunmakers took real pride in the quality of their products, rather than placing the emphasis on how quickly rifles could be turned out.

By the way, at the outset of this project, I fully intended to checker the stock myself. However, after much practice on many odd pieces of scrap walnut, I finally came to the conclusion that, like the replacement of the bolt handle—any checkering of the stock should best be left to a professional. It is still possible that I might have checkering added in the future. But, even without checkering, the stock is still very pleasing to me.

Next, all metal parts of the rifle – barrel, action, front sight ramp, front swivel stud, grip cap and buttplate – were blued. I chose to use Belgium Blue for this process, a product which I had used before and had liked. Belgium Blue is wiped on after the part to be

blued has been heated in boiling water, so, all the home gunsmith needs in the way of special equipment is a tank large enough to hold the part to be blued and an adequate heating source. After each application of the bluing compound, the part is "carded" (rubbed down) with steel wool to remove the excess bluing solution from the surface of the metal. Once enough successive applications have been made, as per the instructions, a deep, durable, blue finish results.

With the bluing completed, I mounted both the front sight ramp and the front swivel stud to the barrel. Their barrel bands had been ordered with inside diameters slightly smaller than they would need to be, so as to permit a

snug fit on the barrel. To bring them to the proper size, I fastened each in a padded vise and used 200-grit emery cloth (wrapped around a dowel rod) to slowly increase their inside diameters to the dimensions needed. Once this had been done, the inside of the barrel band of the swivel stud was given a light coat of Brownells' Acraglas Gel epoxy and was tapped into place on the barrel. The Acraglas was used, of course, to prevent the stud from moving, and this is much easier than using solder to accomplish

A picture of the author at his 200-yard shooting bench. He was pleased with the appearance, balance and accuracy of his converted Yugo Mauser.

the same result. Any excess epoxy was immediately wiped from the barrel with an oily rag. Once the swivel stud was in place, I used the same method to mount the front sight ramp to the barrel.

At this point, my conversion was basically complete. Of course, conversions of military Mausers can be much more extensive than the one I have just described. For instance, I could have changed the trigger from the original two-stage military one to a crisper single-stage trigger. Many brands of replacement triggers are available, but I do not mind two-stage triggers in the least for the deliberate type of shooting that is generally encountered while hunting. Also, I could have opted to replace the military safety, which is a top-swing safety located at the back of the bolt. Such a safety simply cannot be manipulated as intended when the rifle has a telescopic sight mounted in the usual position. But, again, I had no plans of mounting a scope, and the military safety – a three-position safety – suits me just fine. Further, adding such replacement parts can also cost a lot of extra money, and, the person considering the conversion must decide if the advantage offered by the after-market part is really worth the added expense.

With the work of converting the rifle behind me, the shooting could begin. It was time to fire it for accuracy to determine whether any adjustments were needed. For a test load, I decided to try some Hornady 139-gr. spire-point boattail bullets. The load that I settled on for use with that bullet was 48 grains of H-414 powder with a CCI 250 primer. I seated the bullet just short of the rifling, and the overall length of the cartridge was then 2.85". According to Hornady's 7th Edition of its *Handbook of Cartridge Reloading*, this load is actually a little less than maximum for the 7mm/08 Remington cartridge.

Not only did that load prove to be nicely accurate, it was also fast. When chronographed from my 24-inch barrel, the load gave an average velocity reading of 2920 fps. No indications of excessive pressure were encountered. As far as accuracy was concerned, groups at 200 yards were very near minute-of-angle when fired from my bench. (It's interesting to note that Jack O'Connor's favorite factory load for his 7mm Mausers was the old Western 139-gr. open-point bullet at a velocity of 2850 fps. Regarding that load, O'Connor said,

"I have never seen a hunter who used the 7mm with that load who did not like it." My load develops slightly more velocity with the same weight bullet.)

My goal had been to create a rifle suitable for open-country hunting of medium game such as antelope, sheep, mule deer and caribou. I believed that the 7mm/08 cartridge was fully adequate to handle all such game as long as proper loads were used. Although there are many fine jacketed or monolithic hunting bullets being manufactured today, Hornady's "Interlock" bullet design had proven reliable on medium-sized game for me in the past – with 270- and 30-caliber bullets – and I expected the same fine results with their .284" (7mm) bullets. I believed that the load I had assembled would prove an excellent one for most of the hunting I would be doing with this rifle.

Frankly, I was quite surprised with the velocity of my load. The 2920 fps reading was more than I had hoped to achieve especially at less than maximum pressures. I know that in these days when many hunters seem to be focused on "magnum" cartridges of one kind or another, such ballistics may not seem very impressive. But, let's take a minute to put things in perspective.

The .280 Remington and the .284 Winchester are both hunting cartridges with splendid reputations for effectiveness on game. Being 7mm cartridges, they, naturally, shoot the same bullets as the 7mm/08 Remington. Again, referring to Hornady's 7th Edition *Handbook of Cartridge Reloading*, velocities with the same 139-grain Hornady bullet in the .284 Winchester and .280 Remington cartridges top out at 2900 and 3000 fps, respectively. Those velocities were taken in a 24-inch barrel with the .284 and a 22-inch barrel for the .280. Certainly, the velocity of 2920 fps in my 7mm/08 Mauser – with a less-than-maximum load, remember – is quite on a par with those two older, and widely acclaimed, hunting cartridges.

Another comparison that is interesting to make is with the famous and ubiquitous .270 Winchester. That cartridge has earned its place as one of the most outstanding medium-game hunting rounds ever produced. The same Hornady reloading manual lists a maximum velocity for their flat-base, 130-gr. Spire Point from a 24-inch-barreled .270 at 3100 fps. Although Hornady does not manufacture a 130-gr. 7mm bullet, Speer does, and in Speer's *Reloading Manual Number 12*, top velocity for their flat-base 130-gr. spitzer from a 7mm/08 with a 24-inch barrel is an almost identical 3065 fps. Further, the ballistic coefficients of those two bullets are nearly identical. Thus, for practical hunting purposes, any difference in the performance of these two cartridges when loaded with the above bullets would have to be imagined, because I honestly don't believe it could be perceived in the field.

Before leaving the comparison of the .270 and 7mm/08 cartridges, it must also be considered that while the .270's top bullet weights are 150-160 grains, the 7mm/08 cartridge can be loaded with bullets as heavy as 175 grains. This would seem to give the 7mm/08 an advantage when deeper penetration on heavier game is desired. Such a load that shoots quite well in my rifle is the 175-gr. Hornady with a load of 45 grains of H-414 powder. Although I have not chronographed this load, it should be about 2600 fps, according to the Hornady manual.

In short, on paper, the fitness of the 7mm/08 as a hunting round for medium big game simply cannot be questioned. But, as always, the proof for a hunting cartridge is in the field.

A couple of springs ago, after I finished sporterizing the Mauser, my wife, Linda, and I got to spend a few days on a ranch in Colorado where our friends, Ken and Susan Swick, and their two children, Brandon and Hannah, were working and living. Of course, I had taken the 7mm/08 with me; I had hopes that a coyote might show himself. During that visit, both Ken and Brandon fired some rounds from my newly-finished rifle, and each boosted my ego somewhat when they offered some favorable comments on its balance and appearance.

As it turned out, I didn't see a single coyote during our visit, but Brandon (age 15) and I did spend a couple of hours one day thinning out a colony of rockchucks that were posing some problems on the ranch. (By the way, those rockchucks were fairly large, easily the size of the groundhogs we have back in Kentucky.) Most of my shots were from the standing and sitting positions, without a rest of any kind, and, of course, I was using just the rifle's iron sights. I was delighted at the way the rifle handled in the field. Its comparatively mild recoil seemed out of place,

however, considering the terrific power the 139-gr. Hornady bullets displayed on those rockchucks. That experience certainly made me look forward to using the rifle as it was intended on an open-country hunt for something bigger.

Well, when looking for "open country" and the game that inhabits it, one could not go wrong choosing an antelope hunt in Wyoming. I thought the plains-dwelling pronghorns would offer the perfect hunting challenge for my 7-08. So, in October of 2008, my converted Mauser and I – along with my friend and hunting buddy, Steve Geurin – wound up near Newcastle, Wyoming, for the beginning of antelope season.

On the day before the season was to open, we set up a tent camp on some public land administered by the Bureau of Land Management. After the tent was erected, we relaxed in a couple of lawn chairs and looked over the country around us. Basically, the view revealed a lot of sagebrush and many low-lying, prickly-pear cactus plants, along with a few small hills and some coulees that led toward a small valley with a nearly-dry creek running the length of it. On the far side of the creek was a lone, healthy-looking tree, the only one in sight.

Using our binoculars in the fading light, we could make out a little bunch of antelope milling around. They were on our side of the creek, nearly in line with the tree, and possibly a mile away. Hunting, it seemed, would be interesting here.

The following morning, we left the tent just after dawn and walked toward the area where we had seen the antelope the previous evening. The sun was not yet above the horizon when two doe antelope and one buck appeared just at the edge of a coulee directly in front of me. They ran away from me on a slight downhill grade in the general direction of the little creek in the valley. As they did so, I got in a sitting position and placed the brass post of my front sight on the buck, hoping he would stop within range. When the three antelope had gotten about 150 yards between us, they made a slight left turn and stopped in a rather open area in the sagebrush.

The buck was to the just to the right of the does. He had turned perfectly broadside to me; and, by that time, I had already taken the slack out of the trigger. After making sure that the sights were aligned properly, I put the last bit of pressure on the trigger and the rifle

fired. The wide, gold-colored post of my front sight had been easy to see, even in the low light of the early dawn, and I knew instantly that the hold had been a good one. There was an audible "thunk" when the bullet struck. The buck ran in a tight circle and fell, only three or four seconds after being hit. The bullet had struck just above the heart and exited the chest on the far side, leaving a sizeable exit wound.

The buck was a young one, probably two or three years old, but I was a happy hunter. I have enough horns and antlers at home. After all, to me it is the meat that is most important, and a good shot on a smaller buck is better than a risky shot on a larger one. My homemade custom Mauser conversion – a sporting-rifle project that I had planned for over forty years, which finally made it to completion in my basement workshop – had performed its job perfectly. It had provided a quick, clean kill, and, in the process, had helped to put some fine meat on our family table.

In closing, I would like it to be noted that I must not be the only one who thinks my converted Mauser has the looks of a nice old sporter from the first part of the 1900's. I can say this because of something that happened when I had finished the rifle and took it in to my local gun store to let the fellows look it over. As I handed the rifle to Jeff Furnish, the owner of the store, one of those who happened to be in the store that day, a rifle-lover by the name of Dave Robinson, was standing just a few feet away from Jeff. He looked at my rifle and said, "Hey, what is that—a Westley Richards?"

Well, if my rifle had been in Dave's hands at the time he spoke, instead of being a few feet away, I'm sure he would have quickly noticed that my rifle fell far short of having the quality and workmanship of a Westley Richards-customized Mauser. But, nevertheless, when Dave asked that question, I've got to admit that I couldn't have been prouder. With that one comment, he had recognized, at least from a distance, that there was a strong similarity between the rifle I had built and those classic bolt-actioned sporters of the first part of the 20th century.

And, after all, that was exactly the goal I had in mind for this project—a project that I had planned for over forty years.

Four decades and a lot of handguns later, a searcher seeks his one and only.

Only One

BY **ANDY EWERT**

A t age 16, with a little help from my dad, I bought my first handgun, a 6-1/2-inch-barrelled Smith & Wesson Highway Patrolman .357 Magnum. Almost four decades, dozens of handguns, and thousands of handloads later, I'm looking at the sidearm from a vastly difference perspective. Having crossed the half-century mark and then some in age, logic tells me I own too many handguns. It's time to start thinning their ranks or leave the task to someone less discriminating when I pass on – not

that I'm planning on departing this earth soon.

Mae West reportedly said that too much of a good thing is "simply marvelous." I wholly agree. However, my reality now is more pragmatic. Thoreau's appeal to "simplify, simplify, simplify" better reflects my current state of mind. OK, but how to decide what stays and what goes out of the 25 handguns I currently own? The solution: Find that ideal pistol in my menagerie and, over time, dispose of the rest.

Military pedigree 9mm pistols are well represented in the author's 40-year+ handgun accumulation. They include (top to bottom): an Astra 600, a 1942-vintage Walther P-38 and a 45-year-old Browning Hi-Power. All feature top quality manufacturing, accuracy and reliability. Does a 9mm meet the author's criteria for the idea handgun? He thinks not.

Understand that I'm a shooter, not a collector. My handguns, an eclectic mix of revolvers, semi-automatics, an old, inherited single shot, and a handsome pair of cap and ball sixshooters, were acquired for the pleasure of use. I've shot them all and reload for most of them. Each occupies a specific niche, however obscure and redundant it might be. Calibers range from .22 Long Rifle, .32 ACP, 9mm Parabellum, 9mm Makarov, .38 Special, .357 Magnum, .44 Special, and .44 Magnum to .45 ACP. Almost all these handguns are at least 25 years old. They include specimens by Colt, Smith & Wesson, Ruger, Mauser, Astra, Browning, Walther, and Hopkins & Allen, among others.

What I've learned about handguns in over four decades of burning powder can be summed up thus:

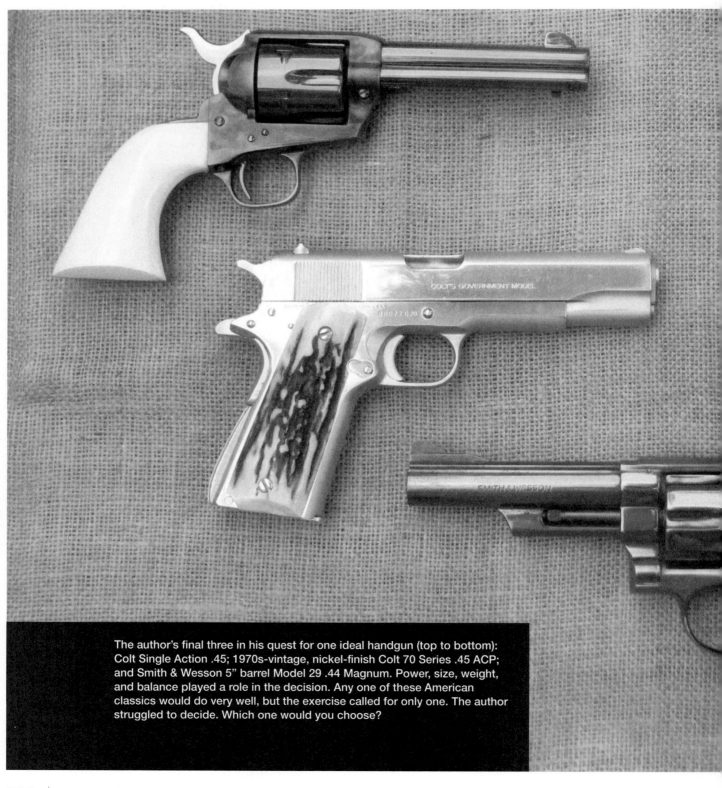

The author's final three in his quest for one ideal handgun (top to bottom): Colt Single Action .45; 1970s-vintage, nickel-finish Colt 70 Series .45 ACP; and Smith & Wesson 5" barrel Model 29 .44 Magnum. Power, size, weight, and balance played a role in the decision. Any one of these American classics would do very well, but the exercise called for only one. The author struggled to decide. Which one would you choose?

Once you've mastered your handgun, practical accuracy is less dependent on the firearm itself than on the fitness of the shooter. Take all the handguns I own and fire, say, six rounds offhand at 25 yards. Group sizes on a good day will vary from the size of a plum (a 1933 vintage Colt Woodsman) to the spread of your hand, fingers extended (a second generation Colt 1860 Army cap and ball).

With practice, a good trigger pull, and – if necessary – optically corrected vision (in my case bifocals), even the most rudimentary sights are usually adequate for shot placement up to 25 yards. This assumes good ammunition, a clean bore, and a steady hold and release. The squared rear- and front-sight configuration seems to work best for me, but others are satisfactory. Because I reload, it isn't vital that handgun sights be adjustable, assuming correct lateral alignment. If necessary, I can load up or down to a 25-yard zero. In my experience, nothing thwarts consistent shot placement more than a bad trigger.

Assuming a Weaver grip, some pistols fit in my hand better than others. Those that fit best usually shoot best. Custom grips can improve shot placement and make shooting a more pleasant experience, especially with hard-kicking magnums.

When striving for shot placement, handgun size and weight matter. Too little or too much stymies practical accuracy. Balance affects placement too.

OK, enough wisdom. Let's get down to business and make those first cuts. My initial battery must include one .22. That's a no-brainer. They're easy to hit with, economical, and fun. Of my four .22s, the keeper is that 60-plus-year-old Woodsman. Even with a six-inch barrel, it's compact, dead accurate, and reliable. The bull-barrel Ruger Target, Smith & Wesson K22 and .22 Combat

Oldies but goodies occupy a special place in the author's heart and handgun hoard. These three fine old Colts are a pleasure to the eye has much as to the hand. They include (top to bottom): .44 Special New Service, ivory-polymer-stocked .357 Magnum New Service and 1960s-vintage .357 Magnum Python. Any one of these beauties could be someone's ideal handgun.

Masterpiece in my possession all fit this bill, but the Woodsman does it best.

My 2-inch barrel, fixed-sight S&W .38 Chiefs Special is a highly specialized pocket pistol for personal defense where concealment is a priority. But the Smith 696 three-inch barrel, adjustable-sight .44 Special is a real seducer. Stuffed with 300-grain lead flat points and Bullseye powder, it's a manstopper par excellence and surprisingly accurate at 25 yards. But at two-pounds-plus it's no pocket pistol. My S&W 2-inch-barrelled, adjustable sight .22 snubby is compact, but its fixed-sight .38 Special rival packs more punch in a comparable size/weight package. If I needed a hideout pistol – I really don't – it probably would be my '60's vintage East German Makarov. Accordingly, all the shorties go.

I'm comfortable parting with two treasured 9mms: a vintage Belgium Browning Hi Power and a Spanish Astra 600. Both are beautifully crafted, accurate sidearms. Their problem is caliber. For defending the hearth and paper punching, the .45 ACP gets the nod, hands down.

With deep regret, I can bid adieu to a fine trio of .357 Magnum revolvers, based solely on my preference for big bores. The 1930s-vintage, five-inch barrel Colt New Service is a classic example of American manufacturing excellence, as is an equally classic six-inch Colt Python, the most elegant, out-of-the-box-perfect handgun I own. The S&W four-inch, fixed-sight, heavy barrel Model 13 fits my mitt and balances best of all my sidearms (with the Colt Single Action Army and Hi Power very close seconds), but in the end the medium bores lose out to their big brothers.

My Mauser 1914 .32 automatic, purchased on a whim after reading about its effective use in the Elliot Tokson thriller *Desert Captive*, is wonderfully crafted and sports excellent fixed sights and a very good trigger. It would be a pocket pistol *par excellence* if it didn't reliably jam. This is too bad because – 3-1/2-inch barrel and all – it's amazingly precise at 25 paces. Still, it never would make the cut.

Likewise for a nickeled, single-shot, 7-inch barrel .22 Hopkins and Allen target pistol my grandparents potted tin cans with in the 1930s. With minicaps and CB and BB caps it excels in friendly basement shootouts, but if I'm going to achieve my goal there's no place for sentimentality or this peculiar, hair-triggered relic.

My second-generation Colt 1851 and 1860 cap and balls are sleek, straight shooting, and a lot of fun. In their day, either one could have been my ideal handgun. With easy-to-clean black powder substitute, I enjoy their company as much as any six-shooter I own. And no handgun points like the 1851 Navy. But in the end, if one is to choose their ideal sidearm for the 21st century, both of them silently slip to the sidelines.

My most recent acquisition, a 1942 vintage Walther P38, was purchased solely on impulse. It's a prime specimen of German technology and craftsmanship. It fits my hand like a glove. I take great pleasure in holding it and imagining the past life this stylish warhorse must have led. Sadly, the time for letting it go is at hand.

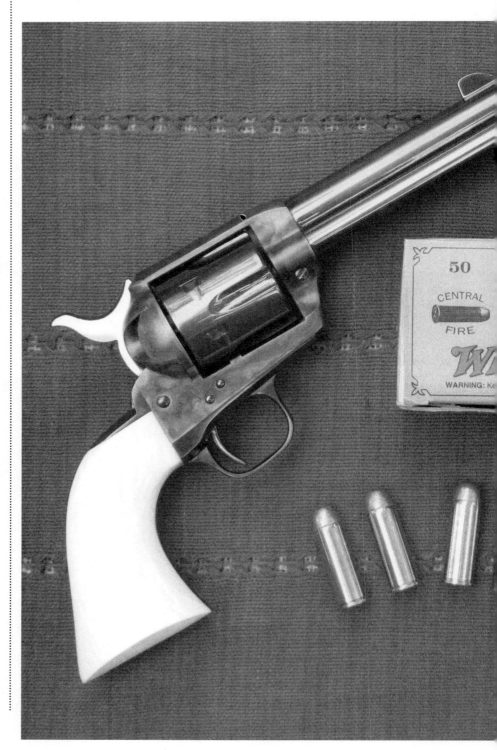

Now we're getting somewhere.

Somehow I own five 45 ACP semi-automatics: a 1930s vintage Colt, an Argentine Model 1927, its successor the Ballaster Molina, and two 1970 Series Colts. My nickeled, stag-gripped 70 Series with a Bar-Sto match barrel outperforms 'em all in accuracy and reliability with lead SWC handloads. It's the keeper of the lot.

Another prize is my 1916-vintage,

Author's surprise choice for his one ideal handgun is this ivory-stocked, 3rd Generation Colt Single Action Army .45. The Peacemaker's power, size, weight, and superior balance make it an ideal choice. At this point in his life, the author doesn't need speedy reloading or brick-busting ballistics. If the Peacemaker's six fat .45 caliber slugs don't do what needs to be done, it's time to grab a 12 gauge or run like hell.

naval-issue Webley Mark IV .45 ACP convert. It's a combat revolver extraordinaire, points like a charm, and perforates paper admirably, all in a most agreeable size/weight package. Still, it goes, only because I have other revolvers that do even better. This Brit is a sentimental favorite. I'd hate to part with it. Likewise, I must say goodbye to a 1930s-vintage Colt New Service .44 Special. It's accurate, superb in fit and finish, and does everything a handgun is called upon to do very nicely. It's a classic American revolver by every measure.

One sixgun that does everything with a little more authority than its peers is my 35-year-old S&W Model 29 .44 Magnum. Two decades ago I had its 6-1/2-inch tube docked to 5 inches, slapped on a set of smooth Herrett Jordan Trooper grips, and never looked back. It has power to spare, is more accurate than I can hold, and parked in a shoulder holster is my absolute field carry limit. With the Model 29, one has extreme flexibility in load selection to accommodate anything from perforating paper to discouraging large, hostile beasts. (Note: If I'm expecting a life-threatening experience, you can bet I won't intentionally make my stand with a handgun.) The .44 Smith makes the first cut.

The final handgun in my battery is a third generation, 4-1/2-inch-barrel Colt Single Action Army. This American classic does its brand proud in looks and performance. Whatever issues Colt purists have with Third Generation SAAs do not apply to this example. Its fit and finish are impeccable. With 255-grain flatpoint handloads at standard velocity, it shoots dead center and point-of-aim at 25 yards. Its trigger pull is just right and the fixed sights work very well for me. This Peacemaker has more than earned its set of genuine ivory grips.

Now we're down to the final four of this exercise: the Colt Woodsman, the Colt 1911A1, the S&W Model 29, and Colt SAA. At this point, each cut is just downright painful.

The first to go is the Woodsman. My personnel preference for big bores prevails. For many, particularly the casual handgunner, this pony is a perfect one and only.

As we're down to the final three, let's refocus our selection criteria from caliber to size, weight, and balance.

The only knocks I have against the Model 29 are its size and 2 lb. 14 oz. heft. Still, if a magnum is on the agenda, who

wants a lightweight .44? Not me. But then, are the .44 Magnum's power and bulk necessary for my regimen of informal paper punching, small game potting, and self defense? No. For that reason, in the most agonizing decision of this exercise, the Model 29 is expendable. If I lived in some wilderness outback where pistol power might carry the day in a pinch, or entertain the possibility of hunting Wisconsin whitetails, it would without debate be my one and only handgun. It's that good.

Now we're down to two Colts: powerful, accurate, and joys to hold and behold. In deciding which one to keep, the focus shifts back to caliber, not capacity or speed of reloading. If I had to rely on one caliber, now that I've eliminated the .44 Magnum/.44 Special tandem, would it be the .45 ACP or .45 Colt? It's a tough call.

After considerable soul-searching, the one handgun I'll carry until the last roundup will be the Colt Peacemaker. Surprised? So am I. Despite my deep affection for Old Hogleg, until this exercise I never considered it as a choice for my final compadre. Since its introduction more than 130 years ago and to this day, the SAA's combination of power, size, weight, and balance make it a solid, all-round contender for the one-gun pistolero. At this point in my life I really don't need magazine loading. If I can't rely on six big, fat .45 caliber slugs to accomplish the task, it's time to grab a 12 gauge or run like hell.

At my self-proclaimed handgun range limit of 35 yards (no disrespect to Elmer Keith), 255 grains of .45 diameter lead at 800-plus fps is all I need. The Single Action Army balances better than any big bore handgun I've ever curled fingers around. It's easy on the hand and hip, and consistently places slugs where I want them to go.

This very subjective exercise is based on personal needs and preferences. Twenty years ago, I suspect the final three probably would have been the same, had I owned a Peacemaker then. However, I'm almost certain my final selection would have been different.

I expect some readers will have issues with my selection methodology and final choice. So be it. Perhaps a good number of you are in a similar position and facing the same hard choices. Set your criteria, conduct your selection process, and let the cards fall as they may.

MARLIN'S 1894-CL CLASSIC

Marlin 1894-CL .25-20 with Bushnell 2-to-7x scope.

Seating a Laser-Cast bullet in a .32-20 case.

BY JOHN W. ROCKEFELLER

Back in the 1890s, the Marlin Firearms Company introduced a short-action, lever action rifle to handle such cartridges as the .25-20, .32-20, .38-40, and .44-40 Winchester, essentially competing with Winchester's Browning-designed Model 1892. While the Marlin Model 1894 has not starred in many Western movies it was, in many ways, superior to the Winchester '92.

Marlin continued to offer their Model 1894 until the mid-1930s or, at best, until the onset of World War II, when so many fine firearms were discontinued so the manufacturers could devote their entire facilities to the war effort. After World War II, manufacture of the neat little Model 1894 was not resumed. Marlin did introduce a new lever action rifle in 1948, their Model 336, in .30-30, .32 Special, and .35 Remington, while their little Model 39 was offered in 22 Long Rifle. That was it.

In 1955, however, Remington introduced a hot new big-bore revolver round, the .44 Remington Magnum, and Smith & Wesson offered their fine Model 29 revolver to handle it. Shortly thereafter, Sturm, Ruger introduced

their Blackhawk single-action for the new round and, in 1961, introduced a neat little gas-operated carbine for the cartridge. Marlin brought out their Model 336-T Texan for the .44 Magnum, while Winchester offered their Model 94 Carbine for the round. My brother-in-law, Bill O'Donnell, had one of these Marlin Texans in .44 Magnum, complete with a brass saddle ring, and it was a lot of fun to shoot with mild .44 Special cast-bullet handloads.

Marlin then decided to go all the way, reintroducing their old Model 1894 lever-gun for the 44 Magnum. The Marlin 1894 has since been offered with 20-inch barrel in calibers .44 Magnum, .41 Magnum, .45 Colt, and .22 Winchester Magnum Rimfire, while a carbine version with 18-1/2-inch barrel was offered for the .357 Magnum. But the neatest of the Marlin 1894s was their rifle version, the 1894-CL Classic, first offered in .32-20 Winchester in 1988, in .25-20 Winchester in 1989, and in .218 Bee a few years later. Sporting a 22-inch barrel and a five-shot half-magazine, it's a pretty gun.

While I have never owned one in .218 Bee, I obtained a pair of 1894-CL Classics

in the early '90s, one each in .25-20 Winchester and .32-20 Winchester. I topped off my rifles with Bushnell Trophy scopes, now discontinued, equipping my .25-20 with a 2-7X variable in Millett engraved steel rings on their two-piece turn-in bases (similar to the old Redfield SR bases), the .32-20 taking the Trophy 4X scope in Millett Angle-Loc rings on a Weaver 63-B one-piece base.

At one time, Remington and Winchester offered "high velocity" loads for the .25-20 Winchester and the .32-20 Winchester, tipped with jacketed, hollow-point bullets and loaded to somewhat higher pressures than the "standard velocity" loads. The .25-20 high velocity loading used a 60-gr. HP bullet at 2,250 fps, while the .32-20 high velocity was tipped with an 80-gr. HP at 2,100 fps. Sadly, the high velocity loads were dropped by the factories since so many gun owners don't read cartridge box labels and were too prone to fire them in the wrong gun! You didn't want to put any of the hotter .25-20s in an old Stevens, for example, or the .32-20 high-velocities in an old Colt or S&W.

Three loads were available for the .32-20 in the early 1990s, including loads with 100-gr. lead bullets from both Remington and Winchester, and a 100-gr. softpoint loading from Remington, all listed at 1,210 fps from a 24-inch barrel. I chronographed all three loads in my Marlin 1894-CL, which has a barrel measuring 21-1/2 inches. Readings from my old PACT PC chronograph were as follows:

.32-20 Winchester, Remington 100-gr. softpoint	**1,327 fps**
.32-20 Winchester, Remington 100-gr. lead	**1,227 fps**
.32-20 Winchester, Winchester 100-gr. lead	**1,198 fps**

I also chronographed some .25-20 Winchester factory loads, both Remington and Winchester makes, with these results:

.25-20 Winchester, Remington 86-gr. softpoint	**1,441 fps**
.25-20 Winchester, Winchester 86-gr. softpoint	**1,431 fps**

(right) Bullets for .32-20 handloads including Hornady 85-gr. HP/XTP, Hornady 100-gr. HP/XTP, Sierra 90-gr. JHC, and Speer 100-gr. FNSP.

(below) Marlin .25-20 with Bushnell 2-7X scope.

Today the Marlin 1894-CL Classic is offered only in .32-20 Winchester, aimed at the "cowboy action" market, with neither the .25-20 Winchester nor the .218 Bee chambering being offered today. Also, factory ammunition for the .32-20 Winchester from both Remington and Winchester is offered only with the 100-gr. lead bullet (which would be "legal" for cowboy action shooting), while the .25-20 Winchester is offered only with the 86-gr. softpoint. The .25-20 with 86-gr. softpoint is listed at 1,460 fps by both makers; the .32-20 Winchester with 100-gr. lead bullet is listed at 1,210 fps.

While I sometimes shoot a little factory ammo, I am primarily a handloader, and I usually "roll my own." I enjoy handloading ammunition, I can save a few bucks on my ammo costs...and I can produce the "high velocity" loads that the factories don't dare offer today, lest some fool fire them in the wrong gun and then sue them silly!

While brass for reloading can be obtained by shooting up factory loads, then reloading the empties, this is not exactly the most cost-effective way to do business, and I much prefer to obtain empty unprimed "virgin" brass and load from scratch. Remington and Winchester offer brass for both the .25-20 and the .32-20 in bags of 100, while Starline offers brass for the .32-20 Winchester in bags of 500 or 1,000.

Lyman and RCBS offer three-die sets for the .32-20 Winchester that include an expander die, which permits "belling"

Marlin 1894-CL 32-20 with Bushnell
4x scope, Winchester factory ammo.

the case so that soft cast lead bullets can be seated without damaging them. Lyman also offers a three-die set for the .25-20 Winchester, while Hornady and RCBS offer two-die sets. If you wish to use cast bullets with either of the two-die sets, you will need to purchase an additional neck-expanding die, which can be had from either Lyman or RCBS.

Jacketed bullets suitable for the Marlin rifle in .32-20 Winchester include the Hornady 85-gr. HP-XTP and 100-gr. HP-XTP, the Sierra 90-gr. JHC, and the Speer #3981, which is listed in the Speer catalog both as a 100-gr. .32 H & R Magnum revolver bullet and as a 100-gr. .32-20 WIN FN HP bullet – same bullet. These bullets are all .312 diameter.

The list of jacketed bullets suitable for the 25-20 Winchester is rather short: the Hornady 60-gr. flatpoint and the Speer .25-20 75-gr. FN SP. Both are .257 diameter and both are cannelured for proper crimping. Hornady introduced the 60-grainer originally for use in the .256 Winchester magnum round, which used a necked-down 357 Magnum case, and was chambered both in the Ruger

Hawkeye single-shot pistol and in the Marlin Model 62 Lever-Matic rifle. The Hornady bullet was not cannelured, but Hornady later changed to the present cannelured version in deference to its use in the Marlin 1894-CL Classic rifles which, with its tubular magazine, required a cannelured bullet. I had some of these older un-cannelured bullets, years ago, but I have long since shot them up.

I like to put up high velocity hand-loads for my two Marlins. I particularly consider my Marlin 32-20 as sort of a "half .30-30" since it is capable of pushing a 100-gr. Hornady HP-XTP to 2,100 fps....the same velocity that a .30-30 can reach with a 170-gr. hunting bullet! Of course, the Marlin .32-20 can reach even higher velocities with the 85-gr. Hornady HP-XTP, up to 2,200 fps, while the Marlin .25-20 can reach up to 2,300 fps with the Hornady 60-gr. flatpoint.

I also like to put up "standard velocity" loads for my .32-20 using cast bullets. When I don't feel like casting my own, I can use the Laser-Cast .32-20 115-gr. FP BB .313 bullet from Oregon Trail

Bullet Company. Otherwise, I can dig out my own bullet moulds and cast up a few, using either the Lyman #311008 115-gr. plain base or the RCBS 32-098-SWC plain base.

Oregon Trail doesn't offer a Laser-Cast bullet for the .25-20, however, and the only suitable bullet mould is Lyman's #257420, which casts a flat-point, gas check bullet of nominal 65 grains...though my own bullets, cast of wheelweight metal, weigh in at 73 grains.

I size my bullets to proper diameter on my new Lyman #4500 lubricator-sizer, using a .312 sizer die for the larger slugs and .258 for the smaller. I also use Lyman Orange Magic bullet lubricant, a high-temperature lube that requires heating. Fortunately, this is easily accomplished with Lyman's electric lube heater, which slips into a well at the rear of the lubricator-sizer casting.

Case necks must be belled when seating cast bullets but, actually, I prefer to bell my cases even when seating jacketed bullets....it helps to avoid crumpling my precious brass! Also, while it is practical to seat and crimp cast bullets in a single operation since cast bullets usually have generous crimping grooves, the skimpy rolled-in cannelure found on jacketed bullets can cause problems if you attempt to seat and crimp the bullet in one operation. When seating jacketed bullets, it is best to back off your seating die so it won't crimp the case mouth, adjust the seating screw and seat all the bullets so the bullet cannelure lines

handloads. Even if you only reload fired cases from factory ammo, though, those factory cardboard cartridge boxes won't last forever.

As for me, I like to use the sturdy plastic Case Gard cartridge boxes from MTM Molded Products, either the fifty-round P50-38 or the hundred-round P-100-3 size, as intended for .38 Special or .357 Magnum. These come in three colors, so I use the clear red boxes for .25-20

Author shooting the .25-20 from the MTM rest.

up with the case mouth. Next, back off the seating screw, readjust the die so it crimps the case mouth, and crimp all the bullets. This takes a little more time but gives better results.

Loading data for the .25-20 and .32-20 Winchester are to be found in most of the major handloading manuals, including the *Accurate Smokeless Powder Loading Guide*, Number Two; the *Hornady Handbook of Cartridge Reloading* 7th Edition; the *Lyman Reloading Handbook*, 49th Edition, and the *Speer Reloading Manual Number 14*. The *Laser-Cast Reloading Manual, First Edition*, lists cast bullet data for the .32-20 only.

If you reload factory ammo, you can store your handloads in the boxes in which the factory loads were originally packaged but if you put up your handloads in virgin brass cases, which come in plastic bags, you will need some good plastic cartridge boxes for your

handloads with softpoints, the clear blue boxes for .32-20 handloads with JHPs, and the opaque green boxes for my .32-20 handloads with cast bullets.

My two Marlin 1894-CL Classics are among my favorite rifles and occupy a favored place in my gun cabinet. Neither rifle is powerful enough for deer or big game, but they are more than adequate for small game, for short-range varmint shooting, or for plinking and paper punching. Unlike some of my more powerful rifles, the little Marlins are very pleasant to shoot. A full-powered deer rifle is, at best, only useful for a once-a-year hunting trip, but these mild-mannered Marlins are year 'round companions.

What more can I say? Good luck, good shooting…and happy handloading!

(This article is dedicated to wildlife photographers and dog lovers Sue and Al Forst of Cody, Wyoming.)

BY ERIC MATHERNE

"You can forget about getting a .22, boy; those things are too dangerous. That bullet can go a mile and hurt somebody. No sir; no .22."

This was dad's opening salvo in the campaign by me to acquire a .22 rifle and it seemed like the end of it also. My father was a Louisiana State Trooper and a man of strong convictions. Like another fellow said, when he said "no," he meant "NO."

Rather than surrendering so early in the battle, I decided to disengage and lick my wounds while planning my next move. Never underestimate the guile of a 16-year old gun nut.

My father was not anti-gun, just anti-.22 rifle. He had bought an Iver Johnson Champion .410 for me when I was 12 and a Winchester Model 12 in 16 gauge was my birthday present at fourteen. He gave me a Colt Official Police .38 Special after nixing the .22. I discovered later that a friend of his had caused the death of a young girl with a ricochet from a .22. This event was the root cause for his antipathy toward rifles, especially .22 rifles.

It eventually came to pass that a

friend had a .22 rifle that he was willing to part with for a reasonable price. It was a Mossberg Model 146B and I fell in love at first sight. This rifle sold for the princely sum of $28.95 when this tale took place in the mid-1950s. It was a bolt-action with a tubular magazine that held thirty Shorts or twenty Long Rifles. The bolt handle was T-shaped and the sights were a marvel to behold. There was a peep sight that could be pivoted aside to allow the use of a rear sight that had four different blades that could be turned to align with a front sight that had four different iterations: two posts, a bead and an aperture. (Whew!) The stock was genuine walnut and was

Ain't it a beauty? Mossberg with Weaver B4 scope – very high-tech in 1953!

The Mossberg 146B

Top: Author's Mossberg 146B with B4 Weaver scope.

Bottom: Winchester 69A with Weaver 3X9 on homemade base, perhaps a step up in prestige from the Mossberg.

equipped with Mossberg's odd but useful sling swivels. In addition, the receiver was grooved for easy attachment of a scope – talk about a boy's dream come true!

It was time to return to the fray with my father but this time I had a secret weapon: a discount.

My friend had agreed to sell me the Mossberg for about one-third off the retail price and I knew this would help me sway dad – that and the fact that he was a strong believer in gun safety and constantly preached it to me. I was in my third year of hunting and he let me hunt by myself most times now. His safety talks were working, and in the end he realized it and relented, buying the rifle for me. His final words on the subject I won't repeat, but they involved what would happen if he ever caught me being unsafe with it.

I had the .22 of my dreams now and I was determined to learn to shoot it well. The sights were a mystery to me because I had a been a shotgun shooter up to now. I tried every combination (and they were many) and achieved some success with them. After several months, and a large number of cartridges, the conclusion was reached that the iron sights had to go. A scope sight was what was needed, but a Weaver B4 sold for close to $10.00. I began a campaign of saving my few spare pennies and by the end of school, I had the Weaver. The summer was spent learning to use the scope. The expenditure in ammo was

high, consuming all my money, but it was worth every cent. After seeing how serious I was about learning to be a rifleman, Dad found a source of Federal Monark Long Rifles at a cost of $3.00 a brick. The rate of fire went up from that point on. The Monarks were standard velocity and it seemed as though you had time to stand up and watch the bullet on its way to the target. Many were the lessons learned that summer, lessons still called upon more than fifty years later.

Came the fall and I decided to do my entire squirrel hunting with the Mossberg. After some more experiments at the local dump, I selected Winchester Super-X Long Rifles as my hunting load and ponied up for a brick at the cost of $5.00. Tough to pay, but worth the expense.

When I informed Dad of my decision, his response was that he would clean every squirrel I killed with the rifle. Despite the fact that I had managed to kill a few squirrels with the iron sights, he had little faith in the Mossberg as a gathering tool for the local tree-climbers. He was very surprised when I presented him with a bag of nine fox squirrels and a smart-alec remark to the effect of "Get busy." True to his word, he cleaned them all. His only complaint was that most of them were shot in the head, thereby spoiling the brain, a delicacy in those days in Cajun country.

That was the start of an informal competition between us as to who was the

better squirrel hunter. For my part, there was no doubt on that subject; he was the champ. I can recall only two times that I managed to top him and I consider them both minor miracles. (They may be major miracles when I consider how good a hunter he really was.)

The old Mossberg has been a real learning tool for me for more years than I care to count, and it is the source of many cherished memories. It's still used a few times every squirrel season and it occasionally sneaks up on a swamp rabbit. My kids learned the basics of rifle shooting with it and now there are grandchildren for it to teach whenever they say they're ready.

Mossberg and other American arms makers at one time had scads of good and inexpensive .22s in their catalogs. I remember drooling over the likes of Winchester Model 69s and Remington 341s and especially the little Mossberg carbines with the fold-down forearm. That one was available as a bolt or semi-auto. These and other makes and models are relegated to closets and attics all over this country. Do yourself a favor if you own one: take it out and shoot it. The smell of that powder and the sharp crack will bring the memories pouring back to your mind, especially if you're lucky enough to have an old buddy along to enjoy it with you. When Cousin Thomas and I get together with our old rifles, it's not long before one of us says "Remember that time....?"

Try it.

There's more than handguns at Smith & Wesson:

The New S&W SHOTGUNS

BY DR. GEORGE E. DVORCHAK, JR.

The three new S&W shotguns used to shoot clay birds as well as hunt with during the quail/pheasant hunts. From top: Elite Gold, Elite Silver, and Model 1012 semiauto.

Smith & Wesson: great semiauto handguns and revolvers! That's the knee-jerk reaction made by most anyone who shoots but today, that assumption needs to expanded upon. When it comes to rifles, they offer what I feel are some of the best semiautos for defense or varmint control, the M&P15 and the M&P15 PC chambered in .223 Remington/5.56 mm NATO. Of course, S&W Holding Corporation (Nasdaq: SWHC) has acquired Thompson/Center Arms, which adds T/C's superb single shot rifles, handguns, slug guns, black powder arms, semiauto rimfire rifles and the new Icon bolt action rifle to S&W's burgeoning product line.

But – shotguns? Yes, shotguns. For those of us old enough to have been interested in firearms in the 1970s, from 1972 until 1984 Smith & Wesson marketed pump and semi-auto shotguns that were manufactured by Howa in

Japan. I fired one of these in a round of skeet years ago and that was all the experience I had with them. Then at the 2007 SHOT Show in Orlando, Florida, at the writer shoot-out the day before the show, writers and guests all had the opportunity to fire the three new shotguns that now carry the Smith & Wesson name. Three years of work went into the market research for these shotguns; by not rushing the introduction, Smith & Wesson management did it right and covered all bases with a side-by-side, an over-under and a gas-operated semi-auto shotgun, all geared to the shooting sports and hunting.

Here is what these S&W shotguns are all about.

ELITE GOLD SIDE-BY-SIDE

This type of shotgun, in years past, has been referred to as a "double-bar-

rel," which is a name that stuck long before over-and-under doubles became popular. As a kid, I remember the old Stevens Model 311 or Fox doubles which were working guns that were used and used hard, with little worry about dings and scratches. (One SXS – i.e., side-by-side – that I used for a round of skeet and *did* worry about scratching was a friend's Winchester Model 21.)

Then came a market shift which saw affordable bread-and-butter doubles being eliminated and classics being retired. The double seemed to fade from the sporting community. Today, I have a new-found respect for fine guns which was strengthened through my hands-on-experience with the Smith & Wesson Elite Gold 2.75-inch and 3-inch side-by-side. I found this double to be both a work of art as well as quite functional in the field. It is also easy to carry, weighing in at around 6.5 lbs. in 20 gauge.

What also stands out is its hand-cut checkering (at 24 lines per inch) and engraving, which covers about 25% of the receiver. Its barrels are either 26 or 28 inches with the overall length being 43.5 or 45.5 inches, respectively. When the Elite Gold was introduced, the triggers were single, which I prefer. New in 2008 was the option for either of two styles of double triggers for the same price as the single-trigger version. For chokes, you have a IC/Mod bores. For those who appreciate a high-quality, well-figured piece of wood, the Elite Gold is available with an English or Prince of Wales stock of AAA grade Turkish Walnut. What is also obvious on the Elite Gold it is the precise metal to wood fit. This is only possible on firearms that are not run-of-the-mill, since fitting takes time and, as you know, time is money.

ELITE SILVER OVER-UNDER

Back in my skeet shooting days when I shot competition, my Browning Superposed Diana had one frame/forend and four gauges of barrels, all balanced exactly. Due to this, they all swung and pointed the same and that became the action type I became accustomed to from thousands of rounds being fired in competition. This is probably why today I shoot an over-under the best.

Being a 12 gauge, the S & W Elite Silver weighs 7.6 to 7.8 pounds and is available with 2-3/4- or 3-inch chambers and 28 or 30 inch barrels. (Alas, the 26-inch length was discontinued in 2008.) There are five choke options: Cylinder, which is for skeet and sporting clays or grouse; Improved Cylinder; Modified; Improved Modified; and Full for those long shots. This newly-designed Elite Silver shares many of the same custom design features as found on the Elite Gold series side-by-side and are also crafted with hand-engraved receivers finished in a bone-charcoal case hardening. Such a finish provides for a distinctive appearance as well as protection for the receiver.

AN ELITE SERIES EXTRA!

We have all heard of lifetime warranties that expire at the end of the original owner's tenure. Smith & Wesson, again taking what many manufacturers had and expanding on it, did it again by coming up with their "Heirloom" warranty: with each purchase of an Elite Series shotgun, you get a lifetime warranty and then, when you pass either of these shotguns to whomever, your heir also has the same warranty protection you originally did. In my experience, a company who does this is one who obviously has the confidence that their product will continue on, trouble-free, into the next generation and then some.

When it comes to cost, the Elite Series models average $2,380 for either the side-by-side Gold or the over/under Silver, which is a lot less than I would have expected. With either purchase you get a fine, classic shotgun that is well-made, functional, practical and a work of art.

1000 SERIES SEMIAUTOS

[Editor's Note: As this edition was going to press, Gun Digest *learned that S&W's 1000-Series semiauto shotguns have been discontinued. However, some will no doubt linger at retail for some time, so we present the following information for its historical value. -DMS.]*

The Models 1012 Super (3-1/2-inch magnum), 1012 (2.75- or 3-inch 12 gauge) and 1020 (2.75- or 3-inch 20 gauge) gas-operated semi-automatics were designed for rough use and display excellent built-in handling characteristics.

Paul Pluff from Smith & Wesson with my favorite of the three, the 12-gauge Elite Silver in 12 gauge.

Before hunting, we were all given a few hours of hands-on shooting time with all three shotguns at clay birds, as author is doing with the Elite Silver.

Point, shoot, and the target goes down! Barrel lengths are 24, 26, and 28 inches as well as a 30-incher with TruGlo sights and ventilated rib. Five different choke tubes and a wrench are also included.

Weight of the 20 gauge, again depending on barrel length (24 or 26 inches) and stock material (wood versus synthetic) runs from 5.5 to 6.1 lbs. Overall lengths begin at 43.0 and go all the way to 50.5 inches for the 30-inch-barreled version that was discontinued in 2008. In 12 gauge, the weights vary from 6.3 to 7.5 lbs. with overall lengths from 45 to 51 inches – again, the latter for the 30-inch-barreled flavor. Magazine capacity also varies, with the 12 gauge magnum holding 3 + 1 and the standard version 4 + 1. In the 20 gauge, it is 4 + 1 for all variations. The price of these shotguns in 2008 varied between $644 to around $735 in 20 gauge and is now slightly higher, primarily because of the falling dollar. The 12 gauge versions averaged between $644 for the 1012 to $882 for the 1012 Super – again, a bit more than that today because of the weak dollar.

FIELD TESTING: AN OKLAHOMA QUAIL HUNT

A hunt to field-test these new shotguns was held for a few writers and personnel from Smith & Wesson/Blue Heron Communications at the famed Selman Ranch in Oklahoma. This is a 14,000-acre ranch located in the northwest part of that state, and it's quite famous. In fact, there was even a book written about this ranch's history. This book, *The Buffalo Creek Chronicles*, by Lantzy and House, tells how the Selman family carved out a living on this land, one rich in game throughout its sagebrush-covered rolling hills.

As we arrived and drove into the ranch area, in certain ways it was like going back in time. As a kid, I remember my grandmother's farm and the machinery of the day, now all gone. It was good to see a lot of the equipment of our past still onsite, reminding us of the jobs it had once accomplished. Then it was time to check in, head to the main house to eat dinner, and then hit the sack in preparation for two days of shooting.

The following morning, we woke up to a great breakfast to begin the day. Then we were directed to a shooting area about a half mile away where Colie Selman, the staff and our group set up clay target throwers to give us all practical experience with the new shotguns. I did shoot all of these at the SHOT Show but

This bird, flushed by the dog, appeared to go straight up. Author shot, and he was then on his way down. This is why it was good to have someone with a camera who was not hunting.

Trying out the Boyt hunting and shooting vests in the Oklahoma fields. It was easy to load game into the vest and later clean it due to its large pouch openings. The large flap pocket pockets with shell loops also made carrying ammo comfortable.

now we could shoot all we desired and fire at targets not confined to "straightaways" but angled or, to add difficulty, launched right off the ground as a quail flies. After a few hours of shooting, we broke up into two groups and with dogs and a skilled handler in tow, it was off to try our luck. After a few hours of hunting, we met for lunch and in the

Due to balance and handling qualities, all of these shotguns pointed naturally. This is a positive quality in any shotgun.

afternoon, we went out to other areas to hunt some more.

When flushed, grouse move and move fast, and here is when a shotgun that fits and naturally swings as the Elite Silver does is necessary to consistently point, shoot and drop that bird. I really appreciated the S&W over-under, an action type I have always done my best with.

The next day, we had the option to go back to quail areas or try fields with pheasants. I opted for the pheasants. Again, the dogs were great and their pointing gave the hunters a few seconds to switch mental gears so to be ready

for that flush that would happen any second. When it did happen, the birds' flight patterns were not as fast as the quails' but seemed to be more erratic. Again, this is where a shotgun that naturally points greatly helped me harvest that bird.

What made a lasting impression on me with these three shotguns, especially the semi-autos, was that even when filthy, they simply did not malfunction. During all that shooting – and gun writers have never been known for being over-protective with test guns – the S&W shotguns continued to work flawlessly. Even though I at times have a mental block with any side-by-side shotgun, the Elite Gold 20 gauge was a pleasure to carry and shoot. With over-under

and semi-autos admittedly being my preference, I was not disappointed with the Elite Silver over/under or the Series 1000 semiautos. The 12-gauge models I shot were on the heavy side but, being so well balanced, they made swinging and point shooting feel natural. When you're hunting and a bird goes up, the shotgun should be shouldered and fired almost instinctively. If your alignment is good, the bird falls out of the sky. When this consistently happens, at least part of the credit should go to the shotgun – and credit is certainly due to the new S&W shotguns.

What was also interesting was that none of the S&W shotguns was a favorite of everyone. Some preferred the 20 gauge side-by-side, others the over-under and others the semi-auto, which just goes to show you that love is ever in the eye of the beholder. It also means that there is something for everyone from Smith & Wesson.

Entering the shotgun market was an adventurous step for a company whose expertise was, and still is, handguns. Yet it was that adventurous attitude that drove S&W to apply for new patents and to build a plant in Turkey dedicated entirely to ensuring the quality of these new shotguns.

Sources for Additional Information:

Boyt Harness Company
www.boytharness.com (800) 550-2698

Smith & Wesson
www.smith-wesson.com (800) 331-0852

Selman Ranch
www.selmanranch.com
(580) 256-2006

The 1000 Series semiautomatic in 12 gauge. As of 2010, this series of shotguns has been dropped from the S&W line-up but can occasionally be found in dealers' gun racks. (S&W photo)

The S&W Elite Gold 20 gauge. (S&W photo)

S&W Elite Silver 12 gauge over-under. (S&W photo)

BY JIM DICKSON

Right and left views of the 4-inch Ruger Redhawk in .45 Colt.

THE 4"-BARREL .45 COLT RUGER REDHAWK REVOLVER

The .45 Colt has always been my favorite revolver cartridge and the new stainless steel Ruger Redhawk allows it to go places it has never gone before. This massive magnum-frame revolver is also chambered for the .454 Casull, among other calibers, so it has far more strength than the old Colt Single Action Army revolver. This strength has engendered a variety of .45 Colt factory loads from sedate 230-grain bullets at 730 fps to 335-grain big-game bullets at 1050 fps, along with 300-grain bullets at 1300 fps. Indeed, the .45 Colt is becoming the 30-06 of the revolver calibers with its wide variety of varying power loads for every purpose.

The use of heavy, deep-penetrating bullets at moderate velocity is much more effective on game than trying to get 2000 fps out of lighter bullets in a handgun. You also get your game without the deafening decibel level that accompanies such velocities in a short-barreled handgun. While ear plugs and ear muffs together cannot guarantee ear protection, you certainly don't dare fire a short-barreled gun with a hot load without them. Hunting and defense rarely allow time for donning your ear protection, so I try to keep the noise down. Anyone who fires a 2000 fps .45 load at a carjacker while he is still in the car or at a burglar in the bedroom can expect permanent hearing loss. It's bad enough to fire a .45 automatic in these confines without hearing protection.

The 4-inch Ruger Redhawk is a near-perfect revolver for the good old .45 Colt. I ordered the 4-inch barrel length because it is easier to carry than longer barrel lengths. Ever try sitting down with a long-barreled revolver in a

holster on your hip? You have to be able to cant the holster to the front or back like a sword or machete and I prefer my pistols not to be moving about lest I end up fumbling for them when I need them in a hurry. As far as accuracy goes, the late Elmer Keith always said he could hit

better with 4-inch barrels than longer ones. He normally carried a 4-inch S&W .44 Magnum revolver and was a very difficult man to outshoot.

When I first picked up the Ruger at Tucker Guns in Tucker, Georgia, I was struck by the sheer massiveness of this beast. At 46 ounces and 9.5 inches long, it is no vest pocket hideout gun. It is a state-of-the-art, modern magnum designed to safely handle the heaviest loads. Handling it was enlightening. It moved with the grace of a prima ballerina, quickly aligning its sights on target and having the weight to hold

steady during fast double action firing, aided by a superbly light and smooth double action trigger pull. Recoil with standard velocity .45 Colt 250- and 255-grain loads was virtually nonexistant. Its 1:16 right-hand twist rifling proved capable of consistently making 1- to 2-1/2-inch groups at 25 yards from a sandbag rest.

This was one of the best-handling revolvers I have seen. It harkens back to the days of the Colt New Service and S&W Triple Lock large-frame revolvers, when "big" meant "steady." Still, my better half Betty found it comfortable to use and she's only 5 feet, 2 inches tall. I quickly realized that this was the ultimate home protection pistol for the average family that wants a revolver because they don't want to bother with the perceived coplexity of a semi-auto. Also, it's built of stainless steel, so it should shrug off the casual maintenance that sometime befalls a home-defense rhandgun.

The Ruger is a natural

4-Inch Ruger Redhawk Specs	
Caliber:	.45 Colt
Capacity:	6
Finish:	Satin Stainless
Grip:	Hogue® Monogrip®
Barrel Length:	4 inches
Groove:	6
Twist:	1:16 RH
Overall Length:	9-1/2 inches
Weight:	46 oz.
Front Sight:	Blade
Rear Sight:	Adjustable
Sugg. Retail Price:	$861.00

pointer, so anyone can learn to hit with it quickly. (The average homeowner will probably practice with it to the extent of putting one box of cartridges through it.) There is nothing simpler than a double action revolver to shoot: you just point and start pulling the trigger when attacked.

But best of all, the Redhawk in .45 Colt is a true manstopper. The standard lead 250-grain .45 Colt is the same load the army used to stop the fanatical Moros in their suicidal jihad charges during the Phillippine Insurrection before the M1911 was adopted. Mayby you don't have Moros in your neighborhood, but there are even worse things in many areas. The .45 Colt has always provided reliable stopping power without much recoil and without the need for hollowpoints or fancy bullet designs. It's big enough to get the job done without needing any help. This is not surprising, considering the history of the cartridge.

There is an old military saying that holds that "if you want to stop a horseman, stop his horse," which led to the development of the .45 Colt around 1873. It was actually designed to bring down a horse so you could more easily deal with his rider. The efficiency of it as a horse killer was borne out by the tens of thousands of cowboys who carried a Colt Single Action Army .45 Colt to shoot the horse with if they were thrown by a bronc and dragged with their high-heeled cowboy boots caught in the stirrups. You could depend on the .45 Colt to stop the horse before he dragged you to death.

Over the years the .45 Colt has proved efficient for defense against bears and was the number one revolver choice for

Though more massive, the Ruger .45 Redhawk has approximately the same footprint as a Colt SAA.

wilderness bear protection in a revolver until the arrival of the .44 Magnum. Now, the Ruger Redhawk can be loaded to equal or exceed the .44 Magnum's performance and it has heavier, deeper-penetrating, larger-diameter bullets available in factory loads for those whose primary worry is bear attack. That is a big difference between the Ruger and the smaller, lighter M1873 Colt SAA, which cannot take these super magnum loads. The Ruger has a longer cylinder than the Colt single action to better accomodate longer, heavier bullets and the cylinder and frame are substantially larger as well. The cylinder walls are also more tightly machined than other .45 Colt revolvers, as befitting a gun intended to take maximum loads. Reloads that have not been full-length resized may not chamber in the Ruger even though they fit other guns.

The revolver itself is a triumph of modern design engineering. It is capable of being disassembed fairly easily by its owner, unlike traditional revolvers that need a gunsmith. That is a most important factor, as anyone who has ever locked up a revolver with debris in the lockwork will agree. This also allows it to have a solid frame (i.e., no lockp!ate) to add strength to the frame. The lockwork is of simple and robust design without any small, delicate parts to batter under recoil or drive you batty as you try to position them for reassembly. Many older designs had overly delicate and complicated parts ill-suited to modern magnum recoil battering. While their steel alloys of 4140 and 4150 were more than adequate, they are eclipsed by the modern steels used in the Redhawk. Carpenter Steel's new Custom 465 stainless is used for the cylinders and the barrels are made from Carpenter Project 7000 15Cr-5Ni stainless steel. These are high-strength steels from one of America's best steel companies.

SHOOTING IMPRESSIONS

We test-fired 1020 rounds of assorted .45 Colt ammunition in the Ruger. Firing the gun produced an unusual problem. The rubber grips were comfortable; recoil was virtually nonexistent, making rapid fire easy; but on firing, the sharp edge of the top of the trigger proceeded to wear a quarter-inch hole in the top of my trigger finger, resulting in blood getting in the gun. While many people have experienced hammer bite from various automatics or had the loading latch of the old S&W Triple Lock cut into them, this was a first for me. Using two hands

The leading edge of the tested Redhawk .45's trigger guard was sharp enough to draw blood under recoil and had to be radiused by Tucker Guns master gunsmith Ken Lundquist.

didn't change anything. I went back to Tucker Guns and had Ken Lundquist, their master gunsmith, polish off the sharp edges on the sides of the trigger. This solved the problem.

The revolver came with a set of Hogue Bantam rubber grips that absorb recoil and have flat sides like those of an automatic, which greatly aided pointing. Curious about the early wood grips on the Redhawk, I got a set of Pachmayr Presentation Wood Grips from Tucker Guns that copied the original wood grips first used on it. (I was amused to read on the package "CAUTION: Firearms are potentially dangerous.") The grips were beautiful but did nothing to absorb recoil and did not point as well as the Hogue Bantams. I also tried a longer set of Hogue grips but found no advantage over the Bantam grips. These are indeed the best grips for this gun, at least for my hands. It should be noted that the wheel with a center pin in the gun that acts to lock the grips on was originally designed as a wheel with a separate pin. This is what is shown in the user's manual, but on current production the wheel is composed of two halves that snap together (or apart, if you want to take it out). As of this writing, this not shown in the manual, which likewise doesn't show anything but the old style wooden grips.

Just as the old Colt Single Action is faster to load than a cap and ball revolver (unless, of course, one has extra cylinders timed to the gun), the Ruger with its swing-out cylinder is faster to load than the Colt single action. For those who want to get almost as fast as an automatic, there are the excellent HKS speedloaders which allow six cartridges to be loaded instantly. The device holds them securely until the knob at the back is twisted, releasing them after the bullet noses are inserted into the cylinder. Waterproof, faux leather carrying cases that accommodate two speedloaders are available, and I highly recommend them as they sure beat laboriously loading each cylinder individually. Anyone who has ever reloaded a revolver one chamber at a time while under fire will not soon forget how agonizingly long it takes. These speedloaders are available from HKS Products (www.hksspeedloaders.com).

For holsters, I have never found anything as good as the pancake design. I have carried a .45 M1911-A1 in one since they were first invented. It hides the gun best, is fast on the draw, and is by far the most comfortable holster ever made. I tried out the Redhawk out in a pancake holster made by Strong Leather Co. and, once again, the pancake design proved the best. The holster was a top-quality, perfectly molded form-fitting job that any custom leather shop would have been proud to claim. For more information, see Strong Leather Company's website at www.strongholster.com.

AMMUNITION ROUNDUP

Ammunition is getting a bit tough to come by these days! Nevertheless, we managed to scrounge a variety of suitable ammo for our test of the Redhawk .45 Colt. The Redhawk was test fired with 100 rounds of Black Hills Ammunition .45 S&W Schofield; 50 rounds of Remington .45 Colt; 150 rounds of Winchester 250-grain Cowboy Action; 60 rounds of 255-grain standard velocity Winchester; 120 rounds of 225-grain Winchester Silvertip hollowpoint; 200 rounds of 265-grain Webley Manstopper rounds and 200 rounds of boattailed 300-grain big game bullets, both from Northwest Custom Projectile and loaded by Reed's Ammunition and Research; 40 rounds of CorBon 200-grain JHP; 40 rounds of CorBon 225-grain DPX;

Accuracy of Loads Tested

MAKE	BULLET WEIGHT	AVG. 5-SHOT GROUP (")
Black Hills .45 Schofield Lead RN	230 gr.	3.00
Remington .45 Colt Lead RN	250 gr.	1.15
Winchester Cowboy Action Lead FN	250 gr.	1.40
Winchester Super-X Lead RN	255 gr.	1.00
Winchester Silvertip HP	225 gr.	2.15
NWCP/Reed	225 gr.	2.35
NWCP/Reed Webley Manstopper	265 gr.	2.50
NWCP/Reed Boattail	300 gr.	1.75
CorBon JHP	200 gr.	1.65
CorBon DPX	225 gr.	2.00
CorBon JSP	300 gr.	2.75
CorBon Hard Cast	335 gr.	2.85

Note: All groups fired off sandbags with iron sights ar 25 yards.

The Ruger handles .45 Colt (right) as well as .45 Schofield (left) – if you happen to have any lying around.

20 rounds of CorBon 300-grain JSP; and 40 rounds of CorBon 335-grain Hard Cast bullets. (See the accompanying table for accuracy results.)

BLACK HILLS

Black Hills Ammunition makes the .45 S&W Schofield, which originally was used in Smith and Wesson's attempt to get their top-break No. 3 revolver adopted by the U.S. Calvalry in 1876. Though unsuccessful, this resulted in the Colt Single Action Army revolver's cartridge being called the .45 Long Colt to differentiate it from the shorter .45 Smith and Wesson Schofield. The Schofield makes an interesting sub-load in ,45 Colt revolvers. Black Hills Ammunition loads it with a 230-grain bullet at 750 fps. They also load .45 Colt ammunition for Cowboy Action

Left to right: .45 Schofield, .45 "Long Colt," Northwest Custom Projectile 260-grain "Manstopper" hollowpoint, CorBon 335-grain hard-cast lead SWC load at 1050 fps.

matches with a 250-grain bullet at 725 fps. Lest anyone think these light loads are ineffectual as manstoppers, I must remind you that in November of 1868, the British adopted the .450 Adams cartridge, which fired a 225-grain bullet at 650 fps. The later Webley .455 revolver cartridges upped the bullet weight to 250 to 265 grains at about 700 fps, while the .455 Webley Automatic fires a 220-grain bullet at 700 fps. The British designed their cartridges as manstoppers while the Americans designed the .45 Long Colt as a horse stopper, hence the difference in the velocities. It should be noted that continued use of the .45 Schofield in a .45 Colt revolver will require regular cleaning of the cylinder to remove the built-up fouling that can make it difficult to chamber the longer .45 Long Colt cartridge. (www.black-hills.com)

REMINGTON

The Remington .45 Colt with a 250-grain bullet at the old standard velocity of 800 fps is the traditional .45 Colt load of the old West (except for its smokeless powder and noncorrosive primer) and the Phillippine campaign against the Moros. The well-proven standard .45 Colt loading is the best all around load. One box of 50 was fired. (www.remington.com)

WINCHESTER

Winchester .45 Colt ammo was tested in three loads: 150 rounds of cowboy action loads at 750 fps with a 255-grain bullet, 60 rounds of their standard 255-grain lead bullet at 800 fps; and 120 rounds of their superb high-tech 225-grain Silvertip hollowpoint ammo at 920 fps. The Silvertip has made a name for itself in the hunting field on deer and boar as well as being a proven manstopper in this caliber. The 255-grain standard velocity load is your basic standard .45 Colt loading. Anytime you are in doubt as to what load to use, just get the old proven standard 255-gr. load. It won't fail you. (www.winchester.com)

NORTHWEST CUSTOM PROJECTILE

Next were two specialty bullets from Northwest Custom Projectile: a 260-grain modern version of the old Webley manstopper bullet and a 300-grain big-game bullet. Both are boattail designs with .020-inch-thick over .999% chemically pure lead cores. The boattail design offers more dramatic improvement in trajectory and penetration (35% more penetration, in fact) at subsonic velocities than at supersonic velocities. When a bullet pushes through the air, it creates a vacuum at its flat base that slows the bullet down. A boattail bullet cuts down on the size of the vaccum the bullet is dragging along with it. Both of these .45 Colt bullets were loaded to 12,500 psi and can also be used in the far lighter 36-ounce Colt Single Action Army revolver, but the 300-grain load must be seated deep enough into the case that it does not extend out the front of the Colt's cylinder. They can be loaded to higher velocity in the Redhawk, of course.

The Webley Manstopper, also by Northwest Custom, is a Victorian-era solution to dumping all the bullet's energy into a fanatical assailant fast. It looks like a hollow base wadcutter that was loaded backward in the case. All you see is one enormous hollowpoint that instantly expands on contact. It is well named and a better manstopper design for an expanding bullet would be hard to imagine. Increasing the velocity would be a bad idea because you would end up losing stopping power to over-penetration. These 260-gr. bullets were loaded with 6.4 grains of Hogden Tight Group Powder for 800 fps. Northwest Custom Projectile's version has proven to expand at velocities as low as 500 fps. Its hollowpoint interior is a tapered hexagon to give controlled expansion to just under one inch with a Gold Dot-style center post to move the balance point further forward for increased bullet stability.

Northwest Custom's 300-grain load is a deep penetrating bullet for hunting anything on the North American continent. At 700 fps the heavy boattail bullet has all the penetration and killing power that you need without the recoil and deafening muzzleblast of supersonic loads (1100 fps or faster). Still, it can be loaded faster if desired. Its boattail design gives better accuracy than flat-based bullets, particularly at long range. My old friend Elmer Keith would have had a field day with these bullets at long range if they had been available when he was alive. 5.8 grains of Hogden Tight Group powder was the the load for 700 fps. (www.customprojectile.com)

The fearsome-looking business end of the Northwest Custom "Manstopper" bullet.

Perfect textbook expansion of the "Manstopper."

CORBON

Next came the high velocity CorBon loads that are intended only for the Redhawk and similar modern designs as they are far too hot for the lightweight M1873 Colt Single Action Army revolver. First was the 200-grain Sierra JHP at 1100 fps designed for fast expansion and 14 inches of penetration in ballistic gelatine. Next came the 225-grain Barnes DPX (Deep Penetrating X bullet), a solid copper projectile at 1200 fps that penetrated 18 inches of ballistic gelatine. Moving right along, we came to the 300-grain JSP at 1300 fps, a big game magnum load that won't expand except on bone. It penetrates 22 to 24 inches in ballistic gelatin.

Finally came the 335-grain hard cast lead semiwadcutter bullet load at 1050 fps for maximum penetration and no expansion on big bear, moose, bison, etc. It goes over 24 inches in ballistic gelatin. How much over? We won't really know until someone rigs up a deeper block of gelatin. For a grizzly load, this would be the best choice. Considering how many people are killed by domestic cattle in this country each year, this would be a good load to tote in the cow pasture as well. Cattle take a lot of stopping when they are riled up. They can also be very treacherous with that docile, friendly old cow or bull suddenly deciding to kill you. I have had a great deal of experience with cattle on my farm and I have learned not to trust any of them. This is my favorite .45 Colt Load for big dangerous game, and 1050 fps is just under the 1100 fps speed of sound so there is no sonic boom to add to the noise. For more info on CorBon loads, visit www.dakotaammo.net.

CONCLUSION

In a way it's surprising that it took the folks at Southport so long to offer it, considering the increasing popularity of the .45 Colt caliber – but better late than never! From home defense to taking most North American game, the 4-inch Redhawk in .45 Colt has "winner" stamped all over it. (Just keep your eyes open for sharp triggers.)

TEST FIRE

BY CHRIS LIBBY

I slowly made my way through the darkness towards the garage, intent on locating the source of the disturbance. It was a humid June night, my window was open, and the sound of rustling garbage had awakened me. I was intent on eliminating the pest that had been strewing the trash all about for the past few weeks.

As I closed the distance to seven yards, I raised the Crosman/Benjamin Model 392 .22 pellet rifle to my shoulder and turned on my D cell Maglite, piercing the pitch black summer night. A large opossum glared back at me, bearing a startling resemblance to a giant, angry rat on steroids. I took aim and squeezed the trigger. The 18.2-gr.

Beeman Crow-Magnum hollowpoint pellet, powered by seven pumps of compressed air, smashed through both sides of the varmint's skull, dropping him in his tracks. The muffled sound of the compressed air being released was quickly swallowed up in the night, not disturbing any of my neighbors in the rural neighborhood, who surely had

THE MODEL 392
BENJAMIN/CROSMAN

(above) The Crosman/Benjamin 392 has more than enough power for hunting and pest control.

(right) The author with a spring woodchuck taken at 18 yards with the 392, a Crosman pointed pellet and seven pumps.

AIR RIFLE

The.22 caliber model 392 is an excellent small game hunting weapon, and due to its short carbine length, it's easy to handle in thick cover and brush.

their windows open as well due to the oppressive heat.

As I looked at the size of the slain critter, I patted the nicely finished hardwood stock. Although I knew how powerful this weapon was, as I had previously test fired a few round nose pellets through both sides of a one-inch pine board, I was still amazed at the lethality of such a quiet and economical arm.

The Crosman-produced Benjamin 392 is advertised as having a velocity of 685 FPS with a standard 14.3 lead pellet at eight pumps, the maximum number recommended by the manufacturer, as any more than that could result in a loss of performance due to an overload of pressure on the air valve. In fact, seven pumps will provide more than enough power for most small game hunting situations at 25 to 30 yards. As few as three or four pumps provide plenty of power for targets and tin can plinking.

I bought my 392 in 2002 after reading James E. House's book, *American Air Rifles*. I would highly recommend Mr. House's book as a must-read to anyone interested in objective airgun reviews and performance data. Since buying my 392 I have used it to successfully hunt numerous small game animals and pests. I have not put a scope on my rifle, as I limit my shots to about 25 yards. The arm is only 36.5 inches long and at 5.5 lbs., it comes up to the shoulder quickly, which is a necessity when hunting rabbits, squirrels and ruffed grouse that one might encounter in the field.

The name Benjamin is synonymous with quality and both old and modern Benjamins possess a reputation for being sturdy and appealing to the eye. The Crosman 392 appears slightly different than older versions produced by Benjamin, sporting

a thick, finished walnut stock, but the high compression air valve encased in a solid brass air chamber is for all intents and purposes the same powerful and dependable system that has been used for decades. In fact, Benjamin was making airguns well over 100 years ago.

I fondly remember my grandfather, long since passed, telling me stories of his childhood growing up on a farm in Dover-Foxcroft, Maine, in the World War I era. He had a Benjamin airgun, a foot valve model that fired round lead shot slightly bigger than a BB. He used his airgun to shoot rats, rabbits and crows around the farm. He claimed that when charged with four or five pumps, the gun would shoot a projectile through both sides of a snowshoe hare at close range, and was just as effective as a .22 Short. (Of course, the old pre-WWII Benjamins had a pump rod at the muzzle. Because of the greater compression of air forced into the valve with each stroke, as the pump rod traveled a longer distance compared to models with a swinging forearm pump mechanism, the gun was fully charged at only four pumps.)

I have used my Benjamin to hunt woodchucks and with Crow-Magnum and Crosman pointed field pellets, it humanely drops them at 25 yards, provided a vital area is hit. No, this pneumatic weapon won't

"Four...Ughhhh!" It takes some muscle to pump up this airgun.

take woodchucks at 150 yards like my old Weaver scoped Remington 722 bolt action .270, but if I do my part and carefully stalk my prey, utilizing any and all available cover to close the distance and hit a vital area, it will do the trick with devastating results and very little noise. Pneumatic arms are noisier than airguns powered with compressed spring power plants, but they are far more economical to own, and as far as I am concerned, not that much noisier and just as effective as break barrel springers for small game hunting and dispatching pests.

I have to stress that the 392 is not a toy; it is an extremely powerful adult airgun fully capable of inflicting serious injury and or death if mishandled. Just because this arm is powered by compressed air, it does not negate the responsibility the user has to follow all gun safety rules, abide by state and local laws and to treat it in the same manner one would a 12 gauge shotgun. Crosman recommends storing the weapon unloaded, and uncharged. I personally keep mine uncocked, unloaded and inaccessible to children, but charged with two pumps, in order to keep the seals firmly seated in the air valve. Prior to the wave of lawsuits in this nation, many airgun manufacturers used to recommend keeping the guns charged with a pump or two, as the air valve will last

The Model 392 will drive .22 pellets into half an inch at 33 feet.

indefinitely if the seals are kept firmly seated to keep out dust particles.

Crosman also makes a .177 caliber version of the Model 392 known as the 397. For small game and pests, I prefer the .22 pellets over the .177. I have owned and used both, and from my experience the bigger caliber has more knockdown power. I have an older Sheridan Blue Streak air rifle in .20 caliber, and have found it to be as hard hitting and accurate as my 392, although much easier to pump. Both .20 and .22 caliber standard weight air gun pellets are 14.3 grains, so there is not much difference in cross sectional density and striking power, all things such as velocity, range, etc., being equal.

The 392 takes some muscle to charge, and more than other pump-up models that are on the market. Although most teenagers and adults can quickly build the strength to pump it to full power, it is tough to close the pump handle after four or five pumps. I find that for small vermin and birds, four or five pumps are more than adequate at 10 to 20 yards. At longer range, or if shooting at bigger game, seven or eight pumps should be used.

The 392 is advertised as having a precision rifled brass barrel that is guaranteed to deliver half-inch groups at 33 feet. This is an understatement! From a rest, at 33 feet, my gun has delivered 1/4-inch groups with match pellets, and this without a scope! These rugged

pneumatic arms are tack drivers.

Pertaining to maintenance: only use Crosman Pellgunoil, and sparingly at that. Every few hundred shots, I put a few drops on the pump lever pivot points, where the metal meets metal, and a drop on the felt plunger. When it comes to oil and airguns, remember that less is more, too much and it can seep into the valve system and ruin it. Replacement parts are available if this does happen, but go easy with the oil and it shouldn't be an issue. The barrel should be wiped down after use with a soft cloth and a light coating of oil to prevent rust. As far as the bore goes, I don't normally clean my airgun barrels with a cleaning rod and brush, as there is too much chance of damaging the rifling. There is no powder residue to deal with, and airgun barrels don't generally get that dirty anyways. I have used a length of fishing line with a cleaning patch attached to clean the barrel after a damp, rainy day afield, however.

Regardless of whether you want a potent .22 caliber airgun for plinking or target practice in your back yard, pest control in an urban or suburban environment, small game hunting, or for sniper work on those pesky rabbits and woodchucks in your garden, the Crosman/Benjamin model 392 will deliver all the accuracy and power you will ever need – and then some.

TEST FIRE

Pocket Parabellum: the 9mm Kel-Tec PF-9 Pistol

BY **JIM DICKSON**

The Kel-Tec PF-9 shown between a Colt .32 and a Savage .32, two f the most popular pocket pistols of all time. The PF-9 is shorter and thinner than both – and it's a 9mm.

Imagine a 9mm Parabellum pistol that is lighter and as small or smaller than most .32 ACP pocket pistols. Want one? Well, you can have one – because that is just what the Kel-Tec PF-9 is. A 14.5 ounce powerhouse only .880 inches thick, 5-3/4 inches long and 4-1/4 inches tall. Compare that to the famous Colt Model M .32 ACP at 24 ounces and 6-1/2 inches long or the Savage 1907 .32 at 19 ounces and 6-1/2 inches long and you will begin to appreciate just what has been done with this 9mm pistol.

Designed to be the smallest possible 9mm, it still is a practical general purpose pistol: not an easy feat to accomplish when dealing with extremes of size and concealability. The Kel-Tec will comfortably perform most anything asked of the average pistol.

While some will point out correctly that a larger, heavier gun is more controllable in rapid fire and steadier to aim and fire, the fact remains that there is always a place for the smallest possible gun. In the first place, there are many people who will not carry a full-size pistol every day and so end up unarmed when their lives depend on having a weapon. A .25 ACP Baby Browning in the hand is better than a Thompson submachinegun in the gunsafe when you are being attacked, and concealability is always easier in direct proportion to gun size and thick-

The PF-9 gobbled up 100 rounds of Remington and 40 rounds of Winchester Supreme hollowpoints without a hitch.

(below) Instinct shooting with the PF-9. The wrist and elbow are straight and the chin rests against the shoulder. The eyes are locked on the target, ignoring the sights, as the gun is fully extended and pointing where the eyes are looking.

ness. That's why you don't find people concealing Barrett .50 caliber rifles on their person, although the idea is not entirely without merit.

The more compact the pistol, the more options you have for different places and ways to conceal it. While we normally think of the .25 ACP when referring to vest pocket pistols, the fact remains that the 9mm PF-9 fits quite nicely in the modern vest pockets and it rides well concealed there. If it were any heavier, it would not.

When my old friend the late Geoffrey Boothroyd was asked by Ian Fleming what pistol his character James Bond should carry, Geoffrey said the Walther PPK. Ian repaid him by promoting the former private Boothroyd of WWII to Major Boothroyd, armorer to James Bond, in the James Bond series of books. Had the Kel-Tec been out then, I strongly suspect Geoffrey would have had James Bond carrying it instead of the Walther.

The PF-9 is a well-made, properly thought-out design that functioned with total reliability during my test firing. The gun is designed with places for dirt, fouling and miscellaneous debris to escape from the action so that it does not jam. There is a gap between the slide and part of the frame that will allow quite a bit of crud to get out at once – a desirable feature, because dirt always finds its way into guns but often is trapped there with no way to get out. Get sand inside the lockwork of a revolver and you will find out just what I mean. It will lock up tighter than a bank vault until you disassemble it to get the sand out. Sadly, many automatics are even worse in this regard, but not the Kel-Tec.While you're not likely to drop your PF-9 into a sand dune in the middle of the Sahara, it's nice to know that it's practically immune to pocket grit.

The PF-9 fits the hand well and does not recoil excessively. The recoil is a bit sharper than on a heavy full-size pistol but nothing that would bother women or children. That's important because children need to grow up shooting and they don't need a vicious kick or muzzle blast to discourage them while you are teaching them to enjoy shooting. The ergonomics of the grip and its texture combine to form a well-pointing gun that properly distributes the felt recoil across the hand comfortably.

The PF-9 has a double action trigger pull like a revolver instead of a safety. That is a very good way to go on a small hideout gun where you don't need to waste time fumbling for a safety. The double action trigger pull is all the safety you need. The trigger requires the slide to be jacked to the rear to reset it so you won't waste time repeatedly snapping on a misfire if you get a bad primer.

The PF-9's trigger pull is light and can be held short just before the hammer falls when you are trying to shoot groups. I began my test session with 40 rounds of Winchester Supreme Elite 147-grain jacketed hollowpoints and 100

rounds of Remington 115-grain jacketed hollowpoints. These two loads are state-of-the-art, modern hollowpoints that give maximum explosive expansion with maximum weight retention. They work very well on coyotes and other varmints, both four-legged and two-legged. I set up a target at 25 yards and began shooting from a sandbag rest. The gun was able to consistently make 2-inch groups, which of course is very good for this type of pistol and far better than most shooters are ever going to be capable of without a sandbagged rest. After all, this is a defensive pistol designed for ease of carry

The pF-9 in a Blackhawk! size 4 nylon pancake holster. The pancake is the most comfortable and concealable holster style ever designed.

and maximum concealability. Firing without the rest proved the gun was fast pointing and easily controllable in rapid fire. The sights are clear and well defined without being so big that they get in the way. The rear sight can be adjusted for windage if necessary. The frame features a rail for a laser sight or a flashlight in the modern style. I don't like either, especially on a subcompact pistol where they add bulk. Flashlights and lasers, like tracers, draw return fire. In my opinion, a laser's not something to be wildly flashing about in the dark.

Unlike many guns I have known, the PF-9 disassembles fast and efficiently. Unload the pistol and pull the slide back, locking it open by pushing up the slide stop. With the rim of a cartridge, pull the assembly pin out of the gun. Holding the slide firmly, release the slide stop and allow the slide to move forward off the frame. Remove the recoil spring and the barrel and you are done. Do not loosen the extractor spring screw.

To put the gun back together, put the barrel back into the slide, push the recoil spring guide with springs into their hole in the slide, and hook the base of the recoil spring onto its half-moon cutout in the barrel. Make certain that the barrel and recoil springs are well-centered when putting them back in the slide. Push the slide onto the frame until the back lines up with the grip. If the slide does not go on easily, make sure that the hammer is half cocked and the barrel and recoil spring guide are centered. While pushing down on the top of the barrel, pull the slide back all the way, compressing the recoil springs, and push up the slide stop to hold the slide in place. Looking into the assembly pin hole, align that hole with its cut in the barrel and insert the assembly pin until it snaps onto the spring. Pull the slide back to release the slide stop and release the slide, working the slide a few times to check the action. Do not dry fire this pistol because you can damage the firing pin and extractor spring screw by dryfiring.

A modern polymer frame pistol, the PF-9 is also very reasonably priced, as are all Kel-Tec firearms. Suggested retail price is $333 for blued guns, $377 for parkerized, and $390 for chrome finished guns. I would recommend the parkerized finish for any pistol that will see hard service. Unlike most specialized pistols, this one can reasonably serve as a family's only pistol, doing double duty as a carry gun and a bedside burgler gun in the same manner as the old topbreak S&W and Iver Johnson revolvers have done for over 100 years.

Since the PF-9 is a pocket pistol, and a very good one, some will choose to carry it directly inside a jacket or pants pocket. I prefer a holster, both because of the extra protection it offers and because it keeps the pistol oriented for immediate access. I have always found the pancake holster design to be the best for comfort, concealment, and gun security. I tried carrying the PF-9 in a

Blackhawk! size 4 nylon pancake holster and was well pleased with the combination. It fit well on both the gun and me. Made from a multi-layer nylon laminate with polymer hardware and stainless steel or brass snaps, the Blackhawk! is ideal for use in wet marine or humid environments. It features an adjustable safety strap system that lets it work on multiple guns within a certain size range. The two polymer safety straps have velcro fasteners on them that, with the aid of a special tool that comes with them, adhere to the velcro in the slots in which they're inserted. They are then permanently in place unless the tool is used to seperate the velcro layers. The system actually works quite well.

Of course the Blackhawk holster works well in everyday concealed-carry service, too. It's an interesting modern answer to age-old holster problems and offer a solution that will give good service in all conditions at a most reasonable price. It's are available from Blackhawk Products Group, 6160 Commander Parkway, Norfolk, Virginia, 23502. You can also check it out at www. BLACKHAWK.com.

While the 9mm Parabellum lacks the authority of the .45 ACP as a manstopper, it holds its own quite nicely with the various .38s and even the .357 Magnum. It nicely eclipses the performance of the 9mm Makarov and the .380, .32, .25 and .22 LR and can be made in a thinner and lighter package than the .45 ACP. Like the 1911-A1, the PF-9 holds seven cartridges in the magazine and one in the chamber for a total of eight rounds. Compare that to the five or six in a bulkier snubnosed .38 and the case for the PF-9 becomes clear. It's available from Kel-Tec CNC Industries, Inc., 1475 Cox Road, Cocoa, Florida, 32926. They probably won't mind if you visit their website at www. kel-tec.com.

The Kel-Tech PF-9 in 9mm Parabellum, right and left views.

A VERSATILE AND ACCURATE .22 LR AMMUNITION:
CCI STANDARD VELOCITY

BY MIKE THOMAS

TEST FIRE

Author at the bench with a Winchester Model 52 reproduction. These rifles shoot quite well as they come from the box. The 6X Unertl scope is ideal for both hunting and informal benchrest work.

Primarily as a means of satisfying a curiosity, I became involved in a ".22 project" several years ago. As is usually the case, it turned into a lengthy piece of work. I summarized my research in an article that appeared in the 2003 *Gun Digest* titled "Practical Accuracy of .22 LR Ammunition" in which 24 different types of ammunition were evaluated for accuracy in six firearms – three rifles and three handguns.

Only by using a sufficient combination of guns and ammunition was I able to come up with what I hoped would be meaningful information for accuracy-oriented .22 rimfire enthusiasts who preferred to fire affordable ammunition in affordable guns. "Affordable" is a relative term, no doubt, and the field here is indeed broad. In fact, it is far broader than the one where shooters buy $10 to $15-per-box ammo that will be fired in $1,500 rifles. (That is in no way intended as a criticism of match shooters and benchrest participants, by the way.)

For the article, I fired five five-shot groups at 50 yards with the rifles and did the same with the handguns but reduced the distance to 25 yards. Shooting was done from a sturdy bench rest. It was all rather simple and straightforward work and sufficient for the purpose of evaluation.

When the article was written, most of the ammunition was available in the larger gun shops or by mail order and could be purchased for $3 or less, often much less, for 50 rounds. The current situation, as most rimfire shooters know, has undergone significant change not only from the price perspective but also from the availability standpoint.

Long guns used in the report were two Winchester reproductions, a scoped Model 52 bolt-action and an open-sighted Model 63 semi-automatic. The third rifle was a scoped Ruger 10/22T (the one that came from the factory with a heavy barrel). The handguns used in the evaluation included a Ruger Mark II Government Model semi-automatic (6-7/8-inch bull barrel), a Smith & Wesson Model 17 revolver (6-inch barrel), and a Rossi Model 84 stainless steel revolver (4-inch barrel).

This bit of background will set the stage for what's coming here. The current project is not, nor was it intended to be, a continuation or update of the earlier piece. In fact, the two works are quite dissimilar.

Like others, over the course of many years, I have accumulated a number of .22 rimfire firearms, both rifles and handguns. Some eventually leave to make room for others that will be gathered farther down the road. With regard to rimfire ammunition, I sometimes have various samples that were leftovers from the conclusion of some article. Others I purchased for informal evaluations with the hope of finding out what is accurate and what is not in various handguns and rifles.

Every time I acquire another .22, I'll shoot a fair number of benchrested groups (50 yards for rifle, 25 yards for handgun) with as many different types of ammunition as possible. From an accuracy standpoint, one ammo almost always stands above the others, though the difference may be a slight one. Mission accomplished. That all sounds good, and it is, until you get the urge to shoot a particular .22 but first must refer to a chart (an abbreviated version of range notes) that indicates which ammo shoots best, second best, and third best in that gun. Oh, and let's not forget the part about point-of-impact versus point-of-aim, another important consideration. Many ammunitions shoot to different points of impact. Like accuracy, the disparity may be ever so slight, not enough for concern. Often, however, it is unacceptable, particularly if shooting at longer distances. Few of us enjoy adjusting sights after they have been set for a particular load.

For a number of years I was content

Rifles used in CCI Standard Velocity project include (from left to right) Winchester Model 52 reproduction w/ 6X Unertl, Winchester Model 61 slide action, Ruger 77/22 w/ 3X Weaver, and Ruger 77/22 Varmint Stainless w/ 4X Weaver.

buying several .22 LR ammos for use in 15 or 20 rimfire guns and referring to my chart prior to every range trip. I referred to the chart without analyzing it. CCI Standard Velocity ammunition had many more entries as first, second, or third choices for different guns than any other. Sometimes, average group sizes of second and third choice ammunition for a particular gun were so close as to be inconsequential. As a matter of interest, I evaluated all my .22 LR rimfire guns with the CCI ammunition. It took a while, but the results were worth the effort. I could not only "get by" with purchasing one ammunition, I found I was giving up little (sometimes nothing) in terms of accuracy. Comparisons were so close, in fact, that I'm hesitant to call converting to a single .22 LR ammo a compromise at all.

at 50 yards. Many will do better, and a few, much better. At 100 yards, average group sizes in the 2- to 2-1/2-inch range can be considered just fine. Frankly, I'm surprised at the number of rifles that will do that well at such a distance. The small, light, and ballistically inefficient .22 rimfire bullets are very susceptible to even slight wind drift and 100 yards is probably 25 yards beyond the maximum useful range of ammunition that quickly loses steam anyway. Even with high-velocity hollow-point ammo, it is hard to tout the .22 Long Rifle cartridge as a dependable and humane 100-yard small game round, despite attempts at such a distance.

It is often said that standard velocity .22 LR ammunition is usually more accurate than high velocity counterparts.

reliably with high velocity ammo. Perhaps they were designed that way or have a particularly heavy recoil spring in anticipation of shooters that prefer the use of high speed ammunition. One example is a personal Walther PPK/S that functions reliably with CCI Standard Velocity, but slide action during the ejection process seems slower than it does when using high velocity .22 LR. Another is my father's WWII-era High Standard Model B that will often jam with almost anything standard velocity but functions fine with high velocity ammunition, even if it's not as accurate.

Lot to lot consistency: I have never rounded up samples of different lots of the same ammunition and compared the accuracy and point of impact. Some have done this and claim that certain

I must emphasize that I neither shoot competitively nor know exactly what makes a "true" competition firearm, even if a couple of the handgun models I have are often referred to as such. I suppose, like many others, I am an informal accuracy enthusiast. Also, like many others, I see no point in buying expensive target ammunition when my guns and I probably won't know or appreciate the comparative difference over what I normally shoot. I shoot all my .22s as I receive them. As far as I am aware, none have been modified, tuned, or worked over by custom gunsmiths or anyone less talented, such as me.

CCI Standard Velocity .22 LR ammunition is capable of very reasonable 50 yard groups. There's nothing wrong with any scope-sighted .22 rifle "shooter" that will consistently group inside one inch

Based on the results of various projects I have been involved with, usually that is a true statement. However, there are several high velocity ammunitions that stand out. One that comes to mind is plain ol' Winchester Super-X High Velocity with a 40-gr. solid bullet. It has displayed good accuracy for me in a number of guns, not just a couple. Same goes for CCI Blazer - this is often among the very cheapest ammo available and the "cheap" part probably keeps some enthusiasts from even trying it. Another is Federal American Eagle, and it's pretty close to Blazer from the price angle.

Another point worthy of mention when comparing standard velocity .22 LR ammunition with the high velocity stuff: some semi-automatic firearms, particularly handguns, function more

The Colt Officer's Model Match revolver hasn't been made in quite a while, but many were produced and are not too difficult to locate even today. A big gun for a .22, these are fine shooters.

lots are better than others in the aforementioned categories. I don't doubt their claims. Realistically, however, the procedure sounds a bit troublesome, time-consuming, and less than practical even for most accuracy enthusiasts, save those with an obsessive interest in the results. Old habits die hard if they die at all, and I must confess that I keep different lots of ammunition separated, even CCI Standard Velocity, though I'm not sure why since the lot-to-lot consistency thus far seems to have no discernible variance. Must be a fanaticism of sorts.

Is sorting .22 ammo worth the trouble? I did an article for the 2009 *Gun Digest* with that very title. According to my results, the short answer to the question is "sometimes." With a rifle/cartridge combination responsive to the process (and not all of them are) the results can be quite noticeable. Other instances can prove nothing more than wasted efforts. The drawbacks to sorting (there are several ways to sort and I chose to do so by rim thickness) are that it takes a lot of time and is quite tedious. By comparison, such a chore almost makes trimming centerfire brass cases seem like an interesting adventure.

There's been some question and confusion as to the packaging of CCI Standard Velocity ammunition. For years, we only saw the clear plastic boxes of 100 rounds. Now there are also 50-round cardboard boxes. This is exactly the same ammunition and all of it is made at the Speer plant in Idaho. Only the packaging differs. To quash rumors that have circulated since the introduction of the smaller cardboard box, this information came straight from the manufacturer. (To quell another rumor, Federal does not make any CCI Standard Velocity .22 ammo.)

What is one giving up by using standard velocity ammo in comparison to a high velocity round? The true answer is that for most purposes besides hunting, probably nothing. Even for some hunting situations carried out within the limits of the .22 LR cartridge, solid round nose 40-gr. standard velocity ammunition would not be a bad choice.

To make the numbers worthwhile for readers, I chose to use four handguns and four rifles for the evaluation of CCI Standard Velocity ammunition. Accuracy results were based on firing five,

The Smith & Wessons used for CCI Standard Velocity ammo evaluation: (top) early Model 41, 7-3/8-inch barrel with muzzle brake removed and Model 17-4, 6-inch barrel.

five-shot groups from a benchrest: 25 yards for the handguns and 50 yards for rifles. Group sizes were measured and rounded to the nearest quarter-inch, then averaged. Average group sizes are summarized in the tables.

Handguns included a Colt Officers Model Match revolver (6-inch barrel); Smith & Wesson Model 17 revolver (6-inch barrel); Smith & Wesson Model 41 semi-automatic (7-3/8-inch barrel); and a Ruger Mark II Government Model semi-automatic (6-7/8-inch bull barrel). Rifles were represented by a Ruger 77/22 Varmint Stainless Laminated (24-inch heavy barrel) with a 4X Weaver scope; another Ruger, an early 77/22 (20-inch barrel) with a 3X Weaver scope; a reproduction Winchester Model 52 (24-inch barrel) with a 6X Unertl Small Game scope; and a Winchester Model

61 slide-action (24-inch barrel) with the factory-equipped open rear sight. The 61 is a particular favorite, despite the difficulty in shooting this rifle rested on a sandbag in the conventional manner. It will likely shoot smaller groups holding the slide by hand and resting the hand on the bag. In the interest of uniform test procedures, however, the 61's forearm (slide) was rested atop the bag like the other rifles.

With regard to the handguns, the procedure I used involved resting only a small portion of the frame / trigger guard area on a sandbag, the gun hand held using both hands rested on top of a sandbag. Gun butts did not come in contact with the rear bag, nor did barrels touch the front bag.

It's sometimes difficult to find an ideal time to shoot in Texas during the

CCI Standard Velocity Accuracy Results

RIFLES (Five, five-shot groups fired at 50 yards from a benchrest, each group measured to the nearest quarter-inch; all groups were then averaged)

Ruger 77/22 Varmint Stainless bolt action, 24-inch heavy barrel, 4X Weaver scope	.85-inch
Ruger 77/22 bolt action, 20-inch barrel, 3X Weaver scope	1.00-inch
Winchester Model 52 bolt action reproduction, 24-inch barrel, 6X Unertl scope	.80-inch
Winchester Model 61 slide action, factory open rear sight	2.00-inch

HANDGUNS (Five, five-shot groups fired at 25 yards from a benchrest, each group measured to the nearest quarter-inch; all groups were then averaged)

Colt Officers Model Match revolver, 6-inch barrel	2.20-inch
Smith & Wesson Model 17-4 revolver, 6-inch barrel	3.00-inch
Smith & Wesson Model 41 semi-automatic, 7 3/8-inch barrel	1.80-inch
Ruger Mark II Government Model semi-automatic, 6 7/8-inch bull barrel	1.40-inch

(top) Ruger Mark II Government Model with 6-7/8-inch bull barrel is certainly a handful, but weight makes this a very forgiving pistol when it comes to accurate shooting. The Officer's Model Match was among the last produced, in 1969.

summer months unless it's at the crack of dawn or just before dark. During the two days I did my range work, the temperature varied from a low of around 80° F to a high that probably exceeded 100°. Slightly windy conditions became a factor for the 50-yard rifle shooting as the point of impact for the scope sighted rifles was a bit off. For the purposes of this article, however, the difference was insignificant. As for the 25-yard handgun shooting, the point of impact was unaffected.

Referring to my assorted range notebooks over a period of several years would show that some .22 LR ammunition is more accurate than CCI Standard Velocity in some of the guns used in these trials. However, averaged overall differences would not amount to much.

What about "fliers"? I cannot deny an occasional flier using CCI Standard Velocity ammunition. And, yes, they can spoil an otherwise good group. However,

fliers have been comparatively few and far between. If one experiences several unexplained fliers in a single shooting session, there is certainly a problem somewhere. If the ammunition is at fault, it's simply unfortunate and there's nothing that will correct the matter short of trying something else.

I have noticed for some time that CCI Standard Velocity ammo chambers with slight difficulty in some bolt action rifles, though it has never been to the point of becoming an annoyance. The Winchester 52 reproduction used here is a good example. I have another of these rifles that chambers the CCI ammo similarly. Putting a micrometer to several rounds confirmed that the bullet is slightly larger in diameter than several other ammunitions that were also measured. Whether the oversize bullet contributes to accuracy, I don't know for certain. However, cast bullet enthusiasts have long known that a slightly oversize

bullet is almost always more accurate than one of groove diameter and an undersized bullet seldom, if ever, shoots accurately.

Smith & Wesson .22 rimfire revolvers have a reputation for tight chambers. Even with perfectly clean cylinders and chambers, many .22 cartridges must be pushed into place, not merely dropped in. In this case, CCI Standard Velocity seems no different than many other ammunition. There has always been speculation that S&W's tight, perhaps even undersized rimfire chambers contribute to accuracy, but there are probably no facts or data to support such a conclusion. I purchased the Model 17-4 used for this report new in 1982. It has been fired considerably and has the typical tight S & W chambers.

As I write this, CCI Standard Velocity .22 LR can be purchased, mail order, for around $6.50 to $8.00 per hundred rounds plus shipping, and in some cases, sales tax. Prices in gun shops may be a little more. That's certainly not cheap, but it's a long way from expensive. It's good ammo for the casual accuracy enthusiast and that includes many of us.

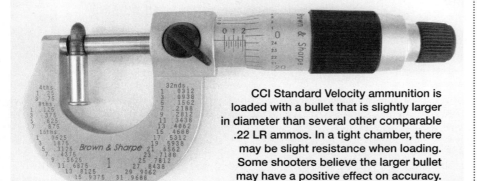

CCI Standard Velocity ammunition is loaded with a bullet that is slightly larger in diameter than several other comparable .22 LR ammos. In a tight chamber, there may be slight resistance when loading. Some shooters believe the larger bullet may have a positive effect on accuracy.

THE LYMAN PLAINS PISTOL

BY **CHRIS LIBBY**
PHOTOS BY **STAN LIBBY**
AND **CHRIS LIBBY**

Perhaps it was watching Robert Redford portray a Mountain Man in the classic 1970s movie *Jeremiah Johnson*. It could have been the opening credits of the Beverly Hillbillies, where the character of Jed Clampett fires a muzzleloader at game, missing and striking oil. Then again it might have been reading and re-reading the book *The Great West* (Charles Neider, 1958), which included many firsthand accounts from explorers and mountain men like Kit Carson and Jim Bridger, who told of exploits in the American Northwest trapping, hunting and battling Indians and grizzly bears. And then again it could just be a deeper, more primal attraction to fire and smoke that first drew my attraction to, and subsequent obsession with, black powder weapons.

Regardless of the source of my affliction in my formative years, my innate attraction to soot-burning firearms only grew stronger over time. To me, the acrid smell of black powder smoke is both intoxicating and satisfying. I have bought, traded, borrowed and shot

The Lyman pistol is an accurate, beautiful and well-built weapon.

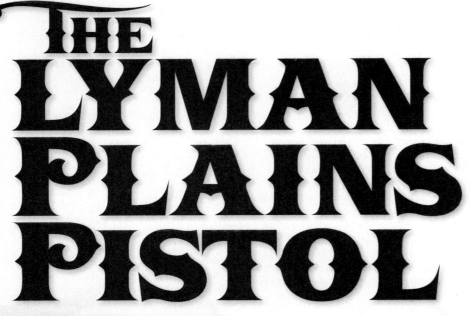

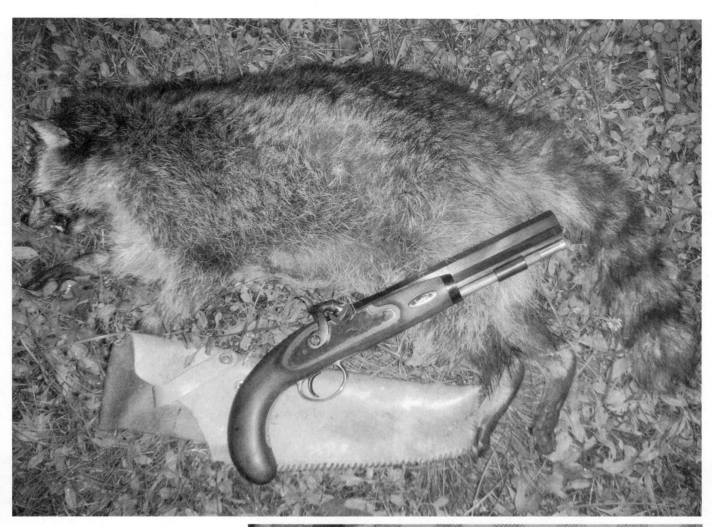

The Lyman Plains Pistol is a superb hunting weapon for small and medium sized game at handgun ranges of under 25 yards. This raccoon was taken with a 225-gr. Speer round ball backed by 30 grains of GOEX FFFG Black Powder. The author made the holster.

countless charcoal-burning rifles, shot-guns. revolvers and pistols over the past 25 years. But there is one that I hope I will never be forced to part with: my beloved 54-caliber Lyman Plains Pistol.

The pistol had first caught my eye as a youth when I read the *Gun Digest*s of the early 1980s. Lyman brought out this fine pistol in 1981, a replica of the mountain man-era Trapper's pistol, a smaller version of their much acclaimed Plains Rifle. Made in Italy by Investarm, this is a rugged and beautiful, well-built tool that, if cared for, should still be in service a century or more from now. Lyman's summery of their product reads;

"The Lyman Plains Pistol recreates

The Lyman .54 caliber percussion pistol, pictured here next to a SIG-Sauer P220 in .45 ACP, outperforms the standard 230-gr. .45 ACP cartridge in both muzzle velocity and energy.

the trapper's pistol of the mid-1800's while incorporating the best of modern steels and technology. It's the perfect companion to a Lyman black powder rifle. This percussion pistol is loaded with quality features. The richly stained walnut stock complements blackened iron furniture, polished brass trigger guard and ramrod tips. The hooked patent breech takes down quickly and easily for cleaning. Just like the originals, the thimble is recessed into the rib and a detachable belt hook provides an alternative to a holster. A spring-loaded trigger and fast 1 in 30" twist make it amazingly accurate."

Offered in either .50 or .54 caliber, this percussion pistol sports a blued 8-inch barrel and weighs about 50 ounces. While there are some low-quality black powder arms out on the market, have no fear: Lyman pistols (and rifles) are quality products and built to last. The name Lyman has been synonymous with quality reloading products and gun sights for several generations of shooters, well over a century in fact (since 1878), and is one of the longstanding giants in the industry. Former *Gun Digest* Editor Ken Ramage had previously worked for Lyman before taking the helm at *Gun Digest* in 2000 and wrote Lyman's *Black Powder Handbook* in 1975. When you examine a Lyman BP arm, you quickly see that the quality control standards put into place long ago for the production of these guns are second to none. When you heft this arm in your hand, you know you are holding a small Italian Dragon built of fine walnut and high carbon steel that spews out fire and brimstone!

I bought my Plains Pistol a few years ago from Dixie Gun Works in Union City, Tennessee. The company has been around since 1954 and has a stellar reputation for customer satisfaction, so I had no qualms pertaining to punching my Visa number into their secure website and placing my order. Within a few days, the big brown truck delivered the gun directly to my doorstep, as there are (at the time of this writing, anyway) no federal restrictions on the shipment of black powder arms in the United States of America. The Gun Control Act of 1968 only applies to modern weapons. The bright orange Lyman box was securely packed inside of a much larger, thick shipping box. As I pulled the pistol out and looked at it, the thought crossed my mind that this weapon would look as much at home on a pirate's belt as it would tucked in a fur trapper's sash in

(below l to r) After snapping a cap or two to clear out any oil in the nipple and wiping a clean patch through the barrel to remove all grease and oil, carefully pour the pre-measured black powder down the barrel.

Once the powder has been gently tamped in place, firmly ram the patched round ball down the barrel, ensuring that it is seated with no air space between it and the powder.

When ready to shoot and the arm is pointed in a safe direction, place the #11 percussion cap on the nipple.

Kayla Nason, donning proper eye and ear protection, draws a bead and prepares to fire the Mountain Man sidearm.

the 1840's.

The gun is equipped with a polished brass trigger guard, a richly blued steel barrel and a nicely finished walnut wood stock. The ramrod is brass tipped. The sights are fixed, simple and tough, just what I expect on a black powder handgun. For hunting, plinking and self defense handguns, I want fixed sights, as I have had adjustable sights get caught on brush and knocked out of kilter in the past. The trigger pull on my gun is a crisp 3.5 lbs. The nipple is 6mmx.75 and the lock is color case hardened. The belt hook, which I at first thought ugly and obtrusive, quickly proved itself on my first rabbit hunt with the gun in deep snow. In Maine, snowshoes are considered seasonal footwear by many, and trying to maneuver in rabbit cover, in deep snow on snowshoes, can prove to be a vigorous endeavor indeed. The belt hook allowed me to securely attach the pistol to my leather belt, cross draw, under my heavy Woolrich hunting coat, which protected the lockwork and percussion cap from brush and snow and left my hands free to maneuver through the thick cover.

In either .50 or .54 caliber, the Lyman is a superb small- to medium-size game-hunting handgun at 20-25 yards. The Lyman, properly loaded, is more than capable of taking deer-sized game and varmints such as coyotes within hand-gun range, provided that the shooter targets a vital zone such as the heart/lung area. The Lyman Plains Pistol can even be used as a short-range shotgun pistol. I have used 3/4 ounce of #7-1/2 birdshot in mine with lubed cardboard wads in front of and behind the shot charge, backed by 35 grains of FFFG. At 15 to 20 feet, this is a potent load for grouse, squirrels and pests. At longer ranges, the shot charge, being fired from a short rifled barrel without a choke, spreads out quickly, with far too many holes in the pattern to be effective. But at close range, this load is bad medicine for vermin and pests! Varmints around the barn or chicken coop won't know the difference at close range between being hit with a black powder-propelled load of birdshot out of the this pistol and being whacked with a modern smokeless load from a .410 shotgun.

My .54 caliber Lyman pistol, charged with a patched Speer 225-gr. round lead ball and 40 grains of FFFG GOEX black powder, will produce a velocity of over 920 fps (feet per second) at the muzzle, and over 425 ft. lbs. of energy! This kind of power will smash that big round lead ball into flesh and bone with devastating and lethal results. To put this in perspective: the average 230-gr. .45 ACP full metal jacket bullet obtains a muzzle velocity of around 830 fps for about 355 ft. lbs of energy. The .45 ACP hardball cartridge and the Colt 1911/1911A1 were used by American forces in two World Wars and many major and minor conflicts across the globe up until 1985 (when it was replaced by the Beretta M-9 9MM) and is still in use by certain elite units in law enforcement and the military today, although +P hollowpoints are quickly gaining favor where permitted. The standard 230-gr. .45 hardball round is still considered by many to be the measuring stick against which all other self defense handgun cartridges are measured – and the .54 Lyman Plains Pistol outmuscles the .45ACP in both velocity and energy. Not bad at all for mountain man-era technology!

This pistol packs a wallop, and the fur trappers in the American northwest of two centuries ago chose virtually

identical weapons for that very reason. The percussion cap became prevalent in the 1820s and gradually its use spread west, eventually replacing the flintlock system. Many rifles and pistols had their lock systems upgraded to accept the percussion cap, which was more reliable. Over four decades ago, Carl P. Russell, Ph. D., wrote in his book *Firearms, Traps, & Tools of the Mountain Men*:

The seldom-mentioned handgun was not the nonentity that its absence from the fur-trade literature might imply. It was the arm of final resort in the "last-ditch stand," and in that connection it receives rare recognition in the records of the trade. But it was also ever-present on the trapper's person and was brought into more frequent unspectacular uses seldom mentioned in the journals. Ballistically it could not compare with the long arms carried by the trapper, but the occasional contemporary records of military tests indicate that even the smoothbore pistol of .525 caliber could inflict deadly wounds at short range. The rifled pistols of the day were still more effective.

Although obsolete for self defense purposes in 21st-century North America, as there are better, more modern and hence more reliable weapons out there, I would feel far from defenseless at home or at camp if this were the only arm I had and I needed protection.

The loading procedure for the Plains Pistol is as follows: after wiping all grease/oil out of the barrel with a dry cleaning patch, fire a number #11 percussion cap or two to ensure that all the oil is out of the nipple. Then with the pistol in the upright position, hammer resting on an empty nipple, carefully pour the pre-measured amount of black powder or Pyrodex into the barrel. Never, under any circumstances, attempt to use smokeless powder in a black powder weapon! These guns are not designed for smokeless powders and can explode. Use the ram rod to gently tamp the powder in place. A patch of proper size (I use .15" thick prelubricated patches) can be placed over the bore and a ball (I prefer .530" Speer) can be seated onto it and started down the bore with a firm grip. A bullet starter makes this job easier, as the first inch can take a lot of pressure to get the lead ball started into the rifling. I have also used pillow ticking and Crisco, but the pre-cut, prelubricated patches provide me with more consistent performance.

The ball should be firmly seated, but not pounded into place, to ensure that no headspace or air is left between the powder and the patched ball. I have my ramrod marked so I know where mark is on the rod is at the muzzle when the gun is charged with patch, ball and 40 grains of powder, as well as the 30-gr. mark. Now that the powder is in, the patched ball is firmly seated and the weapon is pointed in a safe direction, the hammer can be raised to the half cock position and the percussion cap seated on the nipple. The arm is now ready to fire.

I should remind readers of the inherent danger, added responsibility and the increased focus on safety that accompany the use and ownership of blackpowder weapons. Although we are blessed with steels and powders that the old timers would envy, the basic design has changed little since the big martial pistols were originally carried by the trappers and explorers in the early 1800s through the 1840s. These arms were built for survival in an era where personal responsibility and common sense ruled, as opposed to our litigious

The author plinking with the Plains Pistol in the western mountains of Maine. He is wearing a homemade pouch on his belt to hold the powder flask, lead balls, percussion caps and accessories.

society where elected officials often attempt to "legislate morality" by passing restrictive laws and product warning labels abound. The big rabbit ear hammer is susceptible to dropping on a percussion cap and firing if dropped on a hard surface or if it receives a sharp blow. If the gun is going to be used for hunting, either wait until the last moment to place the percussion cap on the nipple or purchase an inexpensive muzzleloading "nipple cap" to provide a level of safety. It be removed instantly when game is spotted and the shooter is ready to fire.

On the .54 caliber model, 40 grains of black powder or substitute is the maximum recommended charge, and often premium accuracy and performance can be obtained with a much smaller charge. Individual results will vary, depending upon the gun and components used. The shooter is encouraged to experiment with different brands and types of balls, patches, powders and lubricants in order to find the best combination. For rabbits, small game and varmints, I find that 30 grains of FFFG provides me with more than enough power and accuracy. I have grouped 4 shots into three inches at 25 yards from a rest, using GOEX FFFG and Speer .530 lead balls, which is better than many modern service weapons achieve and accurate enough for hunting.

Shooting the .54 Lyman is a blast! To anyone accustomed to the sound of centerfire handgun cartridges detonating, this thing sounds like a cannon going off. It is more of a "Boom" than the sharp, earsplitting explosion of centerfire cartridges, although you still need ear protection and shooting glasses. You take aim, squeeze the trigger, the gun roars, flames shoot out of the muzzle, and your target is enveloped in a cloud of thick smoke. As the wind gently pushes the cloud of smoke away, you look to see if you hit your mark. The Lyman will provide many hours of leisurely fun and economical target practice.

There is something special about shooting single shot black powder pistols, either percussion or flintlock. There is a certain nostalgic, eccentric state of mind you have to be in to take a primitive single shot weapon out plinking or for a stroll in the woods. The gun forces you to take your time and slow down, whether you are loading, taking careful aim with your single shot, or cleaning up after shooting, which involves field stripping, lots of hot soapy water, scrub-

bing and grease. When not in use, I keep my pistol coated inside and out with Thompson Center's Natural Lube 1000 Plus, an all-natural lubricant, in order to prevent rust and make cleanup easier in the future.

All this procedure and care necessitates taking time. I find it relaxing to forget about the world for an afternoon, take my pistol outside in the fresh air and sunshine to enjoy some target practice, 1840s style. When I get to escape from the modern world during the hunting season, I can spend a day or more outside with my .54 Lyman

(top) Black powder guns need to be cleaned ASAP after shooting. Here the Plains Pistol is stripped down and ready to be thoroughly cleaned and greased.

(above) Stan Libby, the author's father, explains to his grandson Clint, how a Mountain Man percussion pistol works.

pistol, possibles bag, and my HB Forge Mountain Man throwing knife on my belt. The cool crisp air and smell of pine trees hits my lungs and I am transported back in time, at least for a little while.

Many manufacturers do not supply suggested retail prices. Others did not get their pricing to us before press time. All pricing can vary dependent on the exact brand and style of ammo selected and/or the retail outlet from which you make your purchase. Pricing has been rounded to the nearest dollar and represents our best estimate of average pricing. An * after the cartridge means these loads are available with Nosler Partition or Swift A-Frame bullets. Listed pricing may or may not reflect this bullet type. ** = these are packed 50 to box, all others are 20 to box. Wea. Mag.= Weatherby Magnum. Spfd. = Springfield. A-Sq. = A-Square. N.E.=Nitro Express.

Cartridge	Bullet Wgt. Grs.	VELOCITY (fps)					ENERGY (ft. lbs.)					TRAJ. (in.)				Est. Price/box
		Muzzle	100 yds.	200 yds.	300 yds.	400 yds.	Muzzle	100 yds.	200 yds.	300 yds.	400 yds.	100 yds.	200 yds.	300 yds.	400 yds.	
17, 22																
17 Remington Fireball	20	4000	3380	2840	2360	1930	710	507	358	247	165	1.6	1.5	-2.8	-13.5	NA
17 Remington Fireball	25	3850	3280	2780	2330	1925	823	597	429	301	206	0.9	0.0	-5.4	NA	NA
17 Remington	25	4040	3284	2644	2086	1606	906	599	388	242	143	+2.0	+1.7	-4.0	-17.0	$17
204 Ruger (Fed)	32 Green	4030	3320	2710	2170	1710	1155	780	520	335	205	0.9	0.0	-5.7	-19.1	NA
204 Ruger	32	4225	3632	3114	2652	2234	1268	937	689	500	355	.6	0.0	-4.2	-13.4	NA
204 Ruger	40	3900	3451	3046	2677	2336	1351	1058	824	636	485	.7	0.0	-4.5	-13.9	NA
204 Ruger	45	3625	3188	2792	2428	2093	1313	1015	778	589	438	1.0	0.0	-5.5	-16.9	NA
221 Fireball	50	2800	2137	1580	1180	988	870	507	277	155	109	+0.0	-7.0	-28.0	0.0	$14
22 Hornet (Fed)	30 Green	3150	2150	1390	990	830	660	310	130	65	45	+0.0	-6.6	-32.7	NA	NA
22 Hornet	34	3050	2132	1415	1017	852	700	343	151	78	55	+0.0	-6.6	-15.5	-29.9	NA
22 Hornet	35	3100	2278	1601	1135	929	747	403	199	100	67	+2.75	0.0	-16.9	-60.4	NA
22 Hornet	45	2690	2042	1502	1128	948	723	417	225	127	90	+0.0	-7.7	-31.0	0.0	$27**
218 Bee	46	2760	2102	1550	1155	961	788	451	245	136	94	+0.0	-7.2	-29.0	0.0	$46**
222 Remington	40	3600	3117	2673	2269	1911	1151	863	634	457	324	+1.07	0.0	-6.13	-18.9	NA
222 Remington	50	3140	2602	2123	1700	1350	1094	752	500	321	202	+2.0	-0.4	-11.0	-33.0	$11
222 Remington	55	3020	2562	2147	1773	1451	1114	801	563	384	257	+2.0	-0.4	-11.0	-33.0	$12
22 PPC	52	3400	2930	2510	2130	NA	1335	990	730	525	NA	+2.0	1.4	-5.0	0.0	NA
223 Remington	40	3650	3010	2450	1950	1530	1185	805	535	340	265	+2.0	+1.0	-6.0	-22.0	$14
223 Remington	40	3800	3305	2845	2424	2044	1282	970	719	522	371	0.84	0.0	-5.34	-16.6	NA
223 Remington (Rem)	45 Green	3550	2911	2355	1865	1451	1259	847	554	347	210	2.5	2.3	-4.3	-21.1	NA
223 Remington	50	3300	2874	2484	2130	1809	1209	917	685	504	363	1.37	0.0	-7.05	-21.8	NA
223 Remington	52/53	3330	2882	2477	2106	1770	1305	978	722	522	369	+2.0	+0.6	-6.5	-21.5	$14
223 Remington (Win)	55 Green	3240	2747	2304	1905	1554	1282	921	648	443	295	1.9	0.0	-8.5	-26.7	NA
223 Remington	55	3240	2748	2305	1906	1556	1282	922	649	444	296	+2.0	-0.2	-9.0	-27.0	$12
223 Remington	60	3100	2712	2355	2026	1726	1280	979	739	547	397	+2.0	+0.2	-8.0	-24.7	$16
223 Remington	64	3020	2621	2256	1920	1619	1296	977	723	524	373	+2.0	-0.2	-9.3	-23.0	$14
223 Remington	69	3000	2720	2460	2210	1980	1380	1135	925	750	600	+2.0	+0.8	-5.8	-17.5	$15
223 Remington	75	2790	2554	2330	2119	1926	1296	1086	904	747	617	2.37	0.0	-8.75	-25.1	NA
223 Remington	77	2750	2584	2354	2169	1992	1293	1110	948	804	679	1.93	0.0	-8.2	-23.8	NA
223 WSSM	55	3850	3438	3064	2721	2402	1810	1444	1147	904	704	0.7	0.0	-4.4	-13.6	NA
223 WSSM	64	3600	3144	2732	2356	2011	1841	1404	1061	789	574	1.0	0.0	-5.7	-17.7	NA
222 Rem. Mag.	55	3240	2748	2305	1906	1556	1282	922	649	444	296	+2.0	-0.2	-9.0	-27.0	$14
225 Winchester	55	3570	3066	2616	2208	1838	1556	1148	836	595	412	+2.0	+1.0	-5.0	-20.0	$19
224 Wea. Mag.	55	3650	3192	2780	2403	2057	1627	1244	943	705	516	+2.0	+1.2	-4.0	-17.0	$32
22-250 Rem.	40	4000	3320	2720	2200	1740	1420	980	660	430	265	+2.0	+1.8	-3.0	-16.0	$14
22-250 Rem.	45 Green	4000	3293	2690	2159	1696	1598	1084	723	466	287	1.7	1.7	-3.2	-15.7	NA
22-250 Rem.	50	3725	3264	2641	2455	2103	1540	1183	896	669	491	0.89	0.0	-5.23	-16.3	NA
22-250 Rem.	52/55	3680	3137	2656	2222	1832	1654	1201	861	603	410	+2.0	+1.3	-4.0	-17.0	$13
22-250 Rem.	60	3600	3195	2826	2485	2169	1727	1360	1064	823	627	+2.0	+2.0	-2.4	-12.3	$19
220 Swift	40	4200	3678	3190	2739	2329	1566	1201	904	666	482	+0.51	0.0	-4.0	-12.9	NA
220 Swift	50	3780	3158	2617	2135	1710	1586	1107	760	506	325	+2.0	+1.4	-4.4	-17.9	$20
220 Swift	50	3850	3396	2970	2576	2215	1645	1280	979	736	545	0.74	0.0	-4.84	-15.1	NA
220 Swift	55	3800	3370	2990	2630	2310	1765	1390	1090	850	650	0.8	0.0	-4.7	-14.4	NA
220 Swift	55	3650	3194	2772	2384	2035	1627	1246	939	694	506	+2.0	+2.0	-2.6	-13.4	$19
220 Swift	60	3600	3199	2824	2475	2156	1727	1364	1063	816	619	+2.0	+1.6	-4.1	-13.1	$19
22 Savage H.P.	71	2790	2340	1930	1570	1280	1225	860	585	390	190	+2.0	-1.0	-10.4	-35.7	NA
6mm (24)																
6mm BR Rem.	100	2550	2310	2083	1870	1671	1444	1185	963	776	620	+2.5	-0.6	-11.8	0.0	$22
6mm Norma BR	107	2822	2667	2517	2372	2229	1893	1690	1506	1337	1181	+1.73	0.0	-7.24	-20.6	NA
6mm PPC	70	3140	2750	2400	2070	NA	1535	1175	895	665	NA	+2.0	+1.4	-5.0	0.0	NA
243 Winchester	55	4025	3597	3209	2853	2525	1978	1579	1257	994	779	+0.6	0.0	-4.0	-12.2	NA
243 Winchester	60	3600	3110	2660	2260	1890	1725	1285	945	680	475	+1.8	0.0	-3.3	-15.5	$17
243 Winchester	70	3400	3040	2700	2390	2100	1795	1435	1135	890	685	1.1	0.0	-5.9	-18.0	NA
243 Winchester	75/80	3350	2955	2593	2259	1951	1993	1551	1194	906	676	+2.0	+0.9	-5.0	-19.0	$16
243 W. Superformance	80	3425	3080	2760	2463	2184	2083	1684	1353	1077	847	1.1	0.0	-5.7	-17.1	NA
243 Winchester	85	3320	3070	2830	2600	2380	2080	1770	1510	1280	1070	+2.0	+1.2	-4.0	-14.0	$18
243 Winchester	90	3120	2871	2635	2411	2199	1946	1647	1388	1162	966	1.4	0.0	-6.4	-18.8	NA
243 Winchester*	100	2960	2697	2449	2215	1993	1945	1615	1332	1089	882	+2.5	+1.2	-6.0	-20.0	$16
243 Winchester	105	2920	2689	2470	2261	2062	1988	1686	1422	1192	992	+2.5	+1.6	-5.0	-18.4	$21
243 Light Mag.	100	3100	2839	2592	2358	2138	2133	1790	1491	1235	1014	+1.5	0.0	-6.0	-19.8	NA
243 WSSM	55	4060	3628	3237	2880	2550	2013	1607	1280	1013	794	0.6	0.0	-3.9	-12.0	NA
243 WSSM	95	3250	3000	2763	2538	2325	2258	1898	1610	1359	1140	1.2	0.0	-5.7	-16.9	NA
243 WSSM	100	3110	2838	2583	2341	2112	2147	1789	1481	1217	991	1.4	0.0	-6.6	-19.7	NA
6mm Remington	80	3470	3064	2694	2352	2036	2139	1667	1289	982	736	+2.0	+1.1	-5.0	-17.0	$16
6mm R. Superformance	95	3235	2955	2692	2443	3309	2207	1841	1528	1259	1028	1.2	0.0	-6.1	-18.0	NA
6mm Remington	100	3100	2829	2573	2332	2104	2133	1777	1470	1207	983	+2.5	+1.6	-5.0	-17.0	$16
6mm Remington	105	3060	2822	2596	2381	2177	2105	1788	1512	1270	1059	+2.5	+1.1	-3.3	-15.0	$21
6mm Rem. Light Mag.	100	3250	2997	2756	2528	2311	2345	1995	1687	1418	1186	1.59	0.0	-6.33	-18.3	NA
6.17(.243) Spitfire	100	3350	3122	2905	2698	2501	2493	2164	1874	1617	1389	2.4	3.2	0.0	-8.0	NA
240 Wea. Mag.	87	3500	3202	2924	2663	2416	2366	1980	1651	1370	1127	+2.0	+2.0	-2.0	-12.0	$32
240 Wea. Mag.	100	3395	3106	2835	2581	2339	2559	2142	1785	1478	1215	+2.5	+2.8	-2.0	-11.0	$43

Cartridge	Bullet Wgt. Grs.	VELOCITY (fps)					ENERGY (ft. lbs.)					TRAJ. (in.)				Est. Price/box
		Muzzle	100 yds.	200 yds.	300 yds.	400 yds.	Muzzle	100 yds.	200 yds.	300 yds.	400 yds.	100 yds.	200 yds.	300 yds.	400 yds.	
25-20 Win.	86	1460	1194	1030	931	858	407	272	203	165	141	0.0	-23.5	0.0	0.0	$32**
25-35 Win.	117	2230	1866	1545	1282	1097	1292	904	620	427	313	+2.5	-4.2	-26.0	0.0	$24
250 Savage	100	2820	2504	2210	1936	1684	1765	1392	1084	832	630	+2.5	+0.4	-9.0	-28.0	$17
257 Roberts	100	2980	2661	2363	2085	1827	1972	1572	1240	965	741	+2.5	-0.8	-5.2	-21.6	$20
257 Roberts+P	117	2780	2411	2071	1761	1488	2009	1511	1115	806	576	+2.5	-0.2	-10.2	-32.6	$18
257 R. Superformance	117	2946	2705	2478	2265	2057	2253	1901	1595	1329	1099	1.1	0.0	-5.7	-17.1	NA
257 Roberts+P	120	2780	2560	2360	2160	1970	2060	1750	1480	1240	1030	+2.5	+1.2	-6.4	-23.6	$22
257 Roberts	122	2600	2331	2078	1842	1625	1831	1472	1169	919	715	+2.5	0.0	-10.6	-31.4	$21
25-06 Rem.	87	3440	2995	2591	2222	1884	2286	1733	1297	954	686	+2.0	+1.1	-2.5	-14.4	$17
25-06 Rem.	90	3440	3043	2680	2344	2034	2364	1850	1435	1098	827	+2.0	+1.8	-3.3	-15.6	$17
25-06 Rem.	100	3230	2893	2580	2287	2014	2316	1858	1478	1161	901	+2.0	+0.8	-5.7	-18.9	$17
25-06 Rem.	117	2990	2770	2570	2370	2190	2320	2000	1715	1465	1246	+2.5	+1.0	-7.9	-26.6	$19
25-06 R. Superformance	117	3110	2861	2626	2403	2191	2512	2127	1792	1500	1246	1.4	0.0	-6.4	-18.9	NA
25-06 Rem.*	120	2990	2730	2484	2252	2032	2382	1985	1644	1351	1100	+2.5	+1.2	-5.3	-19.6	$17
25-06 Rem.	122	2930	2706	2492	2289	2095	2325	1983	1683	1419	1189	+2.5	+1.8	-4.5	-17.5	$23
25 WSSM	85	3470	3156	2863	2589	2331	2273	1880	1548	1266	1026	1.0	0.0	-5.2	-15.7	NA
25 WSSM	115	3060	284	2639	2442	2254	2392	2066	1778	1523	1398	1.4	0.0	-6.4	-18.6	NA
25 WSSM	120	2990	2717	2459	2216	1987	2383	1967	1612	1309	1053	1.6	0.0	-7.4	-21.8	NA
257 Wea. Mag.	87	3825	3456	3118	2805	2513	2826	2308	1870	1520	1220	+2.0	+2.7	-0.3	-7.6	$32
257 Wea. Mag.	100	3555	3237	2941	2665	2404	2806	2326	1920	1576	1283	+2.5	+3.2	0.0	-8.0	$32
257 Scramjet	100	3745	3450	3173	2912	2666	3114	2643	2235	1883	1578	+2.1	+2.77	0.0	-6.93	NA
6.5																
6.5x47 Lapua	123	2887	NA	2554	NA	2244	2285	NA	1788	NA	1380	NA	4.53	0.0	-10.7	NA
6.5x50mm Jap.	139	2360	2160	1970	1790	1620	1720	1440	1195	985	810	+2.5	-1.0	-13.5	0.0	NA
6.5x50mm Jap.	156	2070	1830	1610	1430	1260	1475	1155	900	695	550	+2.5	-4.0	-23.8	0.0	NA
6.5x52mm Car.	139	2580	2360	2160	1970	1790	2045	1725	1440	1195	985	+2.5	0.0	-9.9	-29.0	NA
6.5x52mm Car.	156	2430	2170	1930	1700	1500	2045	1630	1285	1005	780	+2.5	-1.0	-13.9	0.0	NA
6.5x52mm Carcano	160	2250	1963	1700	1467	1271	1798	1369	1027	764	574	+3.8	0.0	-15.9	-48.1	NA
6.5x55mm Swe.	93	2625	2350	2090	1850	1630	1425	1140	905	705	550	2.4	0.0	-10.3	-31.1	NA
6.5x55mm Swe.	123	2750	2570	2400	2240	2080	2065	1810	1580	1370	1185	1.9	0.0	-7.9	-22.9	NA
6.5x55mm Swe.	140	2550	NA	NA	NA	NA	2020	NA	NA	NA	NA	0.0	0.0	0.0	0.0	$18
6.5x55mm Swe.*	139/140	2850	2640	2440	2250	2070	2525	2170	1855	1575	1330	+2.5	+1.6	-5.4	-18.9	$18
6.5x55mm Swe.	156	2650	2370	2110	1870	1650	2425	1950	1550	1215	945	+2.5	0.0	-10.3	-30.6	NA
260 Remington	125	2875	2669	2473	2285	2105	2294	1977	1697	1449	1230	1.71	0.0	-7.4	-21.4	NA
260 Remington	140	2750	2544	2347	2158	1979	2351	2011	1712	1448	1217	+2.2	0.0	-8.6	-24.6	NA
6.5 Creedmoor	120	3020	2815	2619	2430	2251	2430	2111	1827	1574	1350	1.4	0.0	-6.5	-18.9	NA
6.5 C. Superformance	129	2950	2756	2570	2392	2221	2492	2175	1892	1639	1417	1.5	0.0	-6.8	-19.7	NA
6.5 Creedmoor	140	2820	2654	2494	2339	2190	2472	2179	1915	1679	1467	1.7	0.0	-7.2	-20.6	NA
6.5-284 Norma	142	3025	2890	2758	2631	2507	2886	2634	2400	2183	1982	1.13	0.0	-5.7	-16.4	NA
6.71 (264) Phantom	120	3150	2929	2718	2517	2325	2645	2286	1969	1698	1440	+1.3	0.0	-6.0	-17.5	NA
6.5 Rem. Mag.	120	3210	2905	2621	2353	2102	2745	2248	1830	1475	1177	+2.5	+1.7	-4.1	-16.3	Disc.
264 Win. Mag.	140	3030	2782	2548	2326	2114	2854	2406	2018	1682	1389	+2.5	+1.4	-5.1	-18.0	$24
6.71 (264) Blackbird	140	3480	3261	3053	2855	2665	3766	3307	2899	2534	2208	+2.4	+3.1	0.0	-7.4	NA
6.8mm Rem.	115	2775	2472	2190	1926	1683	1966	1561	1224	947	723	+2.1	0.0	-3.7	-9.4	NA
27																
270 Winchester	100	3430	3021	2649	2305	1988	2612	2027	1557	1179	877	+2.0	+1.0	-4.9	-17.5	$17
270 Win. (Rem.)	115	2710	2482	2265	2059	NA	1875	1485	1161	896	NA	0.0	4.8	-17.3	0.0	NA
270 Winchester	130	3060	2776	2510	2259	2022	2702	2225	1818	1472	1180	+2.5	+1.4	-5.3	-18.2	$17
270 Win. Supreme	130	3150	2881	2628	2388	2161	2865	2396	1993	1646	1348	1.3	0.0	-6.4	-18.9	NA
270 W. Superformance	130	3200	2984	2788	2582	2393	2955	2570	2228	1924	1653	1.2	0.0	-5.7	-16.7	NA
270 Winchester	135	3000	2780	2570	2369	2178	2697	2315	1979	1682	1421	+2.5	+1.4	-6.0	-17.6	$23
270 Winchester*	140	2940	2700	2480	2260	2060	2685	2270	1905	1590	1315	+2.5	+1.8	-4.6	-17.9	$20
270 Winchester*	150	2850	2585	2336	2100	1879	2705	2226	1817	1468	1175	+2.5	+1.2	-6.5	-22.0	$17
270 Win. Supreme	150	2930	2693	2468	2254	2051	2860	2416	2030	1693	1402	1.7	0.0	-7.4	-21.6	NA
270 WSM	130	3275	3041	2820	2609	2408	3096	2669	2295	1564	1673	1.1	0.0	-5.5	-16.1	NA
270 WSM	140	3125	2865	2619	2386	2165	3035	2559	2132	1769	1457	1.4	0.0	-6.5	-19.0	NA
270 WSM	150	3120	2923	2734	2554	2380	3242	2845	2490	2172	1886	1.3	0.0	-5.9	-17.2	NA
270 Wea. Mag.	100	3760	3380	3033	2712	2412	3139	2537	2042	1633	1292	+2.0	+2.4	-1.2	-10.1	$32
270 Wea. Mag.	130	3375	3119	2878	2649	2432	3287	2808	2390	2026	1707	+2.5	-2.9	-0.9	-9.9	$32
270 Wea. Mag.*	150	3245	3036	2837	2647	2465	3507	3070	2681	2334	2023	+2.5	+2.6	-1.8	-11.4	$47
7mm																
7mm BR	140	2216	2012	1821	1643	1481	1525	1259	1031	839	681	+2.0	-3.7	-20.0	0.0	$23
7mm Mauser*	139/140	2660	2435	2221	2018	1827	2199	1843	1533	1266	1037	+2.5	0.0	-9.6	-27.7	$17
7mm Mauser	145	2690	2442	2206	1985	1777	2334	1920	1568	1268	1017	+2.5	+0.1	-9.6	-28.3	$18
7mm Mauser	154	2690	2490	2300	2120	1940	2475	2120	1810	1530	1285	+2.5	+0.8	-7.5	-23.5	$17
7mm Mauser	175	2440	2137	1857	1603	1382	2313	1774	1340	998	742	+2.5	-1.7	-16.1	0.0	$17

Cartridge	Bullet Wgt. Grs.	VELOCITY (fps)					ENERGY (ft. lbs.)					TRAJ. (in.)				Est. Price/box
		Muzzle	100 yds.	200 yds.	300 yds.	400 yds.	Muzzle	100 yds.	200 yds.	300 yds.	400 yds.	100 yds.	200 yds.	300 yds.	400 yds.	
7x30 Waters	120	2700	2300	1930	1600	1330	1940	1405	990	685	470	+2.5	-0.2	-12.3	0.0	$18
7mm-08 Rem.	120	3000	2725	2467	2223	1992	2398	1979	1621	1316	1058	+2.0	0.0	-7.6	-22.3	$18
7mm-08 Rem.*	140	2860	2625	2402	2189	1988	2542	2142	1793	1490	1228	+2.5	+0.8	-6.9	-21.9	$18
7mm-08 Rem.	154	2715	2510	2315	2128	1950	2520	2155	1832	1548	1300	+2.5	+1.0	-7.0	-22.7	$23
7-08 R. Superformance	139	2950	2857	2571	2393	2222	2686	2345	2040	1768	1524	1.5	0.0	-6.8	-19.7	NA
7x64mm Bren.	140						Not Yet Announced									$17
7x64mm Bren.	154	2820	2610	2420	2230	2050	2720	2335	1995	1695	1430	+2.5	+1.4	-5.7	-19.9	NA
7x64mm Bren.*	160	2850	2669	2495	2327	2166	2885	2530	2211	1924	1667	+2.5	+1.6	-4.8	-17.8	$24
7x64mm Bren.	175						Not Yet Announced									$17
284 Winchester	150	2860	2595	2344	2108	1886	2724	2243	1830	1480	1185	+2.5	+0.8	-7.3	-23.2	$24
280 R. Superformance	139	3090	2890	2699	2516	2341	2946	2578	2249	1954	1691	1.3	0.0	-6.1	-17.7	NA
280 Remington	140	3000	2758	2528	2309	2102	2797	2363	1986	1657	1373	+2.5	+1.4	-5.2	-18.3	$17
280 Remington*	150	2890	2624	2373	2135	1912	2781	2293	1875	1518	1217	+2.5	+0.8	-7.1	-22.6	$17
280 Remington	160	2840	2637	2442	2556	2078	2866	2471	2120	1809	1535	+2.5	+0.8	-6.7	-21.0	$20
280 Remington	165	2820	2510	2220	1950	1701	2913	2308	1805	1393	1060	+2.5	+0.4	-8.8	-26.5	$17
7x61mm S&H Sup.	154	3060	2720	2400	2100	1820	3200	2520	1965	1505	1135	+2.5	+1.8	-5.0	-19.8	NA
7mm Dakota	160	3200	3001	2811	2630	2455	3637	3200	2808	2456	2140	+2.1	+1.9	-2.8	-12.5	NA
7mm Rem. Mag. (Rem.)	140	2710	2482	2265	2059	NA	2283	1915	1595	1318	NA	0.0	-4.5	-1.57	0.0	NA
7mm Rem. Mag.*	139/140	3150	2930	2710	2510	2320	3085	2660	2290	1960	1670	+2.5	+2.4	-2.4	-12.7	$21
7 R.M. Superformance	139	3240	3033	2836	2648	2467	3239	2839	2482	2163	1877	1.1	0.0	-5.5	-15.9	NA
7mm Rem. Mag.	150/154	3110	2830	2568	2320	2085	3221	2667	2196	1792	1448	+2.5	+1.6	-4.6	-16.5	$21
7mm Rem. Mag.*	160/162	2950	2730	2520	2320	2120	3090	2650	2250	1910	1600	+2.5	+1.8	-4.4	-17.8	$34
7 R.M. Superformance	154	3100	2914	2736	2565	2401	3286	2904	2560	2250	1970	1.3	0.0	-5.9	-17.2	NA
7mm Rem. Mag.	165	2900	2699	2507	2324	2147	3081	2669	2303	1978	1689	+2.5	+1.2	-5.9	-19.0	$28
7mm Rem Mag.	175	2860	2645	2440	2244	2057	3178	2718	2313	1956	1644	+2.5	+1.2	-6.5	-20.7	$21
7mm Rem. SA ULTRA MAG	140	3175	2934	2707	2490	2283	3033	2676	2277	1927	1620	1.3	0.0	-6	-17.7	NA
7mm Rem. SA ULTRA MAG	150	3110	2828	2563	2313	2077	3221	2663	2188	1782	1437	2.5	2.1	-3.6	-15.8	NA
7mm Rem. SA ULTRA MAG	160	2960	2762	2572	2390	2215	3112	2709	2350	2029	1743	2.6	2.2	-3.6	-15.4	NA
7mm Rem. WSM	140	3225	3008	2801	2603	2414	3233	2812	2438	2106	1812	1.2	0.0	-5.6	-16.4	NA
7mm Rem. WSM	160	2990	2744	2512	2081	1883	3176	2675	2241	1864	1538	1.6	0.0	-7.1	-20.8	NA
7mm Wea. Mag.	140	3225	2970	2729	2501	2283	3233	2741	2315	1943	1621	+2.5	+2.0	-3.2	-14.0	$35
7mm Wea. Mag.	154	3260	3023	2799	2586	2382	3539	3044	2609	2227	1890	+2.5	+2.8	-1.5	-10.8	$32
7mm Wea. Mag.*	160	3200	3004	2816	2637	2464	3637	3205	2817	2469	2156	+2.5	+2.7	-1.5	-10.6	$47
7mm Wea. Mag.	165	2950	2747	2553	2367	2189	3188	2765	2388	2053	1756	+2.5	+1.8	-4.2	-16.4	$43
7mm Wea. Mag.	175	2910	2693	2486	2288	2098	3293	2818	2401	2033	1711	+2.5	+1.2	-5.9	-19.4	$35
7.21(.284) Tomahawk	140	3300	3118	2943	2774	2612	3386	3022	2693	2393	2122	2.3	3.2	0.0	-7.7	NA
7mm STW	140	3325	3064	2818	2585	2364	3436	2918	2468	2077	1737	+2.3	+1.8	-3.0	-13.1	NA
7mm STW Supreme	160	3150	2894	2652	2422	2204	3526	2976	2499	2085	1727	1.3	0.0	-6.3	-18.5	NA
7mm Rem. Ultra Mag.	140	3425	3184	2956	2740	2534	3646	3151	2715	2333	1995	1.7	1.6	-2.6	-11.4	NA
7mm Firehawk	140	3625	3373	3135	2909	2695	4084	3536	3054	2631	2258	+2.2	+2.9	0.0	-7.03	NA
30																
7.21 (.284) Firebird	140	3750	3522	3306	3101	2905	4372	3857	3399	2990	2625	1.6	2.4	0.0	-6.0	NA
30 Carbine	110	1990	1567	1236	1035	923	977	600	373	262	208	0.0	-13.5	0.0	0.0	$28**
303 Savage	190	1890	1612	1327	1183	1055	1507	1096	794	591	469	+2.5	-7.6	0.0	0.0	$24
30 Remington	170	2120	1822	1555	1328	1153	1696	1253	913	666	502	+2.5	-4.7	-26.3	0.0	$20
7.62x39mm Rus.	123/125	2300	2030	1780	1550	1350	1445	1125	860	655	500	+2.5	-2.0	-17.5	0.0	$13
30-30 Win.	55	3400	2693	2085	1570	1187	1412	886	521	301	172	+2.0	0.0	-10.2	-35.0	$18
30-30 Win.	125	2570	2090	1660	1320	1080	1830	1210	770	480	320	-2.0	-2.6	-19.9	0.0	$13
30-30 Win.	150	2390	2040	1723	1447	1225	1902	1386	989	697	499	0.0	-7.5	-27.0	-63.0	NA
30-30 Win. Supreme	150	2480	2095	1747	1446	1209	2049	1462	1017	697	487	0.0	-6.5	-24.5	0.0	NA
30-30 Win.	160	2300	1997	1719	1473	1268	1879	1416	1050	771	571	+2.5	-2.9	-20.2	0.0	$18
30-30 Win. Lever Evolution	160	2400	2150	1916	1699	NA	2046	1643	1304	1025	NA	3.0	0.2	-12.1	NA	NA
30-30 PMC Cowboy	170	1300	1198	1121			638	474				0.0	-27.0	0.0	0.0	NA
30-30 Win.*	170	2200	1895	1619	1381	1191	1827	1355	989	720	535	+2.5	-5.8	-23.6	0.0	$13
300 Savage	150	2630	2354	2094	1853	1631	2303	1845	1462	1143	886	+2.5	-0.4	-10.1	-30.7	$17
300 Savage	180	2350	2137	1935	1754	1570	2207	1825	1496	1217	985	+2.5	-1.6	-15.2	0.0	$17
30-40 Krag	180	2430	2213	2007	1813	1632	2360	1957	1610	1314	1064	+2.5	-1.4	-13.8	0.0	$18
7.65x53mm Arg.	180	2590	2390	2200	2010	1830	2685	2280	1925	1615	1345	+2.5	0.0	-27.6	0.0	NA
7.5x53mm Argentine	150	2785	2519	2269	2032	1814	2583	2113	1714	1376	1096	+2.0	0.0	-8.8	-25.5	NA
308 Marlin Express	160	2660	2430	2226	2026	1836	2513	2111	1761	1457	1197	3.0	1.7	-6.7	-23.5	NA
307 Winchester	150	2760	2321	1924	1575	1289	2530	1795	1233	826	554	+2.5	-1.5	-13.6	0.0	Disc.
307 Winchester	180	2510	2179	1874	1599	1362	2519	1898	1404	1022	742	+2.5	-1.6	-15.6	0.0	$20
7.5x55 Swiss	180	2650	2450	2250	2060	1880	2805	2390	2020	1700	1415	+2.5	+0.6	-8.1	-24.9	NA
7.5x55mm Swiss	165	2720	2515	2319	2132	1954	2710	2317	1970	1665	1398	+2.0	0.0	-8.5	-24.6	NA
30 Remington AR	123/125	2800	2465	2154	1867	1606	2176	1686	1288	967	716	2.1	0.0	-9.7	-29.4	NA

Cartridge	Bullet Wgt. Grs.	VELOCITY (fps)					ENERGY (ft. lbs.)					TRAJ. (in.)				Est. Price/box
		Muzzle	100 yds.	200 yds.	300 yds.	400 yds.	Muzzle	100 yds.	200 yds.	300 yds.	400 yds.	100 yds.	200 yds.	300 yds.	400 yds.	
308 Winchester	55	3770	3215	2726	2286	1888	1735	1262	907	638	435	-2.0	+1.4	-3.8	-15.8	$22
308 Winchester	150	2820	2533	2263	2009	1774	2648	2137	1705	1344	1048	+2.5	+0.4	-8.5	-26.1	$17
308 W. Superformance	150	3000	2772	2555	2348	1962	2997	2558	2173	1836	1540	1.5	0.0	-6.9	-20.0	NA
308 Winchester	165	2700	2440	2194	1963	1748	2670	2180	1763	1411	1199	+2.5	0.0	-9.7	-28.5	$20
308 Winchester	168	2680	2493	2314	2143	1979	2678	2318	1998	1713	1460	+2.5	0.0	-8.9	-25.3	$18
308 Win. (Fed.)	170	2000	1740	1510	NA	NA	1510	1145	860	NA	NA	0.0	0.0	0.0	0.0	NA
308 Winchester	178	2620	2415	2220	2034	1857	2713	2306	1948	1635	1363	+2.5	0.0	-9.6	-27.6	$23
308 Winchester*	180	2620	2393	2178	1974	1782	2743	2288	1896	1557	1269	+2.5	-0.2	-10.2	-28.5	$17
30-06 Spfd.	55	4080	3485	2965	2502	2083	2033	1483	1074	764	530	+2.0	+1.9	-2.1	-11.7	$22
30-06 Spfd. (Rem.)	125	2660	2335	2034	1757	NA	1964	1513	1148	856	NA	0.0	-5.2	-18.9	0.0	NA
30-06 Spfd.	125	3140	2780	2447	2138	1853	2736	2145	1662	1279	953	+2.0	+1.0	-6.2	-21.0	$17
30-06 Spfd.	150	2910	2617	2342	2083	1853	2820	2281	1827	1445	1135	+2.5	+0.8	-7.2	-23.4	$17
30-06 Superformance	150	3080	2848	2617	2417	2216	3159	2700	2298	1945	1636	1.4	0.0	-6.4	-18.9	NA
30-06 Spfd.	152	2910	2654	2413	2184	1968	2858	2378	1965	1610	1307	+2.5	+1.0	-6.6	-21.3	$23
30-06 Spfd.*	165	2800	2534	2283	2047	1825	2872	2352	1909	1534	1220	+2.5	+0.4	-8.4	-25.5	$17
30-06 Spfd.	168	2710	2522	2346	2169	2003	2739	2372	2045	1754	1497	+2.5	+0.4	-8.0	-23.5	$18
30-06 Spfd. (Fed.)	170	2000	1740	1510	NA	NA	1510	1145	860	NA	NA	0.0	0.0	0.0	0.0	NA
30-06 Spfd.	178	2720	2511	2311	2121	1939	2924	2491	2111	1777	1486	+2.5	+0.4	-8.2	-24.6	$23
30-06 Spfd.*	180	2700	2469	2250	2042	1846	2913	2436	2023	1666	1362	-2.5	0.0	-9.3	-27.0	$17
30-06 Superformance	180	2820	2630	2447	2272	2104	3178	2764	2393	2063	1769	1.8	0.0	-7.6	-21.9	NA
30-06 Spfd.	220	2410	2130	1870	1632	1422	2837	2216	1708	1301	988	+2.5	-1.7	-18.0	0.0	$17
30-06 Light Mag.	150	3100	2815	2548	2295	2058	3200	2639	2161	1755	1410	+1.4	0.0	-6.8	-20.3	NA
30-06 Light Mag.	180	2880	2676	2480	2293	2114	3316	2862	2459	2102	1786	+1.7	0.0	-7.3	-21.3	NA
30-06 High Energy	180	2880	2690	2500	2320	2150	3315	2880	2495	2150	1845	+1.7	0.0	-7.2	-21.0	NA
30 T/C Superformance	150	3000	2772	2555	2348	2151	2997	2558	2173	1836	1540	1.5	0.0	-6.9	-20.0	NA
30 T/C Superformance	165	2850	2644	2447	2258	2078	2975	2560	2193	1868	1582	1.7	0.0	-7.6	-22.0	NA
300 Rem SA Ultra Mag	150	3200	2901	2622	2359	2112	3410	2803	2290	1854	1485	1.3	0.0	-6.4	-19.1	NA
300 Rem SA Ultra Mag	165	3075	2792	2527	2276	2040	3464	2856	2339	1898	1525	1.5	0.0	-7	-20.7	NA
300 Rem SA Ultra Mag	180	2960	2761	2571	2389	2214	3501	3047	2642	2280	1959	2.6	2.2	-3.6	-15.4	NA
7.82 (308) Patriot	150	3250	2999	2762	2537	2323	3519	2997	2542	2145	1798	+1.2	0.0	-5.8	-16.9	NA
300 RCM Superformance	150	3310	3065	2833	2613	2404	3648	3128	2673	2274	1924	1.1	0.0	-5.4	-16.0	NA
300 RCM Superformance	165	3185	2964	2753	2552	2360	3716	3217	2776	2386	2040	1.2	0.0	-5.8	-17.0	NA
300 RCM Superformance	180	3040	2840	2649	2466	2290	3693	3223	2804	2430	2096	1.4	0.0	-6.4	-18.5	NA
300 WSM	150	3300	3061	2834	2619	2414	3628	3121	2676	2285	1941	1.1	0.0	-5.4	-15.9	NA
300 WSM	180	2970	2741	2524	2317	2120	3526	3005	2547	2147	1797	1.6	0.0	-7.0	-20.5	NA
300 WSM	180	3010	2923	2734	2554	2380	3242	2845	2490	2172	1886	1.3	0	-5.9	-17.2	NA
308 Norma Mag.	180	3020	2820	2630	2440	2270	3645	3175	2755	2385	2050	+2.5	+2.0	-3.5	-14.8	NA
300 Dakota	200	3000	2824	2656	2493	2336	3996	3542	3131	2760	2423	+2.2	+1.5	-4.0	-15.2	NA
300 H&H Magnum*	180	2880	2640	2412	2196	1990	3315	2785	2325	1927	1583	+2.5	+0.8	-6.8	-21.7	$24
300 H&H Magnum	220	2550	2267	2002	1757	NA	3167	2510	1958	1508	NA	-2.5	-0.4	-12.0	0.0	NA
300 Win. Mag.	150	3290	2951	2636	2342	2068	3605	2900	2314	1827	1424	+2.5	+1.9	-3.8	-15.8	$22
300 WM Superformance	150	3400	3150	2914	2690	2477	3850	3304	2817	2409	2043	1.0	0.0	-5.1	-15.0	NA
300 Win. Mag.	165	3100	2877	2665	2462	2269	3522	3033	2603	2221	1897	+2.5	+2.4	-3.0	-16.9	$24
300 Win. Mag.	178	2900	2760	2568	2375	2191	3509	3030	2606	2230	1897	+2.5	+1.4	-5.0	-17.6	$29
300 Win. Mag.*	180	2960	2745	2540	2344	2157	3501	3011	2578	2196	1859	+2.5	+1.2	-5.5	-18.5	$22
300 WM Light Mag.	180	3100	2879	2668	2467	2275	3840	3313	2845	2431	2068	+1.39	0.0	-6.45	-18.7	NA
300 WM Superformance	180	3130	2927	2732	2546	2366	3917	3424	2983	2589	2238	1.3	0.0	-5.9	-17.3	NA
300 Win. Mag.	190	2885	1691	2506	2327	2156	3511	3055	2648	2285	1961	+2.5	+1.2	-5.7	-19.0	$26
300 Win. Mag.*	200	2825	2595	2376	2167	1970	3545	2991	2508	2086	1742	-2.5	+1.6	-4.7	-17.2	$36
300 Win. Mag.	220	2680	2448	2228	2020	1823	3508	2927	2424	1993	1623	+2.5	0.0	-9.5	-27.5	$23
300 Rem. Ultra Mag.	150	3450	3208	2980	2762	2556	3964	3427	2956	2541	2175	1.7	1.5	-2.6	-11.2	NA
300 Rem. Ultra Mag.	150	2910	2686	2473	2279	2077	2820	2403	2037	1716	1436	1.7	0.0	-7.4	-21.5	NA
300 Rem. Ultra Mag.	180	3250	3037	2834	2640	2454	4221	3686	3201	2786	2407	2.4	0.0	-3.0	-12.7	NA
300 Rem. Ultra Mag.	180	2960	2774	2505	2294	2093	3501	2971	2508	2103	1751	2.7	2.2	-3.8	-16.4	NA
300 Rem. Ultra Mag.	200	3032	2791	2562	2345	2138	4083	3459	2916	2442	2030	1.5	0.0	-6.8	-19.9	NA
300 Wea. Mag.	100	3900	3441	3038	2652	2305	3714	2891	2239	1717	1297	+2.0	+2.6	-0.6	-8.7	$32
300 Wea. Mag.	150	3600	3307	3033	2776	2533	4316	3642	3064	2566	2137	+2.5	+3.2	0.0	-8.1	$32
300 Wea. Mag.	165	3450	3210	3000	2792	2593	4360	3796	3297	2855	2464	+2.5	+3.2	0.0	-7.8	NA
300 Wea. Mag.	178	3120	2902	2695	2497	2308	3847	3329	2870	2464	2104	+2.5	-1.7	-3.6	-14.7	$43
300 Wea. Mag.	180	3330	3110	2910	2710	2520	4430	3875	3375	2935	2540	+1.0	0.0	-5.2	-15.1	NA
300 Wea. Mag.	190	3030	2830	2638	2455	2279	3873	3378	2936	2542	2190	+2.5	+1.6	-4.3	-16.0	$38
300 Wea. Mag.	220	2850	2541	2283	1964	1736	3967	3155	2480	1922	1471	+2.5	+0.4	-8.5	-26.4	$35
300 Warbird	180	3400	3180	2971	2772	2582	4620	4042	3528	3071	2664	+2.59	+3.25	0.0	-7.95	NA
300 Pegasus	180	3500	3319	3145	2978	2817	4896	4401	3953	3544	3172	+2.28	+2.89	0.0	-6.79	NA

31

32-20 Win.	100	1210	1021	913	834	769	325	231	185	154	131	0.0	-32.3	0.0	0.0	$23**

Cartridge	Bullet Wgt. Grs.	VELOCITY (fps)					ENERGY (ft. lbs.)					TRAJ. (in.)				Est. Price/box
		Muzzle	100 yds.	200 yds.	300 yds.	400 yds.	Muzzle	100 yds.	200 yds.	300 yds.	400 yds.	100 yds.	200 yds.	300 yds.	400 yds.	
303 British	180	2460	2124	1817	1542	1311	2418	1803	1319	950	687	+2.5	-1.8	-16.8	0.0	$18
303 Light Mag.	150	2830	2570	2325	2094	1884	2667	2199	1800	1461	1185	+2.0	0.0	-8.4	-24.6	NA
7.62x54mm Rus.	146	2950	2730	2520	2320	NA	2820	2415	2055	1740	NA	+2.5	+2.0	-4.4	-17.7	NA
7.62x54mm Rus.	180	2580	2370	2180	2000	1820	2650	2250	1900	1590	1100	+2.5	0.0	-9.8	-28.5	NA
7.7x58mm Jap.	150	2640	2399	2170	1954	1752	2321	1916	1568	1271	1022	+2.3	0.0	-9.7	-28.5	NA
7.7x58mm Jap.	180	2500	2300	2100	1920	1750	2490	2105	1770	1475	1225	+2.5	0.0	-10.4	-30.2	NA
8x56 R	205	2400	2188	1987	1797	1621	2621	2178	1796	1470	1196	+2.9	0.0	-11.7	-34.3	NA
8mm																
8x57mm JS Mau.	165	2850	2520	2210	1930	1670	2965	2330	1795	1360	1015	+2.5	+1.0	-7.7	0.0	NA
32 Win. Special	165	2410	2145	1897	1669	NA	2128	1685	1318	1020	NA	2.0	0.0	- 13.0	-19.9	NA
32 Win. Special	170	2250	1921	1626	1372	1175	1911	1393	998	710	521	+2.5	-3.5	-22.9	0.0	$14
8mm Mauser	170	2360	1969	1622	1333	1123	2102	1464	993	671	476	+2.5	-3.1	-22.2	0.0	$18
325 WSM	180	3060	2841	2632	2432	2242	3743	3226	2769	2365	2009	+1.4	0.0	-6.4	-18.7	NA
325 WSM	200	2950	2753	2565	2384	2210	3866	3367	2922	2524	2170	+1.5	0.0	-6.8	-19.8	NA
325 WSM	220	2840	2605	2382	2169	1968	3941	3316	2772	2300	1893	+1.8	0.0	-8.0	-23.3	NA
8mm Rem. Mag.	185	3080	2761	2464	2186	1927	3896	3131	2494	1963	1525	+2.5	+1.4	-5.5	-19.7	$30
8mm Rem. Mag.	220	2830	2581	2346	2123	1913	3912	3254	2688	2201	1787	+2.5	+0.6	-7.6	-23.5	Disc.
33																
338 Federal	180	2830	2590	2350	2130	1930	3200	2670	2215	1820	1480	1.8	0.0	-8.2	-23.9	NA
338 Marlin Express	200	2565	2365	2174	1992	1820	2922	2484	2099	1762	1471	3.0	1.2	-7.9	-25.9	NA
338 Federal	185	2750	2550	2350	2160	1980	3105	2660	2265	1920	1615	1.9	0.0	-8.3	-24.1	NA
338 Federal	210	2630	2410	2200	2010	1820	3225	2710	2265	1880	1545	2.3	0.0	-9.4	-27.3	NA
338-06	200	2750	2553	2364	2184	2011	3358	2894	2482	2118	1796	+1.9	0.0	-8.22	-23.6	NA
330 Dakota	250	2900	2719	2545	2378	2217	4668	4103	3595	3138	2727	+2.3	+1.3	-5.0	-17.5	NA
338 Lapua	250	2963	2795	2640	2493	NA	4842	4341	3881	3458	NA	+1.9	0.0	-7.9	0.0	NA
338 RCM Superformance	185	2980	2755	2542	2338	2143	3647	3118	2653	2242	1887	1.5	0.0	-6.9	-20.3	NA
338 RCM Superformance	200	2950	2744	2547	2358	2177	3846	3342	2879	2468	2104	1.6	0.0	-6.9	-20.1	NA
338 RCM Superformance	225	2750	2575	2407	2245	2089	3778	3313	2894	2518	2180	1.9	0.0	-7.9	-22.7	NA
338 WM Superformance	185	3080	2850	2632	2424	2226	3896	3337	2845	2413	2034	1.4	0.0	-6.4	-18.8	NA
338 Win. Mag.*	210	2830	2590	2370	2150	1940	3735	3130	2610	2155	1760	+2.5	+1.4	-6.0	-20.9	$33
338 Win. Mag.*	225	2785	2517	2266	2029	1808	3871	3165	2565	2057	1633	+2.5	+0.4	-8.5	-25.9	$27
338 WM Superformance	225	2840	2758	2582	2414	2252	4318	3798	3331	2911	2533	1.5	0.0	-6.8	-19.5	NA
338 Win. Mag.	230	2780	2573	2375	2186	2005	3948	3382	2881	2441	2054	+2.5	+1.2	-6.3	-21.0	$40
338 Win. Mag.*	250	2660	2456	2261	2075	1898	3927	3348	2837	2389	1999	+2.5	+0.2	-9.0	-26.2	$27
338 Ultra Mag.	250	2860	2645	2440	2244	2057	4540	3882	3303	2794	2347	1.7	0.0	-7.6	-22.1	NA
8.59(.338) Galaxy	200	3100	2899	2707	2524	2347	4269	3734	3256	2829	2446	3	3.8	0.0	-9.3	NA
340 Wea. Mag.*	210	3250	2991	2746	2515	2295	4924	4170	3516	2948	2455	+2.5	+1.9	-1.8	-11.8	$56
340 Wea. Mag.*	250	3000	2806	2621	2443	2272	4995	4371	3812	3311	2864	+2.5	+2.0	-3.5	-14.8	$56
338 A-Square	250	3120	2799	2500	2220	1958	5403	4348	3469	2736	2128	+2.5	+2.7	-1.5	-10.5	NA
338-378 Wea. Mag.	225	3180	2974	2778	2591	2410	5052	4420	3856	3353	2902	3.1	3.8	0.0	-8.9	NA
338 Titan	225	3230	3010	2800	2600	2409	5211	4524	3916	3377	2898	+3.07	+3.8	0.0	-8.95	NA
338 Excalibur	200	3600	3361	3134	2920	2715	5755	5015	4363	3785	3274	+2.23	+2.87	0.0	-6.99	NA
338 Excalibur	250	3250	2922	2618	2333	2066	5863	4740	3804	3021	2370	+1.3	0.0	-6.35	-19.2	NA
34, 35																
348 Winchester	200	2520	2215	1931	1672	1443	2820	2178	1656	1241	925	+2.5	-1.4	-14.7	0.0	$42
357 Magnum	158	1830	1427	1138	980	883	1175	715	454	337	274	0.0	-16.2	-33.1	0.0	$25**
35 Remington	150	2300	1874	1506	1218	1039	1762	1169	755	494	359	+2.5	-4.1	-26.3	0.0	$16
35 Remington	200	2080	1698	1376	1140	1001	1921	1280	841	577	445	+2.5	-6.3	-17.1	-33.6	$16
35 Rem. Lever Evolution	200	2225	1963	1721	1503	NA	2198	1711	1315	1003	NA	3.0	-1.3	-17.5	NA	NA
356 Winchester	200	2460	2114	1797	1517	1284	2688	1985	1434	1022	732	+2.5	-1.8	-15.1	0.0	$31
356 Winchester	250	2160	1911	1682	1476	1299	2591	2028	1571	1210	937	+2.5	-3.7	-22.2	0.0	$31
358 Winchester	200	2490	2171	1876	1619	1379	2753	2093	1563	1151	844	+2.5	-1.6	-15.6	0.0	$31
358 STA	275	2850	2562	2292	2039	NA	4958	4009	3208	2539	NA	+1.9	0.0	-8.6	0.0	NA
350 Rem. Mag.	200	2710	2410	2130	1870	1631	3261	2579	2014	1553	1181	+2.5	-0.2	-10.0	-30.1	$33
35 Whelen	200	2675	2378	2100	1842	1606	3177	2510	1958	1506	1145	+2.5	-0.2	-10.3	-31.1	$20
35 Whelen	225	2500	2300	2110	1930	1770	3120	2650	2235	1870	1560	+2.6	0.0	-10.2	-29.9	NA
35 Whelen	250	2400	2197	2005	1823	1652	3197	2680	2230	1844	1515	+2.5	-1.2	-13.7	0.0	$20
358 Norma Mag.	250	2800	2510	2230	1970	1730	4350	3480	2750	2145	1655	+2.5	+1.0	-7.6	-25.2	NA
358 STA	275	2850	2562	229*2	2039	1764	4959	4009	3208	2539	1899	+1.9	0.0	-8.58	-26.1	NA
9.3mm																
9.3x57mm Mau.	286	2070	1810	1590	1390	1110	2710	2090	1600	1220	955	+2.5	-2.6	-22.5	0.0	NA
9.3x62mm Mau.	286	2360	2089	1844	1623	NA	3538	2771	2157	1670	1260	+2.5	-1.6	-21.0	0.0	NA
370 Sako Mag.	286	3550	2370	2200	2040	2880	4130	3570	3075	2630	2240	2.4	0.0	-9.5	-27.2	NA
9.3x64mm	286	2700	2505	2318	2139	1968	4629	3984	3411	2906	2460	+2.5	+2.7	-4.5	-19.2	NA
9.3x74Rmm	286	2360	2136	1924	1727	1545	3536	2896	2351	1893	1516	0.0	-6.1	-21.7	-49.0	NA
375																

Cartridge	Bullet Wgt. Grs.	VELOCITY (fps)					ENERGY (ft. lbs.)					TRAJ. (in.)				Est. Price/box
		Muzzle	100 yds.	200 yds.	300 yds.	400 yds.	Muzzle	100 yds.	200 yds.	300 yds.	400 yds.	100 yds.	200 yds.	300 yds.	400 yds.	
375 Winchester	200	2200	1841	1526	1268	1089	2150	1506	1034	714	527	+2.5	-4.0	-26.2	0.0	$27
375 Winchester	250	1900	1647	1424	1239	1103	2005	1506	1126	852	676	+2.5	-6.9	-33.3	0.0	$27
376 Steyr	225	2600	2331	2078	1842	1625	3377	2714	2157	1694	1319	2.5	0.0	-10.6	-31.4	NA
376 Steyr	270	2600	2372	2156	1951	1759	4052	3373	2787	2283	1855	2.3	0.0	-9.9	-28.9	NA
375 Dakota	300	2600	2316	2051	1804	1579	4502	3573	2800	2167	1661	+2.4	0.0	-11.0	-32.7	NA
375 N.E. 2-1/2"	270	2000	1740	1507	1310	NA	2398	1815	1362	1026	NA	+2.5	-6.0	-30.0	0.0	NA
375 Flanged	300	2450	2150	1886	1640		3998	3102	2369	1790	NA	+2.5	-2.4	-17.0	0.0	NA
375 Ruger	270	2840	2600	2372	2156	1951	4835	4052	3373	2786	2283	1.8	0.0	-8.0	-23.6	NA
375 Ruger	300	2660	2344	2050	1780	1536	4713	3660	2800	2110	1572	2.4	0.0	-10.8	-32.6	NA
375 H&H Magnum	250	2670	2450	2240	2040	1850	3955	3335	2790	2315	1905	+2.5	-0.4	-10.2	-28.4	NA
375 H&H Magnum	270	2690	2420	2166	1928	1707	4337	3510	2812	2228	1747	+2.5	0.0	-10.0	-29.4	$28
375 H&H Magnum*	300	2530	2245	1979	1733	1512	4263	3357	2608	2001	1523	+2.5	-1.0	-10.5	-33.6	$28
375 H&H Hvy. Mag.	270	2870	2628	2399	2182	1976	4937	4141	3451	2150	1845	+1.7	0.0	-7.2	-21.0	NA
375 H&H Hvy. Mag.	300	2705	2386	2090	1816	1568	4873	3793	2908	2195	1637	+2.3	0.0	-10.4	-31.4	NA
375 Rem. Ultra Mag.	270	2900	2558	2241	1947	1678	5041	3922	3010	2272	1689	1.9	2.7	-8.9	-27.0	NA
375 Rem. Ultra Mag.	300	2760	2505	2263	2035	1822	5073	4178	3412	2759	2210	2.0	0.0	-8.8	-26.1	NA
375 Wea. Mag.	300	2700	2420	2157	1911	1685	4856	3901	3100	2432	1891	+2.5	-.04	-10.7	0.0	NA
378 Wea. Mag.	270	3180	2976	2781	2594	2415	6062	5308	4635	4034	3495	+2.5	+2.6	-1.8	-11.3	$71
378 Wea. Mag.	300	2929	2576	2252	1952	1680	5698	4419	3379	2538	1881	+2.5	+1.2	-7.0	-24.5	$77
375 A-Square	300	2920	2626	2351	2093	1850	5679	4594	3681	2917	2281	+2.5	+1.4	-6.0	-21.0	NA
38-40 Win.	180	1160	999	901	827	764	538	399	324	273	233	0.0	-33.9	0.0	0.0	$42**
40, 41																
400 A-Square DPM	400	2400	2146	1909	1689	NA	5116	2092	3236	2533	NA	2.98	0.0	-10.0	NA	NA
400 A-Square DPM	170	2980	2463	2001	1598	NA	3352	2289	1512	964	NA	2.16	0.0	-11.1	NA	NA
408 CheyTac	419	2850	2752	2657	2562	2470	7551	7048	6565	6108	5675	-1.02	0.0	1.9	4.2	NA
405 Win.	300	2200	1851	1545	1296		3224	2282	1589	1119		4.6	0.0	-19.5	0.0	NA
450/400-3"	400	2050	1815	1595	1402	NA	3732	2924	2259	1746	NA	0.0	NA	-33.4	NA	NA
416 Ruger	400	2400	2151	1917	1700	NA	5116	4109	3264	2568	NA	0.0	-6.0	-21.6	0.0	NA
416 Dakota	400	2450	2294	2143	1998	1859	5330	4671	4077	3544	3068	+2.5	-0.2	-10.5	-29.4	NA
416 Taylor	400	2350	2117	1896	1693	NA	4905	3980	3194	2547	NA	+2.5	-1.2	15.0	0.0	NA
416 Hoffman	400	2380	2145	1923	1718	1529	5031	4087	3285	2620	2077	+2.5	-1.0	-14.1	0.0	NA
416 Rigby	350	2600	2449	2303	2162	2026	5253	4661	4122	3632	3189	+2.5	-1.8	-10.2	-26.0	NA
416 Rigby	400	2370	2210	2050	1900	NA	4990	4315	3720	3185	NA	+2.5	-0.7	-12.1	0.0	NA
416 Rigby	410	2370	2110	1870	1640	NA	5115	4050	3165	2455	NA	+2.5	-2.4	-17.3	0.0	$110
416 Rem. Mag.*	350	2520	2270	2034	1814	1611	4935	4004	3216	2557	2017	+2.5	-0.8	-12.6	-35.0	$82
416 Wea. Mag.*	400	2700	2397	2115	1852	1613	6474	5104	3971	3047	2310	+2.5	0.0	-10.1	-30.4	$96
10.57 (416) Meteor	400	2730	2532	2342	2161	1987	6621	5695	4874	4147	3508	+1.9	0.0	-8.3	-24.0	NA
404 Jeffrey	400	2150	1924	1716	1525	NA	4105	3289	2614	2064	NA	+2.5	-4.0	-22.1	0.0	NA
425, 44																
425 Express	400	2400	2160	1934	1725	NA	5115	4145	3322	2641	NA	+2.5	-1.0	-14.0	0.0	NA
44-40 Win.	200	1190	1006	900	822	756	629	449	360	300	254	0.0	-33.3	0.0	0.0	$36**
44 Rem. Mag.	210	1920	1477	1155	982	880	1719	1017	622	450	361	0.0	-17.6	0.0	0.0	$14
44 Rem. Mag.	240	1760	1380	1114	970	878	1650	1015	661	501	411	0.0	-17.6	0.0	0.0	$13
444 Marlin	240	2350	1815	1377	1087	941	2942	1753	1001	630	472	+2.5	-15.1	-31.0	0.0	$22
444 Marlin	265	2120	1733	1405	1160	1012	2644	1768	1162	791	603	+2.5	-6.0	-32.2	0.0	Disc.
444 Marlin Light Mag	265	2335	1913	1551	1266		3208	2153	1415	943		2.0	-4.9	-26.5	0.0	NA
444 Mar. Lever Evolution	265	2325	1971	1652	1380	NA	3180	2285	1606	1120	NA	3.0	-1.4	-18.6	NA	NA
45																
45-70 Govt.	300	1810	1497	1244	1073	969	2182	1492	1031	767	625	0.0	-14.8	0.0	0.0	$21
45-70 Govt. Supreme	300	1880	1558	1292	1103	988	2355	1616	1112	811	651	0.0	-12.9	-46.0	-105.0	NA
45-70 Lever Evolution	325	2050	1729	1450	1225	NA	3032	2158	1516	1083	NA	3.0	-4.1	-27.8	NA	NA
45-70 Govt. CorBon	350	1800	1526	1296			2519	1810	1307			0.0	-14.6	0.0	0.0	NA
45-70 Govt.	405	1330	1168	1055	977	918	1590	1227	1001	858	758	0.0	-24.6	0.0	0.0	$21
45-70 Govt. PMC Cowboy	405	1550	1193				1639	1280				0.0	-23.9	0.0	0.0	NA
45-70 Govt. Garrett	415	1850					3150					3.0	-7.0	0.0	0.0	NA
45-70 Govt. Garrett	530	1550	1343	1178	1062	982	2828	2123	1633	1327	1135	0.0	-17.8	0.0	0.0	NA
450 Bushmaster	250	2200	1831	1508	1480	1073	2686	1860	1262	864	639	0.0	-9.0	-33.5	0.0	NA
450 Marlin	350	2100	1774	1488	1254	1089	3427	2446	1720	1222	922	0.0	-9.7	-35.2	0.0	NA
450 Mar. Lever Evolution	325	2225	1887	1585	1331	NA	3572	2569	1813	1278	NA	3.0	-2.2	-21.3	NA	NA
458 Win. Magnum	350	2470	1990	1570	1250	1060	4740	3065	1915	1205	870	+2.5	-2.5	-21.6	0.0	$43
458 Win. Magnum	400	2380	2170	1960	1770	NA	5030	4165	3415	2785	NA	+2.5	-0.4	-13.4	0.0	$73
458 Win. Magnum	465	2220	1999	1791	1601	NA	5088	4127	3312	2646	NA	+2.5	-2.0	-17.7	0.0	NA
458 Win. Magnum	500	2040	1823	1623	1442	1237	4620	3689	2924	2308	1839	+2.5	-3.5	-22.0	0.0	$61
458 Win. Magnum	510	2040	1770	1527	1319	1157	4712	3547	2640	1970	1516	+2.5	-4.1	-25.0	0.0	$41

Cartridge	Bullet Wgt. Grs.	VELOCITY (fps)					ENERGY (ft. lbs.)					TRAJ. (in.)				Est. Price/box
		Muzzle	100 yds.	200 yds.	300 yds.	400 yds.	Muzzle	100 yds.	200 yds.	300 yds.	400 yds.	100 yds.	200 yds.	300 yds.	400 yds.	
450 N.E. 3-1/4"	465	2190	1970	1765	1577	NA	4952	4009	3216	2567	NA	+2.5	-3.0	-20.0	0.0	NA
450 N.E. 3-1/4"	500	2150	1920	1708	1514	NA	5132	4093	3238	2544	NA	+2.5	-4.0	-22.9	0.0	NA
450 No. 2	465	2190	1970	1765	1577	NA	4952	4009	3216	2567	NA	+2.5	-3.0	-20.0	0.0	NA
450 No. 2	500	2150	1920	1708	1514	NA	5132	4093	3238	2544	NA	+2.5	-4.0	-22.9	0.0	NA
458 Lott	465	2380	2150	1932	1730	NA	5848	4773	3855	3091	NA	+2.5	-1.0	-14.0	0.0	NA
458 Lott	500	2300	2062	1838	1633	NA	5873	4719	3748	2960	NA	+2.5	-1.6	-16.4	0.0	NA
450 Ackley Mag.	465	2400	2169	1950	1747	NA	5947	4857	3927	3150	NA	+2.5	-1.0	-13.7	0.0	NA
450 Ackley Mag.	500	2320	2081	1855	1649	NA	5975	4085	3820	3018	NA	+2.5	-1.2	-15.0	0.0	NA
460 Short A-Sq.	500	2420	2175	1943	1729	NA	6501	5250	4193	3319	NA	+2.5	-0.8	-12.8	0.0	NA
460 Wea. Mag.	500	2700	2404	2128	1869	1635	8092	6416	5026	3878	2969	+2.5	+0.6	-8.9	-28.0	$72
475																
500/465 N.E.	480	2150	1917	1703	1507	NA	4926	3917	3089	2419	NA	+2.5	-4.0	-22.2	0.0	NA
470 Rigby	500	2150	1940	1740	1560	NA	5130	4170	3360	2695	NA	+2.5	-2.8	-19.4	0.0	NA
470 Nitro Ex.	480	2190	1954	1735	1536	NA	5111	4070	3210	2515	NA	+2.5	-3.5	-20.8	0.0	NA
470 Nitro Ex.	500	2150	1890	1650	1440	1270	5130	3965	3040	2310	1790	+2.5	-4.3	-24.0	0.0	$177
475 No. 2	500	2200	1955	1728	1522	NA	5375	4243	3316	2573	NA	+2.5	-3.2	-20.9	0.0	NA
50, 58																
505 Gibbs	525	2300	2063	1840	1637	NA	6166	4922	3948	3122	NA	+2.5	-3.0	-18.0	0.0	NA
500 N.E.-3"	570	2150	1928	1722	1533	NA	5850	4703	3752	2975	NA	+2.5	-3.7	-22.0	0.0	NA
500 N.E.-3"	600	2150	1927	1721	1531	NA	6158	4947	3944	3124	NA	+2.5	-4.0	-22.0	0.0	NA
495 A-Square	570	2350	2117	1896	1693	NA	5850	4703	3752	2975	NA	+2.5	-1.0	-14.5	0.0	NA
495 A-Square	600	2280	2050	1833	1635	NA	6925	5598	4478	3562	NA	+2.5	-2.0	-17.0	0.0	NA
500 A-Square	600	2380	2144	1922	1766	NA	7546	6126	4920	3922	NA	+2.5	-3.0	-17.0	0.0	NA
500 A-Square	707	2250	2040	1841	1567	NA	7947	6530	5318	4311	NA	+2.5	-2.0	-17.0	0.0	NA
500 BMG PMC	660	3080	2854	2639	2444	2248	13688	500 yd. zero				+3.1	+3.9	+4.7	+2.8	NA
577 Nitro Ex.	750	2050	1793	1562	1360	NA	6990	5356	4065	3079	NA	+2.5	-5.0	-26.0	0.0	NA
577 Tyrannosaur	750	2400	2141	1898	1675	NA	9591	7633	5996	4671	NA	+3.0	0.0	-12.9	0.0	NA
600, 700																
600 N.E.	900	1950	1680	1452	NA	NA	7596	5634	4212	NA	NA	+5.6	0.0	0.0	0.0	NA
700 N.E.	1200	1900	1676	1472	NA	NA	9618	7480	5774	NA	NA	+5.7	0.0	0.0	0.0	NA

Notes: Blanks are available in 32 S&W, 38 S&W and 38 Special. "V" after barrel length indicates test barrel was vented to produce ballistics similar to a revolver with a normal barrel-to-cylinder gap. Ammo prices are per 50 rounds except when marked with an ** which signifies a 20 round box; *** signifies a 25-round box. Not all loads are available from all ammo manufacturers. Listed loads are those made by Remington, Winchester, Federal, and others. DISC. is a discontinued load.
Prices are rounded to the nearest whole dollar and will vary with brand and retail outlet. † = new bullet weight this year; "c" indicates a change in data.

Cartridge	Bullet Wgt. Grs.	VELOCITY (fps)			ENERGY (ft. lbs.)			Mid-Range Traj. (in.)		Bbl. Lgth. (in).	Est. Price/ box
		Muzzle	50 yds.	100 yds.	Muzzle	50 yds.	100 yds.	50 yds.	100 yds.		
22, 25											
221 Rem. Fireball	50	2650	2380	2130	780	630	505	0.2	0.8	10.5"	$15
25 Automatic	35	900	813	742	63	51	43	NA	NA	2"	$18
25 Automatic	45	815	730	655	65	55	40	1.8	7.7	2"	$21
25 Automatic	50	760	705	660	65	55	50	2.0	8.7	2"	$17
30											
7.5mm Swiss	107	1010	NA	NA	240	NA	NA	NA	NA	NA	NEW
7.62mm Tokarev	87	1390	NA	NA	365	NA	NA	0.6	NA	4.5"	NA
7.62 Nagant	97	790	NA	NA	134	NA	NA	NA	NA	NA	NEW
7.63 Mauser	88	1440	NA	NA	405	NA	NA	NA	NA	NA	NEW
30 Luger	93†	1220	1110	1040	305	255	225	0.9	3.5	4.5"	$34
30 Carbine	110	1790	1600	1430	785	625	500	0.4	1.7	10"	$28
30-357 AeT	123	1992	NA	NA	1084	NA	NA	NA	NA	10"	NA
32											
32 S&W	88	680	645	610	90	80	75	2.5	10.5	3"	$17
32 S&W Long	98	705	670	635	115	100	90	2.3	10.5	4"	$17
32 Short Colt	80	745	665	590	100	80	60	2.2	9.9	4"	$19
32 H&R Magnum	85	1100	1020	930	230	195	165	1.0	4.3	4.5"	$21
32 H&R Magnum	95	1030	940	900	225	190	170	1.1	4.7	4.5"	$19
327 Federal Magnum	85	1400	1220	1090	370	280	225	NA	NA	4-V	NA
327 Federal Magnum	100	1500	1320	1180	500	390	310	-0.2	-4.50	4-V	NA
32 Automatic	60	970	895	835	125	105	95	1.3	5.4	4"	$22
32 Automatic	60	1000	917	849	133	112	96			4"	NA
32 Automatic	65	950	890	830	130	115	100	1.3	5.6	NA	NA
32 Automatic	71	905	855	810	130	115	95	1.4	5.8	4"	$19
8mm Lebel Pistol	111	850	NA	NA	180	NA	NA	NA	NA	NA	NEW
8mm Steyr	112	1080	NA	NA	290	NA	NA	NA	NA	NA	NEW
8mm Gasser	126	850	NA	NA	200	NA	NA	NA	NA	NA	NEW
9mm, 38											
380 Automatic	60	1130	960	NA	170	120	NA	1.0	NA	NA	NA
380 Automatic	85/88	990	920	870	190	165	145	1.2	5.1	4"	$20
380 Automatic	90	1000	890	800	200	160	130	1.2	5.5	3.75"	$10
380 Automatic	95/100	955	865	785	190	160	130	1.4	5.9	4"	$20
38 Super Auto +P	115	1300	1145	1040	430	335	275	0.7	3.3	5"	$26
38 Super Auto +P	125/130	1215	1100	1015	425	350	300	0.8	3.6	5"	$26
38 Super Auto +P	147	1100	1050	1000	395	355	325	0.9	4.0	5"	NA
9x18mm Makarov	95	1000	NA	NA	NA	NA	NA	NA	NA	NA	NEW
9x18mm Ultra	100	1050	NA	NA	240	NA	NA	NA	NA	NA	NEW
9x21	124	1150	1050	980	365	305	265	NA	NA	4	NA
9x23mm Largo	124	1190	1055	966	390	306	257	0.7	3.7	4"	NA
9x23mm Win.	125	1450	1249	1103	583	433	338	0.6	2.8	NA	NA
9mm Steyr	115	1180	NA	NA	350	NA	NA	NA	NA	NA	NEW
9mm Luger	88	1500	1190	1010	440	275	200	0.6	3.1	4"	$24
9mm Luger	90	1360	1112	978	370	247	191	NA	NA	4"	$26
9mm Luger	95	1300	1140	1010	350	275	215	0.8	3.4	4"	NA
9mm Luger	100	1180	1080	NA	305	255	NA	0.9	NA	4"	NA
9mm Luger	115	1155	1045	970	340	280	240	0.9	3.9	4"	$21
9mm Luger	123/125	1110	1030	970	340	290	260	1.0	4.0	4"	$23
9mm Luger	140	935	890	850	270	245	225	1.3	5.5	4"	$23
9mm Luger	147	990	940	900	320	290	265	1.1	4.9	4"	$26
9mm Luger +P	90	1475	NA	NA	437	NA	NA	NA	NA	NA	NA
9mm Luger +P	115	1250	1113	1019	399	316	265	0.8	3.5	4"	$27
9mm Federal	115	1280	1130	1040	420	330	280	0.7	3.3	4"V	$24
9mm Luger Vector	115	1155	1047	971	341	280	241	NA	NA	4"	NA
9mm Luger +P	124	1180	1089	1021	384	327	287	0.8	3.8	4"	NA
38											
38 S&W	146	685	650	620	150	135	125	2.4	10.0	4"	$19
38 Short Colt	125	730	685	645	150	130	115	2.2	9.4	6"	$19
39 Special	100	950	900	NA	200	180	NA	1.3	NA	4"V	NA
38 Special	110	945	895	850	220	195	175	1.3	5.4	4"V	$23
38 Special	110	945	895	850	220	195	175	1.3	5.4	4"V	$23
38 Special	130	775	745	710	175	160	120	1.9	7.9	4"V	$22

Notes: Blanks are available in 32 S&W, 38 S&W and 38 Special. "V" after barrel length indicates test barrel was vented to produce ballistics similar to a revolver with a normal barrel-to-cylinder gap. Ammo prices are per 50 rounds except when marked with an ** which signifies a 20 round box; *** signifies a 25-round box. Not all loads are available from all ammo manufacturers. Listed loads are those made by Remington, Winchester, Federal, and others. DISC. is a discontinued load. Prices are rounded to the nearest whole dollar and will vary with brand and retail outlet. † = new bullet weight this year; "c" indicates a change in data.

Cartridge	Bullet Wgt. Grs.	VELOCITY (fps)			ENERGY (ft. lbs.)			Mid-Range Traj. (in.)		Bbl. Lgth. (in).	Est. Price/ box
		Muzzle	50 yds.	100 yds.	Muzzle	50 yds.	100 yds.	50 yds.	100 yds.		
38 Special Cowboy	140	800	767	735	199	183	168			7.5" V	NA
38 (Multi-Ball)	140	830	730	505	215	130	80	2.0	10.6	4"V	$10**
38 Special	148	710	635	565	165	130	105	2.4	10.6	4"V	$17
38 Special	158	755	725	690	200	185	170	2.0	8.3	4"V	$18
38 Special +P	95	1175	1045	960	290	230	195	0.9	3.9	4"V	$23
38 Special +P	110	995	925	870	240	210	185	1.2	5.1	4"V	$23
38 Special +P	125	975	929	885	264	238	218	1	5.2	4"	NA
38 Special +P	125	945	900	860	250	225	205	1.3	5.4	4"V	#23
38 Special +P	129	945	910	870	255	235	215	1.3	5.3	4"V	$11
38 Special +P	130	925	887	852	247	227	210	1.3	5.50	4"V	NA
38 Special +P	147/150(c)	884	NA	NA	264	NA	NA	NA	NA	4"V	$27
38 Special +P	158	890	855	825	280	255	240	1.4	6.0	4"V	$20

357

Cartridge	Bullet Wgt. Grs.	Muzzle	50 yds.	100 yds.	Muzzle	50 yds.	100 yds.	50 yds.	100 yds.	Bbl. Lgth.	Est. Price
357 SIG	115	1520	NA	NA	593	NA	NA	NA	NA	NA	NA
357 SIG	124	1450	NA	NA	578	NA	NA	NA	NA	NA	NA
357 SIG	125	1350	1190	1080	510	395	325	0.7	3.1	4"	NA
357 SIG	150	1130	1030	970	420	355	310	0.9	4.0	NA	NA
356 TSW	115	1520	NA	NA	593	NA	NA	NA	NA	NA	NA
356 TSW	124	1450	NA	NA	578	NA	NA	NA	NA	NA	NA
356 TSW	135	1280	1120	1010	490	375	310	0.8	3.5	NA	NA
356 TSW	147	1220	1120	1040	485	410	355	0.8	3.5	5"	NA
357 Mag., Super Clean	105	1650									NA
357 Magnum	110	1295	1095	975	410	290	230	0.8	3.5	4"V	$25
357 (Med.Vel.)	125	1220	1075	985	415	315	270	0.8	3.7	4"V	$25
357 Magnum	125	1450	1240	1090	585	425	330	0.6	2.8	4"V	$25
357 (Multi-Ball)	140	1155	830	665	420	215	135	1.2	6.4	4"V	$11**
357 Magnum	140	1360	1195	1075	575	445	360	0.7	3.0	4"V	$25
357 Magnum FlexTip	140	1440	1274	1143	644	504	406	NA	NA	NA	NA
357 Magnum	145	1290	1155	1060	535	430	360	0.8	3.5	4"V	$26
357 Magnum	150/158	1235	1105	1015	535	430	360	0.8	3.5	4"V	$25
357 Mag. Cowboy	158	800	761	725	225	203	185				NA
357 Magnum	165	1290	1189	1108	610	518	450	0.7	3.1	8-3/8"	NA
357 Magnum	180	1145	1055	985	525	445	390	0.9	3.9	4"V	$25
357 Magnum	180	1180	1088	1020	557	473	416	0.8	3.6	8"V	NA
357 Mag. CorBon F.A.	180	1650	1512	1386	1088	913	767	1.66	0.0		NA
357 Mag. CorBon	200	1200	1123	1061	640	560	500	3.19	0.0		NA
357 Rem. Maximum	158	1825	1590	1380	1170	885	670	0.4	1.7	10.5"	$14**

40, 10mm

Cartridge	Bullet Wgt. Grs.	Muzzle	50 yds.	100 yds.	Muzzle	50 yds.	100 yds.	50 yds.	100 yds.	Bbl. Lgth.	Est. Price
40 S&W	135	1140	1070	NA	390	345	NA	0.9	NA	4"	NA
40 S&W	155	1140	1026	958	447	362	309	0.9	4.1	4"	$14***
40 S&W	165	1150	NA	NA	485	NA	NA	NA	NA	4"	$18***
40 S&W	180	985	936	893	388	350	319	1.4	5.0	4"	$14***
40 S&W	180	1015	960	914	412	368	334	1.3	4.5	4"	NA
400 Cor-Bon	135	1450	NA	NA	630	NA	NA	NA	NA	5"	NA
10mm Automatic	155	1125	1046	986	436	377	335	0.9	3.9	5"	$26
10mm Automatic	170	1340	1165	1145	680	510	415	0.7	3.2	5"	$31
10mm Automatic	175	1290	1140	1035	650	505	420	0.7	3.3	5.5"	$11**
10mm Auto. (FBI)	180	950	905	865	361	327	299	1.5	5.4	4"	$16**
10mm Automatic	180	1030	970	920	425	375	340	1.1	4.7	5"	$16**
10mm Auto H.V.	180†	1240	1124	1037	618	504	430	0.8	3.4	5"	$27
10mm Automatic	200	1160	1070	1010	495	510	430	0.9	3.8	5"	$14**
10.4mm Italian	177	950	NA	NA	360	NA	NA	NA	NA	NA	NEW
41 Action Exp.	180	1000	947	903	400	359	326	0.5	4.2	5"	$13**
41 Rem. Magnum	170	1420	1165	1015	760	515	390	0.7	3.2	4"V	$33
41 Rem. Magnum	175	1250	1120	1030	605	490	410	0.8	3.4	4"V	$14**
41 (Med. Vel.)	210	965	900	840	435	375	330	1.3	5.4	4"V	$30
41 Rem. Magnum	210	1300	1160	1060	790	630	535	0.7	3.2	4"V	$33
41 Rem. Magnum	240	1250	1151	1075	833	706	616	0.8	3.3	6.5V	NA

44

Cartridge	Bullet Wgt. Grs.	Muzzle	50 yds.	100 yds.	Muzzle	50 yds.	100 yds.	50 yds.	100 yds.	Bbl. Lgth.	Est. Price
44 S&W Russian	247	780	NA	NA	335	NA	NA	NA	NA	NA	NA
44 S&W Special	180	980	NA	NA	383	NA	NA	NA	NA	6.5"	NA
44 S&W Special	180	1000	935	882	400	350	311	NA	NA	7.5"V	NA
44 S&W Special	200†	875	825	780	340	302	270	1.2	6.0	6"	$13**
44 S&W Special	200	1035	940	865	475	390	335	1.1	4.9	6.5"	$13**

Notes: Blanks are available in 32 S&W, 38 S&W and 38 Special. "V" after barrel length indicates test barrel was vented to produce ballistics similar to a revolver with a normal barrel-to-cylinder gap. Ammo prices are per 50 rounds except when marked with an ** which signifies a 20 round box; *** signifies a 25-round box. Not all loads are available from all ammo manufacturers. Listed loads are those made by Remington, Winchester, Federal, and others. DISC. is a discontinued load. Prices are rounded to the nearest whole dollar and will vary with brand and retail outlet. † = new bullet weight this year; "c" indicates a change in data.

Cartridge	Bullet Wgt. Grs.	VELOCITY (fps)			ENERGY (ft. lbs.)			Mid-Range Traj. (in.)		Bbl. Lgth. (in).	Est. Price/ box
		Muzzle	50 yds.	100 yds.	Muzzle	50 yds.	100 yds.	50 yds.	100 yds.		
44 S&W Special	240/246	755	725	695	310	285	265	2.0	8.3	6.5"	$26
44-40 Win. Cowboy	225	750	723	695	281	261	242				NA
44 Rem. Magnum	180	1610	1365	1175	1035	745	550	0.5	2.3	4"V	$18**
44 Rem. Magnum	200	1400	1192	1053	870	630	492	0.6	NA	6.5"	$20
44 Rem. Magnum	210	1495	1310	1165	1040	805	635	0.6	2.5	6.5"	$18**
44 Rem. Mag. FlexTip	225	1410	1240	1111	993	768	617	NA	NA	NA	NA
44 (Med. Vel.)	240	1000	945	900	535	475	435	1.1	4.8	6.5"	$17
44 R.M. (Jacketed)	240	1180	1080	1010	740	625	545	0.9	3.7	4"V	$18**
44 R.M. (Lead)	240	1350	1185	1070	970	750	610	0.7	3.1	4"V	$29
44 Rem. Magnum	250	1180	1100	1040	775	670	600	0.8	3.6	6.5"V	$21
44 Rem. Magnum	250	1250	1148	1070	867	732	635	0.8	3.3	6.5"V	NA
44 Rem. Magnum	275	1235	1142	1070	931	797	699	0.8	3.3	6.5"	NA
44 Rem. Magnum	300	1200	1100	1026	959	806	702	NA	NA	7.5"	$17
44 Rem. Magnum	330	1385	1297	1220	1406	1234	1090	1.83	0.00	NA	NA
440 CorBon	260	1700	1544	1403	1669	1377	1136	1.58	NA	10"	NA

45, 50

Cartridge	Bullet Wgt. Grs.	Muzzle	50 yds.	100 yds.	Muzzle	50 yds.	100 yds.	50 yds.	100 yds.	Bbl. Lgth. (in).	Est. Price/ box
450 Short Colt/450 Revolver	226	830	NA	NA	350	NA	NA	NA	NA	NA	NEW
45 S&W Schofield	180	730	NA	NA	213	NA	NA	NA	NA	NA	NA
45 S&W Schofield	230	730	NA	NA	272	NA	NA	NA	NA	NA	NA
45 G.A.P.	185	1090	970	890	490	385	320	1.0	4.7	5"	NA
45 G.A.P.	230	880	842	NA	396	363	NA	NA	NA	5"	NA
45 Automatic	165	1030	930	NA	385	315	NA	1.2	NA	5"	NA
45 Automatic	185	1000	940	890	410	360	325	1.1	4.9	5"	$28
45 Auto. (Match)	185	770	705	650	245	204	175	2.0	8.7	5"	$28
45 Auto. (Match)	200	940	890	840	392	352	312	2.0	8.6	5"	$20
45 Automatic	200	975	917	860	421	372	328	1.4	5.0	5"	$18
45 Automatic	230	830	800	675	355	325	300	1.6	6.8	5"	$27
45 Automatic	230	880	846	816	396	366	340	1.5	6.1	5"	NA
45 Automatic +P	165	1250	NA	NA	573	NA	NA	NA	NA	NA	NA
45 Automatic +P	185	1140	1040	970	535	445	385	0.9	4.0	5"	$31
45 Automatic +P	200	1055	982	925	494	428	380	NA	NA	5"	NA
45 Super	185	1300	1190	1108	694	582	504	NA	NA	5"	NA
45 Win. Magnum	230	1400	1230	1105	1000	775	635	0.6	2.8	5"	$14**
45 Win. Magnum	260	1250	1137	1053	902	746	640	0.8	3.3	5"	$16**
45 Win. Mag. CorBon	320	1150	1080	1025	940	830	747	3.47			NA
455 Webley MKII	262	850	NA	NA	420	NA	NA	NA	NA	NA	NA
45 Colt	200	1000	938	889	444	391	351	1.3	4.8	5.5"	$21
45 Colt	225	960	890	830	460	395	345	1.3	5.5	5.5"	$22
45 Colt + P CorBon	265	1350	1225	1126	1073	884	746	2.65	0.0		NA
45 Colt + P CorBon	300	1300	1197	1114	1126	956	827	2.78	0.0		NA
45 Colt	250/255	860	820	780	410	375	340	1.6	6.6	5.5"	$27
454 Casull	250	1300	1151	1047	938	735	608	0.7	3.2	7.5"V	NA
454 Casull	260	1800	1577	1381	1871	1436	1101	0.4	1.8	7.5"V	NA
454 Casull	300	1625	1451	1308	1759	1413	1141	0.5	2.0	7.5"V	NA
454 Casull CorBon	360	1500	1387	1286	1800	1640	1323	2.01	0.0		NA
460 S&W	200	2300	2042	1801	2350	1851	1441	0	-1.60	NA	NA
460 S&W	260	2000	1788	1592	2309	1845	1464	NA	NA	7.5"V	NA
460 S&W	250	1450	1267	1127	1167	891	705	NA	NA	8.375-V	NA
460 S&W	250	1900	1640	1412	2004	1494	1106	0	-2.75	NA	NA
460 S&W	300	1750	1510	1300	2040	1510	1125	NA	NA	8.4-V	NA
460 S&W	395	1550	1389	1249	2108	1691	1369	0	-4.00	NA	NA
475 Linebaugh	400	1350	1217	1119	1618	1315	1112	NA	NA	NA	NA
480 Ruger	325	1350	1191	1076	1315	1023	835	2.6	0.0	7.5"	NA
50 Action Exp.	325	1400	1209	1075	1414	1055	835	0.2	2.3	6"	$24**
500 S&W	275	1665	1392	1183	1693	1184	854	1.5	NA	8.375	NA
500 S&W	325	1800	1560	1350	2340	1755	1315	NA	NA	8.4-V	NA
500 S&W	350	1400	1231	1106	1523	1178	951	NA	NA	10"	NA
500 S&W	400	1675	1472	1299	2493	1926	1499	1.3	NA	8.375	NA
500 S&W	440	1625	1367	1169	2581	1825	1337	1.6	NA	8.375	NA
500 S&W	500	1425	1281	1164	2254	1823	1505	NA	NA	10"	NA

Note: The actual ballistics obtained with your firearm can vary considerably from the advertised ballistics.
Also, ballistics can vary from lot to lot with the same brand and type load.

Cartridge	Bullet Wt. Grs.	Velocity (fps) 22-1/2" Bbl.		Energy (ft. lbs.) 22-1/2" Bbl.		Mid-Range Traj. (in.)	Muzzle Velocity
		Muzzle	100 yds.	Muzzle	100 yds.	100 yds.	6" Bbl.
17 Aguila	20	1850	1267	NA	NA	NA	NA
17 Hornady Mach 2	17	2100	1530	166	88	0.7	NA
17 HMR TNT Green	16	2500	1642	222	96	NA	NA
17 HMR	17	2550	1902	245	136	NA	NA
17 HMR	20	2375	1776	250	140	NA	NA
5mm Rem. Rimfire Mag.	30	2300	1669	352	188	NA	24
22 Short Blank	—	—	—	—	—	—	—
22 Short CB	29	727	610	33	24	NA	706
22 Short Target	29	830	695	44	31	6.8	786
22 Short HP	27	1164	920	81	50	4.3	1077
22 Colibri	20	375	183	6	1	NA	NA
22 Super Colibri	20	500	441	11	9	NA	NA
22 Long CB	29	727	610	33	24	NA	706
22 Long HV	29	1180	946	90	57	4.1	1031
22 LR Pistol Match	40	1070	890	100	70	4.6	940
22 LR Shrt. Range Green	21	1650	912	127	NA	NA	NA
22 LR Sub Sonic HP	38	1050	901	93	69	4.7	NA
22 LR Standard Velocity	40	1070	890	100	70	4.6	940
22 LR AutoMatch	40	1200	990	130	85	NA	NA
22 LR HV	40	1255	1016	140	92	3.6	1060
22 LR Silhoutte	42	1220	1003	139	94	3.6	1025
22 SSS	60	950	802	120	86	NA	NA
22 LR HV HP	40	1280	1001	146	89	3.5	1085
22 Velocitor GDHP	40	1435	0	0	0	NA	NA
22 LR Hyper HP	32/33/34	1500	1075	165	85	2.8	NA
22 LR Expediter	32	1640	NA	191	NA	NA	NA
22 LR Stinger HP	32	1640	1132	191	91	2.6	1395
22 LR Lead Free	30	1650	NA	181	NA	NA	NA
22 LR Hyper Vel	30	1750	1191	204	93	NA	NA
22 LR Shot #12	31	950	NA	NA	NA	NA	NA
22 WRF LFN	45	1300	1015	169	103	3	NA
22 Win. Mag. Lead Free	28	2200	NA	301	NA	NA	NA
22 Win. Mag.	30	2200	1373	322	127	1.4	1610
22 Win. Mag. V-Max BT	33	2000	1495	293	164	0.60	NA
22 Win. Mag. JHP	34	2120	1435	338	155	1.4	NA
22 Win. Mag. JHP	40	1910	1326	324	156	1.7	1480
22 Win. Mag. FMJ	40	1910	1326	324	156	1.7	1480
22 Win. Mag. Dyna Point	45	1550	1147	240	131	2.60	NA
22 Win. Mag. JHP	50	1650	1280	300	180	1.3	NA
22 Win. Mag. Shot #11	52	1000	—	NA	—	—	NA

NOTES: * = 10 rounds per box. ** = 5 rounds per box. Pricing variations and number of rounds per box can occur with type and brand of ammunition. Listed pricing is the average nominal cost for load style and box quantity shown. Not every brand is available in all shot size variations. Some manufacturers do not provide suggested list prices. All prices rounded to nearest whole dollar. The price you pay will vary dependent upon outlet of purchase. # = new load spec this year; "C" indicates a change in data.

Dram Equiv.	Shot Ozs.	Load Style	Shot Sizes	Brands	Avg. Price/box	Velocity (fps)
10 Gauge 3-1/2" Magnum						
4-1/2	2-1/4	premium	BB, 2, 4, 5, 6	Win., Fed., Rem.	$33	1205
Max	2	premium	4, 5, 6	Fed., Win.	NA	1300
4-1/4	2	high velocity	BB, 2, 4	Rem.	$22	1210
Max	18 pellets	premium	00 buck	Fed., Win.	$7**	1100
Max	1-7/8	Bismuth	BB, 2, 4	Bis.	NA	1225
Max	1-3/4	high density	BB, 2	Rem.	NA	1300
4-1/4	1-3/4	steel	TT, T, BBB, BB, 1, 2, 3	Win., Rem.	$27	1260
Mag	1-5/8	steel	T, BBB, BB, 2	Win.	$27	1285
Max	1-5/8	Bismuth	BB, 2, 4	Bismuth	NA	1375
Max	1-1/2	steel	T, BBB, BB, 1, 2, 3	Fed.	NA	1450
Max	1-3/8	steel	T, BBB, BB, 1, 2, 3	Fed., Rem.	NA	1500
Max	1-3/8	steel	T, BBB, BB, 2	Fed., Win.	NA	1450
Max	1-3/4	slug, rifled	slug	Fed.	NA	1280
Max	24 pellets	Buckshot	1 Buck	Fed.	NA	1100
Max	54 pellets	Super-X	4 Buck	Win.	NA	1150
12 Gauge 3-1/2" Magnum						
Max	2-1/4	premium	4, 5, 6	Fed., Rem., Win.	$13*	1150
Max	2	Lead	4, 5, 6	Fed.	NA	1300
Max	2	Copper plated turkey	4, 5	Rem.	NA	1300
Max	18 pellets	premium	00 buck	Fed., Win., Rem.	$7**	1100
Max	1-7/8	Wingmaster HD	4, 6	Rem.	NA	1225
Max	1-7/8	heavyweight	5, 6	Fed.	NA	1300
Max	1-3/4	high density	BB, 2, 4, 6	Rem.		1300
Max	1-7/8	Bismuth	BB, 2, 4	Bis.	NA	1225
Max	1-5/8	Hevi-shot	T	Hevi-shot	NA	1350
Max	1-5/8	Wingmaster HD	T	Rem.	NA	1350
Max	1-5/8	high density	BB, 2	Fed.	NA	1450
Max	1-3/8	Heavyweight	2, 4, 6	Fed.	NA	1450
Max	1-3/8	steel	T, BBB, BB, 2, 4	Fed., Win., Rem.	NA	1450
Max	1-1/2	FS steel	BBB, BB, 2	Fed.	NA	1500
Max	1-1/2	Supreme H-V	BBB, BB, 2, 3	Win.	NA	1475
Max	1-3/8	H-speed steel	BB, 2	Rem.	NA	1550
Max	1-1/4	Steel	BB, 2	Win.	NA	1625
Max	24 pellets	Premium	1 Buck	Fed.	NA	1100
Max	54 pellets	Super-X	4 Buck	Win.	NA	1050
12 Gauge 3" Magnum						
4	2	premium	BB, 2, 4, 5, 6	Win., Fed., Rem.	$9*	1175
4	1-7/8	premium	BB, 2, 4, 6	Win., Fed., Rem.	$19	1210
4	1-7/8	duplex	4x6	Rem.	$9*	1210
Max	1-3/4	turkey	4, 5, 6	Fed., Fio., Win., Rem.	NA	1300
Max	1-3/4	high density	BB, 2, 4	Rem.	NA	1450
Max	1-5/8	high density	BB, 2	Fed.	NA	1450
Max	1-5/8	Wingmaster HD	4, 6	Rem.	NA	1227
Max	1-5/8	high velocity	4, 5, 6	Fed.	NA	1350
4	1-5/8	premium	2, 4, 5, 6	Win., Fed., Rem.	$18	1290
Max	1-1/2	Wingmaster HD	T	Rem.	NA	1300
Max	1-1/2	Hevi-shot	T	Hevi-shot	NA	1300
Max	1-1/2	high density	BB, 2, 4	Rem.	NA	1300
Max	1-5/8	Bismuth	BB, 2, 4, 5, 6	Bis.	NA	1250
4	24 pellets	buffered	1 buck	Win., Fed., Rem.	$5**	1040
4	15 pellets	buffered	00 buck	Win., Fed., Rem.	$6**	1210
4	10 pellets	buffered	000 buck	Win., Fed., Rem.	$6**	1225
4	41 pellets	buffered	4 buck	Win., Fed., Rem.	$6**	1210
Max	1-3/8	heavyweight	5, 6	Fed.	NA	1300
Max	1-3/8	high density	B, 2, 4, 6	Rem. Win.	NA	1450
12 Gauge 3" Magnum (cont.)						
Max	1-3/8	slug	slug	Bren.	NA	1476
Max	1-1/4	slug, rifled	slug	Fed.	NA	1600
Max	1-3/16	saboted slug	copper slug	Rem.	NA	1500
Max	7/8	slug, rifled	slug	Rem.	NA	1875
Max	1-1/8	low recoil	BB	Fed.	NA	850
Max	1-1/8	steel	BB, 2, 3, 4	Fed., Win., Rem.	NA	1550
Max	1-1/16	high density	2, 4	Win.	NA	1400
Max	1	steel	4, 6	Fed.	NA	1330
Max	1-3/8	buckhammer	slug	Rem.	NA	1500
Max	1	slug, rifled	slug, magnum	Win., Rem.	$5**	1760
Max	1	saboted slug	slug	Rem., Win., Fed.	$10**	1550
Max	385 grs.	partition gold	slug	Win.	NA	2000
Max	1-1/8	Rackmaster	slug	Win.	NA	1700
Max	300 grs.	XP3	slug	Win.	NA	2100
3-5/8	1-3/8	steel	BBB, BB, 1, 2, 3, 4	Win., Fed., Rem.	$19	1275
Max	1-1/8	snow goose FS	BB, 2	Fed.	NA	1635
Max	1-1/8	steel	BB, 2, 4	Rem.	NA	1500
Max	1-1/8	steel	T, BBB, BB, 2, 4, 5, 6	Fed., Win.	NA	1450
Max	1-1/8	steel	BB, 2	Fed.	NA	1400
4	1-1/4	steel	T, BBB, BB, 1, 2, 3, 4, 6	Win., Fed., Rem.	$18	1400
Max	1-1/4	FS steel	BBB, BB, 2	Fed.	NA	1450
12 Gauge 2-3/4"						
Max	1-5/8	magnum	4, 5, 6	Win., Fed.	$8*	1250
Max	1-3/8	lead	4, 5, 6	Fiocchi	NA	1485
Max	1-3/8	turkey	4, 5, 6	Fio.	NA	1250
Max	1-3/8	steel	4, 5, 6	Fed.	NA	1400
Max	1-3/8	Bismuth	BB, 2, 4, 5, 6	Bis.	NA	1300
3-3/4	1-1/2	magnum	BB, 2, 4, 5, 6	Win., Fed., Rem.	$16	1260
Max	1-1/4	Supreme H-V	4, 5, 6, 7-1/2	Win. Rem.	NA	1400
3-3/4	1-1/4	high velocity	BB, 2, 4, 5, 6, 7-1/2 & 8	Win., Fed., Rem., Fio.	$13	1330
Max	1-1/4	high density	B, 2, 4	Win.	NA	1450
Max	1-1/4	high density	4, 6	Rem.	NA	1325
3-1/4	1-1/4	standard velocity	6, 7-1/2, 8, 9	Win., Fed., Rem., Fio.	$11	1220
Max	1-1/8	Hevi-shot	5	Hevi-shot	NA	1350
3-1/4	1-1/8	standard velocity	4, 6, 7-1/2, 8, 9	Win., Fed., Rem., Fio.	$9	1255
Max	1-1/8	steel	2, 4	Rem.	NA	1390
Max	1	steel	BB, 2	Fed.	NA	1450
3-1/4	1	standard velocity	6, 7-1/2, 8	Rem., Fed., Fio., Win.	$6	1290
3-1/4	1-1/4	target	7-1/2, 8, 9	Win., Fed., Rem.	$10	1220
3	1-1/8	spreader	7-1/2, 8, 8-1/2, 9	Fio.	NA	1200
3	1-1/8	target	7-1/2, 8, 9, 7-1/2x8	Win., Fed., Rem., Fio.	$7	1200
2-3/4	1-1/8	target	7-1/2, 8, 8-1/2, 9, 7-1/2x8	Win., Fed., Rem., Fio.	$7	1145
2-3/4	1-1/8	low recoil	7-1/2, 8	Rem.	NA	1145
2-1/2	26 grams	low recoil	8	Win.	NA	980
2-1/4	1-1/8	target	7-1/2, 8, 8-1/2, 9	Rem., Fed.	$7	1080
Max	1	spreader	7-1/2, 8, 8-1/2, 9	Fio.	NA	1300
3-1/4	28 grams (1 oz)	target	7-1/2, 8, 9	Win., Fed., Rem., Fio.	$8	1290
3	1	target	7-1/2, 8, 8-1/2, 9	Win., Fio.	NA	1235
2-3/4	1	target	7-1/2, 8, 8-1/2, 9	Fed., Rem., Fio.	NA	1180
3-1/4	24 grams	target	7-1/2, 8, 9	Fed., Win., Fio.	NA	1325
3	7/8	light	8	Fio.	NA	1200
3-3/4	8 pellets	buffered	000 buck	Win., Fed., Rem.	$4**	1325

NOTES: * = 10 rounds per box. ** = 5 rounds per box. Pricing variations and number of rounds per box can occur with type and brand of ammunition. Listed pricing is the average nominal cost for load style and box quantity shown. Not every brand is available in all shot size variations. Some manufacturers do not provide suggested list prices. All prices rounded to nearest whole dollar. The price you pay will vary dependent upon outlet of purchase. # = new load spec this year; "C" indicates a change in data.

Dram Equiv.	Shot Ozs.	Load Style	Shot Sizes	Brands	Avg. Price/box	Velocity (fps)
12 Gauge 2-3/4" (cont.)						
4	12 pellets	premium	00 buck	Win., Fed., Rem.	$5**	1290
3-3/4	9 pellets	buffered	00 buck	Win., Fed., Rem., Fio.	$19	1325
3-3/4	12 pellets	buffered	0 buck	Win., Fed., Rem.	$4**	1275
4	20 pellets	buffered	1 buck	Win., Fed., Rem.	$4**	1075
3-3/4	16 pellets	buffered	1 buck	Win., Fed., Rem.	$4**	1250
4	34 pellets	premium	4 buck	Fed., Rem.	$5**	1250
3-3/4	27 pellets	buffered	4 buck	Win., Fed., Rem.	$4**	1325
		PDX1	1 oz. slug, 3-00 buck	Win.	NA	1150
Max	1	saboted slug	slug	Win., Fed., Rem.	$10**	1450
Max	1-1/4	slug, rifled	slug	Fed.	NA	1520
Max	1-1/4	slug	slug	Lightfield		1440
Max	1-1/4	saboted slug	attached sabot	Rem.	NA	1550
Max	1	slug, rifled	slug, magnum	Rem., Fio.	$5**	1680
Max	1	slug, rifled	slug	Win., Fed., Rem.	$4**	1610
Max	1	sabot slug	slug	Sauvestre		1640
Max	7/8	slug, rifled	slug	Rem.	NA	1800
Max	400	plat. tip	sabot slug	Win.	NA	1700
Max	385 grains	Partition Gold Slug	slug	Win.	NA	1900
Max	385 grains	Core-Lokt bonded	sabot slug	Rem.	NA	1900
Max	325 grains	Barnes Sabot	slug	Fed.	NA	1900
Max	300 grains	SST Slug	sabot slug	Hornady	NA	2050
3	1-1/8	steel target	6-1/2, 7	Rem.	NA	1200
2-3/4	1-1/8	steel target	7	Rem.	NA	1145
3	1#	steel	7	Win.	$11	1235
3-1/2	1-1/4	steel	T, BBB, BB, 1, 2, 3, 4, 5, 6	Win., Fed., Rem.	$18	1275
3-3/4	1-1/8	steel	BB, 1, 2, 3, 4, 5, 6	Win., Fed., Rem., Fio.	$16	1365
3-3/4	1	steel	2, 3, 4, 5, 6, 7	Win., Fed., Rem., Fio.	$13	1390
Max	7/8	steel	7	Fio.	NA	1440
16 Gauge 2-3/4"						
3-1/4	1-1/4	magnum	2, 4, 6	Fed., Rem.	$16	1260
3-1/4	1-1/8	high velocity	4, 6, 7-1/2	Win., Fed., Rem., Fio.	$12	1295
Max	1-1/8	Bismuth	4, 5	Bis.	NA	1200
2-3/4	1-1/8	standard velocity	6, 7-1/2, 8	Fed., Rem., Fio.	$9	1185
2-1/2	1	dove	6, 7-1/2, 8, 9	Fio., Win.	NA	1165
2-3/4	1		6, 7-1/2, 8	Fio.	NA	1200
Max	15/16	steel	2, 4	Fed., Rem.	NA	1300
Max	7/8	steel	2, 4	Win.	$16	1300
3	12 pellets	buffered	1 buck	Win., Fed., Rem.	$4**	1225
Max	4/5	slug, rifled	slug	Win., Fed., Rem.	$4**	1570
Max	.92	sabot slug	slug	Sauvestre	NA	1560
20 Gauge 3" Magnum						
3	1-1/4	premium	2, 4, 5, 6, 7-1/2	Win., Fed., Rem.	$15	1185
Max	1-1/4	Wingmaster HD	4, 6	Rem.	NA	1185
3	1-1/4	turkey	4, 6	Fio.	NA	1200
Max	1-1/4	Hevi-shot	2, 4, 6	Hevi-shot	NA	1250
Max	1-1/8	high density	4, 6	Rem.	NA	1300
Max	18 pellets	buck shot	2 buck	Fed.	NA	1200
Max	24 pellets	buffered	3 buck	Win.	$5**	1150
2-3/4	20 pellets	buck	3 buck	Rem.	$4**	1200
3-1/4	1	steel	1, 2, 3, 4, 5, 6	Win., Fed., Rem.	$15	1330
Max	7/8	steel	2, 4	Win.	NA	1300

Dram Equiv.	Shot Ozs.	Load Style	Shot Sizes	Brands	Avg. Price/box	Velocity (fps)
20 Gauge 3" Magnum (cont.)						
Max	1-1/16	high density	2, 4	Win.	NA	1400
Max	1-1/16	Bismuth	2, 4, 5, 6	Bismuth	NA	1250
Mag	5/8	saboted slug	275 gr.	Fed.	NA	1900
20 Gauge 2-3/4"						
2-3/4	1-1/8	magnum	4, 6, 7-1/2	Win., Fed., Rem.	$14	1175
2-3/4	1	high velocity	4, 5, 6, 7-1/2, 8, 9	Win., Fed., Rem., Fio.	$12	1220
Max	1	Bismuth	4, 6	Bis.	NA	1200
Max	1	Hevi-shot	5	Hevi-shot	NA	1250
Max	1	Supreme H-V	4, 6, 7-1/2	Win. Rem.	NA	1300
Max	7/8	Steel	2, 3, 4	Fio.	NA	1500
2-1/2	1	standard velocity	6, 7-1/2, 8	Win., Rem., Fed., Fio.	$6	1165
2-1/2	7/8	clays	8	Rem.	NA	1200
2-1/2	7/8	promotional	6, 7-1/2, 8	Win., Rem., Fio.	$6	1210
2-1/2	1	target	8, 9	Win., Rem.	$8	1165
Max	7/8	clays	7-1/2, 8	Win.	NA	1275
2-1/2	7/8	target	8, 9	Win., Fed., Rem.	$8	1200
Max	3/4	steel	2, 4	Rem.	NA	1425
2-1/2	7/8	steel - target	7	Rem.	NA	1200
Max	1	buckhammer	slug	Rem.	NA	1500
Max	5/8	Saboted Slug	Copper Slug	Rem.	NA	1500
Max	20 pellets	buffered	3 buck	Win., Fed.	$4	1200
Max	5/8	slug, saboted	slug	Win.,	$9**	1400
2-3/4	5/8	slug, rifled	slug	Rem.	$4**	1580
Max	3/4	saboted slug	copper slug	Fed., Rem.	NA	1450
Max	3/4	slug, rifled	slug	Win., Fed., Rem., Fio.	$4**	1570
Max	.9	sabot slug	slug	Sauvestre		1480
Max	260 grains	Partition Gold Slug	slug	Win.	NA	1900
Max	260 grains	Core-Lokt Ultra	slug	Rem.	NA	1900
Max	260 grains	saboted slug	platinum tip	Win.	NA	1700
Max	3/4	steel	2, 3, 4, 6	Win., Fed., Rem.	$14	1425
Max	250 grains	SST slug	slug	Hornady	NA	1800
Max	1/2	rifled, slug	slug	Rem.	NA	1800
28 Gauge 3"						
Max	7/8	tundra tungsten	4, 5, 6	Fiocchi	NA	TBD
28 Gauge 2-3/4"						
2	1	high velocity	6, 7-1/2, 8	Win.	$12	1125
2-1/4	3/4	high velocity	6, 7-1/2, 8, 9	Win., Fed., Rem., Fio.	$11	1295
2	3/4	target	8, 9	Win., Fed., Rem.	$9	1200
Max	3/4	sporting clays	7-1/2, 8-1/2	Win.	NA	1300
Max	5/8	Bismuth	4, 6	Bis.	NA	1250
Max	5/8	steel	6, 7	NA	NA	1300
410 Bore 3"						
Max	11/16	high velocity	4, 5, 6, 7-1/2, 8, 9	Win., Fed., Rem., Fio.	$10	1135
Max	9/16	Bismuth	4	Bis.	NA	1175
Max	3/8	steel	6	NA	NA	1400
		judge	5 pellets 000 Buck	Fed.	NA	960
		judge	9 pellets #4 Buck	Fed.	NA	1100
410 Bore 2-1/2"						
Max	1/2	high velocity	4, 6, 7-1/2	Win., Fed., Rem.	$9	1245
Max	1/5	slug, rifled	slug	Win., Fed., Rem.	$4**	1815
1-1/2	1/2	target	8, 8-1/2, 9	Win., Fed., Rem., Fio.	$8	1200
Max	1/2	sporting clays	7-1/2, 8, 8-1/2	Win.	NA	1300
Max		Buckshot	5-000 Buck	Win.	NA	1135
		judge	12-bb's, 3 disks	Win.	NA	TBD

2011 Gun Digest
Catalog of Arms & Accessories

ACCU-TEK AT-380 II 380 ACP PISTOL
Caliber: 380 ACP, 6-shot magazine. **Barrel:** 2.8". **Weight:** 23.5 oz. **Length:** 6.125" overall. **Grips:** Textured black composition. **Sights:** Blade front, rear adjustable for windage. **Features:** Made from 17-4 stainless steel, has an exposed hammer, manual firing-pin safety block and trigger disconnect. Magazine release located on the bottom of the grip. American made, lifetime warranty. Comes with two 6-round stainless steel magazines and a California-approved cable lock. Introduced 2006. Made in U.S.A. by Excel Industries.
Price: Satin stainless **$262.00**

AMERICAN CLASSIC 1911-A1
1911-style semiauto pistol chambered in .45 ACP. Features include Series 90 lockwork, 7+1 capacity, walnut grips, 5-inch barrel, blued or hard-chromed steel frame, checkered wood grips, drift adjustable sights.
Price: . . . . **N/A**

AMERICAN CLASSIC COMMANDER
1911-style semiauto pistol chambered in .45 ACP. Features include 7+1 capacity, checkered mahogany grips, 4.25-inch barrel, blued or hard-chromed steel frame, drift adjustable sights.
Price: . . . . **N/A**

ARMALITE AR-24 PISTOL
Caliber: 9mm Para., 10- or 15-shot magazine. **Barrel:** 4.671", 6 groove, right-hand cut rifling. **Weight:** 34.9 oz. **Length:** 8.27" overall. **Grips:** Black polymer. **Sights:** Dovetail front, fixed rear, 3-dot luminous design. **Features:** Machined slide, frame and barrel. Serrations on forestrap and backstrap, external thumb safety and internal firing pin box, half cock. Two 15-round magazines, pistol case, pistol lock, manual and cleaning brushes. Manganese phosphate finish. Compact comes with two 13-round magazines, 3.89" barrel, weighs 33.4 oz. Made in U.S.A. by ArmaLite.
Price: AR-24 Full Size. **$550.00**
Price: AR-24K Compact **$550.00**

ARMSCOR/ROCK ISLAND ARMORY 1911A1-45 FS GI
1911-style semiauto pistol chambered in .45 ACP (8 rounds), 9mm Parabellum, .38 Super (9 rounds). Features include checkered plastic or hardwood grips, 5-inch barrel, parkerized steel frame and slide, drift adjustable sights.
Price: . . . . **N/A**

ARMSCOR/ROCK ISLAND ARMORY 1911A1-45 CS GI
1911-style Officer's-size semiauto pistol chambered in .45 ACP. Features plain hardwood grips, 3.5-inch barrel, parkerized steel frame and slide, drift adjustable sights.
Price: . . . . **N/A**

AUTO-ORDNANCE TA5 SEMI-AUTO PISTOL
Caliber: 45 ACP, 30-round stick magazine (standard), 50- or 100-round drum magazine optional. **Barrel:** 10.5", finned. **Weight:** 6.5 lbs. **Length:** 25" overall. **Features:** Semi-auto pistol patterned after Thompson Model 1927 semi-auto carbine. Horizontal vertical foregrip, aluminum receiver, top cocking knob, grooved walnut pistolgrip.
Price: **$1,143.00**

AUTO-ORDNANCE 1911A1 AUTOMATIC PISTOL
Caliber: 45 ACP, 7-shot magazine. **Barrel:** 5". **Weight:** 39 oz.

Length: 8.5" overall. **Grips:** Brown checkered plastic with medallion. **Sights:** Blade front, rear drift-adjustable for windage. **Features:** Same specs as 1911A1 military guns-parts interchangeable. Frame and slide blued; each radius has non-glare finish. Introduced 2002. Made in U.S.A. by Kahr Arms.
Price: 1911PKZSE Parkerized, plastic grips **$627.00**
Price: 1911PKZSEW Parkerized **$662.00**
Price: 1911PKZMA Parkerized, Mass. Compliant (2008). **$627.00**

BAER H.C. 40 AUTO PISTOL
Caliber: 40 S&W, 18-shot magazine. **Barrel:** 5". **Weight:** 37 oz. **Length:** 8.5" overall. **Grips:** Wood. **Sights:** Low-mount adjustable rear sight with hidden rear leaf, dovetail front sight. **Features:** Double-stack Caspian frame, beavertail grip safety, ambidextrous thumb safety, 40 S&W match barrel with supported chamber, match stainless steel barrel bushing, lowered and flared ejection port, extended ejector, match trigger fitted, integral mag well, bead blast blue finish on lower, polished sides on slide. Introduced 2008. Made in U.S.A. by Les Baer Custom, Inc.
Price: **$2,960.00**

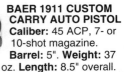

BAER 1911 CUSTOM CARRY AUTO PISTOL
Caliber: 45 ACP, 7- or 10-shot magazine. **Barrel:** 5". **Weight:** 37 oz. **Length:** 8.5" overall. **Grips:** Checkered walnut. **Sights:** Baer improved ramp-style dovetailed front, Novak low-mount rear. **Features:** Baer forged NM frame, slide and barrel with stainless bushing. Baer speed trigger with 4-lb. pull. Partial listing shown. Made in U.S.A. by Les Baer Custom, Inc.
Price: Custom Carry 5", blued **$1,995.00**
Price: Custom Carry 5", stainless **$2,120.00**
Price: Custom Carry 4" Commanche length, blued **$1,995.00**
Price: Custom Carry 4" Commanche length, stainless **$2,120.00**

BAER 1911 ULTIMATE RECON PISTOL
Caliber: 45 ACP, 7- or 10-shot magazine. **Barrel:** 5". **Weight:** 37 oz. **Length:** 8.5" overall. **Grips:** Checkered cocobolo. **Sights:** Baer improved ramp-style dovetailed front, Novak low-mount rear. **Features:** NM Caspian frame, slide and barrel with stainless bushing. Baer speed trigger with 4-lb. pull. Includes integral Picatinny rail and Sure-Fire X-200 light. Made in U.S.A. by Les Baer Custom, Inc. Introduced 2006.
Price: Bead blast blued **$3,070.00**
Price: Bead blast chrome **$3,390.00**

BAER 1911 PREMIER II AUTO PISTOL
Caliber: 38 Super, 400 Cor-Bon, 45 ACP, 7- or 10-shot magazine. **Barrel:** 5". **Weight:** 37 oz. **Length:** 8.5" overall. **Grips:** Checkered rosewood, double diamond pattern. **Sights:** Baer dovetailed front, low-mount Bo-Mar rear with hidden leaf. **Features:** Baer NM forged steel frame and barrel with stainless bushing, deluxe Commander

Prices given are believed to be accurate at time of publication however, many factors affect retail pricing so exact prices are not possible.

hammer and sear, beavertail grip safety with pad, extended ambidextrous safety; flat mainspring housing; 30 lpi checkered front strap. Made in U.S.A. by Les Baer Custom, Inc.

Price: 5" 45 ACP **$1,790.00**
Price: 5" 400 Cor-Bon **$1,890.00**
Price: 5" 38 Super **$2,070.00**
Price: 6" 45 ACP, 400 Cor-Bon, 38 Super, from. **$1,990.00**
Price: Super-Tac, 45 ACP, 400 Cor-Bon, 38 Super, from . . **$2,280.00**

BAER 1911 S.R.P. PISTOL

Caliber: 45 ACP. **Barrel:** 5". **Weight:** 37 oz. **Length:** 8.5" overall. **Grips:** Checkered walnut. **Sights:** Trijicon night sights. **Features:** Similar to the F.B.I. contract gun except uses Baer forged steel frame. Has Baer match barrel with supported chamber, complete tactical action. Has Baer Ultra Coat finish. Introduced 1996. Made in U.S.A. by Les Baer Custom, Inc.
Price: Government or Commanche length **$2,590.00**

BAER 1911 STINGER PISTOL

Caliber: 45 ACP, 7-round magazine. **Barrel:** 5". **Weight:** 34 oz. **Length:** 8.5" overall. **Grips:** Checkered cocobolo. **Sights:** Baer dovetailed front, low-mount Bo-Mar rear with hidden leaf. **Features:** Baer NM frame. Baer Commanche slide, Officer's style grip frame, beveled mag well. Made in U.S.A. by Les Baer Custom, Inc.
Price: Blued **$1,890.00**
Price: Stainless **$1,970.00**

BAER 1911 PROWLER III PISTOL

Caliber: 45 ACP, 8-round magazine. **Barrel:** 5". **Weight:** 34 oz. **Length:** 8.5" overall. **Grips:** Checkered cocobolo. **Sights:** Baer dovetailed front, low-mount Bo-Mar rear with hidden leaf. **Features:** Similar to Premier II with tapered cone stub weight, rounded corners. Made in U.S.A. by Les Baer Custom, Inc.
Price: Blued **$2,580.00**

BERETTA MODEL 92FS PISTOL

Caliber: 9mm Para., 10-shot magazine. **Barrel:** 4.9". **Weight:** 34 oz. **Length:** 8.5" overall. **Grips:** Checkered black plastic. **Sights:** Blade front, rear adjustable for windage. Tritium night sights available. **Features:** Double action. Extractor acts as chamber loaded indicator, squared trigger guard, grooved front and backstraps, inertia firing pin. Matte or blued finish. Introduced 1977. Made in U.S.A.
Price: With plastic grips **$650.00**

BERETTA MODEL 80 CHEETAH SERIES DA PISTOLS

Caliber: 380 ACP, 10-shot magazine (M84); 8-shot (M85); 22 LR, 7-shot (M87). **Barrel:** 3.82". **Weight:** About 23 oz. (M84/85); 20.8 oz. (M87). **Length:** 6.8" overall. **Grips:** Glossy black plastic (wood optional at extra cost). **Sights:** Fixed front, drift-adjustable rear. **Features:** Double action, quick takedown, convenient magazine release. Introduced 1977. Made in U.S.A.
Price: Model 84 Cheetah, plastic grips **$650.00**

BERETTA MODEL 21 BOBCAT PISTOL

Caliber: 22 LR or 25 ACP. Both double action. **Barrel:** 2.4". **Weight:** 11.5 oz.; 11.8 oz. **Length:** 4.9" overall. **Grips:** Plastic. **Features:** Available in nickel, matte, engraved or blue finish. Introduced in 1985.
Price: Bobcat, 22 or 25, blue . . **$335.00**
Price: Bobcat, 22, Inox **$420.00**
Price: Bobcat, 22 or 25, matte **$335.00**

BERETTA MODEL 3032 TOMCAT PISTOL

Caliber: 32 ACP, 7-shot magazine. **Barrel:** 2.45". **Weight:** 14.5 oz. **Length:** 5" overall. **Grips:** Checkered black plastic. **Sights:** Blade front, drift-adjustable rear. **Features:** Double action with exposed hammer; tip-up barrel for direct loading/unloading; thumb safety; polished or matte blue finish. Made in U.S.A. Introduced 1996.
Price: Matte **$435.00**
Price: Inox **$555.00**

BERETTA MODEL U22 NEOS

Caliber: 22 LR, 10-shot magazine. **Barrel:** 4.5"; 6". **Weight:** 32 oz.; 36 oz. **Length:** 8.8"; 10.3". **Sights:** Target. **Features:** Integral rail for standard scope mounts, light, perfectly weighted, 100 percent American made by Beretta.
Price: **$250.00**
Price: Inox **$350.00**

BERETTA MODEL PX4 STORM

Caliber: 9mm Para., 40 S&W. **Capacity:** 17 (9mm Para.); 14 (40 S&W). **Barrel:** 4". **Weight:** 27.5 oz. **Grips:** Black checkered w/3 interchangeable backstraps. **Sights:** 3-dot system coated in Superluminova; removable front and rear sights. **Features:** DA/SA, manual safety/hammer decocking lever (ambi) and automatic firing pin block safety. Picatinny rail. Comes with two magazines (17/10 in 9mm Para. and 14/10 in 40 S&W). Removable hammer unit. American made by Beretta. Introduced 2005.
Price: **$600.00**
Price: 45 ACP **$650.00**

BERETTA MODEL PX4 STORM SUB-COMPACT

Caliber: 9mm, 40 S&W. **Capacity:** 13 (9mm); 10 (40 S&W). **Barrel:** 3". **Weight:** 26.1 oz. **Length:** 6.2" overall. **Grips:** NA. **Sights:** NA. **Features:** Ambidextrous manual safety lever, interchangeable backstraps included, lock breech and tilt barrel system, stainless steel barrel, Picatinny rail.
Price: **$600.00**

BERETTA MODEL M9

Caliber: 9mm Para. **Capacity:** 15. **Barrel:** 4.9". **Weight:** 32.2-35.3 oz. **Grips:** Plastic. **Sights:** Dot and post, low profile, windage adjustable rear. **Features:** DA/SA, forged aluminum alloy frame, delayed locking-bolt system, manual safety doubles as decocking lever, combat-style trigger guard, loaded chamber indicator. Comes with two magazines (15/10). American made by Beretta. Introduced 2005.
Price: **$650.00**

BERETTA MODEL M9A1

Caliber: 9mm Para. Capacity: 15. **Barrel:** 4.9". **Weight:** 32.2-35.3 oz. **Grips:** Plastic. **Sights:** Dot and post, low profile, windage adjustable rear. **Features:** Same as M9, but also includes integral Mil-Std-1913 Picatinny rail, has checkered frontstrap and backstrap. Comes with two magazines (15/10). American made by Beretta. Introduced 2005.

Price: **$750.00**

BERSA THUNDER 45 ULTRA COMPACT PISTOL

Caliber: 45 ACP. **Barrel:** 3.6". **Weight:** 27 oz. **Length:** 6.7" overall. **Grips:** Anatomically designed polymer. **Sights:** White outline rear. **Features:** Double action; firing pin safeties, integral locking system. Available in matte, satin nickel, gold, or duo-tone. Introduced 2003. Imported from Argentina by Eagle Imports, Inc.

Price: Thunder 45, matte blue **$402.00**
Price: Thunder 45, stainless **$480.00**
Price: Thunder 45, satin nickel **$445.00**

BERSA THUNDER 380 SERIES PISTOLS

Caliber: 380 ACP, 7 rounds **Barrel:** 3.5". **Weight:** 23 oz. **Length:** 6.6" overall. **Features:** Otherwise similar to Thunder 45 Ultra Compact. 380 DLX has 9-round capacity. 380 Concealed Carry has 8 round capacity. Imported from Argentina by Eagle Imports, Inc.

Price: Thunder 380 Matte **$310.00**
Price: Thunder 380 Satin Nickel **$336.00**
Price: Thunder 380 Blue DLX **$332.00**
Price: Thunder 380 Matte CC (2006) **$315.00**

BERSA THUNDER 9 ULTRA COMPACT/40 SERIES PISTOLS

Caliber: 9mm Para., 40 S&W. **Barrel:** 3.5". **Weight:** 24.5 oz. **Length:** 6.6" overall. **Features:** Otherwise similar to Thunder 45 Ultra Compact. 9mm Para. High Capacity model has 17-round capacity. 40 High Capacity model has 13-round capacity. Imported from Argentina by Eagle Imports, Inc.

Price: Thunder 9mm Para. Matte **$402.00**
Price: Thunder 40 High Capacity Satin Nickel **$419.00**

BROWNING HI POWER 9MM AUTOMATIC PISTOL

Caliber: 9mm Para., 13-round magazine; 40 S&W, 10-round magazine. **Barrel:** 4-5/8". **Weight:** 32 to 39 oz. **Length:** 7.75" overall. **Metal Finishes:** Blued (Standard); black-epoxy/silver-chrome (Practical); black-epoxy (Mark III). **Grips:** Molded (Mark III); wraparound Pachmayr (Practical); or walnut grips (Standard). **Sights:** Fixed (Practical, Mark III, Standard); low-mount adjustable rear (Standard). Cable lock supplied. **Features:** External hammer with half-cock and thumb safeties. Fixed rear sight model available. Commander-style (Practical) or spur-type hammer, single action. Includes gun lock. Imported from Belgium by Browning.

Price: Mark III **$979.00**
Price: Standard, fixed sights, from **$999.00**
Price: SMark III, Digital green (2009) **$985.00**

BROWNING BUCK MARK PISTOLS

Common Features: Caliber: 22 LR, 10-shot magazine. **Action:** Blowback semi-auto. **Trigger:** Wide grooved style. **Sights:** Ramp front, Browning Pro-Target rear adjustable for windage and elevation.

Grips: Cocobolo, target-style (Hunter, 5.5 Target, 5.5 Field); polymer (Camper, Camper Stainless, Micro Nickel, Standard, STD Stainless); checkered walnut (Challenge); laminated (Plus and Plus Nickel); laminated rosewood (Bullseye Target, FLD Plus); rubber (Bullseye Standard). **Metal finishes:** Matte blue (Hunter, Camper, Challenge, Plus, Bullseye Target, Bullseye Standard, 5.5 Target, 5.5 Field, FLD Plus); matte stainless (Camper Stainless, STD Stainless, Micro Standard); nickel-plated (Micro Nickel, Plus Nickel, and Nickel). **Features:** Machined aluminum frame. Includes gun lock. Introduced 1985. Hunter, Camper Stainless, STD Stainless, 5.5 Target, 5.5 Field all introduced 2005. Multiple variations, as noted below. Made in U.S.A. From Browning.

Price: Hunter, 7.25" heavy barrel, 38 oz., Truglo sight **$429.00**
Price: Camper, 5.5" heavy barrel, 34 oz. **$329.00**
Price: FLD Camper Stainless URX, 5.5" tapered bull barrel, 34 oz. **$359.00**
Price: Standard URX, 5.5" flat-side bull barrel, 34 oz. **$399.00**
Price: Standard Stainless URX, 5.5" flat-side bull barrel, 34 oz. **$439.00**
Price: Micro Standard URX, 4" flat-side bull barrel, 32 oz. . . . **$399.00**
Price: Micro Standard Stainless URX, 4" flat-side bull barrel, 32 oz. **$439.00**
Price: Challenge, 5.5" lightweight taper barrel, 25 oz. **$399.00**
Price: Contour 5.5 URX, 5.5" barrel, 36 oz. **$469.00**
Price: Contour 7.25 URX, 7.25", 39 oz. **$479.00**
Price: Contour Lite 5.5 URX, 5.5" barrel, 28 oz., adj. sights . **$519.00**
Price: Contour Lite 7.25 URX, 7.25" barrel, 30 oz., adj. sights **$529.00**
Price: Bullseye URX, 7.25" fluted bull barrel, 36 oz. **$549.00**
Price: Bullseye Target Stainless, 7.25" fluted bull barrel, 36 oz. **$719.00**
Price: 5.5 Target, 5.5" round bull barrel, target sights, 35.5 oz. **$579.00**
Price: 5.5 Field, 5.5" round bull barrel, 35 oz. **$579.00**
Price: Plus Stainless UDX (2007) **$509.00**
Price: Plus UDX (2007). **$469.00**
Price: FLD Plus Rosewood UDX (2007). **$469.00**
Price: Stainless Camper, 5.5" tapered bull barrel (2008) **$379.00**
Price: Practical URX Fiber-Optic, 5.5" barrel (2009) **$379.00**
Price: Lite Splash 5.5 URX **$489.00**
Price: Lite Splash 7.25 URX **$509.00**

BUSHMASTER CARBON 15 .223 PISTOL

Caliber: 5.56/223, 30-round. **Barrel:** 7.25" stainless steel. **Weight:** 2.88 lbs. **Length:** 20" overall. **Grips:** Pistol grip, Hogue overmolded unit for ergonomic comfort. **Sights:** A2-type front with dual-aperture

Prices given are believed to be accurate at time of publication however, many factors affect retail pricing so exact prices are not possible.

slip-up rear. **Features:** AR-style semi-auto pistol with carbon composite receiver, shortenend handguard, full-length optics rail.
Price: . . . . **N/A**
Price: Type 97 pistol, without handguard **$1,055.00**

CHARLES DALY ENHANCED 1911 PISTOLS
Caliber: 45 ACP. **Barrel:** 5".
Weight: 38 oz. **Length:** 8.75" overall. **Grips:** Checkered double diamond hardwood. **Sights:** Dovetailed front and dovetailed snag-free low profile rear sights, 3-dot system. **Features:** Extended high-rise beavertail grip safety, combat trigger, combat hammer, beveled magazine well, flared and lowered ejection port. Field Grade models are satin-finished blued steel. EMS series includes an ambidextrous safety, 4" barrel, 8-shot magazine. ECS series has a contoured left hand safety, 3.5" barrel, 6-shot magazine. Two magazines, lockable carrying case. Introduced 1998. Empire series are stainless versions. Imported from the Philippines by K.B.I., Inc.
Price: EFS, blued, 39.5 oz., 5" barrel **$649.00**
Price: EMS, blued, 37 oz., 4" barrel **$649.00**
Price: ECS, blued, 34.5 oz., 3.5" barrel **$649.00**

CHARLES DALY M-5 POLYMER-FRAMED HI-CAP 1911 PISTOL
Caliber: 9mm Para., 12-round magazine; 40 S&W 17-round magazine; 45 ACP, 13-round magazine. **Barrel:** 5". **Weight:** 33.5 oz. **Length:** 8.5" overall. **Grips:** Checkered polymer. **Sights:** Blade front, adjustable low-profile rear. **Features:** Stainless steel beaver-tail grip safety, rounded trigger-guard, tapered bull barrel, full-length guide rod, matte blue finish on frame and slide. 40 S&W models in M-5 Govt. 1911, M-5 Commander, and M-5 IPSC introduced 2006; M-5 Ultra X Compact in 9mm Para. and 45 ACP introduced 2006; M-5 IPSC .45 ACP introduced 2006. Made in Israel by BUL, imported by K.B.I., Inc.
Price: M-5 Govt. 1911, 40 S&W/45 ACP, matte blue **$749.00**
Price: M-5 Commander, 40 S&W/45 ACP, matte blue **$749.00**
Price: M-5 Ultra X Compact, 9mm Para., 3.1" barrel,
7" OAL, 28 oz. **$749.00**
Price: M-5 Ultra X Compact, 45 ACP, 3.1" barrel, 7" OAL,
28 oz. **$749.00**

CHIAPPA 1911-22
1911-style semiauto pistol chambered in .22 LR. Features include alloy frame; steel barrel; matte blue-black or bright nickel finish, walnut-like grips, two 10-round magazines, fixed sights. Straight blowback action.
Price: **$295.00**

COBRA ENTERPRISES FS32, FS380 AUTO PISTOL
Caliber: 32 ACP, 380 ACP, 7-shot magazine.
Barrel: 3.5". **Weight:** 2.1 lbs. **Length:** 6-3/8" overall. **Grips:** Black composition. **Sights:** Fixed. **Features:** Choice of bright chrome, satin nickel or black finish. Introduced 2002. Made in U.S.A. by Cobra Enterprises of Utah, Inc.
Price: **$165.00**

COBRA ENTERPRISES PATRIOT 45 PISTOL
Caliber: 45 ACP, 6, 7, or 10-shot magazine. **Barrel:** 3.3". **Weight:** 20 oz. **Length:** 6" overall. **Grips:** Black polymer. **Sights:** Rear adjustable. **Features:** Stainless steel or black melonite slide with

load indicator; Semi-auto locked breech, DAO. Made in U.S.A. by Cobra Enterprises of Utah, Inc.
Price: **$380.00**

COBRA ENTERPRISES CA32, CA380 PISTOL
Caliber: 32 ACP, 380 ACP. **Barrel:** 2.8". **Weight:** 22 oz. **Length:** 5.4".
Grips: Black molded synthetic. **Sights:** Fixed. **Features:** Choice of black, satin nickel, or chrome finish. Made in U.S.A. by Cobra Enterprises of Utah, Inc.
Price: **$157.00**

COLT MODEL 1991 MODEL O AUTO PISTOL
Caliber: 45 ACP, 7-shot magazine. **Barrel:** 5". **Weight:** 38 oz.
Length: 8.5" overall. **Grips:** Checkered black composition. **Sights:** Ramped blade front, fixed square notch rear, high profile. **Features:** Matte finish. Continuation of serial number range used on original G.I. 1911A1 guns. Comes with one magazine and molded carrying case. Introduced 1991.
Price: Blue **$786.00**
Price: Stainless **$839.00**

COLT XSE SERIES MODEL O AUTO PISTOLS
Caliber: 45 ACP, 8-shot magazine.
Barrel: 4.25", 5". **Grips:** Checkered, double diamond rosewood. **Sights:** Drift-adjustable 3-dot combat. **Features:** Brushed stainless finish; adjustable, two-cut aluminum trigger; extended ambidextrous thumb safety; upswept beavertail with palm swell; elongated slot hammer. Introduced 1999. From Colt's Mfg. Co., Inc.
Price: XSE Government (5" bbl.) **$944.00**
Price: XSE Government (4.25" bbl.) **$944.00**

COLT XSE LIGHTWEIGHT COMMANDER AUTO PISTOL
Caliber: 45 ACP, 8-shot. **Barrel:** 4.25". **Weight:** 26 oz. **Length:** 7.75" overall. **Grips:** Double diamond checkered rosewood.
Sights: Fixed, glare-proofed blade front, square notch rear; 3-dot system. **Features:** Brushed stainless slide, nickeled aluminum frame; McCormick elongated slot enhanced hammer, McCormick two-cut adjustable aluminum hammer. Made in U.S.A. by Colt's Mfg. Co., Inc.
Price: Stainless **$944.00**

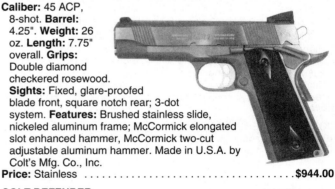

COLT DEFENDER
Caliber: 45 ACP, 7-shot magazine. **Barrel:** 3".
Weight: 22-1/2 oz.
Length: 6.75" overall.
Grips: Pebble-finish rubber wraparound with finger grooves.
Sights: White dot front, snag-free Colt competition rear. **Features:** Stainless finish; aluminum frame; combat-style hammer; Hi Ride grip safety, extended manual safety, disconnect

safety. Introduced 1998. Made in U.S.A. by Colt's Mfg. Co., Inc.
Price: 07000D, stainless **$885.00**

COLT SERIES 70
Caliber: 45 ACP.
Barrel: 5".
Weight: NA.
Length: NA.
Grips: Rosewood with double diamond checkering pattern.
Sights: Fixed. **Features:** Custom replica of the Original Series 70 pistol with a Series 70 firing system, original rollmarks. Introduced 2002. Made in U.S.A. by Colt's Mfg. Co., Inc.
Price: Blued **$919.00**
Price: Stainless **$950.00**

COLT 38 SUPER
Caliber: 38 Super. **Barrel:** 5". **Weight:** NA. **Length:** 8.5" **Grips:** Checkered rubber (stainless and blue models); wood with double diamond checkering pattern (bright stainless model). **Sights:** 3-dot. **Features:** Beveled magazine well, standard thumb safety and service-style grip safety. Introduced 2003. Made in U.S.A. by Colt's Mfg. Co., Inc.
Price: Blued **$837.00**
Price: Stainless **$866.00**
Price: Bright Stainless **$1,090.00**

COLT 1918 WWI REPLICA
Caliber: 45 ACP, 2 7-round magazines. **Barrel:** 5". **Weight:** 38 oz. **Length:** 8.5". **Grips:** Checkered walnut with double diamond checkering pattern. **Sights:** Tapered blade front sight, U-shaped rear notch. **Features:** Reproduction based on original 1911 blueprints. Original rollmarks and inspector marks. Smooth mainspring housing with lanyard loop, WWI-style manual thumb and grip safety, black oxide finish. Introduced 2007. Made in U.S.A. by Colt's Mfg. Co., Inc.
Price: Blued **$990.00**

COLT RAIL GUN
Caliber: 45 ACP (8+1). **Barrel:** NA. **Weight:** NA. **Length:** NA. **Grips:** Rosewood double diamond. **Sights:** White dot front and Novak rear. **Features:** 1911-style semi-auto. Stainless steel frame and slide, front and rear slide serrations, skeletonized trigger, integral; accessory rail, Smith & Alexander upswept beavertail grip palm swell safety, tactical thumb safety, National Match barrel.
Price: . . . . **TO BE ANNOUNCED**

COLT NEW AGENT
Caliber: 45 ACP (7+1). **Barrel:** 3". **Weight:** 25 oz. **Length:** 6.75" overall. **Grips:** Double diamond slim fit. **Sights:** Snag free trench style. **Features:** Semi-auto pistol with blued finish and enhanced black anodized aluminum receiver. Skeletonized aluminum trigger, series 80 firing system, front strap serrations, beveled magazine well.
Price: **$885.00**

COLT DEFENDER PISTOL
1911-style semiauto pistol chambered in .45 ACP and 9mm Parabellum. Features include Series 90 lockwork, 7+1 (.45) or 8+1 (9mm) capacity, wraparound rubber grips, 3-inch barrel, beveled magazine well, aluminum alloy frame with stainless steel slide, white dot carry sights.
Price: **$939.00**

COLT NEW AGENT PISTOL
Similar to Colt Defender but with steel frame and fixed sights.
Price: **$939.00**

COLT SPECIAL COMBAT GOVERNMENT CARRY MODEL
Caliber: 45 ACP (8+1), 38 Super (9+1). **Barrel:** 5". **Weight:** NA. **Length:** NA. **Grips:** Black/silver synthetic. **Sights:** Novak front and rear night. **Features:** 1911-style semi-auto. Skeletonized three-hole trigger, slotted hammer, Smith & Alexander upswept beavertail grip

palm swell safety and extended magazine well, Wilson tactical ambidextrous safety. Available in blued, hard chrome, or blue/satin nickel finish, depending on chambering.
Price: **$1,676.00**

CZ 75 B AUTO PISTOL
Caliber: 9mm Para., 40 S&W, 10-shot magazine. **Barrel:** 4.7". **Weight:** 34.3 oz. **Length:** 8.1" overall. **Grips:** High impact checkered plastic. **Sights:** Square post front, rear adjustable for windage; 3-dot system. **Features:** Single action/double action design; firing pin block safety; choice of black polymer, matte or high-polish blue finishes. All-steel frame. B-SA is a single action with a drop-free magazine. Imported from the Czech Republic by CZ-USA.
Price: 75 B, black polymer, 16-shot magazine **$597.00**
Price: 75 B, dual-tone or satin nickel **$617.00**
Price: 40 S&W, black polymer, 12-shot magazine **$615.00**
Price: 40 S&W, glossy blue, dual-tone, satin nickel **$669.00**
Price: 75 B-SA, 9mm Para./40 S&W, single action **$609.00**

CZ 75 BD Decocker
Similar to the CZ 75B except has a decocking lever in place of the safety lever. All other specifications are the same. Introduced 1999. Imported from the Czech Republic by CZ-USA.
Price: 9mm Para., black polymer **$609.00**

CZ 75 B Compact Auto Pistol
Similar to the CZ 75 B except has 14-shot magazine in 9mm Para., 3.9" barrel and weighs 32 oz. Has removable front sight, non-glare ribbed slide top. Trigger guard is squared and serrated; combat hammer. Introduced 1993. Imported from the Czech Republic by CZ-USA.
Price: 9mm Para., black polymer **$631.00**
Price: 9mm Para., dual tone or satin nickel **$651.00**
Price: 9mm Para. D PCR Compact, alloy frame **$651.00**

CZ 75 Champion Pistol
Similar to the CZ 75 B except has a longer frame and slide, rubber grip to accommodate new heavy-duty magazine. Ambidextrous thumb safety, extended magazine release; three-port compensator. Blued slide and stain nickel frame finish. Introduced 2005. Imported from the Czech Republic by CZ-USA.
Price: 40 S&W, 12-shot mag. **$1,739.00**

CZ 75 Tactical Sport
Similar to the CZ 75 B except the CZ 75 TS is a competition ready pistol designed for IPSC standard division (USPSA limited division). Fixed target sights, tuned single-action operation, lightweight polymer match trigger with adjustments for take-up and overtravel, competition hammer, extended magazine catch, ambidextrous manual safety, checkered walnut grips, polymer magazine well, two tone finish. Introduced 2005. Imported from the Czech Republic by CZ-USA.
Price: 9mm Para., 20-shot mag. **$1,338.00**
Price: 40 S&W, 16-shot mag. **$1,338.00**

CZ 75 SP-01 Pistol
Similar to NATO-approved CZ 75 Compact P-01 model. Features an integral 1913 accessory rail on the dust cover, rubber grip panels, black polycoat finish, extended beavertail, new grip geometry with checkering on front and back straps, and double or single action operation. Introduced 2005. The Shadow variant designed as an IPSC "production" division competition firearm. Includes competition hammer, competition rear sight and fiber-optic front sight, modified slide release, lighter recoil and main spring for use with "minor power

factor" competition ammunition. Includes polycoat finish and slim walnut grips. Finished by CZ Custom Shop. Imported from the Czech Republic by CZ-USA.
Price: SP-01 9mm Para., black polymer, 19+1............**$850.00**

CZ 75 SP-01 Phantom
Similar to the CZ 75 B. 9mm Luger, 19-round magazine, weighs 26 oz. and features a polymer frame with accessory rail, and a forged steel slide with a weight-saving scalloped profile. Two interchangeable grip inserts are included to accommodate users with different-sized hands.
Price: **$695.00**

CZ 85 B/85 Combat Auto Pistol
Same gun as the CZ 75 except has ambidextrous slide release and safety levers; non-glare, ribbed slide top; squared, serrated trigger guard; trigger stop to prevent overtravel. Introduced 1986. The CZ 85 Combat features a fully adjustable rear sight, extended magazine release, ambidextrous slide stop and safety catch, drop free magazine and overtravel adjustment. Imported from the Czech Republic by CZ-USA.
Price: 9mm Para., black polymer **$628.00**
Price: Combat, black polymer **$702.00**
Price: Combat, dual-tone, satin nickel **$732.00**

CZ 75 KADET AUTO PISTOL
Caliber: 22 LR, 10-shot magazine. **Barrel:** 4.88". **Weight:** 36 oz. **Grips:** High impact checkered plastic. **Sights:** Blade front, fully adjustable rear. **Features:** Single action/double action mechanism; all-steel construction. Introduced 1999. Kadet conversion kit consists of barrel, slide, adjustable sights, and magazine to convert the centerfire 75 to rimfire. Imported from the Czech Republic by CZ-USA.
Price: Black polymer **$689.00**
Price: Kadet conversion kit **$412.00**

CZ 83 DOUBLE-ACTION PISTOL
Caliber: 32 ACP, 380 ACP, 12-shot magazine. **Barrel:** 3.8". **Weight:** 26.2 oz. **Length:** 6.8" overall. **Grips:** High impact checkered plastic. **Sights:** Removable square post front, rear adjustable for windage; 3-dot system. **Features:** Single action/double action; ambidextrous magazine release and safety. Blue finish; non-glare ribbed slide top. Imported from the Czech Republic by CZ-USA.
Price: Glossy blue, 32 ACP or 380 ACP **$495.00**
Price: Satin Nickel **$522.00**

CZ 97 B AUTO PISTOL
Caliber: 45 ACP, 10-shot magazine. **Barrel:** 4.85". **Weight:** 40 oz. **Length:** 8.34" overall. **Grips:** Checkered walnut. **Sights:** Fixed. **Features:** Single action/double action; full-length slide rails; screw-in barrel bushing; linkless barrel; all-steel construction; chamber loaded indicator; dual transfer bars. Introduced 1999. Imported from the Czech Republic by CZ-USA.
Price: Black polymer **$779.00**
Price: Glossy blue **$799.00**

CZ 97 BD Decocker
Similar to the CZ 97 B except has a decocking lever in place of the safety lever. Tritium night sights. Rubber grips. All other specifications are the same. Introduced 1999. Imported from the Czech Republic by CZ-USA.
Price: 9mm Para., black polymer **$874.00**

CZ 2075 RAMI/RAMI P AUTO PISTOL
Caliber: 9mm Para., 40 S&W. **Barrel:** 3". **Weight:** 25 oz. **Length:** 6.5" overall. **Grips:** Rubber. **Sights:** Blade front with dot, white outline rear drift adjustable for windage. **Features:** Single-action/double-action; alloy or polymer frame, steel slide; has laser sight mount. Imported from the Czech Republic by CZ-USA.
Price: 9mm Para., alloy frame, 10 and 14-shot magazines . . .**$671.00**
Price: 40 S&W, alloy frame, 8-shot magazine **$671.00**
Price: RAMI P, polymer frame, 9mm Para., 40 S&W **$612.00**

CZ P-01 AUTO PISTOL
Caliber: 9mm Para., 14-shot magazine. **Barrel:** 3.85". **Weight:** 27 oz. **Length:** 7.2" overall. **Grips:** Checkered rubber. **Sights:** Blade front with dot, white outline rear drift adjustable for windage. **Features:** Based on the CZ 75, except with forged aircraft-grade aluminum alloy frame. Hammer forged barrel, decocker, firing-pin block, M3 rail, dual slide serrations, squared trigger guard, re-contoured trigger, lanyard loop on butt. Serrated front and back strap. Introduced 2006. Imported from the Czech Republic by CZ-USA.
Price: CZ P-01 ....**$672.00**

DAN WESSON FIREARMS POINTMAN SEVEN AUTO PISTOL

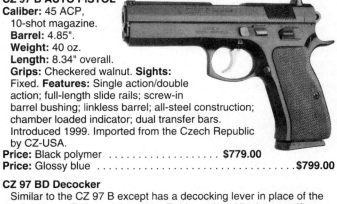

Caliber: 10mm, 40 S&W, 45 ACP. **Barrel:** 5". **Grips:** Diamond checkered cocobolo. **Sights:** Bo-Mar style adjustable target sight. **Weight:** 38 oz. **Features:** Stainless-steel frame and serrated slide. Series 70-style 1911, stainless-steel frame, forged stainless-steel slide. One-piece match-grade barrel and bushing. 20-LPI checkered mainspring housing, front and rear slide cocking serrations, beveled magwell, dehorned by hand. Lowered and flared ejection port, Ed Brown slide stop and memory groove grip safety, tactical extended thumb safety. Commander-style match hammer, match grade sear, aluminum trigger with stainless bow, Wolff springs. Introduced 2000. Made in U.S.A. by Dan Wesson Firearms, distributed by CZ-USA.
Price: 45 ACP, 7+1 ....**$1,158.00**
Price: 10mm, 8+1 ....**$1,191.00**
Price: 40 S&W, stainless **$1,189.00**
Price: 45 ACP, Desert Tan **$1,269.00**

Dan Wesson Commander Classic Bobtail Auto Pistols
Similar to Pointman Seven, a Commander-sized frame with 4.25" barrel. Available with stainless finish, fixed night sights. Introduced 2005. Made in U.S.A. by Dan Wesson Firearms, distributed by CZ-USA.
Price: 45 ACP, 7+1, 33 oz. **$1,191.00**
Price: 10mm, 8+1, 33 oz., stainless **$1,224.00**
Price: 10mm, 33 oz. two-tone **$1,530.00**

DAN WESSON DW RZ-10 AUTO PISTOL
Caliber: 10mm, 9-shot. **Barrel:** 5". **Grips:** Diamond checkered cocobolo. **Sights:** Bo-Mar style adjustable target sight. **Weight:** 38.3 oz. **Length:** 8.8" overall. **Features:** Stainless-steel frame and serrated slide. Series 70-style 1911, stainless-steel frame, forged stainless-steel slide. Commander-style match hammer. Reintroduced 2005. Made in U.S.A. by Dan Wesson Firearms, distributed by CZ-USA.
Price: 10mm, 8+1 ....**$1,191.00**

Dan Wesson DW RZ-10 Sportsman
Similar to the RZ-10 Auto except with 8-shot magazine. Weighs 36 oz., length is 8.8" overall.
Price: **$1,448.00**

Dan Wesson DW RZ-45 Heritage
Similar to the RZ-10 Auto except in 45 ACP with 7-shot magazine. Weighs 36 oz., length is 8.8" overall.
Price: 10mm, 8+1 ....**$1,141.00**

DESERT EAGLE MARK XIX PISTOL
Caliber: 357 Mag., 9-shot; 44 Mag., 8-shot; 50 AE, 7-shot. **Barrel:** 6", 10", interchangeable. **Weight:** 357 Mag.-62 oz.; 44 Mag.-69 oz.; 50 AE-72 oz. **Length:** 10.25" overall (6" bbl.). **Grips:** Polymer; rubber available. **Sights:** Blade on ramp front, combat-style rear. Adjustable available. **Features:** Interchangeable barrels; rotating three-lug bolt; ambidextrous safety; adjustable trigger. Military epoxy finish. Satin, bright nickel, chrome, brushed, matte or black-oxide finishes available. 10" barrel extra. Imported from Israel by Magnum Research, Inc.
Price: Black-6, 6" barrel **$1,475.00**
Price: Black-10, 10" barrel **$1,575.00**
Price: Component System Package, 3 barrels, carrying case, from **$2,801.00**

DESERT BABY MICRO DESERT EAGLE PISTOL
Caliber: 380 ACP, 6-rounds. **Barrel:** 2.22". **Weight:** 14 oz. **Length:** 4.52" overall. **Grips:** NA. **Sights:** Fixed low-profile. **Features:** Small-frame DAO pocket pistol. Steel slide, aluminum alloy frame, nickel-teflon finish.
Price: **$535.00**

DESERT BABY EAGLE PISTOLS
Caliber: 9mm Para., 40 S&W, 45 ACP, 10- or 15-round magazines. **Barrel:** 3.64", 3.93", 4.52". **Weight:** 26.8 to 39.8 oz. **Length:** 7.25" to 8.25" overall. **Grips:** Polymer. **Sights:** Drift-adjustable rear, blade front. **Features:** Steel frame and slide; slide safety; decocker. Reintroduced in 1999. Imported from Israel by Magnum Research, Inc.
Price: **$619.00**

EAA WITNESS FULL SIZE AUTO PISTOL
Caliber: 9mm Para., 38 Super, 18-shot magazine; 40 S&W, 10mm, 15-shot magazine; 45 ACP, 10-shot magazine. **Barrel:** 4.50". **Weight:** 35.33 oz. **Length:** 8.10" overall. **Grips:** Checkered rubber. **Sights:** Undercut blade front, open rear adjustable for windage. **Features:** Double-action/single-action trigger system; round trigger guard; frame-mounted safety. Introduced 1991. Polymer frame introduced 2005. Imported from Italy by European American Armory.
Price: 9mm Para., 38 Super, 10mm, 40 S&W, 45 ACP, full-size steel frame, Wonder finish **$514.00**
Price: 45/22 22 LR, full-size steel frame, blued **$472.00**
Price: 9mm Para., 40 S&W, 45 ACP, full-size polymer frame . **$472.00**

EAA WITNESS COMPACT AUTO PISTOL
Caliber: 9mm Para., 40 S&W, 10mm, 12-shot magazine; 45 ACP, 8-shot magazine. **Barrel:** 3.6". **Weight:** 30 oz. **Length:** 7.3" overall. Otherwise similar to Full Size Witness. Polymer frame introduced 2005. Imported from Italy by European American Armory.
Price: 9mm Para., 10mm, 40 S&W, 45 ACP, steel frame, Wonder finish **$514.00**
Price: 9mm Para., 40 S&W, 45 ACP, polymer frame **$472.00**

EAA WITNESS-P CARRY AUTO PISTOL
Caliber: 10mm, 15-shot magazine; 45 ACP, 10-shot magazine.

Barrel: 3.6". **Weight:** 27 oz. **Length:** 7.5" overall. Otherwise similar to Full Size Witness. Polymer frame introduced 2005. Imported from Italy by European American Armory.
Price: 10mm, 45 ACP, polymer frame, from **$598.00**

EAA ZASTAVA EZ PISTOL
Caliber: 9mm Para., 15-shot magazine; 40 S&W, 11-shot magazine; 45 ACP, 10-shot magazine. **Barrel:** 3.5" or 4." **Weight:** 30-33 oz. **Length:** 7.25" to 7.5" overall. **Features:** Ambidextrous decocker, slide release and magazine release; three dot sight system, aluminum frame, steel slide, accessory rail, full-length claw extractor, loaded chamber indicator. M88 compact has 3.6" barrel, weighs 28 oz. Introduced 2008. Imported by European American Armory.
Price: 9mm Para. or 40 S&W, blued **$547.00**
Price: 9mm Para. or 40 S&W, chromed **$587.00**
Price: 45 ACP, chromed **$587.00**
Price: M88, from **$292.00**

ED BROWN CLASSIC CUSTOM
Caliber: 45 ACP, 7 shot. **Barrel:** 5". **Weight:** 40 oz. **Grips:** Cocobolo wood. **Sights:** Bo-Mar adjustable rear, dovetail front. **Features:** Single-action, M1911 style, custom made to order, stainless frame and slide available. Special mirror-finished slide.
Price: Model CC-BB, blued **$3,155.00**
Price: Model CC-SB, blued and stainless **$3,155.00**
Price: Model   CC-SS, stainless **$3,155.00**

ED BROWN KOBRA AND KOBRA CARRY
Caliber: 45 ACP, 7-shot magazine. **Barrel:** 5" (Kobra); 4.25" (Kobra Carry). **Weight:** 39 oz. (Kobra); 34 oz. (Kobra Carry). **Grips:** Hogue exotic wood. **Sights:** Ramp, front; fixed Novak low-mount night sights, rear. **Features:** Has snakeskin pattern serrations on forestrap and mainspring housing, dehorned edges, beavertail grip safety.
Price: Kobra K-BB, blued **$2,195.00**
Price: Kobra K-SB, stainless and blued **$2,195.00**
Price: Kobra K-SS, stainless **$2,195.00**
Price: Kobra Carry blued, blued/stainless, or stainless from **$2,445.00**

Ed Brown Executive Pistols
Similar to other Ed Brown products, but with 25-lpi checkered frame and mainspring housing.
Price: Elite blued, blued/stainless, or stainless, from **$2,395.00**
Price: Carry blued, blued/stainless, or stainless, from **$2,645.00**
Price: Target blued, blued/stainless, or stainless (2006) from **$2,595.00**

Prices given are believed to be accurate at time of publication however, many factors affect retail pricing so exact prices are not possible.

Ed Brown Special Forces Pistol
Similar to other Ed Brown products, but with ChainLink treatment on forestrap and mainspring housing. Entire gun coated with Gen III finish. "Square cut" serrations on rear of slide only. Dehorned. Introduced 2006.
Price: From **$2,195.00**

Ed Brown Special Forces Carry Pistol
Similar to the Special Forces basic models. Features a 4.25" Commander model slide, single stack commander Bobtail frame. Weighs approx. 35 oz. Fixed dovetail 3-dot night sights with high visibility white outlines.
Price: From **$2,445.00**

EXCEL ARMS ACCELERATOR MP-17/MP-22 PISTOLS
Caliber: 17 HMR, 22 WMR, 9-shot magazine. **Barrel:** 8.5" bull barrel. **Weight:** 54 oz. **Length:** 12.875" overall. **Grips:** Textured black composition. **Sights:** Fully adjustable target sights. **Features:** Made from 17-4 stainless steel, comes with aluminum rib, integral Weaver base, internal hammer, firing-pin block. American made, lifetime warranty. Comes with two 9-round stainless steel magazines and a California-approved cable lock. 22 WMR Introduced 2006. Made in U.S.A. by Excel Arms.
Price: **$433.00**
Price: Camo finishes (2008) **$520.00**

FIRESTORM AUTO PISTOLS
Caliber: 22 LR, 32 ACP, 10-shot magazine; 380 ACP, 7-shot magazine; 9mm Para., 40 S&W, 10-shot magazine; 45 ACP, 7-shot magazine. **Barrel:** 3.5". **Weight:** From 23 oz. **Length:** From 6.6" overall. **Grips:** Rubber. **Sights:** 3-dot. **Features:** Double action. Distributed by SGS Importers International.
Price: 22 LR, matte or duotone, from **$309.95**
Price: 380, matte or duotone, from **$311.95**
Price: Mini Firestorm 9mm Para., matte, duotone, nickel, from **$395.00**
Price: Mini Firestorm 40 S&W, matte, duotone, nickel, from . . **$395.00**
Price: Mini Firestorm 45 ACP, matte, duotone, chrome, from **$402.00**

GLOCK 17/17C AUTO PISTOL
Caliber: 9mm Para., 17/19/33-shot magazines. **Barrel:** 4.49". **Weight:** 22.04 oz. (without magazine). **Length:** 7.32" overall. **Grips:** Black polymer. **Sights:** Dot on front blade, white outline rear adjustable for windage. **Features:** Polymer frame, steel slide; double-action trigger with "Safe Action" system; mechanical firing pin

safety, drop safety; simple takedown without tools; locked breech, recoil operated action. ILS designation refers to Internal Locking System. Adopted by Austrian armed forces 1983. NATO approved 1984. Imported from Austria by Glock, Inc.
Price: Fixed sight **$690.00**

GLOCK 17 GEN4
Similar to Model G17 but with multiple backstrap system allowing three options: a short frame version, medium frame or large frame; reversible, enlarged magazine release catch; dual recoil spring assembly; new Rough Textured Frame (RTF) surface designed to enhance grip traction.
Price: . . . . **N/A**

GLOCK 19/19C AUTO PISTOL
Caliber: 9mm Para., 15/17/19/33-shot magazines. **Barrel:** 4.02". **Weight:** 20.99 oz. (without magazine). **Length:** 6.85" overall. Compact version of Glock 17. Pricing the same as Model 17. Imported from Austria by Glock, Inc.
Price: Fixed sight **$699.00**
Price: 19C Compensated (fixed sight) **$675.00**

GLOCK 20/20C 10MM AUTO PISTOL
Caliber: 10mm, 15-shot magazines. **Barrel:** 4.6". **Weight:** 27.68 oz. (without magazine). **Length:** 7.59" overall. **Features:** Otherwise similar to Model 17. Imported from Austria by Glock, Inc. Introduced 1990.
Price: Fixed sight, from **$700.00**

GLOCK MODEL 20 SF SHORT FRAME PISTOL
Caliber: 10mm. **Barrel:** 4.61" with hexagonal rifling. **Weight:** 27.51 oz. **Length:** 8.07" overall. **Sights:** Fixed. **Features:** Otherwise similar to Model 20 but with short-frame design, extended sight radius.
Price: **$664.00**

GLOCK 21/21C AUTO PISTOL
Caliber: 45 ACP, 13-shot magazines. **Barrel:** 4.6". **Weight:** 26.28 oz. (without magazine). **Length:** 7.59" overall. **Features:** Otherwise similar to Model 17. Imported from Austria by Glock, Inc. Introduced 1991. SF version has tactical rail, smaller diameter grip, 10-round magazine capacity. Introduced 2007.
Price: Fixed sight, from **$700.00**

GLOCK 22/22C AUTO PISTOL
Caliber: 40 S&W, 15/17-shot magazines. **Barrel:** 4.49". **Weight:** 22.92 oz. (without magazine). **Length:** 7.32" overall. **Features:** Otherwise similar to Model 17, including pricing. Imported from Austria by Glock, Inc. Introduced 1990.
Price: Fixed sight, from **$641.00**

GLOCK 22 GEN4
Similar to Model G22 but with multiple backstrap system allowing three options: a short frame version, medium frame or large frame; reversible, enlarged magazine release catch; dual recoil spring assembly; new Rough Textured Frame (RTF) surface designed to enhance grip traction.
Price: . . . . **N/A**

GLOCK 23/23C AUTO PISTOL
Caliber: 40 S&W, 13/15/17-shot magazines. **Barrel:** 4.02". **Weight:** 21.16 oz. (without magazine). **Length:** 6.85" overall. **Features:** Otherwise similar to Model 22, including pricing. Compact version of Glock 22. Imported from Austria by Glock, Inc. Introduced 1990.
Price: Fixed sight **$641.00**
Price: 23C Compensated (fixed sight) **$694.00**

GLOCK 26 AUTO PISTOL

Caliber: 9mm Para. 10/12/15/17/19/33-shot magazines. **Barrel:** 3.46". **Weight:** 19.75 oz. **Length:** 6.29" overall. Subcompact version of Glock 17. Pricing the same as Model 17. Imported from Austria by Glock, Inc.
Price: Fixed sight **$690.00**

GLOCK 27 AUTO PISTOL

Caliber: 40 S&W, 9/11/13/15/17-shot magazines. **Barrel:** 3.46". **Weight:** 19.75 oz. (without magazine). **Length:** 6.29" overall. **Features:** Otherwise similar to Model 22, including pricing. Subcompact version of Glock 22. Imported from Austria by Glock, Inc. Introduced 1996.
Price: Fixed sight **$750.00**

GLOCK 29 AUTO PISTOL

Caliber: 10mm, 10/15-shot magazines. **Barrel:** 3.78". **Weight:** 24.69 oz. (without magazine). **Length:** 6.77" overall. **Features:** Otherwise similar to Model 20, including pricing. Subcompact version of Glock 20. Imported from Austria by Glock, Inc. Introduced 1997.
Price: Fixed sight **$672.00**

GLOCK MODEL 29 SF SHORT FRAME PISTOL

Caliber: 10mm. **Barrel:** 3.78" with hexagonal rifling. **Weight:** 24.52 oz. **Length:** 6.97" overall. **Sights:** Fixed. **Features:** Otherwise similar to Model 29 but with short-frame design, extended sight radius.
Price: **$660.00**

GLOCK 30 AUTO PISTOL

Caliber: 45 ACP, 9/10/13-shot magazines. **Barrel:** 3.78". **Weight:** 23.99 oz. (without magazine). **Length:** 6.77" overall. **Features:** Otherwise similar to Model 21, including pricing. Subcompact version of Glock 21. Imported from Austria by Glock, Inc. Introduced 1997. SF version has tactical rail, octagonal rifled barrel with a 1:15.75 rate of twist, smaller diameter grip, 10-round magazine capacity. Introduced 2008.
Price: Fixed sight **$700.00**

GLOCK 31/31C AUTO PISTOL

Caliber: 357 Auto, 15/17-shot magazines. **Barrel:** 4.49". **Weight:** 23.28 oz. (without magazine). **Length:** 7.32" overall. **Features:** Otherwise similar to Model 17. Imported from Austria by Glock, Inc.
Price: Fixed sight, from **$641.00**

GLOCK 32/32C AUTO PISTOL

Caliber: 357 Auto, 13/15/17-shot magazines. **Barrel:** 4.02". **Weight:** 21.52 oz. (without magazine). **Length:** 6.85" overall. **Features:** Otherwise similar to Model 31. Compact. Imported from Austria by Glock, Inc.
Price: Fixed sight **$669.00**

GLOCK 33 AUTO PISTOL

Caliber: 357 Auto, 9/11/13/15/17-shot magazines. **Barrel:** 3.46". **Weight:** 19.75 oz. (without magazine). **Length:** 6.29" overall. **Features:** Otherwise similar to Model 31. Subcompact. Imported from Austria by Glock, Inc.
Price: Fixed sight, from **$641.00**

GLOCK 34 AUTO PISTOL

Caliber: 9mm Para. 17/19/33-shot magazines. **Barrel:** 5.32". **Weight:** 22.9 oz. **Length:** 8.15" overall. Competition version of Glock 17 with extended barrel, slide, and sight radius dimensions. Imported from Austria by Glock, Inc.
Price: Adjustable sight, from **$648.00**

GLOCK 35 AUTO PISTOL

Caliber: 40 S&W, 15/17-shot magazines. **Barrel:** 5.32". **Weight:** 24.52 oz. (without magazine). **Length:** 8.15" overall. **Features:** Otherwise similar to Model 22. Competition version of Glock 22 with extended barrel, slide, and sight radius dimensions. Imported from Austria by Glock, Inc. Introduced 1996.
Price: Adjustable sight **$648.00**

GLOCK 36 AUTO PISTOL

Caliber: 45 ACP, 6-shot magazines. **Barrel:** 3.78". **Weight:** 20.11 oz. (without magazine). **Length:** 6.77" overall. **Features:** Single-stack magazine, slimmer grip than Glock 21/30. Subcompact. Imported from Austria by Glock, Inc. Introduced 1997.
Price: Adjustable sight **$616.00**

GLOCK 37 AUTO PISTOL

Caliber: 45 GAP, 10-shot magazines. **Barrel:** 4.49". **Weight:** 25.95 oz. (without magazine). **Length:** 7.32" overall. **Features:** Otherwise similar to Model 17. Imported from Austria by Glock, Inc. Introduced 2005.
Price: Fixed sight, from **$562.00**

GLOCK 38 AUTO PISTOL

Caliber: 45 GAP, 8/10-shot magazines. **Barrel:** 4.02". **Weight:** 24.16 oz. (without magazine). **Length:** 6.85" overall. **Features:** Otherwise similar to Model 37. Compact. Imported from Austria by Glock, Inc.
Price: Fixed sight **$614.00**

GLOCK 39 AUTO PISTOL

Caliber: 45 GAP, 6/8/10-shot magazines. **Barrel:** 3.46". **Weight:** 19.33 oz. (without magazine). **Length:** 6.3" overall. **Features:** Otherwise similar to Model 37. Subcompact. Imported from Austria by Glock, Inc.
Price: Fixed sight .. **$614.00**

GLOCK MODEL G17/G22/G19/G23 RTF

Similar to Models G17, G22, G19 and G23 but with rough textured frame.
Price: .... **N/A**

HECKLER & KOCH USP AUTO PISTOL

Caliber: 9mm Para., 15-shot magazine; 40 S&W, 13-shot magazine; 45 ACP, 12-shot magazine. **Barrel:** 4.25-4.41". **Weight:** 1.65 lbs. **Length:** 7.64-7.87" overall. **Grips:** Non-slip stippled black polymer. **Sights:** Blade front, rear adjustable for windage. **Features:** New HK design with polymer frame, modified Browning action with recoil reduction system, single control lever. Special "hostile environment" finish on all metal parts. Available in SA/DA, DAO, left- and right-hand versions. Introduced 1993. 45 ACP Introduced 1995. Imported from Germany by Heckler & Koch, Inc.
Price: USP 45 ....**$919.00**
Price: USP 40 and USP 9mm **$859.00**

HECKLER & KOCH USP COMPACT AUTO PISTOL

Caliber: 9mm Para., 13-shot magazine; 40 S&W and .357 SIG, 12-shot magazine; 45 ACP, 8-shot magazine. Similar to the USP except the 9mm Para., 357 SIG, and 40 S&W have 3.58" barrels, measure

Prices given are believed to be accurate at time of publication however, many factors affect retail pricing so exact prices are not possible.

6.81" overall, and weigh 1.47 lbs. (9mm Para.). Introduced 1996. 45 ACP measures 7.09" overall. Introduced 1998. Imported from Germany by Heckler & Koch, Inc.
Price: USP Compact 45 . . . . . **$959.00**
Price: USP Compact 9mm Para., 40 S&W **$879.00**

HECKLER & KOCH USP45 TACTICAL PISTOL
Caliber: 40 S&W, 13-shot magazine; 45 ACP, 12-shot magazine. **Barrel:** 4.90-5.09". **Weight:** 1.9 lbs. **Length:** 8.64" overall. **Grips:** Non-slip stippled polymer. **Sights:** Blade front, fully adjustable target rear. **Features:** Has extended threaded barrel with rubber O-ring; adjustable trigger; extended magazine floorplate; adjustable trigger stop; polymer frame. Introduced 1998. Imported from Germany by Heckler & Koch, Inc.
Price: USP Tactical 45 . . . . **$1,239.00**
Price: USP Tactical 40 . . . . **$1,179.00**

HECKLER & KOCH USP COMPACT TACTICAL PISTOL
Caliber: 45 ACP, 8-shot magazine. Similar to the USP Tactical except measures 7.72" overall, weighs 1.72 lbs. Introduced 2006. Imported from Germany by Heckler & Koch, Inc.
Price: USP Compact Tactical **$1,179.00**

HECKLER & KOCH MARK 23 SPECIAL OPERATIONS PISTOL
Caliber: 45 ACP, 12-shot magazine. **Barrel:** 5.87". **Weight:** 2.42 lbs. **Length:** 9.65" overall. **Grips:** Integral with frame; black polymer. **Sights:** Blade front, rear drift adjustable for windage; 3-dot. **Features:** Civilian version of the SOCOM pistol. Polymer frame; double action; exposed hammer; short recoil, modified Browning action. Introduced 1996. Imported from Germany by Heckler & Koch, Inc.
Price: **$2,139.00**

HECKLER & KOCH P2000 AUTO PISTOL
Caliber: 9mm Para., 13-shot magazine; 40 S&W and .357 SIG, 12-shot magazine. **Barrel:** 3.62". **Weight:** 1.5 lbs. **Length:** 7" overall. **Grips:** Interchangeable panels. **Sights:** Fixed Patridge style, drift adjustable for windage, standard 3-dot. **Features:** Incorporates features of HK USP Compact pistol, including Law Enforcement Modification (LEM) trigger, double-action hammer system, ambidextrous magazine release, dual slide-release levers, accessory mounting rails, recurved, hook trigger guard, fiber-reinforced polymer frame, modular grip with exchangeable back straps, nitro-carburized finish, lock-out safety device. Introduced 2003. Imported from Germany by Heckler & Koch, Inc.
Price: **$879.00**
Price: P2000 LEM DAO, 357 SIG, intr. 2006 . . . . **$879.00**
Price: P2000 SA/DA, 357 SIG, intr. 2006 . . . . **$879.00**

HECKLER & KOCH P2000 SK AUTO PISTOL
Caliber: 9mm Para., 10-shot magazine; 40 S&W and .357 SIG, 9-shot magazine. **Barrel:** 3.27". **Weight:** 1.3 lbs. **Length:** 6.42"

overall. **Sights:** Fixed Patridge style, drift adjustable. **Features:** Standard accessory rails, ambidextrous slide release, polymer frame, polygonal bore profile. Smaller version of P2000. Introduced 2005. Imported from Germany by Heckler & Koch, Inc.
Price: **$919.00**

HI-POINT FIREARMS MODEL 9MM COMPACT PISTOL
Caliber: 9mm Para., 8-shot magazine. **Barrel:** 3.5". **Weight:** 25 oz. **Length:** 6.75" overall. **Grips:** Textured plastic. **Sights:** Combat-style adjustable 3-dot system; low profile. **Features:** Single-action design; frame-mounted magazine release; polymer frame. Scratch-resistant matte finish. Introduced 1993. Comps are similar except they have a 4" barrel with muzzle brake/compensator. Compensator is slotted for laser or flashlight mounting. Introduced 1998. Made in U.S.A. by MKS Supply, Inc.
Price: C-9 9mm **$155.00**

Hi-Point Firearms Model 380 Polymer Pistol
Similar to the 9mm Compact model except chambered for 380 ACP, 8-shot magazine, adjustable 3-dot sights. Weighs 25 oz. Polymer frame. Action locks open after last shot. Includes 10-shot and 8-shot magazine; trigger lock. Introduced 1998. Comps are similar except they have a 4" barrel with muzzle compensator. Introduced 2001. Made in U.S.A. by MKS Supply, Inc.
Price: CF-380 . . . . **$135.00**

HI-POINT FIREARMS 40SW/POLY AND 45 AUTO PISTOLS
Caliber: 40 S&W, 8-shot magazine; 45 ACP (9-shot). **Barrel:** 4.5". **Weight:** 32 oz. **Length:** 7.72" overall. **Sights:** Adjustable 3-dot. **Features:** Polymer frames, last round lock-open, grip mounted magazine release, magazine disconnect safety, integrated accessory rail, trigger lock. Introduced 2002. Made in U.S.A. by MKS Supply, Inc.
Price: 40SW-B **$186.00**
Price: 45 ACP **$186.00**

HIGH STANDARD VICTOR 22 PISTOL
Caliber: 22 Long Rifle (10 rounds) or .22 Short (5 rounds). **Barrel:** 4.5"-5.5". **Weight:** 45 oz.-46 oz. **Length:** 8.5"-9.5" overall. **Grips:** Freestyle wood. **Sights:** Frame mounted, adjustable. **Features:** Semi-auto with drilled and tapped barrel, tu-tone or blued finish.
Price: **$845.00**

High Standard 10X Custom 22 Pistol
Similar to the Victor model but with precision fitting, black wood grips, 5.5" barrel only. High Standard Universal Mount, 10-shot magazine, barrel drilled and tapped, certificate of authenticity. Overall length is 9.5". Weighs 44 oz. to 46 oz. From High Standard Custom Shop.
Price: **$1,095.00**

HIGH STANDARD SUPERMATIC TROPHY 22 PISTOL
Caliber: 22 Long Rifle (10 rounds) or .22 Short (5 rounds/Citation version), not interchangable. **Barrel:** 5.5", 7.25". **Weight:** 44 oz., 46 oz. **Length:** 9.5", 11.25" overall. **Grips:** Wood. **Sights:** Adjustable. **Features:** Semi-auto with drilled and tapped barrel, tu-tone or blued finish with gold accents.
Price: 5.5" **$845.00**

High Standard Olympic Military 22 Pistol
Similar to the Supermatic Trophy model but in 22 Short only with 5.5" bull barrel, five-round magazine, aluminum alloy frame, adjustable sights. Overall length is 9.5", weighs 42 oz.
Price: **$875.00**

High Standard Supermatic Citation Series 22 Pistol
Similar to the Supermatic Trophy model but with heavier trigger pull, 10" barrel, and nickel accents. 22 Short conversion unit available. Overall length 14.5", weighs 52 oz.
Price: **$895.00**

HIGH STANDARD SUPERMATIC TOURNAMENT 22 PISTOL
Caliber: 22 LR. **Barrel:** 5.5" bull barrel. **Weight:** 44 oz. **Length:** 9.5" overall. **Features:** Limited edition; similar to High Standard Victor

model but with rear sight mounted directly to slide.
Price: **$835.00**

HIGH STANDARD SPORT KING 22 PISTOL
Caliber: 22 LR. **Barrel:** 4.5" or 6.75" tapered barrel. **Weight:** 40 oz. to 42 oz. **Length:** 8.5" to 10.75". **Features:** Sport version of High Standard Supermatic. Two-tone finish, fixed sights.
Price: **$725.00**

HI-STANDARD SPACE GUN
Semiauto pistol chambered in .22 LR. Recreation of famed competition "Space Gun" from 1960s. Features include 6.75- 8- or 10-inch barrel; 10-round magazine; adjustable sights; barrel weight; adjustable muzzle brake; blue-black finish with gold highlights.
Price: **$1095.00**

KAHR K SERIES AUTO PISTOLS
Caliber: K9: 9mm Para., 7-shot; K40: 40 S&W, 6-shot magazine. **Barrel:** 3.5". **Weight:** 25 oz. **Length:** 6" overall. **Grips:** Wraparound textured soft polymer. **Sights:** Blade front, rear drift adjustable for windage; bar-dot combat style. **Features:** Trigger-cocking double-action mechanism with passive firing pin block. Made of 4140 ordnance steel with matte black finish. Contact maker for complete price list. Introduced 1994. Made in U.S.A. by Kahr Arms.
Price: K9093C K9, matte stainless steel **$855.00**
Price: K9093NC K9, matte stainless steel w/tritium
  night sights **$985.00**
Price: K9094C K9 matte blackened stainless steel **$891.00**
Price: K9098 K9 Elite 2003, stainless steel **$932.00**
Price: K4043 K40, matte stainless steel **$855.00**
Price: K4043N K40, matte stainless steel w/tritium
  night sights **$985.00**
Price: K4044 K40, matte blackened stainless steel **$891.00**
Price: K4048 K40 Elite 2003, stainless steel **$932.00**

Kahr MK Series Micro Pistols
Similar to the K9/K40 except is 5.35" overall, 4" high, with a 3.08" barrel. Weighs 23.1 oz. Has snag-free bar-dot sights, polished feed ramp, dual recoil spring system, DA-only trigger. Comes with 5-round flush baseplate and 6-shot grip extension magazine. Introduced 1998. Made in U.S.A. by Kahr Arms.
Price: M9093 MK9, matte stainless steel . . **$855.00**
Price: M9093N MK9, matte stainless steel, tritium
  night sights **$958.00**
Price: M9098 MK9 Elite 2003, stainless steel **$932.00**
Price: M4043 MK40, matte stainless steel **$855.00**
Price: M4043N MK40, matte stainless steel, tritium
  night sights **$958.00**
Price: M4048 MK40 Elite 2003, stainless steel **$932.00**

KAHR P SERIES PISTOLS
Caliber: 380 ACP, 9x19, 40 S&W, 45 ACP. Similar to K9/K40 steel frame pistol except has polymer frame, matte stainless steel slide. Barrel length 3.5"; overall length 5.8"; weighs 17 oz. Includes two 7-shot magazines, hard polymer case, trigger lock. Introduced 2000. Made in U.S.A. by Kahr Arms.
Price: KP9093 9mm Para. **$739.00**
Price: KP4043 40 S&W **$739.00**
Price: KP4543 45 ACP **$805.00**
Price: KP3833 380 ACP (2008) **$649.00**

KAHR PM SERIES PISTOLS
Caliber: 9x19, 40 S&W, 45 ACP. Similar to P-Series pistols except has smaller polymer frame (Polymer Micro). Barrel length 3.08"; overall length 5.35"; weighs 17 oz. Includes two 7-shot magazines, hard polymer case, trigger lock. Introduced 2000. Made in U.S.A. by Kahr Arms.
Price: PM9093 PM9 . . . . **$786.00**
Price: PM4043 PM40 . . . . **$786.00**
Price: PM4543 (2007) **$855.00**

KAHR T SERIES PISTOLS
Caliber: T9: 9mm Para., 8-shot magazine; T40: 40 S&W, 7-shot magazine. **Barrel:** 4". **Weight:** 28.1-29.1 oz. **Length:** 6.5" overall. **Grips:** Checkered Hogue Pau Ferro wood grips. **Sights:** Rear: Novak low profile 2-dot tritium night sight, front tritium night sight. **Features:** Similar to other Kahr makes, but with longer slide and barrel upper, longer butt. Trigger cocking DAO; lock breech; "Browning-type" recoil lug; passive striker block; no magazine disconnect. Comes with two magazines. Introduced 2004. Made in U.S.A. by Kahr Arms.
Price: KT9093 T9 matte stainless steel **$831.00**
Price: KT9093-NOVAK T9, "Tactical 9," Novak night sight . . . **$968.00**
Price: KT4043 40 S&W **$831.00**

KAHR TP SERIES PISTOLS
Caliber: TP9: 9mm Para., 7-shot magazine; TP40: 40 S&W, 6-shot magazine. Barrel: 4". **Weight:** 19.1-20.1 oz. **Length:** 6.5-6.7" overall. **Grips:** Textured polymer. Similar to T-series guns, but with polymer frame, matte stainless slide. Comes with two magazines. TP40s introduced 2006. Made in U.S.A. by Kahr Arms.
Price: TP9093 TP9 . . . . **$697.00**
Price: TP9093-Novak TP9
  (Novak night sights) **$838.00**
Price: TP4043 TP40 . . . . **$697.00**
Price: TP4043-Novak (Novak night sights) . **$838.00**
Price: TP4543 (2007) **$697.00**
Price: TP4543-Novak (4.04 barrel, Novak night sights) **$838.00**

KAHR CW SERIES PISTOL
Caliber: 9mm Para., 7-shot magazine; 40 S&W and 45 ACP, 6-shot magazine. **Barrel:** 3.5-3.64". **Weight:** 17.7-18.7 oz. **Length:** 5.9-6.36" overall. **Grips:** Textured polymer. Similar to P-Series, but CW Series have conventional rifling, metal-injection-molded slide stop lever, no front dovetail cut, one magazine. CW40 introduced 2006. Made in U.S.A. by Kahr Arms.
Price: CW9093 CW9 . . . . **$549.00**
Price: CW4043 CW40 . . . . **$549.00**
Price: CW4543 45 ACP (2008) **$606.00**

KAHR P380

Very small double action only semiauto pistol chambered in .380 ACP. Features include 2.5-inch Lothar Walther barrel; black polymer frame with stainless steel slide; drift adjustable white bar/dot combat/sights; optional tritium sights; two 6+1 magazines. Overall length 4.9 inches, weight 10 oz. without magazine.
Price: Standard sights **$649.00**

KEL-TEC P-11 AUTO PISTOL

Caliber: 9mm Para., 10-shot magazine. **Barrel:** 3.1". **Weight:** 14 oz. **Length:** 5.6" overall. **Grips:** Checkered black polymer. **Sights:** Blade front, rear adjustable for windage. **Features:** Ordnance steel slide, aluminum frame. Double-action-only trigger mechanism. Introduced 1995. Made in U.S.A. by Kel-Tec CNC Industries, Inc.
Price: **$333.00**

KEL-TEC PF-9 PISTOL

Caliber: 9mm Para.; 7 rounds. **Weight:** 12.7 oz. **Sights:** Rear sight adjustable for windage and elevation. **Barrel Length:** 3.1". **Length:** 5.85". **Features:** Barrel, locking system, slide stop, assembly pin, front sight, recoil springs and guide rod adapted from P-11. Trigger system with integral hammer block and the extraction system adapted from P-3AT. MIL-STD-1913 Picatinny rail. Made in U.S.A. by Kel-Tec CNC Industries, Inc.
Price: From **$333.00**

KEL-TEC P-32 AUTO PISTOL

Caliber: 32 ACP, 7-shot magazine. **Barrel:** 2.68". **Weight:** 6.6 oz. **Length:** 5.07" overall. **Grips:** Checkered composite. **Sights:** Fixed. **Features:** Double-action-only mechanism with 6-lb. pull; internal slide stop. Textured composite grip/frame. Now available in 380 ACP. Made in U.S.A. by Kel-Tec CNC Industries, Inc.
Price: From **$318.00**

KEL-TEC P-3AT PISTOL

Caliber: 380 ACP; 7-rounds. **Weight:** 7.2 oz. **Length:** 5.2". **Features:** Lightest 380 ACP made; aluminum frame, steel barrel.
Price: From **$324.00**

KEL-TEC PLR-16 PISTOL

Caliber: 5.56mm NATO; 10-round magazine. **Weight:** 51 oz. **Sights:** Rear sight adjustable for windage, front sight is M-16 blade. **Barrel Length:** 9.2". **Length:** 18.5". **Features:** Muzzle is threaded 1/2"-28 to accept standard attachments such as a muzzle brake. Except for the barrel, bolt, sights, and mechanism, the PLR-16 pistol is made of high-impact glass fiber reinforced polymer. Gas-operated semi-auto. Conventional gas-piston operation with M-16 breech locking system. MIL-STD-1913 Picatinny rail. Made in U.S.A. by Kel-Tec CNC Industries, Inc.
Price: Blued **$665.00**

Kel-Tec PLR-22 Pistol

Semi-auto pistol chambered in 22 LR; based on centerfire PLR-16 by same maker. Blowback action, 26-round magazine. Open sights and picatinny rail for mounting accessories; threaded muzzle. Overall length is 18.5", weighs 40 oz.
Price: **$390.00**

KIMBER CUSTOM II AUTO PISTOL

Caliber: 45 ACP. **Barrel:** 5". **Weight:** 38 oz. **Length:** 8.7" overall. **Grips:** Checkered black rubber, walnut, rosewood. **Sights:** Dovetailed front and rear, Kimber low profile adj. or fixed sights. **Features:** Slide, frame and barrel machined from steel or stainless steel. Match grade barrel, chamber and trigger group. Extended thumb safety, beveled magazine well, beveled front and rear slide serrations, high ride beavertail grip safety, checkered flat mainspring housing, kidney cut under trigger guard, high cut grip, match grade stainless steel barrel bushing, polished breech face, Commander-style hammer, lowered and flared ejection port, Wolff springs, bead blasted black oxide or matte stainless finish. Introduced in 1996. Made in U.S.A. by Kimber Mfg., Inc.
Price: Custom II **$828.00**
Price: Custom II Walnut (double-diamond walnut grips) **$872.00**

Kimber Stainless II Auto Pistols

Similar to Custom II except has stainless steel frame. 9mm Para. chambering and 45 ACP with night sights introduced 2008. Also chambered in 38 Super. Target version also chambered in 10mm.
Price: Stainless II 45 ACP **$964.00**
Price: Stainless II 9mm Para. (2008) **$983.00**
Price: Stainless II 45 ACP w/night sights (2008) **$1,092.00**
Price: Stainless II Target 45 ACP (stainless, adj. sight) **$942.00**

Kimber Pro Carry II Auto Pistol

Similar to Custom II, has aluminum frame, 4" bull barrel fitted directly to the slide without bushing. Introduced 1998. Made in U.S.A. by Kimber Mfg., Inc.
Price: Pro Carry II, 45 ACP **$888.00**
Price: Pro Carry II, 9mm **$929.00**
Price: Pro Carry II w/night sights **$997.00**

Kimber Compact Stainless II Auto Pistol

Similar to Pro Carry II except has stainless steel frame, 4-inch bbl., grip is .400" shorter than standard, no front serrations. Weighs 34 oz. 45 ACP only. Introduced in 1998. Made in U.S.A. by Kimber Mfg., Inc.
Price: **$1,009.00**

Kimber Ultra Carry II Auto Pistol

Lightweight aluminum frame, 3" match grade bull barrel fitted to slide without bushing. Grips .4" shorter. Low effort recoil. Weighs 25 oz. Introduced in 1999. Made in U.S.A. by Kimber Mfg., Inc.
Price: Stainless Ultra Carry II 45 ACP . . . **$980.00**
Price: Stainless Ultra Carry II 9mm Para. (2008) **$1,021.00**
Price: Stainless Ultra Carry II 45 ACP with night sights (2008) **$1,089.00**

Kimber Gold Match II Auto Pistol

Similar to Custom II models. Includes stainless steel barrel with match grade chamber and barrel bushing, ambidextrous thumb safety, adjustable sight, premium aluminum trigger, hand-checkered double diamond rosewood grips. Barrel hand-fitted for target accuracy. Made in U.S.A. by Kimber Mfg., Inc.
Price: Gold Match II **$1,345.00**
Price: Gold Match Stainless II 45 ACP **$1,519.00**
Price: Gold Match Stainless II 9mm Para. (2008) **$1,563.00**

Kimber Team Match II Auto Pistol

Similar to Gold Match II. Identical to pistol used by U.S.A. Shooting Rapid Fire Pistol Team, available in 45 ACP and 38 Super. Standard features include 30 lines-per-inch front strap extended and beveled magazine well, red, white and blue Team logo grips. Introduced 2008.

Price: 45 ACP **$1,539.00**
Price: 9mm $1,546.00

Kimber CDP II Series Auto Pistol

Similar to Custom II, but designed for concealed carry. Aluminum frame. Standard features include stainless steel slide, fixed Meprolight tritium 3-dot (green) dovetail-mounted night sights, match grade barrel and chamber, 30 LPI front strap checkering, two-tone finish, ambidextrous thumb safety, hand-checkered double diamond rosewood grips. Introduced in 2000. Made in U.S.A. by Kimber Mfg., Inc.

Price: Ultra CDP II 9mm Para. (2008) **$1,359.00**
Price: Ultra CDP II 45 ACP **$1,318.00**
Price: Compact CDP II 45 ACP **$1,318.00**
Price: Pro CDP II 45 ACP. **$1,318.00**
Price: Custom CDP II (5" barrel, full length grip) **$1,318.00**

Kimber Eclipse II Series Auto Pistol

Similar to Custom II and other stainless Kimber pistols. Stainless slide and frame, black oxide, two-tone finish. Gray/black laminated grips. 30 lpi front strap checkering. All models have night sights; Target versions have Meprolight adjustable Bar/Dot version. Made in U.S.A. by Kimber Mfg., Inc.

Price: Eclipse Ultra II (3" barrel, short grip) **$1,236.00**
Price: Eclipse Pro II (4" barrel, full length grip) **$1,236.00**
Price: Eclipse Pro Target II (4" barrel, full length grip, adjustable sight) **$1,236.00**
Price: Eclipse Custom II 10mm **$1,291.00**
Price: Eclipse Target II (5" barrel, full length grip, adjustable sight) **$1,345.00**

KIMBER TACTICAL ENTRY II PISTOL

Caliber: 45 ACP, 7-round magazine. **Barrel:** 5". **Weight:** 40 oz. **Length:** 8.7" overall. **Features:** 1911-style semi auto with checkered frontstrap, extended magazine well, night sights, heavy steel frame, tactical rail.
Price: **$1,428.00**

KIMBER TACTICAL CUSTOM HD II PISTOL

Caliber: 45 ACP, 7-round magazine. **Barrel:** 5" match-grade. **Weight:** 39 oz. **Length:** 8.7" overall. **Features:** 1911-style semi auto with night sights, heavy steel frame.
Price: **$1,333.00**

KIMBER SIS AUTO PISTOL

Caliber: 45 ACP, 7-round magazine. **Barrel:** 3", ramped match grade. **Weight:** 31 oz. **Grips:** Stippled black laminate logo grips. **Sights:** SIS fixed tritium Night Sight with cocking shoulder. **Features:** Named for LAPD Special Investigation Section. Stainless-steel slides, frames and serrated mainspring housings. Flat top slide, solid trigger, SIS-pattern slide serrations, gray KimPro II finish, black small parts. Bumped and grooved beavertail grip safety, Kimber Service Melt on slide and frame edges, ambidextrous thumb safety, stainless steel KimPro Tac-Mag magazine. Rounded mainspring housing and frame on Ultra version. Introduced 2007. Made in U.S.A. by Kimber Mfg., Inc.

Price: SIS Ultra (2008) **$1,427.00**
Price: SIS Pro (2008) **$1,427.00**
Price: SIS Custom **$1,427.00**
Price: Custom/RL **$1,522.00**

KIMBER SUPER CARRY PRO

1911-syle semiauto pistol chambered in .45 ACP. Features include 8-round magazine; ambidextrous thumb safety; carry melt profiling; full length guide rod; aluminum frame with stainless slide; satin silver finish; super carry serrations; 4-inch barrel; micarta laminated grips; tritium night sights.
Price: **$1,530.00**

KIMBER CENTENNIAL EDITION 1911

Highly artistic 1911-style semiauto pistol chambered in .45 ACP. Features include color case-hardened steel frame; extended thumb safety; charcoal-blue finished steel slide; 5-inch match grade barrel; special serial number; solid smooth ivory grips; nitre blue pins; adjustable sights; presentation case. Edition limited to 250 units. Finished by Doug Turnbull Restoration.
Price: **$4,352.00**

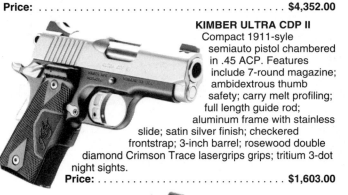

KIMBER ULTRA CDP II

Compact 1911-syle semiauto pistol chambered in .45 ACP. Features include 7-round magazine; ambidextrous thumb safety; carry melt profiling; full length guide rod; aluminum frame with stainless slide; satin silver finish; checkered frontstrap; 3-inch barrel; rosewood double diamond Crimson Trace lasergrips grips; tritium 3-dot night sights.
Price: **$1,603.00**

KIMBER STAINLESS ULTRA TLE II

1911-syle semiauto pistol chambered in .45 ACP. Features include 7-round magazine; full length guide rod; aluminum frame with stainless slide; satin silver finish; checkered frontstrap; 3-inch barrel; tactical gray double diamond grips; tritium 3-dot night sights.
Price: **$1,210.00**

KORTH USA PISTOL SEMI-AUTO

Caliber: 9mm Para., 9x21. **Barrel:** 4", 4.5". **Weight:** 39.9 oz. **Grips:** Walnut, Palisander, Amboinia, Ivory. **Sights:** Fully adjustable. **Features:** DA/SA, 2 models available with either rounded or combat-style trigger guard, recoil-operated, locking block system, forged steel. Available finishes: High polish blue plasma, high polish or matted silver plasma, gray pickled

finish, or high polish blue. "Schalldampfer Modell" has special threaded 4.5" barrel and thread protector for a suppressor, many deluxe options available, 10-shot mag. From Korth USA.

Price: From **$15,000.00**

MAGNUM RESEARCH MICRO DESERT EAGLE PISTOL

Double action only semiauto pistol chambered in .380. Features include steel slide, aluminum allow frame, black polymer grips, nickel silver or blue anodized frame, 6-round capacity, fixed sights, 2.2-inch barrel. Weight less than 14 oz.

Price: **$535.00**

MAGNUM RESEARCH DESERT EAGLE MAGNUM PISTOL

Enormous gas-operated semiauto pistol chambered in .50 AE, .44 Magnum, .357 Magnum. Features include 6- or 10-inch barrel, adjustable sights, variety of finishes. Now made in the USA.

Price: . . . . **$1,650.00 to $2,156.00.**

MOSSBERG INTERNATIONAL MODELS 702 AND 802 PLINKSTER PISTOLS

Semiauto (702) or bolt action (802) pistols chambered in .22 LR. Features include black synthetic or laminated wood stock, 10-inch blued barrel, ergonomic grips, 10-shot detachable box magazine.

Price: . . . . **N/A**

NORTH AMERICAN ARMS GUARDIAN DAO PISTOL

Caliber: 25 NAA, 32 ACP, 380 ACP, 32 NAA, 6-shot magazine. **Barrel:** 2.49". **Weight:** 20.8 oz. **Length:** 4.75" overall. **Grips:** Black polymer. **Sights:** Low profile fixed. **Features:** Double-action only mechanism. All stainless steel construction. Introduced 1998. Made in U.S.A. by North American Arms.

Price: From **$402.00**

OLYMPIC ARMS MATCHMASTER 5 1911 PISTOL

Caliber: 45 ACP, 7-shot magazine. **Barrel:** 5" stainless steel. **Weight:** 40 oz. **Length:** 8.75" overall. **Grips:** Smooth walnut with laser-etched scorpion icon. **Sights:** Ramped blade, LPA adjustable rear. **Features:** Matched frame and slide, fitted and head-spaced barrel, complete ramp and throat jobs, lowered and widened

ejection port, beveled mag well, hand-stoned-to-match hammer and sear, lightweight long-shoe over-travel adjusted trigger, shaped and tensioned extractor, extended thumb safety, wide beavertail grip safety and full-length guide rod. Made in U.S.A. by Olympic Arms, Inc.

Price: **$903.00**

OLYMPIC ARMS MATCHMASTER 6 1911 PISTOL

Caliber: 45 ACP, 7-shot magazine. **Barrel:** 6" stainless steel. **Weight:** 44 oz. **Length:** 9.75" overall. **Grips:** Smooth walnut with laser-etched scorpion icon. **Sights:** Ramped blade, LPA adjustable rear. **Features:** Matched frame and slide, fitted and head-spaced barrel, complete ramp and throat jobs, lowered and widened ejection port, beveled mag well, hand-stoned-to-match hammer and sear, lightweight long-shoe over-travel adjusted trigger, shaped and tensioned extractor, extended thumb safety, wide beavertail grip safety and full length guide rod. Made in U.S.A. by Olympic Arms, Inc.

Price: **$973.00**

OLYMPIC ARMS ENFORCER 1911 PISTOL

Caliber: 45 ACP, 6-shot magazine. **Barrel:** 4" bull stainless steel. **Weight:** 35 oz. **Length:** 7.75" overall. **Grips:** Smooth walnut with etched black widow spider icon. **Sights:** Ramped blade front, LPA adjustable rear. **Features:** Compact Enforcer frame. Bushingless bull barrel with triplex counter-wound self-contained recoil system. Matched frame and slide, fitted and head-spaced barrel, complete ramp and throat jobs, lowered and widened ejection port, beveled mag well, hand-stoned-to-match hammer and sear, lightweight longshoe over-travel adjusted trigger, shaped and tensioned extractor, extended thumb safety, wide beavertail grip safety and full length guide rod. Made in U.S.A. by Olympic Arms.

Price: **$1,033.50**

OLYMPIC ARMS COHORT PISTOL

Caliber: 45 ACP, 7-shot magazine. **Barrel:** 4" bull stainless steel. **Weight:** 36 oz. **Length:** 7.75" overall. **Grips:** Fully checkered walnut. **Sights:** Ramped blade front, LPA adjustable rear. **Features:** Full size 1911 frame. Bushingless bull barrel with triplex counter-wound self-contained recoil system. Matched frame and slide, fitted and head-spaced barrel, complete ramp and throat jobs, lowered and widened ejection port, beveled mag well, hand-stoned-to-match hammer and sear, lightweight long-shoe over-travel adjusted trigger, shaped and tensioned extractor, extended thumb safety, wide beavertail grip safety and full length guide rod. Made in U.S.A. by Olympic Arms.

Price: **$973.70**

OLYMPIC ARMS BIG DEUCE PISTOL

Caliber: 45 ACP, 7-shot magazine. **Barrel:** 6" stainless steel. **Weight:** 44 oz. **Length:** 9.75" overall. **Grips:** Double diamond checkered exotic cocobolo wood. **Sights:** Ramped blade front, LPA adjustable rear. **Features:** Carbon steel parkerized slide with satin bead blast finish full size frame. Matched frame and slide, fitted and head-spaced barrel, complete ramp and throat jobs, lowered and widened

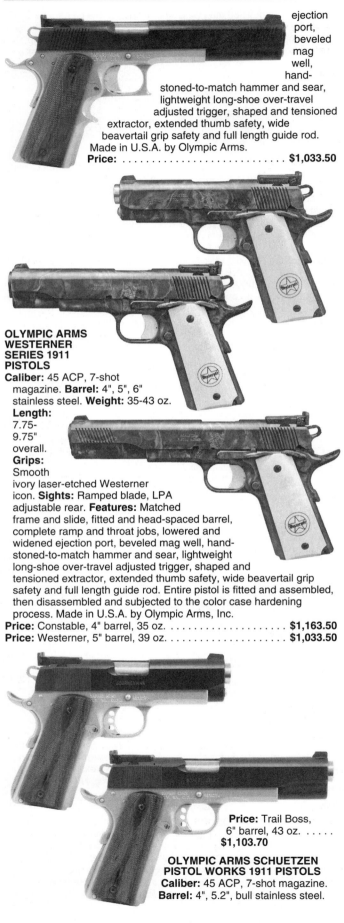

ejection port, beveled mag well, hand-stoned-to-match hammer and sear, lightweight long-shoe over-travel adjusted trigger, shaped and tensioned extractor, extended thumb safety, wide beavertail grip safety and full length guide rod. Made in U.S.A. by Olympic Arms.
Price: **$1,033.50**

OLYMPIC ARMS WESTERNER SERIES 1911 PISTOLS

Caliber: 45 ACP, 7-shot magazine. **Barrel:** 4", 5", 6" stainless steel. **Weight:** 35-43 oz. **Length:** 7.75-9.75" overall. **Grips:** Smooth ivory laser-etched Westerner icon. **Sights:** Ramped blade, LPA adjustable rear. **Features:** Matched frame and slide, fitted and head-spaced barrel, complete ramp and throat jobs, lowered and widened ejection port, beveled mag well, hand-stoned-to-match hammer and sear, lightweight long-shoe over-travel adjusted trigger, shaped and tensioned extractor, extended thumb safety, wide beavertail grip safety and full length guide rod. Entire pistol is fitted and assembled, then disassembled and subjected to the color case hardening process. Made in U.S.A. by Olympic Arms, Inc.
Price: Constable, 4" barrel, 35 oz. **$1,163.50**
Price: Westerner, 5" barrel, 39 oz. **$1,033.50**

Price: Trail Boss, 6" barrel, 43 oz. **$1,103.70**

OLYMPIC ARMS SCHUETZEN PISTOL WORKS 1911 PISTOLS

Caliber: 45 ACP, 7-shot magazine. **Barrel:** 4", 5.2", bull stainless steel.

Weight: 35-38 oz. **Length:** 7.75-8.75" overall. **Grips:** Double diamond checkered exotic cocobolo wood. **Sights:** Ramped blade, LPA adjustable rear. **Features:** Carbon steel parkerized slide with satin bead blast finish full size frame. Matched frame and slide, fitted and head-spaced barrel, complete ramp and throat jobs, lowered and widened ejection port, beveled mag well, hand-stoned-to-match hammer and sear, lightweight long-shoe over-travel adjusted trigger, shaped and tensioned extractor, extended thumb safety, wide beavertail grip safety and full length guide rod. Custom made by Olympic Arms Schuetzen Pistol Works. Parts are hand selected and fitted by expert pistolsmiths. Several no-cost options to choose from. Made in U.S.A. by Olympic Arms Schuetzen Pistol Works.
Price: Journeyman, 4" bull barrel, 35 oz. **$1,293.50**
Price: Street Deuce, 5.2" bull barrel, 38 oz. **$1,293.50**

OLYMPIC ARMS OA-93 AR PISTOL

Caliber: 5.56 NATO. **Barrel:** 6.5" button-rifled stainless steel. **Weight:** 4.46 lbs. **Length:** 17" overall. **Sights:** None. **Features:** Olympic Arms integrated recoil system on the upper receiver eliminates the buttstock, flat top upper, free floating tubular match handguard, threaded muzzle with flash suppressor. Made in U.S.A. by Olympic Arms, Inc.
Price: **$1,202.50**

OLYMPIC ARMS K23P AR PISTOL

Caliber: 5.56 NATO. **Barrel:** 6.5" button-rifled chrome-moly steel. **Length:** 22.25" overall. **Weight:** 5.12 lbs. **Sights:** Adjustable A2 rear, elevation adjustable front post. **Features:** A2 upper with rear sight, free floating tubular match handguard, threaded muzzle with flash suppressor, receiver extension tube with foam cover, no bayonet lug. Made in U.S.A. by Olympic Arms, Inc. Introduced 2007.
Price: **$973.70**

OLYMPIC ARMS K23P-A3-TC AR PISTOL

Caliber: 5.56 NATO. **Barrel:** 6.5" button-rifled chrome-moly steel. **Length:** 22.25" overall. **Weight:** 5.12 lbs. **Sights:** Adjustable A2 rear, elevation adjustable front post. **Features:** Flat-top upper with detachable carry handle, free floating FIRSH rail handguard, threaded muzzle with flash suppressor, receiver extension tube with foam cover, no bayonet lug. Made in U.S.A. by Olympic Arms, Inc. Introduced 2007.
Price: **$1,118.20**

OLYMPIC ARMS WHITNEY WOLVERINE PISTOL

Caliber: 22 LR, 10-shot magazine. **Barrel:** 4.625" stainless steel. **Weight:** 19.2 oz. **Length:** 9" overall. **Grips:** Black checkered with fire/safe markings. **Sights:** Ramped blade front, dovetail rear. **Features:** Polymer frame with natural ergonomics and ventilated rib. Barrel with 6-groove 1x16 twist rate. All metal magazine shell. Made in U.S.A. by Olympic Arms.
Price: **$291.00**

PARA USA PXT 1911 SINGLE-ACTION SINGLE-STACK AUTO PISTOLS

Caliber: 38 Super, 9mm Para., 45 ACP. **Barrel:** 3.5", 4.25", 5". **Weight:** 28-40 oz. **Length:** 7.1-8.5" overall. **Grips:** Checkered cocobolo, textured composition, Mother of Pearl synthetic. **Sights:** Blade front, low-profile Novak Extreme Duty adjustable rear. High visibility 3-dot system. **Features:** Available with alloy, steel or stainless steel frames. Skeletonized trigger, spurred hammer. Manual thumb, grip and firing pin lock safeties. Full-length guide rod. PXT designates new Para Power Extractor throughout the line. Introduced 2004. Made in U.S.A. by Para USA.
Price: 1911 SSP 9mm Para. (2008) **$959.00**
Price: 1911 SSP 45 ACP (2008) **$959.00**

Prices given are believed to be accurate at time of publication however, many factors affect retail pricing so exact pricing is not possible.

PARA USA PXT 1911 SINGLE-ACTION HIGH-CAPACITY AUTO PISTOLS

Caliber: 9mm Para., 45 ACP, 10/14/18-shot magazines. **Barrel:** 3", 5". **Weight:** 34-40 oz. **Length:** 7.1-8.5" overall. **Grips:** Textured composition. **Sights:** Blade front, low-profile Novak Extreme Duty adjustable rear or fixed sights. High visibility 3-dot system. **Features:** Available with alloy, steel or stainless steel frames. Skeletonized match trigger, spurred hammer, flared ejection port. Manual thumb, grip and firing pin lock safeties. Full-length guide rod. Introduced 2004. Made in U.S.A. by Para USA.
Price: PXT P14-45 Gun Rights (2008), 14+1, 5" barrel **$1,149.00**
Price: P14-45 (2008), 14+1, 5" barrel **$919.00**

Para USA PXT Limited Pistols
Similar to the PXT-Series pistols except with full-length recoil guide system; fully adjustable rear sight; tuned trigger with over-travel stop; beavertail grip safety; competition hammer; front and rear slide serrations; ambidextrous safety; lowered ejection port; ramped match-grade barrel; dove-tailed front sight. Introduced 2004. Made in U.S.A. by Para USA.
Price: Todd Jarrett 40 S&W, 16+1, stainless **$1,729.00**

Para USA LDA Single-Stack Auto Pistols
Similar to LDA-series with double-action trigger mechanism. Cocobolo and polymer grips. Available in 45 ACP. Introduced 1999. Made in U.S.A. by Para USA.
Price: SSP, 8+1, 5" barrel **$899.00**

Para USA LDA Hi-Capacity Auto Pistols
Similar to LDA-series with double-action trigger mechanism. Polymer grips. Available in 9mm Para., 40 S&W, 45 ACP. Introduced 1999. Made in U.S.A. by Para USA.
Price: High-Cap 45, 14+1 .... **$1,279.00**

PARA USA WARTHOG
Caliber: 9mm Para., 45 ACP, 6, 10, or 12-shot magazines. **Barrel:** 3". **Weight:** 24 to 31.5 oz. **Length:** 6.5". **Grips:** Varies by model. **Features:** Single action. Big Hawg (2008) is full-size .45 ACP on lightweight alloy frame, 14+1, match grade ramped barrel, Power extractor, three white-dot fixed sights. Made in U.S.A. by Para USA.
Price: Slim Hawg (2006) single stack .45 ACP, stainless, 6+1 .... **$1,099.00**

Price: Nite Hawg .45 ACP, black finish, 10+1 .... **$1,099.00**
Price: Warthog .45 ACP, Regal finish, 10+1 ....**$959.00**
Price: Warthog Stainless **$1,069.00**
Price: Big Hawg (2008)...........................**$959.00**

PHOENIX ARMS HP22, HP25 AUTO PISTOLS

Caliber: 22 LR, 10-shot (HP22), 25 ACP, 10-shot (HP25). **Barrel:** 3". **Weight:** 20 oz. **Length:** 5.5" overall. **Grips:** Checkered composition. **Sights:** Blade front, adjustable rear. **Features:** Single action, exposed hammer; manual hold-open; button magazine release. Available in satin nickel, matte blue finish. Introduced 1993. Made in U.S.A. by Phoenix Arms.
Price: With gun lock **$130.00**
Price: HP Range kit with 5" bbl., locking case and accessories (1 Mag) **$171.00**
Price: HP Deluxe Range kit with 3" and 5" bbls., 2 mags, case **$210.00**

PICUDA .17 MACH-2 GRAPHITE PISTOL

Caliber: 17 HM2, 22 LR, 10-shot magazine. **Barrel:** 10" graphite barrel, "French grey" anodizing. **Weight:** 3.2 pounds. **Length:** 20.5" overall. **Grips:** Barracuda nutmeg laminated pistol stock. **Sights:** None, integral scope base. **Features:** MLP-1722 receiver, target trigger, match bolt kit. Introduced 2008. Made in U.S.A. by Magnum Research, Inc.
Price: **$699.00**

ROCK RIVER ARMS BASIC CARRY AUTO PISTOL

Caliber: 45 ACP. **Barrel:** NA. **Weight:** NA. **Length:** NA. **Grips:** Rosewood, checkered. **Sights:** dovetail front sight, Heinie rear sight. **Features:** NM frame with 20-, 25- or 30-LPI checkered front strap, 5-inch slide with double serrations, lowered and flared ejection port, throated NM Kart barrel with NM bushing, match Commander hammer and match sear, aluminum speed trigger, dehorned, Parkerized finish, one magazine, accuracy guarantee. 3.5 lb. Trigger pull. Introduced 2006. RRA Service Auto 9mm has forged NM frame with beveled mag well, fixed target rear sight and dovetail front sight, KKM match 1:32 twist 9mm Para. barrel with supported ramp. Guaranteed to shoot 1-inch groups at 25 yards with quality 9mm Para. 115-124 grain match ammunition. Intr. 2008. Made in U.S.A. From Rock River Arms.
Price: Basic Carry PS2700 .... **$1,600.00**
Price: Limited Match PS2400 .... **$2,185.00**
Price: RRA Service Auto 9mm Para. PS2715 .... **$1,790.00**

ROCK RIVER ARMS LAR-15/LAR-9 PISTOLS

Caliber: .223/5.56mm NATO chamber 4-shot magazine. **Barrel:** 7", 10.5" Wilson chrome moly, 1:9 twist, A2 flash hider, 1/2-28 thread. **Weight:** 5.1 lbs. (7" barrel), 5.5 lbs. (10.5" barrel). **Length:** 23" overall. **Stock:** Hogue rubber grip. **Sights:** A2 front. **Features:** Forged A2 or A4 upper, single stage trigger, aluminum free-float tube, one magazine. Similar 9mm Para. LAR-9 also available. From Rock River Arms, Inc.
Price: LAR-15 7" A2 AR2115 ....**$955.00**
Price: LAR-15 10.5" A4 AR2120.....................**$945.00**
Price: LAR-9 7" A2 9MM2115.....................**$1,125.00**

ROHRBAUGH R9 SEMI-AUTO PISTOL

Caliber: 9mm Parabellum, 380 ACP. **Barrel:** 2.9". **Weight:** 12.8 oz. **Length:** 5.2" overall. **Features:** Very small double-action-only semi-auto pocket pistol. Stainless steel slide with matte black aluminum frame. Available with or without sights. Available with all-black (Stealth) and partial Diamond Black (Stealth Elite) finish.
Price: **$1,149.00**

RUGER SR9 AUTOLOADING PISTOL

Caliber: 9mm Para. **Barrel:** 4.14". **Weight:** 26.25, 26.5 oz. **Grips:** Glass-filled nylon in two color options—black or OD Green, w/flat or arched reversible backstrap. **Sights:** Adjustable 3-dot, built-in Picatinny-style rail. **Features:** Semi-DA, 6 configurations, striker-fired, through-hardened stainless steel slide, brushed or blackened stainless slide with black grip frame or blackened stainless slide with OD Green grip frame, ambi manual 1911-style safety, ambi mag release, mag disconnect, loaded chamber indicator, Ruger camblock

design to absorb recoil, two 10 or 17-shot mags. Intr. 2008. Made in U.S.A. by Sturm, Ruger & Co.
Price: SR9 (17-Round), SR9-10 (SS) **$525.00**
Price: KBSR9 (17-Round), KBSR9-10 (Blackened SS) **$565.00**
Price: KODBSR9 (17-Round), KODBSR9-10
(OD Green Grip) **$565.00**

RUGER SR9C COMPACT PISTOL

Compact double action only semiauto pistol chambered in 9mm Parabellum. Features include 1911-style ambidextrous manual safety; internal trigger bar interlock and striker blocker; trigger safety; magazine disconnector; loaded chamber indicator; two magazines, one 10-round and the other 17-round; 3.5-inch barrel; 3-dot sights; accessory rail; brushed stainless or blackened allow finish. Weight 23.40 oz.
Price: **$525.00**

RUGER LCP

Caliber: .380 ACP. **Barrel:** 2.75" **Weight:** 9.4 oz. **Grips:** Glass-filled nylon. **Sights:** Fixed. **Features:** SA, one configuration, ultra-light compact carry pistol in Ruger's smallest pistol frame, through-hardened stainless steel slide, blued finish, lock breach design, 6-shot mag. Intr. 2008. Made in U.S.A. by Sturm, Ruger & Co.
Price: LCP. **$347.00**

RUGER P90 MANUAL SAFETY MODEL AUTOLOADING PISTOL

Caliber: 45 ACP, 8-shot magazine. **Barrel:** 4.50". **Weight:** 33.5 oz. **Length:** 7.75" overall. **Grips:** Grooved black synthetic composition. **Sights:** Square post front, square notch rear adjustable for windage, both with white dot. **Features:** Double action; ambidextrous slide-mounted safety-levers. Stainless steel only. Introduced 1991.
Price: KP90 with extra mag, loader, case and gunlock **$617.00**
Price: P90 (blue) **$574.00**

Ruger KP944 Autoloading Pistol

Sized midway between full-size P-Series and compact KP94. 4.2" barrel, 7.5" overall length, weighs about 34 oz. KP94 manual safety model. Slide grip-ping grooves roll over top of slide. KP94 has ambidextrous safety-levers; Stainless slide, barrel, alloy frame. Also blue. Includes hard case and lock, spare magazine. Introduced 1994. Made in U.S.A. by Sturm, Ruger & Co.
Price: P944, blue, manual safety, .40 cal. . . .**$541.00**
Price: KP944 (40-caliber)
(manual safety-stainless) **$628.00**

RUGER P95 AUTOLOADING PISTOL

Caliber: 9mm, 15-shot magazine. **Barrel:** 3.9". **Weight:** 30 oz. **Length:** 7.25" overall. **Grips:** Grooved; integral with frame. **Sights:** Blade front, rear drift adjustable for windage; 3-dot system. **Features:** Molded polymer grip frame, stainless steel or chrome-moly slide. Suitable for +P+ ammunition. Safety model, decocker. Introduced 1996. Made in U.S.A. by Sturm, Ruger & Co. Comes

with lockable plastic case, spare magazine, loader and lock, Picatinny rails.
Price: KP95PR15 safety model, stainless steel **$424.00**
Price: P95PR15 safety model, blued finish **$395.00**
Price: P95PR 10-round model, blued finish **$393.00**
Price: KP95PR 10-round model, stainless steel **$424.00**

RUGER 22 CHARGER PISTOL

Caliber: .22 LR. **Barrel:** 10". **Weight:** 3.5 lbs (w/out bi-pod). **Stock:** Black Laminate. **Sights:** None. **Features:** Rimfire Autoloading, one configuration, 10/22 action, adjustable bi-pod, new mag release for easier removal, precision-rifled barrel, black matte finish, combination Weaver-style and tip-off scope mount, 10-shot mag. Intr. 2008. Made in U.S.A. by Sturm, Ruger & Co.
Price: CHR22-10. . . . .**$380.00**

RUGER MARK III STANDARD AUTOLOADING PISTOL

Caliber: 22 LR, 10-shot magazine. **Barrel:** 4.5", 4.75", 5.5", 6", or 6-7/8". **Weight:** 33 oz. (4.75" bbl.). **Length:** 9" (4.75" bbl.). **Grips:** Checkered composition grip panels. **Sights:** Fixed, fiber-optic front, fixed rear. **Features:** Updated design of original Standard Auto and Mark II series. Hunter models have lighter barrels. Target models have cocobolo grips; bull, target, competition, and hunter barrels; and adjustable sights. Introduced 2005.
Price: MKIII4, MKIII6 (blued) **$352.00**
Price: MKIII512 (blued bull barrel) **$417.00**
Price: KMKIII512 (stainless bull barrel) **$527.00**
Price: MKIII678 (blued) **$417.00**
Price: KMKIII678GC (stainless slabside barrel) **$606.00**
Price: KMKIII678H (stainless fluted barrel) **$620.00**
Price: KMKIII45HCL (Crimson Trace Laser Grips, intr. 2008) .**$787.00**
Price: KMKIII454 (2009) **$620.00**

Ruger 22/45 Mark III Pistol

Similar to other 22 Mark III autos except has Zytel grip frame that matches angle and magazine latch of Model 1911 45 ACP pistol. Available in 4" standard, 4.5", 5.5", 6-7/8" bull barrels. Comes with extra magazine, plastic case, lock. Introduced 1992. Hunter introduced 2006.
Price: P4MKIII, 4" bull barrel, adjustable sights **$380.00**
Price: P45GCMKIII, 4.5" bull barrel, fixed sights **$380.00**
Price: P512MKIII (5.5" bull blued barrel, adj. sights) **$380.00**
Price: KP512MKIII (5.5" stainless bull barrel, adj. sights **$475.00**
Price: Hunter KP45HMKIII 4.5" barrel (2007), KP678HMKIII, 6-7/8" stainless fluted bull barrel, adj. sights **$562.00**

SABRE DEFENCE SPHINX PISTOLS

Caliber: 9mm Para., 45 ACP., 10-shot magazine. **Barrel:** 4.43". **Weight:** 39.15 oz. **Length:** 8.27" overall. **Grips:** Textured polymer. **Sights:** Fixed Trijicon Night Sights. **Features:** CNC engineered from stainless steel billet; grip frame in stainless steel, titanium or high-strength aluminum. Integrated accessory rail, high-cut beavertail, decocking lever. Made in Switzerland. Imported by Sabre Defence Industries.
Price: 45 ACP (2007) **$2,990.00**
Price: 9mm Para. Standard, titanium w/decocker **$2,700.00**

SEECAMP LWS 32/380 STAINLESS DA AUTO

Caliber: 32 ACP, 380 ACP Win. Silvertip, 6-shot magazine. **Barrel:** 2", integral with frame. **Weight:** 10.5 oz. **Length:** 4-1/8" overall. **Grips:** Glass-filled nylon. **Sights:** Smooth, no-snag, contoured slide and barrel top. **Features:** Aircraft quality 17-4 PH stainless steel. Inertia-operated firing pin. Hammer fired double-action-only. Hammer automatically follows slide down to safety rest position after each shot, no manual safety needed. Magazine safety disconnector. Polished stainless. Introduced 1985. From L.W. Seecamp.
Price: 32 . . . .**$446.25**
Price: 380 . . . .**$795.00**

SIG SAUER 250 COMPACT AUTO PISTOL

Caliber: 9mm Para. (16-round magazine), 357 SIG, 40 S&W and 45 ACP. **Barrel:** NA. **Weight:** 24.6 oz. **Length:** 7.2" overall. **Grips:** Interchangeable polymer. **Sights:** Siglite night sights. **Features:** Modular design allows for immediate change in caliber and size; subcompact, compact and full. Six different grip combinations for each size. Introduced 2008. From Sig Sauer, Inc.
Price: P250 . . . .**$750.00**

SIG SAUER 1911 PISTOLS

Caliber: 45 ACP, 8-shot magazine. **Barrel:** 5". **Weight:** 40.3 oz. **Length:** 8.65" overall. **Grips:** Checkered wood grips. **Sights:** Novak night sights. Blade front, drift adjustable rear for windage. **Features:** Single-action 1911. Hand-fitted dehorned stainless-steel frame and slide; match-grade barrel, hammer/sear set and trigger; 25-lpi front strap checkering, 20-lpi mainspring housing checkering. Beavertail grip safety with speed bump, extended thumb safety, firing pin safety and hammer intercept notch. Introduced 2005. XO series has contrast sights, Ergo Grip XT textured polymer grips. Target line features adjustable target night sights, match barrel, custom wood grips, non-railed frame in stainless or Nitron finishes. TTT series is two-tone 1911 with Nitron slide and black controls on stainless frame. Includes burled maple grips, adjustable combat night sights. STX line available from Sig Sauer Custom Shop; two-tone 1911, non-railed, Nitron slide, stainless frame, burled maple grips. Polished cocking serrations, flat-top slide, magwell. Carry line has Novak night sights, lanyard attachment point, gray diamondwood or rosewood grips, 8+1 capacity. Compact series has 6+1 capacity, 7.7" OAL, 4.25" barrel, slim-profile wood grips, weighs 30.3 oz. RCS line (Compact SAS) is Customs Shop version with anti-snag dehorning. Stainless or Nitron finish, Novak night sights, slim-profile gray diamondwood or rosewood grips. 6+1 capacity. 1911 C3 (2008) is a 6+1 compact .45

ACP, rosewood custom wood grips, two-tone and Nitron finishes. Weighs about 30 ounces unloaded, lightweight alloy frame. Length is 7.7". From SIG SAUER, Inc.
Price: Nitron **$1,200.00**
Price: Stainless. **$1,170.00**
Price: XO Black **$1,005.00**
Price: Target Nitron (2006) **$1,230.00**
Price: TTT (2006) **$1,290.00**
Price: STX (2006) **$1,455.00**
Price: Carry Nitron (2006). **$1,200.00**
Price: Compact Nitron. **$1,200.00**
Price: RCS Nitron **$1,305.00**
Price: C3 (2008) **$1,200.00**
Price: Platinum Elite **$1,275.00**
Price: Blackwater (2009) . . . .
$1,290.00

SIG SAUER P220 AUTO PISTOLS

Caliber: 45 ACP, (7- or 8-shot magazine). **Barrel:** 4.4". **Weight:** 27.8 oz. **Length:** 7.8" overall. **Grips:** Checkered black plastic. **Sights:** Blade front, drift adjustable rear for windage. Optional Siglite night sights. **Features:** Double action. Stainless-steel slide, Nitron finish, alloy frame, M1913 Picatinny rail; safety system of decocking lever, automatic firing pin safety block, safety intercept notch, and trigger bar disconnector. Squared combat-type trigger guard. Slide stays open after last shot. Introduced 1976. P220 SAS Anti-Snag has dehorned stainless steel slide, front Siglite Night Sight, rounded trigger guard, dust cover, Custom Shop wood grips. Equinox line is Custom Shop product with Nitron stainless-steel slide with a black hard-anodized alloy frame, brush-polished flats and nickel accents. Truglo tritium fiber-optic front sight, rear Siglite night sight, gray laminated wood grips with checkering and stippling. From SIG SAUER, Inc.
Price: P220 Two-Tone, matte-stainless slide,
      black alloy frame. **$1,110.00**
Price: P220 Elite Stainless (2008) **$1,350.00**
Price: P220 Two-Tone SAO, single action (2006), from . . . **$1,086.00**
Price: P220 DAK (2006) **$853.00**
Price: P220 Equinox (2006) **$1,200.00**
Price: P220 Elite Dark (2009) **$1,200.00**
Price: P220 Elite Dark, threaded barrel (2009) **$1,305.00**

SIG SAUER P220 CARRY AUTO PISTOLS

Caliber: 45 ACP, 8-shot magazine. **Barrel:** 3.9". **Weight:** NA. **Length:** 7.1" overall. **Grips:** Checkered black plastic. **Sights:** Blade front, drift adjustable rear for windage. Optional Siglite night sights. **Features:** Similar to full-size P220, except is "Commander" size. Single stack, DA/SA operation, Nitron finish, Picatinny rail, and either post and dot contrast or 3-dot Siglite night sights. Introduced 2005. Many

variations availble. From SIG SAUER, Inc.
Price: P220 Carry, from . . . . $975.00; w/night sights **$1,050.00**
Price: P220 Carry Elite Stainless (2008) **$1,350.00**

SIG SAUER P229 DA Auto Pistol
Similar to the P220 except chambered for 9mm Para. (10- or 15-round magazines), 40 S&W, 357 SIG (10- or 12-round magazines). Has 3.86" barrel, 7.1" overall length and 3.35" height. Weight is 32.4 oz. Introduced 1991. Snap-on modular grips. Frame made in Germany, stainless steel slide assembly made in U.S.; pistol assembled in U.S. Many variations available. From SIG SAUER, Inc.
Price: P229, from . . . . $975.00; w/night sights **$1,050.00**
Price: P229 Platinum Elite (2008) **$1,275.00**

SIG SAUER P226 Pistols
Similar to the P220 pistol except has 4.4" barrel, measures 7.7" overall, weighs 34 oz. Chambered in 9mm, 357 SIG, or 40 S&W. X-Five series has factory tuned single-action trigger, 5" slide and bar- rel, ergonomic wood grips with beavertail, ambidextrous thumb safety and stainless slide and frame with magwell, low-profile adjustable target sights, front cocking serrations and a 25-meter factory test target. Many variations available. Snap-on modular grips. From SIG SAUER, Inc.
Price: P226, from $975.00
Price: P226 Blackwater Tactical (2009) $1,300.00

SIG SAUER SP2022 PISTOLS
Caliber: 9mm Para., 357 SIG, 40 S&W, 10-, 12-, or 15-shot magazines. **Barrel:** 3.9". **Weight:** 30.2 oz. **Length:** 7.4" overall. **Grips:** Composite and rubberized one-piece. **Sights:** Blade front, rear adjustable for windage. Optional Siglite night sights. **Features:** Polymer frame, stainless steel slide; integral frame accessory rail; replaceable steel frame rails; left- or right-handed magazine release, two interchangeable grips. From SIG SAUER, Inc.
Price: SP2009, Nitron finish $613.00

SIG SAUER P232 PERSONAL SIZE PISTOL
Caliber: 380 ACP, 7-shot. **Barrel:** 3.6". **Weight:** 17.6-22.4 oz. **Length:** 6.6" overall. **Grips:** Checkered black composite. **Sights:** Blade front, rear adjustable for windage. **Features:** Double action/single action or DAO. Blow-back operation, stationary barrel. Introduced 1997. From SIG SAUER, Inc.
Price: P232, from $660.00

SIG SAUER P238 PISTOL
Ultra-cool 1911-styled single action semiauto pistol chambered for .380 Auto. Features include 2.7-inch barrel; 6-round magazine; Siglite night sights or laser sights, polymer or wood grips; alloy frame; stainless slide; stainless, two-tone, rainbow or black nitride finish. Weight: 15.2 oz.
Price: **$643.00**

SIG SAUER P239 PISTOL
Caliber: 9mm Para., 8-shot, 357 SIG 40 S&W, 7-shot magazine. **Barrel:** 3.6". **Weight:** 25.2 oz. **Length:** 6.6" overall. **Grips:** Checkered black composite. **Sights:** Blade front, rear adjustable for windage. Optional Siglite night sights. **Features:** SA/DA or DAO; blackened stainless steel slide, aluminum alloy frame. Introduced 1996. Made in U.S.A. by SIG SAUER, Inc.
Price: P239, from **$840.00**

SIG SAUER MOSQUITO PISTOL
Caliber: 22 LR, 10-shot magazine. **Barrel:** 3.9". **Weight:** 24.6 oz. **Length:** 7.2" overall. **Grips:** Checkered black composite. **Sights:** Blade front, rear adjustable for windage. **Features:** Blowback operated, fixed barrel, polymer frame, slide-mounted ambidextrous safety. Introduced 2005. Made in U.S.A. by SIG SAUER, Inc.
Price: Mosquito, from **$375.00**

SIG SAUER P522 PISTOL
Semiauto blowback pistol chambered in .22 LR. Pistol version of SIG522 rifle. Features include a 10-inch barrel; lightweight polymer lower receiver with pistol grip; ambi mag catch; aluminum upper; faux gas valve; birdcage; 25-round magazine; quad rail or "clean" handguard; optics rail.
Price: . . . .$572.00 to $643.00

SMITH & WESSON M&P AUTO PISTOLS
Caliber: 9mm Para., 40 S&W, 357 Auto. **Barrel:** 4.25". **Weight:** 24.25 oz. **Length:** 7.5" overall. **Grips:** One-piece Xenoy, wraparound with straight backstrap. **Sights:** Ramp dovetail mount front; tritium sights optional; Novak Lo-mount Carry rear. **Features:** Zytel polymer frame, embedded stainless steel chassis; stainless steel slide and barrel, stainless steel structural components, black Melonite finish, reversible magazine catch, 3 interchangeable palmswell grip sizes, universal rail, sear deactivation lever, internal lock system, magazine disconnect. Ships with 2 magazines. Internal lock models available. Overall height: 5.5"; width: 1.2"; sight radius: 6.4". Introduced November 2005. 45 ACP version introduced 2007, 10+1 or 14+1 capacity. **Barrel:** 4.5". **Length:** 8.05". **Weight:** 29.6 ounces. **Features:** Picatinny-style equipment rail; black or bi-tone, dark-earth-brown frame. Bi-tone M&P45 includes ambidextrous,

Prices given are believed to be accurate at time of publication however, many factors affect retail pricing so exact prices are not possible.

frame-mounted thumb safety, take down tool with lanyard attachment. Compact 9mm Para./357 SIG/40 S&W versions introduced 2007. Compacts have 3.5" barrel, OAL 6.7". 10+1 or 12+1 capacity. **Weight:** 21.7 ounces. **Features:** Picatinny-style equipment rail. Made in U.S.A. by Smith & Wesson.
Price: Full Size, from **$719.00**
Price: Compacts, from **$719.00**
Price: Midsize, from **$758.00**
Price: Crimson Trace Lasergrip models, from . . **$988.00**
Price: Thumb-safety M&P models, from . . . .
$719.00

SMITH & WESSON PRO SERIES MODEL M&P40

Striker-fired DAO semiauto pistol chambered in .40 S&W. Features include 4.25- or 5-inch barrel, matte black polymer frame and stainless steel slide, tactical rail, Novak front and rear sights or two-dot night sights, polymer grips, 15+1 capacity.
Price: **$830.00**

Smith & Wesson Pro Series Model M&P9

Similar to M&P40 but chambered in 9mm Parabellum. Capacity 17+1, 4.25-inch barrel, two-dot night sights.
Price: **$830.00**

SMITH & WESSON MODEL 908 AUTO PISTOL

Caliber: 9mm Para., 8-shot magazine. **Barrel:** 3.5". **Weight:** 24 oz. **Length:** 6-13/16". **Grips:** One-piece Xenoy, wraparound with straight backstrap. **Sights:** Post front, fixed rear, 3-dot system. **Features:** Aluminum alloy frame, matte blue carbon steel slide; bobbed hammer; smooth trigger. Introduced 1996. Made in U.S.A. by Smith & Wesson.
Price: Model 908, black matte finish **$679.00**
Price: Model 908S, stainless matte finish **$679.00**
Price: Model 908S Carry Combo, with holster **$703.00**

SMITH & WESSON MODEL 4013TSW AUTO

Caliber: 40 S&W, 9-shot magazine. **Barrel:** 3.5". **Weight:** 26.8 oz. **Length:** 6 3/4" overall. **Grips:** Xenoy one-piece wraparound. **Sights:** Novak 3-dot system. **Features:** Traditional double-action system; stainless slide, alloy frame; fixed barrel bushing; ambidextrous decocker; reversible magazine catch, equipment rail. Introduced 1997. Made in U.S.A. by Smith & Wesson.
Price: Model 4013TSW **$1,027.00**

SMITH & WESSON MODEL 910 DA AUTO PISTOL

Caliber: 9mm Para., 10-shot magazine. **Barrel:** 4". **Weight:** 28 oz. **Length:** 7-3/8" overall. **Grips:** One-piece Xenoy, wraparound with straight backstrap. **Sights:** Post front with white dot, fixed 2-dot rear. **Features:** Alloy frame, blue carbon steel slide. Slide-mounted decocking lever. Introduced 1995.
Price: **$648.00**

SMITH & WESSON MODEL 3913 TRADITIONAL DOUBLE ACTIONS

Caliber: 9mm Para., 8-shot magazine. **Barrel:** 3.5". **Weight:** 24.8 oz. **Length:** 6.75" overall. **Grips:** One-piece Delrin wraparound, textured surface. **Sights:** Post front with white dot, Novak LoMount Carry with two dots. **Features:** TSW has aluminum alloy frame, stainless slide. Bobbed hammer with no half-cock notch; smooth .304" trigger with rounded edges. Straight backstrap. Equipment rail. Extra magazine included. Introduced 1989. The 3913-LS Ladysmith has frame that is upswept at the front, rounded trigger guard. Comes in frosted stainless steel with matching gray grips. Grips are ergonomically correct for a woman's hand. Novak LoMount Carry rear sight adjustable for windage. Extra magazine included. Introduced 1990.
Price: 3913TSW **$924.00**
Price: 3913-LS **$909.00**

SMITH & WESSON MODEL SW1911 PISTOLS

Caliber: 45 ACP, 8 rounds; 9mm, 11 rounds. **Barrel:** 5". **Weight:** 39 oz. **Length:** 8.7". **Grips:** Wood or rubber. **Sights:** Novak Lo-Mount Carry, white dot front. **Features:** Large stainless frame and slide with matte finish, single-side external safety. No. 108284 has adjustable target rear sight, ambidextrous safety levers, 20-lpi checkered front strap, comes with two 8-round magazines. DK model (Doug Koenig) also has oversized magazine well, Doug Koenig speed hammer, flat competition speed trigger with overtravel stop, rosewood grips with Smith & Wesson silver medallions, oversized magazine well, special serial number run. No. 108295 has olive drab Crimson Trace lasergrips. No. 108299 has carbon-steel frame and slide with polished flats on slide, standard GI recoil guide, laminated double-diamond walnut grips with silver Smith & Wesson medallions, adjustable target sights. Tactical Rail No. 108293 has a Picatinny rail, black Melonite finish, Novak Lo-Mount Carry Sights, scandium alloy frame. Tactical Rail Stainless introduced 2006. SW1911PD gun is Commander size, scandium-alloy frame, 4.25" barrel, 8" OAL, 28.0 oz., non-reflective black matte finish. Gunsite edition has scandium alloy frame, beveled edges, solid match aluminum trigger, Herrett's logoed tactical oval walnut stocks, special serial number run, brass bead Novak front sight. SC model has 4.25" barrel, scandium alloy frame, stainless-steel slide, non-reflective matte finish.
Price: From **$1,130.00**
Price: Crimson Trace Laser Grips **$1,493.00**

SMITH & WESSON MODEL 1911 SUB-COMPACT PRO SERIES

Caliber: 45 ACP, 7 + 1-shot magazine. **Barrel:** 3". **Weight:** 24 oz. **Length:** 6-7/8". **Grips:** Fully stippled synthetic. **Sights:** Dovetail white dot front, fixed white 2-dot rear. **Features:** Scandium frame with stainless steel slide, matte black finish throughout. Oversized external extractor, 3-hole curved trigger with overtravel stop, full-length guide rod, and cable lock. Introduced 2009.
Price: **$1,304.00**

SMITH & WESSON ENHANCED SIGMA SERIES DAO PISTOLS

Caliber: 9mm Para., 40 S&W; 10-, 16-shot magazine. **Barrel:** 4". **Weight:** 24.7 oz. **Length:** 7.25" overall. **Grips:** Integral. **Sights:** White dot front, fixed rear; 3-dot system. Tritium night sights available. **Features:** Ergonomic polymer frame; low barrel centerline; internal striker firing system; corrosion-resistant slide; Teflon-filled,

electroless-nickel coated magazine, equipment rail. Introduced 1994. Made in U.S.A. by Smith & Wesson.
Price: From **$482.00**

SMITH & WESSON MODEL CS9 CHIEF'S SPECIAL AUTO
Caliber: 9mm Para., 7-shot magazine. **Barrel:** 3". **Weight:** 20.8 oz.
Length: 6.25" overall. **Grips:** Hogue wraparound rubber. **Sights:**
White dot front, fixed 2-dot rear. **Features:** Traditional double-action
trigger mechanism. Alloy frame, stainless slide. Ambidextrous safety.
Introduced 1999. Made in U.S.A. by Smith & Wesson.
Price: Stainless **$782.00**

SMITH & WESSON MODEL CS45 CHIEF'S SPECIAL AUTO
Caliber: 45 ACP, 6-shot magazine. **Weight:** 23.9 oz. **Features:**
Introduced 1999. Made in U.S.A. by Smith & Wesson.
Price: From **$787.00**

SPRINGFIELD ARMORY EMP ENHANCED MICRO PISTOL

Caliber: 9mm Para., 40 S&W; 9-round magazine. **Barrel:** 3" stainless steel match grade, fully supported ramp, bull. **Weight:** 26 oz. **Length:** 6.5" overall. **Grips:** Thinline cocobolo hardwood. **Sights:** Fixed low profile combat rear, dovetail front, 3-dot tritium. **Features:** Two 9-round stainless steel magazines with slam pads, long aluminum match-grade trigger adjusted to 5 to 6 lbs., forged aluminum alloy frame, black hardcoat anodized; dual spring full-length guide rod, forged satin-finish stainless steel slide. Introduced 2007. From Springfield Armory.
Price: 9mm Para. Compact Bi-Tone **$1,329.00**
Price: 40 S&W Compact Bi-Tone (2008) **$1,329.00**

SPRINGFIELD ARMORY XD POLYMER AUTO PISTOLS
Caliber: 9mm Para., 40 S&W, 45 ACP. **Barrel:** 3", 4", 5". **Weight:** 20.5-31 oz. **Length:** 6.26-8" overall. **Grips:** Textured polymer. **Sights:** Varies by model; Fixed sights are dovetail front and rear steel 3-dot units. **Features:** Three sizes in X-Treme Duty (XD) line: Sub-Compact (3" barrel), Service (4" barrel), Tactical (5" barrel). Three ported models available. Ergonomic polymer frame, hammer-forged barrel, no-tool disassembly, ambidextrous magazine release, visual/tactile loaded chamber indicator, visual/tactile striker status indicator, grip safety, XD gear system included. Introduced 2004. XD 45 introduced 2006. Compact line introduced 2007. Compacts ship with one extended magazine (13) and one compact magazine (10). From Springfield Armory.
Price: Sub-Compact OD Green 9mm Para./40 S&W, fixed sights **$543.00**
Price: Compact 45 ACP, 4" barrel, Bi-Tone finish (2008) **$589.00**
Price: Compact 45 ACP, 4" barrel, OD green frame, stainless slide (2008) **$653.00**
Price: Service Black 9mm Para./40 S&W, fixed sights **$543.00**
Price: Service Dark Earth 45 ACP, fixed sights **$571.00**

Price: Service Black 45 ACP, external thumb safety (2008) **$571.00**
Price: V-10 Ported Black 9mm Para./40 S&W **$573.00**
Price: Tactical Black 45 ACP, fixed sights **$616.00**
Price: Service Bi-Tone 40 S&W, Trijicon night sights (2008) ..**$695.00**

SPRINGFIELD ARMORY GI 45 1911A1 AUTO PISTOLS
Caliber: 45 ACP; 6-, 7-, 13-shot magazines. **Barrel:** 3", 4", 5". **Weight:** 28-36 oz. **Length:** 5.5-8.5" overall. **Grips:** Checkered double-diamond walnut, "U.S" logo. **Sights:** Fixed GI style. **Features:** Similar to WWII GI-issue 45s at hammer, beavertail, mainspring housing. From Springfield Armory.
Price: GI .45 4" Champion Lightweight, 7+1, 28 oz. **$619.00**
Price: GI .45 5" High Capacity, 13+1, 36 oz. **$676.00**
Price: GI .45 5" OD Green, 7+1, 36 oz. **$619.00**
Price: GI .45 3" Micro Compact, 6+1, 32 oz. **$667.00**

SPRINGFIELD ARMORY MIL-SPEC 1911A1 AUTO PISTOLS
Caliber: 38 Super, 9-shot magazines; 45 ACP, 7-shot magazines. **Barrel:** 5". **Weight:** 35.6-39 oz. **Length:** 8.5-8.625" overall. **Features:** Similar to GI 45s. From Springfield Armory.
Price: Mil-Spec Parkerized, 7+1, 35.6 oz. **$715.00**
Price: Mil-Spec Stainless Steel, 7+1, 36 oz. **$784.00**
Price: Mil-Spec 38 Super, 9+1, 39 oz. **$775.00**

Springfield Armory Custom Loaded Champion 1911A1 Pistol
Similar to standard 1911A1, slide and barrel are 4". 7.5" OAL. Available in 45 ACP only. Novak Night Sights. Delta hammer and cocobolo grips. Parkerized or stainless. Introduced 1989.
Price: Stainless, 34 oz. **$1,031.00**
Price: Lightweight, 28 oz. **$989.00**

Springfield Armory Custom Loaded Ultra Compact Pistol
Similar to 1911A1 Compact, shorter slide, 3.5" barrel, 6+1, 7" OAL. Beavertail grip safety, beveled magazine well, fixed sights. Videki speed trigger, flared ejection port, stainless steel frame, blued slide, match grade barrel, rubber grips. Introduced 1996. From Springfield Armory.
Price: Stainless Steel **$1,031.00**

SPRINGFIELD ARMORY CUSTOM LOADED MICRO-COMPACT 1911A1 PISTOL
Caliber: 45 ACP, 6+1 capacity. **Barrel:** 3" 1:16 LH. **Weight:** 24-32 oz. **Length:** 4.7". **Grips:** Slimline cocobolo. **Sights:** Novak LoMount

Prices given are believed to be accurate at time of publication however, many factors affect retail pricing so exact prices are not possible.

tritium. Dovetail front. **Features:** Aluminum hard-coat anodized alloy frame, forged steel slide, forged barrel, ambi-thumb safety, Extreme Carry Bevel dehorning. Lockable plastic case, 2 magazines.
Price: Lightweight Bi-Tone $992.00

SPRINGFIELD ARMORY CUSTOM LOADED LONG SLIDE 1911A1 PISTOL
Caliber: 45 ACP, 7+1 capacity. **Barrel:** 6" 1:16 LH. **Weight:** 41 oz.
Length: 9.5". **Grips:** Slimline cocobolo. **Sights:** Dovetail front; fully adjustable target rear. **Features:** Longer sight radius, 7.9".
Price: Bi-Tone Operator w/light rail $1,189.00

Springfield Armory Tactical Response Loaded Pistols
Similar to 1911A1 except 45 ACP only, checkered front strap and main-spring housing, Novak Night Sight combat rear sight and matching dove-tailed front sight, tuned, polished extractor, oversize barrel link; lightweight speed trigger and combat action job, match barrel and bushing, extended ambidextrous thumb safety and fitted beavertail grip safety. Checkered cocobolo wood grips, comes with two Wilson 7-shot magazines. Frame is engraved "Tactical" both sides of frame with "TRP." Introduced 1998. TRP-Pro Model meets FBI specifications for SWAT Hostage Rescue Team. From Springfield Armory.
Price: 45 TRP Service Model, black Armory Kote finish, fixed Trijicon night sights **$1,741.00**

SPRINGFIELD ARMORY XDM-3.8
Double action only semiauto pistol chambered in 9mm Parabellum (19+1) and .40 S&W (16+1). Features include 3.8-inch steel full-ramp barrel; dovetail front and rear 3-dot sights (tritium and fiber-optics sights available); polymer frame; stainless steel slide with slip-resistant slide serrations; loaded chamber indicator; grip safety. Black, bi-tone or stainless steel finish. Overall length 7 inches, weight 27.5 oz. (9mm). Also available with 4.5-inch barrel as Model XDM-4.5.
Price: . . . . **N/A**

STI LIMITED EDITION STI 20TH ANNIVERSARY PISTOL
1911-style semiauto pistol chambered in 9x19, .38 Super, .40 S&W, and .45 ACP to commemorate STI's 20th anniversary. Features include ambidextrous thumb safeties and knuckle relief high-rise beavertail grip safety; gold TiN (or Titanium Nitride) coating; full length steel bar stock slide with custom serrations specific to this model; 5-inch fully ramped and supported bull barrel; STI adjustable rear sight and a Dawson fiber optic front sight. STI will only build 200 of these pistols and the serial numbers reflect this (1 of 200, 2 of 200, etc.).
Price: . . . . **N/A**

STI DUTY ONE PISTOL
1911-style semiauto pistol chambered in .45 ACP. Features include government size frame with integral tactical rail and 30 lpi checkered frontstrap; milled tactical rail on the dust cover of the frame; ambidextrous thumb safeties; high rise beavertail grip safety; lowered and flared ejection

port; fixed rear sight; front and rear cocking serrations; 5-inch fully supported STI International ramped bull barrel.
Price: . . . . **N/A**

STI APEIRO PISTOL
1911-style semiauto pistol chambered in 9x19, .40 S&W, and .45 ACP. Features include Schuemann "Island" barrel; patented modular steel frame with polymer grip; high capacity double-stack magazine; stainless steel ambidextrous thumb safeties and knuckle relief high-rise beavertail grip safety; unique sabertooth rear cocking serrations; 5-inch fully ramped, fully supported "island" bull barrel, with the sight milled in to allow faster recovery to point of aim; custom engraving on the polished sides of the (blued) stainless steel slide; stainless steel magwell; STI adjustable rear sight and Dawson fiber optic front sight; blued frame.
Price: . . . . **N/A**

STI EAGLE PISTOL
1911-style semiauto pistol chambered in .45 ACP, 9mm, .40 S&W. Features include modular steel frame with polymer grip; high capacity doule-stack magazines; scalloped slide with front and rear cocking serrations; dovetail front sight and STI adjustable rear sight; stainless steel STI hi-ride grip safety and stainless steel STI ambi-thumb safety; 5- or 6-inch STI stainless steel fully supported, ramped bull barrel or the traditional bushing barrel; blued or stainless finish.
Price: . . . . **N/A**

STI ECLIPSE PISTOL
Compact 1911-tyle semiauto pistol chambered in 9x19, .40 S&W, and .45 ACP. Features include 3-inch slide with rear cocking serrations, oversized ejection port; 2-dot tritium night sights recessed into the slide; high-capacity polymer grip; single sided blued thumb safety; bobbed, high-rise, blued, knuckle relief beavertail grip safety; 3-inch barrel.
Price: . . . . **N/A**

STI ESCORT PISTOL
Similar to STI Eclipse but with aluminum allow frame and chambered in .45 ACP only.
Price: . . . . **N/A**

TAURUS MODEL 800 SERIES
Caliber: 9mm Para., 40 S&W, 45 ACP. **Barrel:** 4". **Weight:** 32 oz.
Length: 8.25". **Grips:** Checkered. **Sights:** Novak. **Features:** DA/SA. Blue and Stainless Steel finish. Introduced in 2007. Imported from Brazil by Taurus International.
Price: 809B, 9mm Para., Blue, 17+1 . . . . **$623.00**

TAURUS MODEL 1911
Caliber: 45 ACP, 8+1 capacity. **Barrel:** 5". **Weight:** 33 oz. **Length:** 8.5". **Grips:** Checkered black. **Sights:** Heinie straight 8. **Features:** SA. Blue, stainless steel, duotone blue, and blue/gray finish.

Standard/picatinny rail, standard frame, alloy frame, and alloy/picatinny rail. Introduced in 2007. Imported from Brazil by Taurus International.

Price: 1911B, Blue **$719.00**
Price: 1911SS, Stainless Steel **$816.00**
Price: 1911SS-1, Stainless Steel **$847.00**
Price: 1911 DT, Duotone Blue **$795.00**

TAURUS MODEL 917

Caliber: 9mm Para., 19+1 capacity. **Barrel:** 4.3". **Weight:** 32.2 oz. **Length:** 8.5". **Grips:** Checkered rubber. **Sights:** Fixed. **Features:** SA/DA. Blue and stainless steel finish. Medium frame. Introduced in 2007. Imported from Brazil by Taurus International.

Price: 917B-20, Blue **$542.00**
Price: 917SS-20, Stainless Steel **$559.00**

TAURUS MODEL PT-22/PT-25 AUTO PISTOLS

Caliber: 22 LR, 8-shot (PT-22); 25 ACP, 9-shot (PT-25). **Barrel:** 2.75". **Weight:** 12.3 oz. **Length:** 5.25" overall. **Grips:** Smooth rosewood or mother-of-pearl. **Sights:** Fixed. **Features:** Double action. Tip-up barrel for loading, cleaning. Blue, nickel, duo-tone or blue with gold accents. Introduced 1992. Made in U.S.A. by Taurus International.

Price: PT-22B or PT-25B, checkered wood grips **$248.00**

Taurus Model 22PLY Small Polymer Frame Pistols

Similar to Taurus Models PT-22 and PT-25 but with lightweight polymer frame. Features include 22 LR (9+1) or 25 ACP (8+1) chambering. 2.33" tip-up barrel, matte black finish, extended magazine with finger lip, manual safety. Overall length is 4.8". Weighs 10.8 oz.
Price: . . . . **TO BE ANNOUNCED**

TAURUS MODEL 24/7

Caliber: 9mm Para., 40 S&W, 45 ACP. **Barrel:** 4". **Weight:** 27.2 oz. **Length:** 7-1/8". **Grips:** "Ribber" rubber-finned overlay on polymer. **Sights:** Adjustable. **Features:** SA/DA; accessory rail, four safeties, blue or stainless finish. One-piece guide rod, flush-fit magazine, flared bushingless barrel, Picatinny accessory rail, manual safety, user changeable sights, loaded chamber indicator, tuned ejector and lowered port, one piece guide rod and flat wound captive spring. Introduced 2003. Long Slide models have 5" barrels, measure 8-1/8" overall, weigh 27.2 oz. Imported from Brazil by Taurus International.

Price: 40BP, 40 S&W, blued, 10+1 or 15+1 . . . .**$452.00**
Price: 24/7-PRO Standard Series; 4" barrel; stainless, duotone or blued finish **$452.00**
Price: 24/7-PRO Compact Series; 3.2" barrel; stainless, titanium or blued finish **$467.00**
Price: 24/7-PRO Long Slide Series; 5.2" barrel; matte stainless, blued or stainless finish **$506.00**
Price: 24/7PLS, 5" barrel, chambered in 9mm Parabellum, 38 Super and 40 S&W **$506.00**

TAURUS 24/7 G2

Double/single action semiauto pistol chambered in 9mm Parabellum (15+1), .40 S&W (13+1), and .45 ACP (10+1). Features include blued or stainless finish; "Strike Two" capability; new trigger safety; low-profile adjustable rear sights for windage and elevation; ambidextrous magazine release; 4.2-inch barrel; Picatinny rail; polymer frame; polymer grip with metallic inserts and three interchangeable backstraps. Also offered in compact model with shorter grip frame and 3.5-inch barrel.
Price: . . . . **N/A**

Taurus Model 2045 Large Frame Pistol

Similar to Taurus Model 24/7 but chambered in 45 ACP only. Features include polymer frame, blued or matte stainless steel slide, 4.2" barrel, ambidextrous "memory pads" to promote safe finger position during loading, ambi three-position safety/decocker. Picatinny rail system, fixed sights. Overall length is 7.34". Weighs 31.5 oz.
Price: **$577.00**

TAURUS MODEL 58 PISTOL

Caliber: 380 ACP (19+1). **Barrel:** 3.25. **Weight:** 18.7 oz. **Length:** 6.125" overall. **Grips:** Polymer. **Sights:** Fixed. **Features:** SA/DA semi-auto. Scaled-down version of the full-size Model 92; steel slide, alloy frame, frame-mounted ambi safety, blued or stainless finish, and extended magazine.
Price: 58HCB **$602.00**
Price: 58HCSS **$617.00**

TAURUS MODEL 92 AUTO PISTOL

Caliber: 9mm Para., 10- or 17-shot mags. **Barrel:** 5". **Weight:** 34 oz. **Length:** 8.5" overall. **Grips:** Checkered rubber, rosewood, mother-of-pearl. **Sights:** Fixed notch rear. 3-dot sight system. Also offered with micrometer-click adjustable night sights. **Features:** Double action, ambidextrous 3-way hammer drop safety, allows cocked & locked carry. Blue, stainless steel, blue with gold highlights, stainless steel with gold highlights, forged aluminum frame, integral key-lock. .22 LR conversion kit available. Imported from Brazil by Taurus International.
Price: 92B **$542.00**
Price: 92SS **$559.00**

Taurus Model 99 Auto Pistol

Similar to Model 92, fully adjustable rear sight.
Price: 99B **$559.00**

Taurus Model 90-Two Semi-Auto Pistol

Similar to Model 92 but with one-piece wraparound grips, automatic disassembly latch, internal recoil buffer, addition slide serrations, picatinny rail with removable cover, 10- and 17-round magazine (9mm) or 10- and 12-round magazines (40 S&W). Overall length is 8.5". Weight is 32.5 oz.
Price: . . . .
$725.00

TAURUS MODEL 100/101 AUTO PISTOL

Caliber: 40 S&W, 10- or 11-shot mags. **Barrel:** 5". **Weight:** 34 oz. **Length:** 8.5". **Grips:** Checkered rubber, rosewood, mother-of-pearl. **Sights:** 3-dot fixed or adjustable; night sights available. **Features:** Single/double action with three-position safety/decocker. Reintroduced in 2001. Imported by Taurus International.
Price: 100B **$542.00**

TAURUS MODEL 111 MILLENNIUM PRO AUTO PISTOL

Caliber: 9mm Para., 10- or 12-shot mags. **Barrel:** 3.25". **Weight:** 18.7 oz. **Length:** 6-1/8" overall. **Grips:** Checkered polymer. **Sights:** 3-dot fixed; night sights available. Low profile, 3-dot combat. **Features:** Double action only, polymer frame, matte stainless or blue steel slide, manual safety, integral key-lock. Deluxe models with wood grip inserts.
Price: 111BP, 111BP-12 . . . .**$419.00**
Price: 111PTi titanium slide . . . . . .
$592.00

TAURUS 132 MILLENNIUM PRO AUTO PISTOL

Caliber: 32 ACP, 10-shot mag. **Barrel:** 3.25". **Weight:** 18.7 oz. **Grips:** Polymer. **Sights:** 3-dot fixed; night sights available. **Features:** Double-action-only, polymer frame, matte stainless or blue steel slide, manual safety, integral key-lock action. Introduced 2001.
Price: 132BP **$419.00**

Prices given are believed to be accurate at time of publication however, many factors affect retail pricing so exact prices are not possible.

TAURUS 138 MILLENNIUM PRO SERIES

Caliber: 380 ACP, 10- or 12-shot mags. **Barrel:** 3.25". **Weight:** 18.7 oz. **Grips:** Polymer. **Sights:** Fixed 3-dot fixed. **Features:** Double-action-only, polymer frame, matte stainless or blue steel slide, manual safety, integral key-lock.
Price: 138BP **$419.00**

TAURUS 140 MILLENNIUM PRO AUTO PISTOL

Caliber: 40 S&W, 10-shot mag. **Barrel:** 3.25". **Weight:** 18.7 oz. **Grips:** Checkered polymer. **Sights:** 3-dot fixed; night sights available. **Features:** Double action only; matte stainless or blue steel slide, black polymer frame, manual safety, integral key-lock action. From Taurus International.
Price: 140BP **$436.00**

TAURUS 145 MILLENNIUM PRO AUTO PISTOL

Caliber: 45 ACP, 10-shot mag. **Barrel:** 3.27". **Weight:** 23 oz. **Stock:** Checkered polymer. **Sights:** 3-dot fixed; night sights available. **Features:** Double-action only, matte stainless or blue steel slide, black polymer frame, manual safety, integral key-lock. Compact model is 6+1 with a 3.25" barrel, weighs 20.8 oz. From Taurus International.
Price: 145BP, blued **$436.00**
Price: 145SSP, stainless, ... **$453.00**

Taurus Model 609Ti-Pro

Similar to other Millennium Pro models but with titanium slide. Chambered in 9mm Parabellum. Weighs 19.7 oz. Overall length is 6.125". Features include 13+1 capacity, 3.25" barrel, checkered polymer grips, and Heinie Straight-8 sights.
Price: **$608.00**

TAURUS SLIM 700 SERIES

Compact double/single action semiauto pistol chambered in 9mm Parabellum (7+1), .40 S&W (6+1), and .380 ACP (7+1). Features include polymer frame; blue or stainless slide; single action/double action trigger pull; low-profile fixed sights. Weight 19 oz., length 6.24 inches, width less than an inch.
Price: . . . . **N/A**

TAURUS MODEL 738 TCP COMPACT PISTOL

Caliber: 380 ACP, 6+1 (standard magazine) or 8+1 (extended magazine). **Barrel:** 3.3". **Weight:** 9 oz. (titanium slide) to 10.2 oz. **Length:** 5.19". **Sights:** Low-profile fixed. **Features:** Lightweight DAO semi-auto with polymer frame; blued (738B), stainless (738SS) or titanium (738Ti) slide; concealed hammer; ambi safety; loaded chamber indicator.
Price: . . . . **$623.00 to $686.00**

TAURUS 800 SERIES COMPACT

Compact double/single action semiauto pistol chambered in 9mm (12+1), .357 SIG (10+1) and .40 cal (10+1). Features include 3.5-inch barrel; external hammer; loaded chamber indicator; polymer frame; blued or stainless slide.
Price: . . . . **N/A**

TAURUS 822

Compact double/single action semiauto pistol chambered in .22 LR (10+1). Features include ambidextrous magazine release; external hammer; checkered grip; adjustable sights; 4.5-inch or 6-inch barrel; loaded chamber indicator; and Picatinny rail. Centerfire-to-rimfire conversion kit also available.
Price: . . . . **N/A**

TAURUS MODEL 911B AUTO PISTOL

Caliber: 9mm Para., 10-shot mag. **Barrel:** 4". **Weight:** 28.2 oz. **Length:** 7" overall. **Grips:** Checkered rubber, rosewood, mother-of-pearl. **Sights:** Fixed, 3-dot blue or stainless; night sights optional. **Features:** Double action, semi-auto ambidextrous 3-way hammer drop safety, allows cocked & locked carry. Blue, stainless steel, blue with gold highlights, or stainless steel with gold highlights, forged aluminum frame, integral key-lock.
Price: From **$584.00**

TAURUS MODEL 940B AUTO PISTOL

Caliber: 40 S&W, 10-shot mag. **Barrel:** 3-5/8". **Weight:** 28.2 oz. **Length:** 7" overall. **Grips:** Checkered rubber, rosewood or mother-of-pearl. **Sights:** Fixed, 3-dot blue or stainless; night sights optional. **Features:** Double action, semi-auto ambidextrous 3-way hammer drop safety, allows cocked & locked carry. Blue, stainless steel, blue with gold highlights, or stainless steel with gold highlights, forged aluminum frame, integral key-lock.
Price: From **$584.00**

TAURUS MODEL 945B/38S SERIES

Caliber: 45 ACP, 8-shot mag. **Barrel:** 4.25". **Weight:** 28.2/29.5 oz. **Length:** 7.48" overall. **Grips:** Checkered rubber, rosewood or mother-of-pearl. **Sights:** Fixed, 3-dot; night sights optional. **Features:** Double-action with ambidextrous 3-way hammer drop safety allows cocked & locked carry. Forged aluminum frame, 945C has ported barrel/slide. Blue, stainless, blue with gold highlights, stainless with gold highlights, integral key-lock. Introduced 1995. 38 Super line based on 945 frame introduced 2005. 38S series is 10+1, 30 oz., 7.5" overall. Imported by Taurus International.
Price: From **$625.00**

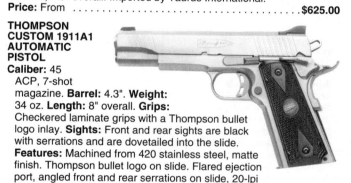

THOMPSON CUSTOM 1911A1 AUTOMATIC PISTOL

Caliber: 45 ACP, 7-shot magazine. **Barrel:** 4.3". **Weight:** 34 oz. **Length:** 8" overall. **Grips:** Checkered laminate grips with a Thompson bullet logo inlay. **Sights:** Front and rear sights are black with serrations and are dovetailed into the slide. **Features:** Machined from 420 stainless steel, matte finish. Thompson bullet logo on slide. Flared ejection port, angled front and rear serrations on slide, 20-lpi checkered mainspring housing and frontstrap. Adjustable trigger, combat hammer, stainless steel full-length recoil guide rod, extended beavertail grip safety; extended magazine release; checkered slide-stop lever. Made in U.S.A. by Kahr Arms.
Price: 1911TC, 5", 39 oz., 8.5" overall, stainless frame **$813.00**

THOMPSON TA5 1927A-1 LIGHTWEIGHT DELUXE PISTOL

Caliber: 45 ACP, 50-round drum magazine. **Barrel:** 10.5" 1:16 right-hand twist. **Weight:** 94.5 oz. **Length:** 23.3" overall. **Grips:** Walnut, horizontal foregrip **Sights:** Blade front, open rear adjustable. **Features:** Based on Thompson machine gun design. Introduced 2008. Made in U.S.A. by Kahr Arms.
Price: TA5 (2008) **$1,237.00**

U.S. FIRE ARMS 1910 COMMERCIAL MODEL AUTOMATIC PISTOL

Caliber: 45 ACP, 7-shot magazine. **Barrel:** 5". **Weight:** NA. **Length:** NA. **Grips:** Browning original wide design, full checkered diamond walnut grips. **Sights:** Fixed. **Features:** High polish Armory Blue, fire blue appointments, 1905 patent dates, grip safety, small contoured checkered thumb safety and round 1905 fire blue hammer with hand cut checkering. Introduced 2006. Made in U.S.A. by United States Fire Arms Mfg. Co.

Price: **$1,895.00**

U.S. FIRE ARMS 1911 MILITARY MODEL AUTOMATIC PISTOL
Caliber: 45 ACP, 7-shot magazine. **Barrel:** 5". **Weight:** NA. **Length:** NA. **Grips:** Browning original wide design, full checkered diamond walnut grips. **Sights:** Fixed. **Features:** Military polish Armory Blue, fire blue appointments, 1905 patent dates, grip safety, small contoured checkered thumb safety and round 1905 fire blue hammer with hand cut checkering. Introduced 2006. Made in U.S.A. by United States Fire Arms Mfg. Co.

Price: **$1,895.00**

U.S. FIRE ARMS SUPER 38 AUTOMATIC PISTOL
Caliber: 38 Auto, 9-shot magazine. **Barrel:** 5". **Weight:** NA. **Length:** NA. **Grips:** Browning original wide design, full checkered diamond walnut grips. **Sights:** Fixed. **Features:** Armory blue, fire blue appointments, 1913 patent date, grip safety, small contoured checkered thumb safety and spur 1911 hammer with hand cut checkering. Supplied with two Super 38 Auto. mags. Super .38 roll mark on base. Introduced 2006. Made in U.S.A. by United States Fire Arms Mfg. Co.

Price: **$1,895.00**

U.S. FIRE ARMS ACE .22 LONG RIFLE AUTOMATIC PISTOL
Caliber: 22 LR, 10-shot magazine. **Barrel:** 5". **Weight:** NA. **Length:** NA. **Grips:** Browning original wide design, full checkered diamond walnut grips. **Sights:** Fixed. **Features:** Armory blue commercial finish, fire blue appointments, 1913 patent date, grip safety, small contoured checkered thumb safety and spur 1911 hammer with hand cut checkering. Supplied with two magazines. Ace roll mark on base. Introduced 2006. Made in U.S.A. by United States Fire Arms Mfg. Co.

Price: **$1,995.00**

WALTHER PPS PISTOL
Caliber: 9mm Para., 40 S&W. 6-, 7-, 8-shot magazines for 9mm Para.; 5-, 6-, 7-shot magazines for 40 S&W. **Barrel:** 3.2". **Weight:** 19.4 oz. **Length:** 6.3" overall. **Stocks:** Stippled black polymer. **Sights:** Picatinny-style accessory rail, 3-dot low-profile contoured sight. **Features:** PPS-"Polizeipistole Schmal," or Police Pistol Slim. Measures 1.04 inches wide. Ships with 6- and 7-round magazines. Striker-fired action, flat slide stop lever, alternate backstrap sizes. QuickSafe feature decocks striker assembly when backstrap is removed. Loaded chamber indicator. First Edition model, limited to 1,000 units, has anthracite grey finish, aluminum gun case. Introduced 2008. Made in U.S.A. by Smith & Wesson.

Price: **$713.00**
Price: First Edition. **$665.00**

WALTHER PPK/S AMERICAN AUTO PISTOL
Caliber: 32 ACP, 380 ACP, 7-shot magazine. **Barrel:** 3.27". **Weight:** 23-1/2 oz. **Length:** 6.1" overall. **Stocks:** Checkered plastic. **Sights:** Fixed, white markings. **Features:** Double action; manual safety blocks firing pin and drops hammer; chamber loaded indicator on 32 and 380; extra finger rest magazine provided. Made in the United States. Introduced 1980. Made in U.S.A. by Smith & Wesson.

Price: **$605.00**

WALTHER P99 AUTO PISTOL
Caliber: 9mm Para., 9x21, 40 S&W, 10-shot magazine. **Barrel:** 4". **Weight:** 25 oz. **Length:** 7" overall. **Grips:** Textured polymer. **Sights:** Blade front (comes with three interchangeable blades for elevation adjustment), micrometer rear adjustable for windage.

Features: Double-action mechanism with trigger safety, decock safety, internal striker safety; chamber loaded indicator; ambidextrous magazine release levers; polymer frame with interchangeable backstrap inserts. Comes with two magazines. Introduced 1997. Made in U.S.A. by Smith & Wesson.

Price: **$799.00**

WALTHER P99AS NIGHT SIGHT DEFENSE KIT
Striker-fired DAO semiauto pistol similar to Walther P99AS but with front and rear tritium sights. Chambered in .40 S&W (12 rounds) or 9mm Parabellum (15 rounds). Features include polymer frame and grip, decocker button, 4-inch (9mm) or 4.17-inch (.40) stainless steel barrel, integral weaver-style accessory rail, black Tenifer finish overall.

Price: . . . . **N/A**

WALTHER PPS NIGHT SIGHT DEFENSE KIT
Striker-fired compact DAO semiauto pistol similar to Walther PPS but with front and rear tritium sights. Chambered in .40 S&W (6 rounds) or 9mm Parabellum (7 rounds). Features include polymer frame and grip, decocker button, loaded chamber indicator, 3.2-inch stainless steel barrel, integral weaver-style accessory rail, black Tenifer finish overall.

Price: . . . . **N/A**

WALTHER P22 PISTOL
Caliber: 22 LR. **Barrel:** 3.4", 5". **Weight:** 19.6 oz. (3.4"), 20.3 oz. (5"). **Length:** 6.26", 7.83". **Grips:** NA. **Sights:** Interchangeable white dot, front, 2-dot adjustable, rear. **Features:** A rimfire version of the Walther P99 pistol, available in nickel slide with black frame, or green frame with black slide versions. Made in U.S.A. by Smith & Wesson.

Price: From **$362.00**

WILSON COMBAT ELITE PROFESSIONAL
Caliber: 9mm Para., 38 Super, 40 S&W; 45 ACP, 8-shot magazine. **Barrel:** Compensated 4.1" hand-fit, heavy flanged cone match grade. **Weight:** 36.2 oz. **Length:** 7.7" overall. **Grips:** Cocobolo. **Sights:** Combat Tactical yellow rear tritium inserts, brighter green tritium front insert. **Features:** High-cut front strap, 30-lpi checkering on front strap and flat mainspring housing, High-Ride Beavertail grip safety. Dehorned, ambidextrous thumb safety, extended ejector, skeletonized ultralight hammer, ultralight trigger, Armor-Tuff finish on frame and slide. Introduced 1997. Made in U.S.A. by Wilson Combat.

Price: From **$2,600.00**

Prices given are believed to be accurate at time of publication however, many factors affect retail pricing so exact prices are not possible.

BAER 1911 ULTIMATE MASTER COMBAT PISTOL

Caliber: 38 Super, 400 Cor-Bon 45 ACP (others available), 10-shot magazine. **Barrel:** 5", 6"; Baer NM. **Weight:** 37 oz. **Length:** 8.5" overall. **Grips:** Checkered cocobolo. **Sights:** Baer dovetail front, low-mount Bo-Mar rear with hidden leaf. **Features:** Full-house competition gun. Baer forged NM blued steel frame and double serrated slide; Baer triple port, tapered cone compensator; fitted slide to frame; lowered, flared ejection port; Baer reverse recoil plug; full-length guide rod; recoil buff; beveled magazine well; Baer Commander hammer, sear; Baer extended ambidextrous safety, extended ejector, checkered slide stop, beavertail grip safety with pad, extended magazine release button; Baer speed trigger. Made in U.S.A. by Les Baer Custom, Inc.

Price: 45 ACP Compensated **$2,790.00**
Price: 38 Super Compensated **$2,940.00**

BAER 1911 NATIONAL MATCH HARDBALL PISTOL

Caliber: 45 ACP, 7-shot magazine. **Barrel:** 5". **Weight:** 37 oz. **Length:** 8.5" overall. **Grips:** Checkered walnut. **Sights:** Baer dovetail front with under-cut post, low-mount Bo-Mar rear with hidden leaf. **Features:** Baer NM forged steel frame, double serrated slide and barrel with stainless bushing; slide fitted to frame; Baer match trigger with 4-lb. pull; polished feed ramp, throated barrel; checkered front strap, arched mainspring housing; Baer beveled magazine well; lowered, flared ejection port; tuned extractor; Baer extended ejector, checkered slide stop; recoil buff. Made in U.S.A. by Les Baer Custom, Inc.

Price: $1,890.00

Baer 1911 Bullseye Wadcutter Pistol

Similar to National Match Hardball except designed for wadcutter loads only. Polished feed ramp and barrel throat; Bo-Mar rib on slide; full length recoil rod; Baer speed trigger with 3-1/2-lb. pull; Baer deluxe hammer and sear; Baer beavertail grip safety with pad; flat mainspring housing checkered 20 lpi. Blue finish; checkered walnut grips. Made in U.S.A. by Les Baer Custom, Inc.

Price: From **$1,890.00**

BF CLASSIC PISTOL

Caliber: Customer orders chamberings. **Barrel:** 8-15" Heavy Match Grade with 11-degree target crown. **Weight:** Approx 3.9 lbs. **Length:** From 16" overall. **Grips:** Thumbrest target style. **Sights:** Bo-Mar/Bond ScopeRib I Combo with hooded post adjustable for height and width, rear notch available in .032", .062", .080" and .100" widths; 1/2-MOA clicks. **Features:** Hand fitted and headspaced, drilled and tapped for scope mount. Etched receiver; gold-colored trigger. Introduced 1988. Made in U.S.A. by E. Arthur Brown Co. Inc.

Price: **$699.00**

COLT GOLD CUP TROPHY PISTOL

Caliber: 45 ACP, 8-shot + 1 magazine. **Barrel:** 5". **Weight:** NA. **Length:** 8.5". **Grips:** Checkered rubber composite with silver-plated medallion. **Sights:** (O5070X) Dovetail front, Champion rear; (O5870CS) Patridge Target Style front, Champion rear. **Features:** Adjustable aluminum trigger, Beavertail grip safety, full length recoil spring and target recoil spring, available in blued finish and stainless steel.

Price: O5070X **$1,022.00**
Price: O5870CS **$1,071.00**

COLT SPECIAL COMBAT GOVERNMENT

Caliber: 45 ACP, 38 Super. **Barrel:** 5". **Weight:** 39 oz. Length: 8.5". **Grips:** Rosewood w/double diamond checkering pattern. **Sights:** Clark dovetail, front; Bo-Mar adjustable, rear. **Features:** A competition-ready pistol with enhancements such as skeletonized trigger, upswept grip safety, custom tuned action, polished feed ramp. Blue or satin nickel finish. Introduced 2003. Made in U.S.A. by Colt's Mfg. Co.

Price: **$1,676.00**

COMPETITOR SINGLE-SHOT PISTOL

Caliber: 22 LR through 50 Action Express, including belted magnums. **Barrel:** 14" standard; 10.5" silhouette; 16" optional. **Weight:** About 59 oz. (14" bbl.). **Length:** 15.12" overall. **Grips:** Ambidextrous; synthetic (standard) or laminated or natural wood. **Sights:** Ramp front, adjustable rear. **Features:** Rotary cannon-type action cocks on opening; cammed ejector; interchangeable barrels, ejectors. Adjustable single stage trigger, sliding thumb safety and trigger safety. Matte blue finish. Introduced 1988. From Competitor Corp., Inc.

Price: 14", standard calibers, synthetic grip **$660.00**

CZ 75 CHAMPION COMPETITION PISTOL

Caliber: 9mm Para., 40 S&W, 16-shot mag. **Barrel:** 4.4". **Weight:** 2.5 lbs. **Length:** 9.4" overall. **Grips:** Black rubber. **Sights:** Blade front, fully adjustable rear. **Features:** Single-action trigger mechanism; three-port compensator (40 S&W, 9mm Para. have two port) full-length guide rod; extended magazine release; ambidextrous safety; flared magazine well; fully adjustable match trigger. Introduced 1999. Imported from the Czech Republic by CZ-USA.

Price: Dual-tone finish **$1,691.00**

EAA WITNESS ELITE GOLD TEAM AUTO

Caliber: 9mm Para., 9x21, 38 Super, 40 S&W, 45 ACP. **Barrel:** 5.1". **Weight:** 44 oz. **Length:** 10.5" overall. **Grips:** Checkered walnut, competition-style. **Sights:** Square post front, fully adjustable rear. **Features:** Triple-chamber cone compensator; competition SA trigger; extended safety and magazine release; competition hammer; beveled magazine well; beavertail grip. Hand-fitted major components. Hard chrome finish. Match-grade barrel. From E.A.A. Custom Shop. Introduced 1992. Limited designed for IPSC Limited Class competition. Features include full-length dust-cover frame, funneled magazine well, interchangeable front sights. Stock (2005) designed for IPSC Production Class competition. Match introduced 2006. Made in Italy, imported by European American Armory.

Price: Gold Team **$1,902.00**
Price: Limited, 4.5" barrel, 18+1 capacity **$1,219.00**
Price: Stock, 4.5" barrel, hard-chrome finish **$930.00**
Price: Match, 4.75" barrel, two-tone finish **$632.00**

FREEDOM ARMS MODEL 83 22 FIELD GRADE SILHOUETTE CLASS

Caliber: 22 LR, 5-shot cylinder. **Barrel:** 10".
Weight: 63 oz. **Length:** 15.5" overall. **Grips:**
Black micarta. **Sights:** Removable Patridge
front blade; Iron Sight Gun Works silhouette rear, click
adjustable for windage and elevation (optional adj. front
sight and hood). **Features:** Stainless steel, matte finish,
manual sliding-bar safety system; dual firing pins, lightened hammer
for fast lock time, pre-set trigger stop. Introduced 1991. Made in
U.S.A. by Freedom Arms.
Price: Silhouette Class **$1,860.00**

FREEDOM ARMS MODEL 83 CENTERFIRE SILHOUETTE MODELS

Caliber: 357 Mag., 41 Mag., 44 Mag.; 5-shot cylinder. **Barrel:** 10",
9" (357 Mag. only). **Weight:** 63 oz. (41 Mag.). **Length:** 15.5", 14.5"
(357 only). **Grips:** Pachmayr Presentation. **Sights:** Iron Sight Gun
Works silhouette rear sight, replaceable adjustable front sight blade
with hood. **Features:** Stainless steel, matte finish, manual sliding-bar
safety system. Made in U.S.A. by Freedom Arms.
Price: Silhouette Models, from **$1,741.65**

HAMMERLI SP 20 TARGET PISTOL

Caliber: 22 LR, 32
S&W. **Barrel:** 4.6".
Weight: 34.6-41.8 oz.
Length: 11.8" overall.
Grips: Anatomically
shaped synthetic Hi-Grip available in five sizes.
Sights: Integral front in three widths, adjustable
rear with changeable notch widths. **Features:** Extremely low-level
sight line; anatomically shaped trigger; adjustable JPS buffer system
for different recoil characteristics. Receiver available in red, blue,
gold, violet or black. Introduced 1998. Imported from Switzerland by
Larry's Guns of Maine.
Price: Hammerli 22 LR **$1,539.00**

HIGH STANDARD SUPERMATIC TROPHY TARGET PISTOL

Caliber: 22 LR, 9-shot mag. **Barrel:**
5.5" bull or 7.25" fluted. **Weight:** 44-46 oz.
Length: 9.5-11.25" overall. **Stock:** Checkered
hardwood with thumbrest. **Sights:** Undercut ramp
front, frame-mounted micro-click rear adjustable for
windage and elevation; drilled and tapped for scope
mounting. **Features:** Gold-plated trigger, slide lock,
safety-lever and magazine release; stippled front grip and backstrap;
adjustable trigger and sear. Barrel weights optional. From High
Standard Manufacturing Co., Inc.
Price: 5.5" barrel, adjustable sights **$795.00**
Price: 7.25", adjustable sights **$845.00**

HIGH STANDARD VICTOR TARGET PISTOL

Caliber: 22 LR, 10-shot magazine. **Barrel:** 4.5" or 5.5" polished blue;
push-button takedown. **Weight:** 46 oz. **Length:** 9.5" overall. **Stock:**
Checkered walnut with thumbrest. **Sights:** Undercut ramp front,
micro-click rear adjustable for windage and elevation. Also available

with
scope mount, rings, no
sights. **Features:** Stainless
steel frame. Full-length vent rib.
Gold-plated trigger, slide lock,
safety-lever and magazine release;
stippled front grip and backstrap; polished blue
slide; adjustable trigger and sear. Comes with
barrel weight. From High Standard Manufacturing
Co., Inc.
Price: 4.5" or 5.5" barrel, vented sight rib,
universal scope base **$795.00**

KIMBER SUPER MATCH II

Caliber: 45
ACP, 8-shot
magazine.
Barrel:
5". **Weight:** 38 oz. **Length:** 8.7"
overall. **Grips:** Rosewood double
diamond. **Sights:** Blade front, Kimber
fully adjustable rear. **Features:** Guaranteed
shoot 1" group at 25 yards. Stainless steel frame,
black KimPro slide; two-piece magazine well;
premium aluminum match-grade trigger; 30 lpi front
strap checkering; stainless match-grade barrel;
ambidextrous safety; special Custom Shop markings.
Introduced 1999. Made in U.S.A. by Kimber Mfg., Inc.
Price: **$2,225.00**

KIMBER RIMFIRE TARGET

Caliber: 22 LR, 10-shot magazine. **Barrel:** 5". **Weight:** 23 oz. **Length:**
8.7" overall. **Grips:** Rosewood, Kimber logo, double diamond
checkering, or black synthetic double diamond. **Sights:** Blade
front, Kimber fully adjustable rear. **Features:** Bumped beavertail
grip safety, extended thumb safety, extended magazine release
button. Serrated flat top slide with flutes, machined aluminum slide
and frame, matte black or satin silver finishes, 30 lines-per-inch
checkering on frontstrap and under trigger guard; aluminum trigger,
test target, accuracy guarantee. No slide lock-open after firing the
last round in the magazine. Introduced 1999. Made in U.S.A. by
Kimber Mfg., Inc.
Price: **$833.00**

RUGER MARK III TARGET MODEL AUTOLOADING PISTOL

Caliber: 22 LR, 10-shot
magazine. **Barrel:** 5.5" to 6-
7/8". **Weight:** 41 to 45 oz. **Length:**
9.75" to 11-1/8" overall. **Grips:** Checkered
cocobolo/laminate. **Sights:** .125" blade front,
micro-click rear, adjustable for windage and
elevation, loaded chamber indicator; integral
lock, magazine disconnect. Plastic case with
lock included. Mark II series introduced 1982,
discontinued 2004. Mark III introduced 2005.
Price: MKIII512 (bull barrel, blued) **$417.00**
Price: KMKIII512 (bull barrel, stainless) **$527.00**
Price: MKIII678 (blued Target barrel, 6-7/8") **$417.00**
Price: KMKIII678GC (stainless slabside barrel) **$606.00**
Price: KMKIII678H (stainless fluted barrel) **$620.00**
Price: KMKIII45HCL (Crimson Trace Laser Grips, intr. 2008) . **$787.00**
Price: KMKIII45H (2009) **$620.00**

SMITH & WESSON MODEL 41 TARGET

Caliber: 22 LR, 10-shot clip. **Barrel:** 5.5", 7". **Weight:** 41 oz. (5.5"
barrel). **Length:** 10.5" overall (5.5" barrel). **Grips:** Checkered walnut
with modified thumbrest, usable with either hand. **Sights:** 1/8"

Patridge on ramp base; micro-click rear adjustable for windage and elevation. **Features:** 3/8" wide, grooved trigger; adjustable trigger stop drilled and tapped.
Price: S&W Bright Blue, either barrel **$1,288.00**

SMITH & WESSON MODEL 22A PISTOLS

Caliber: 22 LR, 10-shot magazine. **Barrel:** 4", 5.5" bull. **Weight:** 28-39 oz. **Length:** 9.5" overall. **Grips:** Dymondwood with ambidextrous thumbrests and flared bottom or rubber soft touch with thumbrest. **Sights:** Patridge front, fully adjustable rear. **Features:** Sight bridge with Weaver-style integral optics mount; alloy frame, stainless barrel and slide; blue/black finish. Introduced 1997. The 22S is similar to the Model 22A except has stainless steel frame. Introduced 1997. Made in U.S.A. by Smith & Wesson.
Price: from **$308.00**
Price: Realtree APG camo finish (2008). **$356.00**

SPRINGFIELD ARMORY LEATHAM LEGEND TGO SERIES PISTOLS

Three models of 5" barrel, 45 ACP 1911 pistols built for serious competition. TGO 1 has deluxe low mount Bo-Mar rear sight, Dawson fiber optics front sight, 3.5 lb. trigger pull.
Price: TGO 1 . . . . **$3,095.00**

Springfield Armory Trophy Match Pistol Similar to Springfield Armory's Full Size model, but designed for bullseye and action shooting competition. Available with a Service Model 5" frame with matching slide and barrel in 5" and 6" lengths. Fully adjustable sights, checkered frame front strap, match barrel and bushing. In 45 ACP only. From Springfield Inc.
Price: **$1,573.00**

STI EAGLE 5.0, 6.0 PISTOL

Caliber: 9mm Para., 9x21, 38 & 40 Super, 40 S&W, 10mm, 45 ACP, 10-shot magazine. **Barrel:** 5", 6" bull. **Weight:** 34.5 oz. **Length:** 8.62" overall. **Grips:** Checkered polymer. **Sights:** STI front, Novak or Heinie rear. **Features:** Standard frames plus 7 others; adjustable match trigger; skeletonized hammer; extended grip safety with locator pad. Introduced 1994. Made in U.S.A. by STI International.
Price: . . . . (5.0 Eagle) **$1,940.12**, (6.0 Eagle), **$1,049.98**

STI EXECUTIVE PISTOL

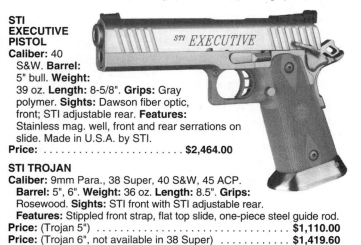

Caliber: 40 S&W. **Barrel:** 5" bull. **Weight:** 39 oz. **Length:** 8-5/8". **Grips:** Gray polymer. **Sights:** Dawson fiber optic, front; STI adjustable rear. **Features:** Stainless mag. well, front and rear serrations on slide. Made in U.S.A. by STI.
Price: **$2,464.00**

STI TROJAN

Caliber: 9mm Para., 38 Super, 40 S&W, 45 ACP. **Barrel:** 5", 6". **Weight:** 36 oz. **Length:** 8.5". **Grips:** Rosewood. **Sights:** STI front with STI adjustable rear. **Features:** Stippled front strap, flat top slide, one-piece steel guide rod.
Price: (Trojan 5") **$1,110.00**
Price: (Trojan 6", not available in 38 Super) **$1,419.60**

CHARTER ARMS BULLDOG REVOLVER

Caliber: 44 Special. **Barrel:** 2.5". **Weight:** NA. **Sights:** Blade front, notch rear. **Features:** 6-round cylinder, soft-rubber pancake-style grips, shrouded ejector rod, wide trigger and hammer spur. American made by Charter Arms, distributed by MKS Supply.

Price: Blued **$455.00**
Price: Stainless **$465.00**
Price: Target Bulldog, 4" barrel, 23 oz. **$459.00**

CHARTER ARMS OFF DUTY REVOLVER

Caliber: 38 Spec. **Barrel:** 2". **Weight:** 12.5 oz. **Sights:** Blade front, notch rear. **Features:** 5-round cylinder, aluminum casting, DAO. American made by Charter Arms, distributed by MKS Supply.

Price: Aluminum **$438.00**

CHARTER ARMS UNDERCOVER REVOLVER

Caliber: Barrel: 2". **Weight:** 12 oz. **Sights:** Blade front, notch rear. **Features:** 6-round cylinder. American made by Charter Arms, distributed by MKS Supply.

Price: Blued **$438.00**

CHARTER ARMS UNDERCOVER SOUTHPAW REVOLVER

Caliber: 38 Spec. +P. **Barrel:** 2". **Weight:** 12 oz. **Sights:** NA. **Features:** Cylinder release is on the right side and the cylinder opens to the right side. Exposed hammer for both single and double-action firing. 5-round cylinder. American made by Charter Arms, distributed by MKS Supply.

Price: Blued **$469.00**

CHARTER ARMS MAG PUG REVOLVER

Caliber: 357 Mag. **Barrel:** 2.2". **Weight:** 23 oz. **Sights:** Blade front, notch rear. **Features:** Five-round cylinder. American made by Charter Arms, distributed by MKS Supply.

Price: Blued or stainless **$409.00**

CHARTER ARMS PINK LADY REVOLVER

Caliber: 32 H&R Magnum, 38 Special +P. **Barrel:** 2". **Weight:** 12 oz. **Grips:** Rubber Pachmayr-style. **Sights:** Fixed. **Features:** Snubnose, five-round cylinder. Pink anodized aluminum alloy frame.

Price: **$438.00**
Price: Lavender Lady, lavender frame **$438.00**
Price: Goldfinger, gold anodized frame, matte black barrel and cylinder assembly **$438.00**

CHARTER ARMS SOUTHPAW REVOLVER

Caliber: 38 Special +P. **Barrel:** 2". **Weight:** 12 oz. **Grips:** Rubber Pachmayr-style. **Sights:** NA. **Features:** Snubnose, five-round cylinder, matte black aluminum alloy frame with stainless steel cylinder. Cylinder latch and crane assembly are on right side of frame for convenience to left-hand shooters.

Price: **$469.00**

CHIAPPA RHINO

Ugly-as-hell revolver chambered in .357 Magnum. Features include 2-, 4-, 5- or 6-inch barrel; fixed or adjustable sights; visible hammer or hammerless design. Weight 24 to 33 oz. Walnut or synthetic grips with black frame; hexagonal-shaped cylinder. Unique design fires from bottom chamber of cylinder.

Price: . . . . **N/A**

COMANCHE I, II, III DA REVOLVERS

Caliber: 22 LR, 9 shot. 38 Spec., 6 shot. 357 Mag, 6 shot. **Barrel:** 6", 22 LR; 2" and 4", 38 Spec.; 2" and 3", 357 Mag. **Weight:** 39 oz. **Length:** 10.8" overall. **Grips:** Rubber. **Sights:** Adjustable rear. **Features:** Blued or stainless. Distributed by SGS Importers.

Price: I Blue **$236.95**
Price: I Alloy **$258.95**
Price: II 38 Spec., 3" bbl., 6-shot, stainless, intr. 2006 . . . . **$236.95**
Price: II 38 Spec., 4" bbl., 6-shot, stainless **$219.95**
Price: III 357 Mag. 3" bbl., 6-shot, blue **$253.95**
Price: III 357 Mag. 4" bbl., 6-shot, blue **$274.95**

EAA WINDICATOR REVOLVERS

Caliber: 38 Spec., 6-shot; 357 Mag., 6-shot. **Barrel:** 2", 4". **Weight:** 30 oz. (4"). **Length:** 8.5" overall (4" bbl.). **Grips:** Rubber with finger grooves. **Sights:** Blade front, fixed or adjustable on rimfires; fixed only on 32, 38. **Features:** Swing-out cylinder; hammer block safety; blue finish. Introduced 1991. Imported from Germany by European American Armory.

Price: 38 Spec. 2" barrel, alloy frame **$277.00**
Price: 38 Spec. 4" barrel, alloy frame **$292.00**
Price: 357 Mag. 2" barrel, steel frame **$292.00**
Price: 357 Mag. 4" barrel, steel frame **$311.00**

KORTH USA REVOLVERS

Caliber: 22 LR, 22 WMR, 32 S&W Long, 38 Spec., 357 Mag., 9mm Para. **Barrel:** 3", 4", 5.25", 6". **Weight:** 36-52 oz. Grips, Combat, Sport: Walnut, Palisander, Amboinia, Ivory. Grips, Target: German Walnut, matte with oil finish, adjustable ergonomic competition style. **Sights:** Adjustable Patridge (Sport) or Baughman (Combat), interchangeable and adjustable rear w/Patridge front (Target) in blue and matte. **Features:** DA/SA, 3 models, over 50 configurations, externally adjustable trigger stop and weight, interchangeable cylinder, removable wide-milled trigger shoe on Target model. Deluxe models are highly engraved editions. Available finishes include high polish blue finish, plasma coated in high polish or matted silver, gold, blue, or charcoal. Many deluxe options available. 6-shot. From Korth USA.

Price: From **$8,000.00**
Price: Deluxe Editions, from **$12,000.00**

ROSSI R461/R462

Caliber: .357 Mag. **Barrel:** 2". **Weight:** 26-35 oz. **Grips:** Rubber. **Sights:** Fixed. **Features:** DA/SA, +P rated frame, blue carbon or high polish stainless steel, patented Taurus Security System, 6-shot.

Price: From **$352.00**

ROSSI MODEL R351/R352/R851 REVOLVERS

Caliber: .38 Spec. **Barrel:** 2" (R35), 4" (R851). **Weight:** 24-32 oz. **Grips:** Rubber. **Sights:** Fixed (R35), Fully Adjustable (R851). **Features:** DA/SA, 3 models available, +P rated frame, blue carbon or high polish stainless steel, patented Taurus Security System, 5-shot (R35) 6-shot (R851).

Price: From **$352.00**

ROSSI MODEL R971/R972 REVOLVERS

Caliber: 357 Mag. +P, 6-shot. **Barrel:** 4", 6". **Weight:** 32 oz. **Length:** 8.5" or 10.5" overall. **Grips:** Rubber. **Sights:** Blade front, adjustable rear. **Features:** Single/double action. Patented key-lock Taurus Security System; forged steel frame. Introduced 2001. Made in Brazil by Amadeo Rossi. Imported by BrazTech/Taurus.

Prices given are believed to be accurate at time of publication however, many factors affect retail pricing so exact prices are not possible.

Price: Model R971
(blued finish,
4" bbl.) **$406.00**
Price: Model R972 (stainless steel
finish, 6" bbl.) **$460.00**

Rossi Model 851
Similar to Model
R971/R972,
chambered for
38 Spec. +P.
Blued finish, 4" barrel. Introduced
2001. Made in Brazil by Amadeo
Rossi. From BrazTech/Taurus.
Price: **$352.00**

**RUGER GP-100
REVOLVERS**
Caliber: 327 Federal,
38 Spec. +P, 357 Mag., 6-shot.
Barrel: 3" full shroud, 4" full shroud,
6" full shroud. **Weight:** 3" full shroud-
36 oz., 4" full shroud-38 oz. **Sights:**
Fixed; adjustable on 4" full shroud, all 6" barrels. **Grips:** Ruger
Santoprene Cushioned Grip with Goncalo Alves inserts. **Features:**
Uses action, frame features of both the Security-Six and Redhawk
revolvers. Full length, short ejector shroud. Satin blue and stainless
steel.
Price: GP-141 (357, 4" full shroud, adj. sights, blue) **$616.00**
Price: GP-161 (357, 6" full shroud, adj. sights, blue), 46 oz. . . **$616.00**
Price: KGP-141 (357, 4" full shroud, adj. sights, stainless) . . . **$680.00**
Price: KGP-161 (357, 6" full shroud, adj. sights, stainless)
46 oz. **$680.00**
Price: KGPF-331 (357, 3" full shroud, stainless) **$659.00**

**RUGER SP-101
REVOLVERS**
Caliber: 327 Federal,
6-shot; 38 Spec.
+P, 357 Mag., 5-shot.
Barrel: 2.25", 3-1/16". **Weight:**
(38 & 357 mag models) 2.25"-25
oz.; 3-1/16"-27 oz. **Sights:** Adjustable
on 327, fixed on others. **Grips:** Ruger
Cushioned Grip with inserts. **Features:** Compact, small
frame, double-action revolver. Full-length ejector shroud.
Stainless steel only. Introduced 1988.

Price: KSP-321X (2.25", 357 Mag.) **$589.00**
Price: KSP-331X (3-1/16", 357 Mag.) **$589.00**
Price: KSP-821X (2.25", 38 Spec.) **$589.00**
Price: KSP-32731X (3-1/16", 327 Federal, intr. 2008) **$589.00**
Price: KSP-321X-LG (Crimson Trace Laser Grips, intr. 2008) . **$839.00**

Ruger SP-101 Double-Action-Only Revolver
Similar to standard SP-101 except double-action-only with no single-
action sear notch. Spurless hammer, floating firing pin and transfer
bar safety system. Available with 2.25" barrel in 357 Mag. Weighs
25 oz., overall length 7". Natural brushed satin, high-polish stainless
steel. Introduced 1993.
Price: KSP321XL (357 Mag.) **$589.00**
Price: KSP321XL-LG (357 Mag., Crimson Trace Laser Grips,
intr. 2008) **$839.00**

RUGER REDHAWK
Caliber: 44 Rem. Mag., 45 Colt, 6-shot.
Barrel: 4", 5.5", 7.5". **Weight:** About 54
oz. (7.5" bbl.). **Length:** 13" overall (7.5"
barrel). **Grips:** Square butt cushioned grip
panels. **Sights:** Interchangeable Patridge-type front,
rear adjustable for windage and elevation. **Features:**
Stainless steel, brushed satin finish, blued ordnance
steel. 9.5" sight radius. Introduced 1979.
Price: KRH-44, stainless, 7.5" barrel **$861.00**
Price: KRH-44R, stainless 7.5" barrel w/scope mount **$915.00**
Price: KRH-445, stainless 5.5" barrel **$861.00**
Price: KRH-444, stainless 4" barrel (2007) **$861.00**
Price: KRH-45-4, Hogue Monogrip, 45 Colt (2008) **$861.00**

**RUGER SUPER REDHAWK
REVOLVER**
Caliber: 44 Rem. Mag., 45 Colt, 454
Casull, 480 Ruger, 5 or 6-shot. **Barrel:**
2.5", 5.5", 7.5", 9.5". **Weight:** About 54
oz. (7.5" bbl.). **Length:** 13" overall (7.5" barrel). **Grips:**
Hogue Tamer Monogrip. **Features:** Similar to standard
Redhawk except has heavy extended frame with Ruger
Integral Scope Mounting System on wide topstrap. Wide
hammer spur lowered for better scope clearance. Incorporates
mechanical design features and improvements of GP-100. Ramp
front sight base has Redhawk-style Interchangeable Insert sight
blades, adjustable rear sight. Satin stainless steel and low-glare
stainless finishes. Introduced 1987.
Price: KSRH-2454, 2.5" 454 Casull/45 Colt, Hogue Tamer
Monogrip, Alaskan Model **$992.00**
Price: KSRH-7, 7.5" 44 Mag, Ruger grip **$915.00**
Price: KSRH-7454, 7.5" 45 Colt/454 Casull **$992.00**
Price: KSRH-9, 9" 44 Mag, Ruger grip **$915.00**
Price: KSRH-9480-5, 9.5", 480 Ruger, intr. 2008 . . . . **$963.00**
Price: KSRH-2, 2.5" 44 Mag, Alaskan Model, intr. 2008 . . . . . **$992.00**

SMITH & WESSON MODEL 14 CLASSIC
Caliber: 38 Spec. +P, 6-shot. **Barrel:** 6". **Weight:** 35 oz. **Length:** 11.5".
Grips: Wood. **Sights:** Pinned Patridge front, micro adjustable rear.
Features: Recreation of the vintage Model 14 revolver. Carbon steel
frame and cylinder with blued finish.
Price: **$995.00**
Price: Model 14 150253, nickel finish **$1,074.00**

SMITH & WESSON M&P REVOLVERS
Caliber: 38 Spec., 357 Mag., 5 rounds (Centennial), 8 rounds (large frame). **Barrel:** 1.87" (Centennial), 5" (large frame). **Weight:** 13.3 oz. (Centennial), 36.3 oz. (large frame). **Length:** 6.31" overall (small frame), 10.5" (large frame). **Grips:** Synthetic. **Sights:** Integral U-Notch rear, XS Sights 24/7 Tritium Night. **Features:** Scandium alloy frame, stainless steel cylinder, matte black finish. Made in U.S.A. by Smith & Wesson.
Price: M&P 340, double action **$869.00**
Price: M&P 340CT, Crimson Trace Lasergrips. **$1,122.00**
Price: M&P R8 large frame **$1,311.00**

SMITH & WESSON NIGHT GUARD REVOLVERS
Caliber: 357 Mag., 38 Spec. +P, 5-, 6-, 7-, 8-shot. **Barrel:** 2.5 or 2.75" (45 ACP). **Weight:** 24.2 oz. (2.5" barrel). **Length:** 7.325" overall (2.5" barrel). **Grips:** Pachmayr Compac Custom. **Sights:** XS Sight 24/7 Standard Dot Tritium front, Cylinder & Slide Extreme Duty fixed rear. **Features:** Scandium alloy frame, stainless PVD cylinder, matte black finish. Introduced 2008. Made in U.S.A. by Smith & Wesson.
Price: Model 310, 10mm/40 S&W (interchangeable), 2.75" barrel, large-frame snubnose **$1,153.00**
Price: Model 315, 38 Special +P, 2.5" barrel, medium-frame snubnose **$995.00**
Price: Model 325, 45 ACP, 2.75" barrel, large-frame snubnose **$1,153.00**
Price: Model 327, 38/357, 2.5" barrel, large-frame snubnose **$1,153.00**
Price: Model 329, 44 Magnum/38 Special (interchangeable), 2.5" barrel, large-frame snubnose **$1,153.00**
Price: Model 357, 41 Magnum, 2.75" barrel, large-frame snubnose **$1,153.00**
Price: Model 386, 357 Magnum/44 Special +P (interchangeable), 2.5" barrel, medium-frame snubnose. **$1,074.00**
Price: Model 396, 44 Special, 2.5" barrel, medium-frame snubnose **$1,074.00**

SMITH & WESSON J-FRAME REVOLVERS
The smallest S&W wheelguns come in a variety of chamberings, barrel lengths, and materials, as noted in the individual model listings.

SMITH & WESSON 60LS/642LS LADYSMITH REVOLVERS
Caliber: .38 Spec. +P, 357 Mag., 5-shot. **Barrel:** 1-7/8" (642LS); 2-1/8" (60LS) **Weight:** 14.5 oz. (642LS); 21.5 oz. (60LS); **Length:** 6.6" overall (60LS); . **Grips:** Wood. **Sights:** Black blade, serrated ramp front, fixed notch rear. **Features:** 60LS model has a Chiefs Special-style frame. 642LS has Centennial-style frame, frosted matte finish, smooth combat wood grips. Introduced 1996. Comes in a fitted carry/storage case. Introduced 1989. Made in U.S.A. by Smith & Wesson.
Price: From **$782.00**

SMITH & WESSON MODEL 63
Caliber: 22 LR, 8-shot. **Barrel:** 5". **Weight:** 28.8 oz. **Length:** 9.5" overall. **Grips:** Black rubber. **Sights:** Black ramp front sight, adjustable black blade rear sight. **Features:** Stainless steel construction throughout. Made in U.S.A. by Smith & Wesson.
Price: **$845.00**

SMITH & WESSON MODEL 442/637/638/642 AIRWEIGHT REVOLVERS
Caliber: 38 Spec. +P, 5-shot. **Barrel:** 1-7/8", 2-1/2". **Weight:** 15 oz. (37, 442); 20 oz. (3); 21.5 oz.; **Length:** 6-3/8" overall. **Grips:** Soft rubber. **Sights:** Fixed, serrated ramp front, square notch rear. **Features:** Aluminum-alloy

frames. Models 37, 637; Chiefs Special-style frame with exposed hammer. Introduced 1996. Models 442, 642; Centennial-style frame, enclosed hammer. Model 638, Bodyguard style, shrouded hammer. Comes in a fitted carry/storage case. Introduced 1989. Made in U.S.A. by Smith & Wesson.
Price: From **$600.00**

SMITH & WESSON MODELS 637 CT/638 CT/642 CT
Similar to Models 637, 638 and 642 but with Crimson Trace Laser Grips.
Price: **$920.00**

SMITH & WESSON MODEL 60 CHIEF'S SPECIAL
Caliber: 357 Mag., 38 Spec. +P, 5-shot. **Barrel:** 2-1/8", 3" or 5". **Weight:** 22.5 oz. (2-1/8" barrel). **Length:** 6-5/8" overall (2-1/8" barrel). **Grips:** Rounded butt synthetic grips. **Sights:** Fixed, serrated ramp front, square notch rear. **Features:** Stainless steel construction, satin finish, internal lock. Introduced 1965. The 5"-barrel model has target semi-lug barrel, rosewood grip, red ramp front sight, adjustable rear sight. Made in U.S.A. by Smith & Wesson.
Price: 2-1/8" barrel, intr. 2005 . . . . **$798.00**
Price: 3" barrel, 7.5" OAL, 24 oz. **$830.00**

SMITH & WESSON MODEL 317 AIRLITE REVOLVERS
Caliber: 22 LR, 8-shot. **Barrel:** 1-7/8", 3". **Weight:** 10.5 oz. **Length:** 6.25" overall (1-7/8" barrel). **Grips:** Rubber. **Sights:** Serrated ramp front, fixed notch rear. **Features:** Aluminum alloy, carbon and stainless steels, Chiefs Special-style frame with exposed hammer. Smooth combat trigger. Clear Cote finish. Introduced 1997. Made in U.S.A. by Smith & Wesson.
Price: Model 317, 1-7/8" barrel **$766.00**
Price: Model 317 w/HiViz front sight, 3" barrel, 7.25 OAL **$830.00**

SMITH & WESSON MODEL 340/340PD AIRLITE SC CENTENNIAL
Caliber: 357 Mag., 38 Spec. +P, 5-shot. **Barrel:** 1-7/8". **Weight:** 12 oz. **Length:** 6-3/8" overall (1-7/8" barrel). **Grips:** Rounded butt rubber. **Sights:** Black blade front, rear notch **Features:** Centennial-style frame, enclosed hammer. Internal lock. Matte silver finish. Scandium alloy frame, titanium cylinder, stainless steel barrel liner. Made in U.S.A. by Smith & Wesson.
Price: Model 340 . . . . **$1,051.00**
Price: Model 340PD **$1,122.00**

SMITH & WESSON MODEL 351PD REVOLVER
Caliber: 22 Mag., 7-shot. **Barrel:** 1-7/8". **Weight:** 10.6 oz. **Length:** 6.25" overall (1-7/8" barrel). **Sights:** HiViz front sight, rear notch. **Grips:** Wood. **Features:** Seven-shot, aluminum-alloy frame. Chiefs Special-style frame with exposed hammer. Nonreflective matte-black finish. Internal lock. Made in U.S.A. by Smith & Wesson.
Price: **$830.00**

SMITH & WESSON MODEL 360/360PD AIRLITE CHIEF'S SPECIAL
Caliber: 357 Mag., 38 Spec. +P, 5-shot. **Barrel:** 1-7/8". **Weight:** 12 oz. **Length:** 6-3/8" overall (1-7/8" barrel). **Grips:** Rounded butt rubber. **Sights:** Black blade front, fixed rear notch.

Prices given are believed to be accurate at time of publication however, many factors affect retail pricing so exact prices are not possible.

Features: Chief's Special-style frame with exposed hammer. Internal lock. Scandium alloy frame, titanium cylinder, stainless steel barrel. Made in U.S.A. by Smith & Wesson.
Price: 360PD **$988.00**

SMITH & WESSON MODEL M&P360
Single/double-action J-frame revolver chambered in .357 Magnum. Features include 3-inch barrel, 5-round cylinder, fixed XS tritium sights, scandium frame, stainless steel cylinder, matte black finish, synthetic grips.
Price: **$980.00**

SMITH & WESSON MODEL 438
Caliber: 38 Spec. +P, 5-shot. **Barrel:** 1-7/8". **Weight:** 15.1 oz. **Length:** 6.31" overall. **Grips:** Synthetic. **Sights:** Fixed front and rear. **Features:** Aluminum alloy frame, stainless steel cylinder. Matte black finish throughout. Made in U.S.A. by Smith & Wesson.
Price: **$624.00**

SMITH & WESSON MODEL 632 POWERPORT PRO SERIES
Caliber: 327 Mag., 6-shot. **Barrel:** 3". **Weight:** 24.5 oz. **Length:** 7.5". **Grips:** Synthetic. **Sights:** Pinned serrated ramp front, adjustable rear. **Features:** Full-lug ported barrel with full-length extractor. Stainless steel frame and cylinder. Introduced 2009.
Price: **$980.00**

SMITH & WESSON MODEL 640 CENTENNIAL DA ONLY
Caliber: 357 Mag., 38 Spec. +P, 5-shot. **Barrel:** 2-1/8". **Weight:** 23 oz. **Length:** 6.75" overall. **Grips:** Uncle Mike's Boot grip. **Sights:** Serrated ramp front, fixed notch rear. **Features:** Stainless steel. Fully concealed hammer, snag-proof smooth edges. Internal lock. Introduced 1995 in 357 Mag.
Price: **$798.00**

SMITH & WESSON MODEL 649 BODYGUARD REVOLVER
Caliber: 357 Mag., 38 Spec. +P, 5-shot. **Barrel:** 2-1/8". **Weight:** 23 oz. **Length:** 6-5/8" overall. **Grips:** Uncle Mike's Combat. **Sights:** Black pinned ramp front, fixed notch rear. **Features:** Stainless steel construction, satin finish. Internal lock. Bodyguard style, shrouded hammer. Made in U.S.A. by Smith & Wesson.
Price: **$798.00**

SMITH & WESSON MODEL 442/642/640/632 PRO SERIES REVOLVERS

Double action only J-frame with concealed hammers chambered in .38 Special +P (442 & 642), .357 Magnum (640) or .327 Federal (632). Features include 5-round cylinder, matte stainless steel frame, fixed sights or dovetail night sights (632, 640), synthetic grips, cylinder cut for moon clips (442, 642, 640).
Price: . . . . **$640.00 (standard) to $916.00 (night sights)**

SMITH & WESSON K-FRAME/L-FRAME REVOLVERS
These mid-size S&W wheelguns come in a variety of chamberings, barrel lengths, and materials, as noted in individual model listings.

SMITH & WESSON MODEL 10 CLASSIC
Single/double action K frame revolver chambered in .38 Special. Features include bright blue steel frame and cylinder, checkered wood grips, 4-inch barrel, adjustable patridge-style sights.
Price: **$814.00**

SMITH & WESSON MODEL 48 CLASSIC
Single/double action K frame revolver chambered in .22 Magnum Rimfire (.22 WMR). Features include bright blue steel frame and cylinder, checkered wood grips, 4- or 6-inch barrel, adjustable patridge-style sights.
Price: . . . . **$1,043.00 to $1,082.00**

SMITH & WESSON MODEL 10 REVOLVER
Caliber: 38 Spec. +P, 6-shot. **Barrel:** 4". **Weight:** 36 oz. **Length:** 8-7/8" overall. **Grips:** Soft rubber; square butt. **Sights:** Fixed; black blade front, square notch rear. Blued carbon steel frame.
Price: Blue **$758.00**

SMITH & WESSON MODEL 64/67 REVOLVERS
Caliber: 38 Spec. +P, 6-shot. **Barrel:** 3". **Weight:** 33 oz. **Length:** 8-7/8" overall. **Grips:** Soft rubber. **Sights:** Fixed, 1/8" serrated ramp front, square notch rear. Model 67 (**Weight:** 36 oz. **Length:** 8-7/8") similar to Model 64 except for adjustable sights. **Features:** Satin finished stainless steel, square butt.
Price: From **$758.00**

SMITH & WESSON MODEL 617 REVOLVERS
Caliber: 22 LR, 6- or 10-shot. **Barrel:** 4". **Weight:** 41 oz. (4" barrel). **Length:** 9-1/8" (4" barrel). **Grips:** Soft rubber. **Sights:** Patridge front, adjustable rear. Drilled and tapped for scope mount. **Features:** Stainless steel with satin finish; 4" has .312" smooth trigger, .375" semi-target hammer; 6" has either .312" combat or .400" serrated trigger, .375" semi-target or .500" target hammer; 8-3/8" with .400" serrated trigger, .500" target hammer. Introduced 1990.
Price: From **$916.00**

SMITH & WESSON MODELS 620 REVOLVERS
Caliber: 38 Spec. +P; 357 Mag., 7 rounds. **Barrel:** 4". **Weight:** 37.5 oz. **Length:** 9.5". **Grips:** Rubber. **Sights:** Integral front blade, fixed rear notch on the 619; adjustable white-outline target style rear, red ramp front on 620. **Features:** Replaces Models 65 and 66. Two-piece semi-lug barrel. Satin stainless frame and cylinder. Made in U.S.A. by Smith & Wesson.
Price: . . . . **$893.00** . . . .

SMITH & WESSON MODEL 386 XL HUNTER
Single/double action L-frame revolver chambered in .357 Magnum. Features include 6-inch full-lug barrel, 7-round cylinder, Hi-Viz fiber optic front sight, adjustable rear sight, scandium frame, stainless steel cylinder, black matte finish, synthetic grips.
Price: **$1,019.00**

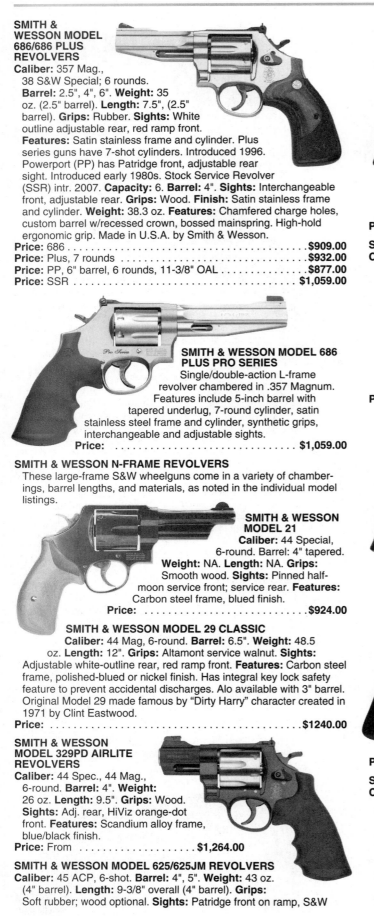

SMITH & WESSON MODEL 686/686 PLUS REVOLVERS

Caliber: 357 Mag., 38 S&W Special; 6 rounds. **Barrel:** 2.5", 4", 6". **Weight:** 35 oz. (2.5" barrel). **Length:** 7.5", (2.5" barrel). **Grips:** Rubber. **Sights:** White outline adjustable rear, red ramp front. **Features:** Satin stainless frame and cylinder. Plus series guns have 7-shot cylinders. Introduced 1996. Powerport (PP) has Patridge front, adjustable rear sight. Introduced early 1980s. Stock Service Revolver (SSR) intr. 2007. **Capacity:** 6. **Barrel:** 4". **Sights:** Interchangeable front, adjustable rear. **Grips:** Wood. **Finish:** Satin stainless frame and cylinder. **Weight:** 38.3 oz. **Features:** Chamfered charge holes, custom barrel w/recessed crown, bossed mainspring. High-hold ergonomic grip. Made in U.S.A. by Smith & Wesson.
Price: 686 . . . .**$909.00**
Price: Plus, 7 rounds **$932.00**
Price: PP, 6" barrel, 6 rounds, 11-3/8" OAL **$877.00**
Price: SSR **$1,059.00**

SMITH & WESSON MODEL 686 PLUS PRO SERIES

Single/double-action L-frame revolver chambered in .357 Magnum. Features include 5-inch barrel with tapered underlug, 7-round cylinder, satin stainless steel frame and cylinder, synthetic grips, interchangeable and adjustable sights.
Price: **$1,059.00**

SMITH & WESSON N-FRAME REVOLVERS

These large-frame S&W wheelguns come in a variety of chamberings, barrel lengths, and materials, as noted in the individual model listings.

SMITH & WESSON MODEL 21

Caliber: 44 Special, 6-round. **Barrel:** 4" tapered. **Weight:** NA. **Length:** NA. **Grips:** Smooth wood. **Sights:** Pinned half-moon service front; service rear. **Features:** Carbon steel frame, blued finish.
Price: **$924.00**

SMITH & WESSON MODEL 29 CLASSIC

Caliber: 44 Mag, 6-round. **Barrel:** 6.5". **Weight:** 48.5 oz. **Length:** 12". **Grips:** Altamont service walnut. **Sights:** Adjustable white-outline rear, red ramp front. **Features:** Carbon steel frame, polished-blued or nickel finish. Has integral key lock safety feature to prevent accidental discharges. Alo available with 3" barrel. Original Model 29 made famous by "Dirty Harry" character created in 1971 by Clint Eastwood.
Price: **$1240.00**

SMITH & WESSON MODEL 329PD AIRLITE REVOLVERS

Caliber: 44 Spec., 44 Mag., 6-round. **Barrel:** 4". **Weight:** 26 oz. **Length:** 9.5". **Grips:** Wood. **Sights:** Adj. rear, HiViz orange-dot front. **Features:** Scandium alloy frame, blue/black finish.
Price: From **$1,264.00**

SMITH & WESSON MODEL 625/625JM REVOLVERS

Caliber: 45 ACP, 6-shot. **Barrel:** 4", 5". **Weight:** 43 oz. (4" barrel). **Length:** 9-3/8" overall (4" barrel). **Grips:** Soft rubber; wood optional. **Sights:** Patridge front on ramp, S&W

---

micrometer click rear adjustable for windage and elevation. **Features:** Stainless steel construction with .400" semi-target hammer, .312" smooth combat trigger; full lug barrel. Glass beaded finish. Introduced 1989. "Jerry Miculek" Professional (JM) Series has .265"-wide grooved trigger, special wooden Miculek Grip, five full moon clips, gold bead Patridge front sight on interchangeable front sight base, bead blast finish. Unique serial number run. Mountain Gun has 4" tapered barrel, drilled and tapped, Hogue Rubber Monogrip, pinned black ramp front sight, micrometer click-adjustable rear sight, satin stainless frame and barrel, weighs 39.5 oz.
Price: 625JM **$1,074.00**

SMITH & WESSON MODEL 629 REVOLVERS

Caliber: 44 Magnum, 44 S&W Special, 6-shot. **Barrel:** 4", 5", 6.5". **Weight:** 41.5 oz. (4" bbl.). **Length:** 9-5/8" overall (4" bbl.). **Grips:** Soft rubber; wood optional. **Sights:** 1/8" red ramp front, white outline rear, internal lock, adjustable for windage and elevation. Classic similar to standard Model 629, except Classic has full-lug 5" barrel, chamfered front of cylinder, interchangeable red ramp front sight with adjustable white outline rear, Hogue grips with S&W monogram, drilled and tapped for scope mounting. Factory accurizing and endurance packages. Introduced 1990. Classic Power Port has Patridge front sight and adjustable rear sight. Model 629CT has 5" barrel, Crimson Trace Hoghunter Lasergrips, 10.5" OAL, 45.5 oz. weight. Introduced 2006.
Price: From **$1,035.00**

SMITH & WESSON MODEL 329 XL HUNTER

Similar to Model 386 XL Hunter but built on large N-frame and chambered in .44 Magnum. Other features include 6-round cylinder and 6.5-barrel.
Price: **$1,138.00**

SMITH & WESSON X-FRAME REVOLVERS

These extra-large X-frame S&W wheelguns come in a variety of chamberings, barrel lengths, and materials, as noted in individual model listings.

SMITH & WESSON MODEL S&W500 (163565)

Caliber: 500 S&W Mag., 5 rounds. **Barrel:** 6.5". **Weight:** 60.7 oz. **Length:** 12.875". **Grips:** Synthetic. **Sights:** Red Ramp front sights, adjustable white outline rear. **Features:** Similar to other S&W500 models but with integral compensator and half-length ejector shroud. Made in U.S.A. by Smith & Wesson.
Price: From **$1,375.00**

SMITH & WESSON MODEL 460V REVOLVERS

Caliber: 460 S&W Mag., 5-shot. Also chambers 454 Casull, 45 Colt. **Barrel:** 8-3/8" gain-twist rifling. **Weight:** 62.5 oz. **Length:** 11.25". **Grips:** Rubber. **Sights:** Adj. rear, red ramp front. **Features:** Satin stainless steel frame and cylinder, interchangeable compensator. 460XVR (X-treme Velocity Revolver) has black blade front sight with interchangeable green Hi-Viz tubes, adjustable rear sight. 7.5"-barrel version has Lothar-Walther barrel, 360-degree recoil compensator, tuned Performance Center action, pinned sear, integral Weaver base, non-glare surfaces, scope mount accessory kit for mounting full-size scopes, flashed-chromed hammer and trigger, Performance Center gun rug and shoulder sling. Interchangeable Hi-Viz green dot

---

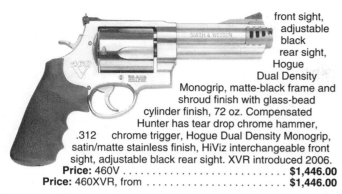

front sight, adjustable black rear sight, Hogue Dual Density Monogrip, matte-black frame and shroud finish with glass-bead cylinder finish, 72 oz. Compensated Hunter has tear drop chrome hammer, .312 chrome trigger, Hogue Dual Density Monogrip, satin/matte stainless finish, HiViz interchangeable front sight, adjustable black rear sight. XVR introduced 2006.
Price: 460V **$1,446.00**
Price: 460XVR, from **$1,446.00**

SMITH & WESSON MODEL 500 REVOLVERS
Caliber: 500 S&W Mag., 5 rounds. **Barrel:** 4", 8-3/8". **Weight:** 72.5 oz. **Length:** 15" (8-3/8" barrel). **Grips:** Hogue Sorbothane Rubber. **Sights:** Interchangeable blade, front, adjustable rear. **Features:** Recoil compensator, ball detent cylinder latch, internal lock. 6.5"-barrel model has orange-ramp dovetail Millett front sight, adjustable black rear sight, Hogue Dual Density Monogrip, .312" chrome trigger with over-travel stop, chrome tear-drop hammer, glassbead finish. 10.5"-barrel model has red ramp front sight, adjustable rear sight, .312 chrome trigger with overtravel stop, chrome tear drop hammer with pinned sear, hunting sling. Compensated Hunter has .400 orange ramp dovetail front sight, adjustable black blade rear sight, Hogue Dual Density Monogrip, glassbead finish w/black clear coat. Made in U.S.A. by Smith & Wesson.
Price: From $1,375.00

SUPER SIX CLASSIC BISON BULL
Caliber: 45-80 Government, 6-shot. **Barrel:** 10" octagonal with 1:14 twist. **Weight:** 6 lbs. **Length:** 17.5"overall. **Grips:** NA. **Sights:** Ramp front sight with dovetailed blade, click-adjustable rear. **Features:** Manganese bronze frame. Integral scope mount, manual crossbolt safety.
Price: . . . . **Appx. $1,100.00**

TAURUS MODEL 17 "TRACKER"

Caliber: 17 HMR, 7-shot. **Barrel:** 6.5". **Weight:** 45.8 oz. **Grips:** Rubber. **Sights:** Adjustable. **Features:** Double action, matte stainless, integral key-lock.
Price: From $453.00

TAURUS MODEL 44 REVOLVER
Caliber: 44 Mag., 6-shot. **Barrel:** 4", 6.5", 8-3/8". **Weight:** 44-3/4 oz. **Grips:** Rubber. **Sights:** Adjustable. **Features:** Double-action. Integral key-lock. Introduced 1994. New Model 44S12 has 12" vent rib barrel. Imported from Brazil by Taurus International Manufacturing, Inc.
Price: From $633.00

TAURUS MODEL 65 REVOLVER
Caliber: 357 Mag., 6-shot. **Barrel:** 4". **Weight:** 38 oz. **Length:** 10.5" overall. **Grips:** Soft rubber. **Sights:** Fixed. **Features:** Double action, integral key-lock. Seven models for 2006 Imported by Taurus International.
Price: From $419.00

Taurus Model 66 Revolver
Similar to Model 65, 4" or 6" barrel, 7-shot cylinder, adjustable rear sight. Integral key-lock action. Imported by Taurus International.
Price: From $469.00

TAURUS MODEL 82 HEAVY BARREL REVOLVER
Caliber: 38 Spec., 6-shot. **Barrel:** 4", heavy. **Weight:** 36.5 oz. **Length:** 9-1/4" overall (4" bbl). **Grips:** Soft black rubber. **Sights:** Serrated ramp front, square notch rear. **Features:** Double action, solid rib, integral key-lock. Imported by Taurus International.
Price: From $403.00

TAURUS MODEL 85 REVOLVER
Caliber: 38 Spec., 5-shot. **Barrel:** 2". **Weight:** 17-24.5 oz., titanium 13.5-15.4 oz. **Grips:** Rubber, rosewood or mother-of-pearl. **Sights:** Ramp front, square notch rear. **Features:** Blue, matte stainless, blue with gold accents, stainless with gold accents; rated for +P ammo. Integral keylock. Some models have titantium frame. Introduced 1980. Imported by Taurus International.
Price: From $403.00

TAURUS PROTECTOR POLYMER
Single/double action revolver chambered in .38 Special +P. Features include 5-round cylinder; polymer frame; faux wood rubber-feel grips; fixed sights; shrouded hammer with cocking spur; blued finish; 2.5-inch barrel. Weight 18.2 oz.
Price: . . . . **N/A**

Taurus 851 & 651 Revolvers
Small frame SA/DA revolvers similar to Taurus Model 85 but with Centennial-style concealed-hammer frame. Chambered in 38 Special +P (Model 851) or 357 Magnum (Model 651). Features include five-shot cylinder; 2" barrel; fixed sights; blue, matte blue, titanium or stainless finish; Taurus security lock. Overall length is 6.5". Weighs 15.5 oz. (titanium) to 25 oz. (blued and stainless).
Price: From $411.00

TAURUS MODEL 94 REVOLVER
Caliber: 22 LR, 9-shot cylinder; 22 Mag, 8-shot cylinder **Barrel:** 2", 4", 5". **Weight:** 18.5-27.5 oz. **Grips:** Soft black rubber. **Sights:** Serrated ramp front, click-adjustable rear. **Features:** Double action, integral key-lock. Introduced 1989. Imported by Taurus International.
Price: From $369.00

TAURUS MODEL 4510 JUDGE
Caliber: 3" .410/45 LC, 2.5" .410/45 LC. **Barrel:** 3", 6.5" (blued finish). **Weight:** 35.2 oz., 22.4 oz. **Length:** 7.5". **Grips:** Ribber. **Sights:** Fiber Optic. **Features:** DA/SA. Matte Stainless and Ultra-Lite Stainless finish. Introduced in 2007. Imported from Brazil by Taurus International.
Price: 4510T TrackerSS Matte Stainless $569.00
Price: 4510TKR-3B Judge $558.00
Price: 4510TKR-SSR, ported barrel, tactical rail $608.00

TAURUS JUDGE PUBLIC DEFENDER POLYMER
Single/double action revolver chambered in .45 Colt/.410 (2-1/2). Features include 5-round cylinder; polymer frame; Ribber rubber-feel grips; fiber-optic front sight; adjustable rear sight; blued or

stainless cylinder; shrouded hammer with cocking spur; blued finish; 2.5-inch barrel. Weight 27 oz.
Price: . . . . **N/A**

TAURUS JUDGE PUBLIC DEFENDER ULTRA-LITE

Single/double action revolver chambered in .45 Colt/.410 (2-1/2). Features include 5-round cylinder; lightweight aluminum frame; Ribber rubber-feel grips; fiber-optic front sight; adjustable rear sight; blued or stainless cylinder; shrouded hammer with cocking spur; blued finish; 2.5-inch barrel. Weight 20.7 oz.
Price: . . . . **N/A**

TAURUS RAGING JUDGE MAGNUM

Single/double action revolver chambered for .454 Casull, .45 Colt, 2.5-inch and 3-inch .410. Features include 3- or 6-inch barrel; fixed sights with fiber-optic front; blued or stainless steel finish; vent rib for scope mounting (6-inch only); cushioned Raging Bull grips.
Price: . . . . **N/A**

TAURUS RAGING JUDGE MAGNUM ULTRA-LITE

Single/double action revolver chambered for .454 Casull, .45 Colt, 2.5-inch and 3-inch .410. Features include 3- or 6-inch barrel; aluminum alloy frame; fixed sights with fiber-optic front; blued or stainless steel finish; cushioned Raging Bull grips. Weight: 41.4 oz. (3-inch barrel).
Price: . . . . **N/A**

TAURUS RAGING BULL MODEL 416

Caliber: 41 Magnum, 6-shot. **Barrel:** 6.5". **Weight:** 61.9 oz. **Grips:** Rubber. **Sights:** Adjustable. **Features:** Double-action, ported, ventilated rib, matte stainless, integral key-lock.
Price: **$706.00**

TAURUS MODEL 425 TRACKER REVOLVERS

Caliber: 357 Mag., 7-shot; 41 Mag., 5-shot. **Barrel:** 4" and 6". **Weight:** 28.8-40 oz. (titanium) 24.3-28. (6"). **Grips:** Rubber. **Sights:** Fixed front, adjustable rear. **Features:** Double-action stainless steel, Shadow Gray or Total Titanium; vent rib (steel models only); integral key-lock action. Imported by Taurus International.
Price: From **$569.00**

TAURUS MODEL 444 ULTRA-LIGHT

Caliber: 44 Mag, 5-shot. **Barrel:** 4". **Weight:** 28.3 oz. **Length:** 9.8" overall. **Grips:** Cushioned inset rubber. **Sights:** Fixed red-fiber optic front, adjustable rear. **Features:** UltraLite titanium blue finish, titanium/alloy frame built on Raging Bull design. Smooth trigger shoe, 1.760" wide, 6.280" tall. Barrel rate of twist 1:16", 6 grooves. Introduced 2005. Imported by Taurus International.
Price: **$666.00**

TAURUS MODEL 416/444/454 RAGING BULL REVOLVERS

Caliber: 41 Mag., 44 Mag., 454 Casull. **Barrel:** 2.25" (454 Casull only), 5", 6.5", 8-3/8". **Weight:** 53-63 oz. **Length:** 12" overall (6.5" barrel). **Grips:** Soft black rubber. **Sights:** Patridge front, adjustable rear. **Features:** Double-action, ventilated rib, ported, integral key-lock. Introduced 1997. Imported by Taurus International.
Price: From **$641.00**

TAURUS MODEL 605 REVOLVER

Caliber: 357 Mag., 5-shot. **Barrel:** 2". **Weight:** 24 oz. **Grips:** Rubber. **Sights:** Fixed. **Features:** Double-action, blue or stainless or titanium, concealed hammer models DAO, porting optional, integral key-lock. Introduced 1995. Imported by Taurus International.
Price: From **$403.00**

TAURUS MODEL 608 REVOLVER

Caliber: 357 Mag. 38 Spec., 8-shot. **Barrel:** 4", 6.5", 8-3/8". **Weight:** 44-57 oz. **Length:** 9-3/8" overall. **Grips:** Soft black rubber. **Sights:** Adjustable. **Features:** Double-action, integral key-lock action. Available in blue or stainless. Introduced 1995. Imported by Taurus International.
Price: From **$584.00**

TAURUS MODEL 617 REVOLVER

Caliber: 357 Mag., 7-shot. **Barrel:** 2". **Weight:** 28.3 oz. **Length:** 6.75" overall. **Grips:** Soft black rubber. **Sights:** Fixed. **Features:** Double-action, blue, Shadow Gray, bright spectrum blue or matte stainless steel, integral key-lock. Available with porting, concealed hammer. Introduced 1998. Imported by Taurus International.
Price: **$436.00**

TAURUS MODEL 650 CIA REVOLVER

Caliber: 357 Mag., 5-shot. **Barrel:** 2". **Weight:** 24.5 oz. **Grips:** Rubber. **Sights:** Ramp front, square notch rear. **Features:** Double-action only, blue or matte stainless steel, integral key-lock, internal hammer. Introduced 2001. From Taurus International.
Price: From **$411.00**

TAURUS MODEL 651 PROTECTOR REVOLVER

Caliber: 357 Mag., 5-shot. **Barrel:** 2". **Weight:** 17-24.5 oz. **Grips:** Rubber. **Sights:** Fixed. **Features:** Concealed single-action/double-action design. Shrouded cockable hammer, blue, matte stainless, Shadow Gray, Total Titanium, integral key-lock. Made in Brazil. Imported by Taurus International Manufacturing, Inc.
Price: From **$411.00**

Taurus Model 731 Revolver

Similar to the Taurus Model 605, except in .32 Magnum.
Price: **$469.00**

TAURUS MODEL 817 ULTRA-LITE REVOLVER
Caliber: 38 Spec., 7-shot. **Barrel:** 2". **Weight:** 21 oz. **Length:** 6.5"
overall. **Grips:** Soft rubber. **Sights:** Fixed. **Features:** Double-action,
integral key-lock. Rated for +P ammo. Introduced 1999. Imported
from Brazil by Taurus International.
Price: From **$436.00**

TAURUS MODEL 850 CIA REVOLVER
Caliber: 38 Spec., 5-shot. **Barrel:** 2". **Weight:** 17-24.5 oz. **Grips:**
Rubber, mother-of-pearl. **Sights:** Ramp front, square notch rear.
Features: Double-action only, blue or matte stainless steel, rated for
+P ammo, integral key-lock, internal hammer. Introduced 2001. From
Taurus International.
Price: From **$411.00**

TAURUS MODEL 941 REVOLVER
Caliber: 22 LR (Mod. 94), 22 WMR (Mod. 941), 8-shot. **Barrel:** 2", 4",
5". **Weight:** 27.5 oz. (4" barrel). **Grips:** Soft black rubber. **Sights:**
Serrated ramp front, rear adjustable. **Features:** Double-action,
integral key-lock. Introduced 1992. Imported by Taurus International.
Price: From **$386.00**

TAURUS MODEL 970/971 TRACKER REVOLVERS
Caliber: 22 LR (Model 970), 22 Magnum
(Model 971); 7-shot. **Barrel:** 6". **Weight:**
53.6 oz. **Grips:** Rubber. **Sights:** Adjustable. **Features:**
Double barrel, heavy barrel with ventilated rib; matte
stainless finish, integral key-lock. Introduced 2001. From
Taurus International.
Price: **$453.00**
Price: Model 17SS6, chambered in 17 HMR **$453.00**

BERETTA STAMPEDE SINGLE-ACTION REVOLVER

Caliber: 357 Mag, 45 Colt, 6-shot. **Barrel:** 4.75", 5.5", 7.5", blued. **Weight:** 36.8 oz. (4.75" barrel). **Length:** 9.5" overall (4.75" barrel). **Grips:** Wood, walnut, black polymer. **Sights:** Blade front, notch rear. **Features:** Transfer-bar safety. Introduced 2003. Stampede Inox (2004) is stainless steel with black polymer grips. Compact Stampede Marshall (2004) has birdshead-style walnut grips, 3.5" barrel, color-case-hardened frame, blued barrel and cylinder. Manufactured for Beretta by Uberti.

Price: Nickel, 45 Colt $630.00
Price: Blued, 45 Colt, 357 Mag, 4.75", 5-1/2" $575.00
Price: Deluxe, 45 Colt, 357 Mag. 4.75", 5-1/2" $675.00
Price: Marshall, 45 Colt, 357 Mag. 3.5" $575.00
Price: Bisley nickel, 4.75", 5.5" $775.00
Price: Bisley, 4.75", 5.5" $675.00
Price: Stampede Deluxe, 45 Colt 7.5" $775.00
Price: Stampede Blued, 45 Colt 7.5" $575.00
Price: Marshall Old West, 45 Colt 3.5" $650.00

CHARTER ARMS DIXIE DERRINGER

Caliber: 22 LR, 22 Magnum, 22 LR/Magnum convertible. **Barrel:** 1-1/8". **Weight:** 6 oz. **Grips:** NA. **Sights:** NA. **Features:** Single-action minigun, five-round cylinder, hammer block safety, stainless steel construction.

Price: $469.00

CIMARRON LIGHTNING SA

Caliber: 22 LR, 32-20, 32 H&R, 38 Colt, **Barrel:** 3.5", 4.75", 5.5". **Grips:** Smooth or checkered walnut. **Sights:** Blade front. **Features:** Replica of the Colt 1877 Lightning DA. Similar to Cimarron Thunderer, except smaller grip frame to fit smaller hands. Standard blue, charcoal blue or nickel finish with forged, old model, or color case hardened frame. Introduced 2001. From Cimarron F.A. Co.

Price: From...$480.70

CIMARRON MODEL P

Caliber: 32 WCF, 38 WCF, 357 Mag., 44 WCF, 44 Spec., 45 Colt, 45 LC and 45 ACP. **Barrel:** 4.75", 5.5", 7.5". **Weight:** 39 oz. **Length:** 10" overall (4" barrel). **Grips:** Walnut. **Sights:** Blade front, fixed or adjustable rear. **Features:** Uses "old model" black powder frame with "Bullseye" ejector or New Model frame. Imported by Cimarron F.A. Co.

Price: From...$494.09
Price: Laser Engraved, from $879.00
Price: New Sheriff, from $494.09

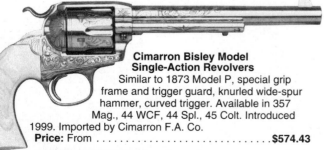

Cimarron Bisley Model Single-Action Revolvers

Similar to 1873 Model P, special grip frame and trigger guard, knurled wide-spur hammer, curved trigger. Available in 357 Mag., 44 WCF, 44 Spl., 45 Colt. Introduced 1999. Imported by Cimarron F.A. Co.

Price: From $574.43

CIMARRON MODEL "P" JR.

Caliber: 32-20, 32 H&R, **Barrel:** 3.5", 4.75", 5.5". **Grips:** Checkered walnut. **Sights:** Blade front. **Features:** Styled after 1873 Colt Peacemaker, except 20 percent smaller. Blue finish with color case-

hardened frame; Cowboy action. Introduced 2001. From Cimarron F.A. Co.

Price: $400.36

CIMARRON U.S.V. ARTILLERY MODEL SINGLE-ACTION

Caliber: 45 Colt. **Barrel:** 5.5". **Weight:** 39 oz. **Length:** 11.5" overall. **Grips:** Walnut. **Sights:** Fixed. **Features:** U.S. markings and cartouche, case-hardened frame and hammer; 45 Colt only. Imported by Cimarron F.A. Co.

Price: $547.65

CIMARRON 1872 OPEN TOP REVOLVER

Caliber: 38, 44 Special, 44 Colt, 44 Russian, 45 LC, 45 S&W Schofield. **Barrel:** 5.5" and 7.5". **Grips:** Walnut. **Sights:** Blade front, fixed rear. **Features:** Replica of first cartridge-firing revolver. Blue, charcoal blue, nickel or Original finish; Navy-style brass or steel Army-style frame. Introduced 2001 by Cimarron F.A. Co.

Price: $467.31

CIMARRON THUNDERER REVOLVER

Caliber: 357 Mag., 44 WCF, 45 Colt, 6-shot. **Barrel:** 3.5", 4.75", with ejector. **Weight:** 38 oz. (3.5" barrel). **Grips:** Smooth or checkered walnut. **Sights:** Blade front, notch rear. **Features:** Thunderer grip. Introduced 1993. Imported by Cimarron F.A. Co.

Price: Stainless $534.26

COLT SINGLE-ACTION ARMY REVOLVER

Caliber: 357 Mag., 38 Spec., .32/20, 44-40, 45 Colt, 6-shot. **Barrel:** 4.75", 5.5", 7.5". **Weight:** 40 oz. (4.75" barrel). **Length:** 10.25" overall (4.75" barrel). **Grips:** Black Eagle composite. **Sights:** Blade front, notch rear. **Features:** Available in full nickel finish with nickel grip medallions, or Royal Blue with color case-hardened frame. Reintroduced 1992. Sheriff's Model and Frontier Six introduced 2008, available in nickel in 2010.

Price: P1540, 32-20, 4.75" barrel, color case-hardened/blued
    finish $1,290.00
Price: P1656, 357 Mag., 5.5" barrel, nickel finish.........$1,490.00
Price: P1876, 45 LC, 7.5" barrel, nickel finish $1,490.00
Price: P2830S SAA Sheriff's, 3" barrel, 45 LC (2008) $1,290.00
Price: P2950FSS Frontier Six Shooter, 5.5" barrel, 44-40
    (2008) $1,350.00

Prices given are believed to be accurate at time of publication however, many factors affect retail pricing so exact prices are not possible.

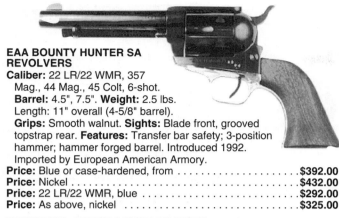

EAA BOUNTY HUNTER SA REVOLVERS

Caliber: 22 LR/22 WMR, 357 Mag., 44 Mag., 45 Colt, 6-shot. **Barrel:** 4.5", 7.5". **Weight:** 2.5 lbs. Length: 11" overall (4-5/8" barrel). **Grips:** Smooth walnut. **Sights:** Blade front, grooved topstrap rear. **Features:** Transfer bar safety; 3-position hammer; hammer forged barrel. Introduced 1992. Imported by European American Armory.
Price: Blue or case-hardened, from $392.00
Price: Nickel $432.00
Price: 22 LR/22 WMR, blue $292.00
Price: As above, nickel $325.00

EMF MODEL 1873 FRONTIER MARSHAL

Caliber: 357 Mag., 45 Colt. **Barrel:** 4.75", 5-1/2", 7.5". **Weight:** 39 oz. **Length:** 10.5" overall. **Grips:** One-piece walnut. **Sights:** Blade front, notch rear. Features: Bright brass trigger guard and backstrap, color case-hardened frame, blued barrel and cylinder. Introduced 1998. Imported from Italy.
Price: $485.00

EMF HARTFORD SINGLE-ACTION REVOLVERS

Caliber: 357 Mag., 32-20, 38-40, 44-40, 44 Spec., 45 Colt. **Barrel:** 4.75", 5.5", 7.5". **Weight:** 45 oz. **Length:** 13" overall (7.5" barrel). **Grips:** Smooth walnut. **Sights:** Blade front, fixed rear. **Features:** Identical to the original Colts. All major parts serial numbered using original Colt-style lettering, numbering. Bullseye ejector head and color case-hardening on old model frame and hammer. Introduced 1990. Imported by E.M.F. Co.
Price: Old Model $489.90
Price: Case-hardened New Model frame $489.90

EMF Great Western II Express Single-Action Revolver

Same as the regular model except uses grip of the Colt Lightning revolver. Barrel lengths of 4.75". Introduced 2006. Imported by E.M.F. Co.
Price: Stainless, Ultra Ivory grips $715.00
Price: Walnut grips $690.00

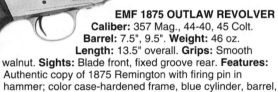

EMF 1875 OUTLAW REVOLVER

Caliber: 357 Mag., 44-40, 45 Colt. **Barrel:** 7.5", 9.5". **Weight:** 46 oz. **Length:** 13.5" overall. **Grips:** Smooth walnut. **Sights:** Blade front, fixed groove rear. **Features:** Authentic copy of 1875 Remington with firing pin in hammer; color case-hardened frame, blue cylinder, barrel, steel backstrap and trigger guard. Also available in nickel, factory engraved. Imported by E.M.F. Co.
Price: All calibers $479.90
Price: Laser Engraved $684.90

EMF 1890 Police Revolver

Similar to the 1875 Outlaw except has 5.5" barrel, weighs 40 oz., with 12.5" overall length. Has lanyard ring in butt. No web under barrel. Calibers: 45 Colt. Imported by E.M.F. Co.
Price: $489.90

EMF 1873 GREAT WESTERN II

Caliber: .357, 45 LC, 44/40. **Barrel:** 4 3/4", 5.5", 7.5". **Weight:** 36 oz. **Length:** 11" (5.5"). **Grips:** Walnut. **Sights:**

Blade front, notch rear. **Features:** Authentic reproduction of the original 2nd generation Colt single-action revolver. Standard and bone case hardening. Coil hammer spring. Hammer-forged barrel.
Price: 1873 Californian $520.00
Price: 1873 Custom series, bone or nickel, ivory-like grips . . **$689.90**
Price: 1873 Stainless steel, ivory-like grips $589.90

FREEDOM ARMS MODEL 83 PREMIER GRADE REVOLVER

Caliber: 357 Mag., 41 Mag., 44 Mag., 454 Casull, 475 Linebaugh, 500 Wyo. Exp., 5-shot. **Barrel:** 4.75", 6", 7.5", 9" (357 Mag. only), 10" (except 357 Mag. and 500 Wyo. Exp. **Weight:** 53 oz. (7.5" bbl. In 454 Casull). **Length:** 13" (7.5" bbl.). **Grips:** Impregnated hardwood. **Sights:** Adjustable rear with replaceable front sight. Fixed rear notch and front blade. **Features:** Stainless steel construction with brushed finish; manual sliding safety bar. Micarta grips optional. 500 Wyo. Exp. Introduced 2006. Lifetime warranty. Made in U.S.A. by Freedom Arms, Inc.
Price: From $2,099.00

FREEDOM ARMS MODEL 83 FIELD GRADE REVOLVER

Caliber: 22 LR, 357 Mag., 41 Mag., 44 Mag., 454 Casull, 475 Linebaugh, 500 Wyo. Exp., 5-shot. **Barrel:** 4.75", 6", 7.5", 9" (357 Mag. only), 10" (except 357 Mag. and 500 Wyo. Exp.) **Weight:** 56 oz. (7.5" bbl. In 454 Casull). **Length:** 13.1" (7.5" bbl.). **Grips:** Pachmayr standard, impregnated hardwood or Micarta optional. **Sights:** Adjustable rear with replaceable front sight. Model 83 frame. All stainless steel. Introduced 1988. Made in U.S.A. by Freedom Arms Inc.
Price: From $1,623.00

FREEDOM ARMS MODEL 97 PREMIER GRADE REVOLVER

Caliber: 17 HMR, 22 LR, 32 H&R, 357 Mag., 6-shot; 41 Mag., 44 Special, 45 Colt, 5-shot. **Barrel:** 4.25", 5.5", 7.5", 10" (17 HMR, 22 LR & 32 H&R). **Weight:** 40 oz. (5.5" 357 Mag.). **Length:** 10.75" (5.5" bbl.). **Grips:** Impregnated hardwood; Micarta optional. **Sights:** Adjustable rear, replaceable blade front. Fixed rear notch and front blade. **Features:** Stainless steel construction, brushed finish, automatic transfer bar safety system. Introduced in 1997. Lifetime warranty. Made in U.S.A. by Freedom Arms.
Price: From $1,772.00

HERITAGE ROUGH RIDER REVOLVER

Caliber: 17 HMR, 17 LR, 32 H&R, 32 S&W, 32 S&W Long, 357 Mag,

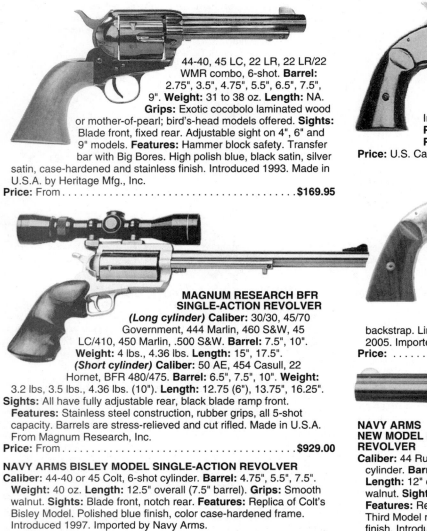

44-40, 45 LC, 22 LR, 22 LR/22 WMR combo, 6-shot. **Barrel:** 2.75", 3.5", 4.75", 5.5", 6.5", 7.5", 9". **Weight:** 31 to 38 oz. **Length:** NA. **Grips:** Exotic cocobolo laminated wood or mother-of-pearl; bird's-head models offered. **Sights:** Blade front, fixed rear. Adjustable sight on 4", 6" and 9" models. **Features:** Hammer block safety. Transfer bar with Big Bores. High polish blue, black satin, silver satin, case-hardened and stainless finish. Introduced 1993. Made in U.S.A. by Heritage Mfg., Inc.

Price: From **$169.95**

MAGNUM RESEARCH BFR SINGLE-ACTION REVOLVER

(Long cylinder) **Caliber:** 30/30, 45/70 Government, 444 Marlin, 460 S&W, 45 LC/410, 450 Marlin, .500 S&W. **Barrel:** 7.5", 10". **Weight:** 4 lbs., 4.36 lbs. **Length:** 15", 17.5". *(Short cylinder)* **Caliber:** 50 AE, 454 Casull, 22 Hornet, BFR 480/475. **Barrel:** 6.5", 7.5", 10". **Weight:** 3.2 lbs, 3.5 lbs., 4.36 lbs. (10"). **Length:** 12.75 (6"), 13.75", 16.25". **Sights:** All have fully adjustable rear, black blade ramp front. **Features:** Stainless steel construction, rubber grips, all 5-shot capacity. Barrels are stress-relieved and cut rifled. Made in U.S.A. From Magnum Research, Inc.

Price: From **$929.00**

NAVY ARMS BISLEY MODEL SINGLE-ACTION REVOLVER

Caliber: 44-40 or 45 Colt, 6-shot cylinder. **Barrel:** 4.75", 5.5", 7.5". **Weight:** 40 oz. **Length:** 12.5" overall (7.5" barrel). **Grips:** Smooth walnut. **Sights:** Blade front, notch rear. **Features:** Replica of Colt's Bisley Model. Polished blue finish, color case-hardened frame. Introduced 1997. Imported by Navy Arms.

Price: **$503.00**

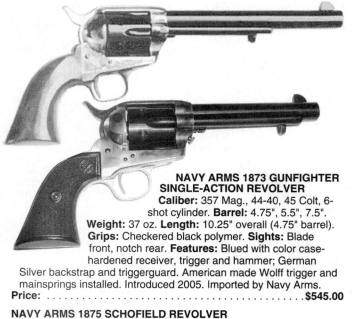

NAVY ARMS 1873 GUNFIGHTER SINGLE-ACTION REVOLVER

Caliber: 357 Mag., 44-40, 45 Colt, 6-shot cylinder. **Barrel:** 4.75", 5.5", 7.5". **Weight:** 37 oz. **Length:** 10.25" overall (4.75" barrel). **Grips:** Checkered black polymer. **Sights:** Blade front, notch rear. **Features:** Blued with color case-hardened receiver, trigger and hammer; German Silver backstrap and triggerguard. American made Wolff trigger and mainsprings installed. Introduced 2005. Imported by Navy Arms.

Price: **$545.00**

NAVY ARMS 1875 SCHOFIELD REVOLVER

Caliber: 44-40, 45 Colt, 6-shot cylinder. **Barrel:** 3.5", 5", 7". **Weight:** 39 oz. **Length:** 10.75" overall (5" barrel). **Grips:** Smooth walnut.

Sights: Blade front, notch rear. **Features:** Replica of Smith & Wesson Model 3 Schofield. Single-action, top-break with automatic ejection. Polished blue finish. Introduced 1994. Imported by Navy Arms.

Price: Hideout Model, 3.5" barrel **$882.00**
Price: Wells Fargo, 5" barrel **$882.00**
Price: U.S. Cavalry model, 7" barrel, military markings **$882.00**

NAVY ARMS FOUNDER'S MODEL SCHOFIELD REVOLVER

Caliber: 45 Colt, 38 Spl., 6-shot cylinder. **Barrel:** 7.5". **Weight:** 41 oz. **Length:** 13.75". **Grips:** Deluxe hand-rubbed walnut with cartouching. **Sights:** Blade front, notch rear. **Features:** Charcoal blued with bone color case-hardened receiver, trigger, hammer and backstrap. Limited production "VF" serial number prefix. Introduced 2005. Imported by Navy Arms.

Price: **$924.00**

NAVY ARMS NEW MODEL RUSSIAN REVOLVER

Caliber: 44 Russian, 6-shot cylinder. **Barrel:** 6.5". **Weight:** 40 oz. **Length:** 12" overall. **Grips:** Smooth walnut. **Sights:** Blade front, notch rear. **Features:** Replica of the S&W Model 3 Russian Third Model revolver. Spur trigger guard, polished blue finish. Introduced 1999. Imported by Navy Arms.

Price: **$924.00**

NAVY ARMS SCOUT SMALL FRAME SINGLE-ACTION REVOLVER

Caliber: 38 Spec., 6-shot cylinder. **Barrel:** 4.75", 5.5". **Weight:** 37 oz. **Length:** 10.75" overall (5.5" barrel). **Grips:** Checkered black polymer. **Sights:** Blade front, notch rear. **Features:** Blued with color case-hardened receiver, trigger and hammer; German silver backstrap and triggerguard. Introduced 2005. Imported by Navy Arms.

Price: **$545.00**

NORTH AMERICAN ARMS MINI REVOLVERS

Caliber: 22 Short, 22 LR, 22 WMR, 5-shot. **Barrel:** 1-1/8", 1-5/8". **Weight:** 4 to 6.6 oz. **Length:** 3-5/8" to 6-1/8" overall. **Grips:** Laminated wood. **Sights:** Blade front, notch fixed rear. **Features:** All stainless steel construction. Polished satin and matte finish. Engraved models available. From North American Arms.

Price: 22 Short, 22 LR **$229.00**

NORTH AMERICAN ARMS MINI-MASTER

Caliber: 22 LR, 22 WMR, 5-shot cylinder. **Barrel:** 4". **Weight:** 10.7 oz. **Length:** 7.75" overall. **Grips:** Checkered hard black rubber. **Sights:** Blade front,

Prices given are believed to be accurate at time of publication however, many factors affect retail pricing so exact prices are not possible.

white outline rear adjustable for elevation, or fixed. **Features:** Heavy vented barrel; full-size grips. Non-fluted cylinder. Introduced 1989.
Price: Fixed sight **$284.00**
Price: Adjustable sight **$314.00**

North American Arms Black Widow Revolver
Similar to Mini-Master, 2" heavy vent barrel. Built on 22 WMR frame. Non-fluted cylinder, black rubber grips. Available with Millett Low Profile fixed sights or Millett sight adjustable for elevation only. Overall length 5-7/8", weighs 8.8 oz. From North American Arms.
Price: Adjustable sight, 22 LR or 22 WMR . . .**$299.00**
Price: Fixed sight, 22 LR or 22 WMR **$269.00**

NORTH AMERICAN ARMS "THE EARL" SINGLE-ACTION REVOLVER
Caliber: 22 Magnum with 22 LR accessory cylinder, 5-shot cylinder. **Barrel:** 4" octagonal. **Weight:** 6.8 oz. **Length:** 7-3/4" overall. **Grips:** Wood. **Sights:** Barleycorn front and fixed notch rear. **Features:** Single-action mini-revolver patterned after 1858-style Remington percussion revolver. Includes a spur trigger and a faux loading lever that serves as cylinder pin release.
Price: . . . . **$289.00** (22 Magnum only); **$324.00** (convertible)

RUGER NEW MODEL SINGLE SIX & NEW MODEL .32 H&R SINGLE SIX REVOLVERS
Caliber: 17 HMR, 22 LR, 22 Mag. **Barrel:** 4-5/8", 5.5", 6.5", 7.5", 9.5". 6-shot. **Grips:** Rosewood, black laminate. **Sights:** Adjustable or fixed. **Features:** Blued or stainless metalwork, short grips available, convertible models available. Introduced 2003 in 17 HMR.
Price: 17 HMR (blued) **$519.00**
Price: 22 LR/22 Mag., from **$506.00**

RUGER NEW MODEL BLACKHAWK/BLACKHAWK CONVERTIBLE
Caliber: 30 Carbine, 327 Federal, 357 Mag./38 Spec., 41 Mag., 44 Special, 45 Colt, 6-shot. **Barrel:** 4-5/8", 5.5", 6.5", 7.5" (30 carbine and 45 Colt). **Weight:** 36 to 45 oz. **Lengths:** 10-3/8" to 13.5". **Grips:** Rosewood or black checkered. **Sights:** 1/8" ramp front, micro-click rear adjustable for windage and elevation. **Features:** Rosewood grips, Ruger transfer bar safety system, independent firing pin, hardened chrome-moly steel frame, music wire springs throughout. Case and lock included. Convertibles come with extra cylinder.
Price: 30 Carbine, 7.5" (BN31, blued) **$541.00**
Price: 357 Mag. (blued or satin stainless), from **$541.00**
Price: 41 Mag. (blued) **$541.00**
Price: 45 Colt (blued or satin stainless), from **$541.00**
Price: 357 Mag./9mm Para. Convertible (BN34XL, BN36XL) .**$617.00**
Price: 45 Colt/45 ACP Convertible (BN44X, BN455XL) **$617.00**

Ruger Bisley Single-Action Revolver
Similar to standard Blackhawk, hammer is lower with smoothly curved, deeply checkered wide spur. The trigger is strongly curved with wide smooth surface. Longer grip frame. Adjustable rear sight, ramp-style front. Unfluted cylinder and roll engraving, adjustable sights. Chambered for 44 Mag. and 45 Colt; 7.5" barrel; overall length 13.5"; weighs 48-51 oz. Plastic lockable case. Orig. fluted cylinder introduced 1985; discontinued 1991. Unfluted cylinder introduced 1986.
Price: RB-44W (44 Mag) RB45W (45 Colt) **$683.00**

RUGER NEW MODEL SUPER BLACKHAWK
Caliber: 44 Mag., 6-shot. Also fires 44 Spec. **Barrel:** 4-5/8", 5.5", 7.5", 10.5" bull. **Weight:** 45-55 oz. **Length:** 10.5" to 16.5" overall. **Grips:** Rosewood. **Sights:** 1/8" ramp front, micro-click rear adjustable for windage and elevation. **Features:** Ruger transfer bar safety system, fluted or unfluted cylinder, steel grip and cylinder frame, round or square back trigger guard, wide serrated trigger, wide spur hammer. With case and lock.
Price: Blue, 4-5/8", 5.5", 7.5"
(S-458N, S-45N, S-47N) **$650.00**
Price: Blue, 10.5" bull barrel (S-411N) **$667.00**
Price: Stainless, 4-5/8", 5.5", 7.5" (KS-458N, KS-45N,
KS-47N) **$667.00**
Price: Stainless, 10.5" bull barrel (KS-411N) **$694.00**
Price: Super Blackhawk 50th Anniversary: Gold highlights, ornamentation; commemorates 50-year anniversary of Super Blackhawk **$729.00**

RUGER NEW MODEL SUPER BLACKHAWK HUNTER
Caliber: 44 Mag., 6-shot. **Barrel:** 7.5", full-length solid rib, unfluted cylinder. **Weight:** 52 oz. **Length:** 13-5/8". **Grips:** Black laminated wood. **Sights:** Adjustable rear, replaceable front blade. **Features:** Reintroduced Ultimate SA revolver. Includes instruction manual, high-impact case, set 1" medium scope rings, gun lock, ejector rod as standard.
Price: Hunter model, satin stainless, 7.5" (KS-47NHNN) **$781.00**
Price: Hunter model, Bisley frame, satin stainless 7.5"
(KS-47NHB) **$781.00**

RUGER NEW VAQUERO SINGLE-ACTION REVOLVER
Caliber: 357 Mag., 45 Colt, 6-shot. **Barrel:** 4-5/8", 5.5", 7.5". **Weight:** 39-45 oz. **Length:** 10.5" overall (4-5/8" barrel). **Grips:** Rubber with Ruger medallion. **Sights:** Fixed blade front, fixed notch rear. **Features:** Transfer bar safety system and loading gate interlock. Blued model color case-hardened finish on frame, rest polished and blued. Engraved model available. Gloss stainless. Introduced 2005.
Price: 357 Mag., blued or stainless **$659.00**
Price: 45 Colt, blued or stainless **$659.00**
Price: 357 Mag., 45 Colt, ivory grips, 45 oz. (2009) **$729.00**

Ruger New Model Bisley Vaquero
Similar to New Vaquero but with Bisley-style hammer and grip frame. Chambered in 357 and 45 Colt. Features include a 5.5" barrel, simulated ivory grips, fixed sights, six-shot cylinder. Overall length is 11.12", weighs 45 oz.
Price: **$729.00**

RUGER NEW BEARCAT SINGLE-ACTION
Caliber: 22 LR, 6-shot. **Barrel:** 4". **Weight:** 24 oz. **Length:** 9" overall. **Grips:** Smooth rosewood with Ruger medallion. **Sights:** Blade front, fixed notch rear. **Features:** Reintroduction of the Ruger Bearcat with slightly lengthened frame, Ruger transfer bar safety system.

Available in blue only. Rosewood grips. Introduced 1996 (blued), 2003 (stainless). With case and lock.
Price: SBC-4, blued **$501.00**
Price: KSBC-4, satin stainless . **$540.00**

STI TEXICAN SINGLE-ACTION REVOLVER
Caliber: 45 Colt, 6-shot. **Barrel:** 5.5", 4140 chrome-moly steel by Green Mountain Barrels. 1:16 twist, air gauged to .0002". Chamber to bore alignment less than .001". Forcing cone angle, 3 degrees. **Weight:** 36 oz. **Length:** 11". **Grips:** "No crack" polymer. **Sights:** Blade front, fixed notch rear. **Features:** Parts made by ultra-high speed or electron discharge machined processes from chrome-moly steel forgings or bar stock. Competition sights, springs, triggers and hammers. Frames, loading gates, and hammers are color case hardened by Turnbull Restoration. Frame, back strap, loading gate, trigger guard, cylinders made of 4140 re-sulphurized Maxell 3.5 steel. Hammer firing pin (no transfer bar). S.A.S.S. approved. Introduced 2008. Made in U.S.A. by STI International.
Price: 5.5" barrel **$1,299.99**

TAURUS SINGLE-ACTION GAUCHO REVOLVERS
Caliber: 38 Spl, 357 Mag, 44-40, 45 Colt, 6-shot. **Barrel:** 4.75", 5.5", 7.5", 12". **Weight:** 36.7-37.7 oz. **Length:** 13". **Grips:** Checkered black polymer. **Sights:** Blade front, fixed notch rear. **Features:** Integral transfer bar; blue, blue with case hardened frame, matte stainless and the hand polished "Sundance" stainless finish. Removable cylinder, half-cock notch. Introduced 2005. Imported from Brazil by Taurus International.
Price: S/A-357-B, 357 Mag., Sundance blue finish,
5.5" barrel **$520.00**
Price: S/A-357-S/S7, 357 Mag., polished stainless,
7.5" barrel **$536.00**
Price: S/A-45-B7 . . . . **$520.00**

UBERTI 1851-1860 CONVERSION REVOLVERS
Caliber: 38 Spec., 45 Colt, 6-shot engraved cylinder. **Barrel:** 4.75", 5.5", 7.5", 8" **Weight:** 2.6 lbs. (5.5" bbl.). **Length:** 13" overall (5.5" bbl.). **Grips:** Walnut. **Features:** Brass backstrap, trigger guard; color case-hardened frame, blued barrel, cylinder. Introduced 2007. Imported from Italy by Stoeger Industries.
Price: 1851 Navy **$519.00**
Price: 1860 Army **$549.00**

UBERTI 1871-1872 OPEN TOP REVOLVERS
Caliber: 38 Spec., 45 Colt, 6-shot engraved cylinder. **Barrel:** 4.75", 5.5", 7.5". **Weight:** 2.6 lbs. (5.5" bbl.). **Length:** 13" overall (5.5" bbl.). **Grips:** Walnut. **Features:** Blued backstrap, trigger guard; color case-hardened frame, blued barrel, cylinder. Introduced 2007. Imported from Italy by Stoeger Industries.
Price: **$499.00**

UBERTI 1873 CATTLEMAN SINGLE-ACTION
Caliber: 45 Colt; 6-shot fluted cylinder. **Barrel:** 4.75", 5.5", 7.5". **Weight:** 2.3 lbs. (5.5" bbl.). **Length:** 11" overall (5.5" bbl.). **Grips:**

Styles: Frisco (pearl styled); Desperado (buffalo horn styled); Chisholm (checkered walnut); Gunfighter (black checkered), Cody (ivory styled), one-piece walnut. **Sights:** Blade front, groove rear. **Features:** Steel or brass backstrap, trigger guard; color case-hardened frame, blued barrel, cylinder. NM designates New Model plunger style frame; OM designates Old Model screw cylinder pin retainer. Imported from Italy by Stoeger Industries.
Price: 1873 Cattleman Frisco **$789.00**
Price: 1873 Cattleman Desperado (2006) **$789.00**
Price: 1873 Cattleman Chisholm (2006) **$539.00**
Price: 1873 Cattleman NM, blued 4.75" barrel **$479.00**
Price: 1873 Cattleman NM, Nickel finish, 7.5" barrel **$609.00**
Price: 1873 Cattleman Cody. **$789.00**

UBERTI 1873 CATTLEMAN BIRD'S HEAD SINGLE ACTION
Caliber: 357 Mag., 45 Colt; 6-shot fluted cylinder **Barrel:** 3.5", 4", 4.75", 5.5". **Weight:** 2.3 lbs. (5.5" bbl.). **Length:** 10.9" overall (5.5" bbl.). **Grips:** One-piece walnut. **Sights:** Blade front, groove rear. **Features:** Steel or brass backstrap, trigger guard; color case-hardened frame, blued barrel, cylinder. Imported from Italy by Stoeger Industries.
Price: 1873 Cattleman Bird's Head OM 3.5" barrel **$539.00**

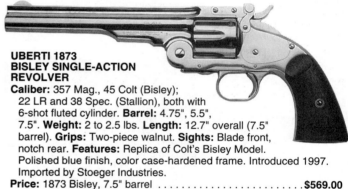

UBERTI 1873 BISLEY SINGLE-ACTION REVOLVER
Caliber: 357 Mag., 45 Colt (Bisley); 22 LR and 38 Spec. (Stallion), both with 6-shot fluted cylinder. **Barrel:** 4.75", 5.5", 7.5". **Weight:** 2 to 2.5 lbs. **Length:** 12.7" overall (7.5" barrel). **Grips:** Two-piece walnut. **Sights:** Blade front, notch rear. **Features:** Replica of Colt's Bisley Model. Polished blue finish, color case-hardened frame. Introduced 1997. Imported by Stoeger Industries.
Price: 1873 Bisley, 7.5" barrel **$569.00**

UBERTI 1873 BUNTLINE AND REVOLVER CARBINE SINGLE-ACTION
Caliber: 357 Mag., 44-40, 45 Colt; 6-shot fluted cylinder **Barrel:** 18". **Length:** 22.9" to 34". **Grips:** Walnut pistol grip or rifle stock. **Sights:** Fixed or adjustable. **Features:** Imported from Italy by Stoeger Industries.
Price: 1873 Revolver Carbine, 18" barrel, 34" OAL **$729.00**
Price: 1873 Cattleman Buntline Target, 18" barrel, 22.9" OAL **$639.00**

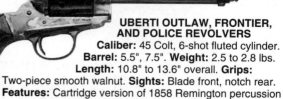

UBERTI OUTLAW, FRONTIER, AND POLICE REVOLVERS
Caliber: 45 Colt, 6-shot fluted cylinder. **Barrel:** 5.5", 7.5". **Weight:** 2.5 to 2.8 lbs. **Length:** 10.8" to 13.6" overall. **Grips:** Two-piece smooth walnut. **Sights:** Blade front, notch rear. **Features:** Cartridge version of 1858 Remington percussion revolver. Nickel and blued finishes. Imported by Stoeger Industries.
Price: 1875 Outlaw nickel finish **$629.00**
Price: 1875 Frontier, blued finish **$539.00**
Price: 1890 Police, blued finish **$549.00**

UBERTI 1870 SCHOFIELD-STYLE TOP BREAK REVOLVER
Caliber: 38, 44 Russian, 44-40, 45 Colt, 6-shot cylinder. **Barrel:** 3.5", 5", 7". **Weight:** 2.4 lbs. (5" barrel) **Length:** 10.8" overall (5" barrel).

Prices given are believed to be accurate at time of publication however, many factors affect retail pricing so exact prices are not possible.

Grips: Two-piece smooth walnut or pearl. **Sights:** Blade front, notch rear. **Features:** Replica of Smith & Wesson Model 3 Schofield. Single-action, top break with automatic ejection. Polished blue finish (first model). Introduced 1994. Imported by Stoeger Industries.
Price: No. 3-2nd Model, nickel finish $1,369.00

U.S. FIRE ARMS U.S. PRE-WAR
Caliber: 45 Colt (standard); 32 WCF, 38 WCF, 38 Spec., 44 WCF, 44 Special. **Barrel:** 4.75", 5.5", 7.5". **Grips:** Hard rubber. **Features:** Armory bone case/Armory blue finish standard, cross-pin or black powder frame. Introduced 2002. Made in U.S.A. by United States Firearms Mfg. Co.
Price: $1,270.00

U.S. FIRE ARMS SINGLE-ACTION REVOLVER
Caliber: 45 Colt (standard); 32 WCF, 38 WCF, 38 Spec., 44 WCF, 44 Special, 6-shot cylinder. **Barrel:** 4.75", 5.5", 7.5". **Weight:** 37 oz. **Length:** NA. **Grips:** Hard rubber. **Sights:** Blade front, notch rear. **Features:** Recreation of original guns; 3" and 4" have no ejector. Available with all-blue, blue with color case-hardening, or full nickel-plate finish. Other models include Custer Battlefield Gun ($1,625, 7.5" barrel), Flattop Target ($1,625), Sheriff's Model ($875, with barrel lengths starting at 2"), Snubnose ($1,475, barrel lengths 2", 3", 4"), Omni-Potent Six-Shooter and Omni-Target Six-Shooter (from $1,625), Bisley ($1,350, introduced 2006). Made in U.S.A. by United States Fire Arms Mfg. Co.
Price: Blue/cased-colors $875.00
Price: Nickel $1,220.00

U.S. FIRE ARMS RODEO COWBOY ACTION REVOLVER
Caliber: 45 Colt, **Barrel:** 4.75", 5.5".
Grips: Rubber. **Features:** Historically correct Armory bone case hammer, blue satin finish, transfer bar safety system, correct solid firing pin. Entry level basic cowboy SASS gun. Other models include the Gunslinger ($1,145). 2006 version includes brown-rubber stocks.
Price: $550.00
Price: New Rodeo 2 (2007) $605.00

BOND ARMS TEXAS DEFENDER DERRINGER

Caliber: From 22 LR to 45 LC/410 shotshells. **Barrel:** 3". **Weight:** 20 oz. **Length:** 5". **Grips:** Rosewood. **Sights:** Blade front, fixed rear. **Features:** Interchangeable barrels, stainless steel firing pins, cross-bolt safety, automatic extractor for rimmed calibers. Stainless steel construction, brushed finish. Right or left hand.
Price: $399.00
Price: Interchangeable barrels, 22 LR thru 45 LC, 3" . . **$139.00**
Price: Interchangeable barrels, 45 LC, 3.5" . **$159.00 to $189.00**

BOND ARMS RANGER

Caliber: 45 LC/.410 shotshells. **Barrel:** 4.25". **Weight:** 23.5 oz. **Length:** 6.25". **Features:** Similar to Snake Slayer except no trigger guard. Intr. 2008. From Bond Arms.
Price: $649.00

BOND ARMS CENTURY 2000 DEFENDER

Caliber: 45 LC/.410 shotshells. **Barrel:** 3.5". **Weight:** 21 oz. **Length:** 5.5". **Features:** Similar to Defender series.
Price: $420.00

BOND ARMS COWBOY DEFENDER

Caliber: From 22 LR to 45 LC/.410 shotshells. **Barrel:** 3". **Weight:** 19 oz. **Length:** 5.5". **Features:** Similar to Defender series. No trigger guard.
Price: $399.00

BOND ARMS SNAKE SLAYER

Caliber: 45 LC/.410 shotshell (2.5" or 3"). **Barrel:** 3.5". **Weight:** 21 oz. **Length:** 5.5". **Grips:** Extended rosewood. **Sights:** Blade front, fixed rear. **Features:** Single-action; interchangeable barrels; stainless steel firing pin. Introduced 2005.
Price: $469.00

BOND ARMS SNAKE SLAYER IV

Caliber: 45 LC/410 shotshell (2.5" or 3"). **Barrel:** 4.25". **Weight:** 22 oz. **Length:** 6.25". **Grips:** Extended rosewood. **Sights:** Blade front, fixed rear. **Features:** Single-action; interchangeable barrels; stainless steel firing pin. Introduced 2006.
Price: $499.00

CHARTER ARMS DIXIE DERRINGERS

Caliber: 22 LR, 22 WMR. **Barrel:** 1.125". **Weight:** 6 oz. **Length:** 4" overall. **Grips:** Black polymer **Sights:** Blade front, fixed notch rear. **Features:** Stainless finish. Introduced 2006. Made in U.S.A. by Charter Arms, distributed by MKS Supply.
Price: $215.00

COBRA BIG BORE DERRINGERS

Caliber: 22 WMR, 32 H&R Mag., 38 Spec., 9mm Para., 380 ACP. **Barrel:** 2.75". **Weight:** 14 oz. **Length:** 4.65" overall. **Grips:** Textured black or white synthetic or laminated rosewood. **Sights:** Blade front, fixed notch rear. **Features:** Alloy frame, steel-lined barrels, steel breech block. Plunger-type safety with integral hammer block. Black, chrome or satin finish. Introduced 2002. Made in U.S.A. by Cobra Enterprises of Utah, Inc.
Price: $165.00

COBRA STANDARD SERIES DERRINGERS

Caliber: 22 LR, 22 WMR, 25 ACP, 32 ACP. **Barrel:** 2.4". **Weight:** 9.5 oz. Length: 4" overall. **Grips:** Laminated wood or pearl. **Sights:** Blade front, fixed notch rear. **Features:** Choice of black powder coat, satin nickel or chrome finish. Introduced 2002. Made in U.S.A. by Cobra Enterprises of Utah, Inc.
Price: $145.00

COBRA LONG-BORE DERRINGERS

Caliber: 22 WMR, 38 Spec., 9mm Para. **Barrel:** 3.5". **Weight:** 16 oz.

Length: 5.4" overall. **Grips:** Black or white synthetic or rosewood. **Sights:** Fixed. **Features:** Chrome, satin nickel, or black Teflon finish. Introduced 2002. Made in U.S.A. by Cobra Enterprises of Utah, Inc.
Price: **$165.00**

COMANCHE SUPER SINGLE-SHOT PISTOL

Caliber: 45 LC, .410 **Barrel:** 10". **Sights:** Adjustable. **Features:** Blue finish, not available for sale in CA, MA. Distributed by SGS Importers International, Inc.
Price: $200.00

MAXIMUM SINGLE-SHOT PISTOL

Caliber: 22 LR, 22 Hornet, 22 BR, 22 PPC, 223 Rem., 22-250, 6mm BR, 6mm PPC, 243, 250 Savage, 6.5mm-35M, 270 MAX, 270 Win., 7mm TCU, 7mm BR, 7mm-35, 7mm INT-R, 7mm-08, 7mm Rocket, 7mm Super-Mag., 30 Herrett, 30 Carbine, 30-30, 308 Win., 30x39, 32-20, 350 Rem. Mag., 357 Mag., 357 Maximum, 358 Win., 375 H&H, 44 Mag., 454 Casull. **Barrel:** 8.75", 10.5", 14". **Weight:** 61 oz. (10.5" bbl.); 78 oz. (14" bbl.). **Length:** 15", 18.5" overall (with 10.5" and 14" bbl., respectively). **Grips:** Smooth walnut stocks and forend. Also available with 17" finger groove grip. **Sights:** Ramp front, fully adjustable open rear. **Features:** Falling block action; drilled and tapped for M.O.A. scope mounts; integral grip frame/receiver; adjustable trigger; Douglas barrel (interchangeable). Introduced 1983. Made in U.S.A. by M.O.A. Corp.
Price: Stainless receiver, blue barrel $839.00
Price: Stainless receiver, stainless barrel $937.00

THOMPSON/CENTER ENCORE PISTOL

Caliber: 22-250, 223, 204 Ruger, 6.8 Rem., 260 Rem., 7mm-08, 243, 308, 270, 30-06, 375 JDJ, 204 Ruger, 44 Mag., 454 Casull, 480 Ruger, 444 Marlin single shot, 450 Marlin with muzzle tamer, no sights. **Barrel:** 12", 15", tapered round. **Weight:** NA. **Length:** 21" overall with 12" barrel. **Grips:** American walnut with finger grooves, walnut forend. **Sights:** Blade on ramp front, adjustable rear, or none. **Features:** Interchangeable barrels; action opens by squeezing the trigger guard; drilled and tapped for scope mounting; blue finish. Announced 1996. Made in U.S.A. by Thompson/Center Arms.
Price: $615.00

THOMPSON/CENTER G2 CONTENDER PISTOL

A second generation Contender pistol maintaining the same barrel interchangeability with older Contender barrels and their corresponding forends (except Herrett forend). The G2 frame will not accept old-style grips due to the change in grip angle. Incorporates an automatic hammer block safety with built-in interlock. Features include trigger adjustable for overtravel, adjustable rear sight; ramp front sight blade, blued steel finish.
Price: $600.00

Prices given are believed to be accurate at time of publication however, many factors affect retail pricing so exact prices are not possible.

ARMALITE M15A2 CARBINE

Caliber: 223 Rem., 30-round magazine. **Barrel:** 16" heavy chrome lined; 1:9" twist. **Weight:** 7 lbs. **Length:** 35-11/16" overall. **Stock:** Green or black composition. **Sights:** Standard A2. **Features:** Upper and lower receivers have push-type pivot pin; hard coat anodized; A2-style forward assist; M16A2-type raised fence around magazine release button. Made in U.S.A. by ArmaLite, Inc.
Price: Green **$1,150.00**
Price: Black. **$1,150.00**

ARMALITE AR-10A4 SPECIAL PURPOSE RIFLE

Caliber: 308 Win., 10- and 20-round magazine. **Barrel:** 20" chrome-lined, 1:11.25" twist. **Weight:** 9.6 lbs. **Length:** 41" overall. **Stock:** Green or black composition. **Sights:** Detachable handle, front sight, or scope mount available; comes with international style flattop receiver with Picatinny rail. **Features:** Forged upper receiver with case deflector. Receivers are hard-coat anodized. Introduced 1995. Made in U.S.A. by ArmaLite, Inc.
Price: Green **$1,557.00**
Price: Black. **$1,557.00**

ArmaLite AR-10A2

Utilizing the same 20" double-lapped, heavy barrel as the ArmaLite AR10A4 Special Purpose Rifle. Offered in 308 Win. only. Made in U.S.A. by ArmaLite, Inc.
Price: AR-10A2 rifle or carbine **$1,561.00**

ARMALITE AR-10B RIFLE

Caliber: 308 Win. **Barrel:** 20" chrome lined. **Weight:** 9.5 lbs. **Length:** 41". **Stock:** Synthetic. **Sights:** Rear sight adjustable for windage, small and large apertures. **Features:** Early-style AR-10. Lower and upper receivers made of forged aircraft alloy. Brown Sudanese-style furniture, elevation scale window. Charging handle in carry handle. Made in U.S.A. by Armalite.
Price: **$1,699.00**

ARSENAL, INC. SLR-107F

Caliber: 7.62x39mm. **Barrel:** 16.25". **Weight:** 7.3 lbs. **Stock:** Left-side folding polymer stock. **Sights:** Adjustable rear. **Features:** Stamped receiver, 24mm flash hider, bayonet lug, accessory lug, stainless steel heat shield, two-stage trigger. Introduced 2008. Made in U.S.A. by Arsenal, Inc.
Price: SLR-107FR, includes scope rail. **$1,035.00**

ARSENAL, INC. SLR-107CR

Caliber: 7.62x39mm. **Barrel:** 16.25". **Weight:** 6.9 lbs. **Stock:** Left-side folding polymer stock. **Sights:** Adjustable rear. **Features:** Stamped receiver, front sight block/gas block combination, 500-meter rear sight, cleaning rod, stainless steel heat shield, scope rail, and removable muzzle attachment. Introduced 2007. Made in U.S.A. by Arsenal, Inc.
Price: SLR-107CR **$1,200.00**

ARSENAL, INC. SLR-106CR

Caliber: 5.56 NATO. **Barrel:** 16.25", Steyr chrome-lined barrel, 1:7 twist rate. **Weight:** 6.9 lbs. **Stock:** Black polymer folding stock with cutout for scope rail. Stainless-steel heatshield handguard. **Sights:** 500-meter rear sight and rear sight block calibrated for 5.56 NATO.

Warsaw Pact scope rail. **Features:** Uses Arsenal, Bulgaria, Mil-Spec receiver, two-stage trigger, hammer and disconnector. Polymer magazines in 5- and 10-round capacity in black and green, with Arsenal logo. Others are 30-round black waffles, 20- and 30-round versions in clear/smoke waffle, featuring the "10" in a double-circle logo of Arsenal, Bulgaria. Ships with 5-round magazine, sling, cleaning kit in a tube, 16" cleaning rod, oil bottle. Introduced 2007. Made in U.S.A. by Arsenal, Inc.
Price: SLR-106CR **$1,200.00**

AUTO-ORDNANCE 1927A-1 THOMPSON

Caliber: 45 ACP. **Barrel:** 16.5". **Weight:** 13 lbs. **Length:** About 41" overall (Deluxe). **Stock:** Walnut stock and vertical forend. **Sights:** Blade front, open rear adjustable for windage. **Features:** Recreation of Thompson Model 1927. Semi-auto only. Deluxe model has finned barrel, adjustable rear sight and compensator; Standard model has plain barrel and military sight. From Auto-Ordnance Corp.
Price: Deluxe **$1,420.00**
Price: Lightweight model (9.5 lbs.) **$1,145.00**

Auto-Ordnance Thompson M1/M1-C

Similar to the 1927 A-1 except is in the M-1 configuration with side cocking knob, horizontal forend, smooth unfinned barrel, sling swivels on butt and forend. Matte-black finish. Introduced 1985.
Price: M1 semi-auto carbine. **$1,334.00**
Price: M1-C lightweight semi-auto **$1,065.00**

Auto-Ordnance 1927 A-1 Commando

Similar to the 1927 A-1 except has Parkerized finish, black-finish wood butt, pistol grip, horizontal forend. Comes with black nylon sling. Introduced 1998. Made in U.S.A. by Auto-Ordnance Corp.
Price: T1-C **$1,393.00**

BARRETT MODEL 82A-1 SEMI-AUTOMATIC RIFLE

Caliber: 50 BMG, 10-shot detachable box magazine. **Barrel:** 29". **Weight:** 28.5 lbs. **Length:** 57" overall. **Stock:** Composition with energy-absorbing recoil pad. **Sights:** Scope optional. **Features:** Semi-automatic, recoil operated with recoiling barrel. Three-lug locking bolt; muzzle brake. Adjustable bipod. Introduced 1985. Made in U.S.A. by Barrett Firearms.
Price: From **$8,900.00**

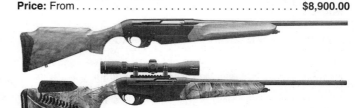

BENELLI R1 RIFLE

Caliber: 300 Win. Mag., 300 WSM, 270 WSM (24" barrel); 30-06 Spfl., 308 Win. (22" barrel); 300 Win. Mag., 30-06 Spfl., (20" barrel). **Weight:** 7.1 lbs. **Length:** 43.75" to 45.75". **Stock:** Select satin walnut or synthetic. **Sights:** None. **Features:** Auto-regulating gas-operated system, three-lug rotary bolt, interchangeable barrels, optional recoil pads. Introduced 2003. Imported from Italy by Benelli USA.
Price: Synthetic with ComforTech gel recoil pad **$1,549.00**
Price: Satin walnut **$1,379.00**
Price: APG HD camo, 30-06 (2008) **$1,689.00**

BENELLI MR1 RIFLE

Gas-operated semiauto rifle chambered in 5.56 NATO. Features include 16-inch 1:9 hard chrome-lined barrel, synthetic stock with pistol grip, rotating bolt, military-style aperture sights with picatinny rail. Comes equipped with 5-round detachable magazine but accepts M16 magazines.

Price: **$1299.00**

BERETTA CX4/PX4 STORM CARBINE

Caliber: 9mm Para., 40 S&W, 45 ACP. **Weight:** 5.75 lbs. **Barrel Length:** 16.6", chrome lined, rate of twist 1:16 (40 S&W) or 1:10 (9mm Para.). **Length:** NA. **Stock:** Black synthetic. **Sights:** NA. **Features:** Introduced 2005. Imported from Italy by Beretta USA.

Price: **$900.00**

BROWNING BAR SAFARI AND SAFARI W/BOSS SEMI-AUTO RIFLES

Caliber: Safari: 243 Win., 25-06 Rem., 270 Win., 7mm Rem. Mag., 30-06 Spfl., 308 Win., 300 Win. Mag., 338 Win. Mag. Safari w/BOSS: 270 Win., 7mm Rem. Mag., 30-06 Spfl., 300 Win. Mag., 338 Win. Mag., plus 270 WSM, 7mm WSM, 300 WSM. **Barrel:** 22-24" round tapered. **Weight:** 7.4-8.2 lbs. **Length:** 43-45" overall. **Stock:** French walnut pistol grip stock and forend, hand checkered. **Sights:** No sights. **Features:** Has new bolt release lever; removable trigger assembly with larger trigger guard; redesigned gas and buffer systems. Detachable 4-round box magazine. Scroll-engraved receiver is tapped for scope mounting. BOSS barrel vibration modulator and muzzle brake system available. Mark II Safari introduced 1993. Imported from Belgium by Browning.

Price: BAR MK II Safari, from **$1,109.00**
Price: BAR Safari w/BOSS, from **$1,229.00**

BROWNING BAR SHORTTRAC/LONGTRAC AUTO RIFLES

Caliber: (ShortTrac models) 270 WSM, 7mm WSM, 300 WSM, 243 Win., 308 Win., 325 WSM; (LongTrac models) 270 Win., 30-06 Spfl., 7mm Rem. Mag., 300 Win. Mag. **Barrel:** 23". **Weight:** 6 lbs. 10 oz. to 7 lbs. 4 oz. **Length:** 41.5" to 44". **Stock:** Satin-finish walnut, pistol-grip, fluted forend. **Sights:** Adj. rear, bead front standard, no sights on BOSS models (optional). **Features:** Designed to handle new WSM chamberings. Gas-operated, blued finish, rotary bolt design (LongTrac models).

Price: BAR ShortTrac, 243 Win., 308 Win. from **$1,079.00**
Price: BAR ShortTrac Left-Hand, intr. 2007, from **$1,129.00**
Price: BAR ShortTrac Mossy Oak New Break-up
. . . . **$1,249.00 to $1,349.00**
Price: BAR LongTrac Left Hand, 270 Win., 30-06 Spfl.,
from **$1,129.00**
Price: BAR LongTrac, from. **$1,079.00**
Price: BAR LongTrac Mossy Oak Break Up, intr. 2007,
from **$1,249.00**
Price: Bar LongTrac, Digital Green camo (2009)
. . . . **$1,247.00 to $1,347.00**

BROWNING BAR STALKER AUTO RIFLES

Caliber: 243 Win., 308 Win., 270 Win., 30-06 Spfl., 270 WSM, 7mm WSM, 300 WSM, 300 Win. Mag., 338 Win. Mag. **Barrel:** 20-24". **Weight:** 7.1-7.75 LBS. **Length:** 41-45" overall. **Stock:** Black composite stock and forearm. **Sights:** Hooded front and adjustable rear. **Features:** Gas-operated action with seven-lug rotary bolt; dual action bars; 2-, 3- or 4-shot magazine (depending on cartridge). Introduced 2001. Imported by Browning.

Price: BAR ShortTrac or LongTrac Stalker, from **$1,119.00**
Price: BAR Lightweight Stalker, from **$1,099.00**

BUSHMASTER SUPERLIGHT CARBINES

Caliber: 223 Rem., 30-shot magazine. **Barrel:** 16", heavy; 1:9" twist. **Weight:** 6.25 lbs. **Length:** 31.25-34.5" overall. **Stock:** 6-position telestock or Stubby (7.25" length). **Sights:** Fully adjustable M16A2 sight system. **Features:** Adapted from original G.I. pencil-barrel profile. Chrome-lined barrel with manganese phosphate finish. "Shorty" handguards. Has forged aluminum receivers with pushpin. Made in U.S.A. by Bushmaster Firearms, Inc.

Price: From **$1, 250.00**

Bushmaster XM15 E2S Dissipator Carbine

Similar to the XM15 E2S Shorty carbine except has full-length "Dissipator" handguards. Weighs 7.6 lbs.; 34.75" overall; forged aluminum receivers with push-pin style takedown. Made in U.S.A. by Bushmaster Firearms, Inc.

Price: From **$1,240.00**

Bushmaster XM15 E25 AK Shorty Carbine

Similar to the XM15 E2S Shorty except has 14.5" barrel with an AK muzzle brake permanently attached giving 16" barrel length. Weighs 7.3 lbs. Introduced 1999. Made in U.S.A. by Bushmaster Firearms, Inc.

Price: From **$1,215.00**

Bushmaster M4 Post-Ban Carbine

Similar to the XM15 E2S except has 14.5" barrel with Mini Y compensator, and fixed telestock. MR configuration has fixed carry handle.

Price: **$1,190.00**

BUSHMASTER VARMINTER RIFLE

Caliber: 223 Rem., 5-shot. **Barrel:** 24", 1:9" twist, fluted, heavy, stainless. **Weight:** 8.75 lbs. **Length:** 42.25". **Stock:** Rubberized pistol grip. **Sights:** 1/2" scope risers. **Features:** Gas-operated, semi-auto, two-stage trigger, slotted free floater forend, lockable hard case.

Price: **$1,360.00**
Price: Bushmaster Predator: 20" 1:8 barrel, 223 Rem. **$1,245.00**
Price: Bushmaster Stainless Varmint Special: Same as
Varminter but with 24" stainless barrel **$1,277.00**

BUSHMASTER 6.8 SPC CARBINE

Caliber: 6.8 SPC, 26-shot mag. **Barrel:** 16" M4 profile. **Weight:** 6.57 lbs. **Length:** 32.75" overall. **Features:** Semi-auto AR-style with Izzy muzzle brake, six-position telestock. Available in A2 (fixed carry handle) or A3 (removable carry handle) configuration.

. . . . **$1,500.00**

BUSHMASTER ORC CARBINE

Caliber: 5.56/223. **Barrel:** 16" M4 profile. **Weight:** 6 lbs. **Length:** 32.5" overall. **Features:** AR-style carbine with chrome-lined barrel,

fixed carry handle, receiver-length picatinny optics rail, heavy oval M4-style handguards.
Price: **$1,085.00**

BUSHMASTER 11.5" BARREL CARBINE
Caliber: 5.56/223, 30-shot mag. **Barrel:** 11.5". **Weight:** 6.46 lbs. or 6.81 lbs. **Length:** 31.625" overall. **Features:** AR-style carbine with chrome-lined barrel with permanently attached BATF-approved 5.5" flash suppressor, fixed or removable carry handle, optional optics rail.
Price: **$1,215.00**

BUSHMASTER HEAVY-BARRELED CARBINE
Caliber: 5.56/223. **Barrel:** 16". **Weight:** 6.93 lbs. to 7.28 lbs. **Length:** 32.5" overall. **Features:** AR-style carbine with chrome-lined heavy profile vanadium steel barrel, fixed or removable carry handle, six-position telestock.
Price: **$1,215.00**

BUSHMASTER MODULAR CARBINE
Caliber: 5.56/223, 30-shot mag. **Barrel:** 16". **Weight:** 7.3 lbs. **Length:** 36.25" overall. **Features:** AR-style carbine with chrome-lined chrome-moly vanadium steel barrel, skeleton stock or six-position telestock, clamp-on front sight and detachable flip-up dual aperature rear.
Price: **$1,745.00**

BUSHMASTER CARBON 15 TOP LOADER RIFLE
Caliber: 5.56/223, internal 10-shot mag. **Barrel:** 16" chrome-lined M4 profile. **Weight:** 5.8 lbs. **Length:** 32.75" overall. **Features:** AR-style carbine with standard A2 front sight, dual aperture rear sight, receiver-length optics rail, lightweight carbon fiber receiver, six-position telestock. Will not accept detachable box magazines.
Price: **$1,070.00**

BUSHMASTER CARBON 15 FLAT-TOP CARBINE
Caliber: 5.56/223, 30-shot mag. **Barrel:** 16" M4 profile. **Weight:** 5.77 lbs. **Length:** 32.75" overall. **Features:** AR-style carbine Izzy flash suppressor, AR-type front sight, dual aperture flip, lightweight carbon composite receiver with receiver-length optics rail.
Price: **$1,155.00**
Price: Carbon 15 9mm, chambered in 9mm Parabellum . . . **$1,025.00**

BUSHMASTER 450 RIFLE AND CARBINE
Caliber: 450 Bushmaster. **Barrel:** 20" (rifle), 16" (carbine), five-round mag. **Weight:** 8.3 lbs. (rifle), 8.1 lbs. (carbine). **Length:** 39.5" overall (rifle), 35.25" overall (carbine). **Features:** AR-style with chrome-lined chrome-moly barrel, synthetic stock, Izzy muzzle brake.
Price: **$1,350.00**

BUSHMASTER GAS PISTON RIFLE
Caliber: 223, 30-shot mag. **Barrel:** 16". **Weight:** 7.46 lbs. **Length:** 32.5" overall. **Features:** Semi-auto AR-style with telescoping stock, carry handle, piston assembly rather than direct gas impingement.
Price: **$1,795.00**

BUSHMASTER TARGET RIFLE
Caliber: 5.56/223, 30-shot mag. **Barrel:** 20" or 24" heavy or standard. **Weight:** 8.43 lbs. to 9.29 lbs. **Length:** 39.5" or 43.5" overall. **Features:** Semi-auto AR-style with chrome-lined or stainless steel 1:9 barrel, fixed or removable carry handle, manganese phosphate finish.
Price: **$1,195.00**

BUSHMASTER M4A3 TYPE CARBINE
Caliber: 5.56/223, 30-shot mag. **Barrel:** 16". **Weight:** 6.22 to 6.7 lbs. **Length:** 31" to 32.5" overall. **Features:** AR-style carbine with chrome-moly vanadium steel barrel, Izzy-type flash-hider, six-position telestock, various sight options, standard or multi-rail handguard, fixed or removable carry handle.
Price: **$1,270.00**
Price: Patrolman's Carbine: Standard mil-style sights **$1,270.00**
Price: State Compliance Carbine: Compliant with various state regulations **$1,270.00**

CENTURY INTERNATIONAL AES-10 HI-CAP RIFLE
Caliber: 7.62x39mm. 30-shot

magazine. **Barrel:** 23.2". **Weight:** NA. **Length:** 41.5" overall. **Stock:** Wood grip, forend. **Sights:** Fixed-notch rear, windage-adjustable post front. **Features:** RPK-style, accepts standard double-stack AK-type mags. Side-mounted scope mount, integral carry handle, bipod. Imported by Century Arms Int'l.
Price: AES-10, from **$450.00**

CENTURY INTERNATIONAL GP WASR-10 HI-CAP RIFLE
Caliber: 7.62x39mm. 30-shot
magazine. **Barrel:** 16.25", 1:10 right-hand twist. **Weight:** 7.2 lbs. **Length:** 34.25" overall. **Stock:** Wood laminate or composite, grip, forend. **Sights:** Fixed-notch rear, windage-adjustable post front. **Features:** Two 30-rd. detachable box magazines, cleaning kit, bayonet. Version of AKM rifle; U.S.-parts added for BATFE compliance. Threaded muzzle, folding stock, bayonet lug, compensator, Dragunov stock available. Made in Romania by Cugir Arsenal. Imported by Century Arms Int'l.
Price: GP WASR-10, from **$350.00**

CENTURY INTERNATIONAL WASR-2 HI-CAP RIFLE
Caliber: 5.45x39mm. 30-shot
magazine. **Barrel:** 16.25". **Weight:** 7.5 lbs. **Length:** 34.25" overall. **Stocks:** Wood laminate. **Sights:** Fixed-notch rear, windage-adjustable post front. **Features:** 1 30-rd. detachable box magazine, cleaning kit, sling. WASR-3 HI-CAP chambered in 223 Rem. Imported by Century Arms Int'l.
Price: GP WASR-2/3, from **$250.00**

CENTURY INTERNATIONAL M70AB2 SPORTER RIFLE
Caliber: 7.62x39mm. 30-shot magazine. **Barrel:** 16.25". **Weight:** 7.5 lbs.
Length: 34.25" overall. **Stocks:** Metal grip, wood forend. **Sights:** Fixed-notch rear, windage-adjustable post front. **Features:** 2 30-rd. double-stack magazine, cleaning kit, compensator, bayonet lug and bayonet. Paratrooper-style Kalashnikov with under-folding stock. Imported by Century Arms Int'l.
Price: M70AB2, from **$480.00**

COLT MATCH TARGET MODEL RIFLE
Caliber: 223 Rem., 5-shot magazine.
Barrel: 16.1" or 20". **Weight:** 7.1 to 8.5 lbs. **Length:** 34.5" to 39" overall. **Stock:** Composition stock, grip, forend. **Sights:** Post front, rear adjustable for windage and elevation. **Features:** 5-round detachable box magazine, flash suppressor, sling swivels. Forward bolt assist included. Introduced 1991. Made in U.S.A. by Colt's Mfg. Co., Inc.
Price: Match Target HBAR MT6601 . . . . **$1,182.00**

Colt Match Target M4
Similar to above but with carbine-length barrel.
Price: . . . . **NA**

DPMS PANTHER ARMS AR-15 RIFLES
Caliber: 223 Rem., 7.62x39. **Barrel:** 16" to 24". **Weight:** 7.75 to 11.75 lbs. **Length:** 34.5" to 42.25" overall. **Stock:** Black Zytel composite. **Sights:** Square front post, adjustable A2 rear. **Features:** Steel or stainless steel heavy or bull barrel; hardcoat anodized receiver; aluminum free-float tube handguard; many options. From DPMS Panther Arms.

Price: Panther Bull Twenty (20" stainless bull bbl.) **$920.00**
Price: Arctic Panther. **$1,099.00**
Price: Panther Classic **$799.00**
Price: Panther Bull Sweet Sixteen (16" stainless bull bbl.) . . .**$885.00**
Price: DCM Panther (20" stainless heavy bbl., n.m. sights) **$1,099.00**
Price: Panther 7.62x39 (20" steel heavy bbl.) **$859.00**

DPMS PANTHER ARMS CLASSIC AUTO RIFLE
Caliber: 5.56x45mm. **Barrel:** Heavy 16" to 20" w/flash hider. **Weight:** 7 to 9 lbs. **Length:** 34-11/16" to 38-7/16". **Sights:** Adj. rear and front. **Stock:** Black Zytel w/trap door assembly. **Features:** Gas operated rotating bolt, mil spec or Teflon black finish.
Price: Panther A2 Tactical 16" **$814.00**
Price: Panther Lite 16 . . . .**$725.00**
Price: Panther Carbine **$799.00**
Price: Panther The Agency Rifle. **$1,999.00**

DPMS PANTHER ARMS 5.56 PANTHER ORACLE
Semiauto AR-style rifle chambered in 5.56 NATO. Features include 16-inch 4140 chrome-moly 1:9 barrel; phosphated steel bolt; oval GlacierGuard handguard; flattop upper with Picatinny rail; aluminum lower; two 30-round magazines; Pardus 6-position telescoping stock. Also available on larger platform in .308 Winchester/7.62 NATO.
Price: **$759.00**

DPMS PANTHER ARMS PANTHER 3G1
Semiauto AR-style rifle chambered in 5.56 NATO. Features include 18-inch 416 stainless 1:9 barrel; phosphated steel bolt; VTAC modular handguard; flattop upper with Picatinny rail; aluminum lower; two 30-round magazines; Magpul CTR adjustable stock.
Price: **$1,499.00**

DPMS PANTHER ARMS PRAIRIE PANTHER
Semiauto AR-style rifle chambered in 5.56 NATO. Features include 20-inch 416 stainless fluted heavy 1:8 barrel; phosphated steel bolt; free-floated carbon fiber handguard; flattop upper with Picatinny rail; aluminum lower; two 30-round magazines; skeletonized Zytel stock; finished in King's Desert Shadow camo overall.
Price: **$1,249.00**

DPMS PANTHER ARMS PANTHER RAPTR
Semiauto AR-style rifle chambered in 5.56 NATO. Features include 16-inch 4140 chrome-moly 1:9 barrel; phosphated steel bolt; ERGO Z-Rail 4-rail handguard; front vertical grip; standard A2 sights; aluminum lower; four 30-round magazines.
Price: **$1,649.00**

DPMS PANTHER ARMS PANTHER REPR
Semiauto AR-style rifle chambered in .308 Win./7.62 NATO. Features include 18-inch 416 stainless steel 1:10 barrel; phosphated steel bolt; 4-rail free-floated handguard; no sights; aluminum lower; two 19-round magazines; Coyote Brown camo finish overall.
Price: **$2,549.00**

DPMS PANTHER ARMS PANTHER 308 MK12
Semiauto AR-style rifle chambered in .308 Win./7.62 NATO. Features include 16-inch 4140 chrome-moly heavy 1:10 barrel; phosphated steel bolt; 4-rail free-floated handguard; flip-up front and rear sights; aluminum lower; two 19-round magazines; matte black finish overall; Magpul CTR adjustable stock.
Price: **$2,549.00**

DSA Z4 GTC CARBINE WITH C.R.O.S.
Caliber: 5.56 NATO **Barrel:** 16" 1:9 twist M4 profile fluted chrome lined heavy barrel with threaded Vortec flash hider. **Weight:** 7.6 lbs. **Stock:** 6 position collapsible M4 stock, Predator P4X free float tactical rail. **Sights:** Chrome lined Picatinny gas block w/removable front sight. **Features:** The Corrosion Resistant Operating System incorporates the new P.O.F. Gas Trap System with removable gas plug eliminates problematic features of standard AR gas system, Forged 7075T6 DSA lower receiver. Introduced 2006. Made in U.S.A. by DSA, Inc.
Price: **$1,800.00**

DSA CQB MRP, STANDARD MRP
Caliber: 5.56 NATO **Barrel:** 16" or 18" 1:7 twist chrome-lined or stainless steel barrel with A2 flash hider **Stock:** 6 position collapsible M4 stock. **Features:** LMT 1/2" MRP upper receiver with 20.5" Standard quad rail or 16.5" CQB quad rail, LMT-enhanced bolt with dual extractor springs, free float barrel, quick change barrel system, forged 7075T6 DSA lower receiver. EOTech and vertical grip additional. Introduced 2006. Made in U.S.A. by DSA, Inc.
Price: CQB MRP w/16" chrome-lined barrel **$2,420.00**
Price: CQB MRP w/16" stainless steel barrel. **$2,540.00**
Price: Standard MRP w/16" chrome-lined barrel **$2,620.00**
Price: Standard MRP w/16" or 18" stainless steel barrel . . .**$2,740.00**

DSA STD CARBINE
Caliber: 5.56 NATO. **Barrel:** 16" 1:9 twist D4 w/A2 flash hider. **Weight:** 6.25 lbs. **Length:** 31". **Stock:** A2 buttstock, D4 handguard w/heatshield. **Sights:** Forged A2 front sight with lug. **Features:** Forged 7075T6 DSA lower receiver, forged A2 or flattop upper receiver. Introduced 2006. Made in U.S.A. by DSA, Inc.
Price: A2 or Flattop STD Carbine **$1,025.00**
Price: With LMT SOPMOD stock **$1,267.00**

DSA 1R CARBINE
Caliber: 5.56 NATO. **Barrel:** 16" 1:9 twist D4 w/A2 flash hider. **Weight:** 6.25 lbs. **Length:** Variable. **Stock:** 6 position collapsible M4 stock, D4 handguard w/heatshield. **Sights:** Forged A2 front sight with lug. **Features:** Forged 7075T6 DSA lower receiver, forged A2 or

flattop upper receiver. Introduced 2006. Made in U.S.A. by DSA, Inc.
Price: A2 or Flattop 1R Carbine **$1,055.00**
Price: With VLTOR ModStock **$1,175.00**

DSA XM CARBINE
Caliber: 5.56 NATO. **Barrel:** 11.5" 1:9 twist D4 with 5.5" permanently attached flash hider. **Weight:** 6.25 lbs. **Length:** Variable. **Stock:** Collapsible, Handguard w/heatshield. **Sights:** Forged A2 front sight with lug. **Features:** Forged 7075T6 DSA lower receiver, forged A2 upper receiver. Introduced 2006. Made in U.S.A. by DSA, Inc.
Price: **$1,055.00**

DSA STANDARD
Caliber: 5.56 NATO. **Barrel:** 20" 1:9 twist heavy barrel w/A2 flash hider. **Weight:** 6.25 lbs. **Length:** 38-7/16". **Stock:** A2 buttstock, A2 handguard w/heatshield. **Sights:** Forged A2 front sight with lug. **Features:** Forged 7075T6 DSA lower receiver, forged A2 or flattop upper receiver. Introduced 2006. Made in U.S.A. by DSA, Inc.
Price: A2 or Flattop Standard **$1,025.00**

DSA DCM RIFLE
Caliber: 223 Wylde Chamber. **Barrel:** 20" 1:8 twist chrome moly match grade Badger Barrel. **Weight:** 10 lbs. **Length:** 39.5". **Stock:** DCM freefloat handguard system, A2 buttstock. **Sights:** Forged A2 front sight with lug. **Features:** NM two stage trigger, NM rear sight, forged 7075T6 DSA lower receiver, forged A2 upper receiver. Introduced 2006. Made in U.S.A. by DSA, Inc.
Price: **$1,520.00**

DSA S1
Caliber: 223 Rem. Match Chamber. **Barrel:** 16", 20" or 24" 1:8 twist stainless steel bull barrel. **Weight:** 8.0, 9.5 and 10 lbs. **Length:** 34.25", 38.25" and 42.25". **Stock:** A2 buttstock with free float aluminum handguard. **Sights:** Picatinny gas block sight base. **Features:** Forged 7075T6 DSA lower receiver, Match two stage trigger, forged flattop upper receiver, fluted barrel optional. Introduced 2006. Made in U.S.A. by DSA, Inc.
Price: **$1,155.00**

DSA SA58 CONGO, PARA CONGO
Caliber: 308 Win. **Barrel:** 18" w/short Belgian short flash hider. **Weight:** 8.6 lbs. (Congo); 9.85 lbs. (Para Congo). **Length:** 39.75" **Stock:** Synthetic w/military grade furniture (Congo); Synthetic with non-folding steel para stock (Para Congo). **Sights:** Elevation adjustable protected post front sight, windage adjustable rear peep (Congo); Belgian type Para Flip Rear (Para Congo). **Features:** Fully-adjustable gas system, high-grade steel upper receiver with carry handle. Made in U.S.A. by DSA, Inc.
Price: Congo. **$1,850.00**
Price: Para Congo **$2,095.00**

DSA SA58 GRAY WOLF
Caliber: 308 Win. **Barrel:** 21" match-grade bull w/target crown. **Weight:** 13 lbs. **Length:** 41.75". **Stock:** Synthetic. **Sights:** Elevation-adjustable post front sight, windage-adjustable match rear peep. **Features:** Fully-adjustable gas system, high-grade steel upper receiver, Picatinny scope mount, DuraCoat finish. Made in U.S.A. by DSA, Inc.
Price: **$2,120.00**

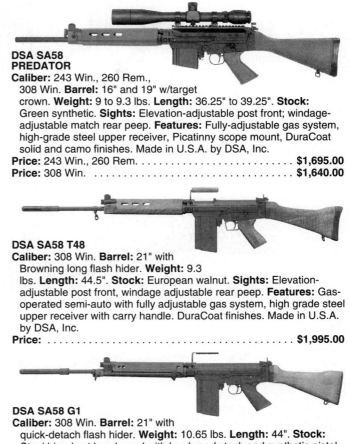

DSA SA58 PREDATOR
Caliber: 243 Win., 260 Rem., 308 Win. **Barrel:** 16" and 19" w/target crown. **Weight:** 9 to 9.3 lbs. **Length:** 36.25" to 39.25". **Stock:** Green synthetic. **Sights:** Elevation-adjustable post front; windage-adjustable match rear peep. **Features:** Fully-adjustable gas system, high-grade steel upper receiver, Picatinny scope mount, DuraCoat solid and camo finishes. Made in U.S.A. by DSA, Inc.
Price: 243 Win., 260 Rem. **$1,695.00**
Price: 308 Win. **$1,640.00**

DSA SA58 T48
Caliber: 308 Win. **Barrel:** 21" with Browning long flash hider. **Weight:** 9.3 lbs. **Length:** 44.5". **Stock:** European walnut. **Sights:** Elevation-adjustable post front, windage adjustable rear peep. **Features:** Gas-operated semi-auto with fully adjustable gas system, high grade steel upper receiver with carry handle. DuraCoat finishes. Made in U.S.A. by DSA, Inc.
Price: **$1,995.00**

DSA SA58 G1
Caliber: 308 Win. **Barrel:** 21" with quick-detach flash hider. **Weight:** 10.65 lbs. **Length:** 44". **Stock:** Steel bipod cut handguard with hardwood stock and synthetic pistol grip. **Sights:** Elevation-adjustable post front, windage adjustable rear peep. **Features:** Gas-operated semi-auto with fully adjustable gas system, high grade steel upper receiver with carry handle, original GI steel lower receiver with GI bipod. DuraCoat finishes. Made in U.S.A. by DSA, Inc.
Price: **$1,850.00**

DSA SA58 STANDARD
Caliber: 308 Win. **Barrel:** 21" bipod cut w/threaded flash hider. **Weight:** 8.75 lbs. **Length:** 43". **Stock:** Synthetic, X-Series or optional folding para stock. **Sights:** Elevation-adjustable post front, windage-adjustable rear peep. **Features:** Fully adjustable short gas system, high grade steel or 416 stainless upper receiver. Made in U.S.A. by DSA, Inc.
Price: High-grade steel **$1,595.00**
Price: Folding para stock **$1,845.00**

DSA SA58 CARBINE
Caliber: 308 Win. **Barrel:** 16.25" bipod cut w/threaded flash hider. **Weight:** 8.35 lbs. **Length:** 37.5". **Stock:** Synthetic, X-Series or optional folding para stock. **Sights:** Elevation-adjustable post front, windage-adjustable rear peep. **Features:** Fully adjustable short gas system, high grade steel or 416 stainless upper receiver. Made in U.S.A. by DSA, Inc.
Price: High-grade steel **$1,595.00**
Price: Stainless steel **$1,850.00**

DSA SA58 TACTICAL CARBINE
Caliber: 308 Win. **Barrel:** 16.25" fluted with A2 flash hider. **Weight:** 8.25 lbs. **Length:** 36.5". **Stock:** Synthetic, X-Series or optional folding para stock. **Sights:** Elevation-adjustable post front, windage-adjustable match rear peep. **Features:** Shortened fully adjustable short gas system, high grade steel or 416 stainless upper receiver. Made in U.S.A. by DSA, Inc.
Price: High-grade steel $1,595.00
Price: Stainless steel $1,850.00

DSA SA58 MEDIUM CONTOUR
Caliber: 308 Win. **Barrel:** 21" w/threaded flash hider. **Weight:** 9.75 lbs. **Length:** 43". **Stock:** Synthetic military grade. **Sights:** Elevation-adjustable post front, windage-adjustable match rear peep. **Features:** Gas-operated semi-auto with fully adjustable gas system, high grade steel receiver. Made in U.S.A. by DSA, Inc.
Price: $1,595.00

DSA SA58 BULL BARREL RIFLE
Caliber: 308 Win. **Barrel:** 21". **Weight:** 11.1 lbs. **Length:** 41.5". **Stock:** Synthetic, free floating handguard. **Sights:** Elevation-adjustable windage-adjustable post front, match rear peep. **Features:** Gas-operated semi-auto with fully adjustable gas system, high grade steel or stainless upper receiver. Made in U.S.A. by DSA, Inc.
Price: $1,745.00
Price: Stainless steel $1,995.00

DSA SA58 MINI OSW
Caliber: 308 Win. **Barrel:** 11" or 13" w/A2 flash hider. **Weight:** 9 to 9.35 lbs. **Length:** 32.75" to 35". **Stock:** Fiberglass reinforced short synthetic handguard, para folding stock and synthetic pistol grip. **Sights:** Adjustable post front, para rear sight. **Features:** Semi-auto or select fire with fully adjustable short gas system, optional FAL rail handguard, SureFire Vertical Foregrip System, EOTech HOLOgraphic Sight and ITC cheekrest. Made in U.S.A. by DSA, Inc.
Price: $1,845.00

EXCEL ARMS ACCELERATOR RIFLES
Caliber: 17 HMR, 22 WMR, 17M2, 22 LR, 9-shot magazine. **Barrel:** 18" fluted stainless steel bull barrel. **Weight:** 8 lbs. **Length:** 32.5" overall. **Grips:** Textured black polymer. **Sights:** Fully adjustable target sights. **Features:** Made from 17-4 stainless steel, aluminum shroud w/Weaver rail, manual safety, firing-pin block, last-round bolt-hold-open feature. Four packages with various equipment available. American made, lifetime warranty. Comes with one 9-round stainless steel magazine and a California-approved cable lock. Introduced 2006. Made in U.S.A. by Excel Arms.
Price: MR-17 17 HMR $488.00
Price: MR-22 22 WMR $523.00

HECKLER & KOCH USC CARBINE
Caliber: 45 ACP, 10-shot magazine. **Barrel:** 16". **Weight:** 8.6 lb. **Length:** 35.4" overall. **Stock:** Skeletonized polymer thumbhole. **Sights:** Blade front with integral hood, fully adjustable diopter. **Features:** Based on German UMP submachine gun. Blowback operation; almost entirely constructed of carbon fiber-reinforced polymer. Free-floating heavy target barrel. Introduced 2000. From H&K.
Price: $1,249.00

HI-POINT 9MM CARBINE
Caliber: 9mm Para., 40 S&W, 10-shot magazine. **Barrel:** 16.5" (17.5" for 40 S&W). **Weight:** 4.5 lbs. **Length:** 31.5" overall. **Stock:** Black polymer, camouflage. **Sights:** Protected post front, aperture rear. Integral scope mount. **Features:** Grip-mounted magazine release. Black or chrome finish. Sling swivels. Available with laser or red dot sights. Introduced 1996. Made in U.S.A. by MKS Supply, Inc.
Price: 995-B (black) $220.00
Price: 995-CMO (camo) $235.00

LES BAER CUSTOM ULTIMATE AR 223 RIFLES
Caliber: 223. **Barrel:** 18", 20", 22", 24". **Weight:** 7.75 to 9.75 lb. **Length:** NA. **Stock:** Black synthetic. **Sights:** None furnished; Picatinny-style flattop rail for scope mounting. **Features:** Forged receiver; Ultra single-stage trigger (Jewell two-stage trigger optional); titanium firing pin; Versa-Pod bipod; chromed National Match carrier; stainless steel, hand-lapped and cryo-treated barrel; guaranteed to shoot 1/2 or 3/4 MOA, depending on model. Made in U.S.A. by Les Baer Custom Inc.
Price: Super Varmint Model $2,390.00
Price: Super Match Model (introduced 2006) $2,490.00
Price: M4 Flattop model $2,360.00
Price: Police Special 16" (2008) $1,690.00
Price: IPSC Action Model $2,640.00

LR 300 RIFLES
Caliber: 5.56 NATO, 30-shot magazine. **Barrel:** 16.5"; 1:9" twist. **Weight:** 7.4-7.8 lbs. **Length:** NA. **Stock:** Folding. **Sights:** YHM flip front and rear. **Features:** Flattop receive, full length top picatinny rail. Phantom flash hider, multi sling mount points, field strips with no tools. Made in U.S.A. from Z-M Weapons.

Prices given are believed to be accurate at time of publication however, many factors affect retail pricing so exact prices are not possible.

Price: AXL, AXLT **$2,139.00**
Price: NXL **$2,208.00**

MERKEL MODEL SR1 SEMI-AUTOMATIC RIFLE

Caliber: 308 Win., 300 Win Mag. **Features:** Streamlined profile, checkered walnut stock and forend, 19.7- (308) or 20-8" (300 SM) barrel, two- or five-shot detachable box magazine. Adjustable front and rear iron sights with Weaver-style optics rail included. Imported from Germany by Merkel USA.
Price: **$1,595.00**

OLYMPIC ARMS K9, K10, K40, K45 PISTOL-CALIBER AR15 CARBINES

Caliber: 9mm Para., 10mm, 40 S&W, 45 ACP; 32/10-shot modified magazines. **Barrel:** 16" button rifled stainless steel, 1x16 twist rate. **Weight:** 6.73 lbs. **Length:** 31.625" overall. **Stock:** A2 grip, M4 6-point collapsible stock. **Features:** A2 upper with adjustable rear sight, elevation adjustable front post, bayonet lug, sling swivel, threaded muzzle, flash suppressor, carbine length handguards. Made in U.S.A. by Olympic Arms, Inc.
Price: K9GL, 9mm Para., Glock lower **$1,092.00**
Price: K10, 10mm, modified 10-round Uzi magazine **$1,006.20**
Price: K40, 40 S&W, modified 10-round Uzi magazine **$1,006.20**
Price: K45, 45 ACP, modified 10-round Uzi magazine **$1,006.20**

OLYMPIC ARMS K3B SERIES AR15 CARBINES

Caliber: 5.56 NATO, 30-shot magazines. **Barrel:** 16" button rifled chrome-moly steel, 1x9 twist rate. **Weight:** 5-7 lbs. **Length:** 31.75" overall. **Stock:** A2 grip, M4 6-point collapsible buttstock. **Features:** A2 upper with adjustable rear sight, elevation adjustable front post, bayonet lug, sling swivel, threaded muzzle, flash suppressor, carbine length handguards. Made in U.S.A. by Olympic Arms, Inc.
Price: K3B base model, A2 upper. **$815.00**
Price: K3B-M4 M4 contoured barrel & handguards **$1,038.70**
Price: K3B-M4-A3-TC A3 upper, M4 barrel, FIRSH rail handguard. **$1,246.70**
Price: K3B-CAR 11.5" barrel with 5.5" permanent flash suppressor **$968.50**
Price: K3B-FAR 16" featherweight contoured barrel **$1,006.20**

OLYMPIC ARMS PLINKER PLUS AR15 MODELS

Caliber: 5.56 NATO, 30-shot magazine. Barrel 16" or 20" button-rifled chrome-moly steel, 1x9 twist. **Weight:** 7.5-8.5 lbs. **Length:** 35.5"-39.5" overall. **Stock:** A2 grip, A2 buttstock with trapdoor. **Sights:** A1 windage rear, elevation-adjustable front post. **Features:** A1 upper, fiberlite handguards, bayonet lug, threaded muzzle and flash suppressor. Made in U.S.A. by Olympic Arms, Inc.
Price: Plinker Plus. **$713.70**
Price: Plinker Plus 20 . . . . **$843.70**

OLYMPIC ARMS GAMESTALKER

Sporting AR-style rifle chambered in .223, .243 and .25 WSSM and .300 OSSM. Features include forged aluminum upper and lower; flat top receiver with Picatinny rail; gas block front sight; 22-inch stainless steel fluted barrel; free-floating slotted tube handguard; camo finish overall; ACE FX skeleton stock.
Price: **$1,359.00**

REMINGTON MODEL R-15 MODULAR REPEATING RIFLE

Caliber: 223, 450 Bushmaster and 30 Rem. AR, five-shot magazine. **Barrel:** 18" (carbine), 22", 24". **Weight:** 6.75 to 7.75 lbs. **Length:** 36.25" to 42.25". **Stock:** Camo. **Features:** AR-style with optics rail, aluminum alloy upper and lower.
Price: R-15 Hunter: 30 Rem. AR, 22" barrel, Realtree AP HD camo **$1,225.00**
Price: R-15 VTR Byron South Edition: 223, 18" barrel, Advantage MAX-1 HD camo **$1,772.00**
Price: R-15 VTR SS Varmint: Same as Byron South Edition but with 24" stainless steel barrel **$1,412.00**
Price: R-15 VTR Thumbhole: Similar to R-15 Hunter but with thumbhole stock **$1,412.00**
Price: R-15 VYR Predator: 204 Ruger or .223, 22" barrel . . **$1,225.00**
Price: R-15 Predator Carbine: Similar to above but with 18" barrel **$1,225.00**

REMINGTON MODEL R-25 MODULAR REPEATING RIFLE

Caliber: 243, 7mm-08, 308 Win., four-shot magazine. **Barrel:** 20" chrome-moly. **Weight:** 7.75 lbs. **Length:** 38.25" overall. **Features:** AR-style semi-auto with single-stage trigger, aluminum alloy upper and lower, Mossy Oak Treestand camo finish overall.
Price: **$1,567.00**

REMINGTON MODEL 750 WOODSMASTER

Caliber: 243 Win., 270 Win., 308 Win., 30-06 Spfl., 35 Whelen. 4-shot magazine. **Barrel:** 22" round tapered. **Weight:** 7.5 lbs. **Length:** 42.6" overall. **Stock:** Restyled American walnut forend and stock with machine-cut checkering. Satin finish. **Sights:** Gold bead front sight on ramp; step rear sight with windage adjustable. **Features:** Replaced wood-stocked Model 7400 line introduced 1981. Gas action, SuperCell recoil pad. Positive cross-bolt safety. Carbine chambered in 308 Win., 30-06 Spfl., 35 Whelen. Receiver tapped for scope mount. Introduced 2006. Made in U.S.A. by Remington Arms Co.
Price: 750 Woodsmaster **$879.00**
Price: 750 Woodsmaster Carbine (18.5" bbl.) **$879.00**
Price: 750 Synthetic stock (2007) **$773.00**

ROCK RIVER ARMS STANDARD A2 RIFLE

Caliber: 45 ACP. **Barrel:** NA. **Weight:** 8.2 lbs. **Length:** NA. **Stock:** Thermoplastic. **Sights:** Standard AR-15 style sights. **Features:** Two-stage, national match trigger; optional muzzle brake. Pro-Series Government package includes side-mount sling swivel, chrome-lined 1:9 twist barrel, mil-spec forged lower receiver, Hogue rubber grip, NM two-stage trigger, 6-position tactical CAR stock, Surefire M73 quad rail handguard, other features. Made in U.S.A. From Rock River Arms.
Price: Standard A2 AR1280 . . . . **$945.00**
Price: Pro-Series Government Package GOVT1001 (2008) **$2,290.00**
Price: Elite Comp AR1270 (2008). **$1,145.00**

RUGER SR-556

AR-style semiauto rifle chambered in 5.56 NATO. Feature include two-stage piston; quad rail handguard; Troy Industries sights; black synthetic fixed or telescoping buttstock; 16.12-inch 1:9 steel barrel with birdcage; 10- or 30-round detachable box magazine; black matte finish overall.
Price: **$1,995.00**

RUGER MINI-14 RANCH RIFLE AUTOLOADING RIFLE

Caliber: 223 Rem., 5-shot detachable box magazine. **Barrel:** 18.5". Rifling twist 1:9". **Weight:** 6.75 to 7 lbs. **Length:** 37.25" overall. **Stock:** American hardwood, steel reinforced, or synthetic. **Sights:** Protected blade front, fully adjustable Ghost Ring rear. **Features:** Fixed piston gas-operated, positive primary extraction. New buffer system, redesigned ejector system. Ruger S100RM scope rings included on Ranch Rifle. Heavier barrels added in 2008, 20-round magazine added in 1009.

Price: Mini-14/5, Ranch Rifle, blued, scope rings **$855.00**
Price: K-Mini-14/5, Ranch Rifle, stainless, scope rings **$921.00**
Price: K-Mini-6.8/5P, All-Weather Ranch Rifle, stainless, synthetic stock (2008) **$921.00**
Price: Mini-14 Target Rifle: laminated thumbhole stock, heavy crowned 22" stainless steel barrel, other refinements **$1,066.00**
Price: Mini-14 ATI Stock: Tactical version of Mini-14 but with six-position collapsible stock or folding stock, grooved pistol grip. multiple picatinny optics/accessory rails . . . **$872.00**
Price: Mini-14 Tactical Rifle: Similar to Mini-14 but with 16-21" barrel with flash hider, black synthetic stock, adjustable sights **$894.00**

Ruger NRA Mini-14 Rifle

Similar to the Mini-14 Ranch Rifle except comes with two 20-round magazines and special Black Hogue OverMolded stock with NRA gold-tone medallion in grip cap. Special serial number sequence (NRA8XXXXX). For 2008 only.
Price: M-14/20C-NRA **$1,035.00**
Price: M-14/5C-NRA (5-round magazines) **$1,035.00**

Ruger Mini Thirty Rifle

Similar to the Mini-14 Ranch Rifle except modified to chamber the 7.62x39 Russian service round. **Weight:** 6.75 lbs. Has 6-groove barrel with 1:10" twist, Ruger Integral Scope Mount bases and protected blade front, fully adjustable Ghost Ring rear. Detachable 5-shot staggered box magazine. Available 2010 with two 30-round magazines. Stainless w/synthetic stock. Introduced 1987.
Price: Stainless, scope rings **$921.00**

SABRE DEFENCE SABRE RIFLES

Caliber: 5.56 NATO, 6.5 Grendel, 30-shot magazines. **Barrel:** 20" 410 stainless steel, 1x8 twist rate; or 18" vanadium alloy, chrome-lined barrel with Sabre Gill-Brake. **Weight:** 6.77 lbs. **Length:** 31.75"

overall. **Stock:** SOCOM 3-position stock with Samson M-EX handguards. **Sights:** Flip-up front and rear sights. **Features:** Fluted barrel, Harris bipod, and two-stage match trigger, Ergo Grips; upper and matched lower CNC machined from 7075-T6 forgings. SOCOM adjustable stock, Samson tactical handguards, M4 contour barrels available in 14.5" and 16" are made of MIL-B-11595 vanadium alloy and chrome lined. Introduced 2002. From Sabre Defence Industries.

Price: 6.5 Grendel, from **$1,409.00**
Price: Competition Extreme, 20" barrel, from **$2,189.00**
Price: Competition Deluxe, from **$2,299.00**
Price: Competition Special, 5.56mm, 18" barrel, from **$1,899.00**
Price: SPR Carbine, from **$2,499.00**
Price: M4 Tactical, from **$1,969.00**
Price: M4 Carbine, 14.5" barrel, from **$1,399.00**
Price: M4 Flat-top Carbine, 16" barrel, from **$1,349.00**
Price: M5 Flat-top, 16" barrel, from **$1,399.00**
Price: M5 Tactical, 14.5" barrel, from **$2,099.00**
Price: M5 Carbine, from **$1,309.00**
Price: Precision Marksman, 20" barrel, from **$2,499.00**
Price: A4 Rifle, 20" barrel, from **$1,349.00**
Price: A3 National Match, 20" barrel **$1,699.00**
Price: Heavy Bench Target, 24" barrel, from **$1,889.00**
Price: Varmint, 20" barrel **$1,709.00**

SIG 556 AUTOLOADING RIFLE

Caliber: 223 Rem., 30-shot detachable box magazine. **Barrel:** 16". Rifling twist 1:9". **Weight:** 6.8 lbs. **Length:** 36.5" overall. **Stock:** Polymer, folding style. **Sights:** Flip-up front combat sight, adjustable for windage and elevation. **Features:** Based on SG 550 series rifle. Two-position adjustable gas piston operating rod system, accepts standard AR magazines. Polymer forearm, three integrated Picatinny rails, forward mount for right- or left-side sling attachment. Aircraft-grade aluminum alloy trigger housing, hard-coat anodized finish; two-stage trigger, ambidextrous safety, 30-round polymer magazine, battery compartments, pistol-grip rubber-padded watertight adjustable butt stock with sling-attachment points. SIG 556 SWAT model has flat-top Picatinny railed receiver, tactical quad rail. SIG 556 HOLO sight options include front combat sight, flip-up rear sight, and red-dot style holographic sighting system with four illuminated reticle patterns. DMR features a 24" military grade cold hammer-forged heavy contour barrel, 5.56mm NATO, target crown. Imported by Sig Sauer, Inc.
Price: SIG 556 . . . . **$2,099.00**

Price: SIG 556 HOLO (2008) **$1,832.00**
Price: SIG 556 DMR (2008) **$2,400.00**
Price: SIG 556 SWAT **$2,000.00**
Price: SIG 556 SCM **$1,838.00**

SIG-SAUER SIG516 GAS PISTON RIFLE

AR-style rifle chambered in 5.56 NATO. Features include 14.5-, 16-, 18- or 20-inch chrome-lined barrel; free-floating, aluminum quad rail fore-end with four M1913 Picatinny rails; threaded muzzle with a standard (0.5x28TPI) pattern; aluminum upper and lower receiver is machined; black anodized finish; 30-round magazine; flattop upper; various configurations available.
Price: . . . . **N/A**

SIG-SAUER SIG716 TACTICAL PATROL RIFLE

AR-10 type rifle chambered in 7.62 NATO/.308 Winchester. Features include gas-piston operation with 3 round-position (4-position optional) gas valve; 16-, 18- or 20-inch chrome-lined barrel with threaded muzzle and nitride finish; free-floating aluminum quad rail fore-end with four M1913 Picatinny rails; telescoping buttstock; lower receiver is machined from a 7075-T6 Aircraft grade aluminum forging; upper receiver, machined from 7075-T6 aircraft grade aluminum with integral M1913 Picatinny rail.
Price: . . . . **N/A**

SMITH & WESSON M&P15 RIFLES

Caliber: 5.56mm NATO/223, 30-shot steel magazine. **Barrel:** 16", 1:9 **Weight:** 6.74 lbs., w/o magazine. **Length:** 32-35" overall. **Stock:** Black synthetic. **Sights:** Adjustable post front sight, adjustable dual aperture rear sight. **Features:** 6-position telescopic stock, thermo-set M4 handguard. 14.75" sight radius. 7-lbs. (approx.) trigger pull. 7075 T6 aluminum upper, 4140 steel barrel. Chromed barrel bore, gas key, bolt carrier. Hard-coat black-anodized receiver and barrel finish. Introduced 2006. Made in U.S.A. by Smith & Wesson.
Price: M&P15 No. 811000 . . . . **$1,406.00**
Price: M&P15T No. 811001, free float modular rail forend . **$1,888.00**
Price: M&P15A No. 811002, folding battle rear sight **$1,422.00**
Price: M&P15A No. 811013, optics ready compliant (2008) **$1,169.00**

SMITH & WESSON MODEL M&P15VTAC VIKING TACTICS MODEL

Caliber: 223 Remington/5.56 NATO, 30-round magazine. **Barrel:** 16". **Weight:** 6.5 lbs. **Length:** 35" extended, 32" collapsed, overall. **Features:** Six-position CAR stock. Surefire flash-hider and G2 light with VTAC light mount; VTAC/JP handguard; JP single-stage match trigger and speed hammer; three adjustable picatinny rails; VTAC padded two-point adjustable sling.
Price: **$2,196.00**

SMITH & WESSON M&P15PC CAMO

Caliber: 223 Rem/5.56 NATO, A2 configuration, 10-round mag. **Barrel:** 20" stainless with 1:8 twist. **Weight:** 8.2 lbs. **Length:** 38.5" overall. **Features:** AR-style, no sights but integral front and rear optics rails. Two-stage trigger, aluminum lower. Finished in Realtree Advantage Max-1 camo.
Price: **$2,046.00**

Smith & Wesson M&p15 Piston Rifle

Similar to AR-derived M&P15 but with gas piston. Chambered in 5.56 NATO. Features include adjustable gas port, optional Troy quad mount handguard, chromed bore/gas key/bolt carrier/chamber, 6-position telescoping or MagPul MOE stock, flattop or folding MBUS sights, aluminum receiver, alloy upper and lower, black anodized finish, 30-round magazine, 16-inch barrel with birdcage.
Price Standard handguard. **$1,531.00**
Price: Troy quad mount handguard **$1,692.00**

SPRINGFIELD ARMORY M1A RIFLE

Caliber: 7.62mm NATO (308), 5- or 10-shot box magazine. **Barrel:** 25-1/16" with flash suppressor, 22" without suppressor. **Weight:** 9.75 lbs. **Length:** 44.25" overall. **Stock:** American walnut with walnut-colored heat-resistant fiberglass handguard. Matching walnut handguard available. Also available with fiberglass stock. **Sights:** Military, square blade front, full click-adjustable aperture rear. **Features:** Commercial equivalent of the U.S. M-14 service rifle with no provision for automatic firing. From Springfield Armory
Price: SOCOM 16. . . . . **$1,855.00**
Price: SOCOM II, from **$2,090.00**
Price: Scout Squad, from **$1,726.00**
Price: Standard M1A, from **$1,608.00**
Price: Loaded Standard, from **$1,759.00**
Price: National Match, from **$2,249.00**
Price: Super Match (heavy premium barrel) about **$2,818.00**
Price: Tactical, from **$3,780.00**

STI SPORTING COMPETITION RIFLE

AR-style semiauto rifle chambered in 5.56 NATO. Features include 16-inch 410 stainless 1:8 barrel; mid-length gas system; Nordic Tactical Compensator and JP Trigger group; custom STI Valkyrie hand guard and gas block; flat-top design with picatinny rail; anodized finish with black Teflon coating. Also available in Tactical configuration.
Price: . . . . **N/A**

STONER
SR-15 M-5 RIFLE

Caliber: 223. **Barrel:** 20". **Weight:** 7.6 lbs. **Length:** 38" overall. **Stock:** Black synthetic. **Sights:** Post front, fully adjustable rear (300-meter sight). **Features:** Modular weapon system; two-stage trigger. Black finish. Introduced 1998. Made in U.S.A. by Knight's Mfg.
Price: **$1,695.00**

STONER SR-25 CARBINE

Caliber: 7.62 NATO, 10-shot steel magazine. **Barrel:** 16" free-floating **Weight:** 7.75 lbs. **Length:** 35.75" overall. **Stock:** Black synthetic. **Sights:** Integral Weaver-style rail. Scope rings, iron sights optional. **Features:** Shortened, non-slip handguard; removable carrying handle. Matte black finish. Introduced 1995. Made in U.S.A. by Knight's Mfg. Co.
Price: **$3,345.00**

WILSON COMBAT TACTICAL RIFLES

Caliber: 5.56mm NATO, accepts all M-16/AR-15 Style Magazines, includes one 20-round magazine. **Barrel:** 16.25", 1:9 twist, match-grade fluted. **Weight:** 6.9 lbs. **Length:** 36.25" overall. **Stock:** Fixed or collapsible. **Features:** Free-float ventilated aluminum quad-rail handguard, Mil-Spec parkerized barrel and steel components, anodized receiver, precision CNC-machined upper and lower receivers, 7075 T6 aluminum forgings. Single stage JP Trigger/ Hammer Group, Wilson Combat Tactical Muzzle Brake, nylon tactical rifle case. M-4T version has flat-top receiver for mounting optics, OD green furniture, 16.25" match-grade M-4 style barrel. SS-15 Super Sniper Tactical Rifle has 1-in-8 twist, heavy 20" match-grade fluted stainless steel barrel. Made in U.S.A by Wilson Combat.
Price: UT-15 Tactical Carbine. **$1,785.00**
Price: M4-TP Tactical Carbine **$1,575.00**
Price: SS-15P Super Sniper. **$1,795.00**

WINCHESTER SUPER X RIFLE

Caliber: 270 WSM, 30-06 Spfl., 300 Win. Mag., 300 WSM, 4-shot steel magazine. **Barrel:** 22", 24", 1:10", blued. **Weight:** 7.25 lbs. **Length:** up to 41-3/8". **Stock:** Walnut, 14-1/8"x 7/8"x 1.25". **Sights:** None. **Features:** Gas operated, removable trigger assembly, detachable box magazine, drilled and tapped, alloy receiver, enlarged trigger guard, crossbolt safety. Reintroduced 2008. Made in U.S.A. by Winchester Repeating Arms.
Price: Super X Rifle, from. **$949.00**

BERETTA 1873 RENEGADE SHORT LEVER-ACTION RIFLE

Caliber: 45 Colt, 357 Magnum. **Barrel:** 20" round or 24-1/2" octagonal. **Features:** Blued finish, checkered walnut buttstock and forend, adjustable rear sight and fixed blade front, ten-round tubular magazine.

Price: **$1,350.00**

BERETTA GOLD RUSH SLIDE-ACTION RIFLE AND CARBINE

Caliber: 357 Magnum, 45 Colt. **Barrel:** 20" round or 24-1/2"octagonal. **Features:** External replica of old Colt Lightning Magazine Rifle. Case-hardened receiver, walnut buttstock and forend, crescent buttplate, 13-round (rifle) or 10-round (carbine) magazine. Available as Standard Carbine, Standard Rifle, or Deluxe Rifle.

Price: Standard Carbine **$1,375.00**
Price: Standard Rifle **$1,425.00**
Price: Deluxe Rifle **$11,950.00**

BIG HORN ARMORY MODEL 89 RIFLE AND CARBINE

Lever action rifle or carbine chambered for .500 S&W Magnum. Features include 22-or 18-inch barrel; walnut or maple stocks with pistol grip; aperture rear and blade front sights; recoil pad; sling swivels; enlarged lever loop; magazine capacity 5 (rifle) or 7 (carbine) rounds.

Price: **$1,889.00**

BROWNING BLR RIFLES

Action: Lever action with rotating bolt head, multiple-lug breech bolt with recessed bolt face, side ejection. Rack-and-pinion lever. Flush-mounted detachable magazines, with 4+1 capacity for magnum cartridges, 5+1 for standard rounds. **Barrel:** Button-rifled chrome-moly steel with crowned muzzle. **Stock:** Buttstocks and forends are American walnut with grip and forend checkering. Recoil pad installed. **Trigger:** Wide-groove design, trigger travels with lever. Half-cock hammer safety; fold-down hammer. **Sights:** Gold bead on ramp front; low-profile square-notch adjustable rear. **Features:** Blued barrel and receiver, high-gloss wood finish. Receivers are drilled and tapped for scope mounts, swivel studs included. Action lock provided. Introduced 1996. Imported from Japan by Browning.

BROWNING BLR LIGHTWEIGHT W/PISTOL GRIP, SHORT AND LONG ACTION; LIGHTWEIGHT '81, SHORT AND LONG ACTION

Calibers: Short Action, 20" Barrel: 22-250 Rem., 243 Win., 7mm-08 Rem., 308 Win., 358, 450 Marlin. Calibers: Short Action, 22" Barrel: 270 WSM, 7mm WSM, 300 WSM, 325 WSM. Calibers: Long Action 22" Barrel: 270 Win., 30-06. Calibers: Long Action 24" Barrel: 7mm Rem. Mag., 300 Win. Mag. **Weight:** 6.5-7.75 lbs. **Length:** 40-45" overall. **Stock:** New checkered pistol grip and Schnabel forearm. Lightweight '81 differs from Pistol Grip models with a Western-style straight grip stock and banded forearm. Lightweight w/Pistol Grip Short Action and Long Action introduced 2005. Model '81 Lightning Long Action introduced 1996.

Price: Lightweight w/Pistol Grip Short Action, from **$879.00**
Price: Lightweight w/Pistol Grip Long Action **$929.00**
Price: Lightweight '81 Short Action **$839.00**
Price: Lightweight '81 Long Action **$889.00**
Price: Lightweight '81 Takedown Short Action, intr. 2007,
  from **$949.00**
Price: Lightweight '81 Takedown Long Action, intr. 2007,
  from **$999.00**

CHARLES DALY MODEL 1892 LEVER-ACTION RIFLES

Caliber: 45 Colt; 5-shot magazine with removable plug. **Barrel:** 24.25" octagonal. **Weight:** 6.8 lbs. **Length:** 42" overall. **Stock:** Two-piece American walnut, oil finish. **Sights:** Post front, adjustable open rear. **Features:** Color case-hardened receiver, lever, buttplate, forend cap. Introduced 2007. Imported from Italy by K.B.I., Inc.

Price: 1892 Rifle **$1,094.00**
Price: Take Down Rifle **$1,249.00**

CIMARRON 1860 HENRY RIFLE CIVIL WAR MODEL

Caliber: 44 WCF, 45 LC; 12-shot magazine. **Barrel:** 24" (rifle). **Weight:** 9.5 lbs. **Length:** 43" overall (rifle). **Stock:** European walnut.

Sights: Bead front, open adjustable rear. **Features:** Brass receiver and buttplate. Uses original Henry loading system. Copy of the original rifle. Charcoal blue finish optional. Introduced 1991. Imported by Cimarron F.A. Co.

Price: From **$1,444.78**

CIMARRON 1866 WINCHESTER REPLICAS

Caliber: 38 Spec., 357, 45 LC, 32 WCF, 38 WCF, 44 WCF. **Barrel:** 24" (rifle), 20" (short rifle), 19" (carbine), 16" (trapper). **Weight:** 9 lbs. **Length:** 43" overall (rifle). **Stock:** European walnut. **Sights:** Bead front, open adjustable rear. **Features:** Solid brass receiver, buttplate, forend cap. Octagonal barrel. Copy of the original Winchester '66 rifle. Introduced 1991. Imported by Cimarron F.A. Co.

Price: 1866 Sporting Rifle, 24" barrel, from **$1,096.64**
Price: 1866 Short Rifle, 20" barrel, from **$1,096.64**
Price: 1866 Carbine, 19" barrel, from **$1,123.42**
Price: 1866 Trapper, 16" barrel, from **$1,069.86**

CIMARRON 1873 SHORT RIFLE

Caliber: 357 Mag., 38 Spec., 32 WCF, 38 WCF, 44 Spec., 44 WCF, 45 Colt. **Barrel:** 20" tapered octagon. **Weight:** 7.5 lbs. **Length:** 39" overall. **Stock:** Walnut. **Sights:** Bead front, adjustable semi-buckhorn rear. **Features:** Has half "button" magazine. Original-type markings, including caliber, on barrel and elevator and "Kings" patent. From Cimarron F.A. Co.

Price: **$1,203.76**

Cimarron 1873 Deluxe Sporting Rifle

Similar to the 1873 Short Rifle except has 24" barrel with half-magazine.

Price: **$1,324.70**

CIMARRON 1873 LONG RANGE RIFLE

Caliber: 44 WCF, 45 Colt. **Barrel:** 30", octagonal. **Weight:** 8.5 lbs. **Length:** 48" overall. **Stock:** Walnut. **Sights:** Blade front, semi-buckhorn ramp rear. Tang sight optional. **Features:** Color case-hardened frame; choice of modern blue-black or charcoal blue for other parts. Barrel marked "Kings Improvement." From Cimarron F.A. Co.

Price: **$1,284.10**

DIXIE ENGRAVED 1873 SPORTING RIFLE

Caliber: 44-40, 13-shot magazine. **Barrel:** 24.25", tapered octagon. **Weight:** 8.25 lbs. **Length:** 43.25" overall. **Stock:** Walnut. **Sights:** Blade front, adjustable rear. **Features:** Engraved frame polished bright (casehardened on plain). Replica of Winchester 1873. Made in Italy. From Dixie Gun Works.

Price: Plain, blued rifle in .44/40, .45 LC, .32/20, .38/40. . . . **$ 1,050.00**

DIXIE 1873 DELUXE SPORTING RIFLE

Caliber: .44-40, .45 LC, .32-20 and .38-40, 13-shot magazine. **Barrel:** 24.25", tapered octagon. **Weight:** 8.25 lbs. **Length:** 43.25" overall. **Stock:** Walnut. Checkered pistol grip buttstock and forearm. **Sights:** Blade front, adjustable rear. **Features:** Color casehardened frame. Engraved frame polished bright. Replica of Winchester 1873. Made in Italy. From Dixie Gun Works.

Price: . . . . **$ 1,050.00 to $ 1,100.00**

DIXIE LIGHTNING RIFLE AND CARBINE

Caliber: .44-40 or .45 LC, 10-shot magazine. **Barrel:** 26" round or octagon, 1:16" or 1:36" twist. **Weight:** 7.25 lbs. **Length:** 43" overall. **Stock:** Walnut. **Sights:** Blade front, open adjustable rear. **Features:** Checkered forearm, blued steel furniture. Made by Pedersoli in Italy. Imported by Dixie Gun Works.

Price: **$1,095.00**
Price: Carbine **$1,225.00**

Prices given are believed to be accurate at time of publication however, many factors affect retail pricing so exact prices are not possible.

EMF 1860 HENRY RIFLE
Caliber: 44-40 or 45 Colt. **Barrel:** 24". **Weight:** About 9 lbs. **Length:** About 43.75" overall. **Stock:** Oil-stained American walnut. **Sights:** Blade front, rear adjustable for elevation. **Features:** Reproduction of the original Henry rifle with brass frame and buttplate, rest blued. Imported by EMF.
Price: Brass frame **$1,149.90**
Price: Casehardened frame **$1,229.90**

EMF 1866 YELLOWBOY LEVER ACTIONS
Caliber: 38 Spec., 44-40, 45 LC. **Barrel:** 19" (carbine), 24" (rifle). **Weight:** 9 lbs. **Length:** 43" overall (rifle). **Stock:** European walnut. **Sights:** Bead front, open adjustable rear. **Features:** Solid brass frame, blued barrel, lever, hammer, buttplate. Imported from Italy by EMF.
Price: Rifle **$1,044.90**
Price: Border Rifle, Short **$969.90**

EMF MODEL 1873 LEVER-ACTION RIFLE
Caliber: 32/20, 357 Mag., 38/40, 44-40, 45 Colt. **Barrel:** 18", 20", 24", 30". **Weight:** 8 lbs. **Length:** 43.25" overall. **Stock:** European walnut. **Sights:** Bead front, rear adjustable for windage and elevation. **Features:** Color case-hardened frame (blue on carbine). Imported by EMF.
Price: **$1,099.90**

EMF MODEL 1873 REVOLVER CARBINE
Caliber: 357 Mag., 45 Colt. **Barrel:** 18". **Weight:** 4 lbs., 8 oz. **Length:** 43-3/4" overall. **Stock:** One-piece walnut. **Sights:** Blade front, notch rear. **Features:** Color case-hardened frame, blue barrel, backstrap and trigger guard. Introduced 1998. Imported from Italy by EMF.
Price: Standard . . . . **$979.90 to $1,040.00**

HENRY BIG BOY LEVER-ACTION CARBINE
Caliber: 357 Magnum, 44 Magnum, 45 Colt, 10-shot tubular magazine. **Barrel:** 20" octagonal, 1:38 right-hand twist. **Weight:** 8.68 lbs. **Length:** 38.5" overall. **Stock:** Straight-grip American walnut, brass buttplate. **Sights:** Marbles full adjustable semi-buckhorn rear, brass bead front. **Features:** Brasslite receiver not tapped for scope mount. Made in U.S.A. by Henry Repeating Arms.
Price: H006 44 Magnum, walnut, blued barrel **$899.95**
Price: H006DD Deluxe 44 Magnum, engraved receiver. . . . **$1,995.95**

Henry .30/30 Lever-Action Carbine
Same as the Big Boy except has straight grip American walnut, 30-30 only, 6-shot. Receivers are drilled and tapped for scope mount. Made in U.S.A. by Henry Repeating Arms.
Price: H009 Blued receiver, round barrel **$749.95**
Price: H009B Brass receiver, octagonal barrel. **$969.95**

MARLIN MODEL 336C LEVER-ACTION CARBINE
Caliber: 30-30 or 35 Rem., 6-shot tubular magazine. **Barrel:** 20" Micro-Groove. **Weight:** 7 lbs. **Length:** 38.5" overall. **Stock:** Checkered American black walnut, capped pistol grip. Mar-Shield finish; rubber buttpad; swivel studs. **Sights:** Ramp front with Wide-Scan hood, semi-buckhorn folding rear adjustable for windage and elevation. **Features:** Hammer-block safety. Receiver tapped for scope mount, offset hammer spur; top of receiver sandblasted to prevent glare. Includes safety lock.
Price: **$530.00**

Marlin Model 336SS Lever-Action Carbine
Same as the 336C except receiver, barrel and other major parts are machined from stainless steel. 30-30 only, 6-shot; receiver tapped for scope. Includes safety lock.
Price: **$650.00**

Marlin Model 336W Lever-Action Rifle
Similar to the Model 336C except has walnut-finished, cut-checkered Maine birch stock; blued steel barrel band has integral sling swivel; no front sight hood; comes with padded nylon sling; hard rubber buttplate. Introduced 1998. Includes safety lock. Made in U.S.A. by Marlin.

Price: **$452.00**
Price: With 4x scope and mount **$495.00**

MARLIN 336BL
Lever action rifle chambered for .30-30. Features include 6-shot full length tubular magazine; 18-inch blued barrel with Micro-Groove rifling (12 grooves); big-loop finger lever; side ejection; blued steel receiver; hammer block safety; brown laminated hardwood pistol-grip stock with fluted comb; cut checkering; deluxe recoil pad; blued swivel studs.
Price: . . . . **N/A**

MARLIN 336 DELUXE
Lever action rifle chambered in .30-30. Features include 6-shot tubular magazine; side ejection; solid top receiver; highly polished deep blue finish; hammer block safety; #1 grade full fancy American black walnut stock and forend; 20-inch barrel with Micro-Groove rifling (12 grooves); adjustable semi-buckhorn folding rear, ramp front sight with brass bead and Wide-Scan™ hood. Solid top receiver tapped for scope mount; offset hammer spur (right or left hand) for scope use.
Price: . . . . **N/A**

Marlin Model XLR Lever-Action Rifles
Similar to Model 336C except has an 24" stainless barrel with Ballard-type cut rifling, stainless steel receiver and other parts, laminated hardwood stock with pistol grip, nickel-plated swivel studs. Chambered for 30-30 Win. with Hornady spire-pointed Flex-Tip cartridges. Includes safety lock. Introduced 2006. Similar models chambered for 308 Marlin Express introduced in 2007
Price: Model 336XLR **$816.00**

MARLIN MODEL 338MXLR
Caliber: 338 Marlin Express. **Barrel:** 24" stainless steel. **Weight:** 7.5 lbs. **Length:** 42.5" overall. **Features:** Stainless steel receiver, lever and magazine tube. Black/gray laminated checkered stock and forend. Hooded ramp front sight and adjustable semi-buckhorn rear; drilled and tapped for scope mounts. Receiver-mounted crossbolt safety.
Price: Model 338MXLR **$806.00**
Price: Model 308MXLR: 308 Marlin Express **$806.00**
Price: Model 338MX: Similar to Model 338MXLR but with blued metal and walnut stock and forend **$611.00**
Price: Model 308MX: 308 Marlin Express **$611.00**

MARLIN MODEL 444 LEVER-ACTION SPORTER
Caliber: 444 Marlin, 5-shot tubular magazine. **Barrel:** 22" deep cut Ballard rifling. **Weight:** 7.5 lbs. **Length:** 40.5" overall. **Stock:** Checkered American black walnut, capped pistol grip, rubber rifle buttpad. Mar-Shield finish; swivel studs. **Sights:** Hooded ramp front, folding semi-buckhorn rear adjustable for windage and elevation. **Features:** Hammer-block safety. Receiver tapped for scope mount; offset hammer spur. Includes safety lock.
Price: **$619.00**

Marlin Model 444XLR Lever-Action Rifle
Similar to Model 444 except has an 24" stainless barrel with Ballard-type cut rifling, stainless steel receiver and other parts, laminated hardwood stock with pistol grip, nickel-plated swivel studs. Chambered for 444 Marlin with Hornady Evolution spire-pointed Flex-Tip cartridges. Includes safety lock. Introduced 2006.
Price: (Model 444XLR) **$816.00**

MARLIN MODEL 1894 LEVER-ACTION CARBINE

Caliber: 44 Spec./44 Mag., 10-shot tubular magazine. **Barrel:** 20" Ballard-type rifling. **Weight:** 6 lbs. **Length:** 37.5" overall. **Stock:** Checkered American black walnut, straight grip and forend. Mar-Shield finish. Rubber rifle buttpad; swivel studs. **Sights:** Wide-Scan hooded ramp front, semi-buckhorn folding rear adjustable for windage and elevation. **Features:** Hammer-block safety. Receiver tapped for scope mount, offset hammer spur, solid top receiver sand blasted to prevent glare. Includes safety lock.

Price: $576.00

Marlin Model 1894C Carbine

Similar to the standard Model 1894 except chambered for 38 Spec./357 Mag. with full-length 9-shot magazine, 18.5" barrel, hammer-block safety, hooded front sight. Introduced 1983. Includes safety lock.

Price: $576.00

MARLIN MODEL 1894 COWBOY

Caliber: 357 Mag., 44 Mag., 45 Colt, 10-shot magazine. **Barrel:** 20" tapered octagon, deep cut rifling. **Weight:** 7.5 lbs. **Length:** 41.5" overall. **Stock:** Straight grip American black walnut, hard rubber buttplate, Mar-Shield finish. **Sights:** Marble carbine front, adjustable Marble semi-buckhorn rear. **Features:** Squared finger lever; straight grip stock; blued steel forend tip. Designed for Cowboy Shooting events. Introduced 1996. Includes safety lock. Made in U.S.A. by Marlin.

Price: $822.00

Marlin Model 1894SS

Similar to Model 1894 except has stainless steel barrel, receiver, lever, guard plate, magazine tube and loading plate. Nickel-plated swivel studs.

Price: $704.00

MARLIN 1894 DELUXE

Lever action rifle chambered in .44 Magnum/.44 Special. Features include 10-shot tubular magazine; squared finger lever; side ejection; richly polished deep blued metal surfaces; solid top receiver; hammer block safety; #1 grade fancy American black walnut straight-grip stock and forend; cut checkering; rubber rifle butt pad; Mar-Shield finish; blued steel fore-end cap: swivel studs; deep-cut Ballard-type rifling (6 grooves).

Price: .... **N/A**

MARLIN 1894CSS

Lever action rifle chambered in .357 Magnum/.38 Special. Features include 9-shot tubular magazine; stainless steel receiver, barrel, lever, trigger and hammer; squared finger lever; side ejection; solid top receiver; hammer block safety; American black walnut straight-grip stock and forend; cut checkering; rubber rifle butt pad; Mar-Shield finish.

Price: .... **N/A**

MARLIN MODEL 1895 LEVER-ACTION RIFLE

Caliber: 45-70 Govt., 4-shot tubular magazine. **Barrel:** 22" round. **Weight:** 7.5 lbs. **Length:** 40.5" overall. **Stock:** Checkered American black walnut, full pistol grip. Mar-Shield finish; rubber buttpad; quick detachable swivel studs. **Sights:** Bead front with Wide-Scan hood, semi-buckhorn folding rear adjustable for windage and elevation. **Features:** Hammer-block safety. Solid receiver tapped for scope mounts or receiver sights; offset hammer spur. Includes safety lock.

Price: $619.00

Marlin Model 1895G Guide Gun Lever-Action Rifle

Similar to Model 1895 with deep-cut Ballard-type rifling; straight-grip walnut stock. Overall length is 37", weighs 7 lbs. Introduced 1998. Includes safety lock. Made in U.S.A. by Marlin.

Price: $630.00

Marlin Model 1895GS Guide Gun

Similar to Model 1895G except receiver, barrel and most metal parts are machined from stainless steel. Chambered for 45-70 Govt., 4-shot, 18.5" barrel. Overall length is 37", weighs 7 lbs. Introduced 2001. Includes safety lock. Made in U.S.A. by Marlin.

Price: $752.00

Marlin Model 1895 SBLR

Similar to Model 1895GS Guide Gun but with stainless steel barrel (18.5"), receiver, large loop lever and magazine tube. Black/gray laminated buttstock and forend, XS ghost ring rear sight, hooded ramp front sight, receiver/barrel-mounted top rail for mounting accessory optics. Chambered in 45-70 Government. Overall length is 42.5", weighs 7.5 lbs.

Price: $979.00

Marlin Model 1895 Cowboy Lever-Action Rifle

Similar to Model 1895 except has 26" tapered octagon barrel with Ballard-type rifling, Marble carbine front sight and Marble adjustable semi-buckhorn rear sight. Receiver tapped for scope or receiver sight. Overall length is 44.5", weighs about 8 lbs. Introduced 2001. Includes safety lock. Made in U.S.A. by Marlin.

Price: $785.00

Marlin Model 1895XLR Lever-Action Rifle

Similar to Model 1895 except has an 24" stainless barrel with Ballard-type cut rifling, stainless steel receiver and other parts, laminated hardwood stock with pistol grip, nickel-plated swivel studs. Chambered for 45-70 Govt. Government with Hornady Evolution spire-pointed Flex-Tip cartridges. Includes safety lock. Introduced 2006.

Price: (Model 1895MXLR) $816.00

Marlin Model 1895M Lever-Action Rifle

Similar to Model 1895G except has an 18.5" barrel with Ballard-type cut rifling. Chambered for 450 Marlin. Includes safety lock.

Price: (Model 1895M) $678.00

Marlin Model 1895MXLR Lever-Action Rifle

Similar to Model 1895M except has an 24" stainless barrel with Ballard-type cut rifling, stainless steel receiver and other parts, laminated hardwood stock with pistol grip, nickel-plated swivel studs. Chambered for 450 Marlin with Hornady Evolution spire-pointed Flex-Tip cartridges. Includes safety lock. Introduced 2006.

Price: (Model 1895MXLR) $874.00

MARLIN 1895GBL

Lever action rifle chambered in .45-70 Government. Features include 6-shot, full-length tubular magazine; 18-1/2-inch barrel with deep-cut Ballard-type rifling (6 grooves); big-loop finger lever; side ejection; solid-top receiver; deeply blued metal surfaces; hammer block safety; pistol-grip two tone brown laminate stock with cut checkering; ventilated recoil pad; Mar-Shield finish, swivel studs.

Price: .... **N/A**

MOSSBERG 464 LEVER ACTION RIFLE

Caliber: 30-30 Win., 6-shot tubular magazine. **Barrel:** 20" round. **Weight:** 6.7 lbs. **Length:** 38.5" overall. **Stock:** Hardwood with straight or pistol grip, quick detachable swivel studs. **Sights:** Folding rear sight, adjustable for windage and elevation. **Features:** Blued receiver and barrel, receiver drilled and tapped, two-position top-tang safety. Available with straight grip or semi-pistol grip. Introduced 2008. From O.F. Mossberg & Sons, Inc.

Price: $497.00

NAVY ARMS 1874 SHARPS #2 CREEDMORE RIFLE
Caliber: .45-70 Govt. **Barrel:** 30" octagon. **Weight:** 10 lbs. **Length:** 48" overall. **Sights:** Soule target grade rear tang sight, front globe with 12 inserts. **Features:** Highly polished nickel receiver and action, double-set triggers. From Navy Arms.
Price: Model SCR072 (2008) **$1,816.00**

NAVY ARMS MILITARY HENRY RIFLE
Caliber: 44-40 or 45 Colt, 12-shot magazine. **Barrel:** 24.25". **Weight:** 9 lbs., 4 oz. **Stock:** European walnut. **Sights:** Blade front, adjustable ladder-type rear. **Features:** Brass frame, buttplate, rest blued. Replica of the model used by cavalry units in the Civil War. Has full-length magazine tube, sling swivels; no forend. Imported from Italy by Navy Arms.
Price: **$1,199.00**

Navy Arms Iron Frame Henry
Similar to the Military Henry Rifle except receiver is blued or color case-hardened steel. Imported by Navy Arms.
Price: Blued **$1,247.00**

NAVY ARMS 1866 YELLOW BOY RIFLE
Caliber: 38 Spec., 44-40, 45 Colt, 12-shot magazine. **Barrel:** 20" or 24", full octagon. **Weight:** 8.5 lbs. **Length:** 42.5" overall. **Stock:** Walnut. **Sights:** Blade front, adjustable ladder-type rear. **Features:** Brass frame, forend tip, buttplate, blued barrel, lever, hammer. Introduced 1991. Imported from Italy by Navy Arms.
Price: Yellow Boy Rifle, 24.25" barrel **$915.00**
Price: Yellow Boy Carbine, 19" barrel **$882.00**

NAVY ARMS 1873 WINCHESTER-STYLE RIFLE
Caliber: 357 Mag., 44-40, 45 Colt, 12-shot magazine. **Barrel:** 24.25". **Weight:** 8.25 lbs. **Length:** 43" overall. **Stock:** European walnut. **Sights:** Blade front, buckhorn rear. **Features:** Color case-hardened frame, rest blued. Full-octagon barrel. Imported by Navy Arms.
Price: **$1,047.00**
Price: 1873 Carbine, 19" barrel **$1,024.00**
Price: 1873 Sporting Rifle (octagonal bbl., checkered walnut stock and forend) **$1,183.00**
Price: 1873 Border Model, 20" octagon barrel **$1,047.00**
Price: 1873 Deluxe Border Model **$1,183.00**

PUMA MODEL 92 RIFLES AND CARBINES
Caliber: 17 HMR (XP and Scout models, only; intr. 2008), 38 Spec./357 Mag., 44 Mag., 45 Colt, 454 Casull, 480 Ruger (.44-40 in 20" octagonal barrel). **Barrel:** 16" and 20" round; 20" and 24" octagonal. 1:30" rate of twist (exc. 17 HMR is 1:9"). **Weight:** 7.7 lbs. **Stock:** Walnut stained hardwood. **Sights:** Blade front, V rear, buckhorn sights sold separately. **Features:** Finishes available in blue/blue, blue/case colored and stainless/stainless with matching crescent butt plates. .454 and .480 calibers have rubber recoil pads. Full-length magazines, thumb safety. Large lever loop or HiViz sights available on select models. Magazine capacity is 12 rounds with 24" bbl.; 10 rounds with 20" barrel; 8 rounds in 16" barrel. Introduced in 2002. Scout includes long-eye-relief scope, rail, elevated cheekpiece, intr. 2008. XP chambered in 17 HMR, 38 Spec./357 Mag. and 44 Mag., loads through magazine tube or loading gate, intr. 2008. Imported from Brazil by Legacy Sports International.
Price: From **$959.00**
Price: Scout Model, w/2.5x32 Nikko-Stirling Nighteater scope, intr. 2008, from **$739.00**
Price: XP Model, tube feed magazine, intr. 2008, from **$613.00**

REMINGTON MODEL 7600/7615 PUMP ACTION
Caliber: 243 Win., 270 Win., 30-06 Spfl., 308; 223 Rem. (7615 only). **Barrel:** 22" round tapered. **Weight:** 7.5 lbs. **Length:** 42.6" overall. **Stock:** Cut-checkered walnut pistol grip and forend, Monte Carlo with full cheekpiece. Satin or high-gloss finish. Also, black synthetic. **Sights:** Gold bead front sight on matted ramp, open step adjustable sporting rear. **Features:** Redesigned and improved version of the Model 760. Detachable 4-shot clip. Cross-bolt safety. Receiver tapped for scope mount. Introduced 1981. Model 7615 Tactical chambered in 223 Rem. **Features:** Knoxx SpecOps NRS (Non Recoil Suppressing) adjustable stock, parkerized finish, 10-round detachable magazine box, sling swivel studs. Introduced 2007.
Price: 7600 Wood **$792.00**
Price: 7600 Synthetic **$665.00**
Price: 7615 Ranch Carbine **$955.00**
Price: 7615 Camo Hunter **$1,009.00**
Price: 7615 Tactical 223 Rem., 16.5" barrel, 10-rd. magazine (2008) **$932.00**

ROSSI R92 LEVER-ACTION CARBINE
Caliber: 38 Special/357 Mag, 44 Mag., 44-40 Win., 45 Colt, 454 Casull. **Barrel:** 16" or 20" with round barrel, 20" or 24" with octagon barrel. **Weight:** 4.8 lbs. to 7 lbs. **Length:** 34" to 41.5". **Features:** Blued or stainless finish. Various options available in selected chamberings (large lever loop, fiber optic sights, cheekpiece, etc.).
Price: From **$499.00**

TAURUS THUNDERBOLT PUMP ACTION
Caliber: 38/.357, 45 Long Colt, 12 or 14 rounds. **Barrel:** 26" blue or polished stainless. **Weight:** 8.1 lbs. **Length:** 43" overall. **Stock:** Hardwood stock and forend. Gloss finish. **Sights:** Longhorn adjustable rear. Introduced 2004. Imported from Brazil by Taurus International.
Price: C45BR (blued) **$705.00**
Price: C45SSR (stainless) **$813.00**

TRISTAR SHARPS 1874 SPORTING RIFLE
Caliber: 45-70 Govt. **Barrel:** 28", 32", 34" octagonal. **Weight:** 9.75 lbs. **Length:** 44.5" overall. **Stock:** Walnut. **Sights:** Dovetail front, adjustable rear. **Features:** Cut checkering, case colored frame finish.
Price: **$1,099.00**

UBERTI 1873 SPORTING RIFLE
Caliber: 357 Mag., 44-40, 45 Colt. **Barrel:** 19" to 24.25". **Weight:** Up to 8.2 lbs. **Length:** Up to 43.3" overall. **Stock:** Walnut, straight grip and pistol grip. **Sights:** Blade front adjustable for windage, open rear adjustable for elevation. **Features:** Color case-hardened frame, blued barrel, hammer, lever, buttplate, brass elevator. Imported by Stoeger Industries.
Price: 1873 Carbine, 19" round barrel **$1,199.00**
Price: 1873 Short Rifle, 20" octagonal barrel **$1,249.00**
Price: 1873 Special Sporting Rifle, 24.25" octagonal barrel **$1,379.00**

UBERTI 1866 YELLOWBOY CARBINE, SHORT RIFLE, RIFLE
Caliber: 38 Spec., 44-40, 45 Colt. **Barrel:** 24.25", octagonal. **Weight:** 8.2 lbs. **Length:** 43.25" overall. **Stock:** Walnut. **Sights:** Blade front adjustable for windage, rear adjustable for elevation. **Features:** Frame, buttplate, forend cap of polished brass, balance charcoal blued. Imported by Stoeger Industries.
Price: 1866 Yellowboy Carbine, 19" round barrel **$1,079.00**
Price: 1866 Yellowboy Short Rifle, 20" octagonal barrel . . . **$1,129.00**
Price: 1866 Yellowboy Rifle, 24.25" octagonal barrel **$1,129.00**

UBERTI 1860 HENRY RIFLE
Caliber: 44-40, 45 Colt. **Barrel:** 24.25", half-octagon. **Weight:** 9.2 lbs. **Length:** 43.75" overall. **Stock:** American walnut. **Sights:** Blade front, rear adjustable for elevation. Imported by Stoeger Industries.
Price: 1860 Henry Trapper, 18.5" barrel, brass frame **$1,329.00**
Price: 1860 Henry Rifle Iron Frame, 24.25" barrel **$1,419.00**

UBERTI LIGHTNING RIFLE
Caliber: 357 Mag., 45 Colt, 10+1. **Barrel:** 20" to 24.25". **Stock:** Walnut. Finish: Blue or case-hardened. Introduced 2006. Imported by Stoeger Industries.
Price: 1875 Lightning Rifle, 24.25" barrel **$1,259.00**
Price: 1875 Lightning Short Rifle, 20" barrel **$1,259.00**
Price: 1875 Lightning Carbine, 20" barrel **$1,179.00**

UBERTI SPRINGFIELD TRAPDOOR RIFLE
Caliber: 4-70, single shot. **Barrel:** 22" or 32.5". **Stock:** Walnut. Finish: Blue and case-hardened. Introduced 2006. Imported by Stoeger Industries.
Price: Springfield Trapdoor Carbine, 22" barrel **$1,429.00**
Price: Springfield Trapdoor Army, 32.5" barrel **$1,669.00**

U.S. FIRE ARMS STANDARD LIGHTNING MAGAZINE RIFLE
Caliber: 45 Colt, 44 WCF, 44 Spec., 38 WCF, 15-shot. **Barrel:** 26". **Stock:** Oiled walnut. Finish: High polish blue. Nickel finish also available. Introduced 2002. Made in U.S.A. by United States Fire-Arms Manufacturing Co.
Price: Round barrel. **$1,480.00**
Price: Octagonal barrel, checkered forend **$1,750.00**
Price: Half-round barrel, checkered forend **$1,995.00**
Price: Premium Carbine, 20" round barrel **$1,480.00**
Price: Baby Carbine, 20" special taper barrel **$1,995.00**
Price: Deluxe Lightning **$2,559.00**

WINCHESTER MODEL 1895 SAFARI CENTENNIAL HIGH GRADE
Caliber: 405 Win. **Barrel:** 24" blued round, four-round box mag. **Weight:** 8 lbs. **Length:** NA. **Features:** Patterned after original Winchester Model 1895. Commemorates Theodore Roosevelt's 1909 African safari. Checkered walnut forend and buttstock with inlaid "TR" medallion, engraved and silvered receiver.
Price: **$1,749.00**
Price: Custom Grade: Jeweled hammer, fancier wood and angraving, gold-filled highlights and numerous accessories. Production limited to 100 sets **$3,649.00**

WINCHESTER MODEL 1894 CUSTOM GRADE
Lever-action rifle chambered in .30-30. Features include 24-inch half-round, half octagon deeply blued barrel; buckhorn rear sight with Marble's gold bead front sight; Grade IV/V walnut stock and forend with a rich, high gloss finish; deep scroll engraving on both sides of the blued receiver. Commemorates the 200th anniversary of Oliver F. Winchester's birth. An early Winchester Repeating Arms crest graces the left side of the receiver, with the right side bearing the words, "Two Hundred Years, Oliver F. Winchester," and the dates, "1810 — 2010," in gold. The barrel is deeply polished, with the signature of Oliver F. Winchester in gold on the top of the bolt. Sold individually in limited quantities and in 500 sets with the High Grade.
Price (single rifle): **$1,959.00**

WINCHESTER MODEL 1894 HIGH GRADE
Lever-action rifle chambered in .30-30. Features include 24-inch half-round, half octagon deeply blued barrel; buckhorn rear sight with Marble's gold bead front sight; silver nitride receiver; Grade II/III high gloss walnut stock and forend with a rich, high gloss finish; delicate scroll work, with Oliver F. Winchester's signature in gold on top of the bolt. The left side of receiver bears an early Winchester Repeating Arms crest; on right side are the words, "Two Hundred Years, Oliver F. Winchester," and the dates, "1810 — 2010." Sold individually in limited quantities and in 500 sets with the Custom Grade.
Price (single rifle): **$1,469.00**

Prices given are believed to be accurate at time of publication however, many factors affect retail pricing so exact prices are not possible.

BARRETT MODEL 95 BOLT-ACTION RIFLE

Caliber: 50 BMG, 5-shot magazine. **Barrel:** 29". **Weight:** 23.5 lbs. **Length:** 45" overall. **Stock:** Energy-absorbing recoil pad. **Sights:** Scope optional. **Features:** Bolt-action, bullpup design. Disassembles without tools; extendable bipod legs; match-grade barrel; muzzle brake. Introduced 1995. Made in U.S.A. by Barrett Firearms Mfg., Inc.

Price: From $6,500.00

BLASER R93 BOLT-ACTION RIFLE

Caliber: 22-250 Rem., 243 Win., 6.5x55, 270 Win., 7x57, 7mm-08 Rem., 308 Win., 30-06 Spfl., 257 Wby. Mag., 7mm Rem. Mag., 300 Win. Mag., 300 Wby. Mag., 338 Win. Mag., 375 H&H, 416 Rem. Mag. **Barrel:** 22" (standard calibers), 26" (magnum). **Weight:** 7 lbs. **Length:** 40" overall (22" barrel). **Stock:** Two-piece European walnut. **Sights:** None furnished; drilled and tapped for scope mounting. **Features:** Straight pull-back bolt action with thumb-activated safety slide/cocking mechanism; interchangeable barrels and bolt heads. Introduced 1994. Imported from Germany by Blaser USA.

Price: R93 Prestige, wood grade 3 . . . . $3,275.00
Price: R93 Luxus $4,460.00
Price: R93 Professional $2,950.00
Price: R93 Grand Luxe $8,163.00
Price: R93 Attache $6,175.00

BROWNING A-BOLT RIFLES

Common Features: Short-throw (60°) fluted bolt, three locking lugs, plunger-type ejector; adjustable trigger is grooved. Chrome-plated trigger sear. Hinged floorplate, detachable box magazine. Slide tang safety. Receivers are drilled and tapped for scope mounts, swivel studs included. Barrel is free-floating and glass-bedded, recessed muzzle. Safety is top-tang sliding button. Engraving available for bolt sleeve or rifle body. Introduced 1985. Imported from Japan by Browning.

BROWNING A-BOLT HUNTER

Calibers: 22" Barrel: 223 Rem., 22-250 Rem., 243 Win., 270 Win., 30-06 Spfl., 7mm-08 Rem., 308 Win. **Barrel:** 270 WSM, 7mm WSM, 300 WSM, 325 WSM (intr. 2005). **Calibers:** 24" Barrel: 25-06 Rem. **Calibers:** 26" Barrel: 7mm Rem. Mag., 300 Win. Mag., 338 Win. Mag. **Weight:** 6.25-7.2 lbs. **Length:** 41.25-46.5" overall. **Stock:** Sporter-style walnut; checkered grip and forend. **Metal Finish:** Low-luster blueing.

Price: Hunter, left-hand, from $819.00

BROWNING A-BOLT HUNTER FLD

Caliber: 23" Barrel: 270 WSM, 7mm WSM, 300 WSM, 325 WSM (intr. 2005). **Weight:** 6.6 lbs. **Length:** 42.75" overall. **Features:** FLD has low-luster blueing and select Monte Carlo stock with right-hand palm swell, double-border checkering. Otherwise similar to A-Bolt Hunter.

Price: FLD $899.00

Browning A-Bolt Target
Similar to A-Bolt Hunter but with 28" heavy bull blued barrel, blued receiver, satin finish gray

laminated stock with adjustable comb and semi-beavertail forend. Chambered in 223, 308 Winchester and 300 WSM. Available also with stainless receiver and barrel.

Price: From $1,269.00
Price: Stainless, from $1,489.00

BROWNING A-BOLT MOUNTAIN TI

Caliber: 223 WSSM, 243 WSSM, 25 WSSM (all added 2005); 270 WSM, 7mm WSM, 300 WSM. **Barrel:** 22" or 23". **Weight:** 5.25-5.5 lbs. **Length:** 41.25-42.75" overall. **Stock:** Lightweight fiberglass Bell & Carlson model in Mossy-Oak New Break Up camo. Metal Finish: Stainless barrel, titanium receiver. **Features:** Pachmayr Decelerator recoil pad. Introduced 1999.

Price: From $1,819.00

BROWNING A-BOLT MICRO HUNTER AND MICRO HUNTER LEFT-HAND

Calibers: 20" Barrel: 22-250 Rem., 243 Win., 308 Win., 7mm-08. 22" Barrel: 22 Hornet, 270 WSM, 7mm WSM, 300 WSM, 325 WSM (2005). **Weight:** 6.25-6.4 lbs. **Length:** 39.5-41.5" overall. **Features:** Classic walnut stock with 13.3" LOP. Otherwise similar to A-Bolt Hunter.

Price: Micro Hunter, from $759.00
Price: Micro Hunter left-hand, from $799.00

BROWNING A-BOLT MEDALLION

Calibers: 22" Barrel: 223 Rem., 22-250 Rem., 243 Win., 308 Win., 270 Win., 280 Rem., 30-06.; 23" Barrel: 270 WSM, 7mm WSM, 300 WSM, 325 WSM (intr. 2005); 24" Barrel: 25-06 Rem.; 26" Barrel: 7mm Rem. Mag., 300 Win. Mag., 338 Win. Mag., 375 H&H. **Weight:** 6.25-7.1 lbs. **Length:** 41.25-46.5" overall. **Stock:** Select walnut stock, glossy finish, rosewood grip and forend caps, checkered grip and forend. Metal Finish: Engraved high-polish blued receiver.

Price: Medallion, from $909.00
Price: Medallion WSM $959.00
Price: Medallion w/BOSS, intr. 1987, from $1,009.00

BROWNING A-BOLT WHITE GOLD MEDALLION, RMEF WHITE GOLD, WHITE GOLD MEDALLION W/BOSS

Calibers: 22" Barrel: 270 Win., 30-06. Calibers: 23" Barrel: 270 WSM, 7mm WSM, 300 WSM, 325 WSM (intr. 2005). Calibers: 26" Barrel: 7mm Rem. Mag., 300 Win. Mag. **Weight:** 6.4-7.7 lbs. **Length:** 42.75-46.5" overall. **Stock:** select walnut stock with brass spacers between rubber recoil pad and between the rosewood gripcap and forend tip; gold-filled barrel inscription; palm-swell pistol grip, Monte Carlo comb, 22 lpi checkering with double borders. **Metal Finish:** Engraved high-polish stainless receiver and barrel. BOSS version chambered in 270 Win. and 30-06 (22" barrel) and 7mm Rem. Mag. and 300 Win. Mag. (26" barrel). Introduced 1988. RMEF version has engraved gripcap, continental cheekpiece; gold engraved, stainless receiver and bbl. Introduced 2004.

Price: White Gold Medallion, from $1,309.00
Price: Rocky Mt. Elk Foundation White Gold, 325 WSM, intr. 2007 . . . . $1,399.00

BROWNING A-BOLT STAINLESS STALKER, STAINLESS STALKER LEFT-HAND

Calibers: 22" Barrel: 223 Rem., 243 Win., 270 Win., 280 Rem., 7mm-08 Rem., 30-06 Spfl., 308 Win. Calibers: 23" Barrel: 270 WSM, 7mm WSM, 300 WSM, 325 WSM (intr. 2005). Calibers: 24" Barrel: 25-06 Rem. Calibers: 26" Barrel: 7mm Rem. Mag., 300 Win. Mag., 338 Win. Mag., 375 H&H. **Weight:** 6.1-7.2 lbs. **Length:** 40.9-46.5" overall. **Features:** Similar to the A-Bolt Hunter model except receiver and barrel are made of stainless steel; other exposed metal surfaces are finished silver-gray matte. Graphite-fiberglass composite textured

stock. No sights are furnished, except on 375 H&H, which comes with open sights. Introduced 1987.
Price: Stainless Stalker left-hand, from **$1,029.00**
Price: Stainless Stalker w/Boss, from **$1,119.00**

BROWNING A-BOLT COMPOSITE STALKER
Calibers: 22 Barrel: 270 Win., 30-06 Sprg.; 23" Barrel: 270 WSM, 7mm WSM, 300 WSM, 325 WSM; 24" Barrel: 25-06 Rem.; 26" Barrel: 7mm Rem. Mag., 300 Win. Mag., 338 Win. Mag. **Weight:** 6.6-7.3 lbs. **Length:** 42.5-46.5" overall. **Features:** Similar to the A-Bolt Stainless Stalker except has black composite stock with textured finish and matte-blued finish on all exposed metal surfaces except bolt sleeve. No sights are furnished.
Price: Composite Stalker w/BOSS, from $869.00
Price: Stainless Stalker **$1,009.00**
Price: Stainless Stalker w/Boss, from **$1,079.00**

BROWNING A-BOLT ECLIPSE HUNTER W/ BOSS, M-1000 ECLIPSE W/BOSS, M-1000 ECLIPSE WSM, STAINLESS M-1000 ECLIPSE WSM
Calibers: 22" Barrel: 270 Win., 30-06. Calibers: 26" Barrel: 7mm Rem. Mag., 300 Win. Mag., 270 WSM, 7mm WSM, 300 WSM. **Weight:** 7.5-9.9 lbs. **Length:** 42.75-46.5" overall. **Features:** All models have gray/black laminated thumbhole stock. Introduced 1996. Two versions have BOSS barrel vibration modulator and muzzle brake. Hunter has sporter-weight barrel. M-1000 Eclipses have long actions and heavy target barrels, adjustable triggers, bench-style forends, 3-shot magazines. Introduced 1997.
Price: Eclipse Hunter w/BOSS, from **$1,259.00**
Price: M-1000 Eclipse, from **$1,169.00**
Price: M-1000 Eclipse w/BOSS, from **$1,259.00**
Price: Stainless M-1000 Eclipse WSM, from **$1,399.00**
Price: Stainless M-1000 Eclipse w/BOSS, from **$1,489.00**

BROWNING X-BOLT HUNTER
Calibers: 223, 22-250, 243 Win., 25-06 Rem., 270 Win., 270 WSM, 280 Rem., 30-06 Spfl., 300 Win. Mag., 300 WSM, 308 Win., 325 WSM, 338 Win. Mag., 375 H&H Mag., 7mm Rem. Mag., 7mm WSM, 7mm-08 Rem. **Barrels:** 22", 23", 24", 26", varies by model. Matte blued or stainless free-floated barrel, recessed muzzle crown. **Weight:** 6.3-7 lbs. **Stock:** Hunter and Medallion models have wood stocks; Composite Stalker and Stainless Stalker models have composite stocks. Inflex Technology recoil pad. **Sights:** None, drilled and tapped receiver, X-Lock scope mounts. **Features:** Adjustable three-lever Feather Trigger system, polished hard-chromed steel components, factory pre-set at 3.5 lbs., alloy trigger housing. Bolt unlock button, detachable rotary magazine, 60-degree bolt lift, three locking lugs, top-tang safety, sling swivel studs. Medallion has metal engraving, gloss finish walnut stock, rosewood fore-end grip and pistol grip cap. Introduced 2008. From Browning.

Browning X-Bolt Micro Hunter
Similar to Browning X-Bolt Hunter but with compact dimensions (13-15/16 length of pull, 41-1/4 overall length).
Price: Standard chamberings **$839.00**
Price: Magnum **$869.00**

Browning X-Bolt Varmint Stalker
Similar to Browning X-Bolt Stalker but with medium-heavy free-floated barrel, target crown, composite stock. Chamberings available: 223, 22-250, 243 Winchester and 308 Winchester only.
Price: **$1,019.00**

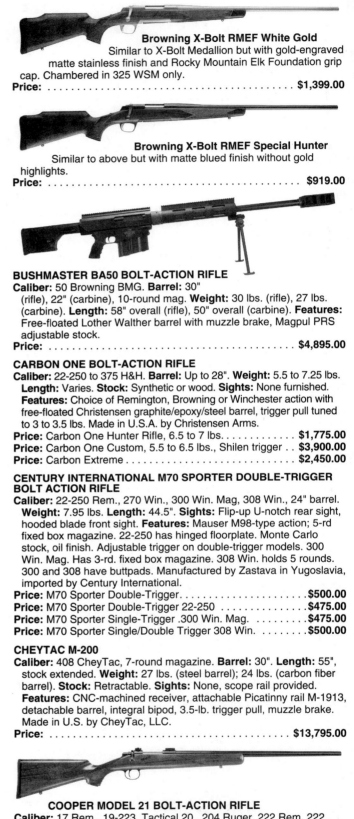

Browning X-Bolt RMEF White Gold
Similar to X-Bolt Medallion but with gold-engraved matte stainless finish and Rocky Mountain Elk Foundation grip cap. Chambered in 325 WSM only.
Price: **$1,399.00**

Browning X-Bolt RMEF Special Hunter
Similar to above but with matte blued finish without gold highlights.
Price: **$919.00**

BUSHMASTER BA50 BOLT-ACTION RIFLE
Caliber: 50 Browning BMG. **Barrel:** 30" (rifle), 22" (carbine), 10-round mag. **Weight:** 30 lbs. (rifle), 27 lbs. (carbine). **Length:** 58" overall (rifle), 50" overall (carbine). **Features:** Free-floated Lother Walther barrel with muzzle brake, Magpul PRS adjustable stock.
Price: **$4,895.00**

CARBON ONE BOLT-ACTION RIFLE
Caliber: 22-250 to 375 H&H. **Barrel:** Up to 28". **Weight:** 5.5 to 7.25 lbs. **Length:** Varies. **Stock:** Synthetic or wood. **Sights:** None furnished. **Features:** Choice of Remington, Browning or Winchester action with free-floated Christensen graphite/epoxy/steel barrel, trigger pull tuned to 3 to 3.5 lbs. Made in U.S.A. by Christensen Arms.
Price: Carbon One Hunter Rifle, 6.5 to 7 lbs. **$1,775.00**
Price: Carbon One Custom, 5.5 to 6.5 lbs., Shilen trigger . . **$3,900.00**
Price: Carbon Extreme **$2,450.00**

CENTURY INTERNATIONAL M70 SPORTER DOUBLE-TRIGGER BOLT ACTION RIFLE
Caliber: 22-250 Rem., 270 Win., 300 Win. Mag., 308 Win., 24" barrel. **Weight:** 7.95 lbs. **Length:** 44.5". **Sights:** Flip-up U-notch rear sight, hooded blade front sight. **Features:** Mauser M98-type action; 5-rd fixed box magazine. 22-250 has hinged floorplate. Monte Carlo stock, oil finish. Adjustable trigger on double-trigger models. 300 Win. Mag. Has 3-rd. fixed box magazine. 308 Win. holds 5 rounds. 300 and 308 have buttpads. Manufactured by Zastava in Yugoslavia, imported by Century International.
Price: M70 Sporter Double-Trigger. $500.00
Price: M70 Sporter Double-Trigger 22-250 . . . .$475.00
Price: M70 Sporter Single-Trigger .300 Win. Mag. $475.00
Price: M70 Sporter Single/Double Trigger 308 Win. $500.00

CHEYTAC M-200
Caliber: 408 CheyTac, 7-round magazine. **Barrel:** 30". **Length:** 55", stock extended. **Weight:** 27 lbs. (steel barrel); 24 lbs. (carbon fiber barrel). **Stock:** Retractable. **Sights:** None, scope rail provided. **Features:** CNC-machined receiver, attachable Picatinny rail M-1913, detachable barrel, integral bipod, 3.5-lb. trigger pull, muzzle brake. Made in U.S. by CheyTac, LLC.
Price: **$13,795.00**

COOPER MODEL 21 BOLT-ACTION RIFLE
Caliber: 17 Rem., 19-223, Tactical 20, .204 Ruger, 222 Rem, 222 Rem. Mag., 223 Rem, 223 Rem A.I., 6x45, 6x47. **Barrel:** 22" or 24" in Classic configurations, 24"-26" in Varminter configurations. **Weight:** 6.5-8.0 lbs., depending on type. **Stock:** AA-AAA select claro walnut, 20 lpi checkering. **Sights:** None furnished. **Features:** Three front locking-lug bolt-action single shot. Action: 7.75" long, Sako extractor. Button ejector. Fully adjustable single-stage trigger.

Prices given are believed to be accurate at time of publication however, many factors affect retail pricing so exact prices are not possible.

Options include wood upgrades, case-color metalwork, barrel fluting, custom LOP, and many others.

Price: From $1,395.00

COOPER MODEL 22 BOLT-ACTION RIFLE

Caliber: 22-250 Rem., 22-250 Rem. AI, 25-06 Rem., 25-06 Rem. AI, 243 Win., 243 Win. AI, 220 Swift, 250/3000 AI, 257 Roberts, 257 Roberts AI, 7mm-08 Rem., 6mm Rem., 260 Rem., 6 x 284, 6.5 x 284, 22 BR, 6mm BR, 308 Win. **Barrel:** 24" or 26" stainless match in Classic configurations. 24" or 26" in Varminter configurations. **Weight:** 7.5 to 8.0 lbs. depending on type. **Stock:** AA-AAA select claro walnut, 20 lpi checkering. **Sights:** None furnished. **Features:** Three front locking-lug bolt-action single shot. Action: 8.25" long, Sako style extractor. Button ejector. Fully adjustable single-stage trigger. Options include wood upgrades, case-color metalwork, barrel fluting, custom LOP, and many others.

Price: From $1,495.00

COOPER MODEL 38 BOLT-ACTION RIFLE

Caliber: 17 Squirrel, 17 He Bee, 17 Ackley Hornet, 17 Mach IV, 19 Calhoon, 20 VarTarg, 221 Fireball, 22 Hornet, 22 K-Hornet, 22 Squirrel, 218 Bee, 218 Mashburn Bee. **Barrel:** 22" or 24" in Classic configurations, 24" or 26" in Varminter configurations. **Weight:** 6.5-8.0 lbs. depending on type. **Stock:** AA-AAA select claro walnut, 20 lpi checkering. **Sights:** None furnished. **Features:** Three front locking-lug bolt-action single shot. Action: 7" long, Sako style extractor. Button ejector. Fully adjustable single-stage trigger. Options include wood upgrades, case-color metalwork, barrel fluting, custom LOP, and many others.

Price: From $1,395.00

CZ 527 LUX BOLT-ACTION RIFLE

Caliber: 204 Ruger, 22 Hornet, 222 Rem., 223 Rem., detachable 5-shot magazine. **Barrel:** 23.5"; standard or heavy barrel. **Weight:** 6 lbs., 1 oz. **Length:** 42.5" overall. **Stock:** European walnut with Monte Carlo. **Sights:** Hooded front, open adjustable rear. **Features:** Improved mini-Mauser action with non-rotating claw extractor; single set trigger; grooved receiver. Imported from the Czech Republic by CZ-USA.

Price: Brown laminate stock $718.00
Price: Model FS, full-length stock, cheekpiece $827.00

CZ 527 American Bolt-Action Rifle

Similar to the CZ 527 Lux except has classic-style stock with 18 lpi checkering; free-floating barrel; recessed target crown on barrel. No sights furnished. Introduced 1999. Imported from the Czech Republic by CZUSA.

Price: From $751.00

CZ 550 AMERICAN CLASSIC BOLT-ACTION RIFLE

Caliber: 22-250 Rem., 243 Win., 6.5x55, 7x57, 7x64, 308 Win., 9.3x62, 270 Win., 30-06. **Barrel:** free-floating barrel; recessed target crown. **Weight:** 7.48 lbs. **Length:** 44.68" overall. **Stock:** American classic-style stock with 18 lpi checkering or FS (Mannlicher). **Sights:** No sights furnished. **Features:** Improved Mauser-style action with claw extractor, fixed ejector, square bridge dovetailed receiver; single set trigger. Introduced 1999. Imported from the Czech Republic by CZ-USA.

Price: FS (full stock) $894.00
Price: American, from $827.00

CZ 550 Safari Magnum/American Safari Magnum Bolt-Action Rifles

Similar to CZ 550 American Classic. Chambered for 375 H&H Mag., 416 Rigby, 458 Win. Mag., 458 Lott. Overall length is 46.5"; barrel

length 25"; weighs 9.4 lbs., 9.9 lbs (American). Hooded front sight, express rear with one standing, two folding leaves. Imported from the Czech Republic by CZ-USA.

Price: $1,179.00
Price: American $1,261.00
Price: American Kevlar $1,714.00

CZ 550 Varmint Bolt-Action Rifle

Similar to CZ 550 American Classic. Chambered for 308 Win. and 22-250. Kevlar, laminated stocks. Overall length is 46.7"; barrel length 25.6"; weighs 9.1 lbs. Imported from the Czech Republic by CZ-USA.

Price: $841.00
Price: Kevlar $1,037.00
Price: Laminated $966.00

CZ 550 Magnum H.E.T. Bolt-Action Rifle

Similar to CZ 550 American Classic. Chambered for 338 Lapua, 300 Win. Mag., 300 RUM. Overall length is 52"; barrel length 28"; weighs 14 lbs. Adjustable sights, satin blued barrel. Imported from the Czech Republic by CZ-USA.

Price: $3,673.00

CZ 550 Ultimate Hunting Bolt-Action Rifle

Similar to CZ 550 American Classic. Chambered for 300 Win Mag. Overall length is 44.7"; barrel length 23.6"; weighs 7.7 lbs. Imported from the Czech Republic by CZ-USA.

Price: $4,242.00

CZ 750 SNIPER RIFLE

Caliber: 308 Winchester, 10-shot magazine. **Barrel:** 26". **Weight:** 11.9 lbs. **Length:** 48" overall. **Stock:** Polymer thumbhole. **Sights:** None furnished; permanently attached Weaver rail for scope mounting. **Features:** 60-degree bolt throw; oversized trigger guard and bolt handle for use with gloves; full-length equipment rail on forend; fully adjustable trigger. Introduced 2001. Imported from the Czech Republic by CZ-USA.

Price: $2,404.00

DAKOTA 76 TRAVELER TAKEDOWN RIFLE

Caliber: 257 Roberts, 25-06 Rem., 7x57, 270 Win., 280 Rem., 30-06 Spfl., 338-06, 35 Whelen (standard length); 7mm Rem. Mag., 300 Win. Mag., 338 Win. Mag., 416 Taylor, 458 Win. Mag. (short magnums); 7mm, 300, 330, 375 Dakota Magnums. **Barrel:** 23". **Weight:** 7.5 lbs. **Length:** 43.5" overall. **Stock:** Medium fancy-grade walnut in classic style. Checkered grip and forend; solid buttpad. **Sights:** None furnished; drilled and tapped for scope mounts. **Features:** Threadless disassembly. Uses modified Model 76 design with many features of the Model 70 Winchester. Left-hand model also available. Introduced 1989. African chambered for 338 Lapua Mag., 404 Jeffery, 416 Rigby, 416 Dakota, 450 Dakota, 4-round magazine, select wood, two stock cross-bolts. 24" barrel, weighs 9-10 lbs. Ramp front sight, standing leaf rear. Introduced 1989.Made in U.S.A. by Dakota Arms, Inc.

Price: Classic $6,095.00
Price: Safari $7,895.00
Price: African $9,495.00

DAKOTA 76 CLASSIC BOLT-ACTION RIFLE

Caliber: 257 Roberts, 270 Win., 280 Rem., 30-06 Spfl., 7mm Rem. Mag., 338 Win. Mag., 300 Win. Mag., 375 H&H Mag., 458 Win. Mag. **Barrel:** 23". **Weight:** 7.5 lbs. **Length:** 43.5" overall. **Stock:** Medium fancy grade walnut in classic style. Checkered pistol grip and forend; solid buttpad. **Sights:** None furnished; drilled and tapped for scope mounts. **Features:** Has many features of the original Winchester Model 70. One-piece rail trigger guard assembly; steel gripcap. Model 70-style trigger. Many options available. Left-hand rifle available at same price. Introduced 1988. From Dakota Arms, Inc.

Price: From $4,595.00

DAKOTA LONGBOW T-76 TACTICAL RIFLE

Caliber: 300 Dakota Magnum, 330 Dakota Magnum, 338 Lapua Magnum. **Barrel:** 28", .950" at muzzle **Weight:** 13.7 lbs. **Length:** 50" to 52" overall. **Stock:** Ambidextrous McMillan A-2 fiberglass, black or olive green color; adjustable cheekpiece and buttplate. **Sights:** None furnished. Comes with Picatinny one-piece optical rail. **Features:** Uses the Dakota 76 action with controlled-round feed; three-position firing pin block safety, claw extractor; Model 70-style trigger. Comes with bipod, case tool kit. Introduced 1997. Made in U.S.A. by Dakota Arms, Inc.

Price: **$4,795.00**

DAKOTA MODEL 97 BOLT-ACTION RIFLE

Caliber: 22-250 to 330. **Barrel:** 22" to 24". **Weight:** 6.1 to 6.5 lbs. **Length:** 43" overall. **Stock:** Fiberglass. **Sights:** Optional. **Features:** Matte blue finish, black stock. Right-hand action only. Introduced 1998. Made in U.S.A. by Dakota Arms, Inc.

Price: From **$3,395.00**

DAKOTA PREDATOR RIFLE

Caliber: 17 VarTarg, 17 Rem., 17 Tactical, 20 VarTarg, 20 Tactical, .20 PPC, 204 Ruger, 221 Rem Fireball, 222 Remington, 22 PPC, 223 Rem., 6mm PPC, 6.5 Grendel. **Barrel:** 22" match grade stainless;. **Weight:** NA. **Length:** NA. **Stock:** Special select walnut, sporter-style stock, 23 lpi checkering on forend and grip. **Sights:** None furnished. Drilled and tapped for scope mounting. **Features:** 13-5/8" LOP, 1/2" black presentation pad, 11" recessed target crown. Serious Predator includes XXX walnut varmint style stock w/semi-beavertail forend, stainless receiver. All-Weather Predator includes varmint style composite stock w/semi-beavertail forend, stainless receiver. Introduced 2007. Made in U.S.A. by Dakota Arms, Inc.

Price: Classic **$4,295.00**
Price: Serious **$3,295.00**
Price: All-Weather. **$1,995.00**

DSA DS-MP1

Caliber: 308 Win. match chamber. **Barrel:** 22", 1:10 twist, hand-lapped stainless-steel match-grade Badger Barrel with recessed target crown. **Weight:** 11.5 lbs. **Length:** 41.75". **Stock:** Black McMillan A5 pillar bedded in Marine-Tex with 13.5" length of pull. **Sights:** Tactical Picatinny rail. **Features:** Action, action threads and action bolt locking shoulder completely trued, Badger Ordnance precision ground heavy recoil lug, machined steel Picatinny rail sight mount, trued action threads, action bolt locking shoulder, bolt face and lugs, 2.5-lb. trigger pull, barrel and action finished in Black DuraCoat, guaranteed to shoot 1/2 MOA at 100 yards with match-grade ammo. Introduced 2006. Made in U.S.A. by DSA, Inc.

Price: **$2,800.00**

EAA/ZASTAVA M-93 BLACK ARROW RIFLE

Caliber: 50 BMG. **Barrel:** 36". **Weight:** 7 to 8.5 lbs. **Length:** 60". **Stock:** Synthetic. **Sights:** Scope rail and iron sights. **Features:** **Features:** Mauser action, developed in early 1990s by Zastava Arms Factory. Fluted heavy barrel with recoil reducing muzzle brake, self-leveling and adjustable folding integral bipod, back up iron sights, heavy duty carry handle, detachable 5 round box magazine, and quick detachable scope mount. Imported by EAA. Imported from Russia by EAA Corp.

Price: **$6,986.25**

ED BROWN HUNTING SERIES RIFLES

Caliber: Many calibers available. **Barrel:** 24" (Savanna, Express, Varmint); 23-24" (Damara); 22" (Compact Varmint). **Weight:** 8 to 8.5 lbs. (Savanna); 6.2 to 6.9 lbs. (Damara); 9 lbs. (Express); 10 lbs. (Varmint), 8.75 lbs. (Compact Varmint). **Stock:** Fully glass-bedded McMillan fiberglass sporter. **Sights:** None furnished. Talley scope mounts utilizing heavy-duty 8-40 screws. **Features:** Custom action with machined steel trigger guard and hinged floor plate.

Price: Savanna **$3,895.00**
Price: Damara . . . . **$3,995.00 to $4,095.00**
Price: Express **$4,995.00**
Price: Varmint & Compact Varmint. **$3,895.00**

ED BROWN MODEL 704 BUSHVELD

Caliber: 338 Win. Mag., 375 H&H, 416 Rem. Mag., 458 Win. Mag., 458 Lott and all Ed Brown Savanna long action calibers. **Barrel:** 24" medium or heavy weight. **Weight:** 8.25 lbs. **Stock:** Fully bedded McMillan fiberglass with Monte Carlo style cheekpiece, Pachmayr Decelerator recoil pad. **Sights:** None furnished. Talley scope mounts utilizing heavy-duty 8-40 screws. **Features:** Stainless steel barrel, additional calibers: iron sights.

Price: From **$2,995.00**

ED BROWN MODEL 704 EXPRESS

Caliber: 375 H&H, 416 Rem, 458 Lott, other calibers available. **Barrel:** 24" #4 Stainless barrel with black Gen III coating for superior rust protection. **Weight:** 9 lbs. **Stocks:** Hand-bedded McMillan fiberglass stock. Monte Carlo style with cheek piece and full 1" thick Pachmayr Decel recoil pad. **Sights:** Adjustable iron sights. **Features:** Ed Brown controlled feed action. A special dropped box magazine ensures feeding and allows a full four-round capacity in the magazine, plus one in the chamber. Barrel band is standard for lower profile when carrying the rifle through heavy brush.

Price: From **$3,695.00**

HOWA M-1500 RANCHLAND COMPACT

Caliber: 223 Rem., 22-250 Rem., 243 Win., 308 Win. and 7mm-08. **Barrel:** 20" #1 contour, blued finish. **Weight:** 7 lbs. **Stock:** Hogue Overmolded in black, OD green, Coyote Sand colors. 13.87" LOP. **Sights:** None furnished; drilled and tapped for scope mounting. **Features:** Three-position safety, hinged floor plate, adjustable trigger, forged one-piece bolt, M-16 style extractor, forged flat-bottom receiver. Also available with Nikko-Stirling Nighteater 3-9x42 riflescope. Introduced in 2008. Imported from Japan by Legacy Sports International.

Price: Rifle Only, (2008) **$479.00**
Price: Rifle with 3-9x42 Nighteater scope (2008) **$599.00**

HOWA M-1500 THUMBHOLE SPORTER

Caliber: 204, 223 Rem., 22-250 Rem., 243 Win., 6.5x55 (2008) 25-06 Rem., 270 Win., 7mm Rem. Mag., 308 Win., 30-06 Spfl., 300 Win. Mag., 338 Win. Mag., 375 Ruger. Similar to Camo Lightning except stock. **Weight:** 7.6 to 7.7 lbs. **Stock:** S&K laminated wood in nutmeg (brown/black) or pepper (grey/black) colors, raised comb with forward taper, flared pistol grip and scalloped thumbhole. **Sights:** None furnished; drilled and tapped for scope mounting. **Features:** Three-position safety, hinged floor plate, adjustable trigger, forged one-piece bolt, M-16 style extractor, forged flat-bottom receiver. Introduced in 2001. Imported from Japan by Legacy Sports International.

Price: Blue/Nutmeg, standard calibers . . . . **$649.00 to $669.00**
Price: Stainless/Pepper, standard calibers. . . . . . . **$749.00 to $769.00**

HOWA M-1500 VARMINTER SUPREME AND THUMBHOLE VARMINTER SUPREME

Caliber: 204, 223 Rem., 22-250 Rem., 243 Win., 308 Win. **Stock:** Varminter Supreme: Laminated wood in nutmeg (brown), pepper (grey) colors, raised comb and rollover cheekpiece, full pistol grip with palm-filling swell and broad beavertail forend with six vents for barrel cooling. Thumbhole Varminter Supreme similar, adds a high, straight comb, more vertical pistol grip. **Sights:** None furnished; drilled and tapped for scope mounting. **Features:** Three-position safety, hinged floor plate, adjustable trigger, forged one-piece bolt, M-16 style extractor, forged flat-bottom receiver, hammer forged bull barrel and recessed muzzle crown; overall length, 43.75", 9.7 lbs. Introduced 2001. Barreled actions imported by Legacy Sports International; stocks by S&K Gunstocks.

Price: Varminter Supreme, Blue/Nutmeg **$679.00**
Price: Varminter Supreme, Stainless/Pepper **$779.00**

Prices given are believed to be accurate at time of publication however, many factors affect retail pricing so exact prices are not possible.

Price: Thumbhole Varminter Supreme, Blue/Nutmeg **$679.00**
Price: Thumbhole Varminter Supreme, Stainless/Pepper **$779.00**

HOWA CAMO LIGHTNING M-1500
Caliber: 204, 223 Rem., 22-250 Rem., 243 Win., 25-06 Rem., 270 Win., 308 Win., 30-06 Spfl., 300 Win. Mag., 338 Win. Mag., 7mm Rem. Mag. **Barrel:** 22" standard calibers; 24" magnum calibers; #2 and #6 contour; blue and stainless. **Weight:** 7.6 to 9.3 lbs. **Length:** 42" to 44.5" overall. **Stock:** Synthetic with molded cheek piece, checkered grip and forend. **Sights:** None furnished; drilled and tapped for scope mounting. **Features:** Three-position safety, hinged floor plate, adjustable trigger, forged one-piece bolt, M-16 style extractor, forged flat bottom receiver. Introduced in 1993. Barreled actions imported by Legacy Sports International.
Price: Blue, #2 barrel, standard calibers **$377.00**
Price: Stainless, #2 barrel, standard calibers **$479.00**
Price: Blue, #2 barrel, magnum calibers **$390.00**
Price: Stainless, #2 barrel, magnum calibers **$498.00**
Price: Blue, #6 barrel, standard calibers **$425.00**
Price: Stainless, #6 barrel, standard calibers **$498.00**

HOWA/HOGUE M-1500
Caliber: 204, 223 Rem., 22-250 Rem., 243 Win., 6.5x5 (2008), 25-06 Rem., 270 Win., 308 Win., 30-06 Spfl., 300 Win. Mag., 338 Win. Mag., 7mm Rem. Mag., 375 Ruger (2008). **Barrel:** Howa barreled action; stainless or blued, 22" #2 contour. **Weight:** 7.4 to 7.6 lbs. **Stock:** Hogue Overmolded, black, or OD green; ambidextrous palm swells. **Sights:** None furnished; drilled and tapped for scope mounting. **Length:** 42" to 44.5" overall. **Features:** Three-position safety, hinged floor plate, adjustable trigger, forged one-piece bolt, M-16 style extractor, forged flat bottom receiver, aluminum pillar bedding and free-floated barrels. Introduced in 2006. Available w/3-10x42 Nikko-Stirling Nighteater scope, rings, bases (2008). from Imported from Japan by Legacy Sports International.
Price: Blued, rifle only . . . . **$479.00 to $499.00**
Price: Blue, rifle with scope package (2008) . . . . . **$599.00 to $619.00**
Price: Stainless, rifle only . . . . **$625.00 to $675.00**

HOWA/HOGUE M-1500 COMPACT HEAVY BARREL VARMINTER
Chambered in 223 Rem., 308 Win., has 20" #6 contour heavy barrel, recessed muzzle crown. **Stock:** Hogue Overmolded, black, or OD green; ambidextrous palm swells. **Sights:** None furnished; drilled and tapped for scope mounting. **Length:** 44.0" overall. **Features:** Three-position safety, hinged floor plate, adjustable trigger, forged one-piece bolt, M-16 style extractor, forged flat bottom receiver, aluminum pillar bedding and free-floated barrels. **Weight:** 9.3 lbs. Introduced 2008. Imported from Japan by Legacy Sports International.
Price: From **$559.00**

HOWA/AXIOM M-1500
Caliber: 204, 223 Rem., 22-250 Rem., 243 Win., 6.5x55 (2008), 25-06 Rem. (2008), 270 Win., 308 Win., 30-06 Spfl., 7mm Rem, 300 Win. Mag., 338 Win. Mag., 375 Ruger standard barrel; 204, 223 Rem., 243 Win. and 308 Win. heavy barrel. **Barrel:** Howa barreled action, 22" #6 contour standard barrel, 20" #6 contour heavy barrel, and 24" #6 contour heavy barrel. **Weight:** 8.6-10 lbs. **Stock:** Knoxx Industries Axiom V/S synthetic, black or camo. Adjustable length of pull from 11.5" to 15.5". **Sights:** None furnished; drilled and tapped for scope mounting. **Features:** Three-position safety, adjustable trigger, hinged floor plate, forged receiver with large recoil lug, forged one-piece bolt with dual locking lugs Introduced in 2007. Standard-barrel scope packages come with 3-10x42 Nikko-Stirling Nighteater scope, rings, bases (2008). Heavy barrels come with 4-16x44 Nikko-Stirling scope. Imported from Japan by Legacy Sports International.
Price: Axiom Standard Barrel, black stock, from **$699.00**
Price: Axiom 20" and 24" Varminter, black or
camo stock, from **$799.00**
Price: Axiom 20" and 24" Varminter, camo stock
w/scope (2008), from **$819.00**

HOWA M-1500 ULTRALIGHT 2-N-1 YOUTH
Caliber: 223 Rem., 22-250 Rem., 243 Win., 308 Win., 7mm-08. **Barrel:** 20" #1 contour, blued. **Weight:** 6.8 lbs. **Length:** 39.25" overall. **Stock:** Hogue Overmolded in black, 12.5" LOP. Also includes adult-size Hogue Overmolded in OD green. **Sights:** None furnished; drilled and tapped for scope mounting. **Features:** Bolt and

receiver milled to reduce weight, three-position safety, hinged floor plate, adjustable trigger, forged one-piece bolt, M-16 style extractor, forged flat-bottom receiver. Scope package includes 3-9x42 Nikko-Stirling riflescope with bases and rings. Imported from Japan by Legacy Sports International.
Price: Blue, Youth Rifle. **$539.00**
Price: w/Scope package (2008) **$589.00**

H-S PRECISION PRO-SERIES BOLT-ACTION RIFLES
Caliber: 30 chamberings, 3- or 4-round magazine. **Barrel:** 20", 22", 24" or 26", sporter contour Pro-Series 10X match-grade stainless steel barrel. Optional muzzle brake on 30 cal. or smaller. **Weight:** 7.5 lbs. **Length:** NA. **Stock:** Pro-Series synthetic stock with full-length bedding block chassis system, sporter style. **Sights:** None; drilled and tapped for bases. **Features:** Accuracy guarantee: up to 30 caliber, 1/2 minute of angle (3 shots at 100 yards), test target supplied. Stainless steel action, stainless steel floorplate with detachable magazine, matte black Teflon finish. Made in U.S.A. by H-S Precision, Inc.
Price: SPR **$2,680.00**
Price: SPL Lightweight (2008) **$2,825.00**

KEL-TEC RFB
Caliber: 7.62 NATO (308 Win.). **Barrels:** 18" to 32". **Weight:** 11.3 lbs. (unloaded). **Length:** 40" overall. **Features:** Gas-operated semi-auto bullpup-style, forward-ejecting. Fully ambidextrous controls, adjustable trigger mechanism, no open sights, four-sided picatinny forend. Accepts standard FAL-type magazines. Production of the RFB has been delayed due to redesign but was expected to begin first quarter 2009.
Price: **$1,800.00**

KENNY JARRETT BOLT-ACTION RIFLE
Caliber: 223 Rem., 243 Improved, 243 Catbird, 7mm-08 Improved, 280 Remington, .280 Ackley Improved, 7mm Rem. Mag., 284 Jarrett, 30-06 Springfield, 300 Win. Mag., .300 Jarrett, 323 Jarrett, 338 Jarrett, 375 H&H, 416 Rem., 450 Rigby., other modern cartridges. **Barrel:** NA. **Weight:** NA. **Length:** NA. **Stock:** NA. **Features:** Tri-Lock receiver. Talley rings and bases. Accuracy guarantees and custom loaded ammunition.
Price: Signature Series. **$7,640.00**
Price: Wind Walker **$7,380.00**
Price: Original Beanfield (customer's receiver) **$5,380.00**
Price: Professional Hunter **$10,400.00**
Price: SA/Custom **$6,630.00**

KIMBER MODEL 8400 BOLT-ACTION RIFLE
Caliber: 25-06 Rem., 270 Win., 7mm, 30-06 Spfl., 300 Win. Mag., 338 Win. Mag., or 325 WSM, 4 shot. **Barrel:** 24". **Weight:** 6 lbs. 3 oz. to 6 lbs 10 oz. **Length:** 43.25". **Stock:** Claro walnut or Kevlar-reinforced fiberglass. **Sights:** None; drilled and tapped for bases. **Features:** Mauser claw extractor, two-position wing safety, action bedded on aluminum pillars and fiberglass, free-floated barrel, match grade adjustable trigger set at 4 lbs., matte or polished blue or matte stainless finish. Introduced 2003. Sonora model (2008) has brown laminated stock, hand-rubbed oil finish, chambered in 25-06 Rem., 30-06 Spfl., and 300 Win. Mag. Weighs 8.5 lbs., measures 44.50" overall length. Front swivel stud only for bipod. Stainless steel bull barrel, 24" satin stainless steel finish. Made in U.S.A. by Kimber Mfg. Inc.
Price: Classic **$1,172.00**
Price: Classic Select Grade, French walnut stock (2008) . . . **$1,359.00**
Price: SuperAmerica, AAA walnut stock. **$2,240.00**
Price: Sonora **$1,359.00**
Price: Police Tactical, synthetic stock, fluted barrel
(300 Win. Mag only) **$2,575.00**

Kimber Model 8400 Caprivi Bolt-Action Rifle
Similar to 8400 bolt rifle, but chambered for .375 H&H and 458 Lott, 4-shot magazine. Stock is Claro walnut or Kevlar-reinforced fiberglass. Features twin steel crossbolts in stock, AA French walnut,

pancake cheekpiece, 24 lines-per-inch wrap-around checkering, ebony forend tip, hand-rubbed oil finish, barrel-mounted sling swivel stud, 3-leaf express sights, Howell-type rear sling swivel stud and a Pachmayr Decelerator recoil pad in traditional orange color. Introduced 2008. Made in U.S.A. by Kimber Mfg. Inc.

Price: **$3,196.00**

Kimber Model 8400 Talkeetna Bolt-Action Rifle

Similar to 8400 bolt rifle, but chambered for .375 H&H, 4-shot magazine. Weighs 8 lbs, overall length is 44.5". Stock is synthetic. Features free-floating match grade barrel with tapered match grade chamber and target crown, three-position wing safety acts directly on the cocking piece for greatest security, and Pacmayr Decelerator. Made in U.S.A. by Kimber Mfg. Inc.

Price: **$2,108.00**

KIMBER MODEL 84M BOLT-ACTION RIFLE

Caliber: 22-250 Rem., 204 Ruger, 223 Rem., 243 Win., 260 Rem., 7mm-08 Rem., 308 Win., 5-shot. **Barrel:** 22", 24", 26". **Weight:** 5 lbs., 10 oz. to 10 lbs. **Length:** 41" to 45". **Stock:** Claro walnut, checkered with steel gripcap; synthetic or gray laminate. **Sights:** None; drilled and tapped for bases. **Features:** Mauser claw extractor, three-position wing safety, action bedded on aluminum pillars, free-floated barrel, match-grade trigger set at 4 lbs., matte blue finish. Includes cable lock. Introduced 2001. Montana (2008) has synthetic stock, Pachmayr Decelerator recoil pad, stainless steel 22" sporter barrel. Made in U.S.A. by Kimber Mfg. Inc.

Price: Classic (243 Win., 260, 7mm-08 Rem., 308) **$1,114.00**
Price: Varmint (22-250) **$1,224.00**
Price: Montana **$1,276.00**
Price: Classic Stainless, matte stainless steel receiver
    and barrel (243 Win., 7mm-08, 308 Win.) **$1,156.00**

KIMBER MODEL 84L CLASSIC RIFLE

Bolt action rifle chambered in .270 Win. and .30-06. Features include 24-inch sightless matte blue sporter barrel; hand-rubbed A-grade walnut stock with 20 lpi panel checkering; pillar and glass bedding; Mauser claw extractor; 3-position M70-style safety; 5-round magazine; adjustable trigger.

Price: **$1,172.00**

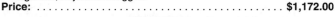

KIMBER MODEL 8400 PATROL RIFLE

Bolt action tactical rifle chambered in .308 Win. Features include 20-inch 1:12 fluted sightless matte blue heavy barrel; black epoxy-coated laminated wood stock with 20 lpi panel checkering; pillar and glass bedding; Mauser claw extractor; 3-position M70-style safety; 5-round magazine; adjustable trigger.

Price: **$1,476.00**

L.A.R. GRIZZLY 50 BIG BOAR RIFLE

Caliber: 50 BMG, single shot. **Barrel:** 36". **Weight:** 30.4 lbs. **Length:** 45.5" overall. **Stock:** Integral. Ventilated rubber recoil pad. **Sights:** None furnished; scope mount. **Features:** Bolt-action bullpup design, thumb and bolt stop safety. All-steel construction. Introduced 1994. Made in U.S.A. by L.A.R. Mfg., Inc.

Price: From **$2,350.00**

MAGNUM RESEARCH MOUNTAIN EAGLE MAGNUMLITE RIFLES

Caliber: .22-250, .223, .224, .243, .257, 7mm Rem. Mag., 7mm WSM, .280, .300 Win. Mag., .300 WSM, .30-06, 3-shot magazine. **Barrel:** 24" sport taper graphite; 26" bull barrel graphite. **Weight:** 7.1-9.2 lbs. **Length:** 44.5-48.25" overall (adjustable on Tactical model). **Stock:** Hogue OverMolded synthetic, H-S Precision Tactical synthetic, H-S

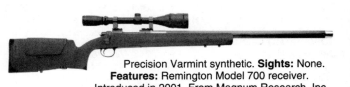

Precision Varmint synthetic. **Sights:** None. **Features:** Remington Model 700 receiver. Introduced in 2001. From Magnum Research, Inc.

Price: MLR3006ST24 Hogue stock **$2,295.00**
Price: MLR7MMBST24 Hogue stock **$2,295.00**
Price: MLRT22250 H-S Tactical stock, 26" bull barrel **$2,400.00**
Price: MLRT300WI Tactical **$2,400.00**

MARLIN XL7 BOLT ACTION RIFLE

Caliber: 25-06 Rem. 270 Win., 30-06 Spfl., 4-shot magazine. **Barrel:** 22" 1:10" right-hand twist, recessed barrel crown. **Weight:** 6.5 lbs. **Length:** 42.5" overall. **Stock:** Black synthetic or Realtree APG-HD camo, Soft-Tech recoil pad, pillar bedded. **Sights:** None. **Features:** Pro-Fire trigger is user adjustable down to 2.5 lbs. Fluted bolt, steel sling swivel studs, high polished blued steel, checkered bolt handle, molded checkering, one-piece scope base. Introduced in 2008. From Marlin Firearms, Inc.

Price: Black Synthetic **$326.00**
Price: Camouflaged **$356.00**

Marlin XS7 Short-Action Bolt-Action Rifle

Similar to Model XL7 but chambered in 7mm-08, 243 Winchester and 308 Winchester.

Price: .... **NA**
Price: XS7Y Youth **$341.00**
Price: XS7C Camo, Realtree APG HD camo stock **$341.00**
Price: XS7S Stainless .... **NA**

MERKEL KR1 BOLT-ACTION RIFLE

Caliber: 223 Rem., 243 Rem., 6.5x55, 7mm-08, 308 Win., 270 Win., 30-06, 9.3x62, 7mm Rem. Mag., 300 Win. Mag., 270 WSM, 300 WSM, 338 Win. Mag. **Features:** Short lock, short bolt movement, take-down design with interchangeable barrel assemblies, three-position safety, detachable box magazine, fine trigger with set feature, checkered walnut pistol-grip semi-schnabel stock. Adjustable iron sights with quick release mounts. Imported from Germany by Merkel USA.

Price: **$1,995.00**
Price: Model KR1 Stutzen Antique: 20.8" barrel, case-colored
    receiver, Mannlicher-style stock **$3,395.00**

MOSSBERG 100 ATR BOLT-ACTION RIFLE

Caliber: 243 Win. (2006), 270 Win., 308 Win. (2006), 30-06 Spfl., 4-round magazine. **Barrel:** 22", 1:10" twist, free-floating, button-rifled, recessed muzzle crown. **Weight:** 6.7 to 7.75 lbs. **Length:** 42"-42.75" overall. **Stock:** Black synthetic, walnut, Mossy Oak New Break Up camo, Realtree AP camo. **Sights:** Factory-installed Weaver-style scope bases; scoped combos include 3x9 factory-mounted, bore-sighted scopes. **Features:** Marinecote and matte blue metal finishes, free gun lock, side lever safety. Introduced 2005. Night Train (2008)comes with Picatinny rail and factory-mounted 4-16x50mm variable scope. From O.F. Mossberg & Sons, Inc.

Price: Short-Action 243 Win., wood stock, matte blue, from. . **$424.00**
Price: Long-Action 270 Win., Mossy Oak New Break Up
    camo, matte blue, from **$424.00**
Price: Scoped Combo 30-06 Spfl., Walnut-Dura-Wood stock,
    Marinecote finish, from **$481.00**
Price: Bantam Short Action 308 Win., 20" barrel **$471.00**
Price: Night Train Short-Action Scoped Combo (2008) **$567.00**

MOSSBERG 4X4 BOLT-ACTION RIFLE

Caliber: 25-06 Rem, 270 Win., 30-06 Spfl., 7mm Rem. Mag., .300 Win. Mag., .338 Win. Mag., detachable box magazine, 4 rounds

Prices given are believed to be accurate at time of publication however, many factors affect retail pricing so exact prices are not possible.

standard, 3 rounds magnum. **Barrel:** 24", 1:10 twist, free-floating, button-rifled, recessed muzzle crown. **Weight:** 7+ lbs. **Length:** 42" overall. **Stock:** Skeletonized synthetic laminate (2008); black synthetic, laminated, select American black walnut. **Sights:** Factory-installed Weaver-style scope bases. **Features:** Marinecote and matte blue metal finishes, free gun lock, side lever safety. Scoped combos include factory-mounted, bore-sighted 3-9x40mm variable. Introduced 2007. From O.F. Mossberg & Sons, Inc.

Price: 25-06 Rem., walnut stock, matte blue, from **$505.00**
Price: 300 Win. Mag., synthetic laminate stock (2008), from . . **$505.00**
Price: 4X4 Classic Stock Synthetic: Black synthetic stock and Marinecote metal surfaces **$654.00**
Price: 4X4 Scoped Combo: Matte blue finish and 3x9 scope **$654.00**
Price: 4X4 Classic Walnut Stock: Checkered walnut stock . . **$654.00**

REMINGTON MODEL 700 CDL CLASSIC DELUXE RIFLE

Caliber: 223 Rem., 243 Win., 25-06 Rem., 270 Win., 7mm-08 Rem., 280 Remington, 7mm Rem. Mag., 7mm Rem. Ultra Mag., 30-06 Spfl., 300 Rem. Ultra Mag., 300 Win. Mag., 35 Whelen. **Barrel:** 24" or 26" round tapered. **Weight:** 7.4 to 7.6 lbs. **Length:** 43.6" to 46.5" overall. **Stock:** Straight-comb American walnut stock, satin finish, checkering, right-handed cheek piece, black fore-end tip and grip cap, sling swivel studs. **Sights:** None. **Features:** Satin blued finish, jeweled bolt body, drilled and tapped for scope mounts. Hinged-floorplate magazine capacity: 4, standard calibers; 3, magnum calibers. SuperCell recoil pad, cylindrical receiver, integral extractor. Introduced 2004. CDL SF (stainless fluted) chambered for 260 Rem., 257 Wby. Mag., 270 Win., 270 WSM, 7mm-08 Rem., 7mm Rem. Mag., 30-06 Spfl., 300 WSM. Left-hand versions introduced 2008 in six calibers. Made in U.S. by Remington Arms Co., Inc.

Price: Standard Calibers: 24" barrel **$959.00**
Price: Magnum Calibers: 26" barrel **$987.00**
Price: CDL SF (2007), from **$1,100.00**
Price: CDL LH (2008), from **$987.00**
Price: CDL High Polish Blued (2008), from **$959.00**
Price: CDL SF (2009), 257 Roberts . . . . **NA**

REMINGTON MODEL 700 BDL RIFLE

Caliber: 243 Win., 270 Win., 7mm Rem. Mag. 30-06 Spfl., 300 Rem Ultra Mag. **Barrel:** 22, 24, 26" round tapered. **Weight:** 7.25-7.4 lbs. **Length:** 41.6-46.5" overall. **Stock:** Walnut. Gloss-finish pistol grip stock with skip-line checkering, black forend tip and gripcap with white line spacers. Quick-release floorplate. **Sights:** Gold bead ramp front; hooded ramp, removable step-adjustable rear with windage screw. **Features:** Side safety, receiver tapped for scope mounts, matte receiver top, quick detachable swivels.

Price: 243 Win., 270 Win., 30-06 . . . .**$927.00**
Price: 7mm Rem. Mag. 300 Rem Ultra Mag. **$955.00**

REMINGTON MODEL 700 SPS RIFLES

Caliber: 17 Rem. Fireball, 204 Ruger, 22-250 Rem., 6.8 Rem SPC, 223 Rem., 243 Win., 270 Win. 270 WSM, 7mm-08 Rem., 7mm Rem. Mag., 7mm Rem. Ultra Mag., 30-06 Spfl., 308 Win., 300 WSM, 300 Win. Mag., 300 Rem. Ultra Mag. **Barrel:** 20", 24" or 26" carbon steel. **Weight:** 7 to 7.6 lbs. **Length:** 39.6" to 46.5" overall. **Stock:** Black

synthetic, sling swivel studs, SuperCell recoil pad. **Sights:** None. Introduced 2005. SPS Stainless replaces Model 700 BDL Stainless Synthetic. **Barrel:** Bead-blasted 416 stainless steel. **Features:** Plated internal fire control component. SPS DM features detachable box magazine. Buckmaster Edition versions feature Realtree Hardwoods HD camouflage and Buckmasters logo engraved on floorplate. SPS Varmint includes X-Mark Pro trigger, 26" heavy contour barrel, vented beavertail forend, dual front sling swivel studs. Made in U.S. by Remington Arms Co., Inc.

Price: SPS, from **$639.00**
Price: SPS DM (2005) **$672.00**
Price: SPS Youth, 20" barrel (2007) 243 Win., 7mm-08. . . . . **$604.00**
Price: SPS Varmint (2007) **$665.00**
Price: SPS Stainless, (2005), from **$732.00**
Price: SPS Buckmasters Youth (2008), 243 Win. **$707.00**
Price: SPS Youth LH (2008), 243 Win., 7mm-08 . . . .**$620.00**
Price: SPS Varmint LH (2008) **$692.00**
Price: SPS Synthetic Left-Hand . . . . **NA**

REMINGTON 700 SPS TACTICAL

Bolt action rifle chambered in .223 and .308 Win. Features include 20-inch heavy-contour tactical-style barrel; dual-point pillar bedding; black synthetic stock with Hogue overmoldings; semi-beavertail fore-end; X-Mark Pro adjustable trigger system; satin black oxide metal finish; hinged floorplate magazine; SuperCell recoil pad.

Price **$734.00**

REMINGTON 700 VTR A-TACS CAMO WITH SCOPE

Bolt action rifle chambered in .223 and .308 Win. Features include ATACS camo finish overall; triangular contour 22-inch barrel has an integral muzzle brake; black overmold grips; 1:9 (.223 caliber) 0r 1:12 (.308) twist; factory-mounted scope.

Price: . . . .**NA**

REMINGTON MODEL 700 MOUNTAIN LSS RIFLES

Caliber: 270 Win., 280 Rem., 7mm-08 Rem., 30-06. **Barrel:** 22" satin stainless steel. **Weight:** 6.6 lbs. **Length:** 41.6" to 42.5" overall. **Stock:** Brown laminated, sling swivel studs, SuperCell recoil pad, black forend tip. **Sights:** None. **Barrel:** Bead-blasted 416 stainless steel, lightweight contour. Made in U.S. by Remington Arms Co., Inc.

Price: **$1,052.00**

REMINGTON MODEL 700 ALASKAN TI

Caliber: 25-06 Rem., 270 Win., 270 WSM, 280 Rem., 7mm-08 Rem., 7mm Rem. Mag., 30-06 Spfl., 300 WSM, 300 Win. Mag. **Barrel:** 24" round tapered. **Weight:** 6 lbs. **Length:** 43.6" to 44.5" overall. **Stock:** Bell & Carlson carbon-fiber synthetic, sling swivel studs, SuperCell gel recoil pad. **Sights:** None. **Features:** Formerly Model 700 Titanium, introduced 2001. Titanium receiver, spiral-cut fluted bolt, skeletonized bolt handle, X-Mark Pro trigger, satin stainless finish. Drilled and tapped for scope mounts. Hinged-floorplate magazine capacity: 4, standard calibers; 3, magnum calibers. Introduced 2007. Made in U.S. by Remington Arms Co., Inc.

Price: From **$2,225.00**

REMINGTON MODEL 700 VLS/VLSS TH RIFLES

Caliber: 204 Ruger, 223 Rem., 22-250 Rem., 243 Win., 308 Win. **Barrel:** 26" heavy contour barrel (0.820" muzzle O.D.), concave

target-style barrel crown **Weight:** 9.4 lbs. **Length:** 45.75" overall. **Stock:** Brown laminated stock, satin finish, with beavertail forend, gripcap, rubber buttpad. **Sights:** None. **Features:** Introduced 1995. VLSS TH (varmint laminate stock stainless) thumbhole model introduced 2007. Made in U.S. by Remington Arms Co., Inc.
Price: VLS $979.00
Price: VL SS TH $1,085.00

REMINGTON MODEL 700 VSSF-II/SENDERO SF II RIFLES
Caliber: 17 Rem. Fireball, 204 Ruger, 220 Swift, 223 Rem., 22-250 Rem., 308 Win. **Barrel:** satin blued 26" heavy contour (0.820" muzzle O.D.). VSSF has satin-finish stainless barreled action with 26" fluted barrel. **Weight:** 8.5 lbs. **Length:** 45.75" overall. **Stock:** H.S. Precision composite reinforced with aramid fibers, black (VSSF-II) Contoured beavertail fore-end with ambidextrous finger grooves, palm swell, and twin front tactical-style swivel studs. **Sights:** None. **Features:** Aluminum bedding block, drilled and tapped for scope mounts, hinged floorplate magazines. Introduced 1994. Sendero model is similar to VSSF-II except chambered for 264 Win. Mag, 7mm Rem. Mag., 7mm Rem. Ultra Mag., 300 Win. Mag., 300 Rem. Ultra Mag. Polished stainless barrel. Introduced 1996. Made in U.S. by Remington Arms Co., Inc.
Price: VSSF-II $1,332.00
Price: Sendero SF II $1,359.00

REMINGTON MODEL 700 XCR RIFLE
Caliber: 25-06 Rem., 270 Win., 270 WSM, 7mm-08 Rem., 7mm Rem. Mag., 7mm Rem Ultra Mag., 30-06 Spfl., 300 WSM, 300 Win. Mag., 300 Rem. Ultra Mag., 338 Rem. Ultra Mag., 338 Win. Mag., 375 H&H Mag., 375 Rem. Ultra Mag. **Barrel:** 24" standard caliber; 26" magnum. **Weight:** 7.4 to 7.6 lbs. **Length:** 43.6" to 46.5" overall. **Stock:** Black synthetic, SuperCell recoil pad, rubber overmolded grip and forend. **Sights:** None. **Features:** XCR (Xtreme Conditions Rifle) includes TriNyte Corrosion Control System; drilled and tapped for scope mounts. 375 H&H Mag., 375 Rem. Ultra Mag. chamberings come with iron sights. Introduced 2005. XCR Tactical model introduced 2007. **Features:** Bell & Carlson OD green tactical stock, beavertail forend, recessed thumbhook behind pistol grip, TriNyte coating over stainless steel barrel, LTR fluting. Chambered in 223 Rem., 300 Win. Mag., 308 Win. 700XCR Left Hand introduced 2008 in 270 Win., 7mm Rem. Mag., 30-06 Spfl., 300 Rem Ultra Mag. Made in U.S. by Remington Arms Co., Inc.
Price: From $1,065.00
Price: XCR Tactical (2007) $1,407.00
Price: XCR Left Hand (2008) $1,092.00
Price: XCR Compact Tactical (2008), 223 Rem., 308 Win. . . $1,434.00

Remington Model 700 XCR Camo RMEF
Similar to Model 700 XCR but with stainless barrel and receiver, AP HD camo stock, TriNyte coating overall, 7mm Remington Ultra Mag chambering.
Price: $1,199.00

REMINGTON 700 XCR II
Bolt action rifle chambered in .25-06 Remington, .270 Win, .280 Remington, 7mm Remington Mag., 7mm Remington Ultra Mag., .300 WSM, .300 Win Mag., .300 Remington Ultra Mag, .338 Win. Mag., .338 Remington Ultra Mag, .375 H&H, .375 Remington Ultra Mag., .30-06 Springfield. Features include black TriNyte corrosion control system coating; coated stainless steel barrel and receiver; olive drab green Hogue overmolded synthetic stock; SuperCell recoil pad; X-Mark Pro Trigger System; 2- or 26-inch barrel, depending on chambering.
Price: $970.00

REMINGTON 700 XCR II - BONE COLLECTOR EDITION
Similar to Remington 700 XCR II but with Realtree AP HD camo stock.
Price: $1,063.00

REMINGTON 700 XHR EXTREME HUNTING RIFLE
Caliber: 243 Win., 25-06, 270 Win., 7mm-08, 7mm Rem. Mag., 300 Win. Mag, 7mm Rem. Ultra Mag. **Barrel:** 24", 25", or 26" triangular magnum-contour counterbored. **Weight:** 7-1/4 to 7-5/8 lbs. **Length:** 41-5/8 to 46-1/2 overall. **Features:** Adjustable trigger, synthetic stock finished in Realtree AG HD camo, satin black oxide finish on exposed metal surfaces, hinged floorplate, SuperCell recoil pad.
Price: . . . . $879.00 to $927.00

REMINGTON MODEL 700 XCR TARGET TACTICAL RIFLE
Caliber: 308 Win. **Barrel:** 26" triangular counterbored, 1:11-1/2 rifling. **Weight:** 11.75 lbs. **Length:** 45-3/4" overall. **Features:** Textured green Bell & Carlson varmint/tactical stock with adjustable comb and length of pull, adjustable trigger, satin black oxide finish on exposed metal surfaces, hinged floorplate, SuperCell recoil pad, matte blue on exposed metal surfaces.
Price: $1,407.00

REMINGTON MODEL 700 VTR VARMINT/TACTICAL RIFLE
Caliber: 17 Rem. Fireball, 204 Ruger, 22-250, 223 Rem., 243 Win., 308 Win. **Barrel:** 22" triangular counterbored. **Weight:** 7.5 lbs. **Length:** 41-5/8" overall. **Features:** Olive drab overmolded or Digital Tiger TSP Desert Camo stock with vented semi-beavertail forend, tactical-style dual swivel mounts for bipod, matte blue on exposed metal surfaces.
Price: $1,972.00
Price: VTR Desert Recon, Digital Desert Camo stock, 223 and 308 Win. only $1,972.00

REMINGTON MODEL 700 VARMINT SF RIFLE
Caliber: 17 Rem. Fireball, 204 Ruger, 22-250, 223, 220 Swift. **Barrel:** 26" stainless steel fluted. **Weight:** 8.5 lbs. **Length:** 45.75". **Features:** Synthetic stock with ventilated forend, stainless steel/triggerguard/floorplate, dual tactical swivels for bipod attachment.
Price: $825.00

REMINGTON MODEL 770 BOLT-ACTION RIFLE
Caliber: 243 Win., 270 Win., 7mm Rem. Mag., 7mm-08 Rem., 308 Win., 30-06 Spfl., 300 Win. Mag. **Barrel:** 22" or 24", button rifled. **Weight:** 8.5 lbs. **Length:** 42.5" to 44.5" overall. **Stock:** Black synthetic. **Sights:** Bushnell Sharpshooter 3-9x scope mounted and bore-sighted. **Features:** Upgrade of Model 710 introduced 2001. Unique action locks bolt directly into barrel; 60-degree bolt throw; 4-shot dual-stack magazine; all-steel receiver. Introduced 2007. Made in U.S.A. by Remington Arms Co.
Price: $460.00
Price: Youth, 243 Win. $460.00
Price: Stainless Camo (2008), stainless barrel, nickel-plated bolt, Realtree camo stock $540.00

Prices given are believed to be accurate at time of publication however, many factors affect retail pricing so exact prices are not possible.

REMINGTON MODEL SEVEN CDL/CDL MAGNUM

Caliber: 17 Rem. Fireball, 243 Win., 260 Rem., 270 WSM, 7mm-08 Rem., 308 Win., 300 WSM, 350 Rem. Mag. **Barrel:** 20"; 22" magnum. **Weight:** 6.5 to 7.4 lbs. **Length:** 39.25" to 41.25" overall. **Stock:** American walnut, SuperCell recoil pad, satin finished. **Sights:** None. **Features:** Satin finished carbon steel barrel and action, 3- or 4-round magazine, hinged magazine floorplate. Furnished with iron sights and sling swivel studs, drilled and tapped for scope mounts. CDL versions introduced 2007. Made in U.S.A. by Remington Arms Co.

Price: CDL **$959.00**
Price: CDL Magnum **$1,01200**
Price: Predator (2008) **$825.00**
Price: 25th Anniversary (2008), 7mm-08 . . . .**$969.00**

REMINGTON MODEL 798/799 BOLT-ACTION RIFLES

Caliber: 243 Win., 270 Win., 7mm Rem. Mag., 308 Win., .30-06 Spfl., .300 Win. Mag., .375 H&H Mag., .458 Win. Mag. **Barrel:** 20" to 26". **Weight:** 7.75 lbs. **Length:** 39.5" to 42.5" overall. **Stock:** Brown or green laminated, 1-inch rubber butt pad. **Sights:** None. Receiver drilled and tapped for standard Mauser 98 (long- and short-action) scope mounts. **Features:** Model 98 Mauser action (square-bridge Mauser 98). Claw extractor, sporter style 2-position safety, solid steel hinged floorplate magazine. Introduced 2006. Made in U.S.A. by Remington Arms Co.

Price: Model 798 SPS, black synthetic stock (2008), from **$527.00**
Price: Model 798 Satin Walnut Stock (2008), from **$648.00**
Price: Model 798 Safari Grade (2008), from **$1,141.00**
Price: Model 799, from **$648.00**

REMINGTON 40-XB TACTICAL

Bolt action rifle chambered in .308 Winchester. Features include stainless steel bolt with Teflon coating; hinged floorplate; adjustable trigger; 27-1/4-inch tri-fluted 1:14 barrel; H-S precision pro series tactical stock, black color with dark green spiderweb; two front swivel studs; one rear swivel stud; vertical pistol grip.
Price: . . . .**NA**

REMINGTON 40-XS TACTICAL - 338LM SYSTEM

Bolt action rifle chambered in .338 Lapua Magnum. Features include 416 stainless steel Model 40-X 24-inch 1:12 barreled action; black polymer coating; McMillan A3 series stock with adjustable length of pull and adjustable comb; adjustable trigger and Sunny Hill heavy duty, all-steel trigger guard; Harris bi-pod with quick adjust swivel lock Leupold Mark IV 3.5-10x40mm long range M1 scope with Mil Dot reticle; Badger Ordnance all-steel Picatinny scope rail and rings.
Price: . . . .**NA**

RUGER MAGNUM RIFLE

Caliber: 375 H&H, 416 Rigby, 458 Lott. **Barrel:** 23". **Weight:** 9.5 to 10.25 lbs. **Length:** 44". **Stock:** AAA Premium Grade Circassian walnut with live-rubber recoil pad, metal gripcap, and studs for mounting sling swivels. **Sights:** Blade, front; V-notch rear express sights (one stationary, two folding) drift-adjustable for windage. **Features:** Floorplate latch secures the hinged floorplate against accidental dumping of cartridges; one-piece bolt has a non-rotating Mauser-type controlled-feed extractor; fixed-blade ejector.
Price: M77RSM MKII **$2,334.00**

RUGER COMPACT MAGNUMS

Caliber: .338 RCM, .300 RCM; 3-shot magazine. **Barrel:** 20". **Weight:** 6.75 lbs. **Length:** 39.5-40" overall. **Stock:** American walnut and black synthetic; stainless steel and Hawkeye Matte blued finishes. **Sights:** Adjustable Williams "U" notch rear sight and brass bead front sight. **Features:** Based on a shortened .375 Ruger case, the .300 and .338 RCMs match the .300 and .338 Win. Mag. in performance; RCM stock is 1/2 inch shorter than standard M77 Hawkeye stock; LC6 trigger; steel floor plate engraved with Ruger logo and "Ruger Compact Magnum"; Red Eagle recoil pad; Mauser-type controlled feeding; claw extractor; 3-position safety; hammer-forged steel barrels; Ruger scope rings. Walnut stock includes extensive cut-checkering and rounded profiles. Intr. 2008. Made in U.S.A. by Sturm, Ruger & Co.

Price: HM77RCM (walnut/Hawkeye matte blued) **$995.00**
Price: HKM77PRCM (synthetic/SS) **$995.00**

RUGER 77/22 BOLT-ACTION RIFLE

Caliber: 22 Hornet, 6-shot rotary magazine. **Barrel:** 20" or 24". **Weight:** About 6.25 to 7.5 lbs. **Length:** 39.5" to 43.5" overall. **Stock:** Checkered American walnut, black rubber buttpad; brown laminate. **Sights:** None. **Features:** Same basic features as rimfire model except slightly lengthened receiver. Uses Ruger rotary magazine. Three-position safety. Comes with 1" Ruger scope rings. Introduced 1994.

Price: 77/22-RH (rings only, no sights) **$754.00**
Price: K77/22-VHZ Varmint, laminated stock, no sights **$836.00**

RUGER M77 HAWKEYE RIFLES

Caliber: 204 Ruger, 223 Rem., 22-250 Rem., 243 Win., 257 Roberts, 25-06 Rem., 270 Win., 280 Rem., 7mm/08, 7mm Rem. Mag., 308 Win., 30-06 Spfl., 300 Win. Mag., 338 Win. Mag., 338 Federal, 358 Win. Mag., 416 Ruger, 375 Ruger, 300 Ruger Compact Magnum, 338 Ruger Compact Magnum; 4-shot magazine, except 3-shot magazine for magnums; 5-shot magazine for 204 Ruger and 223 Rem. **Barrel:** 22", 24". **Weight:** 6.75 to 8.25 lbs. **Length:** 42-44.4" overall. **Stock:** American walnut. **Sights:** None furnished. Receiver has Ruger integral scope mount base, Ruger 1" rings. **Features:** Includes Ruger LC6 trigger, new red rubber recoil pad, Mauser-type controlled feeding, claw extractor, 3-position safety, hammer-forged steel barrels, Ruger scope rings. Walnut stock includes wrap-around cut checkering on the forearm and, more rounded contours on stock and top of pistol grips. Matte stainless version features synthetic stock. Hawkeye Alaskan and African chambered in 375 Ruger. Alaskan features matte-black finish, 20" barrel, Hogue OverMolded synthetic stock. African has 23" blued barrel, checkered walnut stock, left-handed model. 375's have windage-adjustable shallow "V" notch rear sight, white bead front sights. Introduced 2007. Left-hand models available 2008.

Price: Standard, right- and left-hand. **$803.00**
Price: All-Weather. **$803.00**
Price: Laminate, left-hand **$862.00**
Price: Ultra Light. **$862.00**

Price: All-Weather Ultra Light $803.00
Price: Compact $803.00
Price: Laminate Compact $862.00
Price: Compact Magnum $899.00
Price: African $1,079.00
Price: Alaskan $1,079.00
Price: Sporter $862.00
Price: Tactical $1,138.00
Price: Predator $935.00
Price: International $939.00

RUGER M77VT TARGET RIFLE
Caliber: 22-250 Rem., 223 Rem., 204 Ruger, 243 Win., 25-06 Rem., 308 Win. **Barrel:** 26" heavy stainless steel with target grey finish. **Weight:** 9 to 9.75 lbs. **Length:** Approx. 45.75" to 46.75" overall. **Stock:** Laminated American hardwood with beavertail forend, steel swivel studs; no checkering or gripcap. **Sights:** Integral scope mount bases in receiver. **Features:** Ruger diagonal bedding system. Ruger steel 1" scope rings supplied. Fully adjustable trigger. Steel floorplate and trigger guard. New version introduced 1992.
Price: KM77VT MKII $935.00

SAKO A7 AMERICAN BOLT-ACTION RIFLE
Caliber: 22-250, 243 Win., 25-06, 260 Rem., 270 Win., 270 WSM, 300 WSM, 30-06, 300 WM, 308 Win., 338 Federall, 7mm Rem. Mag., 7mm-08. **Barrel:** 22-7/16" standard, 24-3/8" magnum. **Weight:** 6 lbs. 3 oz. to 6 lbs. 13 oz. **Length:** 42-5/16" to 44-5/16" overall. **Features:** Blued or stainless barrel and receiver, black composite stock with sling swivels and recoil pad, two-position safety, adjustable trigger, detachable 3+1 box magazine.
Price: From . . . . **$850.00** (blued); **$950.00** (stainless)

SAKO TRG-22 AND TRG-42 TACTICAL RIFLES
Bolt action rifles chambered in .308 Winchester (TRG-22) or .338 Lapua Magnum (TRG-42). Features include target grade Cr-Mo or stainless barrels with muzzle brake; three locking lugs; 60° bolt throw; adjustable two-stage target trigger; adjustable or folding synthetic stock; receiver-mounted integral 17mm axial optics rails with recoil stop-slots; tactical scope mount for modern three turret tactical scopes (30 and 34 mm tube diameter); optional bipod.
Price: . . . .$2,850.00 to $4,400.00

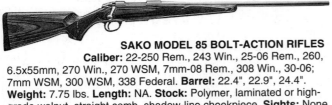

SAKO MODEL 85 BOLT-ACTION RIFLES
Caliber: 22-250 Rem., 243 Win., 25-06 Rem., 260, 6.5x55mm, 270 Win., 270 WSM, 7mm-08 Rem., 308 Win., 30-06; 7mm WSM, 300 WSM, 338 Federal. **Barrel:** 22.4", 22.9", 24.4". **Weight:** 7.75 lbs. **Length:** NA. **Stock:** Polymer, laminated or high-grade walnut, straight comb, shadow-line cheekpiece. **Sights:** None furnished. **Features:** Controlled-round feeding, adjustable trigger, matte stainless or nonreflective satin blue. Quad model is polymer/stainless with four interchangeable barrels in 22 LR, 22 WMR 17 HMR and 17 Mach 2; 50-degree bolt-lift, ambidextrous palm-swell, adjustable butt-pad. Introduced 2006. Imported from Finland by Beretta USA.
Price: Sako 85 Hunter, walnut/blued $1,700.00
Price: Sako 85 Grey Wolf, laminated/stainless $1,575.00
Price: Sako 85 Quad, polymer/stainless $925.00
Price: Sako 85 Quad Combo, four barrels $2,175.00

Sako 85 Finnlight
Similar to Model 85 but chambered in 243 Win., 25-06, 260 Rem., 270 Win., 270 WSM, 300 WSM, 30-06, 300 WM, 308 Win., 6.5x55mm, 7mm Rem Mag.,

7mm-08. Weighs 6 lbs., 3 oz. to 6 lbs. 13 oz. Stainless steel barrel and receiver, black synthetic stock.
Price: **$1,600.00**

SAKO 75 HUNTER BOLT-ACTION RIFLE
Caliber: 223 Rem., 22-250 Rem., 243 Win., 25-06 Rem., 260, 270 Win., 270 WSM, 280 Rem., 300 Win. Mag., 30-06; 7mm-08 Rem., 308 Win., 270 Wby. Mag., 7mm Rem. Mag., 7mm STW, 7mm Wby. Mag., 300 Wby. Mag., 338 Win. Mag., 340 Wby. Mag., 375 H&H. **Barrel:** 22", standard calibers; 24", 26" magnum calibers. **Weight:** About 6 lbs. **Length:** NA. **Stock:** European walnut with matte lacquer finish. **Sights:** None furnished; dovetail scope mount rails. **Features:** New design with three locking lugs and a mechanical ejector, key locks firing pin and bolt, cold hammer-forged barrel is free-floating, two-position safety, hinged floorplate or detachable magazine that can be loaded from the top, short 70-degree bolt lift. Five action lengths. Introduced 1997. Imported from Finland by Beretta USA.
Price: From **$1,375.00**

Sako 75 Deluxe Rifle
Similar to 75 Hunter except select wood rosewood gripcap and forend tip. Available in 17 Rem., 222, 223 Rem., 25-06 Rem., 243 Win., 7mm-08 Rem., 308 Win., 25-06 Rem., 270 Win., 280 Rem., 30-06; 270 Wby. Mag., 7mm Rem. Mag., 7mm STW, 7mm Wby. Mag., 300 Win. Mag., 300 Wby. Mag., 338 Win. Mag., 340 Wby. Mag., 375 H&H, 416 Rem. Mag. Introduced 1997. Imported from Finland by Beretta USA.
Price: From **$2,175.00**

Sako 75 Varmint Rifle
Similar to Model 75 Hunter except chambered only for 17 Rem., 222 Rem., 223 Rem., 22-250 Rem., 22 PPC and 6mm PPC, 24" heavy barrel with recessed crown; set trigger; beavertail forend. Introduced 1998. Imported from Finland by Beretta USA.
Price: **$1,850.00**

SAVAGE EDGE BOLT ACTION RIFLE
Entry-level bolt-action repeating rifle chambered in .223, .22-250, .243 Win., 7mm-08, .308 Win., .25-06, .270 Win., and .30-06. Features include 22-inch matte black barrel, synthetic black stock, 4-round capacity; detachable box magazine, drilled and tapped for scope mounts. Also available in camo finish (Edge Camo); XP variation (with 3x9 scope); and Camo XP (with camo finish and scope).
Price: . . . .$329.00 to $424.00

SAVAGE MODEL 25 BOLT ACTION RIFLES
Caliber: 204 Ruger, 223 Rem., 4-shot magazine. **Barrel:** 24", medium-contour fluted barrel with recessed target crown, free-floating sleeved barrel, dual pillar bedding. **Weight:** 8.25 lbs. **Length:** 43.75" overall. **Stock:** Brown laminate with beavertail-style forend. **Sights:** Weaver-style bases installed. **Features:** Diameter-specific action built around the 223 Rem. bolthead dimension. Three locking lugs, 60-degree bolt lift, AccuTrigger adjustable from 2.5 to 3.25 lbs. Model 25 Classic Sporter has satin lacquer American walnut with contrasting forend tip, wraparound checkering, 22" blued barrel. **Weight:** 7.15 lbs. **Length:** 41.75". Introduced 2008. Made in U.S.A. by Savage Arms, Inc.
Price: Model 25 Lightweight Varminter $641.00
Price: Model 25 Lightweight Varminter Thumbhole $691.00
Price: Model 25 Classic Sporter $672.00

SAVAGE CLASSIC SERIES MODEL 14/114 RIFLES
Caliber: 204 Ruger, 223 Rem., 22-250 Rem., 243 Win., 7mm-08 Rem., 308 Win., 270 WSM, 300 WSM (short action Model 14), 2- or 4-shot magazine; 270 Win., 7mm Rem. Mag., 30-06 Spfl., 300 Win. Mag. (long action Model 114), 3- or 4-shot magazine. **Barrel:** 22" or 24". **Weight:** 7 to 7.5 lbs. **Length:** 41.75" to 43.75" overall (Model 14); 43.25" to 45.25" overall (Model 114). **Stock:** Satin lacquer American walnut with ebony forend, wraparound checkering, Monte Carlo Comb

Prices given are believed to be accurate at time of publication however, many factors affect retail pricing so exact prices are not possible.

and cheekpiece. **Sights:** None furnished. Receiver drilled and tapped for scope mounting. **Features:** AccuTrigger, high luster blued barreled action, hinged floorplate. From Savage Arms, Inc.
Price: Model 14 or 114 Classic, from $826.00
Price: Model 14 or 114 American Classic, detachable box magazine, from. $779.00
Price: Model 14 or 114 Euro Classic, oil finish, from $875.00
Price: Model 14 Left Hand, 250 Savage and 300 Savage only $779.00

SAVAGE MODEL 12 SERIES VARMINT RIFLES
Caliber: 204 Ruger, 223 Rem., 22-250 Rem. 4-shot magazine. **Barrel:** 26" stainless barreled action, heavy fluted, free-floating and button-rifled barrel. **Weight:** 10 lbs. **Length:** 46.25" overall. **Stock:** Dual pillar bedded, low profile, laminated stock with extra-wide beavertail forend. **Sights:** None furnished; drilled and tapped for scope mounting. **Features:** Recessed target-style muzzle. AccuTrigger, oversized bolt handle, detachable box magazine, swivel studs. Model 112BVSS has heavy target-style prone laminated stock with high comb, Wundhammer palm swell, internal box magazine. Model 12FVSS has black synthetic stock, additional chamberings in 308 Win., 270 WSM, 300 WSM. Model 12FV has blued receiver. Model 12BTCSS has brown laminate vented thumbhole stock. Made in U.S.A. by Savage Arms, Inc.
Price: Model 12 Varminter, from. $991.00
Price: Model 12BVSS. $899.00
Price: Model 12FVSS, from $815.00
Price: Model 12FV $658.00
Price: Model 12BTCSS (2008) $1,041.00
Price: Model 12 Long Range (2008). $1,239.00
Price: Model 12 LRPV, single-shot only with right bolt/left port or left load/right eject receiver $1,273.00

SAVAGE MODEL 16/116 WEATHER WARRIORS
Caliber: 204 Ruger, 223 Rem., 22-250 Rem., 243 Win., 7mm-08 Rem., 308 Win., 270 WSM, 7mm WSM, 300 WSM (short action Model 16), 2- or 4-shot magazine; 270 Win., 7mm Rem. Mag., 30-06 Spfl., 300 Win. Mag., 338 Win. Mag. (long action Model 116), 3- or 4-shot magazine. **Barrel:** 22", 24"; stainless steel with matte finish, free-floated barrel. **Weight:** 6.5 to 6.75 lbs. **Length:** 41.75" to 43.75" overall (Model 16); 42.5" to 44.5" overall (Model 116). **Stock:** Graphite/fiberglass filled composite. **Sights:** None furnished; drilled and tapped for scope mounting. **Features:** Quick-detachable swivel studs; laser-etched bolt. Left-hand models available. Model 116FSS introduced 1991; 116FSAK introduced 1994. Made in U.S.A. by Savage Arms, Inc.
Price: Model 16FHSS or 116FHSS, hinged floorplate magazine, from. $755.00
Price: Model 16FLHSS or 116FLHSS, left hand models, from.$755.00
Price: Model 16FSS or 116FSS, internal box magazine, from .$678.00
Price: Model 16FCSS or 116FCSS, detachable box magazine, from. $755.00
Price: Model 16FHSAK or 116FHSAK, adjustable muzzle brake. $822.00

SAVAGE MODEL 10GXP3, 110GXP3 PACKAGE GUNS
Caliber: 223 Rem., 22-250 Rem., 243 Win., 7mm-08 Rem., 308 Win., 300 WSM (10GXP3). 25-06 Rem., 270 Win., 30-06 Spfl., 7mm Rem. Mag., 300 Win. Mag., 300 Rem. Ultra Mag. (110GXP3). **Barrel:** 22" 24", 26". **Weight:** 7.5 lbs. average. **Length:** 43" to 47". **Stock:** Walnut Monte Carlo with checkering. **Sights:** 3-9x40mm scope, mounted & bore sighted. **Features:** Blued, free floating and button rifled, internal box magazines, swivel studs, leather sling. Left-hand available.
Price: AccuTrigger, from. $669.00

SAVAGE MODEL 11FXP3, 111FXP3, 111FCXP3, 11FYXP3 (YOUTH) PACKAGE GUNS
Caliber: 223 Rem., 22-250 Rem., 243 Win., 308 Win., 300 WSM (11FXP3). 270 Win., 30-06 Spfl., 25-06 Rem., 7mm Rem. Mag., 300 Win. Mag., 338 Win. Mag., 300 Rem. Ultra Mag. (11FCXPE & 111FXP3). **Barrel:** 22" to 26". **Weight:** 6.5 lbs. **Length:** 41" to 47". **Stock:** Synthetic checkering, dual pillar bed. **Sights:** 3-9X40mm scope, mounted & bore sighted. **Features:** Blued, free floating and button rifled, Top loading internal box mag (except 111FXCP3 has detachable box magazine). Nylon sling and swivel studs. Some left-hand available.
Price: Model 11FXP3, from. $640.00
Price: Model 111FCXP3 . . . .$519.00
Price: Model 11FYXP3, 243 Win., 12.5" pull (youth) $519.00
Price: Model 11FLYXP3 Youth: Left-handed configuration of Model 11FYXP3 Youth $640.00

SAVAGE MODEL 16FXP3, 116FXP3 SS ACTION PACKAGE GUNS
Caliber: 223 Rem., 243 Win., 6.5x.284, 308 Win., 300 WSM, 270 Win., 30-06 Spfl., 7mm Rem. Mag., 300 Win. Mag., 338 Win. Mag., 375 H&H, 7mm S&W, 7mm Rem. Ultra Mag., 300 Rem. Ultra Mag. **Barrel:** 22", 24", 26". **Weight:** 6.75 lbs. average. **Length:** 41" to 46". **Stock:** Synthetic checkering, dual pillar bed. **Sights:** 3-9X40mm scope, mounted & bore sighted. **Features:** Free floating and button rifled. Internal box magazine, nylon sling and swivel studs.
Price: From. $736.00

SAVAGE MODEL 11/111 HUNTER SERIES BOLT ACTIONS
Caliber: 223 Rem., 22-250 Rem., 243 Win., 7mm-08 Rem., 308 Win., 270 WSM, 7mm WSM, 300 WSM (short action Model 11), 2- or 4-shot magazine; 25-06 Rem., 270 Win., 7mm Rem. Mag., 30-06 Spfl., 300 Win. Mag., (long action Model 111), 3- or 4-shot magazine. **Barrel:** 22" or 24"; blued free-floated barrel. **Weight:** 6.5 to 6.75 lbs. **Length:** 41.75" to 43.75" overall (Model 11); 42.5" to 44.5" overall (Model 111). **Stock:** Graphite/fiberglass filled composite or hardwood. **Sights:** Ramp front, open fully adjustable rear; drilled and tapped for scope mounting. **Features:** Three-position top tang safety, double front locking lugs. Introduced 1994. Made in U.S.A. by Savage Arms, Inc.
Price: Model 11FL or 111FL $564.00
Price: Model 11FL or 111FL, left hand models, from $564.00
Price: Model 11FCNS or 111FCNS, detachable box magazine, from. $591.00
Price: Model 11FLNS or 111FLNS $564.00
Price: Model 11G or 111G, hardwood stock, from $582.00
Price: Model 11BTH or 111BTH, laminate thumbhole stock (2008). $779.00
Price: Model 11FNS Model FLNS $591.00
Price: Model 11FHNS or 111FHNS. $656.00
Price: Model 11FYCAK Youth $691.00
Price: Model 11GNS or 111GNS $618.00
Price: Model 11GLNS or 111GLSN $618.00
Price: Model 11GCNS or 111GCNS $659.00
Price: Model 11/111 Long-Range Hunter $934.00

SAVAGE MODEL 10 BAS LAW ENFORCEMENT BOLT-ACTION RIFLE
Caliber: 380 Win. **Barrel:** 24" fluted heavy with muzzle brake. **Weight:** 13.4 lbs. **Length:** NA.

Features: Bolt-action repeater based on Model 10 action but with M4-style collapsible buttstock, pistolgrip with palm swell, all-aluminum Accustock, picatinny rail for mounting optics.
Price: **$1,852.00**
Price: 10 BAT/S, multi-adjustable buttstock **$1,991.00**

SAVAGE MODEL 10FP/110FP LAW ENFORCEMENT SERIES RIFLES

Caliber: 223 Rem., 308 Win. (Model 10), 4-shot magazine; 25-06 Rem., 300 Win. Mag., (Model 110), 3- or 4-shot magazine. **Barrel:** 24"; matte blued free-floated heavy barrel and action. **Weight:** 6.5 to 6.75 lbs. **Length:** 41.75" to 43.75" overall (Model 10); 42.5" to 44.5" overall (Model 110). **Stock:** Black graphite/fiberglass composition, pillar-bedded, positive checkering. **Sights:** None furnished. Receiver drilled and tapped for scope mounting. **Features:** Black matte finish on all metal parts. Double swivel studs on the forend for sling and/or bipod mount. Right- or left-hand. Model 110FP introduced 1990. Model 10FP introduced 1998. Model 10FCPXP has HS Precision black synthetic tactical stock with molded alloy bedding system, Leupold 3.5-10x40mm black matte scope with Mil Dot reticle, Farrell Picatinny Rail Base, flip-open lens covers, 1.25" sling with QD swivels, Harris bipod, Storm heavy duty case. Made in U.S.A. by Savage Arms, Inc.
Price: Model 10FP, 10FLP (left hand), 110FP **$649.00**
Price: Model 10FP folding Choate stock. **$896.00**
Price: Model 10FCP McMillan, McMillan fiberglass tactical
  stock **$1,178.00**
Price: Model 10FCP-HS HS Precision, HS Precision tactical
  stock **$984.00**
Price: Model 10FPXP-HS Precision **$2,715.00**
Price: Model 10FCP **$866.00**
Price: Model 10FLCP, left-hand model, standard stock
  or Accu-Stock **$866.00**
Price: Model 110FCP **$866.00**
Price: Model 10 Precision Carbine, 20" medium contour barrel,
  synthetic camo Accu-Stock, 223/308 . . . . **$829.00**
Price: Model 10 FCM Scout **$646.00**

Savage Model 110-50th Anniversary Rifle

Same action as 110-series rifles, except offered in 300 Savage, limited edition of 1,000 rifles. Has high-luster blued barrel and action, unique checkering pattern, high-grade hinged floorplate, scroll pattern on receiver, 24-karat gold-plated double barrel bands, 24-karat gold-plated AccuTrigger, embossed recoil pad. Introduced 2008. Made in U.S.A. from Savage Arms, Inc.
Price: Model 110 50th Anniversary. **$1,724.00**

SAVAGE 110 BA LAW ENFORCEMENT RIFLE

Bolt action rifle chambered .300 Win. Mag. And .338 Lapua Mag. Features include aluminum stock that features Savage's innovative three-dimensional bedding system; interchangeable buttstocks and pistol grips; three-sided accessory rail; 5-round detachable magazine; high-efficiency muzzlebrake; Magpul PRS adjustable stock; 26-inch carbon steel barrel.
Price: **$2,267.00**

SAVAGE MODEL 10 PREDATOR SERIES

Caliber: 223, 22-250, 243, 204 Ruger. **Barrel:** 22", medium-contour. **Weight:** 7.25 lbs. **Length:** 43"overall. **Stock:** Synthetic with rounded forend and oversized bolt handle. **Features:** Entirely covered in either Mossy Oak Brush or Realtree Hardwoods Snow pattern camo. Also features AccuTrigger, AccuStock, detachable box magazine.
Price: **$806.00**

Savage Model 10XP Predator Hunting Bolt-Action Rifle Package

Similar to Model 10 but chambered in 223, 204, 22-250 or 243 Win. Includes 4-12x40 scope, 22" barrel, AccuTrigger, choice of Realtree Snow or Mossy Oak Brush camo overall.
Price: **$839.00**

SAVAGE MODEL 12 PRECISION TARGET SERIES BENCHREST RIFLE

Caliber: 308 Win, 6.5x284 Norman, 6mm Norma BR. **Barrel:** 29" ultra-heavy. **Weight:** 12.75 lbs. **Length:** 50" overall. **Stock:** Gray laminate. **Features:** New Left-Load, Right-Eject target action, Target AccuTrigger adjustable from approx 6 oz to 2.5 lbs, oversized bolt handle, stainless extra-heavy free-floating and button-rifled barrel.
Price: **$1,375.00**

Savage Model 12 Precision Target Palma Rifle

Similar to Model 12 Benchrest but in 308 Palma only, 30" barrel, multi-adjustable stock, weighs 13.3 lbs.
Price: **$1,798.00**

Savage Model 12 F Class Target Rifle

Similar to Model 12 Benchrest but in 6.5x284 Norma, 6 Norma BR, 30" barrel, weighs 11.5 lbs.
Price: **$1,341.00**

Savage Model 12 F/TR Target Rifle

Similar to Model 12 Benchrest but in 308 Win. only, 30" barrel, weighs 12.65 lbs.
Price: **$1,265.00**

SMITH & WESSON I-BOLT RIFLES

Caliber: 25-06 Rem., 270 Win., 30-06 Win. (4-round magazine), 7mm Rem. Mag., 300 Win. Mag. (3-round magazine). **Barrel:** 23", 1:10" right-hand twist, 1:9" right-hand twist for 7mm Mag. Thompson/Center barrel. Blued and stainless. **Weight:** 6.75 lbs. **Stock:** Black synthetic, Realtree AP camo, walnut. Length of pull, 13-5/8", drop at comb, 7/8". Monte Carlo cheekpiece. **Sights:** Adjustable post front sight, adjustable dual aperture rear sight. **Features:** Adjustable Tru-Set Trigger. Introduced 2008. Made in U.S.A. by Smith & Wesson.
Price: Black synthetic stock, weather shield finish **$588.00**
Price: Camo stock, weather shield finish **$658.00**

STEVENS MODEL 200 BOLT-ACTION RIFLES

Caliber: 223, 22-250, 243, 7mm-08, 308 Win. (short action) or 25-06, 270 Win., 30-06, 7mm Rem. Mag., 300 Win Mag. **Barrel:** 22" (short action) or 24" (long action blued). **Weight:** 6.5 lbs. **Length:** 41.75" overall. **Stock:** Black synthetic or camo. **Sights:** None. **Features:** Free-floating and button-rifled barrel, top loading internal box magazine, swivel studs.
Price: . . . . **$399.00** (standard); **$439.00** (camo)
Price: Model 200XP Long or Short Action
  Package Rifle with 4x12 scope. **$449.00**
Price: Model 200XP Camo, camo stock **$499.00**

STEYR MANNLICHER CLASSIC RIFLE

Caliber: 222 Rem., 223 Rem., 243 Win., 25-06 Rem., 308 Win., 6.5x55, 6.5x57, 270 Win., 270 WSM, 7x64 Brenneke, 7mm-08 Rem., 7.5x55, 30-06 Spfl., 9.3x62, 6.5x68, 7mm Rem. Mag., 300 WSM, 300 Win. Mag., 8x68S, 4-shot magazine. **Barrel:** 23.6" standard; 26" magnum; 20" full stock standard calibers. **Weight:** 7 lbs. **Length:** 40.1" overall. **Stock:** Hand-checkered fancy European oiled walnut with standard forend. **Sights:** Ramp front adjustable for elevation, V-notch rear adjustable for windage. **Features:** Single adjustable trigger; 3-position roller safety with "safe-bolt" setting; drilled and tapped for Steyr factory scope mounts. Introduced 1997. Imported from Austria by Steyr Arms, Inc.
Price: Half stock, standard calibers **$3,799.00**
Price: Full stock, standard calibers **$4,199.00**

Steyr Pro Hunter Rifle

Similar to the Classic Rifle except has ABS synthetic stock with adjustable butt spacers, straight comb without cheekpiece, palm swell, Pachmayr 1" swivels. Special 10-round magazine conversion kit available. Introduced 1997. Imported from Austria by Steyr Arms, Inc.
Price: From **$1,500.00**

STEYR SCOUT BOLT-ACTION RIFLE

Caliber: 308 Win., 5-shot magazine. **Barrel:** 19", fluted. **Weight:** NA. **Length:** NA. **Stock:** Gray Zytel. **Sights:** Pop-up front & rear, Leupold M8 2.5x28 IER scope on Picatinny optic rail with Steyr mounts. **Features:** luggage case, scout sling, two stock spacers, two magazines. Introduced 1998. Imported from Austria by Steyr Arms, Inc.
Price: From **$2,199.00**

STEYR SSG 69 PII BOLT-ACTION RIFLE

Caliber: 22-250 Rem., 243 Win., 308 Win., detachable 5-shot rotary magazine. **Barrel:** 26". **Weight:** 8.5 lbs. **Length:** 44.5" overall. **Stock:** Black ABS Cycolac with spacers for length of pull adjustment. **Sights:** Hooded ramp front adjustable for elevation, V-notch rear adjustable for windage. **Features:** Sliding safety; NATO rail for bipod; 1" swivels; Parkerized finish; single or double-set triggers. Imported from Austria by Steyr Arms, Inc.
Price: **$1,889.00**

THOMPSON/CENTER ICON BOLT-ACTION RIFLE

Caliber: 22-250 Rem., 243 Win., 308 Win., 30TC, 3-round box magazine. **Barrel:** 24", button rifled. **Weight:** 7.5 lbs. **Length:** 44.5" overall. **Stock:** Walnut, 20-lpi grip and forend cut checkering with ribbon detail. **Sights:** None; integral Weaver style scope mounts. **Features:** Interchangeable bolt handle, 60-degree bolt lift, Interlok Bedding System, 3-lug bolt with T-Slot extractor, cocking indicator, adjustable trigger, preset to 3 to 3.5 lbs of pull. Introduced 2007. From Thompson/Center Arms.
Price: **$1,025.00**

Thompson/Center ICON Precision Hunter Rifle

Similar to the basic ICON model. Available in 204 Ruger, 223 Rem., 22-250 Rem., 243 Win. and 308 Win. 22" heavy barrel, blued finish, varminter-style stock. Introduced 2009.
Price: **$1,149.00**

THOMPSON/CENTER VENTURE BOLT-ACTION RIFLE

Caliber: 270 Win., 7mm Rem. Mag., 30-06 Springfield, 300 Win. Mag., 3-round magazine. **Barrel:** 24". **Weight:** NA. **Length:** NA. **Stock:** Composite. **Sights:** NA. **Features:** Nitride fat bolt design, externally adjustable trigger, two-position safety, textured grip. Introduced 2009.
Price: **$489.00**

THOMPSON/CENTER VENTURE MEDIUM ACTION RIFLE

Bolt action rifle chambered in .204, .22-250, .223, .243, 7mm-08, .308 and 30TC. Features include a 24-inch crowned medium weight barrel, classic styled composite stock with inlaid traction grip panels, adjustable 3.5 to 5 pound trigger along with a drilled and tapped receiver (bases included). 3+1 detachable nylon box magazine. **Weight:** 7 lbs. **Length:** 43.5 inches.
Price: **$499.00**

THOMPSON/CENTER VENTURE PREDATOR PDX RIFLE

Bolt action rifle chambered in .204, .22-250, .223, .243, .308. Similar to Venture Medium action but with heavy, deep-fluted 22-inch barrel and Max-1 camo finish overall. **Weight:** 8 lbs. **Length:** 41.5 inches.

Price: .... **$549.00 to $599.00**

TIKKA T3 HUNTER

Caliber: 223 Rem., 22-250 Rem., 243 Win., 308 Win., 25-06 Rem., 270 Win., 30-06 Spfl., 300 Win. Mag., 338 Win. Mag., 270 WSM, 300 WSM, 6.5x55 Swedish Mauser, 7mm Rem. Mag. **Stock:** Walnut. **Sights:** None furnished. **Barrel:** 22-7/16", 24-3/8". **Features:** Detachable magazine, aluminum scope rings. Introduced 2005. Imported from Finland by Beretta USA.
Price: **$675.00**

Tikka T3 Stainless Synthetic

Similar to the T3 Hunter except stainless steel, synthetic stock. Available in 243 Win., 2506, 270 Win., 308 Win., 30-06 Spfl., 270 WSM, 300 WSM, 7mm Rem. Mag., 300 Win. Mag., 338 Win. Mag. Introduced 2005. Imported from Finland by Beretta USA.
Price: **$700.00**

Tikka T3 Lite Bolt-Action Rifle

Similar to the T3 Hunter, available in 223 Rem., 22-250 Rem., 308 Win., 243 Win., 25-06 Rem., 270 Win., 270 WSM, 30-06 Sprg., 300 Win Mag., 300 WSM, 338 Federal, 338 Win Mag., 7mm Rem. Mag., 7mm-08 Rem. Barrel lengths vary from 22-7/16" to 24-3/8". Made in Finland by Sako. Imported by Beretta USA.
Price: **$695.00**
Price: Stainless steel synthetic **$600.00**
Price: Stainless steel synthetic, left-hand **$700.00**

Tikka T3 Varmint/Super Varmint Rifle

Similar to the T3 Hunter, available in 223 Rem., 22-250 Rem., 308 Win. Length is 23-3/8" (Super Varmint). Made in Finland by Sako. Imported by Beretta USA.
Price: **$900.00**
Price: Super Varmint **$1,425.00**

ULTRA LIGHT ARMS BOLT-ACTION RIFLES

Caliber: 17 Rem. to 416 Rigby. **Barrel:** Douglas, length to order. **Weight:** 4.75 to 7.5 lbs. **Length:** Varies. **Stock:** Kevlar graphite composite, variety of finishes. **Sights:** None furnished; drilled and tapped for scope mounts. **Features:** Timney trigger, hand-lapped action, button-rifled barrel, hand-bedded action, recoil pad, sling-swivel studs, optional Jewell trigger. Made in U.S.A. by New Ultra Light Arms.
Price: Model 20 (short action)...................... **$3,000.00**
Price: Model 24 (long action) **$3,100.00**
Price: Model 28 (magnum action) **$3,400.00**
Price: Model 40 (300 Wby. Mag., 416 Rigby) **$3,400.00**
Price: Left-hand models, add **$100.00**

WEATHERBY MARK V BOLT-ACTION RIFLES

Caliber: Deluxe version comes in all Weatherby calibers plus 243 Win., 270 Win., 7mm-08 Rem., 30-06 Spfl., 308 Win. **Barrel:** 24", 26", 28". **Weight:** 6.75 to 10 lbs. **Length:** 44" to 48.75" overall. **Stock:** Walnut, Monte Carlo with cheekpiece; high luster finish; checkered pistol grip and forend; recoil pad. **Sights:** None furnished. **Features:** 4 models with Mark V action and wood stocks; other common elements include cocking indicator; adjustable trigger; hinged floorplate; thumb safety; quick detachable sling swivels. Ultramark has hand-selected exhibition-grade walnut stock, maplewood/ebony spacers, 20-lpi checkering. Chambered for 257 and 300 Wby Mags. Lazermark same as Mark V Deluxe except stock

has extensive oak leaf pattern laser carving on pistol grip and forend; chambered in Wby. Magnums—257, 270 Win., 7mm., 300, 340, with 26" barrel. Introduced 1981. Sporter is same as the Mark V Deluxe without the embellishments. Metal has low-luster blue, stock is Claro walnut with matte finish, Monte Carlo comb, recoil pad. Chambered for these Wby. Mags: 257, 270 Win., 7mm, 300, 340. Other chamberings: 7mm Rem. Mag., 300 Win. Introduced 1993. Six Mark V models come with synthetic stocks. Ultra Lightweight rifles weigh 5.75 to 6.75 lbs.; 24", 26" fluted stainless barrels with recessed target crown; Bell & Carlson stock with CNC-machined aluminum bedding plate and tan "spider web" finish, skeletonized handle and sleeve. Available in 243 Win., Wby. Mag., 25-06 Rem., 270 Win., 7mm-08 Rem., 7mm Rem. Mag., 280 Rem, 308 Win., 30-06 Spfl., 300 Win. Mag. Wby. Mag chamberings: 240, 257, 270 Win., 7mm, 300. Introduced 1998. Accumark uses Mark V action with heavy-contour 26" and 28" stainless barrels with black oxidized flutes, muzzle diameter of .705". No sights, drilled and tapped for scope mounting. Stock is composite with matte gel-coat finish, full length aluminum bedding Hasblock. Weighs 8.5 lbs. Chambered for these Wby. Mags: 240 (2007), 257, 270, 7mm, 300, 340, 338-378, 30-378. Other chamberings: 22-250 (2007), 243 Win. (2007), 25-06 Rem. (2007), 270 Win. (2007), 308 Win.(2007), 7mm Rem. Mag., 300 Win. Mag. Introduced 1996. SVM (Super VarmintMaster) has 26" fluted stainless barrel, spiderweb-pattern tan laminated synthetic stock, fully adjustable trigger. Chambered for 223 Rem., 22-250 Rem., 243. Mark V Synthetic has lightweight injection-molded synthetic stock with raised Monte Carlo comb, checkered grip and forend, custom floorplate release. Weighs 6.5-8.5 lbs., 24-28" barrels. Available in 22-250 Rem., 243 Win., 25-06 Rem., 270 Win., 7mm-08 Rem., 7mm Rem., Mag., 280 Rem., 308 Win., 30-06 Spfl., 308 Win., 300 Win. Mag., 375 H&H Mag, and these Wby. Magnums: 240, 257, 270 Win., 7mm, 300, 30-378, 338-378, 340. Introduced 1997. Fibermark composites are similar to other Mark V models except has black Kevlar and fiberglass composite stock and bead-bead-blast blue or stainless finish. Chambered for 9 standard and magnum calibers. Introduced 1983; reintroduced 2001. SVR comes with 22" button-rifled chrome-moly barrel, .739 muzzle diameter. Composite stock w/bedding block, gray spiderweb pattern. Made in U.S.A. From Weatherby.

Price: Mark V Deluxe $2,199.00
Price: Mark V Ultramark $2,979.00
Price: Mark V Lazermark $2,479.00
Price: Mark V Sporter $1,499.00
Price: Mark V SVM $1,959.00
Price: Mark V Ultra Lightweight $1,879.00
Price: Mark V Ultra Lightweight LH. $1,911.00
Price: Mark V Accumark. $1,879.00
Price: Mark V Synthetic $1,209.00
Price: Mark V Fibermark Composite $1,449.00
Price: Mark V SVR Special Varmint Rifle $1,259.00

WEATHERBY VANGUARD BOLT-ACTION RIFLES

Caliber: 257, 300 Wby Mags; 223 Rem., 22-250 Rem., 243 Win., 25-06 Rem. (2007), 270 Win., 270 WSM, 7mm Rem. Mag., 308 Win., 30-06 Spfl., 300 Win. Mag., 300 WSM, 338 Win. Mag. **Barrel:** 24" barreled action, matte black. **Weight:** 7.5 to 8.75 lbs. **Length:** 44" to 46-3/4" overall. **Stock:** Raised comb, Monte Carlo, injection-molded composite stock. **Sights:** None furnished. **Features:** One-piece forged, fluted bolt body with three gas ports, forged and machined receiver, adjustable trigger, factory accuracy guarantee. Vanguard Stainless has 410-Series stainless steel barrel and action, bead blasted matte metal finish. Vanguard Deluxe has raised comb, semi-fancy grade Monte Carlo walnut stock with maplewood spacers, rosewood forend and grip cap, polished action with high-

gloss-blued metalwork. Vanguard Synthetic Package includes Vanguard Synthetic rifle with Bushnell Banner 3-9x40mm scope mounted and boresighted, Leupold Rifleman rings and bases, Uncle Mikes nylon sling, and Plano PRO-MAX injection-molded case. Sporter has Monte Carlo walnut stock with satin urethane finish, fineline diamond point checkering, contrasting rosewood forend tip, matte-blued metalwork. Sporter SS metalwork is 410 Series bead-blasted stainless steel. Vanguard Youth/Compact has 20" No. 1 contour barrel, short action, scaled-down non-reflective matte black hardwood stock with 12.5" length of pull and full-size, injection-molded composite stock. Chambered for 223 Rem., 22-250 Rem., 243 Win., 7mm-08 Rem., 308 Win. Weighs 6.75 lbs.; OAL 38.9". Sub-MOA Matte and Sub-MOA Stainless models have pillar-bedded Fiberguard composite stock (Aramid, graphite unidirectional fibers and fiberglass) with 24" barreled action; matte black metalwork, Pachmayr Decelerator recoil pad. Sub-MOA Stainless metalwork is 410 Series bead-blasted stainless steel. Sub-MOA Varmint guaranteed to shoot 3-shot group of .99" or less when used with specified Weatherby factory or premium (non-Weatherby calibers) ammunition. Hand-laminated, tan Monte Carlo composite stock with black spiderwebbing; CNC-machined aluminum bedding block, 22" No. 3 contour barrel, recessed target crown. Varmint Special has tan injection-molded Monte Carlo composite stock, pebble grain finish, black spiderwebbing. 22" No. 3 contour barrel (.740 muzzle dia.), bead blasted matte black finish, recessed target crown. Made in U.S.A. From Weatherby.

Price: Vanguard Synthetic **$399.00**
Price: Vanguard Stainless **$709.00**
Price: Vanguard Deluxe, 7mm Rem. Mag., 300 Win. Mag. (2007) **$989.00**
Price: Vanguard Synthetic Package, 25-06 Rem. (2007) **$552.00**
Price: Vanguard Sporter **$689.00**
Price: Vanguard Sporter SS **$869.00**
Price: Vanguard Youth/Compact **$649.00**
Price: Vanguard Sub-MOA Matte, 25-06 Rem. (2007) **$929.00**
Price: Vanguard Sub-MOA Stainless, 270 WSM **$1,079.00**
Price: Vanguard Sub-MOA Varmint, 204 Ruger (2007) **$1,009.00**

WINCHESTER MODEL 70 BOLT-ACTION RIFLES

Caliber: Varies by model. **Barrel:** Blued, or free-floating, fluted stainless hammer-forged barrel, 22", 24", 26". Recessed target crown. **Weight:** 6.75 to 7.25 lbs. **Length:** 41 to 45.75 " overall. **Stock:** Walnut (three models) or Bell and Carlson composite; textured charcoal-grey matte finish, Pachmayr Decelerator recoil pad. **Sights:** None. **Features:** Claw extractor, three-position safety, M.O.A. three-lever trigger system, factory-set at 3.75 lbs. Super Grade features fancy grade walnut stock, contrasting black fore-end tip and pistol grip cap, and sculpted shadowline cheekpiece. Featherweight Deluxe has angled-comb walnut stock, Schnabel fore-end, satin finish, cut checkering. Sporter Deluxe has satin-finished walnut stock, cut checkering, sculpted cheekpiece. Extreme Weather SS has composite stock, drop @ comb, 0.5"; drop @ heel, 0.5". Introduced 2008. Made in U.S.A. from Winchester Repeating Arms.

Price: Extreme Weather SS, 270 Win., 270 WSM, 30-06 Spfl., 300 Win. Mag., 300 WSM, 308 Win., 325 WSM, 243 Winchester, 7mm WSM, from **$1,069.00**
Price: Super Grade, 30-06 Sprg., 300 Win. Mag., 270 WSM, 300 WSM, 270 Winchester, from **$1,139.00**
Price: Featherweight Deluxe, 243 Win., 270 Win., 270 WSM, 30-06 Spfl., 300 Win. Mag., 300 WSM, 308 Win., 325 WSM, 7mm-08 Rem., from **$999.00**
Price: Sporter Deluxe, 270 Win., 270 WSM, 30-06 Spfl., 300 Win. Mag., 300 WSM, 325 WSM, from **$999.00**

WINCHESTER MODEL 70 COYOTE LIGHT

Caliber: 22-250, 243 Winchester, 308 Winchester, 270 WSM, 300 WSM and 325 WSM, five-shot magazine (3-shot in 270 WSM, 300

WSM and 325 WSM). **Barrel:** 22" fluted stainless barrel (24" in 270 WSM, 300 WSM and 325 WSM). **Weight:** 7.5 lbs. **Length:** NA. **Features:** Composite Bell and Carlson stock, Pachmayr Decelerator pad. Controlled round feeding. No sights but drilled and tapped for mounts.

Price: **$1,099.00**

WINCHESTER MODEL 70 FEATHERWEIGHT
    Caliber: 22-250, 243, 7mm-08, 308, 270 WSM, 7mm WSM, 300 WSM, 325 WSM, 25-06, 270, 30-06, 7mm Rem. Mag., 300 Win. Mag., 338 Win. Mag. Capacity 5 rounds (short action) or 3 rounds (long action). **Barrel:** 22" blued barrel (24" in magnum chamberings). **Weight:** 6-1/2 to 7-1/4 lbs. **Length:** NA. **Features:** Satin-finished checkered Grade I walnut stock, controlled round feeding. Pachmayr Decelerator pad. No sights but drilled and tapped for scope mounts.

Price: Short action **$799.00**
Price: Long action and magnum) **$839.00**

WINCHESTER MODEL 70 SPORTER
    Caliber: 270 WSM, 7mm WSM, 300 WSM, 325 WSM, 25-06, 270, 30-06, 7mm Rem. Mag., 300 Win. Mag., 338 Win. Mag. Capacity 5 rounds (short action) or 3 rounds (long action). Barrel: 22", 24" or 26" blued. Weight: 6-1/2 to 7-1/4 lbs. Length: NA. Features: Satin-finished checkered Grade I walnut stock with sculpted cheekpiece, controlled round feeding. Pachmayr Decelerator pad. No sights but drilled and tapped for scope mounts.

Price: Short action **$799.00**
Price: Long action and magnum) **$839.00**

WINCHESTER MODEL 70 ULTIMATE SHADOW
Caliber: 243, 308, 270 WSM, 7mm WSM, 300 WSM, 325 WSM, 270, 30-06, 7mm Rem. Mag., 300 Win. Mag. Capacity 5 rounds (short action) or 3 rounds (long action). **Barrel:** 22" matte stainless (24" or 26" in magnum chamberings). **Weight:** 6-1/2 to 7-1/4 lbs. **Length:** NA. **Features:** Synthetic stock with WinSorb recoil pad, controlled round feeding. Pachmayr Decelerator pad. No sights but drilled and tapped for scope mounts.

Price: Standard **$739.00**
Price: Magnum **$769.00**

ARMALITE AR-50 RIFLE
Caliber: 50 BMG **Barrel:** 31". **Weight:** 33.2 lbs. **Length:** 59.5" **Stock:** Synthetic. **Sights:** None furnished. **Features:** A single-shot bolt-action rifle designed for long-range shooting. Available in left-hand model. Made in U.S.A. by Armalite.
Price: **$3,359.00**

BALLARD 1875 1 1/2 HUNTER RIFLE
Caliber: NA. **Barrel:** 26-30". **Weight:** NA **Length:** NA. **Stock:** Hand-selected classic American walnut. **Sights:** Blade front, Rocky Mountain rear. **Features:** Color case-hardened receiver, breechblock and lever. Many options available. Made in U.S.A. by Ballard Rifle & Cartridge Co.
Price: **$3,250.00**

BALLARD 1875 #3 GALLERY SINGLE SHOT RIFLE
Caliber: NA. **Barrel:** 24-28" octagonal with tulip. **Weight:** NA. **Length:** NA. **Stock:** Hand-selected classic American walnut. **Sights:** Blade front, Rocky Mountain rear. **Features:** Color case-hardened receiver, breechblock and lever. Many options available. Made in U.S.A. by Ballard Rifle & Cartridge Co.
Price: **$3,300.00**

BALLARD 1875 #4 PERFECTION RIFLE
Caliber: 22 LR, 32-40, 38-55, 40-65, 40-70, 45-70 Govt., 45-90, 45-110, 50-70, 50-90. **Barrel:** 30" or 32" octagon, standard or heavyweight. **Weight:** 10.5 lbs. (standard) or 11.75 lbs. (heavyweight bbl.). **Length:** NA. **Stock:** Smooth walnut. **Sights:** Blade front, Rocky Mountain rear. **Features:** Rifle or shotgun-style buttstock, straight grip action, single or double-set trigger, "S" or right lever, hand polished and lapped Badger barrel. Made in U.S.A. by Ballard Rifle & Cartridge Co.
Price: **$3,950.00**

BALLARD 1875 #7 LONG RANGE RIFLE
Caliber: 32-40, 38-55, 40-65, 40-70 SS, 45-70 Govt., 45-90, 45-110. **Barrel:** 32", 34" half-octagon. **Weight:** 11.75 lbs. **Stock:** Walnut; checkered pistol grip shotgun butt, ebony forend cap. **Sights:** Globe front. **Features:** Designed for shooting up to 1000 yards. Standard or heavy barrel; single or double-set trigger; hard rubber or steel buttplate. Introduced 1999. Made in U.S.A. by Ballard Rifle & Cartridge Co.
Price: From **$3,600.00**

BALLARD 1875 #8 UNION HILL RIFLE
Caliber: 22 LR, 32-40, 38-55, 40-65 Win., 40-70 SS. **Barrel:** 30" half-octagon. **Weight:** About 10.5 lbs. **Length:** NA. **Stock:** Walnut; pistol grip butt with cheekpiece. **Sights:** Globe front. **Features:** Designed for 200-yard offhand shooting. Standard or heavy barrel; double-set triggers; full loop lever; hook Schuetzen buttplate. Introduced 1999. Made in U.S.A. by Ballard Rifle & Cartridge Co.
Price: From **$4,175.00**

BALLARD MODEL 1885 LOW WALL SINGLE SHOT RIFLE
Caliber: NA. **Barrel:** 24-28". **Weight:** NA. **Length:** NA. **Stock:** Hand-selected classic American walnut. **Sights:** Blade front, sporting rear. **Features:** Color case hardened receiver, breech block and lever. Many options available. Made in U.S.A. by Ballard Rifle & Cartridge Co.
Price: **$3,300.00**

BALLARD MODEL 1885 HIGH WALL STANDARD SPORTING SINGLE SHOT RIFLE
Caliber: 17 Bee, 22 Hornet, 218 Bee, 219 Don Wasp, 219 Zipper, 22 Hi-Power, 225 Win., 25-20 WCF, 25-35 WCF, 25 Krag, 7mmx57R, 30-30, 30-40 Krag, 303 British, 33 WCF, 348 WCF, 35 WCF, 35-30/30, 9.3x74R, 405 WCF, 50-110 WCF, 500 Express, 577 Express. **Barrel:** Lengths to 34". **Weight:** NA. **Length:** NA. **Stock:** Straight-grain American walnut. **Sights:** Buckhorn or flattop rear, blade front. **Features:** Faithful copy of original Model 1885 High Wall; parts interchange with original rifles; variety of options available. Introduced 2000. Made in U.S.A. by Ballard Rifle & Cartridge Co.
Price: **$3,300.00**

BALLARD MODEL 1885 HIGH WALL SPECIAL SPORTING SINGLE SHOT RIFLE
Caliber: NA. **Barrel:** 28-30" octagonal. **Weight:** NA. **Length:** NA. **Stock:** Hand-selected classic American walnut. **Sights:** Blade front, sporting rear. **Features:** Color case hardened receiver, breech block and lever. Many options available. Made in U.S.A. by Ballard Rifle & Cartridge Co.
Price: **$3,600.00**

BARRETT MODEL 99 SINGLE SHOT RIFLE
Caliber: 50 BMG. **Barrel:** 33". **Weight:** 25 lbs. **Length:** 50.4" overall. **Stock:** Anodized aluminum with energy-absorbing recoil pad. **Sights:** None furnished; integral M1913 scope rail. **Features:** Bolt action; detachable bipod; match-grade barrel with high-efficiency muzzle brake. Introduced 1999. Made in U.S.A. by Barrett Firearms.
Price: From **$4,000.00**

BROWN MODEL 97D SINGLE SHOT RIFLE
Caliber: 17 Ackley Hornet through 45-70 Govt. **Barrel:** Up to 26", air gauged match grade. **Weight:** About 5 lbs., 11 oz. **Stock:** Sporter style with pistol grip, cheekpiece and Schnabel forend. **Sights:** None furnished; drilled and tapped for scope mounting. **Features:** Falling block action gives rigid barrel-receiver matting; polished blue/black finish. Hand-fitted action. Many options. Made in U.S.A. by E. Arthur Brown Co., Inc.
Price: From **$999.00**

BROWNING MODEL 1885 HIGH WALL SINGLE SHOT RIFLE
Caliber: 22-250 Rem., 30-06 Spfl., 270 Win., 7mm Rem. Mag., 454 Casull, 45-70 Govt. **Barrel:** 28". **Weight:** 8 lbs., 12 oz. **Length:** 43.5" overall. **Stock:** Walnut with straight grip, Schnabel forend. **Sights:** None furnished; drilled and tapped for scope mounting. **Features:** Replica of J.M. Browning's high-wall falling block rifle. Octagon barrel with recessed muzzle. Imported from Japan by Browning. Introduced 1985.
Price: **$1,260.00**

C. SHARPS ARMS MODEL 1875 TARGET & SPORTING RIFLE
Caliber: 38-55, 40-65, 40-70 Straight or Bottlenecks, 45-70, 45-90. Barrel: 30" heavy taperred round. Weight: 11 lbs. Length: NA. Stock: American walnut. Sights: Globe with post front sight. Features: Long Range Vernier tang sight with windage adjustments. Pistol grip stock with cheek rest; checkered steel buttplate. Introduced 1991. From C. Sharps Arms Co.
Price: Without sights **$1,325.00**
Price: With blade front & Buckhorn rear barrel sights **$1,420.00**
Price: With standard Tang & Globe w/post & ball front sights **$1,615.00**
Price: With deluxe vernier Tang & Globe w/spirit level & aperture sights **$1,730.00**
Price: With single set trigger, add **$125.00**

C. Sharps Arms 1875 Classic Sharps
Similar to New Model 1875 Sporting Rifle except 26", 28" or 30" full octagon barrel, crescent buttplate with toe plate, Hartford-style forend with cast German silver nose cap. Blade front sight, Rocky Mountain buckhorn rear. Weighs 10 lbs. Introduced 1987. From C. Sharps Arms Co.
Price: **$1,670.00**

C. SHARPS ARMS 1874 BRIDGEPORT SPORTING RIFLE
Caliber: 38-55 TO 50-3.25. **Barrel:** 26", 28", 30" tapered octagon. **Weight:** 10.5 lbs. **Length:** 47". **Stock:** American black walnut; shotgun butt with checkered steel buttplate; straight grip, heavy forend with Schnabel tip. **Sights:** Blade front, buckhorn rear. Drilled and tapped for tang sight. **Features:** Double-set triggers. Made in U.S.A. by C. Sharps Arms.
Price: **$1,895.00**

C. SHARPS ARMS NEW MODEL 1885 HIGHWALL RIFLE
Caliber: 22 LR, 22 Hornet, 219 Zipper, 25-35 WCF, 32-40 WCF, 38-55 WCF, 40-65, 30-40 Krag, 40-50 ST or BN, 40-70 ST or BN, 40-90 ST or BN, 45-70 Govt. 2-1/10" ST, 45-90 2-4/10" ST, 45-100 2-6/10" ST, 45-110 2-7/8" ST, 45-120 3-1/4" ST. **Barrel:** 26", 28", 30", tapered full octagon. **Weight:** About 9 lbs., 4 oz. **Length:** 47" overall. **Stock:** Oil-finished American walnut; Schnabel-style forend. **Sights:** Blade front, buckhorn rear. Drilled and tapped for optional tang sight. **Features:** Single trigger; octagonal receiver top; checkered steel buttplate; color case-hardened receiver and buttplate, blued barrel. Many options available. Made in U.S.A. by C. Sharps Arms Co.
Price: From **$1,750.00**

C. SHARPS ARMS CUSTOM NEW MODEL 1877 LONG RANGE TARGET RIFLE

Caliber: 44-90 Sharps/Rem., 45-70 Govt., 45-90, 45-100 Sharps. **Barrel:** 32", 34" tapered round with Rigby flat. **Weight:** About 10 lbs. **Stock:** Walnut checkered. Pistol grip/forend. **Sights:** Classic long range with windage. **Features:** Custom production only.
Price: From **$7,250.00**

CABELA'S 1874 SHARPS SPORTING RIFLE

Caliber: 45-70. **Barrel:** 32", tapered octabon. **Weight:** 10.5 lbs. **Length:** 49.25" overall. **Stock:** Checkered walnut. **Sights:** Blade front, open adjustable rear. **Features:** Color case-hardened receiver and hammer, rest blued. Introduced 1995. Imported by Cabela's.
Price: 45-70 . . . . **$1,399.99**
Price: Quigley Sharps, 45-70 Govt., 45-120, 45-110 . . . . . **$1,699.99**

CIMARRON BILLY DIXON 1874 SHARPS SPORTING RIFLE

Caliber: 40-40, 50-90, 50-70, 45-70 Govt. **Barrel:** 32" tapered octagonal. **Weight:** NA. **Length:** NA. **Stock:** European walnut. **Sights:** Blade front, Creedmoor rear. **Features:** Color case-hardened frame, blued barrel. Hand-checkered grip and forend; hand-rubbed oil finish. Introduced 1999. Imported by Cimarron F.A. Co.
Price: From **$1,987.70**

CIMARRON QUIGLEY MODEL 1874 SHARPS SPORTING RIFLE

Caliber: 45-110, 50-70, 50-40, 45-70 Govt., 45-90, 45-120. **Barrel:** 34" octagonal. **Weight:** NA. **Length:** NA. **Stock:** Checkered walnut. **Sights:** Blade front, adjustable rear. **Features:** Blued finish; double-set triggers. From Cimarron F.A. Co.
Price: From **$2,156.70**

CIMARRON SILHOUETTE MODEL 1874 SHARPS SPORTING RIFLE

Caliber: 45-70 Govt. **Barrel:** 32" octagonal. **Weight:** NA. **Length:** NA. **Stock:** Walnut. **Sights:** Blade front, adjustable rear. **Features:** Pistol-grip stock with shotgun-style buttplate; cut-rifled barrel. From Cimarron F.A. Co.
Price: **$1,597.70**

CIMARRON MODEL 1885 HIGH WALL RIFLE

Caliber: 38-55, 40-65, 45-70 Govt., 45-90, 45-120, 30-40 Krag, 348 Winchester. **Barrel:** 30" octagonal. **Weight:** NA. **Length:** NA. **Stock:** European walnut. **Sights:** Bead front, semi-buckhorn rear. **Features:** Replica of the Winchester 1885 High Wall rifle. Color case-hardened receiver and lever, blued barrel. Curved buttplate. Optional double-set triggers. Introduced 1999. Imported by Cimarron F.A. Co.
Price: From **$1,002.91**
Price: With pistol grip, from **$1,136.81**

DAKOTA MODEL 10 SINGLE SHOT RIFLE

Caliber: Most rimmed and rimless commercial calibers. **Barrel:** 23". **Weight:** 6 lbs. **Length:** 39.5" overall. **Stock:** Medium fancy grade walnut in classic style. Checkered grip and forend. **Sights:** None furnished. Drilled and tapped for scope mounting. **Features:** Falling block action with underlever. Top tang safety. Removable

trigger plate for conversion to single set trigger. Introduced 1990. Made in U.S.A. by Dakota Arms.
Price: From **$4,695.00**
Price: Action only **$1,875.00**
Price: Magnum action only **$1,875.00**

EMF PREMIER 1874 SHARPS RIFLE

Caliber: 45/70, 45/110, 45/120. **Barrel:** 32", 34". **Weight:** 11-13 lbs. **Length:** 49", 51" overall. **Stock:** Pistol grip, European walnut. **Sights:** Blade front, adjustable rear. **Features:** Superb quality reproductions of the 1874 Sharps Sporting Rifles; casehardened locks; double-set triggers; blue barrels. Imported from Pedersoli by EMF.
Price: Business Rifle. **$1,199.90**
Price: "Quigley", Patchbox, heavy barrel **$1,799.90**
Price: Silhouette, pistol-grip **$1,499.90**
Price: Super Deluxe Hand Engraved **$3,500.00**

HARRINGTON & RICHARDSON ULTRA VARMINT/ULTRA HUNTER RIFLES

Caliber: 204 Ruger, 22 WMR, 22-250 Rem., 223 Rem., 243 Win., 25-06 Rem., 30-06. **Barrel:** 22" to 26" heavy taper. **Weight:** About 7.5 lbs. **Stock:** Laminated birch with Monte Carlo comb or skeletonized polymer. **Sights:** None furnished. Drilled and tapped for scope mounting. **Features:** Break-open action with side-lever release, positive ejection. Scope mount. Blued receiver and barrel. Swivel studs. Introduced 1993. Ultra Hunter introduced 1995. From H&R 1871, Inc.
Price: Ultra Varmint Fluted, 24" bull barrel, polymer stock **$406.00**
Price: Ultra Hunter Rifle, 26" bull barrel in 25-06 Rem., laminated stock **$357.00**
Price: Ultra Varmint Rifle, 22" bull barrel in 223 Rem., laminated stock **$357.00**

HARRINGTON & RICHARDSON/NEW ENGLAND FIREARMS STAINLESS ULTRA HUNTER WITH THUMBHOLE STOCK

Caliber: 45-70 Govt. **Barrel:** 24". **Weight:** 8 lbs. **Length:** 40". **Features:** Stainless steel barrel and receiver with scope mount rail, hammer extension, cinnamon laminate thumbhole stock.
Price: **$439.00**

HARRINGTON & RICHARDSON/NEW ENGLAND FIREARMS HANDI-RIFLE/SLUG GUN COMBOS

Chamber: 44 Mag./12-ga. rifled slug and 357 Mag./20-ga. rifled slug. **Barrel:** Rifle barrel 22" for both calibers; shotgun barrels 28" (12 ga.) and 40" (20 ga.) fully rifled. **Weight:** 7-8 lbs. **Length:** 38" overall (both rifle chamberings). **Features:** Single-shot break-open rifle/shotgun combos (one rifle barrel, one shotgun barrel per combo). Rifle barrels are not interchangeable; shotgun barrels are interchangeable. Stock is black matte high-density polymer with sling swivel studs, molded checkering and recoil pad. No iron sights; scope rail included.
Price: **$362.00**

HARRINGTON & RICHARDSON CR-45LC

Caliber: 45 Colt. **Barrel:** 20". **Weight:** 6.25 lbs. **Length:** 34"overall. **Features:** Single-shot break-open carbine. Cut-checkered American black walnut with case-colored crescent steel buttplate, open sights, case-colored receiver.
Price: **$407.00**

HARRINGTON & RICHARDSON BUFFALO CLASSIC RIFLE

Caliber: 45-70 Govt. **Barrel:** 32" heavy. **Weight:** 8 lbs. **Length:** 46" overall. **Stock:** Cut-checkered American black walnut. **Sights:**

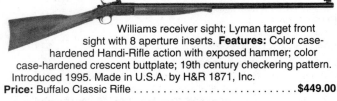

Williams receiver sight; Lyman target front sight with 8 aperture inserts. **Features:** Color case-hardened Handi-Rifle action with exposed hammer; color case-hardened crescent buttplate; 19th century checkering pattern. Introduced 1995. Made in U.S.A. by H&R 1871, Inc.
Price: Buffalo Classic Rifle **$449.00**

KRIEGHOFF HUBERTUS SINGLE-SHOT RIFLE
Caliber: 222, 243 Win., 270 Win., 308 Win., 30-06 Spfl., 5.6x50R Mag., 5.6x52R, 6x62R Freres, 6.5x57R, 6.5x65R, 7x57R, 7x65R, 8x57JRS, 8x75RS, 9.3x74R, 7mm Rem. Mag., 300 Win. Mag. **Barrel:** 23.5". **Weight:** 6.5 lbs. **Length:** 40.5. **Stock:** High-grade walnut. **Sights:** Blade front, open rear. **Features:** Break-open loading with manual cocking lever on top tang; takedown; extractor; Schnabel forearm; many options. Imported from Germany by Krieghoff International Inc.
Price: Hubertus single shot, from **$5,995.00**
Price: Hubertus, magnum calibers **$6,995.00**

MEACHAM HIGHWALL SILHOUETTE OR SCHUETZEN RIFLE
Caliber: any rimmed cartridge. **Barrel:** 26-34". **Weight:** 8-15 lbs. **Sights:** none. Tang drilled for Win. base, 3/8 dovetail slot front. **Stock:** Fancy eastern walnut with cheekpiece; ebony insert in forearm tip. **Features:** Exact copy of 1885 Winchester. With most Winchester factory options available, including double set triggers. Introduced 1994. Made in U.S.A. by Meacham T&H Inc.
Price: From **$4,999.00**

MERKEL K1 MODEL LIGHTWEIGHT STALKING RIFLE
Caliber: 243 Win., 270 Win., 7x57R, 308 Win., 30-06 Spfl., 7mm Rem. Mag., 300 Win. Mag., 9.3x74R. **Barrel:** 23.6". **Weight:** 5.6 lbs. unscoped. **Stock:** Satin-finished walnut, fluted and checkered; sling-swivel studs. **Sights:** None (scope base furnished). **Features:** Franz Jager single-shot break-open action, cocking/uncocking slide-type safety, matte silver receiver, selectable trigger pull weights, integrated, quick detach 1" or 30mm optic mounts (optic not included). Imported from Germany by Merkel USA.
Price: Jagd Stutzen Carbine **$3,795.00**

MERKEL K-2 CUSTOM SINGLE-SHOT "WEIMAR" STALKING RIFLE
Caliber: 308 Win., 30-06 Spfl., 7mm Rem. Mag., 300 Win. Mag. **Features:** Franz Jager single-shot break-open action, cocking. uncocking slide safety, deep relief engraved hunting scenes on silvered receiver, octagin barrel, deluxe walnut stock. Includes front and reare adjustable iron sights, scope rings. Imported from Germany by Merkel USA.
Price: Jagd Stutzen Carbine **$15,595.00**

NAVY ARMS 1874 SHARPS "QUIGLEY" RIFLE
Caliber: .45-70 Govt. **Barrel:** 34" octagon. **Weight:** 10 lbs. **Length:** 50" overall. **Grips:** Walnut checkered at wrist and forend. **Sights:** High blade front, full buckhorn rear. **Features:** Color case-hardened receiver, trigger, military patchbox, hammer and lever. Double-set triggers, German silver gripcap. Reproduction of rifle from "Quigley Down Under" movie.
Price: Model SQR045 (20087) **$2,026.00**

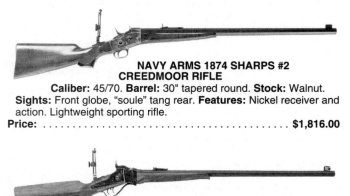

NAVY ARMS 1874 SHARPS #2 CREEDMOOR RIFLE
Caliber: 45/70. **Barrel:** 30" tapered round. **Stock:** Walnut. **Sights:** Front globe, "soule" tang rear. **Features:** Nickel receiver and action. Lightweight sporting rifle.
Price: **$1,816.00**

Navy Arms Sharps Sporting Rifle
Same as the Navy Arms Sharps Plains Rifle except

has pistol grip stock. Introduced 1997. Imported by Navy Arms.
Price: 45-70 Govt. only **$1,711.00**
Price: #2 Sporting with case-hardened receiver **$1,739.00**
Price: #2 Silhouette with full octagonal barrel **$1,739.00**

NAVY ARMS 1885 HIGH WALL RIFLE
Caliber: 45-70 Govt.; others available on special order. **Barrel:** 28" round, 30" octagonal. **Weight:** 9.5 lbs. **Length:** 45.5" overall (30" barrel). **Stock:** Walnut. **Sights:** Blade front, vernier tang-mounted peep rear. **Features:** Replica of Winchester's High Wall designed by Browning. Color case-hardened receiver, blued barrel. Introduced 1998. Imported by Navy Arms.
Price: 28", round barrel, target sights **$1,120.00**
Price: 30" octagonal barrel, target sights **$1,212.00**

NAVY ARMS 1873 SPRINGFIELD CAVALRY CARBINE
Caliber: 45-70 Govt. **Barrel:** 22". **Weight:** 7 lbs. **Length:** 40.5" overall. **Stock:** Walnut. **Sights:** Blade front, military ladder rear. **Features:** Blued lockplate and barrel; color case-hardened breechblock; saddle ring with bar. Replica of 7th Cavalry gun. Officer's Model Trapdoor has single-set trigger, bone case-hardened buttplate, trigger guard and breechblock. Deluxe walnut stock hand-checkered at the wrist and forend. German silver forend cap and rod tip. Adjustable rear peep target sight. Authentic flip-up 'Beech' front target sight. Imported by Navy Arms.
Price: Model STC073 . . . . **$1,261.00**
Price: Officer's Model Trapdoor (2008). **$1,648.00**

NAVY ARMS "JOHN BODINE" ROLLING BLOCK RIFLE
Caliber: 45-70 Govt. **Barrel:** 30" heavy octagonal. **Stock:** Walnut. **Sights:** Globe front, "soule" tang rear. **Features:** Double-set triggers.
Price: **$1,928.00**
Price: (#2 with deluxe nickel finished receiver) **$1,928.00**

NAVY ARMS 1874 SHARPS NO. 3 LONG RANGE RIFLE
Caliber: 45-70 Govt. **Barrel:** 34" octagon. **Weight:** 10 lbs., 14 oz. **Length:** 51.2". **Stock:** Deluxe walnut. **Sights:** Globe target front and match grade rear tang. **Features:** Shotgun buttplate, German silver forend cap, color case hardened receiver. Imported by Navy Arms.
Price: **$2,432.00**

NEW ENGLAND FIREARMS HANDI-RIFLE
Caliber: 204 Ruger, 22 Hornet, 223 Rem., 243 Win., 30-30, 270 Win., 280 Rem., 7mm-08 Rem., 308 Win., 7.62x39 Russian, 30-06 Spfl., 357 Mag., 35 Whelen, 44 Mag., 45-70 Govt., 500 S&W. **Barrel:** From 20" to 26", blued or stainless. **Weight:** 5.5 to 7 lbs. **Stock:** Walnut-finished hardwood or synthetic. **Sights:** Vary by model, but most have ramp front, folding rear, or are drilled and tapped for scope mount. **Features:** Break-open action with side-lever release. Swivel

studs on all models. Blue finish. Introduced 1989. From H&R 1871, Inc.

Price: Various cartridges. **$292.00**
Price: 7.62x39 Russian, 35 Whelen, intr. 2006 . . . .**$292.00**
Price: Youth, 37" OAL, 11.75" LOP, 6.75 lbs. **$292.00**
Price: Handi-Rifle/Pardner combo, 20 ga. synthetic, intr. 2006 . . . .**$325.00**
Price: Handi-Rifle/Pardner Superlight, 20 ga., 5.5 lbs., intr. 2006 . . . .**$325.00**
Price: Synthetic **$302.00**
Price: Stainless **$364.00**
Price: Superlight, 20" barrel, 35.25" OAL, 5.5 lbs. **$302.00**

NEW ENGLAND FIREARMS SURVIVOR RIFLE
Caliber: 223 Rem., 308 Win., .410 shotgun, 45 Colt, single shot. **Barrel:** 20" to 22". **Weight:** 6 lbs. **Length:** 34.5" to 36" overall. **Stock:** Black polymer, thumbhole design. **Sights:** None furnished; scope mount provided. **Features:** Receiver drilled and tapped for scope mounting. Stock and forend have storage compartments for ammo, etc.; comes with integral swivels and black nylon sling. Introduced 1996. Made in U.S.A. by H&R 1871, Inc.
Price: Blue or nickel finish. **$304.00**

NEW ENGLAND FIREARMS SPORTSTER/VERSA PACK RIFLE
Caliber: 17M2, 17 HMR, 22 LR, 22 WMR, .410 bore single shot. **Barrel:** 20" to 22". **Weight:** 5.4 to 7 lbs. **Length:** 33" to 38.25" overall. **Stock:** Black polymer. **Sights:** Adjustable rear, ramp front. **Features:** Receiver drilled and tapped for scope mounting. Made in U.S.A. by H&R 1871, Inc.
Price: Sportster 17M2, 17 HMR **$193.00**
Price: Sportster **$161.00**
Price: Sportster Youth **$161.00**

REMINGTON MODEL SPR18 SINGLE SHOT RIFLES
Caliber: 223 Rem., 243 Win., 270 Win., .30-06 Spfl., 308 Win., 7.62x39mm. **Barrel:** 23.5" chrome-lined hammer forged, all steel receiver, spiral-cut fluting. **Weight:** 6.75 lbs. **Stock:** Walnut stock and fore-end, swivel studs. **Sights:** adjustable, with 11mm scope rail. **Length:** 39.75" overall. **Features:** Made in U.S. by Remington Arms Co., Inc.
Price: Blued/walnut (2008) **$277.00**
Price: Nickel/walnut (2008) **$326.00**

REMINGTON NO. 1 ROLLING BLOCK MID-RANGE SPORTER
Caliber: 45-70 Govt. **Barrel:** 30" round. **Weight:** 8.75 lbs. **Length:** 46.5" overall. **Stock:** American walnut with checkered pistol grip and forend. **Sights:** Beaded blade front, adjustable center-notch buckhorn rear. **Features:** Recreation of the original. Polished blue metal finish. Many options available. Introduced 1998. Made in U.S.A. by Remington.
Price: **$2,927.00**
Price: Silhouette model with single-set trigger, heavy barrel **$3,366.00**

ROSSI SINGLE-SHOT RIFLES
Caliber: 17, 223 Rem., 243 Win., 270 Win., .30-06, 308 Win., 7.62x39, 22-250. **Barrel:** 22" (Youth), 23". **Weight:** 6.25-7 lbs. **Stocks:** Wood, Black Synthetic (Youth). **Sights:** Adjustable sights, drilled and tapped for scope. **Features:** Single-shot break open, 13 models available, positive ejection, internal transfer bar mechanism, manual external safety, trigger

block system, Taurus Security System, Matte blue finish, youth models available.
Price: **$238.00**

ROSSI MATCHED PAIRS
Gauge/Caliber: 12, 20, .410, 22 Mag, 22 LR, 17 HMR, 223 Rem, 243 Win., 270 Win., .30-06, 308 Win., .50 (black powder). **Barrel:** 23", 28". **Weight:** 5-6.3 lbs. **Stocks:** Wood or black synthetic. **Sights:** Bead front on shotgun barrel, fully adjustable front and rear on rifle barrel, drilled and tapped for scope, fully adjustable fiber optic sights (black powder). **Features:** Single-shot break open, 27 models available, internal transfer bar mechanism, manual external safety, blue finish, trigger block system, Taurus Security System, youth models available.
Price: Rimfire/Shotgun, from. **$178.00**
Price: Centerfire/Shotgun **$299.00**
Price: Black Powder Matched Pair, from **$262.00**

ROSSI WIZARD
Single shot rifle chambered in 18 different rimfire/centerfire/shotshell/muzzleloading configurations. Featured include drop-barrel action; quick, toolless barrel interchangeability; fiber optic front sight; adjustable rear sight with barrel-mounted optics rail; hardwood or camo Monte Carlo stock.
Price: . . . .**NA**

RUGER NO. 1-B SINGLE SHOT
Caliber: 223 Rem., 204 Ruger, 25-06 Rem., 6.5 Creedmore, 270 Win., 30-06 Spfl., 7mm Rem. Mag., 300 Win. Mag., 308 Win. **Barrel:** 26" round tapered with quarter-rib; with Ruger 1" rings. **Weight:** 8.25 lbs. **Length:** 42.25" overall. **Stock:** Walnut, two-piece, checkered pistol grip and semi-beavertail forend. **Sights:** None, 1" scope rings supplied for integral mounts. **Features:** Under-lever, hammerless falling block design has auto ejector, top tang safety.
Price: 1-B **$1,093.00**
Price: K1-B-BBZ stainless steel, laminated stock 25-06 Rem., 7mm Rem. Mag., 270, 300 Win. Mag., 243 Win., 30-06 . . . .**$1,186.00**

RUGER NO. 1-A LIGHT SPORTER
Caliber: 243 Win., 270 Win., 7x57, 30-06, 300 Ruger Compact Magnum. **Weight:** 7.25 lbs. Similar to the No. 1-B Standard Rifle except has lightweight 22" barrel, Alexander Henry-style forend, adjustable folding leaf rear sight on quarter-rib, dovetailed ramp front with gold bead.
Price: No. 1A. **$1,147.00**

Ruger No. 1-V Varminter
Similar to the No. 1-B Standard Rifle except has 24" heavy barrel. Semi-beavertail forend, barrel ribbed for target scope block, with 1" Ruger scope rings. Calibers 204 Ruger (26" barrel), 22-250 Rem., 223 Rem., 25-06 Rem. Weight about 9 lbs.
Price: No. 1-V **$1,147.00**

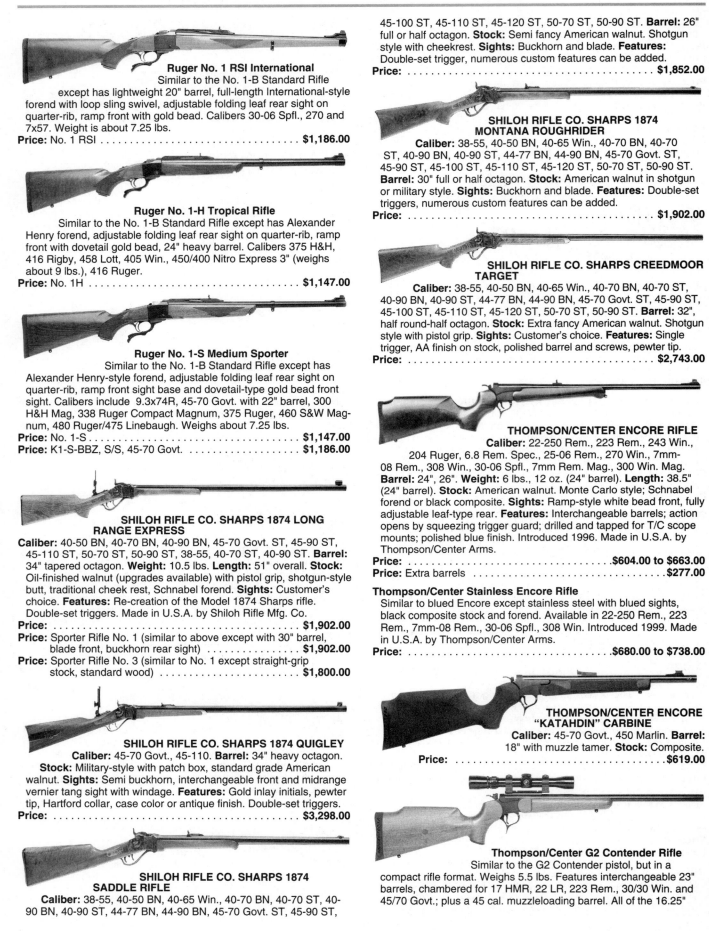

Ruger No. 1 RSI International
Similar to the No. 1-B Standard Rifle except has lightweight 20" barrel, full-length International-style forend with loop sling swivel, adjustable folding leaf rear sight on quarter-rib, ramp front with gold bead. Calibers 30-06 Spfl., 270 and 7x57. Weight is about 7.25 lbs.
Price: No. 1 RSI **$1,186.00**

Ruger No. 1-H Tropical Rifle
Similar to the No. 1-B Standard Rifle except has Alexander Henry forend, adjustable folding leaf rear sight on quarter-rib, ramp front with dovetail gold bead, 24" heavy barrel. Calibers 375 H&H, 416 Rigby, 458 Lott, 405 Win., 450/400 Nitro Express 3" (weighs about 9 lbs.), 416 Ruger.
Price: No. 1H **$1,147.00**

Ruger No. 1-S Medium Sporter
Similar to the No. 1-B Standard Rifle except has Alexander Henry-style forend, adjustable folding leaf rear sight on quarter-rib, ramp front sight base and dovetail-type gold bead front sight. Calibers include 9.3x74R, 45-70 Govt. with 22" barrel, 300 H&H Mag, 338 Ruger Compact Magnum, 375 Ruger, 460 S&W Magnum, 480 Ruger/475 Linebaugh. Weighs about 7.25 lbs.
Price: No. 1-S **$1,147.00**
Price: K1-S-BBZ, S/S, 45-70 Govt. **$1,186.00**

SHILOH RIFLE CO. SHARPS 1874 LONG RANGE EXPRESS
Caliber: 40-50 BN, 40-70 BN, 40-90 BN, 45-70 Govt. ST, 45-90 ST, 45-110 ST, 50-70 ST, 50-90 ST, 38-55, 40-70 ST, 40-90 ST. **Barrel:** 34" tapered octagon. **Weight:** 10.5 lbs. **Length:** 51" overall. **Stock:** Oil-finished walnut (upgrades available) with pistol grip, shotgun-style butt, traditional cheek rest, Schnabel forend. **Sights:** Customer's choice. **Features:** Re-creation of the Model 1874 Sharps rifle. Double-set triggers. Made in U.S.A. by Shiloh Rifle Mfg. Co.
Price: **$1,902.00**
Price: Sporter Rifle No. 1 (similar to above except with 30" barrel, blade front, buckhorn rear sight) **$1,902.00**
Price: Sporter Rifle No. 3 (similar to No. 1 except straight-grip stock, standard wood) **$1,800.00**

SHILOH RIFLE CO. SHARPS 1874 QUIGLEY
Caliber: 45-70 Govt., 45-110. **Barrel:** 34" heavy octagon. **Stock:** Military-style with patch box, standard grade American walnut. **Sights:** Semi buckhorn, interchangeable front and midrange vernier tang sight with windage. **Features:** Gold inlay initials, pewter tip, Hartford collar, case color or antique finish. Double-set triggers.
Price: **$3,298.00**

SHILOH RIFLE CO. SHARPS 1874 SADDLE RIFLE
Caliber: 38-55, 40-50 BN, 40-65 Win., 40-70 BN, 40-70 ST, 40-90 BN, 40-90 ST, 44-77 BN, 44-90 BN, 45-70 Govt. ST, 45-90 ST,

45-100 ST, 45-110 ST, 45-120 ST, 50-70 ST, 50-90 ST. **Barrel:** 26" full or half octagon. **Stock:** Semi fancy American walnut. Shotgun style with cheekrest. **Sights:** Buckhorn and blade. **Features:** Double-set trigger, numerous custom features can be added.
Price: **$1,852.00**

SHILOH RIFLE CO. SHARPS 1874 MONTANA ROUGHRIDER
Caliber: 38-55, 40-50 BN, 40-65 Win., 40-70 BN, 40-70 ST, 40-90 BN, 40-90 ST, 44-77 BN, 44-90 BN, 45-70 Govt. ST, 45-90 ST, 45-100 ST, 45-110 ST, 45-120 ST, 50-70 ST, 50-90 ST. **Barrel:** 30" full or half octagon. **Stock:** American walnut in shotgun or military style. **Sights:** Buckhorn and blade. **Features:** Double-set triggers, numerous custom features can be added.
Price: **$1,902.00**

SHILOH RIFLE CO. SHARPS CREEDMOOR TARGET
Caliber: 38-55, 40-50 BN, 40-65 Win., 40-70 BN, 40-70 ST, 40-90 BN, 40-90 ST, 44-77 BN, 44-90 BN, 45-70 Govt. ST, 45-90 ST, 45-100 ST, 45-110 ST, 45-120 ST, 50-70 ST, 50-90 ST. **Barrel:** 32", half round-half octagon. **Stock:** Extra fancy American walnut. Shotgun style with pistol grip. **Sights:** Customer's choice. **Features:** Single trigger, AA finish on stock, polished barrel and screws, pewter tip.
Price: **$2,743.00**

THOMPSON/CENTER ENCORE RIFLE
Caliber: 22-250 Rem., 223 Rem., 243 Win., 204 Ruger, 6.8 Rem. Spec., 25-06 Rem., 270 Win., 7mm-08 Rem., 308 Win., 30-06 Spfl., 7mm Rem. Mag., 300 Win. Mag. **Barrel:** 24", 26". **Weight:** 6 lbs., 12 oz. (24" barrel). **Length:** 38.5" (24" barrel). **Stock:** American walnut. Monte Carlo style; Schnabel forend or black composite. **Sights:** Ramp-style white bead front, fully adjustable leaf-type rear. **Features:** Interchangeable barrels; action opens by squeezing trigger guard; drilled and tapped for T/C scope mounts; polished blue finish. Introduced 1996. Made in U.S.A. by Thompson/Center Arms.
Price: ....$604.00 to $663.00
Price: Extra barrels **$277.00**

Thompson/Center Stainless Encore Rifle
Similar to blued Encore except stainless steel with blued sights, black composite stock and forend. Available in 22-250 Rem., 223 Rem., 7mm-08 Rem., 30-06 Spfl., 308 Win. Introduced 1999. Made in U.S.A. by Thompson/Center Arms.
Price: ....$680.00 to $738.00

THOMPSON/CENTER ENCORE "KATAHDIN" CARBINE
Caliber: 45-70 Govt., 450 Marlin. **Barrel:** 18" with muzzle tamer. **Stock:** Composite.
Price: **$619.00**

THOMPSON/CENTER G2 CONTENDER RIFLE
Similar to the G2 Contender pistol, but in a compact rifle format. Weighs 5.5 lbs. Features interchangeable 23" barrels, chambered for 17 HMR, 22 LR, 223 Rem., 30/30 Win. and 45/70 Govt.; plus a 45 cal. muzzleloading barrel. All of the 16.25"

and 21" barrels made for the old-style Contender will fit. Introduced 2003. Made in U.S.A. by Thompson/Center Arms.
Price: ....$622.00 to $637.00

THOMPSON/CENTER ENCORE PROHUNTER PREDATOR RIFLE
Contender-style break-action single shot rifle chambered in .204 Ruger, .223 Remington, .22-250 and .308 Winchester. Features include 28-inch deep-fluted interchangeable barrel, composite buttstock and forend with non-slip inserts in cheekpiece, pistol grip and forend. Max 1 camo finish overall. Overall length: 42.5 inches. Weight: 7-3/4 lbs.
Price: $799.00

TRADITIONS 1874 SHARPS DELUXE RIFLE
Caliber: 45-70 Govt. **Barrel:** 32" octagonal; 1:18" twist. **Weight:** 11.67 lbs. **Length:** 48.8" overall. **Stock:** Checkered walnut with German silver nose cap and steel buttplate. **Sights:** Globe front, adjustable Creedmore rear with 12 inserts. **Features:** Color case-hardened receiver; double-set triggers. Introduced 2001. Imported from Pedersoli by Traditions.
Price: $1,545.00

Traditions 1874 Sharps Sporting Deluxe Rifle
Similar to Sharps Deluxe but custom silver engraved receiver, European walnut stock and forend, satin finish, set trigger, fully adjustable.
Price: $2,796.00

Traditions 1874 Sharps Standard Rifle
Similar to 1874 Sharps Deluxe except has blade front and adjustable buckhorn-style rear sight. Weighs 10.67 pounds. Introduced 2001. Imported from Pedersoli by Traditions.
Price: $1,324.00

TRADITIONS ROLLING BLOCK SPORTING RIFLE
Caliber: 45-70 Govt. **Barrel:** 30" octagonal; 1:18" twist. **Weight:** 11.67 lbs. **Length:** 46.7" overall. **Stock:** Walnut. **Sights:** Blade front, adjustable rear. **Features:** Antique silver, color case-hardened receiver, drilled and tapped for tang/globe sights; brass buttplate and trigger guard. Introduced 2001. Imported from Pedersoli by Traditions.
Price: $1,029.00

UBERTI 1874 SHARPS SPORTING RIFLE
Caliber: 45-70 Govt. **Barrel:** 30", 32", 34" octagonal. **Weight:** 10.57 lbs. with 32" barrel. **Length:** 48.9" with 32" barrel. **Stock:** Walnut. **Sights:** Dovetail front, Vernier tang rear. **Features:** Cut checkering, case-colored finish on frame, buttplate, and lever. Imported by Stoeger Industries.
Price: Standard Sharps (2006), 30" barrel $1,459.00
Price: Special Sharps (2006) 32" barrel $1,729.00
Price: Deluxe Sharps (2006) 34" barrel $2,749.00
Price: Down Under Sharps (2006) 34" barrel $2,249.00
Price: Long Range Sharps (2006) 34" barrel $2,279.00
Price: Buffalo Hunters Sharps, 32" barrel $2,219.00
Price: Calvary Carbine Sharps, 22" barrel $1,569.00
Price: Sharps Extra Deluxe, 32" barrel (2009) $4,199.00
Price: Sharps Hunter, 28" barrel $1,459.00

UBERTI 1885 HIGH-WALL SINGLE-SHOT RIFLES
Caliber: 45-70 Govt., 45-90, 45-120 single shot. **Barrel:** 28" to 23". **Weight:** 9.3 to 9.9 lbs. **Length:** 44.5" to 47" overall. **Stock:** Walnut stock and forend. **Sights:** Blade front, fully adjustable open rear.

Features: Based on Winchester High-Wall design by John Browning. Color case-hardened frame and lever, blued barrel and buttplate. Imported by Stoeger Industries.
Price: 1885 High-Wall, 28" round barrel $969.00
Price: 1885 High-Wall Sporting, 30" octagonal barrel $1,029.00
Price: 1885 High-Wall Special Sporting, 32" octagonal barrel $1,179.00

BERETTA EXPRESS SSO O/U DOUBLE RIFLES
Caliber: 375 H&H, 458 Win. Mag., 9.3x74R. **Barrel:** 25.5". **Weight:** 11 lbs. **Stock:** European walnut with hand-checkered grip and forend. **Sights:** Blade front on ramp, open V-notch rear. **Features:** Sidelock action with color case-hardened receiver (gold inlays on SSO6 Gold). Ejectors, double triggers, recoil pad. Introduced 1990. Imported from Italy by Beretta U.S.A.
Price: SSO6 .... **$21,000.00**
Price: SSO6 Gold **$23,500.00**

BERETTA MODEL 455 SXS EXPRESS RIFLE
Caliber: 375 H&H, 458 Win. Mag., 470 NE, 500 NE 3", 416 Rigby. **Barrel:** 23.5" or 25.5". **Weight:** 11 lbs. **Stock:** European walnut with hand-checkered grip and forend. **Sights:** Blade front, folding leaf V-notch rear. **Features:** Sidelock action with easily removable sideplates; color case-hardened finish (455), custom big game or floral motif engraving (455EELL). Double triggers, recoil pad. Introduced 1990. Imported from Italy by Beretta U.S.A.
Price: Model 455 .... **$36,000.00**
Price: Model 455EELL **$47,000.00**

CZ 584 SOLO COMBINATION GUN
Caliber/Gauge: 7x57R; 12, 2-3/4" chamber. **Barrel:** 24.4". **Weight:** 7.37 lbs. **Length:** 45.25" overall. **Stock:** Circassian walnut. **Sights:** Blade front, open rear adjustable for windage. **Features:** Kersten-style double lump locking system; double-trigger Blitz-type mechanism with drop safety and adjustable set trigger for the rifle barrel; auto safety, dual extractors; receiver dovetailed for scope mounting. Imported from the Czech Republic by CZ-USA.
Price: **$851.00**

CZ 589 STOPPER OVER/UNDER GUN
Caliber: 458 Win. Magnum. **Barrels:** 21.7". **Weight:** 9.3 lbs. **Length:** 37.7" overall. **Stock:** Turkish walnut with sling swivels. **Sights:** Blade front, fixed rear. **Features:** Kersten-style action; Blitz-type double trigger; hammer-forged, blued barrels; satin-nickel, engraved receiver. Introduced 2001. Imported from the Czech Republic by CZ USA.
Price: **$2,999.00**
Price: Fully engraved model **$3,999.00**

DAKOTA DOUBLE RIFLE
Caliber: 470 Nitro Express, 500 Nitro Express. **Barrel:** 25". **Stock:** Exhibition-grade walnut. **Sights:** Express-style. **Features:** Round action; selective ejectors; recoil pad; Americase. From Dakota Arms Inc.
Price: **$25,000.00**

GARBI EXPRESS DOUBLE RIFLE
Caliber: 7x65R, 9.3x74R, 375 H&H. **Barrel:** 24.75". **Weight:** 7.75 to 8.5 lbs. **Length:** 41.5" overall. **Stock:** Turkish walnut. **Sights:** Quarter-rib with express sight. **Features:** Side-by-side double; H&H-pattern sidelock ejector with reinforced action, chopper lump barrels of Boehler steel; double triggers; fine scroll and rosette engraving, or full coverage ornamental; coin-finished action. Introduced 1997. Imported from Spain by Wm. Larkin Moore.
Price: **$25,000.00**

HOENIG ROTARY ROUND ACTION DOUBLE RIFLE
Caliber: Most popular calibers from 225 Win. to 9.3x74R. **Barrel:** 22" to 26". **Stock:** English Walnut; to customer specs.

Sights: Swivel hood front with button release (extra bead stored in trap door gripcap), express-style rear on quarter-rib adjustable for windage and elevation; scope mount. **Features:** Round action opens by rotating barrels, pulling forward. Inertia extractor system, rotary safety blocks strikers. Single lever quick-detachable scope mount. Simple takedown without removing forend. Introduced 1997. Made in U.S.A. by George Hoenig.
Price: **$19,980.00**

HOENIG ROTARY ROUND ACTION COMBINATION
Caliber: 28 ga. **Barrel:** 26". **Weight:** 7 lbs. **Stock:** English Walnut to customer specs. **Sights:** Front ramp with button release blades. Foldable aperture tang sight windage and elevation adjustable. Quarter-rib with scope mount. **Features:** Round action opens by rotating barrels, pulling forward. Inertia extractor; rotary safety blocks strikers. Simple takedown without removing forend. Made in U.S.A. by George Hoenig.
Price: **$25,000.00**

KRIEGHOFF CLASSIC DOUBLE RIFLE
Caliber: 7x57R, 7x65R, 308 Win., 30-06 Spfl., 8x57 JRS, 8x75RS, 9.3x74R, 375NE, 500/416NE, 470NE, 500NE. **Barrel:** 23.5". **Weight:** 7.3 to 8 lbs; 10-11 lbs. Big 5. **Stock:** High grade European walnut. Standard model has conventional rounded cheekpiece, Bavaria model has Bavarian-style cheekpiece. **Sights:** Bead front with removable, adjustable wedge (375 H&H and below), standing leaf rear on quarter-rib. **Features:** Boxlock action; double triggers; short opening angle for fast loading; quiet extractors; sliding, self-adjusting wedge for secure bolting; Purdey-style barrel extension; horizontal firing pin placement. Many options available. Introduced 1997. Imported from Germany by Krieghoff International.
Price: With small Arabesque engraving **$8,950.00**
Price: With engraved sideplates **$12,300.00**
Price: For extra barrels **$5,450.00**
Price: Extra 20-ga., 28" shotshell barrels **$3,950.00**

Krieghoff Classic Big Five Double Rifle
Similar to the standard Classic except available in 375 Flanged Mag. N.E., 500/416 NE, 470 NE, 500 NE. Has hinged front trigger, non-removable muzzle wedge (models larger than 375 caliber), Universal Trigger System, Combi Cocking Device, steel trigger guard, specially weighted stock bolt for weight and balance. Many options available. Introduced 1997. Imported from Germany by Krieghoff International. Imperial Model introduced 2006.
Price: **$11,450.00**
Price: With engraved sideplates **$14,800.00**

LEBEAU-COURALLY EXPRESS RIFLE SXS
Caliber: 7x65R, 8x57JRS, 9.3x74R, 375 H&H, 470 N.E. **Barrel:** 24" to 26". **Weight:** 7.75 to 10.5 lbs. **Stock:** Fancy French walnut with cheekpiece. **Sights:** Bead on ramp front, standing left express rear on quarter-rib. **Features:** Holland & Holland-type sidelock with automatic ejectors; double triggers. Built to order only. Imported from Belgium by Wm. Larkin Moore.
Price: **$50,000.00**

MERKEL DRILLINGS
Caliber/Gauge: 12, 20, 3" chambers, 16, 2-3/4" chambers; 22 Hornet, 5.6x50R Mag., 5.6x52R, 222 Rem., 243 Win., 6.5x55, 6.5x57R, 7x57R, 7x65R, 308 Win., 30-06 Spfl., 8x57JRS, 9.3x74R, 375 H&H. **Barrel:** 25.6". **Weight:** 7.9 to 8.4 lbs. depending upon caliber. **Stock:** Oil-finished walnut with pistol grip; cheekpiece on 12-, 16-gauge. **Sights:** Blade front, fixed rear. **Features:** Double barrel locking lug with Greener cross bolt; scroll-engraved, case-hardened

receiver; automatic trigger safety; Blitz action; double triggers. Imported from Germany by Merkel USA.

Price: Model 96K (manually cocked rifle system), from **$8,495.00**
Price: Model 96K engraved (hunting series on receiver) . . . **$9,795.00**

MERKEL BOXLOCK DOUBLE RIFLES

Caliber: 5.6x52R, 243 Winchester, 6.5x55, 6.5x57R, 7x57R, 7x65R, 308 Win., 30-06 Springfield, 8x57 IRS, 9.3x74R. **Barrel:** 23.6". **Weight:** 7.7 oz. **Length:** NA. **Stock:** Walnut, oil finished, pistol grip. **Sights:** Fixed 100 meter. **Features:** Anson & Deely boxlock action with cocking indicators, double triggers, engraved color case-hardened receiver. Introduced 1995. Imported from Germany by Merkel USA.

Price: Model 140-2, from **$11,995.00**
Price: Model 141 Small Frame SXS Rifle; built on smaller frame, chambered for 7mm Mauser, 30-06, or 9.3x74R **$8,195.00**
Price: Model 141 Engraved; fine hand-engraved hunting scenes on silvered receiver **$9,495.00**

RIZZINI EXPRESS 90L DOUBLE RIFLE

Caliber: 30-06 Spfl., 7x65R, 9.3x74R. **Barrel:** 24". **Weight:** 7.5 lbs. **Length:** 40" overall. **Stock:** Select European walnut with satin oil finish; English-style cheekpiece. **Sights:** Ramp front, quarter-rib with express sight. **Features:** Color case-hardened boxlock action; automatic ejectors; single selective trigger; polished blue barrels. Extra 20 gauge shotgun barrels available. Imported for Italy by Wm. Larkin Moore.

Price: With case **$3,850.00**

AMERICAN TACTICAL IMPORTS GSG-522

Semiauto tactical rifle chambered in .22 LR. Features include 16.25-inch barrel; black finish overall; polymer forend and buttstock; backup iron sights; receiver-mounted Picaatinny rail; 10-round magazine. Several other rifle and carbine versions available.

Price: **$475.00**

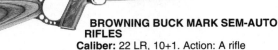

BROWNING BUCK MARK SEM-AUTO RIFLES

Caliber: 22 LR, 10+1. Action: A rifle version of the Buck Mark Pistol; straight blowback action; machined aluminum receiver with integral rail scope mount; manual thumb safety. **Barrel:** Recessed crowns. **Stock:** Stock and forearm with full pistol grip. **Features:** Action lock provided. Introduced 2001. Four model name variations for 2006, as noted below. **Sights:** FLD Target, FLD Carbon, and Target models have integrated scope rails. Sporter has Truglo/Marble fiber optic sights. Imported from Japan by Browning.

Price: FLD Target, 5.5 lbs., bull barrel, laminated stock **$659.00**
Price: Target, 5.4 lbs., blued bull barrel, wood stock **$639.00**
Price: Sporter, 4.4 lbs., blued sporter barrel w/sights **$639.00**

BROWNING SA-22 SEMI-AUTO 22 RIFLES

Caliber: 22 LR, 11+1. **Barrel:** 16.25". **Weight:** 5.2 lbs. **Length:** 37" overall. **Stock:** Checkered select walnut with pistol grip and semi-beavertail forend. **Sights:** Gold bead front, folding leaf rear. **Features:** Engraved receiver with polished blue finish; cross-bolt safety; tubular magazine in buttstock; easy takedown for carrying or storage. The Grade VI is available with either grayed or blued receiver with extensive engraving with gold-plated animals: right side pictures a fox and squirrel in a woodland scene; left side shows a beagle chasing a rabbit. On top is a portrait of the beagle. Stock and forend are of high-grade walnut with a double-bordered cut checkering design. Introduced 1987. Imported from Japan by Browning.

Price: Grade I, scroll-engraved blued receiver **$619.00**
Price: Grade VI BL, gold-plated engraved blued receiver . . **$1,329.00**

CZ 513 RIFLE

Caliber: 22 LR, 5-shot magazine. **Barrel:** 20.9". **Weight:** 5.7 lbs. **Length:** 39" overall. **Stock:** Beechwood. **Sights:** Tangent iron. **Features:** Simplified version of the CZ 452, no checkering on stock, simple non-adjustable trigger. Imported from the Czech Republic by CZ-USA.

Price: **$328.00**

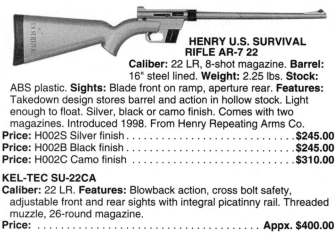

HENRY U.S. SURVIVAL RIFLE AR-7 22

Caliber: 22 LR, 8-shot magazine. **Barrel:** 16" steel lined. **Weight:** 2.25 lbs. **Stock:** ABS plastic. **Sights:** Blade front on ramp, aperture rear. **Features:** Takedown design stores barrel and action in hollow stock. Light enough to float. Silver, black or camo finish. Comes with two magazines. Introduced 1998. From Henry Repeating Arms Co.

Price: H002S Silver finish **$245.00**
Price: H002B Black finish **$245.00**
Price: H002C Camo finish **$310.00**

KEL-TEC SU-22CA

Caliber: 22 LR. **Features:** Blowback action, cross bolt safety, adjustable front and rear sights with integral picatinny rail. Threaded muzzle, 26-round magazine.

Price: . . . . **Appx. $400.00**

MAGNUM RESEARCH MAGNUMLITE RIFLES

Caliber: 22 WMR, 17 HMR, 22 LR 17M2, 10-shot magazine. **Barrel:** 17" graphite. **Weight:** 4.45 lbs. **Length:** 35.5" overall. **Stock:** Hogue OverMolded synthetic or walnut. **Sights:** Integral scope base.

Features: Magnum Lite graphite barrel, French grey anodizing, match bolt, target trigger. 22 LR/17M2 rifles use factory Ruger 10/22 magazines. 4-5 lbs. average trigger pull. Graphite carbon-fiber barrel weighs approx. 13.04 ounces in 22 LR, 1:16 twist. Introduced: 2007. From Magnum Research, Inc.

Price: MLR22H 22 LR. **$640.00**

MARLIN MODEL 60 AUTO RIFLE

Caliber: 22 LR, 14-shot tubular magazine. **Barrel:** 19" round tapered. **Weight:** About 5.5 lbs. **Length:** 37.5" overall. **Stock:** Press-checkered, walnut-finished Maine birch with Monte Carlo, full pistol grip; Mar-Shield finish. **Sights:** Ramp front, open adjustable rear. **Features:** Matted receiver is grooved for scope mount. Manual bolt hold-open; automatic last-shot bolt hold-open. Model 60C is similar except has hardwood Monte Carlo stock with Mossy Oak Break-Up camouflage pattern. From Marlin.

Price: **$179.00**
Price: With 4x scope **$186.00**
Price: Model 60C camo **$211.00**

Marlin Model 60SS Self-Loading Rifle

Same as the Model 60 except breech bolt, barrel and outer magazine tube are made of stainless steel; most other parts are either nickel-plated or coated to match the stainless finish. Monte Carlo stock is of black/gray Maine birch laminate, and has nickel-plated swivel studs, rubber buttpad. Introduced 1993. From Marlin.

Price: **$283.00**

MARLIN 60DLX

Semiauto rifle chambered for .22 LR. Features include 14-shot tubular magazine; side ejection; manual and automatic last-shot bolt hold-opens; receiver top with serrrated, non-glare finish; cross-bolt safety; steel charging handle; Monte Carlo American walnut-finished hardwood; full pistol grip; tough Mar-Shield finish; 19-inch barrel with Micro-Groove® rifling. Limited availability.

Price: . . . . **NA**

MARLIN 70PSS PAPOOSE STAINLESS RIFLE

Caliber: 22 LR, 7-shot magazine. **Barrel:** 16.25" stainless steel, Micro-Groove rifling. **Weight:** 3.25 lbs. **Length:** 35.25" overall. **Stock:** Black fiberglass-filled synthetic with abbreviated forend, nickel-plated swivel studs, molded-in checkering. **Sights:** Ramp front with orange post, cut-away Wide Scan hood; adjustable open rear. Receiver grooved for scope mounting. **Features:** Takedown barrel; cross-bolt safety; manual bolt hold-open; last shot bolt hold-open; comes with padded carrying case. Introduced 1986. Made in U.S.A. by Marlin.

Price: **$284.00**

MARLIN MODEL 795 AUTO RIFLE

Caliber: 22. **Barrel:** 18" with 16-groove Micro-Groove rifling. Ramp front sight, adjustable rear. Receiver grooved for scope mount. **Stock:** Black synthetic, hardwood, synthetic thumbhole, solid pink, pink camo, or Mossy Oak New Break-up camo finish. **Features:** 10-round magazine, last shot hold-open feature. Introduced 1997. SS is similar to Model 795 except stainless steel barrel. Most other parts nickel-plated. Adjustable folding semi-buckhorn rear sights, ramp

Prices given are believed to be accurate at time of publication however, many factors affect retail pricing so exact prices are not possible.

front high-visibility post and removable cutaway wide scan hood. Made in U.S.A. by Marlin Firearms Co.
Price: 795 . . . . **$157.00**
Price: 795SS **$227.00**

MOSSBERG MODEL 702 PLINKSTER AUTO RIFLE

Caliber: 22 LR, 10-round detachable magazine. **Barrel:** 18" free-floating. **Weight:** 4.1 to 4.6 lbs. **Sights:** Adjustable rifle. Receiver grooved for scope mount. **Stock:** Solid pink or pink marble finish synthetic. **Features:** Ergonomically placed magazine release and safety buttons, crossbolt safety, free gun lock. Made in U.S.A. by O.F. Mossberg & Sons, Inc.
Price: Pink Plinkster (2008) **$199.00**

MOSSBERG MODEL 702 PLINKSTER AUTOLOADING RIFLE WITH MUZZLE BRAKE

Semiauto rifle chambered in .22 LR. Features include a black synthetic stock with Schnabel, 10-round detachable box magazine, 21-inch matte blue barrel with muzzle brake, receiver grooved for scope mount.
Price: . . . .

$271.00

REMINGTON MODEL 552 BDL DELUXE SPEEDMASTER RIFLE

Caliber: 22 S (20), L (17) or LR (15) tubular magazine. **Barrel:** 21" round tapered. **Weight:** 5.75 lbs. **Length:** 40" overall. **Stock:** Walnut. Checkered grip and forend. **Sights:** Big game. **Features:** Positive cross-bolt safety, receiver grooved for tip-off mount.
Price: **$593.00**
Price: Smoothbore model (2007) **$633.00**

REMINGTON 597 AUTO RIFLE

Caliber: 22 LR, 10-shot clip; 22 WMR, 8-shot clip. **Barrel:** 20". **Weight:** 5.5 lbs. **Length:** 40" overall. **Stock:** Black synthetic. **Sights:** Big game. **Features:** Matte black finish, nickel-plated bolt. Receiver is grooved and drilled and tapped for scope mounts. Introduced 1997. Made in U.S.A. by Remington.
Price: Synthetic Scope Combo (2007) **$239.00**
Price: Model 597 Magnum **$492.00**
Price: Model 597 w/Mossy Oak Blaze Pink or Orange,
22 LR (2008) **$260.00**
Price: Model 597 Stainless TVP, 22 LR (2008) **$552.00**
Price: Model 597 TVP: Skeletonized laminated stock with
undercut forend, optics rail **$552.00**
Price: Model 597 FLX: Similar to Model 597, Blaze/Pink camo
but with FLX Digital Camo stock **$260.00**

REMINGTON 597 VTR - QUAD RAIL

Semiauto rifle chambered in .22 LR, styled to resemble AR. Features include matte blued finished and black synthetic stock; 16-inch barrel; Pardus A2-style collapsible pistol-grip stock; quad-rail free-floated tube; 10-round magazine.
Price: **$618.00**

REMINGTON 597 VTR A-2 FIXED STOCK

Similar to Remington 597 VTR - Quad Rail but with fixed A2-style stock and standard handguard with quad rail.
Price: **$618.00**

REMINGTON 597 VTR COLLAPSIBLE STOCK

Similar to 597 VTR A-2 Fixed Stock but with Pardus A2-style collapsible pistol-grip stock.
Price: **$618.00**

REMINGTON 597 VTR A-TACS CAMO

Semiauto rifle chambered in .22 LR, styled to resemble AR. Features include ATACS camo finish overall; 16-inch barrel; Pardus A2-style collapsible pistol-grip stock; round handguard without rails; receiver-mounted optics rail; 10-round magazine.
Price: **$618.00**

RUGER 10/22 AUTOLOADING CARBINE

Caliber: 22 LR, 10-shot rotary magazine. **Barrel:** 18.5" round tapered. **Weight:** 5 lbs. **Length:** 37.25" overall. **Stock:** American hardwood with pistol grip and barrel band or synthetic. **Sights:** Brass bead front, folding leaf rear adjustable for elevation. **Features:** Detachable rotary magazine fits flush into stock, cross-bolt safety, receiver tapped and grooved for scope blocks or tip-off mount. Scope base adaptor furnished with each rifle.
Price: Model 10/22-RB (black matte) **$269.00**
Price: Model 10/22-CRR Compact RB (black matte), 2006 . . . **$307.00**

Ruger 10/22 Deluxe Sporter

Same as 10/22 Carbine except walnut stock with hand checkered pistol grip and forend; straight buttplate, no barrel band, has sling swivels.
Price: Model 10/22-DSP **$355.00**

Ruger 10/22-T Target Rifle

Similar to the 10/22 except has 20" heavy, hammer-forged barrel with tight chamber dimensions, improved trigger pull, laminated hardwood stock dimensioned for optical sights. No iron sights supplied. Introduced 1996. Made in U.S.A. by Sturm, Ruger & Co.
Price: 10/22-T **$485.00**
Price: K10/22-T, stainless steel **$533.00**

Ruger K10/22-RPF All-Weather Rifle

Similar to the stainless K10/22/RB except has black composite stock of thermoplastic polyester resin reinforced with fiberglass; checkered grip and forend. Brushed satin, natural metal finish with clear hard-coat finish. Weighs 5 lbs., measures 37" overall. Introduced 1997. From Sturm, Ruger & Co.
Price: **$318.00**

RUGER 10/22VLEH TARGET TACTICAL RIFLE

Semiauto rimfire rifle chambered in .22 LR. Features include precision-rifled, cold hammer-forged, spiral-finished 16-1/8-inch crowned match barrel; Hogue® OverMolded® stock; 10/22T target trigger; precision-adjustable bipod for steady shooting from the bench; 10-round rotary magazine. Weight: 6-7/8 lbs.
Price: **$555.00**

RUGER RUGER SR-22 RIFLE

AR-style semiauto rifle chambered in .22 LR, based on 0/22 action. Features include all-aluminum chassis replicating the AR-platform dimensions between the sighting plane, buttstock height, and grip; Picatinny rail optic mount includes a six-position, telescoping M4-style buttstock (on a Mil-Spec diameter tube); Hogue Monogrip pistol grip; buttstocks and grips interchangeable with any AR-style compatible option; round, mid-

length handguard mounted on a standard-thread AR-style barrel nut; precision-rifled, cold hammer forged 16-1/8-inch alloy steel barrel capped with an SR-556/Mini-14 flash suppressor.
Price: . . . .**NA**

SAVAGE MODEL 64G AUTO RIFLE
Caliber: 22 LR, 10-shot magazine. **Barrel:** 20", 21". **Weight:** 5.5 lbs. **Length:** 40", 41". **Stock:** Walnut-finished hardwood with Monte Carlo-type comb, checkered grip and forend. **Sights:** Bead front, open adjustable rear. Receiver grooved for scope mounting. **Features:** Thumb-operated rotating safety. Blue finish. Side ejection, bolt hold-open device. Introduced 1990. Made in Canada, from Savage Arms.
Price: . . . .**From $187.00**

SAVAGE BRJ SERIES SEMIAUTO RIMFIRE RIFLES
Similar to Mark II, Model 93 and Model 93R17 semiauto rifles but feature spiral fluting pattern on a heavy barrel, blued finish and Royal Jacaranda wood laminate stock.
Price: Mark II BRJ – .22 LR) **$456.00**
Price: Model 93 BRJ – .22 Mag. **$464.00**
Price: Model 93 R17 BRJ – .17 HMR $464 . . . . **$464.00**

SAVAGE TACTICAL SEMIAUTO RIMFIRE RIFLES
Similar to Savage Model BRJ series semiauto rifles but feature heavy barrel, matte finish and a tactical-style wood stock.
Price: Mark II TR – .22 LR) **$469.00**
Price: Mark II TRR – .22 LR with three-way accessory rail) . **$539.00**
Price: Model 93R17 TR – .17 HMR **$477.00**
Price: Model 93R17 TRR – .17 HMR
with three-way accessory rail) **$536.00**

SMITH & WESSON M&P15-22
.22 LR rimfire verson of AR-derived M&P tactical autoloader. Features include blowback action, 15.5- or 16-inch barrel, 6-position telescoping or fixed stock, quad mount picatinny rails, plain barrel or compensator, alloy upper and lower, matte black finish, 10- or 25-round magazine.
Price: **$589.00**

THOMPSON/CENTER 22 LR CLASSIC RIFLE
Caliber: 22 LR, 8-shot magazine. **Barrel:** 22" match-grade. **Weight:** 5.5 pounds. **Length:** 39.5" overall. **Stock:** Satin-finished American walnut with Monte Carlo-type comb and pistol gripcap, swivel studs. **Sights:** Ramp-style front and fully adjustable rear, both with fiber optics. **Features:** All-steel receiver drilled and tapped for scope mounting; barrel threaded to receiver; thumb-operated safety; trigger guard safety lock included. New 22 Classic Benchmark TGT target rifle variant has 18" heavy barrel, brown laminated target stock, blued with matte finish, 10-shot magazine and no sights; drilled and tapped.
Price: T/C 22 LR Classic (blue) **$396.00**
Price: T/C 22 LR   Classic Benchmark . . . . . **$505.00** . . . .

UMAREX COLT TACTICAL RIMFIRE M4 OPS CARBINE
Blowback semiauto rife chambered in .22 LR, styled to resemble Colt M16. Features include 16.2.2-inch barrel; front sight adjustable for elevation; adjustable rear sight; alloy lower; adjustable telestock; flattop receiver with removable carry handle; 10- or 30-round detachable magazine.
Price: **$599.00**

UMAREX COLT TACTICAL RIMFIRE M4 CARBINE
Blowback semiauto rifle chambered in .22 LR, styled to resemble Colt M4. Features include 16.2-inch barrel; front sight adjustable

for elevation; adjustable rear sight; alloy lower; adjustable telestock; flattop receiver with optics rail; 10- or 30-round detachable magazine.
Price: **$640.00**

UMAREX COLT TACTICAL RIMFIRE M16 RIFLE
Blowback semiauto rifle chambered in .22 LR, styled to resemble Colt M16. Features include 21.2-inch barrel; front sight adjustable for elevation; adjustable rear sight; alloy lower; fixed stock; flattop receiver; removable carry handle; 10- or 30-round detachable magazine.
Price: **$599.00**

UMAREX COLT TACTICAL RIMFIRE M16 SPR RIFLE
Blowback semiauto rifle chambered in .22 LR, styled to resemble Colt M16 SPR. Features include 21.2-inch barrel; front sight adjustable for elevation; adjustable rear sight; alloy lower; fixed stock; flattop receiver with optics rail; removable carry handle; 10- or 30-round detachable magazine.
Price: **$670.00**

UMAREX H&K 416-22
Blowback semiauto rife chambered in .22 LR, styled to resemble H&K 416. Features include metal upper and lower receivers; RIS – rail interface system; retractable stock; pistol grip with storage compartment; on-rail sights; rear sight adjustable for wind and elevation; 16.1-inch barrel; 10- or 20-round magazine. Also available in pistol version with 9-inch barrel.
Price: **$675.00**

UMAREX H&K MP5 A5
Blowback semiauto rifle chambered in .22 LR, styled to resemble H&K MP5. Features include metal receiver; compensator; bolt catch; NAVY pistol grip; on-rail sights; rear sight adjustable for wind and elevation; 16.1-inch barrel; 10- or 25-round magazine. Also available in pistol version with 9-inch barrel. Also available with SD-type forend.
Price: **$525.00**

Prices given are believed to be accurate at time of publication however, many factors affect retail pricing so exact prices are not possible.

BROWNING BL-22 RIFLES

Action: Short-throw lever action, side ejection. Rack-and-pinion lever. Tubular magazines, with 15+1 capacity for 22 LR. **Barrel:** Recessed muzzle. **Stock:** Walnut, two-piece straight grip Western style. **Trigger:** Half-cock hammer safety; fold-down hammer. **Sights:** Bead post front, folding-leaf rear. Steel receiver grooved for scope mount. **Weight:** 5-5.4 lbs. **Length:** 36.75-40.75" overall. **Features:** Action lock provided. Introduced 1996. FLD Grade II Octagon has octagonal 24" barrel, silver nitride receiver with scroll engraving, gold-colored trigger. FLD Grade I has satin-nickel receiver, blued trigger, no stock checkering. FLD Grade II has satin-nickel receivers with scroll engraving; gold-colored trigger, cut checkering. Both introduced 2005. Grade I has blued receiver and trigger, no stock checkering. Grade II has gold-colored trigger, cut checkering, blued receiver with scroll engraving. Imported from Japan by Browning.

Price: BL-22 Grade I/II, from $529.00
Price: BL-22 FLD Grade I/II, from $569.00
Price: BL-22 FLD, Grade II Octagon $839.00

HENRY LEVER-ACTION RIFLES

Caliber: 22 Long Rifle (15 shot), 22 Magnum (11 shots), 17 HMR (11 shots). **Barrel:** 18.25" round. **Weight:** 5.5 to 5.75 lbs. **Length:** 34" overall (22 LR). **Stock:** Walnut. **Sights:** Blade front, open adjustable rear. **Features:** Polished blue finish; full-length tubular magazine; side ejection; receiver grooved for scope mounting. Introduced 1997. Made in U.S.A. by Henry Repeating Arms Co.

Price: H001 Carbine 22 LR. $325.00
Price: H001L Carbine 22 LR, Large Loop Lever. $340.00
Price: H001Y Youth model (33" overall, 11-round 22 LR) $325.00
Price: H001M 22 Magnum, 19.25" octagonal barrel, deluxe
    walnut stock $475.00
Price: H001V 17 HMR, 20" octagonal barrel, Williams Fire
    Sights $549.95

Henry Lever Octagon Frontier Model

Same as Lever rifles except chambered in 17 HMR, 22 Short/22 Long/22 LR, 22 Magnum; 20" octagonal barrel **Sights:** Marbles full adjustable semi-buckhorn rear, brass bead front. Weighs 6.25 lbs. Made in U.S.A. by Henry Repeating Arms Co.

Price: H001T Lever Octagon $425.00
Price: H001TM Lever Octagon 22 Magnum $539.95

HENRY GOLDEN BOY 22 LEVER-ACTION RIFLE

Caliber: 17 HMR, 22 LR (16-shot), 22 Magnum. **Barrel:** 20" octagonal. **Weight:** 6.25 lbs. **Length:** 38" overall. **Stock:** American walnut. **Sights:** Blade front, open rear. **Features:** Brasslite receiver, brass buttplate, blued barrel and lever. Introduced 1998. Made in U.S.A. from Henry Repeating Arms Co.

Price: H004 22 LR $515.00
Price: H004M 22 Magnum $595.00
Price: H004V 17 HMR $615.00
Price: H004DD 22 LR Deluxe, engraved receiver $1,200.00

HENRY PUMP-ACTION 22 PUMP RIFLE

Caliber: 22 LR, 15-shot. **Barrel:** 18.25".
Weight: 5.5 lbs. **Length:** NA. **Stock:** American walnut. **Sights:** Bead on ramp front, open adjustable rear. **Features:** Polished blue finish; receiver grooved for scope mount; grooved slide handle; two barrel

bands. Introduced 1998. Made in U.S.A. from Henry Repeating Arms Co.
Price: H003T 22 LR $515.00
Price: H003TM 22 Magnum $595.00

MARLIN MODEL 39A GOLDEN LEVER-ACTION RIFLE

Caliber: 22, S (26), L (21), LR (19), tubular magazine. **Barrel:** 24" Micro-Groove. **Weight:** 6.5 lbs. **Length:** 40" overall. **Stock:** Checkered American black walnut; Mar-Shield finish. Swivel studs; rubber buttpad. **Sights:** Bead ramp front with detachable Wide-Scan hood, folding rear semi-buckhorn adjustable for windage and elevation. **Features:** Hammer block safety; rebounding hammer. Takedown action, receiver tapped for scope mount (supplied), offset hammer spur, gold-colored steel trigger. From Marlin Firearms.
Price: $593.00

MOSSBERG MODEL 464 RIMFIRE LEVER-ACTION RIFLE

Caliber: 22 LR. **Barrel:** 20" round blued. **Weight:** 5.6 lbs. **Length:** 35-3/4" overall. **Features:** Adjustable sights, straight grip stock, 124-shot tubular magazine, plain hardwood straight stock and forend.
Price: . . . . **NA; apparently not yet in production**

REMINGTON 572 BDL DELUXE FIELDMASTER PUMP RIFLE

Caliber: 22 S (20), L (17) or LR (15), tubular magazine. **Barrel:** 21" round tapered. **Weight:** 5.5 lbs. **Length:** 40" overall. **Stock:** Walnut with checkered pistol grip and slide handle. **Sights:** Big game. **Features:** Cross-bolt safety; removing inner magazine tube converts rifle to single shot; receiver grooved for tip-off scope mount.
Price: $607.00

RUGER MODEL 96 LEVER-ACTION RIFLE

Caliber: 22 WMR, 9 rounds; 17 HMR, 9 rounds. **Barrel:** 18.5". **Weight:** 5.25 lbs. **Length:** 37-3/8" overall. **Stock:** Hardwood. **Sights:** Gold bead front, folding leaf rear. **Features:** Sliding cross button safety, visible cocking indicator; short-throw lever action. Introduced 1996. Made in U.S.A. by Sturm, Ruger & Co.
Price: 96/22M, 22 WMR or 17 HMR $451.00

TAURUS MODEL 62 PUMP RIFLE

Caliber: 22 LR, 12- or 13-shot. **Barrel:** 16.5" or 23" round. **Weight:** 72 oz. to 80 oz. **Length:** 39" overall. **Stock:** Premium hardwood. **Sights:** Adjustable rear, bead blade front, optional tang. **Features:** Blue, case hardened or stainless, bolt-mounted safety; pump action, manual firing pin block, integral security lock system. Imported from Brazil by Taurus International.
Price: From $299.00

Taurus Model 72 Pump Rifle

Same as Model 62 except chambered in 22 Magnum or 17 HMR; 16.5" barrel holds 10-12 shots, 23" barrel holds 11-13 shots. Weighs 72 oz. to 80 oz. Introduced 2001. Imported from Brazil by Taurus International.
Price: From $329.00

ANSCHUTZ 1416D/1516D CLASSIC RIFLES

Caliber: 22 LR (1416D888), 22 WMR (1516D), 5-shot clip. **Barrel:** 22.5". **Weight:** 6 lbs. **Length:** 41" overall. **Stock:** European hardwood with walnut finish; classic style with straight comb, checkered pistol grip and forend. **Sights:** Hooded ramp front, folding leaf rear. **Features:** Uses Match 64 action. Adjustable single-stage trigger. Receiver grooved for scope mounting. Imported from Germany by Merkel USA.

Price: 1416D KL, 22 LR **$899.00**
Price: 1416D KL Classic left-hand **$949.00**
Price: 1516D KL, 22 WMR **$919.00**

ANSCHUTZ 1710D CUSTOM RIFLE

Caliber: 22 LR, 5-shot clip. **Barrel:** 24.25". **Weight:** 7-3/8 lbs. **Length:** 42.5" overall. **Stock:** Select European walnut. **Sights:** Hooded ramp front, folding leaf rear; drilled and tapped for scope mounting. **Features:** Match 54 action with adjustable single-stage trigger; roll-over Monte Carlo cheekpiece, slim forend with Schnabel tip, Wundhammer palm swell on pistol grip, rosewood gripcap with white diamond insert; skip-line checkering on grip and forend. Introduced 1988. Imported from Germany by Merkel USA.

Price: **$1,649.00**

BROWNING T-BOLT RIMFIRE RIFLE

Caliber: 22 LR, 10-round rotary box Double Helix magazine. **Barrel:** 22", free-floating, semi-match chamber, target muzzle crown. **Weight:** 4.8 lbs. **Length:** 40.1" overall. **Stock:** Walnut, satin finish, cut checkering, synthetic buttplate. **Sights:** None. **Features:** Straight-pull bolt-action, three-lever trigger adjustable for pull weight, dual action screws, sling swivel studs. Crossbolt lockup, enlarged bolt handle, one-piece dual extractor with integral spring and red cocking indicator band, gold-tone trigger. Top-tang, thumb-operated two-position safety, drilled and tapped for scope mounts. Varmint model has raised Monte Carlo comb, heavy barrel, wide forearm. Introduced 2006. Imported from Japan by Browning. Left-hand models added in 2009.

Price: Sporter **$679.00**
Price: Sporter, left-hand, from **$689.00**
Price: Sporter, 17 HMR, 22 Mag., intr. 2008 . . . . **$709.00**
Price: Target/Varmint, intr. 2007 . . . . **$709.00**
Price: Composite Target/Varmint, intr. 2008 . . . . **$709.00**
Price: Composite Target/Varmint left-hand, from **$689.00**
Price: Composite Sporter, 17 HMR, 22 Mag., intr. 2008 . . . . . **$709.00**
Price: Composite Sporter left-hand, from **$689.00**

BUSHMASTER DCM-XR COMPETITION RIFLE

Caliber: 223 Rem, 10-shot mag. (2). **Barrel:** Heavy 1"-diameter free-floating match. **Weight:** 13.5 lbs. **Length:** 38.5" overall. **Features:** Fitted bolt, aperture rear sight that accepts four different inserts, choice of two front sight blades, two-stage competition trigger, weighted buttstock. Available in pre-and post-ban configurations.

Price: From . . . . **NA**

BUSHMASTER PIT VIPER 3-GUN COMPETITION RIFLE

Caliber: 5.56/223 Rem, 20-shot mag. (2). **Barrel:** Lapped/crowned 18" A2-profile 1:8. **Weight:** 7.5 lbs. **Length:** 38" overall. **Features:** AR-style semi-auto rifle designed for three-gun competition. Hybrid chambering to accept mil-spec ammunition, titanium nitride-coated bolt, free-floating handguard with two 3" rails and two 4" rails, JR tactical sight.

Price: From . . . . **NA**

COOPER MODEL 57-M BOLT-ACTION RIFLE

Caliber: 22 LR, 22 WMR, 17 HMR, 17 Mach 2. **Barrel:** 22" or 24" stainless steel or 4140 match grade. **Weight:** 6.5-7.5 lbs. **Stock:** AA-

AAA select Claro walnut, 22 lpi hand checkering. **Sights:** None furnished. **Features:** Three rear locking lug, repeating bolt-action with 5-shot magazine. for 22 LR and 17M2; 4-shot magazine for 22 WMR and 17 HMR. Fully adjustable trigger. Left-hand models add $150 to base rifle price. 1/4"-group rimfire accuracy guarantee at 50 yards; 0.5"-group centerfire accuracy guarantee at 100 yards. Options include wood upgrades, case-color metalwork, barrel fluting, custom LOP, and many others.

Price: Classic **$1,400.00**
Price: LVT **$1,595.00**
Price: Custom Classic **$2,395.00**
Price: Western Classic **$3,295.00**
Price: TRP-3 (22 LR only, benchrest style) **$1,395.00**
Price: Jackson Squirrel Rifle **$1,595.00**
Price: Jackson Hunter (synthetic) **$1,495.00**

CZ 452 LUX BOLT-ACTION RIFLE

Caliber: 22 LR, 22 WMR, 5-shot detachable magazine. **Barrel:** 24.8". **Weight:** 6.6 lbs. **Length:** 42.63" overall. **Stock:** Walnut with checkered pistol grip. **Sights:** Hooded front, fully adjustable tangent rear. **Features:** All-steel construction, adjustable trigger, polished blue finish. Imported from the Czech Republic by CZ-USA.

Price: 22 LR, 22 WMR **$427.00**

CZ 452 Varmint Rifle

Similar to the Lux model except has heavy 20.8" barrel; stock has beavertail forend; weighs 7 lbs.; no sights furnished. Available in 22 LR, 22 WMR, 17HMR, 17M2. Imported from the Czech Republic by CZ-USA.

Price: From **$497.00**

CZ 452 American Bolt-Action Rifle

Similar to the CZ 452 M 2E Lux except has classic-style stock of Circassian walnut; 22.5" free-floating barrel with recessed target crown; receiver dovetail for scope mounting. No open sights furnished. Introduced 1999. Imported from the Czech Republic by CZ-USA.

Price: 22 LR, 22 WMR **$463.00**

DAVEY CRICKETT SINGLE SHOT RIFLE

Caliber: 22 LR, 22 WMR, single shot. **Barrel:** 16-1/8". **Weight:** About 2.5 lbs. **Length:** 30" overall. **Stock:** American walnut. **Sights:** Post on ramp front, peep rear adjustable for windage and elevation. **Features:** Drilled and tapped for scope mounting using special Chipmunk base ($13.95). Engraved model also available. Made in U.S.A. Introduced 1982. Formerly Chipmunk model. From Keystone Sporting Arms.

Price: From **$220.00**

HENRY ACU-BOLT RIFLE

Caliber: 22, 22 Mag., 17 HMR; single shot. **Barrel:** 20". **Weight:** 4.15 lbs. **Length:** 36". **Stock:** One-piece fiberglass synthetic. **Sights:** Scope mount and 4x scope included. **Features:** Stainless barrel and receiver, bolt-action.

Price: H007 22 LR **$399.95**

Prices given are believed to be accurate at time of publication however, many factors affect retail pricing so exact prices are not possible.

HENRY "MINI" BOLT ACTION 22 RIFLE
Caliber: 22 LR, single shot youth gun. **Barrel:** 16" stainless, 8-groove rifling. **Weight:** 3.25 lbs. **Length:** 30", LOP 11.5". **Stock:** Synthetic, pistol grip, wraparound checkering and beavertail forearm. **Sights:** William Fire sights. **Features:** One-piece bolt configuration manually operated safety.
Price: H005 22 LR, black fiberglass stock **$249.95**
Price: H005S 22 LR, orange fiberglass stock **$249.95**

MARLIN MODEL 917 BOLT-ACTION RIFLES
Caliber: 17 HMR, 4- and 7-shot clip. **Barrel:** 22". **Weight:** 6 lbs., stainless 7 lbs. **Length:** 41". **Stock:** Checkered walnut Monte Carlo SS, laminated black/grey. **Sights:** No sights but receiver grooved. **Features:** Swivel studs, positive thumb safety, red cocking indicator, safety lock, SS 1" brushed aluminum scope rings.
Price: 917 . . . . **$240.00**
Price: 917VS Stainless steel barrel **$287.00**
Price: 917VT Laminated thumbhole stock (2008), from . . . **$382.00**
Price: 917VST, stainless-finish metal, gray/black laminated
    thumbhole stock **$426.00**
Price: 917VSF, fluted barrel **$397.00**
Price: 917VS-CF, carbon fiber-patterned stock **$358.00**

MARLIN MODEL 915YN "LITTLE BUCKAROO"
Caliber: 22 S, L, LR, single shot. **Barrel:** 16.25" Micro-Groove. **Weight:** 4.25 lbs. **Length:** 33.25" overall. **Stock:** One-piece walnut-finished, press-checkered Maine birch with Monte Carlo; Mar-Shield finish. **Sights:** Ramp front, adjustable open rear. **Features:** Beginner's rifle with thumb safety, easy-load feed throat, red cocking indicator. Receiver grooved for scope mounting. Introduced 1989.
Price: **$203.00**
Price: 915YS (stainless steel with fire sights) **$227.00**

MARLIN 981TS
Bolt action rifle chambered in .22 S/L/LR.
Features include tubular magazine (holds 25 Short, 19 Long or 17 Long Rifle cartridges; thumb safety; red cocking indicator; black fiberglass-filled synthetic stock with full pistol grip; molded-in checkering and swivel studs; 22-inch stainless steel barrel with Micro-Groove rifling (16 grooves). Adjustable semi-buckhorn folding rear sight, ramp front with high visibility, orange front sight post; cutaway Wide-Scan hood. Receiver grooved for scope mount; drilled and tapped for scope bases.
Price: . . . . **NA**

MARLIN MODEL 982 BOLT-ACTION RIFLE
Caliber: 22 WMR. **Barrel:** 22" Micro-Groove. **Weight:** 6 lbs. **Length:** 41" overall. **Stock:** Walnut Monte Carlo genuine American black walnut with swivel studs; full pistol grip; classic cut checkering; rubber rifle butt pad; tough Mar-Shield finish. **Sights:** Adjustable semi-buckhorn folding rear, ramp front sight with brass bead and Wide-Scan front sight hood. **Features:** 7-shot clip, thumb safety, red cocking indicator, receiver grooved for scope mount. 982S has stainless steel front breech bolt, barrel, receiver and bolt knob. All other parts are either stainless steel or nickel-plated. Has black Monte Carlo stock of fiberglass-filled polycarbonate with molded-in checkering, nickel-plated swivel studs. Introduced 2005. Made in U.S.A. by Marlin Firearms Co.
Price: 982VS (heavy stainless barrel, 7 lbs) **$309.00**
Price: 982VS-CF (carbon fiber stock) **$350.00**

Marlin Model 925M Bolt-Action Rifles
Similar to the Model 982 except chambered for 22 WMR. Has 7-shot clip magazine, 22" Micro-Groove barrel, checkered walnut-finished Maine birch stock. Introduced 1989.
Price: 925M **$234.00**
Price: 925RM, black fiberglass-filled synthetic stock **$220.95**

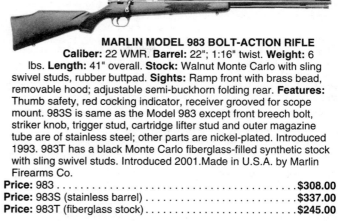

MARLIN MODEL 983 BOLT-ACTION RIFLE
Caliber: 22 WMR. **Barrel:** 22"; 1:16 twist. **Weight:** 6 lbs. **Length:** 41" overall. **Stock:** Walnut Monte Carlo with sling swivel studs, rubber buttpad. **Sights:** Ramp front with brass bead, removable hood; adjustable semi-buckhorn folding rear. **Features:** Thumb safety, red cocking indicator, receiver grooved for scope mount. 983S is same as the Model 983 except front breech bolt, striker knob, trigger stud, cartridge lifter stud and outer magazine tube are of stainless steel; other parts are nickel-plated. Introduced 1993. 983T has a black Monte Carlo fiberglass-filled synthetic stock with sling swivel studs. Introduced 2001. Made in U.S.A. by Marlin Firearms Co.
Price: 983 . . . . **$308.00**
Price: 983S (stainless barrel) **$337.00**
Price: 983T (fiberglass stock) **$245.00**

MEACHAM LOW-WALL RIFLE
Caliber: Any rimfire cartridge. **Barrel:** 26-34". **Weight:** 7-15 lbs. **Sights:** none. Tang drilled for Win. base, 3/8" dovetail slot front. **Stock:** Fancy eastern walnut with cheekpiece; ebony insert in forearm tip. Features; Exact copy of 1885 Winchester. With most Winchester factory options available including double set triggers. Introduced 1994. Made in U.S.A. by Meacham T&H Inc.
Price: From **$4,999.00**

MOSSBERG MODEL 817 VARMINT BOLT-ACTION RIFLE
Caliber: 17 HMR, 5-round magazine. **Barrel:** 21"; free-floating bull barrel, recessed muzzle crown. **Weight:** 4.9 lbs. (black synthetic), 5.2 lbs. (wood). **Stock:** Black synthetic or wood; length of pull, 14.25". **Sights:** Factory-installed Weaver-style scope bases. **Features:** Blued or brushed chrome metal finishes, crossbolt safety, gun lock. Introduced 2008. Made in U.S.A. by O.F. Mossberg & Sons, Inc.
Black synthetic stock, chrome finish (2008) **$279.00**

MOSSBERG MODEL 801/802 BOLT RIFLES
Caliber: 22 LR, 10-round detachable magazine. **Barrel:** 18" free-floating. **Weight:** 4.1 to 4.6 lbs. **Sights:** Adjustable rifle. Receiver grooved for scope mount. **Stock:** Solid pink or pink marble finish synthetic. **Features:** Ergonomically placed magazine release and safety buttons, crossbolt safety, free gun lock. 801 Half Pint has 12.25" length of pull, 16" barrel, and weighs 4 lbs. Hardwood stock; removable magazine plug. Made in U.S.A. by O.F. Mossberg & Sons, Inc.
Price: Pink Plinkster (2008) **$199.00**
Price: Half Pint (2008) **$199.00**

NEW ENGLAND FIREARMS SPORTSTER SINGLE-SHOT RIFLES
Caliber: 22 LR, 22 WMR, 17 HMR, single-shot. **Barrel:** 20". **Weight:** 5.5 lbs. **Length:** 36.25" overall. **Stock:** Black polymer. **Sights:** None furnished; scope mount included. **Features:** Break open, side-lever release; automatic ejection; recoil pad; sling swivel studs; trigger locking system. Introduced 2001. Made in U.S.A. by New England Firearms.
Price: **$149.00**
Price: Youth model (20" barrel, 33" overall, weighs 5-1/3 lbs.) **$149.00**
Price: Sportster 17 HMR **$180.00**

NEW ULTRA LIGHT ARMS 20RF BOLT-ACTION RIFLE
Caliber: 22 LR, single shot or repeater. **Barrel:** Douglas, length to order. **Weight:** 5.25 lbs. **Length:** Varies. **Stock:** Kevlar/graphite composite, variety of finishes. **Sights:** None furnished; drilled and tapped for scope mount. **Features:** Timney trigger, hand-lapped action, button-rifled barrel, hand-bedded action, recoil pad, sling-swivel studs, optional Jewell trigger. Made in U.S.A. by New Ultra Light Arms.
Price: 20 RF single shot **$1,300.00**
Price: 20 RF repeater **$1,350.00**

REMINGTON MODEL FIVE SERIES
Caliber: 17 HMR, 22 LR, 22 WMR. **Barrel:** 16.5" (Youth), 22". **Barrel:** Carbon-steel, hammer-forged barrel, 1:16 twist, polished blue finish. **Weight:** 5.5 to 6.75 lbs. **Stock:** Hardwood, laminate, European Walnut. **Length:** 35.25" to 40.75" overall. **Features:** Detachable, steel

magazine box with five-round capacity; steel trigger guard; chrome-plated bolt body; single stage trigger with manual two-position safety; buttplate; sling swivel studs (excluding Youth version); adjustable big game-style rifle sights; and dovetail-style receiver. Introduced 2006. Model Five Youth (22 LR) has 12.4-inch length of pull, 16.5-inch barrel, single-shot adapter. Model Five Laminate has weather-resistant brown laminate stock. Model Five European Walnut has classic satin-finish stock. Made in U.S.A. by Remington.

Price: Model Five Youth, 22 LR (2008). **$237.00**
Price: Model Five Laminate, 17 HMR (2008), 22 LR, 22 WMR **$363.00**
Price: Model Five European Walnut, 22 LR (2008) **$279.00**

ROSSI MATCHED PAIR SINGLE-SHOT RIFLE/SHOTGUN

Caliber: 17 HMR, 22 LR, 22 Mag. **Barrel:** 18.5" or 23". **Weight:** 6 lbs. **Stock:** Hardwood (brown or black finish). **Sights:** Fully adjustable front and rear. **Features:** Break-open breech, transfer-bar manual safety, includes matched 410-, 20 or 12 gauge shotgun barrel with bead front sight. Introduced 2001. Imported by BrazTech/Taurus.

Price: S121280RS **$160.00**
Price: S121780RS **$200.00**
Price: S122280RS **$160.00**
Price: S201780RS **$200.00**

RUGER K77/22 VARMINT RIFLE

Caliber: 22 LR, 10-shot, 22 WMR, 9-shot detachable rotary magazine. **Barrel:** 24", heavy. **Weight:** 7.25 lbs. **Length:** 43.25" overall. **Stock:** Laminated hardwood with rubber buttpad, quick-detachable swivel studs. **Sights:** None furnished. Comes with Ruger 1" scope rings. **Features:** Stainless steel or blued finish. Three-position safety, dual extractors. Stock has wide, flat forend. Introduced 1993.

Price: K77/22VBZ, 22 LR **$836.00**
Price: K77/22VMBZ, 22 WMR **$836.00**

RUGER 77/22 RIMFIRE BOLT-ACTION RIFLE

Caliber: 22 LR, 10-shot rotary magazine; 22 WMR, 9-shot rotary magazine. **Barrel:** 20". **Weight:** About 6 lbs. **Length:** 39.25" overall. **Stock:** Checkered American walnut, laminated hardwood, or synthetic stocks, stainless sling swivels. **Sights:** Plain barrel with 1" Ruger rings. **Features:** Mauser-type action uses Ruger's rotary magazine. Three-position safety, simplified bolt stop, patented bolt locking system. Uses the dual-screw barrel attachment system of the 10/22 rifle. Integral scope mounting system with 1" Ruger rings. Blued model introduced 1983. Stainless steel and blued with synthetic stock introduced 1989.

Price: 77/22R (no sights, rings, walnut stock). **$754.00**
Price: K77/22RP (stainless, no sights, rings, synthetic stock) . **$754.00**
Price: 77/22RM (22 WMR, blued, walnut stock) **$754.00**
Price: K77/22RMP (22 WMR, stainless, synthetic stock) **$754.00**

RUGER 77/17 RIMFIRE BOLT-ACTION RIFLE

Caliber: 17 HMR (9-shot rotary magazine. **Barrel:** 22" to 24". **Weight:** 6.5-7.5 lbs. **Length:** 41.25-43.25" overall. **Stock:** Checkered American walnut, laminated hardwood; stainless sling swivels. **Sights:** Plain barrel with 1" Ruger rings. **Features:** Mauser-type action uses Ruger's rotary magazine. Three-position safety, simplified bolt stop, patented bolt locking system. Uses the dual-screw barrel attachment system of the 10/22 rifle. Integral scope mounting system with 1" Ruger rings. Introduced 2002.

Price: 77/17-RM (no sights, rings, walnut stock) **$754.00**
Price: K77/17-VMBBZ (Target grey bbl, black laminate stock) **$836.00**

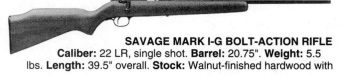

SAVAGE MARK I-G BOLT-ACTION RIFLE

Caliber: 22 LR, single shot. **Barrel:** 20.75". **Weight:** 5.5 lbs. **Length:** 39.5" overall. **Stock:** Walnut-finished hardwood with Monte Carlo-type comb, checkered grip and forend. **Sights:** Bead front, open adjustable rear. Receiver grooved for scope mounting. **Features:** Thumb-operated rotating safety. Blue finish. Rifled or smooth bore. Introduced 1990. Made in Canada, from Savage Arms Inc.

Price: Mark I-G, rifled or smooth bore, right- or left-handed . . .**$226.00**
Price: Mark I-GY (Youth), 19" barrel, 37" overall, 5 lbs. **$226.00**

SAVAGE MARK II BOLT-ACTION RIFLE

Caliber: 22 LR, 10-shot magazine. **Barrel:** 20.5". **Weight:** 5.5 lbs. **Length:** 39.5" overall. **Stock:** Walnut-finished hardwood with Monte Carlo-type comb, checkered grip and forend. **Sights:** Bead front, open adjustable rear. Receiver grooved for scope mounting. **Features:** Thumb-operated rotating safety. Blue finish. Introduced 1990. Made in Canada, from Savage Arms, Inc.

Price: Mark II-BV. **$342.00**
Price: Mark II-GY (youth), 19" barrel, 37" overall, 5 lbs. **$226.00**
Price: Mark II-GL, left-hand **$226.00**
Price: Mark II-F, 17 HM2 . . . . **$202.00**
Price: Mark II XP Camo Scope Package (2008). **$400.00**
Price: Mark II Classic T, thumbhole walnut stock (2008) **$559.00**
Price: Mark II BTV: laminated thumbhole vent stock,
AccuTrigger, blued receiver and bull barrel **$393.00**
Price: Mark II BVTS: stainless barrel/receiver;
available in right- or left-hand (BTVLS) configuration
. . . . **$393.00** (standard); **$441.00** (left hand)

Savage Mark II-FSS Stainless Rifle

Similar to the Mark II except has stainless steel barreled action and black synthetic stock with positive checkering, swivel studs, and 20.75" free-floating and button-rifled barrel with detachable magazine. Weighs 5.5 lbs. Introduced 1997. Imported from Canada by Savage Arms, Inc.

Price: **$273.00**

SAVAGE MODEL 93G MAGNUM BOLT-ACTION RIFLE

Caliber: 22 WMR, 5-shot magazine. **Barrel:** 20.75". **Weight:** 5.75 lbs. **Length:** 39.5" overall. **Stock:** Walnut-finished hardwood with Monte Carlo-type comb, checkered grip and forend. **Sights:** Bead front, adjustable open rear. Receiver grooved for scope mount. **Features:** Thumb-operated rotary safety. Blue finish. Introduced 1994. Made in Canada, from Savage Arms.

Price: Model 93G **$260.00**
Price: Model 93F (as above with black graphite/fiberglass
stock) **$241.00**
Price: Model 93 Classic, American walnut stock (2008) **$566.00**
Price: Model 93 Classic T, American walnut thumbhole stock
(2008) **$604.00**

Savage Model 93FSS Magnum Rifle

Similar to Model 93G except stainless steel barreled action and black synthetic stock with positive checkering. Weighs 5.5 lbs. Introduced 1997. Imported from Canada by Savage Arms, Inc.

Price: **$306.00**

Savage Model 93FVSS Magnum Rifle

Similar to Model 93FSS Magnum except 21" heavy barrel with recessed target-style crown, satin-finished stainless barreled action, black graphite/fiberglass stock. Drilled and tapped

for scope mounting; comes with Weaver-style bases. Introduced 1998. Imported from Canada by Savage Arms, Inc.
Price: **$347.00**

Savage Model 93R17 Bolt-Action Rifles

Similar to Model 93G Magnum but chambered in 17 HMR. Features include standard synthetic, hardwood or walnut stock or thumbhole stock with cheekpiece, 21" or 22" barrel, no sights, detachable box magazine.

Price: Model 93R17BTV: Laminted ventilated thumbhole stock, blued barrel/receiver **$393.00**
Price: Model 93R17BV: Standard brown laminate stock, heavy barrel **$342.00**
Price: Model 93R17GV: Checkered hardwood stock **$278.00**
Price: Model 93R17GLV: Left-hand configuration **$278.00**
Price: Model 93R17 Classic T: Checkered walnut thumbhole stock with unvented forend, blued barrel/receiver **$559.00**
Price: Model 93R17 Classic: Standard walnut stock **$559.00**
Price: Model 93R17BTVS: Laminated thumbhole vent stock, stainless steel barrel and receiver **$441.00**
Price: Model 93R17BLTVS: Left-hand **$441.00**
Price: Model 93R17BVSS: Similar to Model 93R17BTVS but with gray laminated non-thumbhole stock **$411.00**
Price: Model 93R17FVS: Black synthetic stock, AccuTrigger, blued or stainless heavy barrel **$347.00**

SAVAGE MODEL 30G STEVENS "FAVORITE"

Caliber: 22 LR, 22 WMR Model 30GM, 17 HMR Model 30R17. **Barrel:** 21". **Weight:** 4.25 lbs. **Length:** 36.75". **Stock:** Walnut, straight grip, Schnabel forend. **Sights:** Adjustable rear, bead post front. **Features:** Lever action falling block, inertia firing pin system, Model 30G half octagonal barrel, Model 30GM full octagonal barrel.
Price: Model 30G **$344.00**
Price: Model 30 Takedown **$360.00**

SAVAGE CUB T MINI YOUTH

Caliber: 22 S, L, LR; 17 Mach 2. **Barrel:** 16". **Weight:** 3.5 lbs. **Length:** 33". **Stock:** Walnut finished hardwood thumbhole stock. **Sights:** Bead post, front; peep, rear. **Features:** Mini single-shot bolt action, free-floating button-rifled barrel, blued finish. From Savage Arms.
Price: Cub T Thumbhole, walnut stained laminated **$266.00**
Price: Cub T Pink Thumbhole (2008) **$280.00**

THOMPSON/CENTER HOTSHOT YOUTH RIFLE

Single-shot dropping-barrel rifle chambered in .22 Long Rifle. Features include a crowned 19-inch steel barrel, exposed hammer, synthetic forend and buttstock, peep sight (receiver drilled and tapped for optics), three stock pattern options (black, Realtree AP and pink AP). Overall weight 3 lbs., 11.5-inch length of pull.
Price: . . . . **$229.00 to $249.00**

WINCHESTER WILDCAT BOLT ACTION 22

Caliber: 22 S, L, LR; one 5-round and three 10-round magazines. **Barrel:** 21". **Weight:** 6.5 lbs. **Length:** 38-3/8". **Stock:**

Checkered hardwood stock, checkered black synthetic Winchester buttplate, Schnabel fore-end. **Sights:** Bead post, front; buckhorn rear. **Features:** Steel sling swivel studs, blued finish. Wildcat Target/Varmint rifle has .866" diameter bull barrel. Receiver drilled, tapped, and grooved for bases. Adjustable trigger, dual front steel swivel studs. Reintroduced 2008. From Winchester Repeating Arms.
Price: **$259.00**
Price: Wildcat/Varmint **$309.00**

ANSCHUTZ 1903 MATCH RIFLE

Caliber: 22 LR, single shot. **Barrel:** 21.25". **Weight:** 8 lbs. **Length:** 43.75" overall. **Stock:** Walnut-finished hardwood with adjustable cheekpiece; stippled grip and forend. **Sights:** None furnished. **Features:** Uses Anschutz Match 64 action. A medium weight rifle for intermediate and advanced Junior Match competition. Available from Champion's Choice.
Price: Right-hand **$965.00**

ANSCHUTZ 64-MP R SILHOUETTE RIFLE

Caliber: 22 LR, 5-shot magazine. **Barrel:** 21.5", medium heavy; 7/8" diameter. **Weight:** 8 lbs. **Length:** 39.5" overall. **Stock:** Walnut-finished hardwood, silhouette-type. **Sights:** None furnished. **Features:** Uses Match 64 action. Designed for metallic silhouette competition. Stock has stippled checkering, contoured thumb groove with Wundhammer swell. Two-stage #5098 trigger. Slide safety locks sear and bolt. Introduced 1980. Available from Champion's Choice.
Price: 64-MP R **$950.00**
Price: 64-S BR Benchrest (2008) **$1,175.00**

Anschutz 2007 Match Rifle

Uses same action as the Model 2013, but has a lighter barrel. European walnut stock in right-hand, true left-hand or extra-short models. Sights optional. Available with 19.6" barrel with extension tube, or 26", both in stainless or blue. Introduced 1998. Available from Champion's Choice.
Price: Right-hand, blue, no sights **$2,410.90**

ANSCHUTZ 1827BT FORTNER BIATHLON RIFLE

Caliber: 22 LR, 5-shot magazine. **Barrel:** 21.7". **Weight:** 8.8 lbs. with sights. **Length:** 40.9" overall. **Stock:** European walnut with cheekpiece, stippled pistol grip and forend. **Sights:** Optional globe front specially designed for Biathlon shooting, micrometer rear with hinged snow cap. **Features:** Uses Super Match 54 action and nine-way adjustable trigger; adjustable wooden buttplate, biathlon butthook, adjustable hand-stop rail. Uses Anschutz/Fortner system straight-pull bolt action, blued or stainless steel barrel. Introduced 1982. Available from Champion's Choice.
Price: Nitride finish with sights, about **$2,895.00**

ANSCHUTZ SUPER MATCH SPECIAL MODEL 2013 RIFLE

Caliber: 22 LR, single shot. **Barrel:** 25.9". **Weight:** 13 lbs. **Length:** 41.7" to 42.9". **Stock:** Adjustable aluminum. **Sights:** None furnished. **Features:** 2313 aluminum-silver/blue stock, 500mm barrel, fast lock time, adjustable cheek piece, heavy action and muzzle tube, w/handstop and standing riser block. Introduced in 1997. Available from Champion's Choice.
Price: Right-hand **$3,195.00**

ANSCHUTZ 1912 SPORT RIFLE

Caliber: 22 LR. **Barrel:** 26" match. **Weight:** 11.4 lbs. **Length:** 41.7" overall. **Stock:** Non-stained thumbhole stock adjustable in length with adjustable butt piece and cheek piece adjustment. Flat forend raiser block 4856 adjustable in height. Hook butt plate. **Sights:** None furnished. **Features:** "Free rifle" for women. Smallbore model 1907 with 1912 **stock:** Match 54 action. Delivered with: Hand stop 6226, forend raiser block 4856, screw driver, instruction leaflet with test target. Available from Champion's Choice.
Price: **$2,595.00**

Anschutz 1913 Super Match Rifle
Same as the Model 1911 except European walnut International-type stock with adjustable cheekpiece, or color laminate, both available with straight or lowered forend, adjustable aluminum hook buttplate, adjustable hand stop, weighs 13 lbs., 46" overall. Stainless or blue barrel. Available from Champion's Choice.
Price: Right-hand, blue, no sights, walnut stock **$2,695.00**

Anschutz 1907 Standard Match Rifle

Same action as Model 1913 but with 7/8" diameter 26" barrel (stainless or blue). Length is 44.5" overall, weighs 10.5 lbs. Choice

of stock configurations. Vented forend. Designed for prone and position shooting ISU requirements; suitable for NRA matches. Also available with walnut flat-forend stock for benchrest shooting. Available from Champion's Choice.
Price: Right-hand, blue, no sights. $1,655.00

ARMALITE AR-10(T) RIFLE

Caliber: 308 Win., 10-shot magazine. **Barrel:** 24" target-weight Rock 5R custom. **Weight:** 10.4 lbs. **Length:** 43.5" overall. **Stock:** Green or black composition; N.M. fiberglass handguard tube. **Sights:** Detachable handle, front sight, or scope mount available. Comes with international-style flattop receiver with Picatinny rail. **Features:** National Match two-stage trigger. Forged upper receiver. Receivers hard-coat anodized. Introduced 1995. Made in U.S.A. by ArmaLite, Inc.
Price: Black **$1,912.00**
Price: AR-10, 338 Federal **$1,912.00**

ARMALITE M15A4(T) EAGLE EYE RIFLE

Caliber: 223 Rem., 10-round magazine. **Barrel:** 24" heavy stainless; 1:8" twist. **Weight:** 9.2 lbs. **Length:** 42-3/8" overall. **Stock:** Green or black butt, N.M. fiberglass handguard tube. **Sights:** One-piece international-style flattop receiver with Weaver-type rail, including case deflector. **Features:** Detachable carry handle, front sight and scope mount (30mm or 1") available. Upper and lower receivers have push-type pivot pin, hard coat anodized. Made in U.S.A. by ArmaLite, Inc.
Price: Green or black furniture **$1,296.00**

ARMALITE M15 A4 CARBINE 6.8 & 7.62X39

Caliber: 6.8 Rem, 7.62x39. **Barrel:** 16" chrome-lined with flash suppressor. **Weight:** 7 lbs. **Length:** 26.6". **Features:** Front and rear picatinny rails for mounting optics, two-stage tactical trigger, anodized aluminum/phosphate finish.
Price: **$1,107.00**

BLASER R93 LONG RANGE SPORTER 2 RIFLE

Caliber: 308 Win., 10-shot detachable box magazine. **Barrel:** 24". **Weight:** 10.4 lbs. **Length:** 44" overall. **Stock:** Aluminum with synthetic lining. **Sights:** None furnished; accepts detachable scope mount. **Features:** Straight-pull bolt action with adjustable trigger; fully adjustable stock; quick takedown; corrosion resistant finish. Introduced 1998. Imported from Germany by Blaser USA.
Price: **$3,848.00**

BUSHMASTER A2/A3 TARGET RIFLE
Caliber: 5.56mm, 223 Rem., 30-round magazine **Barrel:** 20", 24". **Weight:** 8.43 lbs. (A2); 8.78 lbs. (A3). **Length:** 39.5" overall (20" barrel). **Stock:** Black composition; A2 type. **Sights:** Adjustable post front, adjustable aperture rear.

Prices given are believed to be accurate at time of publication however, many factors affect retail pricing so exact prices are not possible.

COMPETITION RIFLES—Centerfire & Rimfire

Features: Patterned after Colt M-16A2. Chrome-lined barrel with manganese phosphate exterior. Available in stainless barrel. Made in U.S.A. by Bushmaster Firearms Co.
Price: (A3 type) **$1,135.00**

BUSHMASTER DCM-XR COMPETITION RIFLE
Caliber: 5.56mm, 223 Rem., 10-round magazine. **Barrel:** 20" extra-heavy (1" diameter) barrel with 1.8" twist for heavier competition bullets. **Weight:** About 12 lbs. with balance weights. **Length:** 38.5". **Stock:** NA. **Sights:** A2 rear sight. **Features:** Has special competition rear sight with interchangeable apertures, extra-fine 1/2- or 1/4-MOA windage and elevation adjustments; specially ground front sight post in choice of three widths. Full-length handguards over free-floater barrel tube. Introduced 1998. Made in U.S.A. by Bushmaster Firearms, Inc.
Price: A2 . . . . **$1,150.00**
Price: A3 . . . . **$1,250.00**

BUSHMASTER VARMINTER RIFLE
Caliber: 5.56mm. **Barrel:** 24", fluted. **Weight:** 8.4 lbs. **Length:** 42.25" overall. **Stock:** Black composition, A2 type. **Sights:** None furnished; upper receiver has integral scope mount base. **Features:** Chrome-lined .950" extra heavy barrel with counter-bored crown, manganese phosphate finish, free-floating aluminum handguard, forged aluminum receivers with push-pin takedown, hard anodized mil-spec finish. Competition trigger optional. Made in U.S.A. by Bushmaster Firearms, Inc.
Price: **$1,360.00**

COLT MATCH TARGET HBAR & M4 RIFLES
Caliber: 223 Rem. **Barrel:** 20". **Weight:** 8 lbs. **Length:** 39" overall. **Stock:** Synthetic. **Sights:** Front: elevation adj. post; rear: 800-meter, aperture adj. for windage and elevation. **Features:** Heavy barrel, rate of rifling twist 1:7. Introduced 1991. Made in U.S.A. by Colt. M4 variant has 16.1" barrel.
Price: Model MT6601, MT6601C **$1,183.00**
Price: Model 6400C **$1,289.00**

Colt Match Target Competition HBAR Rifle
Similar to the Match Target except has removable carry handle for scope mounting, 1:9" rifling twist, 9-round magazine. Weighs 8.5 lbs. Introduced 1991.
Price: Model MT6700C **$1,250.00**

Colt Match Target Competition HBAR II Rifle
Similar to the Match Target Competition HBAR except has 16:1" barrel, overall length 34.5", and weighs 7.1 lbs. Introduced 1995.
Price: Model MT6731 . . . . **$1,172.00**

Colt Accurized Rifle
Similar to the Match Target Model except has 24" barrel. Features flat-top receiver for scope mounting, stainless steel heavy barrel, tubular handguard, and free-floating barrel. Matte black finish. Weighs 9.25 lbs. Made in U.S.A. by Colt's Mfg. Co., Inc.
Price: Model CR6724 . . . . **$1,334.00**

EAA/HW 660 MATCH RIFLE
Caliber: 22 LR. **Barrel:** 26". **Weight:** 10.7 lbs. **Length:** 45.3" overall. **Stock:** Match-type walnut with adjustable cheekpiece and buttplate. **Sights:** Globe front, match aperture rear. **Features:** Adjustable match trigger; stippled pistol grip and forend; forend accessory rail. Introduced 1991. Imported from Germany by European American Armory.
Price: About **$999.00**
Price: With laminate stock **$1,159.00**

ED BROWN MODEL 704, M40A2 MARINE SNIPER
Caliber: 308 Win., 30-06 Springfield. **Barrel:** Match-grade 24". **Weight:** 9.25 lbs. **Stock:** Hand bedded McMillan GP fiberglass tactical stock with recoil pad in special Woodland Camo molded-in colors. **Sights:** None furnished. Leupold Mark 4 30mm scope mounts with heavy-duty screws. **Features:** Steel trigger guard, hinged floor plate, three position safety.
Price: From **$3,695.00**

OLYMPIC ARMS SM SERVICEMATCH AR15 RIFLES
Caliber: 223 Rem. minimum SAAMI spec, 30-shot magazine. **Barrel:** 20" broach-cut Ultramatch stainless steel 1x8 twist rate. **Weight:** 10 lbs. **Length:** 39.5" overall. **Stock:** A2 grip, A2 buttstock with trapdoor. **Sights:** A2 NM rear, elevation adjustable front post. **Features:** DCM-ready AR15, free-floating handguard looks standard, A2 upper, threaded muzzle, flash suppressor. Premium model adds pneumatic recoil buffer, Bob Jones interchangeable sights, two-stage trigger and Turner Saddlery sling. Made in U.S.A. by Olympic Arms, Inc.
Price: SM-1, 20" DCM ready **$1,272.70**
Price: SM-1P, Premium 20" DCM ready **$1,727.70**

OLYMPIC ARMS UM ULTRAMATCH AR15 RIFLES
Caliber: 223 Rem. minimum SAAMI spec, 30-shot magazine. **Barrel:** 20" or 24" bull broach-cut Ultramatch stainless steel 1x10 twist rate. **Weight:** 8-10 lbs. **Length:** 38.25" overall. **Stock:** A2 grip, A2 buttstock with trapdoor. **Sights:** None, flat-top upper and gas block with rails. **Features:** Flat top upper, free floating tubular match handguard, Picatinny gas block, crowned muzzle, factory trigger job and "Ultramatch" pantograph. Premium model adds pneumatic recoil buffer, Harris S-series bipod, hand selected premium receivers and William Set Trigger. Made in U.S.A. by Olympic Arms, Inc.
Price: UM-1, 20" Ultramatch **$1,332.50**
Price: UM-1P **$1,805.70**

OLYMPIC ARMS ML-1/ML-2 MULTIMATCH AR15 CARBINES
Caliber: 223 Rem. minimum SAAMI spec, 30-shot magazine. **Barrel:** 16" broach-cut Ultramatch stainless steel 1x10 twist rate. **Weight:** 7-8 lbs. **Length:** 34-36" overall. **Stock:** A2 grip and varying buttstock. **Sights:** None. **Features:** The ML-1 includes A2 upper

with adjustable rear sight, elevation adjustable front post, free floating tubular match handguard, bayonet lug, threaded muzzle, flash suppressor and M4 6-point collapsible buttstock. The ML-2 includes bull diameter barrel, flat top upper, free floating tubular match handguard, Picatinny gas block, crowned muzzle and A2 buttstock with trapdoor. Made in U.S.A. by Olympic Arms, Inc.

Price: ML-1 or ML-2 . . . . **$1,188.20**

OLYMPIC ARMS K8 TARGETMATCH AR15 RIFLES

Caliber: 5.56 NATO, 223 WSSM, 243 WSSM, .25 WSSM 30/7-shot magazine. **Barrel:** 20", 24" bull button-rifled stainless/chrome-moly steel 1x9/1x10 twist rate. **Weight:** 8-10 lbs. **Length:** 38"-42" overall. **Stock:** A2 grip, A2 buttstock with trapdoor. **Sights:** None. **Features:** Barrel has satin bead-blast finish; flat-top upper, free-floating tubular match handguard, Picatinny gas block, crowned muzzle and "Targetmatch" pantograph on lower receiver. K8-MAG model uses Winchester Super Short Magnum cartridges. Includes 24" bull chrome-moly barrel, flat-top upper, free-floating tubular match handguard, Picatinny gas block, crowned muzzle and 7-shot magazine. Made in U.S.A. by Olympic Arms, Inc.

Price: K8 . . . .**$908.70**
Price: K8-MAG **$1,363.70**

REMINGTON 40-XB RANGEMASTER TARGET CENTERFIRE

Caliber: 15 calibers from 220 Swift to 300 Win. Mag. **Barrel:** 27.25". **Weight:** 11.25 lbs. **Length:** 47" overall. **Stock:** American walnut, laminated thumbhole or Kevlar with high comb and beavertail forend stop. Rubber non-slip buttplate. **Sights:** None. Scope blocks installed. **Features:** Adjustable trigger. Stainless barrel and action. Receiver drilled and tapped for sights. Model 40-XB Tactical (2008) chambered in 308 Win., comes with guarantee of 0.75-inch maximum 5-shot groups at 100 yards. **Weight:** 10.25 lbs. Includes Teflon-coated stainless button-rifled barrel, 1:14 twist, 27.25 inch long, three longitudinal flutes. Bolt-action repeater, adjustable 40-X trigger and precision machined aluminum bedding block. Stock is H-S Precision Pro Series synthetic tactical stock, black with green web finish, vertical pistol grip. From Remington Custom Shop.

Price: 40-XB KS, aramid fiber stock, single shot **$2,780.00**
Price: 40-XB KS, aramid fiber stock, repeater **$2,634.00**
Price: 40-XB Tactical 308 Win. (2008) **$2,927.00**
Price: 40-XB Thumbhole Repeater. **$2,927.00**

REMINGTON 40-XBBR KS

Caliber: Five calibers from 22 BR to 308 Win. **Barrel:** 20" (light varmint class), 24" (heavy varmint class). **Weight:** 7.25 lbs. (light varmint class); 12 lbs. (heavy varmint class). **Length:** 38" (20" bbl.), 42" (24"bbl.). **Stock:** Aramid fiber. **Sights:** None. Supplied with scope blocks. **Features:** Unblued benchrest with stainless steel barrel, trigger adjustable from 1-1/2 lbs. to 3.5 lbs. Special two-oz. trigger extra cost. Scope and mounts extra.

Price: Single shot **$3,806.00**

REMINGTON 40-XC KS TARGET RIFLE

Caliber: 7.62 NATO, 5-shot. **Barrel:** 24", stainless steel. **Weight:** 11 lbs. without sights. **Length:** 43.5" overall. **Stock:** Aramid fiber. **Sights:** None furnished. **Features:** Designed to meet the needs of competitive shooters. Stainless steel barrel and action.

Price: **$3,000.00**

REMINGTON 40-XR CUSTOM SPORTER

Caliber: 22 LR, 22 WM. **Barrel:** 24" stainless steel, no sights. **Weight:** 9.75 lbs. **Length:** 40". **Features:** Model XR-40 Target rifle action. Many options available in stock, decoration or finish.

Price: Single shot **$4,391.00**

Price: 40-XRBR KS, bench rest 22 LR .   **$2,927.00**

SAKO TRG-22 BOLT-ACTION RIFLE

Caliber: 308 Win., 10-shot magazine. **Barrel:** 26". **Weight:** 10.25 lbs. **Length:** 45.25" overall. **Stock:** Reinforced polyurethane with fully adjustable cheekpiece and buttplate. **Sights:** None furnished. Optional quick-detachable, one-piece scope mount base, 1" or 30mm rings. **Features:** Resistance-free bolt, free-floating heavy stainless barrel, 60-degree bolt lift. Two-stage trigger is adjustable for length, pull, horizontal or vertical pitch. Introduced 2000. Imported from Finland by Beretta USA.

Price: TRG-22 folding stock **$4,560.00**

SPRINGFIELD ARMORY M1A SUPER MATCH

Caliber: 308 Win. **Barrel:** 22", heavy Douglas Premium. **Weight:** About 11 lbs. **Length:** 44.31" overall. **Stock:** Heavy walnut competition stock with longer pistol grip, contoured area behind the rear sight, thicker butt and forend, glass bedded. **Sights:** National Match front and rear. **Features:** Has figure-eight-style operating rod guide. Introduced   1987. From Springfield Armory.

Price: About **$2,479.00**

Springfield Armory M1A/M-21 Tactical Model Rifle

Similar to M1A Super Match except special sniper stock with adjustable cheekpiece and rubber recoil pad. Weighs 11.6 lbs. From Springfield Armory.

Price: . . . .

$2,975.00

SPRINGFIELD ARMORY M-1 GARAND AMERICAN COMBAT RIFLES

Caliber: 30-06 Spfl., 308 Win., 8-shot. **Barrel:** 24". **Weight:** 9.5 lbs. **Length:** 43.6". **Stock:** American walnut. **Sights:** Military square post front, military aperture, MOA adjustable rear. **Features:** Limited production, certificate of authenticity, all new receiver, barrel and stock with remaining parts USGI mil-spec. Two-stage military trigger.

Price: About **$2,479.00**

STONER SR-15 MATCH RIFLE

Caliber: 223. **Barrel:** 20". **Weight:** 7.9 lbs. **Length:** 38" overall. **Stock:** Black synthetic. **Sights:** None furnished; flattop upper receiver for scope mounting. **Features:** Short Picatinny rail, two-stage match trigger. Introduced 1998. Made in U.S.A. by Knight's Mfg. Co.

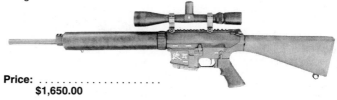

Price: . . . .
$1,650.00

STONER SR-25 MATCH RIFLE
Caliber: 7.62 NATO, 10-shot steel magazine, 5-shot optional. **Barrel:** 24" heavy match; 1:11.25" twist. **Weight:** 10.75 lbs. **Length:** 44" overall. **Stock:** Black synthetic AR-15A2 design. Full floating forend of mil-spec synthetic attaches to upper receiver at a single point. **Sights:** None furnished. Has integral Weaver-style rail. Rings and iron sights optional. **Features:** Improved AR-15 trigger, AR-15-style seven-lug rotating bolt. Introduced 1993. Made in U.S.A. by Knight's Mfg. Co.
Price: **$3,345.00**
Price: SR-25 Lightweight Match (20" medium match target contour barrel, 9.5 lbs., 40" overall) **$3,345.00**

TIME PRECISION 22 RF BENCH REST RIFLE
Caliber: 22 LR, single shot. **Barrel:** Shilen match-grade stainless. **Weight:** 10 lbs. with scope. **Length:** NA. **Stock:** Fiberglass. Pillar bedded. **Sights:** None furnished. **Features:** Shilen match trigger removable trigger bracket, full-length steel sleeve, aluminum receiver. Introduced 2008. Made in U.S.A. by Time Precision.
Price: **$2,200.00**

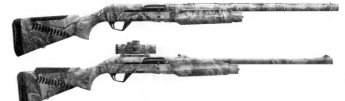

Price: 24", 26", 28" $1,219.00

Price: 24", 26", 28" $1,219.00
Price: Left hand. $1,229.00
Price: 20 ga. $1,219.00
Price: 20 ga. short stock (LOP: 12.5") $1,120.00
Price: Silver (AA walnut; nickel-blue receiver) $1,649.00
Price: Silver 20 ga. $1,649.00

BENELLI LEGACY SHOTGUN

Gauge: 12, 20, 2-3/4" and 3" chamber. **Barrel:** 24", 26", 28" (Full, Mod., Imp. Cyl., Imp. Mod., cylinder choke tubes). Mid-bead sight. **Weight:** 5.8 to 7.4 lbs. **Length:** 49-5/8" overall (28" barrel). **Stock:** Select AA European walnut with satin finish. **Features:** Uses the rotating bolt inertia recoil operating system with a two-piece steel/aluminum etched receiver (bright on lower, blue upper). Drop adjustment kit allows the stock to be custom fitted without modifying the stock. Introduced 1998. Ultralight model has gloss-blued finish receiver. Weight is 6.0 lbs., 24" barrel, 45.5" overall length. WeatherCoat walnut stock. Introduced 2006. Imported from Italy by Benelli USA, Corp.

Price: Legacy $1,689.00
Price: Sport (2008) $2,269.00

BENELLI ULTRA LIGHT SHOTGUN

Gauge: 12, 20, 3" chamber. **Barrel:** 28". Mid-bead sight. **Weight:** 5.2 to 6 lbs. **Features:** Similar to Legacy line. Drop adjustment kit allows the stock to be custom fitted without modifying the stock. WeatherCoat walnut stock. Lightened receiver, shortened magazine tube, carbon-fiber rib and grip cap. Introduced 2008. Imported from Italy by Benelli USA, Corp.

Price: 12 gauge. $1,539.00

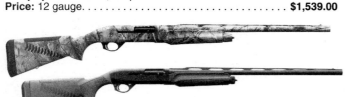

BENELLI M2 FIELD SHOTGUNS

Gauge: 20 ga., 12 ga., 3" chamber. **Barrel:** 21", 24", 26", 28". **Weight:** 5.4 to 7.2 lbs. **Length:** 42.5 to 49.5" overall. **Stock:** Synthetic, Advantage Max-4 HD, Advantage Timber HD, APG HD. **Sights:** Red bar. **Features:** Uses the Inertia Driven bolt mechanism. Vent rib. Comes with set of five choke tubes. Imported from Italy by Benelli USA.

Price: Synthetic ComforTech gel recoil pad $1,319.00
Price: Camo ComforTech gel recoil pad. $1,335.00
Price: Satin walnut $1,229.00
Price: Rifled slug synthetic $1,380.00
Price: Camo turkey model w/SteadyGrip stock $1,429.00
Price: Realtree APG HD ComforTech stock (2007) $1,429.00
Price: Realtree APG HD ComforTech 20 ga. (2007) $1,429.00
Price: Realtree APG HD LH ComforTech (2007) $1,429.00
Price: Realtree APG HD ComforTech Slug (2007). $1,429.00
Price: Realtree APG HD w/SteadyGrip stock (2007) $1,429.00
Price: Black Synthetic Grip Tight 20 ga. (2007) $1,319.00

BENELLI M4 TACTICAL SHOTGUN

Gauge: 12 ga., 3" chamber. **Barrel:** 18.5". **Weight:** 7.8 lbs. **Length:** 40" overall. **Stock:** Synthetic. **Sights:** Ghost Ring rear, fixed blade front. **Features:** Auto-regulating gas-operated (ARGO) action, choke tube, Picatinny rail, standard and collapsible stocks available, optional LE tactical gun case. Introduced 2006. Imported from Italy by Benelli USA.

Price: Pistol grip stock, black synthetic. $1,699.00
Price: Desert camo pistol grip (2007) $1,829.00

BENELLI MONTEFELTRO SHOTGUNS

Gauge: 12 and 20 ga. Full, Imp. Mod, Mod., Imp. Cyl., Cyl. choke tubes. **Barrel:** 24", 26", 28". **Weight:** 5.3 to 7.1 lbs. **Stock:** Checkered walnut with satin finish. **Length:** 43.6 to 49.5" overall. **Features:** Uses the Inertia Driven rotating bolt system with a simple inertia recoil design. Finish is blue. Introduced 1987.

BENELLI SUPER BLACK EAGLE II SHOTGUNS

Gauge: 12, 3-1/2" chamber. **Barrel:** 24", 26", 28" (Cyl. Imp. Cyl., Mod., Imp. Mod., Full choke tubes). **Weight:** 7.1 to 7.3 lbs. **Length:** 45.6 to 49.6" overall. **Stock:** European walnut with satin finish, polymer, or camo. Adjustable for drop. **Sights:** Red bar front. **Features:** Uses Benelli inertia recoil bolt system. Vent rib. Advantage Max-4 HD, Advantage Timber HD camo patterns. Features ComforTech stock. Introduced 1991. Left-hand models available. Imported from Italy by Benelli USA.

Price: Satin walnut, non-ComforTech. $1,549.00
Price: Camo stock, ComforTech gel recoil pad $1,759.00
Price: Black Synthetic stock $1,649.00
Price: Max-4 HD Camo stock $1,759.00
Price: Timber HD turkey model w/SteadyGrip stock. $1,680.00
Price: Realtree APG HD w/ComforTech stock (2007) $1,759.00
Price: Realtree APG HD LH ComforTech stock (2007) $1,759.00
Price: Realtree APG HD Slug Gun (2007) $1,730.00

BENELLI CORDOBA SHOTGUN

Gauge: 20; 12; 3" chamber. **Barrel:** 28" and 30", ported, 10mm sporting rib. **Weight:** 7.2 to 7.3 lbs. **Length:** 49.6 to 51.6". **Features:** Designed for high-volume sporting clays and Argentina dove shooting. Inertia-driven action, Extended Sport CrioChokes, 4+1 capacity. Ported. Imported from Italy by Benelli USA.

Price: Black synthetic GripTight ComforTech stock $1,869.00
Price: Black synthetic GripTight ComforTech stock, 20 ga., (2007) $1,869.00
Price: Max-4 HD ComforTech stock (2007) $2,039.00

BENELLI SUPERSPORT & SPORT II SHOTGUNS

Gauge: 20; 12; 3" chamber. **Barrel:** 28" and 30", ported, 10mm sporting rib. **Weight:** 7.2 to 7.3 lbs. **Length:** 49.6 to 51.6". **Stock:** Carbon fiber, ComforTech (Supersport) or walnut (Sport II). **Sights:** Red bar front, metal midbead. Sport II is similar to the Legacy model except has nonengraved dual tone blue/silver receiver, ported wide-rib barrel, adjustable buttstock, and functions with all loads. Walnut stock with satin finish. Introduced 1997. **Features:** Designed for high-volume sporting clays. Inertia-driven action, Extended CrioChokes, 4+1 capacity. Ported. Imported from Italy by Benelli USA.

Price: Carbon fiber ComforTech stock $1,979.00
Price: Carbon fiber ComforTech stock, 20 ga. (2007) $1,979.00
Price: Sport II 20 ga. (2007) $1,699.00

BENELLI VINCI

Gas-operated semiauto shotgun chambered for 2-3/4- and 3-inch 12-gauge. Features include modular disassembly; interchangeable choke tubes; 24- to 28-inch ribbed barrel; black, MAX-4HD or APG HD finish; synthetic contoured stocks; optional Steady-Grip model;. Weight 6.7 to 6.9 lbs.

Price: .... $1379.00 to $1599.00

BENELLI LEGACY SPORT

Gas-operated semiauto shotgun chambered for 12, 20 (2-3/4- and 3-inch) gauge. Features include Inertia Driven system; sculptured lower receiver with classic game scene etchings; highly polished

blued upper receiver; AA-Grade walnut stock; gel recoil pad; ported 24- or 26-inch barrel, Crio chokes. Weight 7.4 to 7.5 lbs.

Price: **$2,369.00**

BERETTA 3901 SHOTGUNS

Gauge: 12, 20 gauge; 3" chamber, semiauto. **Barrel:** 26", 28". **Weight:** 6.55 lbs. (20 ga.), 7.2 lbs. (12 ga.). **Length:** NA. **Stock:** Wood, X-tra wood (special process wood enhancement), and polymer. **Features:** Based on A390 shotgun introduced in 1996. Mobilchokes, removable trigger group. 3901 Target RL uses gas operating system; Sporting style flat rib with steel front bead and mid-bead, walnut stock and forearm, satin matte finish, adjustable LOP from 12P13", adjustable for cast on/off, Beretta's Memory System II to adjust the parallel comb. Weighs 7.2 lbs. 3901 Citizen has polymer stock. 3901 Statesman has basic wood and checkering treatment. 3901 Ambassador has X-tra wood stock and fore end; high-polished receiver with engraving, Gel-Tek recoil pad, optional TruGlo fiber-optic front sight. 3901 Rifled Slug Shotgun has black high-impact synthetic stock and fore end, 24" barrel,1:28 twist, Picatinny cantilever rail. Introduced 2006. Made in U.S. by Beretta USA.

Price: 3901 Target RL............................... **$900.00**
Price: 3901 Citizen, synthetic or wood, from **$750.00**
Price: 3901 Statesman **$900.00**
Price: 3901 Rifled Slug Shotgun...................... **$800.00**

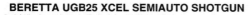

BERETTA UGB25 XCEL SEMIAUTO SHOTGUN

Gauge: 12, 2-3/4" chambers. **Barrel:** 28", 30", 32"; competition-style interchangeable vent rib; Optima choke tubes. **Weight:** 7.7-9 lbs. **Stock:** High-grade walnut with oil finish; hand-checkered grip and forend, adjustable. **Features:** Break-open semiautomatic. High-resistance fiberglass-reinforced technopolymer trigger plate, self-lubricating firing mechanism. Rounded alloy receiver, polished sides, external cartridge carrier and feeding port, bottom eject. two technopolymer recoil dampers on breech bolt, double recoil dampers located in the receiver, Beretta Recoil Reduction System, recoil-absorbing Beretta Gel Tek recoil pad. Optima-Bore barrel with a lengthened forcing cone, Optimachoke and Extended Optimachoke tubes. Steel-shot capable, interchangeable aluminum alloy top rib. Introduced 2006. Imported from Italy by Beretta USA.

Price: **$3,875.00**

BERETTA A400 XPLOR UNICO SEMIAUTO SHOTGUN

Self-regulation gas-operated shotgun chambered to shoot all 12-ga. loads from 2-3/4 to 3.5 inches. Features include Kick-Off3 hydraulic damper; 26- or 28-inch "Steelium" barrel with interchangeable choke tubes; anodized aluminum receiver; sculpted, checkered walnut buttstock and forend.

Price: **$1625.00**

BERETTA AL391 TEKNYS SHOTGUNS

Gauge: 12, 20 gauge; 3" chamber, semiauto. **Barrel:** 26", 28". **Weight:** 5.9 lbs. (20 ga.), 7.3 lbs. (12 ga.). **Length:** NA. **Stock:** X-tra wood (special process wood enhancement). **Features:** Flat 1/4 rib, TruGlo Tru-Bead sight, recoil reducer, stock spacers, overbored bbls., flush choke tubes. Comes with fitted, lined case.
Price: From.. **$2,050.00**

BERETTA AL391 URIKA AND URIKA 2 AUTO SHOTGUNS

Gauge: 12, 20 gauge; 3" chamber. **Barrel:** 22", 24", 26", 28", 30"; five Mobilchoke choke tubes. **Weight:** 5.95 to 7.28 lbs. **Length:** Varies by model. **Stock:** Walnut, black or camo synthetic; shims, spacers and interchangeable recoil pads allow custom fit. **Features:** Self-

compensating gas operation handles full range of loads; recoil reducer in receiver; enlarged trigger guard; reduced-weight receiver, barrel and forend; hard-chromed bore. Introduced 2000. AL391 Urika 2 (2007) has self-cleaning action, X-Tra Grain stock finish. AL391 Urika 2 Gold has higher-grade select oil-finished wood stock, upgraded engraving (gold-filled gamebirds on field models, gold-filled laurel leaf on competition version). Kick-Off recoil reduction system available in Synthetic, Realtree Advantage Max-4 and AP models. Imported from Italy by Beretta USA.

Price: Urika 2 X-tra Grain, from **$1,400.00**
Price: Urika 2 Gold, from **$1,550.00**
Price: Urika 2 Synthetic **$975.00**
Price: Urika 2 Realtree AP Kick-Off,............... **$1,350.00**

BERETTA A391 XTREMA2 3.5 AUTO SHOTGUNS

Gauge: 12 ga. 3.5" chamber. **Barrel:** 24", 26", 28". **Weight:** 7.8 lbs. **Stock:** Synthetic. **Features:** Semiauto goes with two-lug rotating bolt and self-compensating gas valve, extended tang, cross bolt safety, self-cleaning, with case.
Price: From **$1,250.00**

BREDA GRIZZLY

Gauge: 12, 3.5" chamber. **Barrel:** 28". **Weight:** 7.2 lbs. **Stock:** Black synthetic or Advantage Timber with matching metal parts. **Features:** Chokes tubes are Mod., IC, Full; inertia-type action, four-round magazine. Imported from Italy by Legacy Sports International.
Price: Blued/black (2008) **$1,826.00**
Price: Advantage Timber Camo (2008) **$2,121.00**

BREDA XANTHOS

Gauge: 12, 3" chamber. **Barrel:** 28". **Weight:** 6.5 lbs. **Stock:** High grade walnut. **Features:** Chokes tubes are Mod., IC, Full; inertia-type action, four-round magazine, spark engraving with hand-engraved details and hand-gilding figures on receiver. Blued, Grey or Chrome finishes. Imported from Italy by Legacy Sports International.
Price: Blued (2007).............................. **$2,309.00**
Price: Grey (2007) **$2,451.00**
Price: Chrome (2007) **$3,406.00**

BREDA ECHO

Gauge: 12, 20. 3" chamber. **Barrel:** 28". **Weight:** 6.0-6.5 lbs. **Stock:** Walnut. **Features:** Chokes tubes are Mod., IC, Full; inertia-type action, four-round magazine, blue, grey or nickel finishes, modern engraving, fully checkered pistol grip. Imported from Italy by Legacy Sports International.
Price: Blued, 12 ga. (2008).......................... **$1,897.00**
Price: Grey, 12 ga. (2008) **$1,969.00**
Price: Nickel, 12 ga. (2008) **$2,214.00**
Price: Nickel, 20 ga. (2008) **$2,214.00**

BREDA ALTAIR

Gauge: 12, 20. 3" chamber. **Barrel:** 28". **Weight:** 5.7-6.1 lbs. **Stock:** Oil-rubbed walnut. **Features:** Chokes tubes are Mod., IC, Full; gas-actuated action, four-round magazine, blued finish, lightweight frame. Imported from Italy by Legacy Sports International.
Price: Blued, 12 ga. (2008).......................... **$1,320.00**
Price: Grey, 20 ga. (2008) **$1,320.00**

BROWNING GOLD AUTO SHOTGUNS

Gauge: 12, 3" or 3-1/2" chamber; 20, 3" chamber. **Barrel:** 12 ga.-26", 28", 30", Invector Plus choke tubes; 20 ga.-26", 30", Invector choke tubes. **Weight:** 7 lbs., 9 oz. (12 ga.), 6 lbs., 12 oz. (20 ga.). **Length:** 46.25" overall (20 ga., 26" barrel). **Stock:** 14"x1.5"x2-1/3"; select walnut with gloss finish; palm swell grip. **Features:** Self-regulating, self-cleaning gas system shoots all loads; lightweight receiver with special non-glare deep black finish; large reversible safety button;

SHOTGUNS—Autoloaders

large rounded trigger guard, gold trigger. The 20 gauge has slightly smaller dimensions; 12 gauge have back-bored barrels, Invector Plus tube system. Introduced 1994. Gold Evolve shotguns have new rib design, HiViz sights. Imported by Browning.

Price: Gold Evolve Sporting, 12 ga., 2-3/4" chamber **$1,326.00**
Price: Gold Superlite Hunter, 12 or 20 ga., 26" or
28" barrel, 6.6 lbs **$1,161.00**

BROWNING GOLD NWTF TURKEY SERIES AND MOSSY OAK SHOTGUNS

Gauge: 12, 10, 3-1/2" chamber. Similar to the Gold Hunter except has specialized camouflage patterns, including National Wild Turkey Federation design. Includes extra-full choke tube and HiViz fiber-optic sights on some models and Dura-Touch coating. Camouflage patterns include Mossy Oak New Break-Up (NBU) or Mossy Oak New Shadow Grass (NSG). NWTF models include NWTF logo on stock. Introduced 2001. From Browning.

Price: NWFT Gold Ultimate Turkey, 24" barrel, 12 ga.
3-1/2" chamber **$1,513.00**
Price: NWFT Gold 10 Gauge, 24" barrel, 3-1/2" chamber . . **$1,639.00**

BROWNING GOLD GOLDEN CLAYS AUTO SHOTGUNS

Gauge: 12, 2-3/4" chamber. **Barrel:** 28", 30", Invector Plus choke tubes. **Weight:** about 7.75 lbs. **Length:** From 47.75 to 50.5". **Stock:** Select walnut with gloss finish; palm swell grip, shim adjustable. **Features:** Ported barrels, "Golden Clays" models feature gold inlays and engraving. Imported by Browning.

Price: Gold "Golden Clays" Sporting Clays, intr. 2005 . . . . . **$1,941.00**

Browning Gold Light 10 Gauge Auto Shotgun

Similar to the Gold Hunter except has an alloy receiver that is 1 lb. lighter than standard model. Offered in 26" or 28" bbls. With Mossy Oak Break-Up or Shadow Grass coverage; 5-shot magazine. Weighs 9 lbs., 10 oz. (28" bbl). Introduced 2001. Imported by Browning.

Price: Camo model only **$1,509.00**

BROWNING SILVER AUTO SHOTGUNS

Gauge: 12, 3" or 3-1/2" chamber; 20, 3" chamber. **Barrel:** 12 ga.-26", 28", 30", Invector Plus choke tubes. **Weight:** 7 lbs., 9 oz. (12 ga.), 6 lbs., 7 oz. (20 ga.). Stock: Satin finish walnut. Features: Active Valve gas system, semi-humpback receiver. Invector Plus tube system, three choke tubes. Imported by Browning.

Price: Silver Hunter, 12 ga., 3.5" chamber **$1,239.00**
Price: Silver Hunter, 20 ga., 3" chamber, intr. 2008 . . . . . . **$1,079.00**
Price: Silver Micro, 20 ga., 3" chamber, intr. 2008 . . . . **$1,079.00**
Price: Silver Sporting, 12 ga., 2-3/4" chamber,
intr. 2009 . . . . **$1,199.00**
Price: Silver Sporting Micro, 12 ga., 2-3/4" chamber,
intr. 2008 . . . . **$1,199.00**
Price: Silver Rifled Deer, Mossy Oak New Break-Up,
12 ga., 3" chamber, intr. 2008 . . . . **$1,319.00**
Price: Silver Rifled Deer Stalker, 12 ga., 3" chamber,
intr. 2008 . . . . **$1,169.00**
Price: Silver Rifled Deer Satin, satin-finished aluminum
alloy receiver and satin-finished walnut buttstock
and forend **$1,229.00**
Price: Silver Stalker, black composite buttstock and forend **$1,179.00**

BROWNING MAXUS

Gauge: 12; 3" or 3.5" chambers. **Barrel:** 26" or 28". **Weight:** 6-7/8 lbs. **Length:** 47.25" to 49.25". **Stock:** Composite with close radius pistol grip. **Features:** Aluminum receiver, lightweight profile barrel with

---

vent rib, Vector Pro lengthened forcing cone, DuraTouch Armor Coating overall. Handles shorter shells interchangeably.

Price: Stalker, matte black finish overall, 3-1/2" **$1,379.00**
Price: Stalker, matte black finish overall, 3" **$1,199.00**
Price: Mossy Oak Duck Blind overall, 3-1/2" **$1,499.00**
Price: Mossy Oak Duck Blind overall, 3" **$1,339.00**

CHARLES DALY FIELD SEMIAUTO SHOTGUNS

Gauge: 12, 20, 28. **Barrel:** 22", 24", 26", 28" or 30". **Stock:** Synthetic black, Realtree Hardwoods or Advantage Timber. **Features:** Interchangeable barrels handle all loads including steel shot. Slug model has adjustable sights. Maxi-Mag is 3.5" chamber.

Price: Field Hunter, from **$489.00**

CHARLES DALY SUPERIOR II SEMIAUTO SHOTGUNS

Gauge: 12, 20, 28. **Barrel:** 26", 28" or 30". **Stock:** Select Turkish walnut. **Features:** Factory ported interchangeable barrels; wide vent rib on Trap and Sport models; fluorescent red sights.

Price: Superior II Hunter, from **$649.00**
Price: Superior II Sport **$709.00**
Price: Superior II Trap **$739.00**

ESCORT SEMIAUTO SHOTGUNS

Gauge: 12, 20; 3" or 3.5" chambers. **Barrel:** 22" (Youth), 26" and 28". **Weight:** 6.7-7.8 lbs. **Stock:** Polymer in black, Shadow Grass® or Obsession® camo finish, Turkish walnut, select walnut. **Sights:** Optional HiViz Spark front. **Features:** Black-chrome or dipped-camo metal parts, top of receiver dovetailed for sight mounts, gold plated trigger, trigger guard safety, magazine cut-off. Three choke tubes (IC, M, F) except the Waterfowl/Turkey Combo, which adds a .665 turkey choke to the standard three. Waterfowl/Turkey combo is two-barrel set, 24"/26" and 26"/28". Several models have Trio recoil pad. Models are: AS, AS Select, AS Youth, AS Youth Select, PS, PS Spark and Waterfowl/Turkey. Introduced 2002. Camo introduced 2003. Youth, Slug and Obsession camo introduced 2005. Imported from Turkey by Legacy Sports International.

Price: . . . . **$425.00 to $589.00**

FRANCHI INERTIA I-12 SHOTGUN

Gauge: 12, 3" chamber. **Barrel:** 24", 26", 28" (Cyl., IC, Mod., IM, F choke tubes). **Weight:** 7.5 to 7.7 lbs. **Length:** 45" to 49". **Stock:** 14-3.8" LOP, satin walnut with checkered grip and forend, synthetic, Advantage Timber HD or Max-4 camo patterns. **Features:** Inertia-Driven action. AA walnut stock. Red bar front sight, metal mid sight. Imported from Italy by Benelli USA.

Price: Synthetic **$839.00**
Price: Camo **$949.00**
Price: Satin walnut **$949.00**

FRANCHI MODEL 720 SHOTGUNS

Gauge: 20, 3" chamber. **Barrel:** 24", 26", 28" w/(IC, Mod., F choke tubes). **Weight:** 5.9 to 6.1 lbs. **Length:** 43.25" to 49". **Stock:** WeatherCoat finish walnut, Max-4 and Timber HD camo. **Sights:** Front bead. **Features:** Made in Italy and imported by Benelli USA.

Price: **$1,049.00**
Price: Walnut, 12.5" LOP, 43.25" OAL **$999.00**

Prices given are believed to be accurate at time of publication however, many factors affect retail pricing so exact prices are not possible.

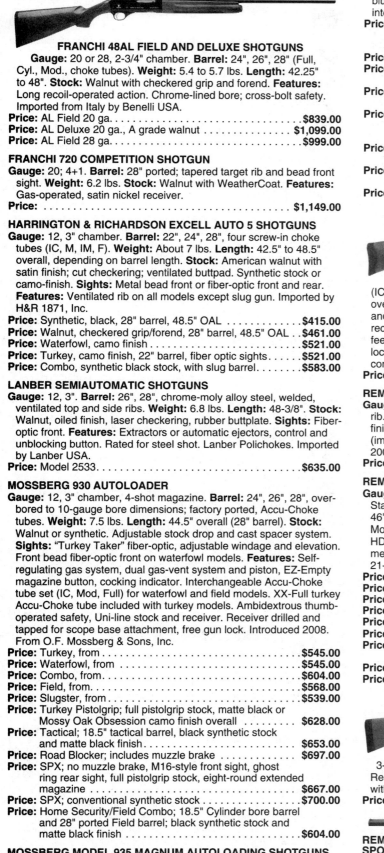

FRANCHI 48AL FIELD AND DELUXE SHOTGUNS
Gauge: 20 or 28, 2-3/4" chamber. **Barrel:** 24", 26", 28" (Full, Cyl., Mod., choke tubes). **Weight:** 5.4 to 5.7 lbs. **Length:** 42.25" to 48". **Stock:** Walnut with checkered grip and forend. **Features:** Long recoil-operated action. Chrome-lined bore; cross-bolt safety. Imported from Italy by Benelli USA.
Price: AL Field 20 ga. $839.00
Price: AL Deluxe 20 ga., A grade walnut $1,099.00
Price: AL Field 28 ga. $999.00

FRANCHI 720 COMPETITION SHOTGUN
Gauge: 20; 4+1. **Barrel:** 28" ported; tapered target rib and bead front sight. **Weight:** 6.2 lbs. **Stock:** Walnut with WeatherCoat. **Features:** Gas-operated, satin nickel receiver.
Price: $1,149.00

HARRINGTON & RICHARDSON EXCELL AUTO 5 SHOTGUNS
Gauge: 12, 3" chamber. **Barrel:** 22", 24", 28", four screw-in choke tubes (IC, M, IM, F). **Weight:** About 7 lbs. **Length:** 42.5" to 48.5" overall, depending on barrel length. **Stock:** American walnut with satin finish; cut checkering; ventilated buttpad. Synthetic stock or camo-finish. **Sights:** Metal bead front or fiber-optic front and rear. **Features:** Ventilated rib on all models except slug gun. Imported by H&R 1871, Inc.
Price: Synthetic, black, 28" barrel, 48.5" OAL $415.00
Price: Walnut, checkered grip/forend, 28" barrel, 48.5" OAL . .$461.00
Price: Waterfowl, camo finish $521.00
Price: Turkey, camo finish, 22" barrel, fiber optic sights $521.00
Price: Combo, synthetic black stock, with slug barrel $583.00

LANBER SEMIAUTOMATIC SHOTGUNS
Gauge: 12, 3". **Barrel:** 26", 28", chrome-moly alloy steel, welded, ventilated top and side ribs. **Weight:** 6.8 lbs. **Length:** 48-3/8". **Stock:** Walnut, oiled finish, laser checkering, rubber buttplate. **Sights:** Fiber-optic front. **Features:** Extractors or automatic ejectors, control and unblocking button. Rated for steel shot. Lanber Polichokes. Imported by Lanber USA.
Price: Model 2533. . . . .$635.00

MOSSBERG 930 AUTOLOADER
Gauge: 12, 3" chamber, 4-shot magazine. **Barrel:** 24", 26", 28", over-bored to 10-gauge bore dimensions; factory ported, Accu-Choke tubes. **Weight:** 7.5 lbs. **Length:** 44.5" overall (28" barrel). **Stock:** Walnut or synthetic. Adjustable stock drop and cast spacer system. **Sights:** "Turkey Taker" fiber-optic, adjustable windage and elevation. Front bead fiber-optic front on waterfowl models. **Features:** Self-regulating gas system, dual gas-vent system and piston, EZ-Empty magazine button, cocking indicator. Interchangeable Accu-Choke tube set (IC, Mod, Full) for waterfowl and field models. XX-Full turkey Accu-Choke tube included with turkey models. Ambidextrous thumb-operated safety, Uni-line stock and receiver. Receiver drilled and tapped for scope base attachment, free gun lock. Introduced 2008. From O.F. Mossberg & Sons, Inc.
Price: Turkey, from $545.00
Price: Waterfowl, from $545.00
Price: Combo, from. $604.00
Price: Field, from. $568.00
Price: Slugster, from $539.00
Price: Turkey Pistolgrip; full pistolgrip stock, matte black or Mossy Oak Obsession camo finish overall $628.00
Price: Tactical; 18.5" tactical barrel, black synthetic stock and matte black finish. $653.00
Price: Road Blocker; includes muzzle brake $697.00
Price: SPX; no muzzle brake, M16-style front sight, ghost ring rear sight, full pistolgrip stock, eight-round extended magazine $667.00
Price: SPX; conventional synthetic stock $700.00
Price: Home Security/Field Combo; 18.5" Cylinder bore barrel and 28" ported Field barrel; black synthetic stock and matte black finish $604.00

MOSSBERG MODEL 935 MAGNUM AUTOLOADING SHOTGUNS
Gauge: 12; 3" and 3.5" chamber, interchangeable. **Barrel:** 22", 24", 26", 28". **Weight:** 7.25 to 7.75 lbs. **Length:** 45" to 49" overall. **Stock:** Synthetic. **Features:** Gas-operated semiauto models in

blued or camo finish. Fiber optics sights, drilled and tapped receiver, interchangeable Accu-Mag choke tubes.
Price: 935 Magnum Turkey: Realtree Hardwoods, Mossy Oak New Break-up or Mossy Oak Obsession camo overall, 24" barrel $732.00
Price: 935 Magnum Turkey Pistolgrip; full pistolgrip stock . . $831.00
Price: 935 Magnum Grand Slam: 22" barrel, Realtree Hardwoods or Mossy Oak New Break-up camo overall $747.00
Price: 935 Magnum Flyway: 28" barrel and Advantage Max-4 camo overall $781.00
Price: 935 Magnum Waterfowl: 26"or 28" barrel, matte black, Mossy Oak New Break-up, Advantage Max-4 or Mossy Oak Duck Blind cam overall . . . . $613.00 to $725.00
Price: 935 Magnum Slugster: 24" fully rifled barrel, rifle sights, Realtree AP camo overall $747.00
Price: 935 Magnum Turkey/Deer Combo: interchangeable 24" Turkey barrel, Mossy Oak New Break-up camo overall $807.00
Price: 935 Magnum Waterfowl/Turkey Combo: 24" Turkey and 28" Waterfowl barrels, Mossy Oak New Break-up finish overall $807.00

REMINGTON MODEL 105 CTI SHOTGUN
Gauge: 12, 3" chamber, 4-shot magazine. **Barrel:** 26", 28" (IC, Mod., Full ProBore chokes). **Weight:** 7 lbs. **Length:** 46.25" overall (26" barrel). **Stock:** Walnut with satin finish. Checkered grip and forend. **Sights:** Front bead. **Features:** Aircraft-grade titanium receiver body, skeletonized receiver with carbon fiber shell. Bottom feed and eject, target grade trigger, R3 recoil pad, FAA-approved lockable hard case, .735" overbored barrel with lengthened forcing cones. TriNyte coating; carbon/aramid barrel rib. Introduced 2006.
Price: $1,559.00

REMINGTON MODEL SPR453 SHOTGUN
Gauge: 12; 3.5" chamber, 4+1 capacity. **Barrel:** 24", 26", 28" vent rib. **Weight:** 8 to 8.25 lbs. **Stock:** Black synthetic. **Features:** Matte finish, dual extractors, four extended screw-in SPR choke tubes (improved cylinder, modified, full and super-full turkey. Introduced 2006. From Remington Arms Co.
Price: Black synthetic $497.00

REMINGTON MODEL 11-87 SPORTSMAN SHOTGUNS
Gauge: 12, 20, 3" chamber. **Barrel:** 26", 28", RemChoke tubes. Standard contour, vent rib. **Weight:** About 7.75 to 8.25 lbs. **Length:** 46" to 48" overall. **Stock:** Black synthetic or Mossy Oak Break Up Mossy Oak Duck Blind, and Realtree Hardwoods HD and AP Green HD camo finishes. **Sights:** Single bead front. **Features:** Matte-black metal finish, magazine cap swivel studs. Sportsman Deer gun has 21-inch fully rifled barrel, cantilever scope mount.
Price: Sportsman Camo (2007), 12 or 20 ga. $879.00
Price: Sportsman black synthetic, 12 or 20 ga. $772.00
Price: Sportsman Deer FR Cantilever, 12 or 20 ga. $892.00
Price: Sportsman Youth Synthetic 20 ga., (2008). $772.00
Price: Sportsman Youth Camo 20 ga., (2008) $879.00
Price: Sportsman Super Magnum 12 ga., 28" barrel (2008) . . .$825.00
Price: Sportsman Super Magnum Shurshot Turkey 12 ga., (2008) $972.00
Price: Sportsman Super Magnum Waterfowl 12 ga., (2008) . .$959.00
Price: Sportsman Compact Synthetic; black synthetic but with reduced overall dimensions $772.00

REMINGTON 11-87 SPORTSMAN FIELD
Semiauto shotgun chambered in 12 and 20 ga., 2-3/4- and 3-inch. Features include 26- (20) or 28-inch (12) barrel; vent rib; RemChokes (one supplied); satin-finished walnut stock and forend with fleur-de-lis pattern; dual sights; nickel-plated bolt and trigger.
Price: . . . . **Starting at $845.00**

REMINGTON 11-87 SPORTSMAN SUPER MAG SYNTHETIC
Semiauto shotgun chambered in 12-ga. 3-1/2-inch. Features include black matte synthetic stock and forend; rubber overmolded grip panels on the stock and forend; black

padded sling; HiViz sights featuring interchangeable light pipe; 28-inch vent rib barrel; SuperCell recoil pad; RemChoke.
Price: **$859.00**

REMINGTON 11-87 SPORTSMAN SUPER MAG SHURSHOT TURKEY

Similar to 11-87 Sportsman Super Mag Synthetic but with ambidextrous ShurShot pistol-grip stock; full Realtree APG HD coverage; 23-inch barrel with fully adjustable TruGlo rifle sights. Wingmaster HD Turkey Choke included.
Price: **$972.00**

REMINGTON MODEL 1100 G3 SHOTGUN

Gauge: 20, 12; 3" chamber. **Barrel:** 26", 28". **Weight:** 6.75-7.6 lbs. **Stock:** Realwood semi-fancy carbon fiber laminate stock, high gloss finish, machine cut checkering. **Features:** Gas operating system, pressure compensated barrel, solid carbon-steel engraved receiver, titanium coating. Action bars, trigger and extended carrier release, action bar sleeve, action spring, locking block, hammer, sear and magazine tube have nickel-plated, Teflon coating. R3 recoil pad, overbored (.735" dia.) vent rib barrels, ProBore choke tubes. 20 gauge have Rem Chokes. Comes with lockable hard case. Introduced 2006.
Price: G3, 12 or 20 ga. **$1,239.00**
Price: G3 Left Hand, 12 ga. 28" barrel (2008) **$1,329.00**

REMINGTON MODEL 1100 TARGET SHOTGUNS

Gauge: .410 bore, 28, 20, 12. **Barrel:** 26", 27", 28", 30" light target contoured vent rib barrel with twin bead target sights. **Stock:** Semi-fancy American walnut stock and forend, cut checkering, high gloss finish. **Features:** Gold-plated trigger. Four extended choke tubes: Skeet, Improved Cylinder, Light Modified and Modified. 1100 Tournament Skeet (20 and 12 gauge) receiver is roll-marked with "Tournament Skeet." 26" light contour, vent rib barrel has twin bead sights, Extended Target Choke Tubes (Skeet and Improved Cylinder). Model 1100 Premier Sporting (2008) has polished nickel receiver, gold accents, light target contoured vent rib Rem Choke barrels. Wood is semi-fancy American walnut stock and forend, high-gloss finish, cut checkering, sporting clays-style recoil pad. Gold trigger, available in 12, 20, 28 and .410 bore options, Briley extended choke tubes, Premier Sporting hard case. Competition model (12 gauge) has overbored (0.735" bore diameter) 30" barrel. **Weight:** 8 lbs. 10mm target-style rib with twin beads. Extended ProBore choke tubes in Skeet, Improved Cylinder, Light-Modified, Modified and Full. Semi-fancy American walnut stock and forend. Classic Trap model has polished blue receiver with scroll engraving, gold accents, 30" low-profile, light-target contoured vent rib barrel with standard .727" dimensions. Comes with specialized Rem Choke trap tubes: Singles (.027"), Mid Handicap (.034"), and Long Handicap (.041"). Monte Carlo stock of semi-fancy American walnut, deep-cut checkering, high-gloss finish.
Price: Sporting 12, 28" barrel, 8 lbs. **$1,105.00**
Price: Sporting 20, 28" barrel, 7 lbs. **$1,105.00**
Price: Sporting 28, 27" barrel, 6.75 lbs. **$1,159.00**
Price: Sporting 410, 27" barrel, 6.75 lbs. **$1,159.00**
Price: Classic Trap, 12 ga. 30" barrel **$1,159.00**
Price: Premier Sporting (2008), from. **$1,359.00**
Price: Competition, standard stock, 12 ga. 30" barrel **$1,692.00**
Price: Competition, adjustable comb **$1,692.00**

Remington Model 1100 TAC-4

Similar to Model 1100 but with 18" or 22" barrel with ventilated rib; 12 gauge 2-3/4"only; standard black synthetic stock or Knoxx SpecOps

SpeedFeed IV pistolgrip stock; RemChoke tactical choke tube; matte black finish overall. Length is 42-1/2" and weighs 7-3/4 lbs.
Price: **$945.00**

REMINGTON MODEL SP-10 MAGNUM SHOTGUN

Gauge: 10, 3-1/2" chamber, 2-shot magazine. **Barrel:** 23", 26", 30" (full and mod. RemChokes). **Weight:** 10.75 to 11 lbs. **Length:** 47.5" overall (26" barrel). **Stock:** Walnut with satin finish (30" barrel) or camo synthetic (26" barrel). Checkered grip and forend. **Sights:** Twin bead. **Features:** Stainless steel gas system with moving cylinder; 3/8" vent rib. Receiver and barrel have matte finish. Brown recoil pad. Comes with padded Cordura nylon sling. Introduced 1989. SP-10 Magnum Camo has buttstock, forend, receiver, barrel and magazine cap covered with Mossy Oak Duck Blind Obsession camo finish; bolt body and trigger guard have matte black finish. RemChoke tube, 26" vent rib barrel with mid-rib bead and Bradley-style front sight, swivel studs and quick-detachable swivels, non-slip Cordura carrying sling. Introduced 1993.
Price: SP-10 Magnum, satin finish walnut stock. **$1,772.00**
Price: SP-10 Magnum Full Camo **$1,932.00**
Price: SP-10 Magnum Waterfowl **$1,945.00**

SAIGA AUTOLOADING SHOTGUN

Gauge: 12, 20, .410; 3" chamber. **Barrel:** 19", 24". **Weight:** 7.9 lbs. **Length:** **Stock:** Black synthetic. **Sights:** Fixed or adjustable leaf. **Features:** Magazine fed, 2- or 5-round capacity. Imported from Russia by Russian American Armory Co.
Price: **$347.95**

SMITH & WESSON 1000/1020/1012 SUPER SEMIAUTO SHOTGUNS

Gauge: 12, 20; 3" in 1000; 3-1/2" chamber in Super. **Barrel:** 24", 26", 28", 30". **Stock:** Walnut. Synthetic finishes are satin, black, Realtree MAX-4, Realtree APG. **Sights:** TruGlo fiber-optic. **Features:** 29 configurations. Gas operated, dual-piston action; chrome-lined barrels, five choke tubes, shim kit for adjusting stock. 20-ga. models are Model 1020 or Model 1020SS (short stock). Lifetime warranty. Introduced 2007. Imported from Turkey by Smith & Wesson.
Price: From **$623.00**

STOEGER MODEL 2000 SHOTGUNS

Gauge: 12, 3" chamber, set of five choke tubes (C, IC, M, F, XFT). **Barrel:** 24", 26", 28", 30". **Stock:** Walnut, synthetic, Timber HD, Max-4. **Sights:** Red bar front. **Features:** Inertia-recoil. Minimum recommended load: 3 dram, 1-1/8 oz. Imported by Benelli USA.
Price: Walnut **$499.00**
Price: Synthetic. **$499.00**
Price: Max-4 .... **$549.00**
Price: Black synthetic pistol grip (2007) **$499.00**
Price: APG HD camo pistol grip (2007), 18.5" barrel **$549.00**

TRISTAR VIPER SEMIAUTOMATIC SHOTGUNS

Gauge: 12, 20; shoots 2-3/4" or 3" interchangeably. **Barrel:** 26", 28" barrels (carbon fiber only offered in 12-ga. 28" and 20-ga. 26"). **Stock:** Wood, black synthetic, Mossy Oak Duck Blind camouflage, faux carbon fiber finish (2008) with the new Comfort Touch technology. **Features:** Magazine cut-off, vent rib with matted sight plane, brass front bead (camo models have fiber-optic front sight), five round magazine-shot plug included, and 3 Beretta-style choke tubes (IC, M, F). Viper synthetic, Viper camo have swivel studs. Five-year warranty. Viper Youth models have shortened length of pull and 24" barrel. Imported by Tristar Sporting Arms Ltd.

Price: From **$469.00**
Price: Camo models (2008), from **$569.00**

TRADITIONS ALS 2100 SERIES SEMIAUTOMATIC SHOTGUNS

Gauge: 12, 3" chamber; 20, 3" chamber. **Barrel:** 24", 26", 28" (Imp. Cyl., Mod. and Full choke tubes). **Weight:** 5 lbs., 10 oz. to 6 lbs., 5 oz. **Length:** 44" to 48" overall. **Stock:** Walnut or black composite. **Features:** Gas-operated; vent rib barrel with Beretta-style threaded muzzle. Introduced 2001 by Traditions.

Price: Field Model (12 or 20 ga., 26" or 28" bbl., walnut stock) **$479.00**
Price: Youth Model (12 or 20 ga., 24" bbl., walnut stock) **$479.00**
Price: (12 or 20 ga., 26" or 28" barrel, composite stock) **$459.00**

Traditions ALS 2100 Turkey Semiautomatic Shotgun

Similar to ALS 2100 Field Model except chambered in 12 gauge, 3" only with 26" barrel and Mossy Oak Break Up camo finish. Weighs 6 lbs.; 46" overall.

Price: **$519.00**

Traditions ALS 2100 Waterfowl Semiautomatic Shotgun

Similar to ALS 2100 Field Model except chambered in 12 gauge, 3" only with 28" barrel and Advantage Wetlands camo finish. Weighs 6.25 lbs.; 48" overall. Multi chokes.

Price: **$529.00**

Traditions ALS 2100 Hunter Combo

Similar to ALS 2100 Field Model except 2 barrels, 28" vent rib and 24" fully rifled deer. Weighs 6 to 6.5 lbs.; 48" overall. Choice TruGlo adj. sights or fixed cantilever mount on rifled barrel. Multi chokes.

Price: Walnut, rifle barrel **$609.00**
Price: Walnut, cantilever. **$629.00**
Price: Synthetic. **$579.00**

Traditions ALS 2100 Slug Hunter Shotgun

Similar to ALS 2100 Field Model, 12 ga., 24" barrel, overall length 44"; weighs 6.25 lbs. Designed specifically for the deer hunter. Rifled barrel has 1 in 36" twist. Fully adjustable fiber-optic sights.

Price: Walnut, rifle barrel **$529.00**
Price: Synthetic, rifle barrel. **$499.00**
Price: Walnut, cantilever. **$549.00**
Price: Synthetic, cantilever **$529.00**

Traditions ALS 2100 Home Security Shotgun

Similar to ALS 2100 Field Model, 12 ga., 20" barrel, overall length 40", weighs 6 lbs. Can be reloaded with one hand while shouldered and ontarget. Swivel studs installed in stock.

Price: **$399.00**

VERONA MODEL 401 SERIES SEMIAUTO SHOTGUNS

Gauge: 12. **Barrel:** 26", 28". **Weight:** 6.5 lbs. **Stock:** Walnut, black composite. **Sights:** Red dot. **Features:** Aluminum receivers, gas-operated, 2-3/4" or 3" Magnum shells without adj. or Mod., 4 screw-in chokes and wrench included. Sling swivels, gold trigger. Blued barrel. Imported from Italy by Legacy Sports International.

Price: **$1,199.00**
Price: 406 Series **$1,199.00**

WINCHESTER SUPER X3 SHOTGUNS

Gauge: 12, 3" and 3.5" chambers. **Barrel:** 26", 28", .742" back-bored; Invector Plus choke tubes. **Weight:** 7 to 7.25 lbs. **Stock:** Composite, 14.25"x1.75"x2". Mossy Oak New Break-Up camo with Dura-Touch Armor Coating. Pachmayr Decelerator buttpad with hard heel insert, customizable length of pull. **Features:** Alloy magazine tube, gunmetal grey Perma-Cote UT finish, self-adjusting Active Valve gas action, lightweight recoil spring system. Electroless nickel-plated bolt, three choke tubes, two length-of-pull stock spacers, drop and cast adjustment spacers, sling swivel studs. Introduced 2006. Made in Belgium, assembled in Portugal by U.S. Repeating Arms Co.

Price: Composite . . . . **$1,119.00 to $1,239.00**
Price: Cantilever Deer. **$1,179.00**

Price: Waterfowl w/Mossy Oak Brush camo, intr. 2007 . . . . **$1,439.00**
Price: Field model, walnut stock, intr. 2007 . . . . **$1,439.00**
Price: Gray Shadow **$1,299.00**
Price: All-Purpose Field **$1,439.00**
Price: Classic Field **$1,159.00**
Price: NWTF Cantiliever Extreme Turkey **$1,499.00**

WINCHESTER SUPER X3 FLANIGUN EXHIBITION/SPORTING

Similar to X3 but .742" backbored barrel, red-toned receiver, black Dura-Touch Armor Coated synthetic stock.

Price: **$1,459.00**

WINCHESTER SUPER X2 AUTO SHOTGUNS

Gauge: 12, 3", 3-1/2" chamber. **Barrel:** Belgian, 24", 26", 28"; Invector Plus choke tubes. **Weight:** 7-1/4 to 7.5 lbs. **Stock:** 14.25"x1.75"x2". Walnut or black synthetic. **Features:** Gas-operated action shoots all loads without adjustment; vent rib barrels; 4-shot magazine. Introduced 1999. Assembled in Portugal by U.S. Repeating Arms Co.

Price: Universal Hunter T **$1,252.00**
Price: NWTF Turkey, 3-1/2", Mossy Oak Break-Up camo . . **$1,236.00**
Price: Universal Hunter Model **$1,252.00**

Winchester Super X2 Sporting Clays Auto Shotguns

Similar to the Super X2 except has two gas pistons (one for target loads, one for heavy 3" loads), adjustable comb system and high-post rib. Back-bored barrel with Invector Plus choke tubes. Offered in 28" and 30" barrels. Introduced 2001. From U.S. Repeating Arms Co.

Price: Super X2 sporting clays **$999.00**
Price: Signature red stock. **$1,015.00**
Price: Practical MK I, composite stock, TruGlo sights **$1,116.00**

BENELLI SUPERNOVA PUMP SHOTGUNS

Gauge: 12; 3.5" chamber. **Barrel:** 24", 26", 28". **Length:** 45.5-49.5". **Stock:** Synthetic; Max-4 , Timber, APG HD (2007). **Sights:** Red bar front, metal midbead. **Features:** 2-3/4", 3" chamber (3-1/2" 12 ga. only). Montefeltro rotating bolt design with dual action bars, magazine cut-off, synthetic trigger assembly, adjustable combs, shim kit, choice of buttstocks. 4-shot magazine. Introduced 2006. Imported from Italy by Benelli USA.

Price: Synthetic ComforTech **$499.00**
Price: Camo ComforTech **$599.00**
Price: SteadyGrip . . . . **$599.00 to $619.00**
Price: Tactical, Ghost Ring sight. . . . . **$459.00 to $499.00**
Price: Rifled Slug ComforTech, synthetic stock (2007) **$670.00**
Price: Tactical desert camo pistol grip, 18" barrel (2007). **$589.00**

BENELLI NOVA PUMP SHOTGUNS

Gauge: 12, 20. **Barrel:** 24", 26", 28". **Stock:** Black synthetic, Max-4, Timber and APG HD. **Sights:** Red bar. **Features:** 2-3/ 4", 3" chamber (3-1/2" 12 ga. only). Montefeltro rotating bolt design with dual action bars, magazine cut-off, synthetic trigger assembly, 4-shot magazine. Introduced 1999. Field & Slug Combo has 24" barrel and rifled bore; open rifle sights; synthetic stock; weighs 8.1 lbs. Imported from Italy by Benelli USA.

PrPrice: Max-4 HD camo stock **$499.00**
Price: H₂0 model, black synthetic, matte nickel finish. **$599.00**

Price: APG HD stock , 20 ga. (2007) **$529.00**
Price: Tactical, 18.5" barrel, Ghost Ring sight **$429.00**
Price: Black synthetic youth stock, 20 ga. **$429.00**
Price: APG HD stock (2007), 20 ga.. . . . . **$529.00**

BROWNING BPS PUMP SHOTGUNS

Gauge: 10, 12, 3-1/2" chamber; 12, 16, or 20, 3" chamber (2-3/4" in target guns), 28, 2-3/4" chamber, 5-shot magazine, .410, 3" chamber. **Barrel:** 10 ga.-24" Buck Special, 28", 30", 32" Invector; 12, 20 ga.-22", 24", 26", 28", 30", 32" (Imp. Cyl., Mod. or Full), .410-26" barrel. (Imp. Cyl., Mod. and Full choke tubes.) Also available with Invector choke tubes, 12 or 20 ga.; Upland Special has 22" barrel with Invector tubes. BPS 3" and 3-1/2" have back-bored barrel. **Weight:** 7 lbs., 8 oz. (28" barrel). **Length:** 48.75" overall (28" barrel). **Stock:** 14.25"x1.5"x2.5". Select walnut, semi-beavertail forend, full pistol grip stock. **Features:** All 12 gauge 3" guns except Buck Special and game guns have back-bored barrels with Invector Plus choke tubes. Bottom feeding and ejection, receiver top safety, high post vent rib. Double action bars eliminate binding. Vent rib barrels only. All 12 and 20 gauge guns with 3" chamber available with fully engraved receiver flats at no extra cost. Each gauge has its own unique game scene. Introduced 1977. Stalker is same gun as the standard BPS except all exposed metal parts have a matte blued finish and the stock has a black finish with a black recoil pad. Available in 10 ga. (3-1/2") and 12 ga. with 3" or 3-1/2" chamber, 22", 28", 30" barrel with Invector choke system. Introduced 1987. Rifled Deer Hunter is similar to the standard BPS except has newly designed receiver/magazine tube/barrel mounting system to eliminate play, heavy 20.5" barrel with rifle-type sights with adjustable rear, solid receiver scope mount, "rifle" stock dimensions for scope or open sights, sling swivel studs. Gloss or matte finished wood with checkering, polished blue metal. Introduced 1992. Imported from Japan by Browning.

Price: Stalker (black syn. stock), 12 ga., from **$549.00**
Price: Rifled Deer Hunter (22" rifled bbl., cantilever mount),
    intr. 2007. . . . . **$699.00**
Price: Trap, intr. 2007 . . . . **$729.00**
Price: Hunter, 16 ga., intr. 2008 . . . . **$569.00**
Price: Upland Special, 16 ga., intr. 2008 . . . . **$569.00**
Price: Mossy Oak New Breakup, 3", 12 ga. only **$679.00**
Price: Mossy Oak New Breakup, 3-1/2", 12 ga. only **$799.00**

Price: Mossy Oak Duck Blind finish overall, 3" **$679.00**
Price: Mossy Oak Duck Blind finish overall, 3-1/2" **$799.00**
Price: Rifled Deer Mossy Oak New Break-Up, 12 ga. **$719.00**
Price: Rifled Deer Mossy Oak New Break-Up, 20 ga. **$839.00**
Price: Micro Trap, similar to BPS Trap but with compact
    dimensions (13-3/4" length of pull, 48-1/4" overall
    length), 12 gauge only **$729.00**

Browning BPS 10 Gauge Camo Pump Shotgun

Similar to the standard BPS except completely covered with Mossy Oak Shadow Grass camouflage. Available with 26" and 28" barrel. Introduced 1999. Imported by Browning
Price: **$799.00**

Browning BPS NWTF Turkey Series Pump Shotgun

Similar to the standard BPS except has full coverage Mossy Oak Break-Up camo finish on synthetic stock, forearm and exposed metal parts. Offered in 12 gauge, 3" or 3-1/2" chamber; 24" bbl. has extra-full choke tube and HiViz fiber-optic sights. Introduced 2001. From Browning.
Price: 12 ga., 3-1/2" chamber. **$859.00**
Price: 12 ga., 3" chamber **$709.00**

Browning BPS Micro Pump Shotgun

Similar to the BPS Stalker except 20 ga. only, 22" Invector barrel, stock has pistol grip with recoil pad. Length of pull is 13.25"; weighs 6 lbs., 12 oz. Introduced 1986.
Price: **$569.00**

CHARLES DALY FIELD PUMP SHOTGUNS

Gauge: 12, 20. **Barrel:** Interchangeable 18.5", 24", 26", 28", 30" multi-choked. **Weight:** NA. **Stock:** Synthetic, various finishes, recoil pad. **Receiver:** Machined aluminum. **Features:** Field Tactical and Slug models come with adustable sights; Youth models may be upgraded to full size. Imported from Turkey by K.B.I., Inc.
Price: Field Tactical **$274.00**
Price: Field Hunter **$499.00**
Price: Field Hunter, Realtree Hardwood **$289.00**
Price: Field Hunter Advantage **$289.00**

CHARLES DALY MAXI-MAG PUMP SHOTGUNS

Gauge: 12 gauge, 3-1/2". **Barrel:** 24", 26", 28"; multi-choke system. **Weight:** NA. **Stock:** Synthetic black, Realtree Hardwoods, or Advantage Timber receiver, aluminum alloy. **Features:** Handles 2-3/4", 3" and 3-1/2" loads. Interchangeable ported barrels; Turkey package includes sling, HiViz sights, XX Full choke. Imported from Turkey by K.B.I., Inc.
Price: Field Hunter **$329.00**
Price: Field Hunter Advantage **$319.00**
Price: Field Hunter Hardwoods. **$319.00**
Price: Field Hunter Turkey **$434.00**

EMF OLD WEST PUMP (SLIDE ACTION) SHOTGUN

Gauge: 12. **Barrel:** 20". **Weight:** 7 lbs. **Length:** 39-1/2" overall. **Stock:** Smooth walnut with cushioned pad. **Sights:** Front bead. **Features:** Authentic reproduction of Winchester 1897 pump shotgun;

Prices given are believed to be accurate at time of publication however, many factors affect retail pricing so exact prices are not possible.

blue receiver and barrel; standard modified choke. Introduced 2006. Imported from China for EMF by TTN.
Price: **$449.90**

ESCORT PUMP SHOTGUNS

Gauge: 12, 20; 3" chamber. **Barrel:** 18" (AimGuard and MarineGuard), 22" (Youth Pump), 26", and 28" lengths. **Weight:** 6.7-7.0 lbs. **Stock:** Polymer in black, Shadow Grass® camo or Obsession® camo finish. Two adjusting spacers included. Youth model has Trio recoil pad. **Sights:** Bead or Spark front sights, depending on model. AimGuard and MarineGuard models have blade front sights. **Features:** Black-chrome or dipped camo metal parts, top of receiver dovetailed for sight mounts, gold plated trigger, trigger guard safety, magazine cut-off. Three choke tubes (IC, M, F) except AimGuard/MarineGuard which are cylinder bore. Models include: FH, FH Youth, AimGuard and Marine Guard. Introduced in 2003. Imported from Turkey by Legacy Sports International.
Price: . . . .**$389.00 to $469.00**

HARRINGTON & RICHARDSON PARDNER PUMP FIELD GUN FULL-DIP CAMO

Gauge: 12, 20; 3" chamber. **Barrel:** 28" fully rifled. **Weight:** 7.5 lbs. **Length:** 48-1/8" overall. **Stock:** Synthetic or hardwood. **Sights:** NA. **Features:** Steel receiver, double action bars, cross-bolt safety, easy takedown, vent rib, screw-in Modified choke tube. Ventilated recoil pad and grooved forend with Realtree APG-HDTM full camo dip finish.
Price: Full camo version **$278.00**

IAC MODEL 87W-1 LEVER-ACTION SHOTGUN

Gauge: 12; 2-3/4" chamber only. **Barrel:** 20" with fixed Cylinder choke. **Weight:** NA. **Length:** NA. **Stock:** American walnut. **Sights:** Bead front. **Features:** Modern replica of Winchester Model 1887 lever-action shotgun. Includes five-shot tubular magazine, pivoting split-lever design to meet modern safety requirements. Imported by Interstate Arms Corporation.
Price: **$429.95**

ITHACA GUN COMPANY DEERSLAYER III SLUG SHOTGUN

Gauge: 12, 20; 3" chamber. **Barrel:** 26" fully rifled, heavy fluted with 1:28 twist for 12 ga.; 1:24 for 20 ga. **Weight:** 8.14 lbs. to 9.5 lbs. with scope mounted. **Length:** 45.625" overall. **Stock:** Fancy black walnut stock and forend. **Sights:** NA. **Features:** Updated, slug-only version of the classic Model 37. Bottom ejection, blued barrel and receiver.
Price: **$1,189.00**

ITHACA GUN COMPANY MODEL 37 28 GAUGE SHOTGUN

Gauge: 28. **Barrel:** 26" or 28". **Weight:** NA. **Length:** NA. **Stock:** Black walnut stock and forend. **Sights:** NA. **Features:** Scaled down receiver with traditional Model 37 bottom ejection and easy takedown. Available in Fancy "A," Fancy "AA," and Fancy "AAA" grades with increasingly elaborate receiver engraving and decoration. Special order only.
Price: Fancy "A" grade **$999.00**

MOSSBERG MODEL 835 ULTI-MAG PUMP SHOTGUNS

Gauge: 12, 3-1/2" chamber. **Barrel:** Ported 24" rifled bore, 24", 28", Accu-Mag choke tubes for steel or lead shot. **Weight:** 7.75 lbs. **Length:** 48.5" overall. **Stock:** 14"x1.5"x2.5". Dual Comb. Cut-checkered hardwood or camo synthetic; both have recoil pad. **Sights:** White bead front, brass mid-bead; fiber-optic rear. **Features:** Shoots 2-3/4", 3" and 3-1/2" shells. Back-bored and ported barrel to reduce recoil, improve patterns. Ambidextrous thumb safety, twin extractors, dual slide bars. Mossberg Cablelock included. Introduced 1988.

Price: Thumbhole Turkey **$674.00**
Price: Tactical Turkey **$636.00**
Price: Synthetic Thumbhole Turkey, from **$493.00**
Price: Turkey, from **$487.00**
Price: Waterfowl, from **$437.00**
Price: Combo, from **$559.00**

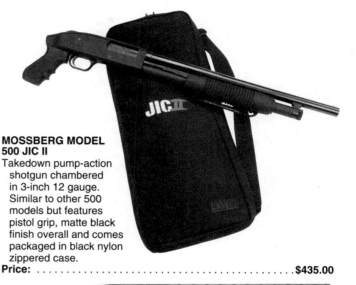

MOSSBERG MODEL 500 JIC II

Takedown pump-action shotgun chambered in 3-inch 12 gauge. Similar to other 500 models but features pistol grip, matte black finish overall and comes packaged in black nylon zippered case.
Price: **$435.00**

MOSSBERG MODEL 500 SPORTING PUMP SHOTGUNS

Gauge: 12, 20, .410, 3" chamber. **Barrel:** 18.5" to 28" with fixed or Accu-Choke, plain or vent rib. **Weight:** 6-1/4 lbs. (.410), 7-1/4 lbs. (12). **Length:** 48" overall (28" barrel). **Stock:** 14"x1.5"x2.5". Walnut-stained hardwood, black synthetic, Mossy Oak Advantage camouflage. Cut-checkered grip and forend. **Sights:** White bead front, brass mid-bead; fiber-optic. **Features:** Ambidextrous thumb safety, twin extractors, disconnecting safety, dual action bars. Quiet Carry forend. Many barrels are ported. From Mossberg.
Price: Turkey **$410.00**
Price: Waterfowl, from **$406.00**
Price: Combo, from **$391.00**
Price: Field, from **$354.00**
Price: Slugster, from **$354.00**

Mossberg Model 500 Bantam Pump Shotgun

Same as the Model 500 Sporting Pump except 12 or 20 gauge, 22" vent rib Accu-Choke barrel with choke tube set; has 1" shorter stock, reduced length from pistol grip to trigger, reduced forend reach. Introduced 1992.
Price: **$354.00**
Price: Super Bantam (2008), from **$338.00**

MOSSBERG 510 MINI BANTAM SHOTGUN

Compact pump-action shotgun based on Model 500 action, chambered in 3-inch 20 gauge and .410. Features include an 18.5-inch vent rib barrel with interchangeable (20) or fixed (.410) choke, black synthetic stock with removable inserts to adjust LOP from 12 to 14+ inches, 4-shot capacity. Weight 5 lbs.
Price: **$364.00**

NEW ENGLAND PARDNER PUMP SHOTGUN

Gauge: 12 ga., 3". **Barrel:** 28" vent rib, screw-in Modified choke tube. **Weight:** 7.5 lbs. **Length:** 48.5". **Stock:** American walnut,

---

grooved forend, ventilated recoil pad. **Sights:** Bead front. **Features:** Machined steel receiver, double action bars, five-shot magazine.
Price: **$200.00**

REMINGTON MODEL 870 WINGMASTER SHOTGUNS
Gauge: 12, 20, 28 ga., .410 bore. **Barrel:** 25", 26", 28", 30" (RemChokes). **Weight:** 7-1/4 lbs. **Length:** 46", 48". **Stock:** Walnut, hardwood. **Sights:** Single bead (Twin bead Wingmaster). **Features:** Light contour barrel. Double action bars, cross-bolt safety, blue finish. LW is 28 gauge and .410-bore only, 25" vent rib barrel with RemChoke tubes, high-gloss wood finish. Limited Edition Model 870 Wingmaster 100th Anniversary Commemorative Edition (2008 only) is 12 gauge with gold centennial logo, "100 Years of Remington Pump Shotguns" banner. Gold-plated trigger, American B Grade walnut stock and forend, high-gloss finish, fleur-de-lis checkering.
Price: Wingmaster, walnut, blued **$785.00**
Price: LW .410-bore **$839.00**
Price: 100th Anniversary (2008), 12 ga., 28" barrel **$1,035.00**

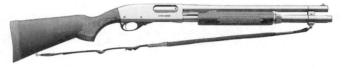

Remington Model 870 Marine Magnum Shotgun
Similar to 870 Wingmaster except all metal plated with electroless nickel, black synthetic stock and forend. Has 18" plain barrel (cyl.), bead front sight, 7-shot magazine. Introduced 1992. XCS version with TriNyte corrosion control introduced 2007.
Price: **$772.00**

REMINGTON MODEL 870 CLASSIC TRAP SHOTGUN
Similar to Model 870 Wingmaster except has 30" vent rib, light contour barrel, singles, mid- and long-handicap choke tubes, semi-fancy American walnut stock, high-polish blued receiver with engraving. Chamber 2.75". From Remington Arms Co.
Price: **$1,039.00**
Price: XCS (2007) **$899.00**

Remington Model 870 Express Shotguns
Similar to Model 870 Wingmaster except laminate, synthetic black, or camo stock with solid, black recoil pad and pressed checkering on grip and forend. Outside metal surfaces have black oxide finish. Comes with 26" or 28" vent rib barrel with mod. RemChoke tube. ShurShot Turkey (2008) has ShurShot synthetic pistol-grip thumbhole design, extended forend, Mossy Oak Obsession camouflage, matte black metal finish, 21" vent rib barrel, twin beads, Turkey Extra Full Rem Choke tube. Receiver drilled and tapped for mounting optics. ShurShot FR CL (Fully Rifled Cantilever, 2008) includes compact 23" fully-rifled barrel with integrated cantilever scope mount.
Price: 12 and 20 ga., laminate or synthetic right-hand stock .. **$383.00**
Price: 12 or 20 ga., laminate or synthetic left-hand stock..... **$409.00**
Price: Express Synthetic, 12 ga., 18" barrel (2007) **$383.00**

Price: Express Synthetic, 20 ga., 7 round capacity, from **$385.00**
Price: Express Synthetic Deer FR 12 ga., rifle sights **$425.00**
Price: Express Laminate Deer FR 12 ga., rifle sights **$416.00**
Price: Express Synthetic or Laminate Turkey 12 ga., 21" barrel **$388.00**
Price: Express Camo Turkey 12 ga., 21" barrel **$445.00**
Price: Express Combo Turkey/Deer Camo 12 ga. **$612.00**
Price: Express Synthetic Youth Combo 20 ga............. **$543.00**
Price: Express Magnum ShurShot Turkey (2008) **$492.00**
Price: Express Magnum ShurShot FR CL (2008) **$500.00**
Price: Express ShurShot Synthetic Cantilever; 12 or 20 ga. with ShurShot stock and cantilever scope mount **$532.00**
Price: Express Compact Deer; 20 ga., similar to 870 Express Laminate Deer but with smaller dimensions **$395.00**
Price: Express Compact Pink Camo; 20 ga. **$429.00**
Price: Express Compact Synthetic; matte black synthetic stock **$383.00**
Price: Express Compact Camo; camo buttstock and forend . **$429.00**
Price: Express Compact Jr.; Shorter barrel and LOP **$383.00**

Remington Model 870 Express Super Magnum Shotgun
Similar to Model 870 Express except 28" vent rib barrel with 3-1/2" chamber, vented recoil pad. Introduced 1998. Model 870 Express Super Magnum Waterfowl (2008) is fully camouflaged with Mossy Oak Duck Blind pattern, 28-inch vent rib Rem Choke barrel, "Over Decoys" Choke tube (.007") fiber-optic HiViz single bead front sight; front and rear sling swivel studs, padded black sling.
Price: **$431.00**
Price: Super Magnum synthetic, 26" **$431.00**
Price: Super Magnum turkey camo (full-coverage RealTree Advantage camo), 23" **$564.00**
Price: Super Magnum combo (26" with Mod. RemChoke and 20" fully rifled deer barrel with 3" chamber and rifle sights; wood stock) **$577.00**
Price: Super Magnum Waterfowl (2008)................. **$577.00**

Remington Model 870 Special Purpose Shotguns (SPS)
Similar to the Model 870 Express synthetic, chambered for 12 ga. 3" and 3-1/2" shells, has Realtree Hardwoods HD or APG HD camo-synthetic stock and metal treatment, TruGlo fiber-optic sights. Introduced 2001. SPS Max Gobbler introduced 2007. Knoxx SpecOps adjustable stock, Williams Fire Sights fiber-optic sights, R3 recoil pad, Realtree APG HD camo. Drilled and tapped for Weaver-style rail
Price: SPS 12 ga. 3" **$671.00**
Price: SPS Super Mag Max Gobbler (2007)............. **$819.00**
Price: SPS Super Mag Max Turkey ShurShot 3-1/2" (2008) .. **$644.00**
Price: SPS Synthetic ShurShot FR Cantilever 3" (2008) **$671.00**

Remington Model 870 Express Tactical
Similar to Model 870 but in 12 gauge only (2-2/4" and 3" interchangeably) with 18.5" barrel, Tactical RemChoke extended/ported choke tube, black synthetic buttstock and forend, extended magazine tube, gray powdercoat finish overall. 38.5" overall length, weighs 7.5 lbs.
Price: **$372.00**
Price: Model 870 TAC Desert Recon; desert camo stock and sand-toned metal surfaces **$692.00**
Price: Model 870 Express Tactical with Ghost Ring Sights; Top-mounted accessories rail and XS ghost ring rear sight **$505.00**

REMINGTON MODEL 870 SPS SHURSHOT SYNTHETIC SUPER SLUG
Gauge: 12; 2-3/4" and 3" chamber, interchangeable. **Barrel:** 25.5" extra-heavy, fully rifled pinned to receiver. **Weight:** 7-7/8 lbs. **Length:** 47" overall. **Features:** Pump-action model based on 870 platform. SuperCell recoil pad. Drilled and tapped for scope mounts with Weaver rail included. Matte black metal surfaces, Mossy Oak Treestand Shurshot buttstock and forend.

Prices given are believed to be accurate at time of publication however, many factors affect retail pricing so exact prices are not possible.

Price: .... **NA**
Price: 870 SPS ShurShot Synthetic Cantilever; cantilever scope mount and Realtree Hardwoods camo buttstock and forend **$532.00**
Price: 870 SPS ShurShot Synthetic Turkey; adjustable sights and APG HD camo buttstock and forend **$532.00**

REMINGTON 870 EXPRESS SYNTHETIC SUPER MAG TURKEY-WATERFOWL CAMO

Pump action shotgun chambered in 12-ga., 2-3/4 to 3-1/2 inch. Features include full Mossy Oak Bottomland camo coverage; 26-inch barrel with HiViz fiber-optics sights; Wingmaster HD Waterfowl and Turkey Extra Full RemChokes; SuperCell recoil pad; drilled and tapped receiver.
Price: **$601.00**

REMINGTON 870 EXPRESS SYNTHETIC TURKEY CAMO

Pump action shotgun chambered for 2-3/4 and 3-inch 12-ga. Features include 21-inch vent rib bead-sighted barrel; standard Express finish on barrel and receiver; Turkey Extra Full RemChoke; synthetic stock with integrated sling swivel attachment.
Price: **$445.00**

REMINGTON 870 SUPER MAG TURKEY-PREDATOR CAMO WITH SCOPE

Pump action shotgun chambered in 12-ga., 2-3/4 to 3-1/2 inch. Features include 20-inch barrel; TruGlo red/green selectable illuminated sight mounted on pre-installed Weaver-style rail; black padded sling; Wingmaster HD™ Turkey/Predator RemChoke; full Mossy Oak Obsession camo coverage; ShurShot pistol grip stock with black overmolded grip panels; TruGlo 30mm Red/Green Dot Scope pre-mounted.
Price: **$679.00**

REMINGTON MODEL 887 NITRO MAG PUMP SHOTGUN

Gauge: 12; 3.5", 3", and 2-3/4" chambers. **Barrel:** 28". **Features:** Pump-action model based on the Model 870. Interchangeable shells, black matte ArmoLokt rustproof coating throughout. SuperCell recoil pad. Solid rib and Hi-Viz front sight with interchangeable light tubes. Black synthetic stock with contoured grip panels.
Price: **$399.00**
Price: Model 887 Nitro Mag Waterfowl, Advantage Max-4 camo overall **$532.00**

REMINGTON 887 BONECOLLECTOR EDITION

Pump action shotgun chambered in 12-ga., 2-3/4 to 3-1/2 inch. Features include ArmorLokt rustproof coating; synthetic stock and forend; 26-inch barrel; full camo finish; integral swivel studs; SuperCell recoil pad; solid rib and HiViz front sight. Bone Collector logo.
Price: **$623.00**

REMINGTON 887 NITRO MAG CAMO COMBO

Pump action shotgun chambered in 12-ga., 2-3/4 to 3-1/2 inch. Features include 22-inch turkey barrel with HiViz fiber-optic rifle sights and 28-inch waterfowl with a HiViz sight; extended Waterfowl and Super Full Turkey RemChokes are included; SuperCell recoil pad; synthetic stock and forend with specially contoured grip panels; full camo coverage.
Price: **$693.00**

STEVENS MODEL 350 PUMP SHOTGUN

Pump-action shotgun chambered for 2.5- and 3-inch 12-ga. Features include all-steel barrel and receiver; bottom-load and -eject design; black synthetic stock; 5+1 capacity.
Price: Field Model with 28-inch barrel, screw-in choke **$267.00**
Price: Security Model with 18-inch barrel, fixed choke **$241.00**
Price: Combo Model with Field and Security barrels **$307.00**
Price: Security Model with 18.25-inch barrel w/ghost ring rear sight. **$254.00**

STOEGER MODEL P350 SHOTGUNS

Gauge: 12, 3.5" chamber, set of five choke tubes (C, IC, M, IM, XF). **Barrel:** 18.5",24", 26", 28". **Stock:** Black synthetic, Timber HD, Max-4 HD, APG HD camos. **Sights:** Red bar front. **Features:** Inertia-recoil, mercury recoil reducer, pistol grip stocks. Imported by Benelli USA.
Price: Synthetic. **$329.00**
Price: Max-4, Timber HD **$429.00**
Price: Black synthetic pistol grip (2007) **$329.00**
Price: APG HD camo pistol grip (2007) **$429.00**

WINCHESTER SUPER X PUMP SHOTGUNS

Gauge: 12, 3" chambers. **Barrel:** 18"; 26" and 28" barrels are .742" back-bored, chrome plated; Invector Plus choke tubes. **Weight:** 7 lbs. **Stock:** Walnut or composite. **Features:** Rotary bolt, four lugs, dual steel action bars. Walnut Field has gloss-finished walnut stock and forearm, cut checkering. Black Shadow Field has composite stock and forearm, non-glare matte finish barrel and receiver. Speed Pump Defender has composite stock and forearm, chromed plated, 18" cylinder choked barrel, non-glare metal surfaces, five-shot magazine, grooved forearm. Weight, 6.5 lbs. Reintroduced 2008. Made in U.S.A. from Winchester Repeating Arms Co.
Price: Black Shadow Field **$359.00**
Price: Defender. **$319.00**

BERETTA DT10 TRIDENT SHOTGUNS
Gauge: 12, 2-3/4", 3" chambers. **Barrel:** 28", 30", 32", 34"; competition-style vent rib; fixed or Optima choke tubes. **Weight:** 7.9 to 9 lbs. **Stock:** High-grade walnut stock with oil finish; hand-checkered grip and forend, adjustable stocks available. **Features:** Detachable, adjustable trigger group, raised and thickened receiver, forend iron has adjustment nut to guarantee wood-to-metal fit. Introduced 2000. Imported from Italy by Beretta USA.
Price: DT10 Trident Trap, adjustable stock. **$7,400.00**
Price: DT10 Trident Skeet **$7,900.00**
Price: DT10 Trident Sporting, from **$6,975.00**

BERETTA SV10 PERENNIA O/U SHOTGUN
Gauge: 12, 3" chambers. **Barrel:** 26", 28", 30". Optima-Bore profile, polished blue. Bore diameter 18.6mm (0.73 in.) Self-adjusting dual conical longitudinal locking lugs, oversized monobloc bearing shoulders, replaceable hinge pins. Ventilated top rib, 6x6mm. Long guided extractors, automatic ejection or mechanical extraction. Optimachoke tubes. **Weight:** 7.3 lbs. **Stock:** Quick take-down stock with pistol grip or English straight stock. Kick-off recoil reduction system available on request on Q-Stock. **Length of pull:** 14.7", drop at comb, 1.5", drop at heel, 2.36" or 1.38"/2.17". Semibeavertail forend with elongated forend lever. New checkering pattern, matte oil finish, rubber pad. **Features:** Floral motifs and game scenes on side panels; nickel-based protective finish, arrowhead-shaped sideplates, solid steel alloy billet. Kick-Off recoil reduction mechanism available on select models. Fixed chokes on request, removable trigger group, titanium single selective trigger. Manual or automatic safety, newly designed safety and selector lever. Gel-Tek recoil pad available on request. Polypropylene case, 5 chokes with spanner, sling swivels, plastic pad, Beretta gun oil. Introduced 2008. Imported from Italy by Beretta USA.
Price: From. **$3,250.00**

BERETTA SERIES 682 GOLD E SKEET, TRAP, SPORTING O/U SHOTGUNS
Gauge: 12, 2-3/4" chambers. **Barrel:** skeet-28"; trap-30" and 32", Imp. Mod. & Full and Mobilchoke; trap mono shotguns-32" and 34" Mobilchoke; trap top single guns-32" and 34" Full and Mobilchoke; trap combo sets-from 30" O/U, to 32" O/U, 34" top single. **Stock:** Close-grained walnut, hand checkered. **Sights:** White Bradley bead front sight and center bead. **Features:** Receiver has Greystone gunmetal gray finish with gold accents. Trap Monte Carlo stock has deluxe trap recoil pad. Various grades available. Imported from Italy by Beretta USA.
Price: 682 Gold E Trap with adjustable stock. **$4,425.00**
Price: 682 Gold E Trap Unsingle **$4,825.00**
Price: 682 Gold E Sporting **$4,075.00**
Price: 682 Gold E Skeet, adjustable stock **$4,425.00**

BERETTA 686 ONYX O/U SHOTGUNS
Gauge: 12, 20, 28; 3", 3.5" chambers. **Barrel:** 26", 28" (Mobilchoke tubes). **Weight:** 6.8-6.9 lbs. **Stock:** Checkered American walnut. **Features:** Intended for the beginning sporting clays shooter. Has wide, vented target rib, radiused recoil pad.

Polished black finish on receiver and barrels. Introduced 1993. Imported from Italy by Beretta U.S.A.
Price: White Onyx. **$1,975.00**
PPrice: White Onyx Sporting **$2,175.00**

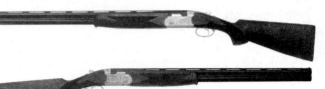

BERETTA SILVER PIGEON O/U SHOTGUNS
Gauge: 12, 20, 28, 3" chambers (2-3/4" 28 ga.). .410 bore, 3" chamber. **Barrel:** 26", 28". **Weight:** 6.8 lbs. **Stock:** Checkered walnut. **Features:** Interchangeable barrels (20 and 28 ga.), single selective gold-plated trigger, boxlock action, auto safety, Schnabel forend.
Price: Silver Pigeon S. **$2,400.00**
Price: Silver Pigeon II **$3,150.00**
Price: Silver Pigeon III **$3,275.00**
Price: Silver Pigeon IV **$3,200.00**
Price: Silver Pigeon V. **$3,675.00**

BERETTA ULTRALIGHT O/U SHOTGUNS
Gauge: 12, 2-3/4" chambers. **Barrel:** 26", 28", Mobilchoke tubes. **Weight:** About 5 lbs., 13 oz. **Stock:** Select American walnut with checkered grip and forend. **Features:** Low-profile aluminum alloy receiver with titanium breech face insert. Electroless nickel receiver with game scene engraving. Single selective trigger; automatic safety. Introduced 1992. Ultralight Deluxe except has matte electroless nickel finish receiver with gold game scene engraving; matte oil-finished, select walnut stock and forend. Imported from Italy by Beretta U.S.A.
Price: **$2,075.00**
Price: Ultralight Deluxe **$2,450.00**

BERETTA COMPETITION SHOTGUNS
Gauge: 12, 20, 28, and .410 bore, 2-3/4", 3" and 3-1/2" chambers. **Barrel:** 26" and 28" (Mobilchoke tubes). **Stock:** Close-grained walnut. **Features:** Highly-figured, American walnut stocks and forends, and a unique, weather-resistant finish on barrels. Silver designates standard 686, 687 models with silver receivers; 686 Silver Pigeon has enhanced engraving pattern, Schnabel forend; Gold indicates higher grade 686EL, 687EL models with full sideplates. Imported from Italy by Beretta U.S.A.
Price: S687 EELL Gold Pigeon Sporting (D.R. engraving). . **$7,675.00**

BILL HANUS 16-GAUGE BROWNING CITORI M525 FIELD
Gauge: 16. **Barrel:** 26" and 28". **Weight:** 6-3/4 pounds. **Stock:** 1-1/2" x 2-3/8" x 14-1/4" and cast neutral. Adjusting for cast-on for left-handed shooters or cast-off for right-handed shooters, $300 extra. Oil finish. **Features:** Full pistol grip with a graceful Schnable forearm and built on a true 16-gauge frame. Factory supplies three Invector choke tubes: IC-M-F and Bill Hanus models come with two Briley-made skeet chokes for close work over dogs and clay-target games.
Price: **$1,795.00**

BROWNING CYNERGY O/U SHOTGUNS
Gauge: 12, 20, 28. **Barrel:** 26", 28", 30", 32". **Stock:** Walnut or composite. **Sights:** White bead front most models; HiViz Pro-Comp sight on some models; mid bead. **Features:** Mono-Lock hinge, recoil-reducing interchangeable Inflex recoil pad, silver nitride receiver; striker-based trigger, ported barrel option. Models include: Cynergy Sporting, Adjustable Comb; Cynergy Sporting Composite CF; Cynergy Field, Composite; Cynergy Classic

Prices given are believed to be accurate at time of publication however, many factors affect retail pricing so exact prices are not possible.

Sporting; Cynergy Classic Field; Cynergy Camo Mossy Oak New Shadow Grass; Cynergy Camo Mossy Oak New Break-Up; and Cynergy Camo Mossy Oak Brush. Imported from Japan by Browning.

Price: Cynergy Classic Field, 12 ga., from **$2,399.00**
Price: Cynergy Classic Field Grade III, similar to Cynergy Classic Field but with full coverage high-relief engraving on reciever and top lever, gloss finish Grade III/IV walnut, from **$3,499.00**
Price: Cyergy Classic Field Grade VI, similar to Cynergy Classic Field Grade III but with more extensive, gold-highlighted engraving, from **$5,229.00**
Price: Cynergy Classic Sporting, from **$3,499.00**
Price: Cynergy Euro Sporting, 12 ga.; 28", 30", or 32" barrels **$3,719.00**
Price: Cynergy Euro Sporting Composite 12 ga. **$3,499.00**
Price: Cynergy Euro Sporting, adjustable comb, intr. 2006 . **$4,079.00**
Price: Cynergy Feather, 12 ga. intr. 2007 . . . . **$2,579.00**
Price: Cynergy Feather, 20, 28 ga., .410, intr. 2008 . . . . . . **$2,599.00**
Price: Cynergy Euro Sporting, 20 ga., intr. 2008 . . . . **$3,739.00**
Price: Cynergy Euro Field, Invector Plus tubes in 12 and 20 gauge, standard Invector tubes on 28 gauge and 410 . . . . **$2,509.00**

BROWNING CITORI O/U SHOTGUNS
Gauge: 12, 20, 28 and .410. **Barrel:** 26", 28" in 28 and .410. Offered with Invector choke tubes. All 12 and 20 gauge models have back-bored barrels and Invector Plus choke system. **Weight:** 6 lbs., 8 oz. (26" .410) to 7 lbs., 13 oz. (30" 12 ga.). **Length:** 43" overall (26" bbl.). **Stock:** Dense walnut, hand checkered, full pistol grip, beavertail forend. Field-type recoil pad on 12 ga. field guns and trap and skeet models. **Sights:** Medium raised beads, German nickel silver. **Features:** Barrel selector integral with safety, automatic ejectors, three-piece takedown. Citori 625 Field (intr. 2008) includes Vector Pro extended forcing cones, new wood checkering patterns, silver-nitride finish with high-relief engraving, gloss oil finish with Grade II/III walnut with radius pistol grip, Schnabel forearm, 12 gauge, three Invector Plus choke tubes. Citori 625 Sporting (intr. 2008) includes standard and adjustable combs, 32", 30", and 28" barrels, five Diamond Grade extended Invector Plus choke tubes. Triple Trigger System allows adjusting length of pull and choice of wide checkered, narrow smooth, and wide smooth canted trigger shoe. HiViz Pro-Comp fiber-optic front sights. Imported from Japan by Browning.
Price: Lightning, from **$1,763.00**
Price: White Lightning, from **$1,836.00**
Price: Superlight Feather **$2,098.00**
Price: Lightning Feather, combo 20 and 28 ga. **$1,869.00**
Price: 625 Field, 12, 20 or 28 ga. and 410. Weighs 6 lbs. 12 oz. to 7 lbs. 14 oz. **$2,339.00**

Price: 625 Sporting, 12, 20 or 28 ga. and 410, standard comb, intr. 2008 . . . . **$3,329.00**
Price: 625 Sporting, 12 ga., adj. comb, intr. 2008 . . . . **$3,639.00**

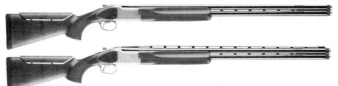

Browning Citori High Grade Shotguns
Similar to standard Citori except has engraved hunting scenes and gold inlays, high-grade, hand-oiled walnut stock and forearm. Introduced 2000. From Browning.
Price: Grade IV Lightning, engraved gray receiver, introduced 2005, from **$2,999.00**
Price: Grade VII Lightning, engraved gray or blue receiver, introduced 2005, from **$4,769.00**
Price: GTS High Grade, intr. 2007 . . . . **$4,309.00**

Browning Citori XS Sporting O/U Shotguns
Similar to the standard Citori except available in 12, 20, 28 or .410 with 28", 30", 32" ported barrels with various screw-in choke combinations: S (Skeet), C (Cylinder), IC (Improved Cylinder), M (Modified), and IM (Improved Modified). Has pistol grip stock, rounded or Schnabel forend. Weighs 7.1 lbs. to 8.75 lbs. Introduced 2004. Ultra XS Prestige (intr. 2008) has silver-nitride finish receiver with gold accented, high-relief Ultra XS Special engraving. Also, single selective trigger, hammer ejectors, gloss oil finish walnut stock with right-hand palm swell, adjustable comb, Schnabel forearm. Comes with five Invector-Plus Midas Grade choke tubes.
Price: XS Special, 12 ga.; 30", 32" barrels **$3,169.00**
Price: XS Skeet, 12 or 20 ga. **$2,829.00**
Price: XS Special High Post Rib, intr. 2007 . . . . **$3,169.00**
Price: Ultra XS Prestige, intr. 2008 . . . . **$4,759.00**

Browning Citori XT Trap O/U Shotgun
Similar to the Citori XS Special except has engraved silver nitride receiver with gold highlights, vented side barrel rib. Available in 12 gauge with 30" or 32" barrels, Invector-Plus choke tubes, adjustable comb and buttplate. Introduced 1999. Imported by Browning.
Price: XT Trap **$2,639.00**
Price: XT Trap w/adjustable comb **$2,959.00**
Price: XT Trap Gold w/adjustable comb, introduced 2005 . . **$4,899.00**

CHARLES DALY MODEL 206 O/U SHOTGUN
Gauge: 12, 3" chambers. **Barrel:** 26", 28", 30", chrome-moly steel. **Weight:** 8 lbs. **Stock:** Checkered select Turkish walnut stocks. **Features:** Single selective trigger, extractors or selective automatic ejectors. Sporting model has 10mm ventilated rib and side ventilated ribs. Trap model comes with 10mm top rib and side ventilated ribs and includes a Monte Carlo Trap buttstock. Both competition ribs have mid-brass bead and front fluorescent sights. Five Multi-Choke tubes. Introduced 2008. Imported from Turkey by K.B.I., Inc.
Price: Field, 26" or 28", extractors **$759.00**
Price: Field, 26" or 28", auto-eject **$884.00**
Price: Sporting, 28" or 30" ported, ... **$999.00**
Price: Trap, 28" or 30" ported, ... **$1,064.00**

CZ SPORTING OVER/UNDER
Gauge: 12, 3" chambers. **Barrel:** 30", 32" chrome-lined, back-bored with extended forcing cones. **Weight:** 9 lbs. **Length:** NA. **Stock:** Neutral cast stock with an adjustable comb, trap style forend, pistol grip and ambidextrous palm swells. #3 grade Circassian walnut. At lowest position, drop at comb: 1-5/8"; drop at heel: 2-3/8"; length of pull: 14-1/2". **Features:** Designed for Sporting Clays and FITASC competition. Hand engraving, satin black-finished receiver. Tapered rib with center bead and a red fiber-optic front bead, 10 choke tubes with wrench, single selective trigger, automatic ejectors, thin rubber pad with slick plastic top. Introduced 2008. From CZ-USA.
Price: **$2,509.00**

CZ CANVASBACK
Gauge: 12, 20, 3" chambers. **Barrel:** 26", 28". **Weight:** 7.3 lbs. **Length:** NA. **Stock:** Round-knob pistol grip, Schnabel forend, Turkish walnut. **Features:** Single selective trigger, set of 5 screw-in chokes, black chrome finished receiver. From CZ-USA.
Price: **$819.00**

CZ MALLARD
Gauge: 12, 20, 28, .410, 3" chambers. **Barrel:** 26". **Weight:** 7.7 lbs. **Length:** NA. **Stock:** Round-knob pistol grip, Schnabel forend, Turkish walnut. **Features:** Double triggers and extractors, coin finished receiver, multi chokes. From CZ-USA.
Price: **$562.00**

CZ REDHEAD
Gauge: 12, 20, 3" chambers. **Barrel:** 28". **Weight:** 7.4 lbs. **Length:** NA. **Stock:** Round-knob pistol grip, Schnabel forend, Turkish walnut. **Features:** Single selective triggers and extractors (12 & 20 ga.), screw-in chokes (12, 20, 28 ga.) choked IC and Mod (.410), coin finished receiver, multi chokes. From CZ-USA.
Price: **$965.00**

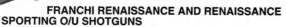

CZ WOODCOCK
Gauge: 12, 20, 28, .410, 3" chambers. **Barrel:** 26". **Weight:** 7.7 lbs. **Length:** NA. **Stock:** Round-knob pistol grip, Schnabel forend, Turkish walnut. **Features:** Single selective triggers and extractors (auto ejectors on 12 & 20 ga.), screw-in chokes (12, 20, 28 ga.) choked IC and Mod (.410), coin finished receiver, multi chokes. The sculptured frame incorporates a side plate, resembling a true side lock, embellished with hand engraving and finished with color casehardening. From CZ-USA.
Price: **$1,246.00**

ESCORT OVER/UNDER SHOTGUNS
Gauge: 12, 3" chamber. **Barrel:** 28". **Weight:** 7.4 lbs. **Stock:** Walnut or select walnut with Trio recoil pad; synthetic stock with adjustable comb. Three adjustment spacers. **Sights:** Bronze front bead. **Features:** Blued barrels, blued or nickel receiver. Trio recoil pad. Five interchangeable chokes (SK, IC, M, IM, F); extractors or ejectors (new, 2008), barrel selector. Hard case available. Introduced 2007. Imported from Turkey by Legacy Sports International.
Price: **$599.00**

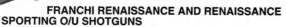

FRANCHI RENAISSANCE AND RENAISSANCE SPORTING O/U SHOTGUNS
Gauge: 12, 20, 28, 3" chamber. **Barrel:** 26", 28". **Weight:** 5.0 to 6.0 lbs. **Length:** 42-5/8" to 44-5/8". **Stock:** 14.5" LOP, European oil-finished walnut with standard grade A grade, and AA grade choices. Prince of Wales grip. **Features:** TSA recoil pad, interchangeable chokes, hard case. Introduced 2006. *Sporting model:* **Gauge:** 12 , 3". **Barrel:** 30" ported. **Weight:** 7.9 lbs. **Length:** 46 5/8". **Stock:** 14.5" LOP, A-grade European oil-finished walnut. **Features:** TSA recoil pad, adjustable comb, lengthened forcing cones, extended choke tubes (C, IC, M and wrench), hard case. Introduced 2007. Imported from Italy by Benelli USA.
Price: Field **$1,729.00**
Price: Classic **$1,899.00**
Price: Elite. **$2,399.00**
Price: Sporting **$2,249.00**

KIMBER MARIAS O/U SHOTGUN
Gauge: 20, 16; 3". **Barrel:** 26", 28", 30". **Weight:** 6.5 lbs. **Length:** NA. **Stock:** Turkish walnut stocks, 24-lpi checkering, oil finish. **LOP:** 14.75". **Features:** Hand-detachable back-action sidelock, bone-charcoal case coloring. Hand-engraving on receiver and locks, Belgian rust blue barrels, chrome lined. Five thinwall choke tubes, automatic ejectors, ventilated rib. Gold line cocking indicators on locks. Grade I has 28" barrels, Prince of Wales stock in grade three Turkish walnut in either 12 or 20 gauge. Grade II shas grade four Turkish walnut stocks, 12 gauge in Prince of Wales and 20 with either Prince of Wales or English profiles. Introduced 2008. Imported from Italy by Kimber Mfg., Inc.
Price: Grade II. **$5,799.00**

KOLAR SPORTING CLAYS O/U SHOTGUNS
Gauge: 12, 2-3/4" chambers. **Barrel:** 30", 32", 34"; extended choke tubes. **Stock:** 14-5/8"x2.5"x1-7/8"x1-3/8". French walnut. Four stock versions available. **Features:** Single selective trigger, detachable, adjustable for length; overbored barrels with long forcing cones; flat tramline rib; matte blue finish. Made in U.S. by Kolar.
Price: Standard. **$9,595.00**
Price: Prestige **$14,190.00**
Price: Elite Gold **$16,590.00**
Price: Legend **$17,090.00**
Price: Select **$22,590.00**
Price: Custom . . . . **Price on request**

Kolar AAA Competition Trap O/U Shotgun
Similar to the Sporting Clays gun except has 32" O/U /34" Unsingle or 30" O/U /34" Unsingle barrels as an over/under, unsingle, or combination set. Stock dimensions are 14.5"x2.5"x1.5"; American or French walnut; step parallel rib standard. Contact maker for full listings. Made in U.S.A. by Kolar.
Price: Over/under, choke tubes, standard **$9,595.00**
Price: Combo (30"/34", 32"/34"), standard **$12,595.00**

Kolar AAA Competition Skeet O/U Shotgun
Similar to the Sporting Clays gun except has 28" or 30" barrels with Kolarite AAA sub gauge tubes; stock of American or French walnut with matte finish; flat tramline rib; under barrel adjustable for point of impact. Many options available. Contact maker for complete listing. Made in U.S.A. by Kolar.
Price: Standard, choke tubes **$10,995.00**
Price: Standard, choke tubes, two-barrel set **$12,995.00**

KRIEGHOFF K-80 SPORTING CLAYS O/U SHOTGUN
Gauge: 12. **Barrel:** 28", 30", 32", 34" with choke tubes. **Weight:** About 8 lbs. **Stock:** #3 Sporting stock designed for gun-down shooting. **Features:** Standard receiver with satin nickel finish and classic scroll engraving. Selective mechanical trigger adjustable for position. Choice of tapered flat or 8mm parallel flat barrel rib. Free-floating barrels. Aluminum case. Imported from Germany by Krieghoff International, Inc.
Price: Standard grade with five choke tubes, from **$9,395.00**

KRIEGHOFF K-80 SKEET O/U SHOTGUNS
Gauge: 12, 2-3/4" chambers. **Barrel:** 28", 30", 32", (skeet & skeet), optional choke tubes). **Weight:** About 7.75 lbs. **Stock:** American skeet or straight skeet stocks, with palm-swell grips. Walnut. **Features:** Satin gray receiver finish. Selective mechanical trigger adjustable for position. Choice of ventilated 8mm parallel flat rib or ventilated 8-12mm tapered flat rib. Introduced 1980. Imported from Germany by Krieghoff International, Inc.
Price: Standard, skeet chokes **$8,375.00**
Price: Skeet Special (28", 30", 32" tapered flat rib,
skeet & skeet choke tubes). **$9,100.00**

KRIEGHOFF K-80 TRAP O/U SHOTGUNS
Gauge: 12, 2-3/4" chambers. **Barrel:** 30", 32" (Imp. Mod. & Full or choke tubes). **Weight:** About 8.5 lbs. **Stock:** Four stock dimensions or adjustable stock available; all have palm-swell grips. Checkered European walnut. **Features:** Satin nickel receiver. Selective mechanical trigger, adjustable for position. Ventilated step rib. Introduced 1980. Imported from Germany by Krieghoff International, Inc.
Price: K-80 O/U (30", 32", Imp. Mod. & Full), from **$8,850.00**
Price: K-80 Unsingle (32", 34", Full), standard, from **$10,080.00**
Price: K-80 Combo (two-barrel set), standard, from **$13,275.00**

Prices given are believed to be accurate at time of publication however, many factors affect retail pricing so exact prices are not possible.

Krieghoff K-20 O/U Shotgun
Similar to the K-80 except built on a 20-gauge frame. Designed for skeet, sporting clays and field use. Offered in 20, 28 and .410; 28", 30" and 32" barrels. Imported from Germany by Krieghoff International Inc.
Price: K-20, 20 gauge, from **$9,575.00**
Price: K-20, 28 gauge, from **$9,725.00**
Price: K-20, .410, from **$9,725.00**

LEBEAU-COURALLY BOSS-VEREES O/U SHOTGUN
Gauge: 12, 20, 2-3/4" chambers. **Barrel:** 25" to 32". **Weight:** To customer specifications. **Stock:** Exhibition-quality French walnut. **Features:** Boss-type sidelock with automatic ejectors; single or double triggers; chopper lump barrels. A custom gun built to customer specifications. Imported from Belgium by Wm. Larkin Moore.
Price: From **$96,000.00**

LJUTIC LM-6 SUPER DELUXE O/U SHOTGUNS
Gauge: 12. **Barrel:** 28" to 34", choked to customer specs for live birds, trap, international trap. **Weight:** To customer specs. **Stock:** To customer specs. Oil finish, hand checkered. **Features:** Custom-made gun. Hollow-milled rib, pull or release trigger, push-button opener in front of trigger guard. From Ljutic Industries.
Price: Super Deluxe LM-6 O/U **$19,995.00**
Price: Over/Under combo (interchangeable single barrel, two trigger guards, one for single trigger, one for doubles) **$27,995.00**
Price: Extra over/under barrel sets, 29"-32" **$6,995.00**

MARLIN L. C. SMITH O/U SHOTGUNS
Gauge: 12, 20. **Barrel:** 26", 28". **Stock:** Checkered walnut w/recoil pad. **Length:** 45". **Weight:** 7.25 lbs. **Features:** 3" chambers; 3 choke tubes (IC, Mod., Full), single selective trigger, selective automatic ejectors; vent rib; bead front sight. Imported from Italy by Marlin. Introduced 2005.
Price: LC12-OU (12 ga., 28" barrel) **$1,254.00**
Price: LC20-OU (20 ga., 26" barrel, 6.25 lbs., OAL 43") . . . **$1,254.00**

MERKEL MODEL 2001EL O/U SHOTGUN
Gauge: 12, 20, 3" chambers, 28, 2-3/4" chambers. **Barrel:** 12-28"; 20, 28 ga.-26.75". **Weight:** About 7 lbs. (12 ga.). **Stock:** Oil-finished walnut; English or pistol grip. **Features:** Self-cocking Blitz boxlock action with cocking indicators; Kersten double cross-bolt lock; silver-grayed receiver with engraved hunting scenes; coil spring ejectors; single selective or double triggers. Imported from Germany by Merkel USA.
Price: **$9,995.00**
Price: Model 2001EL Sporter; full pistol grip stock **$9,995.00**

Merkel Model 2000CL O/U Shotgun
Similar to Model 2001EL except scroll-engraved case-hardened receiver; 12, 20, 28 gauge. Imported from Germany by Merkel USA.
Price: **$8,495.00**
Price: Model 2016 CL; 16 gauge **$8,495.00**

PERAZZI MX8/MX8 SPECIAL TRAP, SKEET O/U SHOTGUNS
Gauge: 12, 2-3/4" chambers. **Barrel:** Trap: 29.5" (Imp. Mod. & Extra Full), 31.5" (Full & Extra Full). Choke tubes optional. Skeet: 27-5/8" (skeet & skeet). **Weight:** About 8.5 lbs. (trap); 7 lbs., 15 oz. (skeet). **Stock:** Interchangeable and custom made to customer specs. **Features:** Has detachable and interchangeable trigger group with flat V springs. Flat 7/16" vent rib. Many options available. Imported from Italy by Perazzi U.S.A., Inc.
Price: MX Trap Single. **$10,934.00**

Perazzi MX8 Special Skeet O/U Shotgun
Similar to the MX8 Skeet except has adjustable four-position trigger, skeet stock dimensions. Imported from Italy by Perazzi U.S.A., Inc.
Price: From **$11,166.00**

PERAZZI MX8 O/U SHOTGUNS
Gauge: 12, 2-3/4" chambers. **Barrel:** 28-3/8" (Imp. Mod. & Extra Full), 29.5" (choke tubes). **Weight:** 7 lbs., 12 oz. **Stock:** Special specifications. **Features:** Has single selective trigger; flat 7/16" x 5/16" vent rib. Many options available. Imported from Italy by Perazzi U.S.A., Inc.
Price: Standard. **$12,532.00**
Price: Sporting **$11,166.00**
Price: Trap Double Trap (removable trigger group) **$15,581.00**
Price: Skeet **$12,756.00**
Price: SC3 grade (variety of engraving patterns) . . . . . . **$23,000.00+**
Price: SCO grade (more intricate engraving, gold inlays). **$39,199.00+**

Perazzi MX8/20 O/U Shotgun
Similar to the MX8 except has smaller frame and has a removable trigger mechanism. Available in trap, skeet, sporting or game models with fixed chokes or choke tubes. Stock is made to customer specifications. Introduced 1993. Imported from Italy by Perazzi U.S.A., Inc.
Price: From **$11,731.00**

PERAZZI MX12 HUNTING O/U SHOTGUNS
Gauge: 12, 2-3/4" chambers. **Barrel:** 26.75", 27.5", 28-3/8", 29.5" (Mod. & Full); choke tubes available in 27-5/8", 29.5" only (MX12C). **Weight:** 7 lbs., 4 oz. **Stock:** To customer specs; interchangeable. **Features:** Single selective trigger; coil springs used in action; Schnabel forend tip. Imported from Italy by Perazzi U.S.A., Inc.
Price: From **$11,166.00**
Price: MX12C (with choke tubes). From. **$11,960.00**

Perazzi MX20 Hunting O/U Shotguns
Similar to the MX12 except 20 ga. frame size. Non-removable trigger group. Available in 20, 28, .410 with 2-3/4" or 3" chambers. 26" standard, and choked Mod. & Full. Weight is 6 lbs., 6 oz. Imported from Italy by Perazzi U.S.A., Inc.
Price: From **$11,166.00**
Price: MX20C (as above, 20 ga. only, choke tubes). From **$11,960.00**

PERAZZI MX10 O/U SHOTGUN
Gauge: 12, 2-3/4" chambers. **Barrel:** 29.5", 31.5" (fixed chokes). **Weight:** NA. **Stock:** Walnut; cheekpiece adjustable for elevation and cast. **Features:** Adjustable rib; vent side rib. Externally selective trigger. Available in single barrel, combo, over/under trap, skeet, pigeon and sporting models. Introduced 1993. Imported from Italy by Perazzi U.S.A., Inc.
Price: MX200410 . . . . **$18,007.00**

PERAZZI MX28, MX410 GAME O/U SHOTGUN
Gauge: 28, 2-3/4" chambers, .410, 3" chambers. **Barrel:** 26" (Imp. Cyl. & Full). **Weight:** NA. **Stock:** To customer specifications. **Features:** Made on scaled-down frames proportioned to the gauge. Introduced 1993. Imported from Italy by Perazzi U.S.A., Inc.
Price: From **$22,332.00**

PIOTTI BOSS

O/U SHOTGUN
Gauge: 12, 20. **Barrel:** 26" to 32", chokes as specified. **Weight:** 6.5 to 8 lbs. **Stock:** Dimensions to customer specs. Best quality figured walnut. **Features:** Essentially a custom-made gun with many options. Introduced 1993. Imported from Italy by Wm. Larkin Moore.
Price: From **$69,000.00**

POINTER OVER/UNDER SHOTGUN
Gauge: 12, 20, 28, .410, 3" chambers. **Barrel:** 28", blued. **Weight:** 6.1 to 7.6 lbs. **Stock:** Turkish Walnut. **Sights:** Fiber-optic front, bronze mid-bead. **Choke:** IC/M/F. **Features:** Engraved nickel receiver, automatic ejectors, fitted hard plastic case. Clays model has

oversized fiber-optic front sight and palm swell pistol grip. Introduced 2007. Imported from Turkey by Legacy Sports International.
Price: . . . .**$1,299.00 to $1,499.00**

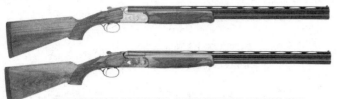

REMINGTON PREMIER OVER/UNDER SHOTGUNS
Gauge: 12, 20, 28, 3" chambers; 28, 2-3/4" chambers. **Barrel:** 26", 28", 30" in 12 gauge; overbored (.735), polished blue; 7mm vent rib. **Sights:** Ivory front bead, steel mid bead. **Weight:** 6.5 to 7.5 lbs. **Stock:** Walnut, cut checkering, Schnabel forends. Checkered pistol grip, checkered forend, satin finish, rubber butt pad. Right-hand palm swell. **Features:** Single selective mechanical trigger, selective automatic ejectors; serrated free-floating vent rib. Five flush mount ProBore choke tubes for 12s and 20s; 28-gauge equipped with 3 flush mount ProBore choke tubes. Hard case included. Introduced 2006. Made in Italy, imported by Remington Arms Co.
Price: Premier Field, nickel-finish receiver, from **$2,086.00**
Price: Premier Upland, case-colored receiver finish, from . . **$2,226.00**
Price: Premier Competition STS (2007) **$2,540.00**
Price: Premier Competition STS Adj. Comb (2007) **$2,890.00**

REMINGTON SPR310 OVER/UNDER SHOTGUNS
Gauge: 12, 20, 28, .410 bore, 3" chambers; 28, 2-3/4" chambers. **Barrel:** 26", 28", 29.5"; blued chrome-lined. **Weight:** 7.25 to 7.5 lbs. **Stock:** Checkered walnut stock and forend, 14.5" LOP; 1.5" drop at comb; 2.5" drop at heel. **Features:** Nickel finish or blued receiver. Single selective mechanical trigger, selective automatic ejectors; serrated free-floating vent rib. SC-4 choke tube set on most models. Sporting has ported barrels, right-hand palm swell, target forend, wide rib. Introduced 2008. Imported by Remington Arms Co.
Price: SPR310, from **$598.00**
Price: SPR310 Sporting **$770.00**

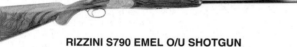

RIZZINI S790 EMEL O/U SHOTGUN
Gauge: 20, 28, .410. **Barrel:** 26", 27.5" (Imp. Cyl. & Imp. Mod.). **Weight:** About 6 lbs. **Stock:** 14"x1.5"x2-1/8". Extra fancy select walnut. **Features:** Boxlock action with profuse engraving; automatic ejectors; single selective trigger; silvered receiver. Comes with Nizzoli leather case. Introduced 1996. Imported from Italy by Wm. Larkin Moore & Co.
Price: From **$14,600.00**

Rizzini S792 EMEL O/U Shotgun
Similar to S790 EMEL except dummy sideplates with extensive engraving coverage. Nizzoli leather case. Introduced 1996. Imported from Italy by Wm. Larkin Moore & Co.
Price: From **$15,500.00**

RIZZINI UPLAND EL O/U SHOTGUN
Gauge: 12, 16, 20, 28, .410. **Barrel:** 26", 27.5", Mod. & Full, Imp. Cyl. & Imp. Mod. choke tubes. **Weight:** About 6.6 lbs. **Stock:** 14.5"x1-1/2"x2.25". **Features:** Boxlock action; single selective trigger; ejectors; profuse engraving on silvered receiver. Comes with fitted case. Introduced 1996. Imported from Italy by Wm. Larkin Moore & Co.
Price: From **$5,200.00**

Rizzini Artemis O/U Shotgun
Same as Upland EL model except dummy sideplates with extensive game scene engraving. Fancy European walnut stock. Fitted case. Introduced 1996. Imported from Italy by Wm. Larkin Moore & Co.
Price: From **$3,260.00**

RIZZINI S782 EMEL O/U SHOTGUN
Gauge: 12, 2-3/4" chambers. **Barrel:** 26", 27.5" (Imp. Cyl. & Imp. Mod.). **Weight:** About 6.75 lbs. **Stock:** 14.5"x1.5"x2.25". Extra fancy select walnut. **Features:** Boxlock action with dummy sideplates, extensive engraving with gold inlaid game birds, silvered receiver,

---

automatic ejectors, single selective trigger. Nizzoli leather case. Introduced 1996. Imported from Italy by Wm. Larkin Moore & Co.
Price: From **$18,800.00**

RUGER RED LABEL O/U SHOTGUNS
Gauge: 12, 20, 3" chambers; 28 2-3/4" chambers. **Barrel:** 26", 28", 30" in 12 gauge. **Weight:** About 7 lbs. (20 ga.); 7.5 lbs. (12 ga.). **Length:** 43" overall (26" barrels). **Stock:** 14"x1.5"x2.5". Straight grain American walnut. Checkered pistol grip or straight grip, checkered forend, rubber butt pad. **Features:** Stainless steel receiver. Single selective mechanical trigger, selective automatic ejectors; serrated free-floating vent rib. Comes with two skeet, one Imp. Cyl., one Mod., one Full choke tube and wrench. Made in U.S. by Sturm, Ruger & Co.
Price: Red Label with pistol grip stock **$1,956.00**
Price: English Field with straight-grip stock **$1,956.00**
Price: Sporting clays (30" bbl.) **$1,956.00**

Ruger Engraved Red Label O/U Shotgun
Similar to Red Label except scroll engraved receiver with 24-carat gold game bird (pheasant in 12 gauge, grouse in 20 gauge, woodcock in 28 gauge). Introduced 2000.
Price: Engraved Red Label, pistol grip only **$2,180.00**

SAVAGE MILANO O/U SHOTGUNS
Gauge: 12, 20, 28, and 410, 2-3/4" (28 ga.) and 3" chambers. **Barrel:** 28"; chrome lined, elongated forcing cones, automatic ejectors. 12, 20, and 28 come with 3 Interchokes (F-M-IC); 410 has fixed chokes (M-IC). **Weight:** 12 ga., 7.5 lbs; 20, 28 gauge, .410, 6.25 lbs. **Length:** NA. **Stock:** Satin finish Turkish walnut stock with laser-engraved checkering, solid rubber recoil pad, Schnabel forend. **Features:** Single selective, mechanical set trigger, fiber-optic front sight with brass mid-rib bead. Introduced 2006. Imported from Italy by Savage Arms, Inc.
Price: **$1,714.00**

SKB MODEL GC7 O/U SHOTGUNS
Gauge: 12 or 20, 3"; 28, 2-3/4"; .410, 3". **Barrel:** 26", 28", Briley internal chokes. **Weight:** NA. **Length:** NA. **Stock:** Grade II and Grade III American black walnut, high-gloss finish, finger-groove forend. **Sights:** Top ventilated rib, sloped with matte surface (Game). **Features:** Low-profile boxlock action; Greener crossbolt locking action, silver-nitride finish; automatic ejectors; single selective trigger. Introduced 2008. Imported from Japan by SKB Shotguns, Inc.
Price: GC7 Game Bird Grade 1, from **$1,569.00**
Price: GC7 Clays Grade 1, from **$1,679.00**

SKB MODEL 85TSS O/U SHOTGUNS
Gauge: 12, 20, .410: 3"; 28, 2-3/4". **Barrel:** Chrome lined 26", 28", 30", 32" (w/choke tubes). **Weight:** 7 lbs., 7 oz. to 8 lbs., 14 oz. **Stock:** Hand-checkered American walnut with matte finish, Schnabel or grooved forend. Target stocks available in various styles. **Sights:** HiViz competition sights. **Features:** Low profile boxlock action with Greener-style cross bolt; single selective trigger; manual safety. Back-bored barrels with lengthened forcing cones. Introduced 2004. Imported from Japan by SKB Shotguns, Inc.
Price: Sporting Clays, Skeet, fixed comb, from **$2,199.00**
Price: Sporting clays, Skeet, adjustable comb, from **$2,429.00**
Price: Trap, standard or Monte Carlo **$2,329.00**
Price: Trap adjustable comb **$2,529.00**
Price: Trap Unsingle (2007) **$2,799.00**

SKB MODEL 585 O/U SHOTGUNS
Gauge: 12 or 20, 3"; 28, 2-3/4"; .410, 3". **Barrel:** 12 ga.-26", 28", (InterChoke tubes); 20 ga.-26", 28" (InterChoke tubes); 28-26", 28" (InterChoke tubes); .410-26", 28" (InterChoke tubes). **Weight:** 6.6 to 8.5 lbs. **Length:** 43" to 51-3/8" overall. **Stock:** 14-1/8"x1.5"x2-3/16".

Prices given are believed to be accurate at time of publication however, many factors affect retail pricing so exact prices are not possible.

Hand checkered walnut with matte finish. **Sights:** Metal bead front (field). **Features:** Boxlock action; silver nitride finish; manual safety, automatic ejectors, single selective trigger. All 12-gauge barrels are back-bored, have lengthened forcing cones and longer choke tube system. Introduced 1992. Imported from Japan by SKB Shotguns, Inc.

Price: Field **$1,699.00**
Price: Two-barrel field set, 12 & 20. . . . . **$2,749.00**
Price: Two-barrel field set, 20 & 28 or 28 & .410 . . . . **$2,829.00**

SMITH & WESSON ELITE SILVER SHOTGUNS

Gauge: 12, 3" chambers. **Barrel:** 26", 28", 30", rust-blued chopper-lump. **Weight:** 7.8 lbs. **Length:** 46-48". **Sights:** Ivory front bead, metal mid-bead. **Stock:** AAA (grade III) Turkish walnut stocks, hand-cut checkering, satin finish. **Features:** Smith & Wesson-designed trigger-plate action, hand-engraved receivers, bone-charcoal case hardening, lifetime warranty. Five choke tubes. Introduced 2007. Made in Turkey, imported by Smith & Wesson.

Price: **$2,380.00**

STEVENS MODEL 512 GOLD WING SHOTGUNS

Gauge: 12, 20, 28, .410; 2-3/4" and 3" chambers. **Barrel:** 26", 28". **Weight:** 6 to 8 lbs. **Sights:** NA. **Features:** Five screw-in choke tubes with 12, 20, and 28 gauge; .410 has fixed M/IC chokes. Black chrome, sculpted receiver with a raised gold pheasant, laser engraved trigger guard and forend latch. Turkish walnut stock finished in satin lacquer and beautifully laser engraved with fleur-de-lis checkering on the side panels, wrist and Schnabel forearm.

Price: **$649.00**

STOEGER CONDOR O/U SHOTGUNS

Gauge: 12, 20, 2-3/4" 3" chambers; 16, .410. **Barrel:** 22", 24", 26", 28", 30". **Weight:** 5.5 to 7.8 lbs. **Sights:** Brass bead. **Features:** IC, M, or F screw-in choke tubes with each gun. Oil finished hardwood with pistol grip and forend. Auto safety, single trigger, automatic extractors.

Price: Condor, 12, 20, 16 ga. or .410 . . . . **$399.00**
Price: Condor Supreme (w/mid bead), 12 or 20 ga. **$599.00**
Price: Condor Combo, 12 and 20 ga. Barrels, from **$549.00**
Price: Condor Youth, 20 ga. or .410 . . . . **$399.00**
Price: Condor Competition, 12 or 20 ga. **$599.00**
Price: Condor Combo, 12/20 ga., RH or LH (2007) **$829.00**
Price: Condor Outback, 12 or 20 ga., 20" barrel. **$369.00**

TRADITIONS CLASSIC SERIES O/U SHOTGUNS

Gauge: 12, 3"; 20, 3"; 16, 2-3/4"; 28, 2-3/4"; .410, 3". **Barrel:** 26" and 28". **Weight:** 6 lbs., 5 oz. to 7 lbs., 6 oz. **Length:** 43" to 45" overall. **Stock:** Walnut. **Features:** Single-selective trigger; chrome-lined barrels with screw-in choke tubes; extractors (Field Hunter and Field I models) or automatic ejectors (Field II and Field III models); rubber butt pad; top tang safety. Imported from Fausti of Italy by Traditions.

Price: Field Hunter: Blued receiver; 12 or 20 ga.; 26" bbl. has IC and Mod. tubes, 28" has mod. and full tubes **$669.00**
Price: Field I: Blued receiver; 12, 20, 28 ga. or .410; fixed chokes (26" has I.C. and mod., 28" has mod. and full). . **$619.00**
Price: Field II: Coin-finish receiver; 12, 16, 20, 28 ga. or .410; gold trigger; choke tubes **$789.00**
Price: Field III: Coin-finish receiver; gold engraving and trigger; 12 ga.; 26" or 28" bbl.; choke tubes **$999.00**
Price: Upland II: Blued receiver; 12 or 20 ga.; English-style straight walnut stock; choke tubes **$839.00**
Price: Upland III: Blued receiver, gold engraving; 20 ga.; high-grade pistol grip walnut stock; choke tubes **$1,059.00**
Price: Upland III: Blued, gold engraved receiver, 12 ga. Round pistol grip stock, choke tubes **$1,059.00**
Price: Sporting Clay II: Silver receiver; 12 ga.; ported barrels with skeet, i.c., mod. and full extended tubes. **$959.00**
Price: Sporting Clay III: Engraved receivers, 12 and 20 ga.; walnut stock, vent rib, extended choke tubes **$1,189.00**

TRADITIONS MAG 350 SERIES O/U SHOTGUNS

Gauge: 12, 3-1/2". **Barrel:** 24", 26" and 28". **Weight:** 7 lbs. to 7 lbs., 4 oz. **Length:** 41" to 45" overall. **Stock:** Walnut or composite with Mossy Oak Break-Up or Advantage Wetlands camouflage. **Features:** Black matte, engraved receiver; vent rib; automatic ejectors; single selective trigger; three screw-in choke tubes; rubber recoil pad; top tang safety. Imported from Fausti of Italy by Traditions.

Price: (Mag Hunter II: 28" black matte barrels, walnut stock, includes I.C., Mod. and Full tubes) **$799.00**
Price: (Turkey II: 24" or 26" camo barrels, Break-Up camo stock, includes Mod., Full and X-Full tubes) **$889.00**
Price: (Waterfowl II: 28" camo barrels, Advantage Wetlands camo stock, includes IC, Mod. and Full tubes) **$899.00**

TRISTAR HUNTER EX O/U SHOTGUN

Gauge: 12, 20, 28, .410. **Barrel:** 26", 28". **Weight:** 5.7 lbs. (.410); 6.0 lbs. (20, 28), 7.2-7.4 lbs. (12). Chrome-lined steel mono-block barrel, five Beretta-style choke tubes (SK, IC, M, IM, F). **Length:** NA. **Stock:** Walnut, cut checkering. 14.25"x1.5"x2-3/8". **Sights:** Brass front sight. **Features:** All have extractors, engraved receiver, sealed actions, self-adjusting locking bolts, single selective trigger, ventilated rib. 28 ga. and .410 built on true frames. Five-year warranty. Imported from Italy by Tristar Sporting Arms Ltd.

Price: From **$619.00**

VERONA 501 SERIES O/U SHOTGUNS

Gauge: 12, 20, 28, .410 (3" chambers). **Barrel:** 28". **Weight:** 6-7 lbs. **Stock:** Enhanced walnut with Scottish net type checkering and oiled finish. **Features:** Select fire single trigger, automatic ejectors, chromed barrels with X-CONE system to reduce felt recoil, and ventilated rubber butt pad. Introduced 1999. Imported from Italy by Legacy Sports International.

Price: Combos 20/28, 28/.410 . . . . **$1,599.00**

Verona 702 Series O/U Shotguns
Same as 501 series model except. with deluxe nickel receiver.
Price: **$1,699.00**

Verona LX692 Gold Hunting O/U Shotguns

Similar to Verona 501 except engraved, silvered receiver with false sideplates showing gold inlaid bird hunting scenes on three sides; Schnabel forend tip; hand-cut checkering; black rubber butt pad. Available in 12 and 20 gauge only, five Interchoke tubes. Introduced 1999. Imported from Italy by B.C. Outdoors.

Price: **$1,295.00**
Price: LX692G Combo 28/.410. . . . . **$2,192.40**

Verona LX680 Sporting O/U Shotgun
Similar to Verona 501 except engraved, silvered receiver; ventilated middle rib; beavertail forend; hand-cut checkering; available in 12 or 20 gauge only with 2-3/4" chambers. Introduced 1999. Imported from Italy by B.C. Outdoors.
Price: **$1,159.68**

Verona LX680 Skeet/Sporting/Trap O/U Shotgun
Similar to Verona 501 except skeet or trap stock dimensions; beavertail forend, palm swell on pistol grip; ventilated center barrel rib. Introduced 1999. Imported from Italy by B.C. Outdoors.
Price: **$1,736.96**

Verona LX692 Gold Sporting O/U Shotgun
Similar to Verona LX680 except false sideplates have gold-inlaid bird hunting scenes on three sides; red high-visibility front sight. Introduced 1999. Imported from Italy by B.C. Outdoors.
Price: Skeet/sporting. **$1,765.12**
Price: Trap (32" barrel, 7-7/8 lbs.) **$1,594.80**

VERONA LX680 COMPETITION TRAP O/U SHOTGUNS

Gauge: 12. **Barrel:** 30" O/U, 32" single bbl. **Weight:** 8-3/8 lbs. combo, 7 lbs. single. **Stock:** Walnut. **Sights:** White front, mid-rib bead.

Features: Interchangeable barrels switch from OU to single configurations. 5 Briley chokes in combo, 4 in single bbl. extended forcing cones, ported barrels 32" with raised rib. By B.C. Outdoors.
Price: Trap Single (LX680TGTSB) $1,736.96
Price: Trap Combo (LX680TC) $2,553.60

VERONA LX702 GOLD TRAP COMBO O/U SHOTGUNS
Gauge: 20/28, 2-3/4" chamber. **Barrel:** 30". **Weight:** 7 lbs. **Stock:** Turkish walnut with beavertail forearm. **Sights:** White front bead. **Features:** 2-barrel competition gun. Color case-hardened side plates and receiver with gold inlaid pheasant. Vent rib between barrels. 5 Interchokes. Imported from Italy by B.C. Outdoors.
Price: Combo $2,467.84
Price: 20 ga. $1,829.12

Verona LX702 Skeet/Trap O/U Shotguns
Similar to Verona LX702. Both are 12 gauge and 2-3/4" chamber. Skeet has 28" barrel and weighs 7.75 lbs. Trap has 32" barrel and weighs 7-7/8 lbs. By B.C. Outdoors.
Price: Skeet $1,829.12
Price: Trap $1,829.12

WEATHERBY ATHENA GRADE V AND GRADE III CLASSIC FIELD O/U SHOTGUNS
Gauge: Grade III and Grade IV: 12, 20, 3" chambers; 28, 2-3/4" chambers. Grade V: 12, 20, 3" chambers. **Barrel:** 26", 28" monobloc, IMC multi-choke tubes. Modified Greener crossbolt action. Matte ventilated top rib with brilliant front bead. **Weight:** 12 ga., 7.25 to 8 lbs.; 20 ga. 6.5 to 7.25 lbs. **Length:** 43" to 45". **Stock:** Rounded pistol grip, slender forend, Old English recoil pad. Grade V has oil-finished AAA American Claro walnut with 20-lpi checkering. Grade III has AA Claro walnut with oil finish, fine-line checkering. **Features:** Silver nitride/gray receivers; Grade III has hunting scene engraving. Grade IV has chrome-plated false sideplates featuring single game scene gold plate overlay. Grade V has rose and scroll engraving with gold-overlay upland game scenes. Top levers engraved with gold Weatherby flying "W". Introduced 1999. Imported from Japan by Weatherby.
Price: Grade III $2,599.00
Price: Grade IV $2,799.00
Price: Grade V $3,999.00

WEATHERBY ORION D'ITALIA O/U SHOTGUNS
Gauge: 12, 20, 3" chambers; 28, 2-3/4" chamber. **Barrel:** 26", 28", IMC multi-choke tubes. Matte ventilated top rib with brilliant bead front sight. **Weight:** 6-1/2 to 8 lbs. **Stock:** 14.25"x1.5"x2.5". American walnut, checkered grip and forend. Old English recoil pad. **Features:** All models have a triggerguard that features Weatherby's "Flying W" engraved with gold fill. D'Italia I available in 12 and 20 gauge, 26" and 28" barrels. Walnut stock with high lustre urethane finish. Metalwork is blued to high lustre finishand has a gold-plated trigger for corrosion protection. D'Italia II available in 12, 20 and 28 gauge with 26" and 28" barrels. Fancy grade walnut stock, hard chrome receiver with sculpted frameheads, elaborate game and floral engraving pattern, and matte vent mid & top rib with brilliant front bead sight. D'Italia III available in 12 and 20 gauge with 26" and 28" barrels. Hand-selected, oil-finished walnut stock wtih 20 LPI

checkering, intricate engraving and gold plate game scene overlay, and damascened monobloc barrel and sculpted frameheads. D'Italia SC available in 12 gauge only with barrel lengths of 28", 30", and 32", weighs 8 lbs. Features satin, oil-finished walnut stock that is adjustable for cheek height with target-style pistol grip and Schnaubel forend, shallow receiver aligns hands for improved balance and pointability, ported barrels reduce muzzle jump, and fiber optic front sight for quick targer acquisition. Introduced 1998. Imported from Japan by Weatherby.
Price: D'Italia I $1,699.00
Price: D'Italia II $1,899.00
Price: D'Italia III $2,199.00
Price: D'Italia SC. $2,599.00

WINCHESTER SELECT MODEL 101 O/U SHOTGUNS
Gauge: 12, 2-3/4", 3" chambers. **Barrel:** 28", 30", 32", ported, Invector Plus choke system. **Weight:** 7 lbs. 6 oz. to 7 lbs. 12. oz. **Stock:** Checkered high-gloss grade II/III walnut stock, Pachmayr Decelerator sporting pad. **Features:** Chrome-plated chambers; back-bored barrels; tang barrel selector/safety; Signature extended choke tubes. Model 101 Field comes with solid brass bead front sight, three tubes, engraved receiver. Model 101 Sporting has adjustable trigger, 10mm runway rib, white mid-bead, Tru-Glo front sight, 30" and 32" barrels. Camo version of Model 101 Field comes with full-coverage Mossy Oak Duck Blind pattern. Model 101 Pigeon Grade Trap has 10mm steel runway rib, mid-bead sight, interchangeable fiber-optic front sight, porting and vented side ribs, adjustable trigger shoe, fixed raised comb or adjustable comb, Grade III/IV walnut, 30" or 32" barrels, molded ABS hard case. Reintroduced 2008. From Winchester Repeating Arms Co.
Price: Model 101 Field $1,739.00
Price: Model 101 Deluxe Field $1,659.00
Price: Model 101 Sporting $2,139.00
Price: Model 101 Pigeon Grade Trap, intr. 2008 . . . . $2,299.00
Price: Model 101 Pigeon Grade Trap w/adj. comb,
intr. 2008. . . . . $2,429.00
Price: Model 101 Light (2009) $1,999.00
Price: Model 101 Pigeon Sporting (2009) $2,579.00

Prices given are believed to be accurate at time of publication however, many factors affect retail pricing so exact prices are not possible.

ARRIETA SIDELOCK DOUBLE SHOTGUNS
Gauge: 12, 16, 20, 28, .410. **Barrel:** Length and chokes to customer specs. **Weight:** To customer specs. **Stock:** To customer specs. Straight English with checkered butt (standard), or pistol grip. Select European walnut with oil finish. **Features:** Essentially custom gun with myriad options. H&H pattern hand-detachable sidelocks, selective automatic ejectors, double triggers (hinged front) standard. Some have selfopening action. Finish and engraving to customer specs. Imported from Spain by Quality Arms, Inc.
Price: Model 557 . . . . **$4,500.00**
Price: Model 570 . . . . **$5,350.00**
Price: Model 578 . . . . **$5,880.00**
Price: Model 600 Imperial **$7,995.00**
Price: Model 601 Imperial Tiro **$9,160.00**
Price: Model 801 . . . . **$14,275.00**
Price: Model 802 . . . . **$14,275.00**
Price: Model 803 . . . . **$9,550.00**
Price: Model 871 . . . . **$6,670.00**
Price: Model 872 . . . . **$17,850.00**
Price: Model 873 . . . . **$16,275.00**
Price: Model 874 . . . . **$13,125.00**
Price: Model 875 . . . . **$19,850.00**
Price: Model 931 . . . . **$20,895.00**

AYA MODEL 4/53 SHOTGUNS
Gauge: 12, 16, 20, 28, 410. **Barrel:** 26", 27", 28", 30". **Weight:** To customer specifications. **Length:** To customer specifications. **Features:** Hammerless boxlock action; double triggers; light scroll engraving; automatic safety; straight grip oil finish walnut stock; checkered butt. Made in Spain. Imported by New England Custom Gun Service, Lt.
Price: **$2,999.00**
Price: No. 2 . . . . **$4,799.00**
Price: No. 2 Rounded Action **$5,199.00**

BERETTA 471 SIDE-BY-SIDE SHOTGUNS
Gauge: 12, 20; 3" chamber. **Barrel:** 24", 26", 28"; 6mm rib. **Weight:** 6.5 lbs. **Stock:** English or pistol stock, straight butt for various types of recoil pads. Beavertail forend. English stock with recoil pad in red or black rubber, or in walnut and splinter forend. Select European walnut, checkered, oil finish. **Features:** Optima-Choke Extended Choke Tubes. Automatic ejection or mechanical extraction. Firing-pin block safety, manual or automatic, open top-lever safety. Introduced 2007. Imported from Italy by Beretta U.S.A.
Price: Silver Hawk **$3,750.00**

BILL HANUS NOBILE III BY FABARM
Gauge: 20. **Barrel:** 28" Tribor® barrels with 3" chambers and extra-long 82mm (3-1/4") internal choke tubes. **Weight:** 5.75 lbs. **Stock:** Upgraded walnut 1-1/2"x2-1/4"x14-3/8", with 1/4" cast-off to a wood butt plate. Altering to 1/4" cast-on for left-handed shooters, $300 extra. **Features:** Tribor® barrels feature extra-long forcing cones along with over-boring, back-boring and extra-long (82mm vs 50mm) choke tubes which put more pellets in the target area. Paradox®-rifled choke tube for wider patterns at short-range targets. Adjustable for automatic ejectors or manual extraction. Adjustable opening tension. Fitted leather case.
Price: **$3,395.00**

CONNECTICUT SHOTGUN MANUFACTURING COMPANY RBL SIDE-BY-SIDE SHOTGUN
Gauge: 12, 16, 20, 28. **Barrel:** 26", 28", 30", 32". **Weight:** NA. **Length:** NA. **Stock:** NA. **Features:** Round-action SXS shotguns made in the USA. Scaled frames, five TruLock choke tubes. Deluxe fancy grade walnut buttstock and forend. Quick Change recoil pad in two lengths. Various dimensions and options available depending on gauge.
Price: 12 gauge **$2,950.00**
Price: 20 gauge **$2,799.00**
Price: 28 gauge **$3,650.00**

CZ BOBWHITE AND RINGNECK SHOTGUNS
Gauge: 12, 20, 28, .410. (5 screw-in chokes in 12 and 20 ga. and fixed chokes in IC and Mod in .410). **Barrel:** 20". **Weight:** 6.5 lbs.

Length: NA. **Stock:** Sculptured Turkish walnut with straight English-style grip and double triggers (Bobwhite) or conventional American pistol grip with a single trigger (Ringneck). Both are hand checkered 20 lpi. **Features:** Both color case-hardened shotguns are hand engraved.
Price: Bobwhite **$789.00**
Price: Ringneck **$1,036.00**

CZ HAMMER COACH SHOTGUNS
Gauge: 12, 3" chambers. **Barrel:** 20". **Weight:** 6.7 lbs. **Length:** NA. **Stock:** NA. **Features:** Following in the tradition of the guns used by the stagecoach guards of the 1880's, this cowboy gun features double triggers, 19th century color case-hardening and fully functional external hammers.
Price: **$904.00**

DAKOTA PREMIER GRADE SHOTGUN
Gauge: 12, 16, 20, 28, .410. **Barrel:** 27". **Weight:** NA. **Length:** NA. **Stock:** Exhibition-grade English walnut, hand-rubbed oil finish with straight grip and splinter forend. **Features:** French grey finish; 50 percent coverage engraving; double triggers; selective ejectors. Finished to customer specifications. Made in U.S. by Dakota Arms.
Price: From **$14,950.00**

Dakota Legend Shotgun
Similar to Premier Grade except has special selection English walnut, full-coverage scroll engraving, oak and leather case. Made in U.S. by Dakota Arms.
Price: From **$19,000.00**

EMF OLD WEST HAMMER SHOTGUN
Gauge: 12. **Barrel:** 20". **Weight:** 8 lbs. **Length:** 37" overall. **Stock:** Smooth walnut with steel butt place. **Sights:** Large brass bead. **Features:** Colt-style exposed hammers rebounding type; blued receiver and barrels; cylinder bore. Introduced 2006. Imported from China for EMF by TTN.
Price: **$474.90**

FOX, A.H., SIDE-BY-SIDE SHOTGUNS
Gauge: 16, 20, 28, .410. **Barrel:** Length and chokes to customer specifications. Rust-blued Chromox or Krupp steel. **Weight:** 5-1/2 to 6.75 lbs. **Stock:** Dimensions to customer specifications. Hand-checkered Turkish Circassian walnut with hand-rubbed oil finish. Straight, semi or full pistol grip; splinter, Schnabel or beavertail forend; traditional pad, hard rubber buttplate or skeleton butt. **Features:** Boxlock action with automatic ejectors; double or Fox single selective trigger. Scalloped, rebated and color case-hardened receiver; hand finished and handengraved. Grades differ in engraving, inlays, grade of wood, amount of hand finishing. Introduced 1993. Made in U.S. by Connecticut Shotgun Mfg.
Price: CE Grade **$14,500.00**
Price: XE Grade **$16,000.00**
Price: DE Grade **$19,000.00**
Price: FE Grade **$24,000.00**
Price: 28/.410 CE Grade **$16,500.00**
Price: 28/.410 XE Grade **$18,000.00**
Price: 28/.410 DE Grade **$21,000.00**
Price: 28/.410 FE Grade **$26,000.00**

GARBI MODEL 100 DOUBLE SHOTGUN
Gauge: 12, 16, 20, 28. **Barrel:** 26", 28", choked to customer specs. **Weight:** 5-1/2 to 7.5 lbs. **Stock:** 14.5"x2.25"x1.5". European walnut. Straight grip, checkered butt, classic forend. **Features:** Sidelock action, automatic ejectors, double triggers standard. Color case-

SHOTGUNS—Side-by-Side

hardened action, coin finish optional. Single trigger; beavertail forend, etc. optional. Five additional models available. Imported from Spain by Wm. Larkin Moore.

Price: From **$4,850.00**

Garbi Model 101 Side-by-Side Shotgun

Similar to the Garbi Model 100 except hand engraved with scroll engraving; select walnut stock; better overall quality than the Model 100. Imported from Spain by Wm. Larkin Moore.

Price: From **$6,250.00**

Garbi Model 103 A & B Side-by-Side Shotguns

Similar to the Garbi Model 100 except has Purdey-type fine scroll and rosette engraving. Better overall quality than the Model 101. Model 103B has nickel-chrome steel barrels, H&H-type easy opening mechanism; other mechanical details remain the same. Imported from Spain by Wm. Larkin Moore.

Price: Model 103A. From **$14,100.00**
Price: Model 103B. From **$21,600.00**

Garbi Model 200 Side-by-Side Shotgun

Similar to the Garbi Model 100 except has heavy-duty locks, magnum proofed. Very fine Continental-style floral and scroll engraving, well figured walnut stock. Other mechanical features remain the same. Imported from Spain by Wm. Larkin Moore.

Price: **$17,100.00**

KIMBER VALIER SIDE-BY-SIDE SHOTGUN

Gauge: 20, 16, 3" chambers. **Barrels:** 26" or 28", IC and M. **Weight:** 6 lbs. 8 oz. **Stock:** Turkish walnut, English style. **Features:** Sidelock design, double triggers, 50-percent engraving; 24 lpi checkering; auto-ejectors (extractors only on Grade I). Color case-hardened sidelocks, rust blue barrels. Imported from Turkey by Kimber Mfg., Inc.

Price: Grade II. **$4,999.00**

LEBEAU-COURALLY BOXLOCK SIDE-BY-SIDE SHOTGUN

Gauge: 12, 16, 20, 28, .410-bore. **Barrel:** 25" to 32". **Weight:** To customer specifications. **Stock:** French walnut. **Features:** Anson & Deely-type action with automatic ejectors; single or double triggers. Custom gun built to customer specifications. Imported from Belgium by Wm. Larkin Moore.

Price: From **$25,500.00**

LEBEAU-COURALLY SIDELOCK SIDE-BY-SIDE SHOTGUN

Gauge: 12, 16, 20, 28, .410-bore. **Barrel:** 25" to 32". **Weight:** To customer specifications. **Stock:** Fancy French walnut. **Features:** Holland & Holland-type action with automatic ejectors; single or double triggers. Custom gun built to customer specifications. Imported from Belgium by Wm. Larkin Moore.

Price: From **$56,000.00**

MARLIN L. C. SMITH SIDE-BY-SIDE SHOTGUN

Gauge: 12, 20, 28, .410. **Stock:** Checkered walnut w/recoil pad. **Features:** 3" chambers, single trigger, selective automatic ejectors; 3 choke tubes (IC, Mod., Full); solid rib, bead front sight. Imported from Italy by Marlin. Introduced 2005.

Price: LC12-DB (28" barrel, 43" OAL, 6.25 lbs) **$1,962.00**
Price: LC28-DB (26" barrel, 41" OAL, 6 lbs) **$1,484.00**

MERKEL MODEL 47E, 147E SIDE-BY-SIDE SHOTGUNS

Gauge: 12, 3" chambers, 16, 2.75" chambers, 20, 3" chambers. **Barrel:** 12, 16 ga.-28"; 20 ga.-26.75" (Imp. Cyl. & Mod., Mod. & Full). **Weight:** About 6.75 lbs. (12 ga.). **Stock:** Oil-finished walnut; straight English or pistol grip. **Features:** Anson & Deeley-type boxlock action with single selective or double triggers, automatic safety, cocking

indicators. Color case-hardened receiver with standard arabesque engraving. Imported from Germany by Merkel USA.

Price: Model 47E (H&H ejectors) **$4,595.00**
Price: Model 147E (as above with ejectors) **$5,795.00**

Merkel Model 47EL, 147EL Side-by-Side Shotguns

Similar to Model 47E except H&H style sidelock action with cocking indicators, ejectors. Silver-grayed receiver and sideplates have arabesque engraving, engraved border and screws (Model 47E), or fine hunting scene engraving (Model 147E). Limited edition. Imported from Germany by Merkel USA.

Price: Model 47EL **$7,195.00**
Price: Model 147EL **$7,695.00**

Merkel Model 280EL, 360EL Shotguns

Similar to Model 47E except smaller frame. Greener cross bolt with double under-barrel locking lugs, fine engraved hunting scenes on silver-grayed receiver, luxury-grade wood, Anson and Deely boxlock action. H&H ejectors, single-selective or double triggers. Introduced 2000. Imported from Germany by Merkel USA.

Price: Model 280EL (28 gauge, 28" barrel, Imp. Cyl. and Mod. chokes) **$7,695.00**
Price: Model 360EL (.410, 28" barrel, Mod. and Full chokes) **$7,695.00**
Price: Model 280EL Combo **$11,195.00**

Merkel Model 280SL and 360SL Shotguns

Similar to Model 280EL and 360EL except has sidelock action, double triggers, English-style arabesque engraving. Introduced 2000. Imported from Germany by Merkel USA.

Price: Model 280SL (28 gauge, 28" barrel, Imp. Cyl. and Mod. chokes) **$10,995.00**
Price: Model 360SL (.410, 28" barrel, Mod. and Full chokes) **$10,995.00**

MERKEL MODEL 1620 SIDE-BY-SIDE SHOTGUN

Gauge: 16. **Features:** Greener crossbolt with double under-barrel locking lugs, scroll-engraved case-hardened receiver, Anson and Deely boxlock aciton, Holland & Holland ejectors, English-style stock, single selective or double triggers, or pistol grip stock with single selective trgger. Imported from Germany by Merkel USA.

Price: **$4,995.00**
Price: Model 1620E; silvered, engraved receiver **$5,995.00**
Price: Model 1620 Combo; 16- and 20-gauge two-barrel set **$7,695.00**
Price: Model 1620EL; upgraded wood **$7,695.00**
Price: Model 1620EL Combo; 16- and 20-gauge two-barrel set **$11,195.00**

PIOTTI KING NO. 1 SIDE-BY-SIDE SHOTGUN

Gauge: 12, 16, 20, 28, .410. **Barrel:** 25" to 30" (12 ga.), 25" to 28" (16, 20, 28, .410). To customer specs. Chokes as specified. **Weight:** 6.5 lbs. to 8 lbs. (12 ga. to customer specs.). **Stock:** Dimensions to customer specs. Finely figured walnut; straight grip with checkered butt with classic splinter forend and hand-rubbed oil finish standard. Pistol grip, beavertail forend. **Features:** Holland & Holland pattern sidelock action, automatic ejectors. Double trigger; non-selective single trigger optional. Coin finish standard; color case-hardened optional. Top rib; level, file-cut; concave, ventilated optional. Very fine, full coverage scroll engraving with small floral bouquets. Imported from Italy by Wm. Larkin Moore.

Price: From **$38,300.00**

Piotti Lunik Side-by-Side Shotgun

Similar to the Piotti King No. 1 in overall quality. Has Renaissance-style large scroll engraving in relief. Best quality Holland & Holland-pattern sidelock ejector double with

Prices given are believed to be accurate at time of publication however, many factors affect retail pricing so exact prices are not possible.

chopper lump (demi-bloc) barrels. Other mechanical specifications remain the same. Imported from Italy by Wm. Larkin Moore.
Price: From $39,900.00

PIOTTI PIUMA SIDE-BY-SIDE SHOTGUN
Gauge: 12, 16, 20, 28, .410. **Barrel:** 25" to 30" (12 ga.), 25" to 28" (16, 20, 28, .410). **Weight:** 5-1/2 to 6-1/4 lbs. (20 ga.). **Stock:** Dimensions to customer specs. Straight grip stock with walnut checkered butt, classic splinter forend, hand-rubbed oil finish are standard; pistol grip, beavertail forend, satin luster finish optional. **Features:** Anson & Deeley boxlock ejector double with chopper lump barrels. Level, file-cut rib, light scroll and rosette engraving, scalloped frame. Double triggers; single non-selective optional. Coin finish standard, color case-hardened optional. Imported from Italy by Wm. Larkin Moore.
Price: From $19,200.00

REMINGTON SPR210 SIDE-BY-SIDE SHOTGUNS
Gauge: 12, 20, 28, .410 bore, 3" chambers; 28, 2-3/4" chambers.
Barrel: 26", 28", blued chrome-lined. **Weight:** 6.75 to 7 lbs. **Stock:** checkered walnut stock and forend, 14.5" LOP; 1.5" drop at comb; 2.5" drop at heel. **Features:** Nickel or blued receiver. Single selective mechanical trigger, selective automatic ejectors; SC-4 choke tube set on most models. Steel receiver/mono block, auto tang safety, rubber recoil pad. Introduced 2008. Imported by Remington Arms Co.
Price: SPR210, from $479.00

REMINGTON SPR220 SIDE-BY-SIDE SHOTGUNS
Gauge: 12, 20, 2-3/4" or 3" chambers. **Barrel:** 20", 26", blued chrome-lined. **Weight:** 6.25 to 7 lbs. Otherwise similar to SPR210 except has double trigger/extractors. Introduced 2008. Imported by Remington Arms Co.
Price: SPR220, from $342.00

RIZZINI SIDELOCK SIDE-BY-SIDE SHOTGUN
Gauge: 12, 16, 20, 28, .410. **Barrel:** 25" to 30" (12, 16, 20 ga.), 25" to 28" (28, .410). To customer specs. Chokes as specified. **Weight:** 6.5 lbs. to 8 lbs. (12 ga. to customer specs). **Stock:** Dimensions to customer specs. Finely figured walnut; straight grip with checkered butt with classic splinter forend and hand-rubbed oil finish standard. Pistol grip, beavertail forend. **Features:** Sidelock action, auto ejectors. Double triggers or non-selective single trigger standard. Coin finish standard. Imported from Italy by Wm. Larkin Moore.
Price: 12, 20 ga. From $106,000.00
Price: 28, .410 bore. From $95,000.00

RUGER GOLD LABEL SIDE-BY-SIDE SHOTGUN
Gauge: 12, 3" chambers. **Barrel:** 28" with skeet tubes. **Weight:** 6.5 lbs. **Length:** 45". **Stock:** American walnut straight or pistol grip. **Sights:** Gold bead front, full length rib, serrated top. **Features:** Spring-assisted break-open, SS trigger, auto eject. Five interchangeable screw-in choke tubes, combination safety/barrel selector with auto safety reset.
Price: $3,226.00

SMITH & WESSON ELITE GOLD SHOTGUNS
Gauge: 20, 3" chambers. **Barrel:** 26", 28", 30", rust-blued chopper-lump. **Weight:** 6.5 lbs. **Length:** 43.5-45.5". **Sights:** Ivory front bead, metal mid-bead. **Stock:** AAA (grade III) Turkish walnut stocks, hand-cut checkering, satin finish. English grip or pistol grip. **Features:** Smith & Wesson-designed trigger-plate action, hand-engraved receivers, bone-charcoal case hardening, lifetime warranty. Five choke tubes. Introduced 2007. Made in Turkey, imported by Smith & Wesson.
Price: $2,380.00

STOEGER UPLANDER SIDE-BY-SIDE SHOTGUNS
Gauge: 16, 28, 2-3/4 chambers. 12, 20, .410, 3" chambers. **Barrel:** 22", 24", 26", 28". **Weight:** 7.3 lbs. **Sights:** Brass bead. **Features:** Double trigger, IC & M fixed choke tubes with gun.
Price: With fixed or screw-in chokes $369.00

Price: Supreme, screw-in chokes, 12 or 20 ga. $489.00
Price: Youth, 20 ga. or .410, 22" barrel, double trigger $369.00
Price: Combo, 20/28 ga. or 12/20 ga. $649.00

STOEGER COACH GUN SIDE-BY-SIDE SHOTGUNS
Gauge: 12, 20, 2-3/4", 3" chambers. **Barrel:** 20". **Weight:** 6.5 lbs. **Stock:** Brown hardwood, classic beavertail forend. **Sights:** Brass bead. **Features:** IC & M fixed chokes, tang auto safety, auto extractors, black plastic buttplate. Imported by Benelli USA.
Price: Supreme blued finish $469.00
Price: Supreme blued barrel, stainless receiver $469.00
Price: Silverado Coach Gun with English synthetic stock $469.00

TRADITIONS ELITE SERIES SIDE-BY-SIDE SHOTGUNS
Gauge: 12, 3"; 20, 3"; 28, 2-3/4"; .410, 3". **Barrel:** 26". **Weight:** 5 lbs., 12 oz. to 6.5 lbs. **Length:** 43" overall. **Stock:** Walnut. **Features:** Chrome-lined barrels; fixed chokes (Elite Field III ST, Field I DT and Field I ST) or choke tubes (Elite Hunter ST); extractors (Hunter ST and Field I models) or automatic ejectors (Field III ST); top tang safety. Imported from Fausti of Italy by Traditions.
Price: Elite Field I DT C 12, 20, 28 ga. or .410; IC and Mod. fixed chokes (F and F on .410); double triggers . . **$789.00 to $969.00**
Price: Elite Field I ST C 12, 20, 28 ga. or .410; same as DT but with single trigger . . . . $969.00 to $1,169.00
Price: Elite Field III ST C 28 ga. or .410; gold-engraved receiver; high-grade walnut stock $2,099.00
Price: Elite Hunter ST C 12 or 20 ga.; blued receiver; IC and Mod. choke tubes $999.00

TRADITIONS UPLANDER SERIES SIDE-BY-SIDE SHOTGUNS
Gauge: 12, 3"; 20, 3". **Barrel:** 26", 28". **Weight:** 6-1/4 lbs. to 6.5 lbs. **Length:** 43" to 45" overall. **Stock:** Walnut. **Features:** Barrels threaded for choke tubes (Improved Cylinder, Modified and Full); top tang safety, extended trigger guard. Engraved silver receiver with side plates and lavish gold inlays. Imported from Fausti of Italy by Traditions.
Price: Uplander III Silver 12, 20 ga. $2,699.00
Price: Uplander V Silver 12, 20 ga. $3,199.00

TRISTAR BRITTANY CLASSIC SIDE-BY-SIDE SHOTGUN
Gauge: 12, 16, 20, 28, .410, 3" chambers. **Barrel:** 27", chrome lined, three Beretta-style choke tubes (IC, M, F). **Weight:** 6.3 to 6.7 lbs. **Stock:** Rounded pistol grip, satin oil finish. **Features:** Engraved case-colored one-piece frame, auto selective ejectors, single selective trigger, solid raised barrel rib, top tang safety. Imported from Spain by Tristar Sporting Arms Ltd.
Price: From $1,419.00

WEATHERBY SBS ATHENA D'ITALIA SIDE-BY-SIDE SHOTGUNS
Gauge: D'Italia: 12, 20, 2-3/4" or 3" chambers, 28, 2-3/4" chambers. **Barrel:** 26" on 20 and 28 gauges; 28" on 12 ga. Chrome-lined, lengthened forcing cones, backbored. **Weight:** 6.75 to 7.25 lbs. **Length:** 42.5" to 44.5". **Stock:** Walnut, 20-lpi laser cut checkering, "New Scottish" pattern. **Features:** All come with foam-lined takedown case. Machined steel receiver, hardened and chromed with coin finish, engraved triggerguard with roll-formed border. D'Italia has double triggers, brass front bead. PG is identical to D'Italia, except for rounded pistol grip and semi-beavertail forearm. Deluxe features sculpted frameheads, Bolino-style engraved game scene with floral engraving. AAA Fancy Turkish walnut, straight grip, 24-lpi hand checkering, hand-rubbed oil finish. Single mechanical trigger; right barrel fires first. Imported from Italy by Weatherby.
Price: SBS Athena D'Italia SBS $3,129.00
Price: SBS Athena D'Italia PG SBS $3,799.00

BERETTA DT10 TRIDENT TRAP TOP SINGLE SHOTGUN

Gauge: 12, 3" chamber. **Barrel:** 34"; five Optima Choke tubes (Full, Full, Imp. Modified, Mod. and Imp. Cyl.). **Weight:** 8.8 lbs. **Stock:** High-grade walnut; adjustable. **Features:** Detachable, adjustable trigger group; Optima Bore for improved shot pattern and reduced recoil; slim Optima Choke tubes; raised and thickened receiver for long life. Introduced 2000. Imported from Italy by Beretta USA.
Price: **$7,400.00**

BROWNING BT-99 TRAP O/U SHOTGUNS

Gauge: 12. **Barrel:** 30", 32", 34". **Stock:** Walnut; standard or adjustable. **Weight:** 7 lbs. 11 oz. to 9 lbs. **Features:** Back-bored single barrel; interchangeable chokes; beavertail forearm; extractor only; high rib.
Price: BT-99 w/conventional comb, 32" or 34" barrels **$1,529.00**
Price: BT-99 w/adjustable comb, 32" or 34" barrels **$1,839.00**
Price: BT-99 Golden Clays w/adjustable comb, 32" or 34" barrels **$3,989.00**
Price: BT-99 Grade III, 32" or 34" barrels, intr. 2008 . . . . . . **$2,369.00**

HARRINGTON & RICHARDSON ULTRA SLUG HUNTER/TAMER SHOTGUNS

Gauge: 12, 20 ga., 3" chamber, .410. **Barrel:** 20" to 24" rifled. **Weight:** 6 to 9 lbs. **Length:** 34.5" to 40". **Stock:** Hardwood, laminate, or polymer with full pistol grip; semi-beavertail forend. **Sights:** Gold bead front. **Features:** Break-open action with side-lever release, automatic ejector. Introduced 1994. From H&R 1871, LLC.
Price: Ultra Slug Hunter, blued, hardwood **$273.00**
Price: Ultra Slug Hunter Youth, blued, hardwood, 13-1/8" LOP **$273.00**
Price: Ultra Slug Hunter Deluxe, blued, laminated **$273.00**
Price: Tamer .410 bore, stainless barrel, black polymer stock . **$173.00**

HARRINGTON & RICHARDSON ULTRA LITE SLUG HUNTER

Gauge: 12, 20 ga., 3" chamber. **Barrel:** 24" rifled. **Weight:** 5.25 lbs. **Length:** 40". **Stock:** Hardwood with walnut finish, full pistol grip, recoil pad, sling swivel studs. **Sights:** None; base included. **Features:** Youth Model, available in 20 ga. has 20" rifled barrel. Deluxe Model has checkered laminated stock and forend. From H&R 1871, LLC.
Price: **$194.00**

Harrington & Richardson Ultra Slug Hunter Thumbhole Stock
Similar to the Ultra Lite Slug Hunter but with laminated thumbhole stock and weighs 8.5 lbs.
Price: . . . . **NA**

HARRINGTON & RICHARDSON TOPPER MODELS

Gauge: 12, 16, 20, .410, up to 3.5" chamber. **Barrel:** 22 to 28". **Weight:** 5-7 lbs. **Stock:** Polymer, hardwood, or black walnut. **Features:** Satin nickel frame, blued barrel. Reintroduced 1992. From H&R 1871, LLC.

Price: Deluxe Classic, 12/20 ga., 28" barrel w/vent rib **$225.00**
Price: Topper Deluxe 12 ga., 28" barrel, black hardwood **$179.00**
Price: Topper 12, 16, 20 ga., .410, 26" to 28", black hardwood **$153.00**
Price: Topper Junior 20 ga., .410, 22" barrel, hardwood **$160.00**
Price: Topper Junior Classic, 20 ga., .410, checkered hardwood **$160.00**

Harrington & Richardson Topper Trap Gun
Similar to other Topper Models but with select checkered walnut stock and forend wtih fluted comb and full pistol grip; 30" barrel with two white beads and screw-in chokes (Improved Modified Extended included); deluxe Pachmayr trap recoil pad.
Price: **$360.00**

KRIEGHOFF K-80 SINGLE BARREL TRAP GUN

Gauge: 12, 2-3/4" chamber. **Barrel:** 32" or 34" Unsingle. Fixed Full or choke tubes. **Weight:** About 8-3/4 lbs. **Stock:** Four stock dimensions or adjustable stock available. All hand-checkered European walnut. **Features:** Satin nickel finish. Selective mechanical trigger adjustable for finger position. Tapered step vent rib. Adjustable point of impact.
Price: Standard grade Full Unsingle, from **$10,080.00**

KRIEGHOFF KX-5 TRAP GUN

Gauge: 12, 2-3/4" chamber. **Barrel:** 32", 34"; choke tubes. **Weight:** About 8.5 lbs. **Stock:** Factory adjustable stock. European walnut. **Features:** Ventilated tapered step rib. Adjustable position trigger, optional release trigger. Fully adjustable rib. Satin gray electroless nickel receiver. Fitted aluminum case. Imported from Germany by Krieghoff International, Inc.
Price: **$5,395.00**

LJUTIC MONO GUN SINGLE BARREL SHOTGUN

Gauge: 12 only. **Barrel:** 34", choked to customer specs; hollow-milled rib, 35.5" sight plane. **Weight:** Approx. 9 lbs. **Stock:** To customer specs. Oil finish, hand checkered. **Features:** Custom gun. Pull or release trigger; removable trigger guard contains trigger and hammer mechanism; Ljutic pushbutton opener on front of trigger guard. From Ljutic Industries.
Price: Std., med. or Olympic rib, custom bbls., fixed choke.. **$7,495.00**
Price: Stainless steel mono gun **$8,495.00**

Ljutic LTX Pro 3 Deluxe Mono Gun
Deluxe, lightweight version of the Mono gun with high quality wood, upgrade checkering, special rib height, screw-in chokes, ported and cased.
Price: **$8,995.00**
Price: Stainless steel model **$9,995.00**

NEW ENGLAND FIREARMS PARDNER AND TRACKER II SHOTGUNS

Gauge: 10, 12, 16, 20, 28, .410, up to 3.5" chamber for 10 and 12 ga. 16, 28, 2-3/4" chamber. **Barrel:** 24" to 30". **Weight:** Varies from 5 to 9.5 lbs. **Length:** Varies from 36" to 48". **Stock:** Walnut-finished hardwood with full pistol grip, synthetic, or camo finish. **Sights:** Bead front on most. **Features:** Transfer bar ignition; break-open action with side-lever release. Introduced 1987. From New England Firearms.
Price: Pardner, all gauges, hardwood stock, 26" to 32" blued barrel, Mod. or Full choke **$140.00**
Price: Pardner Youth, hardwood stock, straight grip, 22" blued barrel **$149.00**
Price: Pardner Screw-In Choke model, intr. 2006 . . . . **$164.00**

Price: Turkey model, 10/12 ga., camo finish
or black . . . .**$192.00 to $259.00**
Price: Youth Turkey, 20 ga., camo finish or black **$192.00**
Price: Waterfowl, 10 ga., camo finish or hardwood **$227.00**
Price: Tracker II slug gun, 12/20 ga., hardwood **$196.00**

REMINGTON SPR100 SINGLE-SHOT SHOTGUNS
Gauge: 12, 20, .410 bore, 3" chambers. **Barrel:** 24", 26", 28", 29.5", blued chrome-lined. **Weight:** 6.25 to 6.5 lbs. **Stock:** Walnut stock and forend. **Features:** Nickel or blued receiver. Cross-bolt safety, cocking indicator, titanium-coated trigger, selectable ejector or extractor. Introduced 2008. Imported by Remington Arms Co.
Price: SPR100, from **$479.00**

ROSSI CIRCUIT JUDGE
Revolving shotgun chambered in .410 (2-1/2- or 3-inch/.45 Colt. Based on Taurus Judge handgun. Features include 18.5-inch barrel; fiber optic front sight; 5-round cylinder; hardwood Monte Carlo stock.
Price: **$475.00**

ROSSI SINGLE-SHOT SHOTGUNS
Gauge: 12, 20, .410. **Barrel:** 22" (Youth), 28".
Weight: 3.75-5.25 lbs. **Stocks:** Wood. **Sights:** Bead front sight, fully adjustable fiber optic sight on Slug and Turkey. **Features:** Single-shot break open, 8 models available, positive ejection, internal transfer bar mechanism, trigger block system, Taurus Security System, blued finish, Rifle Slug has ported barrel.
Price: From **$117.00**

ROSSI TUFFY SHOTGUN
Gauge: .410. **Barrel:** 18-1/2". **Weight:** 3 lbs.
Length: 29.5" overall. **Features:** Single-shot break-open model with black synthetic thumbhole stock in blued or stainless finish.
Price: . . . . **Appx. $150.00**

ROSSI MATCHED PAIRS
Gauge/Caliber: 12, 20, .410, .22 Mag, .22LR, .17HMR, .223 Rem, .243 Win, .270 Win, .30-06, .308 Win, .50 (black powder). **Barrel:** 23", 28". **Weight:** 5-6.3 lbs. **Stocks:** Wood or black synthetic. **Sights:** Bead front on shotgun barrel, fully adjustable front and rear on rifle barrel, drilled and tapped for scope, fully adjustable fiber optic sights (black powder). **Features:** Single-shot break open, 27 models available, internal transfer bar mechanism, manual external safety, blue finish, trigger block system, Taurus Security System, youth models available.
Price: Rimfire/Shotgun, from **$160.00**
Price: Centerfire/Shotgun **$271.95**
Price: Black Powder Matched Pair, from **$262.00**

ROSSI MATCHED SET
Gauge/Caliber: 12, 20, .22 LR, .17 HMR, .243 Win, .270 Win, .50 (black powder). **Barrel:** 33.5". **Weight:** 6.25-6.3 lbs. **Stocks:** Wood. **Sights:** Bead front on shotgun barrel, fully adjustable front and rear on rifle barrel, drilled and tapped for scope, fully adjustable fiber optic sights (black powder). **Features:** Single-shot break open, 4 models available, internal transfer bar mechanism, manual external safety,

blue finish, trigger block system, Taurus Security System, youth models available.
Price: From **$374.00**

TAR-HUNT RSG-12 PROFESSIONAL RIFLED SLUG GUN
Gauge: 12, 2-3/4" or 3" chamber, 1-shot magazine. **Barrel:** 23", fully rifled with muzzle brake. **Weight:** 7.75 lbs. **Length:** 41.5" overall. **Stock:** Matte black McMillan fiberglass with Pachmayr Decelerator pad. **Sights:** None furnished; comes with Leupold windage or Weaver bases. **Features:** Uses rifle-style action with two locking lugs; two-position safety; Shaw barrel; single-stage, trigger; muzzle brake. Many options available. All models have area-controlled feed action. Introduced 1991. Made in U.S. by Tar-Hunt Custom Rifles, Inc.
Price: 12 ga. Professional model **$2,585.00**
Price: Left-hand model add **$110.00**

Tar-Hunt RSG-16 Elite Shotgun
Similar to RSG-12 Professional except 16 gauge; right- or left-hand versions.
Price: **$2,585.00**

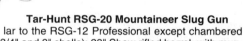

Tar-Hunt RSG-20 Mountaineer Slug Gun
Simi-　lar to the RSG-12 Professional except chambered for 20 gauge (2-3/4" and 3" shells); 23" Shaw rifled barrel, with muzzle brake; two-lug bolt; one-shot blind magazine; matte black finish; McMillan fiberglass stock with Pachmayr Decelerator pad; receiver drilled and tapped for Rem. 700 bases. Right- or left-hand versions. Weighs 6.5 lbs. Introduced 1997. Made in U.S. by Tar-Hunt Custom Rifles, Inc.
Price: **$2,585.00**

THOMPSON/CENTER ENCORE RIFLED SLUG GUN
Gauge: 20, 3" chamber. **Barrel:** 26", fully rifled. **Weight:** About 7 lbs. **Length:** 40.5" overall. **Stock:** Walnut with walnut forearm. **Sights:** Steel; click-adjustable rear and ramp-style front, both with fiber optics. **Features:** Encore system features a variety of rifle, shotgun and muzzle-loading rifle barrels interchangeable with the same frame. Break-open design operates by pulling up and back on trigger guard spur. Composite stock and forearm available. Introduced 2000.
Price: **$684.00**

THOMPSON/CENTER ENCORE TURKEY GUN
Gauge: 12 ga. **Barrel:** 24". **Features:** All-camo finish, high definition Realtree Hardwoods HD camo.
Price: **$763.00**

THOMPSON/CENTER ENCORE PROHUNTER TURKEY GUN
Contender-style break-action single shot shotgun chambered in 12 or 20 gauge 3-inch shells. Features include 24-inch barrel with interchangeable choke tubes (Extra Full supplied), composite buttstock and forend with non-slip inserts in cheekpiece, pistol grip and forend. Adjustable fiber optic sights, Sims recoil pad, AP camo finish overall. Overall length: 40.5 inches. Weight: 6-1/2 lbs.
Price: **$799.00**

BENELLI M3 CONVERTIBLE SHOTGUN

Gauge: 12, 2-3/4", 3" chambers, 5-shot magazine. **Barrel:** 19.75" (Cyl). **Weight:** 7 lbs., 4oz. **Length:** 41" overall. **Stock:** High-impact polymer with sling loop in side of butt; rubberized pistol grip on stock. **Sights:** Open rifle, fully adjustable. Ghost ring and rifle type. **Features:** Combination pump/auto action. Alloy receiver with inertia recoil rotating locking lug bolt; matte finish; automatic shell release lever. Introduced 1989. Imported by Benelli USA. Price with pistol grip, open rifle sights.
Price: With ghost ring sights, pistol grip stock **$1,489.00**

BENELLI M2 TACTICAL SHOTGUN

Gauge: 12, 2-3/4", 3" chambers, 5-shot magazine. **Barrel:** 18.5" IC, M, F choke tubes. **Weight:** 6.7 lbs. **Length:** 39.75" overall. **Stock:** Black polymer. **Sights:** Rifle type ghost ring system, tritium night sights optional. **Features:** Semiauto intertia recoil action. Cross-bolt safety; bolt release button; matte-finish metal. Introduced 1993. Imported from Italy by Benelli USA.
Price: With rifle sights **$1,159.00**
Price: With ghost ring sights, standard stock **$1,269.00**
Price: With ghost ring sights, pistol grip stock **$1,269.00**
Price: With rifle sights, pistol grip stock **$1,159.00**
Price: ComforTech stock, rifle sights **$1,269.00**
Price: Comfortech Stock, Ghost Ring **$1,379.00**

BERETTA TX4 SEMIAUTO SHOTGUN

Gas-operated semiauto shotgun chambered for 3-inch 12-ga. shells. Features include 18-inch barrel with interchangeable choke tubes; adjustable ghost ring rear sight with military-style front sight; adjustable length of pull; integral picatinny rail on receiver; 5+1 capacity; soft rubber grip inlays in buttstock and forend.
Price: **$1450.00**

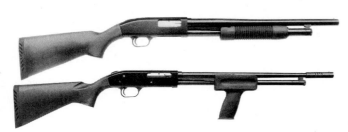

MOSSBERG MODEL 500 SPECIAL PURPOSE SHOTGUNS

Gauge: 12, 20, .410, 3" chamber. **Barrel:** 18.5", 20" (Cyl). **Weight:** 7 lbs. **Stock:** Walnut-finished hardwood or black synthetic. **Sights:** Metal bead front. **Features:** Available in 6- or 8-shot models. Top-mounted safety, double action slide bars, swivel studs, rubber recoil pad. Blue, Parkerized, Marinecote finishes. Mossberg Cablelock included. From Mossberg. The HS410 Home Security model chambered for .410 with 3" chamber; has pistol grip forend, thick recoil pad, muzzle brake and has special spreader choke on the 18.5" barrel. Overall length is 37.5", weight is 6.25 lbs. Blue finish; synthetic field stock. Mossberg Cablelock and video included. Mariner model has Marinecote metal finish to resist rust and corrosion. Synthetic field stock; pistol grip kit included. 500 Tactical 6-shot has black synthetic tactical stock. Introduced 1990.
Price: Rolling Thunder, 6-shot **$471.00**
Price: Tactical Cruiser, 18.5" barrel **$434.00**
Price: Persuader/Cruiser, 6 shot, from **$394.00**
Price: Persuader/Cruiser, 8 shot, from **$394.00**
Price: HS410 Home Security **$404.00**
Price: Mariner 6 or 9 shot, from **$538.00**
Price: Tactical 6 shot, from **$509.00**

MOSSBERG MODEL 590 SPECIAL PURPOSE SHOTGUN

Gauge: 12, 3" chamber, 9 shot magazine. **Barrel:** 20" (Cyl). **Weight:** 7.25 lbs. **Stock:** Synthetic field or Speedfeed. **Sights:** Metal bead front or Ghost Ring. **Features:** Top-mounted safety, double slide action bars. Comes with heat shield, bayonet lug, swivel studs, rubber recoil pad. Blue, Parkerized or Marinecote finish. Mossberg Cablelock included. From Mossberg.
Price: Synthetic stock, from **$471.00**
Price: Speedfeed stock, from **$552.00**

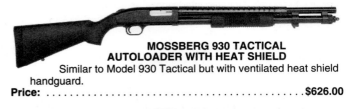

MOSSBERG 930 TACTICAL AUTOLOADER WITH HEAT SHIELD

Similar to Model 930 Tactical but with ventilated heat shield handguard.
Price: **$626.00**

REMINGTON MODEL 870 AND MODEL 1100 TACTICAL SHOTGUNS

Gauge: 870: 12, 2-3/4 or 3" chamber; 1100: 2-3/4". **Barrel:** 18", 20", 22" (Cyl or IC). **Weight:** 7.5-7.75 lbs. **Length:** 38.5-42.5" overall. **Stock:** Black synthetic, synthetic Speedfeed IV full pistol-grip stock, or Knoxx Industries SpecOps stock w/recoil-absorbing spring-loaded cam and adjustable length of pull (12" to 16", 870 only). **Sights:** Front post w/dot only on 870; rib and front dot on 1100. **Features:** R3 recoil pads, LimbSaver technology to reduce felt recoil, 2-, 3- or 4-shot extensions based on barrel length; matte-olive-drab barrels and receivers. Model 1100 Tactical is available with Speedfeed IV pistol grip stock or standard black synthetic stock and forend. Speedfeed IV model has an 18" barrel with two-shot extension. Standard synthetic-stocked version is equipped with 22" barrel and four-shot extension. Introduced 2006. From Remington Arms Co.
Price: 870, Speedfeed IV stock, 3" chamber, 38.5" overall, from. **$587.00**
Price: 870, SpecOps stock, 3" chamber, 38.5" overall, from . . **$587.00**
Price: 1100, synthetic stock, 2-3/4" chamber, 42.5" overall . . . **$945.00**
Price: 870 TAC Desert Recon (2008), 18" barrel, 2-shot **$692.00**

REMINGTON 870 EXPRESS TACTICAL A-TACS CAMO

Pump action shotgun chambered for 2-3/4- and 3-inch 12-ga. Features include full A-TACS digitized camo; 18-1/2-inch barrel; extended ported Tactical RemChoke; SpeedFeed IV pistol-grip stock with SuperCell recoil pad; fully adjustable XS® Ghost Ring Sight rail with removable white bead front sight; 7-round capacity with factory-installed 2-shot extension; drilled and tapped receiver; sling swivel stud.
Price: **$665.00**

REMINGTON 887 NITRO MAG TACTICAL

Pump action shotgun chambered in 12-ga., 2-3/4 to 3-1/2 inch. Features include 18-1/2-inch barrel with ported, extended tactical RemChoke; 2-shot magazine extension; barrel clamp with integral Picatinny rails; ArmorLokt coating; synthetic stock and forend with specially contour grip panels.
Price: **$498.00**

TACTICAL RESPONSE TR-870 STANDARD MODEL SHOTGUNS

Gauge: 12, 3" chamber, 7-shot magazine. **Barrel:** 18" (Cyl). **Weight:** 9 lbs. **Length:** 38" overall. **Stock:** Fiberglass-filled polypropolene with non-snag recoil absorbing butt pad. Nylon tactical forend houses flashlight. **Sights:** Trak-Lock ghost ring sight system. Front sight has Tritium insert. **Features:** Highly modified Remington 870P with

Parkerized finish. Comes with nylon three-way adjustable sling, high visibility non-binding follower, high performance magazine spring, Jumbo Head safety, and Side Saddle extended 6-shot shell carrier on left side of receiver. Introduced 1991. From Scattergun Technologies, Inc.

Price: Standard model **$1,050.00**
Price: Border Patrol model, from **$1,050.00**
Price: Professional model, from **$1,070.00**

TRISTAR COBRA PUMP
Gauge: 12, 3". **Barrel:** 28". **Weight:** 6.7 lbs. Three Beretta-style choke tubes (IC, M, F). **Length:** NA. **Stock:** Matte black synthetic stock and forearm. **Sights:** Vent rib with matted sight plane. **Features:** Five-year warranty. Cobra Tactical Pump Shotgun magazine holds 7, return spring in forearm, 20" barrel, Cylinder choke. Introduced 2008. Imported by Tristar Sporting Arms Ltd.
Price: Tactical **$349.00**

FRENCH-STYLE DUELING PISTOL

Caliber: 44. **Barrel:** 10". **Weight:** 35 oz. **Length:** 15.75" overall. **Stocks:** Carved walnut. **Sights:** Fixed. **Features:** Comes with velvet-lined case and accessories. Imported by Mandall Shooting Supplies.
Price: **$295.00**

HARPER'S FERRY 1805 PISTOL

Caliber: 58 (.570" round ball). **Barrel:** 10". **Weight:** 39 oz. **Length:** 16" overall. **Stocks:** Walnut. **Sights:** Fixed. **Features:** Case-hardened lock, brass-mounted German silver-colored barrel. Replica of the first U.S. gov't.-made flintlock pistol. Imported by Navy Arms, Dixie Gun Works.
Price: Dixie Gun Works RH0225 . . . . **$495.00**
Price: Dixie Kit FH0411. . . . . **$395.00**

KENTUCKY FLINTLOCK PISTOL

Caliber: 45, 50, 54. **Barrel:** 10.4". **Weight:** 37-40 oz. **Length:** 15.4" overall. **Stocks:** Walnut. **Sights:** Fixed. **Features:** Specifications, including caliber, weight and length may vary with importer. Case-hardened lock, blued barrel; available also as brass barrel flintlock Model 1821. Imported by The Armoury.
Price: Single cased set (Navy Arms) **$375.00**

KENTUCKY PERCUSSION PISTOL

Similar to Flint version but percussion lock. Imported by The Armoury, Navy Arms, CVA (50-cal.).
Price: . . . . **$129.95 to $225.00**
Price: Steel barrel (Armoury) **$179.00**
Price: Single cased set (Navy Arms) **$355.00**
Price: Double cased set (Navy Arms) **$600.00**

LE PAGE PERCUSSION DUELING PISTOL

Caliber: .45. **Barrel:** 10.25" octagon, rifled. **Weight:** 36-41 oz. **Length:** 16.9" overall. **Stocks:** Walnut, fluted butt. **Sights:** Blade front, open style rear. **Features:** Double set trigger. Bright barrel, brass furniture (silver plated). Imported by Dixie Gun Works
Price: PH0310 . . . . **$525.00**

LYMAN PLAINS PISTOL

Caliber: 50 or 54. **Barrel:** 8"; 1:30" twist, both calibers. **Weight:** 50 oz. **Length:** 15" overall. **Stocks:** Walnut half-stock. **Sights:** Blade front, square notch rear adjustable for windage. **Features:** Polished brass trigger guard and ramrod tip, color case-hardened coil spring lock, springloaded trigger, stainless steel nipple, blackened iron furniture. Hooked patent breech, detachable belt hook. Introduced 1981. From Lyman Products.
Price: Finished **$349.95**
Price: Kit **$289.95**

PEDERSOLI MANG TARGET PISTOL

Caliber: 38. **Barrel:** 10.5", octagonal; 1:15" twist, **Weight:** 2.5 lbs. **Length:** 17.25" overall. **Stocks:** Walnut with fluted grip. **Sights:** Blade front, open rear adjustable for windage. **Features:** Browned barrel, polished breech plug, remainder color case-

hardened. Imported from Italy by Dixie Gun Works.
Price: PH0503. . . . . **$1,250.00**

QUEEN ANNE FLINTLOCK PISTOL

Caliber: 50 (.490" round ball). **Barrel:** 7.5", smoothbore. **Stocks:** Walnut. **Sights:** None. **Features:** German silver-colored steel barrel, fluted brass trigger guard, brass mask on butt. Lockplate left in the white. Made by Pedersoli in Italy. Introduced 1983. Imported by Dixie Gun Works. **Baby Dragoon 1848**
Price: RH0211 . . . . **$375.00**
Price: Kit FH0421 . . . . **$295.00**

TRADITIONS KENTUCKY PISTOL

Caliber: 50. **Barrel:** 10"; octagon with 7/8" flats; 1:20" twist. **Weight:** 40 oz. **Length:** 15" overall. **Stocks:** Stained beech. **Sights:** Blade front, fixed rear. **Features:** Bird's-head grip; brass thimbles; color case-hardened lock. Percussion only. Introduced 1995. From Traditions.
Price: Finished **$209.00**
Price: Kit **$174.00**

TRADITIONS TRAPPER PISTOL

Caliber: 50. **Barrel:** 9.75"; 7/8" flats; 1:20" twist. **Weight:** 2.75 lbs. **Length:** 16" overall. **Stocks:** Beech. **Sights:** Blade front, adjustable rear. **Features:** Double-set triggers; brass buttcap, trigger guard, wedge plate, forend tip, thimble. From Traditions.
Price: Percussion **$286.00**
Price: Flintlock **$312.00**
Price: Kit **$149.00**

TRADITIONS VEST-POCKET DERRINGER

Caliber: 31. **Barrel:** 2.25"; brass. **Weight:** 8 oz. **Length:** 4.75" overall. **Stocks:** Simulated ivory. **Sights:** Bead front. **Features:** Replica of riverboat gamblers' derringer; authentic spur trigger. From Traditions.
Price: **$165.00**

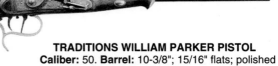

TRADITIONS WILLIAM PARKER PISTOL

Caliber: 50. **Barrel:** 10-3/8"; 15/16" flats; polished steel. **Weight:** 37 oz. **Length:** 17.5" overall. **Stocks:** Walnut with checkered grip. **Sights:** Brass blade front, fixed rear. **Features:** Replica dueling pistol with 1:20" twist, hooked breech. Brass wedge plate, trigger guard, cap guard; separate ramrod. Double-set triggers. Polished steel barrel, lock. Imported by Traditions.
Price: **$381.00**

Prices given are believed to be accurate at time of publication however, many factors affect retail pricing so exact prices are not possible.

ARMY 1860 PERCUSSION REVOLVER

Caliber: 44, 6-shot. **Barrel:** 8". **Weight:** 40 oz. **Length:** 13-5/8" overall. **Stocks:** Walnut. **Sights:** Fixed. **Features:** Engraved Navy scene on cylinder; brass trigger guard; case-hardened frame, loading lever and hammer. Some importers supply pistol cut for detachable shoulder stock, have accessory stock available. Imported by Cabela's (1860 Lawman), EMF, Navy Arms, The Armoury, Cimarron, Dixie Gun Works (half-fluted cylinder, not roll engraved), Euroarms of America (brass or steel model), Armsport, Traditions (brass or steel), Uberti U.S.A. Inc., United States Patent Fire-Arms.

Price: Dixie Gun Works RH0125 . . . . **$240.00**
Price: Brass frame (EMF) **$215.00**
Price: Single cased set (Navy Arms) **$300.00**
Price: Double cased set (Navy Arms) **$490.00**
Price: 1861 Navy: Same as Army except 36-cal., 7.5" bbl., weighs 41 oz., cut for shoulder stock; round cylinder (fluted available), from Cabela's, CVA (brass frame, 44 cal.), United States Patent Fire-Arms . . . . **$99.95 to $385.00**
Price: Steel frame kit (EMF) **$240.00**
Price: Colt Army Police, fluted cyl., 5.5", 36-cal. (Cabela's) . **$229.99**
Price: With nickeled frame, barrel and backstrap, gold-tone fluted cylinder, trigger and hammer, simulated ivory grips (Traditions) **$199.00**

BABY DRAGOON 1848, 1849 POCKET, WELLS FARGO

Caliber: 31. **Barrel:** 3", 4", 5", 6"; seven-groove; RH twist. **Weight:** About 21 oz. **Stocks:** Varnished walnut. **Sights:** Brass pin front, hammer notch rear. **Features:** No loading lever on Baby Dragoon or Wells Fargo models. Unfluted cylinder with stagecoach holdup scene; cupped cylinder pin; no grease grooves; one safety pin on cylinder and slot in hammer face; straight (flat) mainspring. From Armsport, Cimarron F.A. Co., Dixie Gun Works, EMF, Uberti U.S.A. Inc.

Price: 5.5" barrel, 1849 Pocket with loading lever (Dixie) **$250.00**
Price: 4" (Uberti USA Inc.) **$275.00**

DIXIE WYATT EARP REVOLVER

Caliber: 44. **Barrel:** 12", octagon. **Weight:** 46 oz. **Length:** 18" overall. **Stocks:** One-piece hardwood. **Sights:** Fixed. **Features:** Highly polished brass frame, backstrap and trigger guard; blued barrel and cylinder; case-hardened hammer, trigger and loading lever. Navy-size shoulder stock requires minor fitting. From Dixie Gun Works.

Price: RH0130 . . . . **$187.50**

LE MAT REVOLVER

Caliber: 44/20 ga. **Barrel:** 6.75" (revolver); 4-7/8" (single shot). **Weight:** 3 lbs., 7 oz. **Length:** 14" overall. **Stocks:** Hand-checkered walnut. **Sights:** Post front, hammer notch rear. **Features:** Exact reproduction with all-steel construction;

44-cal. 9-shot cylinder, 20-gauge single barrel; color case-hardened hammer with selector; spur trigger guard; ring at butt; lever-type barrel release. From Navy Arms.

Price: Cavalry model (lanyard ring, spur trigger guard) **$750.00**
Price: Army model (round trigger guard, pin-type barrel release) **$750.00**
Price: Naval-style (thumb selector on hammer) **$750.00**

NAVY MODEL 1851 PERCUSSION REVOLVER

Caliber: 36, 44, 6-shot. **Barrel:** 7.5". **Weight:** 44 oz. **Length:** 13" overall. **Stocks:** Walnut finish. **Sights:** Post front, hammer notch rear. **Features:** Brass backstrap and trigger guard; some have 1st Model squareback trigger guard, engraved cylinder with navy battle scene; case-hardened frame, hammer, loading lever. Imported by The Armoury, Cabela's, Cimarron F.A. Co., Navy Arms, EMF, Dixie Gun Works, Euroarms of America, Armsport, CVA (44-cal. only), Traditions (44 only), Uberti U.S.A. Inc., United States Patent Fire-Arms.

Price: Brass frame (Dixie Gun Works RH0100) **$275.00**
Price: Steel frame (Dixie Gun Works RH0210) **$200.00**
Price: Engraved model (Dixie Gun Works RH0110) **$275.00**
Price: Confederate Navy (Cabela's) **$139.99**
Price: Hartford model, steel frame, German silver trim, cartouche (EMF) **$190.00**
Price: Man With No Name Conversion (Cimarron, 2006) . . . **$480.00**

NEW MODEL 1858 ARMY PERCUSSION REVOLVER

Caliber: 36 or 44, 6-shot. **Barrel:** 6.5" or 8". **Weight:** 38 oz. **Length:** 13.5" overall. **Stocks:** Walnut. **Sights:** Blade front, groove-in-frame rear. **Features:** Replica of Remington Model 1858. Also available from some importers as Army Model Belt Revolver in 36-cal., a shortened and lightened version of the 44. Target Model (Uberti U.S.A. Inc., Navy Arms) has fully adjustable target rear sight, target front, 36 or 44. Imported by Cimarron F.A. Co., CVA (as 1858 Army, brass frame, 44 only), Navy Arms, The Armoury, EMF, Euroarms of America (engraved, stainless and plain), Armsport, Traditions (44 only), Uberti U.S.A. Inc.

Price: Steel frame, Dixie RH0220 . . . . **$315.00**
Price: Steel frame kit (Euroarms) . . . . **$115.95 to $150.00**
Price: Stainless steel Model 1858 (Euroarms, Uberti U.S.A. Inc., Navy Arms, Armsport, Traditions) . . . . **$169.95 to $380.00**
Price: Target Model, adjustable rear sight (Cabela's, Euroarms, Uberti U.S.A. Inc., Stone Mountain Arms) . . . . **$95.95 to $399.00**
Price: Brass frame (CVA, Cabela's, Traditions, Navy Arms) . . . . **$79.95 to $199.99**
Price: Buffalo model, 44-cal. (Cabela's) **$119.99**
Price: Hartford model, steel frame, cartouche (EMF) **$225.00**
Price: Improved Conversion (Cimarron) **$492.00**

NORTH AMERICAN COMPANION PERCUSSION REVOLVER

Caliber: 22. **Barrel:** 1-1/8". **Weight:** 5.1 oz. **Length:** 4.5" overall. **Stocks:** Laminated wood. **Sights:** Blade front, notch fixed rear. **Features:** All stainless steel construction. Uses standard #11 percussion caps. Comes with bullets, powder measure, bullet seater, leather clip holster, gun rag. Long Rifle or Magnum frame size. Introduced 1996. Made in U.S. by North American Arms.

Price: Long Rifle frame **$215.00**

North American Super Companion Percussion Revolver

Similar to the Companion except has larger frame. Weighs 7.2 oz., has 1-5/8" barrel, measures 5-7/16" overall. Comes with bullets, powder measure, bullet seater, leather clip holster, gun rag. Introduced 1996. Made in U.S. by North American Arms.

Price: **$230.00**

POCKET POLICE 1862 PERCUSSION REVOLVER

Caliber: 36, 5-shot. **Barrel:** 4.5", 5.5", 6.5", 7.5". **Weight:** 26 oz. **Length:** 12" overall (6.5" bbl.). **Stocks:** Walnut. **Sights:** Fixed. **Features:** Round tapered barrel; half-fluted and rebated cylinder; case-hardened frame, loading lever and hammer; silver or brass trigger guard and backstrap. Imported by Dixie Gun Works, Navy Arms (5.5" only), Uberti U.S.A. Inc. (5.5", 6.5" only), United States Patent Fire-Arms and Cimarron F.A. Co.

Price: Dixie Gun Works RH0422 .... **$315.00**
Price: Hartford model, steel frame, cartouche (EMF) **$300.00**

ROGERS & SPENCER PERCUSSION REVOLVER

Caliber: 44. **Barrel:** 7.5". **Weight:** 47 oz. **Length:** 13.75" overall. **Stocks:** Walnut. **Sights:** Cone front, integral groove in frame for rear. **Features:** Accurate reproduction of a Civil War design. Solid frame; extra large nipple cut-out on rear of cylinder; loading lever and cylinder easily removed for cleaning. From Dixie Gun Works, Euroarms of America (standard blue, engraved, burnished, target models), Navy Arms.

Price: Dixie Gun Works RH1320 .... **$425.00**
Price: Nickel-plated **$215.00**
Price: Engraved (Euroarms) **$430.00**
Price: Target version (Euroarms) .... **$239.00 to $270.00**
Price: Burnished London Gray (Euroarms) ..... **$245.00 to $370.00**

SHERIFF MODEL 1851 PERCUSSION REVOLVER

Caliber: 36, 44, 6-shot. **Barrel:** 5". **Weight:** 40 oz. **Length:** 10.5" overall. **Stocks:** Walnut. **Sights:** Fixed. **Features:** Brass backstrap and trigger guard; engraved navy scene; case-hardened frame, hammer, loading lever. Imported by EMF.

Price: Steel frame **$169.95**
Price: Brass frame **$140.00**

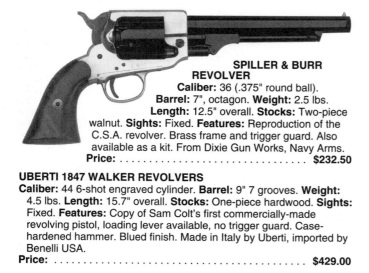

SPILLER & BURR REVOLVER

Caliber: 36 (.375" round ball). **Barrel:** 7", octagon. **Weight:** 2.5 lbs. **Length:** 12.5" overall. **Stocks:** Two-piece walnut. **Sights:** Fixed. **Features:** Reproduction of the C.S.A. revolver. Brass frame and trigger guard. Also available as a kit. From Dixie Gun Works, Navy Arms.

Price: **$232.50**

UBERTI 1847 WALKER REVOLVERS

Caliber: 44 6-shot engraved cylinder. **Barrel:** 9" 7 grooves. **Weight:** 4.5 lbs. **Length:** 15.7" overall. **Stocks:** One-piece hardwood. **Sights:** Fixed. **Features:** Copy of Sam Colt's first commercially-made revolving pistol, loading lever available, no trigger guard. Case-hardened hammer. Blued finish. Made in Italy by Uberti, imported by Benelli USA.

Price: **$429.00**

UBERTI 1848 DRAGOON AND POCKET REVOLVERS

Caliber: 44 6-shot engraved cylinder. **Barrel:** 7.5" 7 grooves. **Weight:** 4.1 lbs. **Stocks:** One-piece walnut. **Sights:** Fixed. **Features:** Copy of Eli Whitney's design for Colt using Walker parts. Blued barrel, backstrap, and trigger guard. Made in Italy by Uberti, imported by Benelli USA.

Price: 1848 Whitneyville Dragoon, 7.5" barrel ... **$429.00**
Price: 1848 Dragoon, 1st-3rd models, 7.5" barrel . **$409.00**
Price: 1848 Baby Dragoon, 4" barrel **$339.00**

UBERTI 1858 NEW ARMY REVOLVERS

Caliber: 44 6-shot engraved cylinder. **Barrel:** 8" 7 grooves. **Weight:** 2.7 lbs. **Length:** 13.6". **Stocks:** Two-piece walnut. **Sights:** Fixed. **Features:** Blued or stainless barrel, backstrap; brass trigger guard. Made in Italy by Uberti, imported by Benelli USA.

Price: 1858 New Army Stainless 8" barrel **$429.00**
Price: 1858 New Army 8" barrel **$349.00**
Price: 1858 Target Carbine 18" barrel **$549.00**
Price: 1862 Pocket Navy 5.5" barrel, 36 caliber **$349.00**
Price: 1862 Police 5.5" barrel, 36 caliber **$349.00**

UBERTI 1861 NAVY PERCUSSION REVOLVER

Caliber: 36, 6-shot. **Barrel:** 7.5", 7-groove, round. **Weight:** 2 lbs., 6 oz. **Length:** 13". **Stocks:** One-piece walnut. **Sights:** German silver blade front sight. **Features:** Rounded trigger guard, "creeping" loading lever, fluted or round cylinder, steel backstrap, trigger guard, cut for stock. Imported by Cimarron F.A. Co., Uberti U.S.A. Inc., Dixie Gun Works.

Price: Dixie RH0420 .... **$295.00**

1862 POCKET NAVY PERCUSSION REVOLVER

Caliber: 36, 5-shot. **Barrel:** 5.5", 6.5", octagonal, 7-groove, LH twist. **Weight:** 27 oz. (5.5" barrel). **Length:** 10.5" overall (5.5" bbl.). **Stocks:** One-piece varnished walnut. **Sights:** Brass pin front, hammer notch rear. **Features:** Rebated cylinder, hinged loading lever, brass or silver-plated backstrap and trigger guard, color-cased frame, hammer, loading lever, plunger and latch, rest blued. Has original-type markings. From Cimarron F.A. Co., Uberti U.S.A. Inc., Dixie Gun Works.

Price: With brass backstrap, trigger guard **$250.00**

WALKER 1847 PERCUSSION REVOLVER

Caliber: 44, 6-shot. **Barrel:** 9". **Weight:** 84 oz. **Length:** 15.5" overall. **Stocks:** Walnut. **Sights:** Fixed. **Features:** Case-hardened frame, loading lever and hammer; iron backstrap; brass trigger guard; engraved cylinder. Imported by Cabela's, Cimarron F.A. Co., Navy Arms, Uberti U.S.A. Inc., EMF, Cimarron, Traditions, United States Patent Fire-Arms.

Price: Dixie RH0200 .... **$385.00**
Price: Dixie Kit RH0400 .... **$300.00**
Price: Hartford model, steel frame, cartouche (EMF) **$350.00**

ARMOURY R140 HAWKEN RIFLE
Caliber: 45, 50 or 54. **Barrel:** 29". **Weight:** 8.75 to 9 lbs. **Length:** 45.75" overall. **Stock:** Walnut, with cheekpiece. **Sights:** Dovetailed front, fully adjustable rear. **Features:** Octagon barrel, removable breech plug; double set triggers; blued barrel, brass stock fittings, color case-hardened percussion lock. From Armsport, The Armoury.
Price: .... **$225.00 to $245.00**

BOSTONIAN PERCUSSION RIFLE
Caliber: 45. **Barrel:** 30", octagonal. **Weight:** 7.25 lbs. **Length:** 46" overall. **Stock:** Walnut. **Sights:** Blade front, fixed notch rear. **Features:** Color case-hardened lock, brass trigger guard, buttplate, patchbox. Imported from Italy by EMF.
Price: **$285.00**

CABELA'S BLUE RIDGE RIFLE
Caliber: 32, 36, 45, 50, .54. **Barrel:** 39", octagonal. **Weight:** About 7.75 lbs. **Length:** 55" overall. **Stock:** American black walnut. **Sights:** Blade front, rear drift adjustable for windage. **Features:** Color case-hardened lockplate and cock/hammer, brass trigger guard and buttplate, double set, double-phased triggers. From Cabela's.
Price: Percussion **$569.99**
Price: Flintlock **$599.99**

CABELA'S TRADITIONAL HAWKEN
Caliber: 50, 54. **Barrel:** 29". **Weight:** About 9 lbs. **Stock:** Walnut. **Sights:** Blade front, open adjustable rear. **Features:** Flintlock or percussion. Adjustable double-set triggers. Polished brass furniture, color case-hardened lock. Imported by Cabela's.
Price: Percussion, right-hand or left-hand **$339.99**
Price: Flintlock, right-hand **$399.99**

CABELA'S KODIAK EXPRESS DOUBLE RIFLE
Caliber: 50, 54, 58, 72. **Barrel:** Length NA; 1:48" twist. **Weight:** 9.3 lbs. **Length:** 45.25" overall. **Stock:** European walnut, oil finish. **Sights:** Fully adjustable double folding-leaf rear, ramp front. **Features:** Percussion. Barrels regulated to point of aim at 75 yards; polished and engraved lock, top tang and trigger guard. From Cabela's.
Price: 50, 54, 58 calibers **$929.99**
Price: 72 caliber **$959.99**

COOK & BROTHER CONFEDERATE CARBINE
Caliber: 58. **Barrel:** 24". **Weight:** 7.5 lbs. **Length:** 40.5" overall. **Stock:** Select walnut. **Features:** Re-creation of the 1861 New Orleans-made artillery carbine. Color case-hardened lock, browned barrel. Buttplate, trigger guard, barrel bands, sling swivels and nosecap of polished brass. From Euroarms of America.
Price: **$563.00**
Price: Cook & Brother rifle (33" barrel) **$606.00**

CVA OPTIMA ELITE BREAK-ACTION RIFLE
Caliber: 45, 50. **Barrel:** 28" fluted. **Weight:** 8.8 lbs. **Stock:** Ambidextrous solid composite in standard or thumbhole. **Sights:** Adj. fiber-optic. **Features:** Break-action, stainless No. 209 breech plug, aluminum loading rod, cocking spur, lifetime warranty.
Price: CR4002 (50-cal., blued/Realtree HD) **$398.95**
Price: CR4002X (50-cal., stainless/Realtree HD) . **$456.95**
Price: CR4003X (45-cal., stainless/Realtree HD) **$456.95**
Price: CR4000T (50-cal), blued/black fiber grip thumbhole) . **$366.95**
Price: CR4000 (50-cal., blued/black fiber grip) **$345.95**
Price: CR4002T (50-cal., blued/Realtree HD thumbhole) ... **$432.95**
Price: CR4002S (50-cal., stainless/Realtree HD thumbhole) **$422.95**
Price: CR4000X (50-cal., stainless/black fiber grip thumbhole) **$451.95**
Price: CR4000S (50-cal., stainless steel/black fiber grip) ... **$400.95**

CVA Optima 209 Magnum Break-Action Rifle
Similar to Optima Elite but with 26" bbl., nickel or blue finish, 50 cal.
Price: PR2008N (nickel/Realtree HD thumbhole) **$345.95**
Price: PR2004N (nickel/Realtree) **$322.95**
Price: PR2000 (blued/black) **$229.95**
Price: PR2006N (nickel/black) **$273.95**

CVA Wolf 209 Magnum Break-Action Rifle
Similar to Optima 209 Mag but with 24 barrel, weighs 7 lbs, and in 50-cal. only.

Price: PR2101N (nickel/camo) **$253.95**
Price: PR2102 (blued/camo) **$231.95**
Price: PR2100 (blued/black) **$180.95**
Price: PR2100N (nickel/black) **$202.95**
Price: PR2100NS (nickel/black scoped package) **$277.95**
Price: PR2100S (blued/black scoped package) **$255.95**

CVA APEX
Caliber: 45, 50. **Barrel:** 27", 1:28 twist. **Weight:** 8 lbs. **Length:** 42". **Stock:** Synthetic. **Features:** Ambi stock with rubber grip panels in black or Realtree APG camo, crush-zone recoil pad, reversible hammer spur, quake claw sling, lifetime warranty.
Price: CR4010S (50-cal., stainless/black) **$576.95**
Price: CR4011S (45-cal., stainless/black) **$576.95**
Price: CR4012S (50-cal., stainless/Realtree HD) **$651.95**
Price: CR4013S (45-cal., stainless/Realtree HD) **$651.95**

CVA ACCURA
Similar to Apex but weighs 7.3 lbs., in stainless steel or matte blue finish, cocking spur.
Price: PR3106S (50-cal, stainless steel/Realtree APG thumbhole) **$495.95**
Price: PR3107S (45-cal., stainless steel/Realtree APG thumbhole) **$495.95**
Price: PR 3104S (50-cal., stainless steel/black fibergrip thumbhole) **$438.95**
Price: PR3100 (50-cal., blued/black fibergrip) **$345.95**
Price: PR3100S (50-cal., stainless steel/black fibergrip) ... **$403.95**
Price: PR3102S (50-cal., stainless steel/Realtree APG) **$460.95**

CVA BUCKHORN 209 MAGNUM
Caliber: 50. **Barrel:** 24". **Weight:** 6.3 lbs. **Sights:** Illuminator fiber-optic. **Features:** Grip-dot stock, thumb-actuated safety; drilled and tapped for scope mounts.
Price: Black stock, blue barrel **$145.00**

CVA KODIAK MAGNUM RIFLE
Caliber: 50. No. 209 primer ignition. **Barrel:** 28"; 1:28" twist. **Stock:** Ambidextrous black or Mossy Oak® camo. **Sights:** Fiber-optic. **Features:** Blue or nickel finish, recoil pad, lifetime warranty. From CVA.
Price: Mossy Oak® camo; nickel barrel **$300.00**
Price: Stainless steel/black fibergrip **$288.95**
Price: Blued/black fibergrip **$229.95**

DIXIE EARLY AMERICAN JAEGER RIFLE
Caliber: 54. **Barrel:** 27.5" octagonal; 1:24" twist. **Weight:** 8.25 lbs. **Length:** 43.5" overall. **Stock:** American walnut; sliding wooden patchbox on butt. **Sights:** Notch rear, blade front. **Features:** Flintlock or percussion. Browned steel furniture. Imported from Italy by Dixie Gun Works.
Price: Flintlock FR0838. .... **$695.00**
Price: Percussion PR0835, case-hardened **$695.00**
Price: Kit **$775.00**

DIXIE DELUXE CUB RIFLE
Caliber: 32, 36, 40, 45. **Barrel:** 28" octagon. **Weight:** 6.25 lbs. **Length:** 44" overall. **Stock:** Walnut. **Sights:** Fixed. **Features:** Short rifle for small game and beginning shooters. Brass patchbox and furniture. Flint or percussion, finished or kit. From Dixie Gun Works
Price: Deluxe Cub (45-cal.) **$525.00**
Price: Deluxe Cub (flint) **$530.00**
Price: Super Cub (50-cal) **$530.00**
Price: Deluxe Cub (32-cal. flint) **$725.00**
Price: Deluxe Cub (36-cal. flint) **$725.00**
Price: Deluxe Cub kit (32-cal. percussion) **$550.00**
Price: Deluxe Cub kit (36-cal. percussion) **$550.00**
Price: Deluxe Cub (45-cal. percussion) **$675.00**
Price: Super Cub (percussion) **$450.00**
Price: Deluxe Cub (32-cal. percussion) **$675.00**
Price: Deluxe Cub (36-cal. percussion) **$675.00**

DIXIE PEDERSOLI 1857 MAUSER RIFLE
Caliber: 54. **Barrel:** 39-3/8". **Weight:** 9.5 lbs. **Length:** 54.75" overall. **Stock:** European walnut with oil finish, sling swivels. **Sights:** Fully adjustable rear, lug front. **Features:** Percussion (musket caps). Armory bright finish with color case-hardened lock and barrel tang, engraved lockplate, steel ramrod. Introduced 2000. Imported from Italy by Dixie Gun Works.
Price: PR1330. .... **$995.00**

BLACKPOWDER MUSKETS & RIFLES

DIXIE SHARPS NEW MODEL 1859 MILITARY RIFLE

Caliber: 54. **Barrel:** 30", 6-groove; 1:48" twist. **Weight:** 9 lbs. **Length:** 45.5" overall. **Stock:** Oiled walnut. **Sights:** Blade front, ladder-style rear. **Features:** Blued barrel, color case-hardened barrel bands, receiver, hammer, nosecap, lever, patchbox cover and buttplate. Introduced 1995. Imported from Italy by Dixie Gun Works.
Price: PR0862. . . . . **$1,100.00**
Price: Carbine (22 barrel, 7-groove, 39-1/4" overall, weighs 8 lbs.) **$925.00**

DIXIE U.S. MODEL 1816 FLINTLOCK MUSKET

Caliber: .69. **Barrel:** 42", smoothbore. **Weight:** 9.75 lbs. **Length:** 56 7/8" overall. **Stock:** Walnut w/oil finish. **Sights:** Blade front. **Features:** All metal finished "National Armory Bright," three barrel bands w/springs, steel ramrod w/button-shaped head. Imported by Dixie Gun Works.
Price: FR0305. . . . . **$1,200.00**
Price: PR0257, Percussion conversion **$995.00**

EMF 1863 SHARPS MILITARY CARBINE

Caliber: 54. **Barrel:** 22", round. **Weight:** 8 lbs. **Length:** 39" overall. **Stock:** Oiled walnut. **Sights:** Blade front, military ladder-type rear. **Features:** Color case-hardened lock, rest blued. Imported by EMF.
Price: **$759.90**

EUROARMS VOLUNTEER TARGET RIFLE

Caliber: 451. **Barrel:** 33" (two-band), 36" (three-band). **Weight:** 11 lbs. (two-band). **Length:** 48.75" overall (two-band). **Stock:** European walnut with checkered wrist and forend. **Sights:** Hooded bead front, adjustable rear with interchangeable leaves. **Features:** Alexander Henry-type rifling with 1:20" twist. Color case-hardened hammer and lockplate, brass trigger guard and nosecap, remainder blued. Imported by Euroarms of America, Dixie Gun Works.
Price: PR1031. . . . . **$925.00**

EUROARMS 1861 SPRINGFIELD RIFLE

Caliber: 58. **Barrel:** 40". **Weight:** About 10 lbs. **Length:** 55.5" overall. **Stock:** European walnut. **Sights:** Blade front, three-leaf military rear. **Features:** Reproduction of the original three-band rifle. Lockplate marked "1861" with eagle and "U.S. Springfield." White metal. Imported by Euroarms of America.
Price: **$730.00**

EUROARMS ZOUAVE RIFLE

Caliber: 54, 58 percussion. **Barrel:** 33". **Weight:** 9.5 lbs. Overall length: 49". **Features:** One-piece solid barrel and bolster. For 54 caliber, .535 R.B., .540 minnie. For 58 caliber, .575 R.B., .577 minnie. 1863 issue. Made in Italy. Imported by Euroarms of America.
Price: **$469.00**

EUROARMS HARPERS FERRY RIFLE

Caliber: 58 flintlock. **Barrel:** 35". **Weight:** 9 lbs. Overall length: 59.5". **Features:** Antique browned barrel. Barrel .575 RB. .577 minnie. 1803 issue. Made in Italy. Imported by Euroarms of America.
Price: **$735.00**

GONIC MODEL 93 M/L RIFLE

Caliber: 45, 50. **Barrel:** 26"; 1:24" twist. **Weight:** 6.5 to 7 lbs. **Length:** 43" overall. **Stock:** American hardwood with black finish. **Sights:** Adjustable or aperture rear, hooded front. **Features:** Adjustable trigger with side safety; unbreakable ramrod; comes with A. Z. scope bases installed. Introduced 1993. Made in U.S. by Gonic Arms, Inc.
Price: Model 93 Standard (blued barrel). **$720.00**
Price: Model 93 Standard (stainless brl., 50 cal. only) **$782.00**

Gonic Model 93 Deluxe M/L Rifle

Similar to the Model 93 except has classic-style walnut or gray laminated wood stock. Introduced 1998. Made in U.S. by Gonic Arms, Inc.
Price: Blue barrel, sights, scope base, choice of stock. **$902.00**
Price: Stainless barrel, sights, scope base, choice of stock (50 cal. only) **$964.00**

Gonic Model 93 Mountain Thumbhole M/L Rifles

Similar to the Model 93 except has high-grade walnut or gray laminate stock with extensive hand-checkered panels, Monte Carlo cheekpiece and beavertail forend; integral muzzle brake. Introduced 1998. Made in U.S. by Gonic Arms, Inc.
Price: Blued or stainless **$2,700.00**

HARPER'S FERRY 1803 FLINTLOCK RIFLE

Caliber: 54 or 58. **Barrel:** 35". **Weight:** 9 lbs. **Length:** 59.5" overall. **Stock:** Walnut with cheekpiece. **Sights:** Brass blade front, fixed steel rear. **Features:** Brass trigger guard, sideplate, buttplate; steel patchbox. Imported by Euroarms of America, Navy Arms (54-cal. only), and Dixie Gun Works.
Price: 54-cal. (Navy Arms) **$625.00**
Price: 54-cal. (Dixie Gun Works), FR0171 . . . . **$995.00**
Price: 54-cal. (Euroarms) **$809.00**

HAWKEN RIFLE

Caliber: 45, 50, 54 or 58. **Barrel:** 28", blued, 6-groove rifling. **Weight:** 8.75 lbs. **Length:** 44" overall. **Stock:** Walnut with cheekpiece. **Sights:** Blade front, fully adjustable rear. **Features:** Coil mainspring, double-set triggers, polished brass furniture. From Armsport and EMF.
Price: . . . . **$220.00 to $345.00**

J.P. HENRY TRADE RIFLE

Caliber: 54. **Barrel:** 34"; 1" flats. **Weight:** 8.5 lbs. **Length:** 45" overall. **Stock:** Premium curly maple. **Sights:** Silver blade front, fixed buckhorn rear. **Features:** Brass buttplate, side plate, trigger guard and nosecap; browned barrel and lock; L&R Large English percussion lock; single trigger. Made in U.S. by J.P. Gunstocks, Inc.
Price: **$965.50**

J.P. MURRAY 1862-1864 CAVALRY CARBINE

Caliber: 58 (.577" Minie). **Barrel:** 23". **Weight:** 7 lbs., 9 oz. **Length:** 39" overall. **Stock:** Walnut. **Sights:** Blade front, rear drift adjustable for windage. **Features:** Blued barrel, color case-hardened lock, blued swivel and band springs, polished brass buttplate, trigger guard, barrel bands. From Dixie Gun Works.
Price: Dixie Gun Works PR0173 . . . . **$750.00**

KENTUCKY FLINTLOCK RIFLE

Caliber: 44, 45, or 50. **Barrel:** 35". **Weight:** 7 lbs. **Length:** 50" overall. **Stock:** Walnut stained, brass fittings. **Sights:** Fixed. **Features:** Available in carbine model also, 28" bbl. Some variations in detail, finish. Kits also available from some importers. Imported by The Armoury.
Price: About . . . . **$217.95 to $345.00**

Kentucky Percussion Rifle

Similar to Flintlock except percussion lock. Finish and features vary with importer. Imported by The Armoury and CVA.
Price: About **$259.95**
Price: 45 or 50 cal. (Navy Arms) **$425.00**
Price: Kit, 50 cal. (CVA) **$189.95**

KNIGHT SHADOW RIFLE

Caliber: 50. **Barrel:** 26". **Weight:** 7 lbs., 12 oz. **Length:** 42" overall. **Stock:** Checkered with recoil pad, swivel studs, Realtree APG HD. or black composite. **Sights:** Fully adjustable, metallic fiber-optic. **Features:** Bolt-action in-line system uses #209 shotshell primer for ignition; primer is held in plastic drop-in Primer Disc. Available in blued or stainless steel. Made in U.S. by Knight Rifles (Modern Muzzleloading).
Price: Blued/black. **$289.99**
Price: Stainless/black **$329.99**
Price: Realtree APG HD camo (2009) **$329.99**

Prices given are believed to be accurate at time of publication however, many factors affect retail pricing so exact prices are not possible.

KNIGHT ROLLING BLOCK RIFLE
Caliber: 50, 52. **Barrel:** 27"; 1:28" twist. **Weight:** 8 lbs. **Length:** 43.5" overall. **Stock:** Brown Sandstone laminate, checkered, recoil pad, sling swivel studs. **Sights:** Fully adjustable, metallic fiber-optic. **Features:** Uses #209 shotshell primer, comes in stainless steel or blued, with walnut or black composite stock. Made in U.S. by Knight Rifles (Modern Muzzleloading).
Price: 50 Stainless/black. **$419.99**
Price: 50 Blued/black **$329.99**
Price: 50 Stainless/Realtree (2009) **$459.99**
Price: 50 Stainless/Brown Sandstone (2009) **$438.88**
Price: 52 Stainless/Next G-1 . . . . **$459.99**

KNIGHT LONG RANGE HUNTER
Caliber: 50. **Barrel:** 27" custom fluted; 1:28" twist. **Weight:** 8 lbs. 6 oz. **Length:** 45.5" overall. **Stock:** Cast-off design thumbhole, checkered, recoil pad, sling swivel studs, in Forest Green or Sandstone. **Sights:** Fully-adjustable, metallic fiber-optic. **Features:** Full plastic jacket ignition system. Made in U.S. by Knight Rifles (Modern Muzzleloading).
Price: SS Forest Green. **$769.99**
Price: SS Forest Green Thumbhole **$799.99**

KNIGHT EXTREME
Caliber: 50, 52. **Barrel:** 26", fluted stainess, 1:28" twist. **Weight:** 7 lbs. 14 oz to 8 lbs. **Length:** 45" overall. **Stock:** Stainless steel laminate, blued walnut, black composite thumbhole with blued or SS, Realtree Hardwoods Green HD with thumbhole. **Sights:** Fully adjustable metallic fiber-optics. **Features:** Full plastic jacket ignition system. Made in U.S. by Knight Rifles (Modern Muzzleloading).
Price: 50 SS/Realtree (2009) **$529.99**
Price: 52 SS/black (2009) **$229.94**
Price: 50 SS/black **$459.99**
Price: 50 SS/black w/thumbhole **$489.99**
Price: 50 SS/brown **$569.99**

KNIGHT BIGHORN
Caliber: 50. **Barrel:** 26"; 1:28" twist. **Weight:** 7 lbs. 3 oz. **Length:** 44.5" overall. **Stock:** Realtree Advantage MAX-1 HD or black composite thumbhole, checkered with recoil pad, sling swivel studs. **Sights:** Fully adjustable metallic fiber-optic. **Features:** Uses 4 different ignition systems (included): #11 nipple, musket nipple, bare 208 shotgun primer and 209 Extreme shotgun primer system (Extreme weatherproof full plastic jacket system); one-piece removable hammer assembly. Made in U.S. by Knight Rifles (Modern Muzzleloading).
Price: Stainless/Realtree w/thumbhole (2009) **$459.99**
Price: Stainless/black **$419.99**
Price: Stainless/black w/thumbhole **$439.99**

KNIGHT 52 MODELS
Caliber: 52. **Barrel:** 26";1:26" twist (composite), 27" 1:28" twist (G-1 camo). **Weight:** 8 lbs. **Length:** 43.5" (G-1 camo); 45" (composite) overall. **Stock:** Standard black composite or Next G-1, checkered with recoil pad, sling swivel studs. **Sights:** Fully adjustable metallic fiber-optic. **Features:** PowerStem breech plug. Made in U.S. by Knight Rifles (Modern Muzzleloading).
Price: Stainless/black (2009) **$299.94**
Price: Stainless/Next G-1 . . . . **$459.99**

LONDON ARMORY 1861 ENFIELD MUSKETOON
Caliber: 58, Minie ball. **Barrel:** 24", round. **Weight:** 7 to 7.5 lbs. **Length:** 40.5" overall. **Stock:** Walnut, with sling swivels. **Sights:** Blade front, graduated military-leaf rear. **Features:** Brass trigger guard, nosecap, buttplate; blued barrel, bands, lockplate, swivels. Imported by Euroarms of America, Navy Arms.
Price: . . . . $300.00 to $521.00
Price: Kit . . . . $365.00 to $402.00

LONDON ARMORY 2-BAND 1858 ENFIELD
Caliber: .577" Minie, .575" round ball. **Barrel:** 33". **Weight:** 10 lbs. **Length:** 49" overall. **Stock:** Walnut. **Sights:** Folding leaf rear adjustable for elevation. **Features:** Blued barrel, color case-hardened lock and hammer, polished brass buttplate, trigger guard, nosecap. From Navy Arms, Euroarms of America, Dixie Gun Works.
Price: PR0330 . . . . **$650.00**

LONDON ARMORY 3-BAND 1853 ENFIELD
Caliber: 58 (.577" Minie, .575" round ball, .580" maxi ball). **Barrel:** 39". **Weight:** 9.5 lbs. **Length:** 54" overall. **Stock:** European walnut. **Sights:** Inverted "V" front, traditional Enfield folding ladder rear. **Features:** Re-creation of the famed London Armory Company Pattern 1853 Enfield Musket. One-piece walnut stock, brass buttplate, trigger guard and nosecap. Lockplate marked "London Armoury Co." and with a British crown. Blued Baddeley barrel bands. From Euroarms of America, Navy Arms.
Price: About . . . . $350.00 to $606.00

LYMAN TRADE RIFLE
Caliber: 50, 54. **Barrel:** 28" octagon;1:48" twist. **Weight:** 10.8 lbs. **Length:** 45" overall. **Stock:** European walnut. **Sights:** Blade front, open rear adjustable for windage or optional fixed sights. **Features:** Fast twist rifling for conical bullets. Polished brass furniture with blue steel parts, stainless steel nipple. Hook breech, single trigger, coil spring percussion lock. Steel barrel rib and ramrod ferrules. Introduced 1980. From Lyman.
Price: 50-cal. percussion **$474.95**
Price: 50-cal. flintlock **$499.95**
Price: 54-cal. percussion **$474.95**
Price: 54-cal. flintlock **$499.95**

LYMAN DEERSTALKER RIFLE
Caliber: 50, 54. **Barrel:** 24", octagonal; 1:48" rifling. **Weight:** 10.4 lbs. **Stock:** Walnut with black rubber buttpad. **Sights:** Lyman #37MA beaded front, fully adjustable fold-down Lyman #16A rear. **Features:** Stock has less drop for quick sighting. All metal parts are blackened, with color case-hardened lock; single trigger. Comes with sling and swivels. Available in flint or percussion. Introduced 1990. From Lyman.
Price: 50-cal. flintlock **$529.95**
Price: 50-, 54-cal., flintlock, left-hand **$569.95**
Price: 54 cal. flintlock **$529.95**
Price: 50-, 54 cal. percussion **$487.95**
Price: 50-, 54-cal. stainless steel **$609.95**

LYMAN GREAT PLAINS RIFLE
Caliber: 50, 54. **Barrel:** 32"; 1:60" twist. **Weight:** 11.6 lbs. **Stock:** Walnut. **Sights:** Steel blade front, buckhorn rear adjustable for windage and elevation and fixed notch primitive sight included. **Features:** Blued steel furniture. Stainless steel nipple. Coil spring lock, Hawken-style trigger guard and double-set triggers. Round thimbles recessed and sweated into rib. Steel wedge plates and toe plate. Introduced 1979. From Lyman.
Price: Percussion **$654.95**
Price: Flintlock **$699.95**
Price: Percussion kit **$519.95**
Price: Flintlock kit **$574.95**
Price: Left-hand percussion **$669.95**
Price: Left-hand flintlock **$709.95**

Lyman Great Plains Hunter Model
Similar to Great Plains model except 1:32" twist shallow-groove barrel and comes drilled and tapped for Lyman 57GPR peep sight.
Price: Percussion **$654.95**
Price: Flintlock **$699.95**
Price: Left-hand percussion **$669.95**

MARKESBERY KM BLACK BEAR M/L RIFLE
Caliber: 36, 45, 50, 54. **Barrel:** 24"; 1:26" twist. **Weight:** 6.5 lbs. **Length:** 38.5" overall. **Stock:** Two-piece American hardwood,

walnut, black laminate, green laminate, black composition, X-Tra or Mossy Oak® Break-up™ camouflage. **Sights:** Bead front, open fully adjustable rear. **Features:** Interchangeable barrels; exposed hammer; Outer-Line Magnum ignition system uses small rifle primer or standard No. 11 cap and nipple. Blue, black matte, or stainless. Made in U.S. by Markesbery Muzzle Loaders.

Price: American hardwood walnut, blue finish	$536.63
Price: American hardwood walnut, stainless	$553.09
Price: Black laminate, blue finish	$539.67
Price: Black laminate, stainless	$556.27
Price: Black composite, blue finish	$532.65
Price: Black composite, stainless	$549.93
Price: Green laminate, blue finish	$539.00
Price: Green laminate, stainless	$556.27

Markesbery KM Brown Bear Rifle
Similar to KM Black Bear except one-piece thumbhole stock with Monte Carlo comb. Stock in Crotch Walnut composite, green or black laminate, black composite or X-Tra or Mossy Oak® Break-Up™ camouflage. Made in U.S. by Markesbery Muzzle Loaders, Inc.

Price: Black composite, blue finish	$658.83
Price: Crotch Walnut, blue finish	$658.83
Price: Walnut wood	$662.81
Price: Black wood	$662.81
Price: Black laminated wood	$662.81
Price: Green laminated wood	$662.81
Price: Black composite, stainless	$676.11
Price: Crotch Walnut composite, stainless	$676.11
Price: Walnut wood, stainless	$680.07
Price: Black wood, stainless	$680.07
Price: Black laminated wood, stainless	$680.07
Price: Green laminate, stainless	$680.07

Markesbery KM Grizzly Bear Rifle
Similar to KM Black Bear except thumbhole buttstock with Monte Carlo comb. Stock in Crotch Walnut composite, green or black laminate, black composite or X-Tra or Mossy Oak® Break-Up camouflage. Made in U.S. by Markesbery Muzzle Loaders, Inc.

Price: Black composite, blue finish	$642.96
Price: Crotch Walnut, blue finish	$642.96
Price: Walnut wood	$646.93
Price: Black wood	$646.93
Price: Black laminate wood	$646.93
Price: Green laminate wood	$646.93
Price: Black composite, stainless	$660.98
Price: Crotch Walnut composite, stainless	$660.98
Price: Black laminate wood, stainless	$664.20
Price: Green laminate, stainless	$664.20
Price: Walnut wood, stainless	$664.20
Price: Black wood, stainless	$664.20

Markesbery KM Polar Bear Rifle
Similar to KM Black Bear except one-piece stock with Monte Carlo comb. Stock in American Hard-wood walnut, green or black laminate, black composite, or X-Tra or Mossy Oak® Break-Up™ camouflage. Interchangeable barrel system, Outer-Line ignition system, cross-bolt double safety. Available in 36, 45, 50, 54 caliber. Made in U.S. by Markesbery Muzzle Loaders, Inc.

Price: American Hardwood walnut, blue finish	$539.01
Price: Black composite, blue finish	$536.63
Price: Black laminate, blue finish	$541.17
Price: Green laminate, blue finish	$541.17
Price: American Hardwood walnut, stainless	$556.27
Price: Black composite, stainless	$556.04
Price: Black laminate, stainless	$570.56
Price: Green laminate, stainless	$570.56

MARKESBERY KM COLORADO ROCKY MOUNTAIN RIFLE
Caliber: 36, 45, 50, 54. **Barrel:** 24"; 1:26" twist. **Weight:** 6.5 lbs. **Length:** 38.5" overall. **Stock:** American hardwood walnut, green or black laminate. **Sights:** Firesight bead on ramp front, fully adjustable open rear. **Features:** Replicates Reed/Watson rifle of 1851. Straight grip stock with or without two barrel bands, rubber recoil pad, large-spur hammer. Made in U.S. by Markesbery Muzzle Loaders, Inc.

Price: American hardwood walnut, blue finish	$545.92

Price: Black or green laminate, blue finish	$548.30
Price: American hardwood walnut, stainless	$563.17
Price: Black or green laminate, stainless	$566.34

MDM BUCKWACKA IN-LINE RIFLES
Caliber: 45 Nitro Mag., 50. **Barrel:** 23", 25". **Weight:** 7 to 7.75 lbs. **Stock:** Black, walnut, laminated and camouflage finishes. **Sights:** Williams Fire Sight blade front, Williams fully adjustable rear with ghost-ring peep aperture. **Features:** Break-open action; Incinerating Ignition System incorporates 209 shotshell primer directly into breech plug; 50-caliber models handle up to 150 grains of Pyrodex; synthetic ramrod; transfer bar safety; stainless or blued finish. Made in U.S. by Millennium Designed Muzzleloaders Ltd.

Price: 45 Nitro, stainless steel, walnut stock	$399.95
Price: 45 Nitro, stainless steel, Mossy Oak Break-up stock	$465.95
Price: 45 Nitro, blued action, walnut stock	$369.95
Price: 45 Nitro, blued action, Mossy Oak Break-up stock	$425.95
Price: 50-cal., stainless steel, walnut stock	$399.95
Price: 50-cal., stainless steel, Mossy Oak Break-up stock	$465.95
Price: 50-cal., blued action, walnut stock	$369.95
Price: 50-cal., blued action, Mossy Oak Break-up stock	$435.95
Price: 50-cal., Youth-Ladies, blued action, walnut stock	$369.95
Price: 50-cal., Youth-Ladies, stainless steel, walnut stock	$399.95

MDM M2K In-Line Rifle
Similar to Buckwacka except adjustable trigger and double-safety mechanism designed to prevent misfires. Made in U.S. by Millennium Designed Muzzleloaders Ltd.

Price:	$529.00 to $549.00

MISSISSIPPI 1841 PERCUSSION RIFLE
Caliber: 54, 58. **Barrel:** 33". **Weight:** 9.5 lbs. **Length:** 48-5/8" overall. **Stock:** One-piece European walnut full stock with satin finish. **Sights:** Brass blade front, fixed steel rear. **Features:** Case-hardened lockplate marked "U.S." surmounted by American eagle. Two barrel bands, sling swivels. Steel ramrod with brass end, browned barrel. From Navy Arms, Dixie Gun Works, Euroarms of America.

Price: Dixie Gun Works PR0870	$825.00

NAVY ARMS 1861 MUSKETOON
Caliber: 58. **Barrel:** 39". **Weight:** NA. **Length:** NA. **Stock:** NA. **Sights:** Front is blued steel base and blade, blued steel lip-up rear adjustable for elevation. **Features:** Brass nosecap, triggerguard, buttplate, blued steel barrel bands, color case-hardened lock with engraved lockplate marked "1861 Enfield" ahead of hammer & crown over "PH" on tail. Barrel is marked "Parker Hale LTD Birmingham England." Imported by Navy Arms.

Price:	$900.00

NAVY ARMS PARKER-HALE 1853 THREE-BAND ENFIELD
Caliber: 58. **Barrel:** 39", tapered, round, blued. **Weight:** NA. **Length:** 55-1/4" overall. **Stock:** Walnut. **Sights:** Front is blued steel base and blade, blued steel lip-up rear adjustable for elevation. **Features:** Meticulously reproduced based on original gauges and patterns. Features brass nosecap, triggerguard, buttplate, blued steel barrel bands, color case-hardened lock with engraved lockplate marked "Parker-Hale" ahead of hammer & crown over "PH" on tail. Barrel is marked "Parker Hale LTD Birmingham England." From Navy Arms.

Price: Finished rifle	$1,050.00

Navy Arms Parker-Hale 1858 Two-Band Enfield
Similar to the Three-band Enfield with 33" barrel, 49" overall length. Engraved lockplate marked "1858 Enfield" ahead of hammer & crown over "PH" on tail. Barrel is marked "Parker Hale LTD Birmingham England."

Price:	$1,050.00

NAVY ARMS PARKER-HALE VOLUNTEER RIFLE
Caliber: 451. **Barrel:** 32", 1:20" twist. **Weight:** 9.5 lbs. **Length:** 49" overall. **Stock:** Walnut, checkered wrist and forend. **Sights:** Globe front, adjustable ladder-type rear. **Features:** Recreation of the type of gun issued to volunteer regiments during the 1860s. Rigby-pattern rifling, patent breech, detented lock. Stock is glass beaded for accuracy. Engraved lockplate marked "Alex Henry" & crown on tail, barrel marked "Parker Hale LTD Birmingham England" and "Alexander Henry Rifling .451" Imported by Navy Arms.

Price:	$1,400.00

Prices given are believed to be accurate at time of publication however, many factors affect retail pricing so exact prices are not possible.

NAVY ARMS PARKER-HALE WHITWORTH MILITARY TARGET RIFLE

Caliber: 45. **Barrel:** 36". **Weight:** 9.25 lbs. **Length:** 52.5" overall. **Stock:** Walnut. Checkered at wrist and forend. **Sights:** Hooded post front, open step-adjustable rear. **Features:** Faithful reproduction of Whitworth rifle. Trigger has detented lock, capable of fine adjustments without risk of the sear nose catching on the half-cock notch and damaging both parts. Engraved lockplate marked "Whitworth" ahead of hammer & crown on tail. Barrel marked "Parker Hale LTD Birmingham England" in one line on front of sight and "Sir Joseph Whitworth's Rifling .451" on left side. Introduced 1978. Imported by Navy Arms.
Price: **$1,550.00**

NAVY ARMS BROWN BESS MUSKET

Caliber: 75, smoothbore. **Barrel:** 41.8". **Weight:** 9 lbs., 5 oz. **Length:** 41.8" overall. **Features:** Brightly polished steel and brass, one-piece walnut stock. Signature of gunsmith William Grice and the date 1762, the crown and alphabetical letters GR (Georgius Rex). Barrel is made of steel, satin finish; the walnut stock is oil finished. From Navy Arms.
Price: **$1,100.00**

NAVY ARMS COUNTRY HUNTER

Caliber: 50. **Barrel:** 28.4", 6-groove, 1:34 twist. **Weight:** 6 lbs. **Length:** 44" overall. **Features:** Matte finished barrel. From Navy Arms.
Price: **$450.00**

NAVY ARMS PENNSYLVANIA RIFLE

Caliber: 32, 45. **Barrel:** 41.6". **Weight:** 7 lbs. 12 oz. to 8 lbs. 6 oz. **Length:** 56.1" overall. **Features:** Extra long rifle finished wtih rust brown color barrel and one-piece oil finished walnut stock. Adjustable double-set trigger. Vertically adjustable steel front and rear sights. From Navy Arms.
Price: **$675.00**

NEW ENGLAND FIREARMS SIDEKICK

Caliber: 50, 209 primer ignition. **Barrel:** 26" (magnum). **Weight:** 6.5 lbs. **Length:** 41.25". **Stock:** Black matte polymer or hardwood. **Sights:** Adjustable fiber-optic open, tapped for scope mounts. **Features:** Single-shot based on H&R break-open action. Uses No. 209 shotgun primer held in place by special primer carrier. Telescoping brass ramrod. Introduced 2004.
Price: Wood stock, blued frame, black-oxide barrel) **$216.00**
Price: Stainless barrel and frame, synthetic stock) **$310.00**

NEW ENGLAND FIREARMS HUNTSMAN

Caliber: 50, 209 primer ignition. **Barrel:** 22" to 26". **Weight:** 5.25 to 6.5 lbs. **Length:** 40" to 43". **Stock:** Black matte polymer or hardwood. **Sights:** Fiber-optic open sights, tapped for scope mounts. **Features:** Break-open action, transfer-bar safety system, breech plug removable for cleaning. Introduced 2004.
Price: Stainless Huntsman **$306.00**
Price: Huntsman **$212.00**
Price: Pardner Combo 12 ga./50 cal muzzleloader **$259.00**
Price: Tracker II Combo 12 ga. rifled slug barrel /50 cal. **$288.00**
Price: Handi-Rifle Combo 243/50 cal. **$405.00**

New England Firearms Stainless Huntsman

Similar to Huntsman, but with matte nickel finish receiver and stainless bbl. Introduced 2003. From New England Firearms.
Price: **$381.00**

PACIFIC RIFLE MODEL 1837 ZEPHYR

Caliber: 62. **Barrel:** 30", tapered octagon. **Weight:** 7.75 lbs. **Length:** NA. **Stock:** Oil-finished fancy walnut. **Sights:** German silver blade front, semi-buckhorn rear. Options available. **Features:** Improved underhammer action. First production rifle to offer Forsyth rifle, with narrow lands and shallow rifling with 1:14" pitch for high-velocity round balls. Metal finish is slow rust brown with nitre blue accents. Optional sights, finishes and integral muzzle brake available. Introduced 1995. Made in U.S. by Pacific Rifle Co.
Price: From **$995.00**

Pacific Rifle Big Bore African Rifles

Similar to the 1837 Zephyr except in 72-caliber and 8-bore. The 72-caliber is available in standard form with 28" barrel, or as the African with flat buttplate, checkered upgraded wood; weight is 9 lbs. The 8-bore African has dual-cap ignition, 24" barrel, weighs 12 lbs., checkered English walnut, engraving, gold inlays. Introduced 1998. Made in U.S. by Pacific Rifle Co.
Price: 72-caliber, from **$1,150.00**
Price: 8-bore, from **$2,500.00**

PEIFER MODEL TS-93 RIFLE

Caliber: 45, 50. **Barrel:** 24" Douglas premium; 1:20" twist in 45; 1:28" in 50. **Weight:** 7 lbs. **Length:** 43.25" overall. **Stock:** Bell & Carlson solid composite, with recoil pad, swivel studs. **Sights:** Williams bead front on ramp, fully adjustable open rear. Drilled and tapped for Weaver scope mounts with dovetail for rear peep. **Features:** In-line ignition uses #209 shotshell primer; fast lock time; fully enclosed breech; adjustable trigger; automatic safety; removable primer holder. Blue or stainless. Made in U.S. by Peifer Rifle Co. Introduced 1996.
Price: Blue, black stock. **$730.00**
Price: Blue, wood or camouflage composite stock, or stainless with black composite stock **$803.00**
Price: Stainless, wood or camouflage composite stock **$876.00**

PRAIRIE RIVER ARMS PRA BULLPUP RIFLE

Caliber: 50. **Barrel:** 28"; 1:28" twist. **Weight:** 7.5 lbs. **Length:** 31.5" overall. **Stock:** Hardwood or black all-weather. **Sights:** Blade front, open adjustable rear. **Features:** Bullpup design thumbhole stock. Patented internal percussion ignition system. Left-hand model available. Dovetailed for scope mount. Introduced 1995. Made in U.S. by Prairie River Arms, Ltd.
Price: 4140 alloy barrel, hardwood stock **$199.00**
Price: All Weather stock, alloy barrel **$205.00**

REMINGTON GENESIS MUZZLELOADER

Caliber: 50. **Barrel:** 28", 1-in-28" twist, blued, camo, or stainless fluted. **Weight:** 7.75 lbs. **Stock:** NA. Black synthetic, Mossy Oak New Break-Up, Realtree Hardwoods HD. **Sights:** Williams fiber-optic sights, drilled and tapped for scope mounts. **Features:** TorchCam action, 209 primer, up to 150-grain charges. Over-travel hammer, crossbolt safety with ambidextrous HammerSpur (right- and left-handed operation). Buckmasters version has stainless fluted barrel with a Realtree Hardwoods HD camo stock, laser-engraved Buckmasters logo. Aluminum anodized ramrod with jag, front and rear swivel studs, removable 7/16" breech plug; optimized for use with Remington Kleanbore 209 Muzzleloading Primers. Introduced 2006. Made in U.S. by Remington Arms Co.
Price: Genesis ML, black synthetic, carbon matte blued **$237.00**
Price: Genesis MLS Overmold synthetic, stainless satin **$307.00**
Price: Genesis ML Camo Mossy Oak Break-Up full camo **$349.00**
Price: Genesis ML Camo Mossy Oak Break-Up matte blue . . . **$293.00**
Price: Genesis MLS Camo, Mossy Oak Break-up, stainless satin **$342.00**
Price: Genesis ML SF Synthetic Thumbhole **$349.00**
Price: Genesis ML SF Synthetic Thumbhole, stainless satin . **$405.00**

Price: Genesis ML SF Buckmasters (2007) $363.00
Price: Genesis ML SF laminate thumbhole, stainless satin . . $538.00

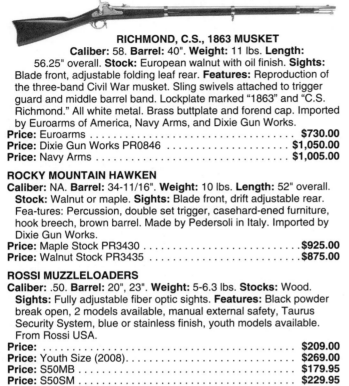

RICHMOND, C.S., 1863 MUSKET
Caliber: 58. **Barrel:** 40". **Weight:** 11 lbs. **Length:**
56.25" overall. **Stock:** European walnut with oil finish. **Sights:**
Blade front, adjustable folding leaf rear. **Features:** Reproduction of
the three-band Civil War musket. Sling swivels attached to trigger
guard and middle barrel band. Lockplate marked "1863" and "C.S.
Richmond." All white metal. Brass buttplate and forend cap. Imported
by Euroarms of America, Navy Arms, and Dixie Gun Works.
Price: Euroarms $730.00
Price: Dixie Gun Works PR0846 . . . . $1,050.00
Price: Navy Arms $1,005.00

ROCKY MOUNTAIN HAWKEN
Caliber: NA. **Barrel:** 34-11/16". **Weight:** 10 lbs. **Length:** 52" overall.
Stock: Walnut or maple. **Sights:** Blade front, drift adjustable rear.
Fea-tures: Percussion, double set trigger, casehard-ened furniture,
hook breech, brown barrel. Made by Pedersoli in Italy. Imported by
Dixie Gun Works.
Price: Maple Stock PR3430 . . . .$925.00
Price: Walnut Stock PR3435 . . . .$875.00

ROSSI MUZZLELOADERS
Caliber: .50. **Barrel:** 20", 23". **Weight:** 5-6.3 lbs. **Stocks:** Wood.
Sights: Fully adjustable fiber optic sights. **Features:** Black powder
break open, 2 models available, manual external safety, Taurus
Security System, blue or stainless finish, youth models available.
From Rossi USA.
Price: $209.00
Price: Youth Size (2008) $269.00
Price: S50MB $179.95
Price: S50SM $229.95
Price: S45YBM (2009) $195.95
Price: S45YSM (2009) $242.95
Price: S50YBN (2009) $195.95
Price: S50YSM (2009) $242.95

SAVAGE MODEL 10ML MUZZLELOADER RIFLE SERIES
Caliber: 50. **Barrel:** 24", 1:24 twist, blue or stainless.
Weight: 7.75 lbs. **Stock:** Black synthetic, Realtree Hardwood
JD Camo, brown laminate. **Sights:** Green adjustable rear, Red
FiberOptic front. **Features:** XP Models scoped, no sights, designed
for smokeless powder, #209 primer ignition. Removeable breech
plug and vent liner.
Price: Model 10ML-II $531.00
Price: Model 10ML-II Camo $569.00
Price: Model 10MLSS-II Camo $628.00
Price: Model 10MLBSS-II $667.00
Price: Model 10ML-IIXP $569.00
Price: Model 10MLSS-IIXP $628.00

SECOND MODEL BROWN BESS MUSKET
Caliber: 75, uses .735" round ball. **Barrel:** 42", smoothbore.
Weight: 9.5 lbs. **Length:** 59" overall. **Stock:** Walnut (Navy); walnut-
stained hardwood (Dixie). **Sights:** Fixed. **Features:** Polished
barrel and lock with brass trigger guard and buttplate. Bayonet and
scabbard available. From Navy Arms, Dixie Gun Works.
Price: Finished . . . . $475.00 to $950.00
Price: Kit, Dixie Gun Works, FR0825 . . . .$875.00
Price: Carbine (Navy Arms) $835.00
Price: Dixie Gun Works FR0810 . . . . $995.00

THOMPSON/CENTER TRIUMPH MAGNUM MUZZLELOADER
Caliber: 50. **Barrel:** 28" Weather Shield coated. **Weight:** NA. **Length:**
NA. **Stock:** Black composite or Realtree AP HD Camo. **Sights:** NA.

Features: QLA 209 shotshell primer ignition. Introduced 2007. Made
in U.S. by Thompson/Center Arms.
Price: $457.00

Thompson/Center Bone Collector
Similar to the Triumph Magnum but with added Flex Tech technol-
ogy and Energy Burners to a shorter stock. Also added is Thompson/
Center's premium fluted barrel with Weather Shield and their patented
Power Rod.
Price: $708.00

THOMPSON/CENTER ENCORE 209X50 MAGNUM
Caliber: 50. **Barrel:** 26"; interchangeable with centerfire calibers.
Weight: 7 lbs. **Length:** 40.5" overall. **Stock:** American walnut butt
and forend, or black composite. **Sights:** TruGlo fiber-optic front
and rear. **Features:** Blue or stainless steel. Uses the stock, frame
and forend of the Encore centerfire pistol; break-open design using
trigger guard spur; stainless steel universal breech plug; uses #209
shotshell primers. Introduced 1998. Made in U.S. by Thompson/
Center Arms.
Price: Stainless with camo stock $772.00
Price: Blue, walnut stock and forend $678.00
Price: Blue, composite stock and forend $637.00
Price: Stainless, composite stock and forend $713.00
Price: All camo Realtree Hardwoods $729.00

THOMPSON/CENTER FIRE STORM RIFLE
Caliber: 50. **Barrel:** 26"; 1:28" twist. **Weight:** 7 lbs. **Length:**
41.75" overall. **Stock:** Black synthetic with rubber recoil pad, swivel
studs. **Sights:** Click-adjustable steel rear and ramp-style front,
both with fiber-optic inserts. **Features:** Side hammer lock is the first
designed for up to three 50-grain Pyrodex pellets; patented Pyrodex
Pyramid breech directs ignition fire 360 degrees around base of
pellet. Quick Load Accurizor Muzzle System; aluminum ramrod.
Flintlock only. Introduced 2000. Made in U.S. by Thompson/Center
Arms.
Price: Blue finish, flintlock model with 1:48" twist for round balls,
conicals $436.00
Price: SST, flintlock $488.00

THOMPSON/CENTER HAWKEN RIFLE
Caliber: 50. **Barrel:** 28" octagon, hooked breech. **Stock:**
American walnut. **Sights:** Blade front, rear adjustable for windage and
elevation. **Features:** Solid brass furniture, double-set triggers, button
rifled barrel, coil-type mainspring. From Thompson/Center Arms.
Price: Percussion model $590.00
Price: Flintlock model $615.00

THOMPSON/CENTER OMEGA
Caliber: 50". **Barrel:** 28", fluted. **Weight:** 7 lbs. **Length:** 42" overall.
Stock: Composite or laminated. **Sights:** Adjustable metal rear sight
with fiber-optics; metal ramp front sight with fiber-optics. **Features:**
Drilled and tapped for scope mounts. Thumbhole stock, sling swivel
studs. From T/C..
Price: $777.00

THOMPSON/CENTER IMPACT MUZZLELOADING RIFLE
50-caliber single shot rifle. Features include 209 primer ignition, sliding
hood to expose removable breechplug, synthetic stock adjustable
from 12.5 to 13.5 inches, 26-inch blued 1:28 rifled barrel, adjustable
fiber optic sights, aluminum ramrod, camo composite stock, QLA
muzzle system. Weight 6.5 lbs.
Price: . . . .$249.00 to $269.00

THOMPSON/CENTER NORTHWEST EXPLORER MUZZLELOADING RIFLE
50-caliber single shot rifle. Features include dropping block action, #11
percussion cap ignition, 28-inch blued or Weathershield 1:48 rifled
barrel, adjustable fiber optic sights, aluminum ramrod, black or camo

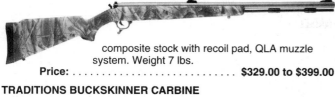

composite stock with recoil pad, QLA muzzle system. Weight 7 lbs.

Price: . . . . **$329.00 to $399.00**

TRADITIONS BUCKSKINNER CARBINE

Caliber: 50. **Barrel:** 21"; 15/16" flats, half octagon, half round; 1:20" or 1:66" twist. **Weight:** 6 lbs. **Length:** 37" overall. **Stock:** Beech or black laminated. **Sights:** Beaded blade front, fiber-optic open rear click adjustable for windage and elevation or fiber-optics. **Features:** Uses V-type mainspring, single trigger. Non-glare hardware; sling swivels. From Traditions.
Price: Flintlock **$249.00**
Price: Flintlock, laminated stock **$303.00**

TRADITIONS DEERHUNTER RIFLE SERIES

Caliber: 32, 50 or 54. **Barrel:** 24", octagonal; 15/16" flats; 1:48" or 1:66" twist. **Weight:** 6 lbs. **Length:** 40" overall. **Stock:** Stained hardwood or All-Weather composite with rubber buttpad, sling swivels. **Sights:** Lite Optic blade front, adjustable rear fiber-optics. **Features:** Flint or percussion with color case-hardened lock. Hooked breech, oversized trigger guard, blackened furniture, PVC ramrod. All-Weather has composite stock and C-nickel barrel. Drilled and tapped for scope mounting. Imported by Traditions, Inc.
Price: Percussion, 50-cal.; blued barrel; 1:48" twist **$228.00**
Price: Flintlock, 50 caliber only; 1:48" twist **$278.00**
Price: 50-cal., synthetic/blued **$224.00**
Price: Flintlock, 50-cal., synthetic/blued **$256.00**
Price: Redi-Pak, 50 cal. flintlock **$308.00**
Price: Flintlock, left-handed hardwood, 50 cal. **$337.00**
Price: 50-cal., hardwood/blued **$264.00**

TRADITIONS PURSUIT BREAK-OPEN MUZZLELOADER

Caliber: 45, 54 and 12 gauge. **Barrel:** 28", tapered, fluted; blued, stainless or Hardwoods Green camo. **Weight:** 8.25 lbs. **Length:** 44" overall. **Stock:** Synthetic black or Hardwoods Green. **Sights:** Steel fiber-optic rear, bead front. Introduced 2004 by Traditions, Inc.
Price: Steel, blued, 45 or 50 cal., synthetic stock **$279.00**
Price: Steel, nickel, 45 or 50 cal., synthetic stock **$309.00**
Price: Steel, nickel w/Hardwoods Green stock **$359.00**
Price: Matte blued; 12 ga., synthetic stock **$369.00**
Price: Matte blued; 12 ga. w/Hardwoods Green stock **$439.00**
Price: Lightweight model, blued, synthetic stock **$199.00**
Price: Lightweight model, blued, Mossy Oak® Break-Up™ Camo stock **$239.00**
Price: Lightweight model, nickel, Mossy Oak® Break-Up™ Camo stock **$279.00**

TRADITIONS EVOLUTION LONG DISTANCE BOLT-ACTION BLACKPOWDER RIFLE

Caliber: 45, 50 percussion. **Barrel:** 26", fluted with porting. **Sights:** Steel fiber-optic. **Weight:** 7 to 7.25 lbs. **Length:** 45" overall. **Features:** Bolt-action, cocking indicator, thumb safety, aluminum ramrod, sling studs. Wide variety of stocks and metal finishes. Introduced 2004 by Traditions, Inc.
Price: 50-cal. synthetic stock **$314.00**
Price: 45-cal. synthetic stock **$259.00**
Price: 50-cal. AW/Adv. Timber HD **$370.00**
Price: 50-cal. synthetic black/blued **$293.00**

TRADITIONS PA PELLET FLINTLOCK

Caliber: 50. **Barrel:** 26", blued, nickel. **Weight:** 7 lbs.

Stock: Hardwood, synthetic and synthetic break-up. **Sights:** Fiber-optic. **Features:** Removeable breech plug, left-hand model with hardwood stock. 1:48" twist.
Price: Hardwood, blued **$343.00**
Price: Hardwood left, blued **$378.00**

TRADITIONS HAWKEN WOODSMAN RIFLE

Caliber: 50. **Barrel:** 28"; 15/16" flats. **Weight:** 7 lbs., 11 oz. **Length:** 44.5" overall. **Stock:** Walnut-stained hardwood. **Sights:** Beaded blade front, hunting-style open rear adjustable for windage and elevation. **Features:** Percussion only. Brass patchbox and furniture. Double triggers. From Traditions.
Price: 50-cal. nickel/black laminate **$299.95**
Price: 50-cal Percussion **$396.00**
Price: 50-cal., left-hand **$415.00**
Price: 50-cal., flintlock **$434.00**

TRADITIONS KENTUCKY RIFLE

Caliber: 50. **Barrel:** 33.5"; 7/8" flats; 1:66" twist. **Weight:** 7 lbs. **Length:** 49" overall. **Stock:** Beech; inletted toe plate. **Sights:** Blade front, fixed rear. **Features:** Full-length, two-piece stock; brass furniture; color case-hardened lock. From Traditions.
Price: **$364.00**

TRADITIONS PENNSYLVANIA RIFLE

Caliber: 50. **Barrel:** 40.25"; 7/8" flats; 1:66" twist, octagon. **Weight:** 9 lbs. **Length:** 57.5" overall. **Stock:** Walnut. **Sights:** Blade front, adjustable rear. **Features:** Brass patchbox and ornamentation. Double-set triggers. From Traditions.
Price: Flintlock **$720.00**
Price: Percussion **$664.00**

TRADITIONS SHENANDOAH RIFLE

Caliber: 36, 50. **Barrel:** 33.5" octagon; 1:66" twist. **Weight:** 7 lbs., 3 oz. **Length:** 49.5" overall. **Stock:** Walnut. **Sights:** Blade front, buckhorn rear. **Features:** V-type mainspring; double-set trigger; solid brass buttplate, patchbox, nosecap, thimbles, trigger guard. Introduced 1996. From Traditions.
Price: Flintlock **$588.00**
Price: Percussion **$551.00**
Price: 36 cal. flintlock, 1:48" twist **$618.00**
Price: 36 cal. percussion, 1:48" twist **$558.00**

TRADITIONS TENNESSEE RIFLE

Caliber: 50. **Barrel:** 24", octagon; 15/16" flats; 1:66" twist. **Weight:** 6 lbs. **Length:** 40.5" overall. **Stock:** Stained beech. **Sights:** Blade front, fixed rear. **Features:** One-piece stock has inletted brass furniture, cheekpiece; double-set trigger; V-type mainspring. Flint or percussion. From Traditions.
Price: Flintlock **$484.00**
Price: Percussion **$439.00**

TRADITIONS TRACKER 209 IN-LINE RIFLES

Caliber: 45, 50. **Barrel:** 22" blued or C-nickel finish; 1:28" twist, 50 cal. 1:20" 45 cal. **Weight:** 6 lbs., 4 oz. **Length:** 41" overall. **Stock:** Black, Advantage Timber® composite, synthetic. **Sights:** Lite Optic blade front, adjustable rear. **Features:** Thumb safety; adjustable trigger; rubber butt pad and sling swivel studs; takes 150 grains of Pyrodex pellets; one-piece breech system takes 209 shotshell primers. Drilled and tapped for scope. From Traditions.
Price: (Black composite or synthetic stock, 22" blued barrel). **$161.00**
Price: (Black composite or synthetic stock, 22" C-nickel barrel) **$184.00**
Price: (Advantage Timber® stock, 22" C-nickel barrel) **$249.00**
Price: (Redi-Pak, black stock and blued barrel, powder flask, capper, ball starter, other accessories) **$219.00**
Price: (Redi-Pak, synthetic stock and blued barrel, with scope) **$265.00**

ULTRA LIGHT ARMS MODEL 209 MUZZLELOADER

Caliber: 45 or 50. **Barrel:** 24" button rifled; 1:32" twist. **Weight:** Under 5 lbs. **Stock:** Kevlar/Graphite. **Features:** Recoil pad, sling swivels included. Some color options available. Adj. Timney trigger, positive primer extraction.

Price: **$1,300.00**

WHITE MODEL 97 WHITETAIL HUNTER RIFLE
Caliber: 45, 50. **Barrel:** 22", 1:20" twist (45 cal.); 1:24" twist (50 cal.). **Weight:** 7.7 lbs. **Length:** 40" overall. **Stock:** Black laminated or black composite. **Sights:** Marble TruGlo fully adjustable, steel rear with white diamond, red bead front with high-visibility inserts. **Features:** In-line ignition with FlashFire one-piece nipple and breech plug that uses standard or magnum No. 11 caps, fully adjustable trigger, double safety system, aluminum ramrod; drilled and tapped for scope. Hard case. Made in U.S.A. by Split Fire Sporting Goods.
Price: Whitetail w/laminated or composite stock. **$499.95**
Price: Adventurer w/26" stainless barrel & thumbhole stock) **$699.95**
Price: Odyssey w/24" carbon fiber wrapped barrel
& thumbhole stock **$1,299.95**

WHITE MODEL 98 ELITE HUNTER RIFLE
Caliber: 45, 50. **Barrel:** 24", 1:24" twist (50 cal.) **Weight:** 8.6 lbs. **Length:** 43.5" overall. **Stock:** Black laminate wtih swivel studs. **Sights:** TruGlo fully adjustable, steel rear with white diamond, red bead front with high-visibility inserts. **Features:** In-line ignition with FlashFire one-piece nipple and breech plug that uses standard or magnum No. 11 caps, fully adjustable trigger, double safety system, aluminum ramrod, drilled and tapped for scope, hard gun case. Made in U.S.A. by Split Fire Sporting Goods.
Price: Composite or laminate wood stock. **$499.95**

White Thunderbolt Rifle
Similar to the Elite Hunter but is designed to handle 209 shotgun primers only. Has 26" stainless steel barrel, weighs 9.3 lbs. and is 45.5" long. Composite or laminate stock. Made in U.S.A. by Split Fire Sporting Goods.
Price: **$599.95**

WHITE MODEL 2000 BLACKTAIL HUNTER RIFLE
Caliber: 50. **Barrel:** 22", 1:24" twist (50 cal.). **Weight:** 7.6 lbs. **Length:** 39-7/8" overall. **Stock:** Black laminated with swivel studs with laser engraved deer or elk scene. **Sights:** TruGlo fully adjustable, steel rear with white diamond, red bead front with high-visibility inserts. **Features:** Teflon finished barrel, in-line ignition with FlashFire one-piece nipple and breech plug that uses standard or magnum No. 11 caps, fully adjustable trigger, double safety system, aluminum ramrod, drilled and tapped for scope. Hard gun case. Made in U.S.A. by Split Fire Sporting Goods.
Price: Laminate wood stock, w/laser engraved game scene . **$599.95**

WHITE LIGHTNING II RIFLE
Caliber: 45 and 50 percussion. **Barrel:** 24", 1:32 twist. **Sights:** Adj. rear. **Stock:** Black polymer. **Weight:** 6 lbs. **Features:** In-line, 209 primer ignition system, blued or nickel-plated bbl., adj. trigger, Delrin ramrod, sling studs, recoil pad. Made in U.S.A. by Split Fire Sporting Goods.
Price: **$299.95**

WHITE ALPHA RIFLE
Caliber: 45, 50 percussion. **Barrel:** 27" tapered, stainless. **Sights:** Marble TruGlo rear, fiber-optic front. **Stock:** Laminated. **Features:** Lever action rotating block, hammerless; adj. trigger, positive safety. All stainless metal, including trigger. Made in U.S.A. by Split Fire Sporting Goods.
Price: **$449.95**

WINCHESTER APEX SWING-ACTION MAGNUM RIFLE
Caliber: 45, 50. **Barrel:** 28". **Stock:** Mossy Oak® Camo, Black Fleck. **Sights:** Adj. fiber-optic. **Weight:** 7 lbs., 12 oz. **Overall length:** 42". **Features:** Monte Carlo cheekpiece, swing-action design, external hammer.
Price: Mossy Oak®/stainless **$489.95**
Price: Black Fleck/stainless **$449.95**
Price: Full Mossy Oak® **$469.95**
Price: Black Fleck/blued **$364.95**

WINCHESTER X-150 BOLT-ACTION MAGNUM RIFLE
Caliber: 45, 50. **Barrel:** 26". **Stock:** Hardwoods or Timber HD, Black Fleck, Break-Up™. **Weight:** 8 lbs., 3 oz. **Sights:** Adj. fiber-optic. **Features:** No. 209 shotgun primer ignition, stainless steel bolt, stainless fluted bbl.

Price: Mossy Oak®, Timber, Hardwoods/stainless. **$349.95**
Price: Black Fleck/stainless **$299.95**
Price: Mossy Oak®, Timber, Hardwoods/blued **$279.95**
Price: Black Fleck/blued **$229.95**

ZOUAVE PERCUSSION RIFLE
Caliber: 58, 59. **Barrel:** 32.5". **Weight:** 9.5 lbs. **Length:** 48.5" overall. **Stock:** Walnut finish, brass patchbox and buttplate. **Sights:** Fixed front, rear adjustable for elevation. **Features:** Color case-hardened lockplate, blued barrel. From Navy Arms, Dixie Gun Works, EMF, Euroarms of America.
Price: Dixie Gun Works PR0853 (58) **$525.00**

Prices given are believed to be accurate at time of publication however, many factors affect retail pricing so exact pricing is not possible.

CABELA'S BLACKPOWDER SHOTGUNS
Gauge: 10, 12, 20. **Barrel:** 10-ga., 30"; 12-ga., 28.5" (Extra-Full, Mod., Imp. Cyl. choke tubes); 20-ga., 27.5" (Imp. Cyl. & Mod. fixed chokes). **Weight:** 6.5 to 7 lbs. **Length:** 45" overall (28.5" barrel). **Stock:** American walnut with checkered grip; 12- and 20-gauge have straight stock, 10-gauge has pistol grip. **Features:** Blued barrels, engraved, color case-hardened locks and hammers, brass ramrod tip. From Cabela's.
Price: 10-gauge **$849.99**
Price: 12-gauge **$719.99**
Price: 20-gauge **$659.99**

DIXIE MAGNUM PERCUSSION SHOTGUN
Gauge: 10, 12, 20. **Barrel:** 30" (Imp. Cyl. & Mod.) in 10-gauge; 28" in 12-gauge. **Weight:** 6.25 lbs. **Length:** 45" overall. **Stock:** Hand-checkered walnut, 14" pull. **Features:** Double triggers; light hand engraving; case-hardened locks in 12-gauge, polished steel in 10-gauge; sling swivels. From Dixie Gun Works.
Price: 12 ga. PS0930 . . . . **$825.00**
Price: 12-ga. Kit PS0940 . . . . **$725.00**
Price: 20-ga. PS0334 . . . . **$825.00**
Price: 10-ga. PS1030 . . . . **$900.00**
Price: 10-ga. kit PS1040 . . . . **$725.00**
Price: Coach Gun, 12 ga. 20" bbl PS0914 . . . . **$800.00**

KNIGHT TK2000 NEXT G-1 CAMO MUZZLELOADING SHOTGUN
Gauge: 12. **Barrel:** 26", extra-full choke tube. **Weight:** 7 lbs., 7 oz. **Length:** 45" overall. **Stock:** Synthetic black or Realtree Hardwoods; recoil pad; swivel studs. **Sights:** Fully adjustable rear, blade front with fiber-optics. **Features:** Receiver drilled and tapped for scope mount; in-line ignition; adjustable trigger; removable breech plug; double safety system; Imp. Cyl. choke tube available. Made in U.S. by Knight Rifles (Modern Muzzleloading)
Price: **$379.99**

NAVY ARMS SIDE-BY-SIDE SHOTGUN
Caliber: 12 smoothbore. **Barrel:** 28.5". **Weight:** 7 lbs. **Length:** 44.3" overall. **Features:** English model reproduction has checkered walnut stock, slightly choked and inside choked blued barrels, engraved locks. From Navy Arms.
Price: **$910.00**

WHITE TOMINATOR SHOTGUN
Caliber: 12. **Barrel:** 25" blue, straight, tapered stainless steel. **Weight:** NA. **Length:** NA. **Stock:** Black laminated or black wood. **Sights:** Drilled and tapped for easy scope mounting. **Features:** Internchangeable choke tubes. Custom vent rib with high visibility front bead. Double safeties. Fully adjustable custom trigger. Recoil pad and sling swivel studs. Made in U.S.A. by Split Fire Sporting Goods.
Price: **$349.95**

ARS HUNTING MASTER AR6 AIR PISTOL
Caliber: .22 (.177 + 20 special order). **Barrel:** 12" rifled. **Weight:** 3 lbs. **Length:** 18.25 overall. **Power:** NA. **Grips:** Indonesian walnut with checkered grip. **Sights:** Adjustable rear, blade front. **Features:** 6 shot repeater with rotary magazine, single or double action, receiver grooved for scope, hammer block and trigger block safeties.
Price: **$659.00**

BEEMAN P1 MAGNUM AIR PISTOL
Caliber: .177, 20. **Barrel:** 8.4". **Weight:** 2.5 lbs. **Length:** 11" overall. **Power:** Top lever cocking; spring-piston. **Grips:** Checkered walnut. **Sights:** Blade front, square notch rear with click micrometer adjustments for windage and elevation. Grooved for scope mounting. **Features:** Dual power for .177 and 20 cal.; low setting gives 350-400 fps; high setting 500-600 fps. All Colt 45 auto grips fit gun. Dry-firing feature for practice. Optional wood shoulder stock. Imported by Beeman.
Price: . . . . **$499.95 to $525.95**

BEEMAN P3 PNEUMATIC AIR PISTOL
Caliber: .177. **Barrel:** NA. **Weight:** 1.7 lbs. **Length:** 9.6" overall. **Power:** Single-stroke pneumatic; overlever barrel cocking. **Grips:** Reinforced polymer. **Sights:** Front and rear fiber-optic sights. **Features:** Velocity 410 fps. Polymer frame; automatic safety; two-stage trigger; built-in muzzle brake.
Price: **$245.95**
Price: With scope **$335.95**

BEEMAN/FEINWERKBAU P44
Caliber: .177, single shot. **Barrel:** 9.17". **Weight:** 2.10 lbs. **Length:** 16.54" overall. **Power:** Pre-charged pneumatic. **Grips:** Walnut grip. **Sights:** front and rear sights. **Features:** 500 fps, sighting line adjustable from 360 to 395mm, adjustable 3-d grip in 3 sizes, adjustable match trigger, delivered in special transport case.
Price: **$2,575.95**
Price: Left-hand model **$2,655.95**

BEEMAN/FEINWERKBAU P56
Caliber: .177, 5-shot magazine. **Barrel:** 8.81". **Weight:** 2.43 lbs. **Length:** 16.54" overall. **Power:** Pre-charged pneumatic. **Grips:** Walnut Morini grip. **Sights:** front and rear sights. **Features:** 500 fps, match-adjustable trigger, adjustable rear sight, front sight accepts interchangeable inserts, delivered in special transport case.
Price: **$2,654.00**

BEEMAN/FWB 103 AIR PISTOL
Caliber: .177. **Barrel:** 10.1", 12-groove rifling. **Weight:** 2.5 lbs. **Length:** 16.5" overall. **Power:** Single-stroke pneumatic, underlever cocking. **Grips:** Stippled walnut with adjustable palm shelf. **Sights:** Blade front, open rear adjustable for windage and elevation. Notch size adjustable for width. Interchangeable front blades. **Features:** Velocity 510 fps. Fully adjustable trigger. Cocking effort 2 lbs. Imported by Beeman.
Price: Right-hand **$2,110.00**
Price: Left-hand **$2,350.00**

BEEMAN HW70A AIR PISTOL
Caliber: .177. **Barrel:** 6-1/4", rifled. **Weight:** 38 oz. **Length:** 12-3/4" overall. **Power:** Spring, barrel cocking. **Grips:** Plastic, with thumbrest. **Sights:** Hooded post front, square notch rear adjustable for windage and elevation. Comes with scope base. **Features:** Adjustable trigger, 31-lb. cocking effort, 440 fps MV; automatic barrel safety. Imported by Beeman.
Price: **$289.95**

BENJAMIN & SHERIDAN CO2 PISTOLS Caliber: .22, single shot. **Barrel:** 6-3/8", brass. **Weight:** 1 lb. 12 oz. **Length:** 9" overall. **Power:** 12-gram CO2 cylinder. **Grips:** American Hardwood. **Sights:** High ramp front, fully adjustable notched rear. **Features:** Velocity to 500 fps. Turnbolt action with cross-bolt safety. Gives about 40 shots per CO2 cylinder. Black or nickel finish. Made in U.S. by Crosman Corp.
Price: EB22 (.22) **$118.59**

BENJAMIN & SHERIDAN PNEUMATIC PELLET PISTOLS
Caliber: .177, .22, single shot. **Barrel:** 9-3/8", rifled brass. **Weight:** 2 lbs., 8 oz. **Length:**12.25" overall. **Power:** Underlever pneumatic, hand pumped. **Grips:** American Hardwood. **Sights:** High ramp front, fully adjustable notch rear. **Features:** Velocity to 525 fps (variable). Bolt action with cross-bolt safety. Choice of black or nickel finish. Made in U.S. by Crosman Corp.
Price: Black finish, HB17 (.177), HB22 (.22) **$133.59**

CROSMAN C11
Caliber: .177, 18-shot BB or pellet. **Weight:** 1.4 lbs. **Length:** 8.5". **Power:** 12g CO2. **Sights:** Fixed. **Features:** Compact semi-automatic BB pistol. Velocity up to 480 fps. Under barrel weaver style rail.
Price: **$52.99**

CROSMAN 2240
Caliber: .22. **Barrel:** Rifled steel. **Weight:** 1 lb. 13 oz. **Length:** 11.125". **Power:** CO2. **Grips:** NA. **Sights:** Blade front, rear adjustable. **Features:** Ergonomically designed ambidextrous grip fits the hand for perfect balance and comfort with checkering and a thumbrest on both grip panels. From Crosman.
Price: **$57.83**

CROSMAN 3576 REVOLVER
Caliber: .177, pellets. **Barrel:** Rifled steel. **Weight:** 2 lbs. **Length:** 11.38". **Power:** CO2. **Grips:** NA. **Sights:** Blade front, rear adjustable. **Features:** Semi-auto 10-shot with revolver styling and finger-molded grip design, 6" barrel for increased accuracy. From Crosman.
Price: **$52.59**

CROSMAN MODEL 1088 REPEAT AIR PISTOL
Caliber: .177, 8-shot pellet clip. **Barrel:** Rifled steel. **Weight:** 17 oz. **Length:** 7.75" overall. **Power:** CO2 Powerlet. **Grips:** Checkered black plastic. **Sights:** Fixed blade front, adjustable rear. **Features:** Velocity about 430 fps. Single or double semi-automatic action. From Crosman.
Price: **$60.99**

CROSMAN PRO77
Caliber: .177, 17-shot BB. **Weight:** 1.31 lbs. **Length:** 6.75". **Power:** 12g CO2. **Sights:** Fixed. **Features:** Compact pistol with realistic recoil. Under the barrel weaver style rail. Velocity up to 325 fps.
Price: Pro77CS **$114.00**

CROSMAN T4
Caliber: .177, 8-shot BB or pellet. **Weight:** 1.32 lbs. **Length:** 8.63". **Power:** 12g CO2. **Sights:** Fixed front, windage adjustable rear. **Features:** Shoots BBs or pellets. Easy patent-pending CO2 piercing mechanism. Under the barrel weaver style rail.
Price: T4CS **$89.59**
Price: T4OPS, includes adjustable Red Dot sight, barrel compensator, and pressure operated tactical flashlight. Comes in foam padeed, hard sided protective case **$167.99**

DAISY POWERLINE® MODEL 15XT AIR PISTOL
Caliber: .177 BB, 15-shot built-in magazine. **Barrel:** NA. **Weight:** NA. **Length:** 7.21". **Power:** CO2. **Grips:** NA. **Sights:** NA. **Features:** Velocity 425 fps. Made in the U.S.A. by Daisy Mfg. Co.
Price: **$50.99**
Price: With electronic point sight **$64.99**

DAISY MODEL 717 AIR PISTOL
Caliber: .177, single shot. **Weight:** 2.25 lbs. **Length:** 13-1/2" overall. **Grips:** Molded checkered woodgrain with contoured thumbrest. **Sights:** Blade and ramp front, open rear with windage and elevation adjustments. **Features:** Single pump pneumatic pistol. Rifled steel barrel. Crossbolt trigger block. Muzzle velocity 360 fps. From Daisy Mfg. Co.
Price: **$220.94**

DAISY MODEL 747 TRIUMPH AIR PISTOL
Caliber: .177, single shot. **Weight:** 2.35 lbs. **Length:** 13-1/2" overall.

Prices given are believed to be accurate at time of publication however, many factors affect retail pricing so exact prices are not possible.

Grips: Molded checkered woodgrain with contoured thumbrest. **Sights:** Blade and ramp front, open rear with windage and elevation adjustments. **Features:** Single pump pneumatic pistol. Lothar Walther rifled high-grade steel barrel; crowned 12 lands and grooves, right-hand twist. Precision bore sized for match pellets. Muzzle velocity 360 fps. From Daisy Mfg. Co.
Price: **$264.99**

DAISY POWERLINE® 201
Caliber: .177 BB or pellet. **Weight:** 1 lb. **Length:** 9.25" overall. **Sights:** Blade and ramp front, fixed open rear. **Features:** Spring-air action, trigger-block safety and smooth-bore steel barrel. Muzzle velocity 230 fps. From Daisy Mfg. Co.
Price: **$29.99**

DAISY POWERLINE® 693 AIR PISTOL
Caliber: .177, single shot. **Weight:** 1.10 lbs. **Length:** 7.9" overall. **Grips:** Molded checkered. **Sights:** Blade and ramp front, fixed open rear. **Features:** Semi-automoatic BB pistol with a nickel finish and smooth bore steel barrel. Muzzle veocity 400 fps. From Daisy Mfg. Co.
Price: **$76.99**

DAISY POWERLINE® 5170 CO2 PISTOL
Caliber: .177 BB. **Weight:** 1 lb. **Length:** 9.5" overall. **Sights:** Blade and ramp front, open rear. **Features:** CO2 semi-automatic action, manual trigger-block safety, upper and lower rails for mounting sights and other accessories and a smooth-bore steel barrel. Muzzle velocity 520 fps. From Daisy Mfg. Co.
Price: **$59.99**

DAISY POWERLINE® 5501 CO2 BLOWBACK PISTOL
Caliber: .177 BB. **Weight:** 1 lb. **Length:** 9.5" overall. **Sights:** Blade and ramp front, open rear. **Features:** CO2 semi-automatic blow-back action, manual trigger-block safety, and a smooth-bore steel barrel. Muzzle velocity 430 fps. From Daisy Mfg. Co.
Price: **$99.99**

EAA/BAIKAL IZH-M46 TARGET AIR PISTOL
Caliber: .177, single shot. **Barrel:** 10". **Weight:** 2.4 lbs. **Length:** 16.8" overall. **Power:** Underlever single-stroke pneumatic. **Grips:** Adjustable wooden target. **Sights:** Micrometer fully adjustable rear, blade front. **Features:** Velocity about 440 fps. Hammer-forged, rifled barrel. Imported from Russia by European American Armory.
Price: **$430.00**

GAMO P-23, P-23 LASER PISTOL
Caliber: .177, 12-shot. **Barrel:** 4.25". **Weight:** 1 lb. **Length:** 7.5". **Power:** CO2 cartridge, semi-automatic, 410 fps. **Grips:** Plastic. **Sights:** NA. **Features:** Walther PPK cartridge pistol copy, optional laser sight. Imported from Spain by Gamo.
Price: . . . . **$89.95**, (with laser) **$139.95**

GAMO PT-80, PT-80 LASER PISTOL
Caliber: .177, 8-shot. **Barrel:** 4.25". **Weight:** 1.2 lbs. **Length:** 7.2". **Power:** CO2 cartridge, semi-automatic, 410 fps. **Grips:** Plastic. **Sights:** 3-dot. **Features:** Optional laser sight and walnut grips available. Imported from Spain by Gamo.
Price: . . . . **$108.95**, (with laser) **$159.95**
Price: (with walnut grip) **$119.95**

HAMMERLI AP-40 AIR PISTOL
Caliber: .177. **Barrel:** 10". **Weight:** 2.2 lbs. **Length:** 15.5". **Power:** NA. **Grips:** Adjustable orthopedic. **Sights:** Fully adjustable micrometer. **Features:** Sleek, light, well balanced and accurate.
Price: **$1,400.00**

MAGNUM RESEARCH DESERT EAGLE
Caliber: .177, 8-shot pellet. 5.7" rifled. **Weight:** 2.5 lbs. 11" overall. **Power:** 12g CO2. **Sights:** Fixed front, adjustable rear. Velocity of 425 fps. 8-shot rotary clip. Double or single action. The first .177 caliber air pistol with BLOWBACK action. Big and weighty, designed in the likeness of the real Desert Eagle.
Price: **$172.31**

MAGNUM BABY DESERT
Caliber: .177, 15-shot BB. 4" **Weight:** 1.0 lbs. 8-1/4" overall. **Power:** 12g CO2. **Sights:** Fixed front and rear. Velocity of 420 fps. Double action BB repeater. Comes with bonus Picatinny top rail and built-in bottom rail.
Price: **$41.54**

MORINI CM 162 EL MATCH AIR PISTOLS
Caliber: .177, single shot. **Barrel:** 9.4". **Weight:** 32 oz. **Length:** 16.1" overall. **Power:** Scuba air. **Grips:** Adjustable match type. **Sights:** Interchangeable blade front, fully adjustable match-type rear. **Features:** Power mechanism shuts down when pressure drops to a preset level. Adjustable electronic trigger.
Price: **$1,075.00**

PARDINI K58 MATCH AIR PISTOLS
Caliber: .177, single shot. **Barrel:** 9". **Weight:** 37.7 oz. **Length:** 15.5" overall. **Power:** Precharged compressed air; single-stroke cocking. **Grips:** Adjustable match type; stippled walnut. **Sights:** Interchangeable post front, fully adjustable match rear. **Features:** Fully adjustable trigger. Short version K-2 available. Imported from Italy by Larry's Guns.
Price: **$819.00**

RWS 9B/9N AIR PISTOLS
Caliber: .177, single shot. **Barrel:** 8". **Weight:** 2.38 lbs. **Length:** 10.4". **Power:** 550 fps. **Grips:** Right hand with thumbrest. **Sights:** Adjustable. **Features:** Spring-piston powered. Black or nickel finish.
Price: 9B/9N **$150.00**

SMITH & WESSON 586
Caliber: .177, 10-shot pellet. Rifled. **Power:** 12g CO2. **Sights:** Fixed front, adjustable rear. 10-shot rotary clip. Double or single action. Replica revolvers that duplicate both weight and handling.
Price: 4" barrel, 2.5 lbs, 400 fps **$215.34**
Price: 6" barrel, 2.8 lbs, 425 fps **$231.49**
Price: 8" barrel, 3.0 lbs, 460 fps **$247.65**
Price: S&W 686 Nickel, 6" barrel, 2.8 lbs, 425 fps **$253.03**

STEYR LP10P MATCH AIR PISTOL
Caliber: .177, single shot. **Barrel:** 9". **Weight:** 38.7 oz. **Length:** 15.3" overall. **Power:** Scuba air. **Grips:** Adjustable Morini match, palm shelf, stippled walnut. **Sights:** Interchangeable blade in 4mm, 4.5mm or 5mm widths, adjustable open rear, interchangeable 3.5mm or 4mm leaves. **Features:** Velocity about 500 fps. Adjustable trigger, adjustable sight radius from 12.4" to 13.2". With compensator. Recoil elimination.
Price: **$1,400.00**

TECH FORCE SS2 OLYMPIC COMPETITION AIR PISTOL
Caliber: .177 pellet, single shot. **Barrel:** 7.4". **Weight:** 2.8 lbs. **Length:** 16.5" overall. **Power:** Spring piston, sidelever. **Grips:** Hardwood. **Sights:** Extended adjustable rear, blade front accepts inserts. **Features:** Velocity 520 fps. Recoilless design; adjustments allow duplication of a firearm's feel. Match-grade, adjustable trigger; includes carrying case. Imported from China by Compasseco, Inc.
Price: **$295.00**

TECH FORCE 35 AIR PISTOL
Caliber: .177 pellet, single shot. **Weight:** 2.86 lbs. **Length:** 14.9" overall. **Power:** Spring-piston, underlever. **Grips:** Hardwood. **Sights:** Micrometer adjustable rear, blade front. **Features:** Velocity 400 fps. Grooved for scope mount; trigger safety. Imported from China by Compasseco, Inc.
Price: **$39.95**

Tech Force S2-1 Air Pistol
Similar to Tech Force 8 except basic grips and sights for plinking.
Price: **$29.95**

WALTHER LP300 MATCH PISTOL
Caliber: .177. **Barrel:** 236mm. **Weight:** 1.018g. **Length:** NA. **Power:** NA. **Grips:** NA. **Sights:** Integrated front with three different widths, adjustable rear. **Features:** Adjustable grip and trigger.
Price: **$1,800.00**

WALTHER PPK/S
Caliber: .177, 15-shot steel BB. 3-1/2". **Weight:** 1.2 lbs. 6-1/4" overall. **Power:** 12g CO2. **Sights:** Fixed front and rear. Velocity of 295 fps. Lookalike of one of the world's most famous pistols. Realistic recoil. Heavyweight steel construction.
Price: **$71.92**
Price: With laser sight **$94.23**
Price: With BiColor pistol, targets, shooting glasses, BBs **$84.62**

WALTHER CP99 COMPACT
Caliber: .177, 17-shot steel BB semi-auto. 3". **Weight:** 1.7 lbs. 6-1/2" overall. **Power:** 12g CO2. **Sights:** Fixed front and rear. Velocity of 345 fps. Realistic recoil, blowback action. Heavyweight steel construction. Built-in Picatinny mount.
Price: **$83.08**

AIRFORCE CONDOR RIFLE

Caliber: .177, .22 single shot. **Barrel:** 24" rifled. **Weight:** 6.5 lbs. **Length:** 38.75" overall. **Power:** Pre-charged pneumatic. **Stock:** NA. **Sights:** Intended for scope use, fiber-optic open sights optional. **Features:** Lothar Walther match barrel, adjustable power levels from 600-1,300 fps. 3,000 psi fill pressure. Automatic safety. Air tank volume: 490cc. An integral extended scope rail allows easy mounting of the largest air-gun scopes. Operates on high-pressure air from scuba tank or hand pump. Manufactured in the U.S.A by AirForce Airguns.
Price: Gun only (.22 or .177) **$631.00**

AIRFORCE TALON AIR RIFLE

Caliber: .177, .22, single shot. **Barrel:** 18" rifled. **Weight:** 5.5 lbs. **Length:** 32.6". **Power:** Pre-charged pneumatic. **Stock:** NA. **Sights:** Intended for scope use, fiber-optic open sights optional. **Features:** Lothar Walther match barrel, adjustable power levels from 400-1,000 fps, 3,000 psi fill pressure. Automatic safety. Air tank volume: 490cc. Operates on high-pressure air from scuba tank or hand pump. Manufactured in the U.S.A. by AirForce Airguns.
Price: Gun only (.22 or .177) **$514.25**

AIRFORCE TALON SS AIR RIFLE

Caliber: .177, .22, single shot. **Barrel:** 12" rifled. **Weight:** 5.25 lbs. **Length:** 32.75". **Power:** Pre-charged pneumatic. **Stock:** NA. **Sights:** Intended for scope use, fiber-optic open sights optional. **Features:** Lothar Walther match barrel, adjustable power levels from 400-1,000 fps. 3,000 psi fill pressure. Automatic safety. Chamber in front of barrel strips away air turbulence, protects muzzle and reduces firing report. Air tank volume: 490cc. Operates on high-pressure air from scuba tank or hand pump. Manufactured in the U.S.A. by AirForce Airguns.
Price: Gun only (.22 or .177) **$535.50**

AIRROW MODEL A-8SRB STEALTH AIR RIFLE

Caliber: .177, .22, .25, 9-shot. **Barrel:** 20"; rifled. **Weight:** 6 lbs. **Length:** 34" overall. **Power:** CO2 or compressed air; variable power. **Stock:** Telescoping CAR-15-type. **Sights:** Variable 3.5-10x scope. **Features:** Velocity 1100 fps in all calibers. Pneumatic air trigger. All aircraft aluminum and stainless steel construction. Mil-spec materials and finishes. From Swivel Machine Works, Inc.
Price: About **$2,299.00**

AIRROW MODEL A-8S1P STEALTH AIR RIFLE

Caliber: #2512 16" arrow. **Barrel:** 16". **Weight:** 4.4 lbs. **Length:** 30.1" overall. **Power:** CO2 or compressed air; variable power. **Stock:** Telescoping CAR-15-type. **Sights:** Scope rings only. 7 oz. rechargeable cylinder and valve. **Features:** Velocity to 650 fps with 260-grain arrow. Pneumatic air trigger. Broadhead guard. All aircraft aluminum and stainless steel construction. Mil-spec materials and finishes. A-8S Models perform to 2,000 PSIG above or below water levels. Waterproof case. From Swivel Machine Works, Inc.
Price: **$1,699.00**

ARS HUNTING MASTER AR6 AIR RIFLE

Caliber: .22, 6-shot repeater. **Barrel:** 25-1/2". **Weight:** 7 lbs. **Length:** 41-1/4" overall. **Power:** Precompressed air from 3000 psi diving tank. **Stock:** Indonesian walnut with checkered grip; rubber buttpad. **Sights:** Blade front, adjustable peep rear. **Features:** Velocity over 1000 fps with 32-grain pellet. Receiver grooved for scope mounting. Has 6-shot rotary magazine. Imported by Air Rifle Specialists.
Price: **$580.00**

BEEMAN HW100

Caliber: .177 or .22, 14-shot magazine. **Barrel:** 21-1/2". **Weight:** 9 lbs. **Length:** 42.13" overall. **Power:** Pre-charged. **Stock:** Walnut Sporter checkering on the pistol grip & forend; walnut thumbhose with lateral finger grooves on the forend & stippling on the pistol grip. **Sights:** None. Grooved for scope mounting. **Features:** 1140 fps .177 caliber; 945 fps .22 caliber. 14-shot magazine, quick-fill cylinder. Two-stage adjustable match trigger and manual safety.
Price: .177 or .22 caliber Sport Stock **$1,649.95**
Price: .177 or .22 caliber Thumbhole Stock **$1,649.95**

BEEMAN R1 AIR RIFLE

Caliber: .177, .20 or .22, single shot. **Barrel:** 19.6", 12-groove rifling. **Weight:** 8.5 lbs. **Length:** 45.2" overall. **Power:** Spring-piston, barrel cocking. **Stock:** Walnut-stained beech; cut-checkered pistol grip; Monte Carlo comb and cheekpiece; rubber buttpad. **Sights:** Tunnel front with interchangeable inserts, open rear click-adjustable for windage and elevation. Grooved for scope mounting. **Features:** Velocity 940-1000 fps (.177), 860 fps (20), 800 fps (.22). Non-drying nylon piston and breech seals. Adjustable metal trigger. Milled steel safety. Right- or left-hand stock. Adjustable cheekpiece and buttplate at extra cost. Custom and Super Laser versions available. Imported by Beeman.
Price: Right-hand **$729.95**
Price: Left-hand **$789.95**

BEEMAN R7 AIR RIFLE

Caliber: .177, .20, single shot. **Barrel:** 17". **Weight:** 6.1 lbs. **Length:** 40.2" overall. **Power:** Spring-piston. **Stock:** Stained beech. **Sights:** Hooded front, fully adjustable micrometer click open rear. **Features:** Velocity to 700 fps (.177), 620 fps (20). Receiver grooved for scope mounting; double-jointed cocking lever; fully adjustable trigger; checkered grip. Imported by Beeman.
Price: .177 . . . . **$409.95**
Price: .20 . . . . **$429.95**

BEEMAN R9 AIR RIFLE

Caliber: .177, .20, single shot. **Barrel:** NA. **Weight:** 7.3 lbs. **Length:** 43" overall. **Power:** Spring-piston, barrel cocking. **Stock:** Stained hardwood. **Sights:** Tunnel post front, fully adjustable open rear. **Features:** Velocity to 1000 fps (.177), 800 fps (20). Adjustable Rekord trigger; automatic safety; receiver dovetailed for scope mounting. Imported from Germany by Beeman Precision Airguns.
Price: .177 . . . . **$499.95**
Price: .20 . . . . **$524.95**

BEEMAN R11 MKII AIR RIFLE

Caliber: .177, single shot. **Barrel:** 19.6". **Weight:** 8.6 lbs. **Length:** 43.5" overall. **Power:** Spring-piston, barrel cocking. **Stock:** Walnut-stained beech; adjustable buttplate and cheekpiece. **Sights:** None furnished. Has dovetail for scope mounting. **Features:** Velocity 910-940 fps. All-steel barrel sleeve. Imported by Beeman.
Price: **$679.95**

BEEMAN RX-2 GAS-SPRING MAGNUM AIR RIFLE

Caliber: .177, .20, .22, .25, single shot. **Barrel:** 19.6", 12-groove rifling. **Weight:** 8.8 lbs. **Power:** Gas-spring piston air; single stroke barrel cocking. **Stock:** Laminated wood stock. **Sights:** Tunnel front, click-adjustable rear. **Features:** Velocity adjustable to about 1200 fps. Imported by Beeman.
Price: .177, right-hand **$889.95**
Price: .20, right-hand **$909.95**
Price: .22, right-hand **$889.95**
Price: .25, right-hand **$909.95**

BEEMAN R1 CARBINE

Caliber: .177, .20, .22 single shot. **Barrel:** 16.1". **Weight:** 8.6 lbs. **Length:** 41.7" overall. **Power:** Spring-piston, barrel cocking. **Stock:** Stained beech; Monte Carlo comb and checkpiece; cut checkered pistol grip; rubber buttpad. **Sights:** Tunnel front with interchangeable inserts, open adjustable rear; receiver grooved for scope mounting. **Features:** Velocity up to 1000 fps (.177). Non-drying nylon piston and breech seals. Adjustable metal trigger. Machined steel receiver end cap and safety. Right- or left-hand stock. Imported by Beeman.
Price: .177, 20, .22, right-hand **$749.95**

BEEMAN/FEINWERKBAU 700 P ALUMINUM OR WOOD STOCK

Caliber: .177, single shot. **Barrel:** 16.6". **Weight:** 10.8 lbs. Aluminum; 9.9 lbs. Wood. **Length:** 43.3-46.25" Aluminum; 43.7" Wood. **Power:** Pre-charged pneumatic. **Stock:** Aluminum stock P laminated hardwood. **Sights:** Tunnel front sight with interchangeable inserts, click micrometer match aperture rear sight. **Features:** Velocity 570 fps. Recoilless action. Anatomical grips can be tilted and pivoted to the barrel axis. Adjustable buttplate and cheekpiece.
Price: Aluminum 700, right, blue or silver **$3,934.95**
Price: Aluminum 700, universal **$3,069.95**

BEEMAN/FEINWERKBAU P70 FIELD TARGET

Caliber: .177, single shot. **Barrel:** 24.6". **Weight:** 10.6 lbs. **Length:** 43.3" overall. **Power:** Pre-charged pneumatic. **Stock:** Aluminum stock (red or blue) anatomical grips, buttplate & cheekpiece. **Sights:**

Prices given are believed to be accurate at time of publication however, many factors affect retail pricing so exact prices are not possible.

None, receiver grooved for scope mounting. **Features:** 870 fps velocity. At 50 yards, this air rifle is capable of achieving 1/2-inch groups. Match adjustable trigger. 2001 US Field Target National Champion.
Price: P70FT, precharged, right (red or blue) **$3,819.95**
Price: P70FT, precharged, left (red or blue) **$3,964.95**

BEEMAN/HW 97 AIR RIFLE
Caliber: .177, .20, .22, single shot. **Barrel:** 17.75". **Weight:** 9.2 lbs. **Length:** 44.1" overall. **Power:** Spring-piston, underlever cocking. **Stock:** Walnut-stained beech; rubber buttpad. **Sights:** None. Receiver grooved for scope mounting. **Features:** Velocity 830 fps (.177). Fixed barrel with fully opening, direct loading breech. Adjustable trigger. Imported by Beeman Precision Airguns.
Price: .177 . . . . **$779.95**
Price: .20, .22 . . . . **$799.95**

BENJAMIN & SHERIDAN PNEUMATIC (PUMP-UP) AIR RIFLE
Caliber: .177 or .22, single shot. **Barrel:** 19-3/8", rifled brass. **Weight:** 5-1/2 lbs. **Length:** 36-1/4" overall. **Power:** Underlever pneumatic, hand pumped. **Stock:** American walnut stock and forend. **Sights:** High ramp front, fully adjustable notched rear. **Features:** Variable velocity to 800 fps. Bolt action with ambidextrous push-pull safety. Black or nickel finish. Made in the U.S. by Benjamin Sheridan Co.
Price: 392 or 397 . . . . **$249.40**

BERETTA CX4 STORM
Caliber: .177, 30-shot semi-auto. 17-1/2", rifled. **Weight:** 5.25 lbs. **Length:** 30.75" overall. **Power:** 88g CO2. **Stock:** Replica style. **Sights:** Adjustable front and rear. Blowback action. Velocity of 600 fps. Accessory rails.
Price: **$276.92**

BSA SUPERTEN MK3 AIR RIFLE
Caliber: .177, .22 10-shot repeater. **Barrel:** 17-1/2". **Weight:** 7 lbs., 8 oz. **Length:** 37" overall. **Power:** Precharged pneumatic via buddy bottle. **Stock:** Oil-finished hardwood; Monte Carlo with cheekpiece, cut checkered grip; adjustable recoil pad. **Sights:** No sights; intended for scope use. **Features:** Velocity 1000+ fps (.177), 1000+ fps (.22). Patented 10-shot indexing magazine, bolt-action loading. Left-hand version also available. Imported from U.K.
Price: **$599.95**

BSA SUPERTEN MK3 BULLBARREL
Caliber: .177, .22, .25, single shot. **Barrel:** 18-1/2". **Weight:** 8 lbs., 8 oz. **Length:** 43" overall. **Power:** Spring-air, underlever cocking. **Stock:** Oil-finished hardwood; Monte Carlo with cheekpiece, checkered at grip; recoil pad. **Sights:** Ramp front, micrometer adjustable rear. **Features:** Velocity 950 fps (.177), 750 fps (.22), 600 fps (25). Patented rotating breech design. Maxi-Grip scope rail protects optics from recoil; automatic anti-beartrap plus manual safety. Imported from U.K.
Price: Rifle, MKII Carbine (14" barrel, 39-1/2" overall) **$349.95**

BSA MAGNUM SUPERSPORT AIR RIFLE, CARBINE
Caliber: .177, .22, .25, single shot. **Barrel:** 18-1/2". **Weight:** 6 lbs., 8 oz. **Length:** 41" overall. **Power:** Spring-air, barrel cocking. **Stock:** Oil-finished hardwood; Monte Carlo with cheekpiece, recoil pad. **Sights:** Ramp front, micrometer adjustable rear. Maxi-Grip scope rail. **Features:** Velocity 950 fps (.177), 750 fps (.22), 600 fps (25). Patented Maxi-Grip scope rail protects optics from recoil; automatic anti-beartrap plus manual tang safety. Muzzle brake standard. Imported for U.K.
Price: **$194.95**
Price: Carbine, 14" barrel, muzzle brake **$214.95**

BSA METEOR AIR RIFLE
Caliber: .177, .22, single shot. **Barrel:** 18-1/2". **Weight:** 6 lbs. **Length:** 41" overall. **Power:** Spring-air, barrel cocking. **Stock:** Oil-finished hardwood. **Sights:** Ramp front, micrometer adjustable rear.

Features: Velocity 650 fps (.177), 500 fps (.22). Automatic anti-beartrap; manual tang safety. Receiver grooved for scope mounting. Imported from U.K.
Price: Rifle **$144.95**
Price: Carbine **$164.95**

CROSMAN MODEL POWERMASTER 664SB AIR RIFLES
Caliber: .177 (single shot pellet) or BB, 200-shot reservoir. **Barrel:** 20", rifled steel. **Weight:** 2 lbs. 15 oz. **Length:** 38-1/2" overall. **Power:** Pneumatic; hand-pumped. **Stock:** Wood-grained ABS plastic; checkered pistol grip and forend. **Sights:** Fiber-optic front, fully adjustable open rear. **Features:** Velocity about 645 fps. Bolt action, cross-bolt safety. From Crosman.
Price: **$105.50**

CROSMAN MODEL PUMPMASTER 760 AIR RIFLES
Caliber: .177 pellets (single shot) or BB (200-shot reservoir). **Barrel:** 19-1/2", rifled steel. **Weight:** 2 lbs., 12 oz. **Length:** 33.5" overall. **Power:** Pneumatic, hand-pump. **Stock:** Walnut-finished ABS plastic stock and forend. **Features:** Velocity to 590 fps (BBs, 10 pumps). Short stroke, power determined by number of strokes. Fiber-optic front sight and adjustable rear sight. Cross-bolt safety. From Crosman.
Price: Model 760 . . . . **$40.59**

CROSMAN MODEL REPEATAIR 1077 RIFLES
Caliber: .177 pellets, 12-shot clip. **Barrel:** 20.3", rifled steel. **Weight:** 3 lbs., 11 oz. **Length:** 38.8" overall. **Power:** CO2 Powerlet. **Stock:** Textured synthetic or hardwood. **Sights:** Blade front, fully adjustable rear. **Features:** Velocity 590 fps. Removable 12-shot clip. True semi-automatic action. From Crosman.
Price: **$73.99**

CROSMAN MODEL .2260 AIR RIFLE
Caliber: .22, single shot. **Barrel:** 24". **Weight:** 4 lbs., 12 oz. **Length:** 39.75" overall. **Power:** CO2 Powerlet. **Stock:** Hardwood. **Sights:** Blade front, adjustable rear open or peep. **Features:** Variable pump power; three pumps give 395 fps, six pumps 530 fps, 10 pumps 600 fps (average). Full-size adult air rifle. From Crosman.
Price: **$83.84**

CROSMAN MODEL CLASSIC 2100 AIR RIFLE
Caliber: .177 pellets (single shot), or BB (200-shot BB reservoir). **Barrel:** 21", rifled. **Weight:** 4 lbs., 13 oz. **Length:** 39-3/4" overall. **Power:** Pump-up, pneumatic. **Stock:** Wood-grained checkered ABS plastic. **Features:** Three pumps give about 450 fps, 10 pumps about 755 fps (BBs). Cross-bolt safety; concealed reservoir holds over 200 BBs. From Crosman.
Price: Model 2100B **$62.99**

DAISY 1938 RED RYDER AIR RIFLE
Caliber: BB, 650-shot repeating action. **Barrel:** Smoothbore steel with shroud. **Weight:** 2.2 lbs. **Length:** 35.4" overall. **Stock:** Wood stock burned with Red Ryder lariat signature. **Sights:** Post front, adjustable open rear. **Features:** Walnut forend. Saddle ring with leather thong. Lever cocking. Gravity feed. Controlled velocity. From Daisy Mfg. Co.
Price: **$55.99**

DAISY MODEL 840B GRIZZLY AIR RIFLE
Caliber: .177 pellet single shot; or BB 350-shot. **Barrel:** 19", smoothbore, steel. **Weight:** 2.25 lbs. **Length:** 36.8" overall. **Power:** Single pump pneumatic. **Stock:** Molded wood-grain stock and forend. **Sights:** Ramp front, open, adjustable rear. **Features:** Muzzle velocity 320 fps (BB), 300 fps (pellet). Steel buttplate; straight pull bolt action; cross-bolt safety. Forend forms pump lever. From Daisy Mfg. Co.
Price: **$60.99**
Price: (840C in Mossy Oak Breakup Camo) **$64.99**

DAISY MODEL 4841 GRIZZLY
Caliber: .177 pellet single shot. **Barrel:** NA. **Weight:** NA. **Length:** 36.8" overall. **Power:** Single pump pneumatic. **Stock:** Composite camo. **Sights:** Blade and ramp front. **Features:** Muzzle velocity 350 fps. Fixed Daisy Model 808 scope. From Daisy Mfg. Co.
Price: **$69.99**

DAISY MODEL 105 BUCK AIR RIFLE
Caliber: .177 or BB. **Barrel:** Smoothbore steel. **Weight:** 1.6 lbs. **Length:** 29.8" overall. **Power:** Lever cocking, spring air. **Stock:** Stained solid wood. **Sights:** TruGlo fiber-optic, open fixed rear.

Features: Velocity to 275. Crossbolt trigger block safety. From Daisy Mfg. Co.
Price: **$39.99**

DAISY AVANTI MODEL 888 MEDALIST
Caliber: .177, pellet. **Barrel:** Lothar Walther rifled high-grade steel, crowned, 12 lands and grooves, right-hand twist. Precision bore sized for match pellets. **Weight:** 6.9 lbs. **Length:** 38.5" overall. **Power:** CO2 single shot bolt. **Stock:** Sporter-style multicolored laminated hardwood. **Sights:** Hooded front with interchangeable aperture inserts; micrometer adjustable rear peep sight. **Features:** Velocity to 500. Crossbolt trigger block safety. From Daisy Mfg. Co.
Price: **$525.99**

DAISY AVANTI MODEL 887 GOLD MEDALIST
Caliber: 177, pellet. **Barrel:** Lothar Walther rifled high-grade steel, crowned, 12 lands and grooves, right hand twist. Precision bore sized for match pellets. **Weight:** 7.3 lbs. **Length:** 39.5" overall. **Power:** CO2 power single shot bolt. **Stock:** Laminated hardwood. **Sights:** Front globe sight with changeable aperture inserts: rear diopter sight with micrometer click adjustment for windage and elevation. **Features:** Velocity to 500. Crossbolt trigger block safety. Includes rail adapter. From Daisy Mfg. Co.
Price: **$599.99**

DAISY MODEL 853 LEGEND
Caliber: .177, pellet. **Barrel:** Lothar Walther rifled high-grade steel barrel, crowned, 12 lands and grooves, right-hand twist. Precision bore sized for match pellets. **Weight:** 5.5 lbs. **Length:** 38.5" overall. **Power:** Single-pump pneumatic, straight pull-bolt. **Stock:** Full-length, sporter-style hardwood with adjustable length. **Sights:** Hooded front with interchangeable aperture inserts; micrometer adjustable rear. **Features:** Velocity to 510. Crossbolt trigger block safety with red indicator. From Daisy Mfg. Co.
Price: **$432.00**
Price: Model 835 Legend EX; velocity to 490 . . . . **$432.00**

DAISY MODEL 753 ELITE
Caliber: .177, pellet. **Barrel:** Lothar Walther rifled high-grade steel barrel, crowned, 12 lands and grooves, right-hand twist. Precision bore sized for match pellets. **Weight:** 6.4 lbs. **Length:** 39.75" overall. **Power:** Recoilless single pump pneumatic, straight pull bolt. **Stock:** Full length match-style hardwood stock with raised cheek piece and adjustable length. **Sights:** Front globe sight with changeable aperture inserts, diopter rear sight with micrometer adjustable rear. **Features:** Velocity to 510. Crossbolt trigger block safety with red indicator. From Daisy Mfg. Co.
Price: **$558.99**

DAISY MODEL 105 BUCK AIR RIFLE
Caliber: .177 or BB. **Barrel:** Smoothbore steel. **Weight:** 1.6 lbs. **Length:** 29.8" overall. **Power:** Lever cocking, spring air. **Stock:** Stained solid wood. **Sights:** TruGlo fiber-optic, open fixed rear. **Features:** Velocity to 275. Cross-bolt trigger block safety. From Daisy Mfg. Co.
Price: **$39.99**

DAISY POWERLINE® TARGETPRO 953 AIR RIFLE
Caliber: .177 pellets, single shot. **Weight:** 6.40 lbs. **Length:** 39.75" overall. **Power:** Pneumatic single-pump cocking lever; straight-pull bolt. **Stock:** Full-length, match-style black composite. **Sights:** Front and rear fiber optic. **Features:** Rifled high-grade steel barrel with 1:15 twist. Max. Muzzle Velocity of 560 fps. From Daisy Mfg. Co.
Price: **$29.99**

DAISY POWERLINE® 500 BREAK BARREL
Caliber: .177 pellet, single shot. **Barrel:** Rifled steel. **Weight:** 6.6 lbs. **Length:** 45.7" overall. **Stock:** Stained solid wood. **Sights:** Truglo® fiber-optic front, micro-adjustable open rear, adjustable 4x32 riflescope. **Features:** Auto rear-button safety. Velocity to 490 fps. Made in U.S.A. by Daisy Mfg. Co.
Price: **$120.99**

DAISY POWERLINE® 800 BREAK BARREL
Caliber: .177 pellet, single shot. **Barrel:** Rifled steel. **Weight:** 6.6 lbs. **Length:** 46.7" overall. **Stock:** Black composite. **Sights:** Truglo fiber-optic front, micro-adjustable open rear, adjustable 4x32 riflescope.

Features: Auto rear-button safety. Velocity to 800 fps. Made in U.S.A. by Daisy Mfg. Co.
Price: **$120.99**

DAISY POWERLINE® 880 AIR RIFLE
Caliber: .177 pellet or BB, 50-shot BB magazine, single shot for pellets. **Barrel:** Rifled steel. **Weight:** 3.7 lbs. **Length:** 37.6" overall. **Power:** Multi-pump pneumatic. **Stock:** Molded wood grain; Monte Carlo comb. **Sights:** Hooded front, adjustable rear. **Features:** Velocity to 685 fps. (BB). Variable power (velocity, range) increase with pump strokes; resin receiver with dovetailed scope mount. Made in U.S.A. by Daisy Mfg. Co.
Price: **$71.99**

DAISY POWERLINE® 901 AIR RIFLE
Caliber: .177. **Barrel:** Rifled steel. **Weight:** 3.7 lbs. **Length:** 37.5" overall. **Power:** Multi-pump pneumatic. **Stock:** Advanced composite. **Sights:** Fiber-optic front, adjustable rear. **Features:** Velocity to 750 fps. (BB); advanced composite receiver with dovetailed mounts for optics. Made in U.S.A. by Daisy Mfg. Co.
Price: **$83.99**

DAISY POWERLINE® 1000 BREAK BARREL
Caliber: .177 pellet, single shot. **Barrel:** Rifled steel. **Weight:** 6.6 lbs. **Length:** 46.7" overall. **Stock:** Black composite. **Sights:** Truglo® fiber-optic front, micro-adjustable open rear, adjustable 4x32 riflescope. **Features:** Auto rear-button safety. Velocity to 750 fps (BB). Made in U.S.A. by Daisy Mfg. Co.
Price: **$231.99**

EAA/BAIKAL IZH61 AIR RIFLE
Caliber: .177 pellet, 5-shot magazine. **Barrel:** 17.8". **Weight:** 6.4 lbs. **Length:** 31" overall. **Power:** Spring-piston, side-cocking lever. **Stock:** Black plastic. **Sights:** Adjustable rear, fully hooded front. **Features:** Velocity 490 fps. Futuristic design with adjustable stock. Imported from Russia by European American Armory.
Price: **$122.65**

GAMO VIPER AIR RIFLE
Caliber: .177. **Barrel:** NA. **Weight:** 7.25 lbs. **Length:** 43.5". **Power:** Single-stroke pneumatic, 1200 fps. **Stock:** Synthetic. **Sights:** 3-9x40IR scope. **Features:** 30-pound cocking effort. Imported from Spain by Gamo.
Price: **319.95**

GAMO SHADOW AIR RIFLES
Caliber: .177. **Barrel:** 18", fluted polymer bull. **Weight:** 6.1 to 7.15 lbs. **Length:** 43" to 43.3". **Power:** Single-stroke pneumatic, 850-1,000 fps. **Stock:** Tough all-weather molded synthetic. **Sights:** NA. **Features:** Single shot, manual safety,
Price: Sport **$219.95**
Price: Hunter **$219.95**
Price: Big Cat 1200 . . . . **$169.95**
Price: Fox **$279.95**

GAMO HUNTER AIR RIFLES
Caliber: .177. **Barrel:** NA. **Weight:** 6.5 to 10.5 lbs. **Length:** 43.5-48.5". **Power:** Single-stroke pneumatic, 850-1,000 fps. **Stock:** Wood. **Sights:** Varies by model **Features:** Adjustable two-stage trigger, rifled barrel, raised scope ramp on receiver. Realtree camo model available.
Price: Sport **$219.95**
Price: Pro **$279.95**
Price: Extreme (.177), Extreme .22 . . . . **$529.95**

GAMO WHISPER AIR RIFLES
Caliber: .177, .22. **Barrel:** 18", fluted polymer bull. **Weight:** 5.28 to 7.4 lbs. **Length:** 45.7" to 46". **Stock:** Tough all-weather molded synthetic. **Sights:** Fiber-optic front with sight guard, adjustable rear.

Prices given are believed to be accurate at time of publication however, many factors affect retail pricing so exact prices are not possible.

Features: Single shot, manual trigger safety. Non-removable noise dampener (with up to 52 percent reduction).

Price: Whisper	**$279.95**
Price: Whisper Deluxe	**$319.95**
Price: Whisper VH (Varmint Hunter/Whisper in one rifle)	**$329.95**
Price: Whisper .22	**$299.95**
Price: CSI Camo (.177)	**$329.95**
Price: CSI Camo (.22)	**$329.95**

HAMMERLI AR 50 AIR RIFLE

Caliber: .177. **Barrel:** 19.8". **Weight:** 10 lbs. **Length:** 43.2" overall. **Power:** Compressed-air. **Stock:** Anatomically-shaped universal and right-hand; match style; multi-colored laminated wood. **Sights:** Interchangeable element tunnel front, adjustable Hammerli peep rear. **Features:** Vibration-free firing release; adjustable match trigger and trigger stop; stainless air tank, built-in pressure gauge. Gives 270 shots per filling. Imported from Switzerland by SIG SAUER, Inc.

Price: **$1,653.00**

HAMMERLI MODEL 450 MATCH AIR RIFLE

Caliber: .177, single shot. **Barrel:** 19.5".
Weight: 9.8 lbs. **Length:** 43.3" overall. **Power:** Pneumatic. **Stock:** Match style with stippled grip, rubber buttpad. Beech or walnut. **Sights:** Match tunnel front, Hammerli diopter rear. **Features:** Velocity about 560 fps. Removable sights; forend sling rail; adjustable trigger; adjustable comb. Imported from Switzerland by SIG SAUER, Inc.

Price: Beech stock **$1,355.00**
Price: Walnut stock **$1,395.00**

HAMMERLI 850 AIR MAGNUM

Caliber: .177, .22, 8-shot repeater. 23-1/2", rifled. **Weight:** 5.8 lbs. 41" overall. **Power:** 88g CO_2. **Stock:** All-weather polymer, Monte Carlo, textured grip and forearm. **Sights:** Hooded fiber optic front, fiber optic adjustable rear. Velocity of 760 fps (.177), 655 (22). Blue finish. Rubber buttpad. Bolt-action. Scope compatible.

Price: .177, .22 .... **$235.99**

HAMMERLI STORM ELITE

Caliber: .177, single shot. 19-1/2", rifled. **Weight:** 6.8 lbs. 45-1/2" overall. **Power:** Spring-air, break-barrel cocking. **Stock:** Synthetic, burled wood look, checkered grip and forearm, cheekpiece. **Sights:** Hooded fiber optic front, fiber optic adjustable rear. Velocity of 1000 fps. 24 lbs. cocking effort. Nickel finish. Rubber buttpad. Scope compatible.

Price: **$165.90**

HAMMERLI RAZOR

Caliber: .177, .22, single shot. **Barrel:** 19", rifled. **Weight:** 17.5 lbs. **Length:** 45-1/2" overall. **Power:** Spring-air, break-barrel cocking. **Stock:** Vaporized beech wood, checkered grip and forearm, cheekpiece. Sleek curves. **Sights:** Hooded fiber optic front, fiber optic adjustable rear. **Features:** Velocity of 1000 fps (.177), 820 (.22). 35 lbs. cocking effort. Blued finish. Rubber buttpad. Scope compatible.

Price: **$219.99**

HAMMERLI NOVA

Caliber: .177, single shot. 18", rifled. **Weight:** 7.8 lbs. 45-1/2" overall. **Power:** Spring-air, under-lever cocking. **Stock:** Vaporized beech wood competition, checkered grip and forearm, cheekpiece. **Sights:** Hooded fiber optic front, fiber optic adjustable rear. **Features:** Velocity of 1000 fps. 36 lbs. cocking effort. Blued finish. Rubber buttpad. Scope compatible.

Price: **$342.00**

HAMMERLI QUICK

Caliber: .177, single shot. 18-1/4", rifled. **Weight:** 5.5 lbs. 41" overall. **Power:** Spring-air, break-barrel cocking. **Stock:** Synthetic impact proof, checkered grip and forearm, cheekpiece. **Sights:** Hooded fiber optic front, fiber optic adjustable rear. Compact, lightweight. Velocity of 620 fps. 18 lbs. cocking effort. Blued finish. Rubber buttpad. Scope compatible. Automatic safety.

Price: **$120.00**

RWS 460 MAGNUM

Caliber: .177, .22, single shot. 18-7/16", rifled. **Weight:** 8.3 lbs. 45" overall. **Power:** Spring-air, underlever cocking. **Stock:** American Sporter, checkered grip and forearm. **Sights:** Ramp front, adjustable rear. Velocity of 1350 fps (.177), 1150 (.22). 36 lbs. cocking effort. Blue finish. Rubber buttpad. Top-side loading port. Scope compatible.

Price: .177, .22 .... **$630.99**

RWS MODEL 34

Caliber: .177, .22, single shot. **Barrel:** 19-1/2", rifled. **Weight:** 7.3 lbs. **Length:** 45" overall. **Power:** Spring-air, break-barrel cocking. **Stock:** Wood. **Sights:** Hooded front, adjustable rear. **Features:** Velocity of 1000 fps (.177), 800 (.22). 33 lbs. cocking effort. Blued finish. Scope compatible.

Price: .177, .22 .... **$202.00**

RWS 34 PANTHER

Caliber: .177, .22, single shot. 19-3/4", rifled. **Weight:** 7.7 lbs. 46" overall. **Power:** Spring-air, break-barrel cocking. **Stock:** Synthetic black. **Sights:** Ramp fiber optic front, adjustable fiber optic rear. Velocity of 1000 fps (.177), 800 (.22). 33 lbs. cocking effort. Blued finish. Scope compatible. Automatic safety.

Price: .177, .22 .... **$192.00**

RWS 48

Caliber: .177, .22, single shot. 17", rifled, fixed. **Weight:** 9.0 lbs. 42-1/2" overall. **Power:** Spring-air, side-lever cocking. **Stock:** Wood stock. **Sights:** Adjustable front, adjustable rear. Velocity of 1100 fps (.177), 900 (.22). 39 lbs. cocking effort. Blued finish. Scope compatible. Automatic safety.

Price: .177, .22 .... **$330.00**

TECH FORCE 6 AIR RIFLE

Caliber: .177 pellet, single shot. **Barrel:** 14". **Weight:** 6 lbs. **Length:** 35.5" overall. **Power:** Spring-piston, sidelever action. **Stock:** Paratrooper-style folding, full pistol grip. **Sights:** Adjustable rear, hooded front. **Features:** Velocity 800 fps. All-metal construction; grooved for scope mounting. Imported from China by Compasseco, Inc.

Price: **$69.95**

TECH FORCE 99 AIR RIFLE

Caliber: .177, .22, single shot. **Barrel:** 18", rifled. **Weight:** 8 lbs. **Length:** 44.5" overall. **Power:** Spring piston. **Stock:** Beech wood; raised cheek piece and checkering on pistol grip and forearm, plus soft rubber recoil pad. **Sights:** Insert type front. **Features:** Velocity 1,100 fps (.177; 900 fps: .22); fixed barrel design has an underlever cocking mechanism with an anti-beartrap lock and automatic safety. Imported from China by Compasseco, Inc.

Price: 177 or .22 caliber **$152.96**

WALTHER LEVER ACTION

Caliber: .177, 8-shot lever action. **Barrel:** 19", rifled. **Weight:** 7.5 lbs. **Length:** 38" overall. **Power:** Two 12g CO_2. **Stock:** Wood. **Sights:** Fixed front, adjustable rear. **Features:** Classic design. Velocity of 630 fps. Scope compatible.

Price: **$475.50**

WINCHESTER MODEL 1000SB

Caliber: .177, pellet, break-barrel spring air. **Barrel:** Rifled steel. **Weight:** 6.6 lbs. **Length:** 44.5" overall. **Stock:** Sporter style black composite. **Sights:** TRUGLO fiber optic with hooded front and micro adjustable rear. **Features:** Velocity of 1000 fps. 4 X 32 adjustable objective, fog proof/shockproof scope with crosshair reticle. From Daisy Mfg. Co.

Price: **$231.99**

WINCHESTER MODEL 1000B

Caliber: .177, pellet, break-barrel spring air. **Barrel:** Rifled steel, solid steel shroud. **Weight:** 6.6 lbs. **Length:** 44.5" overall. **Stock:** Black composite. **Sights:** TRUGLO fiber optic with hooded front and micro adjustable rear. **Features:** Velocity of 1000 fps. From Daisy Mfg. Co.

Price: **$184.99**

WINCHESTER MODEL 1000XS
Caliber: .177, pellet, break-barrel spring air. **Barrel:** Rifled steel, solid steel shroud. **Weight:** 6.6 lbs. **Length:** 46.7" overall. **Stock:** Walnut. **Sights:** Hooded front with blade and ramp, micro-adjustable rear. **Features:** Velocity of 1000 fps, uniquely designed 4 X 32 scope with adjustable objective. From Daisy Mfg. Co.
Price: **$269.99**

WINCHESTER MODEL 1000X
Caliber: .177, pellet, break-barrel spring air. **Barrel:** Rifled steel, solid steel shroud. **Weight:** 6.6 lbs. **Length:** 46.7" overall. **Stock:** Walnut. **Sights:** Hooded front with blade and ramp, micro-adjustable rear. **Features:** Velocity of 1000 fps. From Daisy Mfg. Co.
Price: **$228.99**

WINCHESTER MODEL 800XS
Caliber: .177, pellet, break-barrel spring air. **Barrel:** Rifled steel, solid steel shroud. **Weight:** 6.6 lbs. **Length:** 46.7" overall. **Stock:** Walnut. **Sights:** Hooded front with blade and ramp, micro-adjustable rear. **Features:** Velocity of 800 fps. Scope is fogproof and shockproof with fully adjustable windage and elevation and cross hair reticle. Also includes mounting rings. From Daisy Mfg. Co.
Price: **$201.99**

WINCHESTER MODEL 800X
Caliber: .177, pellet, break-barrel spring air. **Barrel:** Rifled steel, solid steel shroud. **Weight:** 6.6 lbs. **Length:** 46.7" overall. **Stock:** Walnut. **Sights:** Hooded front with blade and ramp, micro-adjustable rear. **Features:** Velocity of 800 fps. From Daisy Mfg. Co.
Price: **$164.99**

THE 2011 GUN DIGEST
Web directory

BY HOLT BODINSON

The *Gun Digest* Web Directory is now in its twelfth year of publication and grows with every edition. The firearms industry is doing a remarkably good job of adapting to e-commerce.

The Internet is a dynamic environment. One of the most interesting developments since our last edition is the emergence of social network marketing. Companies are increasingly coupling their websites to social sites such as YouTube, Twitter, Facebook, Flicker, Linkedin and MySpace. A parallel development is the posting of a company blog on the internet. Two excellent examples are Remington's webpage,: www.remington. com, that features an active selection box reading "Follow Us on Twitter," "See us on Facebook and YouTube" and Federal's interactive social site,: www.stormchasersnetwork.com.

For the first time in history, companies are actually spending more on internet than print advertising. Concurrently, companies are investing in internet presence management and using the social network as a completely new advertising and outreach vehicle. It's good business since the latest estimate indicates that 74% of the residents in North America have access to the internet.

A new category has been added to our web directory this year: "Firearm Auction Sites." Increasingly, internet auction sites are being used to sell firearms and firearm-related items as well as major, historically significant collections. It is a trend that will surely increase over time. Bidding over the internet is relatively easy and never before have collectors and shooters

had so many opportunities to find exactly what they are looking for on a worldwide basis.

The following index of web addresses is offered to our readers as a convenient jumping-off point. Half the fun is just exploring what's out there. Considering that most of the web pages have hot links to other firearm-related web pages, the Internet trail just goes on-and-on once you've taken the initial step to go online.

Here are a few pointers:

If the website you desire is not listed, try using the full name of the company or product, typed without spaces, between: www.-and-.com, for example,: www.krause.com. Probably 95% of current Web sites are based on this simple, self-explanatory format.

Try a variety of search engines such as Google, Bing, Yahoo, Ask.com, Dogpile.com, Metacrawler, GoTo.com, HotBot, AltaVista, Lycos, Excite, InfoSeek, Looksmart, and WebCrawler while using key words such as gun, firearm, rifle, pistol, blackpowder, shooting, hunting — frankly, any word that relates to the sport. Each search engine combs through their indices in a different fashion and produces different results. Google is currently the dominant general search engine. Accessing the various search engines is simple. Just type: www.google.com for example, and you're on your way.

Welcome to the digital world of firearms. *A journey of a thousand sites begins with a single click.*

Ammunition and Components

A-Square Co.: **www.asquarecompany.com**
3-D Ammunition: **www.3dammo.com**
Accurate Arms Co. Inc: **www.accuratepowder.com**
ADCO/Nobel Sport Powder: **www.adcosales.com**
Aguila Ammunition: **www.aguilaammo.com**
Alexander Arms: **www.alexanderarms.com**
Alliant Powder: **www.alliantpowder.com**
American Ammunition: **www.a-merc.com**
American Derringer Co.: **www.amderringer.com**
American Pioneer Powder: **www.americanpioneerpowder.com**
Ammo Depot: **www.ammodepot.com**
Arizona Ammunition, Inc.: **www.arizonaammunition.com**
Ballistic Products,Inc.: **www.ballisticproducts.com**
Barnaul Cartridge Plant: **www.ab.ru/~stanok**
Barnes Bullets: **www.barnesbullets.com**
Baschieri & Pellagri: **www.baschieri-pellagri.com**
Beartooth Bullets: **www.beartoothbullets.com**
Bell Brass: **www.bellbrass.com**

Berger Bullets, Ltd.: **www.bergerbullets.com**
Berry's Mfg., Inc.: **www.berrysmfg**
Big Bore Bullets of Alaska: **www.awloo.com/bbb/index.htm**
Big Bore Express: **www.powerbeltbullets.com**
Bismuth Cartridge Co.: **www.bismuth-notox.com**
Black Dawge Cartridge: **www.blackdawgecartridge.com**
Black Hills Ammunition, Inc.: **www.black-hills.com**
BlackHorn209: **www.blackhorn209.com**
Brenneke of America Ltd.: **www.brennekeusa.com**
Buffalo Arms: **www.buffaloarms.com**
Calhoon, James, Bullets: **www.jamescalhoon.com**
Cartuchos Saga: **www.saga.es**
Cast Performance Bullet: **www.castperformance.com**
CCI: **www.cci-ammunition.com**
Centurion Ordnance: **www.aguilaammo.com**
Century International Arms: **www.centuryarms.com**
Cheaper Than Dirt: **www.cheaperthandirt.com**
Cheddite France: **www.cheddite.com**

Claybuster Wads: **www.claybusterwads.com**
Clean Shot Powder: **www.cleanshot.com**
Cole Distributing: **www.cole-distributing.com**
Combined Tactical Systems: **www.less-lethal.com**
Cor-Bon/Glaser: **www.cor-bon.com**
Cowboy Bullets: **www.cowboybullets.com**
Defense Technology Corp.: **www.defense-technology.com**
Denver Bullet Co. denbullets@aol.com
Dillon Precision: **www.dillonprecision.com**
Dionisi Cartridge: **www.dionisi.com**
DKT, Inc.: **www.dktinc.com**
Down Range Mfg.: **www.downrangemfg.com**
Dynamit Nobel RWS Inc.: **www.dnrws.com**
Elephant/Swiss Black Powder: **www.elephantblackpowder.com**
Eley Ammunition: **www.eleyusa.com**
Eley Hawk Ltd.: **www.eleyhawk.com**
Environ-Metal: **www.hevishot.com**
Estate Cartridge: **www.estatecartridge.com**
Extreme Shock Munitions: **www.extremeshockusa.net**
Federal Cartridge Co.: **www.federalpremium.com**
Fiocchi of America: **www.fiocchiusa.com**
Fowler Bullets: **www.benchrest.com/fowler**
Gamebore Cartridge: **www.gamebore.com**
Garrett Cartridges: **www.garrettcartridges.com**
Gentner Bullets: **www.benchrest.com/gentner/**
Glaser Safety Slug, Inc.: **www.corbon.com**
GOEX Inc.: **www.goexpowder.com**
GPA: **www.cartouchegpa.com**
Graf & Sons: **www.grafs.com**
Hastings: **www.hastingsammunition.com**
Hawk Bullets: **www.hawkbullets.com**
Hevi.Shot: **www.hevishot.com**
Hi-Tech Ammunition: **www.iidbs.com/hitech**
Hodgdon Powder: **www.hodgdon.com**
Hornady: **www.hornady.com**
Hull Cartridge: **www.hullcartridge.com**
Huntington Reloading Products: **www.huntingtons.com**
Impact Bullets: **www.impactbullets.com**
IMR Smokeless Powders: **www.imrpowder.com**
International Cartridge Corp: **www.iccammo.com**
Israel Military Industries: **www.imisammo.co.il**
ITD Enterprise: **www.itdenterpriseinc.com**
Kent Cartridge America: **www.kentgamebore.com**
Knight Bullets: **www.benchrest.com/knight/**
Kynoch Ammunition: **www.kynochammunition.com**
Lapua: **www.lapua.com**
Lawrence Brand Shot: **www.metalico.com**
Lazzeroni Arms Co.: **www.lazzeroni.com**
Leadheads Bullets: **www.proshootpro.com**
Lightfield Ammunition Corp: **www.lightfieldslugs.com**
Lomont Precision Bullets: **www.klomont.com/kent**
Lost River Ballistic Technologies,Inc.: **www.lostriverballistic.com**
Lyman: **www.lymanproducts.com**
Magkor Industries.: **www.magkor.com**
Magnum Muzzleloading Products: **www.mmpsabots.com**
Magnus Bullets: **www.magnusbullets.com**

MagSafe Ammunition: **www.realpages.com/magsafeammo**
Magtech: **www.magtechammunition.com**
Masterclass Bullet Co.: **www.mastercast.com**
Meister Bullets: **www.meisterbullets.com**
Midway USA: **www.midwayusa.com**
Miltex,Inc.: **www.miltexusa.com**
Mitchell Mfg. Co.: **www.mitchellsales.com**
MK Ballistic Systems: **www.mkballistics.com**
Mullins Ammunition: **www.mullinsammunition.com**
National Bullet Co.: **www.nationalbullet.com**
Navy Arms: **www.navyarms.com**
Nobel Sport: **www.nobelsportammo.com**
Norma: **www.norma.cc**
North Fork Technologies: **www.northforkbullets.com**
Nosler Bullets,Inc.: **www.nosler.com**
Old Western Scrounger: **www.ows-ammunition.com**
Oregon Trail/Trueshot Bullets: **www.trueshotbullets.com**
Pattern Control: **www.patterncontrol.com**
PMC: **www.pmcammo.com**
Polywad: **www.polywad.com**
PowerBelt Bullets: **www.powerbeltbullets.com**
PR Bullets: **www.prbullet.com**
Precision Ammunition: **www.precisionammo.com**
Precision Reloading: **www.precisionreloading.com**
Pro Load Ammunition: **www.proload.com**
Quality Cartridge: **www.qual-cart.com**
Rainier Ballistics: **www.rainierballistics.com**
Ram Shot Powder: **www.ramshot.com**
Reloading Specialties Inc.: **www.reloadingspecialties.com**
Remington: **www.remington.com**
Rio Ammunition: **www.rioammo.com**
Rocky Mountain Cartridge: **www.rockymountaincartridge.com**
RUAG Ammotec: **www.ruag.com**
Samco Global Arms: **www.samcoglobal.com**
Schuetzen Powder: **www.schuetzenpowder.com**
Sellier & Bellot USA inc.: **www.sb-usa.com**
Shilen: **www.shilen.com**
Sierra: **www.sierrabullets.com**
Simunition.: **www.simunition.com**
SinterFire, Inc.: **www.sinterfire.com**
Speer Bullets: **www.speer-bullets.com**
Sporting Supplies Int'l Inc.: **www.ssiintl.com**
Starline: **www.starlinebrass.com**
Swift Bullets Co.: **www.swiftbullet.com**
Ten-X Ammunition: **www.tenxammo.com**
Top Brass: **www.top-brass.com**
Triton Cartridge: **www.a-merc.com**
Trueshot Bullets: **www.trueshotbullets.com**
Tru-Tracer: **www.trutracer.com**
Ultramax Ammunition: **www.ultramaxammunition.com**
Vihtavuori Lapua: **www.vihtavuori-lapua.com**
Weatherby: **www.weatherby.com**
West Coast Bullets: **www.westcoastbullet.com**
Western Powders Inc.: **www.westernpowders.com**
Widener's Reloading & Shooters Supply: **www.wideners.com**
Winchester Ammunition: **www.winchester.com**

Windjammer Tournament Wads.: **www.windjammer-wads.com**
Wolf Ammunition: **www.wolfammo.com**
Woodleigh Bullets: **www.woodleighbullets.com.au**
Zanders Sporting Goods: **www.gzanders.com**

Cases, Safes, Gun Locks, and Cabinets

Ace Case Co.: **www.acecase.com**
AG English Sales Co.: **www.agenglish.com**
All Americas' Outdoors: **www.innernet.net/gunsafe**
Alpine Cases: **www.alpinecases.com**
Aluma Sport by Dee Zee: **www.deezee.com**
American Security Products: **www.amsecusa.com**
Americase: **www.americase.com**
Assault Systems: **www.elitesurvival.com**
Avery Outdoors, Inc.: **www.averyoutdoors.com**
Bear Track Cases: **www.beartrackcases.com**
Boyt Harness Co.: **www.boytharness.com**
Bulldog Gun Safe Co.: **www.gardall.com**
Cannon Safe Co.: **www.cannonsafe.com**
CCL Security Products: **www.cclsecurity.com**
Concept Development Corp.: **www.saf-t-blok.com**
Doskocil Mfg. Co.: **www.doskocilmfg.com**
Fort Knox Safes: **www.ftknox.com**
Franzen Security Products: **www.securecase.com**
Frontier Safe Co.: **www.frontiersafe.com**
Granite Security Products: **www.granitesafe.com**
Gunlocker Phoenix USA Inc.: **www.gunlocker.com**
GunVault: **www.gunvault.com**
Hakuba USA Inc.: **www.hakubausa.com**
Heritage Safe Co.: **www.heritagesafecompany.com**
Hide-A-Gun: **www.hide-a-gun.com**
Homak Safes: **www.homak.com**
Hunter Company: **www.huntercompany.com**
Kalispel Case Line: **www.kalispelcaseline.com**
Knouff & Knouff, Inc.: **www.kkair.com**
Knoxx Industries: **www.knoxx,com**
Kolpin Mfg. Co.: **www.kolpin.com**
Liberty Safe & Security: **www.libertysafe.com**
New Innovative Products: **www.starlightcases**
Noble Security Systems Inc.: **www.noble.co.ll**
Phoenix USA Inc.: **www.gunlocker.com**
Plano Molding Co.: **www.planomolding.com**
Rhino Gun Cases: **www.rhinoguns.com**
Rhino Safe: **www.rhinosafe.com**
Rotary Gun Racks: **www.gun-racks.com**
Safe Tech, Inc.: **www.safrgun.com**
Saf-T-Hammer: **www.saf-t-hammer.com**
Saf-T-Lok Corp.: **www.saf-t-lok.comww**
Securecase: **www.securecase.com**
Shot Lock Corp.: **www.shotlock.com**
Smart Lock Technology Inc.: **www.smartlock.com**
Sportsmans Steel Safe Co.: **www.sportsmansteelsafes.com**
Stack-On Products Co.: **www.stack-on.com**
Starlight Cases: **www.starlightcases.com**
Sun Welding: **www.sunwelding.com**
Technoframes: **www.technoframes.com**

T.Z. Case Int'l: **www.tzcase.com**
Versatile Rack Co.: **www.versatilegunrack.com**
V-Line Industries: **www.vlineind.com**
Winchester Safes: **www.fireking.com**
Ziegel Engineering: **www.ziegeleng.com**
Zonetti Armor: **www.zonettiarmor.com**

Choke Devices, Recoil Reducers, Suppressors and Accuracy Devices

Advanced Armament Corp.: **www.advanced-armament.com**
100 Straight Products: **www.100straight.com**
Answer Products Co.: **www.answerrifles.com**
Briley Mfg: **www.briley.com**
Carlson's: **www.choketube.com**
Colonial Arms: **www.colonialarms.com**
Comp-N-Choke: **www.comp-n-choke.com**
Gemtech: **www.gem-tech.com**
Hastings: **www.hastingsbarrels.com**
Kick's Industries: **www.kicks-ind.com**
LimbSaver: **www.limbsaver.com**
Mag-Na-Port Int'l Inc.: **www.magnaport.com**
Metro Gun: **www.metrogun.com**
Patternmaster Chokes: **www.patternmaster.com**
Poly-Choke: **www.poly-choke.com**
Sims Vibration Laboratory: **www.limbsaver.com**
Teague Precision Chokes: **www.teague.ca**
Truglo: **www.truglo.com**

Chronographs and Ballistic Software

Barnes Ballistic Program: **www.barnesbullets.com**
Ballisticard Systems: **www.ballisticards.com**
Competition Electronics: **www.competitionelectronics.com**
Competitive Edge Dynamics: **www.cedhk.com**
Hodgdon Shotshell Program: **www.hodgdon.com**
Lee Shooter Program: **www.leeprecision.com**
Load From A Disk: **www.loadammo.com**
Oehler Research Inc.: **www.oehler-research.com**
PACT: **www.pact.com**
ProChrony: **www.competitionelectronics.com**
Quickload: **www.neconos.com**
RCBS Load: **www.rcbs.com**
Shooting Chrony Inc: **www.shootingchrony.com**
Sierra Infinity Ballistics Program: **www.sierrabullets.com**
Winchester Ballistics Calculator: **www.winchester.com**

Cleaning Products

Accupro: **www.accupro.com**
Ballistol USA: **www.ballistol.com**
Battenfeld Technologies: **www.battenfeldtechnologies.com**
Birchwood Casey: **www.birchwoodcasey.com**
Blue Wonder: **www.bluewonder.com**
Bore Tech: **www.boretech.com**
Break-Free, Inc.: **www.break-free.com**
Bruno Shooters Supply: **www.brunoshooters.com**
Butch's Bore Shine: **www.lymanproducts.com**

C.J. Weapons Accessories: **www.cjweapons,com**
Clenzoil: **www.clenzoil.com**
Corrosion Technologies: **www.corrosionx.com**
Dewey Mfg.: **www.deweyrods.com**
DuraCoat: **www.lauerweaponry.com**
Eezox Inc.: **www.xmission.com**
G 96: **www.g96.com**
Gunslick Gun Care: **www.gunslick.com**
Gunzilla: **www.topduckproducts.com**
Hollands Shooters Supply: **www.hollandgun.com**
Hoppes: **www.hoppes.com**
Hydrosorbent Products: **www.dehumidify.com**
Inhibitor VCI Products: **www.theinhibitor.com**
Iosso Products: **www.iosso.com**
KG Industries: **www.kgcoatings.com**
Kleen-Bore Inc.: **www.kleen-bore.com**
L&R Mfg.: **www.lrultrasonics.com**
Lyman: **www.lymanproducts.com**
Mil-Comm Products: **www.mil-comm.com**
Militec-1: **www.militec-1.com**
Mpro7 Gun Care: **www.mp7.com**
Old West Snake Oil: **www.oldwestsnakeoil.com**
Otis Technology, Inc.: **www.otisgun.com**
Outers: **www.outers-guncare.com**
Ox-Yoke Originals Inc.: **www.oxyoke.com**
Parker-Hale Ltd.: **www.parker-hale.com**
Prolix Lubricant: **www.prolixlubricant.com**
ProShot Products: **www.proshotproducts.com**
ProTec Lubricants: **www.proteclubricants.com**
Rusteprufe Labs: **www.rusteprufe.com**
Sagebrush Products: **www.sagebrushproducts.com**
Sentry Solutions Ltd.: **www.sentrysolutions.com**
Shooters Choice Gun Care: **www.shooters-choice.com**
Silencio: **www.silencio.com**
Slip 2000: **www.slip2000.com**
Stony Point Products: **www.uncle-mikes.com**
Tetra Gun: **www.tetraproducts.com**
The TM Solution thetmsolution@comsast.net
Top Duck Products: **www.topduckproducts.com**
Ultra Bore Coat: **www.ultracoatingsinc.com**
World's Fastest Gun Bore Cleaner: **www.michaels-oregon.com**

Firearms Auction Sites

A&S Auction Co.: **www.asauction.com**
Alderfer Austion: **www.alderferauction.com**
Amoskeag Auction Co.: **www.amoskeagauction.com**
Antique Guns: **www.antiqueguns.com**
Auction Arms: **www.auctionarms.com**
Batterman's Auctions: **www.battermans.com**
Bonhams & Butterfields: **www.bonhams.com/usarms**
Cowan's: **www.cowans.com**
Fontaine's Auction Gallery: **www.fontainesauction.net**
Greg Martin Auctions: **www.gregmartinauctions.com**
Guns America: **www.gunsamerica.com**
Gun Broker: **www.gunbroker.com**

Guns International: **www.gunsinternational.com**
Heritage Auction Gallaries: **www.ha.com**
James D. Julia, Inc.: **www.jamesdjulia.com**
J.C. Devine, Inc.: **www.jcdevine.com**
Little John's Auction Service: **www.littlejohnsauctionservice.com**
Morphy Auctions: **www.morphyauctions.com**
Poulin Auction Co.: **www.poulinantiques.com**
Rock Island Auction Co.: **www.rockislandauction.com**
Wallis & Wallis: **www.wallisandwallis.org**

Firearms Manufacturers and Importers

AAR, Inc.: **www.iar-arms.com**
A-Square: **www.asquarecompany.com**
Accuracy Int'l North America: **www.accuracyinternational.org**
Accuracy Rifle Systems: **www.mini-14.net**
Ace Custom 45's: **www.acecustom45.com**
Advanced Weapons Technology: **www.AWT-Zastava.com**
AIM: **www.aimsurplus.com**
AirForce Airguns: **www.airforceairguns.com**
Air Gun, Inc.: **www.airrifle-china.com**
Airguns of Arizona: **www.airgunsofarizona.com**
Airgun Express: **www.airgunexpress.com**
Alchemy Arms: **www.alchemyltd.com**
Alexander Arms: **www.alexanderarms.com**
American Derringer Corp.: **www.amderringer.com**
American Spirit Arms Corp.: **www.gunkits.com**
American Tactical Imports: **www.americantactical.us**
American Western Arms: **www.awaguns.com**
Anics Corp.: **www.anics.com**
Anschutz: **www.anschutz-sporters.com**
Answer Products Co.: **www.answerrifles.com**
AR-7 Industries,LLC: **www.ar-7.com**
Ares Defense Systems: **www.aresdefense.com**
Armalite: **www.armalite.com**
Armi Sport: **www.armisport.com**
Armory USA: **www.globaltraders.com**
Armsco: **www.armsco.net**
Armscorp USA Inc.: **www.armscorpusa.com**
Arnold Arms: **www.arnoldarms.com**
Arsenal Inc.: **www.arsenalinc.com**
Arthur Brown Co.: **www.eabco.com**
Atlanta Cutlery Corp.: **www.atlantcutlery.com**
Auction Arms: **www.auctionarms.com**
Autauga Arms,Inc.: **www.autaugaarms.com**
Auto-Ordnance Corp.: **www.tommygun.com**
AWA Int'l: **www.awaguns.com**
Axtell Rifle Co.: **www.riflesmith.com**
Aya: **www.aya-fineguns.com**
Baikal: **www.baikalinc.ru/eng/**
Ballard Rifles,LLC: **www.ballardrifles.com**
Barrett Firearms Mfg.: **www.barrettrifles.com**
Beeman Precision Airguns: **www.beeman.com**
Benelli USA Corp.: **www.benelliusa.com**
Benjamin Sheridan: **www.crosman.com**
Beretta U.S.A. Corp.: **www.berettausa.com**

Bernardelli: **www.bernardelli.com**
Bersa: **www.bersa-llama.com**
Bill Hanus Birdguns: **www.billhanusbirdguns.com**
Blaser Jagdwaffen Gmbh: **www.blaser.de**
Bleiker: **www.bleiker.ch**
Bluegrass Armory: **www.bluegrassarmory.com**
Bond Arms: **www.bondarms.com**
Borden's Rifles, Inc.: **www.bordensrifles.com**
Boss & Co.: **www.bossguns.co.uk**
Bowen Classic Arms: **www.bowenclassicarms.com**
Briley Mfg: **www.briley.com**
BRNO Arms: **www.zbrojovka.com**
Brown, David McKay: **www.mckaybrown.com**
Brown, Ed Products: **www.brownprecision.com**
Browning: **www.browning.com**
BRP Corp.: **www.brpguns.com**
BSA Guns: **www.bsaguns.com**
BUL Ltd.: **www.bultransmark.com**
Bushmaster Firearms/Quality Parts: **www.bushmaster.com**
BWE Firearms: **www.bwefirearms.com**
Caesar Guerini USA: **www.gueriniusa.com**
Cape Outfitters: **www.doublegun.com**
Carbon 15: **www.professional-ordnance.com**
Caspian Arms, Ltd.: **www.caspianarmsltd.8m.com**
Casull Arms Corp.: **www.casullarms.com**
Calvary Arms: **www.calvaryarms.com**
CDNN Investments, Inc.: **www.cdnninvestments.com**
Century Arms: **www.centuryarms.com**
Chadick's Ltd.: **www.chadicks-ltd.com**
Champlin Firearms: **www.champlinarms.com**
Chapuis Arms: **www.doubleguns.com/chapuis.htm**
Charles Daly: **www.charlesdaly.com**
Charter Arms: **www.charterfirearms.com**
CheyTac USA: **www.cheytac.com**
Christensen Arms: **www.christensenarms.com**
Cimarron Firearms Co.: **www.cimarron-firearms.com**
Clark Custom Guns: **www.clarkcustomguns.com**
Cobra Enterprises: **www.cobrapistols.com**
Cogswell & Harrison: **www.cogswell.co.uk/home.htm**
Colt's Mfg Co.: **www.colt.com**
Compasseco, Inc.: **www.compasseco.com**
Connecticut Valley Arms: **www.cva.com**
Cooper Firearms: **www.cooperfirearms.com**
Corner Shot: **www.cornershot.com**
CPA Rifles: **www.singleshotrifles.com**
Crosman: **www.crosman.com**
Crossfire, L.L.C.: **www.crossfirelle.com**
C.Sharp Arms Co.: **www.csharparms.com**
CVA: **www.cva.com**
Czechp Int'l: **www.czechpoint-usa.com**
CZ USA: **www.cz-usa.com**
Daisy Mfg Co.: **www.daisy.com**
Dakota Arms Inc.: **www.dakotaarms.com**
Dan Wesson Firearms: **www.danwessonfirearms.com**
Davis Industries: **www.davisindguns.com**
Detonics USA: **www.detonicsusa.com**

Diana: **www.diana-airguns.de**
Dixie Gun Works: **www.dixiegunworks.com**
Dlask Arms Corp.: **www.dlask.com**
D.P.M.S., Inc.: **www.dpmsinc.com**
D.S.Arms,Inc.: **www.dsarms.com**
Dumoulin: **www.dumoulin-herstal.com**
Dynamit Noble: **www.dnrws.com**
EAA Corp.: **www.eaacorp.com**
Eagle Imports,Inc.: **www.bersa-llama.com**
Ed Brown Products: **www.edbrown.com**
EDM Arms: **www.edmarms.com**
E.M.F. Co.: **www.emf-company.com**
Enterprise Arms: **www.enterprise.com**
E R Shaw: **www.ershawbarrels.com**
European American Armory Corp.: **www.eaacorp.com**
Evans, William: **www.williamevans.com**
Excel Arms: **www.excelarms.com**
Fabarm: **www.fabarm.com**
FAC-Guns-N-Stuff: **www.gunsnstuff.com**
Falcon Pneumatic Systems: **www.falcon-airguns.com**
Fausti Stefano: **www.faustistefanoarms.com**
Firestorm: **www.firestorm-sgs.com**
Flodman Guns: **www.flodman.com**
FN Herstal: **www.fnherstal.com**
FNH USA: **www.fnhusa.com**
Franchi: **www.franchiusa.com**
Freedom Arms: **www.freedomarms.com**
Galazan: **www.connecticutshotgun.com**
Gambo Renato: **www.renatogamba.it**
Gamo: **www.gamo.com**
Gary Reeder Custom Guns: **www.reeder-customguns.com**
Gazelle Arms: **www.gazellearms.com**
German Sport Guns: **www.germansportguns.com**
Gibbs Rifle Company: **www.gibbsrifle.com**
Glock: **www.glock.com**
Griffin & Howe: **www.griffinhowe.com**
Grizzly Big Boar Rifle: **www.largrizzly.com**
GSI Inc.: **www.gsifirearms.com**
Guerini: **www.gueriniusa.com**
Gunbroker.Com: **www.gunbroker.com**
Hammerli: **www.carl-walther.com**
Hatfield Gun Co.: **www.hatfield-usa.com**
Hatsan Arms Co.: **www.hatsan.com.tr**
Heckler and Koch: **www.hk-usa.com**
Henry Repeating Arms Co.: **www.henryrepeating.com**
Heritage Mfg.: **www.heritagemfg.com**
Heym: **www.heym-waffenfabrik.de**
High Standard Mfg.: **www.highstandard.com**
Hi-Point Firearms: **www.hi-pointfirearms.com**
Holland & Holland: **www.hollandandholland.com**
H&R 1871 Firearms: **www.hr1871.com**
H-S Precision: **www.hsprecision.com**
Hunters Lodge Corp.: **www.hunterslodge.com**
IAR Inc.: **www.iar-arms.com**
Imperial Miniature Armory: **www.1800miniature.com**
Interarms: **www.interarms.com**

International Military Antiques, Inc.: **www.ima-usa.com**
Inter Ordnance: **www.interordnance.com**
Intrac Arms International LLC: **www.hsarms.com**
Israel Arms: **www.israelarms.com**
Iver Johnson Arms: **www.iverjohnsonarms.com**
Izhevsky Mekhanichesky Zavod: **www.baikalinc.ru**
James River Mfg.: **www.jamesriverarmory.com**
Jarrett Rifles,Inc.: **www.jarrettrifles.com**
J&G Sales, Ltd.: **www.jgsales.com**
Johannsen Express Rifle: **www.johannsen-jagd.de**
Jonathan Arthur Ciener: **www.22lrconversions.com**
JP Enterprises, Inc.: **www.jprifles.com**
Kahr Arms/Auto-Ordnance: **www.kahr.com**
K.B.I.: **www.kbi-inc.com**
Kel-Tec CNC Ind., Inc.: **www.kel-tec.com**
Kifaru: **www.kifaru.net**
Kimber: **www.kimberamerica.com**
Knight's Armament Co.: **www.knightsarmco.com**
Knight Rifles: **www.knightrifles.com**
Korth: **www.korthwaffen.de**
Krebs Custom Guns: **www.krebscustom.com**
Krieghoff Int'l: **www.krieghoff.com**
KY Imports, Inc.: **www.kyimports.com**
K-VAR: **www.k-var.com**
L.A.R Mfg: **www.largrizzly.com**
Lazzeroni Arms Co.: **www.lazzeroni.com**
Legacy Sports International: **www.legacysports.com**
Les Baer Custom, Inc.: **www.lesbaer.com**
Lewis Machine & Tool Co.: **www.lewismachine.net**
Linebaugh Custom Sixguns: **www.sixgunner.com/linebaugh**
Ljutic: **www.ljuticgun.com**
Llama: **www.bersa-llama.com**
Lone Star Rifle Co.: **www.lonestarrifle.com**
LRB Arms: **www.lrbarms.com**
LWRC Int'l: **www.lwrifles.com**
Magnum Research: **www.magnumresearch.com**
Majestic Arms: **www.majesticarms.com**
Markesbery Muzzleloaders: **www.markesbery.com**
Marksman Products: **www.marksman.com**
Marlin: **www.marlinfirearms.com**
Mauser: **www.mauser.com**
McMillan Bros Rifle Co.: **www.mcfamily.com**
MDM: **www.mdm-muzzleloaders.com**
Meacham Rifles: **www.meachamrifles.com**
Merkel: **www.hk-usa.com**
Miller Arms: **www.millerarms.com**
Miltech: **www.miltecharms.com**
Miltex, Inc.: **www.miltexusa.com**
Mitchell's Mausers: **www.mitchellsales.com**
MK Ballistic Systems: **www.mkballistics.com**
M-Mag: **www.mmag.com**
Montana Rifle Co.: **www.montanarifleman.com**
Mossberg: **www.mossberg.com**
Navy Arms: **www.navyarms.com**
Nesika: **www.nesika.com**
New England Arms Corp.: **www.newenglandarms.com**

New England Custom Gun Svc, Ltd.: **www.newenglandcustomgun.com**
New England Firearms: **www.hr1871.com**
New Ultra Light Arms: **www.newultralight.com**
Nighthawk Custom: **www.nighthawkcustom.com**
North American Arms: **www.northamericanarms.com**
Nosler Bullets,Inc.: **www.nosler.com**
Nowlin Mfg. Inc.: **www.nowlinguns.com**
O.F. Mossberg & Sons: **www.mossberg.com**
Ohio Ordnance Works: **www.ohioordnanceworks.com**
Olympic Arms: **www.olyarms.com**
Panther Arms: **www.dpmsinc.com**
Para-USA: **www.para-usa.com**
Pedersoli Davide & Co.: **www.davide-pedersoli.com**
Perazzi: **www.perazzi.com**
Pietta: **www.pietta.it**
PKP Knife-Pistol: **www.sanjuanenterprise.com**
Power Custom: **www.powercustom.com**
Professional Arms: **www.professional-arms.com**
PTR 91,Inc.: **www.ptr91.com**
Purdey & Sons: **www.purdey.com**
Remington: **www.remington.com**
Republic Arms Inc.: **www.republicarmsinc.com**
Rhineland Arms, Inc.: **www.rhinelandarms.com**
Rigby: **www.johnrigbyandco.com**
Rizzini USA: **www.rizziniusa.com**
Robar Companies, Inc.: **www.robarguns.com**
Robinson Armament Co.: **www.robarm.com**
Rock River Arms, Inc.: **www.rockriverarms.com**
Rogue Rifle Co. Inc.: **www.chipmunkrifle.com**
Rohrbaugh Firearms: **www.rohrbaughfirearms.com**
Rossi Arms: **www.rossiusa.com**
RPM: **www.rpmxlpistols.com**
Russian American Armory: **www.raacfirearms.com**
RUAG Ammotec: **www.ruag.com**
Sabatti SPA: **www.sabatti.com**
Sabre Defense Industries: **www.sabredefense.com**
Saco Defense: **www.sacoinc.com**
Safari Arms: **www.olyarms.com**
Sako: **www.berettausa.com**
Samco Global Arms Inc.: **www.samcoglobal.com**
Sarco Inc.: **www.sarcoinc.com**
Savage Arms Inc.: **www.savagearms.com**
Scattergun Technologies Inc.: **www.wilsoncombat.com**
Searcy Enterprises: **www.searcyent.com**
Shiloh Rifle Mfg.: **www.shilohrifle.com**
SIGARMS,Inc.: **www.sigarms.com**
Simpson Ltd.: **www.simpsonltd.com**
SKB Shotguns: **www.skbshotguns.com**
Smith & Wesson: **www.smith-wesson.com**
SOG International, Inc: **www.soginternational.com**
Sphinx System: **www.sphinxarms.com**
Springfield Armory: **www.springfield-armory.com**
SSK Industries: **www.sskindustries.com**
Stag Arms: **www.stagarms.com**
Steyr Arms, Inc.: **www.steyrarms.com**
Stoeger Industries: **www.stoegerindustries.com**

Strayer-Voigt Inc.: **www.sviguns.com**
Sturm,Ruger & Company: **www.ruger-firearms.com**
Tactical Rifles: **www.tacticalrifles.com**
Tactical Solutions: **www.tacticalsol.com**
Tar-Hunt Slug Guns, Inc.: **www.tar-hunt.com**
Taser Int'l: **www.taser.com**
Taurus: **www.taurususa.com**
Taylor's & Co., Inc.: **www.taylorsfirearms.com**
Tennessee Guns: **www.tennesseeguns.com**
TG Int'l: **www.tnguns.com**
The 1877 Sharps Co.: **www.1877sharps.com**
Thompson Center Arms: **www.tcarms.com**
Tikka: **www.berettausa.com**
TNW, Inc.: **www.tnwfirearms.com**
Traditions: **www.traditionsfirearms.com**
Tristar Sporting Arms: **www.tristarsportingarms.com**
Uberti: **www.ubertireplicas.com**
Ultralite 50: **www.ultralite50.com**
Ultra Light Arms: **www.newultralight.com**
Umarex: **www.umarex.com**
U.S. Firearms Mfg. Co.: **www.usfirearms.com**
Valkyrie Arms: **www.valkyriearms.com**
Vektor Arms: **www.vektorarms.com**
Verney-Carron: **www.verney-carron.com**
Volquartsen Custom Ltd.: **www.volquartsen.com**
Vulcan Armament: **www.vulcanarmament.com**
Walther USA: **www.waltheramerica.com**
Weatherby: **www.weatherby.com**
Webley and Scott Ltd.: **www.webley.co.uk**
Westley Richards: **www.westleyrichards.com**
Widley: **www.widleyguns.com**
Wild West Guns: **www.wildwestguns.com**
William Larkin Moore & Co.: **www.doublegun.com**
Wilson Combat: **www.wilsoncombat.com**
Winchester Rifles and Shotguns: **www.winchesterguns.com**

Gun Parts, Barrels, Aftermarket Accessories

300 Below: **www.300below.com**
Accuracy Int. of North America: **www.accuracyinternational.org**
Accuracy Speaks, Inc.: **www.accuracyspeaks.com**
Accurary Systems: **www.accuracysystemsinc.com**
Advanced Barrel Systems: **www.carbonbarrels.com**
Advantage Arms: **www.advantagearms.com**
Aim Surplus: **www.aimsurplus.com**
AK-USA: **www.ak-103.com**
American Spirit Arms Corp.: **www.gunkits.com**
Amhurst-Depot: **www.amherst-depot.com**
AMT Gun Parts: **www.amt-gunparts.com**
Armatac Industries: **www.armatac.com**
Badger Barrels, Inc.: **www.badgerbarrels.com**
Bar-Sto Precision Machine: **www.barsto.com**
Battenfeld Technologies: **www.battenfeldtechnologies.com**
Bellm TC's: **www.bellmtcs.com**
Belt Mountain Enterprises: **www.beltmountain.com**
Bergara Barrels: **www.bergarabarrels.com**

Briley: **www.briley.com**
Brownells: **www.brownells.com**
B-Square: **www.b-square.com**
Buffer Technologies: **www.buffertech.com**
Bullberry Barrel Works: **www.bullberry.com**
Bulldog Barrels: **www.bulldogbarrels.com**
Bushmaster Firearms/Quality Parts: **www.bushmaster.com**
Butler Creek Corp: **www.butler-creek.com**
Cape Outfitters Inc.: **www.capeoutfitters.com**
Caspian Arms Ltd.: **www.caspianarms.com**
Cheaper Than Dirt: **www.cheaperthandirt.com**
Chesnut Ridge: **www.chestnutridge.com/**
Chip McCormick Corp: **www.chipmccormickcorp.com**
Choate Machine & Tool Co.: **www.riflestock.com**
Cierner, Jonathan Arthur: **www.22lrconversions.com**
CJ Weapons Accessories: **www.cjweapons.com**
Colonial Arms: **www.colonialarms.com**
Comp-N-Choke: **www.comp-n-choke.com**
Cylinder & Slide Shop: **www.cylinder-slide.com**
Daniel Defense: **www.danieldefense.com**
Dave Manson Precision Reamers.: **www.mansonreamers.com**
Digi-Twist: **www.fmtcorp.com**
Dixie Gun Works: **www.dixiegun.com**
Douglas Barrels: **www.benchrest.com/douglas/**
DPMS: **www.dpmsinc.com**
D.S.Arms,Inc.: **www.dsarms.com**
eBay: **www.ebay.com**
Ed Brown Products: **www.edbrown.com**
EFK Marketing/Fire Dragon Pistol Accessories: **www.flmfire.com**
E.R. Shaw: **www.ershawbarrels.com**
Forrest Inc.: **www.gunmags.com**
Fulton Armory: **www.fulton-armory.com**
Galazan: **www.connecticutshotgun.com**
Gemtech: **www.gem-tech.com**
Gentry, David: **www.gentrycustom.com**
GG&G: **www.gggaz.com**
Green Mountain Rifle Barrels: **www.gmriflebarrel.com**
Gun Parts Corp.: **www.e-gunparts.com**
Harris Engineering: **www.harrisbipods.com**
Hart Rifle Barrels: **www.hartbarrels.com**
Hastings Barrels: **www.hastingsbarrels.com**
Heinie Specialty Products: **www.heinie.com**
Holland Shooters Supply: **www.hollandgun.com**
H-S Precision: **www.hsprecision.com**
100 Straight Products: **www.100straight.com**
I.M.A.: **www.ima-usa.com**
Jack First Gun Shop: **www.jackfirstgun.com**
Jarvis, Inc.: **www.jarvis-custom.com**
J&T Distributing: **www.jtdistributing.com**
John's Guns: **www.johnsguns.com**
John Masen Co.: **www.johnmasen.com**
Jonathan Arthur Ciener, Inc.: **www.22lrconversions.com**
JP Enterprises: **www.jpar15.com**
Keng's Firearms Specialities: **www.versapod.com**
KG Industries: **www.kgcoatings.com**
Kick Eez: **www.kickeez.com**

Kidd Triggers: **www.coolguyguns.com**
King's Gunworks: **www.kingsgunworks.com**
Knoxx Industries: **www.knoxx.com**
Krieger Barrels: **www.kriegerbarrels.com**
K-VAR Corp.: **www.k-var.com**
LaRue Tactical: **www.laruetactical.com**
Les Baer Custom, Inc.: **www.lesbaer.com**
Lilja Barrels: **www.riflebarrels.com**
Lone Star Rifle Co.: **www.lonestarrifles.com**
Lone Wolf Dist.: **www.lonewolfdist.com**
Lothar Walther Precision Tools Inc.: **www.lothar-walther.de**
M&A Parts, Inc.: **www.m-aparts.com**
MAB Barrels: **www.mab.com.au**
Majestic Arms: **www.majesticarms.com**
Marvel Products, Inc.: **www.marvelprod.com**
MEC-GAR SrL: **www.mec-gar.it**
Mesa Tactical: **www.mesatactical.com**
Michaels of Oregon Co.: **www.michaels-oregon.com**
North Mfg. Co.: **www.rifle-barrels.com**
Numrich Gun Parts Corp.: **www.e-gunparts.com**
Pachmayr: **www.pachmayr.com**
Pac-Nor Barrels: **www.pac-nor.com**
Para Ordinance Pro Shop: **www.ltms.com**
Point Tech Inc.: **www.pointtech.com**
Promag Industries: **www.promagindustries.com**
Power Custom, Inc.: **www.powercustom.com**
Precision Reflex: **www.pri-mounts.com**
Red Star Arms: **www.redstararms.com**
Rocky Mountain Arms: **www.rockymountainarms.com**
Royal Arms Int'l: **www.royalarms.com**
R.W. Hart: **www.rwhart.com**
Sarco Inc.: **www.sarcoinc.com**
Scattergun Technologies Inc.: **www.wilsoncombat.com**
Schuemann Barrels: **www.schuemann.com**
Seminole Gunworks Chamber Mates: **www.chambermates.com**
Shilen: **www.shilen.com**
Sims Vibration Laboratory: **www.limbsaver.com**
Smith & Alexander Inc.: **www.smithandalexander.com**
Speed Shooters Int'l: **www.shooternet.com/ssi**
Sprinco USA Inc.: **www.sprinco.com**
Springfield Sporters, Inc.: **www.ssporters.com**
STI Int'l: **www.stiguns.com**
S&S Firearms: **www.ssfirearms.com**
SSK Industries: **www.sskindustries.com**
Sun Devil Mfg.: **www.sundevilmfg.com**
Sunny Hill Enterprises: **www.sunny-hill.com**
Tac Star: **www.lymanproducts.com**
Tactical Innovations: **www.tacticalinc.com**
Tapco: **www.tapco.com**
Trapdoors Galore: **www.trapdoors.com**
Triple K Manufacturing Co. Inc.: **www.triplek.com**
U.S.A. Magazines Inc.: **www.usa-magazines.com**
Verney-Carron SA: **www.verney-carron.com**
Volquartsen Custom Ltd.: **www.volquartsen.com**
W.C. Wolff Co.: **www.gunsprings.com**
Waller & Son: **www.wallerandson.com**

Weigand Combat Handguns: **www.weigandcombat.com**
Western Gun Parts: **www.westerngunparts.com**
Wilson Arms: **www.wilsonarms.com**
Wilson Combat: **www.wilsoncombat.com**
Wisner's Inc.: **www.wisnerinc.com**
Z-M Weapons: **www.zmweapons.com/home.htm**

Gunsmithing Supplies and Instruction

American Gunsmithing Institute: **www.americangunsmith.com**
Battenfeld Technologies: **www.battenfeldtechnologies.com**
Bellm TC's: **www.bellmtcs.com**
Blue Ridge Machinery & Tools: **www.blueridgemachinery.com**
Brownells, Inc.: **www.brownells.com**
B-Square Co.: **www.b-square.com**
Clymer Mfg. Co.: **www.clymertool.com**
Craftguard Metal Finishing: **www.craftguard.com**
Dem-Bart: **www.dembartco.com**
Doug Turnbull Restoration: **www.turnbullrestoration,com**
Du-Lite Corp.: **www.dulite.com**
Dvorak Instruments: **www.dvorakinstruments.com**
Gradiant Lens Corp.: **www.gradientlens.com**
Grizzly Industrial: **www.grizzly.com**
Gunline Tools: **www.gunline.com**
Harbor Freight: **www.harborfreight.com**
JGS Precision Tool Mfg. LLC: **www.jgstools.com**
Mag-Na-Port International: **www.magnaport.com**
Manson Precision Reamers: **www.mansonreamers.com**
Midway: **www.midwayusa.com**
Murray State College: **www.mscok.edu**
Olympus America Inc.: **www.olympus.com**
Pacific Tool & Gauge: **www.pacifictoolandgauge.com**
Trinidad State Junior College: **www.trinidadstate.edu**

Handgun Grips

A&G Supply Co.: **www.gripextender.com**
Ajax Custom Grips, Inc.: **www.ajaxgrips.com**
Altamont Co.: **www.altamontco.com**
Aluma Grips: **www.alumagrips.com**
Badger Grips: **www.pistolgrips.com**
Barami Corp.: **www.hipgrip.com**
Blu Magnum Grips: **www.blumagnum.com**
Buffalo Brothers: **www.buffalobrothers.com**
Crimson Trace Corp.: **www.crimsontrace.com**
Eagle Grips: **www.eaglegrips.com**
Falcon Industries: **www.ergogrips.net**
Herrett's Stocks: **www.herrettstocks.com**
Hogue Grips: **www.getgrip.com**
Kirk Ratajesak: **www.kgratajesak.com**
Lett Custom Grips: **www.lettgrips.com**
N.C. Ordnance: **www.gungrip.com**
Nill-Grips USA: **www.nill-grips.com**
Pachmayr: **www.pachmayr.com**
Pearce Grips: **www.pearcegrip.com**
Trausch Grips Int.Co.: **www.trausch.com**
Tyler-T Grips: **www.t-grips.com**
Uncle Mike's:: **www.uncle-mikes.com**

Holsters and Leather Products

Akah: **www.akah.de**
Aker Leather Products: **www.akerleather.com**
Alessi Distributor R&F Inc.: **www.alessiholsters.com**
Alfonso's of Hollywood: **www.alfonsogunleather.com**
Armor Holdings: **www.holsters.com**
Bagmaster: **www.bagmaster.com**
Bianchi International: **www.bianchi-intl.com**
Blackhawk Outdoors: **www.blackhawk.com**
Blackhills Leather: **www.blackhillsleather.com**
BodyHugger Holsters: **www.nikolais.com**
Boyt Harness Co.: **www.boytharness.com**
Brigade Gun Leather: **www.brigadegunleather.com**
Chimere: **www.chimere.com**
Clipdraw: **www.clipdraw.com**
Conceal It: **www.conceal-it.com**
Concealment Shop Inc.: **www.theconcealmentshop.com**
Coronado Leather Co.: **www.coronadoleather.com**
Covert Carry: **www.covertcarry.com**
Creedmoor Sports, Inc.: **www.creedmoorsports.com**
Custom Leather Wear: **www.customleatherwear.com**
Defense Security Products: **www.thunderwear.com**
Dennis Yoder: **www.yodercustomleather.com**
DeSantis Holster: **www.desantisholster.com**
Dillon Precision: **www.dillonprecision.com**
Don Hume Leathergoods, Inc.: **www.donhume.com**
Ernie Hill International: **www.erniehill.com**
Fist: **www.fist-inc.com**
Fobus USA: **www.fobusholster.com**
Galco: **www.usgalco.com**
Gilmore's Sports Concepts: **www.gilmoresports.com**
Gould & Goodrich: **www.gouldusa.com**
Gunmate Products: **www.gun-mate.com**
Hellweg Ltd.: **www.hellwegltd.com**
Hide-A-Gun: **www.hide-a-gun.com**
High Noon Holsters: **www.highnoonholsters.com**
Holsters.Com: **www.holsters.com**
Horseshoe Leather Products: **www.horseshoe.co.uk**
Humphrey Custom Leather: **www.humphreycustomleather.com**
Hunter Co.: **www.huntercompany.com**
Kirkpatrick Leather Company: **www.kirkpatrickleather.com**
KNJ: **www.knjmfg.com**
Kramer Leather: **www.kramerleather.com**
Law Concealment Systems: **www.handgunconcealment.com**
Levy's Leathers Ltd.: **www.levysleathers.com**
Mernickle Holsters: **www.mernickleholsters.com**
Michaels of Oregon Co.: **www.michaels-oregon.com**
Milt Sparks Leather: **www.miltsparks.com**
Mitch Rosen Extraordinary Gunleather: **www.mitchrosen.com**
Old World Leather: **www.gun-mate.com**
Pacific Canvas & Leather Co.:**www.pacificcanvasandleather.com**
Pager Pal: **www.pagerpal.com**
Phalanx Corp.: **www.smartholster.com**
PWL: **www.pwlusa.com**
Rumanya Inc.: **www.rumanya.com**

S.A. Gunleather: **www.elpasoleather.com**
Safariland Ltd. Inc.: **www.safariland.com**
Shooting Systems Group Inc.: **www.shootingsystems.com**
Strictly Anything Inc.: **www.strictlyanything.com**
Strong Holster Co.: **www.strong-holster.com**
The Belt Co.: **www.conceal-it.com**
The Leather Factory Inc.: **www.tandyleatherfactory.com**
The Outdoor Connection: **www.outdoorconnection.com**
Top-Line USA inc.: **www.toplineusa.com**
Triple K Manufacturing Co.: **www.triplek.com**
Wilson Combat: **www.wilsoncombat.com**

Miscellaneous Shooting Products

10X Products Group: **www.10Xwear.com**
Aero Peltor: **www.aearo.com**
American Body Armor: **www.americanbodyarmor.com**
Armor Holdings Products: **www.armorholdings.com**
Battenfeld Technologies: **www.battenfeldtechnologies.com**
Beamhit: **www.beamhit.com**
Beartooth: **www.beartoothproducts.com**
Bodyguard by S&W: **www.yourbodyguard.com**
Burnham Brothers: **www.burnhambrothers.com**
Collectors Armory: **www.collectorsarmory.com**
Dalloz Safety: **www.cdalloz.com**
Deben Group Industries Inc.: **www.deben.com**
Decot Hy-Wyd Sport Glasses: **www.sportyglasses.com**
E.A.R., Inc.: **www.earinc.com**
First Choice Armor: **www.firstchoicearmor.com**
Gunstands: **www.gunstands.com**
Howard Leight Hearing Protectors: **www.howardleight.com**
Hunters Specialities: **www.hunterspec.com**
Johnny Stewart Wildlife Calls: **www.hunterspec.com**
Merit Corporation: **www.meritcorporation.com**
Michaels of Oregon: **www.michaels-oregon.com**
MPI Outdoors: **www.mpioutdoors.com**
MTM Case-Gard: **www.mtmcase-gard.com**
North Safety Products: **www.northsafety-brea.com**
Plano Molding: **www.planomolding.com**
Pro-Ears: **www.pro-ears.com**
Second Chance Body Armor Inc.: **www.secondchance.com**
Silencio: **www.silencio.com**
Smart Lock Technologies: **www.smartlock.com**
Surefire: **www.surefire.com**
Taser Int'l: **www.taser.com**
Walker's Game Ear Inc.: **www.walkersgameear.com**

Muzzleloading Firearms and Products

American Pioneer Powder: **www.americanpioneerpowder.com**
Armi Sport: **www.armisport.com**
Barnes Bullets: **www.barnesbullets,com**
Black Powder Products: **www.bpiguns.com**
Buckeye Barrels: **www.buckeyebarrels.com**
Cabin Creek Muzzleloading: **www.cabincreek.net**
CVA: **www.cva.com**
Caywood Gunmakers: **www.caywoodguns.com**

Davide Perdsoli & co.: **www.davide-pedersoli.com**
Dixie Gun Works, Inc.: **www.dixiegun.com**
Elephant/Swiss Black Powder: **www.elephantblackpowder.com**
Goex Black Powder: **www.goexpowder.com**
Green Mountain Rifle Barrel Co.: **www.gmriflebarrel.com**
Gunstocks Plus: **www.gunstocksplus.com**
Harvester Bullets: **www.harvesterbullets.com**
Hornady: **www.hornady.com**
Jedediah Starr Trading Co.: **www.jedediah-starr.com**
Jim Chambers Flintlocks: **www.flintlocks.com**
Kahnke Gunworks: **www.powderandbow.com/kahnke/**
Knight Rifles: **www.knightrifles.com**
Knob Mountain Muzzleloading: **www.knobmountainmuzzleloading.com**
The leatherman: **www.blackpowderbags.com**
Log Cabin Shop: **www.logcabinshop.com**
L&R Lock Co.: **www.lr-rpl.com**
Lyman: **www.lymanproducts.com**
Magkor Industries: **www.magkor.com**
MDM Muzzleloaders: **www.mdm-muzzleloaders.com**
Middlesex Village Trading: **www.middlesexvillagetrading.com**
Millennium Designed Muzzleloaders: **www.mdm-muzzleloaders.com**
MSM, Inc.: **www.msmfg.com**
Muzzleloader Builders Supply: **www.muzzleloadersbuilderssupply.com**
Muzzleload Magnum Products: **www.mmpsabots.com**
Muzzleloading Technologies, Inc.: **www.mtimuzzleloading.com**
Navy Arms: **www.navyarms.com**
Northwest Trade Guns: **www.northstarwest.com**
Nosler, Inc.: **www.nosler.com**
October Country Muzzleloading: **www.oct-country.com**
Ox-Yoke Originals Inc.: **www.oxyoke.com**
Palmetto Arms: **www.palmetto.it**
Pietta: **www.pietta.it**
Powerbelt Bullets: **www.powerbeltbullets.com**
PR Bullets: **www.prbullets.com**
Precision Rifle Dead Center Bullets: **www.prbullet.com**
R.E. Davis CVo.: **www.redaviscompany.com**
Remington: **www.remington.com**
Rightnour Mfg. Co. Inc.: **www.rmcsports.com**
The Rifle Shop trshoppe@aol.com
Savage Arms, Inc.: **www.savagearms.com**
Schuetzen Powder: **www.schuetzenpowder.com**
TDC: **www.tdcmfg.com**
Tennessee Valley Muzzleloading: **www.avsia.com/tvm**
Thompson Center Arms: **www.tcarms.com**
Tiger Hunt Stocks: **www.gunstockwood.com**
Track of the Wolf: **www.trackofthewolf.com**
Traditions Performance Muzzleloading: **www.traditionsfirearms.com**
Vernon C. Davis & Co.: **www.stonewallcreekoutfitters.com**

Publications, Videos and CDs

Arms and Military Press: **www.skennerton.com**
A&J Arms Booksellers: **www.ajarmsbooksellers.com**
American Cop: **www.americancopmagazine.com**
American Firearms Industry: **www.amfire.com**
American Handgunner: **www.americanhandgunner.com**

American Hunter: **www.nrapublications.org**
American Pioneer Video: **www.americanpioneervideo.com**
American Rifleman: **www.nrapublications.org**
American Shooting Magazine: **www.americanshooting.com**
Backwoodsman: **www.backwoodsmanmag.com**
Black Powder Cartridge News: **www.blackpowderspg.com**
Blue Book Publications: **www.bluebookinc.com**
Combat Handguns: **www.combathandguns.com**
Concealed Carry: **www.uscca.us**
Cornell Publications: **www.cornellpubs.com**
Countrywide Press: **www.countrysport.com**
DBI Books/Krause Publications: **www.krause.com**
Fouling Shot: **www.castbulletassoc.org**
George Shumway Publisher: **www.shumwaypublisher.com**
Gun List: **www.gunlist.com**
Gun Video: **www.gunvideo.com**
GUNS Magazine: **www.gunsmagazine.com**
Guns & Ammo: **www.gunsandammomag.com**
Gun Week: **www.gunweek.com**
Gun World: **www.gunworld.com**
Harris Publications: **www.harrispublications.com**
Heritage Gun Books: **www.gunbooks.com**
Krause Publications: **www.krause.com**
Law and Order: **www.hendonpub.com**
Man at Arms: **www.manatarmsbooks.com**
Muzzleloader: **www.muzzleloadermag.com**
Paladin Press: **www.paladin-press.com**
Precision Shooting: **www.precisionshooting.com**
Ray Riling Arms Books: **www.rayrilingarmsbooks.com**
Rifle and Handloader Magazines: **www.riflemagazine.com**
Safari Press Inc.: **www.safaripress.com**
Scurlock Publishing: **www.muzzleloadingmag.com**
Shoot! Magazine: **www.shootmagazine.com**
Shooting Illustrated: **www.nrapublications.org**
Shooting Industry: **www.shootingindustry.com**
Shooting Sports Retailer: **www.shootingsportsretailer.com**
Shooting Sports USA: **www.nrapublications.org**
Shotgun News: **www.shotgunnews.com**
Shotgun Report: **www.shotgunreport.com**
Shotgun Sports Magazine: **www.shotgun-sports.com**
Single Shot Rifle Journal: **www.assra.com**
Small Arms Review: **www.smallarmsreview.com**
Small Caliber News: **www.smallcaliber.com**
Sporting Clays Web Edition: **www.sportingclays.net**
Sports Afield: **www.sportsafield.comm**
Sportsmen on Film: **www.sportsmenonfilm.com**
SWAT Magazine: **www.swatmag.com**
The Single Shot Exchange Magazine: **www.singleshotexchange.com**
The Sixgunner: **www.sskindustries.com**
Varmint Hunter: **www.varminthunter.org**
VSP Publications: **www.gunbooks.com**

Reloading Tools

Antimony Man: **www.theantimonyman.com**
Ballisti-Cast Mfg.: **www.ballisti-cast.com**

Battenfeld Technologies: **www.battenfeldtechnologies.com**
Bruno Shooters Supply: **www.brunoshooters.com**
Buffalo Arms: **www.buffaloarms.com**
CabineTree: **www.castingstuff.com**
Camdex, Inc.: **www.camdexloader.com**
CH/4D Custom Die: **www.ch4d.com**
Colorado Shooters Supply: **www.hochmoulds.com**
Corbin Mfg & Supply Co.: **www.corbins.com**
Dillon Precision: **www.dillonprecision.com**
Forster Precision Products: **www.forsterproducts.com**
GSI International, Inc.: **www.gsiinternational.com**
Hanned Line: **www.hanned.com**
Harrell's Precision: **www.harrellsprec.com**
Holland's Shooting Supplies: **www.hollandgun.com**
Hornady: **www.hornady.com**
Huntington Reloading Products: **www.huntingtons.com**
J & J Products Co.: **www.jandjproducts.com**
Lead Bullet Technology: **www.lbtmoulds.com**
Lee Precision, Inc.: **www.leeprecision.com**
Littleton Shotmaker: **www.leadshotmaker.com**
Load Data: **www.loaddata.com**
Lyman: **www.lymanproducts.com**
Magma Engineering: **www.magmaengr.com**
Mayville Engineering Co. (MEC): **www.mecreloaders.com**
Midway: **www.midwayusa.com**
Moly-Bore: **www.molybore.com**
Montana Bullet Works: **www.montanabulletworks.com**
MTM Case-Guard: **www.mtmcase-guard.com**
NECO: **www.neconos.com**
NEI: **www.neihandtools.com**
Neil Jones Custom Products: **www.neiljones.com**
Ponsness/Warren: **www.reloaders.com**
Quinetics Corp.: **www.quineticscorp.com**
Ranger Products: **www.pages.prodigy.com/rangerproducts.home.htm**
Rapine Bullet Mold Mfg Co.: **www.bulletmoulds.com**
RCBS: **www.rcbs.com**
Redding Reloading Equipment: **www.redding-reloading.com**
Russ Haydon's Shooting Supplies: **www.shooters-supply.com**
Sinclair Int'l Inc.: **www.sinclairintl.com**
Stoney Point Products Inc: **www.stoneypoint.com**
Thompson Bullet Lube Co.: **www.thompsonbulletlube.com**
Vickerman Seating Die: **www.castingstuff.com**
Wilson (L.E. Wilson): **www.lewilson.com**

Rests: Bench, Portable, Attachable

Battenfeld Technolgies: **www.battenfeldtechnologies.com**
Bench Master: **www.bench-master.com**
B-Square: **www.b-square.com**
Bullshooter: **www.bullshooterssightingin.com**
Desert Mountain Mfg.: **www.benchmasterusa.com**
Harris Engineering Inc.: **www.harrisbipods**
Kramer Designs: **www.snipepod.com**
L Thomas Rifle Support: **www.ltsupport.com**
Level-Lok: **www.levellok.com**
Midway: **www.midwayusa.com**

Predator Sniper Styx: **www.predatorsniperstyx.com**
Ransom International: **www.ransom-intl.com**
Rotary Gun Racks: **www.gun-racks.com**
R.W. Hart: **www.rwhart.com**
Sinclair Intl, Inc.: **www.sinclairintl.com**
Stoney Point Products: **www.uncle-mikes.com**
Target Shooting: **www.targetshooting.com**
Varmint Masters: **www.varmintmasters.com**
Versa-Pod: **www.versa-pod.com**

Scopes, Sights, Mounts and Accessories

Accumount: **www.accumounts.com**
Accusight: **www.accusight.com**
ADCO: **www.shooters.com/adco/index/htm**
Adirondack Opitcs: **www.adkoptics.com**
Advantage Tactical Sight: **www.advantagetactical.com**
Aimpoint: **www.aimpoint.com**
Aim Shot, Inc.: **www.miniosprey.com**
Aimtech Mount Systems: **www.aimtech-mounts.com**
Alpec Team, Inc.: **www.alpec.com**
Alpen Outdoor Corp.: **www.alpenoutdoor.com**
American Technologies Network, Corp.: **www.atncorp.com**
AmeriGlo, LLC: **www.ameriglo.net**
ArmaLaser: **www.armalaser.com**
ARMS: **www.armsmounts.com**
Aro-Tek, Ltd.: **www.arotek.com**
ATN: **www.atncorp.com**
Badger Ordnance: **www.badgerordnance.com**
Barrett: **www.barrettrifles.com**
Beamshot-Quarton: **www.beamshot.com**
BSA Optics: **www.bsaoptics.com**
B-Square Company, Inc.: **www.b-square.com**
Burris: **www.burrisoptics.com**
Bushnell Performance Optics: **www.bushnell.com**
Carl Zeiss Optical Inc.: **www.zeiss.com**
Carson Optical: **www.carson-optical.com**
CenterPoint Precision Optics: **www.centerpointoptics.com**
Centurion Arms: **www.centurionarms.com**
C-More Systems: **www.cmore.com**
Conetrol Scope Mounts: **www.conetrol.com**
Crimson Trace Corp.: **www.crimsontrace.com**
Crossfire L.L.C.: **www.amfire.com/hesco/html**
Cylinder & Slide, Inc.: **www.cylinderslide.com**
DCG Supply Inc.: **www.dcgsupply.com**
D&L Sports: **www.dlsports.com**
DuraSight Scope Mounting Systems: **www.durasight.com**
EasyHit, Inc.: **www.easyhit.com**
EAW: **www.eaw.de**
Elcan Optical Technologies: **www.armament.com,: www.elcan.com**
Electro-Optics Technologies: **www.eotechmdc.com/holosight**
EoTech: www.eotech-inc.com
Europtik Ltd.: **www.europtik.com**
Fujinon, Inc.: **www.fujinon.com**
GG&G: **www.w.gggaz.com**
Gilmore Sports: **www.gilmoresports.com**

Gradient Lens Corp.: **www.gradientlens.com**
Hakko Co. Ltd.: **www.hakko-japan.co.jp**
Hahn Precision: **www.hahn-precision.com**
Hesco: **www.hescosights.com**
Hi-Lux Optics: **www.hi-luxoptics.com**
Hitek Industries: **www.nightsight.com**
HIVIZ: **www.hivizsights.com**
Hollands Shooters Supply: **www.hollandguns.com**
Horus Vision: **www.horusvision.com**
Hunter Co.: **www.huntercompany.com**
Innovative Weaponry,Inc.: **www.ptnightsights.com**
Insight: **www.insighttechnology.com**
Ironsighter Co.: **www.ironsighter.com**
ITT Night Vision: **www.ittnightvision.com**
Kahles: **www.kahlesoptik.com**
Knight's Armament: **www.knightarmco.com**
Kowa Optimed Inc.: **www.kowascope.com**
Kwik-Site Co.: **www.kwiksitecorp.com**
L-3 Communications-Eotech: **www.l-3com.com**
LaRue Tactical: **www.laruetactical.com**
Laser Bore Sight: **www.laserboresight.com**
Laser Devices Inc.: **www.laserdevices.com**
Lasergrips: **www.crimsontrace.com**
LaserLyte: **www.laserlytesights.com**
LaserMax Inc.: **www.lasermax.com**
Laser Products: **www.surefire.com**
Leapers, Inc.: **www.leapers.com**
Leatherwood: **www.hi-luxoptics.com**
Legacy Sports: **www.legacysports.com**
Leica Camera Inc.: **www.leica-camera.com/usa**
Leupold: **www.leupold.com**
Lewis Machine & Tool: **www.lewismachine.net**
LightForce/NightForce USA: **www.nightforcescopes.com**
Lyman: **www.lymanproducts.com**
Lynx: **www.b-square.com**
MaTech: **www.adcofirearms.com**
Marble's Outdoors: **www.marblesoutdoors.com**
MDS,Inc.: **www.mdsincorporated.com**
Meopta: **www.meopta.com**
Meprolight: **www.kimberamerica.com**
Micro Sight Co.: **www.microsight.com**
Millett: **www.millettsights.com**
Miniature Machine Corp.: **www.mmcsight.com**
Mini-Scout-Mount: **www.amegaranges.com**
Montana Vintage Arms: **www.montanavintagearms.com**
Moro Vision: **www.morovision.com**
Mounting Solutions Plus: **www.mountsplus.com**
NAIT: **www.nait.com**
Newcon International Ltd.: **www.newcon-optik.com**
Night Force Optics: **www.nightforcescopes.com**
Night Optics USA, Inc.: **www.nightoptics.com**
Night Owl Optics: **www.nightowloptics.com**
Night Vision Systems: **www.nightvisionsystems.com**
Nikon Inc.: **www.nikonusa.com**
North American Integrated Technologies: **www.nait.com**
O.K. Weber, Inc.: **www.okweber.com**

Optolyth-Optic: **www.optolyth.de**
Osprey Optics: **www.osprey-optics.com**
Pentax Corp.: **www.pentaxlightseeker.com**
Precision Reflex: **www.pri-mounts.com**
Pride Fowler, Inc.: **www.rapidreticle.com**
Premier Reticles: **www.premierreticles.com**
Redfield: **www.redfieldoptics.com**
Rifle Electronics: **www.theriflecam.com**
R&R Int'l Trade: **www.nightoptic.com**
Schmidt & Bender: **www.schmidt-bender.com**
Scopecoat: **www.scopecoat.com**
Scopelevel: **www.scopelevel.com**
Segway Industries: **www.segway-industries.com**
Shepherd Scope Ltd.: **www.shepherdscopes.com**
Sig Sauer: **www.sigsauer.com**
Sightron: **www.sightron.com**
Simmons: **www.simmonsoptics.com**
S&K: **www.scopemounts.com**
Springfield Armory: **www.springfield-armory.com**
Sure-Fire: **www.surefire.com**
Swarovski/Kahles: **www.swarovskioptik.com**
Swift Optics: **www.swiftoptics.com**
Talley Mfg. Co.: **www.talleyrings.com**
Target Scope Blocks-Steve Earl Products: **www.steveearlproducts.com**
Tasco: **www.tascosales.com**
Tech Sights: **www.tech-sights.com**
Trijicon Inc.: **www.trijicon.com**
Troy Industries: **www.troyind.com**
Truglo Inc.: **www.truglo.com**
Ultimak: **www.ultimak.com**
UltraDot: **www.ultradotusa.com**
Unertl Optical Co.: **www.unertlopics.com**
US Night Vision: **www.usnightvision.com**
U.S. Optics Technologies Inc.: **www.usoptics.com**
Valdada-IOR Optics: **www.valdada.com**
Viridian Green Laser Sights: **www.viridiangreenlaser.com**
Warne: **www.warnescopemounts.com**
Weaver Mounts: **www.weaver-mounts.com**
Weaver Scopes: **www.weaveroptics.com**
Wilcox Industries Corp: **www.wilcoxind.com**
Williams Gun Sight Co.: **www.williamsgunsight.com**
Wilson Combat: **www.wilsoncombat.com**
XS Sight Systems: **www.xssights.com**
Zeiss: **www.zeiss.com**

Shooting Organizations, Schools and Ranges

Amateur Trapshooting Assoc.: **www.shootata.com**
American Custom Gunmakers Guild: **www.acgg.org**
American Gunsmithing Institute: **www.americangunsmith.com**
American Pistolsmiths Guild: **www.americanpistol.com**
American Shooting Sports Council: **www.assc.com**
American Single Shot Rifle Assoc.: **www.assra.com**
Antique Shooting Tool Collector's Assoc.: **www.oldshootingtools.org**
Assoc. of Firearm & Tool Mark Examiners: **www.afte.org**
BATF: **www.atf.ustreas.gov**

Blackwater Lodge and Training Center: **www.blackwaterlodge.com**
Boone and Crockett Club: **www.boone-crockett.org**
Buckmasters, Ltd.: **www.buckmasters.com**
Cast Bullet Assoc.: **www.castbulletassoc.org**
Citizens Committee for the Right to Keep & Bear Arms: **www.ccrkba.org**
Civilian Marksmanship Program: **www.odcmp.com**
Colorado School of Trades: **www.gunsmith-school.com**
Cylinder & Slide Pistolsmithing Schools: **www.cylinder-slide.com**
Ducks Unlimited: **www.ducks.org**
4-H Shooting Sports Program: **www.4-hshootingsports.org**
Fifty Caliber Institute: **www.fiftycal.org**
Fifty Caliber Shooters Assoc.: **www.fcsa.org**
Firearms Coalition: **www.nealknox.com**
Front Sight Firearms Training Institute: **www.frontsight.com**
German Gun Collectors Assoc.: **www.germanguns.com**
Gun Clubs: **www.associatedgunclubs.org**
Gun Owners' Action League: **www.goal.org**
Gun Owners of America: **www.gunowners.org**
Gun Trade Asssoc. Ltd.: **www.brucepub.com/gta**
Gunsite Training Center, Inc.: **www.gunsite.com**
Handgun Hunters International: **www.sskindustries.com**
Hunting and Shooting Sports Heritage Fund: **www.huntandshoot.org**
I.C.E. Traing: **www.icetraining.com**
International Defense Pistol Assoc.: **www.idpa.com**
International Handgun Metallic Silhouette Assoc.: **www.ihmsa.org**
International Hunter Education Assoc.: **www.ihea.com**
Int'l Law Enforcement Educators and Trainers Assoc.: **www.ileeta.com**
International Single Shot Assoc.: **www.issa-schuetzen.org**
Jews for the Preservation of Firearms Ownership: **www.jpfo.org**
Mule Deer Foundation: **www.muledeer.org**
Muzzle Loaders Assoc. of Great Britain: **www.mlagb.com**
National 4-H Shooting Sports: **www.4-hshootingsports.org**
National Assn. of Sporting Goods Wholesalers: **www.nasgw.org**
National Benchrest Shooters Assoc.: **www.benchrest.com**
National Muzzle Loading Rifle Assoc.: **www.nmlra.org**
National Reloading Manufacturers Assoc: **www.reload-nrma.com**
National Rifle Assoc.: **www.nra.org**
National Rifle Assoc. ILA: **www.nraila.org**
National Shooting Sports Foundation: **www.nssf.org**
National Skeet Shooters Association: **www.nssa-nsca.com**
National Sporting Clays Assoc.: **www.nssa-nsca.com**
National Wild Turkey Federation: **www.nwtf.com**
NICS/FBI: **www.fbi.gov**
North American Hunting Club: **www.huntingclub.com**
Order of Edwardian Gunners (Vintagers): **www.vintagers.org**
Outdoor Industry Foundation: **www.outdoorindustryfoundation.org**
Pennsylvania Gunsmith School: **www.pagunsmith.com**
Piedmont Community College: **www.piedmontcc.edu**
Quail Unlimited: **www.qu.org**
Remington Society of America: **www.remingtonsociety.com**
Right To Keep and Bear Arms: **www.rkba.org**
Rocky Mountain Elk Foundation: **www.rmef.org**
SAAMI: **www.saami.org**
Safari Club International: **www.scifirstforhunters.org**
Scholastic Clay Target Program: **www.nssf.org/sctp**
Second Amendment Foundation: **www.saf.org**

Second Amendment Sisters: **www.2asisters.org**
Shooting Ranges Int'l: **www.shootingranges.com**
Sig Sauer Academy: **www.sigsauer.com**
Single Action Shooting Society: **www.sassnet.com**
Students for Second Amendment: **www.sf2a.org**
Suarez Training: **www.warriortalk.com**
S&W Academy and Nat'l Firearms Trng. Center: **www.sw-academy.com**
Tactical Defense Institute: **www.tdiohio.com**
Tactical Life: **www.tactical-life.com**
Ted Nugent United Sportsmen of America: **www.tnugent.com**
Thunder Ranch: **www.thunderranchinc.com**
Trapshooters Homepage: **www.trapshooters.com**
Trinidad State Junior College: **www.trinidadstate.edu**
U.S. Concealed Carry Association: **www.uscca.us**
U.S. Int'l Clay Target Assoc.: **www.usicta.com**
United States Fish and Wildlife Service: **www.fws.gov**
U.S. Practical Shooting Assoc.: **www.uspsa.org**
USA Shooting: **www.usashooting.com**
Varmint Hunters Assoc.: **www.varminthunter.org**
U.S. Sportsmen's Alliance: **www.ussportsmen.org**
Winchester Arms Collectors Assoc.: **www.winchestercollector.com**
Women Hunters: **www.womanhunters.com**
Women's Shooting Sports Foundation: **www.wssf.org**

Stocks, Grips, Forearms

Ace, Ltd.: **www.aceltdusa.com**
Advanced Technology: **www.atigunstocks.com**
Battenfeld Technologies: **www.battenfeldtechnologies.com**
Bell & Carlson, Inc.: **www.bellandcarlson.com**
Boyd's Gunstock Industries, Inc.: **www.boydgunstocks.com**
Butler Creek Corp: **www.butler-creek.com**
Cadex: **www.vikingtactics.com**
Calico Hardwoods, Inc.: **www.calicohardwoods.com**
Choate Machine: **www.riflestock.com**
Command Arms: **www.commandarms.com**
C-More Systems: **www.cmore.com**
D&L Sports: **www.dlsports.com**
Duo Stock: **www.duostock.com**
Elk Ridge Stocks: **www.reamerrentals.com/elk_ridge.htm**
FAB Tactical: **www.botachtactical.com**
Fajen: **www.battenfeldtechnologies.com**
Falcon Ergo Grip: **www.ERGOGRIPS.COM**
Great American Gunstocks: **www.gunstocks.com**
Grip Pod: **www.grippod.com**
Gun Stock Blanks: **www.gunstockblanks.com**
Herrett's Stocks: **www.herrettstocks.com**
High Tech Specialties: **www.bansnersrifle.com/hightech**
Hogue Grips: **www.getgrip.com**
Holland's Shooting Supplies: **www.hollandgun.com**
Knight's Mfg. Co.: **wwwknightarmco.com**
Knoxx Industries: **www.blackhawk.com**
KZ Tactical: **www.kleyzion.com**
LaRue Tactical: **www.laruetactical.com**
Lewis Machine & Tool: **www.lewismachine.net**
Lone Wolf: **www.lonewolfriflestocks.com**

Magpul: **www.magpul.com**
McMillan Fiberglass Stocks: **www.mcmfamily.com**
MPI Stocks: **www.mpistocks.com**
Precision Gun Works: **www.precisiongunstocks.com**
Ram-Line: **www.outers-guncare.com**
Richards Microfit Stocks: **www.rifle-stocks.com**
Rimrock Rifle Stock: **www.rimrockstocks.com**
Royal Arms Gunstocks: **www.imt.net/~royalarms**
S&K Industries: **www.sandkgunstocks.com**
Speedfeed, Inc.: **www.speedfeedinc.com**
TacStar/Pachmayr: **www.tacstar.com**
Tango Down: **www.tangodown.com**
TAPCO: **www.tapco.com**
Surefire: **www.surefire.com**
Tiger-Hunt Curly Maple Gunstocks: **www.gunstockwood.com**
Vltor: **www.vltor.com**
Wenig Custom Gunstocks Inc.: **www.wenig.com**
Wilcox Industries: **www.wilcoxind.com**
Yankee Hill: **www.yhm.net**

Targets and Range Equipment

Action Target Co.: **www.actiontarget.com**
Advanced Interactive Systems: **www.ais-sim.com**
Birchwood Casey: **www.birchwoodcasey.com**
Bullet Proof Electronics: **www.thesnipertarget.com**
Caswell Meggitt Defense Systems: **www.mds-caswell.com**
Champion Traps & Targets: **www.championtarget.com**
Handloader/Victory Targets: **www.targetshandloader.com**
Just Shoot Me Products: **www.ballistictec.com**
Laser Shot: **www.lasershot.com**
Mountain Plains Industries: **www.targetshandloader.com**
MTM Products: **www.mtmcase-gard.com**
Natiional Target Co.: **www.nationaltarget.com**
Newbold Target Systems: **www.newboldtargets.com**
Porta Target,Inc.: **www.portatarget.com**
Range Management Services Inc.: **www.casewellintl.com**
Range Systems: **www.shootingrangeproducts.com**
ShatterBlast Targets: **www.daisy.com**
Super Trap Bullet Containment Systems: **www.supertrap.com**
Thompson Target Technology: **www.thompsontarget.com**
Tombstone Tactical Targets: **www.tttargets.com**
Visible Impact Targets: **www.crosman.com**
White Flyer: **www.whiteflyer.com**

Trap and Skeet Shooting Equipment and Accessories

Auto-Sporter Industries: **www.auto-sporter.com**
10X Products Group: **www.10Xwear.com**
Claymaster Traps: **www.claymaster.com**
Do-All Traps, Inc.: **www.doalloutdoors.com**
Laporte USA: **www.laporte-shooting.com**
Outers: **www.blount.com**
Trius Products Inc.: **www.triustraps.com**
White Flyer: **www.whiteflyer.com**

Triggers

American Trigger Corp.: **www.americantrigger.com**
Brownells: **www.brownells.com**
Chip McCormick Corp.: **www.chipmccormickcorp.com**
Huber Concepts: **www.huberconcepts.com**
Kidd Triggers.: **www.coolguyguns.com**
Shilen: **www.shilen.com**
Timney Triggers: **www.timneytrigger.com**
Williams Trigger Specialties: **www.williamstriggers.com**

Major Shooting Websites and Links

24 Hour Campfire: **www.24hourcampfire.com**
Alphabetic Index of Links: **www.gunsgunsguns.com**
Auction Arms: **www.auctionarms.com**
Benchrest Central: **www.benchrest.com**
Big Game Hunt: **www.biggamehunt.net**
Bullseye Pistol: **www.bullseyepistol.com**
Firearms History: **www.researchpress.co.uk/firearms**
Glock Talk: **www.glocktalk.com**
Gun Broker Auctions: **www.gunbroker.com**
Gun Industry: **www.gunindustry.com**
Gun Blast: **www.gunblast.com**
Gun Boards: **www.gunboards.com**
GunsAmerica.com: **www.gunsamerica.com**
Guns Unified Nationally Endorsing Dignity: **www.guned.com**
Gun Shop Finder: **www.gunshopfinder.com**
GUNS and Hunting: **www.gunsandhunting.com**
Hunt and Shoot (NSSF): **www.huntandshoot.org**
Keep and Bear Arms: **www.keepandbeararms.com**
Leverguns: **www.leverguns.com**
Load Swap: **www.loadswap.com**
Outdoor Press Room: **www.outdoorpressroom.com**
Real Guns: **www.realguns.com**
Ruger Forum: **www.rugerforum.com**
SavageShooters: **www.savageshooters.com**
Shooters Forum: **www.shootersforum.com**
Shotgun Sports Resource Guide: **www.shotgunsports.com**
Sixgunner: **www.sixgunner.com**
Sniper's Hide: **www.snipershide.com**
Sportsman's Web: **www.sportsmansweb.com**
Surplus Rifles: **www.surplusrifle.com**
Tactical-Life: **www.tactical-life.com**
Wing Shoooting USA: **www.wingshootingusa.org**

FOR COLLECTOR • HUNTER • SHOOTER • OUTDOORSMAN
IMPORTANT NOTICE TO BOOK BUYERS

Books listed here may be bought from Ray Riling Arms Books Co., 6844 Gorsten St., Philadelphia, PA 19119, Phone 215-438-2456; FAX: 215-438-5395. E-mail: sales@rayrilingarmsbooks.com. Larry Riling is the researcher and compiler of "The Arms Library" and a seller of gun books for over 65 years. The Riling stock includes books classic and modern, many hard-to-find items, and many not obtainable elsewhere. These pages list a portion of the current stock. They offer prompt, complete service, with delayed shipments occurring only on out-of-print or out-of-stock books.

Visit our Web site at www.rayrilingarmsbooks.com and order all of your favorite titles online from our secure site.

NOTICE FOR ALL CUSTOMERS: Remittance in U.S. funds must accompany all orders. For your convenience we accept VISA, MasterCard, Discover & American Express. For shipments in the U.S., add $7.00 for the 1st book and $2.00 for each additional book for postage and insurance. Minimum order $10.00. International Orders add $13.00 for the 1st book and $5.00 for each additional book. All International orders are shipped at the buyer's risk unless an additional $5 for insurance is included. USPS does not offer insurance to all countries unless shipped Air-Mail. Please e-mail or call for pricing.

Payments in excess of order or for "Backorders" are credited or fully refunded at request. Books "As-Ordered" are not returnable except by permission and a handling charge on these of 10% or $2.00 per book, whichever is greater, is deducted from refund or credit. Only Pennsylvania customers must include current sales tax.

A full variety of arms books also available from Rutgers Book Center, 127 Raritan Ave., Highland Park, NJ 08904/732-545-4344; FAX: 732-545-6686 or I.D.S.A. Books, 3220 E. Galbraith Rd., Cincinnati, OH 45236. Email IDSABooks@IDSABooks.com; www.IDSABooks.com.

BALLISTICS AND HANDLOADING

ABC's of Reloading, 7th Edition, by Bill Chevalier, Iola, WI, Krause Publications, 2005. 288 pp., illustrated with 550 b&w photos. Softcover. $21.95

American Cartridge, The, by Charles Suydam, Borden Publishing Co. Alhambra, CA, 1986. 184 pp., illus. Softcover $24.95
An illustrated study of the rimfire cartridge in the United States.

Ammo and Ballistics II, by Robert W. Forker, Safari Press, Inc., Huntington Beach, CA, 2002. 298 pp., illus. Paper covers. $19.95
Ballistic data on 125 calibers and 1,400 loads out to 500 yards.

Barnes Bullets Reloading Manual Number 3, Barnes Bullets, American Fork, UT, 2003. 668 pp., illus. $29.95
Features data and trajectories on the new weight X, XBT and Solids in calibers from .22 to .50 BMG.

Black Powder, Pig Lead and Steel Silhouettes, by Paul A. Matthews, Prescott, AZ, Wolfe Publishing, 2002. 132 pp., illustrated with b&w photographs and detailed drawings and diagrams. Softcover. $16.95

Cartridge Reloading Tools of the Past, by R.H. Chamberlain, and Tom Quigley, Castle Rock, WA, 1998. 167 pp., illus. Paper covers. $25.00
A detailed treatment of the extensive Winchester and ideal line of handloading tools and bullet molds, plus Remington, Marlin, Ballard, Browning, Maynard, and many others.

Cast Bullets for the Black Powder Rifle, by Paul A. Matthews, Wolfe Publishing Co., Prescott, AZ, 1996. 133 pp., illus. Paper covers. $22.50
The tools and techniques used to make your cast bullet shooting a success.

Complete Blackpowder Handbook, 5th Edition, by Sam Fadala, DBI Books, a division of Krause Publications, Iola, WI, 2006. 448 pages, with over 650 b&w photos. Paper covers. $26.95
More than 650 detailed photos illustrating new gear and demonstrating effective techniques. Written for every blackpowder enthusiast-hunters, war re-enactors, collectors, cowboy action shooters, target shooters and DIY blackpowder hobbyists.

Complete Reloading Manual, One Book / One Caliber, CA, Load Books USA, 2000. $7.95 each
Contains unabridged information from U.S. bullet and powder makers. With thousands of proven and tested loads, plus dozens of various bullet designs and different powders. Spiral bound. Available in all calibers.

Designing and Forming Custom Cartridges for Rifles and Handguns, by Ken Howell. Precision Shooting, Manchester, CT. 2002. 600 pp., illus. $59.95
The classic work in its field, out of print for the last few years and virtually unobtainable on the used book market, now returns in an exact reprint of the original. Full size (8½" x 11"), hardcovers. Dozens of cartridge drawings never published anywhere before–dozens you've never heard of (guaranteed!). Precisely drawn to the dimensions specified by the men who designed them, the factories that made them, and the authorities that set the standards. All drawn to the same format and scale (1.5x) for most, how to form them from brass. Other practical information included.

Early Gunpowder Artillery 1300-1600 by John Norris, London, The Crowood Press, 2003. 1st edition. 141 pp., with 160 b&w photos. Hardcover. New in new dust jacket. $34.95

Early Loading Tools & Bullet Molds, Pioneer Press, 1988. 88 pp., illus. Softcover. $7.50

Handbook for Shooters and Reloaders, by P.O. Ackley, Salt Lake City, UT, 1998, (Vol. I), 567 pp., illus. Includes a separate exterior ballistics chart. $24.95; (Vol. II), a new printing with specific new material. 495 pp., illus. $21.95

Handgun Stopping Power; The Definitive Study, by Marshall & Sandow. Boulder, CO, Paladin Press, 1992. 240 pp. $45.00
Offers accurate predictions of the stopping power of specific loads in calibers from 380 Auto to 45 ACP, as well as such specialty rounds as the Glaser Safety Slug, Federal Hydra-Shok, MagSafe, etc. This is the definitive methodology for predicting the stopping power of handgun loads, the first to take into account what really happens when a bullet meets a man.

Handloader's Digest: 18th Edition edited by Ken Ramage, Iola, WI, Krause Publications, 2003. 300 b&w photos, 256 pp. Softcover. $19.95

Handloader's Manual of Cartridge Conversions, Revised 3rd edition, by John Donnelly, and Bryce Towsley, Accokeek, MD, Stoeger Publications, 2004. 609pp, Hardcover. NEW $39.95

Over 900 cartridges described in detail, complete with dimensions, and accurate drawings. Includes case capacities and all physical data.

Hatcher's Notebook, by S. Julian Hatcher, Stackpole Books, Harrisburg, PA, 1992. 488 pp., illus. $39.95
A reference work for shooters, gunsmiths, ballisticians, historians, hunters and collectors.

Headstamped Cartridges and Their Variations; Volume 1, by Daniel L. Shuey, W.R.A. Co., Rockford, IL, WCF Publications, 2003. 351 pp. illustrated with b&w photos. Hardcover. $55.00

Headstamped Cartridges and Their Variations; Volume 2, by Daniel L. Shuey, W.R.A. Co., Rockford, IL, WCF Publications, 2003. 351 pp. illustrated with b&w photos. Hardcover. $55.00

History & Development of Small Arms Ammunition, Volume 1, Second Edition–With A Value Guide, Martial Long Arms, Flintlock through Rimfire, by George A. Hoyem, Missoula, MI, Armory Publications, 2005. Hardcover. New in new dust jacket. $60.00

Hornady Handbook of Cartridge Reloading, 7th Edition, edited by Larry Steadman, Hornady Mfg. Co., Grand Island, NE, 2007, 978 pages, illus. $44.95
This completely revised and updated manual contains load data for almost every cartridge available, including the latest developments like the 204 Ruger and 500 S&W. Includes tips on basic reloading, rifle and handgun load data and an illustrated glossary.

How-To's for the Black Powder Cartridge Rifle Shooter, by Paul A. Matthews, Wolfe Publishing Co., Prescott, AZ, 1995. 45 pp. Paper covers. $22.50
Covers lube recipes, good bore cleaners and over-powder wads. Tips include compressing powder charges, combating wind resistance, improving ignition and much more.

Loading the Black Powder Rifle Cartridge, by Paul A. Matthews, Wolfe Publishing Co., Prescott, AZ, 1993. 121 pp., illus. Paper covers. $22.50
Author Matthews brings the blackpowder cartridge shooter valuable information on the basics, including cartridge care, lubes and moulds, powder charges and developing and testing loads in his usual authoritative style.

Lyman 48th Reloading Handbook, No. 48. Connecticut, Lan Publishing Corporation, 2003. 48th edition. 480 pp. Softcover. $26.95

Lyman Cast Bullet Handbook, 3rd Edition, edited by C. Kenneth Ramage, Lyman Publications, Middlefield, CT, 1980. 416 pp., illus. Paper covers. $19.95
Information on more than 5000 tested cast bullet loads and 19 pages of trajectory and wind drift tables for cast bullets.

Lyman Black Powder Handbook, 2nd Edition, edited by Sam Fadala, Lyman Products for Shooters, Middlefield, CT, 2000. 239 pp., illus. Paper covers. $19.95
Comprehensive load information for the modern blackpowder shooter.

Lyman Shotshell Handbook, 5th Edition, edited by Edward A. Matunas, Lyman Products Co., Middlefield, CT, 2007. 330 pp., illus. Paper covers. $25.95
This new 5th edition covers cases, wads and primers currently offered by all leading manufacturers in all gauges from .410 to 10 gauge. In addition, the latest and also the most popular powders from Alliant, Hodgdon, Accurate, IMR, VihtaVuori, Ramshot, Winchester are included.

Make It Accurate-Get the Maximum Performance from Your Hunting Rifle, by Craig Boddington, Long Beach, CA, Safari Press, 1999. Hardcover. New in new dust jacket. $24.95

Metallic Cartridge Conversions: The History of the Guns and Modern Reproductions, by Dennis Adler, Foreword by R. L. Wilson, Iola, WI, Krause Publications, 2003. 1st edition. 208 pp. 250 color photos. Hardcover. New in new dust jacket. $39.95

Modern Exterior Ballistics, by Robert L. McCoy, Schiffer Publishing Co., Atglen, PA, 1999. 128 pp. $95.00
Advanced students of exterior ballistics and flight dynamics will find this comprehensive textbook on the subject a useful addition to their libraries.

Modern Reloading 2nd Edition, by Richard Lee, Inland Press, 2003. 623 pp., illus. $29.95
The how-to's of rifle, pistol and shotgun reloading plus load data for rifle and pistol calibers.

Mr. Single Shot's Cartridge Handbook, by Frank de Haas, Mark de Haas, Orange City, IA, 1996. 116 pp., illus. Paper covers. $22.50
This book covers most of the cartridges, both commercial and wildcat, that the author has known and used.

Norma Reloading Manual, by Norma Precision AB, 2004, 1st edition. Data for over 2,000 loads in 73 calibers. 432pp, hardcover, $34.95

Nosler Reloading Manual #5, edited by Gail Root, Nosler Bullets, Inc., Bend, OR, 2002. 516 pp., illus. $29.99
Combines information on their ballistic tip, partition and handgun bullets with traditional powders and new powders never before used, plus trajectory information from 100 to 500 yards.

Reloading for Shotgunners, 4th Edition, by Kurt D. Fackler, and M.L. McPherson, DBI Books, a division of Krause Publications, Iola, WI, 1997. 320 pp., illus. Paper covers. $19.95
Expanded reloading tables with over 11,000 loads. Bushing charts for every major press and component maker. All new presentation on all aspects of shotshell reloading by two of the top experts in the field.

Reloading Tools, Sights and Telescopes for S/S Rifles, by Gerald O. Kelver, Brighton, CO, 1982. 163 pp., illus. Softcover. $15.00
A listing of most of the famous makers of reloading tools, sights and telescopes with a brief description of the products they manufactured.

Rimfire Cartridge in the United States and Canada, Illustrated History of Rimfire Cartridges, Manufacturers, and the Products Made from 1857-1984, by John L. Barber, Thomas Publications, Gettysburg, PA 2000. 1st edition. Profusely illus. 221 pp. $50.00
The author has written an encyclopedia of rimfire cartridges from the 22 to the massive 1.00 in. Gatling. Fourteen chapters, six appendices and an excellent bibliography.

Round Ball to Rimfire: Civil War Small Arms Ammunition, Vol. 1, by Dean S. Thomas, Gettysburg, PA, Thomas Publications, 2003. 344 pp. Hardcover. $40.00
Federal Ordnance Dept., Arsenals, Smoothbores & Rifle Muskets. Detailed information on the Ordnance Department, Northern arsenals, patents, designers, & manufacturers of Federal musket ammunition.

Round Ball to Rimfire: Civil War Small Arms Ammunition, Vol. 2, by Dean S. Thomas, Gettysburg, PA, Thomas Publications, 2004. 528 pp. Hardcover. $49.95
Federal Breechloading Carbines and Rifles. Federal carbine and rifle ammunition. Detailed information on patents, designers, & manufacturers of Federal breechloaders and their ammunition.

Round Ball to Rimfire: Civil War Small Arms Ammunition, Vol. 3, by Dean S. Thomas, Gettysburg, PA, Thomas Publications, 2005. 488 pp. Hardcover. $49.95
Federal pistols, revolvers and miscellaneous essays. Detailed information on patents, designers, & manufacturers. Miscellaneous essays wrap-up the Northern side of the story.

Shotshells & Ballistics, Safari Press, 2002. 275 pp., photos. Softcover, $19.95
Accentuated with photos from the field and the range, this is a reference book unlike any other.

Sierra Reloading Manual, 5th Edition: Rifle and Handgun Manual of Reloading Data. Sedalia, MO, Sierra Bullets, 2003. Hardcover. $39.95

Speer Reloading Manual No. 13, edited by members of the Speer research staff, Omark Industries, Lewiston, ID, 1999. 621 pp., illus. $29.95
With 13 new sections containing the latest technical information and reloading trends for both novice and expert in this latest edition. More than 9,300 loads are listed, including new propellant powders from Accurate Arms, Alliant, Hodgdon and Vihtavuori.

Stopping Power: A Practical Analysis of the Latest Handgun Ammunition, by Marshall & Sanow, Paladin Press, 2002. 600+ photos, 360 pp. Softcover, $49.95
Stopping Power bases its conclusions on real-world facts from real-world gunfights. It provides the latest street results of actual police and civilian shootings in all of the major handgun calibers, from 22 LR to 45 ACP, plus more than 30 chapters of vital interest to all gun owners.

Street Stoppers, The Latest Handgun Stopping Power Street Results, by Marshall & Lanow, Boulder, CO, Paladin Press, 1996. 374 pp., illus. Softcover. $42.95
Street Stoppers is the long-awaited sequel to *Handgun Stopping Power.* It provides the latest results of real-life shootings in all of the major handgun calibers, plus more than 25 thought-provoking chapters that are vital to anyone interested in firearms, wound ballistics, and combat shooting. This book also covers the street results of the hottest new caliber to hit the shooting world in years, the 40 Smith & Wesson, plus updated street results of the latest exotic ammunition.

Understanding Firearm Ballistics, 6th Edition, by Robert A. Rinker, Mulberry House Corydon, IN, 2005. 437 pp., illus. Paper covers. New, revised and expanded. $24.95
Explains basic to advanced firearm ballistics in understandable terms.

Why Not Load Your Own?, by Col. T. Whelen, Gun Room Press, Highland Park, NJ 1996, 4th ed., rev. 237 pp., illus. $20.00
A basic reference on handloading, describing each step, materials and equipment. Includes loads for popular cartridges.

Wildcat Cartridges, "Reloader's Handbook of Wildcat Cartridge Design", by Fred Zeglin, privately printed, 2005. 1st edition. 287 Pages, Hard back book. Forward by Wayne van Zwoll. Pictorial Hardcover. $39.95
Twenty-two chapters cover wildcatting from every possible angle. History, dimensions, load data, and how to make or use reloading tool and reamers. If you're interested in reloading or wildcatting this is a must have book.

Wildcat Cartridges Volumes 1 & 2 Combination, by the editors of *Handloaders* magazine, Wolfe Publishing Co., Prescott, AZ, 1997. 350 pp., illus. Paper covers. $39.95
A profile of the most popular information on wildcat cartridges that appeared in the *Handloaders* magazine.

W.R.A. Co.; Headstamped Cartridges and their Variations; Volume 1, by Daniel Shuey, Rockford, IL, WCF Publications, 2001. 298pp illustrated with b&w photos, Hardcover, $55.00

W.R.A. Co.; Headstamped Cartridges and their Variations; Volume 2, by Daniel Shuey, Rockford, IL, WCF Publications, 2003. 351pp illustrated with b&w photos, Hardcover, $50.00

COLLECTORS

1 October 1934 SS Dienstalterliste, by the Ulric of England Research Unit San Jose, CA, R. James Bender Publishing, 1994. Reprint softcover. $29.95

10. Panzer Division: In Action in the East, West and North Africa 1939-1943, by Jean Resta and N. Moller, Canada, J.J. Fedorowicz Publishing Inc., 2003. 1st edition. Hardcover. $89.95

18th Century Weapons of the Royal Welsh Fuziliers from Flixton Hall, by Erik Goldstein, Thomas Publications, Gettysburg, PA, 2002. 1st edition. 126 pp., illustrated with b&w photos. Softcover. $19.95

.45-70 Springfield Book I, by Albert Frasca and Robert Hill, Frasca Publishing, 2000. Memorial edition. Hardback with gold embossed cover and spine. $95.00
The Memorial edition reprint of the .45-70 Springfield was done to honor Robert H. Hill who was an outstanding Springfield collector, historian, researcher, and gunsmith. Only 1,000 of these highly regarded books were printed, using the same binding and cover material as the original 1980 edition. The book is considered the bible for 45-70 Springfield Trapdoor collectors.

.45-70 Springfield Book II 1865-1893, by Albert Frasca, Frasca Publishing, Springfield, Ohio 1997, 400+ pp. and 400+ photographs which cover ALL the trapdoor Springfield models. Hardback with gold embossed cover and spine. A MUST for the trapdoor collector! $85.00

.45-70 Springfield 4th Ed. Revised & Expanded, The, by Joe Poyer and Craig Riesch, North Cape Publications, Tustin, CA, 2006. 274 pp., illus. Paper covers. $19.95
Every part and every change to that part made by the Ordnance Department is described in photos and drawings. Dimensions and finishes are listed for each part in both the text and tables.

'51 Colt Navies, by Nathan L. Swayze, The Gun Room Press, Highland Park, NJ, 1993. 243 pp., illus. $59.95
The Model 1851 Colt Navy, its variations and markings.

1862 U.S. Cavalry Tactics, by Philip St. George Cooke, Mechanicsburg, PA, Stackpole Books, 2004. 416 pp. Hardcover. New in new dust jacket. $19.89

A Collector's Guide to the '03 Springfield, by Bruce N. Canfield, Andrew Mowbray Inc., Lincoln, RI, 2004. 160 pp., illus. Paper covers. $22.00
A comprehensive guide follows the '03 through its unparalleled tenure of service. Covers all of the interesting variations, modifications and accessories of this highly collectible military rifle.

An Illustrated Guide To The '03 Springfield Service Rifle, by Bruce N. Canfield Andrew Mowbray, Inc., Pictorial Hardcover 2005. $49.95
Your ultimate guide to the military '03 Springfield! Three times as large as the author's previous best selling book on this topic. Covers all models, all manufacturers and all conflicts, including WWI, WWII and beyond. Heavily illustrated. Serial number tables, combat photos, sniper rifles and more! 240 pages, illustrated with over 450 photos.

Complete Guide To The United States Military Combat Shotguns, by Bruce N. Canfield Andrew Mowbray, Inc., 2007. 1st edition. 312 Pages. $49.95
From the famed Winchester M97 to the Mossberg and beyond! Expanded and updated covereage of American combat shotguns with three times the information found in the author's pervious best-selling book on this topic. Hundreds of detailed photographs show you the specific features that you need to recognize in order to identify fakes and assembled guns. Special, in-depth historical coverage of WWI, WWII, Korea, Vietnam and Iraq!

A Collector's Guide to United States Combat Shotguns, by Bruce N. Canfield, Andrew Mowbray Inc., Lincoln, RI, 1992. 184 pp., illus. Paper covers. $24.00
This book provides full coverage of combat shotguns, from the earliest examples right up to the Gulf War and beyond.

A Collector's Guide to Winchester in the Service, by Bruce N. Canfield, Andrew Mowbray, Inc., Lincoln, RI, 1991. 192 pp., illus. Paper covers. $24.00
The firearms produced by Winchester for the national defense. From Hotchkiss to the M14, each firearm is examined and illustrated.

A Concise Guide to the Artillery at Gettysburg, by Gregory Coco, Thomas Publications, Gettysburg, PA, 1998. 96 pp., illus. Paper covers. $10.00
Coco's book on Gettysburg is a beginner's guide to artillery and its use at the battle. It covers the artillery batteries, describing the types of cannons, shells, fuses, etc. using interesting narrative and human interest stories.

A Glossary of the Construction, Decoration and Use of Arms and Armor in All Countries and in All Times, by George Cameron Stone, Dover Publishing, New York 1999. Softcover. $39.95
An exhaustive study of arms and armor in all countries through recorded history-from the Stone Age up to WWII. With over 4,500 b&w illustrations, this Dover edition is an unabridged republication of the work originally published in 1934 by the Southworth Press, Portland, MA. A new Introduction has been specially prepared for this edition.

A Guide to American Trade Catalogs 1744-1900, by Lawrence B. Romaine, Dover Publications, New York, NY. 422 pp., illus. Paper covers. $12.95

A Guide to Ballard Breechloaders, by George J. Layman, Pioneer Press, Union City, TN, 1997. 261 pp., illus. Paper covers. $19.95
Documents the saga of this fine rifle from the first models made by Ball & Williams of Worchester, to its production by the Marlin Firearms Co., to the cessation of 19th century manufacture in 1891, and finally to the modern reproductions made in the 1990s.

A Guide to the Maynard Breechloader, by George J. Layman, George J. Layman, Ayer, MA, 1993. 125 pp., illus. Paper covers. $14.95
The first book dedicated entirely to the Maynard family of breech-loading firearms. Coverage of the arms is given from the 1850s through the 1880s.

A Guide to U.S. Army Dress Helmets 1872-1904, by Kasal and Moore, North Cape Publications, 2000. 88 pp., illus. Paper covers. $15.95
This thorough study provides a complete description of the Model 1872 and 1881 dress helmets worn by the U.S. Army.

A Study of Remington's Smoot Patent and Number Four Revolvers, by Parker Harry, Parker Ora Lee, and Joan Reisch, Foreword by Roy M. Marcot, Santa Ana, CA, Armslore Press, Graphic Publishers, 2003. 1st edition. 120 pp., profusely illus., plus 8-page color section. Softcover. $17.95
A detailed, pictorial essay on Remington's early metallic cartridge-era pocket revolvers: their design, development, patents, models, identification and variations. Includes the biography of arms inventor Wm. S. Smoot, as well as a mini-history of the Remington Arms Company.

Accoutrements of the United States Infantry, Riflemen, and Dragoons 1834-1839, by R.T. Huntington, Historical Arms Series No. 20. Canada, Museum Restoration. 58 pp. illus. Softcover. $8.95

Although the 1841 edition of the U.S. Ordnance Manual provides ample information on the equipment that was in use during the 1840s, it is evident that the patterns of equipment that it describes were not introduced until 1838 or 1839. This guide is intended to fill this gap in our knowledge by providing an overview of what we now know about the accoutrements that were issued to the regular infantryman, rifleman, and dragoon, in the 1830s with excursions into earlier and later years.

Ackermann Military Prints: Uniforms of the British and Indian Armies 1840-1855, by William Y. Carman with Robert W. Kenny Jr., Schiffer Publications, Atglen, PA, 2002. 1st edition. 176 pp., with over 160 color images. $69.95

Afrikakorps: Rommel's Tropical Army in Original Color, by Bernd Peitz, Gary Wilkins. Atglen, PA, Schiffer Publications, 2004. 1st edition. 192 pp., with over 200 color and b&w photographs. Hardcover. New in new dust jacket. $59.95

Air Guns, by Eldon G. Wolff, Duckett's Publishing Co., Tempe, AZ, 1997. 204 pp., illus. Paper covers. $35.00

Historical reference covering many makers, European and American guns, canes and more.

All About Southerners, by Lionel J. Bogut, White Star, Inc., 2002. A limited edition of 1,000 copies. Signed and numbered. 114 pp., including bibliography, and plenty of b&w photographs and detailed drawings. Hardcover. $29.95

Detailed look at the characteristics and design of the "Best Little Pistol in the World."

Allgemeine-SS The Commands, Units and Leaders of the General SS, by Mark C. Yerger, Atglen, PA, Schiffer Publications, 1997. 1st edition. Hardcover. New in new dust jacket. $49.95

Allied and Enemy Aircraft: May 1918; Not to be Taken from the Front Lines, Historical Arms Series No. 27. Canada, Museum Restoration. Softcover. $8.95

The basis for this title is a very rare identification manual published by the French government in 1918 that illustrated 60 aircraft with three or more views: French, English American, German, Italian, and Belgian, which might have been seen over the trenches of France. Each is described in a text translated from the original French. This is probably the most complete collection of illustrations of WWI aircraft that has survived.

American Beauty; The Prewar Colt National Match Government Model Pistol, by Timothy J. Mullin, Collector Grade Publications, Cobourg, Ontario, Canada. 72 pp., illus. $34.95

Includes over 150 serial numbers, and 20 spectacular color photos of factory engraved guns and other authenticated upgrades, including rare "double-carved" ivory grips.

American Civil War Artillery 1861-65: Field Artillery, by Philip Oxford Katcher, United Kingdom, Osprey Publishing, 2001. 1st edition. 48 pp. Softcover. $14.95

Perhaps the most influential arm of either army in the prosecution of the American Civil War, the artillery of both sides grew to be highly professional organizations. This book covers all the major artillery pieces employed, including the Napoleon, Parrott Rifle and Mountain Howitzer.

American Military and Naval Belts, 1812-1902, by R. Stephen Dorsey, Eugene, OR, Collectors Library, 2002. 1st edition. Hardcover. $80.00

With introduction by Norm Flayderman, this massive work is the NEW key reference on sword belts, waist belts, sabre belts, shoulder belts and cartridge belts (looped and non-looped). At over 460 pp., this 8½" x 11" book offers over 840 photos (primarily in color) and original period drawings. In addition, this work offers the first, comprehensive research on the Anson Mills woven cartridge belts, the belt-related patents and the government contracts from 1880 through 1902. This book is a "must" for all accoutrements collectors, military historians and museums.

American Military Headgear Insignia, by Michael J. O'Donnell and J. Duncan, Campbell, Alexandria, VA, O'Donnell Publishing, 2004. 1st edition. 311 pp., 703 photo figures, 4 sketches. Hardcover. New in new dust jacket. $89.95

American Military Saddle, 1776-1945, The, by R. Stephen Dorsey and Kenneth L. McPheeters, Collector's Library, Eugene, OR, 1999. 400 pp., illus. $67.00

The most complete coverage of the subject ever written on the American Military Saddle. Nearly 1,000 actual photos and official drawings, from the major public and private collections in the U.S. and Great Britain.

American Police Collectibles; Dark Lanterns and Other Curious Devices, by Matthew G. Forte, Turn of the Century Publishers, Upper Montclair, NJ, 1999. 248 pp., illus. $24.95

For collectors of police memorabilia (handcuffs, police dark lanterns, mechanical and chain nippers, rattles, billy clubs and nightsticks) and police historians.

American Thunder II: The Military Thompson Submachine Guns, by Frank Iannamico, Harmony, ME, Moose Lake Publishing, 2004, 2nd edition. Many great photographs that show detail markings and features of the various models, as well as vintage WW11 photographs showing the Thompson in action. 536 pages, Soft cover, $29.95

An Introduction to the Civil War Small Arms, by Earl J. Coates and Dean S. Thomas, Thomas Publishing Co., Gettysburg, PA, 1990. 96 pp., illus. Paper covers. $10.00

The small arms carried by the individual soldier during the Civil War.

Arming the Glorious Cause; Weapons of the Second War for Independence, by James B. Whisker, Daniel D. Hartzler and Larry W. Tantz, Old Bedford Village Press, Bedford, PA., 1998. 175 pp., illus. $45.00

A photographic study of Confederate weapons.

Arms & Accoutrements of the Mounted Police 1873-1973, by Roger F. Phillips, and Donald J. Klancher, Museum Restoration Service, Ont., Canada, 1982. 224 pp., illus. $49.95 Also, available in paperback, $29.95

A definitive history of the revolvers, rifles, machine guns, cannons, ammunition, swords, etc. used by the NWMP, the RNWMP and the RCMP during the first 100 years of the Force.

Arms and Armor in Colonial America 1526-1783, by Harold Peterson, Dover Publishing, New York, 2000. 350 pp. with over 300 illustrations, index, bibliography and appendix. Softcover. $34.95

Over 200 years of firearms, ammunition, equipment and edged weapons.

Arms and Armor in the Art Institute of Chicago, by Waltler J. Karcheski, Bulfinch, New York 1999. 128 pp., 103 color photos, 12 b&w illustrations. $50.00

The George F. Harding Collection of arms and armor is the most visited installation at the Art Institute of Chicago–a testament to the enduring appeal of swords, muskets and the other paraphernalia of medieval and early modern war. Organized both chronologically and by type of weapon, this book captures the best of this astonishing collection in 115 striking photographs-most in color–accompanied by illuminating text.

Arms Makers of Western Pennsylvania, by James B. Whisker, Old Bedford Village Press. 1st edition. Deluxe hardbound edition, 176 pp., $50.00

Printed on fine coated paper with many large photographs and detailed text describing the period, lives, tools, and artistry of the Arms Makers of Western Pennsylvania.

Arsenal of Freedom: The Springfield Armory 1890-1948, by Lt. Col. William Brophy, Andrew Mowbray, Inc., Lincoln, RI,1997. 20 pgs. of photos. 400 pp. As new, Softcover. $29.95

A year-by-year account drawn from offical records. Reports, charts, tables and line drawings.

Art of Remington Arms, by Tom Davis, Sporting Classics, 2004, 1st edition. Large format book, featuring 200 paintings by Remington Arms over the years on it's calendars, posters, shell boxes, etc. 50 full-color by Bob Kuhn alone. Hardcover. NEW $54.95

Astra Automatic Pistols, by Leonardo M. Antaris, FIRAC Publishing Co., Sterling, CO, 1989. 248 pp., illus. $55.00

Charts, tables, serial ranges, etc. The definitive work on Astra pistols.

Ballard: The Great American Single Shot Rifle, by John T. Dutcher. Denver, CO, privately printed, 2002. 1st edition. 380 pp., illustrated with b&w photos, with 8-page color insert. Hardcover. New in new dust jacket. $79.95

Basic Documents on U.S. Martial Arms, commentary by Col. B.R. Lewis, reissue by Ray Riling, Phila., PA, 1956 and 1960. Rifle Musket Model 1855. Each $10.00

The first issue rifle of musket caliber, a muzzleloader equipped with the Maynard Primer, 32 pp. Rifle Musket Model 1863. The typical Union muzzleloader of the Civil War, 26 pp. Breech-Loading Rifle Musket Model 1866. The first of our 50-caliber breechloading rifles, 12 pp. Remington Navy Rifle Model 1870. A commercial type breech-loader made at Springfield, 16 pp. Lee Straight Pull Navy Rifle Model 1895. A magazine cartridge arm of 6mm caliber, 23 pp. Breech-Loading Arms (five models) 27 pp. Ward-Burton Rifle Musket 1871, 16 pp.

Battle Colors: Insignia and Aircraft Markings of the Eighth Air Force in World War II, by Robert A. Watkins, Atglen, PA, Schiffer Publications, 2004. Hardcover. $45.00

This book is an invaluable tool for anyone with an interest in the history of the U.S. Eighth Air Force in World War II. 128 pages, with over 500 color illustrations.

Battle Colors: Insignia and Aircraft Markings of the Eighth Air Force in World War II, Vol. 2, by Robert A. Watkins, Atglen, PA, Schiffer Publications, 2006. $45.00

This work includes diagrams showing approved specifications for the size and placement of all versions of the U.S. insignia as applied to USAAF P-38, P-47 and P-51 fighter aircraft. Also included are all unit airfield location maps and order-of-battle charts for all combat air elements assigned to the 8th AAF from June 1942 through June 1945. 144 pages, with over 600 color profiles, insignia, photographs, and maps. Hardcover

Battle Weapons of the American Revolution, by George C. Neuman, Scurlock Publishing Co., Texarkana, TX, 2001. 400 pp. Illus. Softcovers. $44.95

The most extensive photographic collection of Revolutionary War weapons ever in one volume. More than 1,600 photos of over 500 muskets, rifles, swords, bayonets, knives and other arms used by both sides in America's War for Independence.

Bedford County Rifle and Its Makers, by Calvin Hetrick, Introduction by George Shumway, George Shumway Pub., 1975. 40 pp. illus. Softcover. $10.00

The author's study of the graceful and distinctive muzzle-loading rifles made in Bedford County, Pennsylvania, stands as a milestone on the long path to the understanding of America's longrifles.

Belgian Rattlesnake; The Lewis Automatic Machine Gun, by William M. Easterly, Collector Grade Publications, Cobourg, Ontario, Canada, 1998. 584 pp., illus. $79.95

The most complete account ever published on the life and times of Colonel Isaac Newton Lewis and his crowning invention, the Lewis Automatic machine gun.

Best of Holland & Holland, England's Premier Gunmaker, by Michael McIntosh and Jan G. Roosenburg. Safari Press, Inc., Long Beach, CA, 2002. 1st edition. 298 pp. Profuse color illustrations. $69.95

Holland & Holland has had a long history of not only building London's "best" guns but also providing superior guns–the ultimate gun in finish, engraving, and embellishment.

Big Guns, Civil War Siege, Seacoast, and Naval Cannon, by Edwin Olmstead, Wayne E. Stark, and Spencer C. Tucker, Museum Restoration Service, Bloomfield, Ontario, Canada, 1997. 360 pp., illus. $80.00

This book is designed to identify and record the heavy guns available to both sides by the end of the Civil War.

Blue Book of Air Guns, 6th Edition, edited by S.P. Fjestad, Blue Book Publications, Inc. Minneapolis, MN 2007. $29.95

It contains most of the popular 2007 and vintage makes and models with detailed descriptions and up-to-date pricing! There are also hundreds of b&w images, and the Color Photo Grading System™ allows readers to stop guessing at airgun condition factors.

Blue Book of Gun Values, 28th Edition, edited by S.P. Fjestad, Blue Book Publications, Inc. Minneapolis, MN 2007. $39.95

This new edition simply contains more firearm values and information than any other single publication. Expanded to 2,080 pages featuring over 100,000 firearms prices, up-to-date pricing and information on thousands of firearms, including new 2007 makes/models. Completely revised 80 page color Photo Percentage Grading System.

Blue Book of Modern Black Powder Values, 4th Edition, by Dennis Adler, Blue Book Publications, Inc. Minneapolis, MN 2005. 271 pp., illus. 41 color photos. $24.95

This new title contains more up-to-date blackpowder values and related information than any other single publication and will keep you up-to-date on modern blackpowder models and prices, including most makes and models introduced by 2005!

Blunderbuss 1500-1900, The, by James D. Forman, Historical Arms Series No. 32. Canada, Museum Restoration, 1994. 40 pp., illus. Softcover. $8.95

An excellent and authoritative booklet giving tons of information on the Blunderbuss, a very neglected subject.

Boarders Away Volume I: With Steel-Edged Weapons & Polearms, by William Gilkerson, Andrew Mowbray, Inc. Publishers, Lincoln, RI, 1993. 331 pp. $48.00

Contains the essential 24-page chapter "War at Sea" which sets the historical and practical context for the arms discussed. Includes chapters on Early Naval Weapons, Boarding Axes, Cutlasses, Officers Fighting Swords and Dirks, and weapons at hand of Random Mayhem.

Boarders Away, Volume II: Firearms of the Age of Fighting Sail, by William Gilkerson, Andrew Mowbray, Inc. Publishers, Lincoln, RI, 1993. 331 pp., illus. $65.00

Covers the pistols, muskets, combustibles and small cannons used aboard American and European fighting ships, 1626-1826.

Boston's Gun Bible, by Boston T. Party, Ignacio, CO, Javelin Press, August 2000. Expanded edition. Softcover. $28.00

This mammoth guide for gun owners everywhere is a completely updated and expanded edition (more than 500 new pages!) of Boston T. Party's classic Boston on Guns and Courage. Boston gives new advice on which shoulder weapons and handguns to buy and why, before exploring such topics as why you should consider not getting a concealed carry permit, what guns and gear will likely be outlawed next and much more.

Bren Gun Saga, by Thomas B. Dugelby, Collector Grade Publications, Cobourg, Ontario, Canada, 1999, revised and expanded edition. 406 pp., illus. $65.95

A modern, definitive book on the Bren in this revised expanded edition, which in terms of numbers of pages and illustrations is nearly twice the size of the original.

British Board of Ordnance Small Arms Contractors 1689-1840, by De Witt Bailey, Rhyl, England, W. S. Curtis, 2000. 150 pp. $18.00

Thirty years of research in the Archives of the Ordnance Board in London has identified more than 600 of these suppliers. The names of many can be found marking the regulation firearms of the period. In the study, the contractors are identified both alphabetically and under a combination of their date period together with their specialist trade.

British Enfield Rifles, Volume 1, The SMLE MK I and MK III Rifles, by Charles R. Stratton, North Cape Pub., Tustin, CA, 1997. 150 pp., illus. Paper covers. $16.95

A systematic and thorough examination on a part-by-part basis of the famous British battle rifle that endured for nearly 70 years as the British Army's number one battle rifle.

British Enfield Rifles, Volume 2, No. 4 and No. 5 Rifles, by Charles R. Stratton, North Cape Publications, Tustin, CA, 1999. 150 pp., illus. Paper covers. $16.95

The historical background for the development of both rifles describing each variation and an explanation of all the marks, numbers and codes found on most parts.

British Enfield Rifles, Volume 4, The Pattern 1914 and U. S. Model 1917 Rifles, by Charles R. Stratton, North Cape Publications, Tustin, CA, 2000. Paper covers. $16.95

One of the least known American and British collectible military rifles is analyzed on a part by part basis. All markings and codes, refurbishment procedures and WWII upgrade are included as are the various sniper rifle versions.

British Falling Block Breechloading Rifle from 1865, by Jonathan Kirton, Tom Rowe Books, Maynardsville, TN, 2nd edition, 1997. 380 pp., illus. $70.00

Expanded edition of a comprehensive work on the British falling block rifle.

British Gun Engraving, by Douglas Tate, Safari Press, Inc., Huntington Beach, CA, 1999. 240 pp., illus. Limited, signed and numbered edition, in a slipcase. $80.00

A historic and photographic record of the last two centuries.

British Gunmakers: Volume One – London, by Nigel Brown, London, Quiller, 2004. 280 pp., 33 colour, 43 b&w photographs, line drawings. Hardcover. $99.95

British Gunmakers: Volume Two-Birmingham, Scotland, And the Regions, by Nigel Brown, London, Quiller, 2005. 1st edition. 439pp, hardcover. $99.95

With this book, read in conjunction with Volume One, the reader or scholar should be able to trace the history and likely age of any shotgun or rifle made in this region since 1800.

British Military Flintlock Rifles 1740-1840, With a Remarkable Wealth of Data about the Riflemen and Regiments that Carried These Weapons, by De Witt Bailey, Andrew Mowbray, Inc. Lincoln, RI, 2002. 1st edition. 264 pp. with over 320 photographs. Hardcover. $47.95

Pattern 1776 Rifles, the Ferguson Breechloader, the famous Baker Rifle, rifles of the Hessians and other German Mercenaries, American Loyalist rifles, rifles given to Indians, Cavalry rifles and rifled carbines, bayonets, accoutrements, ammunition and more.

British Service Rifles and Carbines 1888-1900, by Alan M. Petrillo, Excaliber Publications, Latham, NY, 1994. 72 pp., illus, Paper covers. $11.95

A complete review of the Lee-Metford and Lee-Enfield rifles and carbines.

British Single Shot Rifles, Volume 1, Alexander Henry, by Wal Winfer, Tom Rowe, Maynardsville, TN, 1998, 200 pp., illus. $50.00

Detailed study of the single shot rifles made by Henry. Illustrated with hundreds of photographs and drawings.

British Single Shot Rifles, Volume 3, Jeffery, by Wal Winfer, Rowe Publications, Rochester, N.Y., 1999. 260 pp., illus. $60.00

The Farquharsen as made by Jeffery and his competitors, Holland & Holland, Bland, Westley, Manton. Large section on the development of nitro cartridges including the 600.

British Single Shot Rifles, Volume 4; Westley Richards, by Wal Winfer, Rowe Publications, Rochester, N.Y., 2000. 265 pp., illus., photos. $60.00

In this 4th volume, Winfer covers a detailed study of the Westley Richards single shot rifles, including Monkey Tails, Improved Martini, 1872, 1873, 1878, 1881, 1897 Falling Blocks. He also covers Westley Richards cartridges, history and reloading information.

British Single Shot Rifles, Volume 5; Holland & Holland, by Winfer, Wal, Rochester, NY: Rowe Publications, 2004. 1st edition. ISBN: 097076085X. 218 pages. Hardcover. New in new dust jacket. (12063)

Volume 5 of the never ending study of the British single shot. One of the rarest and finest quality single shots made by any British firm is described. A large section is devoted to the cartridge developments carried on by Hollands with a large section on their Paradox cartridges.

Broad Arrow: British & Empire Factory Production, Proof, Inspection, Armourers, Unit & Issue Markings, by Ian Skennerton. Australia, Arms & Militaria Press, 2001. 140 pp., circa 80 illus. Stiff paper covers. $29.95

Thousands of service markings are illustrated and their applications described. Invaluable reference on units, also ideal for medal collectors.

Browning Dates of Manufacture, compiled by George Madis, Art and Reference House, Brownsboro, TX, 1989. 48 pp. $8.00

Gives the date codes and product codes for all models from 1824 to the present.

Browning Sporting Firearms: Dates of Manufacture, by D. R. Morse. Phoenix, AZ, Firing Pin Enterprizes, 2003. 37 pp. Softcover. New. $6.95

Covers their pistols, revolvers, rifles, shotguns and commemoratives, plus, models and serial numbers.

Browning Machine Gun Volume 1-Rifle Caliber Brownings in U.S. Service, by Dolf Goldsmith, Canada: Collector Grade Publications, 2005. 1st Edition, 552 pages, 568 illustrations. Hardcover. $79.95

This profusely illustrated history covers all models of the U.S. Browning, from the first "gas hammer" Model 1895 and the initial recoil-operated Models of 1901 and 1910, through the adoption and manufacture of the famous water-cooled heavy Model 1917 during World War I and the numerous Interwar experimental tank and aircraft guns, most of which were built up on surplus M1917 receivers.

Browning Machine Gun Volume 2-Rifle Caliber Brownings Abroad, by Dolf Goldsmith, Canada: Collector Grade Publications, 2006. 1st Edition, 392 pages, with over 486 illustrations. Hardcover, $69.95

This second volume of Dolf Goldsmith's series on Browning machine guns proves beyond doubt that the rifle-caliber Browning was simply the most popular and most-used machine gun ever designed. In some ways this book is even more engrossing than Volume I, as it describes and illustrates in considerable detail the many variations on the basic Browning which were manufactured and/or used by over twenty countries, in virtually every corner of the world, in both World Wars, in Korea and in Vietnam.

Browning–Sporting Arms of Distinction 1903-1992, by Matt Eastman, Long Beach, CA, Safari Press, 2004. 428 pp., profuse illus. Hardcover. $50.00

Bullard Firearms, by G. Scott Jamieson, Schiffer Publications, Atglen, PA 2002. 400 pp., with over 1100 color and b&w photos, charts, diagrams. Hardcover. $100.00

Bullard Firearms is the story of a mechanical genius whose rifles and cartridges were the equal of any made in America in the 1880s, yet little of substance had been written about James H. Bullard or his arms prior to 1988 when the first edition, called ***Bullard Arms***, was published. This greatly expanded volume, with over 1,000 b&w and 150 color plates, most not previously published, answers many of the questions posed in the first edition. The final chapter outlines, in chart form, almost 500 Bullard rifles by serial number, caliber and type. Quick and easy to use, this book is a real benefit for collectors and dealers alike.

Burning Powder, compiled by Major D.B. Wesson, Wolfe Publishing Company, Prescott, AZ, 1992. 110 pp. Soft cover. $10.95

A rare booklet from 1932 for Smith & Wesson collectors.

Burnside Breech Loading Carbines, The, by Edward A. Hull, Andrew Mowbray, Inc., Lincoln, RI, 1986. 95 pp., illus. $16.00

No. 1 in the "Man at Arms Monograph Series." A model-by-model historical/technical examination of one of the most widely used cavalry weapons of the American Civil War based upon important and previously unpublished research.

C.S. Armory Richmond: History of the Confederate States Armory, Richmond, VA and the Stock Shop at the C.S. Armory, Macon, GA., by Paul Davies, privately printed, 2000. 368 pp., illustrated with b&w photos. Hardcover. $75.00

The American Society of Arms Collectors is pleased to recommend C.S. Armory Richmond as a useful and valuable reference for collectors and scholars in the field of antique firearms. Gives fantastic explanations of machinery, stocks, barrels, and every facet of the production process during the timeframe covered in this book.

Cacciare A Palla: Uso E Tecnologia Dell'arma Rigata, by Marco E. Nobili, Italy, Il Volo Srl, 1994. 4th Edition-1st printing. 397 pp., illustrated with b&w photographs. Hardcover. New in new dust jacket. $75.00

Call of Duty; Military Awards and Decorations of the United States of America, by John E. Strandberg, LTC and Roger James Bender, San Jose, CA, R. James Bender Publishing, 2005. (New expanded edition). 559 pp. illustrated with 1,293 photos (most in color). Hardcover. $67.95

Camouflage Uniforms of European and NATO Armies; 1945 to the Present, by J. F. Borsarello, Atglen, PA, Schiffer Publications. Over 290 color and b&w photographs, 120 pp. Softcover. $29.95

This full-color book covers nearly all of the NATO, and other European armies' camouflaged uniforms, and not only shows and explains the many patterns, but also their efficacy of design. Described and illustrated are the variety of materials tested in over 40 different armies, and includes the history of obsolete trial tests from 1945 to the present time. This book provides a superb reference for the historian, reenactor, designer, and modeler.

Camouflage Uniforms of the Waffen-SS A Photographic Reference, by Michael Beaver, Schiffer Publishing, Atglen, PA. Over 1,000 color and b&w photographs and illustrations, 296 pp. $69.95

Finally a book that unveils the shroud of mystery surrounding Waffen-SS camouflage clothing. Illustrated here, both in full color and in contemporary b&w photographs, this unparalleled look at Waffen-SS combat troops and their camouflage clothing will benefit both the historian and collector.

Canadian Colts for the Boer War, by Col. Robert D. Whittington III. Hooks, TX, Brownlee Books, 2003. A limited edition of 1,000 copies. Numbered. 5 pp. Paper covers. New. $15.00

A study of Colt Revolvers issued to the First and Second Canadian Contingents Special Service Force.

Canadian Colts for the Boer War, Part 2, Col. Robert D. by Whittington III, Hooks, TX, Brownlee Books, 2005. A limited edition of 1,000 copies. Numbered. 5 pp. Paper covers, $5.00

Canadian Gunsmiths from 1608: A Checklist of Tradesmen, by John Belton, Historical Arms Series No. 29. Canada, Museum Restoration, 1992. 40 pp., 17 illustrations. Softcover. $8.95

This checklist is a greatly expanded version of HAS No. 14, listing the names, occupation, location, and dates of more than 1,500 men and women who worked as gunmakers, gunsmiths, armorers, gun merchants, gun patent holders, and a few other gun related trades.

Canadian Miliitaria Directory & Sourcebook Second Edition, by Clive M. Law, Ont. Canada, Service Publications, 1998. pp. 90. Softcover. $14.95

Cap Guns, by James Dundas, Schiffer Publishing, Atglen, PA, 1996. 160 pp., illus. Paper covers. $29.95

Over 600 full-color photos of cap guns and gun accessories with a current value guide.

Carbines of the Civil War, by John D. McAulay, Pioneer Press, Union City, TN, 1981. 123 pp., illus. Paper covers. $12.95

A guide for the student and collector of the colorful arms used by the Federal cavalry.

Carbines of the U.S. Cavalry 1861-1905, by John D. McAulay, Andrew Mowbray Publishers, Lincoln, RI, 1996. $35.00

Covers the crucial use of carbines from the beginning of the Civil War to the end of the cavalry carbine era in 1905.

Cartridge Carbines of the British Army, by Alan M. Petrillo, Excalibur Publications, Latham, NY, 1998. 72 pp., illus. Paper covers. $11.95

Begins with the Snider-Enfield which was the first regulation cartridge carbine introduced in 1866 and ends with the 303 caliber No.5, Mark 1 Enfield.

Cartridges for Collectors, by Fred Datig, Pioneer Press, Union City, TN, 1999. Three volumes of 176 pp. each. Vol. 1 (Centerfire); Vol. 2 (Rimfire and Misc.) types. Volume 1, softcover only, $19.95. Volumes 2 and 3, hardcover. $19.95

Vol. 3 (Additional Rimfire, Centerfire, and Plastic). All illustrations are shown in full-scale drawings.

Civil War Arms Makers and Their Contracts, edited by Stuart C. Mowbray and Jennifer Heroux, Andrew Mowbray Publishing, Lincoln, RI, 1998. 595 pp. $39.50

A facsimile reprint of the Report by the Commissioner of Ordnance and Ordnance Stores, 1862.

Civil War Arms Purchases and Deliveries, edited by Stuart C. Mowbray, Andrew Mowbray Publishing, Lincoln, RI, 1998. 300pp., illus. $39.50

A facsimile reprint of the master list of Civil War weapons purchases and deliveries including Small Arms, Cannon, Ordnance and Projectiles.

Civil War Cartridge Boxes of the Union Infantryman, by Paul Johnson, Andrew Mowbray, Inc., Lincoln, RI, 1998. 352 pp., illus. $45.00

There were four patterns of infantry cartridge boxes used by Union forces during the Civil War. The author describes the development and subsequent pattern changes to these cartridge boxes. All updated prices, scores of new listings, and hundreds of new pictures! It's the one reference work no collector should be without. An absolute must.

Civil War Collector's Price Guide; 11th Edition, Orange, VA, Publisher's Press, 2006. 300 pps., softbound, heavily illustrated, full color cover. $37.95

Our newly released 11th edition of the popular Civil War Collector's Price Guide! Expanded to include new images and new listings.

Civil War Commanders, by Dean Thomas, Thomas Publications, Gettysburg, PA. 1998. 72 pp., illus., photos. Paper covers. $9.95

138 photographs and capsule biographies of Union and Confederate officers. A convenient personalities reference guide.

Civil War Heavy Explosive Ordnance: A Guide to Large Artillery Projectiles, Torpedoes, and Mines, by Jack Bell, Denton, TX, University of North Texas Press, 2003. 1,016 b&w photos. 537 pp. Hardcover. New in new dust jacket. $50.00

Civil War Infantryman: In Camp, on the March, and in Battle, by Dean Thomas, Thomas Publications, Gettysburg, PA. 1998. 72 pp., illus. Softcovers. $12.95

Uses first-hand accounts to shed some light on the "common soldier" of the Civil War from enlistment to muster-out, including camp, marching, rations, equipment, fighting, and more.

Civil War Pistols, by John D. McAulay, Andrew Mowbray Inc., Lincoln, RI, 1992. 166 pp., illus. $38.50

A survey of the handguns used during the American Civil War.

Civil War Relic Hunting A to Z, by Robert Buttafuso, Sheridan Books, 2000. 1st edition. illus., 91 pp., b&w illustrations. Softcover. $21.95

Civil War Sharps Carbines and Rifles, by Earl J. Coates and John D. McAulay, Thomas Publications, Gettysburg, PA, 1996. 108 pp., illus. Paper covers. $12.95

Traces the history and development of the firearms including short histories of specific serial numbers and the soldiers who received them.

Civil War Small Arms of the U.S. Navy and Marine Corps, by John D. McAulay, Mowbray Publishing, Lincoln, RI, 1999. 186 pp., illus. $39.00

The first reliable and comprehensive guide to the firearms and edged weapons of the Civil War Navy and Marine Corps.

Collecting Military Headgear; A Guide to 5000 Years of Helmet History, by Robert Atglen Attard, PA, Schiffer Publications, 2004. 1st edition. Hardcover. New in new dust jacket. $69.95

Collecting Third Reich Recordings, by Stuart McKenzie, San Jose, CA, R. James Bender Publishing, 2001. 1st edition. Softcover. $29.95

Collector's Illustrated Encyclopedia of the American Revolution, by George C. Neumann and Frank J. Kravic, Rebel Publishing Co., Inc., Texarkana, TX, 1989. 286 pp., illus. $42.95

A showcase of more than 2,300 artifacts made, worn, and used by those who fought in the War for Independence.

Colonel Thomas Claiborne Jr. and the Colt Whitneyville-Walker Pistol, by Col. Robert D. Whittington III, Hooks, TX, Brownlee Books, 2005. A limited edition of 1,000 copies. Numbered. 8 pp. Paper covers, $7.50

Colonels in Blue: Union Army Colonels of the Civil War, by Roger Hunt, New York, Atglen, PA, Schiffer Publications, 2003. 1st edition. 288 pp., with over 640 b&w photographs. Hardcover. New in new dust jacket. $59.95

Colonial Frontier Guns, by T.M. Hamilton, Pioneer Press, Union City, TN, 1988. 176 pp., illus. Paper covers. $17.50

A complete study of early flint muskets of this country.

Colt 1909 Military Revolvers; The 1904 Thompson-Lagarde Report, and General John J. Pershing, by Col. Robert D. Whittington III. Hooks, TX, Brownlee Books, 2003. A limited edition of 1,000 copies. Numbered. 10 pp. Paper covers. New. $10.00

The 1904 Thompson-Lagarde Report, and General John J. Pershing.

Colt and Its Collectors Exhibition Catalog for Colt: The Legacy of A Legend, Buffalo Bill Historical Center, Cody, Wyoming. Colt Collectors Association, 2003. 1st edition. Hardcover. New in new dust jacket. $125.00

Colt and Its Collectors accompanies the upcoming special exhibition, Colt: The Legacy of a Legend, opening at the Buffalo Bill Historical Center in May 2003. Numerous essays, over 750 color photographs by Paul Goodwin.

Colt Armory, by Ellsworth Grant, Man-at-Arms Bookshelf, Lincoln, RI, 1996. 232 pp., illus. $35.00

A history of Colt's Manufacturing Company.

Colt Engraving Book, Volumes I & II, by R. L. Wilson. Privately printed, 2001. Each volume is appx. 500 pp., with 650 illustrations, most in color. $390.00

This third edition from the original texts of 1974 and 1982 has been fine-tuned and dramatically expanded, and is by far the most illuminating and complete. With over 1,200 illustrations, more than 2/3 of which are in color, this book joins the author's The Book of Colt Firearms, and Fine Colts as companion volumes. Approximately 1,000 pages in two volumes, each signed by the author, serial numbered, and strictly limited to 3000 copies. Volume I covers from the Paterson and pre-Paterson period through c.1921 (end of the Helfricht period). Volume II commences with Kornbrath, and Glahn, and covers Colt embellished arms from c.1919 through 2000.

Colt Model 1905 Automatic Pistol, by John Potocki, Andrew Mowbray Publishing, Lincoln, RI, 1998. 191 pp., illus. $28.00

Covers all aspects of the Colt Model 1905 Automatic Pistol, from its invention by the legendary John Browning to its numerous production variations.

Colt Peacemaker British Model, by Keith Cochran, Cochran Publishing Co., Rapid City, SD, 1989. 160 pp., illus. $35.00

Covers those revolvers Colt squeezed in while completing a large order of revolvers for the U.S. Cavalry in early 1874, to those magnificent cased target revolvers used in the pistol competitions at Bisley Commons in the 1890s.

Colt Peacemaker Encyclopedia, by Keith Cochran, Cochran Publishing Co., Rapid City, SD, 1986. 434 pp., illus. $60.00

A must-have book for the Peacemaker collector.

Colt Peacemaker Encyclopedia, Volume 2, by Keith Cochran, Cochran Publishing Co., SD, 1992. 416 pp., illus. $60.00

Included in this volume are extensive notes on engraved, inscribed, historical and noted revolvers, as well as those revolvers used by outlaws, lawmen, movie and television stars.

Colt Pistols, Texas, And The U.S. Army 1847-1861, by Col. Robert D. Whittington III. Hooks, TX, Brownlee Books, 2003. A limited edition of 1,000 copies. Numbered. 8 pp. Paper covers. New. $7.50

A study of the Colt pistols used in Texas by the U.S. Army between 1847-1861. A remarkable detailed report.

Colt Presentations: From the Factory Ledgers 1856-1869, by Herbert G. Houze. Lincoln, RI, Andrew Mowbray, Inc., 2003. 112 pp., 45 b&w photos. Softcover. $21.95

Samuel Colt was a generous man. He also used gifts to influence government decision makers. But after Congress investigated him in 1854, Colt needed to hide the gifts from prying eyes, which makes it very difficult for today's collectors to document the many revolvers presented by Colt and the factory. Using the original account journals of the Colt's Patent Fire Arms Manufacturing Co., renowned arms authority Herbert G. Houze finally gives us the full details behind hundreds of the most exciting Colts ever made.

Colt Single Action Army Revolver Study: New Discoveries, by Kenneth Moore, Lincoln, RI, Andrew Mowbray, Inc., 2003. 1st edition. 200 pp., with 77 photos and illustrations. Hardcover. New. $49.95

Twenty-five years after co-authoring the classic Study of the Colt Single Action Army Revolver, Ken fills in the gaps and sets the record straight. The serial number data alone will astound you. Includes, ejector models, special section on low serial numbers, U.S. Army testing data, new details about militia S.A.A.'s plus a true wealth of cartridge info.

Colt Single Action Army Revolvers: The Legend, the Romance and the Rivals, by "Doc" O'Meara, Krause Publications, Iola, WI, 2000. 160 pp., illustrated with 250 photos in b&w and a 16-page color section. $22.95

Production figures, serial numbers by year, and rarities.

Colt Single Action Army Revolvers and Alterations, by C. Kenneth Moore, Mowbray Publishers, Lincoln, RI, 1999. 112 pp., illus. $35.00

A comprehensive history of the revolvers that collectors call "Artillery Models." These are the most historical of all S.A.A. Colts, and this new book covers all the details.

Colt Single Action Army Revolvers and the London Agency, by C. Kenneth Moore, Andrew Mowbray Publishers, Lincoln, RI, 1990. 144 pp., illus. $35.00

Drawing on vast documentary sources, this work chronicles the relationship between the London Agency and the Hartford home office.

Colt Sporting Firearms: Dates of Manufacture, by D.R. Morse, Phoenix, AZ, Firing Pin Enterprizes, 2003. 82 pp. Softcover. New. $6.95

Covers their pistols, revolvers, rifles, shotguns and commemoratives, plus models and serial numbers.

Colt U.S. General Officers' Pistols, by Horace Greeley IV, Andrew Mowbray Inc., Lincoln, RI, 1990. 199 pp., illus. $38.00

These unique weapons, issued as a badge of rank to General Officers in the U.S. Army from WWII onward, remain highly personal artifacts of the military leaders who carried them. Includes serial numbers and dates of issue.

Colt Walker's, Walkers Controversy is Solved, by Col. Robert D. Whittington III. Hooks, TX, Brownlee Books, 2005. A limited edition of 1,000 copies. Numbered. 17 pp. Paper covers. New. $15.00

The truth about serial numbers on the Colt Whitneyville-Walker Pistols presented to Captain Samuel Hamilton Walker by Sam Colt and J. B. Colt on July 28th, 1847.

Colts from the William M. Locke Collection, by Frank Sellers, Andrew Mowbray Publishers, Lincoln, RI, 1996. 192 pp., illus. $55.00

This important book illustrates all of the famous Locke Colts, with captions by arms authority Frank Sellers.

Colt's Dates of Manufacture 1837-1978, by R.L. Wilson, published by Maurie Albert, Coburg, Australia; N.A. distributor Madis Books, TX, 1997. 61 pp. $8.50

An invaluable pocket guide to the dates of manufacture of Colt firearms up to 1978.

Colt's Pocket '49: Its Evolution Including the Baby Dragoon and Wells Fargo, by Robert Jordan and Darrow Watt, privately printed, Loma Mar, CA 2000. 304 pp., with 984 color photos, illus. Beautifully bound in a deep blue leather-like case. $125.00

Detailed information on all models and covers engaving, cases, accoutrements, holsters, fakes, and much more. Included is a summary booklet containing information such as serial numbers, production ranges and identifing photos. This book is a masterpiece on its subject.

Colt's SAA Post War Models, by George Garton, The Gun Room Press, Highland Park, NJ, 1995. 166 pp., illus. $39.95

Complete facts on the post-war Single Action Army revolvers. Information on calibers, production numbers and variations taken from factory records.

Combat Helmets of the Third Reich: A Study in Photographs, by Thomas Kibler, Pottsboro, TX, Reddick Enterprises, 2003. 1st edition. 96 pp., illustrated in full color. Pictorial softcover. $19.95

Combat Perspective The Thinking Man's Guide to Self-Defense, by Gabriel Suarez, Boulder, CO, Paladin Press, 2003. 1st edition. 112 pp. Softcover. $15.00

Complete Guide to United States Military Medals 1939 to Present, 6th Edition, by Colonel Frank C. Foster, Medals of America Press, Fountain Inn, SC, 2006. 168 pp., illus., photos. $29.95

Complete criteria for every Army, Navy, Marine, Air Force, Coast Guard, and Merchant Marine award since 1939. All decorations, service medals, and ribbons shown in full color and accompanied by dates and campaigns, as well as detailed descriptions on proper wear and display.

Complete Guide to the M1 Garand and the M1 Carbine, by Bruce N. Canfield, 2nd printing, Andrew Mowbray Inc., Lincoln, RI, 1999. 296 pp., illus. $39.50

Expanded and updated coverage of both the M1 Garand and the M1 Carbine, with more than twice as much information as the author's previous book on this topic.

Complete Guide to U.S. Infantry Weapons of the First War, by Bruce Canfield, Andrew Mowbray, Publisher, Lincoln, RI, 2000. 304 pp., illus. $39.95

The definitive study of the U.S. Infantry weapons used in WWI.

Complete Guide to U.S. Infantry Weapons of World War Two, by Bruce Canfield, Andrew Mowbray, Publisher, Lincoln, RI, 1995. 303 pp., illus. $39.95

A definitive work on the weapons used by the United States Armed Forces in WWII.

Confederate Belt Buckles & Plates, by Steve E. Mullinax, O'Donnell Publishing, Alexandria, VA, 1999. Expanded edition. 247 pp., illus. Hardcover. $34.00

Hundreds of crisp photographs augment this classic study of Confederate accoutrement plates.

Confederate Carbines & Musketoons Cavalry Small Arms Manufactured in and for the Southern Confederacy 1861-1865, by John M. Murphy, Santa Ana, CA, privately printed, 2002. Reprint. Hardcover. New in new dust jacket. $79.95

Confederate Rifles & Muskets: Infantry Small Arms Manufactured in the Southern Confederacy 1861-1865, by John M. Murphy. Santa Ana, CA, privately printed, 1996. Reprint. 768 pp., 8 pp. color plates, profusely illustrated. Hardcover. $119.95

The first in-depth and academic analysis and discussion of the "long" longarms produced in the South by and for the Confederacy during the American Civil War. The collection of Dr. Murphy is doubtless the largest and finest grouping of Confederate longarms in private hands today.

Confederate Saddles & Horse Equipment, by Ken R. Knopp, Orange, VA, Publisher's Press, 2002. 194 pps., illus. Hardcover. $39.95

A pioneer work on the subject. After 10 years of research Ken Knopp has compiled a thorough and fascinating study of the little-known field of Confederate saddlery and equipment. An indispensable source for collectors and historians.

Cooey Firearms, Made in Canada 1919-1979, by John A. Belton, Museum Restoration, Canada, 1998. 36pp., with 46 illus. Paper covers. $8.95

More than 6 million rifles and at least 67 models were made by this small Canadian riflemaker. They have been identified from the first 'Cooey Canuck' through the last variations made by the 'Winchester-Cooey'. Each is descibed and most are illustrated in this first book on the Cooey.

Cowboy and Gunfighter Collectible, by Bill Mackin, Mountain Press Publishing Co., Missoula, MT, 1995. 178 pp., illus. Paper covers. $25.00

A photographic encyclopedia with price guide and makers' index.

Cowboy Collectibles and Western Memorabilia, by Bob Bell and Edward Vebell, Schiffer Publishing, Atglen, PA, 1992. 160 pp., illus. Paper covers. $29.95

The exciting era of the cowboy and the wild west collectibles including rifles, pistols, gun rigs, etc.

Cowboy Culture: The Last Frontier of American Antiques, by Michael Friedman, Schiffer Publishing, Ltd., West Chester, PA, 2002. 300 pp., illus. $89.95

Covers the artful aspects of the old west, the antiques and collectibles. Illustrated with clear color plates of over 1,000 items such as spurs, boots, guns, saddles, etc.

Cowboys and the Trappings of the Old West, by William Manns and Elizabeth Clair Flood, Zon International Publishing Co., Santa Fe, NM, 1997, 1st edition. 224 pp., illus. $45.00

A pictorial celebration of the cowboy dress and trappings.

Custom Firearms Engraving, by Tom Turpin, Krause Publications, Iola, WI, 1999. 208 pp., illus. $49.95

Over 200 four-color photos with more than 75 master engravers profiled. Engravers directory with addresses in the U.S. and abroad.

Daisy Air Rifles & BB Guns: The First 100 Years, by Neal Punchard. St. Paul, MN, Motorbooks, 2002. 1st edition. 10" x 10", 156 pp., 300 color. Hardcover. $29.95

Flash back to the days of your youth and recall fond memories of your Daisy. Daisy Air Rifles and BB Guns looks back fondly on the first 100 years of Daisy BB rifles and pistols, toy and cork guns, accessories, packaging, period advertising and literature.

Death From Above: The German FG42 Paratrooper Rifle, New Expanded Edition, by Blake Stevens, Collector Grade Publications, Canada, 2007. 228 pages, 278 illustrations. $59.95

This book depicts and describes seven basic models of the FG42, from the earliest prototype (the Type 'A') through the first or 'early' production series (the Type 'E') with its distinctively swept-back handgrip and intricately machined receiver, then the initial Rheinmetall redesign utilizing a stamped receiver (the Type 'F'), followed by the ultimate if extremely short-lived final series-production model, the Type 'G'. Amazingly, virtually none of the Type 'G' components will interchange with their lookalike Type 'F' counterparts. This includes magazines.

Decorations, Medals, Ribbons, Badges and Insignia of the United States Navy; World War II to Present, by James G. Thompson, Medals of America Press, Fountain Inn, SC. 2005. 124 pp., illus. $29.95

The most complete guide to United States Army medals, ribbons, rank, insignia and patches from WWII to the present day. Each medal and insignia shown in full color. Includes listing of respective criteria and campaigns.

Defending the Dominion, Canadian Military Rifles, 1855-1955, by David Edgecombe. Service Publications, Ont., Canada, 2003. 168 pp., with 60+ illustrations. Hardcover. $39.95

This book contains much new information on the Canadian acquisition, use and disposal of military rifles during the most significant century in the development of small arms. In addition to the venerable Martini-Henry, there are chapters on the Winchester, Snider, Starr, Spencer, Peabody, Enfield rifles and others.

Derringer in America, Volume 1, The Percussion Period, by R.L. Wilson and L.D. Eberhart, Andrew Mowbray Inc., Lincoln, RI, 1985. 271 pp., illus. $48.00

A long awaited book on the American percussion derringer.

Derringer in America, Volume 2, the Cartridge Period, by L.D. Eberhart and R.L. Wilson, Andrew Mowbray Inc., Publishers, Lincoln, RI, 1993. 284 pp., illus. $65.00

Comprehensive coverage of cartridge derringers organized alphabetically by maker. Includes all types of derringers known by the authors to have been offered in the American market.

Devil's Paintbrush: Sir Hiram Maxim's Gun, by Dolf Goldsmith, 3rd Edition, expanded and revised, Collector Grade Publications, Toronto, Canada, 2002. 384 pp., illus. $79.95

The classic work on the world's first true automatic machine gun.

Dressed For Duty: America's Women in Uniform, 1898-1973 Volume I, by Jill Halcomb Smith, San Nose, CA, Bender Publishing, 2002. 1st edition. 480 pages-1,089 photos & illustrations (many in color), deluxe binding. Hardcover. $54.95

Dressed For Duty: America's Women in Uniform, 1898-1973 Volume II, by Jill Halcomb Smith, San Nose, CA, Bender Publishing, 2004. 1st edition. 544 pages-1,300 photos & illustrations (many in color), deluxe binding. Hardcover. $59.95

Dr. Josephus Requa Civil War Dentist and the Billinghurst-Requa Volley Gun, by John M. Hyson Jr., and Margaret Requa DeFrancisco, Museum Restoration Service, Bloomfield, Ont., Canada, 1999. 36 pp., illus. Paper covers. $8.95

The story of the inventor of the first practical rapid-fire gun to be used during the American Civil War.

Dutch Luger (Parabellum) A Complete History, by Bas J. Martens and Guus de Vries, Ironside International, Alexandria, VA, 1995. 268 pp., illus. $49.95

The history of the Luger in the Netherlands. An extensive description of the Dutch pistol and trials and the different models of the Luger in the Dutch service.

E.C. Prudhomme's Gun Engraving Review, by E. C. Prudhomme, R&R Books, Livonia, NY, 1994. 164 pp., illus. $60.00

As a source for engravers and collectors, this book is an indispensable guide to styles and techniques of the world's foremost engravers.

Eagle on U.S. Firearms, by John W. Jordan, Pioneer Press, Union City, TN, 1992. 140 pp., illus. Paper covers. $17.50

Stylized eagles have been stamped on government owned or manufactured firearms in the U.S. since the beginning of our country. This book lists and illustrates these various eagles in an informative and refreshing manner.

Emblems of Honor; Patches and Insignia of the U.S. Army from the Great War to the Early Cold War Vol. IV Armor-Cavalry-Tank Destroyer, by Kurt Keller, Constabulary, PA, privately printed, 2005. 1st edition, signed. 232 pp., with over 600 color photos. Hardcover. New in new dust jacket. $59.95

Emma Gees, by Capt. Herbert W. McBride, Mt. Ida, AR, Lancer Publishing, 2003. 224 pp., b&w photos. Softcover. $19.95

Encyclopedia of Rifles & Handguns; A Comprehensive Guide to Firearms, edited by Sean Connolly, Chartwell Books, Inc., Edison, NJ., 1996. 160 pp., illus. $26.00

Encyclopedia of United States Army Insignia and Uniforms, by William Emerson, OK, University of Oklahoma Press, 1996. Hardcover. $134.95

Enemies Foreign and Domestic, by Matthew Bracken, San Diego, CA, Steelcutter Publishing, 2003. Softcover. $19.89

Eprouvettes: A Comprehensive Study of Early Devices for the Testing of Gunpowder, by R.T.W. Kempers, Royal Armouries Museum, Leeds, England, 1999. 352 pp., illustrated with 240 b&w and 28 color plates. $125.00

Equipment of the WWII Tommy, by David Gordon, Missoula, MT, Pictorial Histories Publishing, 2004. 1st edition. Softcover. $24.95

Fifteen Years in the Hawken Lode, by John D. Baird, The Gun Room Press, Highland Park, NJ, 1976. 120 pp., illus. $24.95

A collection of thoughts and observations gained from many years of intensive study of the guns from the shop of the Hawken brothers.

Fighting Colors: The Creation of Military Aircraft Nose Art, by Gary Velasco, Paducah, KY, Turner Publishing, 2005. 1st edition. Hardcover. New in new dust jacket. $57.95

Fighting Iron, by Art Gogan, Andrew Mowbray, Inc., Lincoln, R.I., 2002. 176 pp., illus. $28.00

It doesn't matter whether you collect guns, swords, bayonets or accoutrement–sooner or later you realize that it all comes down to the metal. If you don't understand the metal, you don't understand your collection.

Fine Art of the West, by Byron Price, New York, Abbeville Press, 2004, 2nd revised edition. $75.00

A glossary and bibliography complete this first comprehensive look at one of America's most fascinating forms of artistic expression. 276 pages illustrated with color photos.

Firearm Suppressor Patents; Volume 1: United States Patents, by N.R. Parker, Foreword by Alan C. Paulson, Boulder, CO, Paladin Press, 2004. 392 pp., illus. Softcover. $45.00

Firearms from Europe, 2nd Edition, by David Noe, Larry W. Yantz, Dr. James B. Whisker, Rowe Publications, Rochester, N.Y., 2002. 192 pp., illus. $45.00

A history and description of firearms imported during the American Civil War by the United States of America and the Confederate States of America.

Firearms of the American West 1803-1865, Volume 1, by Louis A. Garavaglia and Charles Worman, University of Colorado Press, Niwot, CO, 1998. 402 pp., illus. $79.95

Traces the development and uses of firearms on the frontier during this period.

Firearms of the American West 1866-1894, Volume 2, by Louis A. Garavaglia and Charles G. Worman, University of Colorado Press, Niwot, CO, 1998. 416 pp., illus. $79.95

A monumental work that offers both technical information on all of the important firearms used in the West during this period and a highly entertaining history of how they were used, who used them, and why.

Firepower from Abroad, by Wiley Sword, Andrew Mowbray Publishing, Lincoln, R.I., 2000. 120 pp., illus. $23.00

The Confederate Enfield and the LeMat revolver and how they reached the Confederate market.

Flayderman's Guide to Antique American Firearms and Their Values, 8th Edition, edited by Norm Flayderman, Krause Publications, Iola, WI, 2001. 692 pp., illus. Paper covers. $34.95

A completely updated and new edition with more than 3,600 models and variants extensively described with all marks and specifications necessary for quick identification.

Flintlock Fowlers: The First Guns Made in America, by Tom Grinslade, Texarkana, TX: Scurlock Publishing Co., 2005. 1st edition. 248 pages. Hardcover. New in new dust jacket. $75.00 Paperback $38.00

The most complete compilation of fowlers ever in one book. Essential resource for collectors, builders and flintlock enthusiasts!

F.N. F.A.L. Assembly, Disassembly Manual 7.62mm, by Skennerton & Riling, Ray Riling Arms Books Co. Philadelphia, PA 2004. 36 pages, $5.00

Over 60 photos & line drawings. Ideal workshop reference for stripping & assembly with exploded parts drawings, specifications, service accessories, historical information and recommended reading references. Triple saddle-stitched binding with durable plastic laminated cover makes this an ideal workshop guide.

FN-FAL Rifle, et al, by Duncan Long, Paladin Press, Boulder, CO, 1999. 144 pp., illus. Paper covers. $18.95

Detailed descriptions of the basic models produced by Fabrique Nationale and the myriad variants that evolved as a result of the firearms' universal acceptance.

Freund & Bro. Pioneer Gunmakers to the West, by F.J. Pablo Balentine, Graphic Publishers, Newport Beach, CA, 1997. 380 pp., illus. $69.95

The story of Frank W. and George Freund, skilled German gunsmiths who plied their trade on the Western American frontier during the final three decades of the nineteenth century.

Full Circle: A Treatise On Roller Locking, by Blake Stevens, Collector Grade Publications, Toronto, Canada, 2006. 536 pages, with over 737 illustrations. $79.95

After the war the roller lock was taken from Germany first to France; then to Spain, and Switzerland; through Holland; and finally back "Full Circle" to Germany again, where it was used in the G3, the service rifle of the Bundeswehr, from 1959 through to the adoption of the 5.56mm G36 in 1995. The classic work on the world's first true automatic machine gun.

Fusil de Tulole in New France, 1691-1741, by Russel Bouchard, Museum Restorations Service, Bloomfield, Ontario, Canada, 1997. 36 pp., illus. Paper covers. $8.95

The development of the company and the identification of their arms.

Gas Trap Garand, by Billy Pyle, Collector Grade Publications, Cobourg, Ontario, Canada, 1999 316 pp., illus. $59.95

The in-depth story of the rarest Garands of them all, the initial 80 Model Shop rifles made under the personal supervision of John Garand himself in 1934 and 1935, and the first 50,000 plus production "gas trap" M1's manufactured at Springfield Armory between August, 1937 and August, 1940.

George Schreyer, Sr. and Jr., Gunmakers of Hanover, Pennsylvania, by George Shumway, George Shumway Publishers, York, PA, 1990. 160pp., illus. $50.00

This monograph is a detailed photographic study of almost all known surviving longrifles and smoothbore guns made by highly regarded gunsmiths George Schreyer, Sr. and George Schreyer Jr.

German and Austrian Gunmakers Trade Catalogs, by George Hoyem, Jaeger Press, 2002. This is a 252 page 11" x 8.5" case bound book with a four color dust jacket, compiled by Hans E. Pfingsten and George A. Hoyem, containing five illustrated gunmakers trade catalogues dating from 1914 to 1935, three of them export issues in German, English, French and Spanish. Hardcover. New in new dust jacket. $60.00

German Anti-Tank Weapons-Panzerbuchse, Panzerfaust and Panzerschrek: Propaganda Series Volume 5, by DeVries and Martens. Alexandria,VA, Ironside Intl., 2005. 1st edition. 152pp, illustrated with 200 high quality b&w photos, most never published before. Hardcover, $38.95

German Assault Rifle 1935-1945, The, by Peter R. Senich, Paladin Press, Boulder, CO, 1987. 328 pp., illus. $60.00

A complete review of machine carbines, machine pistols and assault rifles employed by Hitler's Wehrmacht during WWII.

German Belt Buckles 1845-1945: Buckles of the Enlisted Soldiers, by Peter Nash Atglen, PA, Schiffer Publications, 2003. 1st edition. Hardcover. New in new dust jacket. $59.95

German Camouflaged Helmets of the Second World War; Volume 1: Painted and Textured Camouflage, by Branislav Atglen Radovic, PA, Schiffer Publications, 2004. 1st edition. Hardcover. New in new dust jacket. $79.95

German Camouflaged Helmets of the Second World War; Volume 2: Wire, Netting, Covers, Straps, Interiors, Miscellaneous, by Branislav Atglen Radovic, PA, Schiffer Publications, 2004. 1st edition. Hardcover. New in new dust jacket. $79.95

German Cross in Gold-Holders of the SS and Police, by Mark Yerger, San Jose, CA, Bender Publishing, 2004. 1st edition. 432 pp., 295 photos and illustrations, deluxe binding. Hardcover. $44.95

German Cross in Gold-Holders of the SS and Police Volume 2-"Das Reich", by Mark Yerger, San Jose, CA, Bender Publishing, 2005. 1st edition. 432 pp., 295 photos and illustrations, deluxe binding. Hardcover. $44.95

German K98k Rifle, 1934-1945: The Backbone of the Wehrmacht, by Richard D. Law, Collector Grade Publications, Toronto, Canada, 1993. 336 pp., illus. $69.95

The most comprehensive study ever published on the 14,000,000 bolt-action K98k rifles produced in Germany between 1934 and 1945.

German Machine Guns, by Daniel D. Musgrave, revised edition, Ironside International Publishers, Inc. Alexandria, VA, 1992. 586 pp., 650 illus. $49.95

The most definitive book ever written on German machine guns. Covers the introduction and development of machine guns in Germany from 1899 to the rearmament period after WWII.

German Military Abbreviations, by Military Intelligence Service, Canada, Service Publications. 268 pp. Stiff paper covers. $16.95

German Paratroops: Uniforms, Insignia & Equipment of the Fallschirmjager in World War II, by Robert Atglen Kurtz, PA, Schiffer Publications, 2003. 1st edition. Hardcover. New in new dust jacket. $59.95

German Tanks of World War II in Color, by Michael Green; Thomas Anderson; Frank Schultz, St. Paul, MN, MBI Publishing Company, 2000. 1st edition. Softcover. $14.95

Government Issue: U.S. Army European Theater of Operations Collector Guide, by Henry-Paul Enjames, Philippe Charbonnier, France, Histoire & Collections, 2004. Hardcover, $49.89

Government Models, by William H.D. Goddard, Andrew Mowbray Publishing, Lincoln, RI, 1998. 296 pp., illus. $58.50

The most authoritative source on the development of the Colt model of 1911.

Grasshoppers and Butterflies, by Adrian B. Caruana, Museum Restoration Service, Alexandria Bay, N.Y., 1999. 32 pp., illus. Paper covers. $8.95

No.39 in the Historical Arms Series. The light 3 pounders of Pattison and Townsend.

Greenhill Dictionary of Guns and Gunmakers: From Colt's First Patent to the Present Day, 1836-2001, by John Walter, Greenhill Publishing, 2001, 1st edition, 576 pp., illustrated with 200 photos, 190 trademarks and 40 line drawings, Hardcover. $59.95

Covers military small arms, sporting guns and rifles, air and gas guns, designers, inventors, patentees, trademarks, brand names and monograms. A famed book of great value, truly encyclopedic in scope and sought after by firearms collectors.

Gun Powder Cans & Kegs, by Ted and David Bacyk and Tom Rowe, Rowe Publications, Rochester, NY, 1999. 150 pp., illus. $65.00

The first book devoted to powder tins and kegs. All cans and kegs in full color. With a price guide and rarity scale.

Gun Tools, Their History and Identification, by James B. Shaffer, Lee A. Rutledge and R. Stephen Dorsey, Collector's Library, Eugene, OR, 1992. 375 pp., illus. $30.00

Written history of foreign and domestic gun tools from the flintlock period to WWII.

Gun Tools, Their History and Identifications, Volume 2, by Stephen Dorsey and James B. Shaffer, Collectors' Library, OR, 1997. 396 pp., illus. Paper covers. $30.00

Gun tools from the Royal Armouries Museum in England, Pattern Room, Royal Ordnance Reference Collection in Nottingham and from major private collections.

Gunmakers of London 1350-1850 with Supplement, by Howard L. Blackmore, Museum Restoration Service, Alexandria Bay, NY, 1999. 222 pp., illus. Two volumes. Slipcased. $135.00

A listing of all the known workmen of gunmaking in the first 500 years, plus a history of the guilds, cutlers, armourers, founders, blacksmiths, etc. 260 gunmarks are illustrated. Supplement is 156 pages, and begins with an introductory chapter on "foreign" gunmakers followed by records of all the new information found about previously unidentified armourers, gunmakers and gunsmiths.

Guns of Dagenham: Lanchester, Patchett, Sterling, by Peter Laidler and David Howroyd, Collector Grade Publications, Inc., Canada, 1995. 310 pp. illus. $39.95

An in-depth history of small arms made by the Sterling Company of Dagenham, England, from 1940 until Sterling was purchased by British Aerospace in 1989 and closed.

Guns of Remington: Historic Firearms Spanning Two Centuries, compiled by Howard M. Madaus, Biplane Productions, Publisher, in cooperation with Buffalo Bill Historical Center, Cody, WY, 1998. 352 pp., illustrated with over 800 color photos. $79.95

A complete catalog of the firearms in the exhibition, "It Never Failed Me: The Arms & Art of Remington Arms Company" at the Buffalo Bill Historical Center, Cody, Wyoming.

Guns of the Third Reich, by John Walter, Pennsylvania, Stackpole Books, 2004. 1st edition. 256pp, 60 illust. Hardcover. $34.95

John Walter examines the full range of guns used by the Third Reich from the commercially successful Walter PP and PPK, to the double-action, personal defense pistols Mauser HSc and Sauer M38.

Guns of the Western Indian War, by R. Stephen Dorsey, Collector's Library, Eugene, OR, 1997. 220 pp., illus. Paper covers. $30.00

The full story of the guns and ammunition that made western history in the turbulent period of 1865-1890.

Gunsmiths of Illinois, by Curtis L. Johnson, George Shumway Publishers, York, PA, 1995. 160 pp., illus. $50.00

Genealogical information is provided for nearly 1,000 gunsmiths. Contains hundreds of illustrations of rifles and other guns, of handmade origin, from Illinois.

Gunsmiths of Manhattan, 1625-1900: A Checklist of Tradesmen, by Michael H. Lewis, Museum Restoration Service, Bloomfield, Ont., Canada, 1991. 40 pp., illus. Paper covers. $8.95

This listing of more than 700 men in the arms trade in New York City prior to about the end of the 19th century will provide a guide for identification and further research.

Gunsmiths of Maryland, by Daniel D. Hartzler and James B. Whisker, Old Bedford Village Press, Bedford, PA, 1998. 208 pp., illus. $45.00

Covers firelock Colonial period through the breech-loading patent models. Featuring longrifles.

Gunsmiths of Virginia, by Daniel D. Hartzler and James B. Whisker, Old Bedford Village Press, Bedford, PA, 1992. 206 pp., illus. $40.00

A photographic study of American longrifles.

Gunsmiths of West Virginia, by Daniel D. Hartzler and James B. Whisker, Old Bedford Village Press, Bedford, PA, 1998. 176 pp., illus. $40.00

A photographic study of American longrifles.

Gunsmiths of York County, Pennsylvania, by Daniel D. Hartzler and James B. Whisker, Old Bedford Village Press, Bedford, PA, 1998. 160 pp., illus. $40.00

Photographs and research notes on the longrifles and gunsmiths of York County, Pennsylvania.

Hand Forged for Texas Cowboys, by Kurt House, an Antonio, TX, Three Rivers Publishing, 2005. This beautifully illustrated book features color photos as well as b&w period photos, and will be a welcome addition to the library of any reader. 160 pages. Hardcover. New in new dust jacket. $69.95

Harrington & Richardson Sporting Firearms: Dates of Manufacture 1871-1991, by D.R. Morse. Phoenix, AZ, Firing Pin Enterprizes, 2003. 14 pp. Softcover. $6.95

Covers their pistols, revolvers, rifles, shotguns and commemoratives, plus models.

Hawken Rifle: Its Place in History, by Charles E. Hanson Jr., The Fur Press, Chadron, NE, 1979. 104 pp., illus. Paper covers. $15.00

A definitive work on this famous rifle.

Hi-Standard Sporting Firearms: Dates of Manufacture, by D.R. Morse. 1926-1992. Phoenix, AZ, Firing Pin Enterprizes, 2003. 22 pp. Softcover. New. $6.95

Covers their pistols, revolvers, rifles, shotguns and commemoratives, plus models and serial numbers.

High Standard: A Collector's Guide to the Hamden & Hartford Target Pistols, by Tom Dance, Andrew Mowbray, Inc., Lincoln, RI, 1991. 192 pp. Paper covers. $24.00

From Citation to Supermatic, all of the production models and specials made from 1951 to 1984 are covered according to model number or series.

History of Modern U.S. Military Small Arms Ammunition, Volume 1, 1880-1939, revised by F.W. Hackley, W.H. Woodin and E.L. Scranton, Thomas Publications, Gettysburg, PA, 1998. 328 pp., illus. $49.95

This revised edition incorporates all publicly available information concerning military small arms ammunition for the period 1880 through 1939 in a single volume.

History of Modern U.S. Military Small Arms Ammunition, Volume 2, 1940-1945, by F.W. Hackley, W.H. Woodin and E.L. Scranton, Gun Room Press, Highland Park, NJ, 1998. 297 pages, illustrated. $49.95

Based on decades of original research conducted at the National Archives, numerous military, public and private museums and libraries, as well as individual collections, this edition incorporates all publicly available information concerning military small arms ammunition for the period 1940 through 1945.

History of Smith & Wesson Firearms, by Dean Boorman, Lyons Press, New York, NY, 2002. 44 pp., illustrated in full color. Hardcover. $29.95

The definitive guide to one of the world's best-known firearms makers. Takes the story through the years of the Military and Police 38 and of the Magnum cartridge, to today's wide range of products for law-enforcement customers.

History of Winchester Rifles, by Dean Boorman, Lyons Press, New York, NY, 2001. 144 pp., illus. 150 full-color photos. $29.95

A captivating and wonderfully photographed history of one of the most legendary names in gun lore.

History of Colt Firearms, by Dean Boorman, Lyons Press, New York, NY, 2001. 144 pp., illus. $29.95

Discover the fascinating story of the world's most famous revolver, complete with more than 150 stunning full-color photographs.

Holsters and Shoulder Stocks of the World, by Anthony Vanderlinden, Greensboro, NC, Wet Dog Publications, 2005. 1st edition. Hardcover $45.95

About 500 holsters and shoulder-stocks will be documented in this first edition. Pistols are listed by make and model. The user guide references the countries that used the holsters so that collectors can instantly refer to either a pistol model or country or use. 204 pages, with over 1000 b& w photos.

Honour Bound: The Chauchat Machine Rifle, by Gerard Demaison and Yves Buffetaut, Collector Grade Publications, Inc., Cobourg, Ont., Canada, 1995. $39.95

The story of the CSRG (Chauchat) machine rifle, the most manufactured automatic weapon of WWI.

Hunting Weapons from the Middle Ages to the Twentieth Century, by Howard L. Blackmore, Dover Publications, Meneola, NY, 2000. 480 pp., illus. Paper covers. $16.95

Dealing mainly with the different classes of weapons used in sport: swords, spears, crossbows, guns, and rifles, from the Middle Ages until the present day.

Illustrations of United States Military Arms 1776-1903 and Their Inspector's Marks, compiled by Turner Kirkland, Pioneer Press, Union City, TN, 1988. 37 pp., illus. Paper covers. $7.00

Reprinted from the 1949 Bannerman catalog. Valuable information for both the advanced and beginning collector.

Imperial German Military Officers' Helmets and Headdress 1871-1918, by Thomas N.G. Stubbs, Atglen, PA, Schiffer Publications, 2003. 1st edition. Hardcover. New in new dust jacket. $79.95

Imperial Japanese Grenade Rifles and Launchers, by Gregory A. Babich and Thomas A. Keep Lemont, PA, Dutch Harlow Publishing, 2004. 1st edition. Hardcover. New in new dust jacket. $75.00

Indian Trade Relics, by Lar Hothem, Paducah, KY, Collector Books, 2003. 1st edition. 320pp. Pictorial Hardcover. $29.95

Indian War Cartridge Pouches, Boxes and Carbine Boots, by R. Stephen Dorsey, Collector's Library, Eugene, OR, 1993. 156 pp., illus. Paper covers. $20.00

The key reference work to the cartridge pouches, boxes, carbine sockets and boots of the Indian War period 1865-1890.

Individual Gear and Personal Items of the GI in Europe 1942-1945; From Pro-Kits to Pin-Up, by James Klokner, Atglen., PA, Schiffer Publications, 2005. 224 pages with over 470 color and b&w photographs. Hardcover. $59.95

This book is by far the best and most complete study available of personal items of the American soldier during World War II and truly an indispensable resource.

International Armament, with History, Data, Technical Information and Photographs of Over 800 Weapons, 2nd edition, new printing, by George B. Johnson, Alexandria, VA, Ironside International, 2002. Hardcover. New in new dust jacket. $59.95

The development and progression of modern military small arms. Over 800 photographs and illustrations with both historical and technical data. Two volumes are now bound into one book.

Jaeger Rifles, collected articles published in Muzzle Blasts, by George Shumway, York PA, 2003. Reprint. 108 pp., illus. Stiff paper covers. New. $30.00

Thirty-six articles previously published in ***Muzzle Blasts*** are reproduced here.

Japanese Rifles of World War Two, by Duncan O. McCollum, Excalibur Publications, Latham, NY, 1996. 64 pp., illus. Paper covers. $18.95

A sweeping view of the rifles and carbines that made up Japan's arsenal during the conflict.

Kentucky Rifle, by Captain John G.W. Dillin, George Shumway Publisher, York, PA, 1993. 221 pp., illus. $50.00

This well-known book was the first attempt to tell the story of the American longrifle. This edition retains the original text and illustrations with supplemental footnotes provided by Dr. George Shumway.

Legends and Reality of the AK, by Val Shilin and Charlie Cutshaw, Paladen Press, Boulder, CO, 2000. 192 pp., illus. Paper covers. $35.00

A behind-the-scenes look at history, design and impact of the Kalashnikov family of weapons.

Light 6-Pounder Battalion Gun of 1776, by Adrian Caruana, Museum Restoration Service, Bloomfield, Ontario, Canada, 2001. 76 pp., illus. Paper covers. $8.95

London Gun Trade, 1850-1920, by Joyce E. Gooding, Museum Restoration Service, Bloomfield, Ontario, Canada, 2001. 48 pp., illus. Paper covers. $8.95

Names, dates and locations of London gunmakers working between 1850 and 1920 are listed. Compiled from the original Kelly's post office directories of the City of London.

London Gunmakers and the English Duelling Pistol, 1770-1830, by Keith R. Dill, Museum Restoration Service, Bloomfield, Ontario, Canada, 1997. 36 pp., illus. Paper covers. $8.95

Ten gunmakers made London one of the major gunmaking centers of the world. This book examines how the design and construction of their pistols contributed to that reputation and how these characteristics may be used to date flintlock arms.

Longrifles of Pennsylvania, Volume 1, Jefferson, Clarion & Elk Counties, by Russel H. Harringer, George Shumway Publisher, York, PA, 1984. 200 pp., illus. $50.00

First in series that will treat in great detail the longrifles and gunsmiths of Pennsylvania.

M1 Garand .30 Assembly, Disassembly Manual, by Skennerton & Riling, Ray Riling Arms Books Co. Philadelphia, PA 2004. 36 pages, $5.00

With over 60 photos & line drawings. Ideal workshop reference for stripping & assembly with exploded parts drawings, specifications, service accessories, historical information and recommended reading references.

M1 Carbine .30 M1, M1A1, M2 & M3 Assembly, Disassembly Manual, by Skennerton & Riling, Ray Riling Arms Books Co. Philadelphia, PA 2004. 36 pages, $5.00

With over 60 photos & line drawings. Ideal workshop reference for stripping & assembly with exploded parts drawings, specifications, service accessories, historical information and recommended reading references.

M1 Carbine: A Revolution in Gun-Stocking, by Grafton H. Cook II and Barbara W. Cook, Lincoln, RI, Andrew Mowbray, Inc., 2002. 1st edition. 208 pp., heavily illustrated with 157 rare photographs of the guns and the men and women who made them. Softcover. $29.95

Shows you, step by step, how M1 carbine stocks were made, right through to assembly with the hardware. Also contains lots of detailed information about other military weapons, like the M1A1, the M1 Garand, the M14 and much, much more.

M1 Carbine: Design, Development, and Production, by Larry Ruth, Gun Room Press, Highland Park, NJ, 1987. 291 pp., illus. Paper $19.95

The origin, development, manufacture and use of this famous carbine of WWII.

M1 Carbine Owner's Guide, by Larry Ruth and Scott A. Duff, Scott A. Duff Publications, Export, PA, 1997. 126 pp., illus. Paper covers. $21.95

This book answers the questions M1 owners most often ask concerning maintenance activities not encounted by military users.

M1 Garand: Owner's Guide, by Scott A. Duff, Scott A. Duff Publications, Export, PA, 1998. 132 pp., illus. Paper covers. $21.95

This book answers the questions M1 owners most often ask concerning maintenance activities not encounted by military users.

M1 Garand Complete Assembly Guide, Vol 2, by Scott A. Duff, Scott A. Duff Publications, Export, PA, 2006. 162 pp., illus. Paper covers. $20.95

This book goes beyond the military manuals in depth and scope, using words It won't make you an Garand armorer, but it will make you a more knowledgeable owner.

M1 Garand: Post World War, by Scott A. Duff, Scott A. Duff Publications, Export, PA, 1990. 139 pp., illus. Softcover. $21.95

A detailed account of the activities at Springfield Armory through this period. International Harvester, H&R, Korean War production and quantities delivered. Serial numbers.

M1 Garand: World War II, by Scott A. Duff, Scott A. Duff Publications, Export, PA, 2001. 210 pp., illus. Paper covers. $34.95

The most comprehensive study available to the collector and historian on the M1 Garand of WWII.

M1 Garand 1936 to 1957, 4th Edition, Revised & Expanded, by Joe Poyer and Craig Riesch, North Cape Publications, Tustin, CA, 2006. 232 pp., illus. PC. $19.95

Describes the entire range of M1 Garand production in text and quick-scan charts.

M1 Garand Serial Numbers and Data Sheets, by Scott A. Duff, Scott A. Duff Publications, Export, PA, 1995. 101 pp., illus. Paper covers. $11.95

Provides the reader with serial numbers related to dates of manufacture and a large sampling of data sheets to aid in identification or restoration.

Machine Guns, by Ian V. Hogg, Iola, WI, Krause Publications, 2002. 1st edition. 336 pp., illustrated with b&w photos with a 16-page color section. Softcover. $29.95

A detailed history of the rapid-fire gun, 14th Century to present. Covers the development, history and specifications.

Made in the C.S.A.: Saddle Makers of the Confederacy, by Ken R. Knopp, Hattiesburg, MS, privately printed, 2003. 1st edition signed. 205 pp., illus., signed by the author. Softcover. $30.00

Maine Made Guns and Their Makers, by Dwight B. Demeritt Jr., Maine State Museum, Augusta, ME, 1998. 209 pp., illus. $55.00

An authoritative, biographical study of Maine gunsmiths.

Marksmanship in the U.S. Army, by William Emerson, Oklahoma, Univ. of Oklahoma Press, 2004 256 pages Illustrated with b&w photos. Hardcover. $64.95

Marlin Firearms: A History of the Guns and the Company That Made Them, by Lt. Col. William S. Brophy, USAR, Ret., Stackpole Books, Harrisburg, PA, 1989. 672 pp., illus. $89.95

The definitive book on the Marlin Firearms Co. and their products.

Martini-Henry .450 Rifles & Carbines, by Dennis Lewis, Excalibur Publications, Latham, NY, 1996. 72 pp., illus. Paper covers. $11.95

The stories of the rifles and carbines that were the mainstay of the British soldier through the Victorian wars.

Mauser Bolt Rifles, by Ludwig Olson, F. Brownell & Son, Inc., Montezuma, IA, 1999. 364 pp., illus. $64.95

The most complete, detailed, authoritative and comprehensive work ever done on Mauser bolt rifles. Completely revised deluxe 3rd edition.

Mauser Military Rifle Markings, by Terence W. Lapin, Arlington, VA, Hyrax Publishers, LLC, 2001. 167 pp., illus. 2nd edition. Revised and expanded. Softcover. $22.95

A general guide to reading and understanding the often mystifying markings found on military Mauser rifles. Includes German Regimental markings as well as German police markings and WWII German Mauser subcontractor codes. A handy reference to take to gun shows.

Military Holsters of World War II, by Eugene J. Bender, Rowe Publications, Rochester, NY, 1998. 200 pp., illus. $49.95

A revised edition with a new price guide of the most definitive book on this subject.

Military Remington Rolling Block Rifle, The, by George Layman, Pioneer Press, TN, 1998. 146 pp., illus. Paper covers. $24.95

A standard reference for those with an interest in the Remington rolling block family of firearms.

Mortimer, the Gunmakers, 1753-1923, by H. Lee Munson, Andrew Mowbray Inc., Lincoln, RI, 1992. 320 pp., illus. $65.00

Seen through a single, dominant, English gunmaking dynasty, this fascinating study provides a window into the classical era of firearms artistry.

Mossberg Sporting Firearms: Dates of Manufacture, by D.R. Morse, Phoenix, AZ, Firing Pin Enterprizes, 2003. Softcover. $6.95

Covers their pistols, revolvers, rifles, shotguns and commemoratives, plus models and serial numbers.

MP38, 40, 40/1 & 41 Submachine Gun, by de Vries & Martens. Propaganda Photo Series, Volume II. Alexandria, VA, Ironside International, 2001. 1st edition. 150 pp., illustrated with 200 high quality b&w photos. Hardcover. $34.95

Covers all essential information on history and development, ammunition and accessories, codes and markings, and contains photos of nearly every model and accessory. Includes a unique selection of original German WWII propaganda photos, most never published before.

Navy Luger, by Joachim Gortz and John Walter, Handgun Press, Glenview, IL, 1988. 128 pp., illus. $24.95

The 9mm Pistole 1904 and the Imperial German Navy. A concise illustrated history.

New World of Russian Small Arms and Ammunition, by Charlie Cutshaw, Paladin Press, Boulder, CO, 1998. 160 pp., illus. $42.95

Detailed descriptions, specifications and first-class illustrations of the AN-94, PSS silent pistol, Bizon SMG, Saifa-12 tactical shotgun, the GP-25 grenade launcher and more cutting edge Russian weapons.

Number 5 Jungle Carbine, by Alan M. Petrillo, Excalibur Publications, Latham, NY, 1994. 32 pp., illus. Paper covers. $7.95

A comprehensive treatment of the rifle that collectors have come to call the "Jungle Carbine"– the Lee-Enfield Number 5, Mark 1.

Observations on Colt's Second Contract, November 2, 1847, by G. Maxwell Longfield and David T. Basnett, Museum Restoration Service, Bloomfield, Ontario, Canada, 1997. 36 pp., illus. Paper covers. $6.95

This study traces the history and the construction of the Second Model Colt Dragoon supplied in 1848 to the U.S. Cavalry.

Official Soviet SVD Manual, The, by Major James F. Gebhardt (Ret.), Paladin Press, Boulder, CO, 1999. 112 pp., illus. Paper covers. $22.00

Operating instructions for the 7.62mm Dragunov, the first Russian rifle developed from scratch specifically for sniping.

Ordnance Tools, Accessories & Appendages of the M1 Rifle, by Billy Pyle. Houston, TX, privately printed, 2002. 2nd edition. 206 pp., illustrated with b&w photos. Softcover $40.00

OSS Special Weapons II, by John Brunner, Williamstown, NJ, Phillips Publications, 2005, 2nd edition. 276pp. profusely illustrated with photos, some in color. Hardcover, New in New DJ. $59.95

P-08 Parabellum Luger Automatic Pistol, The, edited by J. David McFarland, Desert Publications, Cornville, AZ, 1982. 20 pp., illus. Paper covers. $11.95

Covers every facet of the Luger, plus a listing of all known Luger models.

Packing Iron, by Richard C. Rattenbury, Zon International Publishing, Millwood, NY, 1993. 216 pp., illus. $45.00

The best book yet produced on pistol holsters and rifle scabbards. Over 300 variations of holster and scabbards are illustrated in large, clear plates.

Painted Steel, Steel Pots Volume 2, by Chris Armold, Bender Publishing, San Jose, CA, 2001. 384 pp.-1,053 photos, hundreds in color. $57.95

From the author of ***Steel Pots: The History of America's Steel Combat Helmets*** comes ***Painted Steel: Steel Pots, Vol. II.*** This companion volume features detailed chapters on painted and unit marked helmets of WWI and WWII, plus a variety of divisional, regimental and subordinate markings. Special full-color plates detail subordinate unit markings such as the tactical markings used by the U.S. 2nd Division in WWI.

Parker Gun Catalog 1900, by Parker Brothers, Davis, IL: Old Reliable Publishing, 1996. Reprint. One of the most attractive and sought-after of the Parker gun catalogs, this one shows the complete Parker line circa 1900. This is the only catalog which pictures EH and NH grades, and is the first to picture $50.00 VH grade. A deluxe reprint, 15pp., illustrated. Stiff Paper Covers. Fine. $10.00

Parker Gun Catalog 1910, by Parker Brothers, Davis, IL: Old Reliable Publishing, 1996. Reprint. One of the most attractive and sought-after of the Parker gun catalogs, this one shows the complete Parker line circa 1910. A deluxe reprint, 20pp., illustrated. Stiff Paper Covers. Fine. $10.00

Parker Gun Catalog 1913 (Flying Ducks), by Parker Brothers, Davis, IL: Old Reliable Publishing, 1996. 36pp., illustrated. Stiff Paper Covers. Fine. $20.00

One of the most attractive and sought-after of the Parker gun catalogs, this one shows the complete Parker line circa 1913. A deluxe reprint, it has the same embossed cover as the original "Flying Ducks" catalog.

Pattern Dates for British Ordnance Small Arms, 1718-1783, by DeWitt Bailey, Thomas Publications, Gettysburg, PA, 1997. 116 pp., illus. Paper covers. $20.00

The weapons discussed in this work are those carried by troops sent to North America between 1737 and 1783, or shipped to them as replacement arms while in America.

Percussion Ammunition Packets 1845-1888 Union, Confederate & European, by John J. Malloy, Dean S. Thomas and Terry A. White with Foreward by Norm Flayderman. Gettysburg, PA, Thomas Publications, 2003. 1st edition. 134 pp., illustrated with color photos. Hardcover. New. $75.00

Finally a means to recognize the untold variety of labeled types of ammunition box labels.

Peters & King, by Thomas D. Schiffer. Krause Publications, Iola, WI 2002. 1st edition. 256 pp., 200+ b&w photos with a 32-page color section. Hardcover. $44.95

Discover the history behind Peters Cartridge and King Powder and see how they shaped the arms industry into what it is today and why their products fetch hundreds, even thousands of dollars at auctions. Current values are provided for their highly collectible product packaging and promotional advertising premiums such as powder kegs, tins, cartridge boxes, and calendars.

Presentation and Commercial Colt Walker Pistols, by Col. Robert D. Whittington III. Hooks, TX, Brownlee Books, 2005. A limited edition of 1,000 copies. Numbered. 21 pp. Paper covers. New. $15.00

A study of events at the Whitneyville Armoury and Samuel Colt's Hartford Factory from 1 June 1847 to 29 November 1848.

Presentation and Commercial Colt Walker Pistols, 2nd Revision, by Col. Robert D. Whittington III. Hooks, TX, Brownlee Books, 2006. A limited edition of 1,000 copies. Numbered. 26 pp. Paper covers. New. $20.00

A study of events at the Whitneyville Armoury and Samuel Colt's Hartford Factory from 1 June 1847 to 29 November 1848. Updated.

Price Guide: Orders and Decorations Germany, 1871-1945, Second Edition, by Klaus Lubbe, Germany, Niemann,2004. 2nd edition. German and English text. 817 pages, over 2,000 photos. Hardcover. $104.95

It is a reference for prices as well as on the differences between the various orders, decorations, award documents, award cases of issue, and miniatures. No fantasy pieces are included, or projected orders which were never realized.

Proud Promise: French Autoloading Rifles, 1898-1979, by Jean Huon, Collector Grade Publications, Inc., Cobourg, Ont., Canada, 1995. 216 pp., illus. $39.95

The author has finally set the record straight about the importance of French contributions to modern arms design.

Purdey Gun and Rifle Makers: The Definitive History, by Donald Dallas, Quiller Press, London, 2000. 245 pp., illus. Color throughout. A limited edition of 3,000 copies. Signed and numbered. With a PURDEY book plate. $99.95

Queen Anne Pistol, 1660-1780: A History of the Turn-Off Pistol, by John W. Burgoyne, Bloomfield, Ont., Canada, Museum Restoration Service, 2002. 1st edition-Historical Arms New Series No. 1. 120 pp. Pictorial hardcover. $35.00

A detailed, fast moving, thoroughly researched text and almost 200 cross-referenced illustrations.

Recreating the 18th Century Powder Horn, by Scott and Cathy Sibley, Texarkana, TX, Scurlock Publishing, 2005. 1st edition. 91 pages. Softcover. $19.95

Scott and Cathy Sibley demonstrates every detail and secret of recreating an 18th century powder horn. New and experienced horn makers will enjoy this how-to book. Lavishly illustrated wtih full-color photos and step-by-step illustrations.

Red Shines The Sun: A Pictorial History of the Fallschirm-Infantrie, by Eric Queen. San Jose, CA, R. James Bender Publishing, 2003. 1st edition. Hardcover. $69.95

A culmination of 12 years of research, this reference work traces the history of the Army paratroopers of the Fallschirm-Infanterie from their origins in 1937, to the expansion to battalion strength in 1938, then on through operations at Wola Gulowska (Poland), and Moerdijk (Holland). This 240-page comprehensive look at their history is supported by 600 images, many of which are in full color, and nearly 90% are previously unpublished.

Reloading Tools, Sights and Telescopes for Single Shot Rifles, by Gerald O. Kelver, Brighton, CO, 1982. 163 pp., illus. Paper covers. $13.95

A listing of most of the famous makers of reloading tools, sights and telescopes with a brief description of the products they manufactured.

Remington-Lee Rifle, by Eugene F. Myszkowski, Excalibur Publications, Latham, NY, 1995. 100 pp., illus. Paper covers. $22.50

Features detailed descriptions, including serial number ranges, of each model from the first Lee magazine rifle produced for the U.S. Navy to the last Remington-Lee small bore shipped to the Cuban Rural Guard.

Remington 'America's Oldest Gunmaker', The Official Authorized History of the Remington Arms Company, by Roy Marcot. Madison, NC, Remington Arms Company, 1999. 1st edition. 312 pp., with 167 b&w illustrations, plus 291 color plates. $79.95

This is without a doubt the finest history of that firm ever to have been compiled. Based on firsthand research in the Remington company archives, it is extremely well written.

Remington Sporting Firearms: Dates of Manufacture, by D.R. Morse, Phoenix, AZ, Firing Pin Enterprizes, 2003. 43 pp. Softcover. New. $6.95

Covers their pistols, revolvers, rifles, shotguns and commemoratives, plus models and serial numbers.

Remington's Vest Pocket Pistols, by Robert E. Hatfield, Lincoln, RI, Andrew Mowbray, Inc., 2002. 117 pp. Hardcover. $29.95

While Remington Vest Pocket pistols have always been popular with collectors, very little solid information has been available about them. Inside you will find 100+ photographs, serial number data, exploded views of all four Remington Vest Pocket pistol sizes, component parts lists and a guide to disassembly and reassembly. Also includes a discussion of Vest Pocket Wire-Stocked Buggy/Bicycle rifles, plus the documented serial number story.

Revolvers of the British Services 1854-1954, by W.H.J. Chamberlain and A.W.F. Taylerson, Museum Restoration Service, Ottawa, Canada, 1989. 80 pp., illus. $27.50

Covers the types issued among many of the United Kingdom's naval, land or air services.

Rifles of the U.S. Army 1861-1906, by John D. McAulay, Andrew Mowbray, Inc., Lincoln, RI, 2003. 1st edition. Over 40 rifles covered, 278 pp., illus. Hardcover. New. $47.95

This exciting new book by renowned authority John McAulay gives the reader detailed coverage of the issue and actual field service of America's fighting rifles, both in peacetime and in war, including their military service with the infantry, artillery, cavalry and engineers. One feature that all readers will value is the impressive number of historical photos, taken during the Civil War, the Mexican War, the Indian Wars, the Spanish-American War, the Philippine Insurrection and more. Procurement information, issue details and historical background.

Ruger and his Guns, by R.L. Wilson, Book Sales, New York, NY, 2006. 358 pp., illus. $24.95

A history of the man, the company and their firearms.

Running Recon: A photo Jorney with SOG Special Ops Along the Ho Chi Minh Trail, by Frank Grecco. Boulder, CO: Paladin Press, 2006. Softcover. $50.00

Running Recon is a combination of military memoir and combat photography book. It reflects both the author's experience in Kontum, Vietnam, from April 1969 to April 1970 as part of the top-secret Studies and Observation Group (SOG) and the collective experience of SOG veterans in general.

Russell M. Catron and His Pistols, by Warren H. Buxton, Ucross Books, Los Alamos, NM, 1998. 224 pp., illus. Paper covers. $49.50

An unknown American firearms inventor and manufacturer of the mid-twentieth century. Military, commerical, ammunition.

SAFN-49 and the FAL, by Joe Poyer and Dr. Richard Feirman, North Cape Publications, Tustin, CA, 1998. 160 pp., illus. Paper covers. $14.95

The first complete overview of the SAFN-49 battle rifle, from its pre-WWII beginnings to its military service in countries as diverse as the Belgian Congo and Argentina. The FAL was a "light" version of the SAFN-49 and it became the Free World's most adopted battle rifle.

Sash Hook Smith & Wesson Revolvers, The, by Col. Robert D. Whittington III. & and Kolman A. Gabel, Hooks, TX, Brownlee Books, 2003. A limited edition of 1,000 copies. Numbered. 10 pp. Paper covers. New. $10.00

The true story of the Sash Hook Smith & Wesson Revolvers and how they came to be.

Savage Sporting Firearms: Dates of Manufacture 1907-1997, by D.R. Morse. Phoenix, AZ, Firing Pin Enterprizes, 2003. 22 pp. Softcover. New. $6.95

Covers their pistols, revolvers, rifles, shotguns and commemoratives, plus models and serial numbers.

Scottish Firearms, by Claude Blair and Robert Woosnam-Savage, Museum Restoration Service, Bloomfield, Ont., Canada, 1995. 52 pp., illus. Paper covers. $8.95

This revision of the first book devoted entirely to Scottish firearms is supplemented by a register of surviving Scottish long guns.

Sharps Firearms, by Frank Seller, Denver, CO, 1998. 358 pp., illus. $65.00

Traces the development of Sharps firearms with full range of guns made including all martial variations.

Sight Book; Winchester, Lyman, Marble, and Other Companies, by George Madis, Borwsboro,TX, Art & Reference House, 2005. 1st edition. 183 pages, with over 350 illustrations. Hardcover. $26.95

Silk and Steel: Women at Arms, by R. L. Wilson, New York, Random House, 2003. 1st edition. 300+ Striking four-color images; 8½" x 11", 320 pgs. Hardcover. New in new dust jacket. (9775). $65.00

Beginning with Artemis and Diana, goddesses of hunting, evolving through modern times, here is the first comprehensive presentation on the subject of women and firearms. No object has had a greater impact on world history over the past 650 years than the firearm, and a surprising number of women have been keen on the subject, as shooters, hunters, collectors, engravers, and even gunmakers.

SKS Carbine, by Steve Kehaya and Joe Poyer, North Cape Publications, Tustin, CA, 1997. 150 pp., illus. Paper covers. $16.95

The first comprehensive examination of a major historical firearm used through the Vietnam conflict to the diamond fields of Angola.

SKS Type 45 Carbines, by Duncan Long, Desert Publications, El Dorado, AZ, 1992. 110 pp., illus. Paper covers. $19.95

Covers the history and practical aspects of operating, maintaining and modifying this abundantly available rifle.

Slave Badges and the Slave-Hire System in Charleston, South Carolina, 1783-1865, by Harlan Greene, Harry S. Hutchins Jr., Brian E. Hutchins. Jefferson, NC, McFarland & Company, 2004. 152 pp. Hardcover, $35.00

Smith & Wesson 1857-1945, by Robert J. Neal and Roy G. Jinks, R&R Books, Livonia, NY, 1996. 434 pp., illus. $50.00

The bible for all existing and aspiring Smith & Wesson collectors.

Smith & Wesson Sporting Firearms: Dates of Manufacture, by D.R. Morse, Phoenix, AZ, Firing Pin Enterprizes, 2003. 76 pp. Softcover. $6.95

Covers their pistols, revolvers, rifles, shotguns and commemoratives, plus models and serial numbers.

Sniper Variations of the German K98k Rifle, by Richard D. Law, Collector Grade Publications, Ontario, Canada, 1997. 240 pp., illus. $47.50

Volume 2 of "Backbone of the Wehrmacht" the author's in-depth study of the German K98k rifle. This volume concentrates on the telescopic-sighted rifle of choice for most German snipers during WWII.

Southern Derringers of the Mississippi Valley, by Turner Kirkland, Pioneer Press, Tenn., 1971. 80 pp., illus., paper covers. $10.00

A guide for the collector and a much-needed study.

Soviet Russian Tokarev "TT" Pistols and Cartridges 1929-1953, by Fred Datig, Graphic Publishers, Santa Ana, CA, 1993. 168 pp., illus. $39.95

Details of rare arms and their accessories are shown in hundreds of photos. It also contains a complete bibliography and index.

Spencer Repeating Firearms, by Roy M. Marcot, New York, Rowe Publications, 2002. 316 pp.; numerous b&w photos and illustrations. Hardcover. $65.00

Springfield 1903 Rifles, by Lt. Col. William S. Brophy, USAR, Ret., Stackpole Books Inc., Harrisburg, PA, 1985. 608 pp., illus. $75.00

The illustrated, documented story of the design, development, and production of all the models, appendages, and accessories.

SS Headgear, by Kit Wilson. Johnson Reference Books, Fredericksburg, VA. 72 pp., 15 full-color plates and over 70 b&w photos. $16.50

An excellent source of information concerning all types of SS headgear, to include Allgemeine-SS, Waffen-SS, visor caps, helmets, overseas caps, M-43's and miscellaneous headgear. Also includes a guide on the availability and current values of SS headgear. This guide was compiled from auction catalogs, dealer price lists, and input from advanced collectors in the field.

SS Helmets: A Collector's Guide, Vol 1, by Kelly Hicks, Johnson Reference Books, Fredericksburg, VA. 96 pp., illus. $17.50

Deals only with SS helmets and features some very nice color close-up shots of the different SS decals used. Over 85 photographs, 27 in color. The author has documented most of the known types of SS helmets, and describes in detail all of the vital things to look for in determining the originality, style type, and finish.

SS Helmets: A Collector's Guide, Vol 2, by Kelly Hicks. Johnson Reference Books, Fredericksburg, VA. 2000. 128 pp. 107 full-color photos, 14 period photos. $25.00

Volume II contains dozen of highly detailed, full-color photos of rare and original SS and Field Police helmets, featuring both sides as well as interior view. The outstanding decal section offers detailed close-ups of original SS and Police decals and, in conjunction with Volume I, completes the documentation of virtually all types of original decal variations used between 1934 and 1945.

SS Uniforms, Insignia and Accoutrements, by A. Hayes. Schiffer Publications, Atglen, PA. 1996. 248 pp., with over 800 color and b&w photographs. $69.95

This new work explores in detailed color the complex subject of Allgemeine and Waffen-SS uniforms, insignia, and accoutrements. Hundreds of authentic items are extensively photographed in close-up to enable the reader to examine and study.

Sturmgewehr! From Firepower to Striking Power, by Hans-Dieter Handrich. Canada, Collector Grade, 2004. 1st edition. 600pp., 392 illustrations. Hardcover $79.95

Hans-Dieter spent years researching original documentation held in the military archives of Germany and elsewhere to produce the entire technical and tactical history of the design, development and fielding of the world's first mass-produced assault rifle and the revolutionary 7.92x33mm Kurz cartridge.

Sturm Ruger Sporting Firearms: Dates of Manufacture, by D.R. Morse, Phoenix, AZ, Firing Pin Enterprizes, 2003. 22 pp. Softcover, $6.95

Covers their pistols, revolvers, rifles, shotguns and commemoratives, plus models and serial numbers.

Sumptuous Flaske, by Herbert G. Houze, Andrew Mowbray, Inc., Lincoln, RI, 1989. 158 pp., illus. Softcover. $35.00

Catalog of a recent show at the Buffalo Bill Historical Center bringing together some of the finest European and American powder flasks of the 16th to 19th centuries.

Swedish Mauser Rifles, The, by Steve Kehaya and Joe Poyer, North Cape Publications, Tustin, CA, 1999. 267 pp., illus. Paper covers. $19.95

Every known variation of the Swedish Mauser carbine and rifle is described, all match and target rifles and all sniper versions. Includes serial number and production data.

System Lefaucheaux: Continuing the Study of Pinfire Cartridge Arms Including Their Role in the American Civil War, by Chris C. Curtis, Foreword by Norm Flayderman, Armslore Press, 2002. 1st edition. 312 pp., heavily illustrated with b&w photos. Hardcover. New in new dust jacket. $44.95

Thoughts on the Kentucky Rifle in its Golden Age, by Joe K. Kindig, III. York, PA, George Shumway Publisher, 2002. Annotated second edition. 561 pp.; Illustrated. This scarce title, long out of print, is once again available. Hardcover. $85.00

The definitive book on the Kentucky Rifle, illustrating 266 of these guns in 856 detailed photographs.

Tin Lids–Canadian Combat Helmets, #2 in "Up Close" Series, by Roger V. Lucy, Ottawa, Ontario, Service Publications, 2000. 2nd edition. 48 pp. Softcover. $17.95

Toys That Shoot and Other Neat Stuff, by James Dundas, Schiffer Books, Atglen, PA, 1999. 112 pp., illus. Paper covers. $24.95

Shooting toys from the twentieth century, especially 1920s to 1960s, in over 420 color photographs of BB guns, cap shooters, marble shooters, squirt guns and more. Complete with a price guide.

Trade Guns of the Hudson's Bay Company 1670-1970, Historical Arms New Series No. 2, by S. James Gooding, Bloomfield, Ont. Canada, Museum Restoration Service, 2003. 1st edition. 158 pp., thoroughly researched text. Includes bibliographical references. Pictorial hardcover. $35.00

Trapdoor Springfield, by M.D. Waite and B.D. Ernst, The Gun Room Press, Highland Park, NJ, 1983. 250 pp., illus. $39.95

The first comprehensive book on the famous standard military rifle of the 1873-92 period.

Treasures of the Moscow Kremlin: Arsenal of the Russian Tsars, A Royal Armories and the Moscow Kremlin exhibition, HM Tower of London 13, June 1998 to 11 September, 1998, BAS Printers, Over Wallop, Hampshire, England. XXII plus 192 pp. over 180 color illustrations. Text in English and Russian. $65.00

For this exhibition catalog, each of the 94 objects on display are photographed and described in detail to provide the most informative record of this important exhibition.

U.S. Army Headgear 1812-1872, by John P. Langellier and C. Paul Loane. Atglen, PA, Schiffer Publications, 2002. 167 pp., with over 350 color and b&w photos. Hardcover. $69.95

This profusely illustrated volume represents more than three decades of research in public and private collections by military historian John P. Langellier and Civil War authority C. Paul Loane.

U.S. Army Rangers & Special Forces of World War II Their War in Photographs, by Robert Todd Ross, Atglen, PA, Schiffer Publications, 2002. 216 pp., over 250 b&w and color photographs. Hardcover. $59.95

Never before has such an expansive view of WWII elite forces been offered in one volume. An extensive search of public and private archives unearthed an astonishing number of rare and never before seen images, including color. Most notable are the nearly 20 exemplary photographs of Lieutenant Colonel William O. Darby's Ranger Force in Italy, taken by Robert Capa, considered by many to be the greatest combat photographer of all time.

U.S. Guns of World War II, by Paul Davies, Gettysburg, PA, Thomas Publications, 2004. 1st edition. A record of army ordnance research and the development of small arms. Hundreds of photos. 144pp, Softcover. $17.95

U.S. Handguns of World War II: The Secondary Pistols and Revolvers, by Charles W. Pate, Andrew Mowbray, Inc., Lincoln, RI, 1998. 515 pp., illus. $39.00

This indispensable new book covers all of the American military handguns of WWII except for the M1911A1 Colt automatic.

U.S. Martial Single Shot Pistols, by Daniel D. Hartzler and James B. Whisker, Old Bedford Village Press, Bedford, PA, 1998. 128 pp., illus. $45.00

A photographic chronicle of military and semi-martial pistols supplied to the U.S. Government and the several States.

U.S. Military Arms Dates of Manufacture from 1795, by George Madis, Dallas, TX, 1995. 64 pp. Softcover. $9.95

Lists all U.S. military arms of collector interest alphabetically, covering about 250 models.

U.S. Naval Handguns, 1808-1911, by Fredrick R. Winter, Andrew Mowbray Publishers, Lincoln, RI, 1990. 128 pp., illus. $26.00

The story of U.S. Naval handguns spans an entire century–included are sections on each of the important naval handguns within the period.

U.S. Silent Service-Dolphins & Combat Insignia 1924-1945, by David Jones. Bender Publishing, San Jose, CA, 2001. 224 pp., 532 photos (most in full color). $39.95

This beautiful full-color book chronicles, with period letters and sketches, the developmental history of U.S. submarine insignia prior to 1945. It also contains many rare and never before published photographs, plus interviews with WWII submarine veterans, from enlisted men to famous skippers. All known contractors are covered plus embroidered versions, mess dress variations, the Roll of Honor, submarine combat insignia, battleflags, launch memorabilia and related submarine collectibles (postal covers, match book covers, jewelry, posters, advertising art, postcards.

Uniform and Dress Army and Navy of the Confederate States of America (Official Regulations), by Confederate States of America, Ray Riling Arms Books, Philadelphia, PA, 1960. $20.00

A portfolio containing a complete set of nine color plates especially prepared for framing, reproduced in exactly 200 sets from the very rare Richmond, VA., 1861 regulations.

Uniforms & Equipment of the Austro-Hungarian Army in World War One, by Spencer A. Coil, Atglen, PA, Schiffer Publications, 2003. 1st edition. 352 pp., with over 550 b&w and color photographs. Hardcover. New in new dust jacket. $69.95

Uniforms and Insignia of the Cossacks in the German Wehrmacht in World War II, by Peter Schuster and Harald Tiede, Atglen, PA, Schiffer Publications, 2003. 1st edition. 160 pp., illustrated with over 420 b&w and color photographs. Hardcover. New in new dust jacket. $49.95

Uniforms & Equipment of the Imperial German Army 1900-1918: A Study in Period Photographs, by Charles Woolley, Schiffer Publications, Atglen, PA, 2000. 375 pp., over 500 b&w photographs and 50 color drawings. Fully illustrated. $69.95

Features formal studio portraits of pre-war dress and wartime uniforms of all arms. Includes a 60-page full-color uniform section reproduced from rare 1914 plates.

Uniforms of the Third Reich: A Study in Photographs, by Maguire Hayes, Schiffer Publications, Atglen, PA, 1997. 200 pp., with over 400 color photographs. $69.95

This new book takes a close look at a variety of authentic WWII era German uniforms including examples from the Army, Luftwaffe, Kriegsmarine, Waffen-SS, Allgemeine-SS, Hitler youth and political leaders. Various accoutrements worn with the uniforms are also included to aid the collector.

Uniforms of the United States Army, 1774-1889, by Henry Alexander Ogden, Dover Publishing, Mineola, NY. 1998. 48 pp. of text plus 44 color plates. Softcover. $9.95

A republication of the work published by the quarter-master general, United States army in 1890. A striking collection of lithographs and a marvelous archive of military, social, and costume history portraying the gamut of U.S. Army uniforms from fatigues to full dress, between 1774 and 1889.

Uniforms of the Waffen-SS; Black Service Uniform-LAH Guard Uniform-SS Earth-Grey Service Uniform-Model 1936 Field Service Uniform-1939-1940-1941 Volume 1, by Michael D. Beaver, Schiffer Publications, Atglen, PA, 2002. 272 pp., with 500 color, and b&w photos. $79.95

This spectacular work is a heavily documented record of all major clothing articles of the Waffen-SS. Hundreds of unpublished photographs were used in production. This book is indispensable and an absolute must-have for any serious historian of WWII German uniforms.

Uniforms of the Waffen-SS; Sports and Drill Uniforms-Black Panzer Uniform-Camouflage-Concentration Camp Personnel-SD-SS Female Auxiliaries, Volume 3, by Michael D. Beaver, Schiffer Publications, Atglen, PA, 2002. 272 pp., with 500 color, and b&w photos. $79.95

Uniforms of the Waffen-SS; 1942-1943-1944-1945-Ski Uniforms-Overcoats-White Service Uniforms-Tropical Clothing, Volume 2, by Michael D. Beaver, Schiffer Publications, Atglen, PA, 2002. 272 pp., with 500 color, and b&w photos. $79.95

Uniforms, Organization, and History of the German Police, Volume I, by John R. Angolia and Hugh Page Taylor, San Jose, CA, R. James Bender Publishing, 2004. 704 pp. illustrated with b&w and color photos. Hardcover. $59.95

United States Marine Corps Uniforms, Insignia, and Personal Items of World War II, by Harlan Glenn Atglen, PA: Schiffer Publications, 2005. 1st edition. 272pp. Hardcover. $79.95

Covering in detail the combat and dress uniforms of the United States Marine in World War II, this new volume is destined to become the World War II Marine Corps collector's reference! Shown in detail are the herringbone utilities that Marines wore from Guadalcanal to Okinawa, as well as Summer Service, Winter Service and Dress (Blues) uniforms.

United States Martial Flintlocks, by Robert M. Reilly, Mowbray Publishing Co., Lincoln, RI, 1997. 264 pp., illus. $40.00

A comprehensive history of American flintlock longarms and handguns (mostly military) c. 1775 to c. 1840.

United States Submachine Guns: From the American 180 to the ZX-7, by Frank Iannamico, Harmony, ME, Moose Lake Publishing, 2004. 1st edition. This profusely illustrated new book covers the research and development of the submachine gun in the U.S. from World War I to the present. to1943. Many photos and charts, nearly 500 pages! Soft cover. $29.95

Variations of Colt's New Model Police and Pocket Breech Loading Pistols, by John D. Breslin, William Q. Pirie and David E. Price, Lincoln, RI, Andrew Mowbray Publishers, 2002. 1st edition. 158 pp., heavily illustrated with over 160 photographs and superb technical detailed drawings and diagrams. Pictorial hardcover. $37.95

A type-by-type guide to what collectors call small frame conversions.

Vietnam Order of Battle, by Shelby L. Stanton, William C. Westmoreland. Mechanicsburg, PA, Stackpole Books, 2003. 1st edition. 416 pp., 32 in full color, 101 pp. halftones. Hardcover. New in new dust jacket. $69.95

Visor Hats of the United States Armed Forces 1930-1950, by Joe Tonelli, Atglen, PA, Schiffer Publications, 2003. 1st edition. Hardcover. New in new dust jacket. $79.95

W.F. Cody Buffalo Bill Collector's Guide with Values, The, by James W. Wojtowicz, Collector Books, Paducah, KY, 1998. 271 pp., illus. $24.95

A profusion of colorful collectibles including lithographs, programs, photographs, books, medals, sheet music, guns, etc. and today's values.

Walther: A German Legend, by Manfred Kersten, Safari Press, Inc., Huntington Beach, CA, 2000. 400 pp., illus. $85.00

This comprehensive book covers, in rich detail, all aspects of the company and its guns, including an illustrious and rich history, the WWII years, all the pistols (models 1 through 9), the P-38, P-88, the long guns, 22 rifles, centerfires, Wehrmacht guns, and even a gun that could shoot around a corner.

Walther P-38 Pistol, by Maj. George Nonte, Desert Publications, Cornville, AZ, 1982. 100 pp., illus. Paper covers. $12.95

Complete volume on one of the most famous handguns to come out of WWII. All models covered.

Walther Pistols: Models 1 Through P99, Factory Variations and Copies, by Dieter H. Marschall, Ucross Books, Los Alamos, NM. 2000. 140 pp., with 140 b&w illustrations, index. Paper covers. $19.95

This is the English translation, revised and updated, of the highly successful and widely acclaimed German language edition. This book provides the collector with a reference guide and overview of the entire line of the Walther military, police, and self-defense pistols from the very first to the very latest. Models 1-9, PP, PPK, MP, AP, HP, P.38, P1, P4, P38K, P5, P88, P99 and the Manurhin models. Variations, where issued, serial ranges, calibers, marks, proofs, logos, and design aspects in an astonishing quantity and variety are crammed into this very well researched and highly regarded work.

Walther Models PP & PPK, 1929-1945 – Volume 1, by James L. Rankin, Coral Gables, FL, 1974. 142 pp., illus. $40.00

Complete coverage on the subject as to finish, proofmarks and Nazi Party inscriptions.

Walther Volume II, Engraved, Presentation and Standard Models, by James L. Rankin, J.L. Rankin, Coral Gables, FL, 1977. 112 pp., illus. $40.00

The new Walther book on embellished versions and standard models. Has 88 photographs, including many color plates.

Walther, Volume III, 1908-1980, by James L. Rankin, Coral Gables, FL, 1981. 226 pp., illus. $40.00

Covers all models of Walther handguns from 1908 to date, includes holsters, grips and magazines.

Winchester an American Legend, by R.L. Wilson, New York, Book Sales, 2004. Reprint. Hardcover. New in new dust jacket. $24.95

Winchester Bolt Action Military & Sporting Rifles 1877 to 1937, by Herbert G. Houze, Andrew Mowbray Publishing, Lincoln, RI, 1998. 295 pp., illus. $45.00

Winchester was the first American arms maker to commercially manufacture a bolt action repeating rifle, and this book tells the exciting story of these Winchester bolt actions.

Winchester Book, by George Madis, David Madis Gun Book Distributor, Dallas, TX, 2000. 650 pp., illus. $54.50

A new, revised 25th anniversary edition of this classic book on Winchester firearms. Complete serial ranges have been added.

Winchester Dates of Manufacture 1849-1984, by George Madis, Art & Reference House, Brownsboro, TX, 1984. 59 pp. $8.50

A most useful work, compiled from records of the Winchester factory.

Winchester Engraving, by R.L. Wilson, Beinfeld Books, Springs, CA, 1989. 500 pp., illus. $185.00

A classic reference work of value to all arms collectors.

Winchester Handbook, The, by George Madis, Art & Reference House, Lancaster, TX, 1982. 287 pp., illus. $26.95

The complete line of Winchester guns, with dates of manufacture, serial numbers, etc.

Winchester Lever Action Repeating Firearms, Vol. 1, The Models of 1866, 1873 and 1876, by Arthur Pirkle, North Cape Publications, Tustin, CA, 1995. 112 pp., illus. Paper covers. $19.95

Complete, part-by-part description, including dimensions, finishes, markings and variations throughout the production run of these fine, collectible guns.

Winchester Lever Action Repeating Rifles, Vol. 2, The Models of 1886 and 1892, by Arthur Pirkle, North Cape Publications, Tustin, CA, 1996. 150 pp., illus. Paper covers. $19.95

Describes each model on a part-by-part basis by serial number range complete with finishes, markings and changes.

Winchester Lever Action Repeating Rifles, Vol. 3, The Model of 1894, by Arthur Pirkle, North Cape Publications, Tustin, CA, 1998. 150 pp., illus. Paper covers. $19.95

The first book ever to provide a detailed description of the Model 1894 rifle and carbine.

Winchester Lever Legacy, The, by Clyde "Snooky" Williamson, Buffalo Press, Zachary, LA, 1988. 664 pp., illus. $75.00

A book on reloading for the different calibers of the Winchester lever action rifle.

Winchester Model 1876 "Centennial" Rifle, The, by Herbert G. Houze. Lincoln, RI, Andrew Mowbray, Inc., 2001. Illustrated with over 180 b&w photographs. 192 pp. Hardcover. $45.00

The first authoritative study of the Winchester Model 1876 written using the company's own records. This book dispels the myth that the Model 1876 was merely a larger version of the Winchester company's famous Model 1873 and instead traces its true origins to designs developed immediately after the American Civil War. For Winchester collectors, and those interested in the mechanics of the 19th-century arms industry, this book provides a wealth of previously unpublished information.

Winchester Pocket Guide: Identification & Pricing for 50 Collectible Rifles and Shotguns, by Ned Schwing, Iola, WI, Krause Publications, 2004. 1st edition. 224 pp., illus. Softcover. $12.95

Winchester Repeating Arms Company Its History & Development from 1865 to 1981, by Herbert G. Houze, Iola, WI, Krause Publications, 2004. 1st edition. Softcover. $34.98

Winchester Single-Shot, Volume 1; A History and Analysis, The, by John Campbell, Andrew Mowbray, Inc., Lincoln, RI, 1995. 272 pp., illus. $55.00

Covers every important aspect of this highly-collectible firearm.

Winchester Single-Shot, Volume 2; Old Secrets and New Discoveries, The, by John Campbell, Andrew Mowbray, Inc., Lincoln, RI, 2000. 280 pp., illus. $55.00

An exciting follow-up to the classic first volume.

Winchester Sporting Firearms: Dates of Manufacture, by D.R. Morse, Phoenix, AZ, Firing Pin Enterprizes, 2003. 45 pp. Softcover. $6.95

Covers their pistols, revolvers, rifles, shotguns and commemoratives, plus models and serial numbers.

Winchester-Lee Rifle, The, by Eugene Myszkowski, Excalibur Publications, Tucson, AZ 2000. 96 pp., illus. Paper covers. $22.95

The development of the Lee Straight Pull, the cartridge and the approval for military use. Covers details of the inventor and memorabilia of Winchester-Lee related material.

World War One Collectors Handbook Volumes 1 and 2, by Paul Schulz, Hayes Otoupalik and Dennis Gordon, Missoula, MT, privately printed, 2002. Two volumes in one edition. 110 pp., loaded with b&w photos. Softcover. $21.95

Covers, uniforms, insignia, equipment, weapons, souvenirs and miscellaneous. Includes price guide. For all of you Doughboy collectors, this is a must.

World War II German War Booty, A Study in Photographs, by Thomas M. Johnson, Atglen, PA, Schiffer Publications, 2003. 1st edition. 368 pp. Hardcover. New in new dust jacket. $79.95

Worldwide Webley and the Harrington and Richardson Connection, by Stephen Cuthbertson, Ballista Publishing and Distributing Ltd., Gabriola Island, Canada, 1999. 259 pp., illus. $50.00

A masterpiece of scholarship. Over 350 photographs plus 75 original documents, patent drawings, and advertisements accompany the text.

World's Great Handguns: From 1450 to the Present Day, The, by Roger Ford, Secaucus, NJ, Chartwell Books, Inc., 1997. 1st edition. 176 pp. Hardcover. New in new dust jacket. $19.95

General

331+ Essential Tips and Tricks; A How-To Guide for the Gun Collector, by Stuart Mowbray, Lincoln, RI, 2006. 1st edition, photographs. Full color, 272 pp., 357 photographs. Soft cover. $35.99

Everything from gun photography to detecting refinishes can be found in this comprehensive new reference book.

A Rifleman Went to War, by H. W. McBride, Lancer Militaria, Mt. Ida, AR, 1987. 398 pp., illus. $29.95

The classic account of practical marksmanship on the battlefields of WWI.

Action Shooting: Cowboy Style, by John Taffin, Krause Publications, Iola, WI, 1999. 320 pp., illus. $39.95

Details on the guns and ammunition. Explanations of the rules used for many events.

Advanced Muzzleloader's Guide, by Toby Bridges, Stoeger Publishing Co., So. Hackensack, NJ, 1985. 256 pp., illus. Paper covers. $14.95

The complete guide to muzzle-loading rifles, pistols and shotguns–flintlock and percussion.

Aids to Musketry for Officers & NCOs, by Capt. B.J. Friend, Excalibur Publications, Latham, NY, 1996. 40 pp., illus. Paper covers. $7.95

A facsimile edition of a pre-WWI British manual filled with useful information for training the common soldier.

Airgun Odyssey, by Steve Hanson, Manchester, CT, Precision Shooting, Inc., 2004. 1st edition. 175 pp. Pictorial softcover. $27.95

America's Great Gunmakers, by Wayne van Zwoll, Stoeger Publishing Co., So. Hackensack, NJ, 1992. 288 pp., illus. Paper covers. $16.95

This book traces in great detail the evolution of guns and ammunition in America and the men who formed the companies that produced them.

American Air Rifles, by James E. House, Krause Publications, Iola, WI, 2002. 1st edition. 208 pp., with 198 b&w photos. Softcover. $22.95

Air rifle ballistics, sights, pellets, games, and hunting caliber recommendations are thoroughly explained to help shooters get the most out of their American air rifles. Evaluation of more than a dozen American-made and American-imported air rifle models.

American and Imported Arms, Ammunition and Shooting Accessories, Catalog No. 18 of the Shooter's Bible, Stoeger, Inc., reprinted by Fayette Arsenal, Fayetteville, NC, 1988. 142 pp., illus. Paper covers. $10.95

A facsimile reprint of the 1932 Stoeger's Shooter's Bible.

American B.B. Gun: A Collector's Guide, by Arni T. Dunathan. A.S. Barnes and Co., Inc., South Brunswick, 2001. 154 pp., illustrated with nearly 200 photographs, drawings and detailed diagrams. Hardcover. $35.00

Annie Oakley of the Wild West, by Walter Havighurst, New York, Castle Books, 2000. 246 pp. Hardcover. New in new dust jacket. $10.00

Antique Guns; The Collector's Guide, by Steve Carpenteri, Accokeek, MD: Stoeger Publications, 2005. Revised edition. 260 pages, illus. plus a 32 page color section. Soft cover. New. $22.95

Covers a vast spectrum of pre-1900 firearms: those manufactured by U.S. gun makers as well as Canadian, French, German, Belgian, Spanish and other foreign firms.

Armed Response, by Massad Ayoob, and David Kenik, NY, Merril Press, 2005. These are valuable real-life lessons about preparing to face a lethal threat, winning a gunfight, and surviving the ensuing court battle that can not be found outside of expensive tactical schools. 179 pages, with b&w photos. Foreword by Massad Ayoob. Soft cover. $19.95

Arming & Equipping the United States Cavalry 1865-1902, by Dusan Farrington, Lincoln, RI: Andrew Mowbray, Inc., 2005. 1st edition. $68.95

775 photos!!! Simply packed with serial numbers, issue information, reports from the field and more! Meticulously researched and absolutely up-to-date. A complete reference to all the arms and accoutrements. And at a bargain price to boot! Hardcover. New in new dust jacket. $68.95

Arming the Glorious Cause: Weapons of the Second War for Independence, by James B. Whisker, Daniel D. Hartzler and Larry W. Yantz, R & R Books, Livonia, NY, 1998. 175 pp., illus. $45.00

A photographic study of Confederate weapons.

Arms & Armor in the Art Institute of Chicago, by Walter J. Karcheski Jr., Bulfinch Press, Boston, MA, 1995. 128 pp., illus. $35.00

Now, for the first time, the Art Institute of Chicago's arms and armor collection is presented in the visual delight of 103 color illustrations.

Arms for the Nation: Springfield Longarms, edited by David C. Clark, Scott A. Duff, Export, PA, 1994. 73 pp., illus. Paper covers. $9.95

A brief history of the Springfield Armory and the arms made there.

Arrowmaker Frontier Series Volume 1, by Roy Chandler, Jacksonville, NC, Ron Brigade Armory, 2000. 390 pp. Hardcover. New in new dust jacket. $38.95

Arsenal of Freedom, The Springfield Armory, 1890-1948: A Year-by-Year Account Drawn from Official Records, compiled and edited by Lt. Col. William S. Brophy, USAR Ret., Andrew Mowbray, Inc., Lincoln, RI, 1991. 400 pp., illus. Softcover. $29.95

A "must buy" for all students of American military weapons, equipment and accoutrements.

Art of American Arms Makers Marketing Guns, Ammunition, and Western Adventure During the Golden Age of Illustration, by Richard C., Rattenbury, Oklahoma City, OK, National Cowboy Museum, 2004. 132 pp. of color photos. Softcover. $29.95

Art of American Game Calls, by Russell E. Lewis, Paducah, KY, Collector Books, 2005. 1st edition. 176 pp. Pictorial hardcover. $24.95

Art of Blacksmithing, by Alex W. Bealer, New York, Book Sales, 1996. Revised edition. 440 pp. Hardcover. New in new dust jacket. $10.00

Art of Remington Arms, Sporting Classics, 2004, by Tom Davis. 1st edition. Hardcover. $60.00

Battle of the Bulge: Hitler's Alternate Scenarios, by Peter Tsouras, Mechanicsburg, PA, Stackpole Books, 2004. 1st edition. 256 pp., 24 b&w photos, 10 maps. Hardcover. $34.95

Belgian Rattlesnake: The Lewis Automatic Machine Gun, The, by William M. Easterly, Collector Grade Publications, Inc., Cobourg, Ont. Canada, 1998. 542 pp., illus. $79.95

A social and technical biography of the Lewis automatic machine gun and its inventors.

Benchrest Shooting Primer, The, edited by Dave Brennan, Precision Shooting, Inc., Manchester, CT, 2000. 2nd edition. 420 pp., illustrated with b&w photographs, drawings and detailed diagrams. Pictorial softcover. $24.95

The very best articles on shooting and reloading for the most challenging of all the rifle accuracy disciplines...benchrest shooting.

Black Rifle Frontier Series Volume 2, The, by Roy Chandler, Jacksonville, NC, Iron Brigade Armory, 2002. 226 pp. Hardcover. New in new dust jacket. $42.95

In 1760, inexperienced Jack Elan settles in Sherman's Valley, suffers tragedy, is captured by hostiles, escapes, and fights on. This is the "2nd" book in the Frontier Series.

Blue Book of Airguns 6th Edition, by Robert Beeman and John Allen, Minneapolis, MN, Blue Book Publications, Inc., 2007. Softcover. $29.95

Blue Book of Gun Values, 28th Edition (2007 Edition), by S.P. Fjestad, Minneapolis, MN, Blue Book Publications, Inc., 2080 pp., illus. Paper covers. $39.95

Blue Book of Modern Black Powder Values, 4th Edition, by Dennis Adler, John Allen, Minneapolis, MN, Blue Book Publications, Inc., 2004. Softcover. $24.95

Bodyguard Manual, by Leroy Thompson, Mechanicsburg,PA. Greehnill Books, 2005. 208 pages, 16 pages of plates. Soft cover. $23.95

Bodyguard Manual details the steps a protective team takes to prevent attack as well as the tactics employed when it is necessary to counter one.

British Small Arms of World War II, by Ian D. Skennerton, Arms & Militaria Press, Australia, 1988. 110 pp., 37 illus. $25.00

C Stories, by Jeff Cooper, Sycamore Island Books, 2005. 1st edition. Quite simply, CStories is Jeff Cooper at his best. illus., 316 pp. Hardcover. New in new dust jacket. $49.95

Carbine and Shotgun Speed Shooting: How to Hit Hard and Fast in Combat, by Steve Moses. Paladin Press, Boulder, CO. 2002. 96 pp., illus. Softcover $18.00

In this groundbreaking book, he breaks down the mechanics of speed shooting these weapons, from stance and grip to sighting, trigger control and more, presenting them in a concise and easily understood manner.

Cavalry Raids of the Civil War, by Col. Robert W. Black, Mechanicsburg, PA, Stackpole Books, 2004. 1st edition. 288 pp., 30 b&w drawings. Softcover. $17.95

CO2 Pistols and Rifles, by James E. House, Iola, WI, Krause Publications, 2004. 1st edition 240 pp., with 198 b&w photos. Softcover. $24.95

Combatives FM-3-25.150, by U.S. Army, Boulder, CO, Paladin Press, 2004. Photos, illus., 272 pp. Soft cover. $19.95

This exact reprint of the U.S. Army's most current field manual on hand-to-hand combat (FM 3-25.150) reflects the first major revision to the Army's close-quarters combat program in a decade. This field manual shows them how.

Complete .50-caliber Sniper Course, The, by Dean Michaelis, Paladin Press, Boulder, CO, 2000. 576 pp., illus., $60.00

The history from German Mauser T-Gewehr of WWI to the Soviet PTRD and beyond. Includes the author's Program of Instruction for Special Operations Hard-Target Interdiction Course.

Complete Guide to Game Care and Cookery, 4th Edition, The, by Sam Fadala, Krause Publications, Iola, WI, 2003. 320 pp., illus. Paper covers. $21.95

Over 500 photos illustrating the care of wild game in the field and at home with a separate recipe section providing over 400 tested recipes.

Concealed Handgun Manual, 4th Edition, The, by Chris Bird, San Antonio, TX, Privateer Publications, 2004. 332 pp., illus. Softcover, $21.95

Cowboys & the Trappings of the Old West, by William Manns & Elizabeth Clair Flood, Santa Fe, NM, ZON International Publishing Company, 1997. 224 pp., 550 colorful photos. Foreword by Roy Rogers. Hardcover. $45.00

Big & beautiful book covering: Hats, boots, spurs, chaps, guns, holsters, saddles and more. It's really a pictorial cele bration of the old time buckaroo. This exceptional book presents all the accoutrements of the cowboy life in a comprehensive tribute to the makers. The history of the craftsmen and the evolution of the gear are lavishly illustrated.

Cowgirls, Revised and Expanded 2nd Edition Early Images and Collectibles Price Guide, by Judy Crandall, Atglen, PA, Schiffer Publications, 2005. 2nd edition. Soft cover. $24.95

The First Ladies from the Great American West live again in this comprehensive pictorial chronicle.

Cowgirls: Women of the Wild West, by Elizabeth Clair Flood and William Maims, edited by Helene Helene, Santa Fe, NM, ZON International Publishing Company, 2000. 1st edition. Hardcover. New in new dust jacket. $45.00

Custom Firearms Engraving, by Tom Turpin, Krause Publications, Iola, WI, 1999. 208 pp., illus. $49.95

Provides a broad and comprehensive look at the world of firearms engraving. The exquisite styles of more than 75 master engravers are shown on beautiful examples of handguns, rifles, shotguns, and other firearms, as well as knives.

Custom Gunmakers of the 20th Century, by Michael Pretov, Manchester, CT, Precision Shooting, 2005. 168 pages, illustrated with Photos. Hardcover. $24.95

Daisy Air Rifles & BB Guns: The First 100 Years, by Neal Punchard, St. Paul, MN, Motorbooks, 2002. 1st edition. Hardcover, 10" x 10", 156 pp., 300 color. Hardcover. $29.95

Dead On, by Tony Noblitt and Warren Gabrilska, Paladin Press, Boulder, CO, 1998. 176 pp., illus. Paper covers. $22.00

The long-range marksman's guide to extreme accuracy. ***Defensive Use of Firearms***, by Stephen Wenger, Boulder,CO, Paladin Press, 2005. 5½" x 8½", soft cover, illus., 120 pp. Soft cover. $20.00

This concise and affordable handbook offers the reader a set of common-sense principles, tactics and techniques distilled from hundreds of hours of the author's training, which includes certification as a law-enforcement handgun, shotgun, patrol rifle and tactical shooting instructor.

Do or Die A Supplementary Manual on Individual Combat, by Lieut. Col. A.J. Drexel Biddle, U.S.M.C.R., Boulder, CO, Paladin Press, 2004. 80 pp., illus. Softcover, $15.00

Down to Earth: The 507th Parachute Infantry Regiment in Normandy: June 6-july 11 1944, by Martin Morgan ICA, Atglen, PA, Schiffer Publishing, 2004. 1st edition. 304 pp., color and b&w photos. Hardcover. New in new dust jacket. $69.95

Effective Defense: The Woman, the Plan, the Gun, by Gila Hayes, Onalaska, WA, Police Bookshelf, 2000. 2nd edition. Photos, 264 pp. Softcover. $16.95

Elmer Keith: The Other Side of a Western Legend, by Gene Brown, Precision Shooting, Inc., Manchester, CT 2002. 1st edition. 168 pp., illustrated with b&w photos. Softcover. $19.95

An updated and expanded edition of his original work, incorporating new tales and information that have come to light in the past six years. Gene Brown was a long time friend of Keith, and today is unquestionably the leading authority on Keith's books.

Encyclopedia of Native American Bows, Arrows and Quivers, by Steve Allely and Jim Hamm, The Lyons Press, N.Y., 1999. 160 pp., illus. $29.95

A landmark book for anyone interested in archery history, or Native Americans.

Exercise of Armes, The, by Jacob de Gheyn, Dover Publications, Inc., Mineola, NY, 1999. 144 pp., illus. Paper covers. $14.95

Republications of all 117 engravings from the 1607 classic military manual. A meticulously accurate portrait of uniforms and weapons of the 17th century Netherlands.

Fighting Iron: A Metals Handbook for Arms Collectors, by Art Gogan, Mowbray Publishers, Inc., Lincoln, RI, 2002. 176 pp., illus. $28.00

A guide that is easy to use, explains things in simple English and covers all of the different historical periods that we are interested in.

FBI Guide to Concealable Weapons, by the FBI, Boulder, Co, Paladin Press, 2005. As citizens responsible for our own safety, we must know everything possible about the dangers that face us, and awareness is the first, vital step in this direction. Photos, 88 pp. Soft cover. $15.00

Filipino Fighting Whip: Advanced Training Methods and Combat Applications, The, by Tom Meadows, Boulder, CO, Paladin Press, 2005. This book is a comprehensive guide for advanced training methods and combat applications as practiced and taught by the best fighters and whip practitioners in the world. 216 pp. Soft cover. $20.00

Fine Art of the West, by Byron B. Price and Christopher Lyon, New York, Abbeville Press, 2004. Hardcover. $75.00

Firearm Suppressor Patents, Volume One: United States Patents, by N.R. Parker, Boulder, CO, Paladin Press, 2004. 392 pages, illustrated. Soft cover. $45.00

This book provides never-before-published interviews with three of today's top designers as well as a special section on the evolution of cutting-edge silencer mounting systems.

Firearms Assembly Disassembly; Part 4: Centerfire Rifles (2nd Edition), by J. B. Wood, Iola, WI, Krause Publications, 2004. 2nd edition. 576 pp., 1,750 b&w photos. Softcover. $24.95

Fireworks: A Gunsight Anthology, by Jeff Cooper, Paladin Press, Boulder, CO, 1998. 192 pp., illus. Paper cover. $27.00

A collection of wild, hilarious, shocking and always meaningful tales from the remarkable life of an American firearms legend.

Force-On-Force Gunfight Training: The Interactive, Reality Based Solution, by Gabriel Suarez, Boulder,CO, Paladin Press, 2005. 105 pages, illustrated with photos. Soft cover. $15.00

Fort Robinson, Frontier Series, Volume 4, by Roy Chandler, Jacksonville, NC, Ron Brigade Armory, 2003. 1st edition. 560 pp. Hardcover. New in new dust jacket. $39.95

Frederic Remington: The Color of Night, by Nancy Anderson, Princeton University Press, 2003. 1st edition. 136 color illus, 24 halftones; 10" x 11", 208 pgs. Hardcover, New in new dust jacket. $49.95; UK $52.49

From a Stranger's Doorstep to the Kremlin Gate, by Mikhail Kalashnikov, Ironside International Publishers, Inc., Alexandria, VA, 1999. 460 pp., illus. $34.95

A biography of the most influential rifle designer of the 20th century. His AK-47 assault rifle has become the most widely used (and copied) assault rifle of this century.

Frontier Rifleman, The, by H.B. LaCrosse Jr., Pioneer Press, Union City, TN, 1989. 183 pp., illus. Softcover. $17.50

The Frontier rifleman's clothing and equipment during the era of the American Revolution, 1760-1800.

Galloping Thunder: The Stuart Horse Artillery Battalion, by Robert Trout, Mechanicsburg, PA, Stackpole Books, 2002. 1st edition. Hardcover, $39.95

Gatling Gun: 19th Century Machine Gun to 21st Century Vulcan, The, by Joseph Berk, Paladin Press, Boulder, CO, 1991. 136 pp., illus. $34.95

Here is the fascinating on-going story of a truly timeless weapon, from its beginnings during the Civil War to its current role as a state-of-the-art modern combat system.

German Artillery of World War Two, by Ian V. Hogg, Stackpole Books, Mechanicsburg, PA, 1997, 304 pp., illus. $44.95

Complete details of German artillery use in WWII.

Gone Diggin: Memoirs of a Civil War Relic Hunter, by Toby Law, Orange, VA, Publisher's Press, 2002. 1st edition signed. 151 pp., illustrated with b&w photos. $24.95

The true story of one relic hunter's life-The author kept exacting records of every relic hunt and every relic hunter he was with working with.

Gun Digest 2007, 61st Annual Edition, edited by Ken Ramage, Iola, WI, Krause Publications, 2006. Softcover. $27.95

This all new 61st edition continues the editorial excellence, quality, content and comprehensive cataloguing that firearms enthusiasts have come to know and expect. The most read gun book in the world for the last half century.

Gun Digest Book of Cowboy Action Shooting: Gear, Guns, Tactics, The, edited by Kevin Michalowski, Iola, WI, Krause Publications, 2005. Softcover. 288 pages, plus 200 b&w photos! $24.99

This one-of-a-kind guide offers complete coverage of the sport from the top experts and personalities in the field.

Gun Digest Book of Exploded Firearms Drawings: 975 Isometric Views, The, by Harold Murtz, Iola,WI, Krause Publications, 2005, 3rd edition. 1032pp, 975 photos. Soft cover. $34.95

This book is sure to become a must-have for gunsmiths, shooters and law enforcement officials!

Gun Digest Blackpowder Loading Manual New Expanded 4th Edition, by Sam Fadala, Iola, WI, Krause Publications, 2006. 352 pp., illus. Softcover. $27.95

All blackpowder rifle, pistol, and shotgun users should be equipped with the new information supplied in this seminal reference--complete with loading tutorial and instructive articles expertly written by author Sam Fadala. Loading techniques are covered for more than 250 different modern blackpowder firearms--the illustrations are clear and the text is expertly laid out--easily understandable to even the most novice shooter. Experts will also benefit from the tips and techniques of Sam Fadala. This is the must-have book blackpowder shooters have been craving.

Gun Digest Book of Deer Guns, The, edited by Dan Shideler, Iola, WI, Krause Publications, 2004. 1st edition Softcover, 160pp, 225 b&w photos. $14.99

An illustrated catalog section details deer rifles, shotguns, handguns and muzzleloaders, complete with current pricing information from "Modern Gun Values." A special reference section includes selected portions of the Arms Library, as well as a website directory of state game and fish departments. This practical guide is a must for any deer hunter!

Gun Digest Book of Guns for Personal Defense Arms & Accessories for Self-Defense, The, edited by Kevin Michalowski, Iola, WI, Krause Publications, 2004. 1st edition Softcover. 160pp plus 200 b&w photos! $14.99

Handgun enthusiasts or anyone looking to find out about handguns for personal defense will find everything they need to know in the pages of this comprehensive guide and reference. Readers will learn the basics of selection and use of handguns for personal defense. The book covers uses of revolvers, semi-automatic pistols, ammunition, holsters, firearms training options, buying a used gun and much more. A catalog section contains listings of currently available pistols and revolvers suitable for personal defense, complete with pricing for each.

Gun Digest Book of Sporting Clays, 3rd Edition, The, edited by Rick Sapp, Iola, WI, Krause Publications, 2005. 1st edition Softcover, 288 pages, illustrated. $19.95

New articles cover equipment selection, strategies, technical issues and more. Features a review of the 50 best clay ranges in the country -Includes a fully illustrated catalog of currently available sporting clays shotguns showing complete specifications and retail prices.

Gun Digest Book of Trap & Skeet Shooting, 4th Edition, The, edited by Rick Sapp, Iola, WI, Krause Publications, 2004. 1st edition Softcover, 256 pages, illustrated. $22.95

The book includes comprehensive coverage on choosing and fitting the right shotgun for each sport, explains the hows and whys of chokes in plain language, and provides an in-depth review of shells, loads and reloading. Valuable reference tools include the official rules for each game as well as a manufacturer's directory for guns, ammunition, clothing and accessories.

Gun Engraving, by C. Austyn, Safari Press Publication, Huntington Beach, CA, 1998. 128 pp., plus 24 pp. of color photos. $50.00

A well-illustrated book on fine English and European gun engravers. Includes a fantastic pictorial section that lists types of engravings and prices.

Gun Notes, Volume 1, by Elmer Keith, Safari Press, Huntington Beach, CA, 2002. 219 pp., illus. Softcover. $24.95

A collection of Elmer Keith's most interesting columns and feature stories that appeared in ***"Guns & Ammo"*** magazine from 1961 to the late 1970s.

Gun Notes, Volume 2, by Elmer Keith, Safari Press, Huntington Beach, CA, 2002. 292 pp., illus. Softcover. $24.95

Covers articles from Keith's monthly column in ***"Guns & Ammo"*** magazine during the period from 1971 through Keith's passing in 1982.

Guns & Shooting: A Selected Bibliography, by Ray Riling, Ray Riling Arms Books Co., Phila., PA, 1982. 434 pp., illus. Limited, numbered edition. $75.00

A limited edition of this superb bibliographical work, the only modern listing of books devoted to guns and shooting.

Guns Illustrated 2007: 39th Edition, edited by Ken Ramage, Iola, WI, Krause Publications, 2006. Softcover. $21.95

Highly informative, technical articles on a wide range of shooting topics by some of the top writers in the industry. A catalog section lists more than 3,000 firearms currently manufactured in or imported to the U.S.

Guns of the Gunfighters: Lawmen, Outlaws & TV Cowboys, by Doc O'Meara, Iola, WI, Krause Publications, 2003. 1st edition. 16-page color section, 225 b&w photos. Hardcover. $34.95

Explores the romance of the Old West, focusing on the guns that the good guys & bad guys, real & fictional characters, carried with them. Profiles of more than 50 gunslingers, half from the Old West and half from Hollywood, include a brief biography of each gunfighter, along with the guns they carried. Fascinating stories about the TV and movie celebrities of the 1950s and 1960s detail their guns and the skill–or lack thereof–they displayed.

Guns, Bullets, and Gunfighters, by Jim Cirillo, Paladin Press, Boulder, CO, 1996. 119 pp., illus. Paper covers. $16.00

Lessons and tales from a modern-day gunfighter.

Gunstock Carving: A Step-by-Step Guide to Engraving Rifles and Shotguns, by Bill Janney, East Petersburg, PA, Fox Chapel Publishing, October 2002. 89 pp., illustrated in color. Softcover. $19.95

Learn gunstock carving from an expert. Includes step-by-step projects and instructions, patterns, tips and techniques.

Hands Off! Self Defense for Women, by Maj. Fairbairn, Boulder, CO: Paladin Press, 2004. 56 pages. Soft cover. $15.00

Paladin Press is proud to bring back a work by the inimitable self-defense master W.E. Fairbairn so that a new generation of Americans can enjoy his teachings.

Hand-To-Hand Combat: United States Naval Institute, by U.S. Navy, Boulder, CO, Paladin Press, 2003. 1st edition. 240 pp. Softcover. $25.00

Now you can own one of the classic publications in the history of U.S. military close-quarters combat training. In 11 photo-heavy chapters, Hand-to-Hand Combat covers training tips; vulnerable targets; the brutal fundamentals of close-in fighting; frontal and rear attacks; prisoner search and control techniques; disarming pistols, rifles, clubs and knives; offensive means of "liquidating an enemy"; and much more. After reading this book (originally published by the United States Naval Institute in 1943), you will see why it has long been sought by collectors and historians of hand-to-hand combat.

Hidden in Plain Sight, "A Practical Guide to Concealed Handgun Carry" (Revised 2nd Edition), by Trey Bloodworth and Mike Raley, Paladin Press, Boulder, CO, 1997, softcover, photos, 176 pp. $20.00

This invaluable guide offers the latest advice on what to look for when choosing a CCW, how to dress for comfortable, effective concealed carry, traditional and more unconventional carry modes, accessory holsters, customized clothing and accessories, accessibility data based on draw-time comparisons and new holsters on the market. Includes 40 new manufacturer listings.

HK Assault Rifle Systems, by Duncan Long, Paladin Press, Boulder, CO, 1995. 110 pp., illus. Paper covers. $27.95

The little known history behind this fascinating family of weapons tracing its beginnings from the ashes of WWII to the present time.

Holsters for Combat and Concealed Carry, by R.K. Campbell, Boulder, CO, Paladin Press, 2004. 1st edition. 144 pp. Softcover. $22.00

Hostage Rescue Manual; Tactics of the Counter-Terrorist Professionals, by Leroy Thompson, Mechanicsburg, PA. Greehnill Books, 2005. 208 pages, with 16 pages of photos. Soft cover. $23.95

Incorporating vivid photographs and diagrams of rescue units in action, the Hostage Rescue Manual is the complete reference work on counter-terrorist procedures all over the world.

Hunter's Guide to Accurate Shooting, by Wayne van Zwoll, Guilford, CT, Lyons Press, 2002. 1st edition. 288 pp. Hardcover. $29.95

Firearms expert van Zwoll explains exactly how to shoot the big-game rifle accurately. Taking into consideration every pertinent factor, he shows a step-by-step analysis of shooting and hunting with the big-game rifle.

Hunting Time: Adventures in Pursuit of North American Big Game: A Forty-Year Chronicle, The, by John E. Howard, Deforest, WI, Saint Huberts Press, 2002. 1st edition. 537 pp., illustrated with drawings. Hardcover. $29.95

From a novice's first hunt for whitetailed deer in his native Wisconsin, to a seasoned hunter's pursuit of a Boone and Crockett Club record book caribou in the northwest territories, the author carries the reader along on his forty year journey through the big game fields of North America.

Instinct Combat Shooting; Defensive Handgunning for Police, by Chuck Klein, Flushing, NY, Looseleaf Law, 2004. 54 pages. Soft cover. $22.95

Tactical tips for effective armed defense, helpful definitions and court-ready statements that help you clearly articulate and competently justify your deadly force decision-making.

Jack O'Connor Catalogue of Letters, by Ellen Enzler Herring, Agoura, CA, Trophy Room Books, 2002. 1st edition. Hardcover. 262 pages, 18 illustrations. $55.00

During a sixteen year period beginning in 1960, O'Connor exchanged many letters with his pal, John Jobson. Material from nearly three hundred of these has been assembled and edited by Ellen Enzler Herring and published in chronological order. A number of the letters have been reproduced in full or part. They offer considerable insight into the beloved gun editor and "Dean of Outdoor Writers"over and beyond what we know about him from his books.

Jane's Guns Recognition Guide: 4th Edition, by Ian Hogg, Terry Gander, NY, Harper Collins, 2005. 464 pages, illustrated. Soft cover. $24.95

This book will help you identify them all. Jane's, always known for meticulous detail in the information of military equipment, aircraft, ships and much more!

Kill or Get Killed, by Col. Rex Applegate, Paladin Press, Boulder, CO, 1996. 400 pp., illus. $49.95

The best and longest-selling book on close combat in history.

Living With Terrorism; Survival Lessons from the Streets of Jerusalem, by Howard Linett, Boulder, CO, Paladin Press, 2005. 277 pages, illustrated with photos. Soft cover. $20.00

Before these dangers become a reality in your life, read this book.

Lost Classics of Jack O'Connor, The, edited by Jim Casada, Columbia, SC, Live Oak Press, 2004. 1st edition. Hardcover. New in new dust jacket. 33 photos, 40 illus by Dan Burr; 376 pages, with illustrations and photos. $35.00

You'll find 40 of O'Connor's most fascinating stories in the Trade Edition of Lost Classics. Exciting tales with a twist of humor.

Manual for H&R Reising Submachine Gun and Semi-Auto Rifle, edited by George P. Dillman, Desert Publications, El Dorado, AZ, 1994. 81 pp., illus. Paper covers. $14.95

A reprint of the Harrington & Richardson 1943 factory manual and the rare military manual on the H&R submachine gun and semi-auto rifle.

Manufacture of Gunflints, The, by Sydney B.J. Skertchly, facsimile reprint with new introduction by Seymour de Lotbiniere, Museum Restoration Service, Ontario, Canada, 1984. 90 pp., illus. $24.50

Limited edition reprinting of the very scarce London edition of 1879.

Master Tips, by J. Winokur, Potshot Press, Pacific Palisades, CA, 1985. 96 pp., illus. Paper covers. $11.95

Basics of practical shooting.

Military and Police Sniper, The, by Mike R. Lau, Precision Shooting, Inc., Manchester, CT, 1998. 352 pp., illus. Paper covers. $34.95

Advanced precision shooting for combat and law enforcement.

Military Small Arms of the 20th Century, 7th Edition, by Ian V. Hogg and John Weeks, DBI Books, a division of Krause Publications, Iola, WI, 2000. 416 pp., illus. Paper covers. Over 800 photographs and illustrations. $24.95

Covers small arms of 46 countries.

Modern Guns Identification and Values, 16th Edition, by Steve and Russell Quertermous, Paducah, KY, Collector's Books, 2006. 1800+ illus; 8.5"x11", 575 pgs. Soft cover. $18.95

Updated edition features current market values for over 2,500 models of rifles, shotguns, & handguns. Contains model name, gauge or caliber, action, finish or stock & forearm, barrel, cylinder or magazine, sights, weight & length, & comments.

Modern Gun Values: 13th Edition, edited by Dan Shideler, Krause Publications, Iola, WI, 2006. Softcover. 680 Pages, 3,000+ b&w photos. $24.95

This all-new expanded edition helps collectors identify the firearm, evaluate condition and determine value. Detailed specifications—and current values from specialized experts—are provided for domestic and imported handguns, rifles, shotguns and commemorative firearms. Heavily illustrated. Over 7,500 arms described and valued, in three grades of condition, according to the NRA's Modern standards.

Modern Law Enforcement Weapons & Tactics, 3rd edition, by Patrick Sweeney, Iola, WI, Krause Publications, 2004. Illustrated, b&w photos, 256 pages. $22.99

Sweeney walks you through the latest gear and tactics employed by American law enforcement officers.

Modern Sporting Guns, by Christopher Austyn, Safari Press, Huntington Beach, CA, 1994. 128 pp., illus. $40.00

A discussion of the "best" English guns; round action, over-and-under, boxlocks, hammer guns, bolt action and double rifles as well as accessories.

More Tactical Reality; Why There's No Such Thing as an Advanced Gunfight, by Louis Awerbuck, Boulder, CO, Paladin Press, 2004. 144 pp. Softcover. $25.00

MP-40 Machine Gun, The, Desert Publications, El Dorado, AZ, 1995. 32 pp., illus. Paper covers. $11.95

A reprint of the hard-to-find operating and maintenance manual for one of the most famous machine guns of WWII.

Naval Percussion Locks and Primers, by Lt. J. A. Dahlgren, Museum Restoration Service, Bloomfield, Canada, 1996. 140 pp., illus. $35.00

First published as an Ordnance Memoranda in 1853, this is the finest existing study of percussion locks and primers origin and development.

Official Soviet AKM Manual, translated by Maj. James F. Gebhardt (Ret.), Paladin Press, Boulder, CO, 1999. 120 pp., illus. Paper covers. $18.00

This official military manual, available in English for the first time, was originally published by the Soviet Ministry of Defence. Covers the history, function, maintenance, assembly and disassembly, etc. of the 7.62mm AKM assault rifle.

One-Round War: U.S.M.C. Scout-Snipers in Vietnam, by Peter Senich, Paladin Press, Boulder, CO, 1996. 384 pp., illus. Paper covers. $59.95

Sniping in Vietnam focusing specifically on the Marine Corps program.

Optics Digest: Scopes, Binoculars, Rangefinders, and Spotting Scopes, by Clair Rees, Long Beach, CA, Safari Press, 2005. 189 pp. Softcover. $24.95

OSS Special Operations in China, by Col. F. Mills and John W. Brunner, Williamstown, NJ, Phillips Publications, 2003. 1st edition. 550 pp., illustrated with photos. Hardcover. New in new dust jacket. $34.95

Paintball Digest The Complete Guide to Games, Gear, and Tactics, by Richard Sapp, Iola, WI, Krause Publications, 2004. 1st edition. 272 pp. Softcover. $19.99

Paleo-Indian Artifacts: Identification & Value Guide, by Lar Hothem, Paducah, KY, Collector Books, 2005. 1st edition. 379 pp. Pictorial hardcover. $29.95

Panzer Aces German Tank Commanders of WWII, by Franz Kurowski, translated by David Johnston, Mechanicsburg, PA, Stackpole Books, 2004. 1st edition. 448 pp., 50 b&w photos Softcover. $19.95

Parker Brothers: Knight of the Trigger, by Ed Muderlak, Davis, IL, Old Reliable Publishing, 2002. 223 pp. $25.00

Knight of the Trigger tells the story of the Old West when Parker's most famous gun saleman traveled the country by rail, competing in the pigeon ring, hunting with the rich and famous, and selling the "Old Reliable" Parker shotgun. The life and times of Captain Arthur William du Bray, Parker Brothers' on-the-road sales agent from 1884 to 1926, is described in a novelized version of his interesting life.

Peril in the Powder Mills: Gunpowder & Its Men, by David McMahon & Anne Kelly Lane, West Conshohocken, PA, privately printed, 2004. 1st edition. 118 pp. Softcover. $18.95

Powder Horns and their Architecture; And Decoration as Used by the Soldier, Indian, Sailor and Traders of the Era, by Madison Grant, York, PA, privately printed, 1987. 165 pp., profusely illustrated. Hardcover. $45.00

Covers homemade pieces from the late eighteenth and early nineteenth centuries.

Practically Speaking: An Illustrated Guide-The Game, Guns and Gear of the International Defensive Pistol Association, by Walt Rauch, Lafayette Hills, PA, privately printed, 2002. 1st edition. 79 pp., illustrated with drawings and color photos. Softcover. $24.95

The game, guns and gear of the International Defensive Pistol Association with real-world applications.

Present Sabers: A Popular History of the U.S. Horse Cavalry, by Allan T. Heninger, Tucson, AZ, Excalibur Publications, 2002. 1st edition. 160 pp., with 148 photographs, 45 illustrations and 4 charts. Softcover. $24.95

An illustrated history of America's involvement with the horse cavalry, from its earliest beginnings during the Revolutionary War through its demise in WWII. The book also contains several appendices, as well as depictions of the regular insignia of all the U.S. Cavalry units.

Principles of Personal Defense, by Jeff Cooper, Paladin Press, Boulder, CO, 2006. 80 pp., illus. Paper covers. $14.00

This revised edition of Jeff Cooper's classic on personal defense offers great new illustrations and a new preface while retaining the theory of individual defense behavior presented in the original book.

Queen's Rook: A Soldier's Story, by Croft Barker, Flatonia,TX, Cistern Publishing, 2004. Limited edition of 500 copies. 177 pages, with 50 never before published photographs. Soft cover. $35.00

Men of the U.S. Army were assigned to South Vietnamese Infantry companies and platoons. Many of these men were lost in a war that is still misunderstood. This is their story, written in their own words. These Americans, and the units they lived with, engaged in savage fights against Viet Cong guerillas and North Vietnamese Army Regulars in the dark, deadly jungles north of Saigon.

Quotable Hunter, The, edited by Jay Cassell and Peter Fiduccia, The Lyons Press, N.Y., 1999. 224 pp., illus. $20.00

This collection of more than three hundred memorable quotes from hunters through the ages captures the essence of the sport, with all its joys idiosyncrasies, and challenges.

Real World Self-Defense by Jerry Vancook, Boulder, CO, Paladin Press, 1999. 224 pp. Soft cover. $20.00

Presenting tactics and techniques that are basic, easy to learn and proven effective under the stress of combat, he covers unarmed defense, improvised weapons, edged weapons, firearms and more, photos, illus.

Renaissance Drill Book, by Jacob de Gheyn, edited by David J. Blackmore, Mechanicsburg, PA, Greenhill Books, 2003. 1st edition. 248 pp., 117 illustrations. Hardcover. $24.95

Jacob de Gheyn's Exercise of Armes was an immense success when first published in 1607. It is a fascinating 17th-century military manual, designed to instruct contemporary soldiers how to handle arms effectively, and correctly, and it makes for a unique glimpse into warfare as waged in the Thirty Years War and the English Civil War. In addition, detailed illustrations show the various movements and postures to be adopted during use of the pike.

Running Recon, A Photo Journey with SOG Special Ops Along the Ho Chi Minh Trail, by Frank Greco, Boulder, CO, Paladin Press, 2004. Paper covers. $50.00

Running Recon is a combination of military memoir and combat photography book. It reflects both the author's experience in Kontum, Vietnam, from April 1969 to April 1970 as part of the top-secret Studies and Observation Group (SOG) and the collective experience of SOG veterans in general. What sets it apart from other Vietnam books is its wealth of more than 700 photographs, many never before published, from the author's personal collection and those of his fellow SOG veterans.

Sharpshooting for Sport and War, by W.W. Greener, Wolfe Publishing Co., Prescott, AZ, 1995. 192 pp., illus. $30.00

This classic reprint explores the *first* expanding bullet; service rifles; shooting positions; trajectories; recoil; external ballistics; and other valuable information.

Shooter's Bible 2007 No. 98, by Wayne Van Zwoll, Stoeger Publishing, 2006. New for this edition is a special Web Directory designed to complement the regular Reference section, including the popular Gun finder index. 576 pages. Pictorial Soft cover. $24.95

Shooting Buffalo Rifles of the Old West, by Mike Venturino, MLV Enterprises, Livingston, MT, 2002. 278 pp., illustrated with b&w photos. Softcover. $30.00

This tome will take you through the history, the usage, the many models, and the actual shooting (and how to's) of the many guns that saw service on the Frontier and are lovingly called "Buffalo Rifles" today. If you love to shoot your Sharps, Ballards, Remingtons, or Springfield "Trapdoors" for hunting or competition, or simply love Old West history, your library WILL NOT be complete without this latest book from Mike Venturino!

Shooting Colt Single Actions, by Mike Venturino, MLV Enterprises, Livingston, MT, 1997. 205 pp., illus. Softcover. $25.00

A complete examination of the Colt Single Action including styles, calibers and generations, b&w photos throughout.

Shooting Lever Guns of the Old West, by Mike Venturino, MLV Enterprises, Livingston, MT, 1999. 300 pp., illus. Softcover. $27.95

Shooting the lever action type repeating rifles of our American West.

Shooting Sixguns of the Old West, by Mike Venturino, MLV Enterprises, Livingston, MT, 1997. 221 pp., illus. Paper covers. $26.50

A comprehensive look at the guns of the early West: Colts, Smith & Wesson and Remingtons, plus blackpowder and reloading specs.

Shooting to Live, by Capt. W.E. Fairbairn and Capt. E.A. Sykes, Paladin Press, Boulder, CO, 1997, 4½" x 7", soft cover, illus., 112 pp. $14.00

Shooting to Live is the product of Fairbairn's and Sykes' practical experience with the handgun. Hundreds of incidents provided the basis for the first true book on life-or-death shootouts with the pistol. Shooting to Live teaches all concepts, considerations and applications of combat pistol craft.

Small Arms of World War II, by Chris Chant, St. Paul, MN, MBI Publishing Company, 2001. 1st edition. 96 pp., single page on each weapon with photograph, description, and a specifications table. Hardcover. New. $13.95

Detailing the design and development of each weapon, this book covers the most important infantry weapons used by both Allied and Axis soldiers between 1939 and 1945. These include both standard infantry bolt-action rifles, such as the German Kar 98 and the British Lee-Enfield, plus the automatic rifles that entered service toward the end of the war, such as the Stg 43. As well as rifles, this book also features submachine guns, machine guns and handguns and a specifications table for each weapon.

Sniper Training, FM 23-10, Reprint of the U.S. Army field manual of August, 1994, Paladin Press, Boulder, CO, 1995. 352 pp., illus. Paper covers. $30.00

The most up-to-date U.S. military sniping information and doctrine.

Song of Blue Moccasin, by Roy Chandler, Jacksonville, NC, Ron Brigade Armory, 2004. 231 pp. Hardcover. New in new dust jacket. $45.00

Speak Like a Native; Professional Secrets for Mastering Foreign Languages, by Michael Janich, Boulder CO, Paladin Press, 2005. 136 pages. Soft cover. $19.00

No matter what language you wish to learn or the level of fluency you need to attain, this book can help you learn to speak like a native.

Special Operations: Weapons and Tactics, by Timothy Mullin, London, Greenhill Press, 2003. 1st edition. 176 pp., with 189 illustrations. $39.95

The tactics and equipment of Special Forces explained in full, Contains 200 images of weaponry and training. This highly illustrated guide covers the full experience of special operations training from every possible angle. There is also considerable information on nonfirearm usage, such as specialized armor and ammunition.

Standard Catalog of Firearms 2007, 17th Edition, by Dan Shideler, Iola, WI, Krause Publications, 2006. 1504 pages, 7,100+ b&w photos, plus a 16-page color section. Paper covers. $34.95

Now in its 17th year and completely updated for 2007, this edition of the world famous Standard Catalog of Firearms is bigger and better than ever. With entries for virtually all of the world's commercial firearms from the percussion era to the present day, Standard Catalog of Firearms is the only book you need to identify and price collectible rifles, handguns and shotguns. New for 2007: "Sleepers": Collectible firearms that are outperforming the market. Value Trends: Real-Life auction reports showing value ranges. How to buy and sell on the Internet.

Standard Catalog of Military Firearms 3rd Edition: The Collector's Price & Reference Guide, by Ned Schwing, Iola, WI, Krause Publications, 2005. 480 pp. Softcover. $29.99

A companion volume to Standard Catalog of Firearms, this revised and expanded second edition comes complete with all the detailed information readers found useful and more. Listings beginning with the early cartridge models of the 1870s to the latest high-tech sniper rifles have been expanded to include more models, variations, historical information, and data, offering more detail for the military firearms collector, shooter, and history buff. Identification of specific firearms is easier with nearly 250 additional photographs. Plus, readers will enjoy "snap shots," small personal articles from experts relating real-life experiences with exclusive models. Revised to include every known military firearm available to the U.S. collector. Special feature articles on focused aspects of collecting and shooting.

Street Tough, Hard Core, Anything Goes, Street Fighting Fundamentals, by Phil Giles, Boulder, CO, Paladin Press, 2004. 176 pages. Soft cover. $25.00

A series of intense training drills performed at full power and full speed sets the Street Tough program apart from all other self-defense regimens.

Stress Fire, Vol. 1: Stress Fighting for Police, by Massad Ayoob, Police Bookshelf, Concord, NH, 1984. 149 pp., illus. Paper covers. $11.95

Gunfighting for police, advanced tactics and techniques.

Stress Fire Gunfighting for Police Vol. 2; Advanced Combat Shotgun, by Massad Ayoob, Police Bookshelf, Concord, NH, 1997. 212 pp., illus. Paper covers. $12.95

The long-awaited second volume in Massad Ayoob's series on Advanced Gunfighting for Police. Learn to control the 12-gauge shotgun in the most rapid fire, pain-rree aimed fire from the shoulder, Speed reloads that don't fail under stress, proven jam-response techniques, keys to selecting a good shotgun.

Tactical Advantage, The, by Gabriel Suarez, Paladin Press, Boulder, CO, 1998. 216 pp., illus. Paper covers. $22.00

Learn combat tactics that have been tested in the world's toughest schools.

Tactical Marksman, by Dave M. Lauch, Paladin Press, Boulder, CO, 1996. 165 pp., illus. Paper covers. $35.00

A complete training manual for police and practical shooters.

Tim Murphy Rifleman Frontier Series Volume 3, by Roy Chandler, Jacksonville, NC, Iron Brigade Armory, 2003. 1st edition. 396 pp. Hardcover. $39.95

Tim Murphy may be our young nation's earliest recognized hero. Murphy was seized by Seneca Tribesmen during his infancy. Traded to the Huron, he was renamed and educated by Sir William Johnson, a British colonial officer. Freed during the prisoner exchange of 1764, Murphy discovered his superior ability with a Pennsylvania longrifle. An early volunteer in the Pennsylvania militia, Tim Murphy served valiantly in rifle companies including the justly famed Daniel Morgan's Riflemen. This is Murphy's story.

To Ride, Shoot Straight, and Speak the Truth, by Jeff Cooper, Paladin Press, Boulder, CO, 1997, 5½" x 8½", soft-cover, illus., 384 pp. $32.00

Combat mind-set, proper sighting, tactical residential architecture, nuclear war-these are some of the many subjects explored by Jeff Cooper in this illustrated anthology. The author discusses various arms, fighting skills and the importance of knowing how to defend oneself, and one's honor, in our rapidly changing world.

Trailriders Guide to Cowboy Action Shooting, by James W. Barnard, Pioneer Press, Union City, TN, 1998. 134 pp., plus 91 photos, drawings and charts. Paper covers. $24.95

Covers the complete spectrum of this shooting discipline, from how to dress to authentic leather goods, which guns are legal, calibers, loads and ballistics.

Traveler's Guide to the Firearms Laws of the Fifty States, 2007 Edition, by Scott Kappas, KY, Traveler's Guide, 2007, 64pp,. Softcover. $12.95

U.S. Army Hand-to-Hand Combat: FM 21-150, 1954 Edition, Boulder,CO, Paladin Press, 2005. 192 pp. illus. Soft cover. $20.00

U.S. Infantry Weapons in Combat: Personal Experiences from Wolrd War II and Korea, by Mark Goodwin w/ forward by Scott Duff, Export, PA, Scott Duff Pub., 2005.

237pp, over 50 photos and drawings. Soft cover. $23.50

The stories about U.S. infantry weapons contained in this book are the real hands-on experiences of the men who actually used them for their intended purposes.

U.S. Marine Corp Rifle and Pistol Marksmanship, 1935, reprinting of a government publication, Lancer Militaria, Mt. Ida, AR, 1991. 99 pp., illus. Paper covers. $11.95

The old corps method of precision shooting.

U.S. Marine Corps Scout/Sniper Training Manual, Lancer Militaria, Mt. Ida, AR, 1989. Softcover. $27.95

Reprint of the original sniper training manual used by the Marksmanship Training Unit of the Marine Corps Development and Education Command in Quantico, Virginia.

U.S. Marine Corps Scout-Sniper, World War II and Korea, by Peter R. Senich, Paladin Press, Boulder, CO, 1994. 236 pp., illus. $44.95

The most thorough and accurate account ever printed on the training, equipment and combat experiences of the U.S. Marine Corps Scout-Snipers.

U.S. Marine Corps Sniping, Lancer Militaria, Mt. Ida, AR, 1989. Irregular pagination. Softcover. $18.95

A reprint of the official Marine Corps FMFM1-3B.

U.S. Marine Uniforms-1912-1940, by Jim Moran, Williamstown, NJ, Phillips Publications, 2001. 174 pp., illustrated with b&w photographs. Hardcover. $49.95

Ultimate Sniper: An Advanced Training Manual for Military and Police Snipers, Updated and Expanded Edition, by Major John L. Plaster, Paladin Press, Boulder, CO, 2006. 584 pp., illus. Paper covers. $49.95

Now this revolutionary book has been completely updated and expanded for the 21st century. Through revised text, new photos, specialized illustrations, updated charts and additional information sidebars, The Ultimate Sniper once again thoroughly details the three great skill areas of sniping – marksmanship, fieldcraft and tactics.

Uniforms And Equipment of the Imperial Japanese Army in World War II, by Mike Hewitt, Atglen, PA, Schiffer Publications, 2002. 176 pp., with over 520 color and b&w photos. Hardcover. $59.95

Unrepentant Sinner, by Col. Charles Askins, Paladin Press, Boulder, CO, 2000. 322 pp., illus. $29.95

The autobiography of Colonel Charles Askins.

Vietnam Order of Battle, by Shelby L. Stanton, William C. Westmoreland, Mechanicsburg, PA, Stackpole Books, 2003. 1st edition. 416 pp., 32 in full color, 101 halftones. Hardcover. $69.95

A monumental, encyclopedic work of immense detail concerning U.S. Army and allied forces that fought in the Vietnam War from 1962 through 1973. Extensive lists of units providing a record of every Army unit that served in Vietnam, down to and including separate companies, and also including U.S. Army aviation and riverine units. Shoulder patches and distinctive unit insignia of all divisions and battalions. Extensive maps portraying unit locations at each six-month interval. Photographs and descriptions of all major types of equipment employed in the conflict. Plus much more!

Warriors; On Ilving with Courage, Discipline, and Honor, by Loren Christensen, Boulder, CO, Paladin Press, 2004. 376 pages. Soft cover. $20.00

The writers who contributed to this work are a diverse mix, from soldiers, cops and SWAT officers to martial art masters to experts in the fields of workplace violence, theology and school safety. They are some of the finest warrior authors, warrior trainers and warrior scholars today. Many have faced death, survived and now teach others to do the same. Here they speak candidly on what it's like to sacrifice, to train, to protect.

"Walking Stick" Method of Self-Defence, The, by an officer of the Indian police, Boulder, CO: Paladin Press, 2004. 1st edition. 112 pages. Soft cover. $15.00

The entire range of defensive and offensive skills is discussed and demonstrated, including guards, strikes, combinations, counterattacks, feints and tricks, double-handed techniques and training drills.

Weapons of Delta Force, by Fred Pushies, St. Paul, MN, MBI Publishing Company, 2002. 1st edition. 128 pgs., 100 b&w and 100 color illustrated. Hardcover. $24.95

America's elite counter-terrorist organization, Delta Force, is a handpicked group of the U.S. Army's finest soldiers. Delta uses some of the most sophisticated weapons in the field today, and all are detailed in this book. Pistols, sniper rifles, special mission aircraft, fast attack vehicles, SCUBA and paratrooper gear, and more are presented in this fully illustrated account of our country's heroes and their tools of the trade.

Weapons of the Waffen-SS, by Bruce Quarrie, Sterling Publishing Co., Inc., 1991. 168 pp., illus. $24.95

An in-depth look at the weapons that made Hitler's Waffen-SS the fearsome fighting machine it was.

Weatherby: The Man, The Gun, The Legend, by Grits and Tom Gresham, Cane River Publishing Co., Natchitoches, LA, 1992. 290 pp., illus. $34.95

A fascinating look at the life of the man who changed the course of firearms development in America.

Winchester Era, The, by David Madis, Art & Reference House, Brownsville, TX, 1984. 100 pp., illus. $19.95

Story of the Winchester company, management, employees, etc.

Winchester Pocket Guide; Identification and Pricing for 50 Collectible Rifles and Shotguns, by Ned Schwing, Iola,WI, Krause Publications, 2004. 224 pages, illustrated. Soft cover. $12.95

The Winchester Pocket Guide also features advice on collecting, grading and pricing the collectible firearms.

With British Snipers to the Reich, by Capt. C. Shore, Lander Militaria, Mt. Ida, AR, 1988. 420 pp., illus. $29.95

One of the greatest books ever written on the art of combat sniping.

World's Machine Pistols and Submachine Guns-Vol. 2a 1964 to 1980, The, by Nelson & Musgrave, Ironside International, Alexandria, VA, 2000. 673 pp. $69.95

Containing data, history and photographs of over 200 weapons. With a special section covering shoulder stocked automatic pistols, 100 additional photos.

Wyatt Earp: A Biography of the Legend: Volume 1: The Cowtown Years, by Lee A. Silva, Santa Ana, CA, privately printed, 2002. 1st edition signed. Hardcover. New in new dust jacket. $86.95

GUNSMITHING

Accurizing the Factory Rifle, by M.L. McPhereson, Precision Shooting, Inc., Manchester, CT, 1999. 335 pp., illus. Paper covers. $44.95

A long-awaiting book, which bridges the gap between the rudimentary (mounting sling swivels, scope blocks and that general level of accomplishment) and the advanced (precision chambering, barrel fluting, and that general level of accomplishment) books that are currently available today.

Antique Firearms Assembly Disassembly: The Comprehensive Guide to Pistols, Rifles, & Shotguns, by David Chicoine, Iola, WI, Krause Publications, 2005. 528 pages, 600 b&w photos & illus. Soft cover. $29.95

Create a resource unequaled by any. Features over 600 photos of antique and rare firearms for quick identification.

Art of Engraving, The, by James B. Meek, F. Brownell & Son, Montezuma, IA, 1973. 196 pp., illus. $47.95

A complete, authoritative, imaginative and detailed study in training for gun engraving. The first book of its kind–and a great one.

Checkering and Carving of Gun Stocks, by Monte Kennedy, Stackpole Books, Harrisburg, PA, 1962. 175 pp., illus. $39.95

Revised, enlarged cloth-bound edition of a much sought-after, dependable work.

Firearms Assembly/Disassembly, Part I: Automatic Pistols, 2nd Revised Edition, The Gun Digest Book of, by J.B. Wood, DBI Books, a division of Krause Publications, Iola, WI, 1999. 480 pp., illus. Paper covers. $24.95

Covers 58 popular autoloading pistols plus nearly 200 variants of those models integrated into the text and completely cross-referenced in the index.

Firearms Assembly/Disassembly Part II: Revolvers, Revised Edition, The Gun Digest Book of, by J.B. Wood, DBI Books, a division of Krause Publications, Iola, WI, 1997. 480 pp., illus. Paper covers. $27.95

Covers 49 popular revolvers plus 130 variants. The most comprehensive and professional presentation available to either hobbyist or gunsmith.

Firearms Assembly/Disassembly Part III: Rimfire Rifles 3rd Edition, The Gun Digest Book of, by J. B. Wood, Krause Publications, Iola, WI, 2006. Softcover. 576 Pages, 1,590 b&w photos. $27.95

This redesigned volume provides comprehensive step-by-step disassembly instruction patterns for 74 rifles-nearly 200 firearms when combined with variations. All the hands-on information you need to increase accuracy and speed.

Firearms Assembly/Disassembly Part IV: Centerfire Rifles, 3rd Revised Edition, The Gun Digest Book of, by J.B. Wood, Krause Publications, Iola, WI, 2004. 480 pp., illus. Paper covers. $24.95

Covers 54 popular centerfire rifles plus 300 variants. The most comprehensive and professional presentation available to either hobbyist or gunsmith.

Firearms Assembly/Disassembly, Part V: Shotguns, Revised Edition, The Gun Digest Book of, by J.B. Wood, Krause Publications, Iola, WI, 2002. 480 pp., illus. Paper covers. $24.95

Covers 46 popular shotguns plus over 250 variants with step-by-step instructions on how to dismantle and reassemble each. The most comprehensive and professional presentation available to either hobbyist or gunsmith.

Firearms Assembly: The NRA Guide to Rifle and Shotguns, NRA Books, Wash., DC, 1980. 264 pp., illus. Paper covers. $14.95

Text and illustrations explaining the takedown of 125 rifles and shotguns, domestic and foreign.

Firearms Assembly: The NRA Guide to Pistols and Revolvers, NRA Books, Wash., DC, 1980. 253 pp., illus. Paper covers. $14.95

Text and illustrations explaining the takedown of 124 pistol and revolver models, domestic and foreign.

Firearms Bluing and Browning, by R.H. Angier, Stackpole Books, Harrisburg, PA. 151 pp., illus. $19.95

A world master gunsmith reveals his secrets of building, repairing and renewing a gun, quite literally, lock, stock and barrel. A useful, concise text on chemical coloring methods for the gunsmith and mechanic.

Guns and Gunmaking Tools of Southern Appalachia, by John Rice Irwin, Schiffer Publishing Ltd., 1983. 118 pp., illus. Paper covers. $9.95

The story of the Kentucky rifle.

Gunsmith Kinks, by F.R. (Bob) Brownell, F. Brownell & Son, Montezuma, IA, 1st ed., 1969. 496 pp., well illus. $22.98

A widely useful accumulation of shop kinks, short cuts, techniques and pertinent comments by practicing gunsmiths from all over the world.

Gunsmith Kinks 2, by Bob Brownell, F. Brownell & Son, Publishers, Montezuma, IA, 1983. 496 pp., illus. $22.95

A collection of gunsmithing knowledge, shop kinks, new and old techniques, shortcuts and general know-how straight from those who do them best–the gunsmiths.

Gunsmith Kinks 3, edited by Frank Brownell, Brownells Inc., Montezuma, IA, 1993. 504 pp., illus. $24.95

Tricks, knacks and "kinks" by professional gunsmiths and gun tinkerers. Hundreds of valuable ideas are given in this volume.

Gunsmith Kinks 4, edited by Frank Brownell, Brownells Inc., Montezuma, IA, 2001. 564 pp., illus. 332 detailed illustrations. 560+ pages with 706 separate subject headings and over 5000 cross-indexed entries. $27.75

An incredible gold mine of information.

Gunsmith Machinist, The, by Steve Acker, Village Press Publications Inc, Michigan. 2001. Hardcover, New in new dust jacket. $69.95

Gunsmith of Grenville County: Building the American Longrifle, The, by Peter Alexander, Texarkana, TX, Scurlock Publishing Co., 2002. 400 pp.in, with hundreds of illustrations, and six color photos of original rifles. Stiff paper covers. $45.00

The most extensive how-to book on building longrifles ever published. Takes you through every step of building your own longrifle, from shop set up and tools to engraving, carving and finishing.

Gunsmithing, by Roy F. Dunlap, Stackpole Books, Harrisburg, PA, 1990. 742 pp., illus. $44.95

A manual of firearm design, construction, alteration and remodeling. For amateur and professional gunsmiths and users of modern firearms.

Gunsmithing at Home: Lock, Stock and Barrel, by John Traister, Stoeger Publishing Co., Wayne, NJ, 1997. 320 pp., illus. Paper covers. $19.95

A complete step-by-step fully illustrated guide to the art of gunsmithing.

Gunsmithing Shotguns: The Complete Guide to Care & Repair, by David Henderson, New York, Globe Pequot, 2003. 1st edition. Hardcover. $24.95

Gunsmithing: Guns of the Old West: Expanded 2nd Edition, by David Chicoine, Iola, WI, Krause Publications, 2004. 446 pp.in, illus. Softcover. $29.95

This updated second edition guides collectors, cowboy action shooters, hobbyists and Old West re-enactors through repairing and improving Old West firearms. New additions include 125 high-resolution diagrams and illustrations, five new handgun models, four new long gun models, and an expanded and illustrated glossary. The book offers expanded coverage of the first edition's featured guns (over 40 original and replica models), as well as updated gunsmithing tips and advice. The step-by-step, detailed illustrations demonstrate to both amateur and advanced gunsmiths how to repair and upgrade Old West firearms.

Gunsmithing: Pistols & Revolvers: Expanded 2nd Edition, by Patrick Sweeney, Iola, WI, Krause Publications, 2004. 384 Pages, illustrated, 850 b&w photos. $24.99

Set up an efficient and organized workplace and learn what tools are needed. Then, tackle projects like installing new grips, adjusting trigger pull and sight replacement. Includes a troubleshooting guide, glossary terms and a directory of suppliers and services for most brands of handguns.

Gunsmithing: Rifles, by Patrick Sweeney, Krause Publications, Iola, WI, 1999. 352 pp., illus. Paper covers. $24.95

Tips for lever-action rifles. Building a custom Ruger 10/22. Building a better hunting rifle.

Home Gunsmithing the Colt Single Action Revolvers, by Loren W. Smith, Ray Riling Arms Books, Co., Phila., PA, 2001. 119 pp., illus. $24.95

Affords the Colt Single Action owner detailed, pertinent information on the operating and servicing of this famous and historic handgun.

How to Convert Military Rifles, Williams Gun Sight Co., Davision, MI, new and enlarged seventh edition, 1997. 76 pp., illus. Paper covers. $13.95

This latest edition updated the changes that have occured over the past thirty years. Tips, instructions and illustratons on how to convert popular military rifles as the Enfield, Mauser 96 and SKS just to name a few are presented.

Mauser M98 & M96, by R.A. Walsh, Wolfe Publishing Co., Prescott, AR, 1998. 123 pp., illus. Paper covers. $32.50

How to build your own favorite custom Mauser rifle from two of the best bolt action rifle designs ever produced–the military Mauser Model 1898 and Model 1896 bolt rifles.

Mr. Single Shot's Gunsmithing-Idea-Book, by Frank de Haas, Mark de Haas, Orange City, IA, 1996. 168 pp., illus. Paper covers. $22.50

Offers easy to follow, step-by-step instructions for a wide variety of gunsmithing procedures all reinforced by plenty of photos.

Recreating the American Longrifle, by William Buchele, et al, George Shumway Publisher, York, Pa, 5th edition, 1999. 175 pp., illus. $40.00

Includes full size plans for building a Kentucky rifle.

Story of Pope's Barrels, The, by Ray M. Smith, R&R Books, Livonia, NY, 1993. 203 pp., illus. $39.00

A reissue of a 1960 book whose author knew Pope personally. It will be of special interest to Schuetzen rifle fans, since Pope's greatest days were at the height of the Schuetzen-era before WWI.

Survival Gunsmithing, by J.B. Wood, Desert Publications, Cornville, AZ, 1986. 92 pp., illus. Paper covers. $11.95

A guide to repair and maintenance of the most popular rifles, shotguns and handguns.

Tactical 1911, The, by Dave Lauck, Paladin Press, Boulder, CO, 1998. 137 pp., illus. Paper covers. $20.00

Here is the only book you will ever need to teach you how to select, modify, employ and maintain your Colt.

HANDGUNS

.22 Caliber Handguns; A Shooter's Guide, by D.F. Geiger, Lincoln, RI, Andrew Mowbray, Inc., 2003. 1st edition. Softcover. $21.95

.380 Enfield No. 2 Revolver, The, by Mark Stamps and Ian Skennerton, I.D.S.A. Books, Piqua, OH, 1993. 124 pp., 80 illus. Paper covers. $19.95

9mm Parabellum; The History & Development of the World's 9mm Pistols & Ammunition, by Klaus-Peter Konig and Martin Hugo, Schiffer Publishing Ltd., Atglen, PA, 1993. 304 pp., illus. $39.95

Detailed history of 9mm weapons from Belguim, Italy, Germany, Israel, France, U.S.A., Czechoslovakia, Hungary, Poland, Brazil, Finland and Spain.

A Study of Colt New Army and Navy Pattern Double action Revolvers 1889-1908, by Robert Best. Privately Printed, 2005, 2nd Printing. 276 pages. Hardcover $62.00

A Study..." is a detailed look into Colt's development and production of the Double Action Swing Out Cylinder New Army and Navy series revolvers. Civilian model production, U.S. Army and Navy models and contracts, and other Government organizations using these revolvers are all covered in this book. There are over 150 photographs with 24 pages of color photos to show specific markings and manufacturing changes. Fully documented.

Advanced Master Handgunning, by Charles Stephens, Paladin Press, Boulder, CO, 1994. 72 pp., illus. Paper covers. $14.00

Secrets and surefire techniques for winning handgun competitions.

Advanced Tactical Marksman More High Performance Techniques for Police, Military, and Practical Shooters, by Dave M. Lauck. Paladin Press, Boulder, CO, 2002. 1st edition. 232 pp., photos, illus. Softcover $35.00

Lauck, one of the most respected names in high-performance shooting and gunsmithing, refines and updates his 1st book. Dispensing with overcomplicated mil-dot formulas and minute-of-angle calculations, Lauck shows you how to achieve superior accuracy and figure out angle shots, train for real-world scenarios, choose optics and accessories.

American Beauty: The Prewar Colt National Match Government Model Pistol, by Timothy Mullin, Collector Grade Publications, Canada, 1999. 72 pp., 69 illus. $34.95

69 illustrations, 20 in full color photos of factory engraved guns and other authenticated upgrades, including rare 'double-carved' ivory grips.

Automatic Pistol, The, by J.B.L. Noel, Foreword by Timothy J. Mullin, Boulder, CO, Paladin Press, 2004. 128 pp., illus. Softcover. $14.00

Ayoob Files: The Book, The, by Massad Ayoob, Police Bookshelf, Concord, NH, 1995. 223 pp., illus. Paper covers. $14.95

The best of Massad Ayoob's acclaimed series in *American Handgunner* magazine.

Big Bore Handguns, by John Taffin, Krause Publications, Iola, WI, 2002. 1st edition. 352 pp., 320 b&w photos with a 16-page color section. Hardcover. $39.95

Gives honest reviews and an inside look at shooting, hunting, and competing with the biggest handguns around. Covers handguns from major gunmakers, as well as handgun customizing, accessories, reloading, and cowboy activities. Significant coverage is also given to handgun customizing, accessories, reloading, and popular shooting hobbies including hunting and cowboy activities.

Bill Ruger's .22 Pistol: A Photographic Essay of the Ruger Rimfire Pistol, by Don Findlay, New York, Simon & Schuster, 2000. 2nd printing. Limited edition of 100 copies, signed and numbered. Hardcover, $100.00

Browning High Power Automatic Pistol (Expanded Edition), by Blake R. Stevens, Collector Grade Publications, Canada, 1996. 310 pp., with 313 illus. $49.95

An in-depth chronicle of seventy years of High Power history, from John M. Browning's original 16-shot prototypes to the present. Profusely illustrated with rare original photos and drawings from the FN Archive to describe virtually every sporting and military version of the High Power. The Expanded Edition contains 30 new pages on the interesting Argentine full-auto High Power, the latest FN 'MK3' and BDA9 pistols, plus FN's revolutionary P90 5.7x28mm Personal Defense Weapon, and more!

Browning Hi-Power Assembly, Disassembly Manual 9mm, by Skennerton & Riling, Ray Riling Arms Books Co. Philadelphia, PA, 2005. 36 pages, illustrated. $5.00

Ideal workshop reference for stripping & assembly with exploded parts drawings, specifications, service accessories, historical information and recommended reading references. Ideal workbook for shooters and collectors alike. The binding is triple saddle-stitched with a durable plastic laminated cover.

Browning Hi-Power Pistols, Desert Publications, Cornville, AZ, 1982. 20 pp., illus. Paper covers. $13.95

Covers all facets of the various military and civilian models of the Browning Hi-Power pistol.

Canadian Military Handguns 1855-1985, by Clive M. Law, Museum Restoration Service, Bloomfield, Ont., Canada, 1994. 130pp., illus. $40.00

A long-awaited and important history for arms historians and pistol collectors.

Classic Handguns of the 20th Century, by David Arnold. Iola, WI, Krause Publications, 2004. 144 pages, color photos. Softcover. $24.99

You'll need this book to find out what qualities, contributions and characteristics made each of the twenty handguns found within a "classic" in the eyes of noted gun historian and author, David W. Arnold. Join him on this most fascinating visual walk through the most significant and prolific handguns of the 20th century. From the Colt Single-Action Army Revolver and the German P08 Luger to the Walther P-38 and Beretta Model 92.

Collecting U. S. Pistols & Revolvers, 1909-1945, by J. C. Harrison. The Arms Chest, Oklahoma City, OK, 1999. 2nd edition (revised). 185 pp., illus. Spiral bound. $35.00

Valuable and detailed reference book for the collector of U.S. pistols & revolvers. Identifies standard issue original military models of the M1911, M1911A1 and M1917 Cal .45 pistols and revolvers as produced by all manufacturers from 1911 through 1945. Plus .22 Ace models, National Match models, and similar foreign military models produced by Colt or manufactured under Colt license, plus arsenal repair, refinish and lend-lease models.

Colt .45 Pistol M1911A1 Assembly, Disassembly Manual, by Skennerton & Riling, Ray Riling Arms Books Co. Philadelphia, PA, 2005. 36 pages, illustrated. $5.00

Ideal workshop reference for stripping & assembly with exploded parts drawings, specifications, service accessories, historical information and recommended reading references. Ideal workbook for shooters and collectors alike. The binding is triple saddle-stitched with a durable plastic laminated cover.

Colt .45 Auto Pistol, compiled from U.S. War Dept. Technical Manuals, and reprinted by Desert Publications, Cornville, AZ, 1978. 80 pp., illus. Paper covers. $14.95

Covers every facet of this famous pistol from mechanical training, manual of arms, disassembly, repair and replacement of parts.

Colt Single Action Army Revolver Study: New Discoveries, by Kenneth Moore, Lincoln, RI, Andrew Mowbray, Inc., 2003. 1st edition. Hardcover. $47.95

Combat Perspective; The Thinking Man's Guide to Self-Defense, by Gabriel Suarez, Boulder, CO, Paladin Press, 2003. 1st edition. 112 pp. Softcover. $15.00

In the Combat Perspective, Suarez keys in on developing your knowledge about and properly organizing your mental attitude toward combat to improve your odds of winning – not just surviving – such a fight. In this book he examines each in a logical and scientific manner, demonstrating why, when it comes to defending your life, the mental edge is at least as critical to victory as the tactical advantage.

Complete Encyclopedia of Pistols & Revolvers, by A.E. Hartnik, Knickerbocker Press, New York, NY, 2003. 272 pp., illus. $19.95

A comprehensive encyclopedia specially written for collectors and owners of pistols and revolvers.

Concealable Pocket Pistols: How to Choose and Use Small-Caliber Handguns, by Terence McLeod, Paladin Press, 2001. 1st edition. 80 pp. Softcover. $14.00

Small-caliber handguns are often maligned as too puny for serious self-defense, but millions of Americans own and carry these guns and have used them successfully to stop violent assaults. Find out what millions of Americans already know about these practical self-defense tools.

Concelealed Handgun Manual, The, 4th Edition, by Chris Bird. San Antonio, Privateer Publications, 2004. 332 pages, illus. Softcover. $21.95

If you carry a gun for personal protection, or plan to, you need to read this book. You will learn whether carrying a gun is for you, what gun to choose and how to carry it, how to stay out of trouble, when to shoot and how to shoot, gunfighting tactics, what to expect after you have shot someone, and how to apply for a concealed-carry license in 30 states, plus never-before published details of actual shooting incidents.

Confederate Lemat Revolver; Secret Weapon of the Confederacy?, The, by Doug Adams, Lincoln, RI, Andrew Mowbray, Inc.,2005. 1st edition. Nearly 200 spectacular full-color illustrations and over 70 b&w period photos, illustrations and patent drawings. 112 pages. Softcover. $29.95

This exciting new book describes LeMat's wartime adventures aboard blockade runners and alongside the famous leaders of the Confederacy, as well as exploring, as never before, the unique revolvers that he manufactured for the Southern Cause.

Darling Pepperbox: The Story of Samuel Colt's Forgotten Competitors in Bellingham, The, Mass. and Woonsocket, RI, by Stuart C. Mowbray, Lincoln, RI, Andrew Mowbray, Inc., 2004. 1st edition. 104 pp. Softcover. $19.95

Developmental Cartridge Handguns of .22 Calibre, as Produced in the United States & Abroad from 1855 to 1875, by John S. Laidacker, Atglen, PA, Schiffer Publications, 2003. Reprint. 597 pp., with over 860 b&w photos, drawings, and charts. Hardcover. $100.00

This book is a reprint edition of the late John Laidacker's personal study of early .22 Cartridge Handguns from 1855-1875. Laidacker's primary aim was to offer a quick reference to the collector, and his commentary on the wide variety of types, variations and makers, as well as detailed photography, make this a superb addition to any firearm library.

Effective Handgun Defense, by Frank James, Iola, WI, Krause Publications, 2004. 1st edition. 223 pp, illustated, softcover. NEW $19.95

Effective Handgun Defense, it's readily apparent that he'd have had no problem making his way in an urban environment either. He has a keen mind for the requirements and nuances for "concealed carry" and personal defense, and a fluid style of presenting his material that is neither awkward nor "precious."

Engraved Handguns of .22 Calibre, by John S. Laidacker, Atglen, PA, Schiffer Publications, 2003. 1st edition. 192 pp., with over 400 color and b&w photos. $69.95

Essential Guide to Handguns: Firearms Instruction for Personal Defense and Protection, by Stephen Rementer and Brian Eimer, Phd., Flushing, NY, Looseleaf law Publications, 2005. 1st edition. Over 300 pages plus illustrations. Softcover. $24.89

Farnam Method of Defensive Handgunning, The, by John S. Farnam, Police Bookshelf, 1999. 191 pp., illus. Paper covers. $24.00

A book intended to not only educate the new shooter, but also to serve as a guide and textbook for his and his instructor's training courses.

Fast and Fancy Revolver Shooting, by Ed McGivern, Anniversary Edition, Winchester Press, Piscataway, NJ, 1984. 484 pp., illus. $19.95

A fascinating volume, packed with handgun lore and solid information by the acknowledged dean of revolver shooters.

French Service Handguns: 1858-2004, by Eugene Medlin & Jean Huon, Tommy Gun Publications, 2004. 1st edition. Over 200 pages and more than 125 photographs. Hardcover, $44.95

Over 10 years in the making, this long awaited volume on French handguns is finally here. this book offers in depth coverage on everything from the 11mm Pinfire to the 9mm Parabellum-including various Lefaucheux revolvers, MAB's, Spanish pistols, and revolvers used in WWI, Uniques, plus, many photos of one-of-a-kind prototypes of the French contract Browning, Model 1935s, and 35a pistols used in WWII.

German Handguns: The Complete Book of the Pistols and Revolvers of Germany, 1869 to the Present, by Ian Hogg, Greenhill Publishing, 2001. 320 pp., 270 illustrations. Hardcover. $49.95

Ian Hogg examines the full range of handguns produced in Germany from such classics as the Luger M1908, Mauser HsC and Walther PPK, to more unusual types such as the Reichsrevolver M1879 and the Dreyse 9mm. He presents the key data (length, weight, muzzle velocity, and range) for each weapon discussed and also gives its date of introduction and service record, evaluates and discusses peculiarities, and examines in detail particular strengths and weaknesses.

Glock in Competition, by Robin Taylor, Spokane, WA, Taylor Press, 2006, 2nd edition. 248pp, Softcover. NEW $19.95
Covered topics include reloading, trigger configurations, recalls, and refits, magazine problems, modifying the Glock, choosing factory ammo, and a host of others.

Glock: The New Wave in Combat Handguns, by Peter Alan Kasler, Paladin Press, Boulder, CO, 1993. 304 pp., illus. $27.00
Kasler debunks the myths that surround what is the most innovative handgun to be introduced in some time.

Glock's Handguns, by Duncan Long, Desert Publications, El Dorado, AR, 1996. 180 pp., illus. Paper covers. $19.95
An outstanding volume on one of the world's newest and most successful firearms of the century.

Gun Digest Book of Beretta Pistols, The, by Massad Ayoob, Iola, WI, Krause Publications, 2005. 288 pages, 300+ photos help with identification. Softcover. $27.99
This new release from the publishers of Gun Digest, readers get information including caliber,weight and barrel lengths for modern pistols. A review of the accuracy and function of all models of modern Beretta pistols give active shooters details needed to make the most of this popular firearm. More than 300 photographs, coupled with articles detailing the development of design and style of these handguns, create a comprehensive must-have resource.

Gun Digest Book of Combat Handgunnery 5th Edition, The, Complete Guide to Combat Shooting, by Massad Ayoob, Iola, WI, Krause Publications, 2002. $22.95
Tap into the knowledge of an international combat handgun expert for the latest in combat handgun designs, strengths and limitations; caliber, size, power and ability; training and technique; cover, concealment and hostage situations. Unparalleled!

Gun Digest Book of the 1911, The, by Patrick Sweeney, Krause Publications, Iola, WI, 2002. 336 pp., with 700 b&w photos. Softcover. $27.95
Complete guide of all models and variations of the Model 1911. The author also includes repair tips and information on buying a used 1911.

Gun Digest Book of the 1911 2nd Edition, The, by Patrick Sweeney, Krause Publications, Iola, WI, 2006. 336 pp., with 700 b&w photos. Softcover. $27.95
Complete guide of all models and variations of the Model 1911. The author also includes repair tips and information on buying a used 1911.

Gun Digest Book of the Glock; A Comprehensive Review, Design, History and Use, The, Iola, WI, Krause Publications, 2003. 303 pp., with 500 b&w photos. Softcover. 27.95
Examine the rich history and unique elements of the most important and influential firearms design of the past 50 years, the Glock autoloading pistol. This comprehensive review of the revolutionary pistol analyzes the performance of the various models and chamberings and features a complete guide to available accessories and little-known factory options. You'll see why it's the preferred pistol for law enforcement use and personal protection.

Gun Digest Book of the SIG-Sauer, The, by Massad Ayoob, Iola, WI, Krause Publications, 2005. 1st edition 304pp. Softcover. $27.99
Noted firearms training expert Massad Ayoob takes an in-depth look at some of the finest pistols on the market. If you own a SIG-Sauer pistol, have consdered buying one or just appreciate the fine quality of these pistols, this is the book for you. Ayoob takes a practical look at each of the SIG-Sauer pistols including handling characteristics, and design and performance. Each gun in every caliber is tested and evaluated, giving you all the details you need as you choose and use your SIG-Sauer pistol.

Gun Digest Book of Smith & Wesson, The, by Patrick Sweeney, Iola, WI, Krause Publications, 2005. 1st edition. Covers all categories of Smith & Wesson Guns in both competition and law enforcement. 312pp, 500 b&w photos. Softcover, $27.99

Hand Cannons: The World's Most Powerful Handguns, by Duncan Long, Paladin Press, Boulder, CO, 1995. 208 pp., illus. Paper covers. $22.00
Long describes and evaluates each powerful gun according to their features.

Handgun Combatives, by Dave Spaulding, Flushing, NY, Looseleaf Law Publications,2005. 212pp, with 60 plus photos, softcover. $22.95

Handgun Stopping Power "The Definitive Study," by Evan P. Marshall & Edwin J. Sanow, Paladin Press, Boulder, CO, 1997. 240 pp. photos. Softcover. $45.00
Dramatic first-hand accounts of the results of handgun rounds fired into criminals by cops, storeowners, cabbies and others are the heart and soul of this long-awaited book. This is the definitive methodology for predicting the stopping power of handgun loads, the first to take into account what really happens when a bullet meets a man.

Handguns 2007, 19th Edition, Ken Ramage, Iola WI, Gun Digest Books, 2006, 320pp, 500 b&w photos, Softcover. $24.99
Target shooters, handgun hunters, collectors and those who rely upon handguns for self-defense will want to pack this value-loaded and entertaining volume in their home libraries. Shooters will find the latest pistol and revolver designs and accessories, plus test reports on several models. The handgun becomes an artist's canvas in a showcase of engraving talents. The catalog section—with comprehensive specs on every known handgun in production—includes a new display of semi-custom handguns, plus an expanded, illustrated section on the latest grips, sights, scopes and other aiming devices. Offer easy access to products, services and manufacturers.

Handguns of the Armed Organizations of the Soviet Occupation Zone and German Democratic Republic, by Dieter H. Marschall, Los Alamos, NM, Ucross Books, 2000. Softcover. $29.95
Translated from German this groundbreaking treatise covers the period from May 1945 through 1996. The organizations that used these pistols are described along with the guns and holsters. Included are the P08, P38, PP, PPK, P1001, PSM, Tokarev, Makarov, (including .22 LR, cutaway, silenced, Suhl marked), Stechlin, plus Hungarian, Romanian and Czech pistols.

Heckler & Koch's Handguns, by Duncan Long, Desert Publications, El Dorado, AR, 1996. 142 pp., illus. Paper covers. $19.95
Traces the history and the evolution of H&K's pistols from the company's beginning at the end of WWII to the present.

Hidden in Plain Sight, by Trey Bloodworth & Mike Raley, Paladin Press, Boulder, CO, 2003. Paper covers. $20.00

A practical guide to concealed handgun carry.

High Standard: A Collectors Guide to the Hamden & Hartford Target Pistols, by Tom Dance, Andrew Mowbray, Inc., Lincoln, RI, 1999. 192 pp., heavily illustrated with b&w photographs and technical drawings. $24.00
From Citation to Supermatic, all of the production models and specials made from 1951 to 1984 are covered according to model number or series, making it easy to understand the evolution to this favorite of shooters and collectors.

High Standard Automatic Pistols 1932-1950, by Charles E. Petty, The Gun Room Press, Highland Park, NJ, 1989. 124 pp., illus. $19.95
A definitive source of information for the collector of High Standard arms.

Hi-Standard Pistols and Revolvers, 1951-1984, by James Spacek, Chesire, CT, 1998. 128 pp., illus. Paper covers. $14.95
Technical details, marketing features and instruction/parts manual of every model High Standard pistol and revolver made between 1951 and 1984. Most accurate serial number information available.

History of Smith & Wesson Firearms, by Dean Boorman, New York, Lyons Press, 2002. 1st edition. 144 pp., illustrated in full color. Hardcover. $29.95
The definitive guide to one of the world's best-known firearms makers. Takes the story through the years of the Military & Police .38 & of the Magnum cartridge, to today's wide range of products for law-enforcement customers.

How to Become a Master Handgunner: The Mechanics of X-Count Shooting, by Charles Stephens, Paladin Press, Boulder, CO, 1993. 64 pp., illus. Paper covers. $14.00
Offers a simple formula for success to the handgunner who strives to master the technique of shooting accurately.

How to Customize Your Glock: Step-By-Step Modifications You Can Do at Little Cost, by Robert and Morgan Boatman, Paladin Press, Boulder, CO, 2005, 1st edition. 8½" x 11", photos, 72 pp. Softcover. $20.00
This mini-"Glocksmithing" course by Glock enthusiasts Robert and Morgan Boatman first explains why you would make a specific modification and what you gain in terms of improved performance. The workbook format makes the manual simple to follow as you work on your Glock, andhigh-resolution photos illustrate each part and step precisely. Make your Glock work even more effectively for you bythinking outside the box.

Inglis Diamond: The Canadian High Power Pistol, by Clive M. Law, Collector Grade Publications, Canada, 2001. 312 pp., illus. $49.95
This definitive work on Canada's first and indeed only mass produced handgun, in production for a very brief span of time and consequently made in relatively few numbers, the venerable Inglis-made Browning High Power covers the pistol's initial history, the story of Chinese and British adoption, use post-war by Holland, Australia, Greece, Belgium, New Zealand, Peru, Brasil and other countries. All new information on the famous light-weights and the Inglis Diamond variations. Completely researched through official archives in a dozen countries. Many of the bewildering variety of markings have never been satisfactorily explained until now

Japanese Military Cartridge Handguns 1893-1945, A Revised and Expanded Edition of Hand Cannons of Imperial Japan, by Harry L. Derby III and James D. Brown, Atglen, PA, Schiffer Publications, 2003. 1st edition. Hardcover. New in new dust jacket. $79.95
When originally published in 1981, *The Hand Cannons of Imperial Japan* was heralded as one of the most readable works on firearms ever produced. To arms collectors and scholars, it remains a prized source of information on Japanese handguns, their development, and their history. In this new revised and expanded edition, original author Harry Derby has teamed with Jim Brown to provide a thorough update reflecting twenty years of additional research. An appendix on valuation has also been added, using a relative scale that should remain relevant despite inflationary pressures. For the firearms collector, enthusiast, historian or dealer, this is the most complete and up-to-date work on Japanese military handguns ever written.

Living with Glocks: The Complete Guide to the New Standard in Combat Handguns, by Robert H. Boatman, Boulder, CO, Paladin Press, 2002. 1st edition. 184 pp., illus. Hardcover. $29.95
In addition to demystifying the enigmatic Glock trigger, Boatman describes and critiques each Glock model in production. Separate chapters on the G36, the enhanced G20 and the full-auto G18 emphasize the job-specific talents of these standout models for those seeking insight on which Glock pistol might best meet their needs. And for those interested in optimizing their Glock's capabilities, this book addresses all the peripherals—holsters, ammo, accessories, silencers, modifications and conversions, training programs and more.

Living With the 1911, by Robert Boatman, Boulder, CO, Paladin Press, 2005. 144pp, softcover. NEW $25.00

Luger P'08 Pistol, 9mm Assembly, Disassembly Manual, by Skennerton & Riling, Ray Riling Arms Books Co. Philadelphia, PA, 2005. 36 pages, illustrated. $5.00
Ideal workshop reference for stripping & assembly with exploded parts drawings, specifications, service accessories, historical information and recommended reading references. The binding is triple saddle-stitched with a durable plastic laminated cover.

Luger Handbook, by Aarron Davis, Krause Publications, Iola, WI, 1997. 112 pp., illus. Paper covers. $9.95
Now you can identify any of the legendary Luger variations using a simple decision tree. Each model and variation includes pricing information, proof marks and detailed attributes in a handy, user-friendly format. Plus, it's fully indexed. Instantly identify that Luger!

Lyman Pistol and Revolver Handbook, 3rd edition, by Lyman. Middletown, CT, Lyman Products Corp, 2005. 3rd edition. 272pp, Softcover. NEW $22.95

Makarov Pistol Assembly, Disassembly Manual 9mm, by Skennerton & Riling, Ray Riling Arms Books Co. Philadelphia, PA, 2005. 36 pages, illustrated. $5.00
Ideal workshop reference for stripping & assembly with exploded parts drawings, specifications, ervice accessories, historical information and recommended reading references. The binding is triple saddle-stitched with a durable plastic laminated cover.

Mauser Self-Loading Pistol, by Belford & Dunlap, Borden Publishing Co., Alhambra, CA. Over 200 pp., 300 illus. large format. $29.95
The long-awaited book on the "Broom Handles," covering their inception in 1894 to the end of production. Complete and in detail: pocket pistols, Chinese and Spanish copies.

Mauser Broomhandle Model 1896 Pistol Assembly, Disassembly Manual, by Skennerton & Riling, Ray Riling Arms Books Co. Philadelphia, PA, 2005. 36 pages, illustrated. $5.00

Ideal workshop reference for stripping & assembly with exploded parts drawings, specifications, service accessories, historical information and recommended reading references.

Mental Mechanics of Shooting: How to Stay Calm at the Center, by Vishnu Karmakar and Thomas Whitney, Littleton, CO, Center Vision, Inc., 2001. 144 pp. Softcover. $19.95

Not only will this book help you stay free of trigger jerk, it will help you in all areas of your shooting.

Model 35 Radom Pistol, The, by Terence Lapin, Hyrax Publishers, 2004. 95 pages with b&w photos, Stiff paper covers. $18.95

Model 1911 Automatic Pistol, by Robert Campbell, Accokeek, Maryland, Stoeger Publications, 2004. Hardcover. $24.95

Modern Law Enforcement Weapons & Tactics, 3rd Edition, by Patrick Sweeney, Iola, WI, Krause Publications, 2004. 256 pp. Softcover. $22.99

Official 9mm Markarov Pistol Manual, translated into English by Major James Gebhardt, U.S. Army (Ret.), Desert Publications, El Dorado, AR, 1996. 84 pp., illus. Paper covers. $14.95

The information found in this book will be of enormous benefit and interest to the owner or a prospective owner of one of these pistols.

Operator's Tactical Pistol Shooting Manual; A Practical Guide to Combat Marksmanship, by Erik Lawrence, Linesville, PA, Blackheart Publishing, 2003. 1st edition. 233 pp. Softcover. $24.50

This manual-type book begins with the basics of safety with a pistol and progresses into advanced pistol handling. A self-help guide for improving your capabilities with a pistol at your own pace.

P08 Luger Pistol, by de Vries & Martens, Alexandria, VA, Ironside International, 2002. 152 pp., illustrated with 200 high quality b&w photos. Hardcover. $34.95

Covers all essential information on history and development, ammunition and accessories, codes and markings, and contains photos of nearly every model and accessory. Includes a unique selection of original German WWII propaganda photos, most never published before.

P-08 Parabellum Luger Automatic Pistol, edited by J. David McFarland, Desert Publications, Cornville, AZ, 1982. 20 pp., illus. Paper covers. $14.95

Covers every facet of the Luger, plus a listing of all known Luger models.

P-38 Pistol: Postwar Distributions, 1945-1990, Volume 3, by Warren Buxton, Ucross Books, Los Alamos, MN 1999, plus an addendum to Volumes 1 & 2. 272 pp. with 342 illustrations. $75.00

P-38 Pistol: The Contract Pistols, 1940-1945, Volume 2, by Warren Buxton, Ucross Books, Los Alamos, MN 1999. 256 pp. with 237 illustrations. $75.00

P-38 Pistol: The Walther Pistols, 1930-1945, Volume 1, by Warren Buxton, Ucross Books, Los Alamos, MN 1999. 328 pp. with 160 illustrations. $75.00

A limited run reprint of this scarce and sought-after work on the P-38 Pistol.

Peacemakers: Arms and Adventure in the American West, by RL Wilson. New York, Book Sales, 2004, reprint. 392pp. colored endpapers, 320 full color illustrations. Hardcover in New DJ, $24.89

Percussion Pistols and Revolvers: History, Performance and Practical Use, by Mike Cumpston and Johnny Bates, Texas, Iunivers, Inc, 2005. 1st edition. 208 pages. Softcover. $19.95

With the advent of the revolving pistols came patents that created monopolies in revolver production and the through-bored cylinder necessary for self-contained metallic cartridges. The caplock revolvers took on a separate evolution and remained state of the art long after the widespread appearance of cartridge-firing rifles and shotguns.

Pistol as a Weapon of Defence in the House and on the Road, by Jeff Cooper, Boulder, CO, Paladin Press, 2004. 1st edition. 48pp. Softcover. $9.00

Penned in 1875 and recently discovered collecting dust on a library bookshelf, this primer for the pistol is remarkably timely in its insights and observations. From a historical perspective, it contains striking parallels to the thinking and controversy that swirl about the practical use of the pistol today.

Pistols of the World; Fully Revised, 4th Edition, Iola, WI, Krause Publications, 2005. 432pp, chronicles 2,500 handguns made from 1887-2004. Stiff paper covers, $22.95

More than 1,000 listings and 20 years of coverage were added since the previous edition.

Pistols of World War I, by Robert J. Adamek, Pittsburgh, Pentagon Press, 2001. 1st edition signed and numbered. 296 pp. with illustrations and photos. Softcover. $45.00

Over 90 pistols illustrated, technical data, designers, history, proof marks. Over 25 pistol magazines illustrated with dimensions, serial number ranges. Over 35 cartridges illustrated with dimensions, manufactures, year of introduction. Weapons from 16 countries involved in WWI, statistics, quantities made, identification.

Remington Large-Bore Conversion Revolvers, by R. Phillips. Canada, Prately printed, 2005. Limited printing of 250 signed and numbered copies in leather hardcover. 126pp, with 200 illustrations. NEW $55.00

Ruger .22 Automatic Pistol, Standard/Mark I/Mark II Series, by Duncan Long, Paladin Press, Boulder, CO, 1989. 168 pp., illus. Paper covers. $16.00

The definitive book about the pistol that has served more than 1 million owners so well.

Ruger .22 Automatic Pistols: The Complete Guide for all Models from 1947 to 2003, Grand Rapids, MI, The Ruger Store, 2004. 74 pp., 66 high-resolution grayscale images. Printed in the U.S.A. with card stock cover and bright white paper. Softcover. $12.95

Includes 'rare' complete serial numbers and manufacturing dates from 1949-2004.

Ruger "P" Family of Handguns, by Duncan Long, Desert Publications, El Dorado, AZ, 1993. 128 pp., illus. Paper covers. $14.95

A full-fledged documentary on a remarkable series of Sturm Ruger handguns.

Ruger Pistol Reference Booklet 1949-1982 (Pocket Guide to Ruger Rimfire Pistols Standard and Mark I), by Don Findlay. Lubbock Tx, 2005. Softcover. 24 pages, illustrated with b&w photos. $9.95

Designed for the professional un dealer as well as the collector. Complete list of serial numbers as well as production dates. Also, includes photos of the original boxes the guns came in.

Semi-automatic Pistols in Police Service and Self Defense, by Massad Ayoob, Police Bookshelf, Concord, NH, 1990. 25 pp., illus. Softcover. $11.95

First quantitative, documented look at actual police experience with 9mm and 45 police service automatics.

Shooting Colt Single Actions, by Mike Venturino, Livingston, MT, 1997. 205 pp., illus. Paper covers. $25.00

A definitive work on the famous Colt SAA and the ammunition it shoots.

SIG Handguns, by Duncan Long, Desert Publications, El Dorado, AZ, 1995. 150 pp., illus. Paper covers. $19.95

The history of SIG/Sauer handguns, including Sig, Sig-Hammerli and Sig/Sauer variants.

Smith & Wesson's Automatics, by Larry Combs, Desert Publications, El Dorado, AZ, 1994. 143 pp., illus. Paper covers. $19.95

A must for every S&W auto owner or prospective owner.

Smith & Wesson: Sixguns of the Old West, by David Chicoine. Lincoln, RI., Andrew Mowbray, Inc., 2004. 1st edition. 480 pages, countless photos and detailed technical drawings. Hardcover. New in new dust jacket. $69.49

The Schofields, The Americans, The Russians, The New Model #3s, and The DAs.

Smith & Wesson American Model; In U.S. And Foreign Service, by Charles W. Pate, Mowbray Publishers, Lincoln, RI, 2006. 408 pp., illus. $65.00

This new book is an awesome new collector's guide to the S&W American. A huge resource on the military and western use of this classic large frame revolver.

Spanish Handguns: The History of Spanish Pistols and Revolvers, by Gene Gangarosa Jr., Stoeger Publishing Co., Accokeek, MD, 2001. 320 pp., illustrated, b&w photos. Paper covers. $21.95

Standard Catalog Of Luger, by Aarron Davis, Gun Digest Books, Iola WI, 2006. 256 pages, illustrated with photos. Paper Covers $29.99

This comprehensive identification and price guide goes a long way to giving Luger enthusiasts information to enjoy and be successful in an extremely active collector market. With Standard Catalog of Luger, firearms enthusiasts receive an unrivaled reference that includes: Reproductions of symbols and makers' marks from every model of Luger for use in accurately identifying the hundreds of Luger variations, More than 1,000 detailed photos and line illustrations demonstrating design and performance of Luger pistols, Manufacturing data and model rarity information to aid collectors when buying Lugers as an investment. Perfect for firearms collectors, gun shop owners, auction houses, museums, and appraisers.

Standard Catalog Of Smith & Wesson; 3rd Edition, by Jim Supica, & Richard Nahas, Gun Digest Books, Iola WI, 2006 384 pages, with photos, Hardcover. $39.99

Definitive Smith & Wesson identification and pricing reference, includes 350+ full-color photos for improved identification. Smith & Wesson is one of the hottest manufacturers of handguns, offering more new models than any other maker-39 new products in 2005 alone. Comprehensive coverage of Smith & Wesson firearm line including the only handgun in the world in continuous production since 1899. The 3rd Edition combines full color photos with details collectors need to identify and better appreciate all Smith & Wesson firearms.

Star Firearms, by Leonardo M. Antaris, Davenport, TA, Firac Publications Co., 2002. 1st edition. Hardcover. New in new dust jacket. $119.95

Tactical 1911, by Dave Lauck, Paladin Press, Boulder, CO, 1999. 152 pp., illus. Paper covers. $22.00

The cop's and SWAT operator's guide to employment and maintenance.

Tactical Pistol, by Gabriel Suarez, Foreword by Jeff Cooper, Paladin Press, Boulder, CO, 1996. 216 pp., illus. Paper covers. $25.00

Advanced gunfighting concepts and techniques.

Tactical Pistol Shooting; Your Guide to Tactics that Work, by Erik Lawrence. Iola, WI, Krause Publications, 2005. 1st edition. More than 250 step-by-step photos to illustrate techniques. 233pp, Softcover. NEW $18.95

Thompson/Center Contender Pistol, by Charles Tephens, Paladin Press, Boulder, CO, 1997. 58 pp., illus. Paper covers. $14.00

How to tune and time, load and shoot accurately with the Contender pistol.

U.S. Handguns of World War II, The Secondary Pistols and Revolvers, by Charles W. Pate, Mowbray Publishers, Lincoln, RI, 1997. 368 pp., illus. $39.00

This indispensable new book covers all of the American military handguns of WWII except for the M1911A1.

Walther P-38 Assembly, Disassembly Manual 9mm, by Skennerton & Riling, Ray Riling Arms Books Co. Philadelphia, PA, 2005. 36 pages, illustrated. $5.00

Ideal workshop reference for stripping & assembly with exploded parts drawings, specifications, service accessories, historical information and recommended reading references. The binding is triple saddle-stitched with a durable plastic laminated cover.

Walther Pistols: Models 1 Through P99, Factory Variations and Copies, by Dieter H. Marschall, Ucross Books, Los Alamos, NM. 2000. 140 pp., with 140 b&w illustrations, index. Paper covers. $21.95

This is the English translation, revised and updated, of the highly successful and widely acclaimed German language edition. This book provides the collector with a reference guide and overview of the entire line of the Walther military, police, and self-defense pistols from the very first to the very latest Variations, where issued, serial ranges, calibers, marks, proofs, logos, and design aspects in an astonishing quantity and variety are crammed into this very well researched and highly regarded work.

Hunting

NORTH AMERICA

A Varmint Hunter's Odyssey, by Steve Hanson with guest chapter by Mike Johnson, Precision Shooting, Inc. Manchester, CT, 1999. 279 pp., illus. Paper covers. $39.95

A new classic by a writer who eats, drinks and sleeps varmint hunting and varmint rifles.

Advanced Black Powder Hunting, by Toby Bridges, Stoeger Publishing Co., Wayne, NJ, 1998. 288 pp., illus. Paper covers. $21.95

The first modern day publication to be filled from cover to cover with guns, loads, projectiles, accessories and the techniques to get the most from today's front loading guns.

Adventures of an Alaskan–You Can Do, by Dennis W. Confer, Foreword by Craig Boddington. Anchorage, AK, Wiley Ventures, 2003. 1st edition. 279 pp., illus. Softcover. $24.95

This book is about 45% fishing, 45% hunting, & 10% related adventures; travel, camping and boating. It is written to stimulate, encourage and motivate readers to make happy memories that they can do on an average income and to entertain, educate and inform readers of outdoor opportunities.

Aggressive Whitetail Hunting, by Greg Miller, Krause Publications, Iola, WI, 1995. 208 pp., illus. Paper covers. $14.95

Learn how to hunt trophy bucks in public forests, private farmlands and exclusive hunting grounds from one of America's foremost hunters.

Alaska Safari, by Harold Schetzle & Sam Fadala, Anchorage, AK, Great Northwest Publishing, 2002. Revised 2nd edition. 366 pp., illus. with b&w photos. Softcover. $29.95

The author has brought a wealth of information to the hunter and anyone interested in Alaska. Harold Schetzle is a great guide and has also written another book of stories of Alaska hunting taken from many, many years of hunting and guiding. The most comprehensive guide to Alaska hunting.

Alaskan Adventures-Volume I-The Early Years, by Russell Annabel, Long Beach, CA, Safari Press,2005, 2nd printing. 453pp. illus. Hardcover. New in new dust jacket. $35.00

No other writer has ever been able to capture the spirit of adventure and hunting in Alaska like Russell Annabel.

Alaskan Yukon Trophies Won and Lost, by G.O. Young, Wolfe Publishing, Prescott, AZ, 2002. Softcover. $35.00

.A classic big game hunting tale with 273 pages b&w photographs and a five-page epilogue by the publisher.

American Duck Shooting, by George Bird Grinnell, Stackpole Books, Harrisburg, PA, 1991. 640 pp., illus. Paper covers. $19.95

First published in 1901 at the height of the author's career. Describes 50 species of waterfowl, and discusses hunting methods common at the turn of the century.

Bear Hunting in Alaska: How to Hunt Brown and Grizzly Bears, by Tony Russ, Northern Publishing, 2004. 116 b&w photos, illus. 256 pgs. Soft cover. Excellent. $22.95

Teaches every skill you will need to prepare for, scout, find, select, stalk, shoot and care for one of the most sought-after trophies on earth – the Alaskan brown bear and the Alaskan Grizzly.

Bears of Alaska, by Erwin Bauer, Sasquatch Books, 2002. Soft cover. Excellent . $15.95

Best of Babcock, The, by Havilah Babcock, Introduction by Hugh Grey, The Gunnerman Press, Auburn Hills, MI, 1985. 262 pp., illus. $19.95

A treasury of memorable pieces, 21 of which have never before appeared in book form.

Blacktail Trophy Tactics, by Boyd Iverson, Stoneydale Press, Stevensville, MI, 1992. 166 pp., illus. Paper covers. $14.95

A comprehensive analysis of blacktail deer habits, describing a deer's and man's use of scents, still hunting, tree techniques, etc.

Bowhunter's Handbook, Expert Strategies and Techniques, by M.R. James with Fred Asbell, Dave Holt, Dwight Schuh and Dave Samuel, DBI Books, a division of Krause Publications, Iola, WI, 1997. 256 pp., illus. Paper covers. $19.95

Tips from the top on taking your bowhunting skills to the next level.

Buffalo Harvest, The, by Frank Mayer as told to Charles Roth, Pioneer Press, Union City, TN, 1995. 96 pp., illus. Paper covers. $12.50

The story of a hide hunter during his buffalo hunting days on the plains.

Call of the Quail: A Tribute to the Gentleman Game Bird, by Michael McIntosh, et al., Countrysport Press, Traverse City, MI, 1990. 175 pp., illus. $35.00

A new anthology on quail hunting.

Calling All Elk, by Jim Zumbo, Cody, WY, 1989. 169 pp., illus. Paper covers. $14.95

The only book on the subject of elk hunting that covers every aspect of elk vocalization.

Complete Book of Grouse Hunting, The, by Frank Woolner, The Lyons Press, New York, NY, 2000. 192 pp., illus. Paper covers. $24.95

The history, habits, and habitat of one of America's great game birds–and the methods used to hunt it.

Complete Book of Mule Deer Hunting, The, by Walt Prothero, The Lyons Press, New York, NY, 2000. 192 pp., illus. Paper covers. $24.95

Field-tested practical advice on how to bag the trophy buck of a lifetime.

Complete Book of Wild Turkey Hunting, The, by John Trout Jr., The Lyons Press, New York, NY, 2000. 192 pp., illus. Paper covers. $24.95

An illustrated guide to hunting for one of America's most popular game birds.

Complete Book of Woodcock Hunting, The, by Frank Woolner, The Lyons Press, New York, NY, 2000. 192 pp., illus. Paper covers. $24.95

A thorough, practical guide to the American woodcock and to woodcock hunting.

Complete Guide To Hunting Wild Boar in California, The, by Gary Kramer, Safari Press, 2002. 1st edition. 127 pp., 37 photos. Softcover. $15.95

Gary Kramer takes the hunter all over California, from north to south and east to west. He discusses natural history, calibers, bullets, rifles, pistols, shotguns, black powder, and bow and arrows—even recipes.

Complete Venison Cookbook from Field to Table, The, by Jim & Ann Casada, Krause Publications, Iola, WI, 1996. 208 pp., Comb-bound. $12.95

More than 200 kitchen-tested recipes make this book the answer to a table full of hungry hunters or guests.

Cougar Attacks: Encounters of the Worst Kind, by Kathy Etling, NY, Lyons Press, 2004. 1st edition. 256 pages, illustrated with b&w photos. Soft cover. $14.95

Blood-curdling encounters between the big cats of North America and their most reluctant prey, humans.

Coyote Hunting, by Phil Simonski, Stoneydale Press, Stevensville, MT, 1994. 126 pp., illus. Paper covers. $12.95

Probably the most thorough "how-to-do-it" book on coyote hunting ever written.

Dabblers & Divers: A Duck Hunter's Book, compiled by the editors of *Ducks Unlimited* magazine, Willow Creek Press, Minocqua, WI, 1997. 160 pp., illus. $39.95

A word-and-photographic portrayal of waterfowl hunter's singular intimacy with, and passion for, watery haunts and wildfowl.

Deer & Deer Hunting, by Al Hofacker, Krause Publications, Iola, WI, 1993. 208 pp., illus. $34.95

Coffee-table volume packed full of how-to-information that will guide hunts for years to come.

Dreaming the Lion, by Thomas McIntyre, Countrysport Press, Traverse City, MI, 1994. 309 pp., illus. $35.00

Reflections on hunting, fishing and a search for the wild. Twenty-three stories by *Sports Afield* editor, Tom McIntyre.

Eastern Cougar: Historic Accounts, Scientific Investigations, and New Evidence, by Chris Bolgiano, Mechanicsburg,PA, Stackpole Books, 2005. Soft cover. $19.95

This fascinating anthology probes America's troubled history with large predators and makes a vital contribution to the wildlife management debates of today.

Elk and Elk Hunting, by Hart Wixom, Stackpole Books, Harrisburg, PA, 1986. 288 pp., illus. $34.95

Your practical guide to fundamentals and fine points of elk hunting.

Elk Hunting Guide: Skills, Gear, and Insight, by Tom Airhart, Stackpole Books,2005. A thorough, informative guide to the growing sport of elk hunting with in-depth coverage of current equipment and gear, techniques for tracking elk and staying safe in the wilderness and advice on choosing guides and outfitters. 432pp, 71 b&w photos, 38 illus. $19.95

Elk Hunting in the Northern Rockies, by Ed Wolff, Stoneydale Press, Stevensville, MT, 1984. 162 pp., illus. $18.95

Helpful information about hunting the premier elk country of the northern Rocky Mountain states–Wyoming, Montana and Idaho.

Elk Hunting with the Experts, by Bob Robb, Stoneydale Press, Stevensville, MT, 1992. 176 pp., illus. Paper covers. $15.95

A complete guide to elk hunting in North America by America's top elk hunting expert.

Encyclopedia of Buffalo Hunters and Skinners Volume 1 A-D, by Gilbert Reminger, Pioneer Press, 2003. The first volume in the series. 286 pages, acknowledgements, introduction, preface, illustrated, maps, plates, portraits, appendices, bibliography, index. Hardcover. $35.00

Encyclopedia of Buffalo Hunters and Skinners Volume 2 E-K, by Gilbert Reminger, Pioneer Press, 2006. The 2nd volume in the series. 285 pages, 115 photos, 15 drawings/newspaper items, and 6 maps. Index, Bibliography. Hardcover. $35.00

Vol. II covers hunters and skinners, that have so far surfaced, with surnames that begin with E-K, beginning with skinner William Earl and runs through the Kuykendall brothers, Judge and John, who hunted late (1886-1888) in southeastern New Mexico.

Fair Chase in North America, by Craig Boddington, Long Beach, CA, Safari Press, 2004. 1st edition. Hardcover. New in new dust jacket. $39.95

Getting a Stand, by Miles Gilbert, Pioneer Press, Union City, TN, 1993. 204 pp., illus. Paper covers. $13.95

An anthology of 18 short personal experiences by buffalo hunters of the late 1800s, specifically from 1870-1882.

Greatest Elk; The Complete Historical and Illustrated Record of North America's Biggest Elk, by R. Selner, Safari Press, Huntington Beach, CA, 2000. 209 pp., profuse color illus. $39.95

Here is the book all elk hunters have been waiting for! This oversized book holds the stories and statistics of the biggest bulls ever killed in North America. Stunning, full-color photographs highlight over 40 world-class heads, including the old world records!

Grouse and Woodcock, A Gunner's Guide, by Don Johnson, Krause Publications, Iola, WI, 1995. 256 pp., illus. Paper covers. $14.95

Find out what you need in guns, ammo, equipment, dogs and terrain.

Gunning for Sea Ducks, by George Howard Gillelan, Tidewater Publishers, Centreville, MD, 1988. 144 pp., illus. $14.95

A book that introduces you to a practically untouched arena of waterfowling.

Head Fer the Hills-Volume VI (1934-1960), by Russell Annabel, Long Beach, CA, Safari Press, 2005, Deluxe, Limited, Signed edition. 312pp., photos, drawings. Hardcover in a Slipcase. $60.00

As Tex Cobb, Russell Annabel's famous mentor and eternal companion, was famous for saying, "Head fer the hills," which is exactly what Rusty did.

Heck with Moose Hunting, The, by Jim Zumbo, Wapiti Valley Publishing Co., Cody, WY, 1996. 199 pp., illus. $17.95

Jim's hunts around the continent including encounters with moose, caribou, sheep, antelope and mountain goats.

High Pressure Elk Hunting, by Mike Lapinski, Stoneydale Press Publishing Co., Stevensville, MT, 1996. 192 pp., illus. $19.95

The secrets of hunting educated elk revealed.

Horns in the High Country, by Andy Russell, Alfred A. Knopf, NY, 1973. 259 pp., illus. Paper covers. $12.95

A many-sided view of wild sheep and their natural world.

How to Hunt, by Dave Bowring, Winchester Press, Piscataway, NJ, 1982. 208 pp., illus. Hardcover $15.00

A basic guide to hunting big game, small game, upland birds, and waterfowl.

Hunt High for Rocky Mountain Goats, Bighorn Sheep, Chamois & Tahr, by Duncan Gilchrist, Stoneydale Press, Stevensville, MT, 1992. 192 pp., illus. Paper covers. $19.95

The source book for hunting mountain goats.

Hunter's Alaska, The, by Roy F. Chandler, Iron Brigade, 2005. Hardcover. $49.95

This is a book written by Roy F. Chandler (Rocky). Rocky's Alaskan travels span half a century. Hunters hoping to hunt the "Great Land" will read exactly how it is done and what they can hope for if they ever make it into the Alaskan wilderness. This is a new publication of 2500 signed and numbered copies. Previous books, written by Rocky, about hunting Alaska have become collectors items. This book has some information from the prior books and much more "added" information.

Hunting Adventure of Me and Joe, by Walt Prothero, Safari Press, Huntington Beach, CA, 1995. 220 pp., illus. $22.50

A collection of the author's best and favorite stories.

Hunting America's Wild Turkey, by Toby Bridges, Stoeger Publishing Company, Pocomoke, MD, 2001. 256 pp., illus. $16.95

The techniques and tactics of hunting North America's largest, and most popular, woodland game bird.

Hunting Hard in Alaska, by Marc Taylor, Anchorage, AK, Biblio Distribution, 2003 Softcover. $19.95

Hunting In Alaska: A Comprehensive Guide, by Christopher Batin, Alaska Angler Pubs., 2002. 430 pages. Soft cover. $29.95

Hunting the Land of the Midnight Sun, by Alaska Professional Hunters Assoc., Safari Press, 2005. Hardcover. New in new dust jacket. $29.95
Contains contributions by Rob Holt, Gary King, Gary LaRose, Garth Larsen, Jim Shockey, Jeff Davis, and many others.

Hunting Mature Bucks, by Larry L. Weishuhn, Krause Publications, Iola, WI, 1995. 256 pp., illus. Paper covers. $18.95
One of North America's top white-tailed deer authorities shares his expertise on hunting those big, smart and elusive bucks.

Hunting Open-Country Mule Deer, by Dwight Schuh, Sage Press, Nampa, ID, 1989. 180 pp., illus. $18.95
A guide taking Western bucks with rifle and bow.

Hunting the Rockies, Home of the Giants, by Kirk Darner, Marceline, MO, 1996. 291 pp., illus. $25.00
Understand how and where to hunt Western game in the Rockies.

Hunting Western Deer, by Jim and Wes Brown, Stoneydale Press, Stevensville, MT, 1994. 174 pp., illus. Paper covers. $14.95
A pair of expert Oregon hunters provide insight into hunting mule deer and blacktail deer in the western states.

Hunting Wild Turkeys in the West, by John Higley, Stoneydale Press, Stevensville, MT, 1992. 154 pp., illus. Paper covers. $12.95
Covers the basics of calling, locating and hunting turkeys in the western states.

Hunting with the Twenty-Two, by Charles Singer Landis, R&R Books, Livonia, NY, 1994. 429 pp., illus. $35.00
A miscellany of articles touching on the hunting and shooting of small game.

In Search of the Buffalo, by Charles G. Anderson, Pioneer Press, Union City, TN, 1996. 144 pp., illus. Paper covers. $13.95
The primary study of the life of J. Wright Mooar, one of the few hunters fortunate enough to kill a white buffalo.

In the Turkey Woods, by Jerome B. Robinson, The Lyons Press, N.Y., 1998. 207 pp., illus. $24.95
Practical expert advice on all aspects of turkey hunting–from calls to decoys to guns.

Kodiak Island and its Bears, by Harry Dodge, Anchorage, Great Northwest Publishing, 2004. 364 pages, carefully indexed, thoughtfully footnoted, and lavishly illustrated. $27.50
This is the most significant volume about Kodiak Island and its bears that has been published in at least 20 years. This book now stands to become a new classic for all time.

Lost Classics of Jack O'Connor, by Jim Casada, Live Oak Press, 2004. Exciting tales with a twist of humor. 33 photos, 40 illus. by Dan Burr; 376 pages, with illustrations and photos. Hardcover. New in new dust jacket. $35.00

Montana–Land of Giant Rams, Volume 2, by Duncan Gilchrist, Outdoor Expeditions and Books, Corvallis, MT, 1992. 208 pp., illus. $34.95
The reader will find stories of how many of the top-scoring trophies were taken.

Montana–Land of Giant Rams, Volume 3, by Duncan Gilchrist, Outdoor Expeditions and Books, Corvallis, MT, 1999. 224 pp., illus. Paper covers. $19.95
All new sheep information including over 70 photos. Learn about how Montana became the "Land of Giant Rams" and what the prospects of the future are.

More Tracks: 78 Years of Mountains, People & Happiness, by Howard Copenhaver, Stoneydale Press, Stevensville, MT, 1992. 150 pp., illus. $18.95
A collection of stories by one of the back country's best storytellers about the people who shared with Howard his great adventure in the high places and wild Montana country.

Mostly Huntin', by Bill Jordan, Everett Publishing Co., Bossier City, LA, 1987. 254 pp., illus. $21.95
Jordan's hunting adventures in North America, Africa, Australia, South America and Mexico.

Mule Deer: Hunting Today's Trophies, by Tom Carpenter and Jim Van Norman, Krause Publications, Iola, WI, 1998. 256 pp., illus. Paper covers. $19.95
A tribute to both the deer and the people who hunt them. Includes info on where to look for big deer, prime mule deer habitat and effective weapons for the hunt.

Muzzleloading for Deer and Turkey, by Dave Ehrig, Stackpole Books, 2005. 475 pages, 293 b&w photos. Hardcover. New in new dust jacket. $29.95

My Health is Better in November, by Havilah Babcock, University of S. Carolina Press, Columbia, SC, 1985. 284 pp., illus. $24.95
Adventures in the field set in the plantation country and backwater streams of SC.

North American Waterfowler, The, by Paul S. Bernsen, Superior Publ. Co., Seattle, WA, 1972. 206 pp. Paper covers. $9.95
The complete inside and outside story of duck and goose shooting. Big and colorful, illustrations by Les Kouba.

Old Man and the Boy, The, by Robert Ruark, Henry Holt & Co., New York, NY, 303 pp., illus. $24.95
A timeless classic, telling the story of a remarkable friendship between a young boy and his grandfather as they hunt and fish together.

Old Man's Boy Grows Older, The, by Robert Ruark, Henry Holt & Co., Inc., New York, NY, 1993. 300 pp., illus. $24.95
The heartwarming sequel to the best-selling *The Old Man and the Boy.*

One Man, One Rifle, One Land; Hunting all Species of Big Game in North America, by J.Y. Jones, Safari Press, Huntington Beach, CA, 2000. 400 pp., illus. $59.95
Journey with J.Y. Jones as he hunts each of the big-game animals of North America–from the polar bear of the high Arctic to the jaguar of the low-lands of Mexico–with just one rifle.

Outdoor Pastimes of an American Hunter, by Theodore Roosevelt, Stackpole Books, Mechanicsburg, PA, 1994. 480 pp., illus. Paper covers. $18.95
Stories of hunting big game in the West and notes about animals pursued and observed.

Outlaw Gunner, The, by Harry M. Walsh, Tidewater Publishers, Cambridge, MD, 1973. 178 pp., illus. $22.95
A colorful story of market gunning in both its legal and illegal phases.

Pheasant Days, by Chris Dorsey, Voyageur Press, Stillwater, MN, 1992. 233 pp., illus. $24.95
The definitive resource on ringnecks. Includes everything from basic hunting techniques to the life cycle of the bird.

Pheasant Hunter's Harvest, by Steve Grooms, Lyons & Burford Publishers, New York, NY, 1990. 180 pp. $22.95
A celebration of pheasant, pheasant dogs and pheasant hunting. Practical advice from a passionate hunter.

Pheasant Tales, by Gene Hill et al, Countrysport Press, Traverse City, MI, 1996. 202 pp., illus. $39.00
Charley Waterman, Michael McIntosh and Phil Bourjaily join the author to tell some of the stories that illustrate why the pheasant is America's favorite game bird.

Pheasants of the Mind, by Datus Proper, Wilderness Adventures Press, Bozeman, MT, 1994. 154 pp., illus. $25.00
No single title sums up the life of the solitary pheasant hunter like this masterful work.

Portraits of Elk Hunting, by Jim Zumbo, Safari Press, Huntington Beach, CA, 2001. 222 pp. illus. $39.95
Zumbo has captured in photos as well as in words the essence, charisma, and wonderful components of elk hunting: back-country wilderness camps, sweaty guides, happy hunters, favorite companions, elk woods, and, of course, the majestic elk. Join Zumbo in the uniqueness of the pursuit of the magnificent and noble elk.

Precision Bowhunting: A Year-Round approach to taking Mature Whitetails, by John and Chrs Eberhart, Stackpole Books, 2005. 214pp, b&w photos. Soft cover. $16.95
Packed with vital information and fresh insights, Precision Bow hunting belongs on the bookshelf of every serious bow hunter.

Proven Whitetail Tactics, by Greg Miller, Krause Publications, Iola, WI, 1997. 224 pp., illus. Paper covers. $19.95
Proven tactics for scouting, calling and still-hunting whitetail.

Quest for Dall Rams, by Duncan Gilchrist, Duncan Gilchrist Outdoor Expeditions and Books, Corvallis, MT, 1997. 224 pp., illus. Paper covers. $19.95
The most complete book of Dall sheep ever written. Covers information on Alaska and provinces with Dall sheep and explains hunting techniques, equipment, etc.

Quest for Giant Bighorns, by Duncan Gilchrist, Outdoor Expeditions and Books, Corvallis, MT, 1994. 224 pp., illus. Paper covers. $19.95
How some of the most successful sheep hunters hunt and how some of the best bighorns were taken.

Radical Elk Hunting Strategies, by Mike Lapinski, Stoneydale Press Publishing Co., Stevensville, MT, 1988. 161 pp., illus. $18.95
Secrets of calling elk in close.

Rattling, Calling & Decoying Whitetails, by Gary Clancy, edited by Patrick Durkin, Krause Publications, Iola, WI, 2000. 208 pp., illus. Paper covers. $19.95
How to consistently coax big bucks into range.

Records of North American Caribou and Moose, Craig Boddington et al, The Boone & Crockett Club, Missoula, MT, 1997. 250 pp., illus. $24.95
More than 1,800 caribou listings and more than 1,500 moose listings, organized by the state or Canadian province where they were taken.

Records of North American Elk and Mule Deer, 2nd Edition, edited by Jack and Susan Reneau, The Boone & Crockett Club, Missoula, MT, 1996. 360 pp., illus. Paper cover, $18.95; hardcover $24.95
Updated and expanded edition featuring more than 150 trophy, field and historical photos of the finest elk and mule deer trophies ever recorded.

Records of North American Sheep, Rocky Mountain Goats and Pronghorn, edited by Jack and Susan Reneau, The Boone & Crockett Club, Missoula, MT, 1996. 400 pp., illus. Paper cover, $18.95; hardcover, $24.95
The first B&C Club records book featuring all 3941 accepted wild sheep, Rocky Mountain goats and pronghorn trophies.

Reflections on Snipe, by Worth Mathewson, illustrated by Eldridge Hardie, Camden, ME, Country Sport Press, 2003. Hardcover. 144 pp. $25.00
Reflections on Snipe is a delightful compendium of information on snipe behavior and habitats; gunning history; stories from the field; and the pleasures of hunting with good companions, whether human or canine.

Ringneck; A Tribute to Pheasants and Pheasant Hunting, by Steve Grooms, Russ Sewell and Dave Nomsen, The Lyons Press, New York, NY, 2000. 120 pp., illus. $40.00
A glorious full-color coffee-table tribute to the pheasant and those who hunt them.

Rooster! A Tribute to Pheasant Hunting, by Dale C. Spartas, Riverbend Publishing, 2003. 1st edition. 150+ glorious photos of pheasants, hunting dogs and hunting trips with family and friends. 128 pp. Hardcover. $39.95
A very special, must-have book for the 2.3 million pheasant hunters across the country!

Rub-Line Secrets, by Greg Miller, edited by Patrick Durkin, Krause Publications, Iola, WI, 1999. 208 pp., illus. Paper covers. $19.95
Based on nearly 30 years' experience. Proven tactics for finding, analyzing and hunting big bucks' rub-lines.

Season, The, by Tom Kelly, Lyons & Burford, New York, NY, 1997. 160 pp., illus. $22.95
The delight and challenges of a turkey hunter's spring season.

Secret Strategies from North America's Top Whitetail Hunters, compiled by Nick Sisley, Krause Publications, Iola, WI, 1995. 256 pp., illus. Paper covers. $14.95
Bow and gun hunters share their success stories.

Sheep Hunting in Alaska–The Dall Sheep Hunter's Guide, by Tony Russ, Outdoor Expeditions and Books, Corvallis, MT, 1994. 160 pp., illus. Paper covers. $19.95
A how-to guide for the Dall sheep hunter.

Southern Deer & Deer Hunting, by Larry Weishuhn and Bill Bynum, Krause Publications, Iola, WI, 1995. 256 pp., illus. Paper covers. $14.95
Mount a trophy southern whitetail on your wall with this firsthand account of stalking big bucks below the Mason-Dixon line.

Spring Gobbler Fever, by Michael Hanback, Krause Publications, Iola, WI, 1996. 256 pp., illus. Paper covers. $15.95
Your complete guide to spring turkey hunting.

Stand Hunting for Whitetails, by Richard P. Smith, Krause Publications, Iola, WI, 1996. 256 pp., illus. Paper covers. $14.95
The author explains the tricks and strategies for successful stand hunting.

Successful Black Bear Hunting, by Bill Vaznis, Iola,WI, Krause Publications, 2004. 144 pages, illustrated with full color photographs and drawings. Pictorial Soft cover. $23.99

Sultan of Spring: A Hunter's Odyssey Through the World of the Wild Turkey, The, by Bob Saile, The Lyons Press, New York, NY, 1998. 176 pp., illus. $22.95
A literary salute to the magic and mysticism of spring turkey hunting.

Taking Big Bucks, by Ed Wolff, Stoneydale Press, Stevensville, MT, 1987. 169 pp., illus. $18.95
Solving the whitetail riddle.

Tales of Quails 'n Such, by Havilah Babcock, University of S. Carolina Press, Columbia, SC, 1985. 237 pp. $19.95
A group of hunting stories, told in informal style, on field experiences in the South in quest of small game.

They Left Their Tracks, by Howard Coperhaver, Stoneydale Press Publishing Co., Stevensville, MT, 1990. 190 pp., illus. $18.95
Recollections of 60 years as an outfitter in the Bob Marshall Wilderness.

To Heck with Moose Hunting, by Jim Zumbo, Wapiti Publishing Co., Cody, WY, 1996. 199 pp., illus. $17.95
Jim's hunts around the continent and even an African adventure.

Track Pack: Animal Tracks In Full Life Size, by Ed Gray, Mechanicsburg, PA, Stackpole Books, 2003. 1st edition. Spiral-bound, 34 pp. $7.95
An indispensable reference for hunters, trackers, and outdoor enthusiasts. This handy guide features the tracks of 38 common North American animals, from squirrels to grizzlies.

Trickiest Thing in Feathers, The, by Corey Ford, compiled and edited by Laurie Morrow, illustrated by Christopher Smith, Wilderness Adventures, Gallatin Gateway, MT, 1998. 208 pp., illus. $29.95
Here is a collection of Corey Ford's best wing-shooting stories, many of them previously unpublished.

Upland Equation: A Modern Bird-Hunter's Code, The, by Charles Fergus, Lyons & Burford Publishers, New York, NY, 1996. 86 pp. $18.00
A book that deserves space in every sportsman's library. Observations based on firsthand experience.

Upland Tales, edited by Worth Mathewson, Sand Lake Press, Amity, OR, 1996. 271 pp., illus. $29.95
A collection of articles on grouse, snipe and quail.

Waterfowler's World, by Bill Buckley, Ducks Unlimited, Inc., Memphis, TN, 1999. 192 pp., illustrated in color. $37.50
An unprecedented pictorial book on waterfowl and waterfowlers.

When the Duck Were Plenty, by Ed Muderlak, Safari Press, Inc., Huntington Beach, CA, 2000. 300 pp., illus. $29.95
The golden age of waterfowling and duck hunting from 1840 until 1920. An anthology.

Whitetail: Behavior Through the Seasons, by Charles J. Alsheimer, Krause Publications, Iola, WI, 1996. 208 pp., illus. $34.95
In-depth coverage of whitetail behavior presented through striking portraits of the whitetail in every season.

Whitetail: The Ultimate Challenge, by Charles J. Alsheimer, Krause Publications, Iola, WI, 1995. 228 pp., illus. Paper covers. $14.95
Learn deer hunting's most intriguing secrets–fooling deer using decoys, scents and calls–from America's premier authority.

Whitetails by the Moon, by Charles J. Alsheimer, edited by Patrick Durkin, Krause Publications, Iola, WI, 1999. 208 pp., illus. Paper covers. $19.95
Predict peak times to hunt whitetails. Learn what triggers the rut.

Wildfowler's Season, by Chris Dorsey, Lyons & Burford Publishers, New York, NY, 1998. 224 pp., illus. $37.95
Modern methods for a classic sport.

Wildfowling Tales, by William C. Hazelton, Wilderness Adventures Press, Belgrade, MT, 1999. 117 pp., illustrated with etchings by Brett Smith. In a slipcase. $50.00
Tales from the great ducking resorts of the continent.

Windward Crossings: A Treasury of Original Waterfowling Tales, by Chuck Petrie et al, Willow Creek Press, Minocqua, WI, 1999. 144 pp., 48 color art and etching reproductions. $35.00
An illustrated, modern anthology of previously unpublished waterfowl hunting (fiction and creative nonfiction) stories by America's finest outdoor journalists.

Wings of Thunder: New Grouse Hunting Revisited, by Steven Mulak, Countrysport Books, Selma, AL, 1998. 168 pp. illus. $30.00
The author examines every aspect of New England grouse hunting as it is today–the bird and its habits, the hunter and his dog, guns and loads, shooting and hunting techniques, practice on clay targets, clothing and equipment.

Woodchuck Hunter, The, by Paul C. Estey, R&R Books, Livonia, NY, 1994. 135 pp., illus. $25.00
This book contains information on woodchuck equipment, the rifle, telescopic sights and includes interesting stories.

AFRICA/ASIA/ELSEWHERE

A Bullet Well Placed; One Hunter's Adventures Around the World, by Johnny Chilton, Safari Press, 2004. 245 pages. Hardcover. New in new dust jacket. $34.95
Painting a picture of what it is actually like to be there and do it, this well-written book captures the excitement and emotions of each journey.

A Country Boy in Africa, by George Hoffman, Trophy Room Books, Agoura, CA, 1998. 267 pp., illustrated with over 100 photos. Limited, numbered edition signed by the author. $85.00
In addition to the author's long and successful hunting career, he is known for developing a most effective big game cartridge, the .416 Hoffman.

A Hunter's Africa, by Gordon Cundill, Trophy Room Books, Agoura, CA, 1998. 298 pp., over 125 photographic illustrations. Limited numbered edition signed by the author. $125.00
A good look by the author at the African safari experience-elephant, lion, spiral-horned antelope, firearms, people and events, as well as the clients that make it worthwhile.

A Hunter's Wanderings in Africa, by Frederick Courteney Selous, Alexanders Books, Alexander, NC, 2003. 504 pp., illus. $28.50
A reprinting of the 1920 London edition. A narrative of nine years spent amongst the game of the far interior of South Africa.

A Pioneering Hunter, by B Marsh, Safari Press, 2006. A limited edition of 1,000 copies. Signed and Numbered. 107. 247pp, color photos. Hardcover in a Slipcase. $65.00
Elephant cropping, buffalo tales, and colorful characters—this book has it all.

A Professional Hunter's Journey of Discovery, by Alec McCallum, Agoura, CA, Trophy Room Books, 2003. Limited edition of 1,000. Signed and numbered. 132 pp. Hardcover. New in new dust jacket. $125.00

A View From A Tall Hill: Robert Ruark in Africa, by Terry Wieland, Bristol, CT, Country Sport Press, 2004. Reprint. 432 pp., Hardcover New in new dust jacket $45.00

African Adventures and Misadventures: Escapades in East Africa with Mau Mau and Giant Forest Hogs, by William York, Long Beach, CA, Safari Press, 2003. A limited edition of 1,000 copies. Signed and numbered. 250 pp., color and b&w photos. Hardcover in a slipcase. $70.00
From his early days in Kenya when he and a companion trekked alone through the desert of the NFD and had to fend off marauding lions that ate his caravan ponies to encountering a Mau Mau terrorist who took potshots at his victims with a stolen elephant gun, the late Bill York gives an entertaining account of his life that will keep you turning the pages. As with York's previous book, the pages are loaded with interesting anecdotes, fascinating tales, and well-written prose that give insight into East Africa and its more famous characters.

African Game Trails, by Theodore Roosevelt, Peter Capstick, Series Editor, St. Martin's Press, New York, NY 1988. 583 pp., illus. $26.95
The famed safari of the noted sportsman, conservationist, and president.

African Hunter II, edited by Craig Boddington and Peter Flack, Foreword by Robin Hurt, Introduction by James Mellon, Long Beach, CA, Safari Press, 2004. 606 pp., profuse color and b&w photos. Hardcover. $135.00
James Mellon spent five years hunting in every African country open to hunting during the late 1960s and early 1970s, making him uniquely qualified to write a book of such scope and breadth. Because so much has changed in today's Africa, however, it was necessary to update the original. With over 500 full-color pages, hundreds of photographs, and updated tables on animals and where they are available, this is THE book to consult for the information on Africa today.

African Rifles & Cartridges, by John Taylor, The Gun Room Press, Highland Park, NJ, 1977. 431 pp., illus. $35.00
Experiences and opinions of a professional ivory hunter in Africa describing his knowledge of numerous arms and cartridges for big game. A reprint.

African Twilight, by Robert F. Jones, Wilderness Adventure Press, Bozeman, MT, 1994. 208 pp., illus. $36.00
Details the hunt, danger and changing face of Africa over a span of three decades.

Atkin, Grant & Lang: A Detailed History of Enduring Gunmakers (trade edition), by Don Masters, Safari Press, 2005. 316pp., color and b&w photos. Hardcover. New in new dust jacket. $69.89
The history of three makers and their several relatives making guns under their own names. In the pages of this book you can learn all the details of the gun makers: dates, premises, main employees, rises and declines in sales fortunes, as well as the many interesting historical anecdotes and insights we have come to expect from Don Masters.

Baron in Africa; The Remarkable Adventures of Werner von Alvensleben, by Brian Marsh, Foreword by Ian Player, Safari Press, Huntington Beach, CA, 2001. 288 pp., illus. $35.00
Follow his career as he hunts lion, goes after large kudu, kills a full-grown buffalo with a spear, and hunts for elephant and ivory in some of the densest brush in Africa. The adventure and the experience were what counted to this fascinating character, not the money or fame; indeed, in the end he left Mozambique with barely more than the clothes on his back. This is a must-read adventure story of one of the most interesting characters to have come out of Africa after WWII.

Buffalo!, by Craig Boddington, Safari Books, 2006. 256pp, color photos, Hardcover. $39.95
Craig tells his readers where to hunt, how and when to hunt, and what will happen when they do hunt. He describes what it means to rush the herd, one of his favorite methods of hunting these worthy opponents. He tells of the great bull in Masailand that he almost got, of the perfect hunt he had in Zambia, and of the charge he experienced in Tanzania.

Buffalo, Elephant, & Bongo (trade edition): **Alone in the Savannas and Rain Forests of the Cameroon,** by Reinald Von Meurers, Long Beach, CA, Safari Press, 2004. Hardcover. New in new dust jacket. $39.50

Cottar: The Exception was the Rule, by Pat Cottar, Trophy Room Books, Agoura, CA, 1999. 350 pp., illus. Limited, numbered and signed edition. $135.00
The remarkable big game hunting stories of one of Kenya's most remarkable pioneers.

Dangerous Game, True Stories of Dangerous Hunting on Three Continents, The, Safari Press, 2006. A limited edition of 500 copies. Signed and Numbered. 225pp, photos. Hardcover in a Slipcase. $70.00

Death and Double Rifles, by Mark Sullivan, Nitro Express Safaris, Phoenix, AZ, 2000. 295 pp., illus. $85.00
Sullivan has captured every thrilling detail of hunting dangerous game in this lavishly illustrated book. Full of color pictures of African hunts & rifles.

Death in a Lonely Land, by Peter Capstick, St. Martin's Press, New York, NY, 1990. 284 pp., illus. $22.95
Twenty-three stories of hunting as only the master can tell them.

Death in the Dark Continent, by Peter Capstick, St. Martin's Press, New York, NY, 1983. 238 pp., illus. $22.95
A book that brings to life the suspense, fear and exhilaration of stalking ferocious killers under primitive, savage conditions, with the ever present threat of death.

Death in the Long Grass, by Peter Hathaway Capstick, St. Martin's Press, New York, NY, 1977. 297 pp., illus. $22.95
A big game hunter's adventures in the African bush.

Death in the Silent Places, by Peter Capstick, St. Martin's Press, New York, NY, 1981. 243 pp., illus. $23.95
The author recalls the extraordinary careers of legendary hunters such as Corbett, Karamojo Bell, Stigand and others.

Elephant Hunters, Men of Legend, by Tony Sanchez-Arino, Safari Press, 2005. A limited edition of 1,000 copies. Signed and Numbered. 240 pages. Hardcover in a Slipcase. $100.00
This newest book from Tony Sanchez is the most interesting ever to emerge on that intrepid and now finished breed of man: Elephant Hunters, Men of Legend.

Encounters with Lions, by Jan Hemsing, Trophy Room Books, Agoura, CA, 1995. 302 pp., illus. $75.00
Some stories fierce, fatal, frightening and even humorous of when man and lion meet.

Fodor's African Safari, From Budget to Big Spending Where and How to Find the Best Big Game Adventure in Southern and Eastern Africa, by David Bristow, Julian Harrison, Chris Swiac, New York, Fodor's, 2004. 1st edition. 190 pp. Softcover. $9.95

Frederick Selous: A Hunting Legend-Recollections By and About the Great Hunter (trade edition), by F.C. Selous (edited by James Casada), Safari Press, 2005. 187pp., illus. Hardcover. $34.95
This second book on Selous, edited by Africana expert Dr. James Casada, completes the work on the lost writings by Selous begun in Africa's Greatest Hunter.

From Mt. Kenya to the Cape: Ten Years of African Hunting, by Craig Boddington, Long Beach, CA, Safari Press, 2005. Hardcover. New in new dust jacket. $39.95
This wealth of information makes not only great reading, but the appendixes also provide tips on rifles, cartridges, equipment, and how to plan a safari.

From Sailor to Professional Hunter: The Autobiography of John Northcote, Trophy Room Books, Agoura, CA, 1997. 400 pp., illus. Limited edition, signed and numbered. $125.00
Only a handful of men can boast of having a 50-year professional hunting career throughout Africa as John Northcote has had.

Gone are the Days; Jungle Hunting for Tiger and other Game in India and Nepal 1953-1969, by Peter Byrne, Safari Press, Inc., Huntington Beach, CA, 2001. 225 pp., illus. Limited signed, numbered, slipcased. $70.00

Great Hunters: Their Trophy Rooms and Collections, Volume 1, compiled and published by Safari Press, Inc., Huntington Beach, CA, 1997. 172 pp., illustrated in color. $60.00
A rare glimpse into the trophy rooms of top international hunters. A few of these trophy rooms are museums.

Great Hunters: Their Trophy Rooms & Collections, Volume 2, compiled and published by Safari Press, Inc., Huntington Beach, CA, 1998. 224 pp., illustrated with 260 full-color photographs. $60.00
Volume Two of the world's finest, best produced series of books on trophy rooms and game collections. 46 sportsmen sharing sights you'll never forget on this guided tour.

Great Hunters: Their Trophy Rooms & Collections, Volume 3, compiled and published by Safari Press, Inc., Huntington Beach, CA, 2000. 204 pp., illustrated with 260 full-color photographs. $60.00
At last, the long-awaited third volume in the best photographic series ever published of trophy room collections is finally available. As before, each trophy room is accompanied by an informative text explaining the collection and giving you insights into the hunters who went to such great efforts to create their trophy rooms. All professionally photographed in the highest quality possible.

Great Hunters: Their Trophy Rooms & Collections, Volume 4, compiled and published by Safari Press, Inc., Huntington Beach, CA, 2005. 204 pp., illustrated with 260 full-color photographs. $60.00
At last, the long-awaited fourth volume in the best photographic series ever published of trophy room collections is finally available. Each trophy room is accompanied by an informative text explaining the collection and giving you insights into the hunters who went to such great efforts to create their trophy rooms. All professionally photographed in the highest quality possible.

Heart of an African Hunter, by Peter Flack, Long Beach, CA, Safari Press, 2005. 266 pp. illustrated with b&w photos. Hardcover. $35.00

Hemingway in Africa: The Last Safari, by Christopher Ondaatje, Overlook Press, 2004. 1st edition. 240 pp. Hardcover. New in new dust jacket. $37.50

Horn of the Hunter, by Robert Ruark, Safari Press, Long Beach, CA, 1987. 315 pp., illus. $35.00
Ruark's most sought-after title on African hunting, here in reprint.

Hunter's Tracks, by J.A. Hunter, Safari Press Publications, Huntington Beach, CA, 1999. 240 pp., illus. $24.95
This is the exciting story of John Hunter's efforts to capture the shady head man of a gang of ivory poachers and smugglers. The story is interwoven with the tale of one of East Africa's most grandiose safaris taken with an Indian maharaja.

Hunting in Ethiopia, An Anthology, by Tony Sanchez-Arino, Safari Press, Huntington Beach, CA, 1996. 350 pp., illus. Limited, signed and numbered edition. $135.00
The finest selection of hunting stories ever compiled on hunting in this great game country.

Hunting in Kenya, by Tony Sanchez-Arino, Safari Press, Inc., Huntington Beach, CA, 2000. 350 pp., illus. Limited, signed and numbered edition in a slipcase. $135.00
The finest selection of hunting stories ever compiled on hunting in this great game country make up this anthology.

Hunting in the Sudan, An Anthology, compiled by Tony Sanchez-Arino, Safari Press, Huntington Beach, CA, 1992. 350 pp., illus. Limited, signed and numbered edition in a slipcase. $125.00
The finest selection of hunting stories ever compiled on hunting in this great game country.

Hunting Instinct, The, by Phillip D. Rowter, Safari Press, Inc., Huntington Beach, CA, 2005, trade edition. Hardcover. New in new dust jacket. $29.95
Safari chronicles from the Republic of South Africa and Namibia 1990-1998.

Hunting the Dangerous Game of Africa, by John Kingsley-Heath, Sycamore Island Books, Boulder, CO, 1998. 477 pp., illus. $95.00
Written by one of the most respected, successful, and ethical P.H.'s to trek the sunlit plains of Botswana, Kenya, Uganda, Tanganyika, Somaliland, Eritrea, Ethiopia, and Mozambique. Filled with some of the most gripping and terrifying tales ever to come out of Africa.

Hunting, Settling and Remembering, by Philip H. Percival, Trophy Room Books, Agoura, CA, 1997. 230 pp., illus. Limited, numbered and signed edition. $85.00
If Philip Percival is to come alive again, it will be through this, the first edition of his easy, intricate and magical book illustrated with some of the best historical big game hunting photos ever taken.

Hunting Trips in The Land of the Dragon; Anglo and American Sportsmen in Old China, 1870-1940, by Kenneth Czech, Safari Press, 2005. Hardcover. New in new dust jacket. $34.95
The first part of this anthology takes the reader after duck, pheasant, and other upland game while the second part focuses on the large game of China and the border regions. The latter includes hunts for Manchurian tiger, tufted deer, goral, wild goat, wild yak,

antelope, takin, wild sheep in the Mongolian Altai, wapiti, blue sheep, ibex, Ovis poli of the Pamir, wild sheep of the Tian Shan, brown bear, and panda--all written by such famous names as Major General Kinloch, St. George Littledale, Kermit Roosevelt, and Roy Chapman Andrews.

In the Salt, by Lou Hallamore, Trophy Room Books, Agoura, CA, 1999. 227 pp., illustrated in b&w and full color. Limited, numbered and signed edition. $125.00
A book about people, animals and the big game hunt, about being outwitted and outmaneuvered. It is about knowing that sooner or later your luck will change and your trophy will be "in the salt."

International Hunter 1945-1999, Hunting's Greatest Era, by Bert Klineburger, Sportsmen on Film, Kerrville, TX, 1999. 400 pp., illus. A limited, numbered and signed edition. $125.00
The most important book of the greatest hunting era by the world's preeminent international hunter.

Jim Corbett Collection, by Jim Corbett, Safari press, 2005. 1124 pages, illus, 5 volumes. Hardcover in a Slipcase. $100.00
The complete set of Jim Corbett's works, housed in a printed slipcase and feature the work of the internationally famous wildlife artist Guy Coheleach.

King of the Wa-Kikuyu, by John Boyes, St. Martin Press, New York, NY, 1993. 240 pp., illus. $19.95
In the 19th and 20th centuries, Africa drew to it a large number of great hunters, explorers, adventurers and rogues. Many have become legendary, but John Boyes (1874-1951) was the most legendary of them all.

Kwaheri! On the Spoor of Big Game in East Africa, by Robert von Reitnauer, Long beach, CA, Safari Press, 2005. A limited edition of 1,000 copies. Signed and Numbered. 285 pages, illustrated with photos. Hardcover in a Slipcase. $75.00
This is the story of an immense land in the days before the truly big tuskers all but disappeared. A very good read.

Last Horizons: Hunting, Fishing and Shooting on Five Continents, by Peter Capstick, St. Martin's Press, New York, NY, 1989. 288 pp., illus. $19.95
The first in a two-volume collection of hunting, fishing and shooting tales from the selected pages of *The American Hunter*, *Guns & Ammo* and *Outdoor Life*.

Last of the Ivory Hunters, by John Taylor, Safari Press, Long Beach, CA, 1990. 354 pp., illus. $29.95
Reprint of the classic book "Pondoro" by one of the most famous elephant hunters of all time.

Legends of the Field: More Early Hunters in Africa, by W.R. Foran, Trophy Room Press, Agoura, CA, 1997. 319 pp., illus. Limited edition. $100.00
This book contains the biographies of some very famous hunters: William Cotton Oswell, F.C. Selous, Sir Samuel Baker, Arthur Neumann, Jim Sutherland, W.D.M. Bell and others.

Lives of A Professional Hunting Family, by Gerard Agoura Miller, Trophy Room Books, 2003. A limited edition of 1,000 copies. Signed and numbered. 303 pp., 230 b&w photographic illustrations. Hardcover. $135.00

Lost Classics, by Robert Ruark, Safari Press, Huntington Beach, CA, 1996. 260 pp., illus. $35.00
The magazine stories that Ruark wrote in the 1950s and 1960s finally in print in book form.

Lost Wilderness; True Accounts of Hunters and Animals in East Africa, by Mohamed Ismail and Alice Pianfetti, Safari Press, Inc., Huntington Beach, CA, 2000. 216 pp., photos, illus. Limited edition signed, numbered and slipcased. $60.00

Mahonhboh, by Ron Thomson, Hartbeesport, South Africa, 1997. 312 pp., illus. Limited signed and numbered edition. $50.00
Elephants and elephant hunting in South Central Africa.

Man-Eaters of Tsavo, The, by Lt. Colonel J.H. Patterson, Peter Capstick, series editor, St. Martin's Press, New York, NY, 1986, 5th printing. 346 pp., illus. $22.95

Maneaters and Marauders, by John "Pondoro" Taylor, Long Beach, CA, Safari Press, 2005. 1st edition, Safari edition. Hardcover. New in new dust jacket. $29.95

McElroy Hunts Asia, by C.J. McElroy, Safari Press, Inc., Huntington Beach, CA, 1989. 272 pp., illus. $50.00
From the founder of SCI comes a book on hunting the great continent of Asia for big game: tiger, bear, sheep and ibex. Includes the story of the all-time record Altai Argali as well as several markhor hunts in Pakistan.

Memoirs of A Sheep Hunter, by Rashid Jamsheed, Safari Press, Inc., Huntington Beach, CA, 1996. 330 pp., illus. $70.00
The author reveals his exciting accounts of obtaining world-record heads from his native Iran, and his eventual move to the U.S. where he procured a grand-slam of North American sheep.

Memoirs of An African Hunter (Trade Edition), by Terry Irwin, Safari Press, 2005. 411pp, 95 color and 20 b&w photos, large format. Hardcover $70.00

Memories of Africa; Hunting in Zambia and Sudan, by W. Brach, Safari Press, 2005. 2005. A limited edition of 1,000 copies. Signed and Numbered. Written with an interesting flair and a true graphic perspective of the animals, people, and the hunt, this is a realistic portrayal, not Hollywood-style swaggering and gun-slinging, of hunting the magnificent wildlife of Zambia and Sudan over the last three decades. 285 pages, illustrated with photos. Hardcover in a Slipcase. $85.00

Mundjamba: The Life Story of an African Hunter, by Hugo Seia, Trophy Room Books, Agoura, CA, 1996. 400 pp., illus. Limited, numbered and signed by the author. $125.00
An autobiography of one of the most respected and appreciated professional African hunters.

My Africa: A Professional Hunter's Journey of Discovery, by Alec McCallum, Trouphy Room Books, 2003. Limited Edition: 1000. Signed and numbered. hunting. 232pp. Hardcover. New in new dust jacket. $125.00

My Wanderings Though Africa: The Life and Times of a Professional Hunter, by Mike and James Cameron, Safari Press, 2004. Deluxe, Limited, Signed edition. 208pp, b&w photos. Hardcover in a Slipcase. $75.00
This is a book for readers whose imagination carries them into a world where reality means starry skies, the call of a jackal and the moan of a lion, the smell of gun oil, and smoke from a cooking fire rising into the African night.

On Target, by Christian Le Noel, Trophy Room Books, Agoura, CA, 1999. 275 pp., illus. Limited, numbered and signed edition. $85.00

History and hunting in Central Africa.

One Long Safari, by Peter Hay, Trophy Room Books, Agoura, CA, 1998. 350 pp., with over 200 photographic illustrations and 7 maps. Limited numbered edition signed by the author. $100.00

Contains hunts for leopards, sitatunga, hippo, rhino, snakes and, of course, the general African big game bag.

Optics for the Hunter, by John Barsness, Safari Press, Inc., Huntington Beach, CA, 1999. 236 pp., illus. $24.95

An evaluation of binoculars, scopes, range finders, spotting scopes for use in the field.

Out in the Midday Shade, by William York, Safari Press, Inc., Huntington Beach, CA, 2005. Trade Edition. Hardcover. New in new dust jacket. $35.00

Path of a Hunter, The, by Gilles Tre-Hardy, Trophy Room Books, Agoura, CA, 1997. 318 pp., illus. Limited Edition, signed and numbered. $85.00

A most unusual hunting autobiography with much about elephant hunting in Africa.

Perfect Shot: Mini Edition for Africa, The, by Kevin Robertson, Long Beach, CA, Safari Press, 2004. 2nd printing Softcover. $17.95

Perfect Shot: Shot Placement for African Big Game, The, by Kevin "Doctari" Robertson, Safari Press, Inc., Huntington Beach, CA, 1999. 230 pp., illus. $65.00

The most comprehensive work ever undertaken to show the anatomical features for all classes of African game. Includes caliber and bullet selection, rifle selection and trophy handling.

Peter Capstick's Africa: A Return to the Long Grass, by Peter Hathaway Capstick, St. Martin's Press, N. Y., NY, 1987. 213 pp., illus. $35.00

A first-person adventure in which the author returns to the long grass for his own dangerous and very personal excursion.

Pondoro, by John Taylor, Safari Press, Inc., Huntington Beach, CA, 1999. 354 pp., illus. $39.95

The author is considered one of the best storytellers in the hunting book world, and Pondoro is highly entertaining. A classic African big-game hunting title.

Quotable Hunter, The, by Jay Cassell and Peter Fiduccia, The Lyons Press, N.Y., 1999. 288 pp., illus. $20.00

This collection of more than three hundred quotes from hunters through the ages captures the essence of the sport, with all its joys, idosyncrasies, and challenges.

Return to Toonaklut–The Russell Annabel Story, by Jeff Davis, Long Beach, CA, Safari Press, 2002. 248 pp., photos, illus. $34.95

Those of us who grew up after WW II cannot imagine the Alaskan frontier that Rusty Annabel walked into early in the twentieth century. The hardships, the resourcefulness, the natural beauty, not knowing what lay beyond the next horizon, all were a part of his existence. This is the story of the man behind the legend, and it is as fascinating as any of the tales Rusty Annabel ever spun for the sporting magazines.

Rifles and Cartridges for Large Game–From Deer to Bear–Advice on the Choice of A Rifle, by Layne Simpson, Long Beach, CA, Safari Press, 2002. Illustrated with 100 color photos, oversize book. 225 pp., color illus. $39.95

Layne Simpson, who has been field editor for *Shooting Times* magazine for 20 years, draws from his hunting experiences on five continents to tell you what rifles, cartridges, bullets, loads, and scopes are best for various applications, and he explains why in plain English. Developer of the popular 7mm STW cartridge, Simpson has taken big game with rifle cartridges ranging in power from the .220 Swift to the .460 Weatherby Magnum, and he pulls no punches when describing their effectiveness in the field.

Rifles for Africa; Practical Advice on Rifles and Ammunition for an African Safari, by Gregor Woods, Long Beach, CA, Safari Press, 2002. 1st edition. 430 pp., illus., photos. $39.95

Invaluable to the person who seeks advice and information on what rifles, calibers, and bullets work on African big game, be they the largest land mammals on earth or an antelope barely weighing in at 20 lbs.!

Robert Ruark's Africa, by Robert Ruark, edited by Michael McIntosh, Countrysport Press, Selma, AL, 1999. 256 pp. illustrated with 19 original etchings by Bruce Langton. $32.00

These previously uncollected works of Robert Ruark make this a classic big-game hunting book.

Safari: The Last Adventure, by Peter Capstick, St. Martin's Press, New York, NY, 1984. 291 pp., illus. $22.95

A modern comprehensive guide to the African Safari.

Safari Rifles: Double, Magazine Rifles and Cartridges for African Hunting, by Craig Boddington, Safari Press, Huntington Beach, CA, 1990. 416 pp., illus. $37.50

A wealth of knowledge on the safari rifle. Historical and present double-rifle makers, ballistics for the large bores, and much, much more.

Sands of Silence, by Peter H. Capstick, Saint Martin's Press, New York, NY, 1991. 224 pp., illus. $35.00

Join the author on safari in Nambia for his latest big-game hunting adventures.

Song of the Summits–Hunting Sheep, Ibex, and Markhor in Asia, Europe, and North America, by Jesus Yurén, Long Beach, CA, Safari Press, 2003. Limited edition. Hardcover in a slipcase. $75.00

Sunset Tales of Safariland, by Stan Bleazard, Trophy Room Books, 2006. Deluxe, Limited, Signed edition. Large 8½" x11" format, bound in sumptuous forest green gilt stamped suede binding. 274 pages. 113 b&w photographic illustrations and index. $125.00

Sunset Tales of Safariland will be of considerable interest to anyone interested in big game hunting.

Tales of the African Frontier, by J.A. Hunter, Safari Press Publications, Huntington Beach, CA, 1999. 308 pp., illus. $24.95

The early days of East Africa is the subject of this powerful John Hunter book.

Tanzania Safari: Hei Safari, by Robert DePole, Trophy Room Books, 2004. Sumptuous Burgundy gilt stamped faux suede binding, 343 pages plus 12 page index of people and places. 32 pages of black & white photographic illustrations. The reader will "see" the animals on the pages long enough to remember them forever. Hardcover. $125.00

To Heck With It–I'm Going Hunting–My First Eighteen Years as an International Big-Game Hunter–Limited Edition, by Arnold Alward with Bill Quimby, Long Beach, CA, Safari Press, 2003. Deluxe, 1st edition, limited to 1,000 signed copies. $80.00

Uganda Safaris, by Brian Herne, Winchester Press, Piscataway, NJ, 1979. 236 pp., illus. $24.95

The chronicle of a professional hunter's adventures in Africa.

Under the African Sun, by Dr. Frank Hibben, Safari Press, Inc., Huntington Beach, CA, 1999. Limited edition signed, numbered and in a slipcase. $85.00

Forty-eight years of hunting the African continent.

Under the African Sun, by Dr. Frank Hibben, Safari Press, Inc., Huntington Beach, CA, 2005. Trade edition. 305 pages illustrated with b&w and color photos. Hardcover. New in new dust jacket. $39.95

Under the Shadow of Man Eaters, by Jerry Jaleel, The Jim Corbett Foundation, Edmonton, Alberta, Canada, 1997. 152 pp., illus. A limited, numbered and signed edition. Paper covers. $35.00

The life and legend of Jim Corbett of Kumaon.

Use Enough Gun, by Robert Ruark, Safari Press, Huntington Beach, CA, 1997. 333 pp., illus. $35.00

Robert Ruark on big game hunting.

Warrior: The Legend of Col. Richard Meinertzhagen, by Peter H. Capstick, St. Martins Press, New York, NY, 1998. 320 pp., illus. $23.95

A stirring and vivid biography of the famous British colonial officer Richard Meinertzhagen, whose exploits earned him fame and notoriety as one of the most daring and ruthless men to serve during the glory days of the British Empire.

Waterfowler's World, The, by Bill Buckley, Willow Creek Press, Minocqua, WI, 1999. 176 pp., 225 color photographs. $37.50

Waterfowl hunting from Canadian prairies, across the U.S. heartland, to the wilds of Mexico, from the Atlantic to the Pacific coasts and the Gulf of Mexico.

Weatherby: Stories From the Premier Big-Game Hunters of the World, 1956-2002, The, edited by Nancy Vokins, Long Beach, CA, Safari Press, 2004. Deluxe, limited, signed edition. 434 pp., profuse color and b&w illus. Hardcover in a slipcase. $200.00

Wheel of Life–Bunny Allen, A Life of Safaris and Sex, The, by Bunny Allen, Long Beach, CA, Safari Press, 2004. 1st edition. 300 pp., illus, photos. Hardcover. $34.95

Wind, Dust & Snow-Great Rams of Asia, by Robert M. Anderson, Collectors Covey, 1997. Deluxe Limited edition of 500 copies. Signed and Numbered. 240pp profuse illus. More than 200 photos some on the greatest Asian rams ever taken by sportsmen. $150.00

A complete chronology of modern exploratory and pioneering Asian sheep-hunting expeditions from 1960 until 1996, with wonderful background history and previously untold stories.

With a Gun in Good Country, by Ian Manning, Trophy Room Books, Agoura, CA, 1996. Limited, numbered and signed by the author. $85.00

A book written about that splendid period before the poaching onslaught which almost closed Zambia and continues to the granting of her independence. It then goes on to recount Manning's experiences in Botswana, Congo, and briefly in South Africa.

Yoshi–The Life and Travels of an International Trophy Hunter, by W. Yoshimoto with Bill Quimby, Long Beach, CA, Safari Press, Inc., 2002. A limited edition of 1,000 copies, signed and numbered. 298 pp., color and b&w photos. Hardcover in a slipcase. $85.00

Watson T. Yoshimoto, a native Hawaiian, collected all 16 major varieties of the world's wild sheep and most of the many types of goats, ibex, bears, antelopes, and antlered game of Asia, Europe, North America, South America, and the South Pacific…as well as the African Big Five. Along the way he earned the respect of his peers and was awarded hunting's highest achievement, the coveted Weatherby Award.

Rifles

'03 Springfield Rifles Era, by Clark S. Campbell, Richmond, VA, privately printed, 2003. 1st edition. 368 pp., 146 illustrations, drawn to scale by author. Hardcover. $58.00

A much-expanded version of this author's famous The '03 Springfield (1957) and The '03 Springfields (1971), representing 40 years of research into all things '03. Part I is a complete and verifiably correct study of all standardized and special-purpose models of the U.S. M1903 Springfield rifle, in both .22 and .30 calibers, including those prototypes which led to standard models, and also all standardized .30 caliber cartridges, including National and International Match, and caliber .22. Part II is the result of the author's five years as a Research and Development Engineer with Remington Arms Co., and will be of inestimable value to anyone planning a custom sporter, whether or not based on the '03.

.303 SMLE Rifle No. 1 Assembly, Disassembly Manual, by Skennerton & Riling, Ray Riling Arms Books Co. Philadelphia, PA 2004. 36 pages, $5.00

With over 60 photos & line drawings. Ideal workshop reference for stripping & assembly with exploded parts drawings, specifications, service accessories, historical information and recommended reading references.

.303 British Rifle No. 4 Assembly, Disassembly Manual, by Skennerton & Riling, Ray Riling Arms Books Co. Philadelphia, PA 2004. 36 pages, $5.00

With over 60 photos & line drawings. Ideal workshop reference for stripping & assembly with exploded parts drawings, specifications, service accessories, historical information and recommended reading references.

.577 Snider-Enfield Rifles & Carbines; British Service Longarms, by Ian Skennerton. 1866-C.1880. Australia, Arms & Militaria Press, 2003. 1st edition. 240 pp. plus 8 color plates, 100 illustrations. Marking Ribbon. Hardcover. $39.50

The definitive study of Britain's first breech-loading rifle, at first converted from Enfield muskets, then newly made with Mk III breech. The trials, development, rifle and carbine models are detailed; new information along with descriptions of the cartridges.

1903 Springfield Assembly, Disassembly Manual .30 Model, by Skennerton & Riling, Ray Riling Arms Books Co. Philadelphia, PA 2004. 36 pages, $5.00

With over 60 photos & line drawings. Ideal workshop reference for stripping & assembly with exploded parts drawings, specifications, service accessories, historical information and recommended reading references.

1903 Springfield Rifle and Its Variations, by Joe Poyer, Tustin, CA, North Cape Publications, 2004. 466 pages, illustrated with hundreds of color and b& drawings and photos. Soft cover. $22.95

It covers the entire spectrum of the Model 1903 rifle from the rod bayonet to the M1903A4 sniper rifle.

A Master Gunmaker's Guide to Building Bolt-Action Rifles, by Bill Holmes, Boulder, CO, Paladin Press, 2003. Photos, illus., 152 pp. Softcover. $25.00

Many people today call themselves gunmakers, but very few have actually made a gun. Most buy parts wherever available and simply assemble them. During the past 50 years Bill Holmes has built from scratch countless rifles, shotguns and pistols of amazing artistry, ranging in caliber from .17 to .50.

A Potpourri of Single Shot Rifles and Actions, by Frank de Haas and Mark de Haas, Ridgeway, MO, 1993. 153 pp., illus. Paper covers. $22.50

The author's 6th book on non-bolt-action single shots. Covers more than 40 single-shot rifles in historical and technical detail.

Accurizing & Shooting Lee-Enfields, by Ian Skennerton, Australia, Arms & Militaria Press, 2005. 35pp, saddle-stitched laminated covers. ALL color photos and illustrations. Stiff paper covers. $15.00

This new full color heavily illustrated work by Ian Skennerton answers all those questions regarding the use of the Lee Enfield Rifles. Packed with detailed information covering the guns, the armourer's tools, and the sighting options for this fascinating series.

AK-47 and AK-74 Kalashnikov Rifles and Their Variations, by Joe Poyer, Tustin, CA, North Cape Publications, 2004. 1st edition. Softcover, 188 pages, illustrated. $22.95

This is the newest book in the "Shooter's and Collector's Guide" series. Prepared with the help of members of the Kalashnikov Collectors Association, this 188 page book surveys every variation of the 7.62 AK-47 and the 5.45 AK-74 developed in the old Soviet Union on a part-to-part basis to permit easy identification of original rifles and those made from kits available from various manufacturers in different countries.

AK-47 Assembly, Disassembly Manual 7.62 X 39mm, by Skennerton & Riling, Ray Riling Arms Books Co. Philadelphia, PA 2004. 36 pages, $5.00

With over 60 photos & line drawings. Ideal workshop reference for stripping & assembly with exploded parts drawings, specifications, service accessories, historical information and recommended reading references. Ideal workbook for shooters and collectors alike. Triple saddle-stitched binding with durable plastic laminated cover makes this an ideal workshop guide.

AK-47 Assault Rifle, Desert Publications, Cornville, AZ, 1981. 150 pp., illus. Paper covers. $15.95

Complete and practical technical information on the only weapon in history to be produced in an estimated 30,000,000 units.

American Hunting Rifles: Their Application in the Field for Practical Shooting, by Craig Boddington, Safari Press, Huntington Beach, CA, 1996. 446 pp., illus. Second printing trade edition. Softcover $24.95

Covers all the hunting rifles and calibers that are needed for North America's diverse game.

American Krag Rifle and Carbine, by Joe Poyer, North Cape Publications, Tustin, CA, 2002. 1st edition. 317 pp., illustrated with hundreds of b&w drawings and photos. Softcover. $19.95

Provides the arms collector, historian and target shooter with a part by part analysis of what has been called the rifle with the smoothest bolt action ever designed. All changes to all parts are analyzed in detail and matched to serial number ranges. A monthly serial number chart by production year has been devised that will provide the collector with the year and month in which his gun was manufactured. A new and complete exploded view was produced for this book.

American Percussion Schuetzen Rifle, by J. Hamilton and T. Rowe, Rochester, NY, Rowe Publications, 2005. 1st edition. 388 pp. Hardcover. New in new dust jacket. $98.00

An Illustrated Guide to the '03 Springfield Service Rifle, by Bruce Canfield, Lincoln, RI, Andrew Mowbray, 2005. 240 pages, illustrated with over 450 photos. Pictorial Hardcover. $49.95

Your ultimate guide to the military '03 Springfield! Covers all models, all manufacturers and all conflicts, including WWI, WWII and beyond. Heavily illustrated with professional photography showing the details that separate a great collectible rifle from the rest. Serial number tables, combat photos, sniper rifles and more!

AR-15 & M-16 5.56mm Assembly, Disassembly Manual, by Skennerton & Riling, Ray Riling Arms Books Co. Philadelphia, PA 2004. 36 pages, $5.00

With over 60 photos & line drawings. Ideal workshop reference for stripping & assembly with exploded parts drawings, specifications, service accessories, historical information and recommended reading references.

AR-15 Complete Owner's Guide, Volume 1, 2nd Edition, by Walt Kuleck and Scott Duff, Export, PA, Scott A. Duff Publications, 2002. 224 pp., 164 photographs & line drawings. Softcover. $21.95

This book provides the prospective, new or experienced AR-15 owner with the in-depth knowledge he or she needs to select, configure, operate, maintain and troubleshoot his or her rifle. The Guide covers history, applications, details of components and subassemblies, operating, cleaning, maintenance, and future of perhaps the most versatile rifle system ever produced. A comprehensive Colt model number table and pre-/post-ban serial number information are included.

AR-15 Complete Assembly Guide, Volume 2, by Walt Kuleck and Clint McKee. Export, PA, Scott A. Duff Publications, 2002. 1st edition. 155 pp., 164 photographs & line drawings. Softcover. $19.95

This book goes beyond the military manuals in depth and scope, using words and pictures to clearly guide the reader through every operation required to assemble their AR-15-type rifle. You'll learn the best and easiest ways to build your rifle. It won't make you an AR-15 armorer, but it will make you a more knowledgeable owner. In short, if you build it, you'll know how to repair it.

AR-15/M16, A Practical Guide, by Duncan Long, Paladin Press, Boulder, CO, 1985. 168 pp., illus. Paper covers. $22.00

The definitive book on the rifle that has been the inspiration for so many modern assault rifles.

Argentine Mauser Rifles 1871-1959, by Colin Atglen, Webster, PA, Schiffer Publications, 2003. 1st edition. 304 pp., over 400 b&w and color photographs, drawings, and charts. Hardcover. $79.95

This is the complete story of Argentina's contract Mauser rifles from the purchase of their first Model 1871s to the disposal of the last shipment of surplus rifles received in the United States in May 2002. The Argentine Commission's relentless pursuit of tactical superiority resulted in a major contribution to the development of Mauser's now famous bolt-action system.

Art of Shooting with the Rifle, by Col. Sir H. St. John Halford, Excalibur Publications, Latham, NY, 1996. 96 pp., illus. Paper covers. $12.95

A facsimile edition of the 1888 book by a respected rifleman providing a wealth of detailed information.

Art of the Rifle, by Jeff Cooper, Paladin Press, Boulder, CO, 1997. 104 pp., illus. Paper covers $22.00

Everything you need to know about the rifle whether you use it for security, meat or target shooting.

Assault Rifle, by Maxim Popenker, and Anthony Williams, London, Crowood Press, 2005. 224 pages. Hardcover. New in new dust jacket. $34.95

Includes brief historical summary of the assault rifle, its origins and development; gun design including operating mechanisms and weapon configuration, and more. The second part includes: national military rifle programs since the end of WWII; history of developments in each country including experimental programs; and detailed descriptions of the principal service and experimental weapons.

Ballard: The Great American Single Shot Rifle, by John T. Dutcher, Denver, CO, privately printed, 2002. 1st edition. 380 pp., illustrated with b&w photos, with an 8-page color insert. Hardcover. $79.95

Benchrest Actions and Triggers, by Stuart Otteson. Rohnert Park, CA, Adams-Kane Press, July 2003. Limited edition. 64 pp. Softcover. $27.95

Stuart Otteson's ***Benchrest Actions and Triggers*** is truly a lost classic. Benchrest Actions and Triggers is a compilation of 17 articles Mr. Otteson wrote. The articles contained are of particular interest to the benchrest crowd. Reprinted by permission of Wolfe Publishing.

Black Magic: The Ultra Accurate AR-15, by John Feamster, Precision Shooting, Manchester, CT, 1998. 300 pp., illus. $29.95

The author has compiled his experiences pushing the accuracy envelope of the AR-15 to its maximum potential. A wealth of advice on AR-15 loads, modifications and accessories for everything from NRA Highpower and Service Rifle competitions to benchrest and varmint shooting.

Black Rifle, M16 Retrospective, by R. Blake Stevens and Edward C. Ezell, Collector Grade Publications, Toronto, Canada, 1987. 416 pp., 441 illustrations and photos. $59.95

At the time of this writing, the 5.56mm NATO M16A2 rifle is heir to world wide acceptance after a quarter-century of U.S. service, longer than any other U.S. rifle in this century except the 1903 bolt-action Springfield. Its history has been far from one of calm acceptance.

Black Rifle II: The M16 into the 21st Century, by Christopher R. Bartocci, Canada, Collector Grade Publications, 2004. 408 pages, 626 illustrations. $69.95

This book chronicles all the new third- and fourth-generation rifle and carbine models which have been introduced by Colt and Diemaco since ***The Black Rifle*** was originally published, and describes and depicts the myriad of enhanced sights and rails systems which help make the M16s of today the most versatile, modular and effective combat weapons in the world. Includes an in-depth reference compendium of all Colt military and civilian models and components.

Blitzkrieg!–The MP40 Maschinenpistole of WWII, by Frank Iannamico, Harmony, ME, Moose Lake Publishing, 2003. 1st edition. Over 275 pp., 280 photos and documents. Softcover. $29.95

It's back, now in a new larger 8" x11" format. Lots of new information and many unpublished photos. This book includes the history and development of the German machine pistol from the MP18.I to the MP40.

Bolt Action Rifles, Expanded 4th Edition, by Frank de Haas and Wayne van Zwoll, Krause Publications, Iola, WI 2003. 696 pp., illustrated with 615 b&w photos. Softcover. $29.95

British .22RF Training Rifles, by Dennis Lewis and Robert Washburn, Excaliber Publications, Latham, NY, 1993. 64 pp., illus. Paper covers. $10.95

The story of Britain's training rifles from the early Aiming Tube models to the post-WWII trainers.

Building Double Rifles on Shotgun Actions, by W. Ellis Brown, Ft. Collins, CO, Bunduki Publishing, 2001. 1st edition. 187 pp., including index and b&w photographs. Hardcover. $55.00

Carbine .30 M1, M1A1, M2 & M3 Assembly, Disassembly Manual, by Skennerton & Riling, Ray Riling Arms Books Co. Philadelphia, PA 2004. 36 pages, over 60 photos & line drawings. $5.00

Ideal workshop reference for stripping & assembly with exploded parts drawings, specifications, service accessories, historical information and recommended reading references.

Classic Sporting Rifles, by Christopher Austyn, Safari Press, Huntington Beach, CA, 1997. 128 pp., illus. $50.00

As the head of the gun department at Christie's Auction House the author examines the "best" rifles built over the last 150 years.

Collectable '03, by J.C. Harrison, The Arms Chest, Oklahoma City, OK. 1999. 2nd edition (revised). 234 pp., illustrated with drawings, Spiral bound. $35.00

Valuable and detailed reference book for the collector of the Model 1903 Springfield rifle.

Collecting Classic Bolt Action Military Rifles, by Paul S. Scarlata, Andrew Mowbray, Inc., Lincoln, RI, 2001. 280 pp., illus. $39.95

Over 400 large photographs detail key features you will need to recognize in order to identify guns for your collection. Learn the original military configurations of these service rifles so you can tell them apart from altered guns and bad restorations. The historical sections are particularly strong, giving readers a clear understanding of how and why these rifles were developed, and which troops used them.

Collecting the Garand, by J.C. Harrison, The Arms Chest, Oklahoma City, OK. 2001. 2nd edition (revised). 198 pp., illus. with pictures and drawings. Spiral bound. $35.00

Valuable and detailed reference book for the collector of the Garand.

Collecting the M1 Carbine, by J.C. Harrison, The Arms Chest, Oklahoma City, OK. 2000. 2nd edition (revised). 247 pp., illustrated with pictures and drawings. Spiral bound. $35.00

Valuable and detailed reference book for the collector of the M1 Carbine. Identifies standard issue original military models of M1 and M1A1 Models of 1942, '43, '44, and '45 carbines as produced by each manufacturer, plus arsenal repair, refinish and lend-lease.

Competitive AR15: The Mouse That Roared, by Glenn Zediker, Zediker Publishing, Oxford, MS, 1999. 286 pp., illus. Paper covers. $29.95

A thorough and detailed study of the newest precision rifle sensation.

Complete AR15/M16 Sourcebook, Revised and Updated Edition, by Duncan Long, Paladin Press, Boulder, CO, 2002. 336 pp., illus. Paper covers. $39.95

The latest development of the AR15/M16 and the many spin-offs now available, selective-fire conversion systems for the 1990s, the vast selection of new accessories.

Complete Book of the .22: A Guide to the World's Most Popular Guns, by Wayne van Zwoll, Lyons Press, 2004. 1st edition. 336 pgs. Hardcover. $26.95

Complete Guide to the M1 Garand and the M1 Carbine, by Bruce Canfield, Andrew Mowbray, Inc., Lincoln, RI, 1999. 296 pp., illus. $39.50

Covers all of the manufacturers of components, parts, variations and markings. The total story behind these guns, from their invention through WWII, Korea, Vietnam and beyond! 300+ photos show you features, markings, overall views and action shots. Thirty-three tables and charts give instant reference to serial numbers, markings, dates of issue and proper configurations. Special sections on sniper guns, National Match rifles, exotic variations, and more!

Complete M1 Garand, by Jim Thompson, Paladin Press, Boulder, CO, 1998. 160 pp., illus. Paper cover. $24.00

A guide for the shooter and collector, heavily illustrated.

Crown Jewels: The Mauser In Sweden; A Century of Accuracy and Precision, by Dana Jones, Canada, Collector Grade Publications, 2003. 1st edition. 312 pp., 691 illustrations. Hardcover. $49.95

Here is the first in-depth study of all the Swedish Mausers: the 6.5mm M/94 carbines, M/96 long rifles, M/38 short rifles, Swedish K98Ks (called the M/39 in 7.92x57mm, then, after rechambering to fire the 8x63mm machine un cartridge, the M/40); sniper rifles, and other military adaptations such as grenade launchers and artillery simulators. Also covers a wide variety of the micrometer-adjustment rear sight inserts and "diopter" receiver sights produced for the Swedish Mauser. Full chapters on bayonets and the many accessories, both military and civilian.

Defending the Dominion, Canadian Military Rifles, 1855-1955, by David Edgecombe, Ont. Canada, Service Publications, 2003. 1st edition. 168 pp., with 60+ illustrations. Hardcover. $39.95

Desperate Measures-The Last Ditch Weapons of the Nazi Voksstrurm, by Darrin Weaver, Canada, Collector Grade Publications, 2005. 424 pages, 558 illustrations. $69.50

All are covered in detail, and the book includes many previously unpublished photographs of original Volkssturm weapons, including prototypes and rare presentation examples.

F.N.-F.A.L. Auto Rifles, Desert Publications, Cornville, AZ, 1981. 130 pp., illus. Paper covers. $18.95

A definitive study of one of the free world's finest combat rifles.

FAL Rifle, by R. Blake Stevens and Jean van Rutten, Collector Grade Publications, Cobourg, Canada, 1993. 848 pp., illus. $129.95

Originally published in three volumes, this classic edition covers North American, UK and Commonwealth and the metric FAL's.

Fighting Rifle, by Chuck Taylor, Paladin Press, Boulder, CO, 1983. 184 pp., illus. Paper covers. $25.00

The difference between assault and battle rifles and auto and light machine guns.

FN-49; Last Elegant Old-World Military Rifle, by Wayne Johnson., Greensboro, NC, Wet Dog Pub. 2004. 200 pages with Over 300 quality b&w photographs. $45.95

The FN-49 The Last Elegant old World Military Rifle book contains both information on the SAFN as well as the AFN rifle.

FN-FAL Rifle, The, et al, by Duncan Long, Delta Press, El Dorado, AR, 1998. 148 pp., illus. Paper covers. $18.95

A comprehensive study of one of the classic assault weapons of all times. Detailed descriptions of the basic models plus the myriad of variants that evolved as a result of its universal acceptance.

Forty Years with the .45-70, 2nd Edition, Revised and Expanded, by Paul A. Matthews, Wolfe Publishing Co., Prescott, AZ, 1997. 184 pp., illus. Paper covers. $17.95

This book is pure gun lore of the .45-70. It not only contains a history of the cartridge, but also years of the author's personal experiences.

Garand .30 Assembly, Disassembly Manual, by Skennerton & Riling, Ray Riling Arms Books Co. Philadelphia, PA 2004. 36 pages, $5.00

With over 60 photos & line drawings. Ideal workshop reference for stripping & assembly with exploded parts drawings, specifications, service accessories, historical information and recommended reading references.

German Sniper 1914-1945, by Peter R. Senich, Paladin Press, Boulder, CO, 1997 8½" x 11", hardcover, photos, 468 pp. $79.95

The complete story of Germany's sniping arms development through both world wars. Presents more than 600 photos of Mauser 98's, Selbstladegewehr 41s and 43s, optical sights by Goerz, Zeiss, etc., plus German snipers in action. An exceptional hardcover collector's edition for serious military historians everywhere.

Great Remington 8 and Model 81 Autoloading Rifles, by John Henwood, Canada, Collector Grade Publications, 2003. 1st edition. 304 pp., 291 illustrations, 31 in color. Hardcover. $59.95

Gun Digest Book of the.22 Rimfire, by James House, Iola,WI, Krause Publications, 2005. 288pgs. Soft cover. 250 b&w photos. $24.99

The most comprehensive guide to rimfire weapons & ammo. Info on current & vintage models. Covers the history, sights & sighting, techniques for testing accuracy, options for enhancing models, & more.

Gun-Guides, AK-47 AKM All Variants, Disassembly and Reassembly Guide, by Gun Guides, 2005. 16pp, illustrations, cardstock cover. Bright white paper. Soft cover. $6.99

The complete guide for ALL models.

Gun-Guides, Colt AR15 and All Variants, Disassembly and Reassembly Guide, by Gun Guides, 2005. 16pp, illustrations, cardstock cover. Bright white paper. Soft cover. $6.99

The complete guide for ALL models.

Gun-Guides, 1911 Pistols & All Variants-Disassembly & Reassembly, by Gun Guides, 2006. 16pp, illustrations, cardstock cover. Bright white paper. Soft cover. $6.99

The complete guide for ALL models.

Gun-Guides, Glock, Disassembly and Reassembly for All Models, by Gun Guides, 2005. 16pp, illustrations, cardstock cover. Bright white paper. Soft cover. $6.99

The complete guide for ALL models.

Gun-Guides, Remington 1100, 11-87 Shotguns, Disassembly and Reassembly Guides, by Gun Guides, 2005. The complete guide for ALL models, 16pp, illustrations, Cardstock cover. Bright white paper. Soft cover. $6.99

Gun-Guides, Remington 870 Shotguns, Disassembly and Reassembly Guides, by Gun Guides, 2005. The complete guide for ALL models, 16pp, illustrations, Cardstock cover. Bright white paper. Soft cover. $6.99

Gun-Guides, Ruger .22 Automatic Pistols: The Complete Guide for All Models from 1947 to 2003, by Gun Guides, 2005. 74 pages, 66 high-resolution grayscale images. Cardstock cover. Bright white paper. $11.95

The complete guide for ALL models. Includes "rare" complete serial numbers and manufacturing dates from 1949-2004.

Gun-Guides, Ruger Single Action Revolvers, Blackhawk, Super Blackhawk, Vaquero and Bisley Models Disassembly and Reassembly Guide for All Models, 1955-2005, by Gun Guides, 2005. 16pp, illustrations, cardstock cover. Bright white paper. $6.99

The complete guide for ALL models.

Gun-Guides, Ruger 10/22 & 10/17 Carbines Complete Guide to All Models from 1964-2004, by Gun Guides, 2005. 55 pages & 66 high-resolution grayscale images. Bright white paper. Soft cover. $11.95

Easy to use: Comb binding lies open and flat on your work surface. Includes all serial numbers and manufacture dates for all models from 1964-2004!

Gun-Guides, Ruger Mini-14 Complete Guide to All Models from 1972-2003, by Gun Guides, 2005. 52pp, illustrations, cardstock cover. Bright white paper. Soft cover. $11.95

The complete guide for ALL models.

Gun-Guides, SKS Semi-Automatic Rifles, Disassembly and Reassembly Guide, by Gun Guides, 2005. 16pp, illustrations, cardstock cover. Bright white paper. Soft cover. $6.99

The complete guide for ALL models.

Handbook of Military Rifle Marks 1866-1950 (third edition), by Richard Hoffman, and Noel Schott, Maple leaf Militaria Publications, 2002. 66 pp, with illustrations, signed by the authors. Stiff paper covers. $20.00

An illustrated military rifles and marks. Officially being used as a reference tool by many law enforcement agencies including BATF, the St. Louis and Philadelphia Police Departments and the Illinois State Police.

High Performance Muzzle Loading Big Game Rifles, by Toby Bridges, Maryland, Stoeger Publications, 2004. 160 pages. Pictorial Hardcover. $24.95

Covers all aspects of in-lines including getting top performance, working up loads, choosing projectiles, scope selection, coping with muzzleloader trajectory, tips for maintaining accuracy, plus much, much more.

Historic Henry Rifle: Oliver Winchester's Famous Civil War Repeater, by Wiley Sword, Andrew Mowbray, Inc., Lincoln, RI. 2002. Softcover. $29.95

It was perhaps the most important firearm of its era. Tested and proved in the fiery crucible of the Civil War, the Henry Rifle became the forerunner of the famous line of Winchester Repeating Rifles that "Won the West." Here is the fascinating story from the frustrations of early sales efforts aimed at the government to the inspired purchase of the Henry Rifle by veteran soldiers who wanted the best weapon.

Hitler's Garands: German Self-Loading Rifles of World War II, by Darrin W. Weaver, Collector Grade Publications, Canada, 2001. 392 pp., 590 illustrations. $69.95

Hitler's Wehrmacht began WWII armed with the bolt-action K98k, a rifle only cosmetically different from that with which Imperial Germany had fought the Great War a quarter-century earlier. Then in 1940, the Heereswaffenamt (HWaA, the Army Weapons Office) issued a requirement for a new self-loading rifle.

How-To's for the Black Powder Cartridge Rifle Shooter, by Paul A. Matthews, Wolfe Publishing Co., Prescott, AZ, 1996. 136 pp., illus. Paper covers. $22.50

Practices and procedures used in the reloading and shooting of blackpowder cartridges.

Imperial Japanese Grenade Rifles and Launchers, by Greg Babisch and Thomas Keep, Lemont, PA, Dutch Harlow Publishing, 2004. 247 pages, illustrated with numerous b&w and color photos throughout. Hardcover. New in new dust jacket. $75.00

This book is a must for museums, military historians, and collectors of Imperial Japanese rifles, rifle cartridges, and ordnance.

Jaeger Rifles Collected Articles Published in Muzzle Blasts, by George Shumway, York, PA, George Shumway, 2003. 108 pp., illus. Stiff paper covers. $30.00

Johnson Rifles and Machine Guns: The Story of Melvin Maynard Johnson Jr. and his Guns, by Bruce N. Canfield, Lincoln, RI, Andrew Mowbray, Inc., 2002. 1st edition. 272 pp. with over 285 photographs. Hardcover. $49.95

The M1941 Johnson rifle is the hottest WWII rifle on the collector's market today. From invention and manufacture through issue to the troops, this book covers them all!

Kalashnikov: The Arms and the Man, A Revised and Expanded Edition of the AK47 Story, by Edward C. Ezell, Canada, Collector Grade Publications, 2002. 312 pp., 356 illustrations. Hardcover. $59.95

The original edition of The AK47 Story was published in 1986, and the events of the intervening fifteen years have provided much fresh new material. Beginning with an introduction by Dr. Kalashnikov himself, this is a most comprehensive study of the "life and times" of the AK, starting with the early history of small arms manufacture in Czarist Russia and then the Soviet Union.

Last Enfield: SA80–The Reluctant Rifle, by Steve Raw, Collector Grade Publications, Canada 2003. 1st edition. 360 pp., with 382 illustrations. Hardcover. $49.95

This book presents the entire, in-depth story of its subject firearm, in this case the controversial British SA80, right from the founding of what became the Royal Small Arms Factory (RSAF) Enfield in the early 1800s; briefly through two world wars with Enfield at the forefront of small arms production for British forces; and covering the adoption of the 7.62mm NATO cartridge in 1954 and the L1A1 rifle in 1957.

Last Steel Warrior: The U.S. M14 Rifle, by Frank Iannamico, Moose Lake Pub., 2006. With over 400 pages and 537 photos and illustrations. Soft cover. $29.95

Acclaimed gun author Frank Iannamico's latest book covers history, development and deployment of the influential M14 rifle.

Lee Enfield No. 1 Rifles, by Alan M. Petrillo, Excaliber Publications, Latham, NY, 1992. 64 pp., illus. Paper covers. $10.95

Highlights the SMLE rifles from the Mark 1-VI.

Lee Enfield Number 4 Rifles, by Alan M. Petrillo, Excalibur Publications, Latham, NY, 1992. 64 pp., illus. Paper covers. $10.95

A pocket-sized, bare-bones reference devoted entirely to the .303 WWII and Korean War vintage service rifle.

Legendary Sporting Rifles, by Sam Fadala, Stoeger Publishing Co., So. Hackensack, NJ, 1992. 288 pp., illus. Paper covers. $16.95

Covers a vast span of time and technology beginning with the Kentucky longrifle.

Li'l M1 .30 Cal. Carbine, by Duncan Long, Desert Publications, El Dorado, AZ, 1995. 203 pp., illus. Paper covers. $19.95

Traces the history of this little giant from its original creation.

Living With the Big .50, The Shooter's Guide to the World's Most Powerful Rifle, Robert Boatman, Boulder, CO, Paladin Press, 2004. 176 pp. Soft cover. $29.00

Living with the Big .50 is the most thorough book ever written on this powerhouse rifle.

M1 Carbine Owner's Manual, M1, M2 & M3 .30 Caliber Carbines, Firepower Publications, Cornville, AZ, 1984. 102 pp., illus. Paper covers. $9.95

The complete book for the owner of an M1 carbine.

M1 Carbine Owner's Guide, by Scott A. Duff, Export, PA, Scott Duff Publications, 2002. 144 pages, illustrated. $21.95

Tells you what to look for before you choose a Carbine for collecting or shooting. Identification guide with serial numbers by production quarter for approximate date of manufacture. Illustrated, complete guide to markings, nomenclature of parts, assembly, disassembly and special tools. History and identification guide with serial numbers by production quarter for approximate date of manufacture. Includes troubleshooting, maintenance, cleaning and lubrication guide.

M1 Garand .30 Assembly, Disassembly Manual, by Skennerton & Riling, Ray Riling Arms Books Co. Philadelphia, PA 2004. 36 pages, over 60 photos & line drawings. $5.00

Ideal workshop reference for stripping & assembly with exploded parts drawings, specifications, service accessories, historical information and recommended reading references.

M1 Garand Owners Guide, Vol 1, by Scott A. Duff, Export, PA, Scott Duff Publications, 2002. 126 pages, illustrated. $21.95

Makes shooting, disassembly and maintenance work easier. Contains a brief history as well as production dates and other information to help identify who made it and when. Line drawings identify the components and show their position and relationships plainly.

M1 Garand Complete Assembly Guide, Vol. 2, by Walt Kuleck, and Clint McKee, Export, PA, Scott Duff Publications, 2004. 162 pp. $21.95

You'll learn the best and easiest ways to build your rifle. It won't make you a Garand armorer, but it will make you a more knowledgeable owner. You'll be able to do more with (and to) your rifle.

M1 Garand Serial Numbers & Data Sheets, by Scott A. Duff, Scott A. Duff, Export, PA, 1995. 101 pp. Paper covers. $11.95

This pocket reference book includes serial number tables and data sheets on the Springfield Armory, gas trap rifles, gas port rifles, Winchester Repeating Arms, International Harvester and H&R Arms Co. and more.

M1 Garand: Post World War, by Scott A. Duff, Scott A. Duff Publications, Export, PA, 1990. 139 pp., illus. Softcover. $21.95

A detailed account of the activities at Springfield Armory through this period. International Harvester, H&R, Korean War production and quantities delivered. Serial numbers.

M1 Garand: World War 2, by Scott A. Duff, Scott A. Duff Publications, Export, PA, 1993. 210 pp., illus. Paper covers. $34.95

The most comprehensive study available to the collector and historian on the M1 Garand of WWII.

M14 Rifle Assembly, Disassembly Manual 7.62mm, by Skennerton & Riling, Ray Riling Arms Books Co. Philadelphia, PA 2004. 36 pages, over 60 photos & line drawings. $5.00

Ideal workshop reference for stripping & assembly with exploded parts drawings, specifications, service accessories, historical information and recommended reading references.

M14 Owner's Guide and Match Conditioning Instructions, by Scott A. Duff and John M. Miller, Duff Publications, Export, PA, 1996. 180 pp., illus. Paper covers. $19.95

Traces the history and development from the T44 through the adoption and production of the M14 rifle.

M14 Complete Assembly Guide; Vol. 2, by Walt Kuleck, and Clint McKee, Duff Publications, Export, PA, 1996. 180 pp., illus. Paper covers. $24.95

You'll learn the best and easiest ways to enhance, disassemble and assemble your rifle. It won't make you an M14/M1A armorer, but it will make you a knowledgeable owner. You'll be able to do more with (and to) your rifle.

M14 Rifle, facsimile reprint of FM 23-8, Desert Publications, Cornville, AZ, 50 pp., illus. Paper $11.95

Well illustrated and informative reprint covering the M-14 and M-14E2.

M14-Type Rifle: A Shooter's And Collector's Guide; 3rd Edition Revised and Expanded edition, by Joe Poyer, North Cape Publications, Tustin, CA, 2007. 104 pp., illus. Paper covers. $19.95

This new revised and expanded edition examines the M14 rifle and its two sniper variations on a part-by-part basis but surveys all current civilian semiautomatic M14-type rifles and components available today. It also provides as a guide for shooters who want to restore an M14 to original condition or build a superb match rifle. Included are the Chinese variations of the M14. The history of the development and use of the M14 in Vietnam, and now in Iraq and Afghanistan, is detailed. The book is fully illustrated with photos and drawings that clarify the text. Appendices provide up-to-date information on parts and supplies and gunsmithing services.

M14/M14A1 Rifles and Rifle Marksmanship, Desert Publications, El Dorado, AZ, 1995. 236 pp., illus. Paper covers. $19.95

Contains a detailed description of the M14 and M14A1 rifles and their general characteristics, procedures for disassembly & assembly, operating and functioning of the rifles.

M16/AR15 Rifle, by Joe Poyer, North Cape Publications, Tustin, CA, 1998. 150 pp., illus. Paper covers. $19.95

From its inception as the first American assault battle rifle to the firing lines of the National Matches, the M16/AR15 rifle in all its various models and guises has made a significant impact on the American rifleman.

Major Ned H. Roberts and the Schuetzen Rifle, edited by Gerald O. Kelver, Brighton, CO, 1998. 3rd edition. 122 pp., illus. $13.95

A compilation of the writings of Major Ned H. Roberts which appeared in various gun magazines.

Mannlicher Military Rifles: Straight Pull and Turn Bolt Designs, Paul Scarlata, Lincoln, RI, Andrew Mowbray, 2004. Hardcover, 168 pages 8.5 x 11, filled with black & white photos. Hardcover. NEW $32.49

Profusely illustrated with close-up photos, drawings and diagrams, this book is the most detailed examination of Mannlicher military rifles ever produced in the English language.

Mauser Military Rifles Of The World, 4th Edition, by Robert Ball, Iola, WI, Krause Publications, 2006. 448 pp., with historical data, coupled with detailed color photos. $49.95

The ultimate Mauser military rifle reference, this superior guide is packed with more models, all-color photos and Mauser history tailored to the interests and needs of firearms collectors. With more than 50 countries represented, 75 years of Mauser military rifle production is meticulously cataloged with descriptions, historical details, model specifications and markings, for easy identification by collectors.

Mauser Military Rifle Markings, 2nd Edition, Revised and Expanded, by Terence Lapin, Hyrax Publishers, Arlington, VA. 2005, 167 pages, illustrated. Softcover. $22.95

A general guide to reading and understanding the often mystifying markings found on military Mauser Rifles. Includes German Regimental markings as well as German police markings and W.W. 2 German Mauser subcontractor codes. A handy reference to take to gun shows.

Mauser Rifles & Carbines Assembly, Disassembly Manual, by Skennerton & Riling, Ray Riling Arms Books Co. Philadelphia, PA 2004. 36 pages, over 60 photos & line drawings. $5.00

Ideal workshop reference for stripping & assembly with exploded parts drawings, specifications, service accessories, historical information and recommended reading references.

Mauser Smallbore Sporting, Target and Training Rifles, by Jon Speed, Collector Grade Publications, Inc., Cobourg, Ont., Canada, 1998. 372 pp., illus. $67.50

The history of all the smallbore sporting, target and training rifles produced by the legendary Mauser-Werke of Obendorf am Neckar.

Mauser: Original-Oberndorf Sporting Rifles, by Jon Speed, Collector Grade Publications, Inc., Cobourg, Ont., Canada, 1997. 508 pp., illus. $89.95

The most exhaustive study ever published of the design origins and manufacturing history of the original Oberndorf Mauser Sporter.

MG34-MG42 German Universal Machineguns, by Folke Myrvang, Collector Grade Publications, Canada. 2002. 496 pp., 646 illustrations. $79.95

This is the first-ever COMPETE study of the MG34 & MG42. Here the author presents in-depth coverage of the historical development, fielding, tactical use of and modifications made to these remarkable guns and their myriad accessories and ancillaries, plus authoritative tips on troubleshooting.

Military Bolt Action Rifles, 1841-1918, by Donald B. Webster, Museum Restoration Service, Alexander Bay, NY, 1993. 150 pp., illus. $34.50

A photographic survey of the principal rifles and carbines of the European and Asiatic powers of the last half of the 19th century and the first years of the 20th century.

Military Rifles of Japan, 5th Edition, by F.L. Honeycutt, Julin Books, Lake Park, FL, 1999. 208 pp., illus. $42.00

A new revised and updated edition. Includes the early Murata-period markings, etc.

Mini-14, by Duncan Long, Paladin Press, Boulder, CO, 1987. 120 pp., illus. Paper covers. $17.00

History of the Mini-14, the factory-produced models, specifications, accessories, suppliers, and much more.

MKB 42, MP43, MP44 and the Sturmgewehr 44, by de Vries & Martens. Alexandria, VA, Ironside International, 2003. 1st edition. 152 pp., illustrated with 200 high quality b&w photos. Hardcover. $39.95

Covers all essential information on history and development, ammunition and accessories, codes and markings, and contains photos of nearly every model and accessory. Includes a unique selection of original German WWII propaganda photos, most never published before.

Modern Guns: Fred Adolph Genoa, by Fred Adolph, Oceanside, CA, Armory Publications, 2003. One of only a few catalogs that list 2, 3 and 4 barrel guns. 68 pages, illustrated. Stiff Paper Covers. New. $19.95

Modern Sniper Rifles, by Duncan Long, Paladin Press, Boulder, CO, 1997, 8½" x 11", soft cover, photos, illus., 120 pp. $20.00

Noted weapons expert Duncan Long describes the .22 LR, single-shot, bolt-action, semiautomatic and large-caliber rifles that can be used for sniping purposes, including the U.S. M21, Ruger Mini-14, AUG and HK-94SG1. These and other models are evaluated on the basis of their features, accuracy, reliability and handiness in the field. The author also looks at the best scopes, ammunition and accessories.

More Single Shot Rifles and Actions, by Frank de Haas and Mark de Haas, Orange City, IA, 1996. 146 pp., illus. Paper covers. $22.50

Covers 45 different single shot rifles. Includes the history plus photos, drawings and personal comments.

Mosin-Nagant Assembly, Disassembly Manual 7.62mmR, by Skennerton & Riling, Ray Riling Arms Books Co. Philadelphia, PA 2004. 36 pages, $5.00

With over 60 photos & line drawings. Ideal workshop reference for stripping & assembly with exploded parts drawings, specifications, service accessories, historical information and recommended reading references.

Mosin-Nagant Rifle, by Terence W. Lapin, North Cape Publications, Tustin, CA, 1998. 30 pp., illus. Paper covers. $19.95

The first ever complete book on the Mosin-Nagant rifle written in English. Covers every variation.

Mr. Single Shot's Book of Rifle Plans, by Frank de Haas and Mark de Haas, Orange City, IA, 1996. 85 pp., illus. Paper covers. $22.50

Contains complete and detailed drawings, plans and instructions on how to build four different and unique breech-loading single shot rifles of the author's own proven design.

Muskets of the Revolution and the French & Indian Wars; The Smoothbore Longarm in Early America, Including British, French, Dutch, German, Spanish, and American

Weapons, by Bill Ahearn, Lincoln, RI, Andrew Mowbray, 2005. 248 pages, illustrated. Pictorial hardcover. $49.95

Not just a technical study of old firearms, this is a tribute to the bravery of the men who fought on both sides of that epic conflict and a celebration of the tools of freedom that have become so much a part of our national character. Includes many never-before published photos!

Neutrality Through Marksmanship: A Collector's and Shooter's Guide to Swedish Army Rifles 1867-1942, by Doug Bowser, Camellia City Military Publications, 1996. 1st edition. Stiff paper covers. $20.00

No. 4 (T) Sniper Rifle: An Armourer's Perspective, The, by Peter Laidler with Ian Skennerton, I.D.S.A. Books, Piqua, OH, 1993. 125 pp., 75 illus. Paper covers. $19.95

A reprint of the 1864 London edition. Captain Heaton was one of the great rifle shots from the earliest days of the Volunteer Movement.

Official SKS Manual, Translation by Major James F. Gebhardt (Ret.), Paladin Press, Boulder, CO, 1997. 96 pp., illus. Paper covers. $16.00

This Soviet military manual covering the widely distributed SKS is now available in English.

Official Soviet AK-47 Manual: Operating Instructions for the 5.45mm Kalashnikov Assault Rifle, and Kalashnikov Light Machine Gun, by James Gebhardt, Boulder, CO, Paladin Press, 2006. 8½" x 11", illus., 150 pp. Soft cover. $25.00

Written to teach Russian soldiers every detail of the operation and maintenance of the Kalashnikov Assault Rifle (AK-74) and Kalashnikov Light Machine Gun (RPK-74), this manual includes ballistic tables, zeroing information, combat firing instructions, data for the 5.45mm service cartridge and more.

Old German Target Arms: Alte Schiebenwaffen, by Jesse Thompson, C. Ron Dillon, Allen Hallock and Bill Loos, Rochester, NY, Tom Rowe Publications, 2003. 1st edition. 392 pp. Hardcover. $98.00

History of Schueten shooting from the middle ages through WWII. Hundreds of illustrations, most in color. History & memorabilia of the Bundesschiessen (State or National Shoots), bird target rifles, American shooters in Germany. Schutzen rifles such as matchlocks, wheellocks, flintlocks, percussion, bader, bornmuller, rifles by Buchel and more.

Old German Target Arms: Alte Schiebenwaffen Volume 2, by Jesse Thompson, C. Ron Dillon, Allen Hallock and Bill Loos, Rochester, NY, Tom Rowe Publications, 2004. 1st edition. 392 pp. Hardcover. $98.00

Old German Target Arms: Alte Schiebenwaffen Volume 3, by Jesse Thompson, C. Ron Dillon, Allen Hallock and Bill Loos, Rochester, NY, Tom Rowe Publications, 2005. 1st edition. 392 pp. Hardcover. $98.00

Ordnance Tools, Accessories & Appendages of the M1 Rifle, by Billy Pyle, Houston, TX, privately printed, 2002. 2nd edition. 206 pp., illustrated with b&w photos. Softcover. $40.00

This is the new updated second edition with over 350 pictures and drawings, of which 30 are new. Part I contains accessories, appendages, and equipment. Part II covers ammunition, grenades, and pyrotechnics. Part III shows the inspection gages. Part IV presents the ordnance tools, fixtures, and assemblies. Part V contains miscellaneous items related to the M1.

Police Rifles, by Richard Fairburn, Paladin Press, Boulder, CO, 1994. 248 pp., illus. Paper covers. $35.00

Selecting the right rifle for street patrol and special tactical situations.

Poor Man's Sniper Rifle, by D. Boone, Paladin Press, Boulder, CO, 1995. 152 pp., illus. Paper covers. $18.95

Here is a complete plan for converting readily available surplus military rifles to high-performance sniper weapons.

Precision Shooting with the M1 Garand, by Roy Baumgardner, Precision Shooting, Inc., Manchester, CT, 1999. 142 pp., illus. Paper covers. $12.95

Starts off with the ever popular ten-article series on accurizing the M1 that originally appeared in Precision Shooting in the 1993-95 era. There follows nine more Baumgardner-authored articles on the M1 Garand and finally a 1999 updating chapter.

Remington 700, by John F. Lacy, Taylor Publishing Co., Dallas, TX, 2002. 208 pp., illus. $54.95

Covers the different models, limited editions, chamberings, proofmarks, serial numbers, military models, and much more.

Remington Autoloading and Pump Action Rifles, by Eugene Myszkowski, Tucson, AZ, Excalibur Publications, 2002. 132 pp., with 162 photographs, 6 illustrations and 18 charts. Softcover. $20.95

An illustrated history of Remington's centerfire Models 760, 740, 742, 7400 and 7600. The book is thoroughly researched and features many previously unpublished photos of the rifles, their accessories and accoutrements. Also covers high grade, unusual and experimental rifles. Contains information on collecting, serial numbers and barrel codes.

Rifle Rules: Magic for the Ultimate Rifleman, by Don Paul, Kaua'i, HI, Pathfinder Publications, 2003. 1st edition. 116 pp., illus. Softcover. $14.95

A new method that shows you how to add hundreds of yards to your effective shooting ability. Ways for you to improve your rifle's accuracy which no factory can do. Illustrations & photos added to make new concepts easy.

Rifle Shooter, by G. David Tubb, Oxford, MS, Zediker Publishing, 2004. 1st edition. 416 pp softcover, 7" x 10" size, 400 photos and illustrations, very high quality printing. Softcover. $34.95

This is not just a revision of his landmark "Highpower Rifle" but an all-new, greatly expanded work that reveals David's thoughts and recommendations on all aspects of precision rifle shooting. Each shooting position and event is dissected and taken to extreme detail, as are the topics of ammunition, training, rifle design, event strategies, and wind shooting. You will learn the secrets of perhaps the greatest rifleman ever, and you'll learn how to put them to work for you!

Rifles of the U.S. Army 1861-1906, by John D. McAulay, Lincoln, RI, Andrew Mowbray, Inc., 2003. 1st edition. 278 pp., illus. Hardcover. $45.89

Rifles of the White Death (Valkoisen Kuoleman Kivaarit) A Collector's and Shooter's Guide to Finnish Military Rifles 1918-1944, by Doug Bowser, MS, Camellia City Military Publications, 1998. 1st edition. Stiff paper covers. $35.00

Rock In A Hard Place The Browning Automatic Rifle, by James L. Ballou. Collector Grade, Canada, 2004. 1st edition. 500 pages, with 751 illustrations. Hardcover $79.95

This first-ever in-depth study of the popular BAR includes clear photos of all U.S.-made military and commercial models, experimental models from Britain and France, plus offshore copies and clones from Belgium, Poland and Sweden.

Rock Island Rifle Model 1903, by C.S. Ferris, Export, PA, Scott A. Duff Publications, 2002. 177 pp., illustrated with b&w photographs. Foreword by Scott A. Duff. Softcover. $22.95

S.L.R.–Australia's F.N. F.A.L., by Ian Skennerton and David Balmer, Arms & Militaria Press, 1989. 124 pp., 100 illus. Paper covers. $24.50

Schuetzen Rifles, History and Loading, by Gerald O. Kelver, Pioneer Press, Union City, TN, 1998. 3rd edition. Illus. $13.95

Reference work on these rifles, their bullets, loading, telescopic sights, accuracy, etc. A limited, numbered ed.

Serbian and Yugoslav Mauser Rifles, by Banko Bogdanovich, Tustin, CA, North Cape Publications, 2005. 278pp. Soft cover. $19.95

In Serbian and Yugoslav Mauser Rifles, each model is discussed in its own chapter. All serial numbers are presented by year. All markings are presented and translated and all finishes and changes to all models are described in text and charts and well illustrated with both photographs and excellent drawings for clarity.

Shooting Lever Guns of the Old West, by Mike Venturino, MLV Enterprises, Livingston, MT, 1999. 300 pp., illus. Paper covers. $27.95

Shooting the lever action type repeating rifles of our American west.

Shooting the .43 Spanish Rolling Block, by Croft Barker, Flatonia, TX, Cistern Publishing, 2003. 1st edition. 137 pp. Softcover. $25.50

The source for information on .43 caliber rolling blocks. Lots of photos and text covering Remington & Oveido actions, antique cartridges, etc. Features smokless & black powder loads, rifle disassembly and maintenance, 11mm bullets. Required reading for the rolling block owner.

Shooting the Blackpowder Cartridge Rifle, by Paul A. Matthews, Wolfe Publishing Co., Prescott, AZ, 1994. 129 pp., illus. Paper covers. $22.50

A general discourse on shooting the blackpowder cartridge rifle and the procedure required to make a particular rifle perform.

Single Shot Military Rifle Handbook, by Croft Barker, Flatonia, TX, Cistern Publishing, 2005. Includes over 40 new high quality photos of vintage rifles, antique cartridges and related equipment. 130pp., many b&w photos. Soft cover. $25.50

Contains instruction on preparing authentic ammunition, shooting techniques, the uses of vintage military sights, rifle refurbishing, etc. Evolution of the single shot military rifle and the center fire cartridge is described.

Single Shot Rifles and Actions, by Frank de Haas, Orange City, IA, 1990. 352 pp., illus. Softcover. $27.00

The definitive book on over 60 single shot rifles and actions.

SKS Carbine 7.62 x 39mm Assembly, Disassembly Manual, by Skennerton & Riling, Ray Riling Arms Books Co. Philadelphia, PA 2004. 36 pages, over 60 photos & line drawings. $5.00

Ideal workshop reference for stripping & assembly with exploded parts drawings, specifications, service accessories, historical information and recommended reading references.

Small Arms Identification Series, No. 1–.303 Rifle, No. 1 S.M.L.E. Marks III and III*, by Ian Skennerton, I.D.S.A. Books, Piqua, OH, 1981. 48 pp. $10.50

Small Arms Identification Series, No. 2–.303 Rifle, No. 4 Marks I, & I*, Marks 1/2, 1/3 & 2, by Ian Skennerton, I.D.S.A. Books, Piqua, OH, 1994. 48 pp. $10.50

Small Arms Identification Series, No. 3–9mm Austen Mk I & 9mm Owen Mk I Sub-Machine Guns, by Ian Skennerton, I.D.S.A. Books, Piqua, OH, 1994. 48 pp. $10.50

Small Arms Identification Series, No. 4–.303 Rifle, No. 5 Mk I, by Ian Skennerton, I.D.S.A. Books, Piqua, OH, 1994. 48 pp. $10.50

Small Arms Identification Series, No. 5–.303-in. Bren Light Machine Gun, by Ian Skennerton, I.D.S.A. Books, Piqua, OH, 1994. 48 pp. $10.50

Springfield Rifle M1903, M1903A1, M1903A3, M1903A4, Desert Publications, Cornville, AZ, 1982. 100 pp., illus. Paper covers. $14.95

Covers every aspect of disassembly and assembly, inspection, repair and maintenance.

Still More Single Shot Rifles, by James J. Grant, Pioneer Press, Union City, TN, 1995. 211 pp., illus. $29.95

This is Volume Four in a series of single-shot rifles by America's foremost authority. It gives more in-depth information on those single-shot rifles that were presented in the first three books.

Sturm, Ruger 10/22 Rifle and .44 Magnum Carbine, by Duncan Long, Paladin Press, Boulder, CO, 1988. 108 pp., illus. Paper covers. $15.00

An in-depth look at both weapons detailing the elegant simplicity of the Ruger design. Offers specifications, troubleshooting procedures and ammunition recommendations.

Swedish Mauser Rifles, by Steve Kehaya and Joe Poyer, Tustin, CA, North Cape Publications, 2004. 2nd edition, revised. 267 pp., illus. Softcover. $19.95

Every known variation of the Swedish Mauser carbine and rifle is described including all match and target rifles and all sniper versions. Includes serial number and production data.

Swiss Magazine Loading Rifles 1869 to 1958, by Joe Poyer, Tustin, CA, North Cape Publications, 2003. 1st edition. 317 pp., illustrated with hundreds of b&w drawings and photos. Softcover. $19.95

It covers the K-31 on a part-by-part basis, as well as its predecessor models of 1889 and 1911, and the first repeating magazine rifle ever adopted by a military, the Model 1869 Vetterli rifle and its successor models. Also includes a history of the development and use of these fine rifles. Details regarding their ammunition, complete assembly/disassembly instructions as well as sections on cleaning, maintenance and trouble shooting.

Tactical Rifle, by Gabriel Suarez, Paladin Press, Boulder, CO, 1999. 264 pp., illus. Paper covers. $25.00

The precision tool for urban police operations.

Target Rifle in Australia, by J.E. Corcoran, R&R, Livonia, NY, 1996. 160 pp., illus. $40.00

A most interesting study of the evolution of these rifles from 1860-1900. British rifles from the percussion period through the early smokeless era are discussed.

Total Airguns; The Complete Guide to Huting with Air Rifles, by Peter Wadeson, London, Swan Hill Press, 2005. 300 pages, illustrated with b&w photos. Hardcover. $29.95

This book covers every aspect from choosing a rifle and scope to field craft and hunting techniques, camouflage, decoys, night shooting, and equipment maintenance. Extensive details on all air gun shooting techniques.

U.S. M1 Carbine: Wartime Production, 5th Edition, Revised and Expanded! by Craig Riesch, North Cape Publications, Tustin, CA 2007 237 pages. $19.95

The book contains 38 charts and 212 photographs, and 14 drawings. The book provides a history of the M1 Carbine's development, manufacture and use during World War II, as well as through the Korean War and the war in Vietnam. All variations of the M1 Carbine are discussed - M1, M1A1, and M2 - by manufacturer. Serial number ranges for original manufacture are included.

U.S. Rifle .30 Model 1917 and .303 British Pattern 1914 Assembly, Disassembly Manual, by Skennerton & Riling, Ray Riling Arms Books Co. Philadelphia, PA 2004. 36 pages, over 60 photos & line drawings. $5.00

Ideal workshop reference for stripping & assembly with exploded parts drawings, specifications, service accessories, historical information and recommended reading references. Ideal workbook for shooters and collectors alike. Triple saddle-stitched binding with durable plastic laminated cover makes this an ideal workshop guide.

U.S. Marine Corps AR15/M16 A2 Manual, reprinted by Desert Publications, El Dorado, AZ, 1993. 262 pp., illus. Paper covers. $16.95

A reprint of TM05538C-23&P/2, August, 1987. The A-2 manual for the Colt AR15/M16.

U.S. Marine Corps Rifle Marksmanship, by U.S. Marine Corps, Boulder, CO, Paladin Press, 2002. Photos, illus., 120 pp. Softcover. $20.00

This manual is the very latest Marine doctrine on the art and science of shooting effectively in battle. Its 10 chapters teach the versatility, flexibility and skills needed to deal with a situation at any level of intensity across the entire range of military operations. Topics covered include the proper combat mindset; cleaning your rifle under all weather conditions; rifle handling and marksmanship the Marine way; engaging targets from behind cover; obtaining a battlefield zero; engaging immediate threat, multiple and moving targets; shooting at night and at unknown distances; and much more.

U.S. Rifle M14–From John Garand to the M21, by R. Blake Stevens, Collector Grade Publications, Inc., Toronto, Canada, revised 2nd edition, 1991. 350 pp., illus. $49.50

A classic, in-depth examination of the development, manufacture and fielding of the last wood-and-metal ("lock, stock, and barrel") battle rifle to be issued to U.S. troops.

United States Rifle Model of 1917, by CS Ferris, Export, PA, Scott Duff Pubs., 2004. 213 pages, illustrated with b&w photographs. Foreword by Scott A. Duff. Soft cover. $23.95

If you are interested in the study of the United States Rifle Model of 1917 and have been disappointed by the lack of information available, then this book is for you!

Ultimate in Rifle Accuracy, by Glenn Newick, Stoeger Publishing Co., Wayne, NJ, 1999. 205 pp., illus. Paper covers. $11.95

This handbook contains the information you need to extract the best performance from your rifle.

War Baby! The U.S. Caliber 30 Carbine, Volume 1, by Larry Ruth, Collector Grade Publications, Toronto, Canada, 1992. 512 pp., illus. $69.95

Volume 1 of the in-depth story of the phenomenally popular U.S. caliber 30 carbine. Concentrates on design and production of the military 30 carbine during WWII.

War Baby Comes Home: The U.S. Caliber 30 Carbine, Volume 2, by Larry Ruth, Collector Grade Publications, Toronto, Canada, 1993. 386 pp., illus. $49.95

The triumphant completion of Larry Ruth's two-volume, in-depth series on the most popular U.S. military small arm in history.

Winchester: An American Legend, by R.L. Wilson, NY, Book Sales, 2004, reprint. 404 pages, illustrated with color and b&w photographs. Hardcover. New in new dust jacket. $29.95

Winchester Model 52: Perfection in Design, by Herbert Houze, Iola, WI, Krause Publications, 2006. Soft cover. $22.95

Herbert Houze unravels the mysteries surrounding the development of what many consider the most perfect rifle ever made. The book covers the rifle's improvements through five modifications. Users, collectors and marksmen will appreciate each variation's history, serial number sequences and authentic photos.

Winchester Model 61 Assembly, Disassembly Manual, by Skennerton & Riling, Ray Riling Arms Books Co. Philadelphia, PA 2004. 36 pages, over 60 photos & line drawings. $5.00

Ideal workshop reference for stripping & assembly with exploded parts drawings, specifications, service accessories, historical information and recommended reading references.

Winchester Model 70 Assembly, Disassembly Manual, by Skennerton & Riling, Ray Riling Arms Books Co. Philadelphia, PA 2004. 36 pages, over 60 photos & line drawings. $5.00

Ideal workshop reference for stripping & assembly with exploded parts drawings, specifications, service accessories, historical information and recommended reading references.

Winchester Model 94 Assembly, Disassembly Manual, by Skennerton & Riling, Ray Riling Arms Books Co. Philadelphia, PA 2004. 36 pages, over 60 photos & line drawings. $5.00

Ideal workshop reference for stripping & assembly with exploded parts drawings, specifications, service accessories, historical information and recommended reading references.

Winchester Slide-Action Rifles, Models 61, 62, 1890 & 1906, by Ned Schwing, Iola, WI, Krause Publications, 2004. 456 Pages, illustrated, 300 b&w photos. Soft cover. $39.95

Take a complete historical look at the favorite slide-action guns of America through Ned Schwing's eyes. Explore receivers, barrels, markings, stocks, stampings and engraving in complete detail.

Workbench AR-15 Project; A Step by Step Guide to Building Your Own Legal AR-15 Without Paperwork, The, by D.A. Hanks, Boulder, CO, Paladin Press, 2004. 80 pages, photos. Soft cover. $19.89

Hanks walks you through the entire process with clear text and detailed photos—staying legal, finishing the lower receiver, assembling all the parts and test-firing your completed rifle. For academic study only.

SHOTGUNS

A Collector's Guide to United States Combat Shotguns, by Bruce N. Canfield, Andrew Mowbray Inc., Publishers, Lincoln, RI, 1993. 184 pp., illus. Paper covers. $24.00

Full coverage of the combat shotgun, from the earliest examples to the Gulf War and beyond.

A.H. Fox: "The Finest Gun in the World," revised and enlarged edition, by Michael McIntosh, Countrysport, Inc., New Albany, OH, 1995. 408 pp., illus. $60.00

The first detailed history of one of America's finest shotguns.

Advanced Combat Shotgun: Stress Fire 2, by Massad Ayoob, Police Bookshelf, Concord, NH, 1993. 197 pp., illus. Paper covers. $14.95

Advanced combat shotgun fighting for police.

Best Guns, by Michael McIntosh, Countrysport Press, Selma, AL, 1999, revised edition. 418 pp. $45.00

Combines the best shotguns ever made in America with information on British and Continental makers.

Best of Holland & Holland, England's Premier Gunmaker, by Michael McIntosh and Jan G. Roosenburg. Long Beach, CA, Safari Press, Inc., 2002. 1st edition. 298 pp., profuse color illustrations. Hardcover. $69.95

Holland & Holland has had a long history of not only building London's "best" guns but also providing superior guns–the ultimate gun in finish, engraving, and embellishment. From the days of old in which a maharaja would order 100 fancifully engraved H&H shotguns for his guests to use at his duck shoot to the recent elaborately decorated sets depicting the Apollo 11 moon landing or the history of the British Empire, all of these guns represent the zenith in the art and craft of gunmaking and engraving. Never before have so many superlative guns from H&H– or any other maker for that matter–been displayed in one book.

Better Shot, by Ken Davies, Quiller Press, London, England, 1992. 136 pp., illus. $39.95

Step-by-step shotgun techniques with Holland and Holland.

Black's Buyer's Directory 2007 Wing & Clay, by James Black, Grand View Media, 2006. Soft cover. $17.95

1,637 companies in 62 sections providing shotgun related products and services worldwide. Destinations: 1,412 hunting destinations, 1,279 sporting clays, trap and skeet clubs state by state.

Breaking Clays, by Chris Batha, Stackpole Books, Mechanicsburg, PA, 2005. Hardcover. $29.95

This clear and concise book offers a distillation of the best tips and techniques that really work to improve your scores and give you the knowledge to develop to your full shooting potential

Browning Auto-5 Shotguns: The Belgian FN Production, by H. M. Shirley Jr. and Anthony Vanderlinden, Geensboro, NC, Wet Dog Publications, 2003. Limited edition of 2,000 copies, signed by the author. 233 pp., plus index. Over 400 quality b&w photographs and 24 color photographs. Hardcover $59.95

This is the first book devoted to the history, model variations, accessories and production dates of this legendary gun. This publication is to date the only reference book on the Auto-5 (A-5) shotgun prepared entirely with the extensive cooperation and support of Browning, FN Herstal, the Browning Firearms Museum and the Liege Firearms Museum.

Browning-Sporting Arms of Distinction 1903-1992, by Matt Eastman, Safari Press, 2005. Hardcover. $50.00

Finally, the history of the Browning family, the inventions, the company, and Browning's association with Colt, Winchester, Savage, and others is detailed in this all-inclusive book, which is profusely illustrated with hundreds of pictures and charts.

Cogswell & Harrison; Two Centuries of Gunmaking, by G. Cooley and J. Newton, Safari Press, Long Beach, CA, 2000. 128 pp., 30 color photos, 100 b&w photos. $39.95

The authors have gathered a wealth of fascinating historical and technical material that will make the book indispensable, not only to many thousands of "Coggie" owners worldwide, but also to anyone interested in the general history of British gunmaking.

Defensive Shotgun, The, by Louis Awerbuck, S.W.A.T. Publications, Cornville, AZ, 1989. 77 pp., illus. Softcover. $14.95

Cuts through the myths concerning the shotgun and its attendant ballistic effects.

Ducks Unlimited Guide to Shotgunning, The, by Don Zutz, Willow Creek Press, Minocqua, WI, 2000. 166 pg. Illustrated. $24.50

This book covers everything from the grand old guns of yesterday to today's best shotguns and loads, from the basic shotgun fit and function to expert advice on ballistics, chocks, and shooting techniques.

Fine European Gunmakers: Best Continental European Gunmakers & Engravers, by M. Nobili, Long Beach, CA, Safari Press, 2002. 250 pp., illustated in color. $69.95

Many experts argue that Continental gunmakers produce guns equally as good or better than British makers. Marco Nobili's new work showcases the skills of the best craftsmen from continental Europe. The book covers the histories of the individual firms and looks at the guns they currently build, tracing the developments of their most influential models.

Firearms Assembly/Disassembly, Part V: Shotguns, 2nd Edition, The Gun Digest Book of, by J.B. Wood, Krause Publications, Iola, WI, 2002. 560 pp., illus. $24.95

Covers 54 popular shotguns plus over 250 variants. The most comprehensive and professional presentation available to either hobbyist or gunsmith.

Game Shooting, by Robert Churchill, Countrysport Press, Selma, AL, 1998. 258 pp., illus. $30.00

The basis for every shotgun instructional technique devised and the foundation for all wingshooting and the game of sporting clays.

Greatest Hammerless Repeating Shotgun Ever Built: The Model 12 Winchester 1912-1964 by David Riffle, 1995. Color illustrations. 195 large detailed b&w photos, 298 pgs. Pictorial hardcover. $54.95

This offers an extremely well written and detailed year-by-year study of the gun, its details, inventors, makers, engravers, and star shooters.

Greener Story, by Graham Greener, Safari Press, Long Beach, CA, 2000. 231 pp., color and b&w illustrations. $69.95

The history of the Greener gunmakers and their guns.

Gunsmithing Shotguns: The Complete Guide to Care & Repair, by David Henderson, New York, Globe Pequot, 2003. 1st edition, b&w photos & illus; 6" x 9", 256 pp., illus. Hardcover. $24.95

An overview designed to provide insight, ideas and techniques that will give the amateur gunsmith the confidence and skill to work on his own guns. General troubleshooting, common problems, stocks and woodworking, soldering and brazing, barrel work and more.

Heyday of the Shotgun, by David Baker, Safari Press, Inc., Huntington Beach, CA, 2000. 160 pp., illus. $39.95

The art of the gunmaker at the turn of the last century when British craftsmen brought forth the finest guns ever made.

Holland & Holland: The "Royal" Gunmaker, by Donald Dallas, London, Safari Press, 2004. 1st edition. 311 pp. Hardcover. $75.00

Donald Dallas tells the fascinating story of Holland & Holland from its very beginnings, and the history of the family is revealed for the first time. The terrific variety of the firm's guns and rifles is described in great detail and set within the historical context of their eras. The book is profusely illustrated with 112 color and 355 b&w photographs, mostly unpublished. In addition many rare guns and rifles are described and illustrated.

House of Churchill, by Don Masters, Safari Press, Long Beach, CA, 2002. 512 pp., profuse color and b&w illustrations. $79.95

This marvelous work on the house of Churchill contains serial numbers and dates of manufacture of its guns from 1891 forward, price lists from 1895 onward, a complete listing of all craftsmen employed at the company, as well as the prices realized at the famous Dallas auction where the "last" production guns were sold. It was written by Don Masters, a long-time Churchill employee, who is keeping the flame of Churchill alive.

Italian Gun, by Steve Smith and Laurie Morrow, Wilderness Adventures, Gallatin Gateway, MT, 1997. 325 pp., illus. $49.95

The first book ever written entirely in English for American enthusiasts who own, aspire to own, or simply admire Italian guns.

Ithaca Featherlight Repeater; The Best Gun Going, by Walter C. Snyder, Southern Pines, NC, 1998. 300 pp., illus. $89.95

Describes the complete history of each model of the legendary Ithaca Model 37 and Model 87 Repeaters from their conception in 1930 throught 1997.

Ithaca Gun Company from the Beginning, by Walter C. Snyder, Cook & Uline Publishing Co., Southern Pines, NC, 2nd edition, 1999. 384 pp., illustrated in color and b&w. $90.00

The entire family of Ithaca Gun Company products is described along with new historical information and the serial number/date of manufacturing listing has been improved.

Little Trapshooting Book, by Frank Little, Shotgun Sports Magazine, Auburn, CA, 1994. 168 pp., illus. Paper covers. $19.95

Packed with know-how from one of the greatest trapshooters of all time.

Mental Training for the Shotgun Sports, by Michael J. Keyes, Shotgun Sports, Auburn, CA, 1996. 160 pp., illus. Paper covers. $29.95

The most comprehensive book ever published on what it takes to shoot winning scores at trap, skeet and sporting clays.

More Shotguns and Shooting, by Michael McIntosh, Countrysport Books, Selma, AL, 1998. 256 pp., illus. $30.00

From specifics of shotguns to shooting your way out of a slump, it's McIntosh at his best.

Mossberg Shotguns, by Duncan Long, Delta Press, El Dorado, AR, 2000. 120 pp., illus. $24.95

This book contains a brief history of the company and its founder, full coverage of the pump and semiautomatic shotguns, rare products and a care and maintenance section.

Mysteries of Shotgun Patterns, by George G. Oberfell and Charles E. Thompson, Ray Riling Arms Books, Philadelphia, PA, 2005. 164 pp., illus. Paper covers. $25.00

Shotgun ballistics for the hunter in non-technical language.

Parker Gun, by Larry Baer, Gun Room Press, Highland Park, NJ, 1993. 195 pp., illustrated with b&w and color photos. $35.00

Covers in detail, production of all models on this classic gun. Many fine specimens from great collections are illustrated.

Parker Guns 'The Old Reliable'-A Concise HIsory of the Famous American Shotgun Manufacturing Co., by Ed Muderlak, Long Beach, CA, Safari Press, 2004 results. A must-have for the American shotgun enthusiast. Hardcover. New in new dust jacket. $48.50

Parker Gun Identification & Serialization, by S.P. Fjestad, Minneapolis, MN, Blue Book Publications, 2002. 1st edition. Softcover. $34.95

This new 608-page publication is the only book that provides an easy reference for Parker shotguns manufactured between 1866-1942. Included is a comprehensive 46-page section on Parker identification, with over 100 detailed images depicting serialization location and explanation, various Parker grades, extra features, stock configurations, action types, and barrel identification.

Parker Story: Volumes 1 & 2, by Bill Mullins, "et al." The Double Gun Journal, East Jordan, MI, 2000. 1,025 pp. of text and 1,500 color and monochrome illustrations. Hardbound in a gold-embossed cover. $295.00

The most complete and attractive "last word" on America's preeminent double gun maker. Includes tables showing the number of guns made by gauge, barrel length and special features for each grade.

Pigeon Shooter: The Complete Guide to Modern Pigeon Shooting, by Jon Batley, London, Swan Hill press, 2005. Hardcover. $29.95

Covering everything from techniques to where and when to shoot. This updated edition contains all the latest information on decoys, hides, and the new pigeon magnets as well as details on the guns and equipment required and invaluable hands-on instruction.

Purdey Gun and Rifle Makers: The Definitive History, by Donald Dallas, Quiller Press, London 2000. 245 pp., illus. Signed and numbered. Limited edition of 3,000 copies. With a PURDEY bookplate. $100.00

Re-Creating the Double Barrel Muzzle Loading Shotgun, by William R. Brockway, York, PA, George Shumway, 2003. Revised 2nd edition. 175 pp., illus. Includes full size drawings. Softcover. $40.00

This popular book, first published in 1985 and out of print for over a decade, has been updated by the author. This book treats the making of double guns of classic style, and is profusely illustrated, showing how to do it all. Many photos of old and contemporary shotguns.

Reloading for Shotgunners, 4th Edition, by Kurt D. Fackler and M.L. McPherson, DBI Books, a division of Krause Publications, Iola, WI, 1997. 320 pp., illus. Paper covers. $19.95

Expanded reloading tables with over 11,000 loads. Bushing charts for every major press and component maker. All new presentation on all aspects of shotshell reloading by two of the top experts in the field.

Remington Double Shotguns, by Charles G. Semer, Denver, CO, 1997. 617 pp., illus. $60.00

This book deals with the entire production and all grades of double shotguns made by Remington during the period of their production 1873-1910.

Shotgun Encyclopedia, The, by John Taylor, Safari Press, Inc., Huntington Beach, CA, 2000. 260 pp., illus. $34.95

A comprehensive reference work on all aspects of shotguns and shotgun shooting.

Shotgun Technicana, by Michael McIntosh and David Trevallion, Camden, ME, Down East Books, 2002. 272 pp., with 100 illustrations. Hardcover $28.00

Everything you wanted to know about fine double shotguns by the nation's foremost experts.

Shotgun–A Shooting Instructor's Handbook, by Michael Yardley, Long Beach, CA, Safari Press, 2002. 272 pp., b&w photos, line drawings. Hardcover. $29.95

This is one of the very few books intended to be read by shooting instructors and other advanced shooters. There is practical advice on gun fit, and on gun and cartridge selection.

Shotgunning: The Art and the Science, by Bob Brister, Winchester Press, Piscataway, NJ, 1976. 321 pp., illus. $18.95

Hundreds of specific tips and truly novel techniques to improve the field and target shooting of every shotgunner.

Shotguns and Shooting, by Michael McIntosh, Countrysport Press, New Albany, OH, 1995. 258 pp., illus. $30.00

The art of guns and gunmaking, this book is a celebration no lover of fine doubles should miss.

Shotguns & Shotgunning, by Layne Simpson, Iola, WI, Krause Publications, 2003. 1st edition. High-quality color photography 224 pp., color illus. Hardcover. $36.95

This is the most comprehensive and valuable guide on the market devoted exclusively to shotguns. Part buyer's guide, part technical manual, and part loving tribute, shooters and hunters of all skill levels will enjoy this comprehensive reference tool.

Spanish Best: The Fine Shotguns of Spain, 2nd Edition, by Terry Wieland, Down East Books, Traverse City, MI, 2001. 364 pp., illus. $60.00

A practical source of information for owners of Spanish shotguns and a guide for those considering buying a used shotgun.

Streetsweepers: The Complete Book of Combat Shotguns, Revised and Updated Edition, by Duncan Long, Boulder Co, Paladin Press, 2004. illus., 224 pp. Soft cover. $35.00

Including how to choose the right gauge and shot, decipher the terminology and use special-purpose rounds such as flechettes and tear-gas projectiles; and gives expert instruction on customizing shotguns, telling you what you must know about the assault weapon ban before you choose or modify your gun.

Successful Shotgunning; How to Build Skill in the Field and Take More Birds in Competition, by Peter F. Blakeley, Mechanicsburg, PA, Stackpole Books, 2003. 1st edition. 305 pp., illustrated with 119 b&w photos & 4-page color section with 8 photos. Hardcover. $24.95

Successful Shotgunning focuses on wing-shooting and sporting clays techniques.

Tactical Shotgun, The, by Gabriel Suzrez, Paladin Press, Boulder, CO, 1996. 232 pp., illus. Paper covers. $25.00

The best techniques and tactics for employing the shotgun in personal combat.

Trapshooting is a Game of Opposites, by Dick Bennett, Shotgun Sports, Inc., Auburn, CA, 1996. 129 pp., illus. Paper covers. $19.95

Discover everything you need to know about shooting trap like the pros.

U.S. Winchester Trench and Riot Guns and Other U.S. Military Combat Shotguns, by Joe Poyer, North Cape Publications, Tustin, CA, 1992. 124 pp., illus. Paper covers. $15.95

A detailed history of the use of military shotguns, and the acquisition procedures used by the U.S. Army's Ordnance Department in both world wars.

Uncle Dan Lefever, Master Gunmaker: Guns of Lasting Fame, by Robert W. Elliott, privately printed, 2002. Profusely illustrated with b&w photos, with a 45-page color section. 239 pp. Handsomely bound, with gilt titled spine and top cover. Hardcover. $60.00

Winchester Model 12 Assembly, Disassembly Manual, by Skennerton & Riling, Ray Riling Arms Books Co. Philadelphia, PA 2004. 36 pages, over 60 photos & line drawings. $5.00

Ideal workshop reference for stripping & assembly with exploded parts drawings, specifications, service accessories, historical information and recommended reading references. Ideal workbook for shooters and collectors alike. Triple saddle-stitched binding with durable plastic laminated cover makes this an ideal workshop guide.

Winchester Model Twelve, by George Madis, Art and Reference House, Dallas, TX, 1982. 176 pp., illus. $26.95

A definitive work on this famous American shotgun.

Winchester Model 97 Assembly, Disassembly Manual, by Skennerton & Riling, Ray Riling Arms Books Co. Philadelphia, PA 2004. 36 pages, over 60 photos & line drawings. $5.00

Ideal workshop reference for stripping & assembly with exploded parts drawings, specifications, service accessories, historical information and recommended reading references. Ideal workbook for shooters and collectors alike. Triple saddle-stitched binding with durable plastic laminated cover makes this an ideal workshop guide.

World's Fighting Shotguns, by Thomas F. Swearengen, T.B.N. Enterprises, Alexandria, VA, 1998. 500 pp., illus. $59.95

The complete military and police reference work from the shotgun's inception to date, with up-to-date developments.

MANUFACTURER'S AND PRODUCT DIRECTORY

A

A. Uberti S.p.A., Via Artigiana 1, Gardone Val Trompia, Brescia 25063, ITALY, P: 011 390308341800, F: 011 390308341801, www.ubertireplicas.it
Firearms

A.R.M.S., Inc./Atlantic Research Marketing Systems, Inc., 230 W. Center St., West Bridgewater, MA 02379, P: 508-584-7816, F: 508-588-8045, www.armsmounts.com
Scopes, Sights and Accessories

AA & E Leathercraft, 107 W. Gonzales St., Yoakum, TX 77995, P: 800-331-9092, F: 361-293-9127, www.tandybrands.com
Bags & Equipment Cases; Custom Manufacturing; Hunting Accessories; Knives/Knife Cases; Leathergoods; Shooting Range Equipment; Sports Accessories

ACIGI / Fujiiryoki, 4399 Ingot St., Fremong, CA 94538, P: 888-816-0888, F: 510-651-6188, www.fujichair.com
Wholesaler/Distributor

ACR Electronics, Inc., 5757 Ravenswood Rd., Ft. Lauderdale, FL 33312, P: 800-432-0227, F: 954-983-5087, www.acrelectronics.com
Backpacking; Hunting Accessories; Lighting Products; Sports Accessories; Survival Kits/First Aid; Training and Safety Equipment

Accro-Met, Inc., 3406 Westwood Industrial Drive, Monroe, NC 28110, P: 800-543-4755, F: 704-283-2112, www.accromet.com
Gun Barrels; Wholesaler/Distributor

Accu-Fire, Inc., P.O. Box 121990, Arlington, TX 76012, P: 888-MUZZLEMATE, F: 817-303-4505
Firearms Maintenance Equipment

Accu-Shot/B&T Industries, LLC, P.O. Box 771071, Wichita, KS 67277, P: 316-721-3222, F: 316-721-1021, www.accu-shot.com
Gun Grips & Stocks; Hunting Accessories; Law Enforcement; Scopes, Sights & Accessories; Shooting Range Equipment; Sports Accessories; Training and Safety Equipment

Accuracy International North America, Inc., 35100 North State Highway, Mingus, TX 76463-6405, P: 907-440-4024, www.accuracyinternational.org
Firearms; Firearms Maintenance Equipment; Law Enforcement; Magazines, Cartridge; Scopes, Sights & Accessories; Wholesaler/Distributor

AccuSharp Knife Sharpeners/Fortune Products, Inc., 205 Hickory Creek Road, Marble Falls, TX 78654, P: 800-742-7797, F: 800-600-5373, www.accusharp.com
Archery; Camping; Cooking Equipment/Accessories; Cutlery; Hunting Accessories; Knives/Knife Cases; Sharpeners; Sports Accessories

Action Target, P.O. Box 636, Provo, UT 84603-0636, P: 888-377-8033, F: 801-377-8096, www.actiontarget.com
Law Enforcement; Shooting Range Equipment; Targets; Training & Safety Equipment

AcuSport Corp., One Hunter Place, Bellefontaine, OH 43311, P: 800-543-3150, www.acusport.com
Ammunition; Black Powder Accessories; Firearms; Hunting Accessories; Online Services; Retailer Services; Scopes, Sights & Accessories; Wholesaler/Distributor

Adams Arms/Retrofit Piston Systems, 255 Hedden Court, Palm Harbor, FL 34681, P: 727-853-0550, F: 727-353-0551, www.arisfix.com

ADCO Arms Co., Inc., 4 Draper St., Woburn, MA 01801, P: 800-775-3687, F: 781-935-1011, www.adcosales.com
Ammunition; Firearms; Paintball Accessories; Scopes, Sights & Accessories

ADS, Inc., Pinehurst Centre, 477 Viking Dr., Suite 350, Virginia Beach, VA 23452, P: 800-948-9433, F: 757-481-2039, www.adstactical.com

ADSTAR, Inc., 1390 Jerusalem Ave., North Merrick, NY 11566, P: 516-483-1800, F: 516-483-2590
Emblems & Decals; Outdoor Art, Jewelry, Sculpture

Advanced Armament Corp., 1434 Hillcrest Rd., Norcross, GA 30093, P: 770-925-9988, F: 770-925-9989, www.advanced-armament.com
Firearms; Hearing Protection; Law Enforcement

Advanced Engineered Systems, Inc., 14328 Commercial Parkway, South Beloit, IL 61080, P: 815-624-7797, F: 815-624-8198, www.advengsys.com
Ammunition; Custom Manufacturing

Advanced Technology International, 2733 W. Carmen Ave., Milwaukee, WI 53209, P: 800-925-2522, F: 414-664-3112, www.atigunstocks.com
Books/Industry Publications; Gun Grips & Stocks; Gun Parts/Gunsmithing; Hunting Accessories; Law Enforcement; Scopes, Sights & Accessories

Advanced Training Systems, 4524 Highway 61 North, St. Paul, MN 55110, P: 651-429-8091, F: 651-429-8702, www.duelatron.com
Law Enforcement; Shooting Range Equipment; Targets; Training & Safety Equipment

Advantage® Camouflage, P.O. Box 9638, Columbus, GA 31908, P: 800-992-9968, F: 706-569-9346, www.advantagecamo.com
Camouflage

Advantage Tactical Sight/WrenTech Industries, LLC, 7 Avenida Vista Grande B-7, Suite 510, Sante Fe, NM 87508, F: 310-316-6413 or 505-466-1811, F: 505-466-4735, www.advantagetactical.com
Scopes, Sights & Accessories

Adventure Action Gear/+VENTURE Heated Clothing, 5932 Bolsa Ave., Suite 103, Huntington Beach, CA 92649, P: 310-412-1070, F: 610-423-5257, www.ventureheat.com
Men & Women's Clothing; Export/Import Specialists; Footwear; Gloves, Mitts, Hats; Sports Accessories; Vehicles, Utility & Rec.; Wholesaler/Distributor

Adventure Lights, Inc., 444 Beaconsfield Blvd., Suite 201, Beaconsfield, Quebec H9W 4C1, CANADA, P: 514-694-8477, F: 514-694-2353

Adventure Medical Kits, P.O. Box 43309, Oakland, CA 94624, P: 800-324-3517, F: 510-261-7419, www.adventuremedicalkits.com
Backpacking; Books/Industry Publications; Camping; Custom Manufacturing; Hunting Accessories; Sports Accessories; Survival Kits/First Aid; Training & Safety Equipment

AE Light/Div. of Allsman Enterprises, LLC, P.O. Box 1869, Rogue River, OR 97537, P: 541-471-8988, F: 888-252-1473, www.aelight.com
Camping; Custom Manufacturing; Hunting Accessories; Law Enforcement; Lighting Products; Wholesaler/Distributor

AES Optics, 201 Corporate Court, Senatobia, MS 38668, P: 800-416-0866, F: 662-301-4739, www.aesoutdoors.com
Eyewear

Aetco, Inc., 2825 Metropolitan Place, Pomona, CA 91767, P: 800-982-5258, F: 800-451-2434, www.aetcoinc.com
Firearms; Hearing Protection; Holsters; Law Enforcement; Leathergoods; Lighting Products; Training & Safety Equipment; Wholesaler/Distributor

Africa Sport Hunting Safaries, 11265 E. Edison St., Tucson, AZ 85749, P: 520-440-5384, F: 520-885-8032, www.africasporthuntingsafaris.com
Archery; Outdoor Art, Jewelry, Sculpture; Outfitter; Tours/Travel

AFTCO Bluewater/Al Agnew, 17351 Murphy Ave., Irvine, CA 92614, P: 949-660-8757, F: 949-660-7067, www.aftcobluewater.com

Aftermath Miami/Stunt Studios, 3911 Southwest 47th Ave., Suite 914, Davie, FL 33314, P: 954-581-5822, F: 954-581-3165, www.aftermathairsoft.com
Airsoft Guns & Accessories

Aguila Ammunition/Centurion Ordnance, Inc., 11614 Rainbow Ridge, Helotes, TX 78023, P: 210-695-4602, F: 210-695-4603, www.aguilaammo.com
Ammunition

Aimpoint, Inc., 14103 Mariah Court, Chantilly, VA 20151, 877-246-7646, F: 703-263-9463, www.aimpoint.com
Scopes, Sights & Accessories

AimShot/Osprey International, Inc., 25 Hawks Farm Rd., White, GA 30184, P: 888-448-3247, F: 770-387-0114, www.aimshot.com, www.miniosprey.com
Archery; Binoculars; Holsters; Hunting Accessories; Law Enforcement; Lighting Products; Scopes, Sights & Accessories; Wholesaler/Distributor

Aimtech Mount Systems, P.O. Box 223, Thomasville, GA 31799-0223, P: 229-226-4313, F: 229-227-0222, www.aimtech-mounts.com
Hunting Accessories; Scopes, Sights & Accessories

Air Gun, Inc., 9320 Harwin Dr., Houston, TX 77036, P: 800-456-0022, F: 713-780-4831, www.airrifle-china.com
Airguns; Ammunition; Hunting Accessories; Scopes, Sights & Accessories; Wholesaler/Distributor

AirForce Airguns, P.O. Box 2478, Fort Worth, TX 76113, P: 877-247-4867, F: 817-451-1613, www.airforceairguns.com
Airguns; Hunting Accessories; Law Enforcement; Scopes, Sights & Accessories

Aitec Co., Ltd., Export Dept., Rm. 817, Crystal Beach ok, Jung Dong Haeundae-Gu Busan, 612 010, SOUTH KOREA, P: 011 82517416497, F: 011 82517462194, www.aitec.co.kr

Lighting Products

Ajax Custom Grips, Inc./Ajax Shooter Supply, 9130 Viscount Row, Dallas, TX 75247, P: 800-527-7537, F: 214-630-4942, www.ajaxgrips.com
Gun Grips & Stocks; Gun Parts/Gunsmithing; Holsters; Law Enforcement; Lighting Products; Magazines, Cartridge; Wholesaler/Distributor

AKDAL/Ucyildiz Arms Ind./Blow & Voltran, Bostanci Cd. Uol Sk. No: 14/A, Y. Dudullu-Umraniye, Istanbul, 34775, TURKEY, P: 011-90 216527671011, F: 011-90 2165276705, www.akdalarms.com, www.voltranarms.com
Airguns; Firearms

Aker International, Inc., 2248 Main St., Suite 6, Chula Vista, CA 91911, P: 800-645-AKER, F: 888-300-AKER, www.akerleather.com
Holsters; Hunting Accessories; Law Enforcement; Leathergoods

Al Mar Knives, P.O. Box 2295, Tualatin, OR 97062, P: 503-670-9080, www.almarknives.com
Custom Manufacturing, Knives/Knife Cases

Alexander Arms, U.S. Army Radford Arsenal, Radford, VA 24141, P: 540-639-8356, F: 540-639-8353, www.alexanderarms.com
Ammunition; Firearms; Magazine, Cartridges; Reloading

All-Star Apparel, 6722 Vista Del Mar Ave., Suite C. La Jolla, CA 92037, P: 858-205-7827, F: 858-225-3544, www.all-star.ws
Camouflage; Men & Women's Clothing; Gloves, Mitts, Hats

All Weather Outerwear, 34 35th St., Brooklym, NY 11232, P: 800-965-6550, F: 718-788-2205
Camouflage; Men's Clothing

AllClear, LLC dba Auspit Rotisserie BBQ's, 2050 Russett Way, Carson City, NV 89703, P: 775-468-5665, F: 775-546-6091, www.auspitbbq.com

Allen Company, 525 Burbank St., P.O. Box 445, Broomfield, CO 80020, P: 800-876-8600, F: 303-466-7437, www.allencompany.net
Archery; Black Powder Accessories; Eyewear; Gun Cases; Hearing Protection; Hunting Accessories; Scopes, Sights & Accessories; Shooting Range Equipment

Alliant Powder/ATK Commercial Products, Route 114, Building 229, P.O. Box 6, Radford, VA 24143, P: 800-276-9337, F: 540-639-8496, www.alliantpowder.com
Reloading

Alot Enterprise Company, Ltd., 1503 Eastwood Centre, 5 A Kung Ngam Village Rd., Shaukeiwan, HONG KONG, P: 011 85225199728, F: 011 85225190122, www.alothk.com
Binoculars; Compasses; Eyewear; Hunting Accessories; Photographic Equipment; Scopes, Sights, & Accessories; Sports Accessories; Telescopes

Alpen Outdoor Corp., 10329 Dorset St., Rancho Cucamonga, CA 91730, P: 877-987-8379, F: 909-987-8661, www.alpenoutdoor.com
Backpacking; Binoculars; Camping; Hunting Accessories; Scopes, Sights & Accessories; Shooting Range Equipment; Sports Accessories, Wholesaler/Distributor

Alpine Archery, P.O. Box 319, Lewiston, ID 83501, P: 208-746-4717, F: 208-746-1635

ALPS Mountaineering, 1 White Pine, New Haven, MO 63068, P: 800-344-2577, F: 573-459-2044, www.alpsouthdoorz.com
Backpacking; Camouflage; Camping; Hunting Accessories; Sports Accessories

ALS Technologies, Inc., 1103 Central Blvd., P.O. Box 525, Bull Shoals, AR 72619, P: 877-902-4257, F: 870-445-8746, www.alslesslethal.com
Ammunition; Firearms; Gun Parts/Gunsmithing; Law Enforcement; Training & Safety Equipment

Alta Industries, 1460 Cader Lane, Petaluma, CA 94954, P: 707-347-2900, F: 707-347-2950, www.altaindustries.com

Altama Footwear, 1200 Lake Hearn Dr., Suite 475, Atlanta, GA 30319, P: 800-437-9888, F: 404-260-2889, www.altama.com
Footwear; Law Enforcement

Altamont Co., 291 N. Church St., P.O. Box 309, Thomasboro, IL 61878, P: 800-626-5774, F: 217-643-7973, www.altamontco.com
Gun Grips & Stocks

AlumaGrips, 2851 N. 34th Place, Mesa, AZ 85213, P: 602-690-5459, F: 480-807-3955
Firearms Maintenance Equipment; Gun Grips & Stocks; Gun Parts/Gunsmithing; Law Enforcement

AmChar Wholesale, Inc., 100 Airpark Dr., Rochester, NY 14624, P: 585-328-3951, F: 585-328-3749, www.amchar. com

American COP Magazine/FMG Publications, 12345 World Trade Dr., San Diego, CA 92128, P: 800-537-3006, F: 858-605-0247, www.americancopmagazine.com
Books/Industry Publications; Law Enforcement; Videos

American Cord & Webbing Co., Inc., 88 Century Dr., Woonsocket, RI 02895, P: 401-762-5500, F: 401-762-5514, www.acw1.com
Archery; Backpacking; Bags & Equipment Cases; Custom Manufacturing; Law Enforcement; Pet Supplies

American Defense Systems, Inc., 230 Duffy Ave., Hicksville, NY 11801, P: 516-390-5300, F: 516-390-5308, www. adsiarmor.com
Custom Manufacturing; Shooting Range Equipment; Training & Safety Equipment

American Furniture Classics/Div. of Dawson Heritage Furniture, P.O. Box 111, Webb City, MO 64870, P: 888-673-9080, F: 417-673-9081, www. americanfurnitureclassics.com
Gun Cabinets/Racks/Safes; Gun Cases; Home Furnishings

American Gunsmithing Institute (AGI), 1325 Imola Ave. West, P.O. Box 504, Napa, CA 94559, P: 800-797-0867, F: 707-253-7149, www.americangunsmith.com
Books/Industry Publications; Computer Software; Firearms Maintenance Equipment; Gun Parts/ Gunsmithing; Videos

American Pioneer Powder, Inc., 20423 State Road 7, Suite F6-268, Boca Raton, FL 33498, P: 888-756-7693, F: 888-766-7693, www.americanpioneerpowder.com
Black Powder/Smokeless Powder; Reloading

American Plastics/SEWIT, 1225 N. MacArthur Drive, Suite 200, Tracy, CA 95376, P: 209-834-0287, F: 209-834-0924, www.americanplastics.com
Backpacking; Bags & Equipment Cases; Export/ Import Specialists; Gun Cases; Holsters; Hunting Accessories; Survival Kits/First Aid; Wholesaler/ Distributor

American Security Products Co., 11925 Pacific Ave., Fontana, CA 92337, P: 800-421-6142, F: 951-685-9685, www. amsecusa.com
Gun Cabinets/Racks/Safes

American Tactical Imports, 100 Airpark Dr., Rochester, NY 14624, P: 585-328-3951, F: 585-328-3749

American Technologies Network, Corp./ATN, Corp., 1341 San Mateo Ave., South San Francisco, CA 94080, P: 800-910-2862, F: 650-875-0129, www.atncorp.com
Binoculars; Law Enforcement; Lighting Products; Photographic Equipment; Scopes, Sights & Accessories; Telescopes

Americase, Inc., 1610 E. Main St., Waxahachie, TX 75165, P: 800-972-2737, F: 972-937-8373, www.americase.com
Bags & Equipment Cases; Custom Manufacturing; Gun Cases; Hunting Accessories

AmeriGlo, 5579-B Chamblee Dunwoody Rd., Suite 214, Atlanta, GA 30338, P: 770-390-0554, F: 770-390-9781, www.ameriglo.com
Camping; Law Enforcement; Lighting Products; Scopes, Sights & Accessories; Survival Kits/First Aid; Training & Safety Equipment

Ameristep, 901 Tacoma Court, Clio, MI 48420, P: 800-374-7837, F: 810-686-7121, www.ameristep.com
Archery; Blinds; Hunting Accessories; Training & Safety Equipment; Treestands

Ammo-Loan Worldwide, 815 D, Lewiston, ID 83501, P: 208-746-7012, F: 208-746-1703

Ammo-Up, 10601 Theresa Dr., Jacksonville, FL 32246, P: 800-940-2688, F: 904-645-5918, www.ammoupusa.com
Shooting Range Equipment

AMT/Auto Mag Co./C.G., Inc., 5200 Mitchelldale, Suite E17, Houston, TX 77092, P: 713-686-3232, F: 713-681-5665

Anglers Book Supply/Hunters & Shooters Book & DVD Catalog, 1380 W. 2nd Ave., Eugene, OR 97402, P: 800-260-3869, F: 541-342-1785, www.anglersbooksupply.com
Books/Industry Publications; Computer Software; Videos; Wholesaler/Distributor

ANXO-Urban Body Armor Corp., 7359 Northwest 34 St., Miami, FL 33122, P: 866-514-ANXO, F: 305-593-5498, www.urbanbodyarmor.com
Men & Women's Clothing; Custom Manufacturing; Law Enforcement

Apple Creek Whitetails, 14109 Cty. Rd. VV, Gillett, WI 54124, P: 920-598-0154, F: 920-855-1773, www. applecreekwhitetails.com

ARC/ArcticShield, Inc./X-System, 1700 West Albany, Suite A, Broken Arrow, OK 74012, P: 877-974-4353, F: 918-258-8790, www.arcoutdoors.com
Footwear; Hunting Accessories; Scents & Lures; Sports Accessories

Arc'Teryx, 100-2155 Dollarton Hwy., North Vancouver, British Columbia V7H 3B2, CANADA, P: 604-960-3001, F: 604-904-3692, www.arcteryx.com
Backpacking; Camouflage; Men's Clothing; Custom Manufacturing; Gloves, Mitts, Hats; Law Enforcement; Outfitter

Arctic Adventures, 19950 Clark Graham, Baie D'urfe, Quebec H9X 3R8, CANADA, P: 800-465-9474, F: 514-457-9834, www.arcticadventures.ca
Outfitter

Ares Defense Systems, Inc., P.O. Box 10667, Blacksburg, VA 24062, P: 540-639-8633, F: 540-639-8634, www. aresdefense.com
Firearms; Gun Parts/Gunsmithing; Law Enforcement; Lighting Products; Magazines, Cartridge; Scopes, Sights & Accessories; Shooting Range Equipment; Survival Kits/First Aid

Argentina Ducks & Doves LLC, P.O. Box 129, Pittsview, AL 36871, P: 334-855-9474, F: 334-855-9474, www. argentinaducksanddoves.com
Outfitter; Tours/Travel

ArmaLite, Inc., 745 S. Hanford St., Geneseo, IL 61254, P: 309-944-6939, F: 309-944-6949, www.armalite.com
Firearms; Firearms Maintenance Equipment

Armament Technology, Inc./ELCAN Optical Technologies, 3045 Robie St., Suite 113, Halifax, Nova Scotia B3K 4P6, CANADA, P: 902-454-6384, F: 902-454-4641, www. armament.com
International Exhibitors; Law Enforcement; Scopes, Sights & Accessories; Telescopes; Wholesaler/ Distributor

Armatix GmbH, Feringastrabe. 4, Unterfohring, D 85774, GERMANY, P: 011 498999228140, F: 011 498999228228, www.armatix.de

Armi Sport di Chiappa Silvia e C. SNC-Chiappa Firearms, Via Milano, 2, Azzano Mella (Bs), 25020, ITALY, P: 011-39 0309749065, F: 011-39 0309749232, www. chiappafirearms.com
Black Powder Accessories; Firearms; International Exhibitors

Armor Express, 1554 E. Torch Lake Dr., P.O. Box 21, Central Lake, MI 49622, P: 866-357-3845, F: 231-544-6734, www. armorexpress.com
Law Enforcement

Armorshield USA, LLC, 30 ArmorShield Dr., Stearns, KY 42647, P: 800-386-9455, F: 800-392-9455, www. armorshield.net
Law Enforcement

Arms Corp. of the Philippines/Armscor Precision International, Armscorp Ave., Bgy Fortune, Marikina City, 1800, PHILIPPINES, P: 011 6329416243, F: 011 6329420682, www.armscor.com.ph
Airguns; Ammunition; Bags & Equipment Cases; Custom Manufacturing; Firearms; Gun Barrels; Gun Parts/Gunsmithing; International Exhibitors

Arms Tech, Ltd., 5025 North Central Ave., Suite 459, Phoenix, AZ 85012, P: 602-272-9045, F: 602-272-1922, www. armstechltd.com
Firearms; Law Enforcement

Arno Bernard Custom Knives, 19 Duiker St., Bethlehem, 9700, SOUTH AFRICA, P: 011 27583033196, F: 011 27583033196

Arrieta, mankaiko, 5, Elgoibar, (Guipuzcoa) 20870, SPAIN, P: 011-34 943743150, F: 011-34 943743154, www. arrietashotguns.com
Firearms

Arrow Precision, LLC, 2750 W. Gordon St., Allentown, PA 18104, P: 610-437-7138, F: 610-437-7139, www.arrow-precision.com
Archery; Crossbows & Accessories; Paintballs, Guns & Accessories

ARS Business Solutions, LLC, 940 Industrial Dr., Suite 107, Sauk Rapids, MN 56379, P: 800-547-7120, www.arss.com
Computer Software; Retailer Services

Arsenal, Inc., 3300 S. Decatur Blvd., Suite 10632, Las Vegas, NV 89102, P: 888-539-2220, F: 702-643-8860, www. arsenalinc.com
Firearms

Artistic Plating Co., 405 W. Cherry St., Milwaukee, WI 53212, P: 414-271-8138, F: 414-271-5541, www.artisticplating.net
Airguns; Ammunition; Archery; Cutlery; Firearms; Game Calls; Gun Barrels; Reloading

ARY, Inc., 10301 Hickman Mills Dr., Suite 110, Kansas City, MO 64137, P: 800-821-7849, F: 816-761-0055, www. aryinc.com
Cutlery; Knives/Knife Cases

ASAT Outdoors, LLC, 307 E. Park Ave., Suite 207A, Anaconda, MT 59711, P: 406-563-9336, F: 406-563-7315
Archery; Blinds; Camouflage; Men's Clothing; Gloves, Mitts, Hats; Hunting Accessories; Law Enforcement; Paintball Accessories

Ashbury International Group, Inc., P.O. Box 8024, Charlottesville, VA 22906, P: 434-296-8600, F: 434-296-9260, www.ashburyintlgroup.com

Camouflage; Firearms; Law Enforcement; Scopes, Sights & Accessories; Wholesaler/Distributor

Asociacion Armera, P. I Azitain, 2-J, P.O. Box 277, Eibar, Guipúzcoa 20600, SPAIN, P: 011 34943208493, F: 011 34943700966, www.a-armera.com
Associations/Agencies

ASP, Inc., 2511 E. Capitol Dr., Appleton, WI 54911, P: 800-236-6243, F: 800-236-8601, www.asp-usa.com
Law Enforcement; Lighting Products; Training & Safety Equipment

A-Square Company/A-Square of South Dakota, LLC, 302 Antelope Dr., Chamberlain, SD 57325, P: 605-234-0500, F: 605-234-0510, www.asquareco.com
Ammunition; Books/Industry Publications; Firearms; Reloading

Astra Radio Communications, 2238 N. Glassell St., Suite D., Orange, CA 92865, P: 714-637-2828, F: 714-637-2669, www.arcmics.com
Two-Way Radios

Atak Arms Ind., Co. Ltd., Imes San. Sit. A Blok 107, Sk. No: 70, Y. Dudullu, Umraniye, Istanbul, 34775 TURKEY, P: +902164203996, F: +902164203998, www.atakarms.com
Airguns; Firearms; Training & Safety Equipment

Atascosa Wildlife Supply, 1204 Zanderson Ave., Jourdanton, TX 78026, P: 830-769-9711, F: 830-769-1001

ATK/ATK Commercial Products, 900 Ehlen Dr., Anoka, MN 55303, P: 800-322-2342, F: 763-323-2506, www.atk.com
Ammunition; Binoculars; Clay Targets; Firearms Maintenance Equipment; Reloading; Scopes, Sights & Accessories; Shooting Range Equipment; Targets

ATK /ATK Law Enforcement, 2299 Snake River Ave., Lewiston, ID 83501, P: 800-627-3640, F: 208-798-3392, www.atk. com
Ammunition; Bags & Equipment Cases; Binoculars; Firearms Maintenance Equipment; Reloading; Scopes, Sights & Accessories

Atlanco, 1125 Hayes Industrial Dr., Marietta, GA 30062-2471, P: 800-241-9414, F: 770-427-9011, www.truspec.com
Camouflage; Men's Clothing; Custom Manufacturing; Law Enforcement; Wholesaler/Distributor

Atlanta Cutlery Corp., 2147 Gees Mill Rd., Conyers, GA 30013, P: 800-883-8838, F: 770-760-8993, www. atlantacutlery.com
Custom Manufacturing; Cutlery; Firearms; Holsters; Knives/Knife Cases; Leathergoods; Wholesaler/ Distributor

Atlas Glove Consumer Products/LFS, Inc., 851 Coho Way, Bellingham, WA 98225, P: 800-426-8860, F: 888-571-8175, www.lfsinc.com/atlasoutdoor
Gloves, Mitts, Hats

Atsko, 2664 Russel St., Orangeburg, SC 29115, P: 800-845-2728, F: 803-531-2139, www.atsko.com
Archery; Backpacking; Camouflage; Camping; Custom Manufacturing; Hunting Accessories; Scents & Lures

AuctionArms.com, Inc., 3031 Alhambra Dr., Suite 101, Cameron Park, CA 95682, P: 877-GUN-AUCTION, F: 530-676-2497, www.auctionarms.com
Airguns; Archery; Black Powder Accessories; Black Powder/Smokeless Powder; Camping; Firearms; Online Services

Autumnwood Wool Outfitters, Inc., 828 Upper Pennsylvania Ave., Bangor, PA 18013, P: 610-588-5744, F: 610-588-4868, www.autumnwoodoutfitters.com

Avon Protection Systems, 1369 Brass Mill Rd., Suite A, Belcamp, MD 21017, P: 888-286-6440, F: 410-273-0126, www.avon-protection.com
Law Enforcement; Training & Safety Equipment

A-Way Hunting Products (MI), 3230 Calhoun Rd., P.O. Box 492, Beaverton, MI, 48612, P: 989-435-3879, F: 989-435-8960, www.awayhunting.com
Decoys; Game Calls; Scents & Lures; Videos

AWC Systems Technology, 1515 W. Deer Valley Rd., Suite A-105, Phoenix, AZ 85027, P: 623-780-1050, F: 800-897-5708, www.awcsystech.com

AyA-Aguirre Y Aranzabal, Avda. Otaola, 25-3a Planta, Eibar, (Guipúzcoa) 20600, SPAIN, P: 011-34-943-820437, F: 011-34-943-200133, www.aya-fineguns.com
Firearms

B

B-Square/Div. Armor Holdings, Inc., 8909 Forum Way, Fort Worth, TX 76140, P: 800-433-2909, F: 817-926-7012

BAM Wuxi Bam Co., Ltd., No 37 Zhongnan Rd., Wuxi, JiangSu 214024, CHINA, P: 011-86 51085432361, FL 011-86 51085401258, www.china-bam.com
Airguns; Gun Cases; Scopes, Sights & Accessories

BCS International, 1819 St. George St., Green Bay, WI 54302, P: 888-965-3700, F: 888-965-3701
Bags & Equipment Cases; Camouflage; Men & Women's Clothing; Export/Import Specialists; Leathergoods

B.E. Meyers, 14540 Northeast 91st St., Redmond, WA 98052, P: 800-327-5648, F: 425-867-1759, www.bemeyers.com
Custom Manufacturing; Law Enforcement

B & F System, Inc., The, 3920 S. Walton Walker Blvd., Dallas, TX 75236, P: 214-333-2111, F: 214-333-2137, www.bnfusa.com
Binoculars; Cooking Equipment/Accessories; Cutlery; Gloves, Mitts, Hats; Leathergoods; Scopes, Sights & Accessories; Telescopes; Wholesaler/Distributor

BOGgear, LLC, 111 W. Cedar Lane, Suite A, Payson, AZ 85541, P: 877-264-7637, F: 505-292-9130, www.boggear.com
Binoculars; Firearms; Hunting Accessories; Law Enforcement; Outfitter; Photographic Equipment; Shooting Range Equipment; Training & Safety Equipment

BSA Optics, 3911 S.W. 47th Ave., Suite 914, Ft. Lauderdale, FL 33314, P: 954-581-2144, F: 954-581-3165, www.bsaoptics.com
Binoculars; Scopes, Sights & Accessories; Sports Accessories; Telescopes

B.S.N. Technology Srl, Via Guido Rossa, 46/52, Cellatica (Bs), 25060, ITALY, P: 011 390302522436, F: 011 390302520946, www.bsn.it
Ammunition; Gun Barrels; Reloading

Bad Boy, Inc., 102 Industrial Dr., Batesville, AR 72501, P: 870-698-0090, F: 870-698-2123

Bad Boy Enterprises, LLC/Bad Boy Buggies, 2 River Terminal Rd., P.O. Box 19087, Natchez, MS 39122, P: 866-678-6701, F: 601-442-6707, www.badboybuggies.com
Vehicles, Utility & Rec

Badger Barrels, Inc., 8330 196 Ave., P.O. Box 417, Bristol, WI 53104, P: 262-857-6950, F: 262-857-6988, www.badgerbarrelsinc.com
Gun Barrels

Badger Ordnance, 1141 Swift St., North Kansas City, MO 64116, P: 816-421-4956, F: 816-421-4958, www.badgerordnance.com
Custom Manufacturing; Firearms; Firearms Maintenance Equipment; Gun Parts/Gunsmithing; Law Enforcement; Magazines, Cartridge; Scopes, Sights & Accessories; Telescopes

Badland Beauty, LLC, P.O. Box 151507, Lufkin, TX 75915, P: 936-875-5522, F: 936-875-5525, www.badlandbeauty.com
Women's Clothing

BAE Systems/Mobility & Protection Systems, 13386 International Parkway, Jacksonville, FL 32218, P: 904-741-5600, F: 904-741-9996, www.baesystems.com
Bags & Equipment Cases; Black Powder/Smokeless Powder; Gloves, Mitts, Hats; Holsters; Hunting Accessories; Law Enforcement; Scopes, Sights & Accessories; Training & Safety Equipment

Bandera/Cal-Bind, 1315 Fernbridge Dr., Fortuna, CA 95540, P: 866-226-3378, F: 707-725-1156, www.banderausa.com
Archery; Hunting Accessories; Leathergoods; Sports Accessories; Wholesaler/Distributor

Barbour, Inc., 55 Meadowbrook Dr., Milford, NH 03055-4613, P: 800-338-3474, F: 603-673-6510, www.barbour.com
Bags & Equipment Cases; Men & Women's Clothing; Footwear; Gloves, Mitts, Hats; Leathergoods

Bardin & Marsee Publishing, 1112 N. Shadesview Terrace, Birmingham, AL 35209, P: 205-453-4361, F: 404-474-3086, www.theoutdoorbible.com
Books/Industry Publications

Barnaul Cartridge Plant CJSC, 28 Kulagina St., Barnaul, 656002, RUSSIAN FEDERATION, P: 011 0073852774391, F: 011 0073852771608, www.ab.ru/~stanok
Ammunition

Barnes Bullets, Inc., P.O. Box 620, Mona, UT 84645, P: 801-756-4222, F: 801-756-2465, www.barnesbullets.com
Black Powder Accessories; Computer Software; Custom Manufacturing; Hunting Accessories; Law Enforcement; Recoil Protection Devices & Services; Reloading

Barnett Outdoors, LLC, 13447 Byrd Dr., P.O. Box 934, Odessa, FL 33556, P: 800-237-4507, F: 813-920-5400, www.barnettcrossbows.com
Archery; Crossbows & Accessories; Sports Accessories

Baron Technology, Inc./Baron Engraving, 62 Spring Hill Rd., Trumbull, CT 06611, P: 203-452-0515, F: 203-452-0663, www.baronengraving.com
Custom Manufacturing; Cutlery; Firearms; Gun Parts/Gunsmithing; Knives/Knife Cases; Law Enforcement; Outdoor Art, Jewelry, Sculpture; Sports Accessories

Barrett Firearms Mfg., Inc., P.O. Box 1077, Murfreesboro, TN 37133, P: 615-896-2938, F: 615-896-7313, www.barrettrifles.com
Firearms

Barska Optics, 1721 Wright Ave., La Verne, CA 91750, P: 909-445-8168, F: 909-445-8169, www.barska.com

Bates Footwear/Div. Wolverine World Wide, Inc., 9341 Courtland Dr., Rockford, MI 49351, P: 800-253-2184, F: 616-866-5658, www.batesfootwear.com

Footwear; Law Enforcement

Battenfeld Technologies, Inc., 5885 W. Van Horn Tavern Rd., Columbia, MO 65203, P: 877-509-9160, F: 573-446-6606, www.battenfeldtechnologies.com
Firearms Maintenance Equipment; Gun Grips & Stocks; Gun Parts/Gunsmithing; Hearing Protection; Recoil Protection Devices & Services; Reloading; Shooting Range Equipment; Targets

Battle Lake Outdoors, 203 W. Main, P.O. Box 548, Clarissa, MN 56440, P: 800-243-0465, F: 218-756-2426, www.battlelakeoutdoors.com
Archery; Backpacking; Bags & Equipment Cases; Black Powder Accessories; Camping; Gun Cases; Hunting Accessories; Law Enforcement

Batz Corp., 1524 Highway 291 North, P.O. Box 130, Prattsville, AR 72129, P: 800-637-7627, F: 870-699-4420, www.batzusa.com
Backpacking; Camping; Custom Manufacturing; Hunting Accessories; Knives/Knife Cases; Lighting Products; Pet Supplies; Retail Packaging

Bayco Products, Inc., 640 S. Sanden Blvd., Wylie, TX 75098, P: 800-233-2155, F: 469-326-9401, www.baycoproducts.com

Beamshot-Quarton USA, Inc., 5805 Callaghan Rd., Suite 102, San Antonio, TX 78228, P: 800-520-8435, F: 210-735-1326, www.beamshot.com
Airguns; Archery; Crossbows & Accessories; Hunting Accessories; Law Enforcement; Lighting Products; Paintball Accessories; Scopes, Sights & Accessories

Bear & Son Cutlery, Inc., 1111 Bear Blvd. SW, Jacksonville, AL 36265, P: 800-844-3034, F: 256-435-9348, www.bearandsoncutlery.com
Cutlery; Hunting Accessories; Knives/Knife Cases

Bear Valley Outfitters, P.O. Box 2294, Swan River, Manitoba R0L-1Z0 CANADA, P: 204-238-4342, F: 204-238-4342, www.bearvalleyoutfitters.com

Beeman Precision Airguns, 5454 Argosy Ave., Huntington Beach, CA 92649, P: 714-890-4800, F: 714-890-4808, www.beeman.com
Airguns; Ammunition; Gun Cases; Holsters; Lubricants; Scopes, Sights & Accessories; Targets

Beijing Defense Co., Ltd., 18 B, Unit One, No. 1 Building, Linghangguoji, Guangqumen Nanxiao St., Chongwen District, Beijing, 100061, CHINA, P: 011 861067153626, F: 011 861067152121, www.tacticalgear.com
Backpacking; Bags & Equipment Cases; Gun Cases; Holsters; Training & Safety Equipment

Bell and Carlson, Inc., 101 Allen Rd., Dodge City, KS 67801, P: 620-225-6688, F: 620-225-9095, www.bellandcarlson.com
Camouflage; Custom Manufacturing; Gun Grips & Stocks; Gun Parts/Gunsmithing; Hunting Accessories; Shooting Range Equipment

Bell-Ranger Outdoor Apparel, 1538 Crescent Dr., P.O. Box 14307, Augusta, GA, 30909, P: 800-241-7618, F: 706-738-3608, www.bellranger.com
Camouflage; Men & Women's Clothing; Hunting Accessories

Benchmade Knife Company, Inc., 300 Beavercreek Rd., Oregon City, OR 97045, P: 800-800-7427, F: 503-655-7922, www.benchmade.com
Knives/Knife Cases; Men's Clothing

Benelli Armi S.p.A./Benelli USA, 17603 Indian Head Hwy., Accokeek, MD 20607, P: 301-283-6981, F: 301-283-6986, www.benelli.it, www.benelliusa.com
Firearms

Beretta/Law Enforcement and Defense, 17601 Beretta Dr., Accokeek, MD 20607, P: 800-545-9567, F: 301-283-5111, www.berettale.com
Firearms; Gun Parts/Gunsmithing; Holsters; Law Enforcement; Lighting Products

Beretta U.S.A. Corp., 17601 Beretta Dr., Accokeek, MD 20607, P: 800-636-3420, F: 253-484-3775

Bergan, LLC, 27600 Hwy. 125, Monkey Island, OK 74331, P: 866-217-9606. F: 918-257-8950, www.berganexperience.com
Pet Products

Berger Bullets, 4275 N. Palm St., Fullerton, CA 92835, P: 714-447-5456, F: 714-447-5478, www.bergerbullets.com
Ammunition; Custom Manufacturing; Reloading

Berry's Manufacturing, Inc., 401 N. 3050 East, St. George, UT 84790, P: 800-269-7373, F: 435-634-1683, www.berrysmfg.com
Ammunition; Custom Manufacturing; Export/Import Specialists; Gun Cases; Reloading; Wholesaler/Distributor

Beta Company, The, 2137B Flintstone Dr., Tucker, GA 30084, P: 800-669-2382, F: 770-270-0599, www.betaco.com
Law Enforcement; Magazines, Cartridge

Beyond Clothing/Beyond Tactical, 1025 Conger St., Suite 8, Eugene, OR 97402, P: 800-775-2279, F: 703-997-6581, www.beyondtactical.com
Backpacking; Camouflage; Men & Women's Clothing; Custom Manufacturing; Law Enforcement

BFAST, LLC, 10 Roff Ave., Palasades Park, NJ 07650, P: 973-706-8210, F: 201-943-3546, www.firearmsafetynet.com
Law Enforcement; Shooting Range Equipment; Sports Accessories; Training & Safety Equipment

Bianchi International, 3120 E. Mission Blvd. Ontario, CA 91761, P: 800-347-1200, F: 800-366-1669, www.bianchi-intl.com
Backpacking; Bags & Equipment Cases; Gun Cases; Holsters; Hunting Accessories; Knives/Knife Cases; Leathergoods; Sports Accessories

Big Game Treestands, 1820 N. Redding Ave., P.O. Box 382, Windom, MN 56101, P: 800-268-5077, F: 507-831-4350, www.biggametreestands.com
Blinds; Hunting Accessories; Shooting Range Equipment; Treestands

Big Sky Carvers/Montana Silversmiths, 308 E. Main St., P.O. Box 507, Manhattan, MT 59741, P: 406-284-3193, F: 406-284-4028, www.bigskycarvers.com
Decoys; Home Furnishings; Lighting Products; Outdoor Art, Jewelry, Sculpture; Watches; Wholesaler/Distributor

Big Sky Racks, Inc., 25A Shawnee Way, Bozeman, MT 58715, P: 800-805-8716, F: 406-585-7378, www.bigskyracks.com
Gun Cabinets, Racks, Safes; Gun Locks; Hunting Accessories

BigFoot Bag/PortaQuip, 1215 S. Grant Ave., Loveland, CO 80537, P: 877-883-0200, F: 970-663-5415, www.bigfootbag.com
Bags & Equipment Cases; Camping; Hunting Accessories; Law Enforcement; Paintball Accessories; Sports Accessories; Tours & Travel

Bill's Sewing Machine Co., 301 Main Avenue East, Hildebran, NC 28637, P: 828-397-6941, F: 828-397-6193, www.billsewing.com

Bill Wiseman & Co., Inc., 18456 Hwy. 6 South, College Station, TX 77845, P: 979-690-3456, F: 979-690-0156, www.billwisemanandco.com
Firearms; Gun Barrels; Gun Parts/Gunsmithing

BioPlastics Co., 34655 Mills Rd., North Ridgeville, OH 44039, P: 440-327-0485, F: 440-327-3666, www.bioplastics.us

Birchwood Casey, 7900 Fuller Rd., Eden Prairie, MN 55344, P: 800-328-6156, F: 952-937-7979, www.birchwoodcasey.com
Black Powder Accessories; Camping; Firearms Maintenance Equipment; Gun Cases; Gun Parts/Gunsmithing; Hunting Accessories; Lubricants; Targets

Bison Designs, 735 S. Lincoln St., Longmont, CO 80501, P: 800-536-2476, F: 303-678-9988, www.bisondesigns.com
Backpacking; Men & Women's Clothing; Pet Supplies; Survival Kits/First Aid; Training & Safety Equipment; Wholesaler/Distributor

Black Hills Ammunition, P.O. Box 3090, Rapid City, SD 57709, P: 605-348-5150, F: 605-348-9827, www.black-hills.com
Ammunition

Black Hills Shooters Supply, Inc., 2875 Creek Dr., Rapid City, SD 57703, P: 800-289-2506, F: 800-289-4570, www.bhshooters.com
Reloading; Wholesaler/Distributor

Black Powder Products Group, 5988 Peachtree Corners East, Norcross, GA 30071, P: 800-320-8767, F: 770-242-8546, www.bpiguns.com
Black Powder Accessories; Firearms; Firearms Maintenance Equipment; Hunting Accessories; Scopes, Sights & Accessories

BlackHawk Products Group, 6160 Commander Pkwy., Norfolk, VA 23502, P: 800-694-5263, F: 757-436-3088, www.blackhawk.com
Bags & Equipment Cases; Men's Clothing; Gloves, Mitts, Hats; Holsters; Hunting Accessories; Knives/Knife Cases; Law Enforcement; Recoil Protection Devices & Services

Blackheart International, LLC, RR3, Box 115, Philippi, WV 26416, P: 877-244-8166, F: 304-457-1281, www.bhigear.com
Ammunition; Gun Parts/Gunsmithing; Holsters; Law Enforcement; Magazines, Cartridge; Scopes, Sights & Accessories; Survival Kits/First Aid; Training & Safety Equipment

Blackwater, P.O. Box 1029, Moyock, NC 27958, P: 252-435-2488, F: 252-435-6388, www.blackwaterusa.com
Bags & Equipment Cases; Men's Clothing; Custom Manufacturing; Gun Cases; Holsters; Law Enforcement; Targets; Training & Safety Equipment

Blade-Tech Industries, 2506 104th St. Court S, Suite A, Lakewood, WA 98499, P: 253-581-4347, F: 253-589-0282, www.blade-tech.com
Bags & Equipment Cases; Custom Manufacturing; Cutlery; Holsters; Hunting Accessories; Knives/Knife Cases; Law Enforcement; Sports Accessories

Blaser Jagdwaffen GmbH, Ziegelstadel 1, Isny, 88316, GERMANY, P: 011 4907562702348, F: 011 4907562702343, www.blaser.de
Firearms; Gun Barrels; Gun Cases; Gun Grips & Stocks; Hunting Accessories

Blauer Manufacturing Co. 20 Aberdeen St., Boston, MA 02215, P: 800-225-6715, www.blauer.com
Law Enforcement; Men & Women's Clothing

Blue Book Publications, Inc., 8009 34th Ave. S, Suite 175, Minneapolis, MN 55425, P: 800-877-4867, F: 952-853-1486, www.bluebookinc.com
Books/Industry Publications; Computer Software

Blue Force Gear, Inc., P.O. Box 853, Pooler, GA 31322, P: 877-430-2583, F: 912-964-7701, www.blueforcegear.com
Bags & Equipment Cases; Hunting Accessories; Law Enforcement; Scopes, Sights & Accessories; Sports Accessories

Blue Ridge Knives, 166 Adwolfe Rd., Marion, VA 24354, P: 276-783-6143, F: 276-783-9298, www.blueridgeknives.com
Binoculars; Cutlery; Export/Import Specialists; Knives/Knife Cases; Lighting Products; Scopes, Sights & Accessories; Sharpeners; Wholesaler/Distributor

Blue Stone Safety Products Co., Inc., 2950 W. 63rd St., Chicago, IL 60629, P: 773-776-9472, F: 773-776-9472, www.wolverineholsters.com
Holsters; Law Enforcement

Bluegrass Armory, 145 Orchard St., Richmond, KY 40475, P: 859-625-0874, F: 859-625-0874, www.bluegrassarmory.com
Firearms

Bluestar USA, Inc., 111 Commerce Center Drive, Suite 303, P.O. Box 2903, Huntersville, NC 28078, P: 877-948-7827, F: 704-875-6714, www.bluestar-hunting.com
Archery; Crossbows & Accessories; Hunting Accessories; Law Enforcement; Training & Safety Equipment; Wholesaler/Distributor

BlueWater Ropes/Yates Gear, Inc., 2608 Hartnell Ave., Suite 6, Redding, CA 96002, P: 800-YATES-16 / 530-222-4640, www.yatesgear.com
Law Enforcement; Training & Safety Equipment; Wholesaler/Distributor

Bobster Eyewear, 12220 Parkway Centre Dr., Suite B, Poway, CA 92064, P: 800-603-2662, F: 858-715-0066, www.bobster.com
Eyewear; Hunting Accessories; Law Enforcement; Shooting Range Equipment; Sports Accessories; Training & Safety Equipment

Body Specs Sunglasses & Goggles, 22846 Industrial Place, Grass Valley, CA 95949, P: 800-824-5907, F: 530-268-1751, www.bodyspecs.com
Eyewear; Law Enforcement; Shooting Range Equipment; Training & Safety Equipment

Bogs Footwear/The Combs Co., 16 Oakway Center, Eugene, OR 97401, P: 800-485-2070, F: 541-484-1345, www.bogsfootwear.com or www.raftersfootwear.com
Footwear

Boker USA, Inc., 1550 Balsam St., Lakewood, CO 80214, P: 800-992-6537, F: 303-462-0668, www.bokerusa.com
Cutlery; Knives/Knife Cases

Border Crossing Scents, 8399 Bristol Rd., Davison, MI 48423, P: 888-653-2759, F: 810-653-2809, www.bordercrossingscents.com
Scents & Lures

Boss Buck, Inc., 210 S. Hwy. 175, Seagoville, TX 75159, P: 972-287-1216, F: 972-287-1892, www.bossbuck.com
Blinds; Feeder Equipment; Hunting Accessories; Scents & Lures; Treestands

Boston Leather, Inc., 1801 Eastwood Dr., P.O. Box 1213, Sterling, IL 61081, P: 800-733-1492, F: 800-856-1650, www.bostonleather.com
Bags & Equipment Cases; Custom Manufacturing; Gun Cases; Holsters; Knives/Knife Cases; Law Enforcement; Leathergoods; Pet Supplies

Boyds' Gunstock Industries, Inc., 25376 403rd Ave., Mitchell, SD 57301, P: 605-996-5011, F: 605-996-9878, www.boydsgunstocks.com
Custom Manufacturing; Firearms Maintenance Equipment; Gun Grips & Stocks; Gun Parts/Gunsmithing; Hunting Accessories; Shooting Range Equipment

Boyt Harness/Bob Allen Sportswear, 1 Boyt Dr., Osceola, IA 50213, P: 800-685-7020, www.boytharness.com
Gun Cases; Hunting Accessories; Law Enforcement; Men & Women's Clothing; Pet Supplies; Shooting Accessories

BraeVal, 23 E. Main St., Torrington, CT 06790, P: 860-482-7260, F: 860-482-7247, www.braeval.net
Men's Clothing

Brass Magnet, 5910 S. University Blvd., Suite C 18-330, Greenwood Village, CO 80121, P: 303-347-2636, F: 360-364-2636

Brazos Walking Sticks, 6408 Gholson Rd., Waco, TX 76705, P: 800-880-7119, F: 254-799-7199, www.brazos-walking-sticks.com
Canes; Walking Sticks

Breaching Technologies, Inc., P.O. Box 701468, San Antonio, TX 78270, P: 866-552-7427, F: 210-590-5193, www.breachingtechnologies.com

Law Enforcement; Training & Safety Equipment

Break-Free, 13386 International Parkway, Jacksonville, FL 32218, P: 800-433-2909, F: 800-588-0339, www.break-free.com
Law Enforcement; Lubricants

Brenneke™ of America, L.P., P.O. Box 1481, Clinton, IA 52733, P: 800-753-9733, F: 563-244-7421, www.brennekeusa.com
Ammunition

Brenzovich Firearms & Training Center/dba BFTC, 22301 Texas 20, Fort Hancock, TX 79839, P: 877-585-3775, F: 915-764-2030, www.brenzovich.com
Airguns; Ammunition; Archery; Black Powder Accessories; Export/Import Specialists; Firearms; Training & Safety Equipment; Wholesaler/Distributor

Brigade Quartermasters, Ltd., 1025 Cobb International Dr., Kennesaw, GA 30152, P: 770-428-1248, F: 720-426-7211

Briley Manufacturing, Inc., 1230 Lumpkin Rd., Houston, TX 77043, P: 800-331-5718, F: 713-932-1043
Chokes, Gun Accessories, Gunsmithing

Brite-Strike Technologies, 26 Wapping Rd., Jones River Industrial Park, Kingston, MA 02364, P: 781-585-5509, F: 781-585-5332, www.brite-strike.com
Law Enforcement; Lighting Products

Broco, Inc., 10868 Bell Ct., Rancho Cucamonga, CA 91730, P: 800-845-7259, F: 800-845-7259, www.brocoinc.com
Law Enforcement

Brookwood/Fine Uniform Co., 1125 E. Broadway, Suite 51, Glendale, CA 91205, P: 626-443-3736, F: 626-444-1551, www.brookwoodbags.com
Archery; Backpacking; Bags & Equipment Cases; Camping; Gun Cases; Hunting Accessories; Knives/Knife Cases; Shooting Range Equipment

Brookwood Companies, Inc., 25 W. 45th St., 11th Floor, New York, NY 10036, P: 800-426-5468, F: 646-472-0294, www.brookwoodcos.com

Brownells/Brownells MIL/LE Supply Group, 200 S. Front St., Montezuma, IA 50171, P: 800-741-0015, F: 800-264-3068, www.brownells.com
Export/Import Specialists; Firearms Maintenance Equipment; Gun Grips & Stocks; Gun Parts/Gunsmithing; Lubricants; Magazines, Cartridge; Scopes, Sights & Accessories; Wholesaler/Distributor

Browning, 1 Browning Place, Morgan, UT 84050, P: 801-876-2711, F: 801-876-3331, www.browning.com

Browning Archery, 2727 N. Fairview Ave., Tucson, AZ 85705, P: 520-838-2000, F: 520-838-2019, www.browning-archery.com
Archery

Browning Footwear, 107 Highland St., Martinsburg, PA 16662, P: 800-441-4319, F: 814-793-9272, www.browningfootwear.com
Footwear

Browning Hosiery/Carolina Hosiery, 2316 Tucker St., Burlington, NC 27215, P: 336-226-5581, F: 336-226-9721, www.browninghosiery.com
Men & Women's Clothing, Footwear

Browning Off Road/Polaris Industries, 2100 Hwy. 55, Medina, MN 55340, P: 763-542-0500, F: 763-542-2317, www.browning offroad.com
Vehicles, Utility & Rec

Browning Outdoor Health and Safety Products, 1 Pharmacal Way, Jackson, WI 53037, P: 800-558-6614, F: 262-677-9006, www.browningsupplies.com
Survival Kits/First Aid

Browning Signature Automotive/Signature Products Group, 2550 S. Decker Lake Blvd. Suite 1, Salt Lake City, UT 84119, P: 801-237-0184, F: 801-237-0118, www.spgcompany.com
Emblems & Decals

Bruce Foods/Cajun Injector, Inc., P.O. Box 1030, New Iberia, LA 70562, P: 337-365-8101, F: 337-364-3742, www.brucefoods.com
Camping; Cooking Equipment/Accessories; Food; Online Services

Brunton, 2255 Brunton Ct., Riverton, WY 82501, P: 307-857-4700, F: 307-857-4703, www.brunton.com
Backpacking, Binoculars, Camping, Scopes

Buck Gardner Calls, LLC, 2129 Troyer Ave., Building 249, Suite 104, Memphis, TN 38114, P: 901-946-2996, F: 901-946-8747, www.buckgardner.com
Duck Calls & Accessories; Cooking

Buck Knives, Inc., 660 S. Lochsa St., Post Falls, ID 83854, P: 800-326-2825, www.buckknives.com
Backpacking; Camping; Custom Manufacturing; Cutlery; Hunting Accessories; Knives/Knife Cases; Law Enforcement; Sharpeners

Buckaroo-Stoo/BVM Productions, 2253 Kingsland Ave., Bronx, NY 10469, P: 877-286-4599, F: 718-652-3014, www.buckaroostoo.com
Scents & Lures

Buck Stop Lure Company, Inc., 3600 Grow Rd., P.O. Box 636, Stanton, MI 48888, P: 800-477-2368, F: 989-762-5124, www.buckstopscents.com

Archery; Books/Industry Publications; Hunting Accessories; Pet Supplies; Scents & Lures; Videos

Buck Wear, Inc., 2900 Cowan Ave., Baltimore, MD 21223, P: 800-813-7708, F: 410-646-7700, www.buckwear.com
Men & Women's Clothing

Buffalo Tools/Sportsman Series, 1220 N. Price Rd., St. Louis, MO 63132, P: 800-568-6657, F: 636-537-1055, www.buffalotools.com
Cooking Equipment/Accessories; Export/Import Specialists; Wholesaler/Distributor

Buffer Technologies, P.O. Box 105047, Jefferson City, MO 65110, P: 877-628-3337, F: 573-634-8522, www.buffertech.com
Gun Parts/Gunsmithing; Law Enforcement; Magazines, Cartridge; Recoil Protection Devices & Services

Bug Band, 127 Riverside Dr., Cartersville, GA 30120, P: 800-473-9467, F: 678-721-9279, www.bugband.com
Archery; Backpacking; Camping; Hunting Accessories; Law Enforcement; Outfitter; Survival Kits/First Aid; Wholesaler/Distributor

Bul, Ltd., 10 Rival St., Tel Aviv, 67778, ISRAEL, P: 011 97236392911, F: 011 97236874853, www.bultransmark.com
Firearms; Gun Barrels; Gun Parts/Gunsmithing; Law Enforcement

Bulldog Barrels, LLC, 106 Isabella St., 4 North Shore Center, Suite 110, Pittsburgh, PA 15212, P: 866-992-8553, F: 412-322-1912, www.bulldogbarrels.com
Firearms; Gun Barrels; Gun Parts/Gunsmithing

Bulldog Cases, 830 Beauregard Ave., Danville, VA 24541, P: 800-843-3483, F: 434-793-7504
Bags & Equipment Cases; Camouflage; Gun Cases; Holsters

Bulldog Equipment, 3706 SW 30th Ave., Hollywood, FL 33312, P: 954-581-5510 or 954-448-5221, F: 954-581-4221, www.bulldogequipment.us
Backpacking; Bags & Equipment Cases; Custom Manufacturing; Gloves, Mitts, Hats; Gun Cases; Law Enforcement; Outfitter

Bulls and Beavers, LLC, P.O. Box 2870, Sun Valley, ID 83353, P: 208-726-8217, www.bullsandbeavers.com

Burn Machine, LLC, The, 26305 Glendale, Suite 200, Redford, MI 48239, P: 800-380-6527, F: 313-794-4355, www.theburnmachine.com
Sports Accessories; Training & Safety Equipment; Wholesaler/Distributor

Burris Company, Inc., 331 E. 8th St., Greeley, CO 80631, P: 970-356-1670, F: 970-356-8702, www.burrisoptics.com
Binoculars; Scopes, Sights & Accessories; Targets

Bushido Tactical, LLC, P.O. Box 721289, Orlando, FL 32972, P: 407-454-4256, F: 407-286-4416, www.bushidotactical.com
Law Enforcement; Training

Bushnell Law Enforcement/Bushnell Outdoor Products, 9200 Cody St., Overland Park, KS 66214, P: 800-423-3537, F: 800-548-0446, www.unclemikesle.com
Binoculars; Firearms Maintenance Equipment; Gloves, Mitts, Hats; Gun Cases; Holsters; Law Enforcement; Lubricants; Scopes, Sights & Accessories

Business Control Systems Corp., 1173 Green St., Iselin, NJ 08830, P: 800-233-5876, F: 732-283-1192, www.businesscontrol.com
Archery; Computer Software; Firearms; Law Enforcement; Retailer Services; Shooting Range Equipment; Wholesaler/Distributor

Butler Creek Corp./Bushnell Outdoor Accessories, 9200 Cody St., Overland Park, KS 66214, P: 800-423-3537, F: 800-548-0446, www.butlercreek.com
Firearms Maintenance Equipment; Gun Barrels; Gun Grips & Stocks; Hunting Accessories; Leathergoods; Scopes, Sights & Accessories

C

CAM Commerce Solutions, 17075 Newhope St., Fountain Valley, CA 92708, 866-840-4443, F: 702-564-3206, www.camcommerce.com
Computer Software

CASL Industries/Tanglefree/Remington, P.O. Box 1280, Clayton, CA 94517, P: 925-685-6055, www.tanglefree.com or www.caslinindustries.com
Bags & Equipment Cases; Blinds; Camouflage; Decoys; Gun Cases; Hunting Accessories

CAS Hanwei, 650 Industrial Blvd., Sale Creek, TN 37373-9797, P: 800-635-9366, F: 423-332-7248, www.cashanwei.com
Custom Manufacturing; Cutlery; Knives/Knife Cases; Leathergoods; Wholesaler/Distributor

CCF Race Frames LLC, P.O. Box 29009, Richmond, VA 23242, P: 804-622-4277, F: 804-740-9599, www.ccfraceframes.com
Firearms; Firearms Maintenance Equipment; Gun Parts/Gunsmithing; Law Enforcement

CCI Ammunition/ATK Commercial Products, 2299 Snake River Ave., Lewiston, ID 83501, P: 800-256-8685, F: 208-798-3392, www.cci-ammunition.com
Ammunition

CGTech, 9000 Research Dr., Irvine, CA 92618, P: 949-753-1050, F: 949-753-1053, www.cgtech.com
Computer Software; Custom Manufacturing

CJ Weapons Accessories, 317 Danielle Ct., Jefferson City, MO 65109, P: 800-510-5919, F: 573-634-2355, www.cjweapons.com
Firearms Maintenance Equipment; Gun Parts/Gunsmithing; Hunting Accessories; Law Enforcement; Magazines, Cartridge; Shooting Range Equipment; Sports Accessories; Wholesaler/Distributor

CMMG, Inc., 620 County Rd. 118, P.O. Box 369, Fayette, MO 65248, P: 660-248-2293, F: 660-248-2290, www.cmmginc.com
Firearms; Law Enforcement; Magazines, Cartridge

CTI Industries Corp., 22160 N. Pepper Rd., Barrington, IL 60010, P: 866-382-1707, F: 800-333-1831, www.zipvac.com
Archery; Backpacking; Bags & Equipment Cases; Camping; Cooking Equipment/Accessories; Custom Manufacturing; Food; Hunting Accessories

CVA, 5988 Peachtree Corners East, Norcross, GA 30071, P: 800-320-8767, F: 770-242-8546
Black Powder Accessories; Firearms; Firearms Maintenance Equipment; Gun Barrels

CZ-USA/Dan Wesson, 3327 N. 7th St., Kansas city, KS 66115, P: 800-955-4486, F: 913-321-4901, www.cz-usa.com
Firearms

Cablz, 411 Meadowbrook Lane, Birmingham, AL 35213, P: 205-222-4477, F: 205-870-8847

Caesar Guerini USA, 700 Lake St., Cambridge, MD 21613, P: 866-901-1131, F: 410-901-1137, www.gueriniusa.com
Firearms

CALVI S.p.A., Via Iv Novembre, 2, Merate (LC), 23807, ITALY, P: 011 3903999851, F: 011 390399985240, www.calvi.it
Custom Manufacturing; Firearms; Gun Barrels; Gun Locks; Gun Parts/Gunsmithing

Camdex, Inc., 2330 Alger, Troy, MI 48083, P: 248-528-2300, F: 248-528-0989, www.camdexloader.com
Reloading

Camelbak Products, 2000 S. McDowell Blvd., Petaluma, CA 94954, P: 800-767-8725, F: 707-665-3844, www.camelbak.com
Backpacking; Bags & Equipment Cases; Gloves, Mitts, Hats; Holsters; Law Enforcement

Camerons Products/CM International, Inc., 2547 Durango Dr., P.O. Box 60220, Colorado Springs, CO 80960, P: 888-563-0227, F: 719-390-0946, www.cameronsproducts.com
Backpacking; Camping; Cooking Equipment/Accessories; Hunting Accessories; Retailer Services; Tours/Travel; Wholesaler/Distributor

Camfour, Inc., 65 Westfield Industrial Park Rd., Westfield, MA 01085, P: 800-FIREARM, F: 413-568-9663, www.camfour.com
Ammunition; Black Powder Accessories; Computer Software; Export/Import Specialists; Firearms; Hunting Accessories; Law Enforcement; Wholesaler/Distributor

Cammenga Corp., 100 Aniline Ave. N, Suite 258, Holland, MI 49424, P: 616-392-7999, F: 616-392-9432, www.cammenga.com
Magazines, Cartridge; Reloading; Training & Safety Equipment

Camo Unlimited, 1021 B Industrial Park Dr., Marietta, GA 30062, P: 866-448-CAMO, F: 770-420-2299, www.camounlimited.com
Blinds; Camouflage; Hunting Accessories; Paintball Accessories

C-More Systems, 7553 Gary Rd., P.O. Box 1750, Manassas, VA 20109, P: 888-265-8266, F: 703-361-5881, www.cmore.com
Airguns; Archery; Crossbows & Accessories; Custom Manufacturing; Firearms; Hunting Accessories; Law Enforcement; Scopes, Sights & Accessories; Shooting Range Equipment

CamoSpace, P.O. Box 125, Rhodesdale, MD 21659, P: 410-310-0380, F: 410-943-8849

Camouflage Face Paint, 2832 Southeast Loop 820, Fort Worth, TX 76140, P: 877-625-3879, F: 817-615-8670, www.camofacepaint.com
Archery; Camouflage; Custom Manufacturing; Export/Import Specialists; Hunting Accessories; Online Services; Paintball Accessories; Wholesaler/Distributor

Camowraps, 429 South St., Slidell, LA 70460, P: 866-CAMO-MAN, F: 985-661-1447, www.camowraps.com
Camouflage; Custom Manufacturing; Emblems & Decals; Printing Services

Camp Chef, 675 North 600 West, P.O. Box 4057, Logan, UT 84321, P: 800-783-8347, F: 435-752-1592, www.campchef.com
Cooking Equipment/Accessories

Camp Technologies, LLC/Div. DHS Technologies, LLC, 33 Kings Hwy., Orangeburg, NY 10962, P: 866-969-2400, F: 845-365-2114, www.camprtv.com
Backpacking; Camping; Hunting Accessories; Law Enforcement; Outfitter; Sports Accessories; Vehicles, Utility & Rec

CampCo/Smith & Wesson Watches HUMVEE/UZI, 4625 W. Jefferson Blvd., Los Angeles, CA 90016, P: 888-9-CAMPCO, F: 323-766-2424, www.campco.com
Backpacking; Binocular; Camping; Compasses; Knives/Knife Cases; Law Enforcement; Lighting Products; Wholesaler/Distributor

Canal Street Cutlery Co., 30 Canal St., Ellenville, NY 12428, P: 845-647-5900, F: 845-647-1456, www.canalstreetcutlery.com
Cutlery; Knives/Knife Cases

Cannon Safe, Inc., 216 S. 2nd Ave., Building 932, San Bernardino, CA 92408, P: 800-242-1055, F: 909-382-0707, www.cannonsafe.com
Gun Cabinets/Racks/Safes; Gun Locks

Careco Multimedia, Inc., 5717 Northwest Pkwy., Suite 104, San Antonio, TX 78249, P: 800-668-8081, F: 251-948-3011, www.americanaoutdoors.com, www.outdooraction.com, www.fishingandhuntingtexas.com
Online Services; Videos; Wholesaler/Distributor

Carl Zeiss Optronics GmbH, Gloelstr. 3-5, Wetzlar, 35576, GERMANY, P: 011 4964414040, F: 011 496441404510, www.zeiss.com/optronics
Law Enforcement; Scopes, Sights & Accessories; Shooting Range Equipment; Targets; Telescopes

Carl Zeiss Sports Optics/Zeiss, 13005 N. Kingston Ave., Chester, VA 23836, P: 800-441-3005, F: 804-530-8481, www.zeiss.com/sports
Binoculars; Scopes, Sights & Accessories

Carlson's Choke Tubes, 720 S. Second St., P.O. Box 162, Atwood, KS 67730, P: 785-626-3700, F: 785-626-3999, www.choketube.com
Custom Manufacturing; Firearms Maintenance Equipment; Game Calls; Gun Parts/Gunsmithing; Hunting Accessories; Scopes, Sights & Accessories; Shooting Range Equipment

Carson Optical, 35 Gilpin Ave., Hauppauge, NY 11788, P: 800-967-8427, F: 631-427-6749, www.carsonoptical.com
Binoculars; Export/Import Specialists; Scopes, Sights & Accessories; Telescopes

Cartuchos Saga, Pda. Caparrela s/n, Lleida, 25192, SPAIN, P: 011 34973275000, F: 011 34973275008
Ammunition

Case Cutlery (W.R. Case & Sons Cutlery Co.), Owens Way, Bradford, PA 16701, P: 800-523-6350, F: 814-358-1736, www.wrcase.com
Cutlery; Knives/Knife Cases; Sharpeners

Caspian S.p.A., 75 Cal Foster Dr., Wolcott, VT 05680, P: 802-472-6454, F: 802-472-6709, www.caspianarms.com
Firearms; Gun Parts/Gunsmithing; Law Enforcement

Cass Creek International, LLC, 1881 Lyndon Blvd., Falconer, NY 14733, P: 800-778-0389, F: 716-665-6536, www.casscreek.com
Game Calls; Hunting Accessories

Cejay Engineering, LLC/InfraRed Combat Marking Beacons, 2129 Gen Booth Blvd., Suite 103-284, Virginia Beach, VA 23454, P: 603-880-8501, F: 603-880-8502, www.cejayeng.com
Lighting Products

Celestron, 2835 Columbia St., Torrance, CA 90503, P: 310-328-9560, F: 310-212-5835, www.celestron.com
Binoculars; Scopes, Sights & Accessories; Telescopes

Center Mass, Inc., 6845 Woonsocket, Canton, MI 48187, P: 800-794-1216, F: 734-416-0650, www.centermassinc.com
Bags & Equipment Cases; Emblems & Decals; Hunting Accessories; Law Enforcement; Men's Clothing; Shooting Range Equipment; Targets; Training & Safety Equipment

Century International Arms, Inc., 430 S. Congress Dr., Suite 1, DelRay Beach, FL 33445, P: 800-527-1252, F: 561-265-4520, www.centuryarms.com
Ammunition; Firearms; Firearms Maintenance Equipment; Gun Parts/Gunsmithing; Law Enforcement; Magazines, Cartridge; Scopes, Sights & Accessories; Wholesaler/Distributor

Cequre Composite Technologies, 5995 Shier-Rings Rd., Suite A, Dublin, OH 43016, P: 614-526-0095, F: 614-526-0098, www.wearmor.com
Custom Manufacturing; Law Enforcement; Shooting Range Equipment; Targets

Cerakote/NIC Industries, Inc., 7050 Sixth St., White City, OR 97503, P: 866-774-7628, F: 541-830-6518, www.nicindustries.com
Camouflage; Custom Manufacturing; Firearms; Firearms Maintenance Equipment; Knives/Knife Cases; Law Enforcement; Lubricants; Paintball Guns

Champion Traps and Targets/ATK Commercial Products, N5549 Cty. Trunk Z, Onalaska, WI 54650, P: 800-635-7656, F: 763-323-3890, www.championtargetr.com
Clay Targets; Hearing Protection; Shooting Range Equipment; Targets

Chapin International, P.O. Box 549, Batavia, NY 14020, P: 800-444-3140, F: 585-813-0118, www.chapinmfg.com
Feeder Equipment

Chapman Innovations, 343 W. 400 South, Salt Lake City, UT 84101, P: 801-415-0024, F: 801-415-2001, www.carbonx.com
Gloves, Mitts, Hats; Law Enforcement; Men & Women's Clothing

Charter Arms/MKS Supply, Inc., 8611A North Dixie Dr., Dayton, OH 45414, P: 866-769-4867, F: 937-454-0503, www.charterfirearms.com
Firearms

Cheddite France, 99 Route de Lyon, P.O. Box 112, Bourg-les-Valence, 26500, FRANCE, P: 011 33475564545, F: 011 33475563587, www.cheddite.com
Ammunition

Chengdu Lis Business, 4-3-9, 359 Shuhan Rd., Chengdu, SICH 610036, CHINA, P: 0110862887541867, F: 011 862887578686, www.lisoptics.com
Binoculars; Compasses; Cutlery; Lighting Products; Scopes, Sights & Accessories; Telescopes

CheyTac Associates, LLC, 363 Sunset Dr., Arco, ID 83213, P: 256-325-0622, F: 208-527-3328, www.cheytac.com
Ammunition; Computer Software; Custom Manufacturing; Firearms; Law Enforcement; Training & Safety Equipment

Chiappa Firearms-Armi Sport di Chiappa Silvia e C. SNC, Via Milano, 2, Azzano Mella (Bs), 25020, ITALY, P: 011 390309749065, F: 011 390309749232, www.chiappafirearms.com
Black Powder Accessories; Firearms

China Shenzhen Aimbond Enterprises Co., Ltd., 19D, Building No. 1, China Phoenix Building, No. 2008, Shennan Rd., Futian District, Shenzhen, Guangdong 518026, CHINA, P: 011 8675582522730812, F: 011 8675583760022, www.sino-optics.com
Binoculars; Eyewear; Firearms Maintenance Equipment; Hunting Accessories; Lighting Products; Scopes, Sights & Accessories; Telescopes

Chip McCormick Custom, LLC, 105 Sky King Dr., Spicewood, TX 78669, P: 800-328-2447, F: 830-693-4975, www.cmcmags.com
Gun Parts/Gunsmithing; Magazines, Cartridge

Choate Machine & Tool, 116 Lovers Lane, Bald Knob, AR 72010, P: 800-972-6390, F: 501-724-5873, www.riflestock.com
Gun Grips & Stocks; Law Enforcement

Chongqing Dontop Optics Co., Ltd., No. 5 Huangshan Ave. Middle Beibu New District, Chongqing, 401121, CHINA, P: 011 862386815057, F: 011 862386815100, www.dontop.com
Binoculars; Custom Manufacturing; Scopes, Sights & Accessories; Shooting Range Equipment; Telescopes

Chongqing Jizhou Enterprise Co., Ltd., Rm 8-1, Block A3, Jiazhou Garden, Chongqing, Yubei 401147, CHINA, P: 011 862367625115, F: 011 862367625121, www.cqjizhou.com
Binoculars; Compasses; Scopes, Sights & Accessories; Telescopes

Chonwoo Corp./Chonwoo Case & Cover (Tianjin) Co., Ltd., 4-6, SamJun-Dong Songpa-gu, Seoul, 138-848, SOUTH KOREA, P: 011 8224205094, F: 011 8224236154, www.chonwoo.co.kr
Backpacking; Bags & Equipment Cases; Gun Cases; Holsters; Hunting Accessories; Knives/Knife Cases; Leathergoods

Chris Reeve Knives, 2949 S. Victory View Way, Boise, ID 83709, P: 208-375-0367, F: 208-375-0368, www.chrisreeve.com
Backpacking; Camping; Cutlery; Hunting Accessories; Knives/Knife Cases; Law Enforcement; Sports Accessories

Christensen Arms, 192 E. 100 North, Fayette, UT 84630, P: 888-517-8855, F: 435-528-5773, www.christensenarms.com
Custom Manufacturing; Firearms; Gun Barrels

Christie & Christie Enterprises, Inc., 404 Bolivia Blvd., Bradenton, FL 34207, P: 440-413-0031, F: 440-428-5551
Gun Grips & Stocks; Gun Parts/Gunsmithing; Magazines, Cartridge; Scopes, Sights & Accessories; Wholesaler/Distributor

Cimarron Firearms Co., 105 Winding Oaks Rd., P.O. Box 906, Fredericksburg, TX 78624, P: 830-997-9090, F: 830-997-0802, www.cimarron-firearms.com
Black Powder Accessories; Firearms; Gun Cases; Gun Grips & Stocks; Gun Parts/Gunsmithing; Holsters; Leathergoods; Wholesaler/Distributor

Citadel (Cambodia) Pt., Ltd., Nr 5 Str 285 Tuol Kork, Phnom Penh, BP 440, CAMBODIA, P: 011 85512802676, F: 011 85523880015, www.citadel.com.kh
Cutlery

Clark Textile Co./ASF Group, 624 S. Grand Ave., San Pedro, CA 90731, P: 310-831-2334, F: 310-831-2335, www.asfgroup.com
Camouflage; Printing Services

Classic Accessories, 22640 68th Ave. S, Kent, WA 98032, P: 800-854-2315, F: 253-395-3991, www.classicaccessories.com
Bags & Equipment Cases; Camouflage; Gun Cases; Hunting Accessories; Pet Supplies; Wholesaler/Distributor

Classic Old West Styles, 1712 Texas Ave., El Paso, TX 79901, P: 800-595-COWS, F: 915-587-0616, www.cows.com
Custom Manfacturing; Holsters; Hunting Accessories; Leathergoods; Men's Clothing; Outfitter; Sports Accessories; Wholesaler/Distributor

Claude Dozorme Cutlery, Z.A. de Racine-B.P. 19, La Monnerie, 63650, FRANCE, P: 011 33473514106, F: 011 33473514851, www.dozorme-claude.fr
Cutlery

Claybuster Wads/Harvester Muzzleloading, 635 Bob Posey St., Henderson, KY 42420, P: 800-922-6287, F: 270-827-4972, www.claybusterwads.com
Black Powder Accessories; Reloading

Clever SRL, Via A. Da Legnago, 9/A, I-37141 Ponteflorio, Verona, ITALY, P: 011 390458840770, F: 011 390458840380, www.clevervr.com
Ammunition

Cliff Weil, Inc., 8043 Industrial Park Rd., Mechanicsville, VA 23116, P: 800-446-9345, F: 804-746-2595, www.cliffweil.com
Eyewear

Club Red, Inc./Bone Collector by Michael Waddell, 4645 Church Rd., Cumming, GA 30028, P: 888-428-1630, F: 678-947-1445, www.clubredinc.com
Emblems & Decals; Men & Women's Clothing

Clymer Precision, 1605 W. Hamlin Rd., Rochester Hills, MI 48309, P: 877-REAMERS, F: 248-853-1530, www.clymertool.com
Black Powder Accessories; Books/Industry Publications; Custom Manufacturing; Firearms Maintenance Equipment; Gun Parts/Gunsmithing; Law Enforcement; Reloading

CMere Deer®, 205 Fair Ave., P.O. Box 1336, Winnsboro, LA, 71295, P: 866-644-8600, F: 318-435-3885, www.cmeredeer.com
Scents & Lures

Coastal Boot Co., Inc. 2821 Center Port Circle, Pompano Beach, FL 33064, P: 954-782-3244, F: 954-782-4342, www.coastalboot.com
Footwear

Coast Products/LED Lenser, 8033 NE Holman St., Portland, OR 97218, P: 800-426-5858, F: 503-234-4422, www.coastportland.com
Camping; Compasses; Cutlery; Knives/Knife Cases; Law Enforcement; Lighting Products; Sharpeners

Cobra Enterprises of Utah, Inc., 1960 S. Milestone Dr., Suite F, Salt Lake City, UT 84104, P: 801-908-8300, F: 801-908-8301, www.cobrapistols.net
Firearms

Codet Newport Corp./Big Bill Work Wear, 924 Crawford Rd., Newport, VT 05855, P: 800-992-6338, F: 802-334-8268, www.bigbill.com
Backpacking; Bags & Equipment Cases; Camouflage; Camping; Footwear; Gloves, Mitts, Hats; Men's Clothing

Cold Steel Inc., 3036 Seaborg Ave., Suite A, Ventura, CA 93003, P: 800-255-4716, F: 805-642-9727, www.coldsteel.com
Cutlery; Knives/Knife Cases; Law Enforcement; Sports Accessories; Videos

Collector's Armoury, Ltd., P.O. Box 1050, Lorton, VA 22199, P: 800-336-4572, F: 703-493-9424, www.collectorsarmoury.com
Black Powder Accessories; Books/Industry Publications; Cutlery; Firearms; Holsters; Home Furnishings; Training & Safety Equipment; Wholesaler/Distributor

Colonial Arms, Inc. 1504 Hwy. 31 S, P.O. Box 250, Bay Minette, AL 36507, P: 800-949-8088, F: 251-580-5006, www.colonialarms.com
Firearms; Firearms Maintenance Equipment; Gun Barrels; Gun Parts/Gunsmithing; Hunting Accessories; Lubricants; Recoil Protection Devices & Services; Wholesaler/Distributor

Colt's Manufacturing Co., LLC, P.O. Box 1868, Hartford, CT 06144, P: 800-962-COLT, F: 860-244-1449, www.coltsmfg.com
Custom Manufacturing; Firearms; Gun Parts/Gunsmithing; Law Enforcement

Columbia River Knife and Tool, 18348 SW 126th Pl., Tualatin, OR 97062, P: 800-891-3100, F: 503-682-9680, www.crkt.com
Knives/Knife Cases; Sharpeners

Columbia Sportswear Co., 14375 NW Science Park Dr., Portland, OR 97229, P: 800-547-8066, F: 503-985-5800, www.columbia.com

Bags & Equipment Cases; Binoculars; Footwear; Gloves, Mitts, Hats; Men & Women's Clothing; Pet Supplies; Scopes, Sights & Accessories

Combined Tactical Systems, 388 Kinsman Rd., P.O. Box 506, Jamestown, PA 16134, P: 724-932-2177, F: 724-932-2166, www.less-lethal.com
Law Enforcement

Compass Industries, Inc., 104 E. 25th St., New York, NW 10010, P: 800-221-9904, F: 212-353-0826, www.compassindustries.com
Binoculars; Camping; Compasses; Cutlery; Export/Import Specialists; Eyewear; Hunting Accessories; Wholesaler/Distributor

Competition Electronics, 3469 Precision Dr., Rockford, IL 61109, P: 815-874-8001, F: 815-874-8181, www.competitionelectronics.com
Firearms Maintenance Equipment; Reloading; Shooting Range Equipment; Training & Safety Equipment

Condor Outdoor Products, 1866 Business Center Dr., Duarte, CA 91010, P: 800-552-2554, F: 626-303-3383, www.condoroutdoor.com
Backpacking; Bags & Equipment Cases; Camouflage; Footwear; Gun Cases; Holsters; Wholesaler/Distributor

Condor Tool & Knife, Inc., 6309 Marina Dr., Orlando, FL 32819, P: 407-876-0886, F: 407-876-0994, www.condortk.com
Archery; Camping; Custom Manufacturing; Cutlery; Gun Cases; Hunting Accessories; Knives/Knife Cases; Leathergoods

Connecticut Shotgun Mfg. Co., 100 Burritt St., New Britain, CT 06053, P: 800-515-4867, F: 860-832-8707, www.connecticutshotgun.com
Firearms; Firearms Maintenance Equipment; Gun Cabinets/Racks/Safes; Gun Cases; Gun Parts/Gunsmithing; Hunting Accessories; Knives/Knife Cases; Scopes, Sights & Accessories

Consorzio Armaioli Bresciani, Via Matteotti, 325, Gardone V.T., Brescia 25063, ITALY, P: 011 39030821752, F: 011 39030831425, www.armaiolibresciani.org
Firearms; Gun Parts/Gunsmithing; Videos

Consorzio Cortellinai Maniago SRL, Via Della Repubblica, 21, Maniago, PN 33085, ITALY, P: 011 39042771185, F: 011 390427700440, www.consorziocoltellinai.it
Camping; Cutlery; Hunting Accessories; Knives/Knife Cases; Law Enforcement

Convert-A-Ball Distributing, Inc., 955 Ball St., P.O. Box 199, Sidney, NE 69162, P: 800-543-1732, F: 308-254-7194, www.convert-a-ball.net
Camping; Vehicles, Utility & Rec

Cooper Firearms of MT, Inc./Cooper Arms, 4004 Hwy. 93 North, P.O. Box 114, Stevensville, MT 59870, P: 406-777-0373, F: 406-777-5228, www.cooperfirearms.com
Custom Manufacturing; Firearms

CopShoes.com/MetBoots.com, 6655 Poss Rd., San Antonio, TX 78238, P: 866-280-0400, F: 210-647-1401, www.copshoes.com
Footwear; Hunting Accessories; Law Enforcement

Cor-Bon/Glaser/Div. Dakota Ammo Inc., 1311 Industry Rd., P.O. Box 369, Sturgis, SD 57785, P: 605-347-4544, F: 605-347-5055, www.corbon.com
Ammunition

Cornell Hunting Products, 114 Woodside Dr., Honea Path, SC 29654, P: 864-369-9587, F: 864-369-9587, www.cornellhuntinproducts.com
Backpacking; Game Calls; Hunting Accessories; Wholesaler/Distributor

Corsivia, Poligono El Campillo, Calle Alemania, 59-61, Zuera, (Zaragoza) 50800, SPAIN, P: 011 34976680075, F: 011 34976680124, www.corsivia.com
Clay Targets

Counter Assault Pepper Sprays/Bear Deterrent, Law Enforcement & Personal Defense, 120 Industrial Court, Kalispell, MT 59901, P: 800-695-3394. F: 406-257-6674, www.counterassault.com
Archery; Backpacking; Camping; Hunting Accessories; Law Enforcement; Sports Accessories; Survival Kits/First Aid; Training & Safety Equipment

Crackshot Corp., 2623 E 36th St. N, Tulsa, OK 74110, P: 800-667-1753, F: 918-838-1271, www.crackshotcorp.com
Archery; Backpacking; Camping; Footwear; Hunting Accessories; Men & Women's Clothing; Training & Safety Equipment

Creative Castings/Les Douglas, 12789 Olympic View Rd. NW, Silverdale, WA 98383, P: 800-580-6516, F: 800-580-0495, www.wildlifepins.com
Custom Manufacturing; Emblems & Decals; Outdoor Art, Jewelry, Sculpture; Pet Supplies; Retailer Services; Watches; Wholesaler/Distributor

Creative Pet Products, P.O. Box 39, Spring Valley, WI 54767, P: 888-436-4566, F: 877-269-6911, www.petfirstaidkits.com
Gloves, Mitts, Hats; Pet Supplies; Survival Kits/First Aid; Training & Safety Equipment

Crest Ultrasonics Corp., P.O. Box 7266, Trenton, NJ 08628, P: 800-273-7822, F: 877-254-7939, www.crest-ultrasonics.com
Custom Manufacturing; Firearms Maintenance Equipment; Gun Parts/Gunsmithing; Law Enforcement; Lubricants; Shooting Range Equipment; Wholesaler/Distributor

Crimson Trace Holdings, LLC/Lasergrips, 9780 SW Freeman Dr., Wilsonville, OR 97070, P: 800-442-2406, F: 503-783-5334, www.crimsontrace.com
Firearms; Gun Grips & Stocks; Hunting Accessories; Law Enforcement; Scopes, Sights & Accessories; Training & Safety Equipment

Critter Cribs, P.O. Box 48545, Fort Worth, TX 76148, P: 877-611-2742, F: 866-351-3291, www.crittercribs.com
Camouflage; Hunting Accessories; Law Enforcement; Pet Supplies

Crooked Horn Outfitters, 26315 Trotter Dr., Tehachapi, CA 93561, P: 877-722-5872, F: 661-822-9100, www.crookedhorn.com
Archery; Bags & Equipment Cases; Binoculars; Hunting Accessories

Crosman Corp., Inc., Routes 5 and 20, East Bloomfield, NY 14443, P: 800-724-7486, F: 585-657-5405, www.crosman.com
Airguns; Airsoft; Ammunition; Archery; Crossbows & Accessories; Scopes, Sights & Accessories; Shooting Range Equipment; Targets

Crye Precision, LLC, 63 Flushing Ave., Suite 252, Brooklyn, NY 11205, P: 718-246-3838, F: 718-246-3833, www.cryeprecision.com
Bags & Equipment Cases; Camouflage; Custom Manufacturing; Law Enforcement; Men's Clothing

Cuppa, 3131 Morris St. N, St. Petersburg, FL 33713, P: 800-551-6541, F: 727-820-9212, www.cuppa.net
Custom Manufacturing; Emblems & Decals; Law Enforcement; Outdoor Art, Jewelry, Sculpture; Retailer Services

Custom Leather, 460 Bingemans Centre Dr., Kitchener, Ontario N2B 3X9, CANADA, P: 800-265-4504, F: 519-741-2072, www.customleather.com
Custom Manufacturing; Gun Cases; Hunting Accessories; Leathergoods

Cutting Edge Tactical, 166 Mariners Way, Moyock, NC 27958, P: 800-716-9425, F: 252-435-2284, www.cuttingedgetactical.com
Bags & Equipment Cases; Binoculars; Eyewear; Footwear; Gun Grips & Stocks; Law Enforcement; Lighting Products; Training & Safety Equipment

Cybrics, Ltd., No 68, Xing Yun Rd., Jin San Industrial Area, Yiwu, Zhejiang 322011, CHINA, P: 011 8657985556142, F: 011 8657985556210, www.cybrics.eu
Bags & Equipment Cases; Camouflage; Gloves, Mitts, Hats; Men & Women's Clothing

Cygnus Law Enforcement Group, 1233 Janesville Ave., Fort Atkinson, WI 53538, P: 800-547-7377, F: 303-322-0627, www.officer.com
Law Enforcement

Cylinder & Slide, Inc., 245 E. 4th St., Fremont, NE 68025, P: 800-448-1713, F: 402-721-0263, www.cylinder-slide.com
Firearms; Gun Barrels; Gun Grips & Stocks; Gun Parts/Gunsmithing; Magazines, Cartridge; Scopes, Sights & Accessories; Wholesaler/Distributor

D

DAC Technologies/GunMaster, 12120 Colonel Glenn Rd., Suite 6200, Little Rock, AR 72210, P: 800-920-0098, F: 501-661-9108, www.dactec.com
Black Powder Accessories; Camping; Cooking Equipment/Accessories; Firearms Maintenance Equipment; Gun Cabinets/Racks/Safes; Gun Locks; Hunting Accessories; Wholesaler/Distributor

DMT-Diamond Machine Technology, 84 Hayes Memorial Dr., Marlborough, MA 01752, P: 800-666-4368, F: 508-485-3924, www.dmtsharp.com
Archery; Cooking Equipment/Accessories; Cutlery; Hunting Accessories; Knives/Knife Cases; Sharpeners; Sports Accessories; Taxidermy

D & K Mfg., Co., Inc., 5180 US Hwy. 380, Bridgeport, TX 76426, P: 800-553-1028, F: 940-683-0248, www.d-k.net
Bags & Equipment Cases; Custom Manufacturing; Emblems & Decals; Law Enforcement; Leathergoods

D.S.A., Inc., 27 W. 990 Industrial Ave. (60010), P.O. Box 370, Lake Barrington, IL 60011, P: 847-277-7258, F: 847-277-7263, www.dsarms.com
Ammunition; Books/Industry Publications; Firearms; Gun Grips & Stocks; Gun Parts/Gunsmithing; Law Enforcement; Magazines, Cartridge; Scopes, Sights & Accessories

Daisy Manufacturing Co./Daisy Outdoors Products, 400 W. Stribling Dr., P.O. Box 220, Rogers, AR 72756, P: 800-643-3458, F: 479-636-0573, www.daisy.com
Airguns; Airsoft; Ammunition; Clay Targets; Eyewear; Scopes, Sights & Accessories; Targets; Training & Safety Equipment

Dakota Arms, Inc., 1310 Industry Rd., Sturgis, SD 57785, P: 605-347-4686, F: 605-347-4459, www.dakotaarms.com
Ammunition; Custom Manufacturing; Export/Import Specialists; Firearms; Gun Cases; Gun Grips & Stocks; Gun Parts/Gunsmithing; Reloading

Damascus Protective Gear, P.O. Box 543, Rutland, VT, 05702, P: 800-305-2417, F: 805-639-0610, www.damascusgear.com
Archery; Custom Manufacturing; Gloves, Mitts, Hats; Law Enforcement; Leathergoods

Danalco, Inc., 1020 Hamilton Rd., Suite G, Duarte, CA 91010, P: 800-868-2629, F: 800-216-9938, www.danalco.com
Footwear; Gloves, Mitts, Hats

Dan's Whetstone Co., Inc./Washita Mountain Whetstone Co., 418 Hilltop Rd., Pearcy, AR 71964, P: 501-767-1616, F: 501-767-9598, www.danswhetstone.com
Black Powder Accessories; Camping; Cutlery; Gun Parts/Gunsmithing; Hunting Accessories; Knives/ Knife Cases; Sharpeners; Sports Accessories

Daniel Defense, Inc., 6002 Commerce Blvd., Suite 109, Savannah, GA 31408, P: 866-554-4867, F: 912-964-4237, www.danieldefense.com
Firearms

Danner, Inc., 17634 NE Airport Way, Portland, OR 97230, P: 800-345-0430, F: 503-251-1119
Footwear

Darkwoods Blind, LLC, 1209 SE 44th, Suite 2, Oklahoma City, OK 73129, P: 405-520-6754, F: 405-677-2262, www.darkwoodsblind.com
Archery; Blinds; Camouflage; Custom Manufacturing; Firearms; Hunting Accessories; Outfitter; Vehicles, Utility & Rec

Darn Tough Vermont, 364 Whetstone Dr., P.O. Box 307, Northfield, VT 05663, P: 877-DARNTUFF, F: 802-485-6140, www.darntough.com
Backpacking; Camping; Footwear; Hunting Accessories; Men & Women's Clothing

Davidson's, 6100 Wilkinson Dr., Prescott, AZ, 86301, P: 800-367-4867, F: 928-776-0344, www.galleryofguns.com
Ammunition; Law Enforcement; Magazines, Cartridge; Online Services; Scopes, Sights & Accessories; Wholesaler/Distributor

Day Six Outdoors, 1150 Brookstone Centre Parkway, Columbus, GA 31904, P: 877-DAY-SIX0, F: 706-323-0178, www.day6outdoors.com
Feeder Equipment; Wildlife Management

Del Norte Outdoors, P.O. Box 5046, Santa Maria, CA 93456, P: 805-474-1793, F: 805-474-1793, www.delnorteoutdoors.com
Archery; Hunting Accessories; Sports Accessories

Del-Ton, Inc., 218B Aviation Pkwy., Elizabethtown, NC 28337, P: 910-645-2172, F: 910-645-2244, www.del-ton.com
Firearms; Gun Barrels; Gun Parts/Gunsmithing; Law Enforcement; Wholesaler/Distributor

DeLorme, Two DeLorme Dr., Yarmouth, ME 04096, P: 800-335-1763, F: 800-575-2244, www.delorme.com
Books/Industry Publications; Computer Software; Hunting Accessories; Sports Accessories; Tours/ Travel

Demyan, 10, 2nd Donskoy Ln., Moscow, 119071, RUSSIAN FEDERATION, P: 011 74959847629, F: 011 74959847629, www.demyan.info
Airguns; Firearms

Dengta Sinpraise Weaving & Dressing Co., Ltd., Tai Zihe District, Wangshuitai Pangjiahe, Liao Yang, LiaoNing Province 111000, CHINA, P: 011 864193305888, F: 011 864193990566, www.sinpraise-hunting.com
Camouflage; Camping; Men & Women's Clothing; Sports Accessories

DeSantis Holster and Leather Goods Co., 431 Bayview Ave., Amityville, NY 11701, P: 800-424-1236, F: 631-841-6320, www.desantisholster.com
Bags & Equipment Cases; Gun Cases; Holsters; Hunting Accessories; Law Enforcement; Leathergoods

Desert Tactical Arms, P.O. Box 65816, Salt Lake City, UT 84165, P: 801-975-7272, F: 801-908-6425, www.deserttacticalarms.com
Firearms; Law Enforcement

Desiccare, Inc., 3400 Pomona Blvd., Pomona, CA 91768, P: 800-446-6650, F: 909-444-9045, www.desiccare.com
Food; Footwear; Gun Cabinets/Racks/Safes; Leathergoods; Scents & Lures

Diamondback Tactical, 23040 N. 11th Ave., Bldg. 1, Phoenix, AZ 85027, P: 800-735-7030, F: 623-583-0674, www.diamondbacktactical.com
Law Enforcement

Diana/Mayer & Grammelspacher GmbH & Co. KG, Karlstr, 34, Rastatt, 76437, GERMANY, P: 011 4972227620, F: 011 49722276278, www.diana-airguns.de
Airguns; Scopes, Sights & Accessories

Dillon Precision Products, Inc., 8009 E. Dillon's Way, Scottsdale, AZ 85260, P: 800-223-4570, F: 480-998-2786, www.dillonprecision.com

Bags & Equipment Cases; Feeder Equipment; Hearing Protection; Holsters; Hunting Accessories; Reloading

Dimension 3D Printing, 7655 Commerce Way, Eden Prairie, MN 55344, P: 888-480-3548, F: 952-294-3715, www.dimensionprinting.com
Computer Software; Custom Manufacturing; Gun Parts/Gunsmithing; Hunting Accessories; Scopes, Sights & Accessories

Ding Zing Chemical Products Co., Ltd., No. 8-1 Pei-Lin Rd., Hsiao-Kang Dist., Kaohsiung, 812, TAIWAN, P: 011 88678070166, F: 011 88678071616, www.dingzing.com
Backpacking; Bags & Equipment Cases; Camping; Custom Manufacturing; Footwear; Gloves, Mitts, Hats; Men & Women's Clothing; Sports Accessories

Directex, 304 S. Leighton Ave., Anniston, AL 36207, P: 800-845-3603, F: 256-235-2275, www.directex.net
Archery; Backpacking; Bags & Equipment Cases; Custom Manufacturing; Export/Import Specialists; Gun Cases; Holsters; Hunting Accessories

Dixie Gun Works, Inc., 1412 W. Reelfoot Ave., P.O. Box 130, Union City, TN 38281, P: 800-238-6785, F: 731-885-0440, www.dixiegunworks.com
Black Powder Accessories; Book/Industry Publications; Firearms; Gun Parts/Gunsmithing; Hunting Accessories; Knives/Knife Cases

DNZ Products, LLC/Game Reaper & Freedom Reaper Scope Mounts, 2710 Wilkins Dr., Sanford, NC 27330, P: 919-777-9608, F: 919-777-9609, www.dnzproducts.com
Black Powder Accessories; Custom Manufacturing; Gun Parts/Gunsmithing; Hunting Accessories; Scopes, Sights & Accessories

Do-All Traps, LLC/dba Do-All Outdoors, 216 19th Ave. N, Nashville, TN 37203, P: 800-252-9247, F: 800-633-3172, www.doalloutdoors.com
Clay Targets; Gun Cases; Hunting Accessories; Outdoor Art, Jewelry, Sculpture; Recoil Protection Devices & Services; Shooting Range Equipment; Targets; Taxidermy

Doc's Deer Farm and Scents, 2118 Niles-Cortland Rd., Cortland, OH 44420, P: 330-638-9507, F: 330-638-2772, www.docsdeerscents.com
Archery; Hunting Accessories; Scents & Lures

Docter Optic/Imported by Merkel USA, 7661 Commerce Lane, Trussville, AL 35173, P: 800-821-3021, F: 205-655-7078, www.merkel-usa.com
Binoculars; Scopes, Sights & Accessories

Dogtra Co., 22912 Lockness Ave., Torrance, CA, 90501, P: 888-811-9111, F: 310-534-9111, www.dogtra.com
Hunting Accessories; Pet Supplies; Training & Safety Equipment

Dokken Dog Supply, Inc., 4186 W. 85th St., Northfield, MN 55057, P: 507-744-2616, F: 507-744-5575, www.deadfowltrainer.com
Hunting Accessories; Pet Supplies; Scents & Lures; Training & Safety Equipment

DoubleStar/J&T Distributing, P.O. Box 430, Winchester, KY 40391, P: 888-736-7725, F: 859-745-4638, www.jtdistributing.com
Firearms; Firearms Maintenance Equipment; Gun Barrels; Gun Parts/Gunsmithing; Magazines, Cartridge; Wholesaler/Distributor

Down Range Mfg., LLC, 4170 N. Gun Powder Circle, Hastings, NE 68901, P: 402-463-3415, F: 402-463-3452, www.downrangemfg.com
Ammunition; Clay Targets; Custom Manufacturing; Reloading

Down Wind Scents, LLC, P.O. Box 549, Severna Park, MD 21146, P: 410-647-8451, F: 410-647-7828, www.downwindscents.com
Archery; Firearms Maintenance Equipment; Hunting Accessories; Lubricants; Scents & Lures

DPMS Firearms, LLC, 3312 12th St. SE, St. Cloud, MN 56304, P: 800-578-3767, F: 320-258-4449, www.dpmsinc.com
Firearms; Scopes, Sights & Accessories

Dri Duck Traders, 7007 College Blvd., Suite 700, Overland Park, KS 66211, P: 866-852-8222, F: 913-234-6280, www.driducktraders.com
Camouflage; Men & Women's Clothing

DriFire, LLC, 3151 Williams Rd., Suite E, Columbus, GA 31909, P: 866-266-4035, F: 706-507-7556, www.drifire.com
Camouflage; Men & Women's Clothing; Training & Safety Equipment

DryGuy, LLC, P.O. Box 1102, Mercer Island, WA 98040, P: 888-330-9452, F: 206-232-9830, www.maxxdry.com
Backpacking; Bags & Equipment Cases; Camping; Footwear; Gloves, Mitts, Hats; Hunting Accessories; Sports Accessories; Wholesaler/Distributor

Du-Lite Corp., 171 River Rd., Middletown, CT 06457, P: 860-347-2505, F: 860-344-9404, www.du-lite.com
Gunsmithing; Lubricants

Duck Commander Co., Inc./Buck Commander Co., Inc., 1978 Brownlee Rd., Calhoun, LA 71225, P: 318-396-1126, F: 318-396-1127, www.duckcommander.com, www.buckcommander.com

Camping; Emblems & Decals; Food; Game Calls; Gun Cases; Hunting Accessories, Men & Women's Clothing; Videos

Ducks Unlimited, Inc., One Waterfowl Way, Memphis, TN 38120, P: 800-45-DUCKS, F: 901-758-3850, www.ducks.org
Books/Industry Publications; Camouflage; Decoys; Firearms; Hunting Accessories; Outdoor Art, Jewelry, Sculpture; Wildlife Management

Duk-Inn-Blind, 49750 Alpine Dr., Macomb, MI 48044, P: 586-855-7494, F: 603-626-4672
Blinds; Camouflage; Hunting Accessories; Wholesaler/Distributor

Dummies Unlimited, Inc., 2435 Pine St., Pomona, CA 91767, P: 866-4DUMMIES, F: 909-392-7510, F: 909-392-7510, www.dummiesunlimited.com
Law Enforcement; Shooting Range Equipment; Targets; Training & Safety Equipment

Duostock Designs, Inc., P.O. Box 32, Welling, OK 74471, P: 866-386-7865, F: 918-431-3182, www.duostock.com
Firearms; Gun Grips & Stocks; Law Enforcement; Recoil Protection Devices & Services

Durasight Scope Mounting Systems, 5988 Peachtree Corners East, Norcross, GA 30071, P: 800-321-8767, F: 770-242-8546, www.durasight.com
Scopes, Sights & Accessories

Dynamic Research Technologies, LLC, 405 N. Lyon St., Grant City, MO 64456, P: 660-564-2331, F: 660-564-2103, www.drtammo.com
Ammunition; Reloading

E

E-Z Mount Corp., 1706 N. River Dr., San Angelo, TX 76902, P: 800-292-3756, F: 325-658-4951, www.ezmountcorp@zipnet.us
Gun Cabinets/Racks/Safes

E-Z Pull Trigger, 932 W. 5th St., Centralia, IL 62801, P: 618-532-6964, F: 618-532-5154, www.ezpulltriggerassist.com
Firearms; Gun Parts/Gunsmithing; Hunting Accessories

E.A.R., Inc./Insta-Mold Div., P.O. Box 18888, Boulder, CO 80303, P: 800-525-2690, F: 303-447-2637, www.earinc.com
Eyewear; Hearing Protection; Law Enforcement; Shooting Range Equipment; Wholesaler/Distributor

ER Shaw/Small Arms Mfg., 5312 Thoms Run Rd., Bridgeville, PA 15017, P: 412-221-4343, F: 412-221-4303, www.ershawbarrels.com
Custom Manufacturing; Firearms; Gun Barrels

ECS Composites, 3560 Rogue River Hwy., Grants Pass, OR 97527, P: 541-476-8871, F: 541-474-2479, www.transitcases.com
Custom Manufacturing; Gun Cases; Law Enforcement; Sports Accessories

EMCO Supply, Inc./Red Rock Outdoor Gear, 2601 Dutton Ave., Waco, TX 76711, P: 800-342-4654, F: 254-662-0045
Backpacking; Bags & Equipment Cases; Blinds; Camouflage; Compasses; Game Calls; Hunting Accessories; Law Enforcement

E.M.F. Co., Inc./Purveyors of Fine Firearms Since 1956, 1900 E. Warner Ave., Suite 1-D, Santa Ana, CA 92705, P: 800-430-1310, F: 800-508-1824, www.emf-company.com
Black Powder Accessories; Firearms; Gun Parts/Gunsmithing; Holsters; Leathergoods; Wholesaler/Distributor

EOTAC, 1940 Old Dunbar Rd., West Columbia, SC 29172, P: 803-744-9930, F: 803-744-9933, www.eotac.com
Tactical Clothing

ESS Goggles, P.O. Box 1017, Sun Valley, ID 83353, P: 877-726-4072, F: 208-726-4563
Eyewear; Hunting Accessories; Law Enforcement; Shooting Range Equipment; Training & Safety Equipment

ETL/Secure Logic, 2351 Tenaya Dr., Modesto, CA 95354, P: 800-344-3242, F: 209-529-3854, www.securelogiconline.com
Firearms; Gun Cabinets/Racks/Safes; Training & Safety Equipment

EZ 4473/American Firearms Software, 5955 Edmond St., Las Vegas, NV 89118, P: 702-364-9022, F: 702-364-9063, www.ez4473.com
Computer Software; Retailer Services

EZE-LAP® Diamond Products, 3572 Arrowhead Dr., Carson City, NV 89706, P: 800-843-4815, F: 775-888-9555, www.eze-lap.com
Camping; Cooking Equipment/Accessories; Cutlery; Gun Parts/Gunsmithing; Hunting Accessories; Sharpeners; Sports Accessories

Eagle Grips, Inc., 460 Randy Rd., Carol Stream, IL, 60188, P: 800-323-6144, F: 630-260-0486, www.eaglegrips.com
Gun Grips & Stocks

Eagle Imports, Inc., 1750 Brielle Ave., Suite B-1, Wanamassa, NJ 07712, P: 732-493-0333, F: 732-493-0301, www.bersafirearmsusa.com

Export/Import Specialists; Firearms; Holsters; Magazines, Cartridge; Wholesaler/Distributor

Eagle Industries Unlimited, Inc., 1000 Biltmore Dr., Fenton, MO 63026, P: 888-343-7547, F: 636-349-0321, www. eagleindustries.com
Backpacking; Bags & Equipment Cases; Camping; Gun Cases; Holsters; Hunting Accessories; Law Enforcement; Sports Accessories

Eagle Seed Co., 8496 Swan Pond Rd., P.O. Box 308, Weiner, AR 72479, P: 870-684-7377, F: 870-684-2225, www. eagleseed.com
Custom Manufacturing; Retail Packaging; Wholesaler/Distributor; Wildlife Management

Ear Phone Connection, 25139 Avenue Stanford, Valencia, CA 91355, P: 888-372-1888, F: 661-775-5622, www. earphoneconnect.com
Airsoft; Hearing Protection; Law Enforcement; Paintball Accessories; Two-Way Radios

EarHugger Safety Equipment, Inc., 1819 N. Main St., Suite 8, Spanish Fork, UT 84660, P: 800-236-1449, F: 801-371-8901, www.earhuggersafety.com
Law Enforcement

Easy Loop Lock, LLC, 8049 Monetary Dr., Suite D-4, Riviera Beach, FL 33404, P: 561-304-4990, F: 561-337-4655, www.ellock.com
Camping; Gun Locks; Hunting Accessories; Sports Accessories; Wholesaler/Distributor

E-Z Mount Corp., 1706 N. River Dr., San Angelo, TX 76902, P: 800-292-3756, F: 325-658-4951, www.ezmountcorp@ zipnet.us
Gun Cabinets/Racks/Safes

E-Z Pull Trigger, 932 W. 5th St., Centralia, IL 62801, P: 618-532-6964, F: 618-532-5154, www.ezpulltriggerassist.com
Firearms; Gun Parts/Gunsmithing; Hunting Accessories

Eberlestock, P.O. Box 862, Boise, ID 83701, P: 877-866-3047, F: 240-526-2632, www.eberlestock.com
Archery; Backpacking; Bags & Equipment Cases; Gun Grips & Stocks; Hunting Accessories; Law Enforcement

Ed Brown Products, Inc., P.O. Box 492, Perry, MO 63462, P: 573-565-3261, F: 573-565-2791, www.edbrown.com
Computer Software; Custom Manufacturing; Firearms; Gun Barrels; Gun Parts/Gunsmithing; Magazines, Cartridge; Scopes, Sights & Accessories

EdgeCraft Corp./Chefs Choice, 825 Southwood Rd., Avondale, PA 19311, P: 800-342-3255, F: 610-268-3545, www.edgecraft.com
Cooking Equipment/Accessories; Custom Manufacturing; Cutlery; Export/Import Specialists; Hunting Accessories; Knives/Knife Cases; Sharpeners

Edgemaker Co., The/(formerly) The Jennex Co., 3902 Funston St., Toledo, OH 43612, P: 800-531-EDGE, F: 419-478-0833, www.edgemaker.com
Camping; Cutlery; Hunting Accessories; Sharpeners; Sports Accessories; Wholesaler/Distributor

El Paso Saddlery, 2025 E. Yandell, El Paso, TX 79903, P: 915-544-2233, F: 915-544-2535, www.epsaddlery.com
Holsters; Leathergoods

Elastic Products/Industrial Opportunities, Inc., 2586 Hwy. 19, P.O. Box 1649, Andrews, NC 28901, P: 800-872-4264, F: 828-321-4784, www.elasticproducts.com
Camouflage; Custom Manufacturing; Hunting Accessories; Men's Clothing

ELCAN Optical Technologies, 1601 N. Plano Rd., Richardson, TX 75081, P: 877-TXELCAN, F: 972-344-8260, www. elcan.com
Binoculars; Custom Manufacturing; Law Enforcement; Scopes, Sights & Accessories

Elder Hosiery Mills, Inc., 139 Homewood Ave., P.O. Box 2377, Burlington, NC 27217, P: 800-745-0267, F: 336-226-5846, www.elderhosiery.com
Footwear

Eley Limited/Eley Hawk Limited, Selco Way, First Ave., Minworth Industrial Estate, Minworth, Sutton Coldfield, West Midlands B76 1BA, UNITED KINGDOM, P: 011 4401213134567, F: 011-4401213134568, www. eleyammunition.com, www.eleyhawkltd.com
Ammunition

Elite First Aid, Inc., 700 E. Club Blvd., Durham, NC 27704, P: 800-556-2537, F: 919-220-6071, www.elite1staid.com
Backpacking; Camping; Cooking Equipment/ Accessories; Hunting Accessories; Sports Accessories; Survival Kits/First Aid; Wholesaler/ Distributor

Elite Iron, LLC, 1345 Thunders Trail, Bldg. D, Potomac, MT 59823, P: 406-244-0234, F: 406-244-0135, www.eliteiron. net
Law Enforcement; Scopes, Sights & Accessories

Elite Survival Systems, 310 W. 12th St., P.O. Box 245, Washington, MO 63090, P: 866-340-2778, F: 636-390-2977, www.elitesurvival.com

Backpacking; Bags & Equipment Cases; Custom Manufacturing; Footwear; Gun Cases; Holsters; Knives/Knife Cases; Law Enforcement

Ellett Brothers, 267 Columbia Ave., P.O. Box 128, Chapin, SC 29036, P: 800-845-3711, F: 800-323-3006, www. ellettbrothers.com
Ammunition; Archery; Black Powder Accessories; Firearms; Hunting Accessories; Leathergoods; Scopes, Sights & Accessories; Wholesaler/Distributor

Ellington-Rush, Inc./Cough Silencer/SlingStix, 170 Private Dr., Lula, GA 30554, P: 706-677-2394, F: 706-677-3425, www. coughsilencer.com, www.slingstix.com
Archery; Black Powder Accessories; Game Calls; Hunting Accessories; Law Enforcement; Shooting Range Equipment

Elvex Corp., 13 Trowbridge, Bethel, CT 06801, P: 800-888-6582, F: 203-791-2278, www.elvex.com
Eyewear; Hearing Protection; Hunting Accessories; Law Enforcement; Men's Clothing; Paintball Accessories

Emerson Knives, Inc., 2730 Monterey St., Suite 101, Torrance, CA 90503, P: 310-212-7455, F: 310-212-7289, www. emersonknives.com
Camping; Cutlery; Knives/Knife Cases; Men & Women's Clothing; Wholesaler/Distributor

Empire Pewter Manufacturing, P.O. Box 15, Amsterdam, NY 12010, P: 518-843-0048, F: 518-843-7050
Custom Manufacturing; Emblems & Decals; Outdoor Art, Jewelry, Sculpture

Energizer Holdings, 533 Maryville University Dr., St. Louis, MO 63141, P: 314-985-2000, F: 314-985-2207, www. energizer.com
Backpacking; Camping; Hunting Accessories; Law Enforcement; Lighting Products; Sports Accessories; Survival Kits/First Aid; Training & Safety Equipment

Enforcement Technology Group, Inc., 400 N. Broadway, 4th Floor, Milwaukee, WI 53202, P: 800-873-2872, F: 414-276-1533, www.etgi.us
Custom Manufacturing; Law Enforcement; Online Services; Shooting Range Equipment; Training & Safety Equipment; Wholesaler/Distributor

Entreprise Arms, Inc., 5321 Irwindale Ave., Irwindale, CA 91706-2025, P: 626-962-8712, F: 626-962-4692, www. entreprise.com
Firearms; Gun Parts/Gunsmithing

Environ-Metal, Inc./Hevishot®, 1307 Clark Mill Rd., P.O. Box 834, Sweet Home, OR 97386, P: 541-367-3522, F: 541-367-3552, www.hevishot.com
Ammunition; Law Enforcement; Reloading

EOTAC, 1940 Old Dunbar Rd., West Columbia, SC 29172, P: 888-672-0303, F: 803-744-9933, www.eotac.com
Gloves, Mitts, Hats; Men's Clothing

Epilog Laser, 16371 Table Mountain Pkwy., Golden, CO 80403, P: 303-277-1188, F: 303-277-9669, www. epiloglaser.com

Essential Gear, Inc./eGear, 171 Wells St., Greenfield, MA 01301, P: 800-582-3861, F: 413-772-8947, www. essentialgear.com
Backpacking; Camping; Hunting Accessories; Law Enforcement; Lighting Products; Sports Accessories; Survival Kits/First Aid; Training & Safety Equipment

European American Armory Corp., P.O. Box 560746, Rockledge, FL 32956, P: 321-639-4842, F: 321-639-7006, www.eaacorp.com
Airguns; Firearms

Evans Sports, Inc., 801 Industrial Dr., P.O. Box 20, Houston, MO 65483, P: 800-748-8318, F: 417-967-2819, www. evanssports.com
Ammunition; Bags & Equipment Cases; Camping; Custom Manufacturing; Gun Cabinets/Racks/Safes; Hunting Accessories; Retail Packaging; Sports Accessories

Evolved Habitats, 2261 Morganza Hwy., New Roads, LA 70760, P: 225-638-4016, F: 225-638-4009, www.evolved. com
Archery; Export/Import Specialists; Hunting Accessories; Pet Supplies; Scents & Lures; Wildlife Management

Extendo Bed Co., 223 Roedel Ave., Caldwell, ID 83605, P: 800-752-0706, F: 208-286-0925, www.extendobed.com
Law Enforcement; Training & Safety Equipment

Extreme Dimension Wildlife Calls, LLC, 208 Kennebec Rd., Hampden, ME 04444, P: 866-862-2825, F: 207-862-3925, www.phantomcalls.com
Game Calls

Extreme Shock USA, 182 Camp Jacob Rd., Clintwood, VA 24228, P: 877-337-6772, F: 276-926-6092, www. extremeshockusa.net
Ammunition; Law Enforcement; Lubricants; Reloading

ExtremeBeam Tactical, 2275 Huntington Dr., Suite 872, San Marino, CA 91108, P: 626-372-5898, F: 626-609-0640, www.extremebeamtactical.com
Camping; Law Enforcement; Lighting Products; Outfitter

Exxel Outdoors, Inc., 14214 Atlanta Dr., Laredo, TX 78045, P: 956-724-8933, F: 956-725-2516, www.prestigemfg.com
Camping; Export/Import Specialists; Men's Clothing

F

F&W Media/Krause Publications, 700 E. State St., Iola, WI 54990, P: 800-457-2873, F: 715-445-4087, www. krausebooks.com
Books/Industry Publications; Videos

F.A.I.R. Srl, Via Gitti, 41, Marcheno, 25060, ITALY, P: 011 39030861162, F: 011 390308610179, www.fair.it
Firearms; Gun Barrels; Gun Parts/Gunsmithing; Hunting Accessories

F.A.P. F. LLI Pietta SNC, Via Mandolossa, 102, Gussago, Brescia 25064, ITALY, P: 011 390303737098, F: 011 390303737100, www.pietta.it
Black Powder Accessories; Firearms; Gun Cases; Gun Grips & Stocks; Gun Parts/Gunsmithing; Holsters

F.I.A.V. L. Mazzacchera SPA, Via S. Faustino, 62, Milano, 20134, ITALY, P: 011 390221095411, F: 011 390221095530, www.flav.it
Gun Parts/Gunsmithing

FMG Publications/Shooting Industry Magazine, 12345 World Trade Dr., San Diego, CA 92128, P: 800-537-3006, F: 858-605-0247, www.shootingindustry.com
Books/Industry Publications; Videos

FNH USA, P.O. Box 697, McLean, VA 22101, P: 703-288-1292, F: 703-288-1730, www.fnhusa.com
Ammunition; Firearms; Law Enforcement; Training & Safety Equipment

F.T.C. (Friedheim Tool), 1433 Roosevelt Ave., National City, CA 91950, 619-474-3600, F: 619-474-1300, www.ftcsteamers. com
Firearms Maintenance Equipment

Fab Defense, 43 Yakov Olamy St., Moshav Mishmar Hashiva, 50297, ISRAEL, P: 011 972039603399, F: 011 972039603312, www.fab-defense.com
Gun Grips & Stocks; Law Enforcement; Targets

FailZero, 7825 SW Ellipse Way, Stuart, FL 34997, P: 772-223-6699, F: 772-223-9996
Gun Parts/Gunsmithing

Falcon Industries, P.O. Box 1690, Edgewood, NM 87015, P: 877-281-3783, F: 505-281-3991, www.ergogrips.net
Gun Grips & Stocks; Gun Parts/Gunsmithing; Law Enforcement; Scopes, Sights & Accessories; Sports Accessories

Fasnap® Corp., 3500 Reedy Dr., Elkhart, IN 46514, P: 800-624-2058, F: 574-264-0802, www.fasnap.com
Backpacking; Bags & Equipment Cases; Gun Cases; Holsters; Hunting Accessories; Knives/Knife Cases; Leathergoods; Wholesaler/Distributor

Faulk's Game Call Co., Inc., 616 18th St., Lake Charles, LA 70601, P: 337-436-9726, FL 337-494-7205, www. faulkcalls.com
Game Calls

Fausti Stefano s.r.l., Via Martiri dell'Indipendenza 70, Marcheno (BS), 25060, ITALY, P: 011 390308960220, F: 011 390308610155, www.faustistefanoarms.com
Firearms

Feather Flage "Ducks In A Row Camo"/B & D Garments, LLC, P.O. Box 5326, Lafayette, LA 70502, P: 866-DUK-CAMO, F: 337-896-8137, www.featherflage.com
Camouflage; Wholesaler/Distributor

Federal Premium Ammunition/ATK Commercial Products, 900 Ehlen Dr., Anoka, MN 55303, P: 800-322-2342, F: 763-323-2506, www.federalpremium.com
Ammunition

Feijuang International Corp., 4FI-1/7, No. 177 Min-Sheng West Road, Taipei, TAIWAN, P: 011 886225520169, F: 011 886225578359
Blinds; Camping; Compasses; Eyewear; Hearing Protection; Hunting Accessories; Sports Accessories

Fenix Flashlights, LLC/4Sevens, LLC, 4896 N. Royal Atlanta Dr., Suite 305, Tucker, GA 30084, P: 866-471-0749, F: 866-323-9544, www.4sevens.com
Backpacking; Camping; Law Enforcement; Lighting Products

FenixLightUS/Casualhome Worldwide, Inc., 29 William St., Amityville, NY 11701, P: 877-FENIXUS, F: 631-789-2970, www.fenixlightus.com
Camping; Law Enforcement; Lighting Products; Scopes, Sights & Accessories; Shooting Range Equipment; Wholesaler/Distributor

Field & Stream Watches, 12481 NW 44th St., Coral Springs, FL 33065, P: 954-509-1476, F: 954-509-1479, www. tfg24gold.com
Camping; Hunting Accessories; Outfitter; Sports Accessories; Watches; Wholesaler/Distributor

Filson, 1555 4th Ave. S, Seattle, WA 98134, P: 800-297-1897, F: 206-624-4539, www.filson.com
Bags & Equipment Cases; Footwear; Gloves, Mitts, Hats; Gun Cases; Hunting Accessories; Leathergoods; Men & Women's Clothing

Final Approach/Bushnell Outdoor Accessories, 9200 Cody, Overland Park, KS 66214, P: 800-423-3537, F: 913-752-3539, www.kolpin-outdoors.com
Bags & Equipment Cases; Blinds; Decoys; Gun Cases; Hunting Accessories; Videos

Fiocchi of America, Inc., 6930 N. Fremont Rd., Ozark, MO 65721, P: 800-721-AMMO, 417-725-1039, www.fiocciusa.com
Ammunition; Reloading

First Choice Armor & Equipment, Inc., 209 Yelton St., Spindale, NC 28160, P: 800-88-ARMOR, F: 866-481-4929, www.firstchoicearmor.com
Law Enforcement; Training & Safety Equipment

First-Light USA, LLC, 320 Cty. Rd. 1100 North, Seymour, IL 61875, P: 877-454-4450, F: 877-454-4420, www.first-light-usa.com
Backpacking; Camping; Firearms; Law Enforcement; Lighting Products; Survival Kits/First Aid; Training & Safety Equipment

Flambeau, Inc., P.O. Box 97, Middlefield, OH 44062, P: 440-632-1631, F: 440-632-1581, www.flambeauoutdoors.com
Bags & Equipment Cases; Crossbows & Accessories; Custom Manufacturing; Decoys; Game Calls; Gun Cases

Fleming & Clark, Ltd., 3013 Honeysuckle Dr., Spring Hill, TN 37174, P: 800-373-6710, F: 931-487-9972, www.flemingandclark.com
Bags & Equipment Cases; Footwear; Gun Cases; Hunting Accessories; Knives/Knife Cases; Leathergoods; Men's Clothing; Wholesaler/Distributor

Flitz International, Ltd., 821 Mohr Ave., Waterford, WI 53185, P: 800-558-8611, F: 262-534-2991, www.flitz.com
Black Powder Accessories; Firearms Maintenance Equipment; Gun Barrels; Gun Grips & Stocks; Gun Parts/Gunsmithing; Knives/Knife Cases; Lubricants; Scopes, Sights & Accessories

Fobus Holsters/CAA-Command Arms Accessories, 780 Haunted Lane, Bensalem, PA 19020, P: 267-803-1517, F: 267-803-1002, www.fobusholsters.com, www.commandarms.com
Bags & Equipment Cases; Firearms; Gun Cases; Gun Grips & Stocks; Gun Parts/Gunsmithing; Holsters; Law Enforcement; Scopes, Sights & Accessories

Foiles Migrators, Inc., 101 N. Industrial Park Dr., Pittsfield, IL 62363, P: 866-83-GEESE, F: 217-285-5995, www.foilesstraitmeat.com
Game Calls; Hunting Accessories

FoodSaver/Jarden Consumer Solutions, 24 Latour Ln., Little Rock, AR 72223, P: 501-821-0138, F: 501-821-0139, www.foodsaver.com
Backpacking; Camping; Cooking Equipment/Accessories; Food; Hunting Accessories

Force One, LLC, 520 Commercial Dr., Fairfield, OH 45014, P: 800-462-7880, F: 513-939-1166, www.forceonearmor.com
Custom Manufacturing; Law Enforcement

Forster Products, Inc., 310 E. Lanark Ave., Lanark, IL 61046, P: 815-493-6360, F: 815-493-2371, www.forsterproducts.com
Black Powder Accessories; Custom Manufacturing; Firearms Maintenance Equipment; Gun Parts/Gunsmithing; Lubricants; Reloading; Scopes, Sights & Accessories

Fort Knox Security Products, 993 N. Industrial Park Rd., Orem, UT 84057, P: 800-821-5216, F: 801-226-5493, www.ftknox.com
Custom Manufacturing; Gun Cabinets/Racks/Safes; Home Furnishings; Hunting Accessories

Foshan City Nanhai Weihong Mold Products Co., Ltd./Xinwei Photo Electricity Industrial Co., Ltd., Da Wo District, Dan Zhao Town, Nanhai, Foshan City, GuangZhou, 528216, CHINA, P: 011 8675785444666, F: 011 8675785444111, www.weihongmj.net
Binoculars; Scopes, Sights & Accessories

Fox Knives Oreste Frati SNC, Via La Mola, 4, Maniago, Pordenone 33085, ITALY, P: 011 39042771814, F: 011 390427700514, www.foxcutlery.com
Camouflage; Camping; Cutlery; Hunting Accessories; Knives/Knife Cases; Law Enforcement; Wholesaler/Distributor

Fox Outdoor Products, 2040 N. 15th Ave., Melrose Park, IL 60160, P: 800-523-4332, F: 708-338-9210, www.foxoutdoor.com
Bags & Equipment Cases; Camouflage; Eyewear; Gun Cases; Holsters; Law Enforcement; Men's Clothing; Wholesaler/Distributor

FoxFury Personal Lighting Solutions, 2091 Elevado Hill Dr., Vista, CA 92084, P: 760-945-4231, F: 760-758-6283, www.foxfury.com
Backpacking; Camping; Hunting Accessories; Law Enforcement; Lighting Products; Paintball Accessories; Sports Accessories; Training & Safety Equipment

FOXPRO, Inc., 14 Fox Hollow Dr., Lewistown, PA 17044, P: 866-463-6977, F: 717-247-3594, www.gofoxpro.com
Archery; Decoys; Game Calls; Hunting Accessories

Foxy Huntress, 17 Windsor Ridge, Frisco, TX 75034, P: 866-370-1343, F: 972-370-1343, www.foxyhuntress.com
Camouflage; Women's Clothing

Franchi, 17603 Indian Head Hwy., Accokeek, MD 20607, P: 800-264-4962, www.franchiusa.com
Firearms

Franklin Sports, Inc./Uniforce Tactical Division, 17 Campanelli Pkwy., Stoughton, MA 02072, P: 800-225-8647, F: 781-341-3220, www.uniforcetactical.com
Camouflage; Eyewear; Gloves, Mitts, Hats; Law Enforcement; Leathergoods; Men's Clothing; Wholesaler/Distributor

Franzen Security Products, Inc., 680 Flinn Ave., Suite 35, Moorpark, CA 93021, P: 800-922-7656, F: 805-529-0446, www.securecase.com
Bags & Equipment Cases; Custom Manufacturing; Gun Cases; Gun Locks; Hunting Accessories; Law Enforcement; Shooting Range Equipment; Training & Safety Equipment

Fraternal Blue Line, P.O. Box 260199, Boston, MA 02126, P: 617-212-1288, F: 617-249-0857, www.fraternalblueline.org
Custom Manufacturing; Emblems & Decals; Law Enforcement; Men & Women's Clothing; Wholesaler/Distributor

Freedom Arms, Inc., 314 Hwy. 239, Freedom, WY 83120, P: 800-833-4432, F: 800-252-4867, www.freedomarms.com
Firearms; Gun Cases; Holsters; Scopes, Sights & Accessories

Freelinc, 266 W. Center St., Orem, UT 84057, P: 866-467-1199, F: 801-672-3003, www.freelinc.com
Law Enforcement

Frogg Toggs, 131 Sundown Drive NW, P.O. Box 609, Arab, AL 35016, P: 800-349-1835, F: 256-931-1585, www.froggtoggs.com
Backpacking; Camouflage; Footwear; Hunting Accessories; Men & Women's Clothing

Front Line/Army Equipment, Ltd., 6 Platin St., Rishon-Le-Zion, 75653, ISRAEL, P: 011 97239519460, F: 011 97239519463, www.front-line.co.il
Bags & Equipment Cases; Gun Cases; Holsters

Frost Cutlery Co., 6861 Mountain View Rd., Ooltewah, TN 37363, P: 800-251-7768, F: 423-894-9576, www.frostcutlery.com
Camping; Cooking Equipment/Accessories; Cutlery; Hunting Accessories; Knives/Knife Cases; Retail Packaging; Sharpeners; Wholesaler/Distributor

Fujinon, Inc., 10 High Point Dr., Wayne, NJ 07470, P: 973-633-5600, F: 973-694-8299, www.fujinon.jp.com
Binoculars; Scopes, Sights & Accessories

Fusion Tactical, 4200 Chino Hills Pkwy., Suite 820-143, Chino Hills, CA 91709, P: 909-393-9450, F: 909-606-6834
Custom Manufacturing; Retail Packaging; Sports Accessories; Training & Safety Equipment

G

G24 Innovations, Ltd., Solar Power, Westloog Environmental Centre, Cardiff, CF3 2EE, UNITED KINGDON, 011 442920837340, F: 011 443930837341, www.g24i.com
Bags & Equipment Cases; Camping; Custom Manufacturing; Lighting Products

G96 Products Co., Inc., 85-5th Ave., Bldg. 6, P.O. Box 1684, Paterson, NJ 07544, P: 877-332-0035, F: 973-684-3848, www.g96.com
Black Powder Accessories; Firearms Maintenance Equipment; Lubricants

GG&G, 3602 E. 42nd Stravenue, Tucson, AZ 85713, P: 800-380-2540, F: 520-748-7583, www.gggaz.com
Custom Manufacturing; Firearms; Gun Barrels; Gun Grips & Stocks, Gun Parts/Gunsmithing; Law Enforcement; Lighting Products; Scopes, Sights & Accessories

G.A. Precision, 1141 Swift St., N. Kansas City, MO 64116, P: 816-221-1844, F: 816-421-4958, www.gaprecision.net
Firearms

G.G. Telecom, Inc./Spypoint, 555 78 Rd., Suite 353, Swanton, VT 05488, CANADA, P: 888-SPYPOINT, F: 819-604-1644, www.spy-point.com
Hunting Accessories; Photographic Equipment

G-LOX, 520 Sampson St., Houston, TX 77003, P: 713-228-8944, F: 713-228-8947, www.g-lox.com
Archery; Gun Cabinets/Racks/Safes; Gun Locks; Hunting Accessories; Shooting Range Equipment

GSM Products/Walker Game Ear, 3385 Roy Orr Blvd., Grand Prairie, TX 75050, P: 877-269-8490, F: 760-450-1014, www.gsmoutdoors.com
Archery; Feeder Equipment; Hearing Protection; Hunting Accessories; Lighting Products; Scopes, Sights & Accessories; Wildlife Management

GT Industrial Products, 10650 Irma Dr., Suite 1, Northglenn, CO 80233, P: 303-280-5777, F: 303-280-5778, www.gt-ind.com
Camping; Hunting Accessories; Lighting Products; Survival Kits/First Aid

Galati Gear/Galati International, 616 Burley Ridge Rd., P.O. Box 10, Wesco, MO 65586, P: 877-425-2847, F: 573-775-4308, www.galatigear.com, www.galatiinternational.com
Bags & Equipment Cases; Cutlery; Gun Cases; Holsters; Knives/Knife Cases; Law Enforcement; Sports Accessories

Galileo, 13872 SW 119th Ave., Miami, FL 33186, P: 800-548-3537, F: 305-234-8510, www.galileosplace.com
Binoculars; Photographic Equipment; Scopes, Sights & Accessories; Telescopes

Gamebore Cartridge Co., Ltd., Great Union St., Hull, HU9 1AR, UNITED KINGDOM, P: 011 441482223707, F: 011 4414823252225, www.gamebore.com
Ammunition; Cartridges

Gamehide–Core Resources, 12257C Nicollet Ave. S, Burnsville, MN 55337, P: 888-267-3591, F: 952-895-8845, www.gamehide.com
Archery; Camouflage; Custom Manufacturing; Export/Import Specialists; Gloves, Mitts, Hats; Hunting Accessories; Men & Women's Clothing

Gamo USA Corp., 3911 SW 47th Ave., Suite 914, Fort Lauderdale, FL 33314, P: 954-581-5822, F: 954-581-3165, www.gamousa.com
Airguns; Ammunition; Hunting Accessories; Online Services; Scopes, Sights & Accessories; Targets

Garmin International, 1200 E. 151st St., Olathe, KS 66062, P: 913-397-8200, F: 913-397-8282, www.garmin.com
Backpacking; Camping; Compasses; Computer Software; Hunting Accessories; Sports Accessories; Two-Way Radios; Vehicles, Utility & Rec

Garrett Metal Detectors, 1881 W. State St., Garland, TX 75042, P: 972-494-6151, F: 972-494-1881, www.garrett.com
Law Enforcement; Sports Accessories

Geissele Automatics, LLC, 1920 W. Marshall St., Norristown, PA 19403, P: 610-272-2060, F: 610-272-2069, www.ar15trigger.com
Firearms; Gun Parts/Gunsmithing

Gemstar Manufacturing, 1515 N. 5th St., Cannon Falls, MN 55009, P: 800-533-3631, F: 507-263-3129
Bags & Equipment Cases; Crossbows & Accessories; Custom Manufacturing; Gun Cases; Law Enforcement; Paintball Accessories; Sports Accessories; Survival Kits/First Aid

Gemtech, P.O. Box 140618, Boise, ID 83714, P: 208-939-7222, www.gem-tech.com
Firearms; Hearing Protection; Law Enforcement; Training & Safety Equipment; Wildlife Management

General Inspection, LLC, 10585 Enterprise Dr., Davisburg, MI 48350, P: 888-817-6314, F: 248-625-0789, www.geninsp.com
Ammunition; Custom Manufacturing

General Starlight Co., 250 Harding Blvd. W, P.O. Box 32154, Richmond Hill, Ontario L4C 9S3, CANADA, P: 905-850-0990, www.electrooptic.com
Binoculars; Law Enforcement; Photographic Equipment; Scopes, Sights & Accessories; Telescopes; Training & Safety Equipment; Wholesaler/Distributor

Generation Guns–(G2) ICS, No. 6, Lane 205, Dongihou Rd., Shengang Township, Taichung County, 429, TAIWAN, P: 011 886425256461, F: 011 886425256484, www.icsbb.com
Airsoft; Sports Accessories

Gerber Legendary Blades, 14200 SW 72nd Ave., Portland, OR 97224, P: 800-443-4871, F: 307-857-4702, www.gerbergear.com
Knives/Knife Cases; Law Enforcement; Lighting Products

Gerstner & Sons, Inc., 20 Gerstner Way, Dayton, OH 45402, P: 937-228-1662, F: 937-228-8557, www.gerstnerusa.com
Bags & Equipment Cases; Custom Manufacturing; Gun Cabinets/Racks/Safes; Gun Cases; Home Furnishings; Knives/Knife Cases; Shooting Range Equipment

GH Armor Systems, 1 Sentry Dr., Dover, TN 37058, P: 866-920-5940, F: 866-920-5941, www.gharmorsystems.com
Custom Manufacturing; Law Enforcement; Men & Women's Clothing

Giant International/Motorola Consumer Products, 3495 Piedmont Rd., Suite 920, Bldg. Ten, Atlanta, GA 30305, P: 800-638-5119, F: 678-904-6030, www.giantintl.com
Backpacking; Camouflage; Camping; Hunting Accessories; Training & Safety Equipment; Two-Way Radios

Ginsu Outdoors, 118 E. Douglas Rd., Walnut Ridge, AR 72476, P: 800-982-5233, F: 870-886-9142, www.ginsuoutdoors.com
Cutlery; Hunting Accessories; Knives/Knife Cases

Girsan–Yavuz 16, Batlama Deresi Mevkii Sunta Sok. No 19, Giresun, 28200, TURKEY, P: 011 905332160201, F: 011 904542153928, www.yavuz16.com
Firearms; Gun Parts/Gunsmithing

Glacier Glove, 4890 Aircenter Circle, Suite 210, Reno, NV 89502, P: 800-728-8235, F: 775-825-6544, www.glacierglove.com
  Gloves, Mitts, Hats; Hunting Accessories; Men's Clothing

Glendo Corp./GRS Tools, 900 Overlander Rd., P.O. Box 1153, Emporia, KS 66801, P: 800-835-3519, F: 620-343-9640, www.glendo.com
  Books/Industry Publications; Custom Manufacturing; Lighting Products; Scopes, Sights & Accessories; Videos; Wholesaler/Distributor

Glock, Inc., 6000 Highlands Pkwy., Smyrna, GA 30082, P: 770-432-1202, F: 770-433-8719, www.glock.com, www.teamglock.com, www.glocktraining.com, www.gssfonline.com
  Firearms; Gun Parts/Gunsmithing; Holsters; Knives/Knife Cases; Law Enforcement; Men & Women's Clothing; Retailer Services

Goex, Inc., P.O. Box 659, Doyline, LA 71023, P: 318-382-9300, F: 318-382-9303, www.goexpowder.com
  Ammunition; Black Powder/Smokeless Powder

Gold House Hardware (China), Ltd., Rm 12/H, 445 Tian He Bei Rd., Guangzhou, 510620, CHINA, P: 011 862038801911, F: 011 862038808485, www.ghhtools.com
  Camping; Cutlery; Gun Cases; Hunting Accessories; Knives/Knife Cases; Scopes, Sights & Accessories; Targets

Goldenrod Dehumidifiers, 3600 S. Harbor Blvd., Oxnard, CA 93035, P: 800-451-6797, F: 805-985-1534, www.goldenroddehumidifiers.com
  Gun Cabinets/Racks/Safes

Golight, Inc., 37146 Old Hwy. 17, Culbertson, NE 69024, P: 800-557-0098, F: 308-278-2525, www.golight.com
  Camping; Hunting Accessories; Law Enforcement; Lighting Products; Vehicles, Utility & Rec

Gore & Associates, Inc., W.L., 295 Blue Ball Rd., Elkton, MD 21921, P: 800-431-GORE, F: 410-392-9057, www.gore-tex.com
  Footwear; Gloves, Mitts, Hats; Law Enforcement; Men & Women's Clothing

Gould & Goodrich, Inc., 709 E. McNeil St., Lillington, NC, 27546, P: 800-277-0732, FL 910-893-4742, www.gouldusa.com
  Holsters; Law Enforcement; Leathergoods

Grabber/MPI Outdoors, 5760 N. Hawkeye Ct. SW, Grand Rapids, MI 49509, P: 800-423-1233, F: 616-940-7718, www.warmers.com
  Archery; Backpacking; Camouflage; Camping; Footwear; Gloves, Mitts, Hats; Hunting Accessories; Survival Kits/First Aid

Gradient Lens Corp., 207 Tremont St., Rochester, NY 14608, P: 800-536-0790, F: 585-235-6645, www.gradientlens.com
  Firearms Maintenance Equipment; Gun Barrels; Gun Parts/Gunsmithing; Scopes, Sights & Accessories; Shooting Range Equipment

Grand View Media Group, 200 Croft St., Suite 1, Birmingham, AL 35242, P: 888-431-2877, F: 205-408-3798, www.gvmg.com
  Books/Industry Publications

Granite Security Products, Inc., 4801 Esco Dr., Fort Worth, TX 76140, P: 817-561-9095, F: 817-478-3056, www.winchestersafes.com
  Gun Cabinets/Racks/Safes

Gransfors Bruks, Inc., P.O. Box 818, Summerville, SC 29484. P: 843-875-0240, F: 843-821-2285
  Custom Manufacturing; Law Enforcement; Men's Clothing; Wholesaler/Distributor

Grant Adventures Int'l., 9815 25th St. E, Parrish, FL 34219, P: 941-776-3029, F: 941-776-1092
  Archery; Outfitter

Grauer Systems, 38 Forster Ave., Mount Vernon, NY 10552, P: 415-902-4721, www.grauerbarrel.com
  Firearms; Gun Barrels; Gun Grips & Stocks; Law Enforcement; Lighting Products; Scopes, Sights & Accessories

Graves Recoil Systems, LLC/Mallardtone, LLC, 9115 Crows Nest Dr., Pine Bluff, AR 71603, P: 870-534-3000, F: 870-534-3000, www.stockabsorber.com
  Black Powder Accessories; Firearms; Game Calls; Hunting Accessories; Recoil Protection Devices & Services; Wholesaler/Distributor

Great American Tool Co., Inc./Gatco Sharpeners/Timberline Knives, 665 Hertel Ave., Buffalo, NY 14207, P: 800-548-7427, F: 716-877-2591, www.gatcosharpeners.com
  Cutlery; Knives/Knife Cases; Sharpeners

Green Supply, Inc., 3059 Audrain Rd., Suite 581, Vandalia, MO 63382, P: 800-424-4867, F: 573-594-2211, www.greensupply.com
  Ammunition; Camping; Computer Software; Firearms; Hunting Accessories; Online Services; Retailer Services; Scopes, Sights & Accessories; Wholesaler/Distributor

Grip On Tools, 4628 Amash Industrial Dr., Wayland, MI 49348, P: 616-877-0000, F: 616-877-4346

Grizzly Industrial, 1821 Valencia St., Bellingham, WA 98229, P: 800-523-4777, F: 800-438-5901, www.grizzly.com
  Firearms Maintenance Equipment; Gun Cabinets/Racks/Safes; Gun Parts/Gunsmithing

Grohmann Knives, Ltd., 116 Water St., P.O. Box 40, Pictou, Nova Scotia B0K 1H0, CANADA, P: 888-7-KNIVES, F: 902-485-5872, www.grohmannknives.com
  Backpacking; Camping; Cooking Equipment/Accessories; Custom Manufacturing; Cutlery; Hunting Accessories; Knives/Knife Cases; Sharpeners

GrovTec US, Inc., 16071 SE 98t Ave., Clackamas, OR, 97015, P: 503-557-4689, F: 503-557-4936, www.grovtec.com
  Custom Manufacturing; Firearms Maintenance Equipment; Gun Parts/Gunsmithing; Holsters

Guay Guay Trading Co., Ltd., 11F-3, No. 27, Lane 169, Kangning St., Shijr City, Taipei County 221, TAIWAN, P: 011 886226922000, F: 011 886226924000, www.guay2.com
  Airsoft

Gun Grabber Products, Inc., 3417 E. 54th St., Texarkana, AR 71854, P: 877-486-4722, F: 870-774-2111, www.gungrab.com
  Gun Cabinets/Racks/Safes; Hunting Accessories

Gun Video, 4585 Murphy Canyon Rd., San Diego, CA 92123, P: 800-942-8273, F: 858-569-0505, www.gunvideo.com
  Books/Industry Publications; Gun Parts/Gunsmithing; Law Enforcement; Training & Safety Equipment; Videos

GunBroker.com, P.O. Box 2511, Kennesaw, GA 30156, P: 720-223-2083, F: 720-223-0164, www.gunbroker.com
  Airguns; Computer Software; Firearms; Gun Parts/Gunsmithing; Hunting Accessories; Online Services; Reloading; Retailer Services

GunMate Products/Bushnell Outdoor Accessories, 9200 Cody, Overland Park, KS 66214, P: 800-423-3537, F: 800-548-0446, www.unclemikes.com
  Gun Cases; Holsters; Hunting Accessories; Leathergoods

Gunslick Gun Care/ATK Commercial Products, N5549 Cty. Trunk Z, Onalaska, WI 54650, P: 800-635-7656, F: 763-323-3890, www.gunslick.com
  Firearms Maintenance Equipment; Lubricants

GunVault, Inc., 216 S. 2nd Ave., Bldg. 932, San Bernardino, CA 92408, P: 800-222-1055, F: 909-382-2042, www.gunvault.com
  Gun Cabinets/Racks/Safes; Gun Cases; Gun Locks

H

HKS Products, Inc., 7841 Foundation Dr., Florence, KY 41042, P: 800-354-9814, F: 859-342-5865, www.hksspeedloaders.com
  Hunting Accessories; Law Enforcement

H & C Headware/Capco Sportswear, 5945 Shiloh Rd., Alpharetta, GA 30005, P: 800-381-3331, F: 800-525-2613, www.kccaps.com
  Camouflage

H & M Metal Processing, 1850 Front St., Cuyanoga Falls, OH 44221, P: 330-928-9021, F: 330-928-5472, www.handmmetal.com
  Airguns; Archery; Black Powder Accessories; Custom Manufacturing; Firearms Maintenance Equipment; Gun Barrels; Gun Parts/Gunsmithing

Haas Outdoors, Inc./Mossy Oak, P.O. Box 757, West Point, MS 39773, P: 662-494-8859, F: 662-509-9397
  Hunting Accessories

H-S Precision, Inc., 1301 Turbine Dr., Rapid City, SD 57703, P: 605-341-3006, F: 605-342-8964, www.hsprecision.com
  Firearms; Gun Barrels; Gun Grips & Stocks; Law Enforcement; Magazines, Cartridge; Shooting Range Equipment

Haix®-Schuhe Produktions-u. Vertriebs GmbH, Aufhofstrasse 10, Mainburg, Bavaria 84048, GERMANY, P: 011 49875186250, F: 011 498751862525, www.haix.com
  Footwear; Law Enforcement; Leathergoods

Haix North America, Inc., 157 Venture Ct., Suite 11, Lexington, KY 40511, P: 866-344-4249, F: 859-281-0113, www.haix.com
  Footwear; Law Enforcement; Leathergoods

Haley Vines Outdoor Collection Badland Beauty, P.O. Box 150308, Lufkin, TX 75915, P: 936-875-5522, F: 936-875-5525, www.haleyvines.com
  Bags & Equipment Cases; Gloves, Mitts, Hats; Wholesaler/Distributor; Women's Clothing

Hallmark Dog Training Supplies, 3054 Beechwood Industrial Ct., P.O. Box 97, Hubertus, WI 53033, P: 800-OK4DOGS, F: 262-628-4434, www.hallmarkdogsupplies.com
  Custom Manufacturing; Hunting Accessories; Pet Supplies; Scents & Lures; Videos; Wholesaler/Distributor

Halys, 1205 W. Cumberland, Corbin, KY 40701, P: 606-528-7490, F: 606-528-7497, www.halysgear.com
  Custom Manufacturing; Men & Women's Clothing; Wholesaler/Distributor

Hammerhead Ind./Gear Keeper, 1501 Goodyear Ave., Ventura, CA 93003, P: 888-588-9981, F: 805-658-8833, www.gearkeeper.com
  Backpacking; Camping; Compasses; Game Calls; Hunting Accessories; Law Enforcement; Lighting Products; Sports Accessories

HangZhou Fujie Outdoor Products, Inc., Qinyuanyashe, Shenghuoguan, Suite 1108, 163# Jichang Rd., Hanzhou, ZHJG 310004, CHINA, P: 011 8657181635196, F: 011 8657187718232, www.hangzhou-outdoor.com
  Footwear; Gloves, Mitts, Hats; Gun Cases; Men & Women's Clothing

Hardigg Storm Case, 147 N. Main St., South Deerfield, MA 01373, P: 800-542-7344, F: 413-665-8330
  Bags & Equipment Cases; Gun Cases

Harris Engineering, Inc., 999 Broadway, Barlow, KY 42024, P: 270-334-3633, F: 270-334-3000
  Hunting Accessories; Shooting Range Equipment; Sports Accessories

Harris Publications, Inc./Harris Tactical Group, 1115 Broadway, 8th Floor, New York, NY 10010, P: 212-807-7100, F: 212-807-1479, www.tactical-life.com
  Airguns; Books/Industry Publications; Cutlery; Firearms; Knives/Knife Cases; Law Enforcement; Paintball Guns; Retailer Services

Hastings, 717 4th St., P.O. Box 135, Clay Center, KS 67432, P: 785-632-3169, F: 785-632-6554, www.hastingsammunition.com
  Ammunition; Firearms; Gun Barrels

Hatsan Arms Co., Izmir-Ankara Karayolu 26. Km. No. 289, OSB Kemalpasa, Izmir, 35170, TURKEY, P: 011 902328789100, F: 011 902328789723, www.hatsan.com.tr
  Airguns; Firearms; Scopes, Sights & Accessories

Havalon Knives/Havels Inc., 3726 Lonsdale St., Cincinnati, OH 45227, P: 800-638-4770, F: 513-271-4714, www.havalon.com
  Hunting Accessories; Knives/Knife Cases

Havaser Turizm, Ltd., Nargileci Sokak No. 4, Mercan, Eminonu, 34450, TURKEY, P: 011 90212135452, F: 011 902125128079
  Firearms

Hawke Sport Optics, 6015 Highview Dr., Suite G, Fort Wayne, IN 46818, P: 877-429-5347, F: 260-918-3443, www.hawkeoptics.com
  Airguns; Binoculars; Computer Software; Crossbows & Accessories; Scopes, Sights & Accessories

Haydel's Game Calls, 5018 Hazel Jones Rd., Bossier City, LA 71111, P: 800-HAYDELS, F: 888-310-3711, www.haydels.com
  Archery; Emblems & Decals; Game Calls; Gun Parts/Gunsmithing; Hunting Accessories; Videos

Health Enterprises, 90 George Leven Dr., N. Attleboro, MA 02760, P: 800-633-4243, F: 508-695-3061, www.healthenterprises.com
  Hearing Protection

Heat Factory, Inc., 2390 Oak Ridge Way, Vista, CA 92081, P: 800-993-4328, F: 760-727-8721, www.heatfactory.com
  Archery; Backpacking; Camping; Footwear; Gloves, Mitts, Hats; Hunting Accessories, Men & Women's Clothing

Heatmax, Inc., 505 Hill Rd., Dalton, GA 30721, P: 800-432-8629, F: 706-226-2195, www.heatmax.com
  Archery; Backpacking; Camping; Footwear; Hunting Accessories; Law Enforcement; Pet Supplies; Sports Accessories

Heckler & Koch, Inc., 5675 Transport Blvd., Columbus, GA 31907, P: 706-568-1906, F: 706-568-9151, www.hk-usa.com
  Firearms

Helly Hansen Pro (US), Inc., 3703 I St. NW, Auburn, WA 98001, P: 866-435-5902, F: 253-333-8359, www.hellyhansen.com
  Men's Clothing

Hen & Rooster Cutlery, 6861 Mountain View Rd., Ooltewah, TN 37363, P: 800-251-7768, F: 423-894-9576, www.henandrooster.com
  Camping; Cooking Equipment/Accessories; Cutlery; Hunting Accessories; Retail Packaging; Wholesaler/Distributor

Hendon Publishing Co./Law and Order/Tactical Response Magazines, 130 Waukegan Rd., Suite 202, Deerfield, IL 60015, P: 800-843-9764, F: 847-444-3333, www.hendonpub.com
  Books/Industry Publications; Law Enforcement

Heritage Manufacturing, Inc., 4600 NW 135th St., Opa Locka, FL 33054, P: 305-685-5966, F: 305-687-6721, www.heritagemfg.com
  Firearms

Heros Pride, P.O. Box 10033, Van Nuys, CA 91410, P: 888-492-9122, F: 888-492-9133, www.herospride.com
  Custom Manufacturing; Emblems & Decals; Law Enforcement; Men & Women's Clothing; Wholesaler/Distributor

Hi-Point Firearms/MKS Supply, Inc., 8611-A N. Dixie Dr., Dayton, OH 45414, P: 877-425-4867, F: 937-454-0503, www.hi-pointfirearms.com
Firearms; Holsters; Law Enforcement; Magazines, Cartridge

Hiatt Thompson Corp., 7200 W. 66th St., Bedford Park, IL 60638, P: 708-496-8585, F: 708-496-8618, www.handcuffsusa.com
Law Enforcement

HideAway/Remington Packs/Cerf Bros. Bag Co., 2360 Chaffee Dr., St. Louis, MO 63146, P: 800-237-3224, F: 314-291-5588, www.cerfbag.com
Backpacking; Bags & Equipment Cases; Camouflage; Camping; Gun Cases; Wholesaler/Distributor

High Standard Mfg., Co./F.I., Inc. ATM–AutoMag, 5200 Mitchelldale, Suite E17, Houston, TX 77092, P: 800-272-7816, F: 713-681-5665, www.highstandard.com
Firearms; Gun Barrels; Gun Grips & Stocks; Gun Parts/Gunsmithing; Lubricants; Magazines, Cartridge

Highgear/Highgear USA, Inc., 145 Cane Creek Industrial Park Rd., Suite 200, Fletcher, NC 28732, P: 888-295-4949, F: 828-681-5320, www.highgear.com
Camping; Compasses; Hunting Accessories; Lighting Products; Sports Accessories; Survival Kits/First Aid

Hillman Ltd., No. 62, Tzar Samuil St., Sofia, Sofia 1000, BULGARIA, P: 011 35929882981, F: 011 35929882981, www.hillman.bg
Backpacking; Camouflage; Footwear; Gloves, Mitts, Hats; Gun Cases; Hunting Accessories; Men & Women's Clothing

HitchSafe Key Vault, 18424 Hwy. 99, Lynnwood, WA 98037, P: 800-654-1786, F: 206-523-9876, www.hitchsafe.com
Gun Cabinets/Racks/Safes; Gun Locks; Hunting Accessories; Outfitter; Sports Accessories; Vehicles, Utility & Rec

HiViz Shooting Systems/North Pass, Ltd., 1941 Heath Pkwy., Suite 1, Fort Collins, CO 80524, P: 800-589-4315, F: 970-416-1208, www.hivizsights.com
Black Powder Accessories; Gun Parts/Gunsmithing; Hunting Accessories; Paintball Accessories; Recoil Protection Devices & Services; Scopes, Sights & Accessories; Sports Accessories

Hobie Cat Co./Hobie Fishing/Hobie Kayaks, 4925 Oceanside Blvd., Oceanside, CA 92056, P: 760-758-9100, F: 760-758-1841, www.hobiecat.com
Bags & Equipment Cases; Camping; Hunting Accessories; Sports Accessories; Tours/Travel

Hodgdon Powder Co., 6231 Robinson, Shawnee Mission, KS 66202, P: 913-362-9455, F: 913-362-1307, www.hodgdon.com
Black Powder/Smokeless Powder; Books/Industry Publications; Reloading

Hog Wild, LLC, 221 SE Main St., Portland, OR 97214, P: 888-231-6465, F: 503-233-0960, www.hogwildtoys.com
Sports Accessories; Watches

Hogue, Inc., 550 Linne Rd., Paso Robles, CA 93447, P: 805-239-1440, F: 805-239-2553, www.hogueinc.com
Gun Grips & Stocks; Holsters

Homak Manufacturing Co., Inc., 1605 Old Rt. 18, Suite 4-36, Wampum, PA 16157, P: 800-874-6625, F: 724-535-1081, www.homak.com
Custom Manufacturing; Gun Cabinets/Racks/Safes; Gun Cases; Gun Locks; Hunting Accessories; Reloading; Retail Packaging

HongKong Meike Digital Technology Co., Ltd., No. 12 Jiaye Rd. Pinghu St., Longgang District, Shenzhen, GNGD 518111, CHINA, P: 011 8613424151607, F: 011 8675528494339, www.mkgrip.com
Scopes, Sights & Accessories

Hope Global, 50 Martin St., Cumberland, RI 02864, P: 401-333-8990, F: 401-334-6442, www.hopeglobal.com
Custom Manufacturing; Footwear; Hunting Accessories; Law Enforcement; Pet Supplies; Scopes, Sights & Accessories; Shooting Range Equipment; Sports Accessories

Hoppe's/Bushnell Outdoor Accessories, 9200 Cody, Overland Park, KS 66214, P: 800-221-9035, F: 800-548-0446, www.hoppes.com
Black Powder Accessories; Firearms Maintenance Equipment; Hearing Protection; Law Enforcement; Lubricants; Shooting Range Equipment

Horizon Manufacturing Ent., Inc./RackEm Racks, P.O. Box 7174, Buffalo Grove, IL 60089, P: 877-722-5369 (877-RACKEM-9), F: 866-782-1550, www.rackems.com
Airguns; Custom Manufacturing; Firearms; Firearms Maintenance Equipment; Footwear; Gloves, Mitts, Hats; Gun Cabinets/Racks/Safes; Holsters; Hunting Accessories; Law Enforcement; Shooting Range Equipment

Hornady Manufacturing Co., 3625 Old Potash Hwy., P.O. Box 1848, Grand Island, NE 68803, P: 308-382-1390, F: 308-382-5761, www.hornady.com
Ammunition; Black Powder Accessories; Lubricants; Reloading

Horus Vision, LLC, 659 Huntington Ave., San Bruno, CA 94066, P: 650-588-8862, F: 650-588-6264, www.horusvision.com
Computer Software; Law Enforcement; Scopes, Sights & Accessories; Targets; Watches

Howard Leight by Sperian, 900 Douglas Pike, Smithfield, RI 02917, P: 866-786-2353, F: 401-233-7641, www.howardleightshootingsports.com, www.sperianprotection.com
Eyewear; Hearing Protection; Hunting Accessories; Sports Accessories; Training & Safety Equipment

Huanic Corp., No. 67 Jinye Rd., Hi-tech Zone, Xi'an, SHNX 710077, CHINA, P: 011 862981881001, F: 011 862981881011, www.huanic.com
Hunting Accessories; Scopes, Sights & Accessories; Shooting Range Equipment; Targets

Hubertus Solingen Cutlery, 147 Wuppertaler Strasse, Solingen, D-42653, GERMANY, P: 011 49212591994, F: 011 49212591992, www.hubertus-solingen.de
Custom Manufacturing; Cutlery; Knives/Knife Cases; Survival Kits/First Aid

Hunter Co., Inc./Hunter Wicked Optics, 3300 W. 71st Ave., Westminster, CO 80030, P: 800-676-4868, F: 303-428-3980, www.huntercompany.com
Binoculars; Custom Manufacturing; Gun Cases; Holsters; Hunting Accessories; Knives/Knife Cases; Leathergoods; Scopes, Sights & Accessories

Hunter Dan, 64 N. US 231, P.O. Box 103, Greencastle, IN 46135, P: 888-241-4868, F: 765-655-1440, www.hunterdan.com
Archery; Home Furnishings; Hunting Accessories; Outdoor Art, Jewelry, Sculpture; Sports Accessories; Training & Safety Equipment

Hunter's Edge, LLC, 270 Whigham Dairy Rd., Bainbridge, GA 39817, P: 888-455-0970, F: 912-248-6219, www.hunters-edge.com
Archery; Camouflage; Decoys; Game Calls; Gloves, Mitts, Hats; Hunting Accessories; Men's Clothing; Scents & Lures

Hunter's Specialties, 6000 Huntington Ct. NE, Cedar Rapids, IA 52402, P: 800-728-0321, F: 319-395-0326, www.hunterspec.com
Archery; Blinds; Camouflage; Game Calls; Gloves, Mitts, Hats; Hunting Accessories; Scents & Lures; Videos

Hunterbid.com/Chiron, Inc., 38 Crosby Rd., Dover, NH 03820, P: 603-433-8908, F: 603-431-4072, www.hunterbid.com
Gun Grips & Stocks; Gun Parts/Gunsmithing

Hunting's-A-Drag, 42 Maple St., Rifton, NY 12471, P: 845-658-8557, F: 845-658-8569, www.gamesled.com
Hunting Accessories

Huntington Die Specialties, 601 Oro Dam Blvd., P.O. Box 991, Oroville, CA 95965, P: 866-RELOADS, F: 530-534-1212, huntingtons.com
Black Powder Accessories; Books/Industry Publications; Reloading; Wholesaler/Distributor

HyperBeam, 1504 Sheepshead Bay Rd., Suite 300, Brooklyn, NY 11236, P: 888-272-4620, F: 718-272-1797, www.nightdetective.com
Binoculars; Hunting Accessories; Law Enforcement; Lighting Products; Photographic Equipment; Scopes, Sights & Accessories; Shooting Range Equipment; Telescopes

Hyskore/Power Aisle, Inc., 193 West Hills Rd., Huntington Station, NY 11746, P: 631-673-5975, F: 631-673-5976, www.hyskore.com
Custom Manufacturing; Export/Import Specialists; Eyewear; Firearms Maintenance Equipment; Gun Cabinets/Racks/Safes; Hearing Protection; Shooting Range Equipment

I

I.C.E., 68 Route 125, Kingston, NH 03848, P: 603-347-3005, F: 603-642-9291, www.icesigns.com
Retailer Services

ICS, No. 6, Lane 205, Dongzou Rd., Taichung, Shangang 429, TAIWAN, P: 011-88 6425256461, F: 011-88 6425256484, icsbb.com
Airguns; Sports Accessories; Training & Safety Equipment

IHC, Inc., 12400 Burt Rd., Detroit, MI 48228, P: 800-661-4642, F: 313-535-3220, www.ihccorp.com
Archery; Backpacking; Camping; Crossbows & Accessories; Firearms; Lighting Products; Magazines, Cartridge; Scopes, Sights & Accessories

i-SHOT/S.E.R.T. System, 16135 Kennedy St., Woodbridge, VA 22191, P: 703-670-8001, F: 703-940-9148, www.ishot-inc.com
Bags & Equipment Cases; Custom Manufacturing; Firearms; Law Enforcement; Training & Safety Equipment; Wholesaler/Distributor

Icebreaker, Inc., P.O. Box 236, Clarkesville, GA 30523, P: 800-343-BOOT, F: 706-754-0423, www.icebreakerinc.com
Camouflage; Footwear; Gloves, Mitts, Hats; Hunting Accessories

Impact Gel Sports, P.O. Box 128, Melrose, WI 54642, P: 608-488-3630, F: 608-488-3633, www.impactgel.com
Footwear

Import Merchandiser's Inc./MasterVision Cap Lights, N-11254 Industrial Lane, P.O. Box 337, Elcho, WI 54428, P: 715-275-5132, F: 715-275-5176, www.mastervisionlight.com
Camping; Custom Manufacturing; Gloves, Mitts, Hats; Hunting Accessories; Lighting Products; Sports Accessories

IMR Powder Co., 6231 Robinson, Shawnee Mission, KS 66202, P: 913-362-9455, F: 913-362-1307, www.imrpowder.com
Black Powder/Smokeless Powder; Reloading

Indo-US Mim Tec. Pvt., Ltd., 315 Eisenhower Pkwy., Suite 211, Ann Arbor, MI 48108, P: 734-327-9842, F: 734-327-9873, www.mimindia.com
Airguns; Archery; Crossbows & Accessories; Gun Locks; Gun Parts/Gunsmithing; Knives/Knife Cases; Paintball Guns; Scopes, Sights & Accessories

Industrial Revolution/Light My Fire USA, 9225 151st Ave. NE, Redmond, WA 98052, P: 888-297-6062, F: 425-883-0036, www.industrialrev.com
Camping; Cooking Equipment/Accessories; Cutlery; Knives/Knife Cases; Lighting Products; Photographic Equipment; Survival Kits/First Aid; Wholesaler/Distributor

Indusys Techologies Belgium SPRL (UFA–Belgium), 22 Pas Bayard, Tavier, Liege B-4163, BELGIUM, P: 011 3243835234, F: 011 3243835189, www.indusys.be
Ammunition; Reloading; Shooting Range Equipment; Training & Safety Equipment

Innovative Plastech, Inc., 1260 Kingsland Dr., Batavia, IL 60510, P: 630-232-1808, F: 630-232-1978
Custom Manufacturing; Retail Packaging; Sports Accessories

INOVA/Emissive Energy Corp., 135 Circuit Dr., North Kingstown, RI 02852, P: 401-294-2030, F: 401-294-2050, www.inovalight.com
Backpacking; Camping; Hunting Accessories; Law Enforcement; Lighting Products; Sports Accessories; Survival Kits/First Aid; Training & Safety Equipment

Insight Tech-Gear, 23 Industrial Dr., Londonderry, NH 03053, P: 877-744-4802, F: 603-668-1084, www.insighttechgear.com
Hunting Accessories; Law Enforcement; Lighting Products; Paintball Accessories; Scopes, Sights & Accessories; Training & Safety Equipment

Instant Armor, Inc., 350 E. Easy St., Suite 1, Simi Valley, CA 93065, P: 805-526-3046, F: 805-526-9213, www.instantarmor.com
Law Enforcement

Instrument Technology, Inc., P.O. Box 381, Westfield, MA 10186, P: 413-562-3606, F: 413-568-9809, www.scopes.com
Law Enforcement

InterMedia Outdoors, Inc., 512 7th Ave., 11th Floor, New York, NY 10018, P: 212-852-6600, F: 212-302-4472, www.imoutdoorsmedia.com
Books/Industry Publications

International Cartridge Corp., 2273 Route 310, Reynoldsville, PA 15851, P: 877-422-5332, F: 814-938-6821, www.iccammo.com
Ammunition; Law Enforcement; Reloading; Shooting Range Equipment; Training & Safety Equipment

International Supplies/Seahorse Protective Cases, 945 W. Hyde Park, Inglewood, CA 90302, P: 800-999-1984, F: 310-673-5988, www.internationalsupplies.com
Bags & Equipment Cases; Export/Import Specialists; Eyewear; Gun Cases; Lighting Products; Photographic Equipment; Retailer Services; Wholesaler/Distributor

Interstate Arms Corp., 6 Dunham Rd., Billerica, MA 01821, P: 800-243-3006, F: 978-671-0023, www.interstatearms.com
Firearms

Iosso Products, 1485 Lively Blvd., Elk Grove, IL 60007, P: 888-747-4332, F: 847-437-8478, www.iosso.com
Black Powder Accessories; Crossbows & Accessories; Firearms Maintenance Equipment; Gun Parts/Gunsmithing; Hunting Accessories; Law Enforcement; Lubricants; Reloading

Iowa Rotocast Plastics, Inc., 1712 Moellers Dr., P.O. Box 320, Decorah, IA 52101, P: 800-553-0050, F: 563-382-3016, www.irpoutdoors.com
Backpacking; Blinds; Camping; Custom Manufacturing; Emblems & Decals; Printing Services; Sports Accessories; Wholesaler/Distributor

Irish Setter, 314 Main St., Red Wing, MN 55066, P: 888-SETTER-O, www.irishsetterboots.com
Footwear; Men's Clothing

Ironclad Performance Wear, 2201 Park Place, Suite 101, El Segundo, CA 90245, P: 888-314-3197, F: 310-643-0300
Camouflage; Gloves, Mitts, Hats; Hunting Accessories; Leathergoods; Men & Women's Clothing; Sports Accessories

Itasca by C.O. Lynch Enterprises, 2655 Fairview Ave. N,
Roseville, MN 55113, P: 800-225-2565, F: 651-633-9095,
www.itascacol.com
Footwear

Ithaca Gun Co., LLC, 420 N. Warpole St., Upper Sandusky,
OH 43351, P: 877-648-4222, F: 419-294-3230, www.
ithacagun.com
Firearms

ITT, 7635 Plantation Rd., Roanoke, VA 24019, P: 800-448-
8678, F: 540-366-9015, www.nightvision.com
Binoculars; Scopes, Sights & Accessories

ITW Military Products, 195 E. Algonquin Rd., Des Plaines,
IL 60016, P: 203-240-7110, F: 847-390-8727, www.
itwmilitaryproducts.com
*Backpacking; Bags & Equipment Cases;
Camouflage; Cooking Equipment/Accessories;
Custom Manufacturing; Law Enforcement*

Iver Johnson Arms Inc./Manufacturing Research, 1840
Baldwin St., Suite 10, Rockledge, FL 32955, P: 321-636-
3377, F: 321-632-7745, www.iverjohnsonarms.com
*Firearms; Gun Parts/Gunsmithing; Training & Safety
Equipment*

J

J.F. Griffin Publishing, LLC, 430 Main St., Suite 5,
Williamstown, MA 01267, P: 413-884-1001, F: 413-884-
1039, www.jfgriffin.com
Books/Industry Publications

JBP Holsters/Masters Holsters, 10100 Old Bon Air Pl.,
Richmond, VA 23235, P: 804-320-5653, F: 804-320-5653,
www.jbpholsters.com
*Gun Cases; Holsters; Hunting Accessories; Law
Enforcement; Leathergoods; Sports Accessories;
Training & Safety Equipment; Wholesaler/Distributor*

JGS Precision Tool Mfg., LLC, 60819 Selander Rd., Coos
Bay, OR 97420, P: 541-267-4331, F: 541-267-5996, www.
jgstools.com
*Firearms Maintenance Equipment; Gun Parts/
Gunsmithing*

J & J Armory/Dragon Skin/Pinnacle Armor, 1344 E. Edinger
Ave., Santa Ana, CA 92705, P: 866-9-ARMORY, F: 714-
558-4817, www.jandjarmory.com
*Firearms; Law Enforcement; Training & Safety
Equipment*

J & J Products Co., 9134 Independence Ave., Chatsworth,
CA 91311, P: 626-571-8084, F: 626-571-8704, www.
jandjproducts.com
*Custom Manufacturing; Hunting Accessories; Recoil
Protection Devices & Services; Reloading; Retail
Packaging; Sports Accessories*

J & K Outdoor Products, Inc., 3864 Cty. Rd. Q, Wisconsin
Rapids, WI 54495, P: 715-424-5757, F: 715-424-5757,
www.jkoutdoorproducts.com
*Archery; Hunting Accessories; Law Enforcement;
Paintball Accessories; Scopes, Sights & Accessories*

J-Tech (Steady Flying Enterprise Co., Ltd.), 1F, No. 235
Ta You Rd., Sung Shang, Taipei, 105, TAIWAN, P: 011
886227663986, F: 011 886287874836, www.tacticaljtech.
com
*Backpacking; Custom Manufacturing; Gloves, Mitts,
Hats; Gun Cases; Holsters; Law Enforcement;
Lighting Products; Wholesaler/Distributor*

Jaccard Corp., 3421 N. Benzing Rd., Orchard Park, NY 14127,
P: 866-478-7373, F: 716-825-5319, www.jaccard.com
Cooking Equipment/Accessories

Jack Brittingham's World of Hunting Adventure, 609-A E.
Clinton Ave., Athens, TX 75751, P: 800-440-4515, F: 903-
677-2126, www.jackbrittingham.com
*Hunting Accessories; Training & Safety Equipment;
Videos; Wildlife Management*

Jack Link's Beef Jerky, One Snackfood Ln., P.O. Box 397,
Minong, WI 54859, P: 800-346-6896, F: 715-466-5986,
www.linksnacks.com
Custom Manufacturing

Jackite, Inc., 2868 W. Landing Rd., Virginia Beach, VA 23456,
P: 877-JACKITE, F: 877-JACKFAX, www.jackite.com
*Decoys; Hunting Accessories; Outdoor Art, Jewelry,
Sculpture; Wholesaler/Distributor*

Jackson Rifles X-Treme Shooting Products, LLC, Glenswinton,
Parton, Castle Douglas, SCOTLAND DG7 3NL, P: 011
441644470223, F: 011 441644470227, www.jacksonrifles.
com
*Firearms; Gun Barrels; Gun Parts/Gunsmithing;
Wholesaler/Distributor*

Jacob Ash Holdings, Inc., 301 Munson Ave., McKees Rocks,
PA 15136, P: 800-245-6111, F: 412-331-6347, www.
jacobash.com
*Camouflage; Gloves, Mitts, Hats; Hunting
Accessories; Law Enforcement; Leathergoods; Men
& Women's Clothing; Sports Accessories*

James River Manufacturing, Inc./James River Armory, 3601
Commerce Dr., Suite 110, Baltimore, MD 21227, P: 410-
242-6991, F: 410-242-6995, www.jamesriverarmory.com
Firearms

Japan Optics, Ltd., 2-11-29, Ukima, Kita-ku, Tokyo, 115-0051,
JAPAN, P: 011 81359146680, F: 011 81353722232
Scopes, Sights & Accessories

Jeff's Outfitters, 599 Cty. Rd. 206, Cape Girardeau, MO
63701, P: 573-651-3200, F: 573-651-3207, www.
jeffsoutfitters.com
*Bags & Equipment Cases; Custom Manufacturing;
Gun Cases; Hunting Accessories; Knives/Knife
Cases; Leathergoods; Scopes, Sights & Accessories*

Jest Textiles, Inc./Bucksuede, 13 Mountainside Ave., Mahwah,
NJ 07430, P: 800-778-7918, F: 866-899-4951, www.
jesttex.com
*Bags & Equipment Cases; Camouflage; Custom
Manufacturing; Export/Import Specialists; Gloves,
Mitts, Hats; Home Furnishings; Men & Women's
Clothing*

John Marshall Design, LLC, P.O. Box 46105, Baton Rouge, LA
70895, P: 800-697-2698, F: 225-275-5900
*Camouflage; Home Furnishings; Men & Women's
Clothing*

John's Guns/A Dark Horse Arms Co., 1041 FM 1274,
Coleman, TX 76834.P: 325-382-4885, F: 325-382-4887,
www.darkhorsearms.com
*Custom Manufacturing; Firearms; Hearing
Protection; Law Enforcement*

Johnston Brothers, 623 Meeting St., Bldg. B, P.O. Box 21810,
Charleston, SC 29413, P: 800-257-2595, F: 800-257-2534
*Bags & Equipment Cases; Firearms Maintenance
Equipment; Gun Cases*

Jonathan Arthur Ciener, Inc., 8700 Commerce St., Cap
Canaveral, FL 32920, P: 321-868-2200, F: 321-868-2201,
www.22lrconversions.com
*Firearms; Gun Barrels; Gun Parts/Gunsmithing;
Hunting Accessories; Magazines, Cartridge; Recoil
Protection Devices & Services; Shooting Range
Equipment; Training & Safety Equipment*

Jordan Outdoor Enterprises, Ltd., P.O. Box 9638, Columbus,
GA 31908, P: 800-992-9968, F: 706-569-9346, www.
realtree.com
Camouflage; Videos

Joseph Chiarello & Co., Inc./NSSF Endorsed Insurance
Program, 31 Parker Rd., Elizabeth, NJ 07208, P: 800-526-
2199, F: 908-352-8512, www.guninsurance.com
Insurance; Retailer Services

Joy Enterprises, 1862 Dr., ML King Jr. Blvd., Port Commerce
Center III, Riviera Beach, FL 33404, P: 800-500-FURY, F:
561-863-3277, www.joyenterprises.com
*Binoculars; Camping; Compasses; Cutlery; Knives/
Knife Cases; Law Enforcement; Sharpeners; Sports
Accessories*

JP Enterprises, Inc., P.O. Box 378, Hugo, NN 55038, P: 651-
426-9196, F: 651-426-2472, www.jprifles.com
*Firearms; Gun Parts/Gunsmithing; Recoil Protection
Devices & Services; Scopes, Sights & Accessories*

JS Products, Inc./Snap-on, 5440 S. Procyon Ave., Las Vegas,
NV 89118, P: 702-362-7011, F: 702-362-5084
Lighting Products

K

KA Display Solutions, Inc., P.O. Box 99, 512 Blackman Blvd.
W, Wartrace, TN 37183, P: 800-227-9540, F: 931-389-
6686, www.kadsi.com
*Custom Manufacturing; Gun Cabinets/Racks/Safes;
Gun Cases; Home Furnishings; Knives/Knife Cases;
Retailer Services; Scopes, Sights & Accessories*

K.B.I., Inc./Charles Daly, P.O. Box 6625, Harrisburg, PA 17112,
P: 866-325-9486, F: 717-540-8567, www.charlesdaly.com
*Ammunition; Export/Import Specialists; Firearms;
Hunting Accessories; Law Enforcement; Scopes,
Sights & Accessories*

Ka-Bar Knives, Inc., 200 Homer St., Olean, NY 14760, P: 800-
282-0130, FL 716-790-7188, www.ka-bar.com
Knives/Knife Cases; Law Enforcement

KDF, Inc., 2485 St. Hwy. 46 N, Seguin, TX 78155, P: 800-KDF-
GUNS, P: 830-379-8144
*Firearms; Gun Grips & Stocks; Recoil Protection
Devices & Services; Scopes, Sights & Accessories*

KDH Defense Systems, Inc., 401 Broad St., Johnstown,
PA 15906, P: 814-536-7701, F: 814-536-7716, www.
kdhdefensesystems.com
Law Enforcement

KNJ Manufacturing, LLC, 757 N. Golden Key, Suite D, Gilbert,
AZ 85233, P: 800-424-6606, F: 480-497-8480, www.
knjmfg.com
*Bags & Equipment Cases; Custom Manufacturing;
Gun Cases; Holsters; Hunting Accessories; Law
Enforcement; Wholesaler/Distributor*

KNS Precision, Inc., 112 Marschall Creek Rd., Fredericksburg,
TN 78624, P: 830-997-0000, F: 830-997-1443, www.
knsprecisioninc.com
*Firearms; Gun Grips & Stocks; Gun Parts/
Gunsmithing; Law Enforcement; Lighting Products;
Scopes, Sights & Accessories; Training & Safety
Equipment; Wholesaler/Distributor*

KP Industries, Inc., 3038 Industry St., Suite 108, Oceanside,
CA 92054, P: 800-956-3377, F: 760-722-9884, www.
kpindustries.com
*Export/Import Specialists; Law Enforcement;
Outfitter; Paintball Accessories; Shooting Range
Equipment; Sports Accessories; Training & Safety
Equipment*

K-VAR Corp., 3300 S. Decatur Blvd., Suite 10601, Las Vegas,
NV 89102, P: 702-364-8880, F: 702-307-2303, www.k-var.
com
*Firearms Maintenance Equipment; Gun Barrels;
Gun Grips & Stocks; Magazines, Cartridge; Scopes,
Sights & Accessories*

Kahr Arms, 130 Goddard Memorial Dr., Worcester, MA 01603,
P: 508-795-3919, FL 508-795-7046, www.kahr.com
Firearms; Holsters; Law Enforcement

Kakadu Traders Australia, 12832 NE Airport Way, Portland,
OR 97230, P: 800-852-5288, F: 503-255-7819, www.
kakaduaustralia.com
*Bags & Equipment Cases; Camouflage; Men &
Women's Clothing; Wholesaler/Distributor*

Kalispel Case Line/Cortona Shotguns, 418641 SR 20, P.O.
Box 267, Cusick, WA 99119, P: 509-445-1121, F: 509-
445-1082, www.kalispelcaseline.com
*Archery; Bags & Equipment Cases; Export/Import
Specialists; Firearms; Gun Cases; Law Enforcement;
Wholesaler/Distributor*

Katz Knives, 10924 Mukilteo Speedway, Suite 287, Mukilteo,
WA 98275, P: 800-848-7084, F: 480-786-9338, www.
katzknives.com
*Backpacking; Camping; Custom Manufacturing;
Cutlery; Knives/Knife Cases; Sharpeners;
Wholesaler/Distributor*

Kel-Tec CNC Ind., Inc., 1475 Cox Rd., Cocoa, FL 32926, P:
321-631-0068, F: 321-631-1169, www.kel-tec-cnc.com
Firearms

Kelbly's, Inc., 7222 Dalton Fox Lk. Rd., North Lawrence, OH
44666, P: 330-683-4674, F: 330-682-7349, www.kelbly.
com
Firearms; Scopes, Sights & Accessories

Kenetrek Boots, 237 Quail Run Rd., Suite A, Bozeman, MT,
59718, P: 800-232-6064, F: 406-585-5548, www.kenetrek.
com
Footwear; Men's Clothing

Keng's Firearms Specialty, Inc./Versa-Pod/Champion Gun
Sights, 875 Wharton Dr. SW, P.O. Box 44405, Atlanta,
GA 30336, P: 800-848-4671, F: 404-505-8445, www.
versapod.com
*Gun Grips & Stocks; Hunting Accessories; Scopes,
Sights & Accessories*

KenMar Products, 411 Cameron Rd., Mattawa, Ontario P0H
1V0, CANADA, P: 866-456-5959, F: 705-744-6540, www.
kenmarproducts.com
*Camouflage; Gun Cases; Hunting Accessories;
Leathergoods; Men's Clothing; Scents & Lures;
Sports Accessories*

Kent Cartridge, 727 Hite Rd., P.O. Box 849, Kearneysville,
WV, 25430, P: 888-311-5368, F: 304-725-0454, www.
kentgamebore.com
Ammunition

Kenyon Consumer Products/KCP Acquisition, LLC, 141
Fairgrounds Rd., West Kingston, RI 02892, P: 800-537-
0024, F: 401-782-4870, www.kenyonconsumer.com
*Backpacking; Camping; Law Enforcement; Men &
Women's Clothing*

Kernel Game Call, 13231 Champion Forest Dr., Suite 201,
Houston, TX 77069, P: 830-928-2140, F: 830-792-6215
Feeder Equipment; Game Calls

Kershaw Knives, 18600 SW Teton Ave., Tualatin, OR 97062, P:
800-325-2891, F: 503-682-7168, www.kershawknives.com
Cutlery; Knives/Knife Cases

Kestrel Pocket Weather Meters, 21 Creek Circle, Boothwyn,
PA 19061, P: 800-784-4221, F: 610-447-1577, www.
kestrelweather.com
*Backpacking; Camping; Crossbows & Accessories;
Hunting Accessories; Law Enforcement; Shooting
Range Equipment; Sports Accessories; Training &
Safety Equipment*

Keyes Hunting Gear, P.O. Box 1047, Pagosa Springs,
CO 81147, P: 317-442-8132, F: 317-770-2127, www.
keyeshuntinggear.com
*Archery; Backpacking; Bags & Equipment Cases;
Camouflage; Camping; Hunting Accessories; Men &
Women's Clothing*

Keystone Sporting Arms, LLC, 155 Sodom Rd., Milton, PA
17847, P: 800-742-0455, F: 570-742-1455, www.crickett.
com
*Airsoft; Books/Industry Publications; Firearms; Gun
Grips & Stocks; Hunting Accessories; Shooting
Range Equipment; Targets; Training & Safety
Equipment*

KG Industries, LLC, 16790 US Hwy. 63 S, Bldg. 2, Hayward,
WI 54843, P: 800-348-9558, F: 715-934-3570, www.
kgcoatings.com

Camouflage; Custom Manufacturing; Firearms; Firearms Maintenance Equipment; Gun Barrels; Knives/Knife Cases; Law Enforcement; Lubricants

Kick-EEZ Products, 1819 Schurman Way, Suite 106, Woodland, WA 98674, P: 877-KICKEEZ, F: 360-225-9702, www.kickeezproducts.com
Black Powder Accessories; Clay Targets; Gun Grips & Stocks; Gun Parts/Gunsmithing; Hunting Accessories; Recoil Protection Devices & Services; Targets

Kiesler Distributor of Lewis Machine & Tool Co., 2802 Sable Mill Rd., Jeffersonville, IN 47130, P: 800-444-2950, F: 812-284-6651, www.kiesler.com
Firearms

Kilgore Flares Co., LLC, 155 Kilgore Dr., Toone, TN 38381, P; 731-228-5371, F: 731-228-4173, www.kilgoreflares.com
Ammunition

Kimar Srl/Chiappa Firearms, Via Milano, 2, Azzano Mella, 25020, ITALY, P: 011 390309749065, F: 011 390309749232, www.kimar.com
Airguns; Firearms; Pet Supplies; Training & Safety Equipment

Kimber Mfg., Inc./Meprolight, Inc., One Lawton St., Yonkers, NY 10705, P: 888-243-4522, F: 406-758-2223
Firearms; Law Enforcement

Kingman Training/Kingman Group, 14010 Live Oak Ave., Baldwin Park, CA 91706, P: 888-KINGMAN, F: 626-851-8530, www.kingmantraining.com
Bags & Equipment Cases; Eyewear; Gun Cases; Men's Clothing; Paintball Accessories, Guns & Paintballs

Kingport Industries, LLC, 1303 Shermer Rd., Northbrook, IL 60062, P: 866-303-5463, F: 847-446-5663, www.kingportindustries.com
Bags & Equipment Cases; Custom Manufacturing; Export/Import Specialists; Leathergoods; Wholesaler/Distributor

King's Outdoor World, 1450 S. Blackhawk Blvd., P.O. Box 307, Mt. Pleasant, UT 84647, P: 800-447-6897, F: 435-462-7436, www.kingoutdoorworld.com
Camouflage; Custom Manufacturing; Hunting Accessories; Men's Clothing; Wholesaler/Distributor

Kitasho Co., Ltd./Kanetsune, 5-1-11 Sakae-Machi, Seki-City, Gifu-Pref, 501 3253 JAPAN, P: 11 81575241211, FL 011 81575241210, www.kanetsune.com
Knives/Knife Cases

Knight Rifles/Div. Modern Muzzleloading, 715B Summit Dr., Decatur, AL 52544, P: 800-696-1703, F: 256-260-8951, www.knightrifles.com
Firearms

Knight's Manufacturing Co., 701 Columbia Blvd., Titusville, FL 32780, P: 321-607-9900, F: 321-383-2143, www.knightarmco.com
Firearms; Scopes, Sights & Accessories

Kolpin Outdoors/Bushness Outdoor Accessories, 9200 Cody, Overland Park, KS 66214, P: 800-423-3537, F: 800-548-0446, www.kolpin-outdoors.com
Firearms Maintenance Equipment; Gun Cases; Hunting Accessories

Konus USA Corp., 7530 NW 79th St., Miami, FL 33166, P: 305-884-7618, F: 305-884-7620, www.konususa.com
Binoculars; Compasses; Eyewear; Scopes, Sights & Accessories; Sports Accessories; Telescopes; Watches

Kowa Optimed, Inc., 20001 S. Vermont Ave., Torrance CA 90502, P: 800-966-5692, F: 310-327-4177, www.kowa-usa.com
Binoculars; Scopes, Sights & Accessories; Telescopes

Krause Publications/F&W Media, 700 E. State St., Iola, WI 54990, P: 888-457-2873, F: 715-445-4087, www.krausebooks.com
Books/Industry Publications; Videos

Krieger Barrels, Inc., 2024 Mayfield Rd., Richfield, WI 53076, P: 262-628-8558, F: 262-628-8748, www.kriegerbarrels.com
Gun Barrels

Kriss-TDI, 2697 International Dr., Pkwy. 4, 140, Virginia Beach, VA 23452, P: 202-821-1089, F: 202-821-1094, www.kriss-tdi.com
Firearms; Law Enforcement; Magazines, Cartridge

Kroll International, 51360 Danview Tech Ct., Shelby TWP, MI 48315, P: 800-359-6912, F: 800-359-9721, www.krollcorp.com
Bags & Equipment Cases; Footwear; Gloves, Mitts, Hats; Holsters; Hunting Accessories; Knives/Knife Cases; Law Enforcement; Wholesaler/Distributor

Kruger Optical, LLC, 141 E. Cascade Ave., Suite 208, P.O. Box 532, Sisters, OR 97759, P: 541-549-0770, F: 541-549-0769, www.krugeroptical.com
Binoculars; Scopes, Sights & Accessories

Kunming Yuanda Optical Co., Ltd./Norin Optech Co. Ltd., 9/F Huihua Bldg. No. 80 Xianlie, Zhong Rd., Guangzhou, 51007, CHINA, P: 011 862037616375, F: 011 862037619210, www.norin-optech.com
Binoculars; Compasses; Scopes, Sights & Accessories; Sports Accessories; Telescopes

Kutmaster/Div. Utica Cutlery Co., 820 Noyes St., Utica, NY 13503, P: 800-888-4223, F: 315-733-6602, www.kutmaster.com
Backpacking; Camping; Cooking Equipment & Accessories; Cutlery; Hunting Accessories; Knives/Knife Cases; Sports Accessories; Survival Kits/First Aid

Kwik-Site Co./Ironsighter Co., 5555 Treadwell, Wayne, MI 48184, P: 734-326-1500, F: 734-326-4120, www.kwiksitecorp.com
Black Powder Accessories; Firearms Maintenance Equipment; Hunting Accessories; Scopes, Sights & Accessories; Sporting Accessories

L

L.P.A. Srl di Ghilardi, Via Vittorio Alfieri, 26, Gardone V.T., 25063, ITALY, P: 011 390308911481, F: 011 390308910951, www.lpasights.com
Black Powder Accessories; Gun Parts/Gunsmithing; Scopes, Sights & Accessories

L-3 Communications-Eotech, 1201 E. Ellsworth Rd., Ann Arbor, MI 48108, P: 734-741-8868, F: 734-741-8221, www.l-3com.com/eotech
Law Enforcement; Scopes, Sights & Accessories

L-3 Electro-Optical Systems, 3414 Herrmann Dr., Garland, TX 75041, P: 866-483-9972, F: 972-271-2195, www.l3nightvision.com
Law Enforcement; Scopes, Sights & Accessories

L.A. Lighter, Inc./Viclight, 19805 Harrison Ave., City of Industry, CA 91789, P: 800-499-4708, F: 909-468-1859, www.lalighter.com
Camping; Cooking Equipment/Accessories; Lighting Products; Sports Accessories; Training & Safety Equipment; Wholesaler/Distributor

L.A.R. Manufacturing, 4133 W. Farm Rd., West Jordan, UT 84088, P: 801-280-3505, F: 801-280-1972, www.largrizzly.com
Firearms

La Crosse Technology, Ltd., 2809 Losey Blvd. S, La Crosse, WI 54601, P: 800-346-9544, F: 608-796-1020, www.lacrossetechnology.com
Sports Accessories; Wholesaler/Distributor

LEM Products, 109 May Dr., Harrison, OH 45030, P: 513-202-1188, F: 513-202-9494, www.lemproducts.com
Books/Industry Publications; Cooking Equipment/Accessories; Cutlery; Knives/Knife Cases; Sharpeners; Videos; Wholesaler/Distributor

L&R Ultrasonics, 577 Elm St., Kearny, NJ 07032, P: 201-991-5330, F: 201-991-5870, www.lrultrasonics.com
Decoys; Firearms; Firearms Maintenance Equipment; Gun Parts/Gunsmithing; Lubricants; Reloading; Shooting Range Equipment

LRB Arms, 96 Cherry Lane, Floral Park, NY 11001, P: 516-327-9061, F: 516-327-0246, www.lrbarms.com
Firearms; Wholesaler/Distributor

LRI–Photon Micro Light, 20448 Hwy. 36, Blachly, OR 97412, P: 541-925-3741, F: 541-925-3751, www.laughingrabbitinc.com
Backpacking; Camping; Hunting Accessories; Law Enforcement; Lighting Products; Sports Accessories; Survival Kits/First Aid; Training & Safety Equipment

Lachausee/New Lachaussée, UFA Belgium, Rue de Tige, 13, Herstal, Liège B 4040, BELGIUM, P: 011 3242488811, F: 011 3242488800, www.lachaussee.com
Ammunition; Firearms Maintenance Equipment; Reloading; Shooting Range Equipment

Lakeside Machine, LLC, 1213 Industrial St., Horseshoe Bend, AR 72512, P: 870-670-4999, F: 870-670-4998, www.lakesideguns.com
Custom Manufacturing; Firearms; Hunting Accessories; Law Enforcement

Lanber, Zubiaurre 3, P.O. Box 3, Zaldibar, (Vizcaya) 48250, SPAIN, P: 011 34946827702, F: 011 34946827999, www.lanber.com
Firearms

Lancer Systems, 7566 Morris Ct., Suite 300, Allentown, PA, 18106, P: 610-973-2614, F: 610-973-2615, www.lancer-systems.com
Custom Manufacturing; Gun Parts/Gunsmithing; Magazines, Cartridge

Landmark Outdoors/Yukon Advanced Optics/Sightmark/Mobile Hunter/Trophy Score/Amacker, 201 Regency Pkwy., Mansfield, TX 76063, P: 877-431-3579, F: 817-453-8770, www.landmarkoutdoors.com
Airsoft; Binoculars; Custom Manufacturing; Feeder Equipment; Hunting Accessories; Law Enforcement; Paintball Accessories; Scopes, Sights & Accessories; Shooting Range Equipment; Treestands; Wholesaler/Distributor

Lanigan Performance Products/KG Industries, 10320 Riverburn Dr., Tampa, FL 33467, P: 813-651-5400, F: 813-991-6156, www.thesacskit.com
Gun Parts/Gunsmithing

Lansky Sharpeners, P.O. Box 50830, Henderson, NV 89016, P: 716-877-7511, F: 716-877-6955, www.lansky.com
Archery; Camping; Cooking Equipment/Accessories; Cutlery; Hunting Accessories; Knives/Knife Cases; Law Enforcement; Sharpeners

Lapua/Vihtavuori, 123 Winchester Dr., Sedalia, MO 65301, P: 660-826-3232, F: 660-826-3232, www.lapua.com
Ammunition; Books/Industry Publications; Reloading; Videos

LaRue Tactical, 850 CR 177, Leander, TX 78641, P: 512-259-1585, F: 512-259-1588, www.laruetactical.com
Custom Manufacturing; Scopes, Sights & Accessories; Targets

Laser Ammo, Ltd., #7 Bar Kochva St., Rishon Lezion, 75353, ISRAEL, P: 682-286-3311, www.laser-ammo.com
Ammunition; Firearms; Law Enforcement; Scopes, Sights & Accessories; Shooting Range Equipment; Training & Safety Equipment

Laser Devices, Inc., 2 Harris Ct., Suite A-4, Monterey, CA 93940, P: 800-235-2162, F: 831-373-0903, www.laserdevices.com
Holsters; Law Enforcement; Lighting Products; Scopes, Sights & Accessories; Shooting Range Equipment; Sports Accessories; Targets; Training & Safety Equipment

Laser Shot, Inc., 4214 Bluebonnet Dr., Stafford, TX 77477, P: 281-240-8241, F: 281-240-8241
Law Enforcement; Training & Safety Equipment

LaserLyte, 101 Airpark Rd., Cottonwood, AZ 86326, P: 928-649-3201, F: 928-649-3970, www.laserlyte.com
Hunting Accessories; Scopes, Sights & Accessories

LaserMax, Inc., 3495 Winton Place Bldg. B, Rochester, NY 14623, P: 800-527-3703, F: 585-272-5427, www.lasermax.com
Airsoft; Crossbows & Accessories; Firearms; Law Enforcement; Paintball Accessories; Scopes, Sights & Accessories; Shooting Range Equipment; Training & Safety Equipment

Lauer Custom Weaponry/Duracoat Products, 3601 129th St., Chippewa Falls, WI 54729, P: 800-830-6677, F: 715-723-2950, www.lauerweaponry.com
Camouflage; Custom Manufacturing; Firearms; Hunting Accessories; Law Enforcement; Lubricants; Magazines, Cartridge; Scopes, Sights & Accessories

Law Enforcement Targets, Inc., 8802 W. 35 W. Service Dr. NE, Blaine, MN 55449, P: 800-779-0182, F: 651-645-5360, www.letargets.com
Eyewear; Gun Cabinets/Racks/Safes; Gun Grips & Stocks; Hearing Protection; Law Enforcement; Targets; Training & Safety Equipment

Law Officer Magazine/Div. Elsevier Public Safety/Elsevier, 525 B St., Suite 1900, San Diego, CA 92101, P: 800-266-5367, F: 619-699-6396, www.lawofficer.com
Books/Industry Publications; Law Enforcement

Lawman Leather Goods, P.O. Box 30115, Las Vegas, NV 89173, P: 877-44LAWMAN, F: 702-227-0036, www.lawmanleathergoods.com
Black Powder Accessories; Books/Industry Publications; Holsters; Law Enforcement; Leathergoods; Wholesaler/Distributor

Lazzeroni Arms Co., 1415 S. Cherry Ave., Tuscon, AZ 85713, P: 888-4-WARBIRD, F: 520-624-6202, www.lazzeroni.com
Ammunition; Firearms

Leapers, Inc., 32700 Capitol St., Livonia, MI 48150, P: 734-542-1500, F: 734-542-7095, www.leapers.com
Airguns; Airsoft; Bags & Equipment Cases; Gun Cases; Holsters; Law Enforcement; Lighting Products; Scopes, Sights & Accessories

Leatherman Tool Group, Inc., 12106 NE Ainsworth Circle, Portland, OR 97220, P: 800-847-8665, F: 503-253-7830, www.leatherman.com
Backpacking; Hunting Accessories; Knives/Knife Cases; Lighting Products; Sports Accessories

Leatherwood/Hi-Lux Optics/Hi-Lux, Inc., 3135 Kashiwa St., Torrance, CA 90505, P: 888-445-8912, F: 310-257-8096, www.hi-luxoptics.com
Binoculars; Scopes, Sights & Accessories; Telescopes

Legacy Sports International, 4750 Longley Lane, Suite 208, Reno, NV 89502, P: 775-828-0555, F: 775-828-0565, www.legacysports.com
Firearms; Gun Cabinets/Racks/Safes; Gun Cases; Scopes, Sights & Accessories

Leica Sport Optics/Leica Camera Inc., 1 Peart Ct., Unit A, Allendale, NJ 07401, P: 800-222-0118, F: 201-955-1686, www.leica-camera.com/usa
Binoculars; Photographic Equipment; Scopes, Sights & Accessories

LensPen–Parkside Optical, 650-375 Water St., Vancouver, British Columbia V6B 5C6, CANADA, P: 877-608-0868, F: 604-681-6194, www.lenspens.com
Binoculars; Hunting Accessories; Law Enforcement; Photographic Equipment; Scopes, Sights & Accessories; Sports Accessories; Telescopes

Les Baer Custom, Inc., 1804 Iowa Dr., Leclaire, IA 52753, P: 563-289-2126, F: 563-289-2132, www.lesbaer.com
Custom Manufacturing; Export/Import Specialists; Firearms; Gun Barrels; Gun Parts/Gunsmithing

Leupold & Stevens, Inc., 14400 NW Greenbriar Pkwy. 9700, P.O. Box 688, Beaverton, OR 97006, P: 503-646-9171, F: 503-526-1478, www.leupold.com
Binoculars; Lighting Products; Scopes, Sights & Accessories

Level Lok Shooting System/Div. Brutis Enterprises Inc., 105 S. 12th St., Pittsburgh, PA 15203, P: 888-461-7468, F: 412-488-5440, www.levellok.com
Binoculars; Firearms; Gun Grips & Stocks; Hunting Accessories; Photographic Equipment; Scopes, Sights & Accessories; Shooting Range Equipment; Sports Accessories

Levy's Leathers Limited, 190 Disraeli Freeway, Winnipeg, Manitoba R3B 2Z4, CANADA, P: 800-565-0203, F: 888-329-5389, www.levysleathers.com
Archery; Bags & Equipment Cases; Hunting Accessories; Knives/Knife Cases; Leathergoods

Lew Horton Distributing Co., Inc., 15 Walkup Dr., P.O. Box 5023, Westboro, MA 01581, P: 800-446-7866, F: 508-366-5332, www.lewhorton.com
Ammunition; Firearms; Hunting Accessories; Knives/Knife Cases; Law Enforcement; Magazines, Cartridge; Scopes, Sights & Accessories; Wholesaler/Distributor

Lewis Machine & Tool, 1305 11th St. W, Milan, IL 61264, P: 309-787-7151, F: 309-787-7193, www.lewismachine.net
Firearms

Liberty Mountain, 4375 W. 1980 S, Suite 100, Salt Lake City, UT 84104, P: 800-366-2666, F: 801-954-0766, www.libertymountain.com
Backpacking; Camping; Cooking Equipment/Accessories; Gloves, Mitts, Hats; Knives/Knife Cases; Lighting Products; Survival Kits/First Aid; Wholesaler/Distributor

Liberty Safe & Security Products, Inc., 1199 W. Utah Ave., Payson, UT 84651, P: 800-247-5625, F: 801-465-5880, www.libertysafe.com
Firearms Maintenance Equipment; Gun Cabinets/Racks/Safes; Gun Locks; Home Furnishings; Hunting Accessories; Law Enforcement; Sports Accessories; Training & Safety Equipment

Light My Fire USA, 9225 151st Ave. NE, Redmond, WA 98052, P: 888-297-6062, F: 425-883-0036
Camping; Cooking Equipment/Accessories; Knives/Knife Cases; Survival Kits/First Aid

Lightfield Ammunition Corp., P.O. Box 162, Adelphia, NJ 07710, P: 732-462-9200, F: 732-780-2437, www.lightfieldslugs.com
Ammunition

LightForce USA, Inc/NightForce Optics, 1040 Hazen Ln., Orofino, ID 83544, P: 800-732-9824, F: 208-476-9817, www.nightforceoptics.com
Law Enforcement; Lighting Products; Scopes, Sights & Accessories; Telescopes

LimbSaver, 50 W. Rose Nye Way, Shelton, WA 98584, P: 877-257-2761, F: 360-427-4025, www.limbsaver.com
Archery; Crossbows & Accessories; Hunting Accessories; Men's Clothing; Paintball Accessories; Recoil Protection Devices & Services; Scopes, Sights & Accessories

Linton Cutlery Co., Ltd., 7F, No. 332, Yongji Rd., Sinyi District, Taipei, 110, TAIWAN, P: 011 886227090905, F: 011 886227003978, www.linton-cutlery.com
Cutlery; Export/Import Specialists; Hunting Accessories; Law Enforcement; Sports Accessories; Wholesaler/Distributor

Linville Knife and Tool Co., P.O. Box 71, Bethania, NC 27010, P: 336-923-2062
Cutlery; Gun Grips & Stocks; Knives/Knife Cases

Lipseys, P.O. Box 83280, Baton Rouge, LA 70884, P: 800-666-1333, FL 225-755-3333, www.lipseys.com
Black Powder Accessories; Firearms; Holsters; Hunting Accessories; Magazines, Cartridge; Online Services; Scopes, Sights & Accessories; Wholesaler/Distributor

Little Giant Ladders, 1198 N. Spring Creek Pl., Springville, UT 84663, P: 800-453-1192, F: 801-489-1130, www.littlegiantladders.com
Law Enforcement; Training & Safety Equipment

Little Sportsman, Inc., 315 N. 400 W, P.O. Box 715, Fillmore, UT 84631, P: 435-743-4400, F: 435-846-2132, www.littlesportsman.com
Books/Industry Publications

LockSAF/VMR Capital Group, 2 Gold St., Suite 903, New York, NY 10038, P: 877-568-5625, F: 877-893-4502, www.locksaf.com
Gun Cabinets/Racks/Safes

Loksak, Inc. (formerly Watchful Eye), P.O. Box 980007, Park City, UT 84098, P: 800-355-1126, F: 435-940-0956, www.loksak.com
Bags & Equipment Cases

Lone Wolf Distributors, Inc., 57 Shepard Rd., P.O. Box 3549, Oldtown, ID 83822, P: 888-279-2077, F: 208-437-1098, www.lonewolfdist.com
Books/Industry Publications; Firearms Maintenance Equipment; Gun Barrels; Gun Parts/Gunsmithing; Holsters; Scopes, Sights & Accessories; Videos; Wholesaler/Distributor

Lone Wolf Knives, 9373 SW Barber St., Suite A, Wilsonville, OR 97070, P: 503-431-6777, F: 503-431-6776, www.lonewolfknives.com
Archery; Backpacking; Camouflage; Camping; Cutlery; Hunting Accessories; Knives/Knife Cases; Law Enforcement

Long Perng Co., Ltd., #16, Hejiang Rd., Chung Li Industrial Zone, Chung Li City, Taoyuan Hsien, 320, TAIWAN, P: 011 88634632468, F: 011 88634631948, www.longperng.com.tw
Binoculars; Scopes, Sights & Accessories; Telescopes

Longleaf Camo, 1505 Airport Rd., Flowood, MS 39232, P: 866-751-2266, F: 601-719-0713, www.longleafcamo.com
Camouflage; Footwear; Gloves, Mitts, Hats; Men & Women's Clothing

Loon Lake Decoy Co., Inc., 170 Industrial Ct., Wabasha, MN 55981, P: 800-555-2696, F: 612-565-4871, www.loonlakedecoycompany.com
Custom Manufacturing; Decoys; Home Furnishings; Hunting Accessories; Lighting Products; Outdoor Art, Jewelry, Sculpture; Wholesaler/Distributor

Lorpen North America, Inc., 100 Ironside Crescent, Suite 8, Toronto, Ontario M1X 1M9, CANADA, P: 888-224-9781, F: 416-335-8201, www.lorpen.com
Footwear

Lothar Walther Precision Tools, Inc., 3425 Hutchinson Rd., Cumming, GA 30040, P: 770-889-9998, F: 770-889-4919, www.lothar-walther.com
Custom Manufacturing; Export/Import Specialists; Gun Barrels

Lou's Police Distributor, 7815 W. 4th Ave., Hialeah, FL 33014, P: 305-822-5362, F: 305-822-9603, www.louspolice.com
Ammunition; Firearms; Gun Grips & Stocks; Hearing Protection; Holsters; Law Enforcement; Scopes, Sights & Accessories; Wholesaler/Distributor

LouderThanWords.US/Heirloom Precision, LLC, 2118 E. 5th St., Tempe, AZ 85281, P: 480-804-1911, www.louderthanwords.us
Firearms; Gun Parts/Gunsmithing; Holsters

Lowa Boots, 86 Viaduct Rd., Stamford, CT 06907, P: 888-335-5692, F: 203-353-0311, www.lowaboots.com
Footwear; Men & Women's Clothing

Lowrance–Navico, Eagle–Navico, 12000 E. Skelly Dr., Tulsa, OK 74128, P: 800-352-1356, F: 918-234-1707, www.lowrance.com
Archery; Backpacking; Camping; Hunting Accessories; Law Enforcement; Sports Accessories; Survival Kits/First Aid; Vehicles, Utility & Rec

Lowy Enterprises, Inc., 1970 E. Gladwick St., Rancho Dominguez, CA 90220, P: 310-763-1111, F: 310-763-1112, www.lowyusa.com
Backpacking; Bags & Equipment Cases; Custom Manufacturing; Law Enforcement; Outfitter; Paintball Accessories; Sports Accessories; Wholesaler/Distributor

Luggage-USA, Inc./L A Luggage, 710 Ducommun St., Los Angeles, CA 90012, P: 888-laluggage, F: 213-626-0800, www.luggage-usa.com
Backpacking; Bags & Equipment Cases; Camouflage; Camping; Export/Import Specialists; Gun Cases; Leathergoods; Wholesaler/Distributor

Lumberjack Tools, 9304 Wolf Pack Terrace, Colorado Springs, CO 80920, P: 719-282-3043, F: 719-282-3046, www.lumberjacktools.com
Camping; Crossbows & Accessories; Firearms; Home Furnishings; Hunting Accessories; Taxidermy; Treestands; Wholesaler/Distributor

Luminox Watch Co., 2301 Kerner Blvd., Suite A, San Rafael, CA 94901, P: 415-455-9500, F: 415-482-8215, www.luminox.com
Backpacking; Camping; Custom Manufacturing; Hunting Accessories; Law Enforcement, Outdoor Art, Jewelry, Sculpture; Sports Accessories; Watches

LWRC International, LLC, 815 Chesapeake Dr., Cambridge, MD 21613, P: 410-901-1348, F: 410-228-1799, www.lwrifles.com
Ammunition; Custom Manufacturing; Firearms; Firearms Maintenance Equipment; Gun Barrels; Gun Parts/Gunsmithing; Law Enforcement; Magazines, Cartridge

Lyalvale Express Limited, Express Estate, Whittington, Lichfield, WS13 8XA, UNITED KINGDOM, P: 011-44 1543434400, F: 011-44 1543434420, www.lyalvaleexpress.com
Ammunition

Lyman-Pachmayr-Trius Products/TacStar-A-Zoom-Butchs-Uni-Dot, 475 Smith St., Middletown, CT 06457, P: 800-225-9626, F: 860-632-1699, www.lymanproducts.com

Black Powder Accessories; Books/Industry Publications; Firearms; Firearms Maintenance Equipment; Gun Parts/Gunsmithing; Reloading; Scopes, Sights & Accessories; Shooting Range Equipment

Lyons Press, 246 Goose Ln., Guilford, CT 06437, P: 800-243-0495, F: 800-820-2329, www.glovepequot.com
Books/Industry Publications; Wholesaler/Distributor

M

MDM/Millennium Designed Muzzleloaders, Ltd., RR 1, Box 405, Maidstone, VT 05905, P: 802-676-331, F: 802-676-3322, www.mdm-muzzleloaders.com
Ammunition; Black Powder Accessories; Black Powder/Smokeless Powder; Custom Manufacturing; Firearms Maintenance Equipment; Gun Barrels; Gun Cases; Scopes, Sights & Accessories

MDS Inc., 3429 Stearns Rd., Valrico, FL 33596, P: 800-435-9352, F: 813-684-5953, www.mdsincorporated.com
Firearms Maintenance Equipment; Gun Parts/Gunsmithing; Law Enforcement

MFI, 563 San Miguel, Liberty, KY 42539, P: 606-787-0022, F: 606-787-0059, www.mfiap.com
Custom Manufacturing; Export/Import Specialists; Firearms; Gun Grips & Stocks; Gun Parts/Gunsmithing; Scopes, Sights & Accessories; Sports Accessories; Wholesaler/Distributor

MGI, 102 Cottage St., Bangor, ME 04401, P: 207-945-5441, F: 207-945-4010, www.mgimilitary.com
Firearms; Gun Barrels; Law Enforcement

MGM–Mike Gibson Manufacturing, 17891 Karcher Rd., Caldwell, ID 83607, P: 888-767-7371, F: 208-454-0666, www.mgmtargets.com
Clay Targets; Custom Manufacturing; Firearms; Gun Cabinets/Racks/Safes; Shooting Range Equipment; Targets; Training & Safety Equipment

MG Arms, Inc., 6030 Treaschwig Rd., Spring, TX 77373, P: 281-821-8282, F: 281-821-6387, www.mgarmsinc.com
Ammunition; Custom Manufacturing; Firearms; Gun Grips & Stocks; Wholesaler/Distributor

MPI Outdoors/Grabber, 5760 N. Hawkeye Ct., Grand Rapids, MI 49509, P: 800-423-1233, F: 616-977-7718, www.warmers.com
Backpacking; Camouflage; Camping; Cooking Equipment/Accessories; Gloves, Mitts, Hats; Hunting Accessories; Lighting Products; Survival Kits/First Aid

MPRI, 10220 Old Columbia Rd., Suites A & B, Columbia, MD 21046, P: 800-232-6448, F: 410-309-1506, www.mpri.com
Ammunition; Gun Barrels; Law Enforcement; Shooting Range Equipment; Targets; Training & Safety Equipment

MPT Industries, 6-B Hamilton Business Park, 85 Franklin Rd., Dover, NJ 07801, P: 973-989-9220, F: 973-989-9234, www.mptindustries.com
Airguns; Camping; Firearms; Firearms Maintenance Equipment; Lubricants; Paintball Guns; Sports Accessories

M-Pro 7 Gun Care/Bushnell Outdoor Accessories, 9200 Cody, Overland Park, KS 66214, P: 800-845-2444, F: 800-548-0446, www.mpro7.com
Black Powder Accessories; Firearms Maintenance Equipment; Gun Parts/Gunsmithing; Hunting Accessories; Law Enforcement; Lubricants

M-Pro 7 Gun Care, 225 W. Deer Valley Rd., Suite 4, Phoenix, AZ 85027, P: 888-YES-4MP7, F: 623-516-0414, www.mpro7.com
Black Powder Accessories; Firearms Maintenance Equipment; Gun Parts/Gunsmithing; Hunting Accessories; Law Enforcement; Lubricants

MSA, 121 Gamma Dr., Pittsburgh, PA 15238, P: 800-672-2222, F: 412-967-3373
Bags & Equipment Cases; Eyewear; Hearing Protection; Law Enforcement; Survival Kits/First Aid; Training & Safety Equipment

MSA Safety Works, 121 Gamma Dr., Pittsburgh, PA 15238, P: 800-969-7562, F: 800-969-7563, www.msasafetyworks.com
Eyewear; Hearing Protection; Shooting Range Equipment; Training & Safety Equipment

MT2, LLC/Metals Treatment Technologies, 14045 W. 66th Ave., Arvada, CO 80004, P: 888-435-6645, F: 303-456-5998, www.mt2.com
Firearms Maintenance Equipment; Shooting Range Equipment

MTM Case-Gard Co., P.O. Box 13117, Dayton, OH 45413, P: 800-543-0548, F: 937-890-1747, www.mtmcase-gard.com
Bags & Equipment Cases; Black Powder Accessories; Camping; Firearms Maintenance Equipment; Gun Cases; Hunting Accessories; Reloading; Targets

Mace Security International, 160 Benmont Ave., Bennington, VT 05201, P: 800-255-2634, F: 802-753-1209, www.mace.com

Archery; Camping; Hunting Accessories; Law Enforcement; Sports Accessories; Training & Safety Equipment

Mag Instrument, Inc./Maglite, 2001 S. Hellman Ave., Ontario, CA 91761, P: 800-289-6241, F: 775-719-4586, www.maglite.com
Backpacking; Camping; Hunting Accessories; Lighting Products; Sports Accessories; Survival Kits/First Aid; Training & Safety Equipment

Magellan Navigation, 471 El Camino Real, Santa Clara, CA 94050, P: 408-615-5100, F: 408-615-5200, www.magellangps.com
Backpacking; Camping; Compasses; Computer Software; Hunting Accessories; Sports Accessories; Vehicles, Utility & Rec

Maglula, Ltd., P.O. Box 302, Rosh Ha'ayin, 48103, ISRAEL, P: 011 97239030902, F: 011 97239030902, www.maglula.com
Firearms Maintenance Equipment; Gun Parts/Gunsmithing; Magazines, Cartridge; Shooting Range Equipment

Magnum USA, 4801 Stoddard Rd., Modesto, CA 95356, P: 800-521-1698, F: 209-545-2079, www.magnumboots.com
Footwear; Law Enforcement; Men's Clothing

Magnum Research, Inc., 7110 University Ave. NE, Minneapolis, MN 55432, P: 800-772-6168, F: 763-574-0109, www.magnumresearch.com
Firearms

Magnum Tents, P.O. Box 18127, Missoula, MT 59808, P: 877-836-8226, F: 877-836-8226, www.magnumtents.com
Camping; Hunting Accessories

Magpul Industries Corp., P.O. Box 17697, Boulder, CO 80308, P: 877-462-4785, F: 303-828-3469, www.magpul.com
Firearms; Gun Grips & Stocks; Gun Parts/Gunsmithing; Law Enforcement; Videos

Magtech Ammunition Co., Inc., 248 Apollo Dr., Suite 180, Lino Lakes, MN 55014, P: 800-466-7191, F: 763-235-4004, www.magtechammunition.com
Ammunition; Export/Import Specialists; Law Enforcement; Reloading; Shooting Range Equipment; Wholesaler/Distributor

Mahco, Inc., 1202 Melissa Dr., Bentonville, AR 72712, P: 479-273-0052, F: 479-271-9248
Bags & Equipment Cases; Binoculars; Camouflage; Camping; Hunting Accessories; Knives/Knife Cases; Scopes, Scopes, Sights & Accessories

Majestic Arms, Ltd., 101-A Ellis St., Staten Island, NY 10307, P: 718-356-6765, F: 718-356-6835, www.majesticarms.com
Firearms; Gun Barrels; Gun Parts/Gunsmithing

Mako Group, 74 Rome St., Farmingdale, NY 11735, P: 631-880-3396, F: 631-880-3397, www.themakogroup.com
Custom Manufacturing; Gun Grips & Stocks; Law Enforcement; Lighting Products; Scopes, Sights & Accessories; Targets; Training & Safety Equipment; Wholesaler/Distributor

Mancom Manufacturing Inc., 1335 Osprey Dr., Ancaster, Ontario L9G 4V5, CANADA, P: 888-762-6266, F: 905-304-6137, www.mancom.ca
Custom Manufacturing; Law Enforcement; Shooting Range Equipment; Training & Safety Equipment

Manners Composite Stocks, 1209 Swift, North Kansas City, MO 64116, P: 816-283-3334, www.mannerstock.com
Custom Manufacturing; Firearms Maintenance Equipment; Gun Grips & Stocks; Law Enforcement; Shooting Range Equipment

Dave Manson Precision Reamers/Div. Loon Lake Precision, Inc., 8200 Embury Rd., Grand Blanc, MI 48439, P: 810-953-0732, F: 810-953-0735, www.mansonreamers.com
Black Powder Accessories; Custom Manufacturing; Firearms Maintenance Equipment; Gun Barrels; Gun Parts/Gunsmithing; Recoil Protection Devices & Services; Reloading

Mantis Knives/Famous Trails, 1580 N. Harmony Circle, Anaheim, CA 92807, P: 877-97-SCOPE, F: 714-701-9672, www.mantisknives.com
Binoculars; Camping; Hunting Accessories; Knives/Knife Cases; Law Enforcement; Photographic Equipment; Scopes, Sights & Accessories; Wholesaler/Distributor

Manzella Productions, 80 Sonwil Dr., Buffalo, NY 14225, P: 716-681-8880, F: 716-681-6888
Hunting Accessories; Law Enforcement

Marbles, 420 Industrial Park, Gladstone, MI 49837, P: 906-428-3710, F: 906-428-3711, www.marblescutlery.com
Compasses; Cutlery; Scopes, Sights & Accessories; Sharpeners

Marlin Firearms/H&R, 100 Kenna Dr., P.O. Box 248, North Haven, CT 06473, P: 888-261-1179, F: 336-548-8736, www.marlinfirearms.com
Firearms

Marvel Precision, LLC, P.O. Box 127, Cortland, NE 68331, P: 800-295-1987, F: 402-791-2246, www.marvelprecision.com
Firearms; Wholesaler/Distributor

Masen Co., Inc., John, 1305 Jelmak St., Grand Prairie, TX 75050, P: 972-970-3691, F: 972-970-3691, www.johnmasen.com
Firearms Maintenance Equipment; Gun Grips & Stocks; Gun Parts/Gunsmithing; Magazines, Cartridge; Online Services; Scopes, Sights & Accessories; Wholesaler/Distributor

Maserin Coltellerie SNC, Via dei Fabbri, 19, Maniago, 33085, ITALY, P: 011 39042771335, F: 011 390427700690, www.maserin.com
Cutlery; Hunting Accessories; Knives/Knife Cases; Law Enforcement; Sports Accessories

Master Cutlery, Inc., 700 Penhorn Ave., Secausus, NJ 07094, P: 888-271-7228, F: 888-271-7228, www.mastercutlery.com
Airsoft; Crossbows & Accessories; Custom Manufacturing; Cutlery

Masterbuilt Manufacturing, Inc., 1 Masterbuilt Ct., Columbus, GA 31907, P: 800-489-1581, F: 706-327-5632, www.masterbuilt.com
Camping; Cooking Equipment/Accessories; Hunting Accessories; Vehicles, Utility & Rec

Matterhorn Footwear/Cove Shoe Co., HH Brown Work & Outdoor Group, 107 Highland St., Martinsburg, PA 16662, P: 800-441-4319, F: 814-793-9272, www.matterhornboot.com
Footwear; Law Enforcement; Training & Safety Equipment

Matz Abrasives/Stagecoach, 1209 W. Chestnut St., Burbank, CA 91506, P: 818-840-8042, F: 818-840-8340, www.matzrubber.com
Black Powder Accessories; Custom Manufacturing; Firearms; Firearms Maintenance Equipment; Gun Grips & Stocks; Gun Parts/Gunsmithing; Hunting Accessories; Recoil Protection Devices & Services

Maurice Sporting Goods, Inc., 1910 Techny Rd., Northbrook, IL 60065, P: 866-477-3474, F: 847-715-1419, www.maurice.net
Archery; Camping; Firearms Maintenance Equipment; Game Calls; Gloves, Mitts, Hats; Hunting Accessories; Sports Accessories; Wholesaler/Distributor

Maxit Designs, Inc., P.O. Box 1052, Carmichael, CA 95609, P: 800-556-2948, F: 916-489-7031, www.maxit-inc.com
Footwear; Gloves, Mitts, Hats; Men & Women's Clothing

Maxpedition Hard-Use Gear/Edgygear, Inc., P.O. Box 5008, Palos Verdes, CA 90274, P: 877-629-5556, F: 310-515-5950, www.maxpedition.com
Backpacking; Bags & Equipment Cases; Gun Cases; Holsters; Hunting Accessories; Knives/Knife Cases; Law Enforcement; Sports Accessories

MaxPro Police & Armor, 4181 W. 5800 N, Mountain Green, UT 84050, P: 801-876-3616, F: 801-876-2746, www.maxpropolice.com
Training & Safety Equipment

Mayville Engineering Co. (MEC), 800 Horicon St., Suite 1, Mayville, WI 53050, P: 800-797-4MEC, F: 920-387-5802, www.mecreloaders.com
Reloading

McConkey, Inc./ATV Backpacker Cart, P.O. Box 1362, Seeley Lake, MT 59868, P: 308-641-1085, F: 866-758-9896, www.atvbackpackercart.com
Ammunition; Backpacking; Camping; Hunting Accessories; Sports Accessories; Vehicles, Utility & Rec; Wholesaler/Distributor

McGowan Manufacturing Co., 4854 N. Shamrock Pl., Suite 100, Tucson, AZ 85705, P: 800-342-4810, F: 520-219-9759, www.mcgowanmfg.com
Archery; Camping; Cooking Equipment/Accessories; Crossbows & Accessories; Cutlery; Hunting Accessories; Knives/Knife Cases; Sharpeners

McKeon Products, Inc./Mack's Hearing Protection, 25460 Guenther, Warren, MI 48091, P: 586-427-7560, F: 586-427-7204, www.macksearplugs.com
Camping; Hearing Protection; Hunting Accessories; Sports Accessories; Training & Safety Equipment

McMillan Fiberglass Stocks, 1638 W. Knudsen Dr., Suite A, Phoenix, AZ 85027, P: 877-365-6148, F: 623-581-3825, www.mcmillanusa.com
Firearms; Gun Grips & Stocks

McNett Corp., 1411 Meador Ave., Bellingham, WA 98229, P: 360-671-2227, F: 360-671-4521, www.mcnett.com
Backpacking; Camouflage; Camping; Hunting Accessories; Knives/Knife Cases; Lubricants; Paintball Accessories; Sports Accessories

Mcusta Knives/Mcusta Knives USA, P.O. Box 22901, Portland, OR 97269, P: 877-714-5487, F: 503-344-4631, www.mcustausa.com
Cooking Equipment/Accessories; Cutlery; Hunting Accessories; Knives/Knife Cases; Law Enforcement; Sports Accessories; Wholesaler/Distributor

Mead Industries, Inc., 411 Walnut St., P.O. Box 402, Wood River, NE 68883, P: 308-583-2875, F: 308-583-2002
Ammunition

MEC-GAR SRL, Via Mandolossa, 102/a, Gussago, Brescia, 25064, ITALY, P: 011 390303735413, F: 011 390303733687, www.mec-gar.it
Gun Parts/Gunsmithing; Law Enforcement; Magazine, Cartridge

Medalist/Performance Sports Apparel, 1047 Macarthur Rd., Reading PA, 19605, P: 800-543-8952, F: 610-373-5400, www.medalist.com
Camouflage; Hunting Accessories; Men & Women's Clothing

Meggitt Training Systems/Caswell, 296 Brogdon Rd., Suwanee, GA 30024, P: 800-813-9046, F: 678-288-1515, www.meggitttrainingsystems.com
Custom Manufacturing; Law Enforcement; Shooting Range Equipment; Targets; Training & Safety Equipment

Meissenberg Designs, 7583 MT Hwy. 35, Bigfork, MT 59911, P: 877-974-7446, F: 866-336-2571, www.oldwoodsigns.com
Home Furnishings; Printing Services

Medota Products, Inc., 120 Bridgepoint Way, Suite B, South St. Paul, MN 55075, P: 800-224-1121, F: 651-457-9085, www.mendotaproducts.com
Custom Manufacturing; Hunting Accessories; Pet Supplies; Training & Safety Equipment

Meopta USA, Inc., 50 Davids Dr., Hauppauge, NY, 11788, P: 800-828-8928, F: 631-436-5920, www.meopta.com
Binoculars; Scopes, Sights & Accessories; Telescopes

Meprolight, 2590 Montana Hwy. 35, Suite B, Kalispell, MT 59901, P: 406-758-2222, F: 406-758-2223
Scopes, Sights & Accessories

Meprolight, Ltd., 58 Hazait St., Or-Akiva Industrial Park, Or-Akiva, 30600, ISRAEL, P: 011 97246244111, F: 011 97246244123, www.meprolight.com
Binoculars; Firearms; Gun Parts/Gunsmithing; Hunting Accessories; Law Enforcement; Lighting Products; Scopes, Sights & Accessories; Telescopes

Mercury Luggage Mfg. Co./Code Alpha Tactical Gear, 4843 Victory St., Jacksonville, FL 32207, P: 800-874-1885, F: 904-733-9671, www.mercuryluggage.com
Bags & Equipment Cases; Camouflage; Custom Manufacturing; Export/Import Specialists; Law Enforcement

Merkel USA, 7661 Commerce Ln., Trussville, AL 35173, P: 800-821-3021, F: 205-655-7078, www.merkel-usa.com
Binoculars; Firearms; Scopes, Sights & Accessories

Mesa Tactical, 1760 Monrovia Ave., Suite A14, Costa Mesa, CA 92627, P: 949-642-3337, F: 949-642-3339, www.mesatactical.com
Gun Grips & Stocks; Law Enforcement; Scopes, Sights & Accessories

Metal Ware Corp./Open Country, 1700 Monroe St., P.O. Box 237, Two Rivers, WI 54241, P: 800-624-2949, F: 920-794-3161, www.opencountrycampware.com
Backpacking; Camping; Cooking Equipment/Accessories; Sports Accessories

Meyerco, 4481 Exchange Service Dr., Dallas, TX 75236, P: 214-467-8949, F: 214-467-9241, www.meyercousa.com
Bags & Equipment Cases; Camping; Cutlery; Gun Cases; Hunting Accessories; Knives/Knife Cases; Law Enforcement; Sharpeners

Mick Lacy Game Calls, 628 W. Main St., Princeville, IL 61559, P: 800-681-1070, F: 309-385-1068, www.micklacygamecalls.com
Game Calls; Hunting Accessories

Microsonic, 2960 Duss Ave., Ambridge, PA 15003, P: 724-266-9480, F: 724-266-9482, www.microsonic-inc.com
Hearing Protection

Microtech Knives, Inc./Microtech Small Arms Research, Inc., 300 Chestnut St., Bradford, PA 16701, P: 814-363-9260, F: 814-363-9284, www.msarinc.com
Custom Manufacturing; Cutlery; Firearms; Knives/Knife Cases; Law Enforcement; Sports Accessories

Midland Radio Corp., 5900 Parretta Dr., Kansas City, MO, 64120, P: 816-241-8500, F: 816-241-5713, www.midlandradio.com
Hunting Accessories; Sports Accessories; Training & Safety Equipment; Two-Way Radios

Midwest Industries, Inc., 828 Philip Dr., Suite 2, Waukesha, WI 53186, P: 262-896-6780, F: 262-896-6756, www.midwestindustriesinc.com
Gun Cases; Gun Parts/Gunsmithing; Law Enforcement; Lubricants; Magazines, Cartridge; Scopes, Sights & Accessories

Midwest Quality Gloves, Inc., 835 Industrial Rd., P.O. Box 260, Chillicothe, MO 64601, P: 800-821-3028, F: 660-646-6933, www.midwestglove.com
Archery; Camouflage; Gloves, Mitts, Hats; Hunting Accessories; Men's Clothing

Mil-Comm Products Co., Inc., 2 Carlton Ave., East Rutherford, NJ 07073, P: 888-947-3273, F: 201-935-6059, www.mil-comm.com
Black Powder Accessories; Firearms Maintenance Equipment; Gun Cabinets/Racks/Safes; Gun

Locks; Gun Parts/Gunsmithing; Law Enforcement; Lubricants; Paintball Guns

Mil-Spec Plus/Voodoo Tactical, 435 W. Alondra Blvd., Gardena, CA 90248, P: 310-324-8855, F: 310-324-6909, www.majorsurplus.com
Bags & Equipment Cases; Eyewear; Footwear; Gloves, Mitts, Hats; Gun Cases; Law Enforcement

Mil-Tac Knives & Tools, P.O. Box 642, Wylie, TX 75098, P: 877-MIL-TAC6, F: 972-412-2208, www.mil-tac.com
Cutlery; Eyewear; Gloves, Mitts, Hats; Gun Parts/ Gunsmithing; Hunting Accessories; Knives/Knife Cases; Law Enforcement; Survival Kits/First Aid

Militaria, Inc., Rt. 2, P.O. Box 166, Collins, GA 30421, P: 912-693-6411, F: 912-693-2060
Books/Industry Publications; Emblems & Decals; Firearms Maintenance Equipment; Lubricants; Wholesaler/Distributor

Military Outdoor Clothing, Inc., 1917 Stanford St., Greenville, TX 75401, P: 800-662-6430, F: 903-454-2433, www.militaryoutdoorclothing.com
Bags & Equipment Cases; Camouflage; Gloves, Mitts, Hats; Law Enforcement; Men & Women's Clothing

Milkor USA, Inc., 3735 N. Romero Rd., Suite 2M, Tucson, AZ 85705, P: 520-888-0103, F: 520-888-0122, www.milkorusainc.com
Firearms

Millett Sights/Bushnell Outdoor Products, 6200 Cody, Overland Park, KS 66214, P: 888-276-5945, F: 800-548-0446, www.millettsights.com
Black Powder Accessories; Gun Parts/Gunsmithing; Hunting Accessories; Law Enforcement; Scopes, Sights & Accessories

Minox USA, 438 Willow Brook Rd., Merdien, NH 03770, P: 866-469-3080, F: 603-469-3471, www.minox.com
Binoculars

Mocean, 1635 Monrovia Ave., Costa Mesa, CA 92627, P: 949-646-1701, F: 949-646-1590, www.mocean.net
Custom Manufacturing; Law Enforcement; Men & Women's Clothing; Wholesaler/Distributor

MOJO Outdoors, 2984 New Monroe Rd., P.O. Box 8460, Monroe, LA 71211, P: 318-283-7777, F: 318-283-1127, www.mojooutdoors.com
Decoys

Molehill Mt. Equipment, Inc., 416 Laskspur St., Suite A, Ponderay, ID 83852, P: 800-804-0820, F: 208-263-3056, www.molehillmtn.com
Camouflage; Camping; Footwear; Gloves, Mitts, Hats; Men & Women's Clothing

Montana Canvas, 110 Pipkin Way, Belgrade, MT 59714, P: 800-235-6518, F: 406-388-1039, www.montanacanvas.com
Camping; Hunting Accessories

Montana Decoys, P.O. Box 2377, Colstrip, MT 59323, P: 888-332-6998, F: 406-748-3471, www.montantadecoy.com
Decoys

Montana Rifle Co./Montana Rifleman, Inc., 3172 Montana Hwy. 35, Kalispell, MT 59901, P: 406-755-4867, F: 406-755-9449, www.montanarifle.com
Custom Manufacturing; Firearms; Gun Barrels; Gun Parts/Gunsmithing

Moore Texas Hunting, 108 S. Ranch House Rd., Suite 800, Aledo, TX 76008, P: 817-688-1774, F: 817-441-1606, www.mooretexashunting.com
Custom Manufacturing; Hunting Accessories; Sports Accessories; Wholesaler/Distributor

Morovision Night Vision, Inc., P.O. Box 342, Dana Point, CA 92629, P: 800-424-8222, F: 949-488-3361, www.morovision.com
Binoculars; Camping; Hunting Accessories; Law Enforcement; Lighting Products; Photographic Equipment; Scopes, Sights & Accessories; Wholesaler/Distributor

Morton Enterprises, 35 Pilot Ln., Great Cacapon, WV, 25422, P: 877-819-7280, www.uniquecases.com
Bags & Equipment Cases; Custom Manufacturing; Gun Cases; Hunting Accessories; Law Enforcement; Sports Accessories

Mossy Oak, P.O. Box 757, West Point, MS 39773, P: 662-494-8859, F: 662-494-8837, www.mossyoak.com
Books; Camouflage; Home Furnishings; Hunting Accessories; Men & Women's Clothing; Videos

Mostly Signs, 12993 Los Nietos Rd., Sante Fe Springs, CA 90670, P: 888-667-8595, F: 800-906-9855, www.mostlysigns.com
Home Furnishings; Wholesaler/Distributor

Moteng, Inc., 12220 Parkway Centre Dr., Poway, CA 92064, P: 800-367-5900, F: 800-367-5903, www.moteng.com
Camping; Cutlery; Knives/Knife Cases; Law Enforcement; Lighting Products; Online Services; Training & Safety Equipment; Wholesaler/Distributor

Mothwing Camo/Gameday Camo, P.O. Box 2019, Calhoun, GA 30703, P: 800-668-4946, F: 706-625-2484, www.mothwing.com

Camouflage; Men & Women's Clothing; Vehicles, Utility & Rec

Moultrie Products, LLC, 150 Industrial Rd., Alabaster, AL 35007, P: 800-653-3334, F: 205-664-6706, www.moultriefeeders.com
Feeder Equipment; Photographic Equipment; Wildlife Management

Mountain Corp./Mountain Life, 59 Optical Ave., P.O. Box 686, Keene, NH 03431, P: 800-545-9684, F: 603-355-3702, www.themountain.com
Law Enforcement; Men & Women's Clothing; Outfitter; Retail Packaging; Wholesaler/Distributor

Mountain House/Oregon Freeze Dry, 525 25th SW, Albany, OR 97321, P: 800-547-0244, F: 541-812-6601, www.mountainhouse.com
Backpacking; Camping; Hunting Accessories

Mounting Solutions Plus, 10655 SW 185 Terrace, Miami, FL 33157, P: 800-428-9394, F: 305-232-1247, www.mountsplus.com
Scopes, Sights & Accessories; Wholesaler/Distributor

MTM-Multi Time Machine, Inc., 1225 S. Grand Ave., Los Angeles, CA 90015, P: 213-741-0808, F: 213-741-0840, www.specialopswatch.com
Archery; Backpacking; Camouflage; Hunting Accessories; Law Enforcement; Sports Accessories; Watches

Mud River Dog Products, 355 E. Hwy. 264, Suite D, Bethel Heights, AR 72764, P: 479-927-2447, F: 479-927-2667, www.mudriverdogproducts.com
Bags & Equipment Cases; Blinds; Camping; Custom Manufacturing; Hunting Accessories; Men's Clothing; Pet Supplies, Vehicles, Utility & Rec

Muela, Ctra. N-420, KM 165, 500, Argamasilla De Calatrava, (Ciudad Real) 13440, SPAIN, P: 011 34926477093, F: 011 34926477237, www.mmuela.com
Knives/Knife Cases

Muller Prinsloo Knives, P.O. Box 2263, Bethlehem, 9700, SOUTH AFRICA, P: 011 27824663885, F: 011 27583037111
Knives/Knife Cases

Mystery Ranch, 34156 E. Frontage Rd., Bozeman, MT 59715, P: 406-585-1428, F: 406-585-1792, www.mysteryranch.com
Backpacking; Bags & Equipment Cases; Camping; Law Enforcement; Photographic Equipment

N

Nantong Universal Optical Instruments Co., Ltd., No. 1 Pingchao Industrial Garden, Nantong, Jiangsu 226361, CHINA, P: 011 8651386726888, F: 011 8651386718158, www.zoscn.com
Airguns; Binoculars; Gun Cases; Gun Locks; Scopes, Sights & Accessories; Wholesaler/Distributor

National Emblem, Inc., 17036 S. Avalon Blvd., Carson, CA 90746, P: 800-877-6185, F: 310-515-5966, www.nationalemblem.com
Custom Manufacturing; Emblems & Decals; Gloves, Mitts, Hats

National Geographic Maps, P.O. Box 4357, Evergreen, CO 80437, P: 800-962-1643, F: 800-626-8676, www.nationalgeographic.com/map
Archery; Backpacking; Books/Industry Publications; Camping; Compasses; Computer Software; Sports Accessories

National Muzzle Loading Rifle Association, P.O. Box 67, Friendship, IN 47021, P: 812-667-5131, F: 812-667-5137, www.nmlra.com

National Rifle Association, 11250 Waples Mill Rd., Fairfax, VA 22030, P: 800-672-3888, F: 703-267-3810, www.nra.org

National Wild Turkey Federation, 770 Augusta Rd., P.O. Box 530, Edgefield, SC 29824, P: 800-843-6983, F: 803-637-0034, www.nwtf.org

Nation's Best Sports, 4216 Hahn Blvd., Fort Worth, TX 76117, P: 817-788-0034, F: 817-788-8542, www.nationsbestsports.com
Retailer Services

Nature Coast Laser Creations, 9185 Mercedes Terrace N, Crystal River, FL 34428, P: 352-564-0794, www.laserautotags.com
Custom Manufacturing; Emblems & Decals; Hunting Accessories; Outdoor Art, Jewelry, Sculpture; Paintball Accessories; Sports Accessories; Vehicles, Utility & Rec

N-Vision Optics, 220 Reservior St., Suite 26, Neenham, MA 02494, P: 781-505-8360, F: 781-998-5656, www.nvisionoptics.com
Binoculars; Law Enforcement; Scopes, Sights & Accessories

Navy Arms Co./Forgett Militaria, 219 Lawn St., Martinsburg, WV 25405, P: 304-262-1651, F: 304-262-1658, www.navyarms.com
Firearms

Nester Hosiery, Inc., 1400 Carter St., Mount Airy, NC 27030, P: 888-871-1507, F: 336-789-0626, www.nesteroutdoorsocks.com
Backpacking; Camping; Custom Manufacturing; Footwear; Hunting Accessories; Men & Women's Clothing; Sports Accessories

New Century Science & Tech, Inc., 10302 Olney St., El Monte, CA 91731, P: 866-627-8278, F: 626-575-2478, www.ncstar.com
Binoculars; Crossbows & Accessories; Custom Manufacturing; Export/Import Specialists; Firearms Maintenance Equipment; Gun Cases; Lighting Products; Scopes, Sights & Accessories

New Ultra Light Arms, 214 Price St., P.O. Box 340, Granville, WV 26534, P: 304-292-0600, FL 304-292-9662, www.newultralight.com
Firearms

Newcon Optik, 105 Sparks Ave., Toronto M2H 2S5, CANADA, P: 877-368-6666, F: 416-663-9065, www.newcon-optik.com
Binoculars; Hunting Accessories; Law Enforcement; Paintballs; Photographic Equipment; Scopes, Sights & Accessories; Shooting Range Equipment

Nextorch, Inc., 2401 Viewcrest Ave., Everett, WA 98203, P: 425-290-3092, www.nextorch.com
Hunting Accessories; Knives/Knife Cases; Lighting Products

Night Optics USA, Inc., 5122 Bolsa Ave., Suite 101, Huntington Beach, CA 92649, P: 800-30-NIGHT, F: 714-899-4485, www.nightoptics.com
Binoculars; Camping; Hunting Accessories; Law Enforcement; Scopes, Sights & Accessories; Training & Safety Equipment; Wholesaler/Distributor; Wildlife Management

Night Owl Optics/Bounty Hunter/Fisher Research Labs, 1465-H Henry Brennan, El Paso, TX 79936, P: 800-444-5994, F: 915-633-8529, www.nightowloptics.com
Binoculars; Camping; Hunting Accessories; Law Enforcement; Photographic Equipment; Scopes, Sights & Accessories; Sports Accessories; Telescopes

Night Vision Depot, P.O. Box 3415, Allentown, PA 18106, P: 610-395-9743, F: 610-395-9744, www.nvdepot.com
Binoculars; Hunting Accessories; Law Enforcement; Lighting Products; Scopes, Sights & Accessories; Wholesaler/Distributor

Night Vision Systems (NVS), 542 Kemmerer Ln., Allentown, PA 18104, P: 800-797-2849, F: 610-391-9220, www.nighvisionsystems.com
Law Enforcement; Scopes, Sights & Accessories

Nighthawk Custom, 1306 W. Trimble, Berryville, AR 72616, P: 877-268-4867, F: 870-423-4230, www.nighthawkcustom.com
Firearms; Gun Grips & Stocks; Gun Parts/ Gunsmithing; Hearing Protection; Holsters

Nikon, Inc., 1300 Walt Whitman Rd., Melville, NY 11747, P: 631-547-4200, FL 631-547-4040, www.nikonhunting.com
Binoculars; Hunting Accessories; Scopes, Sights & Accessories

Ningbo Electric and Consumer Goods I/E. Corp., 17/F, Lingqiao Plaza, 31 Yaohang Street, Ningbo, Zhejiang, 315000 CHINA P: 011 8657487194807; F: 011 8657487296214

Nite Ize, Inc., 5660 Central Ave., Boulder, CO 80301, P: 800-678-6483, F: 303-449-2013, www.niteize.com
Bags & Equipment Cases; Camping; Custom Manufacturing; Holsters; Lighting Products; Pet Supplies

Nite Lite Co., 3801 Woodland Heights Rd., Suite 100, Little Rock, AR 72212, P: 800-648-5483, F: 501-227-4892, www.huntsmart.com
Game Calls; Hunting Accessories; Lighting Products; Men's Clothing; Pet Supplies; Scents & Lures; Scopes, Sights & Accessories; Training & Safety Equipment

Nitrex Optics/ATK Commercial Products, N5549 Cty. Tk. Z, Onalaska, WI 54650, P: 800-635-7656, F: 763-323-3890, www.nitrexoptics.com
Binoculars; Scopes, Sights & Accessories

NiViSys Industries LLC, 400 S. Clark Dr., Suite 105, Tempe, AZ 85281, P: 480-970-3222, F: 480-970-3555, www.nivisys.com
Binoculars; Law Enforcement; Lighting Products; Photographic Equipment; Scopes, Sights & Accessories; Wholesaler/Distributor

Norica Laurona, Avda. Otaola, 16, Eibar, (Guipúzcoa) 20600, P: 011 34943207445, F: 011 34943207449, www.norica.es, www.laurona.es
Airguns; Ammunition; Firearms; Hearing Protection; Hunting Accessories; Knives/Knife Cases; Scopes, Sights & Accessories

Norma Precision AB/RUAG Ammotec, Jagargatan, Amotfors, S-67040, SWEDEN, P: 044-46-571-31500, F: 011-46-571-31540, www.norma.cc
Ammunition; Custom Manufacturing; Reloading

North American Arms, Inc., 2150 S. 950 E, Provo, UT 84606, P: 800-821-5783, F: 801-374-9998, www.northamericanarms.com
Firearms

North American Hunter, 12301 Whitewater Dr., Minnetonka, MN 55343, P: 800-688-7611, F: 952-936-9169, www.huntingclub.com
Books/Industry Publications

Northern Lights Tactical, P.O. 10272, Prescott, AZ 86304, P: 310-376-4266, F: 310-798-9278, www.northernlightstactical.com
Archery; Hunting Accessories; Law Enforcement; Paintball Accessories; Shooting Range Equipment; Targets; Training & Safety Equipment; Vehicles, Utility & Rec

Northridge International, Inc., 23679 Calabasas Rd., Suit 406, Calabasas, CA 91302, P: 661-269-2269, www.northridgeinc.com
Camouflage; Compasses; Cutlery; Firearms; Firearms Maintenance Equipment; Gun Barrels; Gun Cases; Survival Kits/First Aid

Northwest Territorial Mint, P.O. Box 2148, Auburn, WA 98071, P: 800-344-6468, F: 253-735-2210, www.nwtmint.com
Custom Manufacturing; Emblems & Decals; Knives/ Knife Cases; Outdoor Art, Jewelry, Sculpture

Northwest Tracker, Inc., 6205 NE 63rd St., Vancouver, WA 98661, P: 360-213-0363, F: 360-693-2212, www.trackeroutpost.com
Gun Cabinets/Racks/Safes; Gun Cases; Hunting Accessories; Treestands

Nosler, Inc., 107 SW Columbia, P.O. Box 671, Bend, OR 97709, P: 800-285-3701, F: 800-766-7537, www.nosler.com
Ammunition; Black Powder Accessories; Books/ Industry Publications; Firearms; Reloading

Not Your Daddy's, 7916 High Heath, Knoxville, TN 37919, P: 865-806-8496, F: 865-690-4555
Gun Cases

Nova Silah Sanayi, Ltd., Merkez Mah. Kultur Cad. No: 22/14, Duzce, TURKEY, P: 011-90 2125140279, F: 011-90 2125111999
Firearms

Novatac, Inc., 300 Carlsbad Village Dr., Suite 108A-100, Carlsbad, CA 92008, P: 760-730-7370, FL 760-730-7375, www.novatac.com
Backpacking; Camping; Hunting Accessories; Law Enforcement; Lighting Products; Survival Kits/First Aid; Training & Safety Equipment

NRA FUD, 11250 Waples Mill Rd., Fairfax, VA 22030, P: 703-267-1300, F: 703-267-3800, www.nrafud.com
Decoys; Hunting Accessories; Wholesaler/Distributor

NTA Enterprise, Inc./Huntworth/Thermologic, R J Casey Industrial Park, Columbus Ave., Pittsburgh, PA 15233, P: 877-945-6837, F: 412-325-7865, www.thermologicgear.com
Archery; Backpacking; Camouflage; Gloves, Mitts, Hats; Hunting Accessories; Men & Women's Clothing; Sports Accessories

Numrich Gun Parts Corp./Gun Parts Corp., 226 Williams Ln., P.O. Box 299, West Hurley, NY 12491, P: 866-686-7424, F: 877-GUN-PART, www.e-gunparts.com
Firearms Maintenance Equipment; Gun Barrels; Gun Cases; Gun Grips & Stocks; Gun Parts/Gunsmithing; Hunting Accessories; Magazines, Cartridge; Scopes, Sights & Accessories

Nutri-Vet, LLC, 495 N. Dupont Ave., Boise, ID 83713, P: 877-728-8668, F: 208-377-1941, www.nutri-vet.com
Pet Supplies

Nuwai International Co., Ltd./Nuwai LED Flashlight, 11 FL., 110 Li Gong St., Bei, Tou Taipei, 11261, TAIWAN, P: 011 886228930199, F: 011 886228930198, www.nuwai.com
Camping; Lighting Products; Outfitter

Nylok Corp., 15260 Hallmark Dr., Macomb, MI 48042, P: 586-786-0100, FL 810-780-0598
Custom Manufacturing; Gun Parts/Gunsmithing; Lubricants

O

O'Keeffe's Co., 251 W. Barclay Dr., P.O. Box 338, Sisters, OR 97759, P: 800-275-2718, F: 541-549-1486, www.okeeffescompany.com
Archery; Backpacking; Camping; Footwear; Outfitter; Sports Accessories; Survival Kits/First Aid

O.F. Mossberg & Sons, Inc., 7 Grasso Ave., North Haven, CT 06473, P: 203-230-5300, F: 203-230-5420, www.mossberg.com
Firearms; Gun Barrels; Hunting Accesories; Law Enforcement

Oakley, Inc., One Icon, Foothill Ranch, CA 92610, P: 800-525-4334, F: 858-459-4336, www.usstandardissue.com
Eyewear; Footwear

Odyssey Automotive Specialty, 317 Richard Mine Rd., Wharton, MJ 07885, P: 800-535-9441, F: 973-328-2601, www.odysseyauto.com

Custom Manufacturing; Gun Cabinets/Racks/Safes; Gun Cases; Law Enforcement; Vehicles, Utility & Rec

Oehler Research, Inc., P.O. Box 9135, Austin, TX 78766, P: 800-531-5125, F: 512-327-6903, www.oehler-research.com
Ammunition; Computer Software; Hunting Accessories; Reloading; Shooting Range Equipment; Targets

Oklahoma Leather Products/Don Hume Leathergoods, 500 26th NW, Miami, OK 74354, P: 918-542-6651, F: 918-542-6653, www.oklahomaleatherproducts.com
Black Powder Accessories; Custom Manufacturing; Cutlery; Holsters; Hunting Accessories; Knives/Knife Cases; Law Enforcement; Leathergoods

Old Western Scrounger, Inc., 50 Industrial Pkwy., Carson City, NV 89706, P: 800-UPS-AMMO, F: 775-246-2095, www.ows-ammunition.com
Ammunition; Reloading

Olivon Manufacturing Co., Ltd./Olivon-Worldwide, 600 Tung Pu Rd., Shanghai, China, Shanghai, Jiangsu, CHINA, P: 604-764-7731, F: 604-909-4951, www.olivonmanufacturing.com
Bag & Equipment Cases; Binoculars; Gun Cabinets/ Racks/Safes; Gun Cases; Hunting Accessories; Scopes, Sights & Accessories; Telescopes

Olympic Arms, Inc., 624 Old Pacific Hwy. SE, Olympia, WA 98513, P: 800-228-3471, F: 360-491-3447, www.olyarms.com
Firearms; Gun Barrels; Gun Grips & Stocks; Gun Parts/Gunsmithing; Law Enforcement; Training & Safety Equipment

On-Target Productions, Inc., 6722 River Walk Dr., Valley City, OH 44280, P: 330-483-6183, F: 330-483-6183, www.ontargetdvds.com
Videos

On Time Wildlife Feeders, 110 E. Railroad Ave., Ruston, LA 71270, P:318-225-1834, F: 315-225-1101

One Shot, 6871 Main St., Newtown, OH 45244, P: 513-233-0885, F: 513-233-0887

Ontario Knife Co./Queen Cutlery Co./Ontario Knife Co., 26 Empire St., P.O. Box 145, Franklinville, NY 14737, P: 800-222-5233, F: 800-299-2618, www.ontarioknife.com
Camping; Custom Manufacturing; Cutlery; Hunting Accessories; Knives/Knife Cases; Law Enforcement; Training & Safety Equipment

Op. Electronics Co., Ltd., 53 Shing-Ping Rd. 5/F, Chungli, 320, TAIWAN, P: 011 88634515131, F: 011 88634615130, www.digi-opto.com
Scopes, Sights & Accessories; Training & Safety Equipment

Opti-Logic Corp., 201 Montclair St., P.O. Box 2002, Tullahoma, TN 37388, P: 888-678-4567, F: 931-455-1229, www.opti-logic.com
Archery; Binoculars; Crossbows & Accessories; Hunting Accessories; Law Enforcement; Scopes, Sights & Accessories

Optisan Corp., Taipei World Trade Center 4B06, 5, Hsin Yi Rd., Section 5, Taipei, 110, TAIWAN, P: 011 8675785799936, F: 011 862081117707
Bags & Equipment Cases; Binoculars; Lighting Products; Photographic Equipment; Scopes, Sights & Accessories; Telescopes

Optolyth/Sill Optics GmbH & Co KG, Johann-Höllfritsch-Straße 13, Wendelstein, 90530, GERMANY, P: 011 499129902352, F: 011 499129902323, www.optolyth.de
Binoculars; Scopes, Sights & Accessories

Original Footwear Co., 4213 Technology Dr., Modesto, CA 95356, P: 888-476-7700, F: 209-545-2739, www.originalswat.com
Footwear; Law Enforcement; Wholesaler/Distributor

Original Muck Boot Co., 1136 2nd St., Rock Island, IL 61201, P: 800-790-9296, F: 800-267-6809, www.muckbootcompany.com
Footwear

Osprey International Inc./AimShot, 25 Hawks Farm Rd., White, GA 30184, P: 888-448-3247, F: 770-387-0114, www.osprey-optics.com
Binoculars; Hunting Accessories; Law Enforcement; Lighting Products; Scopes, Sights & Accessories; Wholesaler/Distributor

Otis Technology, Inc., 6987 Laura St., P.O. Box 582, Lyon Falls, NY 13368, P: 800-OTISGUN, F: 315-348-4332, www.otisgun.com
Black Powder Accessories; Firearms Maintenance Equipment; Gun Parts/Gunsmithing; Hunting Accessories; Lubricants; Paintball Accessories; Scopes, Sights & Accessories; Training & Safety Equipment

Otte Gear, 332 Bleecker St., Suite E10, New York, NY 10014, P: 212-604-0304, F: 773-439-5237, www.ottegear.com
Backpacking; Camouflage; Camping; Gloves, Mitts, Hats; Men's Clothing

Otter Outdoors, 411 W. Congress, Maple Lake, MN 55358, P: 877-466-8837, F: 320-963-6192, www.otteroutdoors.com

Blinds; *Custom Manufacturing; Hunting Accessories; Sports Accessories; Vehicles, Utility & Rec*

Outdoor Cap Co., 1200 Melissa Ln., P.O. Box 210, Bentonville, AR 72712, P: 800-279-3216, F: 800-200-0329, www.outdoorcap.com
Camouflage; Custom Manufacturing; Gloves, Mitts, Hats; Hunting Accessories; Men & Women's Clothing

Outdoor Connection, 424 Neosho, Burlington, NS 66839, P: 888-548-0636, F: 620-364-5563, www.outdoor-connection.com
Outfitter; Tours/Travel

Outdoor Connection, Inc., 7901 Panther Way, Waco, TX 76712, P: 800-533-6076, F: 866-533-6076, www.outdoorconnection.com
Bags & Equipment Cases; Camouflage; Gun Cases; Gun Parts/Gunsmithing; Hunting Accessories; Retail Packaging; Shooting Range Equipment; Sports Accessories

Outdoor Edge Cutlery Corp., 4699 Nautilus Ct. S, Suite 503, Boulder, CO 80301, P: 800-447-3343, F: 303-530-7020, www.outdooredge.com
Cutlery; Hunting Accessories; Sharpeners

Outdoor Kids Club Magazine, P.O. Box 35, Greenville, OH 45331, P: 937-417-0903, www.outdoorkidsclub.com
Books/Industry Publications

Outdoor Research, 2203 First Ave. S, Seattle, WA 98134, P: 888-467-4327, F: 206-467-0374, www.outdoorresearch.com/gov
Gloves, Mitts, Hats; Law Enforcement

OutdoorSportsMarketingCenter.com, 95 Old Stratton Chase, Atlanta, GA 30328, P: 256-653-5087, F: 404-943-1634, www.outdoorsportsmarketingcenter.com
Books/Industry Publications; Computer Software; Emblems & Decals; Online Services; Printing Services; Retail Packaging; Retailer Services

Outers Gun Care/ATK Commercial Products, N5549 Cty. Tk. Z, Onalaska, WI 54650, P: 800-635-7656, F: 763-323-3890, www.outers-guncare.com
Firearms Maintenance Equipment; Lubricants

Over The Hill Outfitters/Adventures Beyond, 4140 Cty. Rd. 234, Durango, CO 81301, P: 970-385-7656, www.overthehilloutfitters.com
Outfitter

Ozonics, 107A This Way, P.O. Box 598, Lake Jackson, TX 77566, P: 979-285-2400, F: 979-297-7744, www.ozonicshunting.com
Scents & Lures

P

PMC/Poongsan, 60-1, Chungmoro - 3ka, Chung-Gu, Seoul 100-705, C.P.O. Box 3537, Seoul, SOUTH KOREA, P: 011 92234065628, F: 011 92234065415, www.pmcammo.com
Ammunition; Law Enforcement

PSC, Pendleton Safe Co., 139 Lee Byrd Rd., Loganville, GA 30052, P: 770-466-6661, F: 678-990-7888
Gun Safes

PSI, LLC, 2 Klarides Village Dr., Suite 336, Seymour, CT 06483, P: 203-262-6484, F: 203-262-6562, www.precisionsalesintl.com
Gun Parts/Gunsmithing; Law Enforcement; Magazines, Cartridge; Scopes, Sights & Accessories

P.S. Products, Inc./Personal Security Products, 414 S. Pulaski St., Suite 1, Little Rock, AR 72201, P: 877-374-7900, F: 501-374-7800, www.psproducts.com
Custom Manufacturing; Export/Import Specialists; Holsters; Law Enforcement; Sports Accessories; Wholesaler/Distributor

Pacific Solution, 14225 Telephone Ave., Suite D, Chino, CA 91710, P: 909-465-9858, F: 909-465-9878
Cutlery; Hunting Accessories; Knives/Knife Cases; Wholesaler/Distributor

Pacific Sun Marketing, 14505 N. 5th St., Bellevue, WA 98007, P: 425-653-3900, F: 425-653-3908
Home Furnishings; Hunting Accessories; Outdoor Art, Jewelry, Sculpture

Pacific Tool & Gauge, Inc., 598 Avenue C, P.O. Box 2549, White City, OR 97503, P: 541-826-5808, F: 541-826-5304, www.pacifictoolandgauge.com
Black Powder Accessories; Books/Industry Publications; Custom Manufacturing; Firearms Maintenance Equipment; Gun Parts/Gunsmithing; Law Enforcement; Reloading

Palco Sports Airsoft, 8575 Monticello Ln. N, Maple Grove, MN 55369-4546, P: 800-882-4656, F: 763-559-2286, www.palcosports.com
Airguns; Airsoft; Crossbows & Accessories; Paintball Guns & Accessories; Sports Accessories

Panthera Outdoors, LLC, 1555 Wedgefield Dr., Rock Hill, SC 29732, P: 276-673-5278

Para USA, Inc., 10620 Southern Loop Blvd., Charlotte, NC 28134-7381, P: 866-661-1911, www.para-usa.com
Firearms

Paragon Luggage, 1111-A Bell Ave., Tustin, CA 92780, P: 714-258-8698, F: 714-258-0018

Paramount Apparel, Inc., 1 Paramount Dr., P.O. Box 98, Bourbon, MO 65441, P: 800-255-4287, F: 800-428-0215, www.paramountoutdoors.com
Camouflage; Custom Manufacturing; Gloves, Mitts, Hats; Hunting Accessories; Men & Women's Clothing; Retailer Services; Sports Accessories

Parker-Hale, Bedford Rd., Petersfield, Hampshire GU32 3XA, UNITED KINGDOM, P: 011-44 1730268011, F: 011-44 1730260074, www.parker-hale.co.uk
Firearms Maintenance Equipment; Law Enforcement; Lubricants

Parmatech Corp., 2221 Pine View Way, Petaluma, CA 94954, P: 800-709-1555, F: 707-778-2262, www.parmatech.com
Custom Manufacturing; Gun Parts/Gunsmithing

Parris Manufacturing, 1825 Pickwick St., P.O. Box 338, Savannah, TN 38372, P: 800-530-7308, F: 731-925-1139, www.parrismfgco.com
Airguns; Archery; Binoculars; Camouflage; Crossbows & Accessories; Wholesaler/Distributor

Passport Sports, Inc., 3545 N. Courtenay Pkwy., P.O. Box 540638, Merritt Island, FL 32953, P: 321-459-0005, F: 321-459-3482, www.passport-holsters.com
Bags & Equipment Cases; Custom Manufacturing; Gun Cases; Holsters; Leathergoods

Patriot3, Inc., P.O. Box 278, Quantico, VA 22134, P: 888-288-0911, F: 540-891-5654, www.patriot3.com
Law Enforcement

Patriot Ordnance Factory, 23623 N. 67th Ave., Glendale, AZ 85310, P: 623-561-9572, F: 623-321-1680, www.pof-usa.com
Custom Manufacturing; Firearms; Gun Barrels; Gun Parts/Gunsmithing; Hunting Accessories; Law Enforcement

PBC, 444 Caribbean Dr., Lakeland, FL 33803, P: 954-304-5948, www.pbccutlery.com
Cutlery; Knives/Knife Cases

Peacekeeper International, 2435 Pine St., Pomona, CA 91767, P: 909-596-6699, F: 909-596-8899, www.peacekeeperproducts.com
Holsters; Law Enforcement; Leathergoods; Targets; Training & Safety Equipment

Peak Beam Systems, Inc., 3938 Miller Rd., P.O. Box 1127, Edgemont, PA 19028, P: 610-353-8505, F: 610-353-8411, www.peakbeam.com
Law Enforcement; Lighting Products

Peca Products, Inc., 471 Burton St., Beloit, WI 53511, P: 608-299-1615, F: 608-229-1827, www.pecaproducts.com
Custom Manufacturing; Firearms Maintenance Equipment; Hunting Accessories; Law Enforcement; Photographic Equipment; Scopes, Sights & Accessories; Sports Accessories; Wholesaler/Distributor

Pedersoli 2 SRL, Via Artigiani, 13, Gardone V.T., 25063, ITALY, P: 011 390308915000, F: 011 390308911019, www.davide-pedersoli.com
Black Powder Accessories; Firearms; Gun Grips & Stocks

Pedersoli Davide & C. SNC, Via Artigiani, 57, Gardone V.T., Brescia 25063, ITALY, P: 011 39308915000, F: 011 39308911019, www.davide-pedersoli.com
Black Powder Accessories; Cutlery; Firearms; Knives/Knife Cases

Peerless Handcuff Co., 95 State St., Springfield, MA 01103, P: 800-732-3705, F: 413-734-5467, www.peerless.net
Law Enforcement

Peet Shoe Dryer, Inc./Peet Dryer, 919 St. Maries River Rd., P.O. Box 618, St. Maries, ID 83861, 800-222-PEET (7338), F: 800-307-4582, www.peetdryer.com
Footwear; Gloves, Mitts, Hats; Hunting Accessories

Pelican Products, Inc., 23215 Early Ave., Torrance, CA 90505, P: 800-473-5422, F: 310-326-3311
Archery; Backpacking; Bags & Equipment Cases; Camping; Crossbows & Accessories; Gun Cases; Hunting Accessories; Paintball Accessories

Peltor, 5457 W. 79th St., Indianapolis, IN 46268, P: 800-327-3431, F: 800-488-8007, www.aosafety.com
Eyewear; Hearing Protection; Shooting Range Equipment; Two-Way Radios

PentagonLight, 151 Mitchell Ave., San Francisco, CA 94080, P: 800-PENTA-15, F: 650-877-9555, www.pentagonlight.com
Holsters; Hunting Accessories; Law Enforcement; Lighting Products; Sports Accessories; Survival Kits/First Aid; Wholesaler/Distributor

Pentax Imaging Co., 600 12th St., Suite 300, Golden, CO 80401, P: 800-877-0155, F: 303-460-1628, www.pentaxsportoptics.com
Binoculars; Photographic Equipment; Scopes, Sights & Accessories

Perazzi U.S.A., Inc., 1010 W. Tenth St., Azusa, CA 91702, P: 626-334-1234, F: 626-334-0344
Firearms

Perfect Fit, 39 Stetson Rd., Ruite 222, P.O. Box 439, Corinna, ME 04928, P: 800-634-9208, F: 800-222-0417, www.perfectfitusa.com
Custom Manufacturing; Emblems & Decals; Law Enforcement; Leathergoods; Training & Safety Equipment; Wholesaler/Distibutor

Permalight (Asia) Co., Ltd./Pila Flashlights, 4/F, Waga Commercial Centre, 99 Wellington St., Central HONG KONG, P: 011 85228150616, F: 011 85225423269, www.pilatorch.com
Camping; Firearms; Hunting Accessories; Law Enforcement; Lighting Products; Training & Safety Equipment; Wholesaler/Distributor

Pete Rickard Co., 115 Walsh Rd., Cobleskill, NY 12043, P: 518-234-2731, F: 518-234-2454, www.peterickard.com
Archery; Game Calls; Hunting Accessories; Leathergoods; Lubricants; Pet Supplies; Scents & Lures; Shooting Range Equipment

Petzl America, Freeport Center M-7, P.O. Box 160447, Clearfield, UT 84016, P: 877-807-3805, F: 801-926-1501, www.petzl.com
Gloves, Mitts, Hats; Law Enforcement; Lighting Products; Training & Safety Equipment

Phalanx Corp., 4501 N. Dixie Hwy., Boca Raton, FL 33431, P: 954-360-0000, F: 561-417-0500, www.smartholster.com
Gun Locks; Holsters; Law Enforcement; Training & Safety Equipment

Phillips Plastics, 1201 Hanley Rd., Hudson, WI 54016, P: 877-508-0252, F: 715-381-3291, www.phillipsplastics.com
Custom Manufacturing

Phoebus Tactical Flashlights/Phoebus Manufacturing, 2800 Third St., San Francisco, CA 94107, P: 415-550-0770, F: 415-550-2655, www.phoebus.com
Lighting Products

Photop Suwtech, Inc., 2F, Building 65, 421 Hong Cao Rd., Shanghai, 200233, CHINA, P: 011 862164853978, F: 011 862164850389, www.photoptech.com
Law Enforcement; Lighting Products; Scopes, Sights & Accessories

Pine Harbor Holding Co., Inc., P.O. Box 336, Chippewa Falls, WI 54729, P: 715-726-8714, F: 715-726-8739
Blinds; Camouflage; Decoys; Hunting Accessories

Pinnacle Ammunition Co., 111 W. Port Plaza, Suite 600, St. Louis, MO 63146, P: 888-702-2660, F: 314-293-1943, www.pinnacleammo.com
Ammunition

PistolCam, Inc., 1512 Front St., Keeseville, NY 12944, P: 518-834-7093, F: 518-834-7061, www.pistolcam.com
Firearms; Gun Parts/Gunsmithing; Law Enforcement; Photographic Equipment; Scopes, Sights & Accessories; Videos

Plano Molding Co., 431 E. South St., Plano, IL 60545, P: 800-226-9868, F: 630-552-9737, www.planomolding.com
Archery; Bags & Equipment Cases; Firearms Maintenance Equipment; Gun Cases; Hunting Accessories

Plotmaster Systems, Ltd., 111 Industrial Blvd., P.O. Box 111, Wrightsville, GA 31096, P: 888-629-4263, F: 478-864-9109, www.theplotmaster.com
Feeder Equipment; Wholesaler/Distributor; Wildlife Management

PlotSpike Wildlife Seeds/Ragan and Massey, Inc., 100 Ponchatoula Pkwy., Ponchatoula, LA 70454, P: 800-264-5281, F: 985-386-5565, www.plotspike.com
Scents & Lures; Wildlife Management

Plymouth Engineered Shapes, 201 Commerce Ct., Hopkinsville, KY 42240, P: 800-718-7590, F: 270-886-6662, www.plymouth.com/engshapes.aspx
Crossbows & Accessories; Firearms; Gun Barrels; Gun Parts/Gunsmithing

Point Blank Body Armor/PACA Body Armor, 2102 SW 2 St., Pompano Beach, FL 33069, P: 800-413-5155, F: 954-414-8118, www.pointblankarmor.com, www.pacabodyarmor.com
Law Enforcement

Point Tech, Inc., 160 Gregg St., Suite 1, Lodi, NJ 07644, P: 201-368-0711, F: 201-368-0133
Firearms; Gun Barrels; Gun Parts/Gunsmithing

Polaris USA, Inc./Signal Mobile USA, 4511 N. O'Connor Rd., Suite 1150, Irving, TX 75062, P: 817-719-1086, F: 817-887-0807, www.polarisvision.com, www.ezsignal.com

Police and Security News, 1208 Juniper St., Quakertown, PA 18951, P: 215-538-1240, F: 215-538-1208, www.policeandsecuritynews.com
Books/Industry Publications; Law Enforcement

Police Magazine/Police Recruit Magazine, 3520 Challenger St., Torrance, CA 90503, P: 480-367-1101, F: 480-367-1102, www.policemag.com
Books/Industry Publications; Law Enforcement

PoliceOne.com, 200 Green St., Second Floor, San Francisco, CA 94111, P: 800-717-1199, F: 480-854-7079, www.policeone.com
Law Enforcement

Port-A-Cool, 709 Southview Circle, P.O. Box 2167, Center, TX 75935, P: 800-695-2942, F: 936-598-8901
Camouflage; Custom Manufacturing; Sports Accessories; Training & Safety Equipment

Portman Security Systems Ltd., 330 W. Cummings Park, Woburn, MA 01801, P: 781-935-9288, F: 781-935-9188, www.portmansecurity.com
Custom Manufacturing; Firearms Maintenance Equipment; Gun Parts/Gunsmithing; Law Enforcement; Pet Supplies; Scopes, Sights & Accessories; Vehicles, Utility & Rec

PowerBelt Bullets, 5988 Peachtree Corners E, Norcross, GA 30071, P: 800-320-8767, F: 770-242-8546, www.powerbeltbullets.com
Ammunition; Black Powder Accessories

PowerFlare, 6489 Camden Ave., Suite 108, San Jose, CA 95120, P: 877-256-6907, F: 408-268-5431, www.powerflare.com
Lighting Products; Survival Kits/First Aid; Training & Safety Equipment; Wholesaler/Distributor

PowerTech, Inc./Smith & Wesson Flashlights, 360 E. South St., Collierville, TN 38017, P: 901-850-9393, F: 901-850-9797, www.powertechinc.com
Camping; Hunting Accessories; Law Enforcement; Lighting Products; Sports Accessories

Practical Air Rifle Training Systems, LLC, P.O. Box 174, Pacific, MO 63069, P: 314-271-8465, F: 636-271-8465, www.smallarms.com
Airguns; Custom Manufacturing; Law Enforcement; Shooting Range Equipment; Targets; Training & Safety Equipment

Precision Ammunition, LLC, 5402 E. Diana St., Tampa, FL 33610, P: 888-393-0694, F: 813-626-0078, www.precisionammo.com
Ammunition; Law Enforcement; Reloading

Precision Metalsmiths, Inc., 1081 E. 200th St., Cleveland, OH 44117, P: 216-481-8900, F: 216-481-8903, www.precisionmetalsmiths.com
Archery; Custom Manufacturing; Firearms; Gun Barrels; Gun Locks; Gun Parts/Gunsmithing; Knives/Knife Cases; Scopes, Sights & Accessories

Precision Reflex, Inc., 710 Streine Dr., P.O. Box 95, New Bremen, OH 45869, P: 419-629-2603, F: 419-629-2173, www.pri-mounts.com
Custom Manufacturing; Firearms; Gun Barrels; Law Enforcement; Magazines, Cartridge; Scopes, Sights & Accessories

Predator, Inc., 2605 Coulee Ave., La Crosse, WI 54601, P: 800-430-3305, F: 608-787-0667, www.predatorcamo.com
Archery; Backpacking; Blinds; Camouflage; Men's Clothing

Predator International, 4401 S. Broadway, Suite 201, Englewood, CO 80113, P: 877-480-1636, F: 303-482-2987, www.predatorpellets.com
Airguns; Airsoft; Ammunition

Predator Sniper Products, 102 W. Washington St., P.O. Box 743, St. Francis, KS 67756, P: 785-332-2731, F: 785-332-8943, www.predatorsniperstyx.com
Custom Manufacturing; Game Calls; Hunting Accessories; Shooting Range Equipment; Wholesaler/Distributor

Predator Trailcams LLC, 10609 W. Old Hwy. 10 R.D., Saxon, WI 54559, P: 715-893-5001, F: 715-893-5005, www.predatortrailcams.com
Archery; Firearms; Hunting Accessories; Outfitter; Photographic Equipment; Sports Accessories; Wildlife Management

Premier Reticles, 175 Commonwealth Ct., Winchester, VA 22602, P: 540-868-2044, F: 540-868-2045 www.premierreticles.com
Scopes, Sights & Accessories; Telescopes

Premierlight, 35 Revenge Rd., Unit 9, Lordswood, Kent ME5 8DW, UNITED KINGDOM, P: 011-44-1634-201284, F: 011-44-1634-201286, www.premierlight-uk.com
Backpacking; Camping; Hunting Accessories; Law Enforcement; Lighting Products; Sports Accessories; Training & Safety Equipment; Wholesaler/Distributor

Prestige Apparel Mfg. Co./Exxel Outdoors, 300 American Blvd., Haleyville, AL 35565, P: 800-221-7452, F: 205-486-9882, www.exxel.com
Camouflage; Camping; Custom Manufacturing; Export/Import Specialists; Gloves, Mitts, Hats; Men's Clothing; Wholesaler/Distributor

Primary Weapons Systems, 800 E. Citation Ct., Suite C, Boise, ID 83716, P: 208-344-5217, F: 208-344-5395, www.primaryweapons.com
Firearms; Firearms Maintenance Equipment; Gun Parts/Gunsmithing; Law Enforcement; Recoil Protection Devices & Services

Primax Hunting Gear Ltd., Rm. 309, 3/F Jiali Mansion, 39-5#, Xingning Rd., Ningbo, Zhejiang 315040, CHINA, P: 011 8657487894016, F: 011 8657487894017, www.primax-hunting.com
Backpacking; Bags & Equipment Cases; Blinds; Camping; Compasses; Gun Cases; Hunting Accessories; Scopes, Sights & Accessories

Primos Hunting Calls, 604 First St., Flora, MS 39071, P: 800-523-2395, F: 601-879-9324, www.primos.com
Archery; Blinds; Camouflage; Decoys; Game Calls; Hunting Accessories; Scents & Lures; Videos

Princeton Tec, P.O. Box 8057, Trenton, NJ 08650, P: 800-257-9080, FL 609-298-9601, www.princetontec.com
Backpacking; Camping; Cooking Equipment/Accessories; Lighting Products; Photographic Equipment; Sports Accessories; Training & Safety Equipment

Pro-Iroda Industries, Inc., No. 68, 32nd Rd., Taichung Industrial Park, Taichung, 407, TAIWAN, P: 888-66-IRODA, F: 440-247-4630, www.pro-iroda.com
Archery; Camping; Cooking Equipment/Accessories; Custom Manufacturing

Pro-Shot Products, P.O. Box 763, Taylorville, IL 62568, P: 217-824-9133, F: 217-824-8861, www.proshotproducts.com
Black Powder Accessories; Firearms Maintenance Equipment; Lubricants

Pro-Systems Spa, Via al Corbé 63, ITALY, P: 011 390331576887, F: 011 390331576295, www.pro-systems.it, www.pro-systems.us
Law Enforcement

Pro Ears/Benchmaster, 101 Ridgeline Dr., Westcliffe, CO 81252, P: 800-891-3660, F: 719-783-4162, www.pro-ears.com
Crossbows & Accessories; Custom Manufacturing; Hearing Protection; Hunting Accessories; Law Enforcement; Shooting Range Equipment; Sports Accessories; Training & Safety Equipment

Pro Line Manufacturing Co., 186 Parish Dr., Wayne, NJ 07470, P: 800-334-4612, F: 973-692-0999, www.prolineboots.com
Camouflage; Footwear; Leathergoods; Wholesaler/Distributor

Professionals Choice/G&A Investments, Inc., 2615 Fruitland Ave., Vernon, CA 90058, P: 323-589-2775, F: 323-589-3511, www.theprofessionalschoice.net
Firearms Maintenance Equipment; Gun Parts/Gunsmithing; Lubricants; Wholesaler/Distributor

Proforce Equipment, Inc./Snugpak USA, 2201 NW 102nd Place, Suite 1, Miami, FL 33172, P: 800-259-5962, F: 800-664-5095, www.proforceequipment.com
Backpacking; Camping; Hunting Accessories; Knives/Knife Cases; Law Enforcement; Men's Clothing; Survival Kits/First Aid; Watches

Prois Hunting Apparel for Women, 28000B W. Hwy. 50, Gunnison, CO 81230, P: 970-641-3355, F: 970-641-6602, www.proishunting.com
Camouflage; Hunting Accessories; Women's Clothing

ProMag Industries, Inc./Archangel Manufacturing, LLC, 10654 S. Garfield Ave., South Gate, CA 90280, P: 800-438-2547, F: 562-861-6377, www.promagindustries.com
Gun Grips & Stocks; Gun Parts/Gunsmithing; Law Enforcement; Magazines, Cartridge; Retail Packaging; Scopes, Sights & Accessories

Promatic, Inc., 7803 W. Hwy. 116, Gower, MO 64454, UNITED KINGDOM, P: 888-767-2529, F: 816-539-0257, www.promatic.biz
Airguns; Clay Targets; Shooting Range Equipment; Targets; Training & Safety Equipment

Propper International Sales, 520 Huber Park Ct., St. Charles, MO 63304, P: 800-296-9690, F: 877-296-9690, www.propper.com
Camouflage; Law Enforcement; Men's Clothing

Protective Products International, 1649 NW 136th Ave., Sunrise, FL 33323, P: 800-509-9111, F: 954-846-0555, www.body-armor.com
Custom Manufacturing; Export/Import Specialists; Law Enforcement; Men & Women's Clothing; Training & Safety Equipment; Vehicles, Utility & Rec

Pumo GmbH IP Solingen, An den Eichen 20-22, Solingen, HMBG 42699, GERMANY, P: 011 492851589655, F: 011 492851589660, www.pumaknives.de
Custom Manufacturing; Cutlery; Hunting Accessories; Knives/Knife Cases; Sharpeners

Pyramex Safety Products, 281 Moore Lane, Collierville, TN 38017, P: 800-736-8673, F: 877-797-2639, www.pyramexsafety.com
Eyewear; Hearing Protection; Training & Safety Equipment

Pyramyd Air, 26800 Fargo Ave., Suite L, Bedford, OH 44146, P: 888-262-4867, F: 216-896-0896, www.pyramydair.com
Airguns, Airsoft

Q

Quail Unlimited, 31 Quail Run, Edgefield, SC 29824, P: 803-637-5731, F: 803-637-5303, www.qu.org
Books/Industry Publications; Firearms; Hunting Accessories; Men & Women's Clothing; Outdoor Art, Jewelry, Sculpture; Wildlife Management

Quake Industries, Inc., 732 Cruiser Ln., Belgrade, MT 59714, P: 770-449-4687, F: 406-388-8810, www.quakeinc.com
Archery; Crossbows & Accessories; Custom Manufacturing; Hunting Accessories; Scopes, Sights & Accessories; Sports Accessories; Treestands

Quaker Boy, Inc., 5455 Webster Rd., Orchard Park, NY 14127, P: 800-544-1600, F: 716-662-9426, www.quakerboy.com
Camouflage; Game Calls; Gloves, Mitts, Hats; Hunting Accessories; Targets; Videos

Quality Cartridge, P.O. Box 445, Hollywood, MD 20636, P: 301-373-3719, F: 301-373-3719, www.qual-cart.com
Ammunition; Custom Manufacturing; Reloading

Quality Deer Management Assoc., 170 Whitetail Way, P.O. Box 160, Bogart, GA 30622, P: 800-209-3337, F: 706-353-0223, www.qdma.com
Books/Industry Publications; Men & Women's Clothing; Videos; Wholesaler/Distributor; Wildlife Management

Quantico Tactical Supply, 109 N. Main St., Raeford, NC 28376, P: 910-875-1672, F: 910-875-3797, www.quanticotactical.com
Eyewear; Firearms; Footwear; Holsters; Knives/Knife Cases; Law Enforcement; Survival Kits/First Aid

Quayside Publishing Group, 400 1st Ave. N, Suite 300, Minneapolis, MN 55401, P: 800-328-0590, F: 612-344-8691, www.creativepub.com
Books/Industry Publications

Quiqlite, Inc., 6464 Hollister Ave., Suite 4, Goleta, CA 93117, P: 866-496-2606, F: 800-910-5711, www.quiqlite.com
Backpacking; Camping; Hunting Accessories; Law Enforcement; Lighting Products; Reloading; Training & Safety Equipment

R

R & R Racing, Inc., 45823 Oak St., Lyons, OR 97358, P: 503-551-7283, F: 503-859-4711, www.randrracingonline.com
Custom Manufacturing; Hearing Protection; Shooting Range Equipment; Targets; Training & Safety Equipment; Wholesaler/Distributor

R & W Rope Warehouse, 39 Tarkiln Pl., P.O. Box 50420, New Bedford, MA 02745, P: 800-260-8599, F: 508-995-1114, www.rwrope.com
Backpacking; Camouflage; Camping; Custom Manufacturing; Hunting Accessories; Law Enforcement; Pet Supplies; Training & Safety Equipment

Rackulator, Inc., P.O. Box 248, Golden Valley, ND 58541, P: 888-791-4213, F: 701-983-4625, www.rackulator.com
Hunting Accessories

Radians, 7580 Bartlett Corp. Dr., Bartlett, TN 38133, P: 877-723-4267, F: 901-266-2558, www.radiansinc.com
Camouflage; Eyewear; Footwear; Gloves, Mitts, Hats; Hearing Protection; Law Enforcement; Sports Accessories; Training & Safety Equipment

Raine, Inc., 6401 S. Madison Ave., Anderson, IN 46013, P: 800-826-5354, F: 765-622-7691, www.raineinc.com
Bags & Equipment Cases; Camping; Custom Manufacturing; Holsters; Knives/Knife Cases; Law Enforcement; Two-Way Radios

Rainer Ballistics, 4500 15th St. E, Tacoma, WA 98424, P: 800-638-8722, F: 253-922-7854, www.rainierballistics.com
Ammunition; Reloading; Wholesaler/Distributor

Ram Mounting Systems, 8410 Dallas Ave. S, Seattle, WA 98108, P: 206-763-8361, F: 206-763-9615, www.ram-mount.com
Hunting Accessories; Law Enforcement; Sports Accessories; Vehicles, Utility & Rec

Ramba, Via Giorgio La Pira, 20 Flero (Bs), Brescia 25020, ITALY, P: 011 390302548522, F: 011 390302549749, www.ramba.it
Ammunition; Reloading

Ranch Products, P.O. Box 145, Malinta, OH 43535, P: 419-966-2881, F: 313-565-8536, www.ranchproducts.com
Gun Parts/Gunsmithing; Scopes, Sights & Accessories

Rancho Trinidad, 4803 Fountainhead, Houston, TX 77066, P: 210-487-1640, F: 210-487-1640, www.ranchotrinidad.com
Outfitter; Tours/Travel

Randolph Engineering, Inc., 26 Thomas Patten Dr., Randolph, MA 02368, P: 800-541-1405, F: 781-986-0337, www.randolphusa.com
Eyewear

Range Systems, 5121 Winnetka Ave. N, Suite 150, New Hope, MN 55428, P: 888-999-1217, F: 763-537-6657, www.range-systems.com
Eyewear; Law Enforcement; Shooting Range Equipment; Targets; Training & Safety Equipment

Ranger/Xtratuf/NEOS Footwear, 1136 2nd St., Rock Island, IL 61201, P: 800-790-9296, F: 800-267-6809, www.npsusa.com
Footwear

Rapid Dominance Corp., 2121 S. Wilmington Ave., Compton, CA 90220, P: 800-719-5260, F: 310-608-3648, www.rapiddominance.com
Bags & Equipment Cases; Gloves, Mitts, Hats; Men's Clothing; Wholesaler/Distributor

Rat Cutlery Co., 60 Randall Rd., Gallant, AL 35972, P: 865-933-8436, F: 256-570-0175, www.ratcutlery.com
Backpacking; Camping; Cutlery; Knives/Knife Cases; Law Enforcement; Survival Kits/First Aid; Tours/Travel; Training & Safety Equipment

Rattlers Brand/Boyt Harness Co., One Boyt Dr., Osceola, IA 50213, P: 800-550-2698, F: 641-342-2703, www.rattlersbrand.com
Camouflage; Sports Accessories

Raza Khalid & Co., 14/8, Haji Pura, P.O. Box 1632, Sailkot, Punjab 51310, PAKISTAN, P: 011 92523264232, F: 011 92523254932, www.razakhalid.com
Bags & Equipment Cases; Gloves, Mitts, Hats; Gun Cases; Hunting Accessories; Law Enforcement; Paintball Accessories; Pet Supplies; Shooting Range Equipment

RBR Tactical Armor, Inc., 3113 Aspen Ave., Richmond, VA 23228, P: 800-672-7667, F: 804-726-6027, www.rbrtactical.com
Custom Manufacturing; Law Enforcement

RCBS/ATK Commercial Products, 605 Oro Dam Blvd., Oroville, CA 95965, P: 800-533-5000, F: 530-533-1647, www.rcbs.com
Reloading

Real Geese/Webfoot-LSP, 130 Cherry St., P.O. Box 675, Bradner, OH 43406, P: 419-800-8104, F: 888-642-6369, www.realgeese.com
Bags & Equipment Cases; Custom Manufacturing; Decoys; Emblems & Decals; Home Furnishings; Hunting Accessories; Printing Services; Retail Packaging

Realtree® Camouflage, P.O. Box 9638, Columbus, GA 31908, P: 800-992-9968, F: 706-569-9346, www.realtree.com
Camouflage; Videos

Recknagel, Landwehr 4, Bergrheinfeld, 97493, GERMANY, P: 011 49972184366, F: 011 49972182969, www.recknagel.de
Gun Parts/Gunsmithing; Scopes, Sights & Accessories

Recognition Services, 8577 Zionsville Rd., Indianapolis, IN 46268, P: 877-808-9400, F: 877-808-3565, www.we-belong.com
Custom Manufacturing; Emblems & Decals; Law Enforcement; Outfitter

ReconRobotics, Inc., 770 W. 78th St., Edina, MN 55439, P: 952-935-5515, F: 952-935-5508, www.reconrobotics.com
Law Enforcement

Redding Reloading Equipment, 1089 Starr Rd., Cortland, NY 13045, P: 607-753-3331, F: 607-756-8445, www.redding-reloading.com
Lubricants; Reloading

Redman Training Gear, 10045 102nd Terrace, Sebastian, FL 32958, P: 800-865-7840, F: 800-459-2598, www.redmangear.com
Law Enforcement; Training & Safety Equipment

Redwolf Airsoft Specialist, 7A-C, V GA Building, 532 Castle Peak Rd., Cheung Sha Wan, HONG KONG, P: 011 85228577665, F: 011 85229758305, www.redwolfairsoft.com
Airsoft

Reel Wings Decoy Co., Inc., 1122 Main Ave., Fargo, ND 58103, P: 866-55DECOY, F: 701-293-8234, www.reelwings.com
Camouflage; Decoys; Wholesaler/Distributor

Reflective Art, Inc., 403 Eastern Ave. SE, Grand Rapids, MI 49508, P: 800-332-1075, F: 616-452-2112, www.reflectiveartinc.com
Home Furnishings

Reliable of Milwaukee, P.O. Box 563, Milwaukee, WI 53201, P: 800-336-6876, F: 414-272-6443, www.reliableofmilwaukee.com
Archery; Bags & Equipment Cases; Camouflage; Footwear; Gloves, Mitts, Hats; Hunting Accessories; Men & Women's Clothing

Reminton Apparel/The Brinkmann Corp., 4215 McEwen Rd., Dallas, TX 75244, P: 877-525-9070, F: 800-780-0109, www.brinkmann.net
Camouflage; Gloves, Mitts, Hats; Hunting Accessories; Men's Clothing

Remington Arms Co., Inc., 870 Remington Dr., P.O. Box 700, Madison, NC 27025, P: 800-243-9700
Ammunition; Cutlery; Firearms; Footwear; Gun Parts/Gunsmithing; Hunting Accessories

Repel Products, P.O. Box 348, Marion, IA 52302, P: 866-921-1810, F: 319-447-0967, www.repelproducts.com
Archery; Hunting Accessories; Sports Accessories; Wildlife Management

Rescomp Handgun Technologies/CR Speed, P.O. Box 11786, Queenswood, 0186, SOUTH AFRICA, P: 011 27123334768, F: 011 27123332112, www.crspeed.co.za
Bags & Equipment Cases; Custom Manufacturing; Holsters; Law Enforcement; Scopes, Sights & Accessories; Sports Accessories; Wholesaler/Distributor

Revision Eyewear, Ltd., 7 Corporate Dr., Essex Junction, VT 05452, CANADA, P: 802-879-7002, F: 802-879-7224, www.revisionready.com
Eyewear; Hunting Accessories; Law Enforcement; Paintball Accessories; Shooting Range Equipment; Sports Accessories; Training & Safety Equipment

Rich-Mar Sports, North 7125 1280 St., River Falls, WI 54022, P: 952-881-6796, F: 952-884-4878, www.richmarsports. com
Cooking Equipment/Accessories; Hunting Accessories; Law Enforcement; Sports Accessories; Training & Safety Equipment

Ridge Outdoors U.S.A., Inc./Ridge Footwear, P.O. Box 389, Eustis, FL 32727-0389, P: 800-508-2668, F: 866-584-2042, www.ridgeoutdoors.com
Footwear; Law Enforcement; Men & Women's Clothing; Sports Accessories

Ring's Manufacturing, 99 East Dr., Melbourne, FL 32904, P: 800-537-7464, F: 321-951-0017, www.blueguns.com
Custom Manufacturing; Law Enforcement; Training & Safety Equipment

Rio Ammunition, Fountainview, Suite 207, Houston, TX 77057, P: 713-266-3091, F: 713-266-3092, www.rioammo.com, www.ueec.es
Ammunition; Black Powder/Smokeless Powder; Law Enforcement

Rio Bonito Ranch, 5309 Rio Bonito Ranch Rd., Junction, TX 76849, P: 800-864-4303, F: 325-446-3859, www.riobonito. com
Outfitter

Rite In The Rain, 2614 Pacific Hwy. E, Tacoma, WA 98424, P: 253-922-5000, F: 253-922-5300, www.riteintherain.com
Archery; Backpacking; Camping; Custom Manufacturing; Law Enforcement; Printing Services; Sports Accessories; Targets

River Oak Outdoors, Inc., 705 E. Market, Warrensburg, MO 64093, P: 660-580-0256, F: 816-222-0427, www. riveroakoutdoors.com
Custom Manufacturing; Game Calls; Gun Cabinets/Racks/Safes; Home Furnishings; Hunting Accessories; Sports Accessories

River Rock Designs, Inc., 900 RR 620 S, Suite C101-223, Austin, TX 78734, P: 512-263-6985, F: 512-263-1277, www.riverrockledlights.com
Backpacking; Camping; Hunting Accessories; Law Enforcement; Lighting Products; Sports Accessories; Training & Safety Equipment

River's Edge Treestands, Inc./Ardisam, Inc./Yukon Tracks, 1690 Elm St., Cumberland, WI 54829, P: 800-450-3343, F: 715-822-2124, www.huntriversedge.com, www.ardisam. com
Archery; Blinds; Camouflage; Gloves, Mitts, Hats; Hunting Accessories; Treestands

Rivers Edge Products, One Rivers Edge Ct., St. Clair, MO 63077, P: 888-326-6200, F: 636-629-7557, www. riversedgeproducts.com
Camouflage; Camping; Home Furnishings; Knives/ Knife Cases; Leathergoods; Lighting Products; Pet Supplies; Wholesaler/Distributor

Rivers West/H2P Waterproof System, 2900 4th Ave. S, Seattle, WA 98134, P: 800-683-0887, F: 206-682-8691, www.riverswest.com
Camouflage; Law Enforcement; Men & Women's Clothing

RM Equipment, 6975 NW 43rd St., Miami, FL 33166, P: 305-477-9312, F: 305-477-9620, www.40mm.com
Firearms; Gun Grips & Stocks; Law Enforcement

RNT Calls, Inc./Buckwild Hunting Products and Quackhead Calls, 2315 Hwy. 63 N, P.O. Box 1026, Stuttgart, AR 72160, P: 877-993-4868, F: 601-829-4072, www.rntcalls. com
Custom Manufacturing; Emblems & Decals; Game Calls; Gloves, Mitts, Hats; Hunting Accessories; Scents & Lures; Videos

Robert Louis Company, Inc., 31 Shepard Hill Rd., Newtown, CT 06470, P: 800-979-9156, F: 203-270-3881, www. shotguncombogauge.com
Gun Parts/Gunsmithing; Shooting Range Equipment; Training & Safety Equipment

Rock Creek Barrels, Inc., 101 Ogden Ave., Albany, WI 53502, P: 608-862-2357, F: 608-862-2356, www.rockcreekbarrels. com
Gun Barrels

Rock River Arms, Inc., 1042 Cleveland Rd., Colona, IL 61241, P: 866-980-7625, F: 309-792-5781, www.rockriverarms. com
Custom Manufacturing; Firearms; Gun Barrels; Gun Grips & Stocks; Gun Parts/Gunsmithing; Law Enforcement; Magazines, Cartridge; Scopes, Sights & Accessories

Rockpoint Apparel, 9925 Aldine Westfield Rd., Houston, TX 77093, P: 713-699-9896, F: 713-699-9856, www. rockpoint-apparel.com
Camouflage; Custom Manufacturing; Export/Import Specialists; Gloves, Mitts, Hats; Men & Women's Clothing

Rocky Brands, 39 E. Canal St., Nelsonville, OH 45764, P: 740-753-9100, F: 740-753-7240, www.rockybrands.com
Footwear

Rocky Mountain Elk Foundation, 5705 Grant Creek Rd., P.O. Box 8249, Missoula, MT 59808, P: 800-CALL-ELK, F: 406-523-4550, www.elkfoundation.org

Books/Industry Publications; Wildlife Management

Rohrbaugh Firearms Corp., P.o. Box 785, Bayport, NY 11705, P: 800-803-2233, F: 631-242-3183, www. rohrbaughfirearms.com
Firearms

ROKON, 50 Railroad Ave., Rochester, NH 03839, P: 800-593-2369, F: 603-335-4400, www.rokon.com
Export/Import Specialists; Hunting Accessories; Sports Accessories; Vehicles, Utility & Rec

ROK Straps, 162 Locust Hill Dr., Rochester, NY 14618, P: 585-244-6451, F: 570-694-0773, www.rokstraps.com
Backpacking; Camouflage; Camping; Hunting Accessories; Pet Supplies; Sports Accessories

Rose Garden, The, 1855 Griffin Rd., Suite C370, Dania Beach, FL 33004, P: 954-927-9590, F: 954-927-9591, www. therosegardendb.com
Export/Import Specialists; Home Furnishings; Outdoor Art, Jewelry, Sculpture; Wholesaler/Distributor

Rose Plastic USA, LP, 525 Technology Dr., P.O. Box 698, California, PA 15419, P: 724-938-8530, F: 724-938-8532, www.rose-plastic.us
Bags & Equipment Cases; Custom Manufacturing; Gun Cases; Retail Packaging

Rossi/BrazTech, 16175 NW 49th Ave., Miami, FL 33014, P: 800-948-8029, F: 305-623-7506, www.rossiusa.com
Black Powder Accessories; Firearms

Rothco, 3015 Veterans Memorial Hwy., P.O. Box 1220, Ronkonkoma, NY 11779, P: 800-645-5195, F: 631-585-9447, www.rothco.com
Bags & Equipment Cases; Camouflage; Hunting Accessories; Knives/Knife Cases; Law Enforcement; Men & Women's Clothing; Survival Kits/First Aid; Wholesaler/Distributor

RPM, Inc./Drymate, 6665 W. Hwy. 13, Savage, MN 55378, P: 800-872-8201, F: 952-808-2277, www.drymate.com
Blinds; Camping; Custom Manufacturing; Firearms Maintenance Equipment; Home Furnishings; Hunting Accessories; Pet Supplies; Sports Accessories; Vehicles, Utility & Rec

RSR Group, Inc., 4405 Metric Dr., Winter Park, FL 32792, P: 800-541-4867, F: 407-677-4489, www.rsrgroup.com
Airguns; Ammunition; Cutlery; Firearms; Gun Cases; Holsters; Scopes, Sights & Accessories; Wholesaler/Distributor

RS International Industry/Hong Kong Co., Ltd., Room 1109, 11F, WingHing Industrial Bldg., Chai Wan Kok St., Tsuen Wan N.T., HONG KONG, P: 011 85224021381, F: 011 85224021385, www.realsword.com.hk
Airsoft

RTZ Distribution/HallMark Cutlery, 4436B Middlebrook Pike, Knoxville, TN 37921, P: 866-583-3912, F: 865-588-0425, www.hallmarkcutlery.com
Cutlery; Knifs/Knife Cases; Law Enforcement; Sharpeners

RUAG Ammotec, Uttigenstrasse 67, Thun, 3602, SWITZERLAND, P: 011 41332282879, F: 011 41332282644, www.ruag.com
Ammunition; Law Enforcement

Ruffed Grouse Society, 451 McCormick Rd., Coraopolis, PA 15108, P: 888-564-6747, F: 412-262-9207, www. ruffedgrousesociety.org
Wildlife Management

Ruger Firearms, 1 Lacey Pl., Southport, CT 06890, P: 203-259-7843, F: 203-256-3367, www.ruger.com
Firearms

Ruko, LLC, P.O. Box 38, Buffalo, NY 14207, P: 716-874-2707, F: 905-826-1353, www.rukoproducts.com
Camping; Compasses; Custom Manufacturing; Cutlery; Export/Import Specialists; Hunting Accessories; Knives/Knife Cases; Sharpeners

Russ Fields Safaris, Gameston, Alicedale Rd., P.O. Box 100, Grahamstown, East Cape, 6140, SOUTH AFRICA, P: 011 27834449753, F: 011 27466225837, www. southafricanhunting.com
Outfitter

Russian American Armory Co., 677 S. Cardinal Ln., Suite A, Scottsburg, IN 47170, P: 877-752-2894, F: 812-752-7683, www.raacfirearms.com
Firearms; Knives/Knife Cases; Magazines, Cartridge

RVJ International/Happy Feet, 6130 W. Flamingo Rd., PMB 460, Las Vegas, NV 89103, P: 702-871-6377, F: 702-222-1212, www.happyfeet.com
Books/Industry Publications; Footwear; Hunting Accessories; Men & Women's Clothing; Sports Accessories

S

S&K Industries, Inc., S. Hwy. 13, Lexington, MO 64067, P: 660-259-4691, F: 660-259-2081, www.sandkgunstocks. com
Custom Manufacturing; Gun Grips & Stocks

Saab Barracuda, LLC, 608 McNeill St., Lillington, NC 27546, P: 910-893-2094, F: 910-893-8807, www.saabgroup.com

Camouflage; Law Enforcement

Sabre Defence Industries, LLC, 450 Allied Dr., Nashville, TN 37211, P: 615-333-0077, F: 615-333-6229, www. sabredefence.com
Firearms; Gun Barrels

Sack-Ups, 1611 Jamestown Rd., Morganton, NC 28655, P: 877-213-6333, F: 828-584-6326, www.sackups.com
Archery; Black Powder Accessories; Firearms Maintenance Equipment; Gun Cases; Hunting Accessories; Knives/Knife Cases; Sports Accessories

Safari Club International, 4800 W. Gates Pass Rd., Tucson, AZ 85745, P: 520-620-1220, F: 520-618-3528, www. safariclub.org
Books/Industry Publications

Safari Nordik, 639 Labelle Blvd., Blainville, Quebec J7C 1V8, CANADA, P: 800-361-3748, F: 450-971-1771, www. safarinordik.com
Outfitter; Tours/Travel

Safari Press, 15621 Chemical Ln., Huntington Beach, CA 92649, P: 714-894-9080, F: 714-894-4949, www. safaripress.com
Books/Industry Publications

Safari Sunsets, 9735 Slater Ln., Overland Park, KS 66212, P: 877-894-1671, F: 913-894-1686, www.safarisunsets.com
Men's Clothing

Safe Guy/Gun Storage Solutions, 18317 N. 2600 East Rd., Cooksville, IL 61730, P: 309-275-1220, www. storemoreguns.com
Gun Cabinets/Racks/Safes

Safety Bullet, Inc., P.O. Box 007, Panama City, FL 32444, P: 850-866-0190, www.safetybullet.com
Gun Locks

Safety Harbor Firearms, Inc., 915 Harbor Lake Dr., Suite D, Safety Harbor, FL 34695, P: 727-725-4700, F: 727-724-1872, www.safetyharborfirearms.com
Firearms

Sage Control Ordnance, Inc./Sage International, Ltd., 3391 E. Eberhardt St., Oscoda, MI 48750, P: 989-739-7000, F: 989-739-7098, www.sageinternationalltd.com
Ammunition; Firearms; Gun Grips & Stocks; Gun Locks; Law Enforcement; Reloading

Salt River Tactical, LLC/Ost-Kraft, LLC, P.O. Box 20397, Mesa, AZ 85277, P: 480-656-2683, www.saltrivertactical.com
Bags & Equipment Cases; Firearms Maintenance Equipment; Hunting Accessories; Law Enforcement; Scopes, Sights & Accessories; Shooting Range Equipment; Wholesaler/Distributor

SAM Medical Products, P.O. Box 3270, Tualatin, OR 97062, P: 800-818-4726, F: 503-639-5425, www.sammedical.com
Backpacking; Camping; Law Enforcement; Outfitter; Shooting Range Equipment; Survival Kits/First Aid; Training & Safety Equipment

Samco Global Arms, Inc., 6995 NW 43rd St., Miami, FL 33166, P: 800-554-1618, F: 305-593-1014, www. samcoglobal.com
Ammunition; Firearms; Sports Accessories

Samson Mfg. Corp., 110 Christian Ln., Whately, MA 01373, P: 888-665-4370, F: 413-665-1163, www.samson-mfg.com
Firearms; Gun Parts/Gunsmithing; Law Enforcement; Scopes, Sights & Accessories

San Angelo/Rio Brands, 10981 Decatur Rd., Philadelphia, PA 19154, P: 800-531-7200, F: 830-393-7621, www. riobrands.com
Backpacking; Blinds; Camping; Cooking Equipment/ Accessories; Gun Cabinets/Racks/Safes; Hunting Accessories; Taxidermy

Sandhurst Safaris, P.O. Box 57, Tosca, 8618, SOUTH AFRICA, P: 011 27824535683, F: 011 27539331002, www. sandhurstsafaris.com
Tours/Travel

Sandpiper of California, 687 Anita St., Suite A, Chula Vista, CA 91911, P: 866-424-6622, F: 619-423-9599, www. pipergear.com
Backpacking; Bags & Equipment Cases; Camouflage; Custom Manufacturing; Law Enforcement

Sandviper, 1611 Jamestown Rd., Morganton, NC 28655, P: 800-873-7225, F: 828-584-6326
Law Enforcement

Sante Fe Stone Works, Inc., 3790 Cerillos Rd., Sante Fe, NM 87507, P: 800-257-7625, F: 505-471-0036, www. santefestoneworks.com
Cutlery

Sargent & Greenleaf, Inc., One Security Dr., Nicholasville, KY 40356, P: 800-826-7652, F: 859-887-2057, www. sargentandgreenleaf.com
Gun Cabinets/Racks/Safes

Sarsilmaz Silah San. A.S, Nargileci Sokak, No. 4, Sarsilmaz Is Merkezi, Mercan, Eminonu, Istanbul, 34116, TURKEY, P: 011 902125133507, F: 011 902125111999, www. sarsilmaz.com
Firearms

Savage Arms, Inc., 118 Mountain Rd., Suffield, CT 06078, P: 866-233-4776, F: 860-668-2168, www.savagearms.com

Black Powder/Smokeless Powder; Firearms; Knives/ Knife Cases; Law Enforcement; Shooting Range Equipment

Savannah Luggage Works, 3428 Hwy. 297 N, Vidalia, GA 30474, P: 800-673-6341, F: 912-537-4492, www. savannahluggage.com
Backpacking; Bags & Equipment Cases; Custom Manufacturing; Holsters; Law Enforcement; Training & Safety Equipment

SBR Ammunition, 1118 Glynn Park Rd., Suite E, Brunswick, GA 31525, P: 912-264-5822, F: 912-264-5888, www. sbrammunition.com
Ammunition; Firearms; Law Enforcement

Sceery Outdoors, LLC, P.O. Box 6520, Sante Fe, NM 87502; P: 800-327-4322 or 505-471-9110; F: 505-471-3476; www.sceeryoutdoors.net
Decoys; Game Calls; Hunting Accessories

Scent-Lok Technologies, 1731 Wierengo Dr., Muskegon, MI 49442, P: 800-315-5799, F: 231-767-2824, www.scentlok. com
Bags & Equipment Cases; Camouflage; Gloves, Mitts, Hats; Men & Women's Clothing; Videos

SCENTite Blinds, P.O. Box 36635, Birmingham, AL 35236, P: 800-828-1554, F: 205-424-4799, www.fargasonoutdoors. com
Archery; Backpacking; Blinds; Crossbows & Accessories; Hunting Accessories; Photographic Equipment; Scents & Lures; Treestands

Scentote, 1221 Keating, Grand Rapids, MI 49503, P: 616-742-0946, F: 616-742-0978, www.scentote.com
Archery; Hunting Accessories; Men's Clothing; Scents & Lures

Scharch Mfg., Inc/Top Brass, 10325 Cty. Rd. 120, Salida, CO 81201, P: 800-836-4683, F: 719-539-3021, www.scharch. com
Ammunition; Magazines, Cartridge; Reloading; Retail Packaging; Shooting Range Equipment

Scherer Supplies, Inc., 205 Four Mile Creek Rd., Tazewell, TN 37879, P: 423-733-2615, F: 423-733-2073
Custom Manufacturing; Magazines, Cartridge; Wholesaler/Distributor

Schmidt & Bender GmbH, Am Grossacker 42, Biebertal, Hessen 35444, GERMANY, P: 011 496409811570, US: 800-468-3450, F: ++49-6409811511, www.schmidt-bender.de, www.schmidtbender.com
Hunting Accessories; Law Enforcement; Scopes, Sights & Accessories; Sports Accessories; Telescopes

Schott Performance Fabrics, Inc., 2850 Gilchrist Rd., Akron, OH 44305, P: 800-321-2178, F: 330-734-0665, www. schottfabrics.com
Camouflage; Export/Import Specialists; Hunting Accessories; Men's Clothing

Scopecoat by Devtron Diversified, 3001 E. Cholla St., Phoenix, AZ 85028, P: 877-726-7328, F: 602-224-9351, www.scopecoat.com
Scopes, Sights & Accessories

SDG Seber Design Group, Inc. 2438 Cades Way, Vista, CA 92081, P: 760-727-5555, F: 760-727-5551, www. severdesigngroup.com
Camping; Cutlery; Knives/Knife Cases; Law Enforcement

Seasonal Marketing, Inc., P.O. Box 1410, La Pine, OR 97739, P: 972-540-1656, www.caddiswadingsystems.net
Footwear; Hunting Accessories

Second Amendment Foundation, 12500 NE Tenth Pl., Bellevue, WA 98005, P: 425-454-7012, F: 425-451-3959, www.saf.org
Books/Industry Publications

SecuRam Systems, Inc., 350 N. Lantana St., Suite 211, Camarillo, CA 93010, P: 805-388-2058, F: 805-383-1728, www.securamsys.com
Gun Cabinets/Racks/Safes

Secure Firearm Products, 213 S. Main, P.O. Box 177, Carl Junction, MO 64834, P: 800-257-8744, F: 417-649-7278, www.securefirearmproducts.com
Bags & Equipment Cases; Custom Manufacturing; Gun Cases; Shooting Range Equipment; Targets

Secure Vault/Boyt Harness Co., One Boyt Dr., Osceola, IA 50213, P: 800-550-2698, F: 641-342-2703
Gun Cabinets/Racks/Safes

Security Equipment Corp., 747 Sun Park Dr., Fenton, MO 63026, P: 800-325-9568, F: 636-343-1318, www.sabrered. com
Backpacking; Camping; Custom Manufacturing; Law Enforcement; Training & Safety Equipment

Seldon Technologies, Inc., P.O. Box 710, Windsor, VT 05089, P: 802-674-2444, F: 802-674-2544, www.seldontech.com
Backpacking; Camping; Hunting Accessories

Self Defense Supply, Inc., 1819 Firman Dr., Suite 101, Richardson, TX 75081, P: 800-211-4186, F: 942-644-6980, www.selfdefensesupply.com
Airguns; Airsoft; Binoculars; Camping; Crossbows & Accessories; Cutlery; Lighting Products; Wholesaler/ Distributor

Sellier & Bellot, USA, Inc., P.O. Box 7307, Shawnee Mission, KS 66207, P: 913-664-5933, F: 913-664-5938, www. sb-usa.com
Ammunition; Law Enforcement

Sentry Group, 900 Linden Ave., Rochester, NY 14625, P: 800-828-1438, F: 585-381-8559, www.sentrysafe.com
Gun Cabinets/Racks/Safes; Home Furnishings; Hunting Accessories; Law Enforcement

Sentry Solutions, Ltd., 5 Souhegan St., P.O. Box 214, Wilton, NH 03086, P: 800-546-8049, F: 603-654-3003, www. sentrysolutions.com
Firearms Maintenance Equipment; Gun Parts/ Gunsmithing; Hunting Accessories; Lubricants; Sharpeners; Sports Accessories

Serbu Firearms, Inc., 6001 Johns Rd., Suite 144, Tampa, FL 33634, P: 813-243-8899, F: 813-243-8899, www.serbu. com
Firearms; Law Enforcement

Sharp Shoot R Precision, Inc., P.O. Box 171, Paola, KS 66071, P: 785-883-4444, F: 785-883-2525, www.sharpshootr.com
Black Powder Accessories; Custom Manufacturing; Firearms Maintenance Equipment; Lubricants; Reloading; Sports Accessories

Shasta Wear, 4320 Mountain Lakes Blvd., Redding, CAR 96003, P: 800-553-2466, F: 530-243-3274, www. shastawear.com
Emblems & Decals; Export/Import Specialists; Gloves, Mitts, Hats; Men & Women's Clothing; Outdoor Art, Jewelry, Sculpture; Retailer Services; Wholesaler/Distributor

SHE Safari, LLC, 15535 W. Hardy, Suite 102, Houston, TX 77060, P: 281-448-4860, F: 281-448-4118, www.shesafari. com
Camouflage; Women's Clothing

Sheffield Equipment, 4569 Mission Gorge Pl., San Diego, CA 92120, P: 619-280-0278, F: 619-280-0011, www. sheffieldcuttingequip.com
Bags & Equipment Cases; Camouflage; Custom Manufacturing; Holsters; Leathergoods; Men & Women's Clothing

Sheffield Tools/GreatLITE Flashlights, 165 E. 2nd St., P.O. Box 3, Mineola, NY 11501, P: 800-457-0600, F: 516-746-5366, www.sheffield-tools.com
Backpacking; Camping; Cutlery; Hunting Accessories; Knives/Knife Cases; Lighting Products

Shelterlogic, 150 Callender Rd., Watertown, CT 06795, P: 800-932-9344, F: 860-274-9306, www.shelterlogic.com
Camouflage; Camping; Custom Manufacturing; Hunting Accessories; Law Enforcement; Pet Supplies; Sports Accessories

Shenzhen Champion Industry Co., Ltd., Longqin Rd. No. 13, Shahu, Pingshan, Longgang Shenzhen City, GNGD 518118, CHINA, P: 011 8675589785877, F: 011 8675589785875, www.championcase.com
Bags & Equipment Cases; Cutlery; Gun Cabinets/ Racks/Safes; Gun Cases; Gun Locks; Gun Parts/ Gunsmithing; Home Furnishings; Knives/Knife Cases

Shepherd Enterprises, Inc., P.O. Box 189, Waterloo, NE 68069, P: 402-779-2424, F: 402-779-4010, www. shepherdscopes.com
Scopes, Sights & Accessories

Sherluk Marketing, Law Enforcement & Military, P.O. Box 156, Delta, OH 43615, P: 419-923-8011, F: 419-923-8120, www.sherluk.com
Firearms; Firearms Maintenance Equipment; Gun Grips & Stocks; Gun Parts/Gunsmithing; Law Enforcement; Wholesaler/Distributor

Shiloh Rifle Manufacturing, 201 Centennial Dr., P.O. Box 279, Big Timber, MT 59011, P: 406-932-4454, F: 406-932-5627, www.shilohrifle.com
Black Powder Accessories; Firearms

Shirstone Optics/Shinei Group, Inc., Komagome-Spancrete Bldg. 8F, Honkomagome 5-4-7, Bunkyo-Ku, Toyko, 113-0021, JAPAN, P: 011 81339439550, F: 011 81339430695, www.shirstone.com
Binoculars; Firearms; Scopes, Sights & Accessories

Shocknife, Inc., 20 Railway St., Winnipeg, Manitoba R2X 2P9, CANADA, P: 866-353-5055, F: 204-586-2049, www. shocknife.com
Knives/Knife Cases; Law Enforcement; Training & Safety Equipment

Shooter's Choice Gun Care/Ventco, Inc., 15050 Berkshire Industrial Pkwy., Middlefield, OH 44062, P: 440-834-8888, F: 440-834-3388, www.shooters-choice.com
Firearms Maintenance Equipment; Gun Parts/ Gunsmithing; Law Enforcement; Lubricants

Shooters Depot, 5526 Leopard St., Corpus Christi, TX 78408, P: 361-299-1299, F: 361-289-9906, www.shootersdepot. com
Firearms; Gun Barrels

Shooters Ridge/ATK Commercial Products, N5549 Cty. Tk. Z, Onalaska, WI 54650, P: 800-635-7656, F: 763-323-3890, www.shootersridge.com
Bags & Equipment Cases; Gun Cabinets/Racks/ Safes; Hunting Accessories; Magazines, Cartridge; Sports Accessories

Shooting Chrony, Inc., 2446 Cawthra Rd., Bldg. 1, Suite 10, Mississauga, Ontario L5A 3K6, CANADA, P: 800-385-3161, F: 905-276-6295, www.shootingchrony.com
Archery; Black Powder Accessories; Computer Software; Hunting Accessories; Lighting Products; Reloading; Shooting Range Equipment; Sports Accessories

Shooting Ranges International, Inc./Advanced Interactive Systems, 3885 Rockbottom St., North Las Vegas, NV 89030, P: 702-362-3623, F: 702-310-6978, www. shootingrangeintl.com
Firearms; Law Enforcement; Shooting Range Equipment

Shooting Sports Retailer, 255 W. 36th St., Suite 1202, New York, NY 10018, P: 212-840-0660, F: 212-944-1884, www. shootingsportsretailer.com
Books/Industry Publications

Sierra Bullets, 1400 W. Henry St., Sedalia, MO 65301, P: 888-223-3006, F: 660-827-4999, www.sierrabullets.com
Books/Industry Publications; Computer Software; Reloading; Videos

SIG SAUER, 18 Industrial Dr., Exeter, NH 03833, P: 603-772-2302, F: 603-772-9082, www.sigsauer.com
Bags & Equipment Cases; Firearms; Holsters; Knives/Knife Cases; Law Enforcement; Training & Safety Equipment

Sightron, Inc., 100 Jeffrey Way, Suite A, Youngville, NC 27596, P: 800-867-7512, F: 919-556-0157, www.sightron.com
Binoculars; Scopes, Sights & Accessories

Silencio/Jackson Safety, 1859 Bowles Ave., Suite 200, Fenton, MO 63026, P: 800-237-4192, F: 636-717-6820, www. jacksonsafety.com
Eyewear; Hearing Protection; Law Enforcement

Silma SRL, Via I Maggio, 74, Zanano Di Sarezzo, Brescia 25068, ITALY, P: 011 390308900505, F: 011 390308900712, www.silma.net
Firearms

Silver Stag, 328 Martin St., Blaine, WA 98230, P: 888-233-7824, F: 360-332-4390, www.silverstag.com
Black Powder Accessories; Camping; Crossbows & Accessories; Custom Manufacturing; Cutlery; Hunting Accessories; Knives/Knife Cases; Outdoor Art, Jewelry, Sculpture

Silver State Armory, LLC, P.O. Box 2902, Pahrump, NV 89041, P: 775-537-1118, F: 775-537-1119
Ammunition; Firearms

Simmons, 9200 Cody St., Overland Park, KS 66214, P: 913-782-3131, F: 913-782-4189
Binoculars; Hunting Accessories; Law Enforcement; Scopes, Sights & Accessories

Simunition Operations, General Dynamics Ordnance & Tactical Systems, 5 Montée des Arsenaux, Le Gardeur, Quebec J5Z 2P4, CANADA, P: 800-465-8255, F: 450-581-0231, www.simunition.com
Ammunition; Gun Barrels; Law Enforcement; Magazines, Cartridge; Training & Safety Equipment

Sinclair International, 2330 Wayne Haven St., Fort Wayne, IN 46803, P: 800-717-8211, F: 260-493-2530, www. sinclairintl.com
Ammunition; Bags & Equipment Cases; Books; Cleaning Products; Reloading; Scopes, Sights & Accessories; Software; Targets, Videos

SISCO, 2835 Ana St., Rancho Dominguez, CA 90221, P: 800-832-5834, F: 310-638-6489, www.honeywellsafes.com
Gun Cabinets/Racks/Safes; Hunting Accessories

Sitka, Inc., 870 Napa Valley Corporate Way, Suite N, Napa, CA 94558, P: 877-SITKA MG, F: 707-253-1121, www. sitkagear.com
Men's Clothing

SKB Corp., 1607 N. O'Donnell Way, Orange, CA 92867, P: 800-654-5992, F: 714-283-0425, www.skbcases.com
Archery; Bags & Equipment Cases; Gun Cases; Hunting Accessories; Knives/Knife Cases; Law Enforcement; Sports Accessories

SKB Shotguns, 4441 S. 134th St., Omaha, NE 68137, P: 800-752-2767, P: 402-330-8040, www.skbshotguns.com
Firearms

Smith & Warren, 127 Oakley Ave., White Plains, NY 10601, P: 800-53-BADGE, F: 914-948-1627, www.smithwarren.com
Custom Manufacturing; Law Enforcement

Smith & Wesson, 2100 Roosevelt Ave., Springfield, MA 01104, P: 800-331-0852, F: 413-747-3317, www.smith-wesson. com
Firearms; Law Enforcement

Smith Optics Elite Division, 280 Northwood Way, P.O. Box 2999, Ketchum, ID 83340, P: 208-726-4477, F: 208-727-6598, www.elite.smithoptics.com
Eyewear; Law Enforcement; Shooting Range Equipment; Training & Safety Equipment

Smith's, 1700 Sleepy Valley Rd., Hot Springs, AR 71901, P: 800-221-4156, F: 501-321-9232, www.smithsedge.com
Backpacking; Camping; Cutlery; Hunting Accessories; Sharpeners

Smith Security Safes, Inc., P.O. Box 185, Tontogany, OH 43565, P: 800-521-0335, F: 419-823-1505, www. smithsecuritysafes.com
Gun Cabinets/Racks/Safes

Sniper's Hide.com/Snipers Hide, LLC, 3205 Fenton St., Wheat Ridge, CO 80212, P: 203-530-3301, F: 203-622-7331, www.snipershide.com
Books/Industry Publications; Firearms; Law Enforcement; Online Services; Training & Safety Equipment

Snow Peak USA, Inc., P.O. Box 2002, Clackamas, OR 97015, P: 503-697-3330, F: 503-699-1396, www.snowpeak.com
Backpacking; Camping; Cooking Equipment/ Accessories; Cutlery

Soft Air USA Inc./Cybergun, 1452 Hughes Rd., Suite 100, Grapevine, TX 76051, P: 480-330-3358, F: 925-906-1360, www.softairusa.com
Airguns; Airsoft; Paintball Guns & Accessories

Sog Armory, Inc., 11707 S. Sam Houston Pkwy. W, Suite R, Houston, TX 77031, P: 281-568-5685, F: 285-568-9191, www.sogarmory.com
Firearms; Firearms Maintenance Equipment; Gun Barrels; Gun Grips & Stocks; Law Enforcement; Scopes, Sights & Accessories; Wholesaler/Distributor

SOG Specialty Knives, 6521 212th St. SW, Lynnwood, WA 98036, P: 888-405-6433, F: 425-771-7689, www. sogknives.com
Cutlery; Hunting Accessories; Knives/Knife Cases; Law Enforcement

Sohn Mfg., Inc., 544 Sohn Dr., Elkhart Lake, WI 53020, P: 920-876-3361, F: 920-876-2952, www.sohnmanufacturing.com
Emblems & Decals; Printing Services

Solkoa, Inc., 3107 W. Colorado Ave., Suite 256, Colorado Springs, CO 80904, P: 719-685-1072, F: 719-623-0067, www.solkoa.com
Bags & Equipment Cases; Compasses; Hunting Accessories; Law Enforcement; Survival Kits/First Aid; Training & Safety Equipment; Wholesaler/ Distributor

Sona Enterprises, 7825 Somerset Blvd., Suite D, Paramount, CA 90723, P: 562-633-3002, F: 562-633-3583
Binoculars; Camouflage; Camping; Compasses; Lighting Products; Survival Kits/First Aid; Wholesaler/ Distributor

SOTech/Special Operations Technologies, 206 Star of India Ln., Carson, CA 90746, P: 800-615-9007, F: 310-202-0880, www.specopstech.com
Backpacking; Bags & Equipment Cases; Custom Manufacturing; Gun Cases; Holsters; Law Enforcement; Shooting Range Equipment; Survival Kits/First Aid

Source One Distributors, 3125 Fortune Way, Suite 1, Wellington, FL 33414, P: 866-768-4327, F: 561-514-1021, www.buysourceone.com
Bags & Equipment Cases; Binoculars; Eyewear; Firearms; Knives/Knife Cases; Men's Clothing; Scopes, Sights & Accessories; Wholesaler/Distributor

Southern Belle Brass, P.O. Box 36, Memphis, TN 38101, P: 800-478-3016, F: 901-947-1924, www.southernbellebrass. com
Firearms Maintenance Equipment; Holsters; Law Enforcement; Men's Clothing; Paintball Guns; Targets; Training & Safety Equipment; Wholesaler/ Distributor

Southern Bloomer Mfg. Co. & Muzzleloader Originals, 1215 Fifth St., P.O. Box 1621, Bristol, TN 37621, P: 800-655-0342, F: 423-878-8761, www.southernbloomer.com
Ammunition; Black Powder Accessories; Firearms Maintenance Equipment; Gun Parts/Gunsmithing; Hunting Accessories; Law Enforcement; Reloading; Shooting Range Equipment

SPA Defense, 3409 NW 9th Ave., Suite 1104, Ft. Lauderdale, FL 33309, P: 954-568-7690, F: 954-630-4159, www.spa-defense.com
Firearms; Law Enforcement; Scopes, Sights & Accessories; Tactical Equipment

Spartan Imports, 213 Lawrence Ave., San Francisco, CA 94080, P: 650-589-5501, F: 650-589-5552, www. spartanimports.com
Airguns; Firearms; Law Enforcement; Paintball Guns; Scopes, Sights & Accessories; Training & Safety Equipment; Wholesaler/Distributor

Spec.-Ops. Brands, 1601 W. 15th St., Monahans, TX 79756, P: 866-773-2677, F: 432-943-5565, www.specopsbrand. com
Bags & Equipment Cases; Custom Manufacturing; Holsters; Knives/Knife Cases; Law Enforcement; Shooting Range Equipment; Sports Accessories; Training & Safety Equipment

Specialty Bar Products Co., 4 N. Shore Center, Suite 110, 106 Isabella St., Pittsburgh, PA 15212, P: 412-322-2747, F: 412-322-1912, www.specialty-bar.com
Firearms; Gun Barrels; Gun Parts/Gunsmithing

Specter Gear, Inc., 1107 E. Douglas Ave., Visalia, CA 93292, P: 800-987-3605, F: 559-553-8835, www.spectergear.com

Bags & Equipment Cases; Gun Cases; Holsters; Law Enforcement

Speer Ammunition/ATK Commercial Products, 2299 Snake River Ave., Lewiston, ID 83501, P: 800-256-8685, F: 208-746-3904, www.speer-bullets.com
Ammunition; Reloading

Spiewak/Timberland Pro Valor, 463 Seventh Ave., 11th Floor, New York, NY 10018, P: 800-223-6850, F: 212-629-4803, www.spiewak.com
Footwear; Law Enforcement

Spitfire, Ltd., 8868 Research Blvd., Suite 203, Austin, TX 78758, P: 800-774-8347, F: 512-453-7504, www.spitfire.us
Backpacking; Camping; Sporting Range Equipment; Sports Accessories; Training & Safety Equipment

SportDOG Brand, 10427 Electric Ave., Knoxville, TN 37932, P: 800-732-0144, F: 865-777-4815, www.sportdog.com
Hunting Accessories; Pet Supplies; Training & Safety Equipment; Videos

SportEAR/HarrisQuest Outdoor Products, 528 E. 800 N, Orem, UT 84097, P: 800-530-0090, F: 801-224-5660, www.harrisquest.com
Clay Targets; Hearing Protection; Hunting Accessories; Law Enforcement; Scopes, Sights & Accessories; Shooting Range Equipment; Sports Accessories; Training & Safety Equipment

SportHill, 725 McKinley St., Eugene, OR 97402, P: 541-345-9623, F: 541-343-7261, www.sporthillhunting.com
Archery; Camouflage; Gloves, Mitts, Hats; Men & Women's Clothing; Sports Accessories

Sporting Clays Magazine, 317 S. Washington Ave., Suite 201, Titusville, FL 32796, P: 321-268-5010, F: 321-267-7216, www.sportingclays.net
Books/Industry Publications

Sporting Supplies International, Inc.®, P.O. Box 757, Placentia, CA 92871, P: 888-757-WOLF (9653), F: 714-632-9232, www.wolfammo.com
Ammunition

Sports Afield Magazine, 15621 Chemical Ln., Huntington Beach, CA 92649, P: 714-894-9080, F: 714-894-4949, www.sportsafield.com
Books/Industry Publications

Sports South, LLC, 1039 Kay Ln., P.O. Box 51367, Shreveport, LA 71115, 800-388-3845, www.internetguncatalog.com
Ammunition; Binoculars; Black Powder Accessories; Firearms; Hunting Accessories; Reloading; Scopes, Sights & Accessories; Wholesaler/Distributor

Spot, Inc., 461 S. Milpitas Blvd., Milpitas, CA 95035, F: 408-933-4543, F: 408-933-4954, www.findmespot.com
Backpacking; Camping; Outfitter; Sports Accessories; Survival Kits/First Aid; Training & Safety Equipment

Springboard Engineering, 6520 Platt Ave., Suite 818, West Hills, CA 91307, P: 818-346-4647, F: 818-346-4647
Backpacking; Law Enforcement; Lighting Products; Sports Accessories; Survival Kits/First Aid; Training & Safety Equipment; Wholesaler/Distributor

Springfield Armory, 420 W. Main St., Geneseo, IL 61254, P: 800-680-6866, F: 309-944-3676, www.springfield-armory. com
Firearms

Spyder Paintball/Kingman Group, 14010 Live Oak Ave., Baldwin Park, CA 91706, P: 888-KINGMAN, F: 626-851-8530, www.spyder.tv
Bags & Equipment Cases; Eyewear; Gun Cases; Men's Clothing; Paintball Guns & Accessories

Spyderco, Inc., 820 Spyderco Way, Golden, CO 80403, P: 800-525-7770, F: 303-278-2229, www.spyderco.com
Knives/Knife Cases

SRT Supply, 4450 60th Ave. N, St. Petersburg, FL 33714, P: 727-526-5451, F: 727-527-6893, www.srtsupply.com
Ammunition; Export/Import Specialists; Firearms; Law Enforcement; Wholesaler/Distributor

Stack-On Products Co., 1360 N. Old Rand Rd., P.O. Box 489, Wauconda, IL 60084, P: 800-323-9601, F: 847-526-6599, www.stack-on.com
Bags & Equipment Cases; Gun Cabinets/Racks/ Safes; Gun Cases; Hunting Accessories; Shooting Range Equipment; Sports Accessories; Training & Safety Equipment

Stackpole Books, Inc., 5067 Ritter Rd., Mechanicsburg, PA 17055, P: 800-732-3669, F: 717-796-0412, www. stackpolebooks.com
Books/Industry Publications

Stag Arms, 515 John Downey Dr., New Britain, CT 06051, P: 860-229-9994, F: 860-229-3738, www.stagarms.com
Firearms; Law Enforcement

Stallion Leather/Helios Systems, 1104 Carroll Ave., South Milwaukee, WI 53172, P: 414-764-7126, F: 414-764-2878, www.helios-sys.com
Bags & Equipment Cases; Holsters; Knives/Knife Cases; Law Enforcement; Leathergoods; Sports Accessories

Stansport, 2801 E. 12th St., Los Angeles, CA 90023, P: 800-421-6131, F: 323-269-2761, www.stansport.com

Backpacking; Bags & Equipment Cases; Camping; Compasses; Cooking Equipment/Accessories; Hunting Accessories; Lighting Products; Survival Kits/First Aid

Stark Equipment Corp., 55 S. Commercial St., 4th Floor, Manchester, NH 03101, P: 603-556-7772, F: 603-556-7344, www.starkequipment.com
Gun Grips & Stocks; Hunting Accessories; Law Enforcement

Starlight Cases™, 2180 Hwy. 70-A E, Pine Level, NC 27568, P: 877-782-7544, F: 919-965-9177, www.starlightcases. com
Bags & Equipment Cases; Custom Manufacturing; Gun Cabinets/Racks/Safes; Gun Cases; Hunting Accessories; Law Enforcement; Scopes, Sights & Accessories; Shooting Range Equipment

Steiner Binoculars, 97 Foster Rd., Suite 5, Moorestown, NJ 08057, P: 800-257-7742, F: 856-866-8615, www.steiner-binoculars.com
Binoculars

SteriPEN/Hydro-Photon, Inc., 262 Ellsworth Rd., Blue Hill, ME 04614, P: 888-783-7473, F: 207-374-5100, www.steripen. com
Backpacking; Camping; Cooking Equipment/ Accessories; Law Enforcement; Sports Accessories; Survival Kits/First Aid; Training & Safety Equipment

Sterling Sharpener, P.O. Box 620547, Woodside, CA 94062, P: 800-297-4277, F: 650-851-1434, www.sterlingsharpener. com
Backpacking; Camping; Cooking Equipment/ Accessories; Hunting Accessories; Knives/Knife Cases; Law Enforcement; Sharpeners; Survival Kits/First Aid

Stewart EFI, LLC, 45 Old Waterbury Rd., Thomaston, CT 06787, P: 800-228-2509, F: 860-283-3174, www. stewartefi.com
Ammunition; Backpacking; Custom Manufacturing; Firearms Hearing Protection; Law Enforcement; Lighting Products; Magazines, Cartridge

Steyr Arms, Inc., P.O. Box 840, Trussville, GA 35173, P: 205-467-6544, F: 205-467-3015, www.steyrarms.com
Firearms; Law Enforcement

STI International, 114 Halmar Cove, Georgetown, TX 78628, P: 512-819-0656, F: 512-819-0465, www.stiguns.com
Firearms; Gun Barrels; Gun Parts/Gunsmithing

Stil Crin SNC, Via Per Gottolengo, 12A, Pavone Mella, Brescia 25020, ITALY, P: 011-390309599496, F: 011-390309959544, www.stilcrin.it
Firearms Maintenance Equipment; Gun Cases; Gun Locks; Lubricants

Stoeger Industries, 17603 Indian Head Hwy., Accokeek, MD 20607, P: 800-264-4962, F: 301-283-6988, www. stoegerindustries.com
Airguns; Firearms

Stoney-Wolf Productions, 130 Columbia Court W, Chaska, MN 55318, P: 800-237-7583, F: 952-361-4217, www. stoneywolf.com
Books/Industry Publications; Computer Software; Food; Videos

Stoney Point Products, Inc., 9200 Cody, Overland Park, KS 66214, P: 800-221-9035, F: 800-548-0446, www. stoneypoint.com
Backpacking; Hearing Protection; Hunting Accessories; Shooting Range Equipment; Sports Accessories

Stormy Kromer Mercantile, 1238 Wall St., Ironwood, MI 49938, P: 888-455-2253, F: 906-932-1579, www. stormykromer.com
Camouflage; Gloves, Mitts, Hats; Men's Clothing

Strangler Chokes, Inc., 7958 US Hwy. 167 S, Winnfield, LA 71483, P: 318-201-3474, F: 318-473-0982
Custom Manufacturing; Firearms; Gun Barrels; Gun Parts/Gunsmithing; Hunting Accessories; Scopes, Sights & Accessories

Streamlight, Inc., 30 Eagleville Rd., Eagleville, PA 19403, P: 800-523-7488, F: 800-220-7007, www.streamlight.com
Hunting Accessories; Law Enforcement; Lighting Products; Training & Safety Equipment

Streamworks, Inc., 3233 Lance Dr., Suite B, Stockton, CA 92505, P: 209-337-3307, F: 209-337-3342, www.hattail. com
Hearing Protection

Streetwise Security Products/Cutting Edge Products, Inc., 235-F Forlines Rd., Winterville, NC 28590, P: 800-497-0539, F: 252-830-5542, www.streetwisesecurity.net
Law Enforcement

Strider Knives, Inc., 120 N. Pacific St., Suite L7, San Marcos, CA 92069, P: 760-471-8275, F: 503-218-7069, www. striderknives.com
Backpacking; Custom Manufacturing; Cutlery; Hunting Accessories; Knives/Knife Cases; Law Enforcement; Training & Safety Equipment

Strike-Hold/MPH System Specialties, Inc., P.O. Box 1923, Dawsonville, GA 30534, P: 866-331-0572, F: 325-204-2550, www.strikehold.com

Black Powder Accessories; Export/Import Specialists; Firearms Maintenance Equipment; Hunting Accessories; Law Enforcement; Lubricants; Paintball Accessories; Wholesaler/Distributor

Strong Leather Co., 39 Grove St., P.O. Box 1195, Gloucester, MA 01930, P: 800-225-0724, F: 866-316-3666, www. strongbadgecase.com
Bags & Equipment Cases; Holsters; Law Enforcement; Leathergoods

Sturm, 430 S. Erwin St., Cartersville, GA 30120, P: 800-441-7367, F: 770-386-6654, www.sturm-miltec.com
Camouflage; Camping; Firearms; Gun Grips & Stocks; Magazines, Cartridge; Men's Clothing; Scopes, Sights & Accessories

Sun Optics USA, 1312 S. Briar Oaks Rd., Cleburne, TX 76031, P: 817-447-9047, F: 817-717-8461
Binoculars; Custom Manufacturer; Gun Parts/ Gunsmithing; Hunting Accessories; Scopes, Sights & Accessories

Sunbuster/Gustbuster, 1966-B Broadhollow Rd., Farmingdale, NY 11735, P: 888-487-8287, F: 631-777-4320, www. sunbuster.info
Clay Targets; Custom Manufacturing; Eyewear; Hunting Accessories; Law Enforcement; Shooting Range Equipment; Sports Accessories; Wholesaler/ Distributor

Sunlite Science & Technology, Inc., 345 N. Iowa St., Lawrence, KS 66044, P: 785-832-8818, F: 913-273-1888, www. powerledlighting.com
Camping; Hunting Accessories; Law Enforcement; Lighting Products; Sports Accessories; Survival Kits/ First Aid; Tours/Travel; Training & Safety Equipment

Sunny Hill Enterprises, Inc., W. 1015 Cty. HHH, Chilton, WI 53014, P: 920-898-4707, F: 920-898-4749, www.sunny-hill.com
Custom Manufacturing; Firearms; Gun Barrels; Gun Parts/Gunsmithing; Law Enforcement; Magazines, Cartridge

Super Seer Corp., P.O. Box 700, Evergreen, CO 80437, P: 800-645-1285, F: 303-674-8540, www.superseer.com
Law Enforcement

Super Six Classic, LLC, 635 Hilltop Trail W, Fort Atkinson, WI 53538, P: 920-568-8299, F: 920-568-8259
Firearms

Superior Arms. 836 Weaver Blvd., Wapello, IA 52653, P: 319-523-2016, F: 319-527-0188, www.superiorarms.com
Firearms

Superior Concepts, Inc., 10791 Oak St., P.O. Box 465, Donald, OR 97020, P: 503-922-0488, F: 503-922-2236, www. laserstock.com
Gun Grips & Stocks; Gun Parts/Gunsmithing; Hunting Accessories; Magazines, Cartridge; Scopes, Sights & Accessories

Sure Site, Inc., 351 Dion St., P.O. Box 335, Emmett, ID 83617, P: 800-627-1576, F: 208-365-6944, www.suresiteinc.com
Shooting Range Equipment; Targets

SureFire, LLC, 18300 Mount Baldy Circle, Fountain Valley, CA 92708, P: 800-828-8809, F: 714-545-9537, www.surefire. com
Knives/Knife Cases; Lighting Products; Scopes, Sights & Accessories

Surgeon Rifles, 48955 Moccasin Trail Rd., Prague, OK 74864, P: 405-567-0183, F: 405-567-0250, www.surgeonrifles. com
Firearms; Gun Parts/Gunsmithing; Law Enforcement

Survival Armor, Inc., 13881 Plantation Rd., International Center I, Suite 8, Ft. Myers, FL 33912, P: 866-868-5001, F: 239-210-0898, www.survivalarmor.com
Law Enforcement; Training & Safety Equipment

Survival Corps, Ltd., Ostashkovskoe Shosse, house 48a, Borodino, Moscow Obl, Mitishinski Region, 143031, RUSSIAN FEDERATION, P: 011 74952257985, F: 011 74952257986, www.survivalcorps.ru
Bags & Equipment Cases; Camouflage; Holsters; Law Enforcement; Outfitter

Swany America Corp., 115 Corporate Dr., Johnstown, NY 12095, P: 518-725-3333, F: 518-725-2026, www. swanyhunting.com
Gloves, Mitts, Hats

Swarovski Optik North America, 2 Slater Rd., Cranston, RI 02920, P: 800-426-3089, F: 401-734-5888, www. swarovskioptik.com
Bags & Equipment Cases; Binoculars; Knives/Knife Cases; Scopes, Sights & Accessories; Telescopes; Wholesaler/Distributor

SWAT Magazine, 5011 N. Ocean Blvd., Suite 5, Ocean Ridge, FL 33435, P: 800-665-7928, F: 561-276-0895, www. swatmag.com
Books/Industry Publications; Law Enforcement; Online Services; Retailer Services; Training & Safety Equipment

Swift Bullet Co., 201 Main St., P.O. Box 27, Quinter, KS 67752, P: 785-754-3959, F: 785-754-2359, www.swiftbullets.com
Ammunition

Switch Pack, LLC, 302 NW 4th St., Grants Pass, OR 97526, P: 541-479-3919, F: 541-474-4573
Backpacking; Blinds; Hunting Accessories; Retailer Services; Sports Accessories; Wholesaler/Distributor

SWR Manufacturing, LLC, P.O. Box 841, Pickens, SC 29671, P: 864-850-3575, F: 864-751-2823, www.swrmfg.com
Firearms; Hearing Protection; Law Enforcement; Recoil Protection Devices & Services; Training & Safety Equipment

Sylvansport, 10771 Greenville Hwy., Cedar Mountain, NC 28718, P: 828-883-4292, F: 828-883-4817, www. sylvansport.com
Backpacking; Camping; Hunting Accessories; Sports Accessories; Tours/Travel; Vehicles, Utility & Rec

Systema Co., 5542 S. Integrity Ln., Fort Mohave, AZ 86426, P: 877-884-0909, F: 267-222-4787, www.systema-engineering.com
Airguns; Airsoft; Law Enforcement; Training & Safety Equipment

Szco Supplies, Inc., 2713 Merchant Dr., P.O. Box 6353, Baltimore, MD 21230, P: 800-232-6998, F: 410-368-9366, www.szco.com
Camping; Custom Manufacturing; Cutlery; Hunting Accessories; Knives/Knife Cases; Pet Supplies; Sharpeners; Wholesaler/Distributor

T

T.Z. Case, 1786 Curtiss Ct., La Verne, CA 91750, P: 888-892-2737, F: 909-392-8406, www.tzcase.com
Airguns; Archery; Custom Manufacturing; Firearms; Gun Cases; Hunting Accessories

Tac Force, 8653 Garvey Ave., Suite 202, Rosemead, CA 91733, P: 626-453-8377, F: 626-453-8378, www.tac-force. com
Backpacking; Bags & Equipment Cases; Gloves, Mitts, Hats; Gun Cases; Holsters; Law Enforcement; Paintball Accessories

Tac Wear, Inc., 700 Progress Ave., Suite 7, Toronto, Ontario M1H 2Z7, CANADA, P: 866-TAC-WEAR, F: 416-289-1522, www.tacwear.com
Gloves, Mitts, Hats; Hunting Accessories; Law Enforcement; Men & Women's Clothing; Sports Accessories; Training & Safety Equipment

Tactical & Survival Specialties, Inc. (TSSI), 3900 Early Rd., P.O. Box 1890, Harrisonburg, VA 22801, P: 877-535-8774, F: 540-434-7796, www.tacsurv.com
Bags & Equipment Cases; Custom Manufacturing; Knives/Knife Cases; Law Enforcement; Men & Women's Clothing; Survival Kits/First Aid; Training & Safety Equipment; Wholesaler/Distributor

Tactical Assault Gear (TAG), 1330 30th St., Suite A, San Diego, CA 92154, P: 888-899-1199, F: 619-628-0126, www. tacticalassaultgear.com
Bags & Equipment Cases; Holsters; Men's Clothing

Tactical Command Industries, Inc., 2101 W. Tenth St., Suite G, Antioch, CA 94509, P: 888-990-1600, F: 925-756-7977, www.tacticalcommand.com
Custom Manufacturing; Hearing Protection; Law Enforcement; Training & Safety Equipment; Two-Way Radios

Tactical Electronics/SPA Defense, P.O. Box 152, Broken Arrow, OK 74013, P: 866-541-7996, F: 918-249-8328, www.tacticalelectronics.com
Photographic Equipment

Tactical Innovations, Inc., 345 Sunrise Rd., Bonners Ferry, ID 83805, P: 208-267-1585, F: 208-267-1597, www. tacticalinc.com
Firearms; Gun Barrels; Gun Grips & Stocks; Holsters; Law Enforcement; Magazines, Cartridge; Wholesaler/ Distributor

Tactical Medical Solutions, Inc., 614 Pinehollow Dr., Anderson, SC 29621, P: 888-TACMED1, F: 864-224-0064
Law Enforcement; Survival Kits/First Aid; Training & Safety Equipment

Tactical Operations Products, 20972 SW Meadow Way, Tualatin, OR 97062, P: 503-638-9873, F: 503-638-0524, www.tacoproducts.com
Airsoft; Backpacking; Bags & Equipment Cases; Camping; Law Enforcement; Lighting Products; Paintball Accessories

Tactical Products Group, Inc., 755 NW 17th Ave., Suite 108, Delray Beach, FL 33445, P: 866-9-TACPRO, F: 561-265-4061, www.tacprogroup.com
Export/Import Specialists; Footwear; Gun Cases; Holsters; Knives/Knife Cases; Law Enforcement; Men's Clothing; Wholesaler/Distributor

Tactical Rifles, 19250 Hwy. 301, Dade City, FL 33523, P: 352-999-0599, F: 352-567-9825, www.tacticalrifles.net
Firearms

Tactical Solutions, 2181 Commerce Ave., Boise, ID 83705, P: 866-333-9901, F: 208-333-9909, www.tacticalsol.com
Firearms; Gun Barrels; Gun Grips & Stocks; Gun Parts/Gunsmithing; Scopes, Sights & Accessories; Wholesaler/Distributor

TacticalTECH1, 251 Beulah Church Rd., Carrollton, GA 30117, P: 800-334-3368, F: 770-832-1676
Bags & Equipment Cases; Eyewear; Law Enforcement; Lighting Products; Training & Safety Equipment

TAG Safari Clothes, 1022 Wirt Rd., Suite 302, Houston, TX 77055, P: 800-TAG-2703, F: 713-688-6806, www.tagsafari. com
Camping; Footwear; Gun Cases; Leathergoods; Men & Women's Clothing; Online Services; Wholesaler/ Distributor

Tagua Gun Leather, 3750 NW 28th St., Miami, FL 33142, P: 866-678-2482, F: 866-678-2482, www.taguagunleather. com
Firearms; Holsters; Hunting Accessories; Law Enforcement; Leathergoods; Wholesaler/Distributor

Talley Manufacturing, Inc., 9183 Old Number Six Hwy., P.O. Box 369, Santee, SC 29142, P: 803-854-5700, F: 803-854-9315, www.talleyrings.com
Black Powder Accessories; Custom Manufacturing; Gun Parts/Gunsmithing; Hunting Accessories; Scopes, Sights & Accessories; Sports Accessories

Tandy Brands Outdoors, 107 W. Gonzales St., Yoakum, TX 77995, P: 800-331-9092, F: 361-293-9127, www. tandybrands.com
Bags & Equipment Cases; Custom Manufacturing; Hunting Accessories; Knives/Knife Cases; Leathergoods; Shooting Range Equipment; Sports Accessories

TangoDown, Inc., 1588 Arrow Hwy., Unit F, La Verne, CA 91750-5334, P: 909-392-4757, F: 909-392-4802, www. tangodown.com
Gun Grips & Stocks; Law Enforcement; Lighting Products; Magazines, Cartridge; Scopes, Sights & Accessories; Targets

TAPCO, Inc.,3615 Kennesaw N. Industrial Pkwy., P.O. Box 2408, Kennesaw, GA 30156-9138, P: 800-554-1445, F: 800-226-1662, www.tapco.com
Custom Manufacturing; Firearms Maintenance Equipment; Gun Grips & Stocks; Gun Parts/ Gunsmithing; Law Enforcement; Magazines, Cartridge; Recoil Protection Devices & Services; Wholesaler/Distributor

Target Shooting, Inc., 1110 First Ave. SE, Watertown, SD 57201, P: 800-611-2164, F: 605-882-8840, www. targetshooting.com
Scopes, Sights & Accessories; Shooting Range Equipment

Tasco/Bushnell Outdoor Products, 9400 Cody, Overland Park, KS 66214, P: 800-221-9035, F: 800-548-0446, www. tasco.com
Binoculars; Scopes, Sights & Accessories; Telescopes

Taser International, 1700 N. 85th St., Scottsdale, AZ 85255, P: 800-978-2737, F: 480-991-0791, www.taser.com
Law Enforcement

Task Holsters, 2520 SW 22nd St., Suite 2-186, Miami, FL 33145, P: 305-335-8647, F: 305-858-9618, www. taskholsters.com
Bags & Equipment Cases; Export/Import Specialists; Gun Cases; Holsters; Hunting Accessories; Law Enforcement; Leathergoods; Wholesaler/Distributor

Taurus International Manufacturing, Inc., 16175 NW 49th Ave., Miami, FL 33014, P: 800-327-3776, F: 305-623-7506, www.taurususa.com
Firearms

Taylor Brands, LLC/Imperial Schrade & Smith & Wesson Cutting Tools, 1043 Fordtown Rd., Kingsport, TN 37663, P: 800-251-0254, F: 423-247-5371, www.taylorbrandsllc.com
Backpacking; Camping; Cutlery; Hunting Accessories; Knives/Knife Cases; Law Enforcement

Taylor's & Co., Inc., 304 Lenoir Dr., Winchester, VA 22603, P: 800-655-5814, F: 540-722-2018, www.taylorsfirearms.com
Black Powder Accessories; Firearms; Firearms Maintenance Equipment; Gun Parts/Gunsmithing; Wholesaler/Distributor

Team Realtree®, P.O. Box 9638, Columbus, GA 31908, P: 800-992-9968, F: 706-569-9346, www.realtree.com
Camouflage; Men & Women's Clothing

Team SD/TSD Sports, 901 S. Fremont Ave., Suite 218, Alhambra, CA 91803, P: 626-281-0979, F: 626-281-0323, www.airsoftsd.com
Airguns; Airsoft; Paintball Guns & Accessories; Scopes, Sights & Accessories; Sports Accessories; Training & Safety Equipment; Wholesaler/Distributor

Team Wendy, 17000 St. Clair Ave., Bldg. 1, Cleveland, OH 44110, P: 877-700-5544, F: 216-738-2510, www. teamwendy.com
Custom Manufacturing; Hunting Accessories; Law Enforcement; Sports Accessories; Training & Safety Equipment

TEARepair, Inc., 2200 Knight Rd., Bldg. 2, P.O. Box 1879, Land O'Lakes, FL 34639, P: 800-937-3716, F: 813-996-4523, www.tear-aid.com

Camping; Hunting Accessories; Retail Packaging; Sports Accessories; Survival Kits/First Aid; Wholesaler/Distributor

Tech Mix, Inc., 740 Bowman St., Stewart, MN 55385, P: 877-466-6455, F: 320-562-2125, www.techmixinc.com
Pet Supplies

Technoframes, Via Aldo Moro 6, Scanzorosciate Bergamo, 24020, ITALY, P: 866-246-1095, F: 011 39035668328, www.technoframes.com
Ammunition; Bags & Equipment Cases; Gun Cases; Hunting Accessories; Magazines, Cartridge; Reloading; Shooting Range Equipment

Tecomate Seed, 33477 Hwy. 99E, Tangent, OR 97389, P: 800-547-4101, F: 541-926-9435, www.tecomateseed.com
Wildlife Management

Teijin Aramid USA, Inc., 801-F Blacklawn Rd., Conyers, GA 30012, P: 800-451-6586, F: 770-929-8138, www.teijinaramid.com
Law Enforcement

Television Equipment Associates, Inc., 16 Mount Ebo Rd. S, P.O. Box 404, Brewster, NY 10509, P: 310-457-7401, F: 310-457-0023, www.swatheadsets.com
Law Enforcement

Temco Communications, Inc., 13 Chipping Campden Dr., South Barrington, IL 60010, P: 847-359-3277, F: 847-359-3743, www.temcom.net
Hearing Protection; Law Enforcement; Two-Way Radios

Ten-X Ammunition, Inc., 5650 Arrow Hwy., Montclair, CA 91763, P: 909-605-1617, F: 909-605-2844, www.tenxammo.com
Ammunition; Custom Manufacturing; Law Enforcement; Reloading; Training & Safety Equipment; Wholesaler/Distributor

TenPoint Crossbow Technologies, 1325 Waterloo Rd., Suffield, OH 44260, P: 800-548-6837, F: 330-628-0999, www.tenpointcrossbows.com
Archery; Crossbows & Accessories

Teton Grill Co., 865 Xenium Lane N, Plymouth, MN 55441, P: 877-838-6643, F: 763-249-6385, www.tetongrills.com
Cooking Equipment/Accessories; Custom Manufacturing; Cutlery; Knives/Knife Cases

Tetra® Gun Care, 8 Vreeland Rd., Florham Park, NJ 07932, P: 973-443-0004, F: 973-443-0263, www.tetraguncare.com
Firearms Maintenance Equipment; Gun Parts/Gunsmithing; Lubricants

Texas Hunt Co., P.O. Box 10, Monahans, TX 79756, P: 888-894-8682, F: 432-943-5565, www.texashuntco.com
Bags & Equipment Cases; Hunting Accessories; Knives/Knife Cases; Vehicles, Utility & Rec; Wholesaler/Distributor

Texsport, P.O. Box 55326, Houston, TX 77255, P: 800-231-1402, F: 713-468-1535, www.texsport.com
Backpacking; Bags & Equipment Cases; Camouflage; Camping; Compasses; Cooking Equipment/Accessories; Lighting Products; Wholesaler/Distributor

Thermacell/The Schawbel Corp., 100 Crosby Dr., Suite 102, Bedford, MA 01730, P: 866-753-3837, F: 781-541-6007, www.thermacell.com
Archery; Backpacking; Camouflage; Camping; Crossbows & Accessories; Holsters; Hunting Accessories; Scents & Lures

Thermore, 6124 Shady Lane SE, Olympia, WA 98503, P: 800-871-6563, www.thermore.com
Gloves, Mitts, Hats; Men & Women's Clothing; Pet Supplies

Thompson/Center Arms, A Smith & Wesson Co., P.O. Box 5002, Rochester, NH 01104, P: 603-332-2333, F: 603-332-5133, www.tcarms.com
Black Powder Accessories; Black Powder/Smokeless Powder; Firearms; Gun Barrels; Hunting Accessories

Thorogood Shoes, 108 S. Polk St., Merrill, WI 54452, P: 800-826-0002, F: 800-569-6817, www.weinbrennerusa.com
Footwear; Law Enforcement; Leathergoods; Men & Women's Clothing

Thunderbolt Customs, Inc., 7296 S. Section Line Rd., Delaware, OH 43015, P: 740-917-9135, www.thunderboltcustoms.com
Backpacking; Black Powder Accessories; Camping; Firearms; Hunting Accessories; Pet Supplies; Scopes, Sights & Accessories; Shooting Range Accessories

Tiberius Arms, 2717 W. Ferguson Rd., Fort Wayne, IN 46809, P: 888-982-2842, F: 260-572-2210, www.tiberiusarms.com
Airguns; Law Enforcement; Paintball Guns & Accessories; Training & Safety Equipment

Tiger-Vac, Inc., 73 SW 12 Ave., Bldg. 1, Suite 7, Dania, FL 33004, P: 800-668-4437, F: 954-925-3626, www.tiger-vac.com
Shooting Range Equipment; Training & Safety Equipment

Timney Manufacturing, Inc., 3940 W. Clarendon Ave., Phoenix, AZ 85019, P: 866-4TIMNEY, F: 602-241-0361, www.timneytriggers.com

Firearms Maintenance Equipment; Gun Locks; Gun Parts/Gunsmithing

Tinks, 10157 Industrial Dr., Covington, GA 30014, P: 800-624-5988, F: 678-342-9973, www.tinks69.com
Archery; Hunting Accessories; Scents & Lures; Videos

Tisas-Trabzon Gun Industry Corp., Degol Cad. No: 13-1 Tandogan Ankara, 06580, TURKEY, P: 011 903122137509, F: 011 903122138570, www.trabzonsilah.com
Firearms; Gun Barrels

TMB Designs, Unit 11, Highgrove Farm Ind Est Pinvin, Pershore, Worchestershire WR10 2LF, UNITED KINGDOM, P: 011 441905840022, F: 011 441905850022, www.cartridgedisplays.com
Ammunition; Custom Manufacturing; Emblems & Decals; Hunting Accessories; Outdoor Art, Jewelry, Sculpture; Sports Accessories

Toadbak, Inc., P.O. Box 18097, Knoxville, TN 37928-8097, P: 865-548-1283
Camouflage; Men's Clothing

Tony's Custom Uppers & Parts, P.O. Box 252, Delta, OH 43515, P: 419-822-9578, F: 419-822-9578
Custom Manufacturing; Gun Barrels; Gun Parts/Gunsmithing; Wholesaler/Distributor

Tool Logic, Inc., 2290 Eastman Ave., Suite 109, Ventura, CA 93003, P: 800-483-8422, F: 805-339-9712, www.toollogic.com
Backpacking; Compasses; Cutlery; Knives/Knife Cases; Lighting Products; Sports Accessories; Survival Kits/First Aid

Top Brass Tackle/dba Cypress Knees Publishing, P.O. Box 209, Starkville, MS 39760, P: 662-323-1559, F: 662-323-7466, www.outdooryouthadventures.com
Books/Industry Publications

TOPS Knives, P.O. Box 2544, Idaho Falls, ID 82403, P: 208-542-0113, F: 208-552-2945, www.topsknives.com
Backpacking; Custom Manufacturing; Hunting Accessories; Knives/Knife Cases; Law Enforcement; Leathergoods; Men's Clothing; Survival Kits/First Aid

Torel, 107 W. Gonzales St., Yoakum, TX 77995, P: 800-331-9092, F: 361-293-9127, www.tandybrands.com
Bags & Equipment Cases; Custom Manufacturing; Hunting Accessories; Knives/Knife Cases; Leathergoods; Shooting Range Equipment; Sports Accessories

Torrey Pines Logic, Inc., 12651 High Bluff Dr., Suite 100, San Diego, CA 92130, P: 858-755-4549, F: 858-350-0007, www.tplogic.com
Binoculars; Law Enforcement; Scopes, Sights & Accessories; Telescopes

Traditions Performance Firearms, 1375 Boston Post Rd., P.O. Box 776, Old Saybrook, CT 06475-0776, P: 800-526-9556, F: 860-388-4657, www.traditionsfirearms.com
Black Powder Accessories; Firearms; Hunting Accessories; Scopes, Sights & Accessories

Transarms Handels GmbH & Co. KG, 6 Im Winkel, Worms, Rheinland Pfalz 67547, GERMANY, P: 011 490624197770, F: 011 4906241977777
Ammunition; Export/Import Specialists; Firearms; Firearms Maintenance Equipment; Gun Barrels; Gun Parts/Gunsmithing; Law Enforcement; Magazines, Cartridge

Traser H3 Watches, 2930 Domingo Ave., Suite 159, Berkeley, CA 94705, P: 510-479-7523, F: 510-479-7532, www.traserusa.com
Custom Manufacturing; Export/Import Specialists; Law Enforcement; Lighting Products; Men's Clothing; Training & Safety Equipment; Wholesaler/Distributor

Tree Talon, 148 Main St., P.O. Box 1370, Bucksport, ME 04416, P: 207-469-1900, F: 207-469-6121, www.treetalon.com
Hunting Accessories

Tri-Tronics, Inc., 1705 S. Research Loop, Tucson, AZ 85710, P: 800-765-2275, F: 800-320-3538, www.tritronics.com
Hunting Accessories; Pet Supplies; Sports Accessories

Trijicon, Inc., 49385 Shafer Ave., P.O. Box 930059, Wixom, MI 48393, P: 800-338-0563, F: 248-960-7725, www.trijicon.com
Scopes, Sights & Accessories

Triple K Manufacturing Co., Inc., 2222 Commercial St., San Diego, CA 92113, P: 800-521-5062, F: 877-486-6247, www.triplek.com
Black Powder Accessories; Gun Parts/Gunsmithing; Holsters; Hunting Accessories; Law Enforcement; Leathergoods; Magazines, Cartridge; Pet Supplies

Tristar Sporting Arms, Ltd., 1816 Linn St., North Kansas City, MO 64116, P: 816-421-1400, F: 816-421-4182, www.tristarsporting.com
Export/Import Specialists; Firearms

Trophy Animal Health Care, 1217 W. 12th St., Kansas City, MO 64101, P: 800-821-7925, F: 816-474-0462, www.trophyanimalcare.com
Pet Supplies

Troy Industries, Inc., 128 Myron St., West Springfield, MA 01089, P: 866-788-6412, F: 413-383-0339, www.troyind.com
Firearms; Gun Grips & Stocks; Gun Parts/Gunsmithing; Law Enforcement; Scopes, Sights & Accessories

Tru Hone Corp., 1721 NE 19th Ave., Ocala, FL 34470, P: 800-237-4663, F: 352-622-9180, www.truhone.com
Sharpeners

TruckVault, Inc., 211 Township St., P.O. Box 734, Sedro Woolley, WA 98284, P: 800-967-8107, F: 800-621-4287, www.truckvault.com
Custom Manufacturing; Gun Cabinets/Racks/Safes; Hunting Accessories; Law Enforcement; Pet Supplies; Sports Accessories; Training & Safety Equipment

True North Tactical, 500 N. Birdneck Rd., Suite 200, Virginia Beach, VA 23451, P: 800-TNT-1478, F: 757-491-9652, www.truenorthtactical.com
Backpacking; Bags & Equipment Cases; Gun Cases; Holsters; Law Enforcement; Wholesaler/Distributor

TrueTimber Outdoors, 150 Accurate Way, Inman, SC 29349, P: 864-472-1720, F: 864-472-1834, www.truetimber.com
Bags & Equipment Cases; Blinds; Camouflage; Footwear; Gloves, Mitts, Hats; Hunting Accessories; Men & Women's Clothing

Truglo, Inc., 710 Presidential Dr., Richardson, TX 75081, P: 888-8-TRUGLO, F: 972-774-0323, www.truglo.com
Archery; Binoculars; Black Powder Accessories; Crossbows & Accessories; Hunting Accessories; Law Enforcement; Scopes, Sights & Accessories; Watches

Trulock Tool, 113 Drayton St. NW, P.O. Box 530, Whigham, GA 39897, P: 800-293-9402, F: 229-762-4050, www.trulockchokes.com
Ammunition; Custom Manufacturing; Firearms Maintenance Equipment; Gun Parts/Gunsmithing; Hunting Accessories; Recoil Protection Devices & Services; Sports Accessories; Wholesaler/Distributor

Trumark Mfg. Co., Inc., 1835 38th St., Boulder, CO 80301, P: 800-878-6272, F: 303-442-1380, www.slingshots.com
Archery; Backpacking; Crossbows & Accessories; Hunting Accessories; Sports Accessories

Tuff-N-Lite, 325 Spencer Rd., Conover, NC 28613, P: 877-883-3654, F: 828-322-7881, www.tuffnlite.com
Gloves, Mitts, Hats; Men & Women's Clothing

TufForce, 1734 Ranier Blvd., Canton, MI 48187, P: 800-382-7989, F: 888-686-0373, www.tufforce.com
Bags & Equipment Cases; Gun Cases; Gun Grips & Stocks; Holsters; Hunting Accessories; Law Enforcement; Scopes, Sights & Accessories; Wholesaler/Distributor

Tunilik Adventure, 11600 Philippe Panneton, Montreal, Quebec H1E 4G4, CANADA, P: 866-648-1595, F: 514-648-1431, www.adventuretunilik.com
Outfitter

TurtleSkin Protective Products, 301 Turnpike Rd., New Ipswich, NH 03071, P: 888-477-4675, F: 603-291-1119, www.turtleskin.com
Gloves, Mitts, Hats; Hunting Accessories; Law Enforcement; Men & Women's Clothing; Sports Accessories

U

U.S. Armament Corp., 121 Valley View Dr., Ephrata, PA 17522, P: 717-721-4570, F: 717-738-4890, www.usarmamentcorp.com
Firearms

U.S. Armor Corp., 16433 Valley View Ave., Cerritos, CA 90703, P: 800-443-9798, F: 562-207-4238, www.usarmor.com
Law Enforcement; Training & Safety Equipment

U.S. Explosive Storage, LLC, 355 Industrial Park Dr., Boone, NC 28607, P: 877-233-1481, F: 800-295-1653, www.usexplosive.com
Custom Manufacturing; Firearms Maintenance Equipment; Gun Cabinets/Racks/Safes; Law Enforcement; Magazines, Cartridge; Training & Safety Equipment

U.S. Fire-Arms Mfg. Co., Inc., P.O. Box 1901, Hartford, CT 06144-1901, P: 860-296-7441, F: 860-296-7688, www.usfirearms.com
Firearms; Gun Parts/Gunsmithing

U.S. Optics, Inc., 150 Arovista Circle, Brea, CA 92821, P: 714-582-1956, F: 714-582-1959, www.usoptics.com
Custom Manufacturing; Law Enforcement; Scopes, Sights & Accessories

U.S. Tactical Supply, Inc., 939 Pacific Blvd. SE, Albany, OR 97321, P: 877-928-8645, F: 541-791-2965, www.ustacticalsupply.com
Bags & Equipment Cases; Gun Parts/Gunsmithing; Holsters; Hunting Accessories; Knives/Knife Cases; Law Enforcement; Scopes, Sights & Accessories; Wholesaler/Distributor

Uberti, A., 17603 Indian Head Hwy., Accokeek, MD 20607-2501, P: 800-264-4962, F: 301-283-6988, www.uberti.com

Firearms

Ultimate Hunter, Inc., 610 Prather, P.O. Box 542, Maryville, MO 64468, P: 660-562-3838, F: 660-582-4377, www.ambushlures.com
Decoys

Ultimate Survival Technologies, LLC, 14428 167th Ave. SE, Monroe, WA 98272, P: 866-479-7994, F: 206-965-9659, www.ultimatesurvival.com
Backpacking; Bags & Equipment Cases; Camping; Hunting Accessories; Law Enforcement; Men's Clothing; Sports Accessories; Survival Kits/First Aid

Ultra Dot Distribution, 6304 Riverside Dr., P.O. Box 362, Yankeetown, FL, 34498, P: 352-447-2255, F: 352-447-2266, www.ultradotusa.com
Scopes, Sights & Accessories

Ultra Lift Corp., 475 Stockton Ave., Unit E, San Jose, CA 95126, P: 800-346-3057, F: 408-297-1199, www.ultralift.com/safes.html
Custom Manufacturing; Gun Cabinets/Racks/Safes; Gun Cases; Retailer Services; Sports Accessories; Training & Safety Equipment

Ultra Paws, 12324 Little Pine Rd. SW, Brainerd, MN 56401, P: 800-355-5575, F: 218-855-6977, www.ultrapaws.com
Backpacking; Hunting Accessories; Law Enforcement; Outfitter; Pet Supplies; Survival Kits/First Aid; Training & Safety Equipment; Wholesaler/Distributor

Ultramax Ammunition/Wideview Scope Mount, 2112 Elk Vale Rd., Rapid City, SD 57701, P: 800-345-5852, F: 605-342-8727, www.ultramaxammunition.com
Ammunition

Ultrec Engineered Products, LLC, 860 Maple Ridge Ln., Brookfield, WI 53045, P: 262-821-2023, F: 262-821-1156, www.ultrec.com
Backpacking; Binoculars; Firearms; Hunting Accessories; Law Enforcement; Photographic Equipment; Shooting Range Equipment; Training & Safety Equipment

Umarex/Umarex, USA/RAM–Real Action Marker, 6007 S. 29th St., Fort Smith, AR 72908, P: 479-646-4210, F: 479-646-4206, www.umarexusa.com, www.trainingumarexusa.com
Airguns; Airsoft; Ammunition; Firearms; Law Enforcement; Paintball Guns; Scopes, Sights & Accessories; Training & Safety Equipment

Uncle Mike's/Bushnell Outdoor Accessories, 9200 Cody St., Overland Park, KS 66214, P: 800-423-3537, F: 800-548-0446, www.unclemikes.com
Bags & Equipment Cases; Gloves, Mitts, Hats; Gun Cases; Holsters; Hunting Accessories

Under Armour Performance, 1020 Hull St., Third Floor, Baltimore, MD 21230, P: 888-427-6687, F: 410-234-1027, www.underarmour.com
Bags & Equipment Cases; Camouflage; Gloves, Mitts, Hats; Law Enforcement; Men & Women's Clothing; Outfitter; Sports Accessories

United Cutlery Corp., 201 Plantation Oak Dr., Thomasville, GA 31792, P: 800-548-0835, F: 229-551-0182, www.unitedcutlery.com
Camping; Compasses; Custom Manufacturing; Cutlery; Knives/Knife Cases; Law Enforcement; Sharpeners; Wholesaler/Distributor

United Shield International, 1606 Barlow St., Suite 1, Traverse City, MI 49686, P: 800-705-9153, F: 231-933-5368, www.unitedshield.net
Law Enforcement

United Weavers of America, Inc., 3562 Dug Gap Rd. SW, Dalton, GA 30721, P: 800-241-5754, F: 706-226-8844, www.unitedweavers.net
Home Furnishings

Universal Power Group, 1720 Hayden, Carrollton, TX 75006, P: 866-892-1122, F: 469-892-1123, www.upgi.com, www.deerfeeder.com
Blinds; Camping; Decoys; Export/Import Specialists; Feeder Equipment; Hunting Accessories; Lighting Products; Wholesaler/Distributor

Urban–E.R.T. Slings, LLC, P.O. Box 429, Clayton, IN 46118, P: 317-223-6509, F: 317-539-2710, www.urbanertslings.com
Firearms; Hunting Accessories; Law Enforcement; Paintball Accessories

US Night Vision Corp., 3845 Atherton Rd., Suite 9, Rocklin, CA 95765, P: 800-500-4020, F: 916-663-5986, www.usnightvision.com
Binoculars; Hunting Accessories; Law Enforcement; Paintball Accessories; Scopes, Sights & Accessories; Sports Accessories; Training & Safety Equipment; Wholesaler/Distributor

US Peacekeeper Products, Inc., W245, N5570 Corporate Circle, Sussex, WI 53089, P: 800-428-0800, F: 262-246-4845, uspeacekeeper.com
Bags & Equipment Cases; Gloves, Mitts, Hats; Hunting Accessories; Men & Women's Clothing

Uselton Arms, 390 Southwinds Dr., Franklin, TN 37064, P: 615-595-2255, F: 615-595-2254, www.useltonarms.com
Custom Manufacturing; Firearms; Gun Barrels; Gun Grips & Stocks; Gun Parts/Gunsmithing; Law Enforcement

V

V.H. Blackinton & Co., Inc., 221 John Dietsch Blvd., P.O. Box 1300, Attleboro Falls, MA 02763, P: 800-699-4436, F: 508-695-5349, www.blackinton.com
Custom Manufacturing; Emblems & Decals; Law Enforcement

V-Line Industries, 370 Easy St., Simi Valley, CA 93065, P: 805-520-4987, F: 805-520-6470, www.vlineind.com
Gun Cabinets; Racks/Safes; Gun Cases

Valdada Optics, P.O. Box 270095, Littleton, CO 80127, P: 303-979-4578, F: 303-979-0256, www.valdada.com
Binoculars; Compasses; Custom Manufacturing; Law Enforcement; Photographic Equipment; Scopes, Sights & Accessories; Telescopes; Wholesaler/Distributor

Valiant Armoury, 3000 Grapevine Mills Pkwy., Suite 101, Grapevine, TX 76051, P: 877-796-7374, F: 972-539-9351, www.valliantarmouryswords.com
Wholesaler/Distributor

Valley Operational Wear, LLC/OP Wear Armor, P.O. Box 9415, Knoxville, TN 37940, P: 865-259-6248, F: 865-259-6255
Law Enforcement

Valley Outdoors, P.O. Box 108, Fort Valley, GA 31030, P: 478-397-0531, F: 478-825-3398, www.valleyoutdoors.us
Outfitter

Valor Corp., 1001 Sawgrass Corporate Pkwy., Sunrise, FL 33323, P: 800-899-VALOR, F: 866-248-9594, www.valorcorp.com
Airguns; Ammunition; Cutlery; Firearms; Knives/Knife Cases; Law Enforcement; Magazines, Cartridge; Wholesaler/Distributor

Vang Comp Systems, 400 W. Butterfield Rd., Chino Valley, AZ 86323, P: 928-636-8455, F: 928-636-1538, www.vangcomp.com
Firearms; Gun Barrels; Gun Parts/Gunsmithing

Vanguard USA, Inc., 9157 E. M-36, Whitmore Lake, MI 48189, P: 800-875-3322, F: 888-426-7008, www.vanguardworld.com
Archery; Bags & Equipment Cases; Binoculars; Gun Cases; Hunting Accessories; Photographic Equipment; Scopes, Sights & Accessories; Shooting Range Equipment

Vector Optics, 3964 Callan Blvd., South San Francisco, CA 94080, P: 415-632-7089, CHINA, P: 011 862154040649, www.vectoroptics.com
Scopes, Sights & Accessories; Sports Accessories; Wholesaler/Distributor

Vega Holster srl, Via Di Mezzo 31 Z.I., Calcinaia (PI), 56031, ITALY, P: 011 390587489190, F: 011 390587489901, www.vegaholster.com
Bags & Equipment Cases; Gun Cases; Holsters; Hunting Accessories; Law Enforcement; Leathergoods; Shooting Range Equipment

Vega Silah Sanayi, Ltd., Tigcilar Sokak No. 1 Mercan, Eminonu, Istanbul, 34450, TURKEY, P: 011 902125200103, F: 011 902125120879
Firearms

Verney-Carron SA, 54 Blvd. Thiers, Boite Postale 72, St. Etienne Cedex 1, 42002, FRANCE, P: 011 33477791500, F: 011 33477790702, www.verney-carron.com
Custom Manufacturing; Firearms; Gun Barrels; Law Enforcement; Wholesaler/Distributor

Versatile Rack Co., 5232 Alcoa Ave., Vernon, CA 90058, P: 323-588-0137, F: 323-588-5067, www.versatilegunrack.com
Firearms Maintenance Equipment; Gun Cabinets/Racks/Safes; Gun Cases; Gun Locks; Hunting Accessories; Reloading; Shooting Range Equipment; Sports Accessories

VibraShine, Inc./Leaf River Outdoor Products, 113 Fellowship Rd., P.O. Box 557, Taylorsville, MS 39168, P: 601-785-9854, F: 601-785-9874, www.myleafriver.com
Firearms Maintenance Equipment; Hunting Accessories; Photographic Equipment; Reloading

Victorinox Swiss Army, 7 Victoria Dr., Monroe, CT 06468, P: 800-243-4032, F: 800-243-4006, www.swissarmy.com
Camping; Cutlery; Hunting Accessories; Knives/Knife Cases; Lighting Products; Sports Accessories

Vintage Editions, Inc., 88 Buff Ln., Taylorsville, NC 28681, P: 800-662-8965, F: 828-632-4187, www.vintageeditions.com
Custom Manufacturing; Home Furnishings; Hunting Accessories; Pet Supplies; Sports Accessories

Virginia Blade, 5177 Boonsboro Rd., Lynchburg, VA 24503, P: 434-384-1282, F: 434-384-4541

Viridian Green Laser Sights/Laser Aiming Systems Corp., 12637 Sable Dr., Burnsville, MN 55337, P: 800-990-9390, F: 952-882-6227, www.viridiangreenlaser.com
Holsters; Law Enforcement; Lighting Products; Scopes, Sights & Accessories

Vixen Optics, 1010 Calle Cordillera, Suite 106, San Clemente, CA 92673, P: 949-429-6363, F: 949-429-6826, www.vixenoptics.com
Binoculars; Scopes, Sights & Accessories; Telescopes; Wholesaler/Distributor

Vltor Weapon Systems, 3735 N. Romero Rd., Tucson, AZ 85705, P: 866-468-5867, F: 520-293-8807, www.vltor.com
Firearms; Gun Grips & Stocks; Gun Parts/Gunsmithing; Law Enforcement; Recoil Protection Devices & Services

Volquartsen Custom, 24276 240th St., P.O. Box 397, Carroll, IA 51401, P: 712-792-4238, F: 712-792-2542, www.volquartsen.com
Custom Manufacturing; Firearms; Gun Barrels; Gun Grips/Stocks; Gun Parts/Gunsmithing

Vortex Optics, 2120 W. Greenview Dr., Middleton, WI 53562, P: 800-426-0048, F: 608-662-7454
Binoculars; Scopes, Sights & Accessories

Vyse-Gelatin Innovations, 5024 N. Rose St., Schiller Park, IL 60176, P: 800-533-2152, F: 800-533-2152, www.vyse.com
Airguns; Ammunition; Firearms; Law Enforcement; Magazines, Cartridge; Paintball Guns & Accessories; Shooting Range Equipment

Vytek, 195 Industrial Rd., Fitchburg, MA 01420, P: 978-342-9800, F: 978-342-0606, www.vy-tek.com
Custom Manufacturing; Emblems & Decals; Retailer Services; Sports Accessories

W

W.R. Case & Sons Cutlery Co., Owens Way, Bradford, PA 16701, P: 800-523-6350, F: 814-368-1736, www.wrcase.com
Cutlery; Knives/Knife Cases; Sharpeners

Walls Industries, Inc., 1905 N. Main, Cleburne, TX 76033, P: 800-433-1765, F: 817-645-8544, www.wallsoutdoors.com
Camouflage; Gloves, Mitts, Hats; Men's Clothing

Walther USA, 2100 Roosevelt Ave., Springfield, MA 01104, P: 800-372-6454, F: 413-747-3317, www.waltheramerica.com
Bags & Equipment Cases; Firearms; Knives/Knife Cases; Law Enforcement; Lighting Products

Warson Group, Inc., 121 Hunter Ave., Suite 204, St. Louis, MO 63124, P: 877-753-2426, F: 314-721-0569, www.warson-group.com
Footwear

Watershed Drybags, 2000 Riverside Dr., Asheville, NC 28804, P: 828-252-7111, F: 828-252-7107, www.drybags.com
Backpacking; Bags & Equipment Cases; Camping; Gun Cases; Hunting Accessories; Law Enforcement; Survival Kits/First Aid; Training & Safety Equipment

WD-40 Co., 1061 Cudahy Pl., San Diego, CA 92110, P: 800-448-9340, F: 619-275-5823, www.wd40.com
Lubricants

Weatherby, Inc., 1605 Commerce Way, Paso Robles, CA 93446, P: 800-227-2016, F: 805-237-0427, www.weatherby.com
Ammunition; Custom Manufacturing; Firearms

Weaver Optics/ATK Commercial Products, N5549 Cty. Tk. Z, Onalaska, WI 54650, P: 800-635-7656, F: 763-323-3890, www.weaveroptics.com
Binoculars; Scopes, Sights & Accessories

Weber's Camo Leather Goods/Wilderness Dreams Lingerie & Swimwear, 615 Nokomis St., Suite 400, Alexandria, MN 56308, P: 320-762-2816, F: 320-763-9762, www.webersleather.com
Bags & Equipment Cases; Camouflage; Footwear; Home Furnishings; Hunting Accessories; Leathergoods; Men & Women's Clothing

Wellco Enterprises, 150 Westwood Circle, P.O. Box 188, Waynesville, NC 28786, P: 800-840-3155, F: 828-456-3547, www.wellco.com
Footwear; Law Enforcement

Wells Creek Outfitters, 803-12 SW 12th St., Bentonville, AR, 72712, P: 479-273-1174, F: 479-273-0137
Camouflage; Hunting Accessories; Men's Clothing

Wenger N.A./Wenger, Maker of the Genuine Swiss Army Knife, 15 Corporate Dr., Orangeburg, NY 10962, P: 800-431-2996, F: 845-425-4700, www.wengerna.com
Backpacking; Camping; Cutlery; Footwear; Hunting Accessories; Knives/Knife Cases; Watches

Western Powders, Inc., P.O. Box 158, Miles City, MT 59301, P: 800-497-1007, F: 406-234-0430, www.blackhorn209.com
Black Powder/Smokeless Powder; Firearms Maintenance Equipment; Lubricants; Reloading; Wholesaler/Distributor

Western Rivers, Inc., 1582 N. Broad St., Lexington, TN 38351, P: 800-967-0998, F: 731-967-1243, www.western-rivers.com
Decoys; Game Calls; Hunting Accessories; Lighting Products; Pet Supplies; Scents & Lures; Scopes, Sights & Accessories

Westfield Outdoor, Inc., 1593 Esprit Dr., Westfield, IN 46074, P: 317-569-0679, F: 317-580-1834, www.westfieldoutdoor.com
Backpacking; Camping

White Flyer Targets/Div. Reagent Chemical & Research, Inc., 115 Route 202/31 S, Ringoes, NJ 08851, P: 800-322-7855, F: 908-284-2113, www.whiteflyer.com
Clay Targets; Firearms; Shooting Range Equipment; Targets

Whites Boots, E. 4002 Ferry Ave., Spokane, WA 99202, P: 509-535-2422, F: 509-535-2423, www.whitesboots.com
Footwear

Whitetails Unlimited, 2100 Michigan St., Sturgeon Bay, WI 54235, P: 920-743-6777, F: 920-743-4658, www.whitetailsunlimited.com
Online Services; Outdoor Art, Jewelry, Sculpture; Videos; Wildlife Management

Wilcox Industries Corp., 25 Piscataque Dr., Newington, NH 03801, P: 603-431-1331, F: 603-431-1221, www.wilcoxind.com
Law Enforcement; Scopes, Sights & Accessories

Wild West Guns, LLC, 7100 Homer Dr., Anchorage, AK 99518-3229, P: 800-992-4570, F: 907-344-4005, www.wildwestguns.com
Custom Manufacturing; Firearms; Gun Parts/Gunsmithing; Outfitter; Recoil Protection Devices & Services; Scopes, Sights & Accessories; Wholesaler/Distributor

Wild Wings, LLC, 2101 S. Hwy. 61, P.O. Box 451, Lake City, MN 55041, P: 800-445-6413, F: 651-345-2981, www.wildwings.com
Decoys; Home Furnishings; Outdoor Art, Jewelry, Sculpture; Wholesaler/Distributor

Wilderness Calls, 12118 Capur St., Orlando, FL 38837, P: 407-620-8833, F: 407-620-8853

Wilderness Mint, P.O. Box 1866, Orting, WA 98360, P: 800-294-9600, F: 360-893-4400, www.wildernessmint.com
Emblems & Decals; Hunting Accessories; Outdoor Art, Jewelry, Sculpture; Watches

Wildfowler Outfitter/Tundra Quest, LLC, 5047 Walnut Grove, San Gabriel, CA 91776, P: 877-436-7177, F: 626-286-9918
Archery; Blinds, Custom Manufacturing; Export/Import Specialists; Feeder Equipment; Men's Clothing; Outfitter; Treestands

Wildlife Research Center, Inc., 14485 Azurite St. NW, Ramsey, MN 55303, P: 800-873-5873, F: 763-427-8354, www.wildlife.com
Scents & Lures

Wildsteer, 9 Avenue Eugene Brisson, Bourges, F-18000, FRANCE, P: 011 33248211380, F: 011 33248211380, www.wildsteer.com
Archery; Knives/Knife Cases; Leathergoods

Wiley X., Inc., 7491 Longard Rd., Livermore, CA 94551, P: 800-776-7842, F: 925-455-8860, www.wileyx.com
Eye Protection

William Henry Studio, 3200 NE Rivergate St., McMinnville, OR 97128, P: 888-563-4500, F: 503-434-9704, www.williamhenrystudio.com
Cutlery; Knives/Knife Cases

Williams Gun Sight Co., 7389 Lapeer Rd., Davison, MI 48423, P: 800-530-9028, F: 810-658-2140, www.williamsgunsight.com
Black Powder Accessories; Books/Industry Publications; Compasses; Gun Parts/Gunsmithing; Hunting Accessories; Scopes, Sights & Accessories

Wilson Arms Co., 97 Leetes Island Rd., Branford, CT 06405, P: 203-488-7297, F: 203-488-0135, www.wilsonarms.com
Custom Manufacturing; Firearms; Gun Barrels

Winchester Ammunition/Div. Olin Corp., 427 N. Shamrock St., East Alton, IL 62024, P: 618-258-2365, F: 618-258-3609, www.winchester.com
Ammunition

Winchester Repeating Arms, 275 Winchester Ave., Morgan, UT 84050, P: 801-876-3440, F: 801-876-3737, www.winchesterguns.com
Firearms

Winchester Safes/Granite Security Products, Inc., 4801 Esco Dr., Fort Worth, TX 76140, P: 817-561-9095, F: 817-478-3056, www.winchestersafes.com
Gun Cabinets/Racks/Safes

Winchester Smokeless Propellant, 6231 Robinson, Shawnee Mission, KS 66202, P: 913-362-9455, F: 913-362-1307
Black Powder/Smokeless Powder; Reloading

Winfield Galleries, LLC, 2 Ladue Acres, Ladue, MO 63124, P: 314-645-7636, F: 314-781-0224, www.winfieldgalleries.com
Computer Software; Outdoor Art, Jewelry, Sculpture

Wing-Sun Trading, Inc., 15501 Heron Ave., La Mirada, CA 90638, P: 866-944-1068, F: 714-522-6417
Backpacking; Binoculars; Camping; Compasses; Lighting Products; Photographic Equipment; Scopes, Sights & Accessories; Wholesaler/Distributor

Witz Sport Cases, 11282 Pyrites Way, Gold River, CA 95670, P: 800-499-1568, F: 916-638-1250, www.witzprod.com
Bags & Equipment Cases

Wolf Peak International, 1221 Marshall Way, Layton, UT 84041, P: 866-953-7325, F: 801-444-9353, www.wolfpeak.net

Airguns; Airsoft; Backpacking; Camouflage; Eyewear; Hunting Accessories; Law Enforcement; Shooting Range Equipment

Wolfe Publishing Co., 2625 Stearman Rd., Suite A, Prescott, AZ 86301, P: 800-899-7810, F: 928-778-5124, www.riflemagazine.com
Books/Industry Publications; Footwear; Gun Cabinets/Racks/Safes; Online Services; Outdoor Art, Jewelry, Sculpture

Wolverine, 9341 Courtland Dr., Rockford, MI 49351, P: 800-253-2184, F: 616-866-5666, www.wolverine.com
Footwear; Gloves, Mitts, Hats; Men's Clothing

Woods Outfitting, P.O. Box 3037, Palmer, AK 99645, P: 907-746-2534, F: 907-745-6283, www.woods-outfitting.com
Outfitter

Woods Wise Products, P.O. Box 681552, Franklin, TN 37068, P: 800-735-8182, F: 931-364-7925, www.woodswise.com
Blinds; Custom Manufacturing; Decoys; Game Calls; Hunting Accessories; Scents & Lures; Videos

Woolrich, Inc./Elite Series Tactical, 1 Mill St., Woolrich, PA 17779, P: 800-996-2299, F: 570-769-7662, www.woolrich.com, www.woolricheliteseriestactical.com
Footwear; Gloves, Mitts, Hats; Home Furnishings; Law Enforcement; Men & Women's Clothing; Wholesaler/Distributor

World Famous Sports, 3625 Dalbergia St., Suite A, San Diego, CA 92113, P: 800-848-9848, F: 619-231-1717, www.worldfamoussports.com
Bags & Equipment Cases; Camouflage; Camping; Gloves, Mitts, Hats; Hunting Accessories; Men & Women's Clothing

Wrangler Rugged Wear/Wrangler ProGear, 400 N. Elm St., Greensboro, NC 27401, P: 336-332-3977, F: 336-332-3518, www.wrangler.com
Men's Clothing

Wycon Safari Inc. (WY)/Wynn Condict, P.O. Box 1126, Saratoga, MY 82331, P: 307-327-5502, F: 307-327-5332, www.wyconsafariinc.com
Outfitter

X

X-Caliber Accuracy Systems, 1837 First St., Bay City, MI 48708, P: 989-893-3961, F: 989-893-0241, www.xcaliberaccuracy.com
Hunting Accessories

X-Caliber Tactical, 1111 Winding Creek Pl., Round Rock, TX 78664, P: 512-524-2621, www.xcalibertactical.com
Airguns; Airsoft; Custom Manufacturing; Export/Import Specialists; Law Enforcement; Wholesaler/Distributor

Xenonics Holdings, Inc., 2236 Rutherford Rd., Suite 123, Carlsbad, CA 92008, P: 760-448-9700, FL 760-929-7571, www.xenonics.com
Law Enforcement; Lighting Products

XGO/Polarmax, 5417 N.C. 211, P.O. Box 968, West End, NC 27376, P: 800-552-8585, F: 910-673-3875, www.xgotech.com
Men & Women's Clothing

Xisico USA, Inc./Rex Optics USA, Inc., 16802 Barker Springs, Suite 550, Houston, TX 77084, P: 281-647-9130, F: 208-979-2848, www.xisicousa.com
Airguns; Ammunition; Binoculars; Scopes, Sights & Accessories

XS Sight Systems, 2401 Ludella St., Fort Worth, TX 76105, P: 888-744-4880, F: 800-734-7939, www.xssights.com
Gun Parts/Gunsmithing; Law Enforcement; Scopes, Sights & Accessories

Y

Yaktrax, 9221 Globe Center Dr., Morrisville, NC 27560, P: 800-446-7587, F: 919-544-0975, www.yaktrax.com
Backpacking; Camping; Footwear; Sports Accessories

Yamaha Motor Corp., U.S.A., 6555 Katella Ave., Cypress, CA 90630, P: 714-761-7300, F: 714-503-7184
Vehicles, Utility & Rec

Yankee Hill Machine Co., Inc., 20 Ladd Ave., Suite 1, Florence, MA 01062, P: 877-892-6533, F: 413-586-1326, www.yhm.net
Firearms; Gun Barrels; Gun Cases; Gun Parts/Gunsmithing; Law Enforcement; Scopes, Sights & Accessories

Yukon Advanced Optics, 201 Regency Pkwy., Mansfield, TX 76063, P: 817-453-9966, F: 817-453-8770
Archery; Backpacking; Binoculars; Camping; Custom Manufacturing; Hunting Accessories; Scopes, Sights & Accessories; Wholesaler/Distributor

Z

Z-Blade, Inc., 28280 Alta Vista Ave., Valencia, CA 91355, P: 800-734-5424, F: 661-295-2615, www.pfimold.com
Custom Manufacturing; Hunting Accessories; Knives/Knife Cases

Zak Tool, 319 San Luis Rey Rd., Arcadia, CA 91007, P: 615-504-4456, F: 931-381-2568, www.zaktool.com
Law Enforcement; Training & Safety Equipment

Zanotti USA, 7907 High Knoll Ln., Houston, TX 77095, P: 281-414-2184, www.zanottiusa.com
Custom Manufacturing; Firearms

Zarc International, Inc., P.O. Box 108, Minonk, IL 61760, P: 800-882-7011, F: 309-432-3490, www.zarc.com
Law Enforcement; Retail Packaging

Zephyr Graf-x, 5443 Earhart Rd., Loveland, CO 80538, P: 970-663-3242, F: 970-663-7695, www.zhats.com
Camouflage; Custom Manufacturing; Gloves, Mitts, Hats; Men & Women's Clothing; Retailer Services

Zero Tolerance Knives, 18600 SW Tetaon Ave., Tualatin, OR 97062, P: 800-325-2891, F: 503-682-7168, www.ztknives.com
Knives/Knife Cases; Law Enforcement

Ziegel Engineering Working Designs, Jackass Field Carts, 2108 Lomina Ave., Long Beach, CA 90815, P: 562-596-9481, F: 562-598-4734, www.ziegeleng.com
Archery; Bags & Equipment Cases; Black Powder Accessories; Custom Manufacturing; Gun Cabinets/Racks/Safes; Gun Cases; Law Enforcement; Shooting Range Equipment

Zippo Manufacturing Co., 33 Barbour St., Bradford, PA 16701, P: 814-368-2700, F: 814-362-1350, www.zippo.com
Camping; Knives/Knife Cases; Lighting Products; Sports Accessories

Zistos Corp., 1736 Church St., Holbrook, NY 11741, P: 631-434-1370, F: 631-434-9104, www.zistos.com
Law Enforcement

Zodi Outback Gear, P.O. Box 4687, Park City, UT 84060, P: 800-589-2849, F: 800-861-8228
Archery; Backpacking; Camping; Cooking Equipment/Accessories; Hunting Accessories; Pet Supplies; Sports Accessories; Training & Safety Equipment

ZOLL Medical Corp., 269 Mill Rd., Chelmsford, MA 01824, P: 800-348-9011, F: 978-421-0025, www.zoll.com
Law Enforcement; Survival Kits/First Aid; Training & Safety Equipment

NUMBERS

10 Minute Deer Skinner, P.O. Box 158, Stillwater, OK 74076; P: 405-377-2222, F: 405-624-6060, www.tenminutedeerskinner.com
Cooking Equipment/Accessories; Hunting Accessories; Outfitter, Videos

32north Corp - STABILicers, 6 Arctic Circle, Buddeford, ME 04005, P: 800-782-2423, F: 207-284-5015, www.32north.com
Backpacking; Footwear; Hunting Accessories; Law Enforcement; Sports Accessories

3M Thinsulate™ Insulation / 3M Scotchgard™ Protector, 3M Center Building 235-2F-06, St. Paul, MN 55144-1000, P: 800-364-3577, F: 651-737-7659, www.thinsulate.com
Men & Women's Clothing; Footwear; Gloves, Mitts, Hats

3Point5.com, 224 South 200 West, Suite 230, Salt Lake City, UT 84101, P: 801-456-6900/2007, F: 801-485-5039, www.3point5.com

5.11 Tactical Series, 4300 Spyres Way, Modesto, CA 95356, P: 866-451-1726/348, F: 209-548-5348, www.511tactical.com
Bags & Equipment Cases; Men & Women's Clothing; Eyewear; Footwear; Gloves, Mitts, Hats; Law Enforcement; Watches

5-Hour Energy, 46570 Humboldt Drive, Novi, MI 48377, P: 248-960-1700/209, F: 248-960-1980, www.fivehour.com
Food; Hunting Accessories; Law Enforcement; Outfitter; Sports Accessories; Wholesaler/Distributor